THE COMPLEAT ASTROLOGER

The Practical Encyclopaedia of Astrological Science.

Incorporating Astrology Ancient and Modern;
How to Cast, Interpret and make Predictions
from your own Birth Chart; Aspects, Progressions;
Planetary Positions and Tables; *Plus* the first ever
Atlas of Astrology explaining in Full Colour the
Secrets of Celestial Mechanics.

by Derek and Julia Parker

Greenwich House New York

THE COMPLEAT ASTROLOGER

Acknowledgments

The Compleat Astrologer was prepared and designed by a team of editors and designers working under the authorship of Derek and Julia Parker and the direction and control of Mitchell Beazley Limited, 14-15 Manette Street, London W1V 5LB.

Editor: Michael Leitch
Art Director: Peter Kindersley
Designer: Martin Bronkhorst

This 1982 edition is published by Greenwich House, a division of Arlington House, Inc., distributed by Crown Publishers, Inc.

Revised edition 1979

Printed in Hong Kong.

Library of Congress Cataloging in Publication Data

Parker, Derek.
The compleat astrologer.

Reprint. Originally published: London: Mitchell Beazley, 1971.
1. Astrology. I. Parker, Julia. II. Title.
BF1708.1.P36 1982 133.5 82-6233
ISBN 0-517-387115 AACR2

h g f e d c b a

The authors and publishers extend grateful thanks to the many individuals and organizations who have contributed to the preparation of *The Compleat Astrologer*. Special thanks go to Jeff Mayo, DF Astrol S, Principal of the Faculty of Astrological Studies, and to the Council of the Faculty; to John Addey, DF Astrol S, and Charles Harvey, DF Astrol S, President and Secretary of the Astrological Association, for their kind and helpful co-operation in making the Association's files freely available for preliminary research, and to John Addey personally for his exclusive account of his theory of celestial harmonics.
We also thank John Filbey, DF Astrol S, who ensured the book's unique comprehensiveness by devising an entirely new table of planetary positions, and supervised the planning of the other astrological tables which appear at the end of the book. The work of compiling the tables was further guided by the existence of Her Majesty's Stationery Office's official reference sources: astronomical data in *The Compleat Astrologer* has been derived from the Nautical Almanac with the permission of the Controller of Her Majesty's Stationery Office. Special acknowledgment is also made to W. Foulsham & Co Ltd whose complete range of astrological publications is recommended to all serious students of the subject.
The authors would like to record their particular gratitude to Roger Elliot, DF Astrol S, Clifford L. Brettelle, DF Astrol S, Mr and Mrs Paul Lethbridge, Mrs Hazel Casimir and Mr David Blair.
The strong visual character of *The Compleat Astrologer* was achieved through the blending of many talents under the overall direction of Peter Kindersley and Martin Bronkhorst. Special artwork was carried out by Barry Evans, Justin Todd, Paul Webb, Paul Harbutt, Diagram, Roger Bristow, Janine Kirwan, Gordon Cramp, Gilchrist Studios, Cecil Misstear and Richard Curthoys. Editorial work was executed by Max Monsarrat, Peter Ford and Christopher Cooper.

The following sources are acknowledged for the supply of photographic material: Aldus Books, London, and in association with Boston Museum of Fine Arts, British Museum, Culver Pictures, Herbert List, Musée du Louvre, Archivo di Stato di Siena; Associated Press; Chris Barker; W. M. Baxter; Bibliothèque Nationale, Paris; Bodleian Library, Oxford; British Museum; BPC Library; Camera Press; Central Press; Robert Cundy; C. M. Dixon; R. Estall; Mary Evans Picture Library; Fox Photos; P. Glaser; E. P. Goldschmidt & Co Ltd; The Hale Observatories (Mt Wilson & Palomar): Sonia Halliday; Hamlyn Group Library; Hirnier Verlag, Munich; Michael Holford; Keystone Press Agency, London; G. P. Kniper; A. Küng; R. D. Küplich; Lincoln Laboratory, MIT; Tony Loftas; Mansell Collection; A. Michaelis; Patrick Moore; National Aeronautics and Space Administration; National Gallery, London; National Portrait Gallery, London; Picturepoint; Pix, New York; Radio Times Hulton Picture Library; Ronan Picture Library; Royal Astronomical Society; Science Museum, London, Crown Copyright; Snark International/Bibliothèque Nationale, Paris; US Naval Observatory; Victoria and Albert Museum, London; Roger Viollet; Zentrale Bibliotek, Zurich.

Tables of Houses for Northern Latitudes © W. Foulsham & Co Ltd reproduced with their permission.

CONTENTS

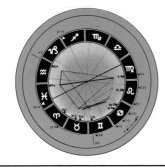

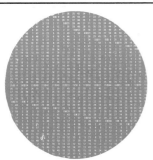

ASTROLOGY IN THE LIFE OF MAN

I

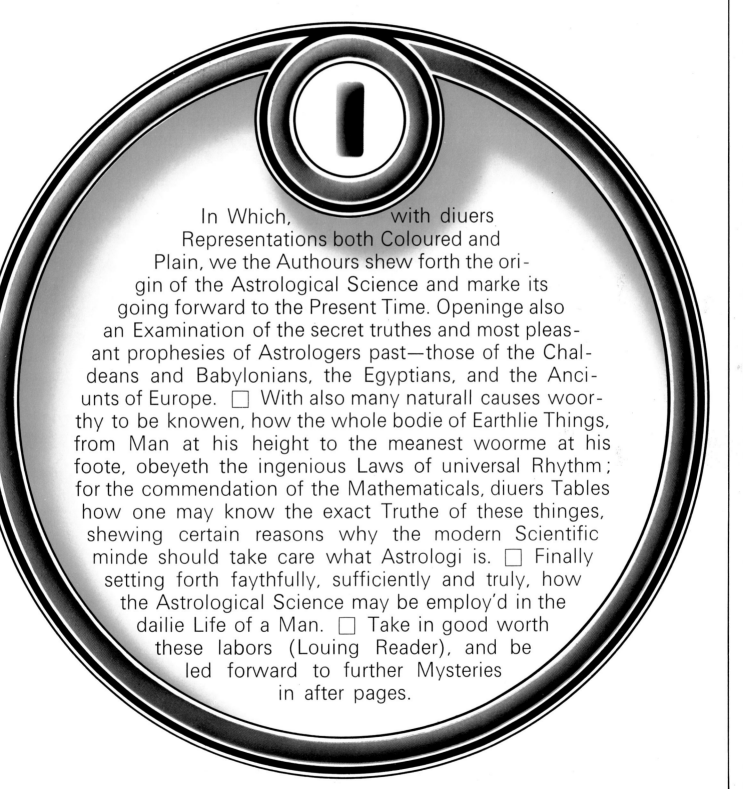

In Which, with diuers Representations both Coloured and Plain, we the Authours shew forth the origin of the Astrological Science and marke its going forward to the Present Time. Openinge also an Examination of the secret truthes and most pleasant prophesies of Astrologers past—those of the Chaldeans and Babylonians, the Egyptians, and the Anciunts of Europe. ☐ With also many naturall causes woorthy to be knowen, how the whole bodie of Earthlie Things, from Man at his height to the meanest woorme at his foote, obeyeth the ingenious Laws of universal Rhythm; for the commendation of the Mathematicals, diuers Tables how one may know the exact Truthe of these thinges, shewing certain reasons why the modern Scientific minde should take care what Astrologi is. ☐ Finally setting forth faythfully, sufficiently and truly, how the Astrological Science may be employ'd in the dailie Life of a Man. ☐ Take in good worth these labors (Louing Reader), and be led forward to further Mysteries in after pages.

Astrology has always served to enlarge our understanding. This opening part of the book is designed to clarify how astrology has achieved its aims in time past, and how they may be applied to our present situation and to the prospect of a new world tomorrow.

Changes have occurred in recent years which promise to have a momentous effect on the progress of astrology, the new directions it can be expected to take, and the attitudes people are likely to adopt towards it.

These changes are at once mysterious and illuminating. What, broadly, has happened is that progressive astrologers, in their natural attempts to relate astrology to a science-orientated society, have reached a point of vital contact with a number of hard-headed scientists approaching the topic of universal motivation from other points of view within their own disciplines. Already common ground has been discovered, most notably in the field of biological rhythms and cycles; more than enough to show that the aims of astrologers and scientists may not be merely compatible but that a profitable partnership may soon result.

Although the coming 'Age of Aquarius' holds a new and special fascination for a younger generation in search of meaning, this story is conceived for men and women of *all* ages and generations. For astrology knows no frontiers, no age differences, is no respecter of divisions between races or colours or creeds or generations. Astrological truths are for all of us, hold us all together as a human family.

But is astrology true? You must discover this for yourself. We know perfectly well that we cannot persuade you that astrology works by simply telling you about it and its history. To discover that astrology works today, what you have to do is join the 150th generation of practitioners in direct line from the astrologer-priests of Babylon!

Astrology is at once a science and an art. The mechanics of its science as well as the techniques of its art must both be understood if you are to become skilled in understanding and interpreting the influence of the heavenly bodies on yourself and mankind. We hope *The Compleat Astrologer* may give you some new insights into the scientific basis for astrology and into contemporary techniques of interpretation and prediction. Some of the ways we have chosen to present these insights are, we believe, new and fresh. We wanted our book to be worthy of the new Renaissance, of the new Age of Aquarius.

In this new Renaissance – which some astrologers had long predicted as the world came under the influence of Aquarius in the Great Year – a more rational, scientific basis for astrology is being discovered and we have tried to tell that story. Equally, we honour and respect the received truths of past masters. So in several ways we have tried to make our book straddle the generations and the generation gap. We wanted our book to be a child of this wonderful moment when Science and Art are meeting again together to cast deeper, clearer light on human life. And we wanted our readers to feel the wonder of the Dawn of Aquarius, the sign of friendliness, of healing, of starting all over again.

The Compleat Astrologer is thus dedicated to the spreading of a deeper harmony in human affairs. It is a book of reconciliation on two levels – the human level where mothers and sons, fathers and daughters, may discover a deeper understanding of their motives and so learn a deeper care and understanding for each other, and the scientific level, where great sciences are drawn together once more.

THE DAWN OF ASTROLOGY

In the ancient Mesopotamian world, as far back as 8000 BC, man lived precariously beneath the open sky. His spirit was almost totally dominated by an upper world of apparently infinite resources: thunder, lightning, burning heat, eclipses – the heavens maintained an unpredictable barrage, spectacular and devastating beyond anything man could contrive for himself. The idea of celestial superiority – of looking *upward* for guidance – soon became part of everyday life.

In his primitive state man did not make allowances for the possibility of accidents; everything that happened was set in motion by some purposeful force. For everything that seemed to defy explanation within his narrow span of experience, a physical source urgently had to be located and named, and a range of behaviour attributed to it. This made him feel less vulnerable.

A star is the ancient Sumerian symbol for divinity. The stars which filled the clear skies in that part of the world were the real founders of astrology. Although their role was, and still is, seen as essentially a passive one, they provided a highly impressive background to the interaction of other celestial bodies. Even today we are naturally aware that the Sun and Moon exert a strong physical influence on our lives. For our primitive ancestor this influence must have been a matter of great and mysterious significance. The Sun kept him warm or faded in the increasing cold of winter; day alternated with night; the sea rose and fell with the tides. Early man, his senses assailed by mysterious processes of growth and decay, the ebb and flow of the natural order, tended naturally towards a physical explanation of the universe.

The Intervention of the Planets

From a viewpoint on Earth the stars turn round us in a pattern that is virtually unchanging from one year to the next. Shifts are of course constantly occurring but they are so slight as to have conveyed little if anything to the earliest observers. What they did notice was the relatively rapid movement against the starry background of seven major bodies. The Sun and Moon we have mentioned. The others were the five visible planets, variously referred to as 'wanderers' or 'goats', and which we now call Mercury, Venus, Mars, Jupiter and Saturn.

In the earliest records we find the idea present that the planets, as well as the Sun and Moon, represented gods with the power to direct or intervene in life. By the time that astronomical observations were being carried out in Babylonia, the pantheon of the gods was well and truly established, each god being allocated power over a particular area of human experience. For example Mercury, a quick, cunning, bisexual god, was held to have a certain calculating wisdom; Mars was the ruler of violence and war; Jupiter was a king-like ruler of men; Saturn, seen as a distant cooling sun in exile, was quick-tempered and cruel. Gradually, as these associations gained in authority, so they were joined to form the basis of astrological lore.

BEFORE THE ZODIAC

Undoubtedly there was a great deal of isolated activity well before the first specifically astrological records to reach us were set down in the 7th century BC. Recent studies of Ice Age bone markings, for example, suggest that men were aware of lunar periodicity as far back as 32,000 years ago. Less remote are the fragments of documents surviving from the reign of Sargon of Agade (*c.*2870 BC), which show that predictions were made according to positions of the Sun, the Moon, the five known planets and a mass of other phenomena, including comets and thunderbolts. From ancient Egypt, star charts have come down to us which have been reliably dated to around 4200 BC. And although in the latter case some scholars believe that the charts were drawn up for exclusively astronomical purposes, it is hard not to impute astrological significance to them. For throughout the history of astrology, until the outbreak of rationalism less than three hundred years ago, astronomy and astrology were an identical subject, the role of scientific techniques being to establish or predict the influences of extra-terrestrial life-forces.

The Twelve Houses of Life

The Chaldeans were astute observers and mathematicians. They saw that events in the sky ran to a pattern: the stars moved in fixed order across the heavens and the planets wandered eccentrically but in much the same plane against the stellar background. It became apparent that the planets also behaved regularly in their own individual fashion, and so the first ephemerides, or tables of planetary movements, were drawn up; the earliest written ephemerides we know about date from the mid-7th century BC, in the time of the Assyrian king Assurbanipal.

In preparing their cosmological system, the Chaldeans made use of the 12 principal constellations through which the Sun and Moon regularly passed, and which were the forerunners of the Zodiac. Every two hours the moving constellations would shift in the sky by 30°, or one-twelfth of the complete circle. For centuries all astronomical observation remained bound up with the rising and setting of heavenly bodies within this pattern. There was also another set of 12 sections, unconnected with the first, and these sections were known as Houses.
They were numbered from the east downward under the horizon, and represented areas of life on the following pattern: 1 Life, 2 Poverty/riches, 3 Brothers, 4 Parents, 5 Children, 6 Illness/health, 7 Wife/husband, 8 Death, 9 Religion, 10 Dignities, 11 Friendship, 12 Enmity. The planets were described according to the Houses they occupied and also in terms of the aspects they formed with each other, the angles between them revealing the kind of influence they were likely to exert.

In the beginning Babylonian astrology was not directly personal: rather it was concerned with large-scale events such as the advent of wars, floods and eclipses, and their possible effect on the king, who embodied the affairs of the state and its well-being.

Divisions of the Sky *below*
In early astrology the sky round the observer (A) was divided into 12 sections.

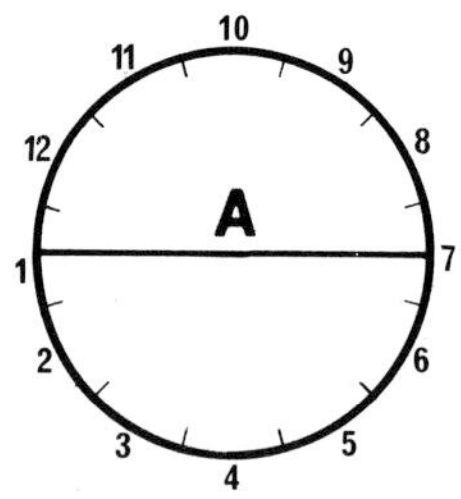

Shamash the Sun-god *above*
The Babylonian Sun-god Shamash, lord of the year, is portrayed on an ancient seal (*c.*2400 BC). Shamash was the son of the Moon-god Sin, who crossed the sky in a boat. Together Shamash and Sin dominated Chaldean mythology.

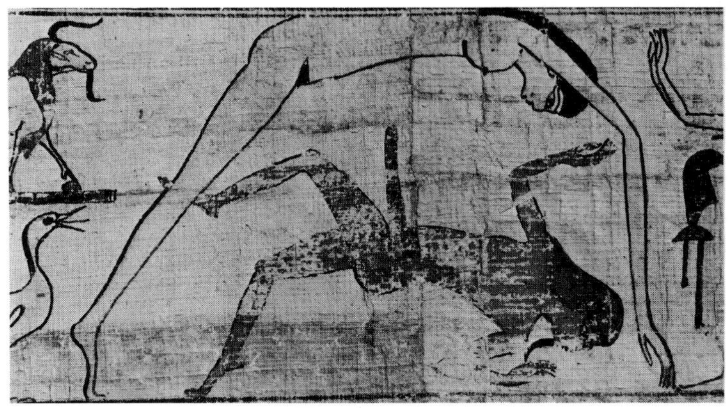

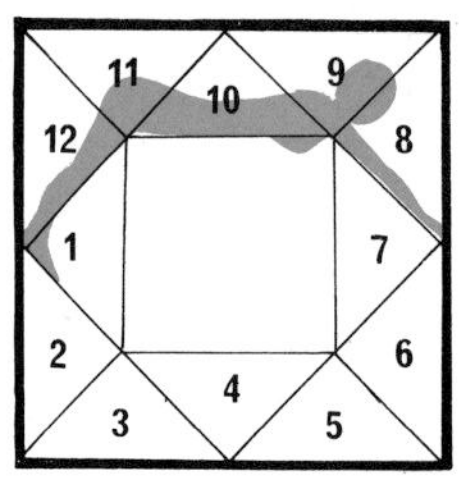

The Upper and Lower Worlds *above*
The separation of the Earth-god Geb and the sky goddess Nut was a key factor in Egyptian cosmology, and is reflected in the square horoscope, left.

Assyrian Astrolabe *below*
A tablet for recording astrological calculations.

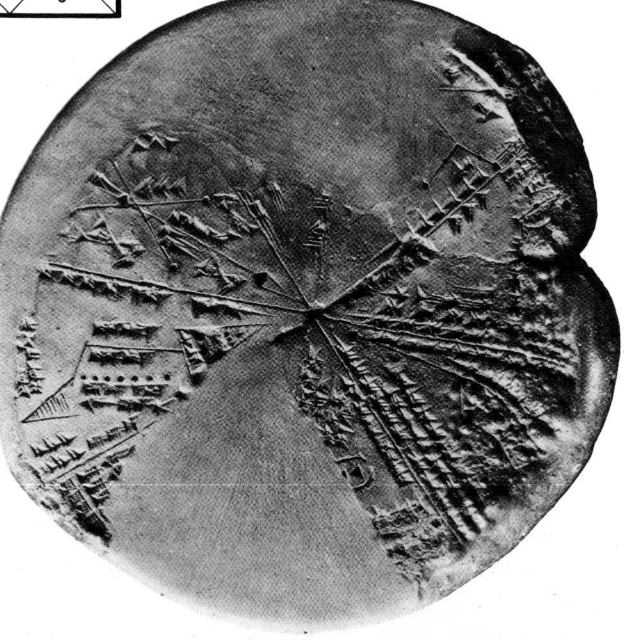

Rameses II and Hathor *right*
Rameses II of Egypt (1300–1236 BC) was responsible for the establishment of the four cardinal Signs of the Zodiac: Aries, Libra, Cancer and Capricorn. His concern for astrology was emphasized for posterity by the astrological symbols which decorated his tomb. In this relief from the Temple of Amon at Karnak, Rameses is shown linking hands with the sky-goddess Hathor.

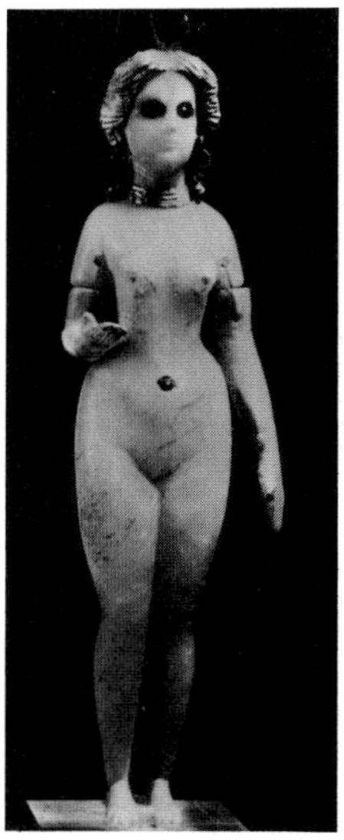

Ishtar *left and below*
In Babylonian mythology Ishtar was the daughter of the Moon-god Sin. She was the goddess of love ruling over fertility and was identified with the planet we now call Venus. The statuette is a relatively late work dating from the 3rd century BC; Ishtar's eight-pointed star emblem shown below is much earlier, dating as it does from *c.*1120 BC, and was carved on an ancient Babylonian boundary stone.

The Ziggurat of Ur *below*
The ziggurats or watch-towers were built in the form of gigantic stepped pyramids; those at Babylon, Uruk and Ur were up to 300 feet high. They afforded the Chaldean observers a massive sweep of horizon and from them they traced the movements of the heavenly bodies with remarkable accuracy. The ziggurat shown below was begun by Ur-Nammu, the king who founded the Third Sumerian Dynasty (2079–1960 BC); in the wing added by King Nebuchadnezzar around 600 BC, indications were found by Sir Leonard Woolley of a shrine in the shape of a boat, such as the Moon-god Sin used for his journeys across the sky.

THE FIRST COMPUTERS

The importance which early man attached to the movements of the Sun, Moon, planets and stars is vividly illustrated by the great megalithic sites distributed throughout Western Europe. In recent years there has been an accumulation of evidence to show that one of their principal functions was to compute the yearly movements of celestial bodies.

The monument at Stonehenge, in England, remains among the most impressive of these sites. Recently revised radio-carbon datings show that its construction may have begun before 2500 BC, predating the Mycenaean civilization. It therefore represents an extraordinary culmination of the achievements of those early Bronze Age inhabitants of Western Europe known to archaeologists as the Beaker People. This apparently barbaric culture possessed, as far as we know, no means of recording its knowledge, yet it evolved a highly sophisticated method of calculating a calendar of great accuracy, pinpointing the solstices and predicting eclipses. Stonehenge went through three main stages of construction, representing a task that Professor G. S. Hawkins has calculated as having taken 1,497,680 man-days.

The Beaker People were, in other words, astrologer/astronomers capable of astonishing technical accomplishments. Many questions remain unanswered, in particular the precise extent to which their knowledge had practical applications – in predicting tides on dangerous coastlines, and the appropriate times to plant crops or make sacrifices, besides more sophisticated astrological inferences.

The Pyramids

The pyramids of Egypt still hold pride of place among ancient astronomical buildings. They are oriented to the north pole of the sky, which now lies close to Polaris, but was in those days near the far fainter star Thuban (Alpha Draconis). The pyramids had a dual purpose as burial places for the pharaohs and astrological calculators.

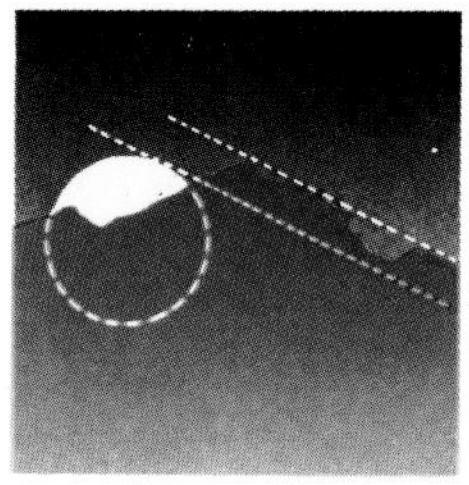

Megalithic Markers *left*
Professor Alexander Thom has shown how menhirs may have served as markers for observing significant astronomical events. In this view a natural landscape feature is taken as a reference point (A). The day when the Moon moves to its furthest north position is the only day when it appears in the notch.

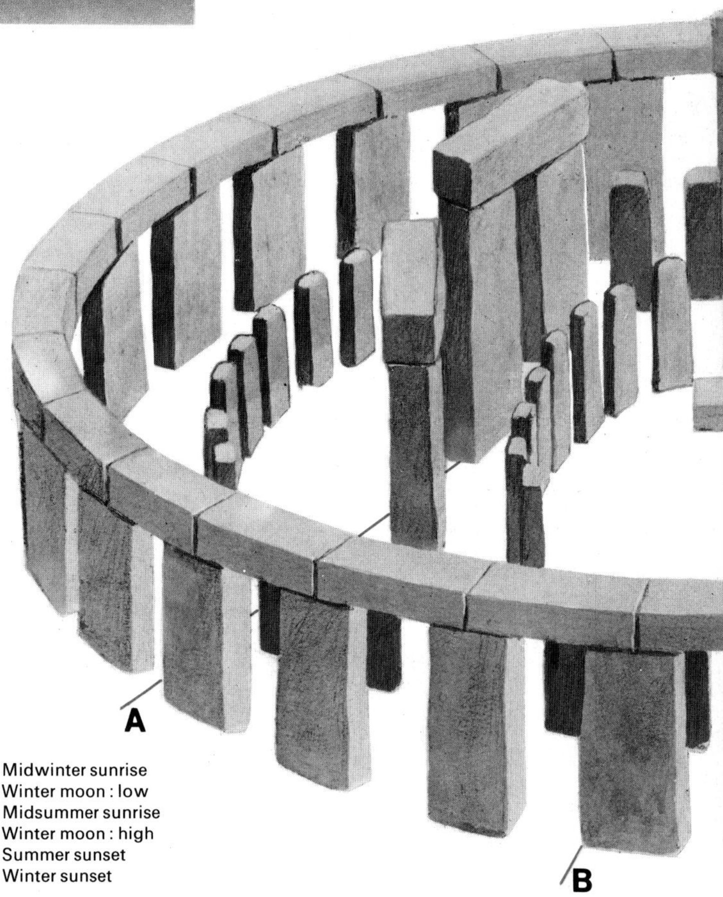

A Midwinter sunrise
B Winter moon: low
C Midsummer sunrise
D Winter moon: high
E Summer sunset
F Winter sunset

The Pyramids at Giza *left*
It used to be one of the world's great mysteries whether the pyramids were only elaborate tombs or whether they had a wider purpose as active spiritual or scientific centres. We now know that the sloping corridors leading from the faces into the interior, were used as sighting tubes, allowing Egyptian astrologers to make naked-eye observations of great accuracy from which astrological calculations were made.

Astrology in Ancient America
Time and the calendar were of central importance to the Maya in pre-Columbian Mexico. In fact they possessed two main calendars: one, plotting the solar year of 365 days, governed the planting of crops and other domestic matters; the other, of 260 days, had a ritual use. Each was linked to an elaborate astrological system to cover every facet of life.

The Mayan priest-interpreters, as with the Aztecs, who later took over the Mayan system, emerged as an all-powerful hierarchy. On the fifth day after the birth of a boy, they would cast his horoscope and say what his profession was to be: soldier, priest, civil servant or sacrificial victim. Under this primitive misapplication of celestial theory, whole peoples found themselves dominated by an inaccurate belief in pre-destiny.

Menhirs at Carnac *right*
At Carnac in Brittany is a series of alignments of about 2,750 menhirs, or great stones. Part of the Kermario alignment is shown at sunset: this group was certainly associated with Sun cults and the summer solstice. The astrological significance of Carnac is now being carefully researched.

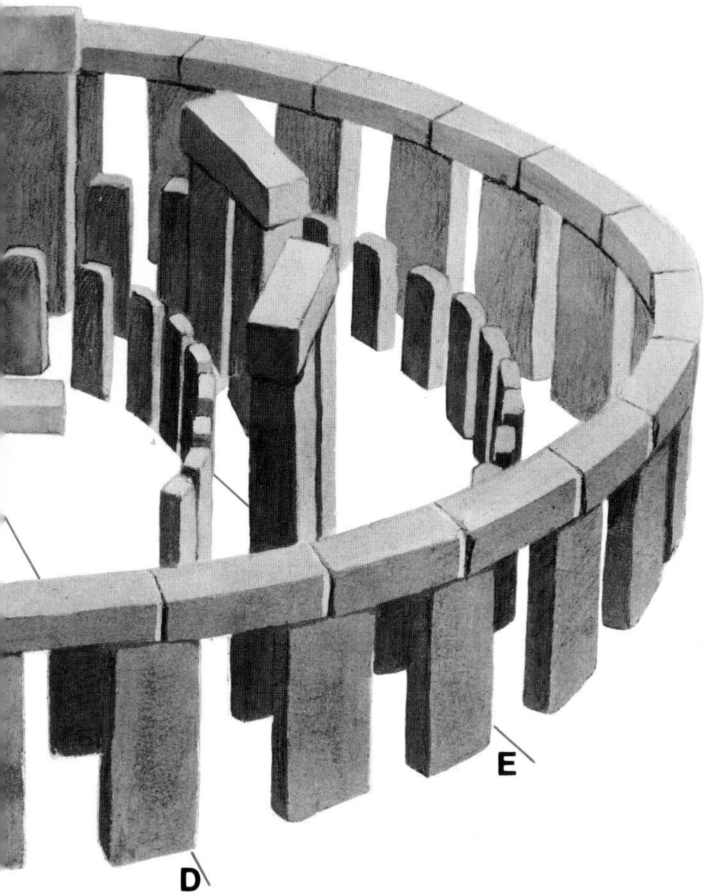

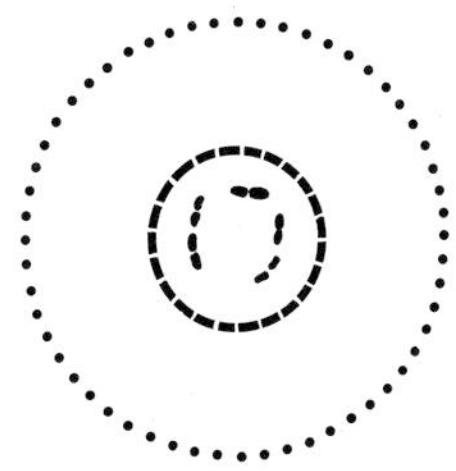

The Aubrey Holes at Stonehenge *left*
Beyond the outer stones at Stonehenge lies a ring of 56 holes known as Aubrey holes after the antiquarian, John Aubrey (1627–97), who rediscovered them. Professor Hawkins has recently shown that, by using a system of four moveable marker stones, errors could be corrected and virtually every eclipse of the Sun or Moon predicted.

Stonehenge
left and above
Stonehenge's layout was submitted to computer analysis by Professor G. S. Hawkins, who uncovered a formidable range of alignments, showing the monument to be nothing more nor less than a gigantic megalithic computer.

Stonehenge Today *above*
The remains of the first astrological computer.

Transporting the Bluestones *right*
The massive 5-ton bluestones at Stonehenge were quarried in the Prescelly mountains and transported along a 240-mile route.

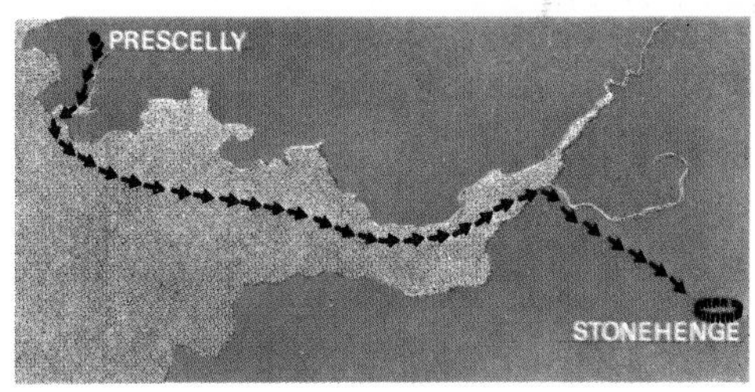

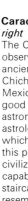

Mayan Astrology
These ancient Mexican codices show, above, the marriage of a city chief, who was also a famous astrologer; a star is descending into position between a forked stick. Left, Mayan representation of an eclipse.

Caracol Observatory
right
The Caracol observatory in the ancient Mayan city of Chichen Itza in Mexico provides a good illustration of the astronomical and astrological skills of which the people of this pre-Columbian civilization were capable. A spiral staircase on the inside, resembling the shape of a shell, leads up to windows which relate to the positions of the planets as they appeared to observers at various times during the year.

EGYPT AND THE CLASSICAL WORLD

From the days of King Assurbanipal in the mid-7th century BC there was virtually no change in astrological theory until Kepler made his mathematical calculations of the planets' orbits some 350 years ago. The planets remained the principal life-forces, their movements being used to reveal the future, and also to explore and elaborate on the present.

Astrology in Egypt

In very ancient times the Egyptians practised a mystical form of astrology which depended on the religious and economic focus of their civilization – the Nile. The great river was the source of all life; floods bringing fertility to an otherwise barren region were activated, the Egyptians believed, by the concerted action of the Sun and Sirius, a bright star which consequently assumed enormous importance.

A remarkable star-map in the shape of a seated man appears on the tomb of Rameses VI, one of the pharoahs who reigned during the 20th Dynasty (1200–1085 BC). According to Dr Margaret Murray, it would have been possible to read from this map the culminations of the stars for each hour of the night throughout the year.

Horoscopes for All—Astrology in Greece and Rome

Astrology came relatively late to Greece. But by about 250 BC the Babylonian astrologer Berosus had made a great impact on the classical world with his astrological writings; as a result he was able to set up a school of astrologers on the island of Cos. In the course of the next four hundred years the Greeks zealously converted Chaldean astrology to their own traditions, making it steadily more formal and more complicated. They also were responsible for popularizing a system of diagnosis which had hitherto been available only to the king: they devised a method of calculating individual destinies based on the moment of birth.

The first modern astrological textbook, the *Tetrabiblos*, is attributed to the great astronomer, mathematician and geographer, Claudius Ptolemy, who was born in Alexandria. Ptolemy, one of the leading intellectuals of his day, worked between AD 150–180, establishing principles of cosmic influence which lie at the heart of modern astrological practice.

Under the Greeks, and Ptolemy in particular, the planets, Houses and Signs of the Zodiac were rationalized and their function set down in a way that has changed remarkably little to this day.

In Imperial Rome astrologers were much in vogue. Their livelihood, however, remained largely subject to the whim of the emperor in power. Tiberius had had his 'lofty destiny' predicted for him at birth, and surrounded himself with astrologers – called by Juvenal his 'herd of Chaldeans'. Claudius, on the other hand, favoured augury, and banned astrologers from the country.

The social standing that astrology enjoyed in Rome was reflected by Juvenal when he recorded in about AD 100 that 'there are people who cannot appear in public, dine or bath, without having first consulted the ephemeris'.

Egyptian Sarcophagus *above*
The Signs of the Zodiac adorn the painted lid of a sarcophagus from the late Egyptian period. These Signs represent the ancient Chaldean Zodiac or 'road of life' after conversion by the Greeks.

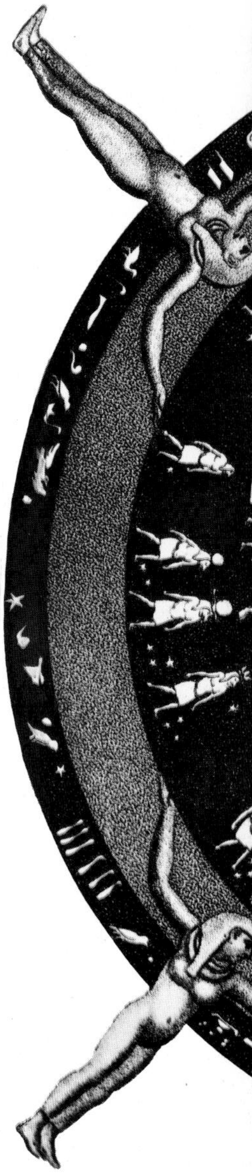

Ptolemy *right*
Claudius Ptolemaeus of Alexandria (AD 120–180), the author of the *Tetrabiblos* which formalized the findings of the Chaldeans, was also the foremost astronomer and geographer of his age; he catalogued 300 new stars and explained the refraction of light. In Book I of the *Tetrabiblos* Ptolemy asserted his belief in the physical effects of the planets, saying that they 'cause heats, winds and storms, to the influence of which earthly things are conformably subjected'. Ptolemy is shown in this medieval woodcut measuring the altitude of the Moon with a quadrant.

Egyptian Zodiac *above*
The earliest known pictorial representation of a Zodiac is this relief on the ceiling of the temple at Denderah. It is later than was once supposed (being now dated *c.*100 BC) and shows a strong Greek influence. It demonstrates the precession of the equinoxes. The vernal equinox was then in Pisces – now it would be in Aquarius. Although the Egyptians had their own mystical beliefs in the stars, the impact of Greek astrology on them was enormous and fundamental after the founding in 322 BC of Alexandria, which became the centre of Mediterranean learning.

Neptune *above*
The Roman god Neptune is seen in this 2nd-century AD mosaic from Chebba, Tunisia, rising from his element, water. Like his Greek counterpart, Poseidon, he is traditionally depicted holding a trident, to raise storms. When the presence of the planet we now know as Neptune was confirmed in 1846, the trident became the planetary glyph.

Aphrodite *above*
The Greek goddess Aphrodite became linked with the goddess Venus in the Roman pantheon – and in turn with the planet. This statue of Aphrodite was sculpted by Menephilos in Myrina, *c.*AD 20.

The Emperor Augustus *above*
The Emperor Augustus published his horoscope and so revealed his death date. He then limited the practice of astrology, presumably in an effort to discourage plots against his life.

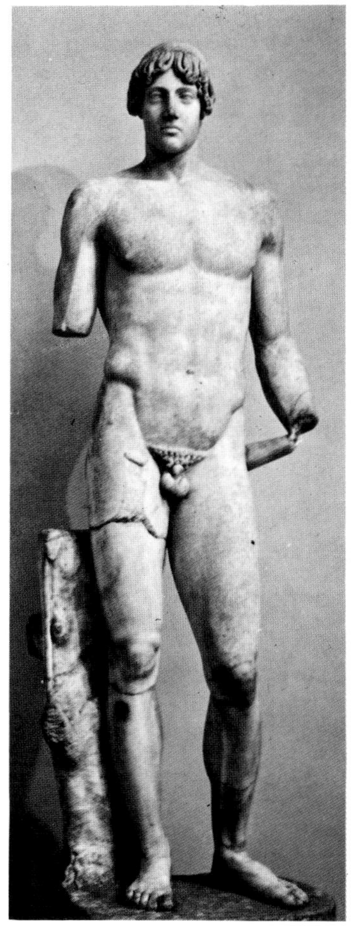

Apollo *above*
This statue of Apollo is a Roman copy of a famous Greek original made *c.*460 BC. Apollo, personifying the Sun, most powerful of the astrologer's planets, was the source of the Earth's fruitfulness.

The Sign of the Sea-Goat *above*
Augustus was a Capricornian. According to Suetonius, he had 'so much confidence in astrology that he made public his natal scheme, and struck silver coinage with the Sign of Capricorn'.

THE CELESTIAL BESTIARY

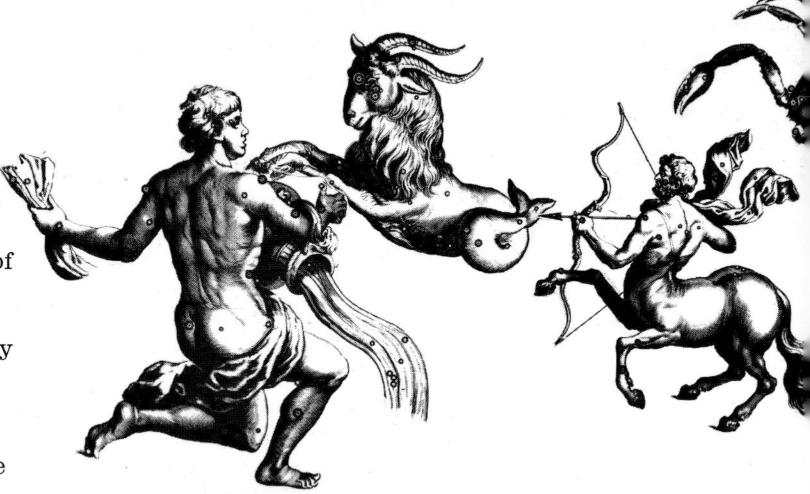

The beasts and human figures which populate the Zodiac appear again and again throughout the mythology of the ancient world; the map and illustrations on these pages show the deep impression which they made on the mind of man, and something of their wide distribution over the Mediterranean region.

In the beginning the Signs of the Zodiac came gradually to be appointed as a result of the Chaldeans' growing appreciation of the heavens. The mass of stars was then divided into bands: particular attention was paid to the Way of Anu, the route followed by Sin and Shamash (the Moon and Sun) across the sky, and consequently to the star-groups through which they passed.

The Signs, and the constellations they represent, serve chiefly as background marker-points to the movements of the planets, and are not in themselves influential. The names the Chaldeans gave to them apparently arose out of their everyday preoccupations, and represent a merging of immediate earthly fears – of bulls, scorpions, lions, etc. – with the potent forces of the sky which so dominated their life. Thirty-six bright stars were named originally; the Chaldeans then selected 12 chiefs of the constellations and these, with modifications, survived until the Western Zodiac was finally established in the early Greek period.

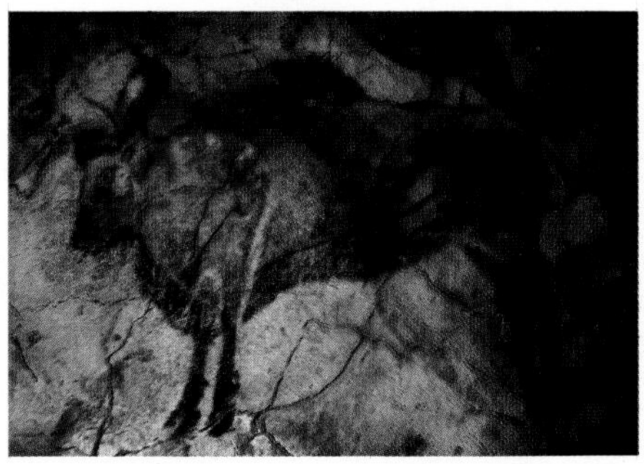

Stone Age Bull *left*
From the caves at Altamira in northern Spain, this bull dates from 12000 BC. Its original purpose is thought to have been magical, either helping in the hunt or ensuring fertility. The caves were not lived in but were perhaps temples.

1

Carthaginian Lion *left*
From Carthage, a stone lion. The Zodiac has seven 'bestial' and four 'human' Signs plus Libra, the 'humane' symbol of justice.

2

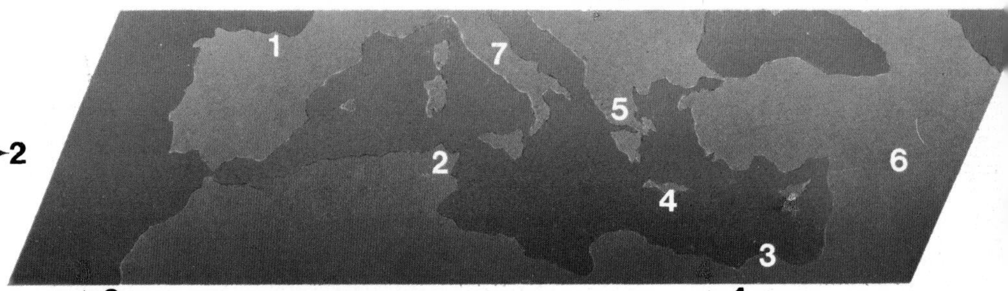

3

4

Egyptian Twins *left*
Two Egyptian water nymphs.

The Sacred Egyptian Ram *right*
Ram-headed images of the god Amon.

Weighing the Dead *below*
Egyptian gods with scales, *c.* 1250 BC.

Minoan Bull *right*
The bull-god of Knossos in Crete, is the symbol of strength and creative energy.

The Fishes *below*
A wall painting from Knossos, *c.*1600 BC. The Greeks believed dolphins brought luck to sailors.

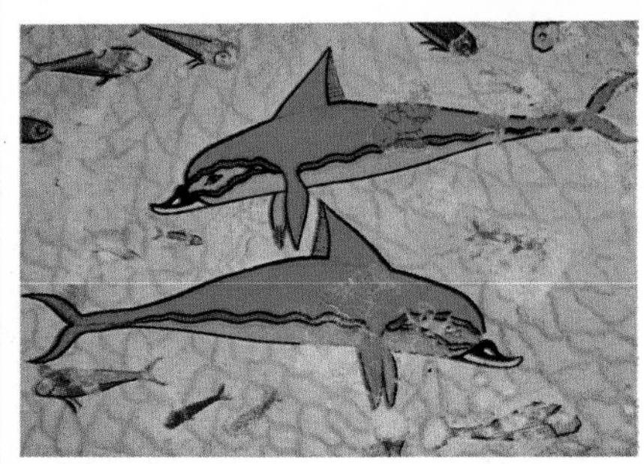

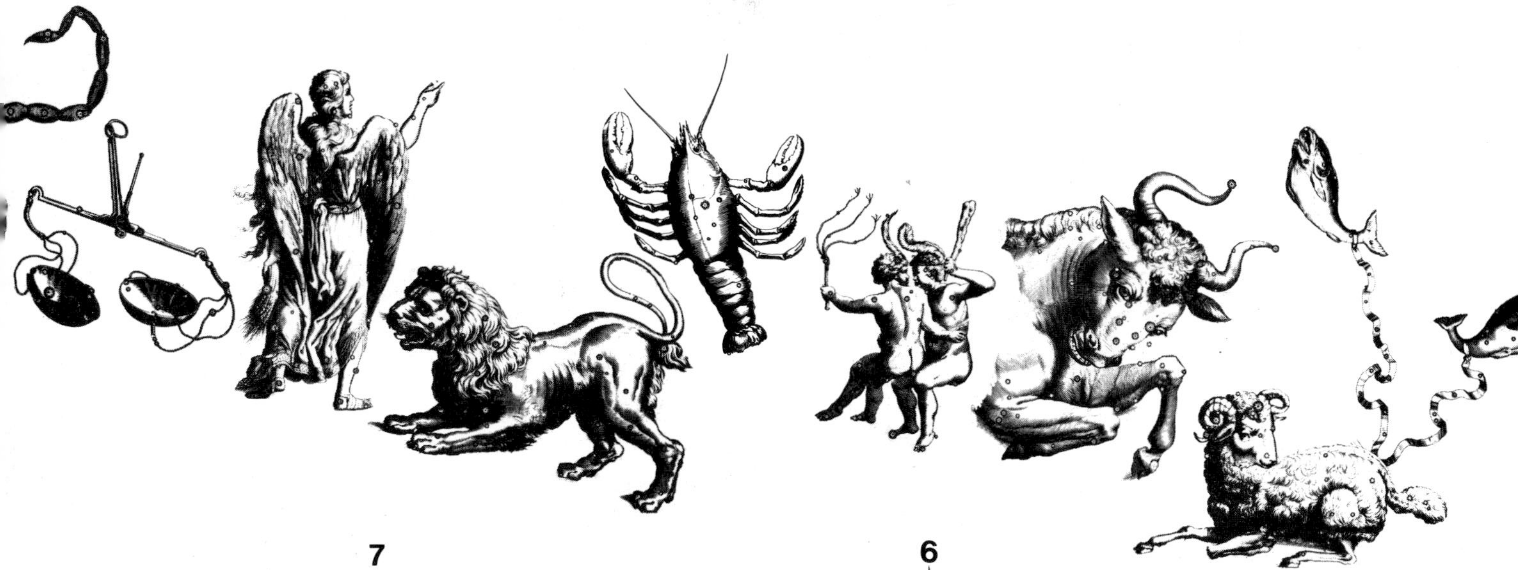

7

Roman Fishes *left*
Fishes and fishermen, from a Roman mosaic; there is strong Egyptian influence in the shape of the boat's bow. At the beginning of the Piscean Age, the fish was identified with the rise of Christianity.

Greek Crab *above*
Crab with sea monster, Scylla.

The Rescuing Ram *below*
Homer's hero Odysseus escapes from the Cyclops' cave strapped to a ram's belly.

Centaur *left*
Part of the famous Elgin Marbles. Half-man, half-horse, the Centaurs are supposed to represent the Thessalians, horse-archers much feared by the Greeks. The sculpture shows the legendary battle between the Centaurs and Lapiths, which the Lapiths finally won. An exhausted Lapith is being trampled to death.

6

Assyrian Goats and Lion
From *c.*740 BC, Assyrian reliefs recording events in the reign of Tiglath-Pileser III. Left, after victory, the Assyrians drive off sheep and goats; above, a lion hunt.

Crab *above*
Assyrian crab in a river, *c.*653 BC.

Babylonian Scorpion *above*
Symbol of Ishtar, goddess of Love.

Sumerian Goat *above*
He-goat in a thicket.

The Water-pourer *left*
This ivory inlay from the kingdom of Sumeria, at the lower end of the Euphrates, may date from 3000 BC. A record of the day-to-day tasks, it emphasizes the role of water through the filling of the King's cup. Special holders had to be made to keep the curved-bottom amphorae upright.

ASTROLOGY IN THE MIDDLE EAST

In Europe the classical tradition died with Ptolemy in AD 180. Astrology also began to decline, mainly because the technical ability to make observations and calculations was lost at the same time. As the Roman empire crumbled, astrology descended temporarily into a corrupt superstition.

The decadent state of astrology was one of the reasons why the early Christian Church attacked its practices – together with all residues of pagan belief – with every means at its disposal. This was despite the appearance in the New Testament of astrological references – one example being the Magi in St Luke's Gospel, and many others occurring throughout the Book of Revelation. All was not totally lost however, and the Eastern Church retained some acquaintance with scientific astrology.

Among the early Church fathers involved in trying to stamp out astrology, the most formidable and effective figure was St Augustine of Hippo (AD 354–430). He had accepted astrology in his youth, but his later condemnation became absolute. Astrology, he proclaimed, was at best a fraud; and if astrologers were sometimes accurate, it could only be because they had invoked those evil spirits which always sought to possess men's minds.

Arab Zodiac *above*
This early Arab Zodiac shows a distinct Persian influence.

Astrology Under the Arabs

Much of the survival of classical science and philosophy is owed to the fact that it was preserved and used by the advanced Arabic cultures of North Africa and the Eastern Mediterranean from about the 8th century.

In the fields of medicine and astronomy in particular, the Arabs soon showed themselves to be outstandingly skilful. Centres of learning were set up in Baghdad and Damascus, and the Caliph al-Mansur of Baghdad (the son of Harun al-Raschid) established a major observatory and library in the city, making it the world's astronomical capital. Arab astronomical studies, moreover, had a strong astrological orientation.

The Arabs defined a new, if dubious, form of practical astrology which could be used for all manner of divination in everyday life, such as the discovery of propitious moments for the undertaking of journeys, etc. Nevertheless, their emphasis on 'favourable' or 'unfavourable' indications, rather than on prophesying categorical events, was later to be a great help to astrology as it rehabilitated itself in the West during the Renaissance.

Albumasur, or Abu Maaschar (805–85), was the greatest of the Arab astrologers. His treatise *Introductorium in Astronomiam* showed a positive Aristotelian influence. 'As the motions of these wandering stars (the seven planets) are never interrupted,' he wrote, 'so the generations and alterations of earthly things never have an end. Only by observing the great diversity of planetary motions can we comprehend the unnumbered varieties of change in this world.'

Albumasur's *Introductorium* was one of the first books to find its way in translation through Spain and into Europe in the early Middle Ages. It was to prove highly influential in the revival of astrology and astronomy.

Albumasur *right*
The leading astrologer of the Arab world, Albumasur (805–85) measures the heavens.

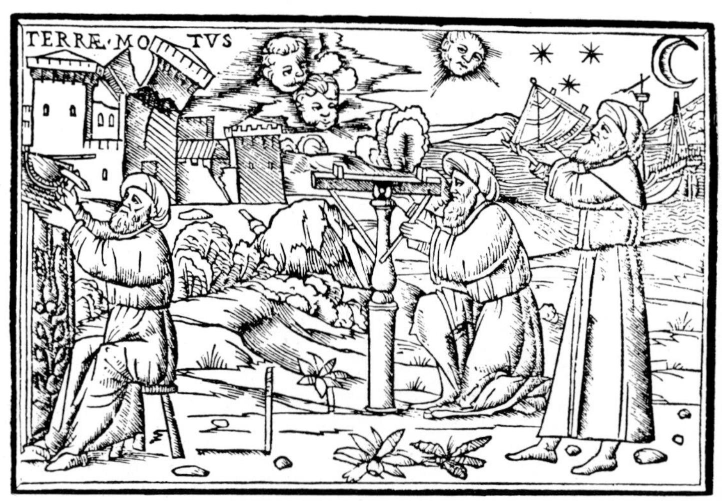

Arab Astrologers *below*
Arab astrologers using astronomical instruments to work out their predictions.

Conjunction of Mars and Jupiter *right*
A 13th-century copy of Albumasur's treatise shows (top) Mars in the Sign of the Ram in conjunction with Jupiter; below are Saturn, Mercury, Venus, Mars and Jupiter.

Arab Water Clock *below*
A water clock surmounted by an Arab Zodiac.

The Major Planets of Christendom *right*
Above the cross in this 11th-century MS the Sun and Moon flank the hand of God.

St Augustine *far right*
St Augustine, formerly a believer in astrology, later violently attacked it as a form of evil magic.

Arab Astrolabe *below*
A planispheric astrolabe made in 1236 by Abd al-Karim Misri for charting the planets.

THE MEDIEVAL CALENDAR

The lunar month, the common basis of many early calendars, was superseded in Roman times. With the help of Egyptian astronomers from Alexandria, Julius Caesar laid down the Julian calendar in 46 BC, which was still in use in Renaissance Europe. Caesar, using the solar rotation as his guide, fixed the length of the year at 365¼ days, and decreed that every fourth year should have 366 days, the others 365. In medieval times the year was also divided between the different Signs. The Zodiacal months did not, however, exactly coincide with solar months, but ran from the Spring equinox at around 21 March; individual months were considered as part of the agricultural year, revealing the extremely important role of agriculture in medieval life. The illustrations arranged round the sun-dial below, from a Norman French Book of Hours of the 15th century, show the months and the occupations that were associated with the Signs.

Cancer the Crab
Approximately 21 June to 21 July. The picture shows a labourer scything grass for the hay harvest. A sharpening stone hangs from his belt.

Gemini the Twins
21 May to 21 June. Hawking on horseback for birds and small animals was a favourite past-time of the aristocracy in the 15th century.

Taurus the Bull
21 April to 21 May. The custom of collecting branches to decorate the streets and houses on May Day still survives in some places.

Aries the Ram
21 March to 21 April. This is the period for clearing away old vines and preparing the ground for new ones.

Leo the Lion
21 July to 21 August. Wheat was harvested by hand with small reaping hooks, gathered into sheaves and built into stooks for drying out.

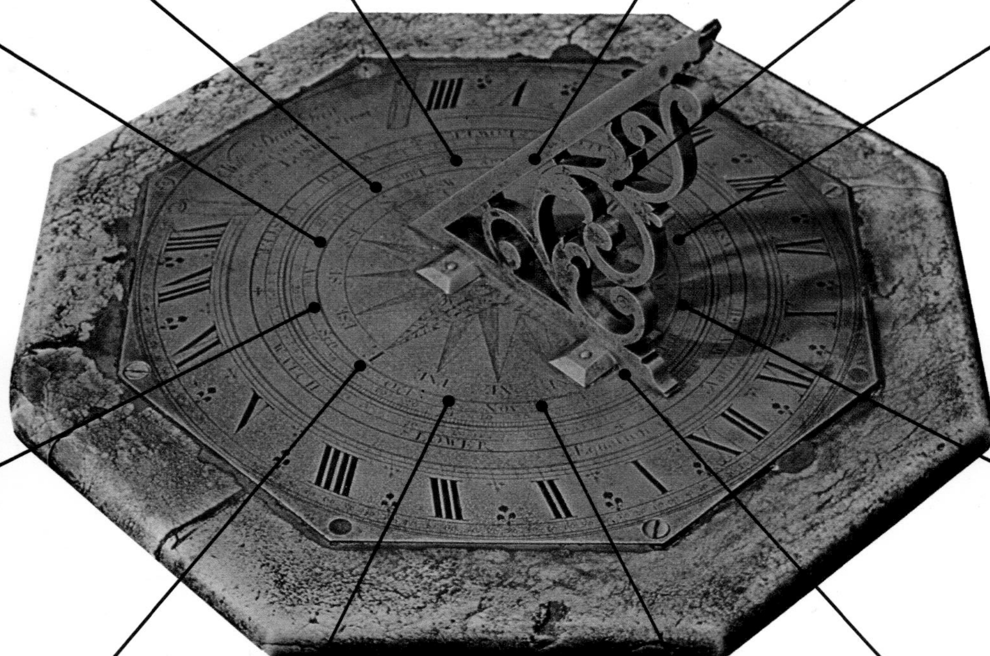

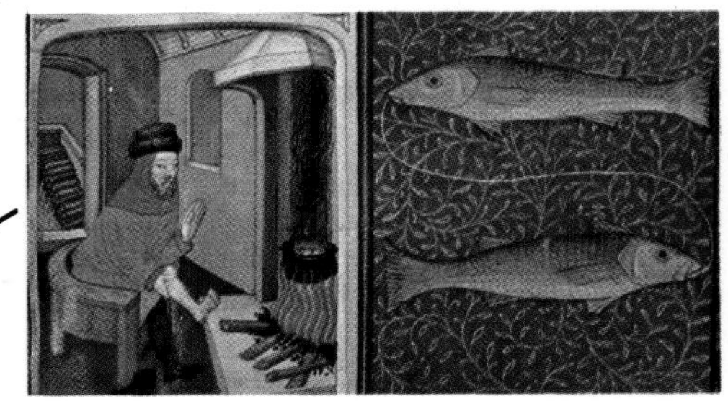

Pisces the Fish
21 February to 21 March. A quiet time on the farm because of the weather. The best thing to do after collecting the firewood is to relax.

Virgo the Virgin

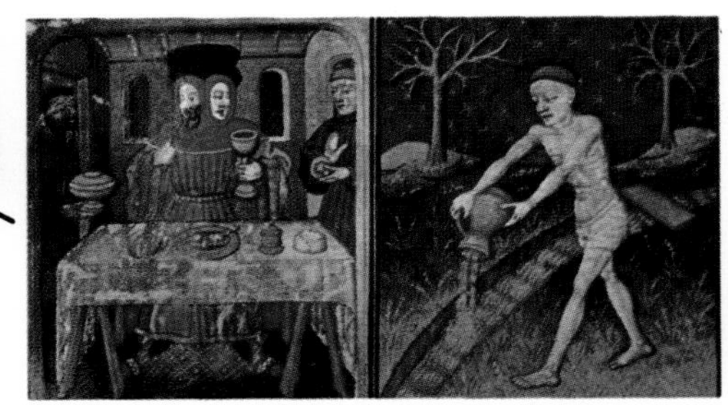

Aquarius the Waterbearer

Libra the Scales
21 September to 21 October. After the grape harvest the grapes are put into wide, shallow barrels and crushed to extract the juice.

Scorpio the Scorpion
21 October to 21 November. This is the best time for sowing, especially on clay land. Note the ridge and furrow strips common in feudal times.

Sagittarius the Archer
21 November to 21 December. It was common practice to let the pigs loose in the woods and fatten them on acorns and sweet chestnuts.

Capricorn the Goat
21 December to 21 January. When winter fodder grew scarce, only the best animals were kept for breeding; all the rest were slaughtered.

The Development of the Calendar

Agriculture provided the main impetus for the earliest calendars. Nearly every task on the farm has to be completed in sequence and at its proper time, in order to make the most of weather conditions, the natural characteristics of plants, etc. It is no use sowing wheat in June, for instance, because it will not have time to ripen before winter. The need to establish a regular pattern and timetable, therefore, was felt almost as soon as man started settled farming. The inspiration came from the visible fixed cycles man saw around him, the solar day, the solar year and the lunar month. Originally, in Sumeria and Assyria, for instance, the year was organized round the 12 lunar revolutions – 354 days – that approximated to one solar rotation of 365 days. However, the gradual but increasing discrepancy between the two necessitated some form of correction; in the case of the Babylonians, an extra month was added. The Egyptian calendar also needed rectifying. The year began with the rising of the star Sirius, which coincided with the flooding of the Nile valley, the fount of Egyptian prosperity. But the system became confused because every four years Sirius rose one day late. The Greeks, when the lunar cycle got out of step, officially slipped in three additional months, though many individuals kept private calendars relying on idiosyncratic systems of pegs stuck in tablets, with the result that one man's Tuesday was, as often as not, another man's Friday week. The Romans, as was seen above, were the first to tackle the problem seriously, instituting the Julian calendar in 46 BC, based on the solar rotation.

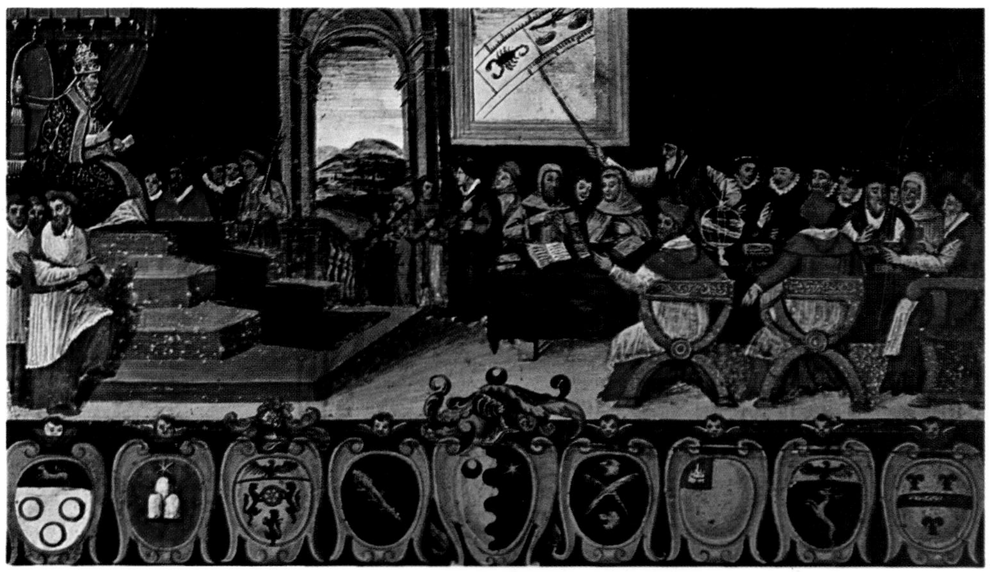

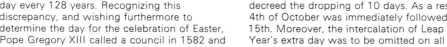

Zodiacal Clock *above*
This ancient clock shows the hours, then the months and finally the Signs of the Zodiac. Phases of the Moon appear in the Sun's halo.

German Calendar *above*
This 15th-century calendar shows the relationships between the seven days of the week (centre) and the planets and their attributes.

The Gregorian Calendar *centre*
The Julian calendar originated by Julius Caesar proved to be 11 minutes 14 seconds a year out of step with the Sun, producing an error of one day every 128 years. Recognizing this discrepancy, and wishing furthermore to determine the day for the celebration of Easter, Pope Gregory XIII called a council in 1582 and decreed the dropping of 10 days. As a result the 4th of October was immediately followed by the 15th. Moreover, the intercalation of Leap Year's extra day was to be omitted on all centenary years except for multiples of 400. The 'loss' was extremely unpopular, the new calendar not being adopted in Britain until 1752, 1918 in Russia and 1923 in Greece.

ASTROLOGY IN THE MIDDLE AGES

'Every astrologer is worthy of praise and honour, because he has found favour with God, his Maker, since by such a doctrine as his astronomy he probably knows many secrets of God, and things which few know' – from the *Liber Introductorius* of Michael Scott (d.1235).

At the beginning of the Middle Ages one problem faced by theologians was whether to class astrology as a legitimate science or as a forbidden divinatory art. John of Salisbury (*c*.1115–80) decided that, in its wider prophetic claims and its apparent denial of free will, astrology usurped the prerogative of the stars' very Creator. It was left to St Albertus Magnus (*c*.1200–80) finally to dissociate astrology from its pagan associations.

Albertus was the first to realize the theological value of Greek and Arab science and philosophy. His great achievement was to make this knowledge available to Western civilization, in particular the teachings of Aristotle; and the doctrine that earthly events were governed by the stellar spheres was central to that teaching. While the stars could not influence the human soul, Albertus concluded, they could certainly influence the body and the human will.

St Thomas Aquinas (*c*.1225–74), perhaps the greatest of all Christian theologians, further crystallized Albertus' work. Astrology, so long as it excluded the elements of necromancy, was now acceptable as a subject worthy of intellectual study; and could, moreover, be seen as complementing the then recognized Church doctrine in its view of the universe.

The Academic Discipline

The academic respectability which astrology now enjoyed was reflected in the great new European universities, where astrological studies acquired a place in the curricula. The University of Bologna, at which Dante and Petrarch studied, had had a chair of astrology since 1125. To become qualified in astrology was quite as much a challenge as any other branch of learning, and the astrologer was regarded with the greatest respect.

Yet, as the Middle Ages proceeded, there was an increasing tendency for astrologers to overstretch their case. Guido Bonatti, perhaps the best-known 13th-century astrologer, who wrote a popular textbook, was in the service of the Count Guido de Montefeltro. At the outset of the count's military campaigns, Bonatti would, by reference to the stars, strike a bell for the army to put on its armour; and again for it to mount; and a third time for it to gallop off. Bonatti and Michael Scott were pilloried by Dante in the *Inferno*. But Dante's complaint was that they mixed necromancy with science; he restored astrology to a dignified position in the later books of *The Divine Comedy*.

When, in 1327, Bologna's Professor of Astrology, Cecco d'Ascoli, was burnt at the stake and provided astrology with one of its few martyrs, he died because of his heretical views, not his profession. As the Renaissance took hold, there was little falling-off in astrology's popularity, indeed support was to come from the papacy itself.

Philosophers and Astronomers *above*
The distrust with which astrology and science were regarded by some orthodox churchmen is shown in this 12th-century MS, which satirizes the vanity of philosophers and astronomers.

Sixtus IV *left*
A number of popes adopted astrological practices with enthusiasm. Sixtus IV (1414–84), seen here in a portrait by Titian, was the first pope to draw up and interpret a horoscope.

Julius II *above*
By the early days of the Renaissance, astrology had won an immense popular following throughout Europe, and particularly in Rome. The scholarly Pope Julius II is known to have consulted an astrologer to help him select the most propitious day for his coronation.

Medieval Shepherd *left*
The shepherd, depicted in this 15th-century woodcut, uses a makeshift rope plumb-line to tell the time at night by reference to the position of a known star.

'The celestial bodies are the cause of all that takes place in the sublunar world.'
St Thomas Aquinas (1225–74)

The Wife of Bath *above*
Chaucer's Wife of Bath, one of the most full-blooded characters in *The Canterbury Tales*, peppered her story with astrological references: 'Venus me yaf my lust, my Likerousness, and Mars yaf me my sturdy Hardinesse. Myn ascendant was Taur, and Mars therinne. Allas! allas! that ever love was sinne!'

A Medieval Cosmology *right*
In this representation of the universe, medieval astrology reaches out of the known world to gain knowledge of the unknown.

St Thomas Aquinas *right*
St Thomas Aquinas was one of the outstanding medieval figures to endorse astrology.

Sun and Moon in Chariots *below*
The Sun drawn by four horses (traditionally the four seasons) and the Moon by two oxen.

Amerigo Vespucci *right*
Vespucci the navigator is shown using an astrolabe to plot the Southern Cross. The four southern stars were earlier described by Dante in his great masterpiece, the *Inferno*, written *c.*1314.

The Planets *above*
This 12th-century illustration shows the five known planets: grouped round the Sun, above, are Mars, Saturn and Jupiter; below, Venus and Mercury flank the Moon.

ANATOMY AND THE ZODIAC

Since time immemorial, each Sign of the Zodiac has had a special relationship to a specific area of the body, from Aries (the head) to Pisces (the feet). More recent astrologically orientated medical thought has underlined relationships between the Signs and the glandular and nervous systems. These often relate through *polarity*: that is, the Arian may be affected by the illnesses tending to affect the parts of the body ruled by the opposite Sign, Libra: so his headaches may be directly related to the kidney functions, which fall under Libran influence.

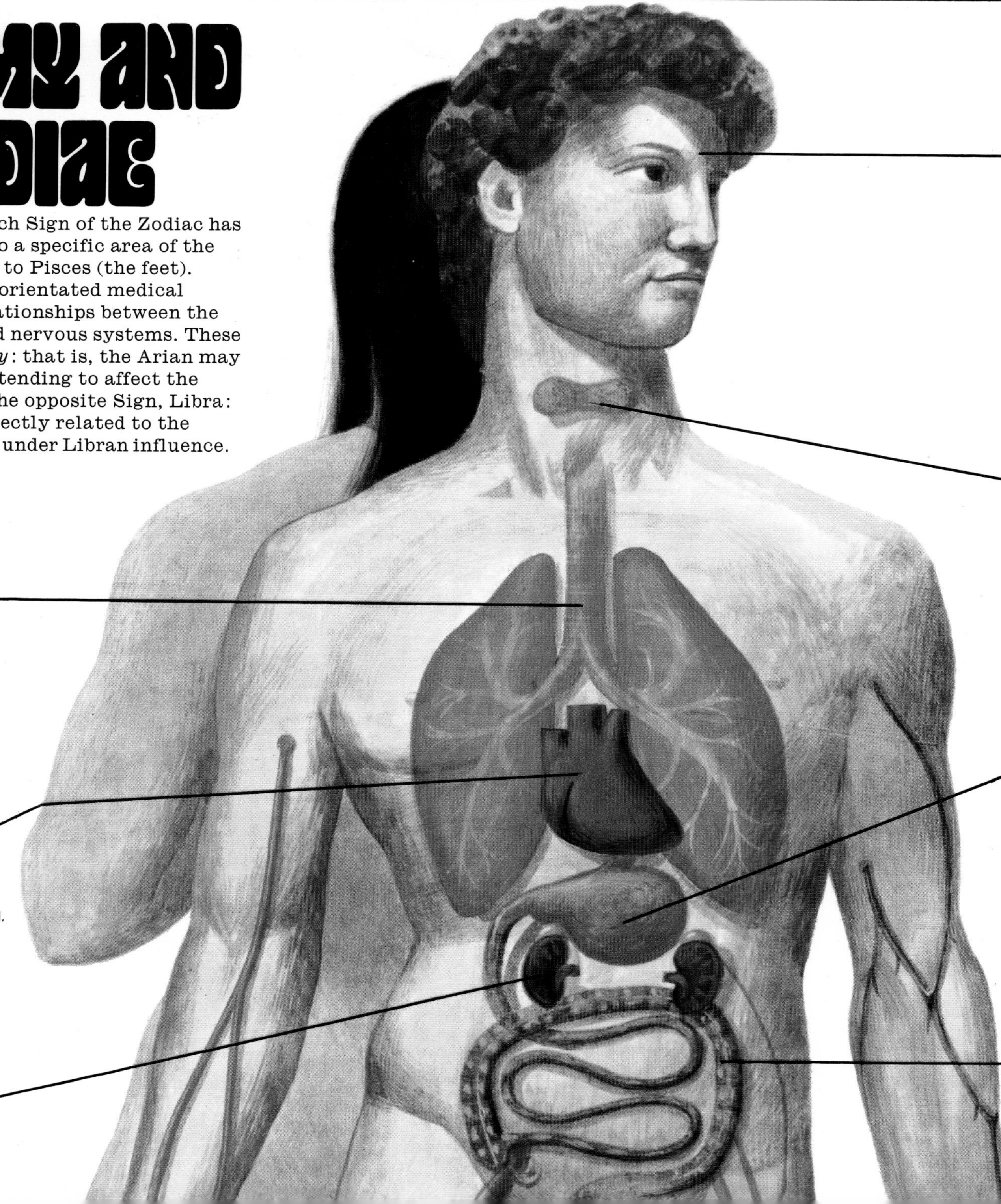

Aries-Libra
Aries rules the head. Arians often, as a result, suffer from headaches. The Arian glands are the subrenals which pump adrenalin into the blood stream in the event of an emergency – such as a rush of Arian anger or energy – giving Arians their reputation for impetuosity.

Taurus-Scorpio
Taurus rules the throat and neck. This makes them particularly vulnerable to colds and chills. The Taurean gland is the thyroid and any malfunction of this will cause serious weight problems.

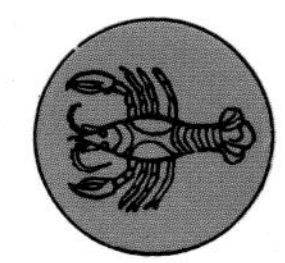

Cancer-Capricorn
Cancer rules the stomach and alimentary canal. With the Cancerian tendency to get upset and worry more than most, they are prone to indigestion and ulcers, which gives them their reputation for delicate health. The mammary glands are attributed to Cancer, the Sign of motherhood.

Virgo-Pisces
Virgo rules the nervous system and intestines. Virgoans suffer from the same bowel and stomach ailments as Cancerians. They tend to worry, again like Cancerians, though in their case the tendency is closely allied to nervous tension. A balanced diet is essential

Gemini-Sagittarius
Gemini rules the nerves, arms and shoulders; Geminians are, therefore, prone to break collar-bones and arms. This Sign also rules the lungs, and colds can often develop into bronchitis. Geminians are restless and 'live on their nerves'.

Leo-Aquarius
Leo rules the heart, spine and back. With the Leonine tendency to live life to the full, they should be especially careful to 'slow up' in middle age: otherwise there is a risk of a heart attack.

Libra-Aries
Libra rules the kidneys. Any disturbance of the usually sensitive and well-balanced Libran way of life, through an accident or argument, is soon reflected in a serious kidney upset.

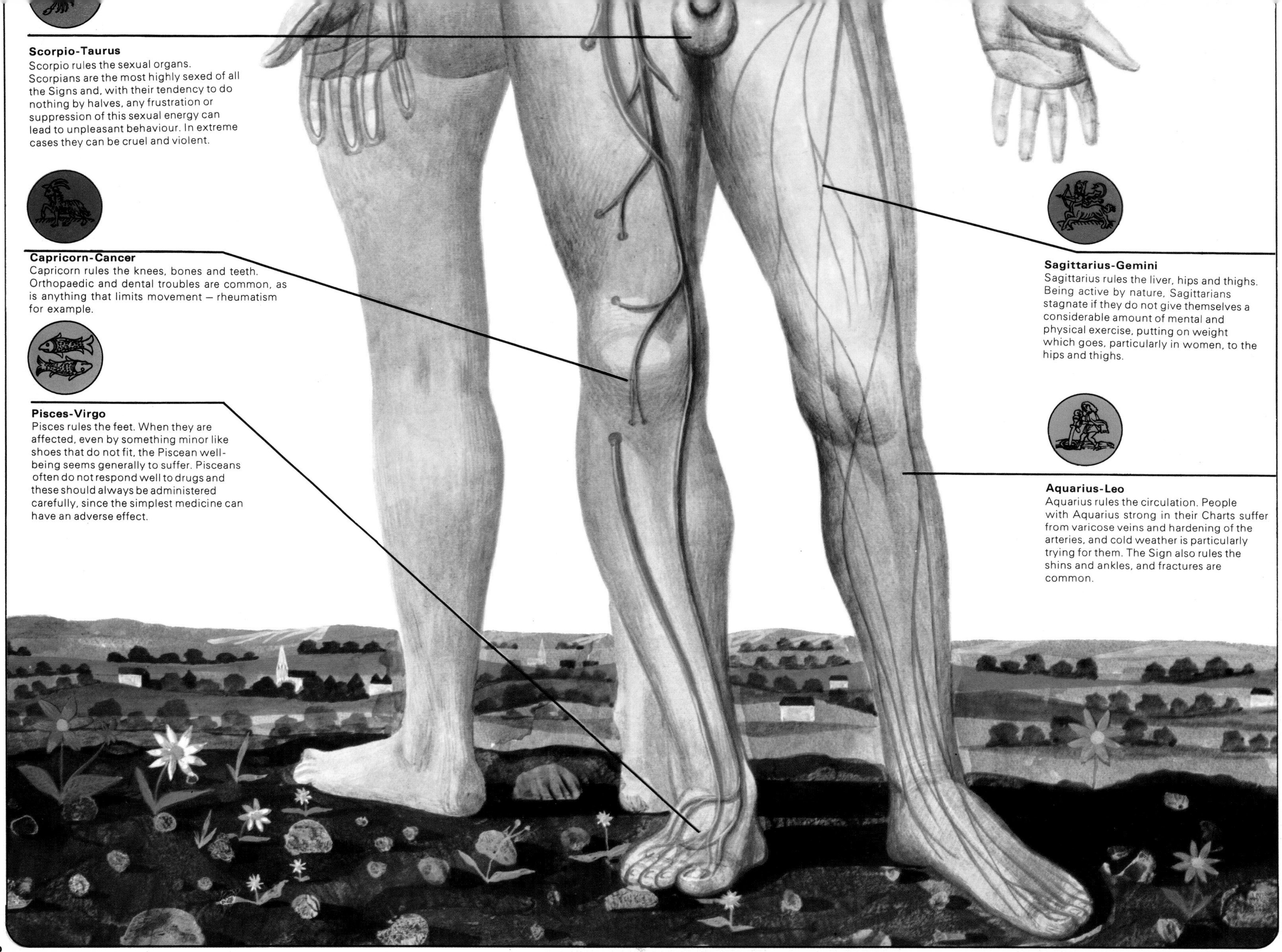

Scorpio-Taurus
Scorpio rules the sexual organs. Scorpians are the most highly sexed of all the Signs and, with their tendency to do nothing by halves, any frustration or suppression of this sexual energy can lead to unpleasant behaviour. In extreme cases they can be cruel and violent.

Capricorn-Cancer
Capricorn rules the knees, bones and teeth. Orthopaedic and dental troubles are common, as is anything that limits movement – rheumatism for example.

Pisces-Virgo
Pisces rules the feet. When they are affected, even by something minor like shoes that do not fit, the Piscean well-being seems generally to suffer. Pisceans often do not respond well to drugs and these should always be administered carefully, since the simplest medicine can have an adverse effect.

Sagittarius-Gemini
Sagittarius rules the liver, hips and thighs. Being active by nature, Sagittarians stagnate if they do not give themselves a considerable amount of mental and physical exercise, putting on weight which goes, particularly in women, to the hips and thighs.

Aquarius-Leo
Aquarius rules the circulation. People with Aquarius strong in their Charts suffer from varicose veins and hardening of the arteries, and cold weather is particularly trying for them. The Sign also rules the shins and ankles, and fractures are common.

ASTROLOGY AND HEALTH

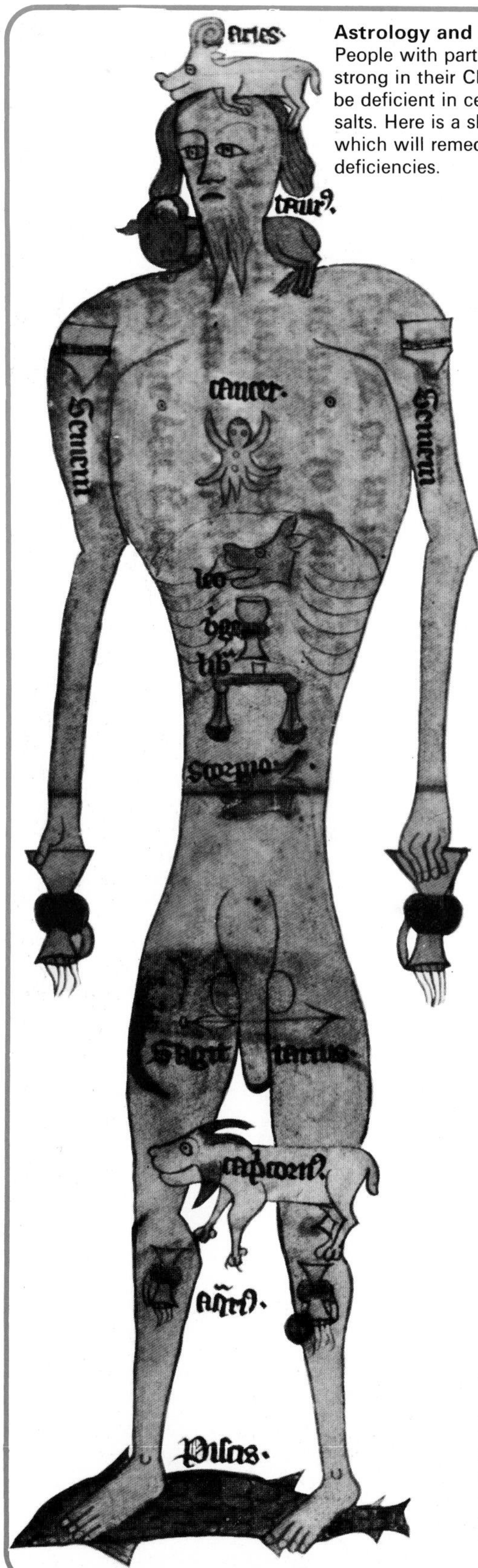

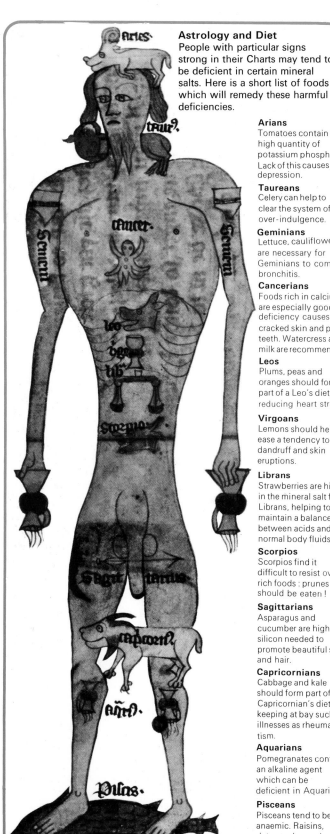

Astrology and Diet
People with particular signs strong in their Charts may tend to be deficient in certain mineral salts. Here is a short list of foods which will remedy these harmful deficiencies.

Arians
Tomatoes contain a high quantity of potassium phosphate. Lack of this causes depression.

Taureans
Celery can help to clear the system of over-indulgence.

Geminians
Lettuce, cauliflower are necessary for Geminians to combat bronchitis.

Cancerians
Foods rich in calcium are especially good; deficiency causes cracked skin and poor teeth. Watercress and milk are recommended.

Leos
Plums, peas and oranges should form part of a Leo's diet, reducing heart strain.

Virgoans
Lemons should help ease a tendency to dandruff and skin eruptions.

Librans
Strawberries are high in the mineral salt for Librans, helping to maintain a balance between acids and normal body fluids.

Scorpios
Scorpios find it difficult to resist over-rich foods: prunes should be eaten!

Sagittarians
Asparagus and cucumber are high in silicon needed to promote beautiful skin and hair.

Capricornians
Cabbage and kale should form part of a Capricornian's diet, keeping at bay such illnesses as rheumatism.

Aquarians
Pomegranates contain an alkaline agent which can be deficient in Aquarians.

Pisceans
Pisceans tend to be anaemic. Raisins, dates and cereals help restore them.

Close bonds have always existed between medicine and astrology. Indeed, until the 18th century the two sciences were inextricably mixed, a study of astrology being, as a matter of course, part of a doctor's training and a vital element in his treatment of disease. A Chart was drawn up for the moment a patient took to his bed, and served as a guide to when the crisis would come and what medicine to give. The various parts of the body were considered to be under the rulership of specific Signs (see p. 26) and planets (p. 30) which were also associated with specific diseases. An individual's health was strongly influenced by his Birth Chart and with due care and attention, eating the right food, for example, he could avoid certain illnesses. However, astrology has over the centuries formed *liaisons dangereuses* with several pseudo-sciences which have often brought it into disrepute.

Hermetic Medicine

Astrological medicine was first formalized in the writings of Hermes Trismegistos, the name the Greeks gave to the Egyptian god, Thoth. Although some of the lore it contained is still adhered to, this collection put forward the view that man reproduced in himself in miniature (microcosm) the structure of the universe (macrocosm). It further held that different ailments were specific to the different decans, or 10° divisions of the Signs. Stomach troubles, for instance, were indicated in the first decanate of Virgo.

The Four Humours

The Greek doctor/philosopher Hippocrates (born *c.*460 BC) proposed that man's character was the result of the balance of four 'humours', blood, phlegm, black bile and yellow bile. These four were loosely linked in astrology with the triplicities – the four groups of Signs: fiery, earthy, airy and watery. These connections have not always been welcomed, however, since at times they are wildly wrong. Gemini, for example, is an 'airy' Sign and therefore 'sanguine'; but the melancholic humour (black bile) is connected with Mercury, the ruler of Gemini, and sorrow, slowness and weakness are scarcely part of the Mercurial character.

Culpeper's Herbal Remedies

The Arabs were the first to link the curative qualities of herbs with specific Signs or planets. Various systems of attribution were used to decide which planet should rule a herb, generally through the triplicities. Mars, for instance, was considered hot and dry and so rules plants with a hot or pungent taste – hellebore, tobacco or mustard. The *Complete Herbal* by Nicholas Culpeper (1616–54) attributes herbs according to the diseases they cured. Agrimony was good for liver complaints; Jupiter rules the liver; therefore Jupiter rules agrimony. Each planet became in turn 'lord of a day'. (Sun/Sunday, Moon/Monday, etc.), and herbs gathered on their planet's 'day', particularly during the first and eighth hour, were at their most effective.

'A physician without a knowledge of astrology has no right to call himself a physician.'
Hippocrates (born *c*.460 BC)

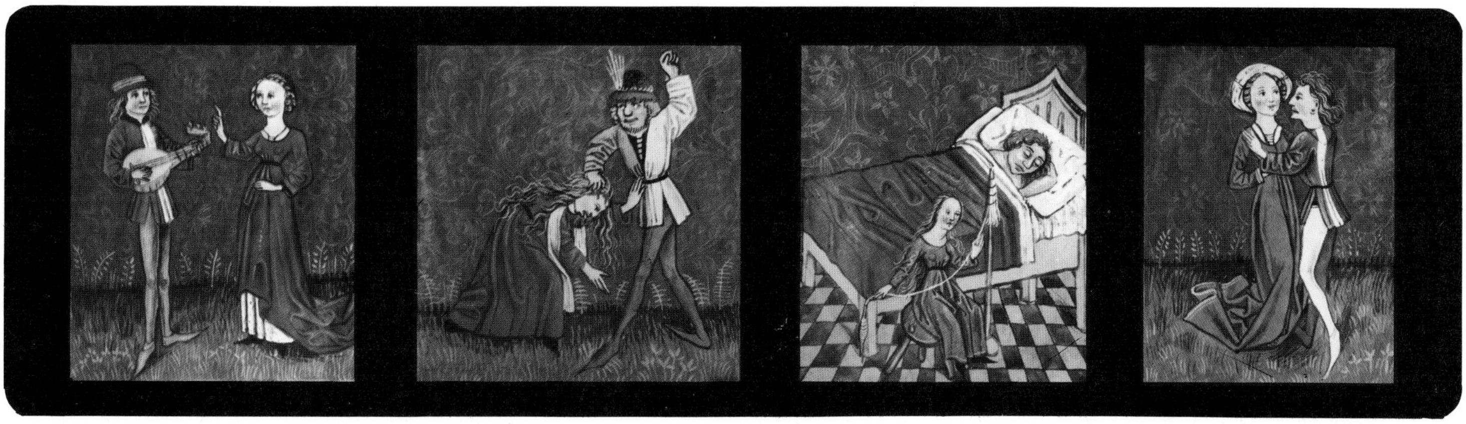

The Four Humours
Interpretations of the four 'humours', as first expounded over two thousand years ago. They are blood, phlegm, yellow bile and black bile, and the combination of them in the body controls the personality. So a man with a preponderance of blood was said to be sanguine, right, being quick, predisposed to pleasant emotions, but weak and given to sudden changes. A phlegmatic man, centre right, was slow, lacking in vivacity, but calm and strong; a choleric man having yellow bile, centre left, was liable to anger, emotionally quick and strong; and, left, a melancholic man (black bile) was given to sadness and weakness.

Culpeper's Herbal
Culpeper insisted that the Chart of an illness should be drawn up for the time of the *first* symptoms. This done and the treatment prescribed, the herbs were collected on the right day and hour, and administered sometimes externally, sometimes powdered, sometimes distilled. The *Herbal* itself must be consulted before any rash experiments!

Aries
Briony (purging; cramps; stitches) (1); crowfoot (drawing a blister); honeysuckle (biliousness) (2); nettles (pleurisy; sore throat); rhubarb (mild purgative).

Taurus
Arrack (swellings of the throat); beans (the water good for the complexion; half a bean will stop a cut bleeding); elder (root cures adder-sting; flowers boiled, water calms sunburn) (3).

Gemini
Carrot (helps conception); fern (swollen spleen; makes ointment for cuts or prickles) (4); haresfoot (diarrhoea and dysentery); lavender (headache, toothache; fainting; apoplexy and dropsy) (5).

Cancer
Flax (inflammation, tumours; diseases of the chest and lungs) (6); privet (sore mouths; treating sores); saxifrage (stomach weakness, cramps, convulsions; the leaves give a good flavour to wine) (6).

Leo
Bay (berries good for cold, rheumatism; 'they mightily expel the wind'); celandine (piles and haemorrhoids) (7); walnuts (pain and inflammation of the ears).

Virgo
Caraway (helps digestion, sharpens the eyesight) (8); horehound (consumption, pain in the side, yellow jaundice) (9); myrtle (stops the spitting of blood; diarrhoea and dysentery).

Libra
Asparagus (expels the stone; 'stirreth up lust'); chestnuts (the cough); daisy (pleurisy and pneumonia) (10); garden mint (hiccoughs).

Scorpio
Broom (clears the chest) (11); furze (jaundice, cleaning the kidneys); hops (cleanse the blood; cure venereal disease) (12); tobacco (rheumatic pains; toothache; powdered, kills lice).

Sagittarius
Betony (removes spots from face and hands) (13); borage (clarifies the blood; fortifies); dandelion (cleans the urinary passages); moss (eases inflammations).

Capricorn
Amaranthus (stops all bleeding) (14); beet (burns, weals, blisters); hemlock (roasted, good for gout and inflammations: very dangerous) (15); onion (coughs; earache; 'increases the sperm').

Aquarius
Heartsease (good for convulsions in children) (16); hemp (expels the wind, but makes men sterile; kills worms); medlar (stops miscarriages); quince (sore mouths).

Pisces
Dock (cleans the blood, strengthens the liver; takes away freckles) (17); fig (removes warts, chilblains); sage (blackens the hair; cures headaches); succory ('drives forth cholera') (18).

ANATOMY AND THE PLANETS

In medieval times it was recognized that each of the planets was connected with a specific part of the body. As medicine has advanced it has discovered a whole new range of small, extremely important endocrine glands that release hormones into the blood. These control body functions as diverse as breathing and erection. Astrologers have established special relationships between these glands and individual planets. Unknown at the time were the three outer planets. Usually associated with 'generation' influences, they have also been linked with specific areas of the body.

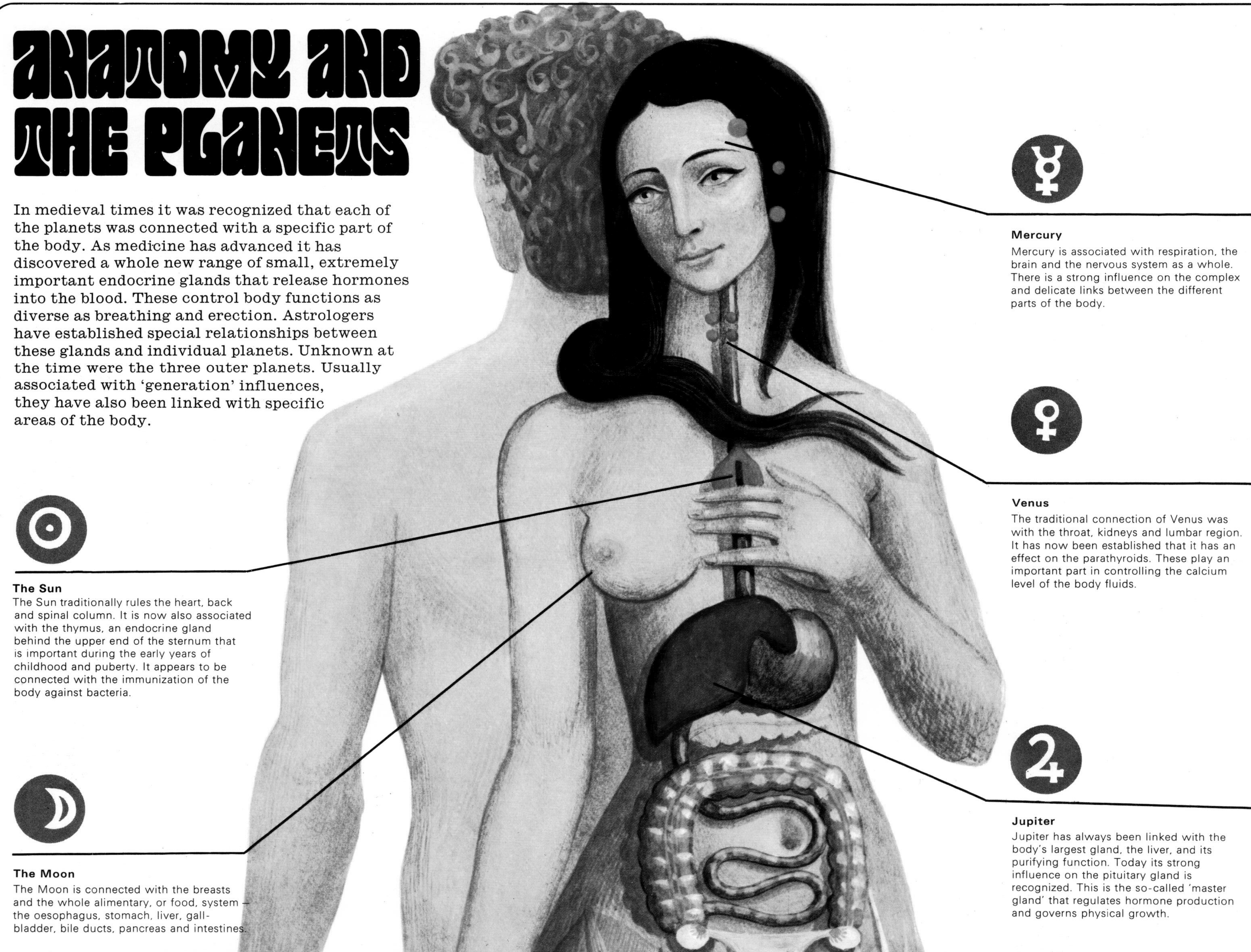

The Sun
The Sun traditionally rules the heart, back and spinal column. It is now also associated with the thymus, an endocrine gland behind the upper end of the sternum that is important during the early years of childhood and puberty. It appears to be connected with the immunization of the body against bacteria.

The Moon
The Moon is connected with the breasts and the whole alimentary, or food, system – the oesophagus, stomach, liver, gall-bladder, bile ducts, pancreas and intestines.

Mercury
Mercury is associated with respiration, the brain and the nervous system as a whole. There is a strong influence on the complex and delicate links between the different parts of the body.

Venus
The traditional connection of Venus was with the throat, kidneys and lumbar region. It has now been established that it has an effect on the parathyroids. These play an important part in controlling the calcium level of the body fluids.

Jupiter
Jupiter has always been linked with the body's largest gland, the liver, and its purifying function. Today its strong influence on the pituitary gland is recognized. This is the so-called 'master gland' that regulates hormone production and governs physical growth.

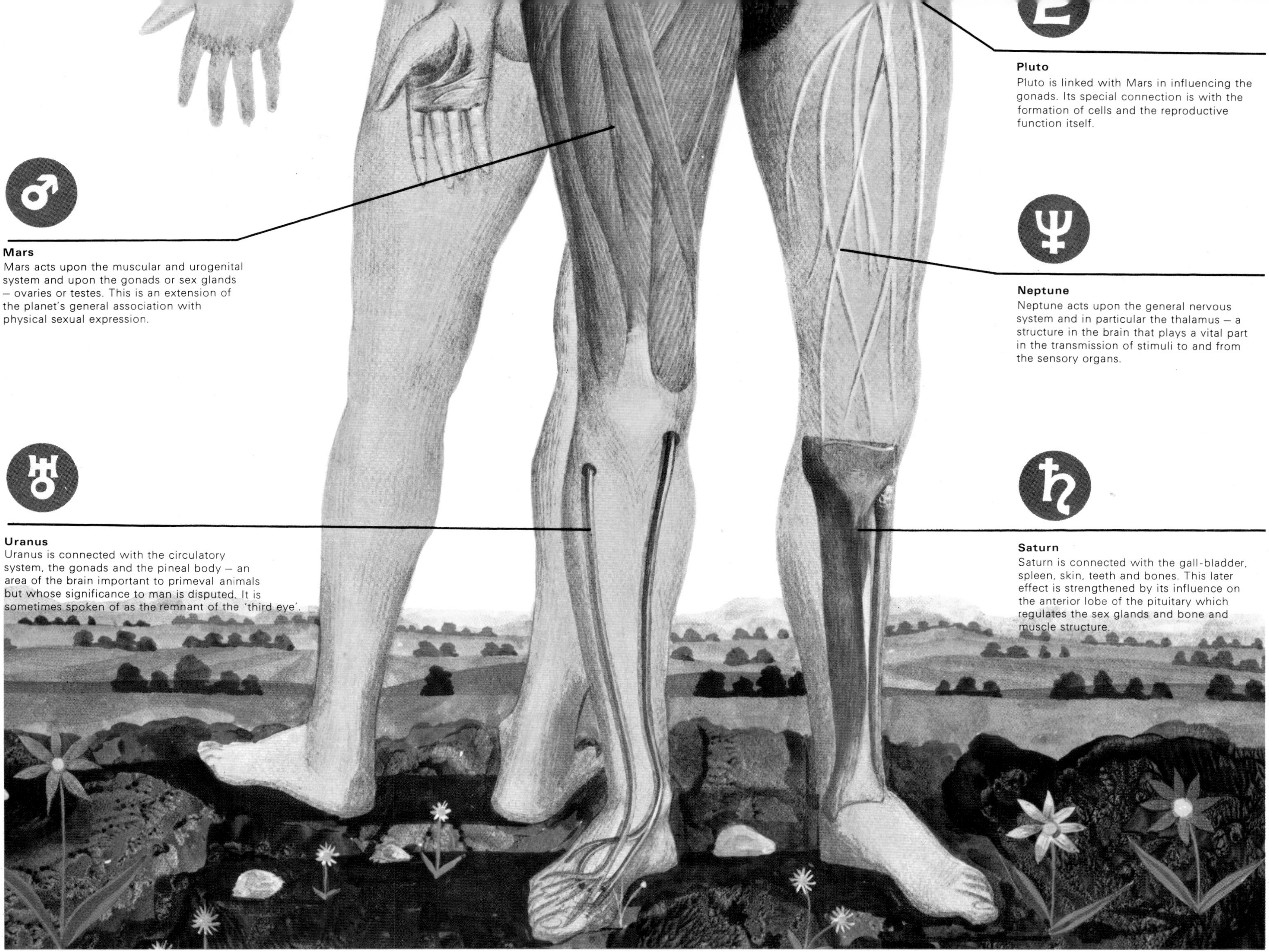

Mars
Mars acts upon the muscular and urogenital system and upon the gonads or sex glands – ovaries or testes. This is an extension of the planet's general association with physical sexual expression.

Uranus
Uranus is connected with the circulatory system, the gonads and the pineal body – an area of the brain important to primeval animals but whose significance to man is disputed. It is sometimes spoken of as the remnant of the 'third eye'.

Pluto
Pluto is linked with Mars in influencing the gonads. Its special connection is with the formation of cells and the reproductive function itself.

Neptune
Neptune acts upon the general nervous system and in particular the thalamus – a structure in the brain that plays a vital part in the transmission of stimuli to and from the sensory organs.

Saturn
Saturn is connected with the gall-bladder, spleen, skin, teeth and bones. This later effect is strengthened by its influence on the anterior lobe of the pituitary which regulates the sex glands and bone and muscle structure.

ASTROLOGY AND SUPERSTITION

Throughout his history, man has tried to interpret signs that he believes might offer him a glimpse round the corner of time and into the future. In practice our ability to predict future events is limited by our incomplete grasp of how the world and, beyond it, the universe works and what are the precise mechanisms that stimulate human action and reaction; also by the existence of free will – the degree to which our deeds are purely the product of conscious decision and how we exercise this choice of action.

Serious astrologers have always accepted these limitations. They predict trends rather than actual events, working in broad areas of time rather than offering specific dates. There are, however, almost as many dishonourable forms of prediction as there are dishonourable practitioners. Given a perpetually curious, often ignorant, certainly superstitious clientele to work on, vast numbers of fakers and flatterers have in the past made a more-than-adequate living out of human weakness and fear of the unknown. Some have used the name of astrology to describe their work; others have devised new cures for uncertainty, or perpetuated the false myths and superstitions of previous generations. Yet others – the supporters of the macrocosm-microcosm theory, for example – have tried to bring order to an unruly universe, but failed badly in the attempt through their own faulty reasoning.

One way of attempting to gain an insight into the future and, by so doing achieve a mastery in some measure over the hidden terrors of the universe, is to obtain information and guidance from extra-terrestial forces. The most common and well-known is perhaps the medium who goes into a trance to bring back a message from the dead. Like the clairvoyant who tries to see the future in a crystal ball, mediums who use this method with some form of glass-rattling, chandelier-quivering or table-tapping as a sign of communication from the desired spirit, are at the end of a long line of occult practitioners. They relate back at least as far as the Greek oracles – those shrines to superstititious activity at which questions about

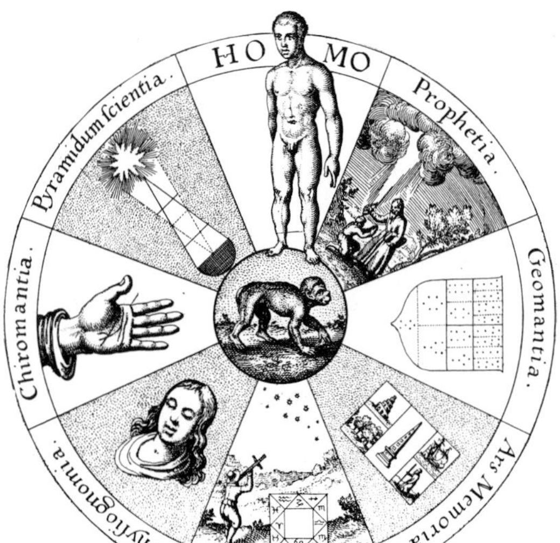

The Street Fortune-Teller *right*
In this 18th-century portrait by Pietro Longhi, a young girl offers her palm to a street fortune-teller. Palmistry, or cheiromancy, was practised 5,000 years ago in China, where the soles of the feet were also examined. In Europe, from the 16th century, palmistry offered a further irresistible avenue to students of the occult and the harmonious notion of macrocosm and microcosm.

The Diviners' Arts *above*
A synopsis of the divinatory arts, including prophecy, geomancy, astrology and palmistry; the diagram is taken from Robert Fludd's *History of the Microcosm* (1617–19).

Early Omens *right*
Part of a 6th-century BC inscription from Ephesus (Turkey), ruled by King Croesus of Lydia, describing omens which were taken from the flight of birds.

Physiognomy
In physiognomy an elaborate code separated, for example, the foreheads of, left, a vicious woman; centre, a sick man and, right, an intelligent man.

anything, from the loss of a jewel to weighty affairs of state such as alliances or declarations of war, could be asked of a particular god and the answer received through the mouth of his priest.

Macrocosm and Microcosm

Seeing man as a microcosm who reflects in his parts the macrocosm or the universe which surrounds him, is a philosophical concept which goes back to before Socrates (*c*.470–399 BC). It was passed down into the Renaissance tradition via the Hermetic texts. Given the dubious hypothesis that man *is* a microcosm, it is then a simple step of the imagination to try and relate his intellect, imagination and senses to specific stellar influences. From this sprang the divinatory art of physiognomy, which seeks to read a man's fate from his facial characteristics. Thus a primarily false notion honourably conceived, degenerated into a pseudo-science having little value, but considerable power to mislead the unwary.

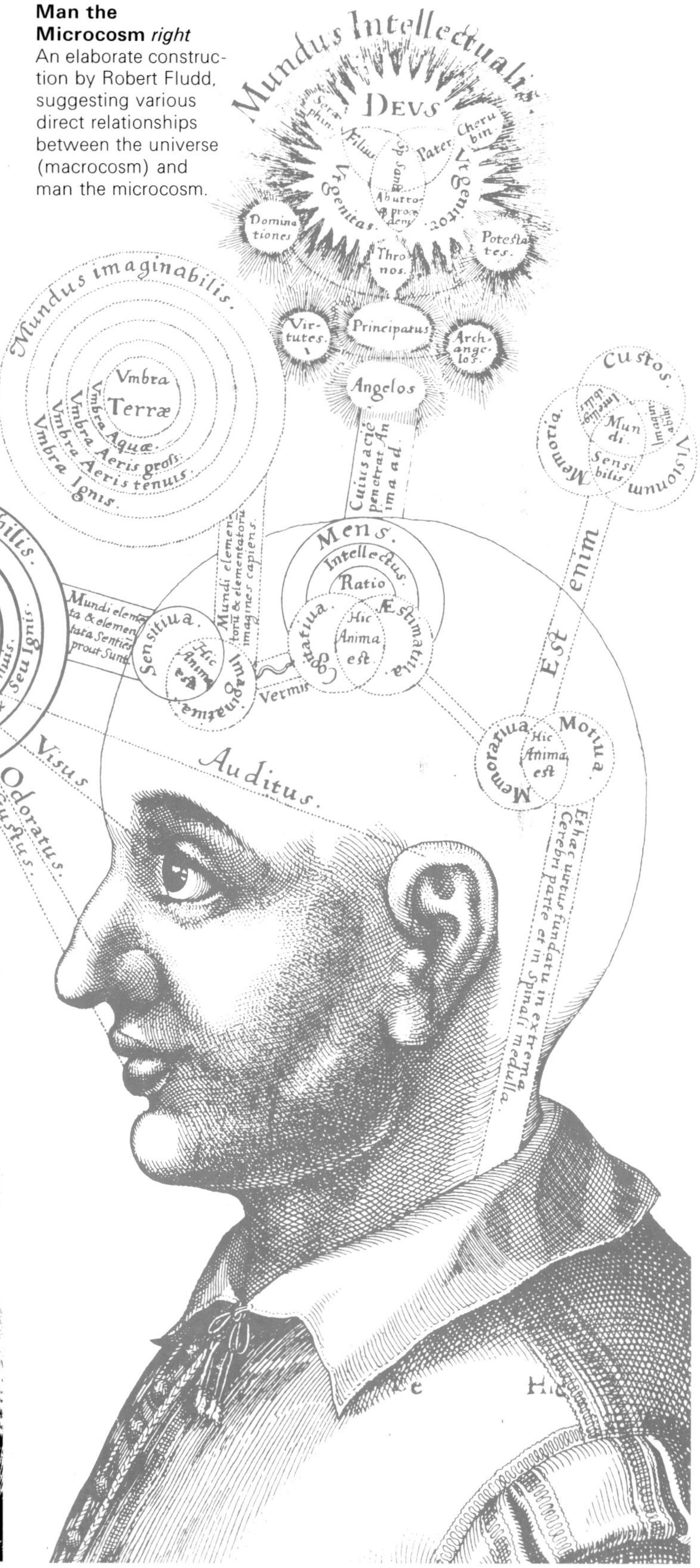

Man the Microcosm *right*
An elaborate construction by Robert Fludd, suggesting various direct relationships between the universe (macrocosm) and man the microcosm.

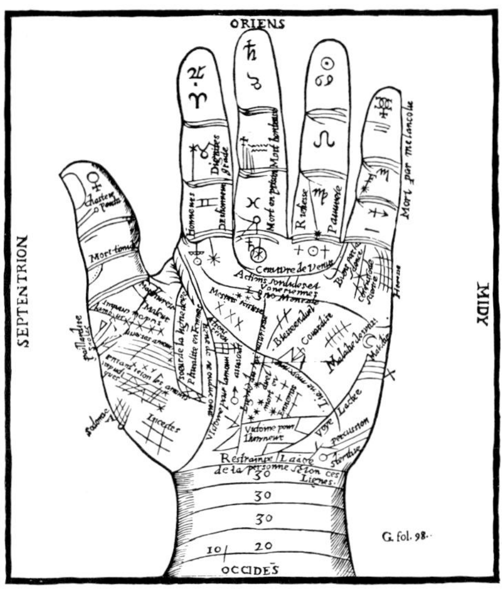

The Celestial Palm *left*
A 17th-century French chart shows the main features interpreted by palmists. Each finger-tip is marked by a planet, from left to right, Venus, Jupiter, Saturn, Sun, Mercury. Other areas of the palm are associated with the Zodiac.

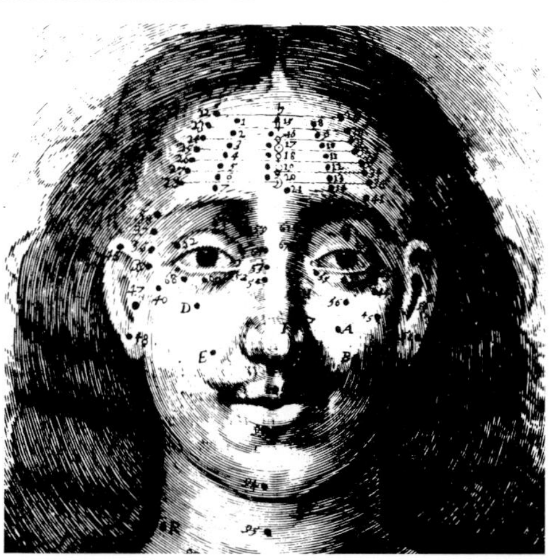

Metoscopy *right*
Lines on the brow and/or moles on the face and body are regarded by adherents of metoscopy as the 'stars of the body', throwing light on the individual's character. Traditionally they are indicated by planetary glyphs. In this 17th-century print the face is built up entirely from circles, perhaps implying a reflection in man of the planets' circular paths round the Sun.

ASTROLOGY IN POWER

Astrology owed its prosperity in the Renaissance period in part at least to the Church and to the positive encouragement it received from several popes. It has been said that one of the reasons why Luther was so opposed to astrology was because it was so much in fashion in the Vatican.

The first popes to engage actively in astrology had been Sixtus IV and Julius II. Julius' successor, Leo X, brought a bevy of astrologers into the papal court to advise him throughout his reign. Paul III (1468–1549), the first pope of the Counter-Reformation, used astrologers to fix the hours for his Consistory. Even Urban VIII (1568–1644), who published a Bull against some aspects of astrology, remained the patron of individual astrologers, who helped him in his private political intrigues.

The example set by the papacy was followed in the leading courts of Europe. In England Queen Elizabeth I took daily advice from the extraordinary Dr Dee, and Christian IV of Denmark, Sigismund III of Sweden and Frederick of Bohemia all employed court astrologers.

A French physician, Nostradamus, became the prophet of his age after predicting the death of the French king Henri II in a tournament four years before it happened. The king's widow, Catherine de Medici, took him into her court circle. Nostradamus, however, was more necromancer than astrologer, and is said to have conducted with the queen a seance which lasted for 45 consecutive nights. Eventually he managed to conjure up a spirit to show her the future. She saw each of her three sons pass briefly across a mirror, once for each year they would reign. Then her son-in-law, the Protestant Henri de Navarre (the future Henri IV), passed across her vision 23 times; much shocked, Catherine at once called off the disturbing experiment.

Astrology and the People

In the popular *Kalendar and Compost of Shepherds*, which first appeared in 1493, astrology was projected as a major influence in the lives of all men; advice was given on matters of health, love and the future. The shepherd of the title represented the wisdom men acquired from their constant observations of the sky, the planets, the Signs of the Zodiac and their natures, informing them on such matters as 'which be good for letting blood, and which be indifferent or evil for the same'.

As the printed word became increasingly available, so a multitude of almanacs appeared throughout Europe. Although they were expensive to buy, many were handed round or their contents passed on by word of mouth. They addressed a mainly agricultural audience, like the *Kalendar*, and recommended propitious times to plant and harvest, when to bathe, marry or undertake a journey. In this way more and more people became aware of astrological beliefs, and could appreciate the astrological allusions of dramatists and poets, agreeing, in most cases, with the character in Webster's *Duchess of Malfi*, who declares: 'We are merely the stars' tennis balls, struck and bandied which way please them'.

The Seven Planets *above*
These German woodcuts by Hans Beham, dated 1531, detail the areas of life governed by the planets: at left, the Sun; top row, left to right, the Moon, Mercury, Venus; below, Mars, Jupiter, Saturn.

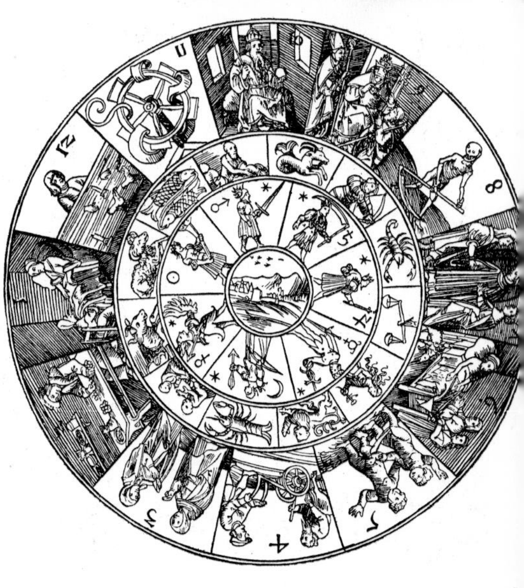

The Astrologer's Wheel *right*
Title-page of Georg von Purbach's astrological treatise of 1515; the planets, Signs and Houses revolve round the Earth which forms the hub of the Chart.

Cesare Borgia (1475–1507) *above*
The famed rival of astrologer-pope Julius II.

Nostradamus (1503–66) *left*
The future kings are revealed to Queen Catherine.

Age of the Alchemists *right*
An illustration from the *Splendor Solis*.

ASTROLOGY AND THE NEW COSMOLOGY

Astrologers in the Renaissance period displayed a restless interest in the mystical elements of their art. Their excursions into alchemy, metoscopy, numerology and other fields, considerably broadened the public's appetite for occult revelation. But their inventiveness sadly dispersed the mainstream of astrological thought.

In 1543 Nicolaus Copernicus, a Polish church official and astronomer, published a book in which he gave reasons for supposing that the Sun, not the Earth, lay in the centre of the Solar System. This heliocentric theory was already known to Renaissance scholars, as it had been to Greek mathematicians, notably Aristarchus, many centuries before, but it had been seen only as an alternative device – not the reality. Copernicus was well aware of risking the wrath of the Church and had refrained from publication until he was on his death-bed. His fears were well founded, and as the implications of Copernicus' work became clear over the next 50 years, the Church indeed proved hostile.

In 1542 the Court of the Inquisition had been renamed the Congregation of the Holy Office, but its repressive techniques were in no way softened. One supporter of Copernicus, Giordano Bruno, was burned at the stake in 1600 for his persistence; and in 1663, almost a century after Copernicus, the great Galileo was forced finally to recant. It seems that the Church, while tolerating symbolic, prophetic forms of astrology, felt more deeply threatened by the new wave of astronomical thinkers.

Copernican Planisphere *above*
In his revolutionary scheme, Copernicus in 1543 placed the Sun at the centre of the universe. In astrology the Earth has remained a symbolic centre from which the apparent motions of the planets are measured and assessed.

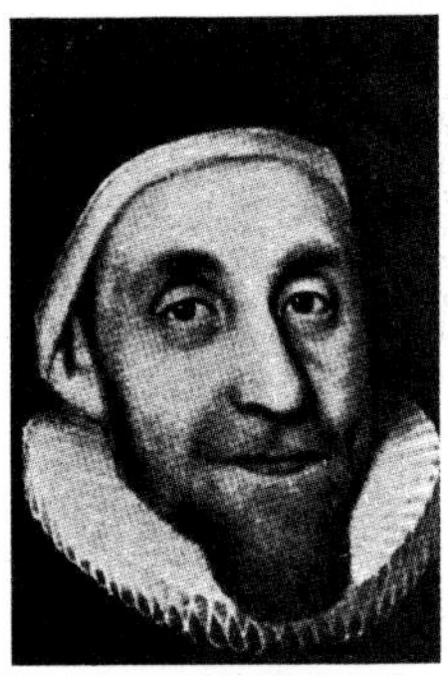

Robert Burton *left*
The scholar Robert Burton (1577–1640), author of the *Anatomy of Melancholy*, took the enlightened view that the stars 'do incline but not compel', thereby allowing for the exercise of free will; he nevertheless predicted his own death with complete accuracy.

The Advent of Tycho Brahe

Copernicus was not correct in all his assertions, and although he lacked the means to prove his case through observation this proof was soon to be provided – ironically by an astrologer violently opposed to Copernicanism. His name was Tycho Brahe; a Danish nobleman, he was the most eccentric figure in the new age of telescopic astronomy.

Tycho flourished during the transitional period when astrology and mechanical astronomy could still exist happily side by side. He was born three years after the death of Copernicus; by 1566 he had become an enthusiastic astrologer, announcing that an eclipse of the Moon foretold the death of the Sultan of Turkey.

Then, in 1572 a new star flared out, brilliant enough to be seen with the naked eye in broad daylight. It was, we now know, a supernova, in which a distant sun (a 'star') suffered a tremendous outburst and blew most of its material into space. Tycho could not know this, but he did comment that the appearance of a new star disproved the traditional dogma that the heavens were unchanging. He also saw an astrological significance: 'The star was at first like Venus and Jupiter, giving pleasing effects; but as it then became like Mars, there will next come a period of wars, seditions, captivity and death of princes, and destruction of cities, together with dryness and fiery meteors in the air, pestilence, and venomous snakes. Lastly the star became like Saturn, and there will finally come a time of want, death, imprisonment and all sorts of sad things.' The supernova made Tycho decide to give his life to astronomy. The King of Denmark financed an

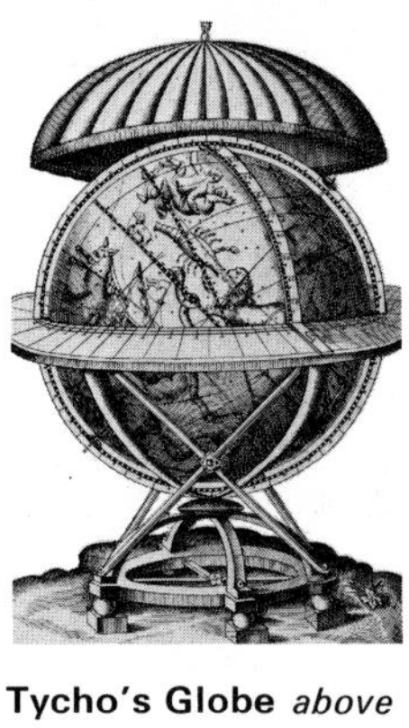

Tycho's Globe *above*
Tycho Brahe's celestial globe (1584).

The Vital Moment *right*
A woodcut of 1587 shows two astrologers preparing the horoscope of the child about to be born.

observatory on the island of Hven, in the Sound near Hamlet's Elsinore, where Tycho worked between 1576 and 1596, drawing up an accurate star catalogue and making observations of the positions of the planets, particularly Mars. Later he became Imperial Mathematician to the Holy Roman Emperor, Rudolph II, in Bohemia. There a German, Johannes Kepler, became his chief assistant.

The End of the Ptolemaic System

Kepler, appointed Imperial Mathematician after Tycho's death in 1601, was also astrologically minded, but, unlike Tycho, he was a Copernican – and he used Tycho's accurate observations to *prove* that the Earth and other planets move round the Sun in ellipses.

Kepler's work gave the death-blow to the Ptolemaic system, though the Church continued its opposition and Copernicus' great book was not removed from the Papal Index until 1835. But the repercussions for astrology itself were not so great as might be supposed. If the Sun now occupied the centre of the universe and the Earth was merely a planet, the astrological influences received by men on Earth would be nevertheless unchanged. Astrologers soon realized that their art was not affected in the slightest.

The Short-sighted Rationalists

When, in 1675, Greenwich, the leading British observatory, was founded, it was put in charge of the Rev. John Flamsteed, the first Astronomer Royal. He cast the Observatory's horoscope, but ended it with the words: 'Risum teneatis, amici?' (Can you help laughing, my friends?) Flamsteed's comment underlines the growing rift between astronomy the science and astrology the mathematical-intuitive art.

Then, in 1687, Isaac Newton's great book the *Principia Mathematica* opened the modern phase of astronomy. It has been described as the greatest mental effort ever made by one man, and as well as laying down the law of gravitation, contained a remarkable number of other fundamental advances. Although Newton set the scene for today's materialistic scientists, he had, as a young man, acquired a conventional grounding in astrology; later he spent many hours over alchemical experiments. He never changed in his respect for the truths inherent in astrology.

In fact Newton's own inquiries into the hidden forces which shape events on a universal scale were not wholly at odds with present-day researches into celestial harmonics. But the new rational spirit had no hesitation in discarding astrology. The rationalists, however, ignored the astrological contributions of men they wished to claim for their own side, most notably Copernicus and Kepler who, with Newton, are commonly labelled by the history books as the chief instigators in the demise of astrology. That astrology suffered a long-lasting decline, at least until the mid-19th century, is undeniable. But curiously, the men held responsible for this fall from favour were in reality more attuned to the potential of serious astrology than its detractors.

The Wisdom of Galileo *above*
The great astronomer in old age, blind and confined to his house by the Inquisition, talks to his son of the new science.

Casting a Horoscope *left*
An astrologer fills in planetary details on a square Birth Chart; from Robert Fludd's *History of the Microcosm.*

The New Cosmology *below*
An astrologer of the new telescopic age begins to interpret the square Birth Chart he has just completed.

THE SEPARATE WAYS

Rather as we are today moved by the sight (quite apart from the significance) of men walking on the Moon, so the spirit of the 18th century was excited by an unprecedented sequence of observational triumphs. In a relatively short period the astronomers of Europe unravelled a vast number of the physical secrets of the universe. In fact, the balance of public and scientific opinion was such that when two new planets, Uranus and Neptune, were discovered in 1781 and 1846 respectively, the world's attention was focused almost totally on the skills of the astronomers alone, while astrology lacked proper support and suffered a decline from which it has only recently recovered. The long-term implications for cosmology as a whole were not seen until much later, when astrologers began to assess the effects of the new planets, not just in terms of their contemporary applications but, more importantly, in determining how they affected past events.

This is, and always has been the true purpose of

Newton's Reflector *left*
The reflector telescope was developed by Newton *c.*1670.

Galileo's Refractor *right*
Galileo, in 1609–10 was the first to exploit the refractor telescope.

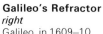

Giant Reflector of the 19th Century *left*
By 1845 Lord Rosse had built a 72-inch reflector; an earlier 48-inch is shown.

Cassini *below*
The Italian G. D. Cassini (1625–1712), was the first accurately to fix the Sun's distance from Earth.

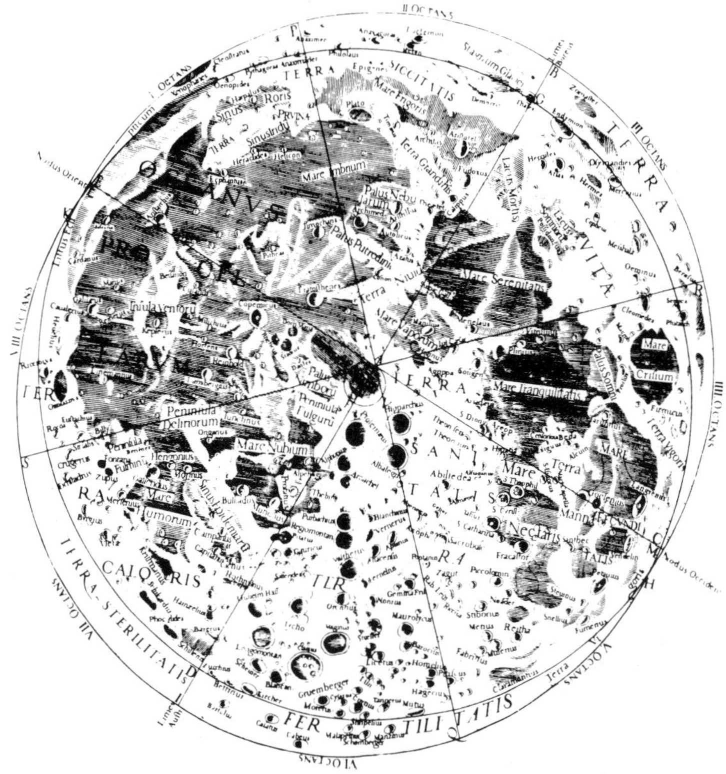

Riccioli's Moon Map *above*
The map which Riccioli, an Italian Jesuit priest, made of the Moon in 1651 established the nomenclature for the Moon's geographical features; not surprisingly he named one prominent crater after himself.

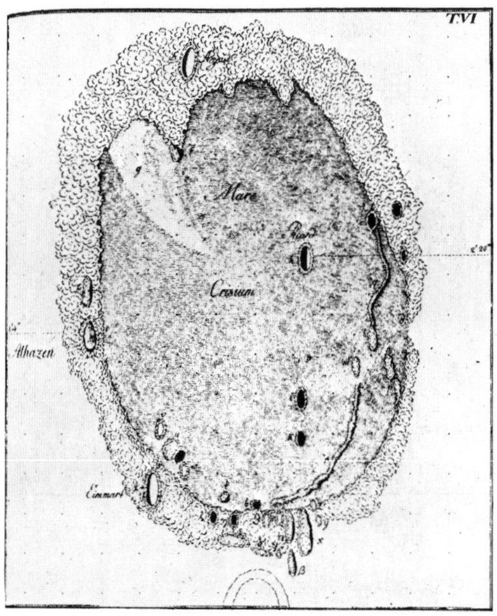

The Mare Crisium *left*
This drawing of the Mare Crisium on the Moon was made by J. H. Schroter, the town magistrate of Lilienthal in Germany. Schroter produced hundreds of sketches of the Moon's features between 1778 and 1814.

'Astrology is astronomy brought to Earth and applied to the affairs of men.'
Ralph Waldo Emerson (1803–82)

astrology in relation to earthly affairs. Sadly, in the 18th and 19th centuries, its real aims became lost in a wilderness of trivia and commercial exploitation. Popular astrological magazines like *The Prophetic Messenger* and *Raphael's Sanctuary of the Astral Art* found their way on to the streets, but were far from being serious publications. Astrology remained at its lowest ebb until, towards the end of the 19th century, it drew the interest of some of the followers of Madame Blavatsky, the founder of Theosophy. Blavatsky was not herself an astrologer, but she believed in the 'occult and mysterious influence' of the stars. Later, Alan Leo and his followers were responsible for broadening the base on which modern astrology is founded.

Today, 250 years after Newton's discoveries, astrology is rightly being taken seriously by the scientific community. Now the case for astrology has been authoritatively established: to ignore the mounting evidence of cosmic interrelations would itself be unscientific.

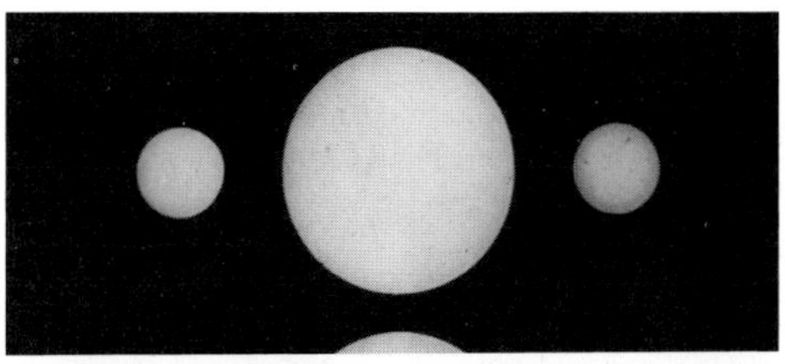

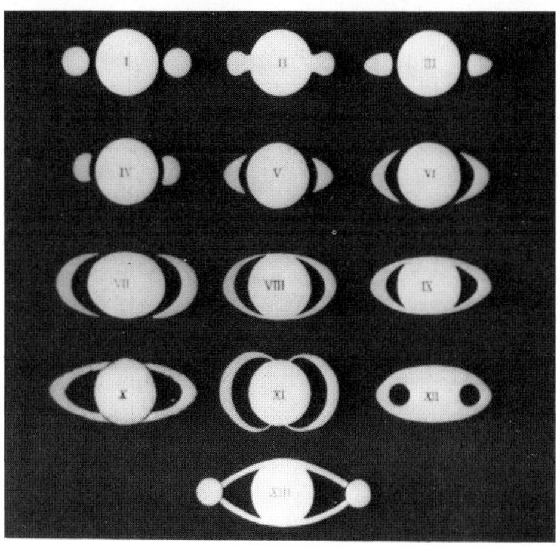

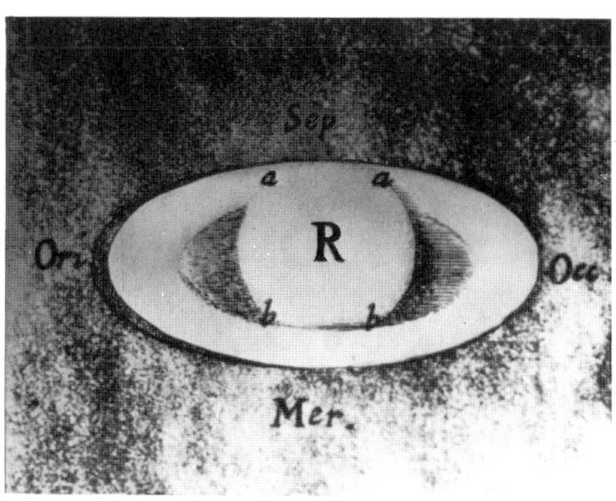

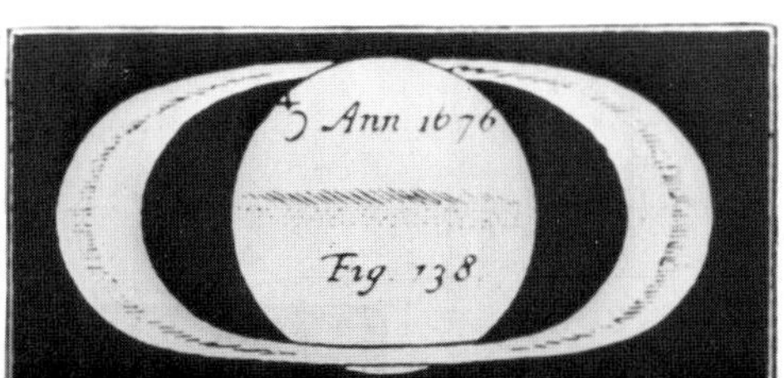

The Observations of Saturn *left*
The observations made of the planet Saturn went through a particularly interesting evolution as is clearly seen in these illustrations, which stretch over approximately 60 years. Its nature gradually came to be more clearly understood only as the technical equipment of astronomers was improved. Galileo's instruments were not strong enough for him to interpret the rings, and his attempts to understand what he was seeing are shown in the top two pictures, of 1620. At one point he believed Saturn to be a triple planet (top picture) but then the two attendant bodies disappeared from view as the rings became turned edge-on to Earth. It was the Dutch astronomer, C. Huygens, who in 1659 first proposed that this curious phenomenon was 'a thin flat ring', which nowhere touches 'the body' of the planet. But astronomers refused to accept this explanation immediately. By 1665, however, the observations of Robert Hooke, who drew the third picture, and the Italian astronomer, Cassini, who drew the bottom one, had provided incontrovertible proof.

Edmond Halley *left*
Halley (1656–1742) succeeded Flamsteed as second Astronomer Royal; he helped to persuade Newton to publish the *Principia.*

Halley's Comet *below*
Halley tracked the comet which now bears his name. The diagram shows its orbit round the Sun and relative to the Earth on its return in 1910, when it was photographed (lower sequence).

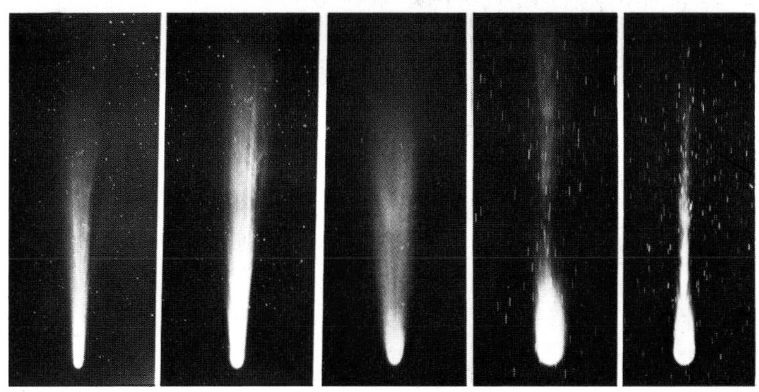

Sir William Herschel *above*
Herschel (1738–1822), the German-born English astronomer, built his own telescope, and with it discovered Uranus, the eighth astrological planet.

Herschel's Mirror *above*
In 1789 Herschel constructed the largest telescope the world had then seen, fitted with a 48-inch mirror. This 8-inch mirror is an example of his early work.

Le Verrier *above*
The new planets are now firmly incorporated into astrological knowledge. It was the French astronomer, Urbain Le Verrier, who enabled the ninth planet, Neptune, to be identified in 1846.

Astrology in History: a Summary

The chart on this page outlines the progress of astrology (right-hand column) from 3000 BC to the present day, comparing it with broader historical developments detailed in the facing column. It is obvious at a glance that man in his struggle with the immediate world around him—not to speak of patterns originating in the outer cosmos—has not advanced at an even pace. Sporadic periods of intense activity, e.g. 1400–1600, seem to exhaust his energy and are follwed by a time, often as long as three or four centuries, of apparent stagnation, when he gathers fresh strength. The great advances made by the early Roman empire were followed by a period when not only were there no new contribution, but even much that had been achieved was shattered and lost. But then the great age of the Renaissance followed and further strides were made. As with political and cultural history so it is with astrology. The early period in Babylon and Greece was enormously fertile, witnessing as it did the foundation and elaboration of the science. Thereafter, however, up to 1400, in Europe at least, there are very few landmarks. After that, as in art, there is a renaissance followed by another eclipse with the growth of science and scepticism. Only now is astrology coming into its own again.

2600 BC, King Snefru, of the fourth Egyptian dynasty, builds the first pyramid.
1728–1686 BC, Hammurabi expands Babylonian empire.
1650–1125 BC, Mycenaean civilization in Greece.

753 BC, Foundation of Rome.
356–323 BC, Alexander the Great builds empire from Athens to India.
27 BC, Augustus, first Roman emperor. Beginning of period of great expansion, particularly in East.

c150, The Pantheon built at Rome: finest example of early domed building.

330, Foundation of Constantinople by the Christian Roman emperor, Constantine.

4th century, Visigoths overrun eastern parts of the Roman empire.

476, Last Roman emperor deposed by Odoacer the Hun. End of western Roman empire.

6th-11th centuries, Romanesque period in European architecture.

c570–632, Mohammed, prophet and founder of Islam.

743–813, Charlemagne, first Holy Roman emperor.

747, Abbasid dynasty of Khalifs defeat Omayyads and move capital of Islam to Baghdad from Damascus.

8th-9th centuries, Arabian Empire disrupts trade with Europe; major cause of the Dark Ages.

9th–10th centuries, Rise of the secular power of the papacy.

10th–11th centuries, Viking raids carried out all over Europe and Russia. Varangian or Viking Guard formed in Constantinople.

1066, Normans, Vikings who had settled in northern France in 10th century, conquer England.
1099, First Crusade captures Jerusalem.

1162–1227, Jenghiz Khan, founder of the largest

c2872 BC, Sargon of Agade uses astrologer priests for purposes of prediction.

1500

c1300–1236 BC, Rameses II fixes cardinal points, Aries, Libra, Cancer and Capricorn.
c668 BC, Earliest surviving horoscope.
c280 BC, Berosos founds school of astrology at Cos. Greek astrologers taught there.
63 BC–14 AD, Augustus has coins stamped

0

with his Sign, Capricorn.

Birth of Christ announced by the Magi, astrologers following a star.

c120–180, Claudius Ptolemy, author of the *Tetrabiblos*, the greatest astrological textbook.

200

204–270, Plotinus, founder of Neoplatonism, accepts validity of astrology, but insists on free-will.

354–430, St Augustine. He accepts astrology when young but then turned violently against it. The arguments he advanced for disbelief are still accepted by churchmen today.

400

c400, The great library of Alexandria is dispersed, with the loss of many astrological texts.
410 485, Proclus, philosopher and successor to Plato, writes paraphrase of Ptolemy's *Tetrabiblos*.
c450, Gaius Julius Solinus writes long interpretation of the horoscope of Rome.
c550, Horapollon publishes *Hieroglyphics*, describing how sacred beetle lives in strict conformity with astrological theory.

600

700–800, Arab scientists and astrologers keep alive Classical learning.

8th century, Ibrahim Al-Fazari invents astrolabe.

800

10th century, Ibn Yunis, Moslem astronomer, compiles at Cairo the Hakimite tables of planetary motions.

940–1020, Firdausi, or Abul-Qasim Mansur, Persia's epic poet, writes the *Shah-Namah* of over 60,000 couplets, containing many astrological references.

b978, Murasaki, author of *The Tale of Genji*, the oldest work of fiction in the world, includes references to Japanese astrology.

1000

1125, University of Bologna founds chair of astrology.

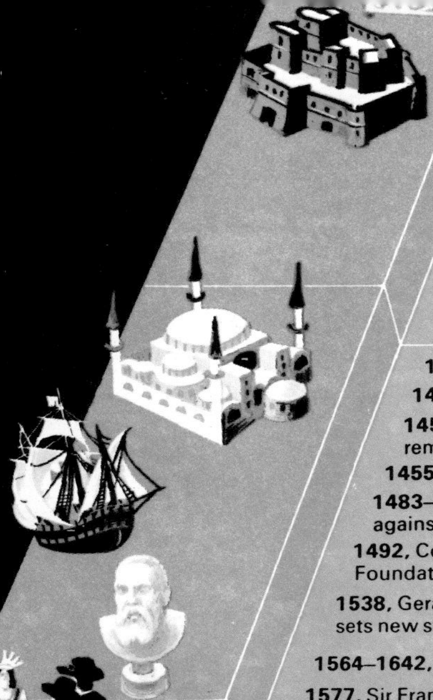

rushing out fire gun', using gunpowder.

1291, Fall of Acre to Egyptian sultan. Last remnants of Crusader kingdoms conquered.

1400–1500, The development of the Renaissance in Italy.

1438, First Hapsburg Holy Roman Emperor.

1453, Constantinople captured by Ottoman Turks. Last remnant of Roman empire destroyed.

1455, Gutenberg publishes his Bible at Mainz.

1483–1536, Martin Luther leads Protestant revolution in Germany against corruption of popes.

1492, Columbus discovers New World. Foundation of the Spanish empire.

1538, Geradius Mercator publishes his map of the world, which sets new standards in cartography.

1564–1642, Galileo Galilei, the first notable user of the telescope.

1577, Sir Francis Drake circumnavigates the world.

16th–17th centuries, Baroque art and architecture symbolize Counter-Reformation

1620, Pilgrim Fathers sail from Plymouth.

1642–1721, Isaac Newton, the great astronomer, publishes the *Principia* in 1687.

1712–1778, Jean Jacques Rousseau, author of the *Contrat Social.*

1738–1822, Sir William Herschel, founder of modern cosmology, discovers Uranus.

1789, Start of the French Revolution.

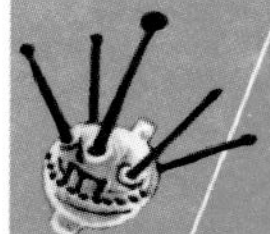

19th century, Rapid growth of British empire.

1802, First steam railway.

1815–1898, Otto von Bismarck, architect of German unification.

1818–1883, Karl Marx, German socialist philosopher.

1846, W. T. G. Morton performs first major operation under anaesthetics at Massachusetts General Hospital in Boston.

1861, American Civil War.

1865, Abraham Lincoln, sixteenth President of the United States, assassinated.

1879–1955, Albert Einstein, German-Jewish physicist, whose *General Theory of Relativity* explained an anomaly in the movement of Mercury.

1893– , Mao Tse-tung, founder of the People's Republic of China.

1903, Wilbur and Orville Wright make first successful powered flight.

1914–1918, World War I.

1917, The Russian Revolution overthrows the last of the Tzars.

1918, Collapse of the Hapsburg and Ottoman empires.

1939–45, World War II.

1959, Sputnik One.

1960s, Growth of radio-telescopy

1969, Americans land first man on the moon.

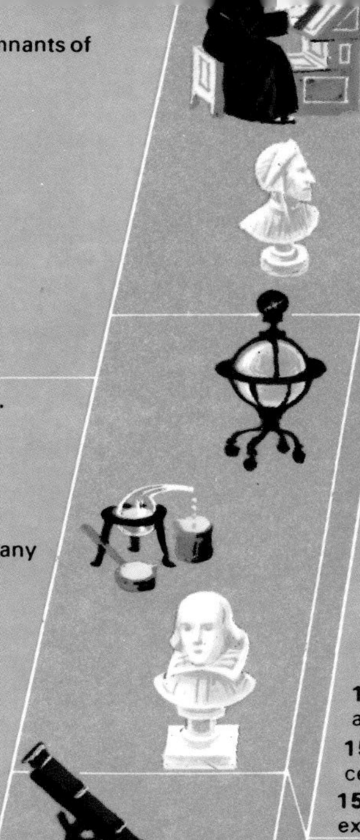

c1214–1294, Roger Bacon, a distinguished Franciscan philosopher, praises the new art of mathematics as essential for the proper practice of astrology.

1225–1230, Cambridge University founded. Astrology taught there from 1250.

c1254–1324, Marco Polo, Venetian explorer, estimates that 5,000 astrologers work in China (Kanbalu) alone.

1265–1321, Dante, author of *Divina Commedia*, uses astrological imagery in his works.

c1280, Johannes Campanus, mathematician and chaplain to Pope Urban IV, devises a new method of House division.

1340–1400, Chaucer, the first great English poet, whose poems contain more direct allusions to astrology than any other great work.

1400

1414–1484, Pope Sixtus IV, first of the great astrologer popes.

1473–1543, Copernicus advances theory that the earth goes round the sun. He dedicates his main work to the astrologer pope, Paul III.

1480–1519, Lucrezia Borgia shares a think-tank of astrologers with her father, Pope Alexander VI.

1527–1608, John Dee, a mysterious and fascinating figure, is connected with astrology, alchemy and the occult; and espionage; reputedly a spy for Queen Elizabeth I, he was certainly her astrological adviser.

1546–1601, Tycho Brahe, court astrologer and astronomer. Says that those who deny astrology 'violate clear evidence', and produces proof of the physical effect of the planets on the earth.

1564–1616, William Shakespeare inserts astrological references in nearly all his plays.

1568–1630, Tommaso Campanella performs magical and astrological ceremonies for Pope Urban VIII.

1571–1630, Johannes Kepler, holds that astrology 'derives from experience which can be denied only by people who have not examined it'.

1600

1602–1681, William Lilly, the best known astrologer of his generation, simultaneously patronized by Cavaliers and Roundheads.

1603–1668, Placidus, a monk and Paduan professor of mathematics, originates best known system of House division (now widely considered impractical).

1749–1832, Johann Wolfgang von Goethe, German poet, dramatist and prose-writer sympathetically disposed to astrological theory.

1781, Uranus becomes the eighth astrological planet.

1795–1873, Richard James Morrison as 'Zadkiel', with Robert Cross Smith ('Raphael'), the most popular astrologers of their time. The popular astrological press is established.

1800

1831–1891, Helena Blavatsky founds the Theosophical Society in 1875: she follows her own brand of astrological thought and has an immense effect on her public.

1846, Neptune discovered after work done by John Couch Adams and U. J. J. Leverrier.

1865–1932, Evangeline Adams, the nationally known American astrologer, starts the first radio astrology column.

1875–1961, Carl Gustav Jung, the great Swiss psychologist, whose astrological experiments do much to revive serious interest.

1887–1968, Charles Carter founds the Faculty of Astrological Studies in England.

1889–1964, Jawaharlal Nehru, first prime minister of India, intent on modernizing India plays down his own interest in astrology, but has Birth Charts cast for all his grandchildren.

1895– Dane Rudhyar, provocative astrological thinker.

1900– , Reinhold Ebertin, founder of Kosmobiologishe Akademie Aalen, astrological theorist and experimenter.

1930, Clyde William Tombaugh discovers Pluto.

1930, Astrological newspaper scoop. British astrologer, R. H. Naylor, writes in the *Daily Express*, of 'serious danger for British aircraft'. A week later the British airship R101 crashes.

1960s, New contact established between astrology and science, notably in field of cosmic rhythms.

1969, Foundation of International Society for Astrological Research in America.

ORIENTAL ASTROLOGY

The earliest known Indian astrological textbook was probably written in about 3000 BC, when an advanced civilization flourished in the Indus valley. The sub-continent remains today the only major area of the world where astrology still has a strong, pervasive influence on everyday life.

Constant invasions from the west have ensured that some of India's astrological theory is familiar to the Western observer. Starting with the Aryans, circa 1500 BC, who brought with them Babylonian ideas, and then the Greeks under Alexander the Great, who added the later Hellenic developments, the interchange of ideas has been regular. The great Hindu texts of 1000 BC, the Vedas, have astrological references, and the Greek Hermetic idea of Catasterism – souls rising into the sky to become stars – is also found. By the third century AD astrology was well developed and had established itself as a popular force.

One of the reasons for its continuing popularity is doubtless that astrology can be related to the concept of Karma, common to most leading Eastern philosophies. Karma is broadly the transmigration of the soul through successive reincarnations to ultimate union with the infinite; behaviour in one life determines the starting point of the next. Astrology is used to establish the stage that a soul has reached on its journey.

One of the major differences between contemporary Western and Indian astrology is the use of the sidereal Zodiac, the planets being observed against the background of the constellations rather than as they lie within the equal fields of the ecliptic. While some Western astrologers have adopted this method, it is usually thought of as an esoteric practice in a European or American context. Western astrologers, however, will find much that is familiar. The Signs govern parts of the body and there are many correspondences: for example, in the relations between Cancer and the breasts, Scorpio and the genitals and Capricorn and the knees. The attributes of the planets, too, are similar. Each month of pregnancy is attributed to a particular planet, except the eighth, the most crucial for the survival of the foetus, which is governed by the complete horoscope.

In Indian domestic matters the influence of astrology seems at times to be all-pervasive. The horoscopes of prospective brides and bridegrooms are examined for signs of mental instability or physical weaknesses – as well as for evidence of intelligence and temperamental compatability – before parents will give their consent.

A man having a house constructed will engage an astrologer along with the architect and builder. The moment to lay the foundation stone, dig the well, tell the owner he can move in, must all be established with great precision. Every object in nature is thought of as radiating some degree of cosmic force, and so where various materials are to be combined into one building, they must come together at the right moment if they are not to interact unfavourably.

With astrology so entrenched, there is no doubt that it will continue to play a dominating role in Indian life.

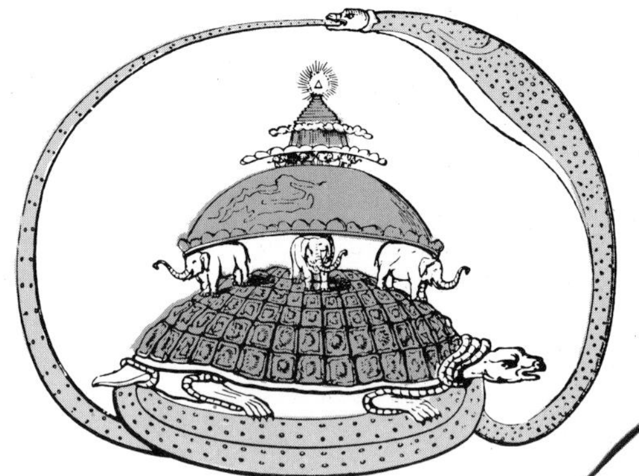

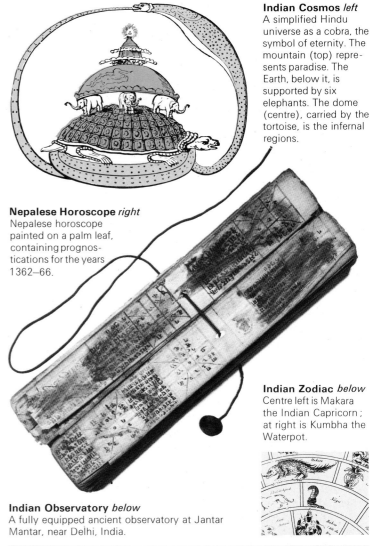

Indian Cosmos *left*
A simplified Hindu universe as a cobra, the symbol of eternity. The mountain (top) represents paradise. The Earth, below it, is supported by six elephants. The dome (centre), carried by the tortoise, is the infernal regions.

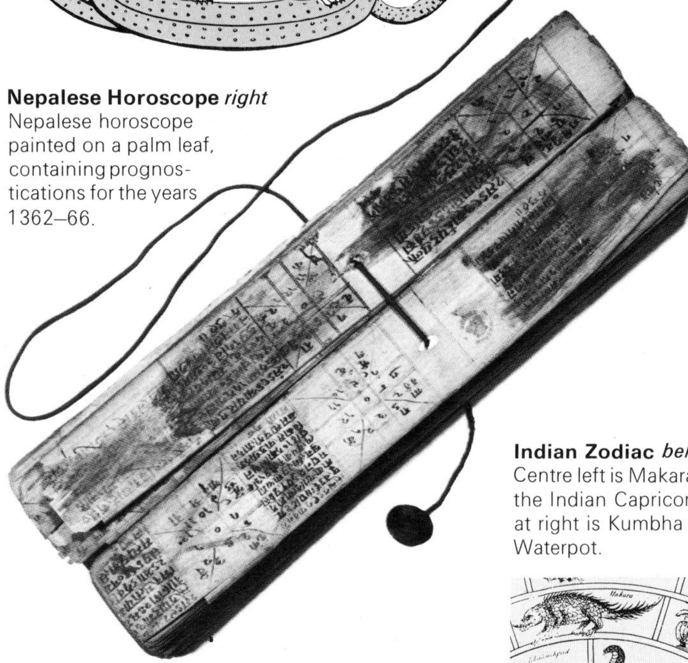

Nepalese Horoscope *right*
Nepalese horoscope painted on a palm leaf, containing prognostications for the years 1362–66.

Indian Zodiac *below*
Centre left is Makara the Indian Capricorn; at right is Kumbha the Waterpot.

Indian Observatory *below*
A fully equipped ancient observatory at Jantar Mantar, near Delhi, India.

'When some new dynasty is going to arise,' wrote Tsou Yen, the famous Chinese astrologer who flourished in about 300 BC, 'heaven exhibits auspicious signs for the people.' Astrology is believed to have been introduced into China along the ancient trade routes through Central Asia in about the third millenium BC. Certainly the philosopher Confucius (551–478 BC) treated planetary predictions with respect: 'Heaven sends down its good or evil symbols and wise men act accordingly.'

Over the centuries, however, Chinese astrology developed its own highly individual flavour. The Chinese concept of the universe and the theory of the principles underlying it became involved with astrology to produce a highly complex, interlocking system, that is very like a set of Chinese boxes. The universe is divided into five 'palaces' (the centre point and the four cardinal regions) and there are five elements (wood, fire, earth, metal and water) and five planets (plus the Sun and Moon). All the various parts of this elaborate structure are interrelated, so that all phenomena – colours, planets, Signs, emotions, elements, etc. – have their special links and associations. In addition, everything is either Yang, male, bright and mobile, or Yin, female, dark and static. The 12 Signs of the Zodiac are all represented by animals – rat, ox, tiger, hare, dragon, snake, horse, goat, monkey, cock, dog and boar. These Signs, however, do not divide the sky, as in the Babylonian system, but the equator. They correspond to one of the 12 double-hours used to measure the day and to one of the twelve months of the year.

The emperors and war-lords made constant demands on their astrologers, seeking to know the most propitious dates for ceremonies and campaigns. With a system as intricate as theirs, the opportunities for error were obviously frequent and since great significance was attached to celestial events, the position of court astrologers was correspondingly dangerous; this may be illustrated by the oft-told story of the two astrologers who were beheaded for failing to predict an eclipse of the Sun. On the other hand, there is at least one instance of an emperor taking the blame for an eclipse upon himself – because of his mismanagement of government affairs.

At all events, the Chinese astrologer's basic equipment until quite recently became the Lo-king magic disc – a horoscope divided into six circles for foretelling the individual's future and after-life. Marco Polo (1254–1324), the Venetian merchant traveller, found them in use during his long stay in China under the Mongol rule of Kublai Khan. They were used, he recorded, to fix dates for cremating deceased dignitaries. The funeral ceremonies could not take place until the subject's birth planets were in the ascendant; and so the corpse might have to remain embalmed and sealed in its coffin for weeks or even months. This persisted well into the 19th century.

Astrology naturally has no official standing in the People's Republic of China, but the birth of the Republic took place under such auspicious signs that many astrologers have felt that Mao Tse-tung must have acted on astrological advice.

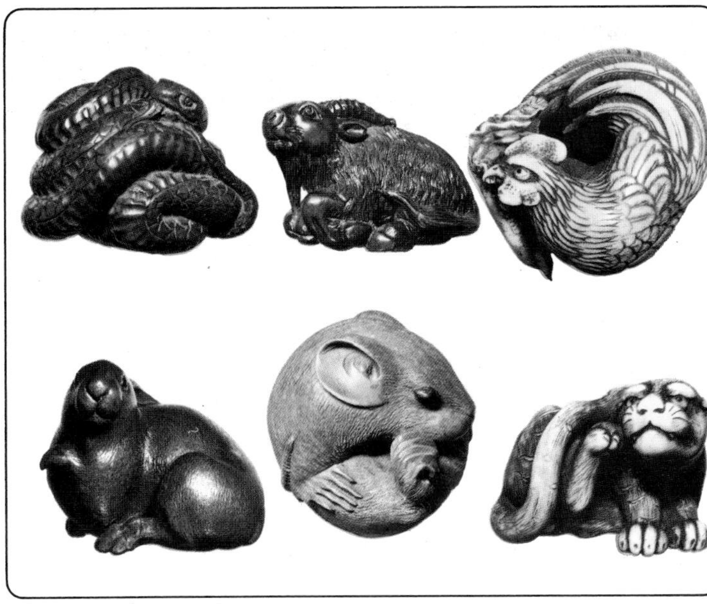

The Japanese Zodiac *above*
All the Signs of the Zodiac in Japan, as in China, are animals. Six are shown here – the cock, hare, tiger, goat, rat and snake – in the form of Netsuke or buttons from a Japanese kimono. They are used to suspend keys, a purse or a writing case.

Chinese Horoscope *left*
An example of the intricate layout of a Chinese horoscope.

Chinese Universe *above*
A mirror showing the animals and elements associated with the four cardinal points.

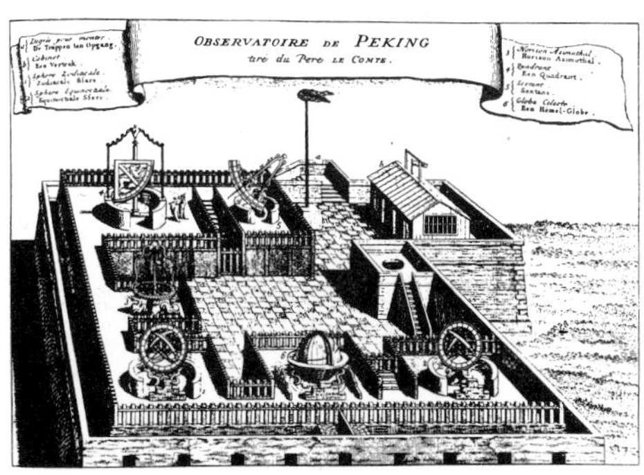

Peking Observatory *left*
An engraving of 1698 shows the observatory that had been in use for centuries before the telescope was known.

THE GREAT YEAR

The Great Year is the period of 25,868 years which the Earth takes to pass through the influence of each of the twelve Signs of the Zodiac in turn, each Great Month lasting for about 2,000 years. Hipparchus of Nicaea (*c.*190–*c.*120 BC), the Greek astronomer, was the first to discover the principle underlying this theory – that of the Precession of the Equinoxes. Due to a slight wobble in the Earth's rotation, the constellation lying behind the Sun at the vernal equinox changes gradually through the centuries and imparts a unique character to the Months.

The Polarities

The influence of a Sign is related to that of its opposite Sign across the Zodiac. This pairing is known as *polarity*. Aries' polarity is with Libra, Taurus' with Scorpio – and so on.

The earliest Month of which we have real knowledge was that of Leo (10000–8000 BC): the Lascaux cave paintings show the Leonine creative influence but the thought-motivation behind the effort is Aquarian in spirit. The Age of Cancer (8000–6000 BC), witnessed the earliest development of settled farming and constructed dwellings – both of which are Capricornian in essence. During the Geminian Age (6000–4000 BC) the founding of the earliest libraries comes under Sagittarius. Perhaps the most striking polarity of all was in the Taurean Age, (4000–2000 BC), for the Egyptians were much preoccupied with death and the after-life, themes strongly related to Scorpio. The war-like Arian age expressed its polarity with Libra in the magnificent beauty and balance of Greek architecture (2000 BC–Birth of Christ). Christian teaching and art, so typical of Virgo, are the most obvious pointers to its polarity with Pisces (Birth of Christ–AD 2000).

The New Great Month

In the Age of Aquarius, we may conjecture that man will consider a system of world government, which will involve the organizational characteristics of Leo.

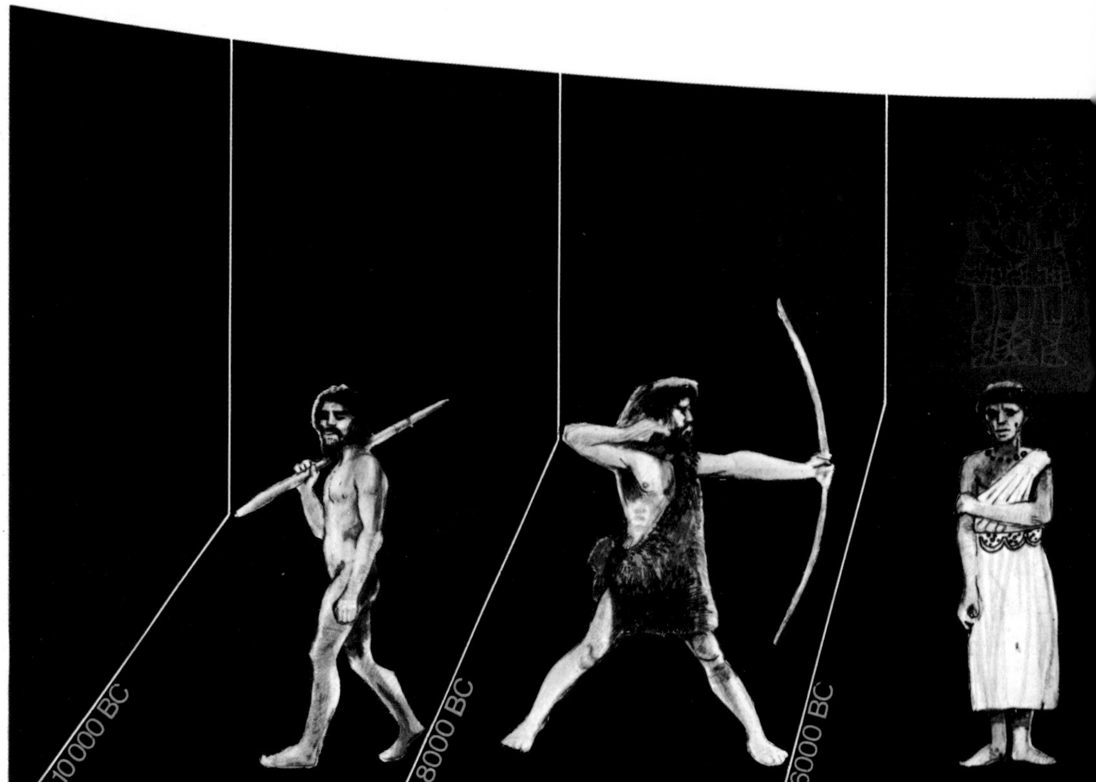

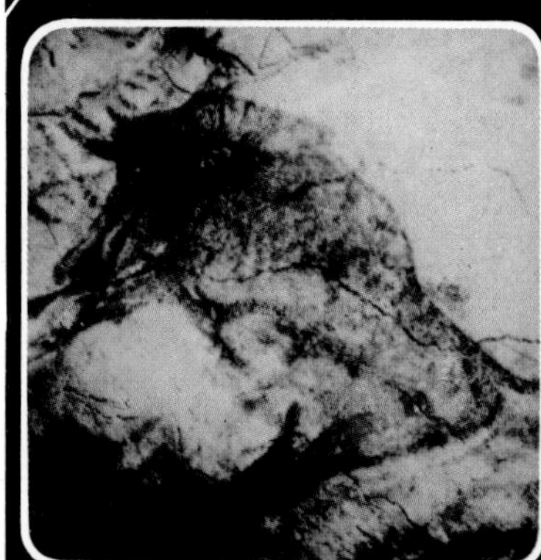

Age of Leo
Although the world has moved through the Great Year many times since it was formed, the effect of the Signs of the Zodiac on the Great Months can only be measured by the developments in man's history – political, cultural, social and technological. Thus the earliest age we can comment on with any degree of certainty is the Age of Leo, circa 10000–8000 BC. The Sun, so important to man in his early primitive state, is the ruler of Leo; and one of its 'keywords' is creativity. This showed itself not only in the many rudimentary inventions typical of the Stone Age, but also in carvings and extraordinarily beautiful and vigorous cave paintings. Above is a still earlier example from northern Spain.

Age of Cancer
With the Leonine Sun gaining in prominence at the end of the Ice Age, *c.*9000 BC, the approach of the Cancerian Age was marked by man's emergence from caves, and the beginning of fixed dwellings in China, Egypt, India and Mesopotamia; which was paralleled by the growth of settled farming. Fertility rites abounded and many carvings of fecund female figures date from this period – the result of the strong influence of Cancer, the Sign of motherhood as well as the home, and its ruling planet, the Moon. Typical of this period are the round, Moon-like carvings made by the men of Lepensky Vir, in Yugoslavia; and the rounded primitive carving of Venus, above, from Catal Huyuk in Turkey.

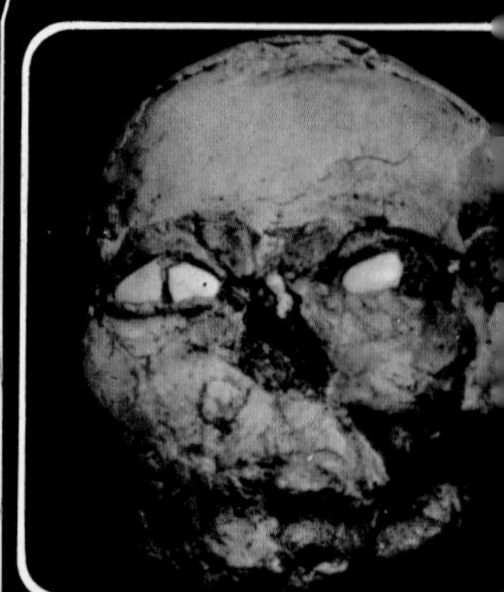

Age of Gemini
The lively, intellectual, mobile anc communicative influence of Gem reflected in the wonder of that Si Great Month – the development writing. This vital link in the expa of man's intellect reveals the neec record and store information. Starting with rough symbols scra in pottery, it was refined by 4000 into the cuneiform and pictogram scripts of China and Egypt. Religi too, took root and became forma and the first groups of men brouc together for the purposes of learr formed something approaching tl university system. The Geminian of movement was combined witr urge for physical communication first widespread use of the wheel Above is a plaster skull from Jeric

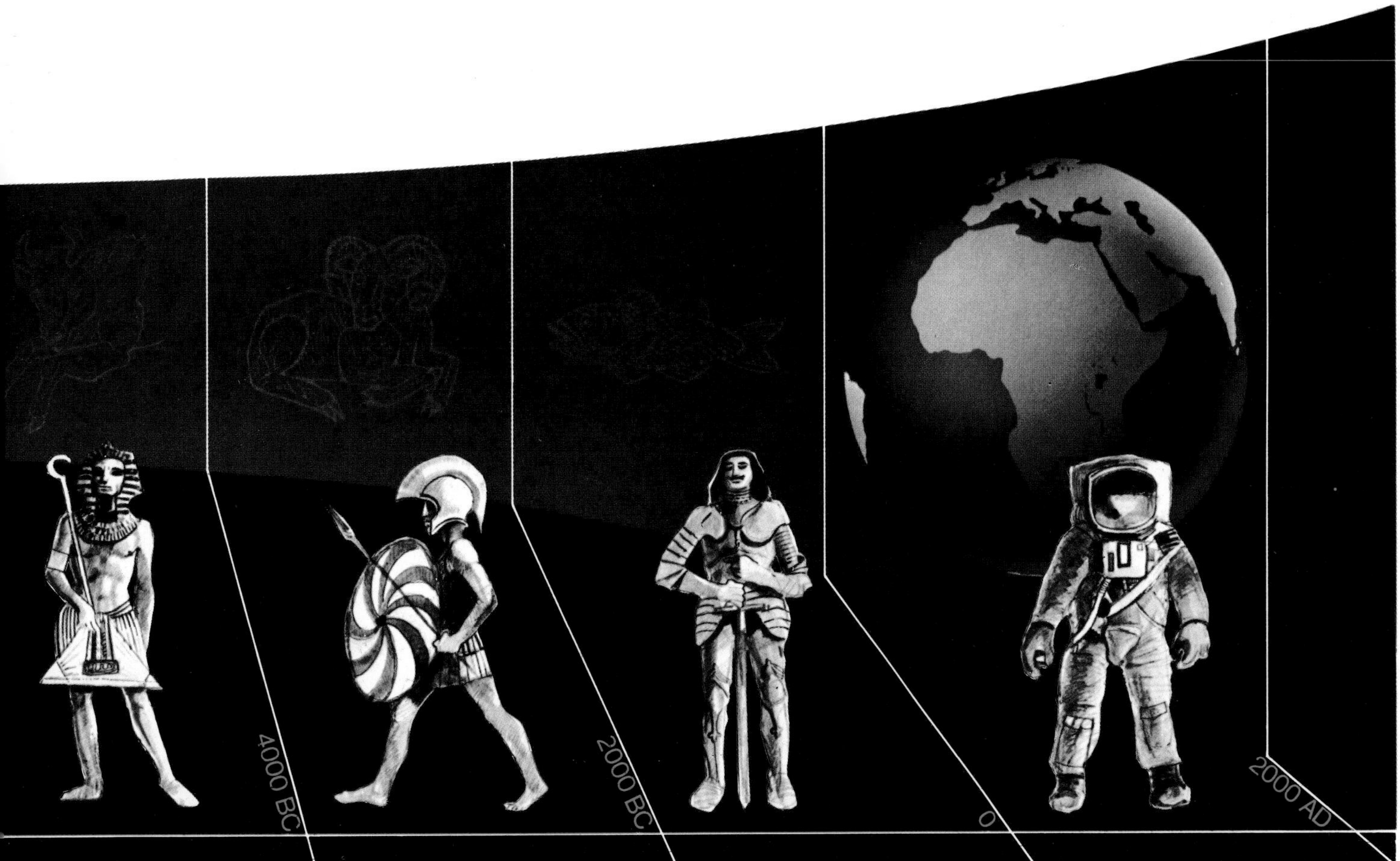

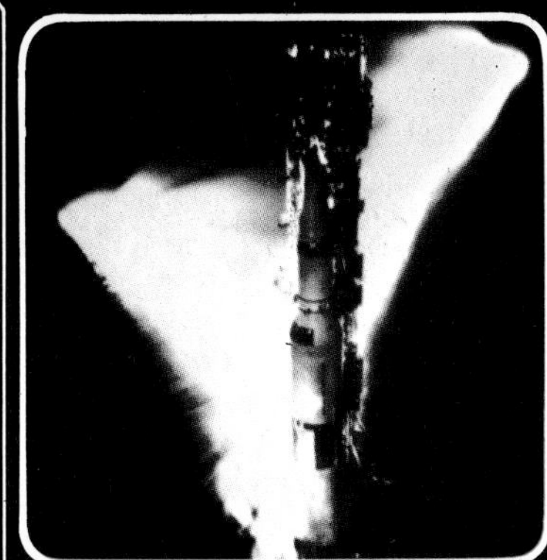

of Taurus
us – the Sign of beauty, of
arity, and a powerful Earth-sign
ongly influenced the early
otian dynasties, and may be seen
eir massive but graceful temples,
h combine lightness and airiness
immense durability. Taurus'
rity (see column on the far left)
Scorpio underlined the Egyptian
ccupation with death as shown in
practice of mummification and care
he dead. The numerous carvings
ll-gods are among the most
ous manifestations of the age. The
cotta model of a bull, above, is
Knossos, Crete, where there was
urishing bull cult. This was also a
period in the evolution of
ology under the clear skies of
opotamia.

Age of Aries

It is obviously impossible to point to a specific decade, or even century, when one Great Age finishes and gives way to the next. One likely clue, however, is the changing of architectural styles and this is well illustrated, in the case of the transition from Taurus to Aries, by the contrast between the Egyptian pyramids and the delicate, poised elegance of such Greek masterpieces as the Parthenon at Athens, Greece. The Arian ram was worshipped by the wandering, warring tribes of Israel, as bloodthirsty as they were religious. The painting, above, a typical example of the style of the time is from a Greek vase, and sums up the war-like tendencies of the age. This violence was reinforced by Aries' ruling planet, Mars.

Age of Pisces

There is no more significant movement in the Age of Pisces than the foundation and development of Christianity and no more central symbol in the history of the religion than the fish. Fish were scratched as secret signs on the walls of the catacombs, near Rome, where the early Christians sheltered in time of persecution, and Christ spoke of his apostles as 'fishers of men'. Reinforcing this connection with Christianity is Pisces' polarity with Virgo which has given rise to its accent on mildness, humility and charity.

It is surely no accident that the Virgin Mary is a central figure in the Christian faith. The illustration, above, is a late Roman mozaic of two fish, from a bath house.

Age of Aquarius

The normal Aquarian preoccupation with rational science is clearly seen in the way that our civilization is becoming increasingly based on, and dominated by, science and technology. However, the keyword of Aquarius is 'humanity', and in the future it is to be hoped that this quality will modify the present over-emphasis on science, harnessing it more to the actual needs of man, than simply to what is technically possible. The moderating influence of Aquarius' polarity with Leo will also be needed to avert the dangers of revolution, and reinforce the growing concern for peace. The illustration, above, from the American space programme, is the symbol of man's striving that will characterize the dawning age.

THE AGE OF AQUARIUS

The keyword for the Age of Aquarius will be Humanity. In the coming years we may hope to see Aquarius preside over a reconciliation between science and humanity, between the newest forms of scientific experiment and discovery and the ageless stream-bed of truths which run through man's unconscious.

The Great Year theory deals with such lengthy periods of time that it is impossible to say precisely when one Great Month gives way to another. The effects of the Piscean Age are undoubtedly still with us in the 1970s; just as undoubtedly, the world is already beginning to feel the influence of Aquarius. One exciting facet of the new dawn is the sudden upsurge of interest in astrology shown by young people. Alan Leo, the 19th-century astrological writer, looking forward to the coming influence of the new Great Month, brought out in his textbooks many Aquarian qualities which strongly apply to the present generation of teenagers: 'They incline towards the unconventional, and therefore make excellent reformers . . . They are always kind, humane . . . exceedingly fond of art, music and literature . . . have a great love for all humanitarian undertakings and concerns that produce harmony for the many . . . When living along purely personal lines they are chaotic, diffuse, deceptive, tricky and clever for their own ends; egotistical, and apt to use their inflexible wills in the direction of selfish mental desires; or inclined to be vacillating and capricious . . . Light and life await those who break away from the personality and live in the individuality of this sign. The inner nature and *destiny* of the sign is expressed in the one word: "humanity".'

Surely those words can be applied to students all over the world – in Japan and the USA, France, Germany, Holland, in Scandinavia and Britain, even perhaps in Russia – who in campus revolutions, peaceful and otherwise, indicate an insistent concern with social conditions, the problem of establishing world peace and the elimination of poverty and hunger, participation in their own education; and unfortunately also with a terse self-interest, foreseen in Leo's words. If the humanity of the present younger generation is seen in the voluntary work done for the Peace Corps, and various United Nations bodies, its chaos and egotism is also marked, though this usually springs from frustration with the status quo, a lack of positive aims and the feeling that any ideas they have will be immediately rejected out of hand.

These are the extremes of the Aquarian instinct. But in applying the 'personality' of the Sign to a two-thousand-year stretch of history, it is necessary to deal in generalities. The strong emphasis the Sign will place on science has already been seen in the scientific experimentation prompted by man's current pollution problems: a concern for environment is one of the strong Aquarian qualities. The polar Sign, Leo, will also contribute to the overall picture of the Age of Aquarius. It may to some extent be a saving force, for the Leonine personality is concerned in applying warm-hearted generosity to practical ends. Leo gives special force to qualities of leadership: combined with the Aquarian concern for humanity, this can be directed to the best kind of international supervision, and may yet rescue the concept of world government which so far in this century has made only faltering progress. This may be because Pisces, the 'watery' Sign which is giving way to Aquarius in the cycle of the Great Year, has been sufficently unsympathetic to the idea of international co-operation to impose its atmosphere of failure, changeability and despondency on these concepts.

Each Great Month has its own disadvantages: and one of the areas of danger which will have to be faced in the coming half-century will result from the conjunction between Uranus and Pluto which fell in Virgo between 1963 and 1969. This is a comparatively infrequent conjunction, and the children born during those years have received its impact linked for the first time with the added influence of the dawning Aquarian age. They will be the hope or despair of their time: they may save or destroy the world. In twenty years or so, when they begin to make their presence felt in society, we can expect to see the beginning of the first real manifestation of Aquarius on a world-wide scale – for these children will of course grow up in China, India, the Americas, Europe, out of vastly different social environments, cultures and political systems.

The individuality of men makes it impossible to say precisely what will occur. Individual babies will continue to be born with individual Birth Charts and will continue to exercise their natural free will both in childhood and in adult life. Science will certainly continue to be the dominating theme of the age. Man, already striding the face of the Moon, will head soon for the planets, and before the end of the Age of Aquarius may have answered the apparently insoluble problem of reaching towards solar systems beyond our own. The Age of Aquarius will be exciting, stimulating, at times dangerous. Whether we make a brilliant new world or destroy what we have already made, the initial responsibility rests with the new Aquarians – ourselves.

'Aquarius is responsible for more inventions
for the benefit of humanity than any of the other Signs.'
Alan Leo (1860–1917)

SCIENCE AND THE NEW ASTROLOGY I

For too long astrology was branded by laymen and experts alike as 'unscientific', a system of belief which they placed somewhere between hobby and cult with roots in man's mystical and superstitious past. How much of the blame for this view lay with the closed minds of the orthodox scientists and how much with the defensive attitudes of astrologers themselves is uncertain. Probably both sides were equally at fault, and it is not hard to see why. The real schism between astrology and its sister science, astronomy, came with the explosive growth of the latter at around the time of Copernicus when it was recognized for the first time that the Earth was a subsidiary unit in the solar complex; telescopic astronomy then revealed that individual members of the Solar System obeyed mysterious but *predictable* laws. The key word here is predictable, for the strength of a science lies in part in its power to plot the future.

In the case of astronomy this strength was soon demonstrated by the increasing grasp of the simpler mechanics of the Heavens – lunar and solar activity, planetary motion, seasonal and climatic shifts – which the Copernican revolution ushered in and which was to pave the way for Newton's great insights and mathematical theories. Astrology, on the other hand, managed to make no striking advance in its ability to predict events reliably. Serious astrologers were aware then – as they are today – that before their subject could hope to gain general acceptance, they would have to cross two major hurdles.

The first and most obvious is that astrology would have to meet this vital requirement of predictability, and not just of a kind acceptable to astrologers, but verifiable by sceptical observers from other scientific disciplines. Secondly, and perhaps the more difficult of the two hurdles, was the requirement that the topic should be logically consistent not only in itself but also within the philosophy of science in general. In other words it should be evident not only that astrology worked, but also that there should be some plausible explanation of *why* it worked. Today, after a long and uphill climb, the first signs are emerging which suggest that the long-awaited marriage between astrology and orthodox science may be about to take place.

The Rhythms of Life

In the past decade or two – it is hard to locate the date precisely – the interest of biologically orientated scientists has increasingly turned towards the study of the fascinating cyclic or rhythmic behaviour patterns displayed by man and many other animals. Most people are to some extent aware of the essentially rhythmic structure of natural events – the daily cycle of day and night, the complex sequence of tidal flow, the Moon's monthly progression, etc. — but few are aware of how profoundly these rhythms permeate not just celestial events but also affect the day-to-day scheme of living things. The brain, for example, as the diagram opposite shows, generates an exceedingly rich output of electrical rhythms, geared in some way to the acts of perception, learning, thinking, etc. Within the body too, apart from such obvious cycles as respiration, cardiac activity and so on, there are recurring patterns of fatigue and revival, of nervous tension and relaxation, and of hormonal and glandular action. On a different level sociologists, economists, anthropologists and ecologists have been detecting in groups and societies other cycles whose periodicity may vary between hours and decades. It is hard to avoid the conclusion that these rhythms have some functional significance, and even more important, that they are set in motion by some external source and 'driven' and controlled by some kind of timing device.

In the case of the 10-cycles-per-second pulses of the brain, the hidden timer is presently considered to be biochemical in origin. The daily cycle of sleep and wakefulness in man is, we know, partly triggered by the coming of light and dark. Similarly the tides are driven by the Moon's recurring phases, and, on an even larger scale, the migratory patterns of birds by the Sun's immense celestial clock. Presumably, other timers must control the rhythms which scientists are today detecting in almost all aspects of nature, whether these concern themselves with the movement of molecules or the rise and fall of economies and nations.

The Hidden Cycles

The reputable journal *Cycles*, the official bulletin of the Foundation for the Study of Cycles, devotes itself exclusively to objective scientific accounts of statistical patterns of various kinds. Most of these cycles are so clearly delineated as to be startling, but few have any identifiable trigger mechanisms or pacemakers to maintain the regularity of the cycle. Why, for example, should clear cycles with four-year 'peaks' be revealed through the study of such amazingly diverse phenomena as US stock prices, plankton yields in Lake Michigan, pork prices in Germany, snowy owl migrations and arctic fox population? Again typical 10-year cycles include such logically unlinked phenomena as cigarette production, cotton prices, prairie chicken abundance and US Post Office revenues. In the August 1970 issue of *The Bulletin*, the Foundation's president, E. R. Dewey, writes that it has now been demonstrated that mankind is subjected to vast, perhaps cosmic forces that determine his actions:

'These forces determine booms and recessions; prosperity and depression. They control to a large extent the ups and downs of production, not only of agricultural commodities but of industrial and mineral production as well. They largely control the ups and downs not only of prices in the mass, but of the prices of individual commodities such as corn, copper and cotton. They largely control interest rates and security prices – again not only of stocks and bonds but in the mass of individual issues. They control or at least influence man's susceptibility to various sorts of disease. They change man's mood from liberal to conservative and back to liberal again.'

To an increasing number of scientists the fact that such cycles exist, both in single living organisms and in major social and historical events, is demonstrated beyond doubt.

The diagram shows a range of activity cycles in the human body geared to acts of perception, breathing, reproduction, etc., from very fast brain rhythms (up to 1000 cycles per second) to the 200-day period of renewal bone.

Cerebral Nerones: 1000 c/sec
Information is transmitted along nerves from the nerve cells by rapid electrical impulses, travelling at several metres a second.

Slower Cerebral Rhythms: 50 c/sec
In each nerve cell are slower rhythms. Alternating bursts of spike activity (above) and slower waves constitute our perception.

Beta Rhythms: 18–22 c/sec
These occur in the frontal lobe of the brain, where the higher and more complex functions of judgment and personality are formed.

Alpha Rhythms: 8–13 c/sec
This rhythm is present when the eyes are closed but not when the eyes are open. It is also stopped or blocked by the act of attention.

Theta Rhythms: 4–7 c/sec
Theta rhythms exist in the memory store inside the temporal lobe; also on the surface of the brain when the level of alertness falls.

Delta Rhythms: 1–3 c/sec
Found on the surface of the brain, these occur naturally only in deep sleep, caused by depression of the reticular formation.

Heart Rhythms: 76 beats/min (first chamber)
The heart contains two natural pacemakers: one in the first chamber (76 beats/min), the other in the second chamber (40–50 beats/min).

Respiratory Cycle: 22 c/min
The lungs move in and out about every three seconds, the exact rate being mainly controlled by the level of gas (carbon dioxide) in the blood.

Kidneys: 24-hour cycle
In its 24-hour cycle, the kidney secretes urine during the daytime and early evening and then reduces the flow during the night.

Stomach and Intestines: 3 c/min and 1 c/min
The stomach contracts about three times every minute and the intestines show waves of contractions about once a minute.

Muscle Cycle: 12 days
Chief among the chemical components of the muscles are the proteins; these are broken down and built up again about every 12 days.

Ovaries: 28-day menstrual cycle
The ovaries release an egg every 28 days; if it is not fertilized the uterine wall is shed, resulting in the menstrual flow.

Red Blood Cell Cycle: 128 days
The bone marrow pours red blood cells or erythrocytes into the blood stream, each cell having a life of about 128 days.

Bone Calcium Cycle: 200 days
Bone is made up mainly of calcium salts, taken from the blood stream. After about 200 days the bone is entirely replaced.

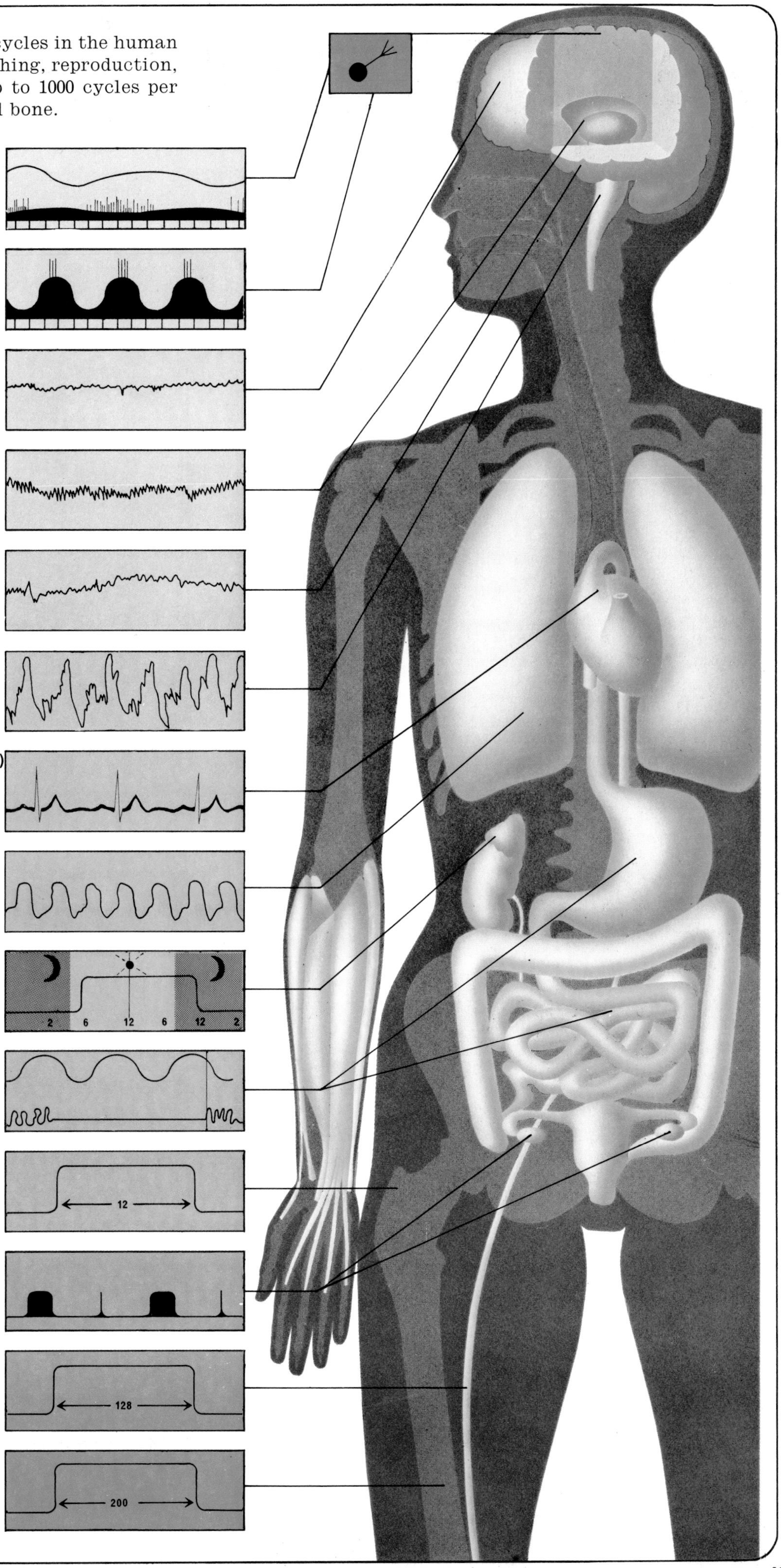

SCIENCE AND THE NEW ASTROLOGY 2

The fascinating questions now raised are (1) what is the function of these rhythms, and (2) what kind of clock or timing mechanism drives them? It is in this area, pioneered by the orthodox scientist, that a growing number of astrologers see their own subject making a significant contribution. For what, after all, have astrologers been studying down the centuries but the link between the stellar and planetary patterns and the behavioural patterns taking place on Earth?

The Work of John Addey

One of the principal protagonists of this point of view, and one of a growing number of similarly-minded students, is the English astrologer John Addey. Mr Addey, who is President of the Astrological Association and editor of its quarterly journal, has, in the course of 30 years of investigations into the topic, found himself moving away from the traditional view that a clear-cut relationship exists between the Signs and planetary aspects and specific human characteristics. In an interesting experiment involving nearly 1,000 nonagenarians (Mr Addey took their relevant statistics from *Who's Who*) he found no evidence that the expected Sun-Saturn aspect assigned to longevity was significantly present, nor again was the supposedly relevant Sign of Capricorn involved more than would be found by chance. A similar experiment involving 1,000 children suffering from paralytic poliomyelitis again failed to produce any indication of a significant dominance of the Sign and aspects which traditional astrological theory would predict.

Deeper analysis of the data, however, revealed an extraordinary wave-pattern in the plots, unlike anything met in previous astrological research. These wave patterns differed markedly from group to group, and Addey later discovered other significant harmonics in data gathered from huge samples of doctors and clergymen. His analysis can be summarized by saying that Addey sees astrological effects as being based on the harmonics of cosmic periods, the waveforms he has discovered as characteristic of, say particular professions, reflecting their harmonious relationship with the distant planetary events. In other words, the universe, whether at cosmic, biological or molecular level, is a complex of waveforms whose periodicity may range from nanoseconds to millions of years, and objects, events, people, nations and even planetary systems may be linked together in ways incomprehensible in terms of traditional astronomy and physics, but explicitly discoverable through astrology.

What is the Driving Force?

Assuming that the study of natural cycles develops at its present pace, providing at last the kind of statistical backing that astrology has long required and allowing astrological ideas to 'make sense' within the framework of current science, then the 'new Copernican revolution' will certainly be upon us. But there still remains the nagging question as to the exact nature of the mechanisms which link events as separate in distance and scale as, say, the

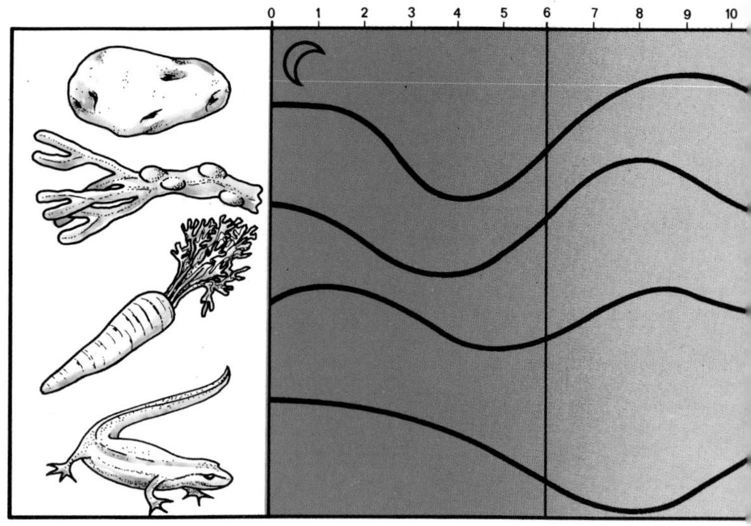

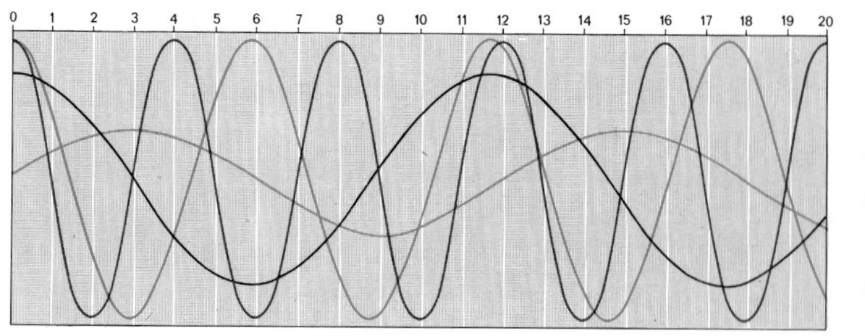

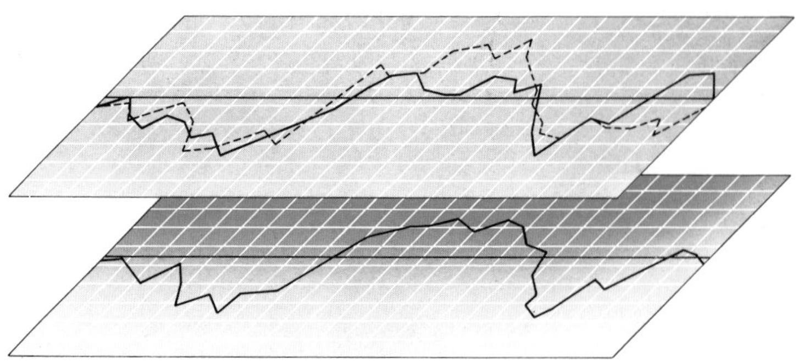

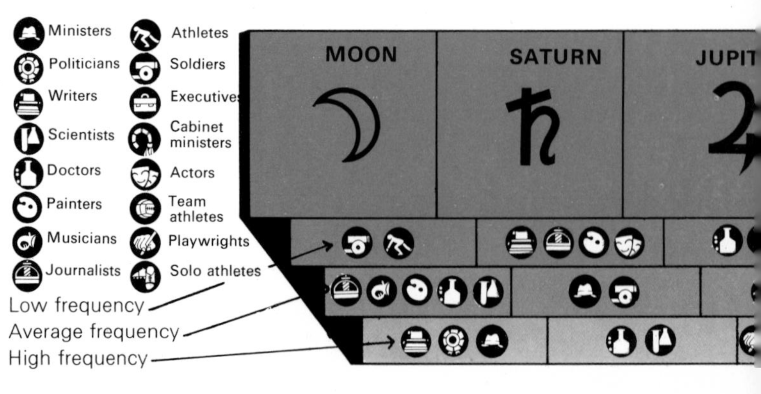

Moon Power *left*
Numerous plants and animals respond in their metabolic activity to the motions of the Moon. The diagram (after F. A. Brown, Jr) shows how he measured the oxygen consumption of potatoes, seaweed, carrots and newts, and plotted the rhythms these produced against the lunar day. Even when the Moon was not visible to particular phenomena, a remarkably similar response was maintained.

Activity Cycles
The US journal *Cycles* reports clearly defined cycles in an extraordinary range of phenomena; left, these reach statistical peaks at precisely maintained intervals, every 4, 5, 9, etc., years. At right, a list of some of the strange 4-year cycles already observed.

Phenomena	Years of Observation	Dates of Crests
Stock Prices, USA, 1837–1958	122	1968·5
Moody's Index of Industrial Bond Yields USA, 1919–1963	45	1968·75
Plankton Yields, Lake Michigan, 1926–1942	17	1969·5
Cheese Consumption, 1867–1953	87	1970·0
Sunspots, Alternate Cycles Reversed, 1749–1954	206	1970·25
Arctic Fox Abundance, Canada, 1872–1931	60	1970·5
Pork Prices, Germany, 1896–1930	35	1970·5
Field Mouse Abundance, 1863–1936	74	1971–72
Industrial Output, USA, 1944–1958	15	1972·5

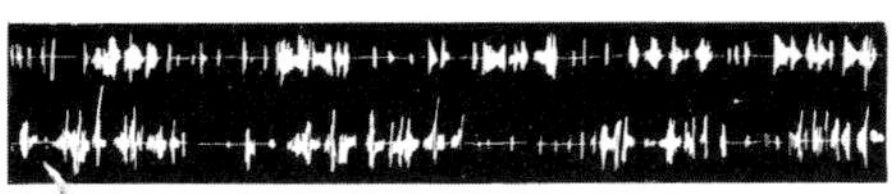

Wave Analysis *left*
John Addey's analyses of the Birth Charts of groups – 1,000 nonagenarians, 1,000 polio victims, etc. – yielded significant wave forms for each. The upper diagram shows the waves obtained from polio victims in two different hospitals; below, a combined graph.

Rat Behaviour *above*
Even in the laboratory confines rats show peaks of activity according to the position of the Moon.

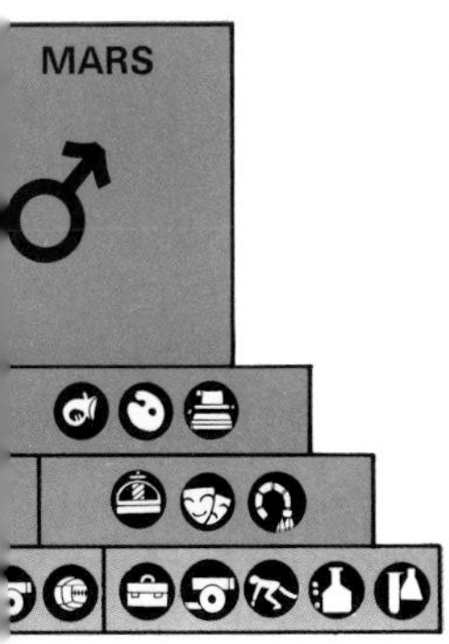

Planets and Professions *left*
The French scientist Michel Gauquelin found remarkable correlations between the Birth Charts of men who later took up the same profession. Saturn, for example, at its rising and zenith positions during the 24-hour cycle, occurred frequently in the Charts of scientists and doctors. The diagram shows the results obtained by Gauquelin in relation to four planets, the Moon, Saturn, Jupiter and Mars. Professions occupying the front row were strongly in evidence; those in the centre row occurred with average frequency, and those in the back row had a low frequency rate.

relative motion of two planets, and the birth of a single human being. In fact, from the strictly scientific point of view, it is not really a valid objection to say that one cannot understand how something works – a demonstration that it *does* work is enough. Obviously, however, an accurate account of the mechanics of any working system, whether it be the inside of a motor-car engine or the subject matter of astrology, would be the biggest step towards a true understanding of it.

The Challenge to Astrology

One of the principal arguments advanced against astrological beliefs relies on the assumption that the mechanics of astrology are either totally unknown or totally incredible. For example the question is often put: 'How can the planets possibly influence day-to-day affairs on earth?' With the possible exception of the hypothesis implicit in Addey's theories that different aspects of life on Earth are driven or set in motion by different 'clocks', some of which will be molecular, others cosmic in scale, few astrologers will pretend to be able to answer this question squarely.

However, a close look at this important question reveals that it is really built on the premise that it is impossible to account for a causal relationship between objects at a distance which are not physically or electromagnetically linked. To make this point a bit clearer, the argument can be rephrased thus: the universe is composed of a vast number of particles of matter, or electromagnetic vibrations, bunched together in the form of planets, suns, people, etc. Events or changes of state in these clusters take place as the result of the impact of one particle of matter (atom) on another. In classical physics the atom with highest energy shoves the lesser about and we say that atom A has 'caused' atom B to move; or that electromagnetic energy has changed from A to B. This notion of causality, fundamental to the whole scientific framework of the moment, may not be as sacrosanct as some people believe – as we shall discuss later when we come to consider the work of the great psychologist Carl Gustav Jung – but we will accept it here for the sake of the argument. What sceptics of astrology are pointing out is that while a causal relationship between two objects close together and physically linked is comprehensible, it is meaningless when the objects are separated by immense gulfs of empty space.

Leaving aside for the moment the peculiar phenomenon known as 'gravity', which seems to act with no direct physical link through 'empty' space, we find that this argument breaks down in more than one way. In the first instance it fails to take into account the dramatic effects of solar light (as opposed to heat) on terrestrial life forms, and secondly it makes the naive assumption that the only possible causal links between distant objects and our own planet are those which we can detect with our normal senses. Before, too, we look at the fascinating data on the effect of light on biological systems, let us first consider the possibility of less obvious forms of 'action at a distance'.

COSMIC ENERGY SYSTEMS I

In our search for a causal link between man, his activities and those of the 'upper world', we are bringing traditional aspects of science to bear on the question: 'Why does astrology work?' Is it due simply to the apparent positions of the planets and other celestial bodies; is it due to their light, to their invisible radiations, or to some other emissions or vibrations which are completely unknown to us?

There seem to be no purely logical reasons to suppose that the positions in themselves can provide a full answer to the problem. It is much more likely that we must turn to radiations of some sort or other. It would be, however, a grave limitation to confine our attention to visible light, for the light we can see is only a very small part of the total electromagnetic spectrum. Below the limit of the visible, we have the short-wavelength ultra-violet rays, X-rays and gamma-rays; above we have infra-red together with microwaves and radio emissions of all kinds. As the diagram shows, the range is tremendous, and apart from the fact that our eyes are sensitive only to the middle octave it is important to remember that the Earth's atmosphere is largely opaque. Only visible light, plus a certain amount of infra-red and radio radiation, can pass through.

Electromagnetic Spectrum *below* Electromagnetic radiation is in the form of a continuous oscillating wave moving through space and varies between low frequency, long-wave length radio waves and high frequency short-wavelength gamma-rays. This is simply illustrated in the diagram below, where the

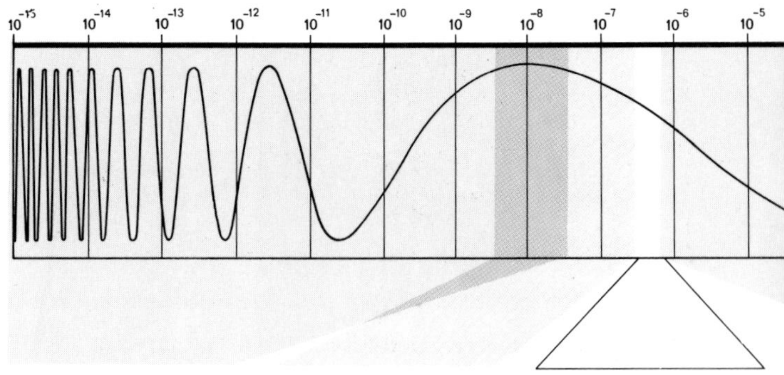

Gamma and X-rays These are short and highly penetrating. Gamma-ray sources have been identified in the sky, but their nature is still uncertain; there are many X-ray sources, one of which is the Crab Nebula below. Since both gamma and X-rays are absorbed in the upper atmosphere, rocket techniques have to be used to study them.

Ultra-Violet Radiation Extending between the X-ray and the visible part of the spectrum, ultra-violet radiations are also absorbed in the upper atmosphere. For this reason little was known about them until recently. In fact all stars send out ultra-violet radiation, but the hotter stars are more powerful. Below is Mars in ultra-violet.

Visible Light Visible light is so limited and restricted that the astronomers with only an optical telescope were bound to have only fragmentary knowledge – like a musician with a piano that only has the notes in the middle octave. Some extension of this range was afforded by photography. Below is Mars in visible light.

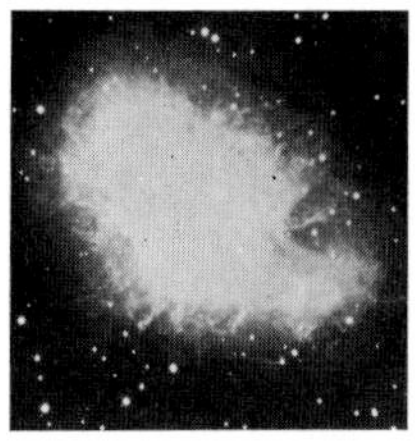

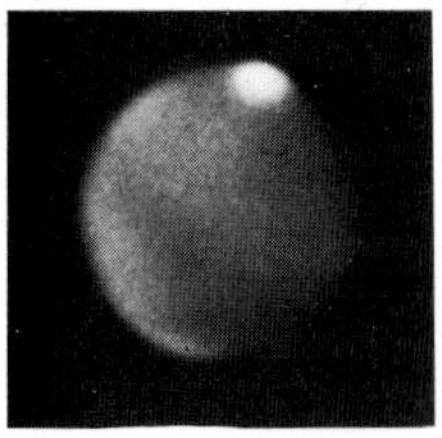

Cosmic Rays and Gravity

We must also bear in mind the fact that the universe contains energy in the form of cosmic rays, which are essentially streams of particles. Our knowledge of them is incomplete; but they may originate in stellar explosions (supernovae). And, as we have said, there is gravity. We have no idea at all of the nature of this weak but vital force. We know how it acts; but we do not know why.

Moreover, we have strong evidence of another force. The outer galaxies (at least, those beyond our local group) are receding from us at high velocities; some attain more than half the speed of light, and if modern theory is to be trusted the strange, enigmatical objects known as quasars may be receding at over 90% of the velocity of light. If gravitation were the only universal force, there would be a steady, inexorable contraction until all the material came together. The fact that this does not happen shows that there is a force whose nature eludes us. It is called cosmic repulsion; but we know nothing about it – except that it exists.

The essential point behind this chain of argument is that we cannot pretend to know about all the various emissions pervading the universe. Some new kinds have been discovered in recent years. Radio astronomy, now such a vital branch of modern science, began only in 1931; it was not till 1954 that the planet Jupiter was found to be such a source. X-rays and gamma-rays from the sky are of even more recent detection. Before these revelations, it was only too easy to dismiss astrology as being false simply because there were no obvious emissions or vibrations which could account for it. Today, any such claim would be most unwise.

The Earth itself has a protecting magnetosphere. The so-called solar wind strikes the boundary of this magnetosphere and sets up a shock-wave, so that the magnetosphere itself is shaped like a tear-drop with its tail pointing away from the Sun. Most of the solar wind particles fail to penetrate the boundary. Those which do so, particularly near the magnetic poles, come into the Van Allen zones, regions of intense radiation discovered initially in 1958.

Quite apart from this protection, there is the Earth's atmosphere itself. In the ionosphere, between 70 and 140 miles above sea level, there are ionized layers which effectively block out all the harmful short-wave radiations which would otherwise bombard us, and would prevent the development of any life on Earth. Most of the long-wavelength emissions, too, are stopped in the ionosphere – as are small solid particles like meteors.

spectrum moves from short/rapid waves on the left to long/slower waves on the right. Although all types of radiation are found in outer space, only two limited ranges are admitted to us via the visible and radio 'windows' in the Earth's atmosphere. The darkly shaded areas show where two bands of radiation overlap.

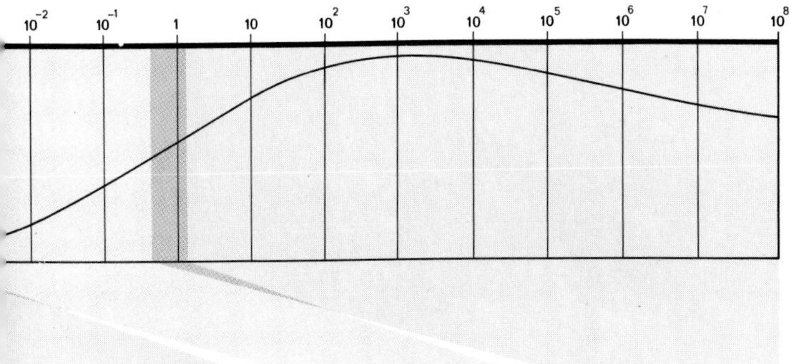

Infra-Red Radiation
Beyond the visible range is the infra-red part of the spectrum, extending to the centimetre range. Again there is absorption in the upper atmosphere (apart from a few 'windows'). Though all stars are infra-red sources, the cool ones are the most powerful; for example, Betelgeux in Orion. Below is Mars in infra-red.

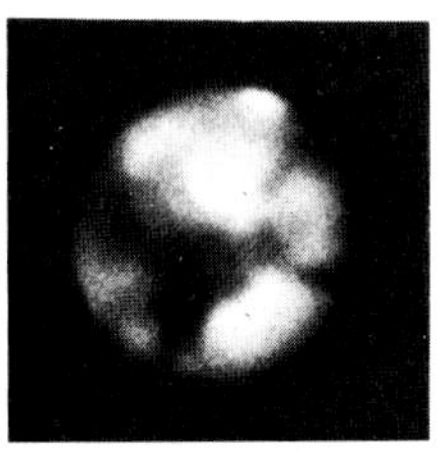

Microwave Radiation
Reaching the Earth through the 'radio window', microwave radiation is collected and focused by radio telescopes. Among sources of microwave radiation are the Sun, the planet Jupiter, and supernova remnants in our Galaxy. By now detailed maps of the 'radio sky' have been drawn up. Below is a contour map of the Sun's emissions.

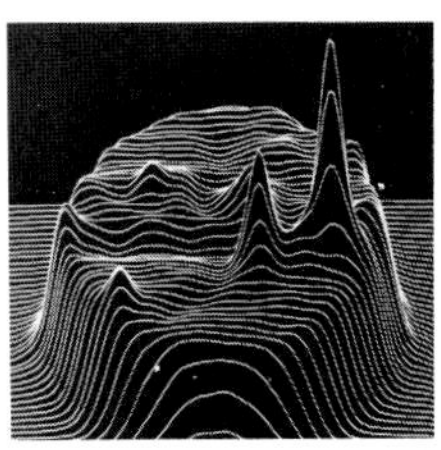

Long-Wave Radio
The ionosphere totally absorbs any extreme long-wave-length radiations. In the future, installations on the surface of the Moon will no doubt be set up to study them. The wavelengths extend from 100 centimetres up to many kilometres from crest to crest. Below is a contour map of the radio source, quasar 3C-47.

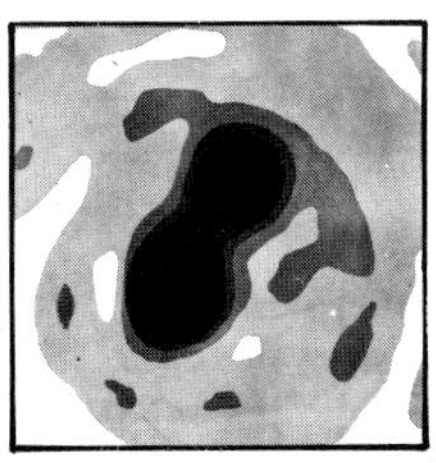

Universal Activity Scale *below*
The idea of activity cycles shown on p. 49 can be applied to every form of cosmic activity. The universal scale below runs from Ångströms (the unit for measuring the wavelength of light and other electromagnetic vibrations) to the time – measured in millions of years – which the Sun takes to complete one cycle of the Galaxy.

Wavelength	Cycles	
0·001 Ångström	10^{23} cycles per second	Cosmic rays
1Å	10^{21}	Gamma rays
500Å	10^{18}	X-rays
3000Å	10^{16}	Ultra-violet rays
6000Å	10^{15}	Visible spectrum
10,000Å	10^{13}	Infra-red rays
Millimetres	10^{12}–10^{7}	Short radio waves
100-1000 metres	10^{6}	Medium radio waves
1000 metres	10^{5}	Long radio waves
	10^{4}	Brain and muscular rhythms
	Seconds per cycle	Slower rhythms of man
	Days per cycle	Rotation of Earth on its axis
	Months per cycle	Rotation of Moon round Earth
	Years per cycle	Rotation of Earth round Sun
	100 years per cycle	Rotation of slow moving planets
	1000 years per cycle	Rotation of star clusters
	Millions of years per cycle	Rotation of Sun round Galaxy

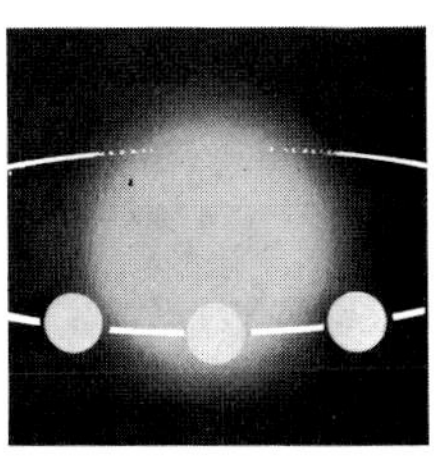

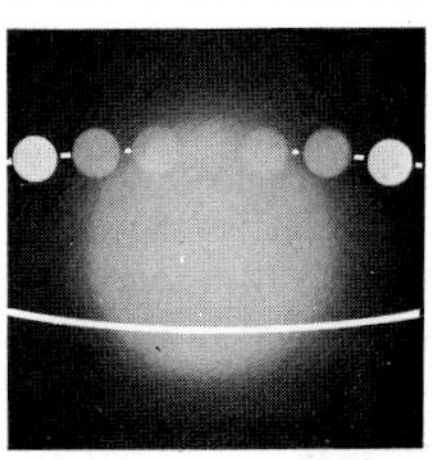

Giants of the Universe *left*
The giant member of the eclipsing binary known as Zeta Aurigae is 180 million miles in diameter. The smaller associated star has a diameter of 2·5 million miles and is shown crossing the disk of the supergiant in the upper illustration; below, when the smaller star is eclipsed the light is so fierce that it shines through the supergiant's atmosphere for three weeks.

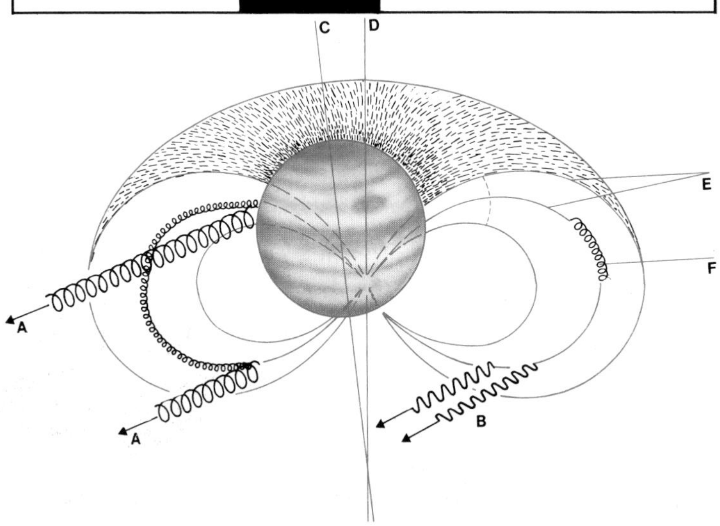

The Magnetosphere of Jupiter *right*
Intense bursts of radio radiation from Jupiter were recorded in 1954. The reasons for this activity are not clear but volcanic shock waves or chemical explosions have been suggested. The diagram is a speculative explanation; A,B Circular-and plane-polarized radiation; C,D Jupiter's rotation and magnetic axis; E Magnetic field lines; F Trapped particles.

COSMIC ENERGY SYSTEMS 2

On Earth, then, we are in some measure screened. Meteors, primary cosmic rays, and lethal emissions from space fail to reach us. Gravity can do so; whether in wave-form or not, it is a force which cannot be blocked.

Now let us consider the possible reasons for astrological effects. The radiations bombarding us from space are of many kinds. They are affected by the positions of the various celestial bodies. No solar X-rays or ultra-violet, and no solar radio emissions, can reach a point on the Earth's surface from which the Sun is below the horizon; the radio waves from Jupiter cannot be detected unless Jupiter is visible in the sky; the rapidly-vibrating pulses from neutron stars, such as that inside the expanding gas-cloud of the Crab Nebula, must also be suitably placed, before we can detect them. Therefore, it is quite logical to suppose that other emissions, unknown to us, are similarly

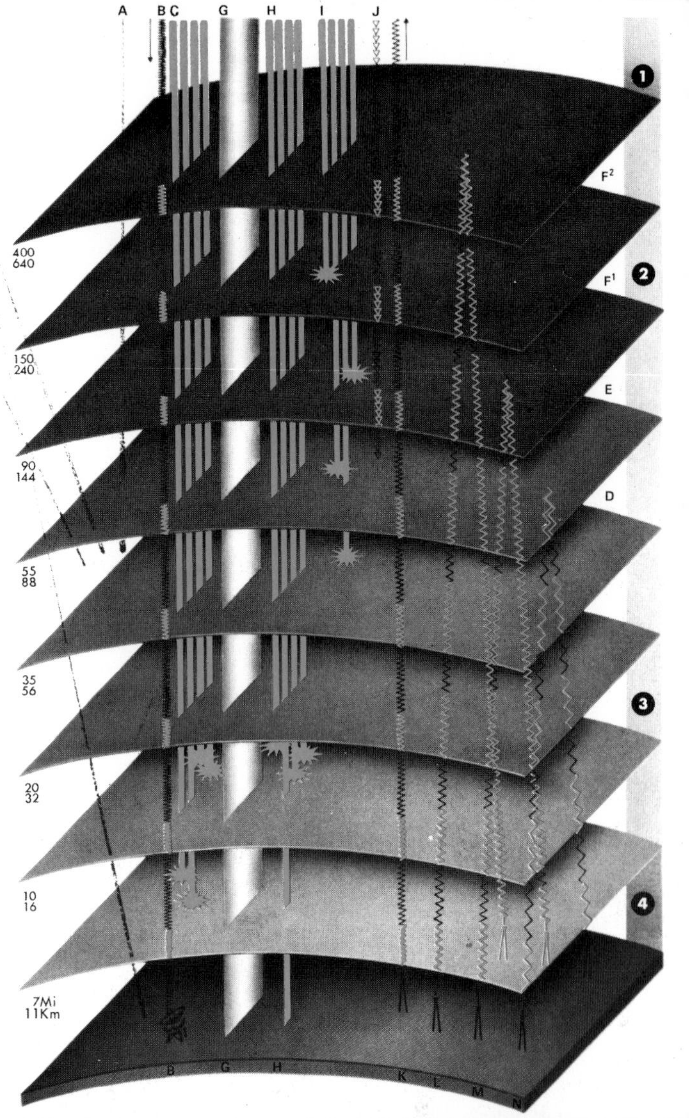

The Earth's Protective Atmosphere *right*
The atmosphere acts as a screen against radiations and cosmic particles. Approximately 450 miles thick, it is made up of four main layers: the outermost is the exosphere; then the ionosphere, vital for communications since it reflects radio waves; then the stratosphere whose ozone, concentrated 16 miles above sea level, protects us from lethal short-wave radiation from space; and finally the troposphere in which all normal weather occurs, and life can flourish.

1 Exosphere **2** Ionosphere; **3** Stratosphere; **4** Troposphere. **A** Meteors; **B** Radio waves from space; **C** Infra-red radiation; **D** D-layer; **E** E-layer; **F** F-layer; **F_2F_2** layer; **G** Visible light; **H** Ultra-violet radiation penetrating atmosphere; **I** Ultra-violet radiation creating ionized layers; **J** X-rays absorbed in ionosphere; **K, L, M, N** VHF, short-wave, medium-wave and long-wave transmissions respectively.

Polar Lights *right*
The 'auroral curtain' is caused by charged particles from the Sun being accelerated downwards after hitting the Earth's upper atmosphere.

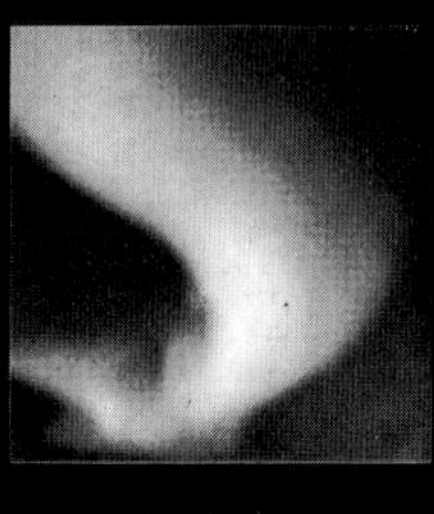

The Earth's Magnetosphere *right*
As a result of its heavy magnetic core the Earth is screened from a range of intensive cosmic rays by its magnetosphere. This forms a barrier against charged particles and traps others, producing what is known as the Van Allen radiation zone discovered only in 1958 by the United States satellite Explorer I. The Van Allen region can be divided into two zones, the inner **1** and the outer **2**. The inner zone, about 3,000 miles above the Earth, is made up of protons caused by cosmic rays **A**. The outer zone, about 10,000 miles above the Earth is made up of electrons **C**, which are due to solar winds **B**. This zone is disturbed by solar flares, which are responsible for the brilliant polar lights (see above). Between the two Van Allen zones is a region, at an altitude of 8,000 miles, of lesser intensity, that is called the 'slot' **3**. The diagram shows the general aspect of the main part of the Earth's magnetosphere. The north and south magnetic poles (X and X) are shown; they are not coincident with the geographical poles (N and S).

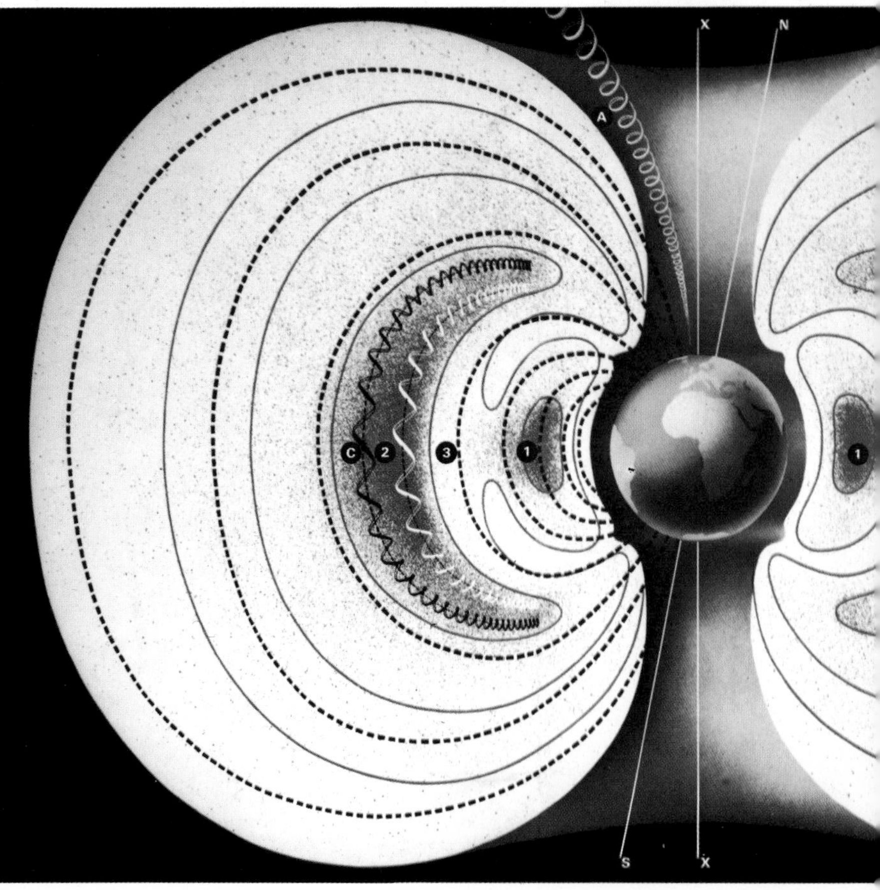

affected. And can it be that these are the cause of astrological influences?

The idea may sound highly speculative; and indeed it is so. But an astronomer of the 1920s, who seriously suggested that the Sun or Jupiter might be sending us radio waves, would have been even more decisively condemned. When we consider the possibilities of invisible radiations, gravitational effects, and unknown emissions, we may have taken a first step towards the answer to our problem. Whether it can ever be solved remains to be seen. At the very least it creates among astrologers and scientists a fresh set of opportunities for profitable dialogue. And this in a field where dialogue was once extremely rare, where both sides tended to issue statements, as of fact, and showed little respect for differing points of view.

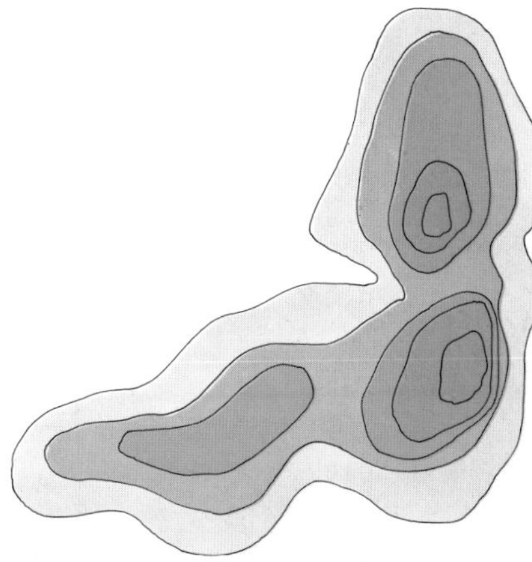

The Radio Sky
Radio telescope's version of Centaurus A, left, covers a wider area than its optical counterpart, above, which is contained in the small rectangle in the centre.

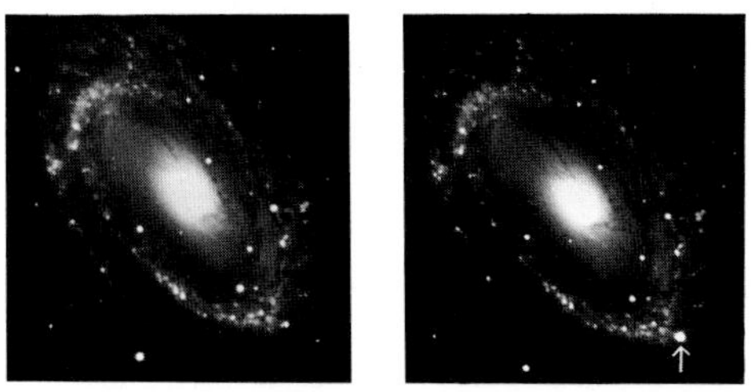

Appearance of a Supernova *above*
An exploding supernova, invisible at left, appears suddenly in this spiral galaxy (arrowed right).

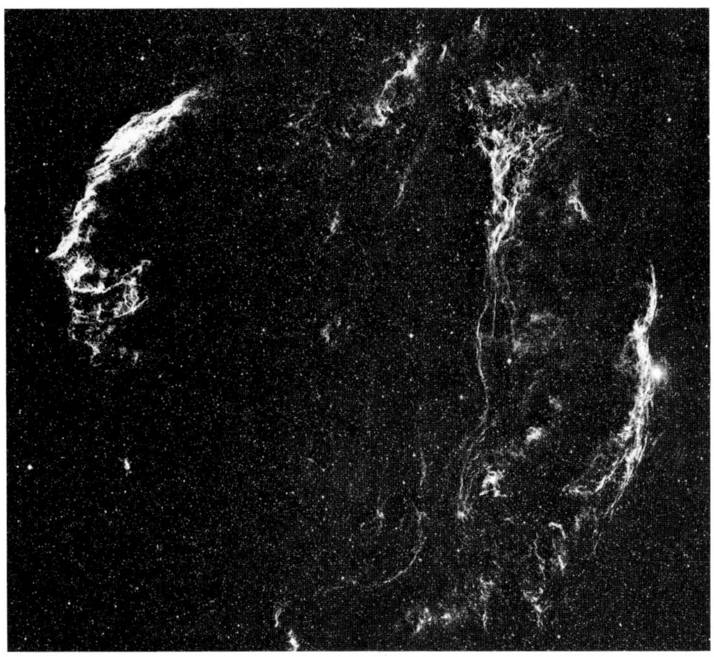

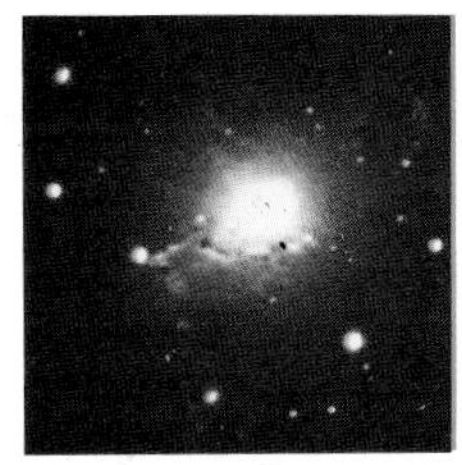

Radio Star *above*
An explosive 'jet' of cosmic energy issues from the main radio source in the constellation, Perseus.

Veil Nebula *left*
A giant gas cloud over 50,000 years old, and still expanding, the Veil Nebula probably resulted from a supernova explosion.

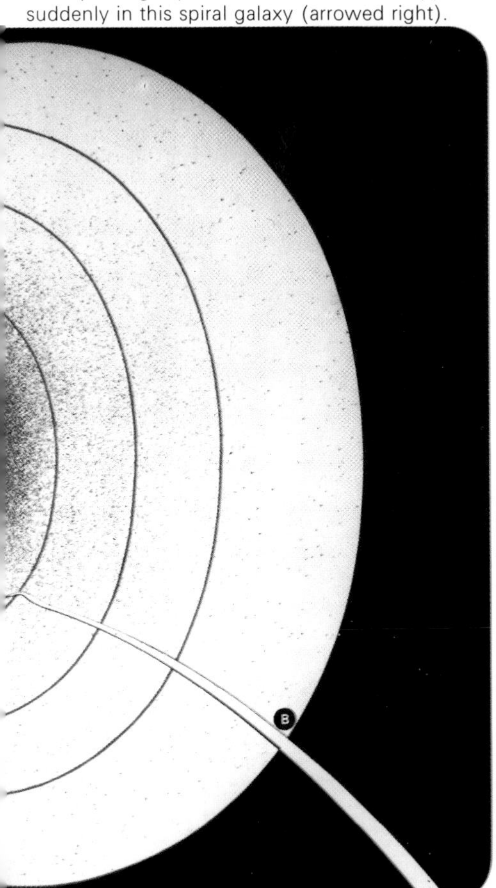

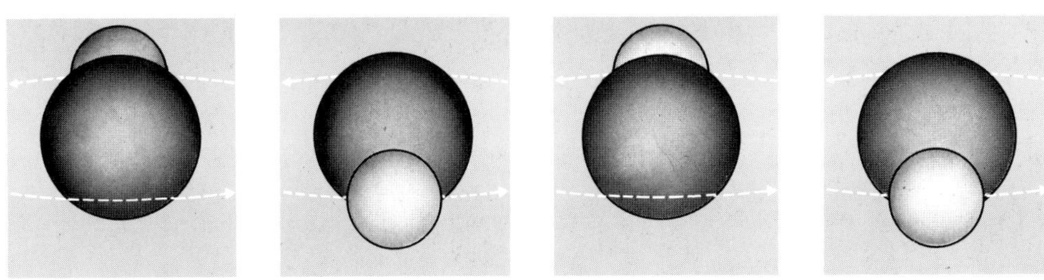

Cosmic Variations *above*
The light-curve diagram shows how the binary or double star Algol varies in cosmic intensity every $2\frac{1}{2}$ days. As the fainter of the two components passes in front of the brighter (1 and 3 above) a marked decrease in brightness occurs. This is known as a primary minimum; a secondary minimum takes place when the brighter body eclipses its partner, and blots out less light.

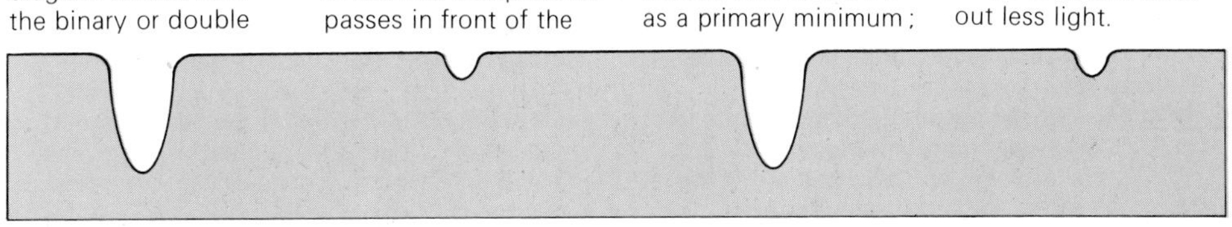

BIOLOGICAL CLOCKS

In recent years the case for astrology has been remarkably strengthened by discoveries made in the context of other, scientifically established disciplines. In the biological sciences the study of rhythms or cycles runs close to the astrological idea in its notion that behaviour patterns are started up and controlled by some kind of timing device or cosmic clock.

The simplest example of this 'photic' control of biological rhythms is one we have already mentioned – the light/dark sequence which controls our feeling of wakefulness. The same sequence involves other bodily functions – digestion, kidney retention, appetite – functions which are severely thrown out of joint when an individual moves rapidly from one part of the world to another; after a transatlantic jet flight a period of days may be needed for readjustment.

Today, thanks to electric light, for example, human beings can introduce artificial control of this photic clock, but by no means the same applies to wild animals which show clear evidence of using the heavenly bodies or other regular natural events in a surprising number of ways. Although care must be taken in drawing too direct conclusions astrologically speaking, it is important to realize the scientific distinction between solar heat and solar light as means of driving terrestrial events: whereas the Sun's heat output is sufficient to cause measurable physical changes in living things, its light output can only control human or higher animal behaviour by acting as some form of clock or timing device. The same argument of course applies even more forcibly to the effects of lunar or stellar light.

Lunar Rhythms

The small Pacific worm *Palolo viridis*, for instance, has an annual swarming date which corresponds not simply with every full Moon, but exactly with one particular new Moon of the year. Another worm, *Convoluta roscoffensis*, apparently uses the tide as its 'clock', appearing on the sand at the ebb in numbers so vast that the surface is coloured green for miles, but rapidly disappearing in the lower level of sand as the tide rises. The presence or absence of water does not provide the clue to what drives the army of worms in unison; rather it is some type of gravity or geotaxic force which scientists are still hard-pressed to understand. Curiously, when single specimens of *Convoluta* are isolated and put in an aquarium, they maintain their rhythm for at least a week in the laboratory even when no mechanical disturbance is given. This has led scientists to assume that these physiologically simple creatures must be equipped with some *internal* clock which in turn has been set by the tides. At this point the astrologer might reasonably point out that this 'explanation' of the worms' cyclic behaviour leaves no fewer questions unanswered than does his own belief in the relationship between planetary patterns and human cycles.

Other examples of rhythmic behaviour of one kind or another can be seen in fireflies (which have a tendency to 'wink' in phase), in grasshoppers, locusts, etc., which tend to swarm according to some unidentifiable stimulus, and schools of fish which display remarkable group behaviour including 'ranking themselves like soldiers on parade' or turning, stopping or starting again in absolute

The Cosmic Triggers
In species as diverse as potatoes, oysters, rats, flatworms and man, evidence is accumulating which shows that many vital functions– breathing, reproduction, etc. – are influenced by extra-terrestrial powers, most notably those emanating from the Sun and Moon, that were undreamed of until a short while ago. Patterns of behaviour in oysters, for example, which were once attributed to the pull of the tides, are now known to result from the changing position of the Moon, new or full, above or below the horizon. Furthermore, these patterns are not brought about by the Moon's light since they are maintained even when the oysters are kept in closed containers in the laboratory.

The presence of unseen influences is the most exciting discovery in this area of biological science, since it illustrates precisely the kind of influence which astrologers have always claimed for the planets. It seems, though, that both sides – the scientist and the astrologer – may need to extend their acceptance of phenomena if a workable union is to be reached. At present, the fact that mice are sensitive to gamma rays is not the kind of information that will excite every astrologer. Nevertheless, astrologers are making use of an increasing mass of cosmic data – and in turn handing back to the traditional sciences entirely fresh predictive data for the scientists to test and utilize.

Lunar Clock of the Pacific Worm *below*
The annual swarming date of the Pacific worm *Palolo viridis* corresponds exactly with one particular new Moon. So predictable is this cycle that local fishermen, guided by their almanacs, arrive in large numbers to harvest it.

The Moon's Influence on Flatworms *right*
F. A. Brown, Jr. found that flatworms (*planaria*) are directed by lunar phases. On leaving their enclosures they turn about 10° to the left at the new Moon (black disk); at full Moon (white disk) they turn to the right.

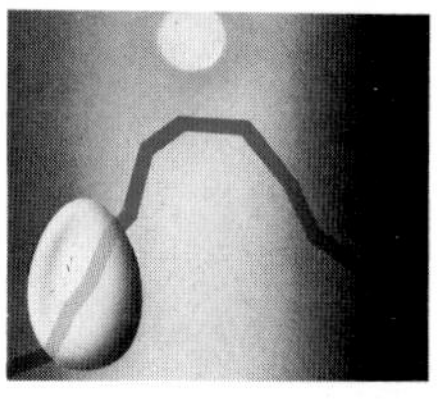

Embryo Chickens *left*
Fertilized hen's eggs respond to the movements of the Sun; thus the 'clock' functions even when the timer is invisible.

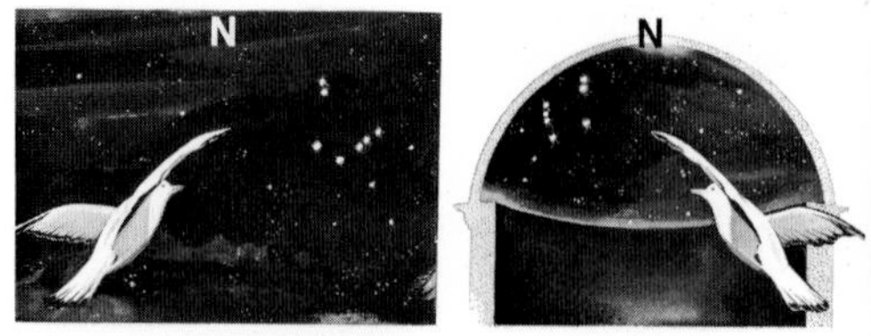

Hamsters Ruled by the Sun and Moon
Hamsters attuned under normal conditions to the movements of the Sun, were then induced to change their pattern. Confined to cages, they adjusted to the longer period of the lunar day, reverting occasionally to the solar clock.

Navigation by the Stars *above*
In a recent experiment a flock of birds released in a planetarium still set off in the 'correct' direction according to the stars; wrong by the compass, they were clearly guided by the constellations.

> 'The Moon feeds oysters, fills sea urchins,
> puts flesh on shellfish and on beasts.'
> Lucilius (180–102 BC)

unison. In case this may seem to have little to do with astrology in the traditional sense, we need to remind ourselves that we are here discussing the driving of human behaviour by some potent, external force which may be either near at hand (as perhaps in the case of the tides) or at an immense distance, as in the case of the lunar clock.

There is clear evidence, which might seem fantastic were it not backed by solid scientific experiment, that the constellations themselves – man's age-old guide to navigation – are used as navigational aids by a number of creatures, notably birds. Homing pigeons released at night, for example, make their way without disaster; and for those who would care to invoke some 'gravitational' explanation it should be pointed out that, in another experiment, birds released in a planetarium set out in the 'correct' direction, thus clearly indicating that it is the very pattern of the constellations which determines their action.

The Powers of Light and Darkness

In man, as we have said, the coming of artificial light and darkness cycles have to some extent overriden the 'natural' pacemakers of the universe. Recent experiments conducted by a leading American Air Force scientist, Dr E. M. Dewan, came with a shock of surprise and highlighted the extent to which this has developed. Dewan, a physicist specializing in the study of linear oscillations, formed the hypothesis that the menstrual periods of the human female were (or should be) related to the 29-day lunar cycle. Why then were so many women irregular in their periods? Dewan suggested that this might be because artificial methods and irregularities of lighting had replaced the light of the Moon, thus slowly reducing the 'power' of the lunar clock. Around the equator the full Moon stays out all night and humans and animals can live outside all year round; and there is a mass of evidence that the fertility cycles of many animals are locked to the full Moon. In Dewan's view the full Moon probably once served as a planetary clock to regulate the fertility cycle of the primitive human female; presumably a racial 'memory' of this was then carried over to *homo sapiens*, long after humans had ceased to live in the warm equatorial outdoors. To test his remarkable idea, the physicist, with a psychiatrist colleague, Dr John Rock, set out to perform an unusual experiment. He arranged for 20 women with a history of chronic irregularity in their menstrual cycle to leave the light on in their bedrooms for three nights commencing on the 14th day after menstruation. The results were dramatic, with all the women regularizing their menstrual cycle. So seriously are these experiments being taken that this method has been proposed to the Roman Catholic ecclesiastical authorities as a method of making the 'safe' period more safe! The results of the experiments, incidentally, have been published in the reputable *American Journal of Obstetrics and Gynaecology*.

It should be clear from these few representative examples, that the essential idea of astrology – the significant and meaningful relationship between celestial events and life in all its forms on Earth – after some centuries in the philosophical wilderness – is slowly but surely finding favour with establishment science. This combination of the two disciplines will strengthen both.

Ovulation of Sea Urchins
Even in Aristotle's day it was known that the gonads of edible marine animals such as clams and sea urchins are fullest at the full Moon, though it was not realized that this was because the lunar light triggered the fertility cycle.

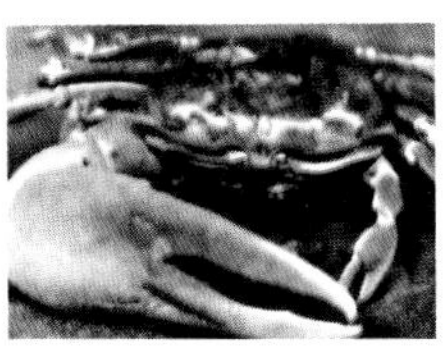

Fiddler Crab *right*
An experiment by Brown showed that the fiddler crab changed colour in relation to the Moon's position.

The Movements of Oysters *right*
Before this test by Brown, it had already been established that oyster shells opened and shut in a distinct rhythm, presumably following the action of the tides. However, Brown removed a batch of oysters from their natural habitat and took them in sealed containers to his laboratory, at Evanston, Illinois, approximately 1,000 miles from the sea. There the oysters continued to behave exactly as though they were still by the sea, opening and closing their shells to the rhythm of their 'home' tides. Then, after about two weeks, a change came about: the oysters adjusted their 'clocks' to a new rhythm, corresponding not to any tide but to the lunar phases at Evanston, thereby proving that it was the Moon's position not the tides, as had always been supposed, which was responsible for the oysters' rhythm cycle.

Fertility Clocks *below*
Dr Dewan, an American scientist, regularized the menstrual cycle of 20 women by persuading them to leave the light on in their bedrooms for three nights from the 14th day after menstruation. This 'Moon substitute' proved 100% successful. In the diagram A represents the beginning of the menstrual cycle.

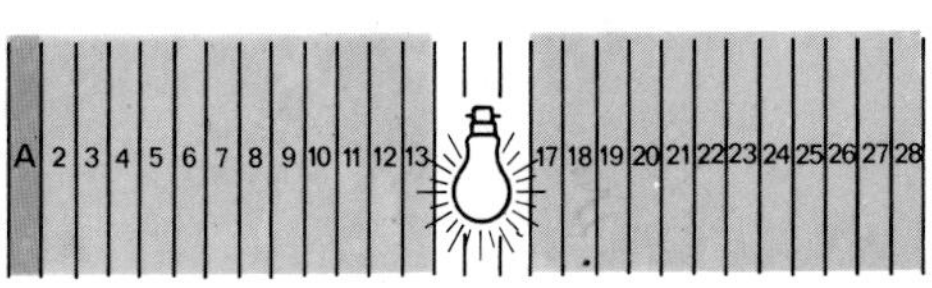

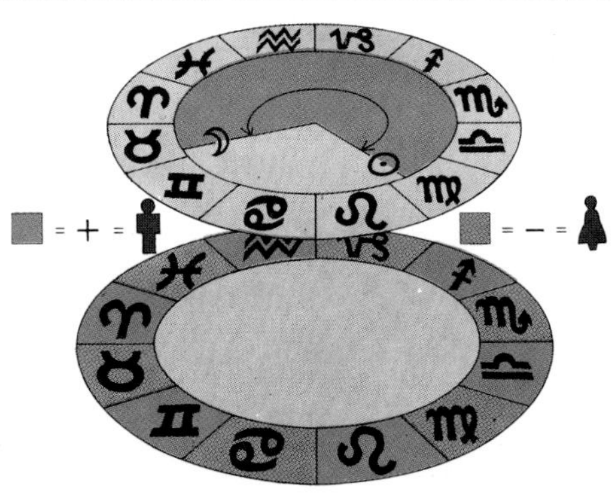

Fertility and the Sun-Moon Axis *left*
Dr Eugen Jonas, a Czech psychiatrist, established with 87% success that women were fertile when the Sun and Moon returned to the exact angular relationship they occupied in the patients' Birth Charts.

Determining the Sex of Unborn Children *left*
Dr Jonas also concluded that the sex of an unborn child was fixed by the Moon's position at conception; against a positive sign of the Zodiac the child would be male; female in a negative sign.

TWO KINDS OF COSMOS

The Causal Chain

Astronomers have suggested that the Sun, Moon and planets may once have been joined in a single body which later exploded. Whether or not this is a valid explanation, astrologers generally regard the 'active' bodies of the Solar System as the sum-total of a single driving force. Within that framework some astrologers believe that the planets are symbolic of the way we think and behave on Earth. On the other hand, many modern astrologers are impressed by the growing weight of scientific evidence to support a causal system. The panels below reveal some of the connections between that evidence and traditional lore.

☉ **The Sun** Most powerful body in the Solar System, a pivotal force in our lives, without which life on Earth could not exist. The Sun is active, associated in astrology with power, energy and self-expression, and human types are assessed largely by their solar characteristics. Sunspots, in the unseen physical sphere, generate magnetic activity; brilliant eruptions, known as solar flares, emit short-wave radiations that cause magnetic storms and interfere with radio transmissions on Earth. During World War II, when our knowledge was less precise, flare outbursts were mistaken for enemy action.

☽ **The Moon** Next to the Sun in astrological importance, the Moon is linked with response to conditions, and fluctuation. In physical terms the Moon is our nearest neighbour and is also an integral part of the terrestrial system, the common centre of gravity being located within the Earth; compare, too, the astrological connection with body fluids to its physical effect on Earth fluids – the oceans – as the main tide-raising force; solar tides are appreciably weaker. The Moon controls the rhythmic behaviour of numerous creatures on Earth, including the feminine rhythm in human life.

☿ **Mercury** In astrology the planet of mentality and nervous reaction, Mercury lies within the outer corona of the Sun; in this zone coronal material is subject to frequent and erratic fluctuations. Mercury is, moreover, the swiftest-moving of the independent planets (not counting the Moon which is 'tied' to the Earth) and makes rapid changes of declination in the sky. At inferior conjunction (when Mercury lies between the Sun and the Earth) its magnetic field deviates the stream of electrified particles sent out from the Sun; these particles have an influence on the human nervous system.

♀ **Venus** Whether we regard the planets as springs of cosmic activity or as symbols, the astrological importance of Venus is easy to understand. It is associated with harmony and unison, qualities borne out by its physical constancy, for Venus has the lowest orbital eccentricity of all the planets, and its distance from the Sun remains almost constant at 67,200,000 miles. Venus is a warm though enclosed world, the carbon dioxide content in its atmosphere tending to shut in the Sun's heat. Venus also shares a special 'partnership' with the Earth, its axial rotation being locked to ours.

♂ **Mars** In astrology Mars is the planet of strength, positivism and liveliness. In a physical sense Mars has none of the barriers which characterize both Venus and the Earth: its atmosphere is essentially transparent to most solar and cosmic radiations. Mars is a reddish colour and this has led to an astrological association with heat. However, the astronomical evidence shows that the redness is not a temperature effect, and the Martian surface is generally thought to be cold, although a recent theory suggests there may be great heat at a level below the planet's outer crust.

♃ **Jupiter** There is a parallel between Jupiter's astrological pre-eminence as an expansive force and its massive nature as a planet. Before 1923 it was even thought that Jupiter might be a miniature sun, radiating heat on its own account; but it was then proved that Jupiter was not nearly massive enough for nuclear reactions to generate energy near its core. The planet is an important source of radio radiations; these were discovered in 1954 and occur in bursts of intense emission. The possible direct effect which these radiations may have is of course fundamental to the new astrology.

♄ **Saturn** This planet poses a major complication in that it has a large satellite, Titan, which may be as much as 3,000 miles in diameter and therefore comparable with Mercury. However, the mainstream of astrology does not at present consider planetary satellites to be significant. On the other hand, Saturn was associated with limitation, the urge to keep within bounds, long before the planet's unique rings were noted by Galileo and correctly interpreted by Huygens in 1655. These are of low mass and have the effect of masking large areas of the planet for long periods of time.

♅ **Uranus,** the planet of eccentricity to astrologers, is a remote body and was discovered only in 1781. It differs physically from its fellow planets in at least one significant respect. Its axial inclination is more than a right angle, so that the seasonal conditions on its surface must be extraordinary. First one pole, then the other, has a 'night' lasting for 21 Earth-years. As such, it is logical that astrologers have classified this massive globe of methane, helium and water as an exceptional, independent entity, endowed with powers over human generations rather than individuals.

♆ **Neptune** was not known until modern times (1846), though information about its astrological influence is now complete. It is regarded as nebulous and, true to this quality, was not immediately discovered, like the planets within its orbit, but was indirectly sensed because of the pull it exerted on Uranus, dragging the latter out of regular orbit. Neptune is a giant, made up largely of hydrogen, with abundant methane and probably a great deal of water; these elements suggest an elusive but subtle strength which future Grand Tour probes to the outermost parts of the Solar System may help to confirm.

♇ **Pluto** is the most distant known planet, discovered in 1930. It is a small, solid body and may once have been a satellite of Neptune with which it shares certain anti-social negative characteristics in astrology. But Pluto is so far from the Earth that its influence is seen as mainly impersonal and having more of a mass effect – unless it is prominently placed in a Birth Chart. Thus the connections with elimination, violence and renewal should be seen as contemporary applications made towards the end of the 1930s (during the planet's 'early' years) which may not be supported in the long term.

The Non-Causal Theory

The theory that the universe is an immense 'super-event' consisting of closely interwoven harmonics and wave-forms, the inter-relationship of which astrologers have been studying, is one which could commend itself to both sides of the scientific fence. However, for those of a rather rigid technical mind, the concepts of astrology may still seem hard to fit into the traditional view of the universe as a collection of causally-linked atomic events. In other words, the same old question can be asked: 'How can a planet such as Saturn, which is millions of miles away, have any meaningful effect on the life of an individual born on the planet Earth on a particular day?' For such people the response that a causal link has been demonstrated but not explained ought to be enough, but there is, as it happens, an interesting alternative view which sidesteps the notion of causality. For this we owe a debt of gratitude to the great philosopher and psychologist, C. G. Jung (1875–1961), whose inquiring mind led him to explore waters which more traditional scientists hesitated to fathom.

For many people Jung's interest and involvement with the principles, if not the practice of astrology, was the first important stage in the slow revival of scientific interest in the topic which we are witnessing today.

Exploring the Spirit of Man

It is important to realize that Jung, apart from fathering a dynamic personal version of psychoanalysis, was also deeply interested in the spiritual nature of man and his place within the vast cosmic arena. He was particularly impressed by the evidence for so-called paranormal faculties such as telepathy, clairvoyance, precognition, etc., which the budding science of parapsychology was beginning to provide, against the tide of current belief. Now the evidence for telepathy, patiently gathered at such establishments as Duke University in North Carolina, at the State University of Utrecht in Holland, and even at some recognized research establishments behind the Iron Curtain is still a matter of scientific controversy. Sufficient to say that Jung, as the result of his own personal experiences in psychoanalytic practice, and in laboratory research, was convinced of the reality of such phenomena, and realized that any theoretical account of the way the universe worked or any useful cosmic model would have to be broad enough to accomodate such data. However, like many other scientists he was impressed by what seemed to be a fatal flaw in the logic of the work on extra-sensory perception – that it appeared to be operating in a way which defied the standard laws of physics and mechanics.

For example, the distance between two people in 'telepathic contact' appeared to be immaterial – it could take place just as well over thousands of miles as over a few feet. In the second place telepathy appeared to be to some extent independent of time as well as space, for there were numerous examples of people becoming aware of events which were to take place in the future. Jung, a man with a logically consistent as well as an adventurous mind, came to the inevitable conclusion that while there appeared to be similar events (thought processes) taking place in separate peoples' minds at similar or significantly related times, this similarity could not have been brought about by information transmission in the usual sense of the word. In other words telepathy was an example not of communication, as most people seemed to be assuming, but of a kind of non-causal but highly significant correspondence, in which physically unrelated events could be synchronously linked together.

From this jumping-off point Jung then began to hypothesize that causality was not the only operating principle at work in the universe, and that a new concept, which he termed 'synchronicity', would have to be introduced. From this time on until his death, Jung searched scientific and philosophical data for other examples of apparently synchronous events which could not possibly have occurred by chance, and this led him to his interest in astrological data and a controversial experiment with married couples.

Jung and the Principle of Astrology

In sum this involved a statistical study of nearly 500 marriages involving 1,000 horoscopes. These were paired off in various ways and comparisons were made of the Charts of individuals both with their spouses and with other members of the group. Jung now looked carefully at the horoscopes of the married and 'unmarried' couples and found a number of interesting correspondences – notably a highly significant tendency in the case of those married for the woman's Moon to be in conjunction with the man's Sun. Jung in fact appeared to be arguing the opposition's case by saying that correspondences of this kind could not possibly be causally related; but, unlike sceptics of astrology, he argued that the correspondences could not be denied and must therefore be accounted for one way or another. For various reasons, which involve rather complex statistical arguments, the great psychiatrist did not count his experiment as in any way conclusive and we will not take it up further here. What is important of course is the fact that a man recognized throughout the world as one of the greatest and most provocative thinkers of the century should have considered the data of astrology sufficiently interesting in principle not only to experiment with it, but also to include it as an integral part of his own cosmological theory.

Jung's interest in astrology and his eventual belief in its reality as an operating principle heartened serious astrologers everywhere, and helped tremendously towards the present developing wave of popular interest in the topic on its own merits. For the first time for centuries, thanks to his unprejudiced approach, and that of many of his scientific colleagues and successors, astrology is being examined with the respect its history and tradition deserves: a vindication and fitting reward for those who upheld its principles and practice in less open-minded times.

THE USES OF ASTROLOGY

What relationship is there between astrology and everyday life in the 20th century? The answer is simple: there is no area of human experience to which astrology cannot be applied. From this page onward, the truth of this statement will become plain. It will also be obvious that there are certain things astrology cannot do: it is not a means of 'foretelling the future' for, in the age-old phrase, 'the stars do not compel'. Many people find something to fear in astrology, because they think that astrologers will tell them of specific accidents, disasters or even the hour of death.

No serious astrologer would ever say that a client will have an accident on a specific day. What he may say is that at such-and-such a time the client may tend to be more accident-prone than at others (just as a doctor will now point out that women are more prone to accidents just before menstruation). No astrological forecast can be absolutely precise, nor are the future events it may describe absolutely inevitable; and the same is true, of course, in conventional medicine, weather forecasting, or any area concerned with relatively intangible topics. Here are some indications of the areas in which astrology can be of special help; of the way astrology 'works' in everyday life.

'Know Thyself'

Goethe said that if he really knew himself, he would run away! But man is endlessly curious about himself. In many ways, our lives reflect our beliefs about ourselves, and our everyday behaviour reflects the person we think we are. But the emphasis must be on the words 'beliefs' and 'think', for we are infinitely capable of self-deception.

Astrology tells the truth about people. It does this because it is an empirical system of judgment relying entirely on those factors which 'make' the personality. An astrologer who meets a client may instinctively believe him to be a realist; his Birth Chart may reveal him to be an incurable romantic. He may think his client to be careless and forgetful; the Chart may show him to be meticulous and the possessor of a keen memory.

The reader who works out and interprets his own Birth Chart according to the instructions in the next part of the book will discover this for himself. He will be told much that he already knows to be true; and this should persuade him to look into himself, and consider whether any unpalatable facts he may find hard to accept, may not also be true.

How he uses his self-knowledge is of course a matter for him. Has self-knowledge a practical value? Is the old biblical injunction to 'know thyself' a valuable one? The authors believe so. As La Rochefoucauld says, 'Not all those who know their minds know their hearts as well'.

Your Children

Many professional astrologers spend a good deal of time working on the Birth Charts of new-born children. Obviously,

the Chart of a new baby is of sentimental interest to the parents. But an astrological report can be of practical help, too. It can have much to say, for instance, about the relationship which will soon begin to develop between parent and child. In some areas of a growing child's life, he will feel closer to his mother than his father; in others, the opposite is true. The astrologer can point out where each parent can best apply persuasion or discipline, and to what extent. He can tell the mother when the child will be most likely to succumb to childish ailments. He can suggest the kind of toys the child will prefer; the kind of games he will most enjoy; the best time to start infants' school, and the type of school best suited to a particular child.

'Progressions' (the astrological term for what the public loosely calls 'predictions') are obviously of limited use early in a child's life. An indication which thirty years later may hint at a marital disturbance will obviously not mean that in the life of a five-year-old! But by the teens, the astrologer will already be able to point out periods when adolescent love affairs, intensive periods of study, or periods of particular laziness, may affect a boy or girl. And from the late teens, full astrological analysis begins to work with accuracy.

Within the growing mind of a baby, various factors are already coming together which will eventually resolve themselves into a preference for one career rather than another. Comparisons of schools' careers advisory reports and astrological reports have shown that astrologers are well able to give reliable advice on this subject. It is very often possible to tell a parent the kind of career that might attract a son or daughter, and – equally important – the degree of success they might expect in it.

Adult Careers

Even when a career has been under way for some years, a man or woman may feel a sudden need for change. A banker may instinctively feel that he wants to drop banking and become a farmer; a grocer may feel the urge to become a racing yachtsman. The astrologer will be able to see whether this is a passing fancy, best channelled into a spare-time interest, or whether indeed a radical change of direction in life is indicated; and whether it is likely to lead to financial success and psychological happiness. In every career astrology is of practical use in timing deals, indicating the best time for buying or selling, starting a new project or discontinuing an old one.

Sex and Love

Statements like 'a Cancerian should not marry a Leo' are, of course, nonsense. A serious astrologer will never say that A should not marry B: that is not his job. What he can say is that there are certain areas of life in which A and B are particularly well-suited, and other areas in which they may find living together something of a strain. Very rarely, the comparison of the two Birth Charts may show such disastrously irreconcilable personalities that the affair is manifestly based solely on physical attraction; he will then invite a client to look very carefully at his true feelings before bringing the affair to the point of marriage.

The Birth Chart reveals much about the sexual and romantic nature – and of course has a great deal to say about relationships with other people. The comparison of the Birth Charts of lovers can be very helpful, especially in the early stages of a relationship. The astrologer can invite his client to look particularly at some aspects of that relationship. Is the man perhaps over-critical of the girl's appearance? Is

'Astrology produces joy by anticipation at the same time that it fortifies people against evil.'
Lucian of Samosata (AD 121–181) *On Astrology*

she perhaps a little too reliant on his good nature? Could they be completely swept away by extravagance? Are they sexually compatible? Lovers who are discovering each other will find in astrology a valuable short cut, revealing instantly some facets of each others' personalities which otherwise might take years to emerge.

An astrologer will advise about a propitious day (or even hour!) for a marriage. But in marriage, there is no denying that the astrologer is at his most helpful at times of crisis. He has to be a tactful and helpful marriage counsellor, and has the advantage that, given the necessary birth date, neither partner can keep any secrets from him! Time and time again, it has been shown that a wife complaining of her husband's behaviour is herself going through a particularly difficult and tense period which contributes to the unhappy state of affairs. But the astrologer can see this. He can also tell when, if at all, the situation is going to ease. He can say to the deserted wife: 'Your husband's affair seems to me to be temporary. The progression which is drawing him closely to the other woman eases in a week or so, and if you want a reconciliation, you will find that it may well be possible at that time.'

Again the astrologer will not tell a client what to do. He can only attempt to clarify the situation, and offer a choice. Every man must make his own decisions in life. No astrologer should ever make a decision for anyone.

Business

Business astrology is an extremely complex area; but specialist astrologers can advise on the proper time to sign contracts; whether a merger with another firm would be profitable, and how executives would be likely to react to each other; at what time a new deal would be most likely to go smoothly through. This is really no area for the amateur, but is for an astrologer who has a good grounding in business and finance, acquired perhaps in a stock exchange or a bank. Nevertheless, even the beginner will discover that astrology has its applications within his business life.

Financial advice is best left to experts: anyone relying on a non-specialist astrologer to indicate profitable shares in which to invest might be expected to have financial recklessness built into his Birth Chart! But the astrologer can indicate the *kind* of investment most likely to be congenial: oil, perhaps, or transport; the motor industry, or entertainment. The rest is up to your broker. The astrologer will be able to indicate spendthrift periods, or times when it would be particularly ill-advised to make investments.

Health

The advantage the astrologer has over the doctor or psychiatrist in dealing with physical and mental health, is that he can tell *when* as well as how a client's health is likely to suffer. The astrologer will as a matter of course tell you when you are likely to be under emotional or physical

stress, when you may catch cold, or when to watch your blood-pressure, slipped disc or weak ankles. He will be able to warn you which parts of your body are most susceptible to weakness. The astrological indications were a prerequisite of medical treatment at medieval universities; today they are linked with the glandular system, for instance, and doctors who use them are impressed by their accuracy.

Weather

Weather forecasts by astrology may eventually become a part of everyday life; professional meteorologists are constantly making new discoveries about the planetary cycles and their effect on terrestrial weather. Some astrological forecasters have remarkable records for accuracy; others are still experimenting, and it is fair to say that a proper rationale remains to be fully worked out.

Travel

In India, an astrologer will warn a client definitely not to travel north on a particular day, or east on another. Western astrology does not go that far: but would warn you that delays might more readily occur at one time than another. If your holiday is not to start with a 12-hour wait at an airport, astrological advice is important; and an astrologer will also say when the family as a whole is likely to relax well, without the internecine strife and squabbling which can ruin even the most sun-soaked month. Ancient astrological tradition links places with specific Zodiacal Signs, and it is often true that people feel particularly happy and at home in countries and cities 'ruled' by Signs emphasized in their own Chart.

Safety

We have already mentioned the extent to which an astrologer can 'predict' periods of tension or of difficulty. No astrologer will tell you that at 4.32 pm on 14 July you will trip on a stair and break an ankle. What he will say is that you may tend to be more prone than usual to have an accident round about that day. The kind of accident is not necessarily predictable – minor cuts and burns have the same indication, for instance; or, warned of a possible motor accident, a client may simply walk into a door. So treat this kind of forecast precisely like a weather forecast: if rain is forecast, you take an umbrella. If an accident is forecast, take care!

Retirement

Those people who are unhappy in retirement are usually bored. Astrology can certainly save you from that, by pointing out new areas of interest – sometimes completely unexpected ones. A man who has never thought about the past may find archaeology absolutely compelling as a hobby in retirement; someone who has spent all his life in the city may find a garden completely absorbing. Retirement may also be the time to explore the subject which in youth was reluctantly disregarded as a career.

Astrology is Fun

Finally, astrology can work at every level, even the most flippant. Guests for dinner? If you know their Birth Charts (or even the barest astrological facts about them), you can decorate the table to their taste – even give them the kind of food they like. You can be sure of always finding a present for the most irascible aunt or difficult uncle. Buying a pet? Buy a Geminian dog if you want a particularly lively companion.

As scientists relax by designing adult toys, as an architect will put all his energy into a garden pagoda, so an astrologer can apply his knowledge to the lighter side of life. It has infinite possibilities as a form of relaxation, as well as applying to the most fundamental problems of life.

CELESTIAL MECHANICS AND INFLUENCES

2

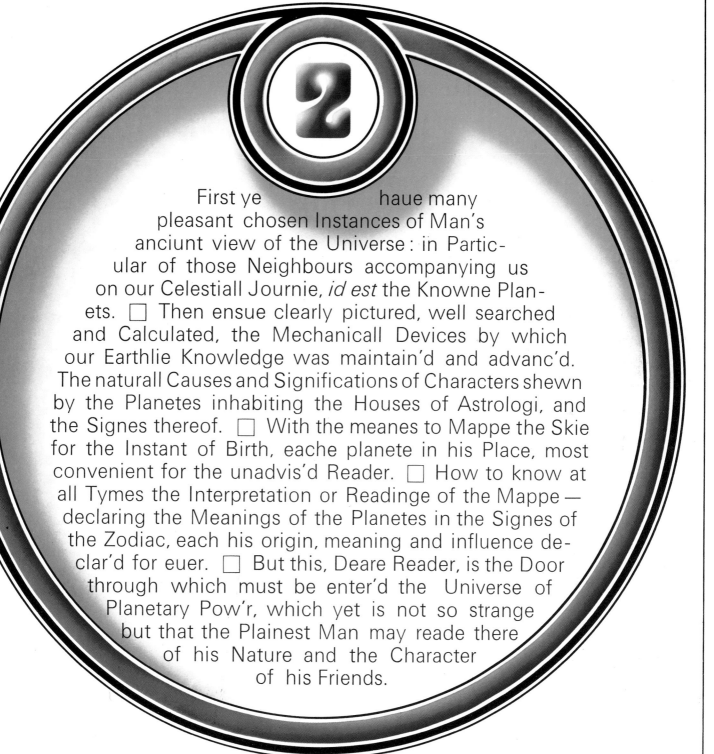

First ye haue many pleasant chosen Instances of Man's anciunt view of the Universe: in Particular of those Neighbours accompanying us on our Celestiall Journie, *id est* the Knowne Planets. □ Then ensue clearly pictured, well searched and Calculated, the Mechanicall Devices by which our Earthlie Knowledge was maintain'd and advanc'd. The naturall Causes and Significations of Characters shewn by the Planetes inhabiting the Houses of Astrologi, and the Signes thereof. □ With the meanes to Mappe the Skie for the Instant of Birth, eache planete in his Place, most convenient for the unadvis'd Reader. □ How to know at all Tymes the Interpretation or Readinge of the Mappe — declaring the Meanings of the Planetes in the Signes of the Zodiac, each his origin, meaning and influence declar'd for euer. □ But this, Deare Reader, is the Door through which must be enter'd the Universe of Planetary Pow'r, which yet is not so strange but that the Plainest Man may reade there of his Nature and the Character of his Friends.

EARLY MAPS OF THE UNIVERSE

When man began to observe the heavens he was enthralled above all else by the moving bodies of the Solar System – the planets. As they shifted against the starry background, he noted their paths and related them to his own predicament. Soon he developed a system, a pattern of celestial events which appeared to have direct parallels with mundane affairs: the Sun and the crops; the Moon and the tides which rose and fell and at intervals flooded his land; positions of the red planet, Mars, seemed to have a bearing on his fortunes in war; in Venus he saw a power to bring harmony and love.

These were some of the notions that formed the core round which astrologers have built their cosmic scheme. It is still evolving today, at a rate perhaps greater than ever before, as our knowledge of universal events grows rapidly more precise and, for the first time, it becomes possible to prove certain physical influences exerted on our Earth by the planets, and by the Sun and the Moon (which astrologers also call planets).

The Astrologer's Viewpoint

The concern of astrology is less with 'the stars' than with the moving bodies of the Solar System. The angular relationships of the planets as seen from Earth are of paramount importance in any astrological assessment of human character, hence the necessity of understanding the precise nature of the heavenly scheme.

Astrology is the most ancient celestial science, and was for many centuries inseparable from astronomy. In fact the two have seemed at odds only since the advent of rationalism in the 17th century when astronomy became more and more a materialist science, believing nothing that could not be ascertained by measurement.

Early man's ideas about the nature of the universe were far from accurate in any physical sense. He believed it to be of limited extent, and that the heavenly bodies were

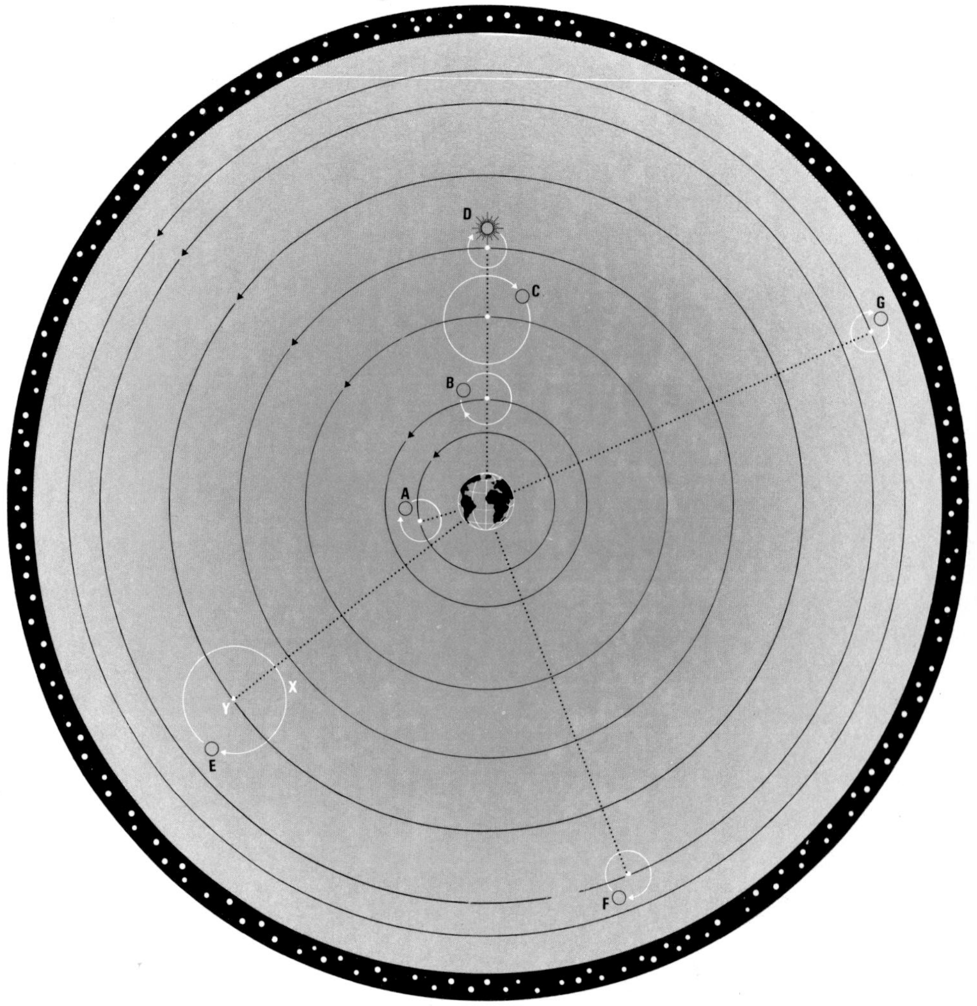

Ptolemy's Universe *above*
The Earth-centred theory of the universe was perfected by Ptolemy. The Earth lay at rest in the centre of the system: around it moved the Moon (A), the planets Mercury (B), Venus (C), Mars (E), Jupiter (F), Saturn (G) and the Sun (D); beyond Saturn were the fixed stars. To make the observed and predicted motions of the planets agree, each was given a constant orbit, the epicycle (X) being centred on the deferent (Y).

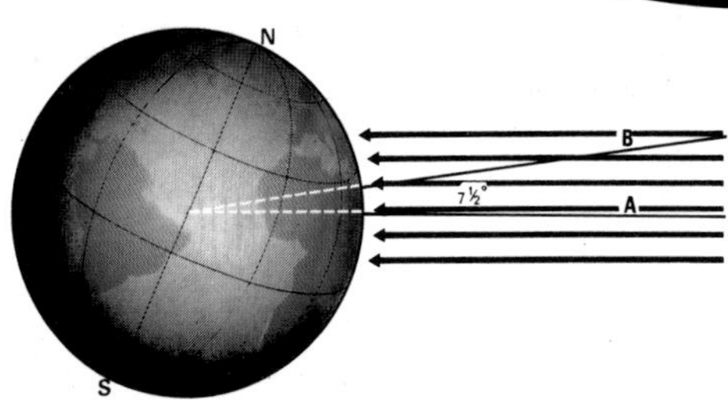

From Square World to Globe *right and above*
The square horoscope persisted long after the Greeks proved that the Earth was spherical, not flat. Eratosthenes, (276–192 BC), the Greek scientific writer who lived in Alexandria and was librarian of the museum, even managed to measure the Earth's circumference, by relating the position of the Sun at its zenith or overhead point in Syene, now better known as Aswan, (A, above) to its simultaneous position 7½° from the zenith at Alexandria (B); then he took the land distance between the two points as a fraction of the 360° circumference, obtaining a better figure than Columbus used more than 1,500 years later.

The Jaipur Observatory *left*
The ancient observatory at Jaipur, India, used for the compilation of star catalogues.

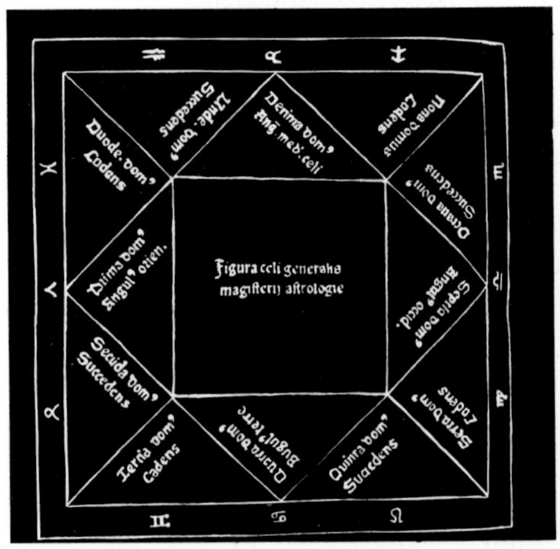

> 'Those who deny the influence of the planets violate clear evidence which for educated people of sane judgment it is not suitable to contradict.'
> Tycho Brahe (1546–1601) *De Disciplinus Mathematicis*

Galileo Galilei *left*
Galileo Galilei, (1564–1642) the Italian scientist who is always remembered as the first great astronomer to use telescopes (in 1609), was also the founder of the science of experimental mechanics.

much smaller than Earth. It was Ptolemy (AD 120–180), an astrologer-mathematician from Alexandria, who eventually put forward a plan of the universe which was to prevail among scientists for many centuries. He taught that the Earth lay at the centre, with the Moon, Mercury, Venus, the Sun, Mars, Jupiter and Saturn moving round it, each in a perfect circle within a solid outer sphere to which the stars were fixed.

Tycho Brahe's Universe *below*
Tycho's scheme had the planets move round the Sun (A), but the Sun in orbit round Earth (B).

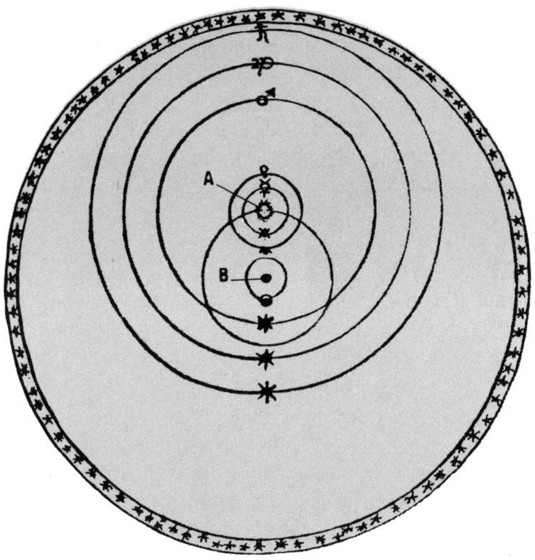

The Triumph of Heresy

During the next centuries, increasingly complex star-maps and catalogues were made for astrological purposes, until in 1543 Copernicus, a Polish churchman, horrified the world by contending that the Sun, not the Earth, lay at the centre of the universe. The next major astrologically-oriented observer, Tycho Brahe (1546–1601), could not accept the basic Copernican point that the Earth was not the centre of all things. He, like most people, saw that as heresy. But his last assistant, Johannes Kepler (1571–1630), used Tycho's observations to prove the theory, and the Ptolemaic system was finally discredited – although the Church waited until 1835 before removing Copernicus' work from the Papal Index.

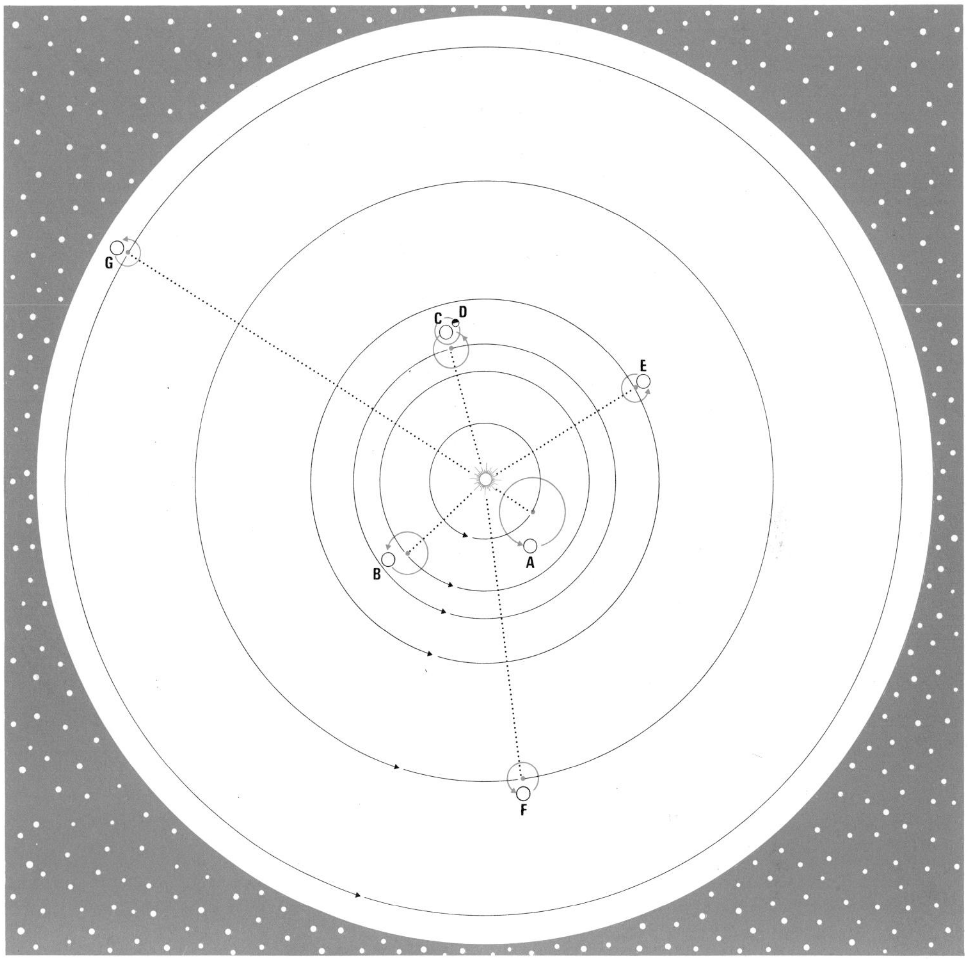

Sir Isaac Newton *right*
In 1687 Sir Isaac Newton, a zealous astrologer, published his *Principia*, in which he laid down the laws of gravitation, and explained many other phenomena, such as the nature of light and tidal movement.

The Copernican System *above*
The Ptolemaic view of the universe was rejected by Copernicus in 1543; he scandalized contemporary thought by placing the Sun in the centre of the Solar System, with the planets moving round it: Mercury (A), Venus (B), Earth (C), Mars (E), Jupiter (F) and Saturn (G); only the Moon (D) remained in orbit round the Earth, hitherto the focal point of all cosmic activity; in common with Ptolemy he retained the false notion of circular orbits and epicycles.

The Astrological Universe *right*
The near-right diagram shows the planets in their orbits as seen from Earth, and demonstrates the nature of the angular relationships used in astrology. Far right, the planets occupy equivalent positions on a conventional Birth Chart.

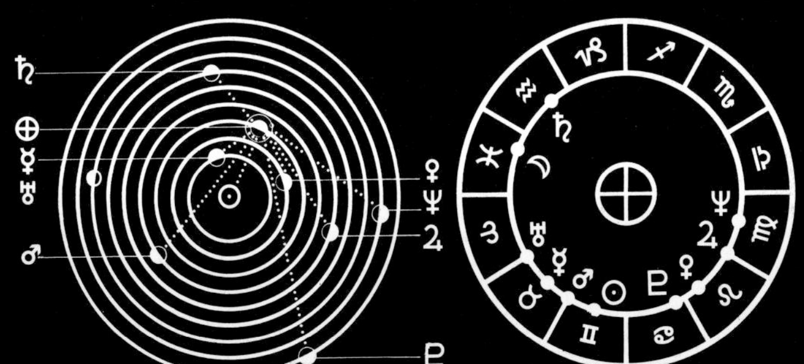

THE CELESTIAL SPHERE

The concept of the celestial sphere evolved gradually from an earlier concept of the sky as a dome rising over a flat Earth. The Ionian philosophers who realized that the Earth itself must be a globe, naturally saw the sky, too, as a hollow globe, its centre coinciding with the centre of the Earth.

The celestial sphere was for some time imagined to be solid, the stars literally stuck to it. For the sake of convenience, this concept can be retained when making certain calculations, both astronomical and astrological. Moreover, the celestial sphere continues to be of great importance, since it provides a standard of reference for positional measures without having to take into account the different distances of the celestial bodies concerned.

The celestial sphere appears to revolve around the Earth, once a day. It is of course the Earth which turns; but this may legitimately be disregarded, since what matters in astrology is the positions the planets appear to take up in the sky. They have their effect on earthly life from those positions and, *in that sense*, they are taken to be real positions.

The stars appear not to move, because they are so far away – the closest is more than 24 million million miles from us – and their 'proper' motions are very slight. The planets, on the other hand, because they are so near, seem to move relatively at speed. In this context the stars may be regarded as reference points only; in calculating and drawing up a Birth Chart, the relevant bodies are the planets: their astrological importance is assessed according to the positions they occupy at a given moment against the Zodiacal segments of the celestial sphere itself.

Other Astrological Centres

Recent research into the nature of the astrological influences has given us new insights into how the planets have the effect they do on human life. If we accept the existence of a causal framework, as outlined earlier in Part 1, it is no doubt proper to infer that the Earth in turn could have some astrological influence on other planets in our relatively tiny Solar System. If it proves possible to colonize another planet, then a Birth Chart would have to be drawn up showing that planet as the centre of the system, and with the Earth in position as a planet seen from it. The centre of the celestial sphere would then coincide with the centre of that planet. It is of course impossible to guess what astrological effect the Earth would have: many years of observation would be needed before a Birth Chart for a child born on, say, Mercury could be drawn up and satisfactorily interpreted.

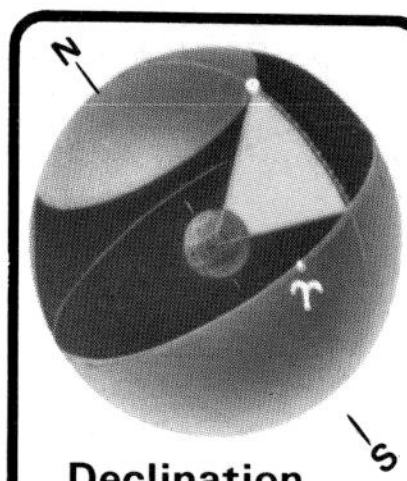

Declination
Just as the terrestrial equator divides the Earth into two hemispheres, so the celestial equator divides the sky. The celestial equator has 'declination 0°'; other objects have declinations measured by their angular distance north and south of the celestial equator. Declination thus corresponds to terrestrial latitude.

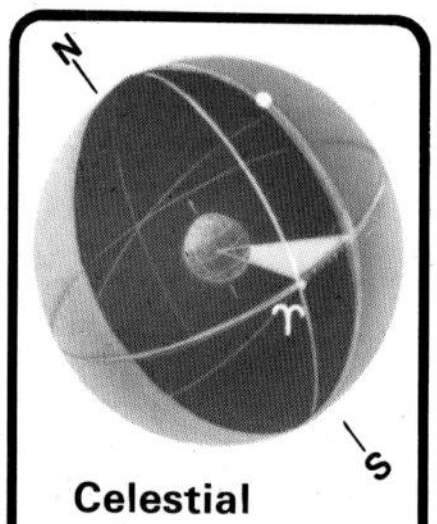

Celestial Longitude
Because the Earth rotates in 23h 56m relative to the stars, the 'sidereal day' is 23h 56m long; as the Sun is in apparent motion, the civil or 'solar day' is slightly longer. In the sky, the angular distance of a planet from 0° Aries gives its celestial longitude; this measure is used by astrologers to plot the celestial bodies in the Birth Chart prior to interpretation.

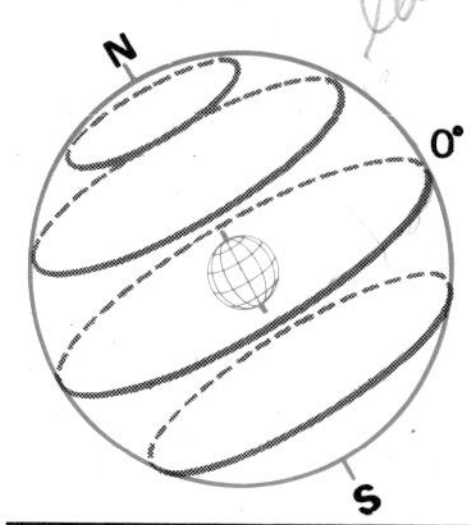

The Celestial Poles and Equator
The projection of the Earth's equator onto the celestial sphere marks the celestial equator (declination 0°). The direction of the Earth's axis indicates the two poles of the sky (declination 90° N and S respectively). The north celestial pole is marked approximately by Polaris, the Pole Star, whose declination is over +89°; the south celestial pole is not marked by a bright star.

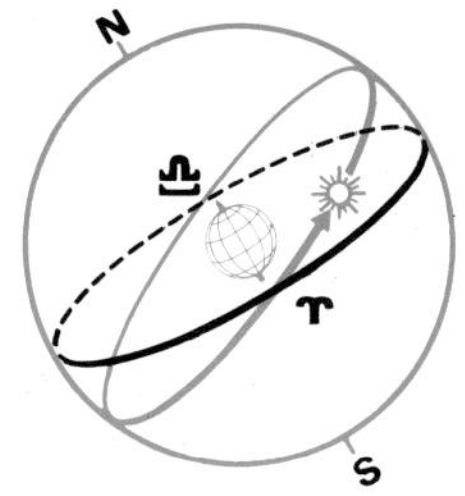

The Ecliptic and the Equinoxes
The apparent yearly path of the Sun in the sky is known as the ecliptic. The ecliptic may also be defined as the projection of the plane of the Earth's orbit onto the celestial sphere. Because of the Earth's $23\frac{1}{2}$° tilt, the angle between the ecliptic and the celestial equator is also $23\frac{1}{2}$°. The two intersect at the vernal equinox (0° Aries) and the autumnal equinox (0° Libra).

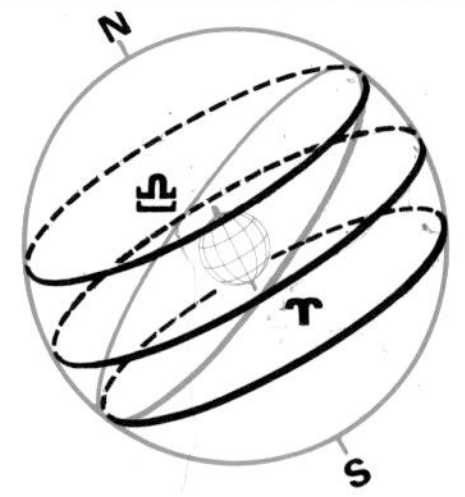

The Solstices
The solstices represent the times when the Sun reaches its maximum declination north or south of the celestial equator. The dates at the present time are about June 22 (summer solstice, from the viewpoint of an observer in the Earth's northern hemisphere) and December 22 (winter solstice). These dates were significant points in the calendars of the first astrologers in Babylon.

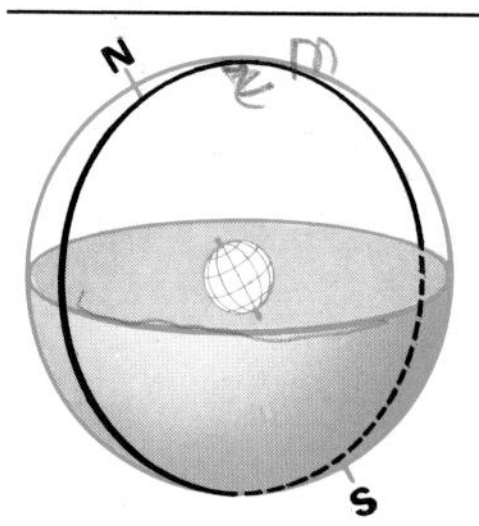

The Horizon and Observer's Meridian
The horizon is a concept familiar to everyone: here it is shown projected onto the celestial sphere. The zenith is the observer's overhead point; his meridian is the great circle on the celestial sphere which passes through the zenith and both celestial poles. Planets are in orbit in all areas of the celestial sphere but are only visible at night and when they are above the horizon.

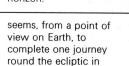

The Sun's Path
Because the Earth makes a complete circuit of the Sun once a year, the Sun seems, from a point of view on Earth, to complete one journey round the ecliptic in the same time span and appears, for example, in Pisces during March, the third month of the year.

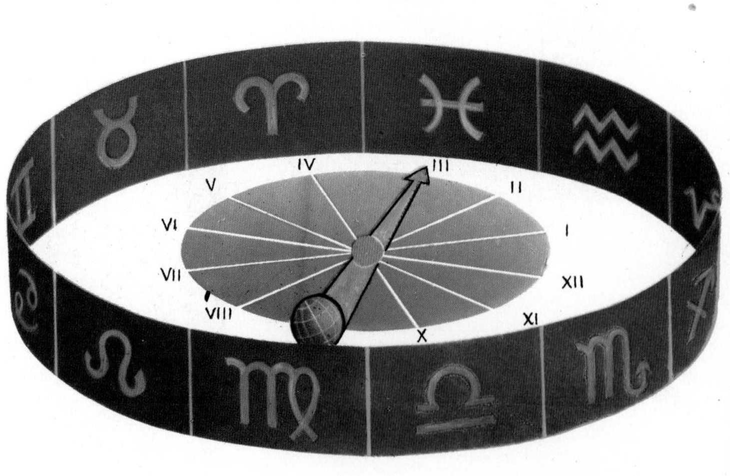

'We need not launch man into interplanetary space, we need not even take him from his own country or home to subject him to the influence of the cosmos. Man is always at the centre of the universe, for the universe is everywhere.'
Professor Giorgio Piccardi

Key
A = Path of ecliptic
B = The fixed Zodiac
C = Earth
N/S = Poles of celestial equator.

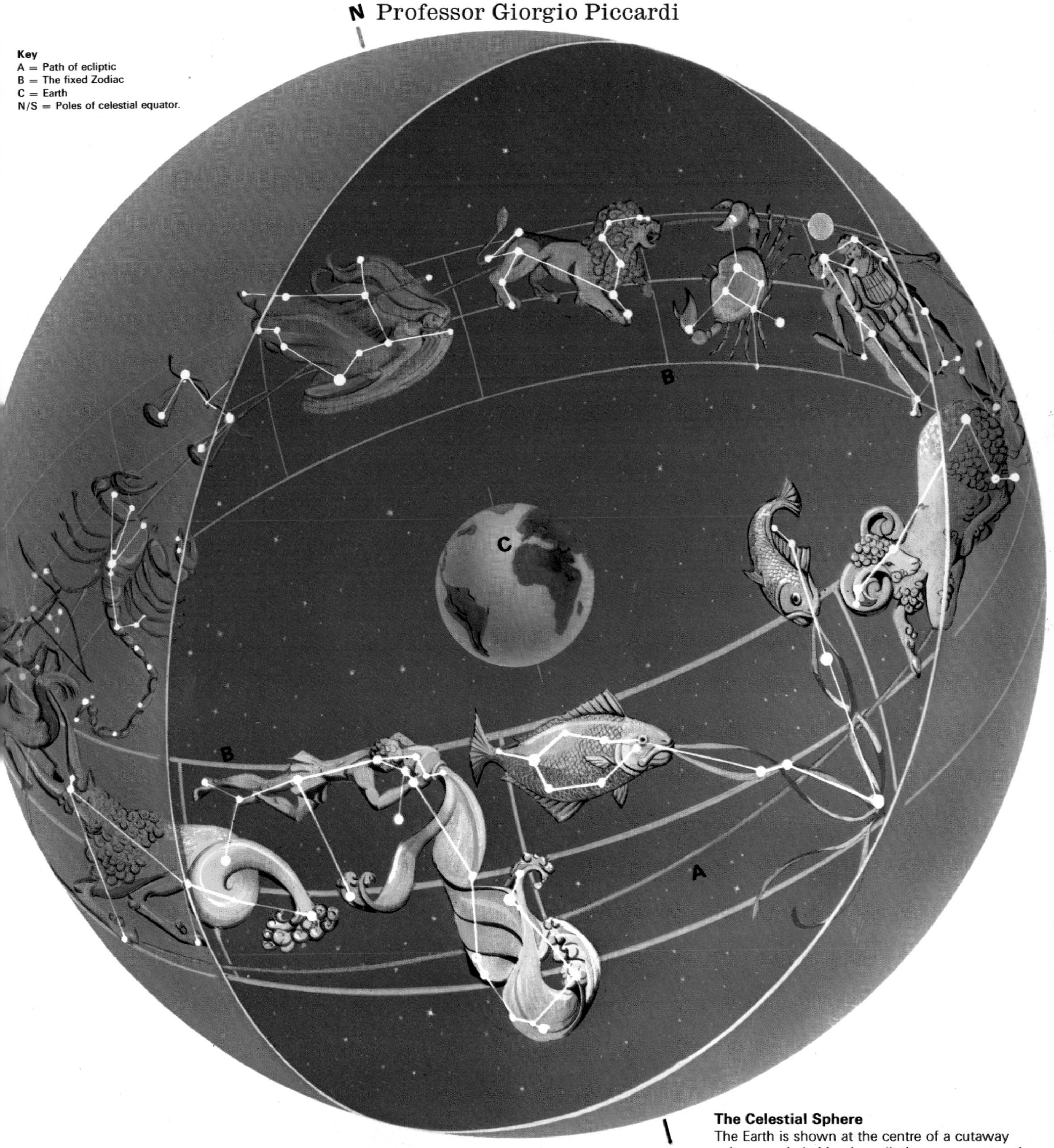

The Celestial Sphere
The Earth is shown at the centre of a cutaway sphere, encircled by the ecliptic or apparent path of the Sun. The Zodiacal band is purely symbolic in astrology; unlike the constellations in the sky, each astrological Sign occupies a fixed 30° segment of the complete circle.

THE ZODIAC

Most of the planets of the Solar System have orbits which are practically in the same plane as that of the Earth. The difference amounts to 7° for Mercury, 3° for Venus, and less than 2° for all the rest. This large measure of uniformity is destroyed by the case of Pluto, which has an inclination of 17° and has an orbit which is altogether exceptional. Two other planets, as yet unsighted, may conceivably exist beyond Pluto: their orbital inclinations are naturally unknown, but it may be logically assumed that they would also move approximately in the same plane as the Earth.

Because of this coincidence in plane, the planets (again excluding Pluto) move only against a definite belt of the sky, stretching all the way round. This belt is known as the Zodiac, and is centred upon the ecliptic – which, as we have seen, is the projection of the Earth's orbit on to the celestial sphere.

The Zodiac is divided up into 12 constellations: Aries (the Ram), Taurus (the Bull), Gemini (the Twins), Cancer (the Crab), Leo (the Lion), Virgo (the Virgin), Libra (the Balance), Scorpio (the Scorpion), Sagittarius (the Archer), Capricorn (the Sea-goat), Aquarius (the Water-bearer) and Pisces (the Fishes). All these constellations are ancient, and were known long before they were listed by Ptolemy in his star-catalogue of circa AD 150. They are not of equal size or brilliance; thus Gemini is large and very bright, while Libra and Pisces are very obscure, with no conspicuous stars.

Intruders in the Zodiac

In fact, two constellations which are not officially classed as Zodiacal enter the belt. A fairly large area of Ophiuchus (the Serpent-bearer) intrudes between Scorpio and Sagittarius, while part of Cetus (the Whale) also approaches the ecliptic – so that the principal planets can enter it. Both these constellations are ancient and they also were listed by Ptolemy. The general consensus of opinion is that they are not significant, but a minority view nevertheless holds that the astrological Zodiac should be enlarged to contain a total of 14 signs.

The essential point, however, is that astrologically the visible constellations are not of primary importance. They serve as names for the fixed astrological signs, each of which occupies an equal 30° area of the ecliptic, beginning at 0° Aries, and is invested with symbolic powers. Thus while Scorpio is far more prominent in the sky than Cancer, the signs of Scorpio and Cancer are equally important. Moreover, owing to the precession of the equinoxes, the signs and the actual constellations no longer correspond; today 0° Aries is found in the astronomical constellation Pisces.

First Point of Aries *right*
The point from which the position of a planet is measured; in the diagrams, the ecliptic runs horizontally, intersected by the celestial equator.

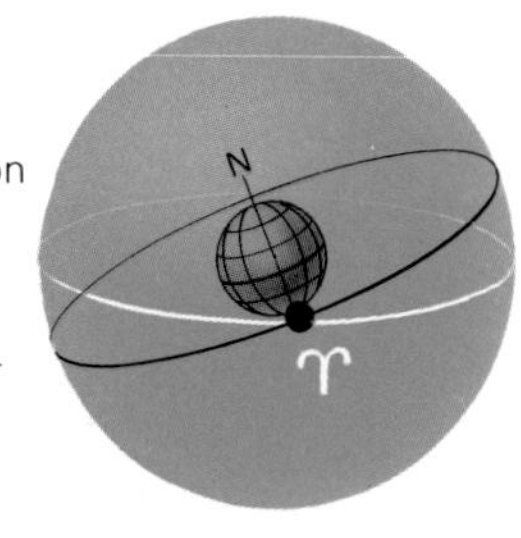

Movement of the First Point of Aries *right*
The First Point of Aries is shown at three points in its progression round the Zodiac. The near-left diagram shows its position near the centre of Aries, approximately correct for the year 900 BC. In the centre diagram, corresponding to AD 1970, it has shifted to a point well advanced in Pisces; by AD 3300 it will appear almost midway through Aquarius. Unlike the fixed 30° signs of astrology, the astronomical constellations vary considerably in size.

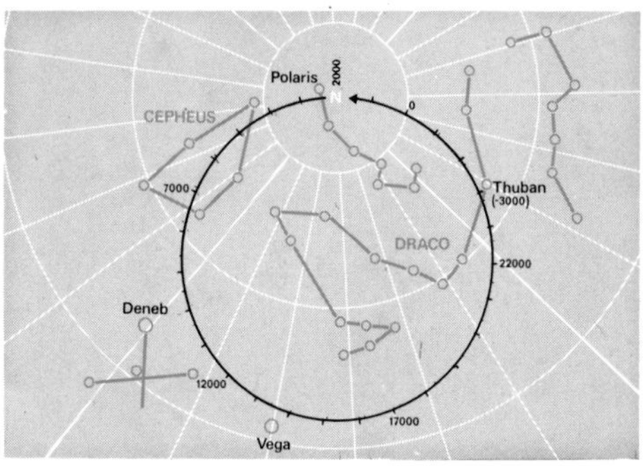

The Precession Circle *left*
Gravitational effects of the Sun, Moon and planets cause the Earth to 'wobble' slightly in much the same way as a top which is running down. This causes a shift in the positions of the celestial poles, and also of the celestial equator and First Point of Aries. In about 25,000 years each pole describes a circle in the sky, 47° in diameter. This diagram shows the precession circle for the north celestial pole. Three thousand years ago it lay near Thuban in Draco (the Dragon); at present it is near Polaris; in 14,000 years' time the pole star will be the brilliant Vega, in Lyra.

The Constellations
1 Aquarius, the Water-bearer
2 Capricorn, the Sea-goat
3 Sagittarius, the Archer
4 Scorpio, the Scorpion
5 Libra, the Scales
6 Virgo, the Virgin
7 Leo, the Lion
8 Cancer, the Crab
9 Gemini, the Twins
10 Taurus, the Bull
11 Aries, the Ram
12 Pisces, the Fishes
A Path of the Ecliptic.

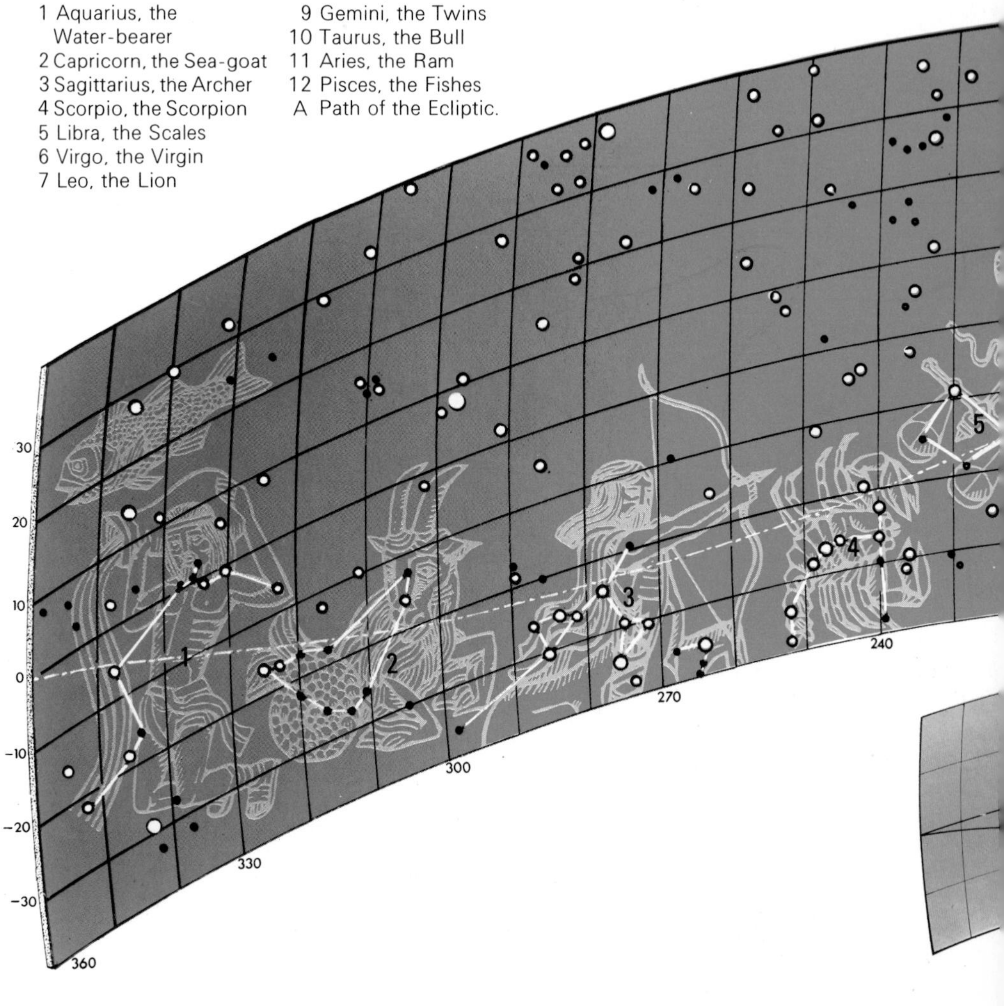

'Nothing exists nor happens in the visible sky that is not sensed in some hidden moment by the faculties of Earth and Nature.'
Johannes Kepler (1571–1630) *De Stella Nova*

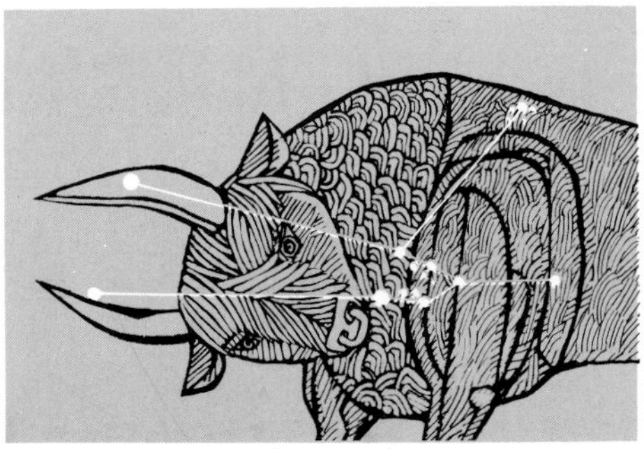

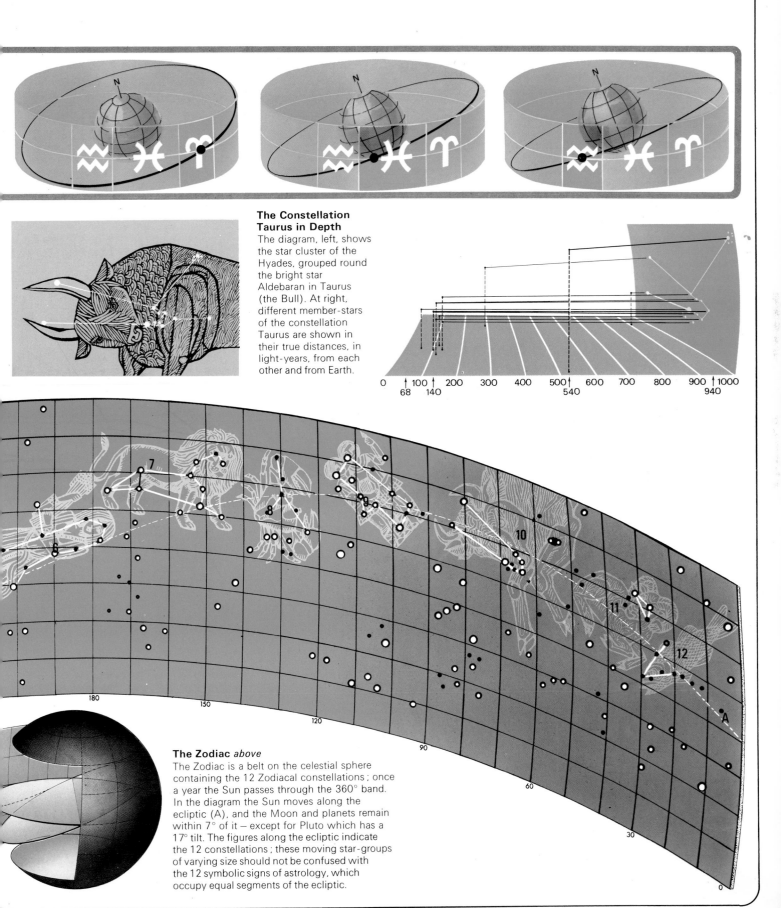

The Constellation Taurus in Depth
The diagram, left, shows the star cluster of the Hyades, grouped round the bright star Aldebaran in Taurus (the Bull). At right, different member-stars of the constellation Taurus are shown in their true distances, in light-years, from each other and from Earth.

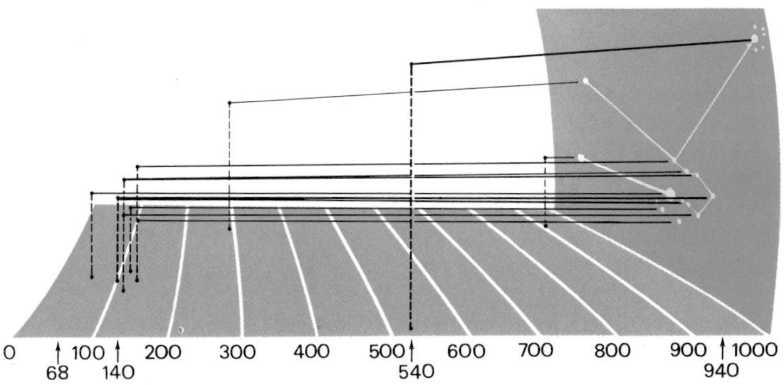

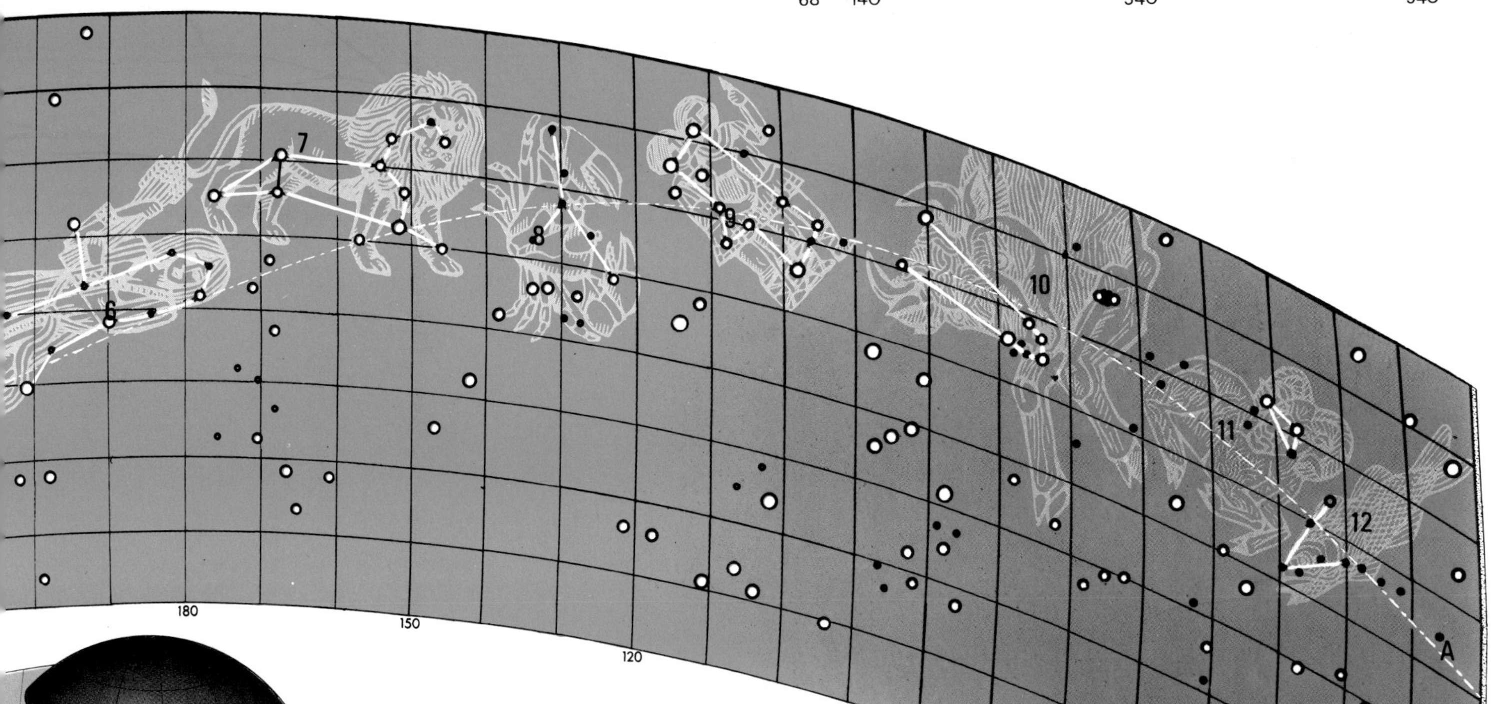

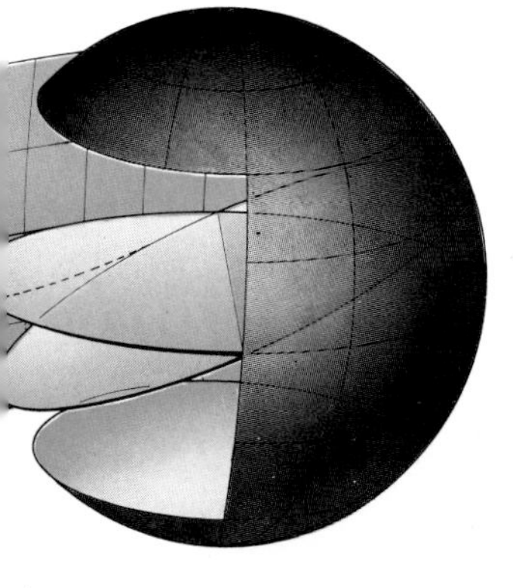

The Zodiac *above*
The Zodiac is a belt on the celestial sphere containing the 12 Zodiacal constellations; once a year the Sun passes through the 360° band. In the diagram the Sun moves along the ecliptic (A), and the Moon and planets remain within 7° of it – except for Pluto which has a 17° tilt. The figures along the ecliptic indicate the 12 constellations; these moving star-groups of varying size should not be confused with the 12 symbolic signs of astrology, which occupy equal segments of the ecliptic.

THE EARTH/MOON SYSTEM

Astrologers assume that the Earth is situated at the centre of the universe. This is a justifiable assumption and compares with the everyday notion that the Sun rises in the east, crosses the sky and sets in the west. In each case we are dealing with the apparent rotation of the celestial sphere, which is in fact a convention arising from the daily rotation of the Earth.

The Earth is a normal planet; the only real difference between it and its fellow-members of the Solar System is that by the combination of certain factors, e.g. atmosphere, water, temperature, etc, conditions are favourable for the growth and continuance of life. The Earth is almost 8,000 miles in diameter, and moves round the Sun at a mean distance of 93 million miles. The actual distance varies through the year, owing to an eccentricity in the Earth's orbit, from approximately 91·4 million miles in December to 94·5 million miles in June. The position of Earth when it is nearest to the Sun is described as perihelion; its farthest position from the Sun is known as aphelion (these terms apply equally to other planets in the Solar System).

Compared with earthly measurements, a distance of 93 million miles seems immense. But in terms of the known universe, with its almost inconceivable size, the area taken up by our Solar System is a minute pinprick in space. And today astologers tend to regard their subject in rather the same way as scientists approach molecular biology, that is, as a study of behaviour-patterns established between relatively small bodies operating within a confined space.

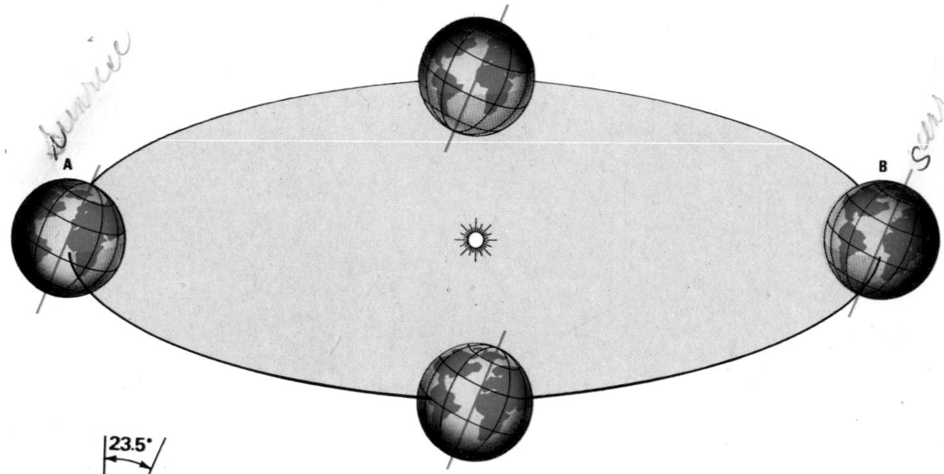

Axial Inclination *left*
The Earth's axis is inclined by $23\frac{1}{2}°$ to the perpendicular to the plane of its orbit round the Sun.

The Earth's Orbit *above*
The Earth's orbit round the Sun is shown: position A marks northern summer, when the north pole is tilted toward the Sun; at position B, when the south pole is tilted toward the Sun, it is summer in the south.

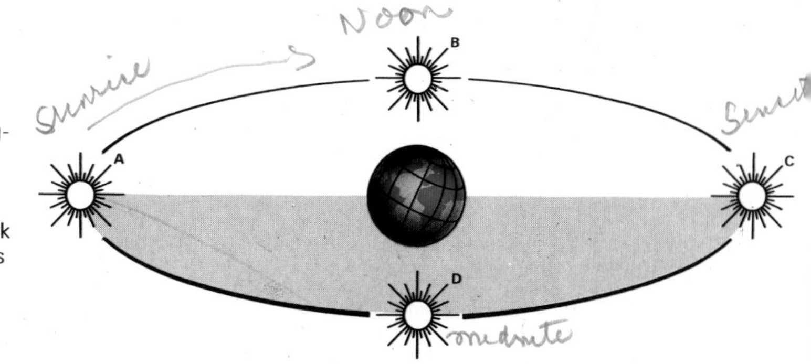

Rotation *right*
On the Earth-centred Birth Chart the starting-point for the Sun's daily rotation is at sunrise (A). The other suns at B, C and D mark the respective positions of noon, sunset and midnight.

Effects of the Moon

The Earth is not a solitary traveller in space. It is accompanied by the Moon, which is of planetary size; indeed, the Earth-Moon system should properly be regarded as a double planet rather than as a planet and a satellite. From the Earth's surface, the Moon naturally ranks as an independent body in the astrological sense, though it is a matter for speculation whether astrology of the future, as practised from the surface of, say, Mercury, will regard it as such. It is possible that an astrologer, in the unlikely event of a horoscope being cast on that planet, will then have to class the Earth and Moon together, even though each will retain independent characteristics.

The movements of the Earth are markedly affected by the presence of the Moon, and the two bodies move round their common centre of gravity. That centre, known as the barycentre, is in fact located within the Earth's surface, since our planet's mass is vastly greater than that of the Moon.

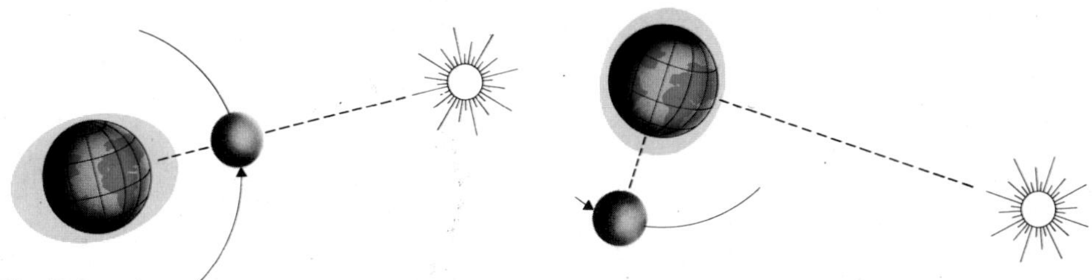

The Tides *above*
The Sun and Moon pull in the same direction to cause spring tides, left; when they pull at right angles their effect is weakened and the neap tides, right, are produced, the difference between high and low tides then being minimal.

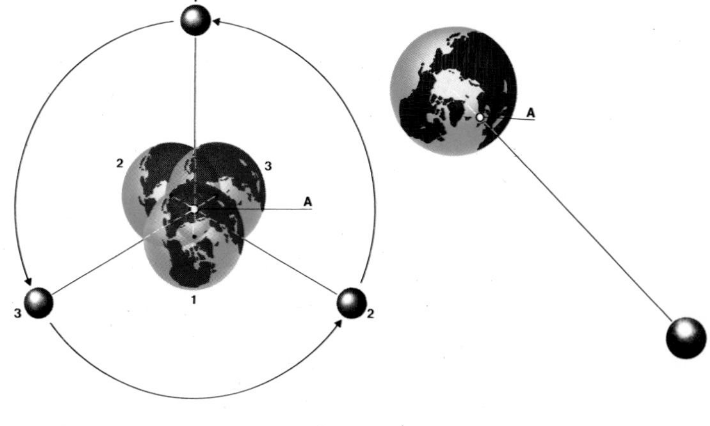

Earth-Moon Gravity *left*
It is wrong to say simply that the Moon travels round the Earth. The two bodies move round their common centre of gravity, or barycentre. However, the Earth has 81 times the mass of the Moon; thus the barycentre lies within the terrestrial globe; in the diagrams the barycentre is marked A.

The Earth in Space
For the very first time the space rockets of the 1950s and 60s allowed the Earth to be seen, above, in its true guise as a planet. The phases of the Moon as it circles the Earth are shown, below, from New Moon (1), when its dark side is turned towards Earth, to full Moon (5) and on to the next new Moon (9) 29.53 days later.

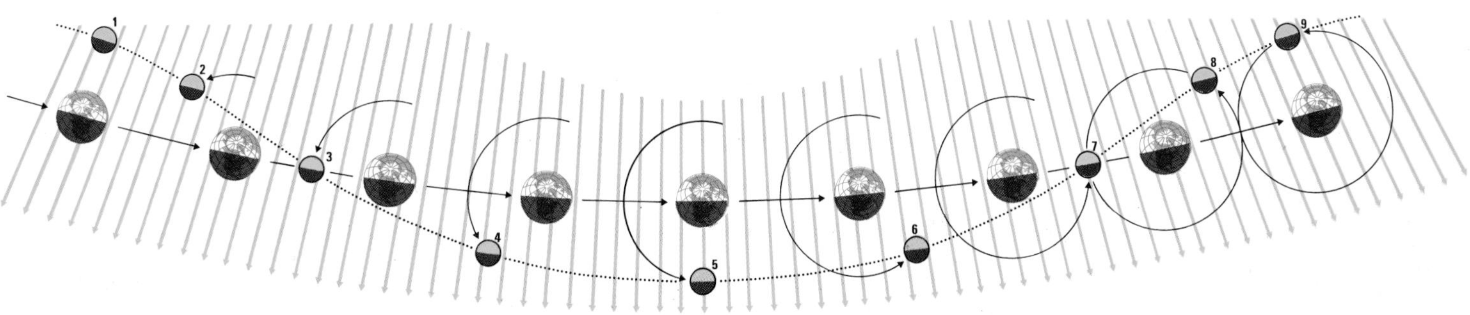

THE SOLAR SYSTEM

This map shows the orbits of the planets around the Sun; the figures at the side show the distances, given in miles (upper figures) and kilometres (lower figures).

The orbits of the planets are virtually circular, except for that of Pluto, which has an exceptional path. It is next due at perihelion in 1989, and for some years on either side of that date it will not be 'the outermost planet'.

The majority of the planets orbit the Sun within 3° of the plane of the Earth's orbit, apart from Mercury, which has a tilt of 7°, and Pluto. Pluto, however, has an exceptionally sharp orbital tilt of 17°.

Despite the enormous scale of the Solar System the planets do not move in complete isolation from one another. Every body has a pull of gravity: the greater the mass, the greater the gravitational pull. Each planet attracts its companions and causes irregularities in motion which are known as 'perturbations'.

Minor and Hypothetical Bodies

The Solar System contains other bodies as well as the Sun, Moon and planets. There are the satellites of the large planets, comets, meteoroids and also the asteroids – a belt of numerous small planets, or perhaps the remains of a larger, old planet which has disintegrated. The asteroids are found between the orbits of Mars and Jupiter. They vary in size from Pallas and Ceres (with diameters of over 400 miles) to unnamed, irregular little worlds of less than ten miles across. The total mass of the asteroids is probably something like 1/500th of the mass of the Earth; and they may, as a whole, have some astrological significance although there is little evidence to support or disprove this.

Some astronomers, as well as astrologers, feel that there may be an undiscovered planet, named Vulcan, within the orbit of Mercury. The astrological significance is as unknown at least as the reality of the planet. Still more doubtful is both the existence and influence of Lilith, said to be a satellite of Earth, one-quarter the size of our Moon, which has been given many mysterious meanings by astrologers in the past. Reputable modern astrologers treat it as sceptically as astronomers; it seems likely that 18th-century astrologers may simply have been confused by asteroid 1181 and mistaken it for a more important body.

Key

A Asteroids
♂ Mars
⊕ Earth
♀ Venus
☿ Mercury
♃ Jupiter
♄ Saturn
♅ Uranus
♆ Neptune
♇ Pluto

‘The universe may be not only queerer than we suppose,
but queerer than we *can* suppose.’
J. S. Haldane (1860–1936)

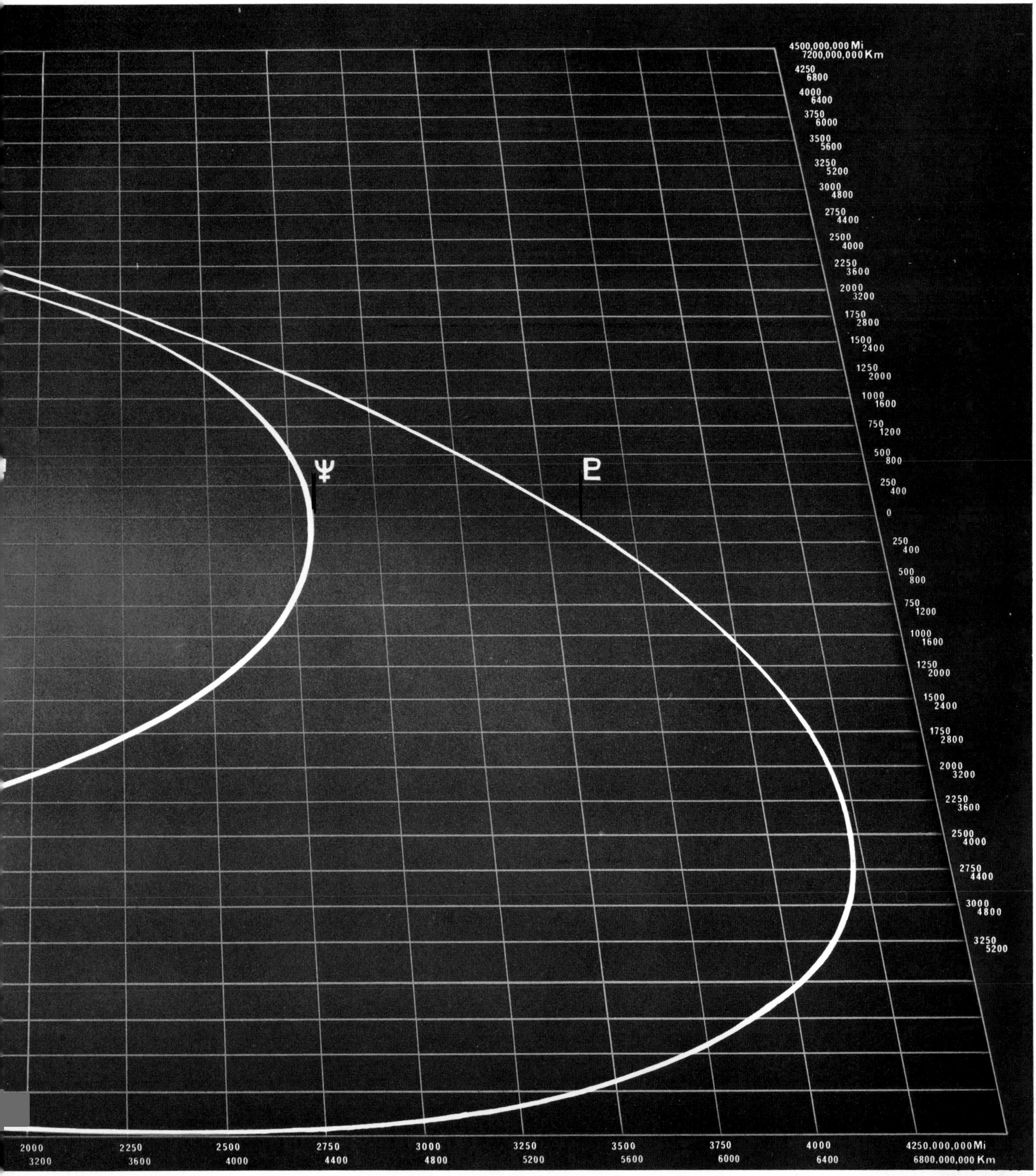

THE ASTROLOSPHERE

Astrologers who base their theories on empirical assumptions rather than on the occult considerations of some of their colleagues, assert that the astrological theory must have its basis in physical influences; that is, the planets must have some kind of physical effect on terrestrial weather, plant and animal life – either by means we can directly sense or via some hitherto undetected emanation.

If this is so, it is reasonable to suppose that spatial relationships within the Solar System are of significance; these are demonstrated in the concept of the Astrolosphere.

The Sun is shown at the centre of the Solar System, the planets extending outward from it. As Newton showed, gravity falls off according to the inverse square law; and one would expect astrological influences to weaken similarly. Evidence of this theory is limited: but there are a few available facts. For instance, figures collected between 1883 and 1941 show that Mercury appears to affect terrestrial temperature in proportion to its distance from the Earth (varying from 38½ million to 36 million miles).

In terms of gravity, the effect of a cosmic body depends not only on distance, but mass; the smaller the distance and the greater the mass, the greater the effect. The Moon, obviously, is of immense importance, its nearness to the Earth (a mere 239,000 miles) counteracting its small size. Jupiter is the most massive of the planets (indeed, would contain all the others); next in order come Saturn, Uranus and Neptune. Scientists have shown conclusively that alignments of these three planets (as they are shown in the illustration) have measurable effects on terrestrial events.

The French scientist Professeur Philippe Lebas stated his conviction many years ago that the planets reacted physically upon one another, and also had a direct influence on the Earth's atmosphere, consequently upon life-patterns and geological events within that atmosphere. Evidence to support this view is now (see Part 1 of this book) flowing in from scientific sources that might in a less imaginative age have been automatically opposed to astrology. For example Dr R. Tomaschek, a distinguished German geophysicist, studied the positions of the planets at the time of 134 earthquakes of greater magnitude than 7, which have taken place in 1904, 1905 and 1906; he found that the placing of Uranus in the charts was significant. The same was true of the famous Tokyo earthquake of 1924, the Assam earthquake of 1950 and the Agadir and Chile earthquakes of 1960. It is surely no coincidence that Uranus has long been regarded by astrologers as the planet of 'tension, explosion and the unexpected'.

The Galaxy *below*
The Galaxy is our local star-system; it contains about 100,000 million stars, and has an overall diameter of 100,000 light-years. The position (A) of the Sun is shown close to the edge of one of the spiral arms and 30,000 light-years from the Galaxy's centre.

The Astrolosphere *right*
The Earth, third planet from the Sun, lies midway between the core and the outer zone of the Astrolosphere's energy-system; beyond it are the slower-moving planets, Jupiter to Pluto, which inhabit a colder, more remote region of the Solar System.

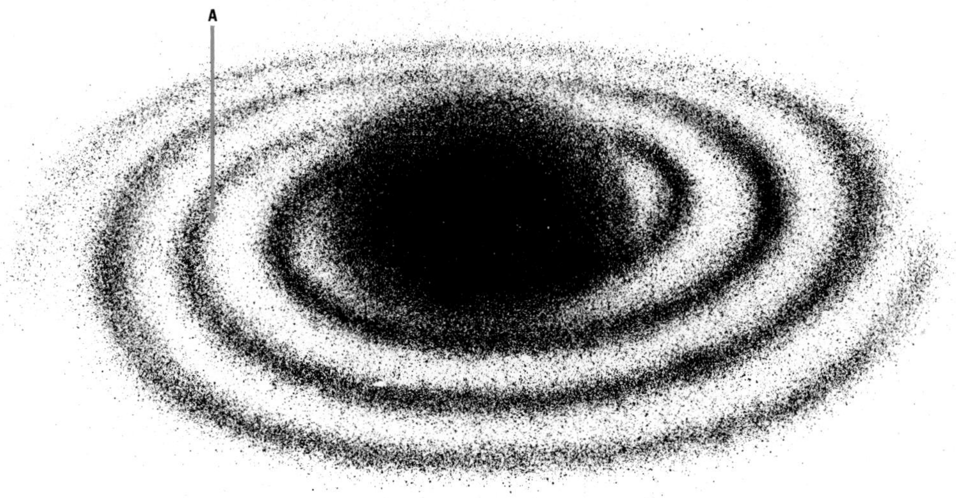

Orbital Speeds *right*
The planets move at differing speeds along the ecliptic from the Moon (13 complete tours a year) to Pluto (1° annually).

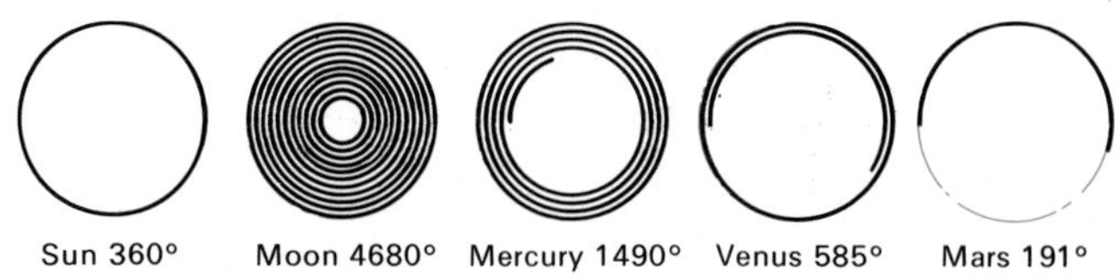

Size of the Planets *below*
The planets are here shown in scale against part of the Sun's curvature. The Moon is not shown.

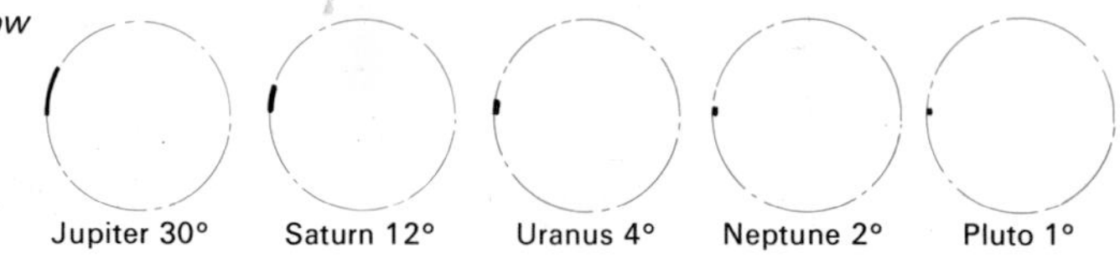

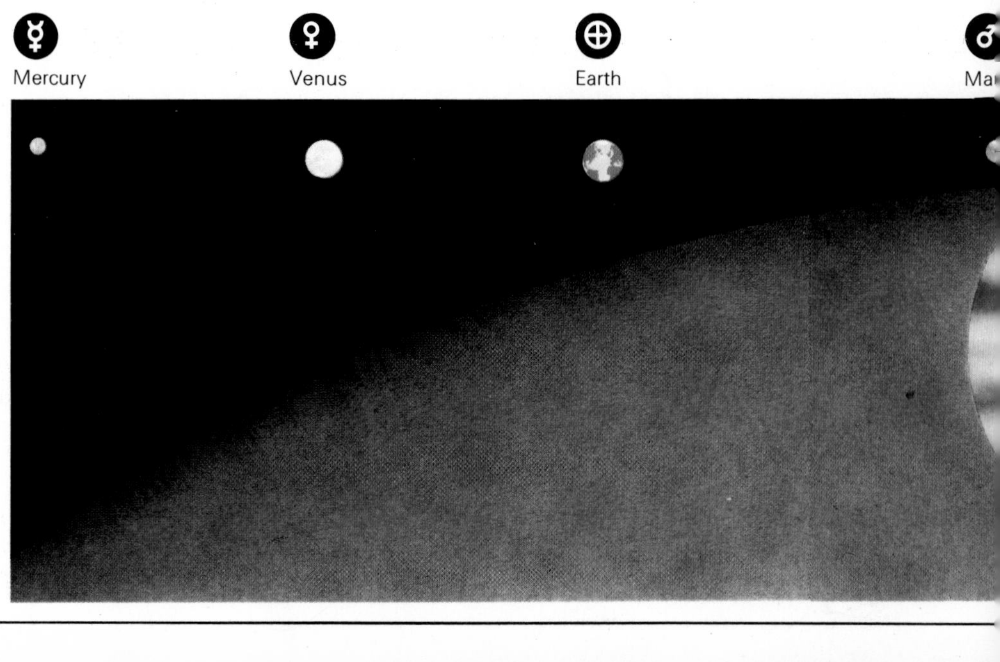

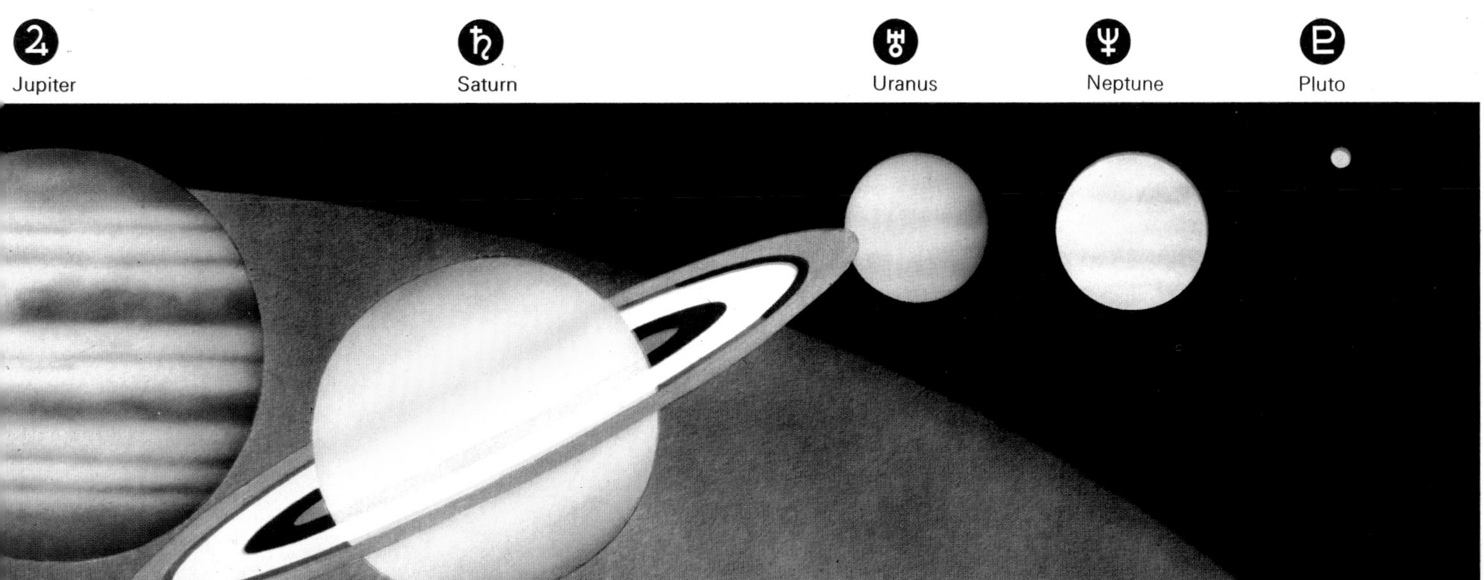

Jupiter
Saturn
Uranus
Neptune
Pluto

THE MOVING PLANETS

The positions of the planets within sections of the ecliptic are all-important to astrologers, and the astrologer-astronomers of ancient times studied these movements with the greatest possible care and exactitude. The equipment they used was of course primitive by modern standards, but the results they achieved by naked-eye methods were remarkably sound.

At first it was thought that the orbits of all celestial bodies must be circular, for the circle was a perfect form, and everything in the heavens must surely be perfect. This was the flaw in the compromise solution arrived at by Ptolemy, and which in reality made his concept of the universe cumbersome and artificial. It was clear to later observers in the post-Copernican age that the planets were irregular in motion – sometimes they stopped, turned and moved backward before resuming their easterly motion.

Johannes Kepler in 1609 made the profound and then astonishing statement that the planets moved not in circles but in ellipses. The ellipses were, nevertheless, almost circular; the eccentricity of orbit of the Earth, for instance, is only 0·017. Again, the speed of the planetary orbits was obviously different: the planets nearest the Sun had the greatest velocities – and Mercury and Venus, the inferior planets, behaved in a somewhat odd manner, different from that of the other members of the Solar System. Astrologically, the eccentricities of Mercury are reflected in the characteristics of its influence.

Retrograde Movement

Not unnaturally, the ancient astrologers suspected that a retrograde planet – one which suddenly moved, or appeared to move, backwards – was involved in some strange and unsatisfactory revolt against the nature of things. Even today some astrologers pay considerable attention to the retrograde planets in a Birth Chart. They claim that the planet's effects will be detrimental or that its positive effect will not be felt if it is retrograde in the natal chart.

We do not feel that this idea is spectacularly proven. But it does seem that perhaps the influence of a planet which was retrograding at the birth date, may be felt with special force when it goes direct again, and crosses over the degree *and minute* it occupied at birth. Astronomically, the Moon returns to its natal position every month; the Sun every year. Astrologers 'progress' a Birth Chart by a special method, explained in Part 3 of the book, and only the Moon can return to its natal position *in a Birth Chart* – once every 30 years. Mercury returns to its natal position after 90 years; but one would have to live to be 360 years old before the Sun would return to its position in the Birth Chart.

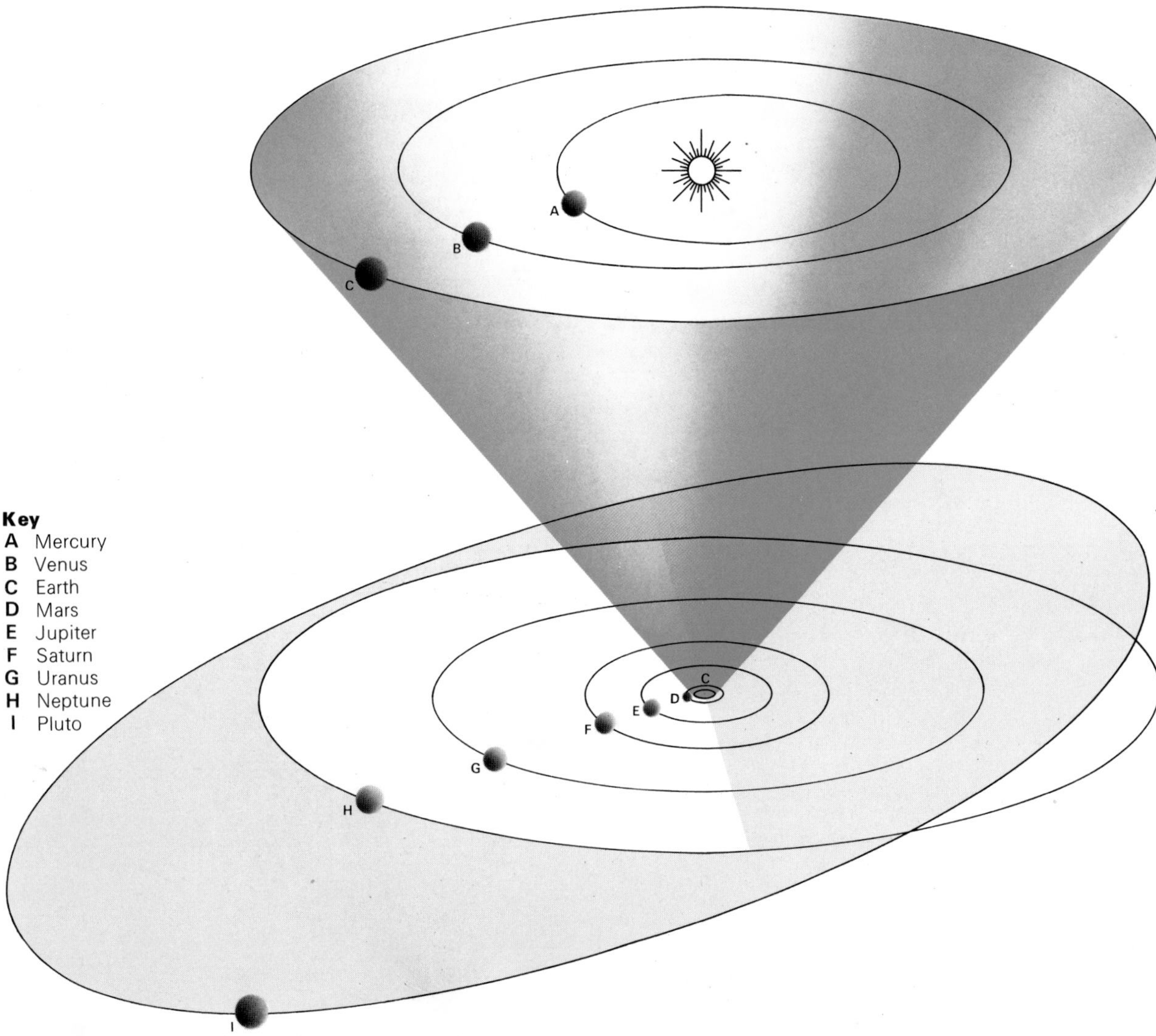

The Inferior Planets *le*
Mercury (A) moves round the Sun at a mean distance of 36,000,000 miles; Venus (B) at 67,000,000 miles; the Earth is shown at (C). The periods are 88 Earth-days and 224.7 Earth-days respectively. The orbit of Venus is practically circular, but that of Mercury is appreciably eccentric. Mercury is never conspicuous with the naked eye; Venus is intensely bright.

The Superior Planets *le*
The term 'superior planet' embraces all the planets beyond the Earth's orbit in the Solar System. However, it is as logical to divide the planets into two groups, terrestrial (Mercury to Mars) and giant (Jupiter to Neptune); Pluto does not seem to fit well into the overall system, and may be an ex-satellite of Neptune. Unlike Mercury and Venus, superior planets do not remain close to the Sun.

'The controls of life are structured as forms and nuclear arrangements, in a relation with the motions of the universe.'
Louis Pasteur (1822–95)

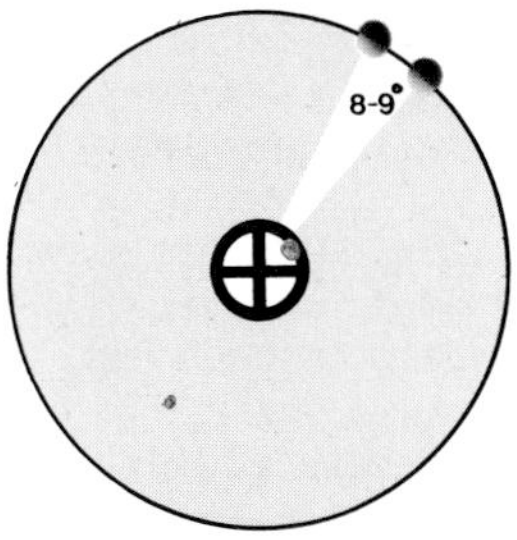

Astrological Conjunctions

An astrological conjunction relates not to the position of other planets vis-à-vis Earth, but to the proximity of two or more planets on the ecliptic as seen from Earth. Conjunctions occur on the Birth Chart when the planet falls within an orb, or arc of tolerance, of up to 8–9°. The conjunction of two planets is a focal point of the Chart, and lays stress according to the characteristics of the houses and signs concerned.

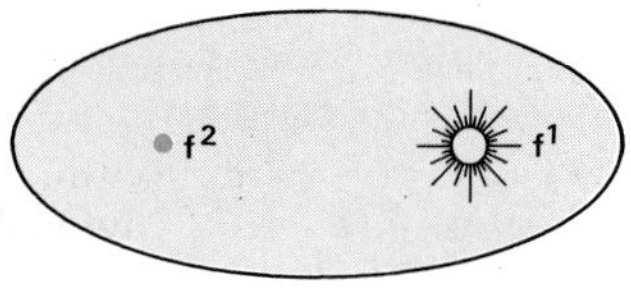

Kepler's Laws

Kepler's First Law (above) states that a planet moves through space in an ellipse, with the Sun at one focus; the Second Law states that the radius vector sweeps out equal areas in equal times. The Third Law relates planetary periods with distance from the Sun.

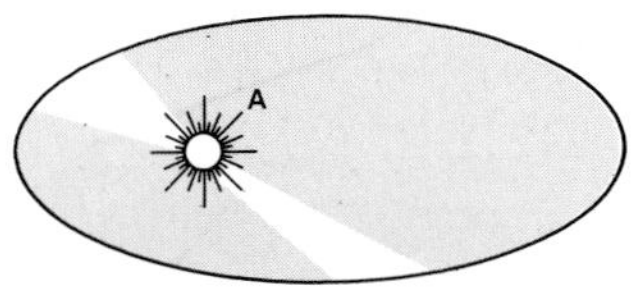

Retrograde Planets

Retrograde motion takes place when an inferior (faster) planet overtakes the Earth, or when a superior (slower) planet is overtaken by the swifter-moving Earth. In the astrological table of planetary positions below, Mercury is seen to go retrograde from 11° Sagittarius on the first day of the month; on the ninth day the planet resumes its forward motion from a position at 3° Sagittarius.

	1	2	3	4	5	6	7	8	9	10	11	12	13	14
☉	♐ 8	9	10	11	12	13	14	15	16	17	18	19	20	21
☿	♐ 11 R	10	9	7	6	5	4	3	3D	3	3	4	5	6
♀	♎ 22	23	24	25	26	27	28	29	29 0	♏ 1	2	4	5	6
♂	♎ 0	1	1	2	3	3	4	4	5	5	6	6	7	7

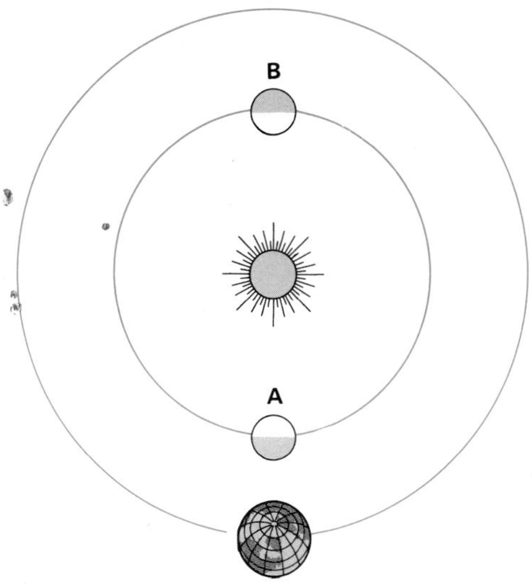

Inferior and Superior Conjunction *left*

This diagram applies equally to both inferior planets, Mercury and Venus. The planet is shown at inferior conjunction (A), between the Earth and Sun and is therefore invisible; and at superior conjunction (B), when it is virtually behind the Sun as seen from Earth.

Apparent Path of an Inferior Planet *right*

The apparent path of Venus (the white line projected onto the background), as seen from Earth; Mercury's path is similar although it moves much more quickly. The numbers indicate the corresponding positions of Venus (A) and Earth (B).

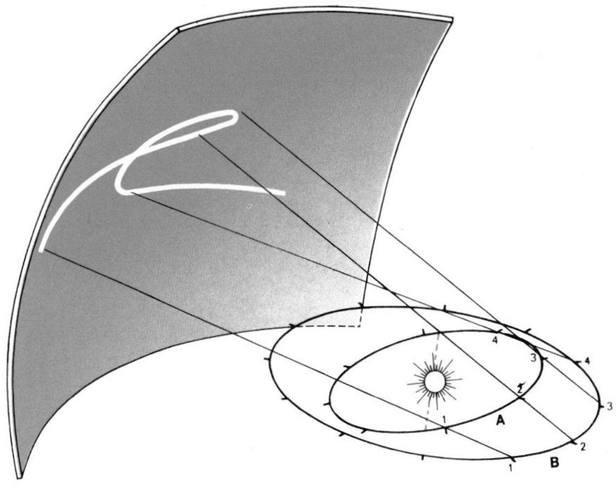

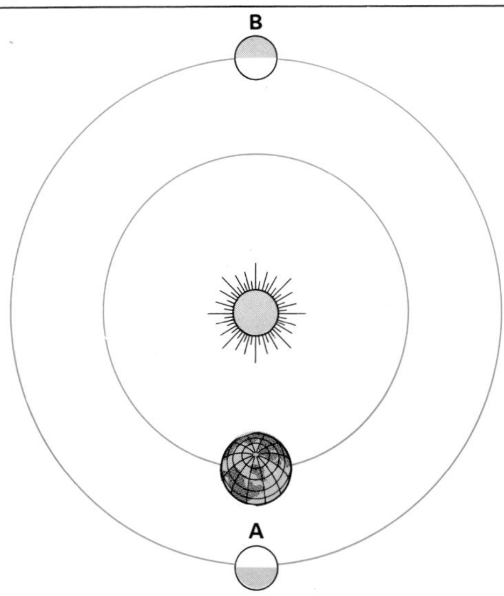

Superior Conjunction and Opposition *left*

This diagram shows a superior planet (one whose orbit round the Sun is beyond that of the Earth) at opposition (A). It is then opposite to the Sun in the sky, and is best placed for astronomical observation. At B it is at superior conjunction, on the far side of the Sun, and is out of view.

Apparent Path of a Superior Planet *right*

The apparent motion of a superior planet (B). Near opposition it seems to 'retrograde', and perform a loop, as seen from the Earth (A). The numbers indicate positions for the two planets. Some astrologers attribute special emphasis to a planet while it is retrograding.

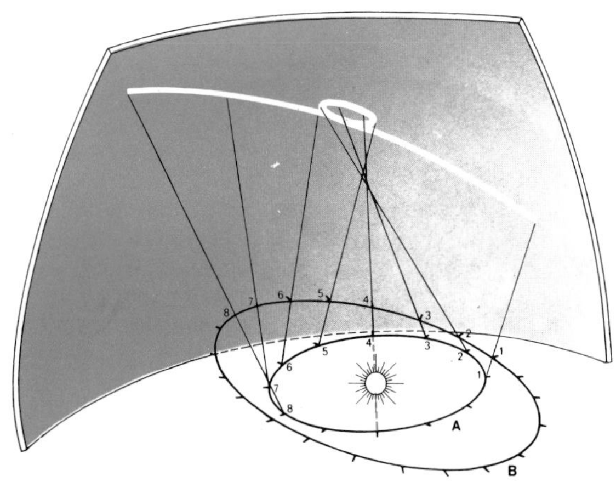

THE BIRTH CHART

How it Works, How to Calculate, Draw up and Prepare a Personal Chart for Interpretation

A Personal Map of the Heavens

A Birth Chart is a map of the heavens as the new-born child would see it at the moment and from the place of his birth – except that it also includes that 'invisible' part of the sky which would be below the horizon. The 'stars' are not included: astrology is chiefly concerned with the ten moving planets.

In the symbolic terms of astrology the small circle in the centre of the Chart represents Earth. This is the map's natural starting-point, since Earth is where we are born and where we live. Around Earth the 12 equal signs of the Zodiac form an encircling band along the ecliptic, each sign occupying a fixed 30° field. Against these fields of the ecliptic move the essential forces of astrology – the planets. They pass, at differing speeds, out of one sign of the Zodiac and into the next in a never-ending circuit.

As the planets move, so the angles they form with Earth can be measured for any given moment. In astrology the moment of birth is taken as the decisive time in the subject's life, and the degree calculations which appear on the Birth Chart record exactly how the planets appeared in the heavens at that moment. In this way the subject's Chart reveals a pattern of cosmic action unique for his time and place of birth.

Ascendant or Rising Sign
The sign rising on the eastern horizon at the moment of birth: here shown as 24° Pisces; once the position of the Ascendant is calculated, the other signs follow in order round the Chart.

Cusp of First House
The inner circle of the Chart is divided into 12 equal Houses; the First House occupies the 30° area below the eastern horizon; the cusp marks its starting-point.

Moon's Nodes
The nodes are the north and south points at which the Moon crosses the ecliptic: the north node is shown here in Pisces, the south node is at the opposite point in Virgo.

Glyphs of Planets
The glyphs of the planets (Saturn is the example marked here) are placed round the Chart and their exact positions at the moment of birth are noted in figures.

MC or Medium Coeli
The MC (Midheaven) is the point at the moment of birth when the ecliptic crosses the subject's meridian; in general terms the MC is the overhead point in the sky.

Glyphs of Signs
The sign glyphs, like that of Scorpio indicated here, are inserted round the Chart once the Ascendant is calculated. The glyphs are an extremely ancient form of shorthand.

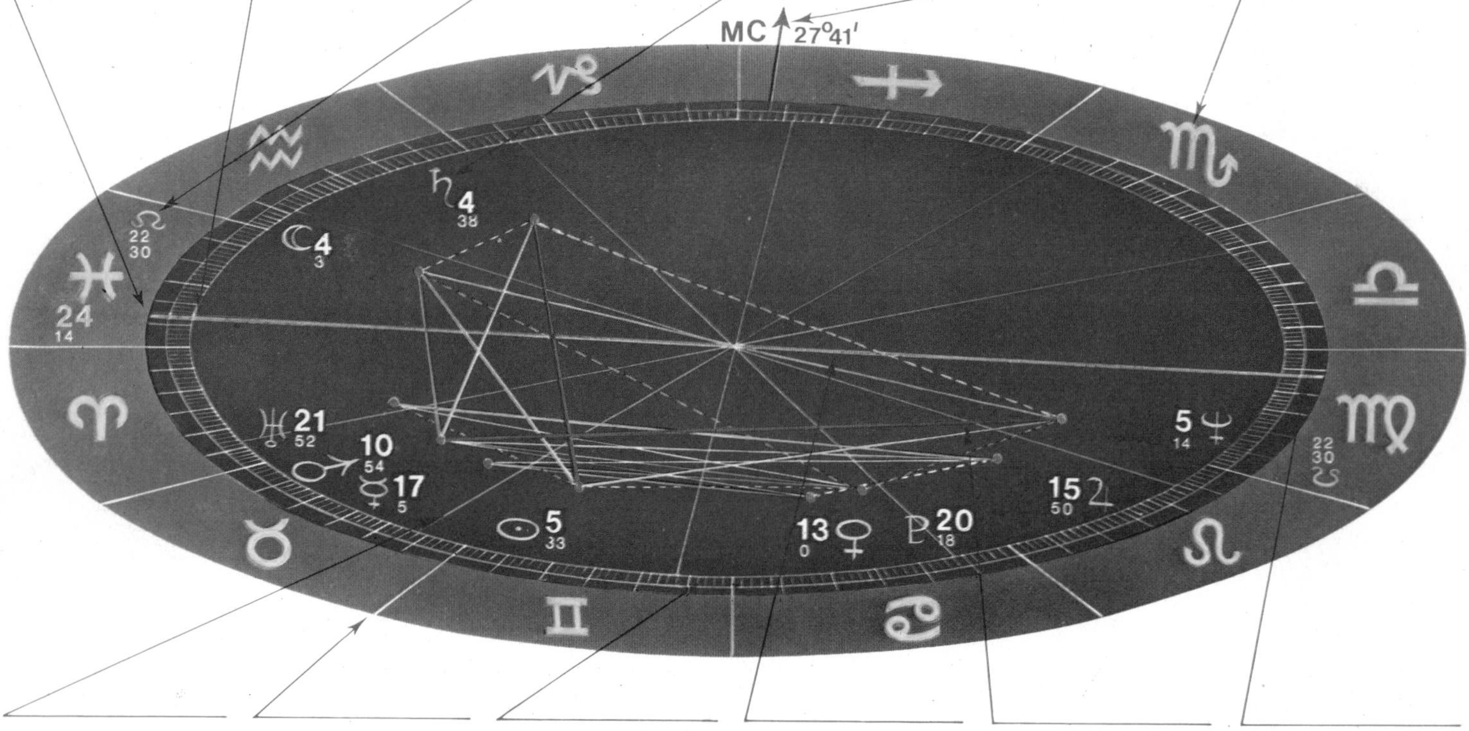

House Divisions
The 12 Houses relate to specific areas of the subject's life, e.g. possessions, career, family, etc.; although other forms exist, the Equal House System is used throughout this book.

Cusp of Sign
The cusp of a sign marks the starting-point of a new sign; a planet appearing precisely on the cusp in our illustration would be placed on 0° Gemini (not 30° Taurus).

IC or Imum Coeli
This is the opposite point on the Chart to the MC or Medium Coeli, i.e. the point in the sky more or less beneath the subject's feet at the moment of his birth.

Line of Horizon
This line divides the Birth Chart in two: planets appear either above the horizon (upper half of Chart) or below it. Here the Sun's position denotes a birth-time after midnight.

Aspect Lines
Aspect lines on the Chart draw attention to specific angular relationships between planets, as seen from Earth. Aspects are of the utmost importance in interpretation.

Descendant
The opposite end of the Horizon line to the Ascendant; i.e. the degree of the Zodiac setting beneath the western horizon, here shown as 24° Virgo.

The Conventions of Astrology

The astrologer assumes that the Earth is a fixed point, and that all other cosmic bodies revolve round it once a day. He then applies this 24-hour system to the Birth Chart. The main circle of the Chart is divided into 12 equal segments; one segment, or House, equals 2 hours out of the total of 24. Outside this circle, the 12 equal signs of the Zodiac are plotted for the moment of birth.

Glyphs of the Signs		Glyphs of the Planets	
♈ Aries	♎ Libra	☉ Sun	♄ Saturn
♉ Taurus	♏ Scorpio	☽ Moon	♅ Uranus
♊ Gemini	♐ Sagittarius	☿ Mercury	♆ Neptune
♋ Cancer	♑ Capricorn	♀ Venus	♇ Pluto
♌ Leo	♒ Aquarius	♂ Mars	☊ Moon's Nodes: North
♍ Virgo	♓ Pisces	♃ Jupiter	☋ South

Preparing the Birth Chart

There are a number of stages to drawing up and interpreting a Birth Chart. The following step-by-step procedure is recommended.

On a sheet of paper draw a circle not less than 4″ in diameter. Inside it, draw another circle, $\frac{1}{4}$″– $\frac{1}{2}$″ smaller in radius. Divide the circumference into 12 equal segments of 30°. Mark off each segment in 5° divisions.

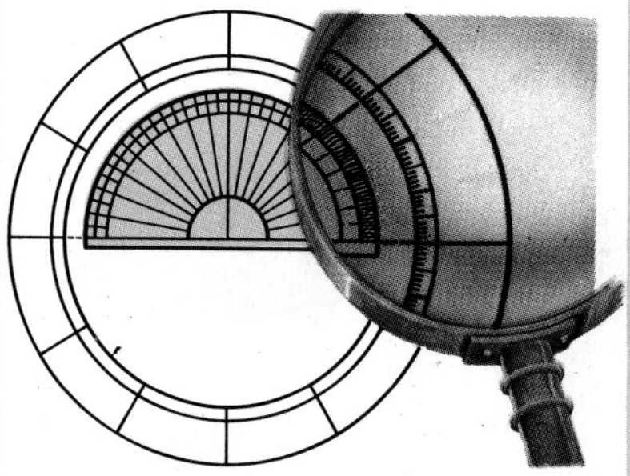

Draw an Aspect grid (see full-scale version on p. 133). Then make the list shown below.

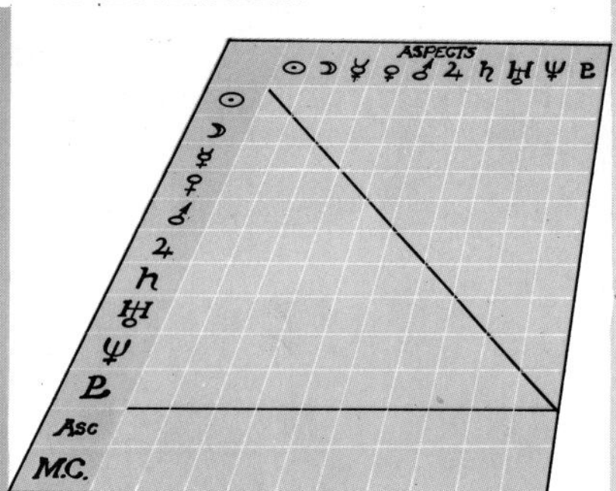

Key List of Traditional Factors

Ruling planet	Planets in their own signs
Rising planet	Exalted planets
Ruler's house	Planets in detriment
Masculine signs	Planets in fall
Feminine signs	Angular planets
Triplicities	**Quadruplicities**
Planets in Fire signs	Planets in Cardinal signs
Earth signs	Fixed signs
Air signs	Mutable signs
Water signs	Planets in Mutual Reception

Establish the date, time and place of birth. If the precise time of birth is not known, take the nearest known time; if no birth-time is known, work from noon – but in that case it will not be possible to ascertain either the Ascendant or Midheaven, or the House positions of the planets. This obviously limits the scope of a Chart.

4

Calculate the Ascendant and Midheaven

The first step in calculating a Birth Chart is to discover the Ascendant and Midheaven. The calculations follow different lines for eastern and western longitudes, and for am and pm birth times. In the examples shown below, our subjects are born at 4 o'clock, am or pm, local time, at longitudes east or west of Greenwich.

For subjects born in southern latitudes, proceed as set out below until you have the local sidereal time at birth; then refer to the note at the foot of the page.

First of all, the local birth-time is converted to Greenwich Mean Time. A careful check should be made to ascertain whether one or two hours had, at the time of birth, been added to local standard time, in the cause of Daylight Saving or Summer Time – schemes which from time to time operate in most parts of the world. The hour (or two) added in this way should be subtracted from the birth-time before calculations begin.

West of Greenwich		East of Greenwich	
The birth occurs in New York (74°00′ West, 40°45′ North) at:		The birth occurs at Frunze, USSR (74°00′ East, 42°00′ North) at:	
4 am	**4 pm**	**4 am**	**4 pm**
To convert these local times to Greenwich Mean Time, refer to the tables on p. 252. These show that 5 hours must be added – the difference between GMT and American Eastern Standard Time.		To convert these local times to Greenwich Mean Time, refer to the tables on p. 252. These show that 5 hours has to be subtracted from the birth-time – the difference between GMT, and local time.	
4 am Eastern Standard Time plus 5 hours = 9 am GMT	4 pm Eastern Standard Time plus 5 hours = 9 pm GMT	4 am, local time minus 5 hours = 11 pm, GMT, the day before.	4 pm, local time minus 5 hours = 11 am, GMT

We have converted the birth-time given us to Greenwich Mean Time. Another conversion now has to take place, in order to discover the equivalent sidereal time at Greenwich. Sidereal time relates to the actual time taken by the Earth to revolve on its axis, as opposed to the rough 24-hour measure we use for daily convenience.

We start this second conversion by referring to the sidereal time at Greenwich at noon on the date of birth. This is given in the tables on p. 234. In this case we will assume that the birth took place on 23 November 1944; the tables tell us that the **sidereal time** at Greenwich at noon on that day was 16h 9m 20s. Now, we find the interval between the GMT birth-time and noon on the same day.

West of Greenwich		East of Greenwich	
If your calculations take you to the subsequent day, find the interval between the GMT time and noon of **that** day, and **not** the birthday.		If your calculations have taken you into the previous day, find the interval between the GMT time and noon of **that day,** and **not** the birthday.	
9 am, GMT count forward to noon = 3 hours	9 pm, GMT count backwards to noon = 9 hours	11 pm, GMT count backwards to noon = 11 hours	11 am, GMT count forward to noon = 1 hour

We have the sidereal time at Greenwich at noon on the day of birth. We now have to discover the sidereal time at Greenwich at the **time** of birth on the day of birth. To do this, we use the interval-time we have just discovered, adding to or subtracting from the sidereal time of 16h 9m 20s: am = subtract, pm = add.

NOTE If your calculations have taken you to the previous or subsequent days, you must work with the sidereal time at noon on **that** day.

Sidereal time at Greenwich for noon on birthday = 16h 9m 20s am so subtract 3 hours = 13h 9m 20s	Sidereal time at Greenwich for noon on birthday = 16h 9m 20s pm so add 9 hours = 25h 9m 20s. **NB** Do not worry if addition results in a total of over 24 hours: it does **not** affect the final calculation.	The calculations have taken us to the previous day – 22 November 1944. The tables on p. 234 tell us that the sidereal time at Greenwich at noon on that day was 16h 5m 23s pm, so add 11 hours = 27h 5m 23s.	Sidereal time at Greenwich for noon on birthday = 16h 9m 20s am so subtract 1 hour = 15h 9m 20s.

Continuing the search for the sidereal time at Greenwich at the time of birth, we now make use of a quantity called 'the acceleration on the interval'. (This is another adjustment which has to be made in order to allow for the difference between sidereal and everyday time.)

The acceleration is found by adding or subtracting ten seconds for every hour and one second for every six minutes of the interval time. Again: am = subtract, pm = add.

am – subtract	**pm – add**	**pm – add**	**am – subtract**
Interval = 3 hours. Ten seconds per hour = 30s. 13h 9m 20s minus 30 seconds = 13h 8m 50s.	Interval = 9 hours. Ten seconds per hour = 1m 30s. 25h 9m 20s plus 1m 30s = 25h 10m 50s.	Interval = 11 hours. Ten seconds per hour = 1m 50s. 27h 5m 23s plus 1m 50s = 27h 7m 13s.	Interval = 1 hour. Ten seconds per hour = 10s. 15h 9m 20s minus 10s = 15h 9m 10s.

We now have the sidereal time at Greenwich for the time of birth. We have to convert this to find the sidereal time at the **place** of birth at the time of birth. The difference in time depends on the distance between the place of birth and Greenwich, and is known as the longitude equivalent in time. This is found by multiplying the longitude of the place of birth by four, calling the result hours, minutes and seconds.

West of Greenwich	East of Greenwich
Longitude of New York is 74°00′ West. Multiply by four = 296′. Divide by 60 = 4h 56m.	Longitude of Frunze is 74°00′ East. Multiply by four = 296′. Divide by 60 = 4h 56m.

To the sidereal time at Greenwich for the time of birth we add or subtract the longitude equivalent in time: East = add, West = subtract.

Sidereal time at Greenwich = 13h 8m 50s. West, so subtract 4h 56m = 8h 12m 50s = LOCAL SIDEREAL TIME AT BIRTH	Sidereal time at Greenwich = 25h 10m 50s. West, so subtract 4h 56m = 20h 14m 50s = LOCAL SIDEREAL TIME AT BIRTH	Sidereal time at Greenwich = 27h 7m 13s. East, so add 4h 56m = 32h 3m 13s. Total is in excess of 24 hours, the equivalent of 8h 3m 13s = LOCAL SIDEREAL TIME AT BIRTH	Sidereal time at Greenwich = 15h 9m 10s. East, so add 4h 56m + 20h 5m 10s = LOCAL SIDEREAL TIME AT BIRTH

The local sidereal time at birth, and at the place of birth, is the essential ingredient for finding the Ascendant and Midheaven. It is now a simple matter of referring to the Tables of Houses on p. 244, which tabulate the Ascendant and Midheaven for every four minutes of local sidereal time for various latitudes. (**NB** These tables give a selection of latitudes, from which the nearest applicable one may be chosen.) Reading off the required degrees for the latitudes we have used, we find:

8h 12m 50s gives **Ascendant:** Libra 26°17′; **Midheaven:** Leo 1°.	20h 14m 50s gives **Ascendant:** Taurus 22°14′; **Midheaven:** Aquarius 1°.	8h 3m 13s gives **Ascendant:** Libra 24° 21′; **Midheaven:** Cancer 29°.	20h 5m 10s gives **Ascendant:** Taurus 20°23′; **Midheaven:** Capricorn 29°.

Southern Latitudes

If the subject was born in a southern latitude, the process after the discovery of the local sidereal time at birth is slightly different, although the same Table of Houses is used, and the latitude read off in the same way as for places north of the equator.

First add, in every case, 12 hours to the local sidereal time. In the case of a subject born south of the Equator at 4 am with a local sidereal time of 8h 12m 50s; add 12h, giving 20h 12m 50s. The Table of Houses gives us **Ascendant**: Taurus 22°14′, **Midheaven**: Aquarius 1°. But, because we are dealing with Southern latitudes, these signs must be **reversed**, according to their order in the horoscope. Thus Taurus, the second sign, becomes Scorpio, the eighth; and Aquarius, the eleventh sign, becomes Leo, the fifth. So finally, we have: **Ascendant**: Scorpio 22°14′, **Midheaven**: Leo 1°.

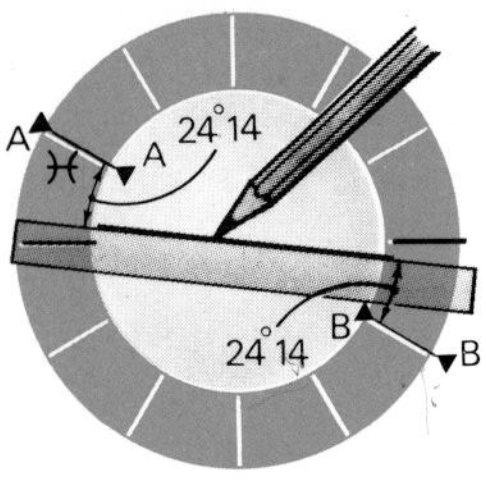

Draw the line of the horizon on the Birth Chart. If the Ascending degree is 24°14′, count 24° down from point A (cusp of the Ascending sign); then count 24° up from B, opposite. Join the two new points in red through the centre of the Chart. Insert the glyph, degree and minute of the Ascending sign.

5

Refer to the tables on p. 194 to discover the positions of the planets on the day of birth, and note these on a separate sheet of paper. The traditional manner of calculating the planets' positions, correct to the nearest degree, minute and second, is given below. In order to complete this more complex operation, the reader will need to obtain a separate astrological ephemeris for his year of birth.

The method used on this page is the 'direct' method as taught by the English Faculty of Astrological Studies. Care must be taken to ensure that the ephemeris used shows planetary positions at noon GMT.

Our subject is born at 2.50 am or 2.50 pm, British Summer Time, on 27 May 1932. **NB** The precise place is immaterial.

The first step in the calculations is to ensure that the time is expressed in Greenwich Mean Time; so check that no local time adjustment system was in operation. In this case, BST had set the clock **forward** one hour. So, subtract one hour. Whether the birth was am or pm, the starting-point is with the planetary positions at **noon on the day of birth**; but if, in converting the birth-time to GMT, your calculation took you forward to the following day or backward to the previous day, then *that day* must be used. The planetary positions are read straight from the ephemeris. In this case, they are:

Sun, 5°57′ Gemini; Moon, 9°18′ Pisces; Mercury, 17°50′ Taurus; Venus, 13°10′ Cancer; Mars, 11°13′ Taurus; Jupiter, 16°3′ Leo; Saturn, 4°38′ (Retrograde) Aquarius; Uranus, 21°53′ Aries; Neptune, 5°14′ Virgo; Pluto, 20°14′ Cancer.

The method employed for am and pm births is now slightly different.

am

To find the position of the Sun at 1.50 am GMT on 27 May, we work from its position at noon on 26 May (for all am births, use the Sun's position on the previous day).

Sun's position, noon, 26 May = 5°0′ Gemini. Subtract this from the Sun's position at noon GMT on 27 May: 5°57′ minus 5°00′ = 0°57′. The Sun has thus moved 0°57′ of celestial longitude between noon on 26 May and noon on 27 May: this is called the Sun's **motion** during that period.

Calculate the interval of time between the hour of birth, and noon on the day of birth. In this case: 12.00 hours less 1.50h = 10.10h of interval.

Use now the table of logarithms (p. 251) to find the log. of the interval. Log. of 10.10h = .3730. Then, from the same table, find the log. of the Sun's motion: Log. of 0°57′ = 1.4025. Add these two results to obtain a total of 1.7755. Find the anti-log of this last total.

Anti-log of 1.7755 = 0°24′.

Now, for an am birth, subtract this anti-log from the position of the Sun at noon on the Birth Day:

5°57′ (Sun at noon on birth day)
−0°24′ (anti-log figure)
5°33′ Gemini = position of Sun at time of birth.

pm

To find the position of the Sun at 1.50 pm GMT on 27 May, we work to its position at noon on 28 May (for all pm births, use the Sun's position on the subsequent day).

Sun's position, noon, 28 May = 6°55′ Gemini. From this, subtract the Sun's position at noon GMT on 27 May: 6°55′ minus 5°57′ = 0°58′. The Sun has thus moved 0°58′ of celestial longitude between noon on 27 May and noon on 28 May: this is called the Sun's **motion** during that period.

Calculate the interval of time between the hour of birth, and noon on the day of birth. In this case: 12.00 hours to 1.50h = 1.50h, interval.

Use now the table of logarithms (p. 251) to find the log. of the interval = 1.1170. Then, from the same table, find the log. of the Sun's motion: Log. of 0°57′ = 1.4025. Add these two results to obtain a total of 2.5195. Find the anti-log of this last total. Anti-log of 2.5195 = 0°04′.

Now, for a pm birth, add this anti-log to the position of the Sun at noon on the birth day:

5°57′ (Sun at noon on birth day)
+0°04′ (Anti-log. figure)
6°01′ Gemini = position of Sun at time of birth.

The same process is followed to find the positions of the Moon, Mercury, Venus and Mars (see examples below). If a planet is Retrograde (marked by a capital 'R' in ephemerides), the process is exactly the same, except that the anti-log is added to the position of the planet at noon on the birthday for an am birth, and subtracted for a pm birth.

NOTE When a planet changes signs, subtract the figure given from 30° (the number of degrees in each sign), and add the result to the position at noon on the birth day if an am birth, or at noon on the following day if a pm birth. In example given below left for the Moon, the Moon position on 27 May = 9°18′. Therefore:

30°00′ (Extent of one sign)
minus 26°53′ (Position at noon on 26 May)
= 3°07′
plus 9°18′ (Position at noon on 27 May)
= 12°25′ = Motion of Moon.

	Moon	Mercury	Venus	Mars
Noon position 27 May	9°18′ Pisces	17°50′ Taurus	13°10′ Cancer	11°13′ Taurus
Noon position 26 May	26°53′ Aquarius	16°05′ Taurus	12°47′ Cancer	10°29′ Taurus
Daily motion	12°25′ (but see note above)	1°45′	0°23′	0°44′
Log of interval	.3730	.3730	.3730	.3730
Log of motion	.2862	1.1372	1.7966	1.5149
Add logs	.6592	1.5102	2.1696	1.8879
Anti-logs	5°15′	0°45′	0°10′	0°19′
Subtract from noon 27 May	9°18′	17°50′	13°10′	11°13′
Positions of planets at time of birth	4°03′ Pisces	17°05′ Taurus	13°00′ Cancer	10°54′ Taurus

Jupiter, during the 24-hour period from 26 May to 27 May, according to the ephemeris, moved from 15°55′ Leo to 16°03′ Leo – a motion of 0°08′ celestial longitude. The interval between the hour of birth and noon on the day of birth is 10.10h, which is almost half a day; therefore subtract half the motion – i.e. 0°04′, giving the position of Jupiter at the time of birth as 15°59′ Leo. Following the same procedure, we have Saturn 4°38′ (Retrograde; Aquarius; Uranus 21°52′ Aries; Neptune 5°14′ Virgo; Pluto 20°18′ Cancer.

	Moon	Mercury	Venus	Mars
Noon position 28 May	21°27′ Pisces	19°37′ Taurus	13°33′ Cancer	11°57′ Taurus
Noon position 27 May	9°18′ Pisces	17°50′ Taurus	13°10′ Cancer	11°13′ Taurus
Daily motion	12°09′	1°47′	0°23′	0°44′
Log of interval	1.1170	1.1170	1.1170	1.1170
Log of motion	.2956	1.1290	1.7966	1.5149
Add logs	1.4126	2.2460	2.9136	2.6319
Anti-logs	0°56′	0°08′	0°02′	0°03′
Add to noon on 27 May	9°18′	17°50′	13°10′	11°13′
Position of planets at time of birth	10°14′ Pisces	17°58′ Taurus	13°12′ Cancer	11°16′ Taurus

Jupiter, during the 24-hour period from 27 May to 28 May, according to the ephemeris, moved from 16°03′ Leo to 16°11′ Leo – a motion of 0°08′ celestial longitude. The interval between noon on the day of birth and the hour of birth itself is 1.50h. During that time, none of the planets will have moved appreciably, so their positions at the time of birth may be taken to be the same as at noon on the day of birth. If the interval is considerable – say 6 or 10 hours – then add the proportionate amount of motion: a quarter for 6 hours, or half for 10 hours.

Calculating the Moon's Nodes

To calculate the moon's nodes refer to the ephemeris, where they are listed for alternate days. The motion is small, and **always retrograde;** so again no calculation is necessary; proceed as for the slow-moving planets.

Declination of the Planets

To calculate this, again use the ephemeris, noting the positions marked under **'Dec'**; the motions are very small except in the case of the Moon, and the positions are usually listed for alternate days. The declinations can therefore be found without calculation by the same process described above for slow-moving plants. In the case of the Moon, logarithms are used, as above; note also whether the Moon is increasing or decreasing (waxing or waning), adding or subtracting as necessary.

6

Mark off the degree of the Ascendant in each segment of the Chart, anti-clockwise around the inner circle, and join each mark to its opposite across the circle. These segments are numbered 1–12 anti-clockwise, the First House being immediately below the Ascendant.

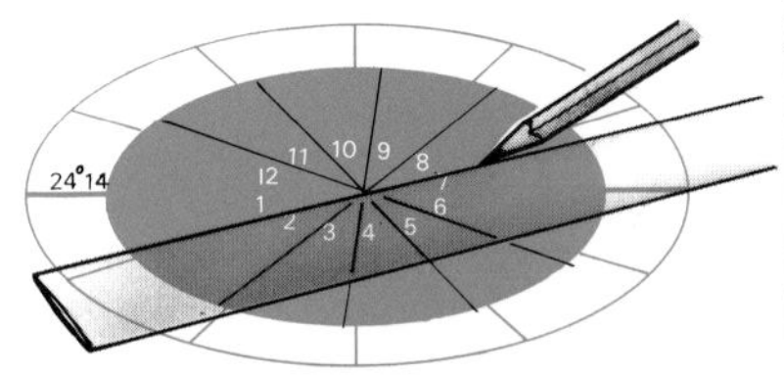

7

Mark the Sign glyphs in the outer circle, in anti-clockwise order, starting from the Ascending Sign.

8

Mark the Midheaven in its appropriate Sign, indicating it with an outward-pointing arrow and the letters MC, and again showing the degree and minute. The IC should be marked at the opposite point on the Chart.

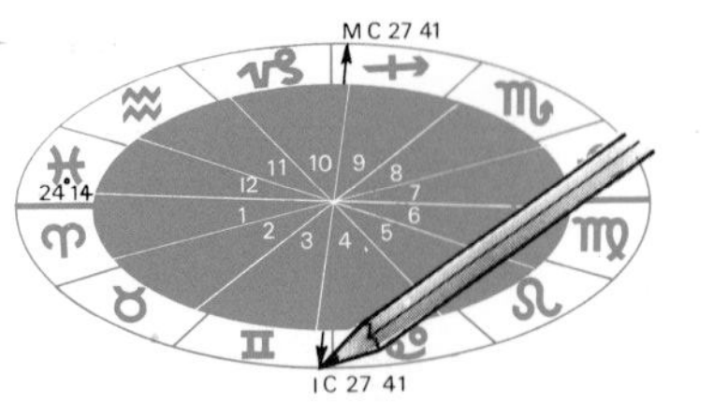

9

Within the inner circle, mark the planetary positions (already calculated or read from the tables) by writing in the relevant glyphs and the degrees.

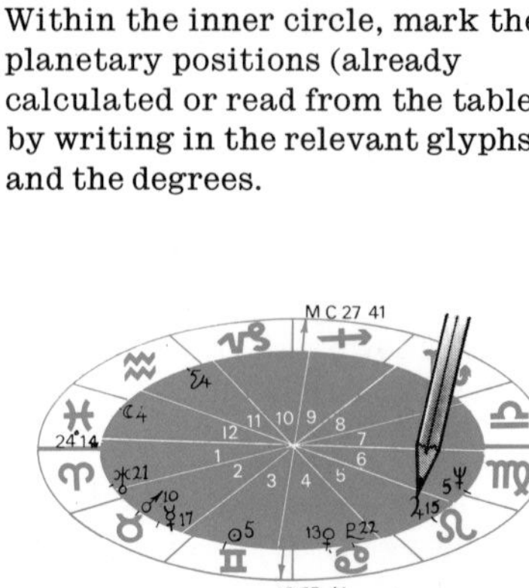

10 Note the Aspects (see p. 132) and register them by their glyphs in the aspect grid (see previous page). Then, inside the inner circle of the Chart, make a series of marks opposite the positions of the planets. The Ascendant and Midheaven are *not* marked in this way.

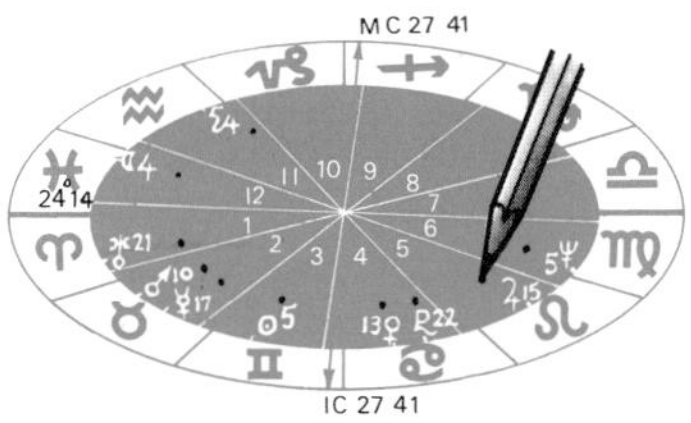

11 Where two planets are in aspect to each other, join the relevant dots. Oppositions or square aspects should be joined with a solid black line; minor aspects should be joined with a dotted black line; trines and sextiles should be joined with a solid red line. This helps to make a Birth Chart clearer. Planets in conjunction are not marked as such; their proximity to each other makes them sufficiently noticeable.

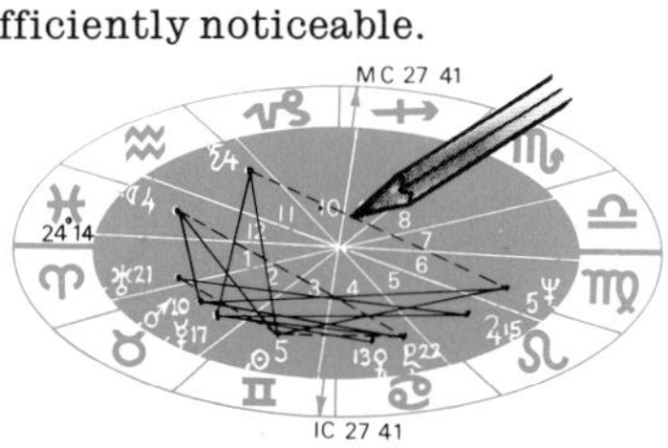

12 Fill in the list of traditional factors, as outlined on p. 79.

13 Refer to the tables of the Moon's nodes (p. 248), and mark their positions on the outer circle.

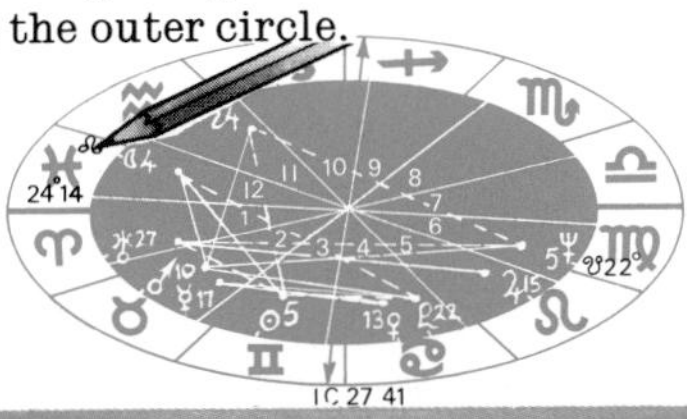

14

Interpreting a Birth Chart

The Birth Chart is now complete and ready for interpretation. Begin your assessment by reading the descriptions of the characteristics of the Ascending Sign and the Sign in which the Sun falls; note the main characteristics. Then note the House position of the Sun, and the sphere of life this indicates (p. 86); note the aspects the Sun makes to the other planets, the Ascendant and Midheaven, and the characteristics these indicate (p. 132). Repeat this process for the Moon and other planets, in order.

The positions of the Sun and Moon are particularly important, and after them the most important factor is the Ruling Planet, the planet which rules the Sign of the Ascendant (pp. 84–103). If the birth-time is accurately known, the aspects made to the Ascendant and Midheaven should be carefully considered; if the birth-time is only roughly known, these should not be emphasized in interpretation.

You will now have a considerable mass of notes relevant to the subject of the Birth Chart. It is in the balancing and combining of these that the art of astrology lies. To help put the facts in order, a 'shorthand' system of key words was devised by Margaret E. Hone. These are given for each planet and Sign.

Example:
Mercury in Leo in the Eleventh House.
Keywords: Mercury, communication; Leo, creatively, powerfully; Eleventh House, clubs, societies, aims in life.

Interpretation
'You have the ability to put over your ideas, which will be creative, to groups of people whose interests you share'.

The keywords for the planets indicate their motivation and principle; those for the Signs show how that motivation or principle is applied. The keywords are related to the affairs of the House in which the planet and Sign fall. By using them, the beginner will be able to make an immediate start on the road to becoming a Compleat Astrologer.

THE TWELVE HOUSES

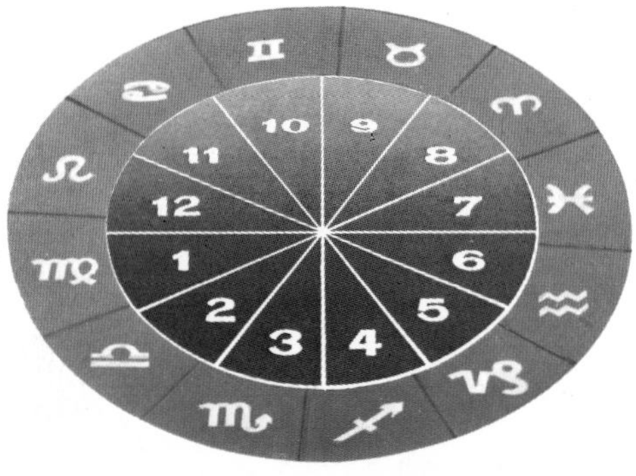

The inner circle of the Birth Chart is divided into 12 sections known as Houses. These are a distinct astrological category and relate to everyday activities, the First House to physical appearance and temperament, the Second to possessions, and so on. Planets and Signs fall within a House's sphere of activity according to their position on the Chart. They are then said to be 'in the Seventh House', for example, which means that their influence will be focused in the area linked with the Seventh House, i.e. in relationships of an emotional and business nature.

A planet (or planets) placed in a particular House on the Birth Chart affects the area of life represented by that House in a manner typical of the planet. If a House is empty of planets this does not mean that the area of life it represents is unimportant or devoid of interest. The House must be considered according to the sign in which the *cusp*, or starting point of the particular House falls.

In this section, the phrase 'under affliction' occurs from time to time. A planet is said to be afflicted when it receives negative or strenuous *aspects* – that is, if it appears at a particular angle to one or more

1ST HOUSE

The personality, disposition, health, temperament, physical build and appearance. This house in essence represents the subject as he or she appears to the outsider. It has a bearing on manners, and forms of outward behaviour. A planet in the First House is very powerful in influence.

2ND HOUSE

Possessions of all kinds, and the subject's attitude towards them; worldly resources which support the physical body. The sign on the cusp may indicate lucrative sources of income. The Second House is also concerned with the feelings, especially in relationship to a planet appearing in this House.

3RD HOUSE

Family ties, brothers, sisters, cousins, etc. School life, education; communications; letters; books. Short journeys, cars, bicycles, public transport. Speech. The mind is also associated with this House, as is the relationship of the subject to his environment, and his self-expression in daily life.

7TH HOUSE

As the First House relates to the personality, so the Seventh indicates those in close relationships of an emotional and business nature. The sign on the cusp of this House often provides a good indication of the marriage partner – as it may be stressed in his or her Chart.

8TH HOUSE

The Second House rules possessions: this House represents money from legacies, shared feelings, life-force elements of sex, birth and death, and attitudes towards death and the after-life. In addition, big business; the stock exchange, insurance companies. The Eighth is also the House of crime.

9TH HOUSE

The educational and intellectual elements of the Third House are extended in the Ninth to further education, study in depth of profound subjects, and mental exploration; also long-distance travel; foreigners; languages. This House also has a bearing on moral ideals, conscience and dreams.

planets as plotted in the Birth Chart.

The areas of life represented by the 12 Houses are shown on these pages. It will be seen that the first six Houses are in some ways related to the second six in the areas of life they represent. This is a traditionally established relationship.

The Midheaven

The Midheaven is found at the meeting point above the horizon of the ecliptic (Sun's apparent path) and the meridian of the place of birth. On the Birth Chart the Midheaven marks the place in the heavens where the Sun is found at midday. The sign occupied by the degree of the ecliptic at this meeting point is of great importance and will have a strong bearing not only on a subject's outward expression of himself in the world – in his work, choice of career and general life-style – but also in events in his life over which he has no direct control. In other words, the things that happen *to* him (e.g. being offered a job rather than applying for one).

The Midheaven also represents the ego, and the characteristics normally associated with the sign in which it is placed are emphasized in an external manner.

THE MIDHEAVEN

The influence of the Midheaven, which has a strong bearing on the outward expression of one's individuality, and also represents the ego, should not be confused with that of the Tenth House. The characteristics of Midheaven and Tenth House can be in alignment, but do not always coincide. The Midheaven is especially important in career matters.

4TH HOUSE

The beginning and end of life; the home, as a base. This House, together with the Tenth, has a certain bearing on parents – their attitude and ability to fulfil their commitments – since personal status and home life depend to some extent on them. Houses, land, and private life are also related to it.

5TH HOUSE

Creativity, children; pleasures, holidays; enterprises and new undertakings. Speculation, games of hazard, sport. Love affairs, and the objects of instinctive affection (pets, playmates, sweethearts). If a planet is seriously afflicted, looseness of behaviour and self-indulgence can easily occur.

6TH HOUSE

This House rules work; also subordinates, providing (in the past) a strong pointer to people's attitudes towards servants. Nowadays, the plumber, electrician, shop assistant and cleaning woman are likely substitutes. This is also the House of health, although physical well-being cannot be entirely assessed from it.

10TH HOUSE

From the 'roots' of the Fourth House we move in the Tenth to aspirations, ambitions, public standing. To all matters outside the home: the career or profession, and attainment in that field; social status and responsibilities, a sense of discipline, and matters affecting outward appearances and the personal image.

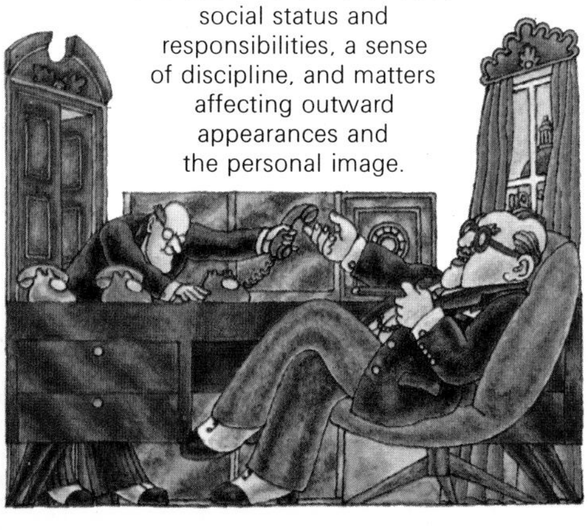

11TH HOUSE

The stress of the Fifth House is on personal pleasures; this House influences friends and acquaintances, clubs and societies. Objectives in life, and the more detached contacts made in day-to-day affairs. Intellectual pleasures, as opposed to the more physical or sporting forms of relaxation.

12TH HOUSE

A need for seclusion; service to others – such as hospital visiting; self-sacrifice, often as a result of a partner's illness. Escapism, the unconscious. The presence of many planets in this House is, at the present time, an indication of negative escapism, making the subject susceptible to drugs.

THE PLANETS

Their Influence and Mythology

The Zodiac and its myths are of secondary importance in astrology. They form a passive background to the action of the planets. It is in fact the positions and movements of the planets along the eclipitic *as seen from Earth* which govern astrological interpretation and prediction.

In ancient times each moving planet was given at least one special relationship with a fixed sign of the Zodiac. The ancient pattern of rulership was both neat and convenient: the Sun and Moon ruled one sign each, and the other planets two signs each.

The influence of Uranus, the first of the three modern planets, discovered in 1781 by William Herschel, was noted gradually at first by astrologers; today, after a long period of some controversy, it is generally accepted that the Uranian principle of disruptive or sudden change is allied to Aquarius. Neptune, discovered in 1846, was associated, after conjecture, with the receptive, diffuse sign Pisces. The newest planet, Pluto, which was discovered in America in February 1930, is linked with Scorpio, although in the 1970s every astrologer is still very conscious of the influence of Mars in Scorpio, even if Pluto has now such a powerful influence on that Sign. By AD 2000, it may be that Mars' link with Scorpio will have been broken: but by then there may be other 'modern' planets to consider, for there is speculation about these among both astronomers and astrologers.

Traditional Factors

Planets can be 'in detriment', 'in exaltation' or 'in fall' if they happen to be placed within the signs which traditionally give them these qualities. It *can* of course happen that no planet in a Chart comes into any of these categories.) A planet *in exaltation* is well-placed, should work well for the subject, and is generally positive. A planet *in detriment* is traditionally ill-placed, and tends to lose some of its power. This is also the case when a planet is *in fall*.

Mutual reception

A planet is 'in mutual reception' with another planet when each falls in the sign ruled by the other: for example, when Mercury is in Libra (traditionally ruled by Venus), and Venus is in Virgo (traditionally ruled by Mercury). Two planets in mutual reception will work together for the subject's benefit, each strengthening and emphasizing the effect of the other.

Angularity

A planet is said to be 'angular' when it falls within 8° of the Ascendant, Descendant, MC or IC. This position strengthens the planet's effect on the subject.

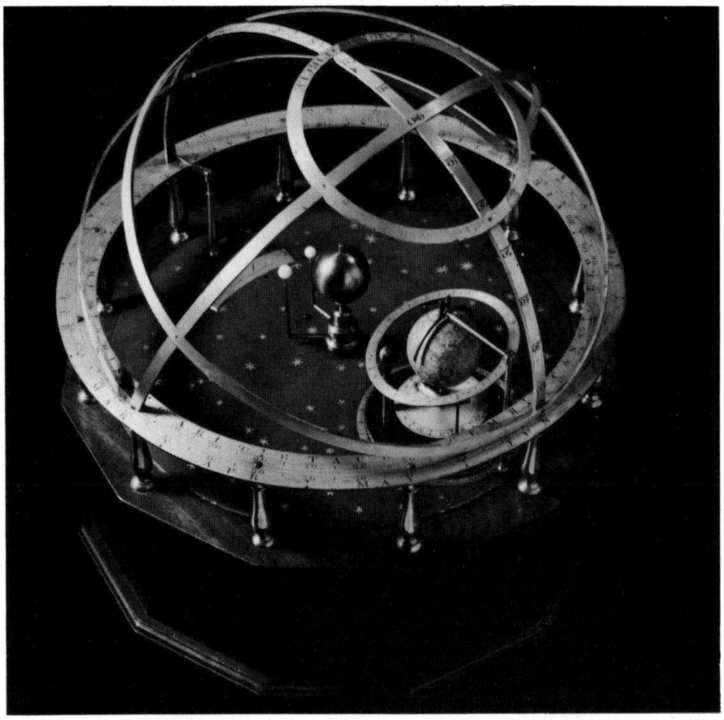

Orrery *left*
Orreries are mechanical instruments showing the relative motions of the Sun, Earth, Moon and planets. They first appeared in the early 18th century and were named after the fourth Earl of Orrery, patron of John Rowley, a London instrument maker. The miniature model illustrated was built by Edward Troughton c. 1800: Mercury and Venus (small white spheres) are in orbit round the central brass sphere of the Sun. The Earth turns round the Sun, its axis inclined at 23½° to the ecliptic; an ivory ball representing the Moon circles the Earth, the hemisphere fa ing away from the Sun being covered to explain the Moon's phases

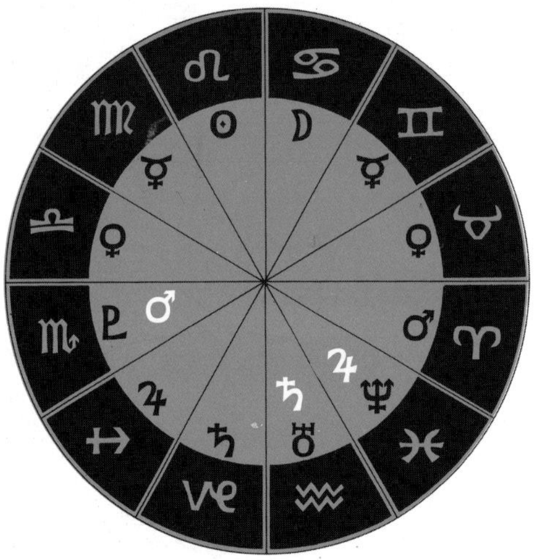

The Planets and Their Signs *left*
By tradition each planet rules at least one sign, e.g. the Sun rules Leo; the Sun is a creative force and Leo is a creative sign. With the discovery of the modern planets the rulers are (black figures in the diagram): Sun (Leo); Moon (Cancer); Mercury (Gemini, Virgo); Venus (Taurus, Libra); Mars (Aries); Jupiter (Sagittarius); Saturn (Capricorn); Uranus (Aquarius); Neptune (Pisces); Pluto (Scorpio). The three former rulerships, Mars (Scorpio), Jupiter (Pisces), Saturn (Aquarius) are in white.

Planet Power *below*
The diagram shows the ten planets ranging outward from the Sun to Pluto. Since ancient times the Sun has been seen as the most powerful energy-system in the sky; on the Birth Chart it is followed in importance by the Moon, then Mercury, Venus, Mars, Jupiter and Saturn. The modern planets are regarded as more remote 'generation influences'.

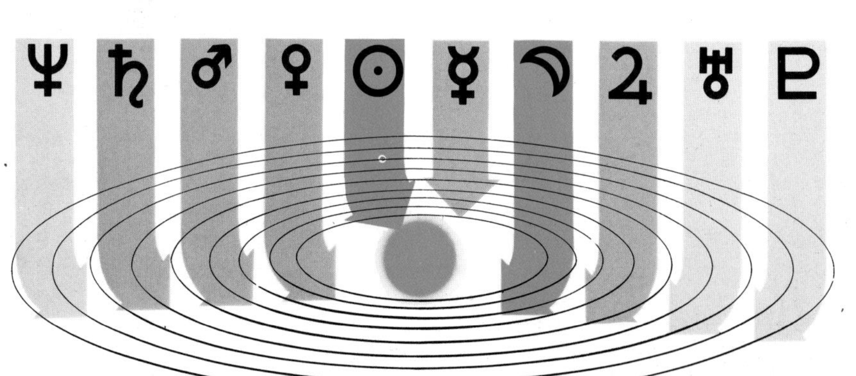

The Sun
Apollo, son of Zeus and second only to him in power, became associated in the 5th century BC with the strength, light and purity of the Sun; the snake which he slew represents the cold darkness of winter, dispersed by his blazing beauty. He governed the seasons, was the god of agriculture, guardian of herds and flocks. Perfectly beautiful, he was supposed to be the first victor in the Olympic Games, and symbolizes Man, most perfect of animals, in his highest form.

The Moon
Myths associated specifically with the Moon are comparatively rare; in general, the Moon is regarded as feminine – although the Albanians and Phrygians believed it to be masculine, and ruled by a male priest. Associated with virginity and purity, the Moon has also been linked with childbearing; bloodthirsty sacrifices were made to her, sometimes in the hope that the entrails of victims would reveal the future. She had no temples in Greece but two in Rome.

Mercury
Mercury became associated with merchandise and merchants when in 495 BC he was introduced into Rome from Greece (where his name was Hermes, and he had been messenger to the other gods). Mercury's temple on the Aventine became a corn exchange, and the corn merchants worshipped him; other merchants were drawn to him, and soon his statue appeared in the business quarters of many Roman towns. His annual festival was on 15 May.

Venus
Venus, a Roman and Latin goddess, was originally goddess of beauty and growth in nature; but later she became associated with Aphrodite, Greek goddess of love, worshipped (often with the most repulsive rites) as far west as Italy and Sicily. She ruled sexuality, fruitfulness, and eventually family life – though in her early days she showed small concern for the conventions! The family of Julius Caesar claimed to be descended from her.

Mars
Although essentially a Roman god, Mars is associated with the Greek god of war, Aries. Rome was the centre of his cult, where he had two temples – one at the army's exercise-ground, for he was always the god of war. His sacred spears were kept in the second temple: during the warm summer season, most suitable for campaigning, they were shaken by the consul, who cried: 'Mars, awake!' His main function was to protect the state.

Jupiter
The most important Roman god, the equivalent of Zeus, Jupiter traditionally owned all places struck by lightning; he cared for the wine harvest, was concerned with treaties and oaths, and the most ancient ceremonies of marriage. He is the archetypal father figure. A great temple to him was raised on the Capitol, and similar temples were found in most Roman cities. Thunderbolts came direct to earth from him, and were used as symbols of his majesty.

Saturn
The Saturnalia, devoted to the worship of Saturn, was the liveliest of all Roman festivals – the equivalent of, and, indeed, an enormous influence on Christmas, with an exchange of presents, criminals set free, and slaves waited on by their masters. The god of sowing or of seedcorn, he was traditionally Uranus' son, who, having castrated his father became supreme lord of the earth, ruling over a Golden Age of innocence and love. Saturday is named after him.

Uranus
At the beginning of all things, Mother Earth gave birth to Uranus (Heaven), who then became incestuously the father of all mankind. His sons, the Titans, included Cronus (known as Saturn), who was incited by Earth to castrate him in revenge for his victimization of his other sons, the Cyclops. Aphrodite was born out of this savage act. The Uranus myth is thought to be pre-Greek – perhaps Hittite. He is generally shown in art as a bewildered old man.

Neptune
Originally an Italian god of fresh water, in the 4th century BC he became linked with Poseidon, and was thence forward known as a sea-god. With his trident, he raised the sea to fury, but was also the god of navigators and the protector of all sea-going people. In spite of this, Neptuniala, his ancient festival, was on 23 July – when droughts were common, and his intercession was desirable. This is obviously a link with his original connection with fresh water.

Pluto
Pluto is one of the many nicknames of Hades, lord of the underworld. Cronus' son, he took part in a lottery dividing the world among his brothers – and won the least desirable prize. Stern and pitiless, god of the dead, unmoved by sacrifices, hung with cypress and narcissus, he carried the key of the lower world, which he ruled with his queen Persephone. He was only once deceived – by Orpheus. He was worshipped as a 'giver of wealth'.

THE SUN

rules Leo; is exalted in Aries; detriment Aquarius; fall Libra
Keywords: Power, vitality, self-expression

The House that the Sun occupies will be strongly emphasized, and the affairs of that House are likely to be of great importance to the subject throughout his life. Generally speaking, the affairs of Houses 7–12 are concerned with adult life; in the interpretation of children's charts, the planets placed in Houses 7–12 will relate to potentialities to be developed in adulthood. (The attributes of the Sun through the Signs are discussed in the Signs section which opens on p. 104.)

Associations
The Sun is associated with the heart and spine; with heads of state or royalty, fatherhood and children; with creativity, especially in the theatre; and with games.

Positive Solar traits
Creative, generous, big-hearted, showing great joie-de-vivre; organizing ability; love of children; affectionate, magnanimous, dignified.

Negative Solar traits
Pompous, arrogant, domineering; gushing and extravagant; condescending, overbearing and bombastic; tends to throw his weight about; 'too big for his boots'.

The Sun Factor *left* **Queen Victoria** and **Richard Wagner** both had the Sun rising in Gemini in their Birth Charts. In the case of Wagner this placing gave him the duality reflected in his work as writer and musician, originating the libretti and the music of his operas; his expansive nature can also be traced to the Sun, which was in the First House at the time of his birth.

Queen Victoria also wrote compulsively, but her Sun, in the Twelfth House, made her shy and introverted, and contributed to the long period of seclusion that followed Prince Albert's death.

The Sun Through the Houses

1 Whether the Sun is well aspected or not, there is always an inward-looking tendency. This can be tinged with selfishness, according to the sign concerned. If the Sun is afflicted, the health may suffer (again, according to the rising sign); if the Sun is free from affliction the health should be robust. Awareness of and kindness to others should be developed in children with this placing. The Sun in this House usually means that both Ascendant and Sun-sign are the same. Therefore all characteristics of this sign are intensified. Sometimes this creates a certain amount of imbalance due to the powerful stress on one sign, and other areas of the Chart – the position of the Moon for instance – will be of great importance in providing the necessary contrasting characteristics.

2 Concentration on financial affairs will be strong; awareness of earning capacity, and a natural desire to increase this, are emphasized. Feelings will be strong, but possessiveness is a common fault. Children with this placing should be encouraged to share their toys with friends.

3 An emphasis on the need to communicate: a good talker; there will be fluent and well-developed writing ability if the Sun is in a creative or intellectual sign. This placing is good for life at school, and while children with the Sun in this house will be extremely lively, they may lack patience and consistency of effort which must be discouraged.

4 Happiness in home and family life, bringing satisfaction and fulfilment, if the Sun is free from affliction. Children with this placing will be keen to help look after brothers and sisters – and may have to be encouraged to spread their wings and find friends outside the family.

5 The Sun is powerful in this House. Much enjoyment, and a desire to get as much as possible out of life. Interest, and possibly creative ability, in the arts, sport, team games. Children will be a great source of pleasure. There may be a propensity to take risks; extreme care should be taken over investment of family funds. Children with this placing will be energetic and sunny, but boisterousness, bossiness and bumptiousness must be checked. Excellent placing for the artist.

6 If the Sun is well aspected in this House, the health should be strengthened by the placing; but the whole Chart should nevertheless be considered carefully. The placing usually shows a good worker, with ability in his or her chosen field. Good organizational ability that will take the subject far in his chosen field, and relationships with subordinates. Under affliction, it is likely that the subject would make a 'difficult' boss. Children with this placing will have many hobbies.

7 The Sun in this House indicates success in marriage. Excellent, too, for business partnerships, which should run smoothly. The subject needs to be given his head in these matters and should be the dominant partner; a feeling of frustration may develop otherwise.

8 The Sun in this House often denotes an interest in mysticism, the occult and psychicism; emotions are deep-rooted and stable. Sometimes there will be involvement with the financial affairs of others. Legacies are common. Thoughts of death and the after-life are kept in perspective, and death, when it comes, should be natural.

9 The Sun in the Ninth House often indicates that a great deal of time is spent abroad. Further education will be particularly successful and should be encouraged, since there is usually a desire to study. Flair for languages sometimes occurs. There is sympathy for other people's customs and points of view, and tolerance for 'quirks'.

10 Career interests will assume a greater than average importance, and the career should be not only successful but will involve the whole personality Perhaps a real sense of vocation. Care is needed when the Sun is in the Tenth House that other spheres of the life do not become neglected. Since the whole personality is likely to be involved in the career, marriage and friendship could suffer. This is especially so if the Sun is in an enthusiastic or very powerful sign such as Leo or Capricorn.

11 Clear-cut objectives and their successful achievement. Much time likely to be spent in societies and group activities. Office in these is likely; a strong organizing ability. Friendships will be rewarding, and the subject himself will probably bring happiness to others

12 A psychological need to withdraw; work often carried on in a study or office at home; the work itself is likely to be of a behind-the-scenes nature. A good placing for the medical profession. The marriage partner should not insist on sharing everything.

Partial Eclipse *above*
Photograph of a partial eclipse of the Sun; a segment of the brilliant solar disk remains visible beyond the obscuring body of the Moon as it passes across the Sun's face.

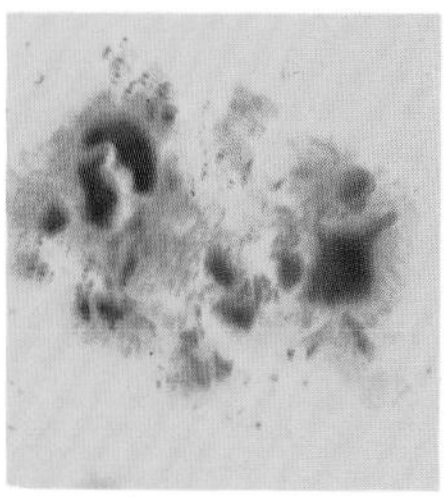

Sunspots *above*
Sunspots, accompanied by violent magnetic activity, operate in an 11-year cycle; a minority of astrologers claim they have a bearing on earthly economics.

The Sun *right*
The Sun is a star, the powerful core of the Solar System; its diameter is 109 times that of the Earth. Because of its mass and its immense light-giving energy, the Sun is a key astrological force, associated with vitality, strength and creative power.

Total Eclipse *right*
The solar disk is totally eclipsed; two eclipses in 1914 were astrologically linked with the outbreak of the Great War.

Solar Prominence *far right*
Prominences are eruptions on the Sun's surface; they sometimes portend economic recession.

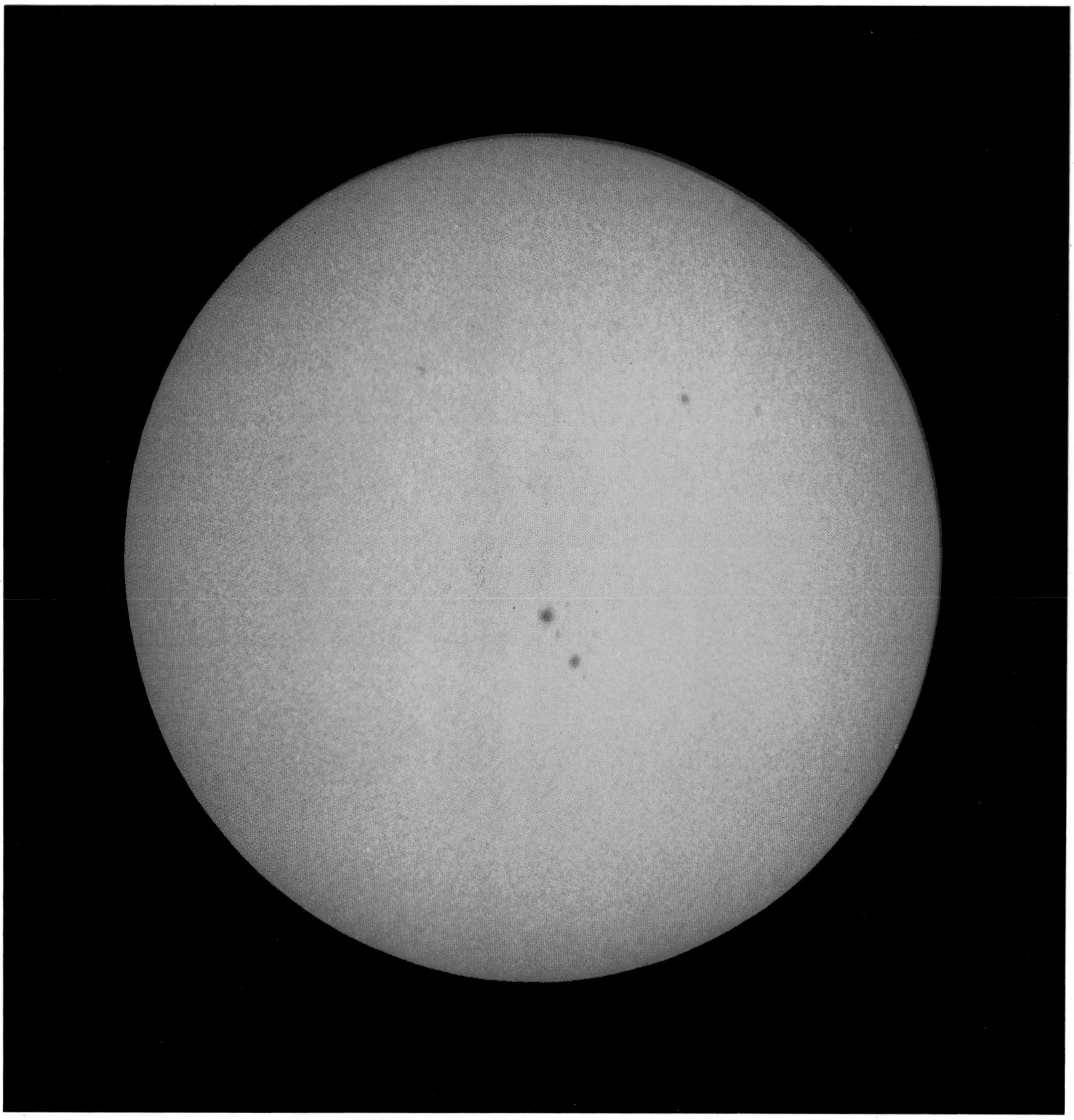

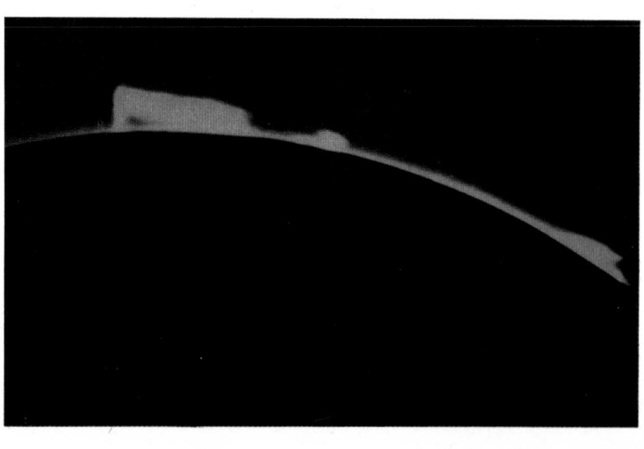

THE MOON

rules Cancer; is exalted in Taurus detriment Capricorn; fall Scorpio Keywords: Response, instinct, fluctuation

Next to the Sun, the Moon is the most important body in the Birth Chart; the characteristics of the sign it occupies form an integral part of the personality. These have a direct bearing on habits and reactions in a given environment and on a person's instinctive behaviour. Characteristics inherited from past generations are related to the Moon and its position.

Associations

The Moon is associated with birth, motherhood; the digestive system, stomach and breasts; the sympathetic nervous system, body fluids, nutrition, emotional disturbance and personal habits; the home, family, ancestors; response, the memory.

Positive Lunar traits

Passive, patient, tenacious; imaginative; sensitive; a maternal nature; sympathetic; receptive; shrewd in business matters; a good memory.

Negative Lunar traits

Moody; clannish; changeable; weak reasoning power; unreliable; gullible; narrow-minded; reluctant to forgive.

The Moon Factor
left
Arturo Toscanini's Chart shows the Moon in the Tenth House in Scorpio, traditionally associated with fame and a career in the public eye. This placing also gives an ability to influence and direct people, which Toscanini put to profitable use in his work as an orchestral conductor.

The brooding **Lord Byron's** Moon was in its own sign, Cancer, at his birth, and gave him the changeable, sensitive imbalance which made personal relationships so difficult for him.

The Moon Through the Houses

1 The Moon in the First House strengthens the characteristics of the rising sign: habits and responses are strongly related to it; the positive and negative qualities of the Moon and ascending sign will be powerfully emphasized. If the Moon is severely afflicted, this can mean that the mother suffered a difficult birth, or that the mother/child relationship was especially close.

2 Possible fluctuations in income, but a shrewd business attitude; there should be an instinctive ability to save.

3 Changeable in ideas; an unsettled early education. This placing makes the subject an excellent elder brother or sister, who will always have a protective attitude.

4 An instinctive and powerful maternal sense. Good placing for the home-maker, but domestic changes can be expected. Under affliction, a clinging attitude towards children, which will be difficult to break. An interest in history or ancestry.

5 Good placing for a kindergarten teacher, securing fast results with young children through creative and artistic interests; also in sport. Perhaps fame through sport.

6 An interest in hygiene and cleanliness, especially in the home. Weakness in health as a young child.

7 Changeable in emotional relationships. Men may choose a motherly kind of wife. In either sex, an emphasis on relationships with women. Shrewd in business, but also inclined to be unsteady (other areas of the Chart need careful consideration).

8 Possible preoccupation with sex, death and the after-life. Excellent for research in psychic matters. Involvement with public finance likely.

9 Able to study serious subjects with tenacity: ancient history or dead languages can attract. Subject may emigrate.

10 Career interests may bring the subject before the public; fame may be fleeting or long-lasting, but such prominence leaves little private life.

11 A liking for societies and lecture groups. Varied and changeable objectives in life.

12 A psychological need for seclusion – which will prove restorative. Good imagination and excellent intuition – needing firm development.

The Moon Through the Signs

Aries When the Moon is 'in' this sign, the 'me first' tendencies of Aries are often asserted, especially in the parent/child relationship. A quick but changeable mind is likely; the temper may be uneven. Much natural, sincere enthusiasm, but patience should be consciously developed. Impetuosity can cause accidents, to which the subject is somewhat prone, burns and cuts being frequent. Feverishness is another health hazard. There is a dislike of conventional behaviour. The subject is commonly headstrong: advice is not listened to, and he finds discipline hard to accept.

Taurus The Moon is at its most stable in Taurus, impulsiveness being balanced by persistence and determination. A hopeful and positive outlook, ambitious and reliable in action. The Moon in this sign is often favourable for financial interests. Usually sociable, sensual and fun-loving, but may be possessive. Sometimes this is inherited from the mother; under affliction, it can be quite serious and needs control. The throat may be vulnerable. Appreciation of, or creative ability in, the arts (especially music) is common.

Gemini If other areas of the Chart lack stability, the subject will have to combat indecision, changeability and physical restlessness. At best, there is a genuine duality which should be recognized and accepted: a preference, even a need to do several things at once being a vital part of the subject's psychological well-being. The intellectual ability of this placing often makes an avid reader or a craftsman. Walking, getting out and about, are particularly beneficial; under affliction, nervous tension is common. Perseverance, deliberation and a capacity to take decisions should be consciously developed. A lively intellectual attitude towards children earns a rewarding response.

Cancer The positive lunar traits are strongly emphasized. The need to cherish and protect, and a powerfully developed family instinct, are prominent. In human relationships a natural tenacity should not be allowed to become negative or clinging – drawing psychological strength from the other person. Sympathy for the feelings of others is common, also sensitivity to surroundings. This placing

The Moon and Earth Compared *above*
Earth has 81 times the lunar mass; but the Moon's nearness to us makes it influential.

The Moon *right*
The Full Moon, showing the dark plains, still called seas; the bright uplands and the walled craters. The Moon's physical effects are numerous: by tradition they include mental disorders and inherited personal traits; recent research links its position (with the Sun) to the fertility of women.

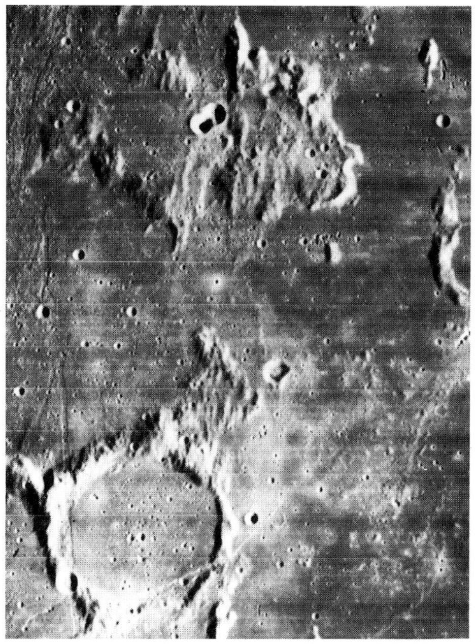

Surface of the Moon *above*
The lunar surface, showing the craters of the Fra Mauro group, suggests by its remoteness some of the Moon's negative, moody characteristics.

usually makes good parents, but a tendency to overstress authority should be watched. A powerful imagination and a high emotional level are always present.

Leo Organizing ability is prominent, but this can become 'bossiness'. The subject has a sunny disposition, being naturally gay and self-confident. Under affliction, conceit, self-satisfaction, ostentatiousness and an overbearing manner are present. The emotions are powerful, affection is generously given. Sophisticated pleasures are usually favoured. Loyalty and a love of luxury are also stressed. Self-indulgence can occur, and personal limitations should be recognized and accepted.

Virgo This position gives a strong tendency to worry which can easily affect the health; the digestion suffers quite seriously as a result. Sometimes timidity and a rather nervous disposition occur. There is good business sense and meticulous attention to detail. This is an excellent position for secretarial work. Fussiness and a lack of self-confidence should be counteracted. An analytical, practical mind and a good memory help the ability to study and work hard – though, again, too much attention may be paid to detail. Health, diet, chemistry, herbalism, horticulture can prove a strong attraction.

Libra There is natural courtesy, charm and a diplomatic manner; a genuine desire to please. The subject is friendly, easy-going and popular; but under affliction, capricious, fickle and inclined to be over-critical. Self-reliance must be consciously developed. Music and poetry are attractive. This placing is excellent for work in the diplomatic corps. The subject is at his best when working with others or in direct partnership, so that decision-making can be shared – decisiveness is not usually a strong point with this planet.

Scorpio The emotional level is high and needs firm, positive direction. Intensity, magnetism and determination are present in this placing. The subject needs to work hard – and also to enjoy life. Pride and obstinacy occur; under affliction, moodiness, resentment, possessiveness, anger and sometimes immorality will mar positive characteristics shown in other areas of the Chart. Sometimes more introvert tendencies appear on the surface; but as a cover for inner turbulence and passion.

Sagittarius Often restless, but generally optimistic, cheerful and a fluent talker. A high degree of independence and a liking for freedom are usual; there is a common tendency to be somewhat off-hand. A strong need for physical exercise is usually expressed through participation in sport. Intuitive powers are highly developed and these often lend the subject a somewhat prophetic air. Carelessness and, sometimes, recklessness are negative traits to be counteracted. Changes of residence are common. A sense of urgency and quickness of movement are characteristic.

Capricorn Reserved, cautious, prudent – these qualities are powerfully in evidence; and while there is much common sense and practical ability, these traits can become extreme, leaning towards over-caution, gloominess and austerity. At the other end of the scale the subject is sometimes ostentatious. At work, he shows application, can take responsibility, and may earn a senior position through persistent effort.

Aquarius Tends to prefer the unconventional and to value his personal independence. Friendliness, humanitarianism and kindness are emphasized. Obstinacy and eccentricity may occur, but these are not normally disagreeable to others. Originality, ingenuity and scientific ability are likely; often there is a flair for astrology. Love of independence can lead to loneliness, and failure with emotional relationships – which may be brushed off with indifference. Nervous tension can occur under affliction. Erratic behaviour, aloofness and unpredictability need conscious control if they are not to outweigh positive qualities.

Pisces The subject is highly receptive, often kind, amicable and gentle. Under affliction, he may be lazy, gullible, restless and impractical, with a strong tendency to change his mind; decision-making can prove a source of conflict. The imaginative powers are well developed, and often there is artistic ability, although this may lack coherent expression. There is a tendency (which should be recognized and resisted) to be too easily discouraged. This placing heightens the emotions. Self-indulgence.

MERCURY

rules Gemini and Virgo; is exalted in Virgo; detriment Sagittarius; fall Pisces Keyword: Communication (mental and physical)

Mercury, moving like Venus inside the Earth's orbit, is an 'inferior' planet. Mercury is the nearest planet to the Sun, and is always found within 28° of it. On a Birth Chart Mercury appears either in the same sign as the Sun, the next sign (ahead of the Sun) or in the previous sign.

Associations
Mercury is associated with the intellect, the brain, co-ordination of the nervous system; the respiratory system; mental perception, the thyroid; also day-to-day travel – your car, motor scooter, bicycle.

Positive Mercurial traits
The urge to acquire knowledge and communicate it to others; good reasoning powers, perceptive, clever, versatile, excellent in debate or argument; intellectual; attentive to detail.

Negative Mercurial traits
Inconsistent, hypercritical; inquisitive, lacking a sense of purpose; uncontrolled nervous energy brings mental strain or stagnation; argumentative, 'slick', bitingly sarcastic, cynical.

The Mercury Factor *lef* **Jules Verne's** Birth Chart shows Mercury conjunct the Midheaven in Aquarius. This is a classic indication of an interest in science fiction and, moreover, creative ability in that field. Verne's prophetic grasp of the principles behind man's future exploration of the universe suggests a spiritual link at least with the presently dawning Age of Aquarius.

Mercury Through the Houses

1 Mercury in the First House puts emphasis on intellectual energy. This needs positive control, to prevent inconsistency. Duality is likely. The need for intellectual challenge is strong but too much self-centred thinking can be dangerous.

2 An interest in financial advancement may lead to over-commitment. Good bargaining powers, perhaps ability in aggressive salesmanship.

3 Emphasis on education, the affairs of brothers and sisters. Nervous system may be a cause of concern, but if the planet is free from affliction all Mercury/Third House matters should flow positively, the mind being applied according to the Sign concerned. Talkative.

4 Strong likelihood of mental activity in home surroundings, perhaps study. May be over-domesticated. Shows forethought, and has a rational attitude towards motherhood.

5 Flair for intellectual games, such as bridge. Ability to get on with children and young people. Great concern with love affairs and pleasure.

6 Tends to worry about health; may have intestinal troubles. Day-to-day work problems can seem over-important. Excellent placing for those engaged in secretarial work.

7 Lively attitude towards marriage, business partnerships. Partner must be intellectually stimulating. Need for continual intellectual rapport.

8 Mental ability, perhaps directed towards big business. The occult may attract: possible pre-occupation with death. Deep-rooted emotions may be aroused by others.

9 Accent on study in depth, languages, further education; application needed to reinforce such abilities. Mercury works well in this House.

10 Career must be intellectually stimulating, otherwise restlessness will mar progress. Business, trade, newspapers – a career in communications may well attract.

11 Many acquaintances, excellent for a lively social life centred around clubs and societies; likely to hold office in them. Intellectual friendships.

12 Secretive tendencies, attraction to mysticism; possibly good intuition. Imagination needs firm external attachments.

Mercury Through the Signs

Aries Quick-thinking, outspoken, sometimes showing a quick wit, an ironic edge. Self-assertiveness must be kept in perspective. Thoughtlessness and a quarrelsome tendency can result if Mercury is afflicted. Mental strain or restlessness may result from a lack of intellectual stimulation. Impulsiveness, hasty speech and insufficient planning of projects can hamper progress, but unless Mercury is badly afflicted the first decision is usually the right one. Study for examinations is put off and usually done at the last moment!

Taurus A practical, steady mind. Needs time to assimilate facts, encouragment to consider others' opinions, and to develop a flexible outlook, since stubbornness and fixed opinions can become powerful negative traits. Generally cheerful and refined in outlook, able to appreciate art and beauty. If the Sun is in Gemini, Mercury in Taurus is often an excellent stabilizer, helping to settle the Geminian restlessness. However, if the Sun is in Taurus the stubborn and fixed tendencies will dominate, and will need counter-balancing in other areas of the Chart.

Gemini Great versatility and duality: will often change his opinions. An inventive and lively mind – usually able to keep prejudice under control. Desire for breadth of knowledge is often only partly fulfilled; although the subject may give the impression that he is well-informed, he tends to settle for a superficial grasp (e.g. the television interviewer who has made a quick check on a few basic facts; the dilettante as opposed to the professional). A good and persistent talker, if verbose and sometimes lacking in emotion.

Cancer Keen memory, powerful imagination which should have some positive, creative outlet; but a strong tendency to live in the past, unconcerned about the future. Considerable tenacity of opinion, but can be changeable in day-to-day matters. Extremely kind and thoughtful. Intuitive and somewhat dreamy, may enjoy lyrical poetry, music; a developed sense of rhythm. Irrational worries, phobias and narrow-mindedness are tendencies to be checked. Tactful and diplomatic, but may harbour resentment and find it hard to forget a slight or injury.

Mercury and Earth Compared *above*
Mercury is fast-moving but small; its 3000-mile diameter makes it closer in size to the Moon than Earth.

Mercury *right*
The face of Mercury, the planet of quick-silver, showing bright and dark areas. Mercury's rapid motion and its generally elusive nature caused it to be associated in astrology with speed and mental agility.

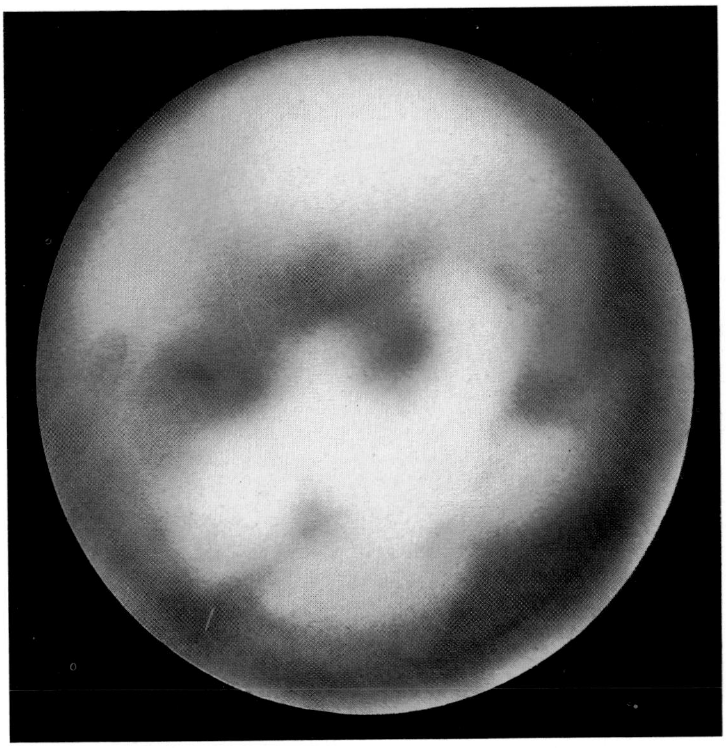

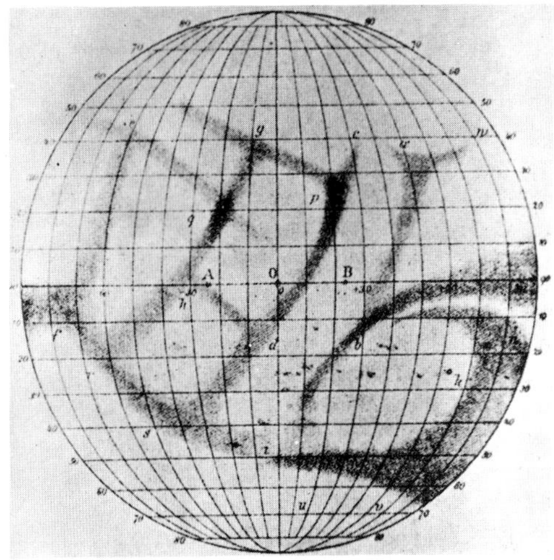

Map of Mercury *above*
The surface features of Mercury have not been well charted as yet; the planet is small and difficult to observe because it always appears in the same part of the sky as the Sun. The map above was drawn by G. V. Schiaparelli in 1888. Mercury's rapid changes of declination in the sky relate directly to the planet's associations first with speed of movement, later with fast-burning nervous energy.

Leo Cheerful and optimistic, but often stubborn and dogmatic; strong-minded, but kind-hearted as well. Loves pleasure, can carry responsibility, usually has good organizing ability. The negative traits are rudeness, prejudice, conceit. This placing of Mercury often shows good intuition, creativity and appreciation of the arts; as well as fondness for, and ability to bring out the best in children. A good position for teachers. Often ambitious and confident; broad-minded, sound at giving orders. However, this can sometimes leave an unfortunate impression of arrogance.

Virgo Versatile, intellectual and discriminating, but may be hypercritical under stress. Analytical and tenacious approach to problems, both traits which will come in useful for long and painstaking research. Meticulous, but can become obsessional. Learns easily and may well have flair for science or critical writing. A sceptic. Considerable interest in health, hygiene and diet; may be vegetarian. Mercury under affliction in this, its own Sign, can cause over-fussiness, pedantry, loss of the general pattern, and old-womanish tendencies in men.

Libra Good reasoning powers, ability to see both sides of a question; but slow to make decisions, tending to shelve them, to wait and see. May lack mental application. Sometimes an intellectual partnership will supply the stimulus needed to balance this failing. At its best, a well-balanced and sympathetic mind. But, under affliction, a weak will possibly lacking in tact.

Scorpio Incisive mind, capable of intuition. Excellent powers of concentration – shrewd, but can be sarcastic, resentful and suspicious, even mentally cruel. A general fascination with criminal activity, the underworld, mystery and 'the forces of darkness' may be present (especially if the Sun occupies the same Sign). Ability to solve difficult problems in a practical way. Knowing the right line of action, taking it and sticking to it, is characteristic of the Scorpian approach. Mental flexibility needs conscious development.

Sagittarius Often this placing indicates the eternal student, with his constant need for intellectual challenge. Generally broad-minded, can grasp a situation quickly; but if Mercury is afflicted, then concentration suffers, and mental restlessness can easily occur. Sincerity and a natural sense of justice are usually in evidence. Writing talent is common. Ability is not always shown during school years – but parents should not press too hard since real progress comes at university or later. Further education is particularly desirable with this placing of Mercury. Duality and versatility are common.

Capricorn A rational, serious mind, cool and calculating. In outlook, ambitious, patient, careful and practical, and, unless the whole personality has been repressed (as may be seen from other areas of the Chart), always aspiring towards particular objectives in life. Methodical and formal – especially where decision-making is concerned. Some hardness and a 'stick-in-the-mud' attitude may be in evidence. Scientific and mathematical ability may be pronounced; prizes may be won at school. Sound grasp of logic and a good memory are usual; but under affliction a certain narrow-mindedness may mar an otherwise dependable and solid character.

Aquarius Original, inventive, with good intuition; although extremely forward-looking – real 'Age of Aquarius' mind – the subject may be reluctant to change his views once they are formed. Interest in and talent for the modern sciences (especially those of a communicative type, such as television); astronomy and astrology could be compelling. Sometimes a love of metaphysics. Eccentricities can occur. Mental application may be erratic, but judgment of human nature is usually excellent. Unemotional but strongly faithful; humanitarian; friendly and kind.

Pisces Kind and charitable: a flexible and easily impressionable mind are usual with this placing. Forgetfulness and absentmindedness can be quite a stumbling-block. The imagination can be extremely creative; but intuition should be checked where it tends to outrun intellectual capacity. There is a tendency to be secretive; a high emotional level requires some positive outlet, perhaps through poetry, creative writing, or dancing. Often good at comedy mime, and generally has a talent for entertaining others. Flair for medicine, religious faith are shown.

VENUS

rules Taurus and Libra; is exalted in Pisces; detriment Aries; fall Virgo
Keywords: Harmony, unison

Venus is the second 'inferior' planet: its orbit, like Mercury's falls, inside that of Earth. Also like Mercury, it is always close to the Sun as seen from Earth, and never travels more than 48° from it along the ecliptic. Venus either occupies the same sign in a Birth Chart as the Sun, or falls within two signs to either side of it.

The Venus Factor *left* **Isadora Duncan,** the well-known American dancer, had Venus rising in the 12th House in Aries, indicating the strong sensuality which revealed itself in her public and private life. It helped to mould her ideas of 'Free Dance' where movement was guided by the rhythm of breathing and the beating of the heart. She founded two schools, one in Berlin, one in Moscow, based on her ideas.

Associations
Venus is associated with the power to love, the feelings, the lumbar region, throat and kidneys, the parathyroids; partnerships, the feminine influence in both sexes; possessions, money; the arts; social life, beauty, adornment, clothes, fashion.

Positive Venusian traits
The urge for harmonious partnership; a gentle, kind and friendly manner; tactful, adept in love and the social arts; adaptable; appreciative of beauty, placid, refined.

Negative Venusian traits
Lazy, gushing; indecisive, excessively romantic, weak-willed, careless, impractical, dependent on others, even parasitical.

Venus Through the Houses

1 Venus in the First House bestows great charm and good looks, but can make the individual lazy, too keen on the social life, liking to be spoilt.

2 A powerful emphasis on possessions and their acquisition. Ability to build up financial resources. Some preference for aesthetic occupations, profiting from an interest in the arts.

3 Good relationships with brothers and sisters, a liking for the social round. Ability to study, if the inclination is present.

4 Domestic surroundings must be visually pleasing as well as comfortable. Pleasure from flower-arranging, interior decoration; but extravagance to this end is likely.

5 Numerous love affairs. Appreciates creativity and the arts, especially the theatre. Enjoys games and social activities.

6 Good health and pleasant working conditions, but if the planet is afflicted, Venusian ailments may be a source of trouble, and work conditions unsavoury. Dirty or hard physical work will not be liked – unless the end product is something beautiful.

7 If well aspected and in a congenial Sign, this is an excellent placing for marriage and business partnerships; but under affliction resentment and a persecution complex may arise from lack of fulfilment.

8 May inherit money. Harmonious sexual relationships. Under affliction, sexual desires may be unsatisfied.

9 A useful and happy period at university. Good relationship with foreigners, even marriage and subsequent residence abroad.

10 Happiness and success in the career. A diplomatic manner, often good relationships with parents, though disappointments are likely to occur under affliction.

11 Excellent at achieving and maintaining good relationships within clubs and societies; friendly and diplomatic under such circumstances, working for the good of the group. Many friends and acquaintances.

12 Attraction to mysticism, the occult. Will be secretive about love affairs – perhaps of necessity. A need for seclusion. Positive integration of unconscious feelings.

Venus Through the Signs

Aries A tendency to fall in love quickly and ardently, with a strong erotic compulsion. Idealistic and imaginative, also persuasive and demonstrative in relationships, but needing to control a self-seeking element. Once in love, great difficulty in restraining affection. A natural and likeable ability to to make friends. Impulsive attitude towards finance, with a strong tendency to sudden money-raising schemes (which often come to nothing). A charming tendency to give small but unexpected presents to loved ones. If Venus is badly afflicted, quarrels and restlessness will constantly upset emotional relationships.

Taurus Although affectionate and passionate in emotional relationships, there is a tendency to think of the loved one as 'mine', and care is needed not to smother the partner by possessiveness which could lead to jealousy. There may be desire for luxury, rich and sweet food, and physical pleasure. Over the years, good looks can be lost through over-weight. Finer elements of Venus in Taurus give appreciation of the arts (especially music) and love of clothes. Financially good, but keeping a balance between pleasures, comfort and acquisitiveness may be difficult.

Gemini Venus is at its most flirtatious in this Sign. The subject tends to approac marriage and emotional relationships lightheartedly. Those with Venus in Gemini usually have a cool attitude towards marriage commitments. There is a need for intellectual rapport with the partner, and sometimes the duality of Gemini is present. Attraction to a cousin or relative can occur. Affection is often charmingly expressed, but inconsistency may spoil relationships. Positive for speculation in trade, but money may be frittered.

Cancer True affection and sympathy are present; expression of love tends to be parental, and may seem claustrophobic and over-tenacious at times, though at its best, cherishing. Home-loving qualities are at their highest, and include good cooking (excellent for entertaining in the home). There is an ability to make the best of surroundings for the partner and children. Emotions can run high and need controlling; tendency to worry about the partner. Safe

Venus and Earth Compared *above*
The two planets are approximately of the same size and mass. Venus has a diameter of 7,700 miles and is thus physically in harmony with Earth.

The Planet *right*
Venus is concealed by a dense, cloudy atmosphere; it has an abnormally long rotation period (243 days) and appears as the most constant, harmonious member of our sky. Venus has always been thought of as a feminine planet.

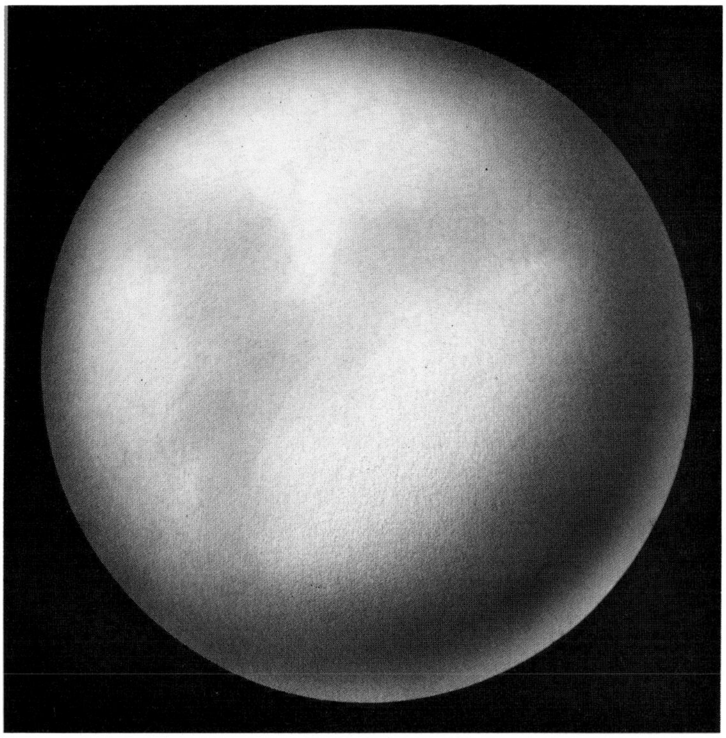

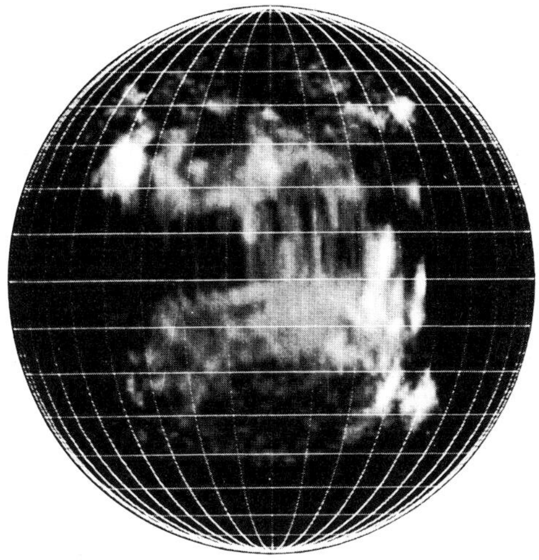

Map of Venus *above*
Since we can never see the surface of Venus, the only possible way to map it is by means of radar: the chart shows the results of pioneer work carried out by American astronomers. From Venus, no observer could see the Sun or stars, because of the planet's dense, cloudy atmosphere. As seen from Earth, Venus is strikingly beautiful, soft in appearance and brightly lit.

investments may be preferred, but in spite of this fluctuation in finances should be expected.

Leo A powerful urge to exalt the loved one and to dominate him as well – often in a charming way. Loyalty, heart-felt warmth and affection are present. Extravagance, especially towards the partner – even if this is financially crippling. A great love of rich clothes, jewellery, furs, expensive theatre seats, and enjoyment of life to the full. A tendency to dramatize can lead to domestic scenes. The subject derives much happiness from children and the arts which will counteract any feelings of claustrophobia the family gives; creative ability.

Virgo The critical and analytical elements of Virgo are directed towards the partner. This can seriously mar emotional relationships or prevent romance from blossoming. Insignificant characteristics of the partner are seen as major faults. Those who have Venus in this sign must recognize these faults and try to compensate for them; sometimes a preoccupation with chastity or virginity is the cause. Often an excellent business sense.

Libra Business and emotional partnerships are powerfully stressed and these bring fulfilment to the personality. Being in love with love can be mistaken for real love. Bonds must not be too hastily formed; it takes little to throw a relationship off-balance. There may be some resentment, but only under serious affliction; usually Venus in Libra means happiness and joy in relationships. Love of creature comforts and generosity lead to extravagance.

Scorpio The action of Venus is at its sexiest in Scorpio; a deeply passionate, highly emotional and satisfying sex life is indicated. Relationships run at a high emotional level and jealousy is common, sometimes aggravated by possessiveness. This needs controlling, but extremes of feeling will not make this easy. Calmer areas of the Chart will show where a balance can be found. Association with big business is likely, and involvement (perhaps in partnership) with insurance, the stock exchange and oil companies may be lucrative. Self indulgence can cause a weight problem in later life, which will not be easy to check.

Sagittarius There is a tendency to stay 'fancy free' longer than most. Although capable of idealistic love, relationships are best formed on the understanding that all freedom is not going to be sacrificed. The partner must be willing to accept this as necessary for those with Venus in Sagittarius. Emphasis elsewhere in the Chart on the sign Scorpio may cause conflict: the love of freedom clashing with jealousy and possessiveness if a partner gives what he gets. Nonchalant with money.

Capricorn This is a chilly position for Venus, and often indicates considerable sacrifice for the loved one or perhaps separation, disappointment or isolation. Affection tends to be expressed rather coolly, but great faithfulness is common. The attitude towards love is very conventional. Sometimes a failure to express feelings makes the individual cold or rather stern. The financial overtones of Venus are strong in this sign, bestowing excellent money-making capabilities. There is a tendency towards social climbing through marriage and advancement is sought in other relationships. Sometimes too demanding as a parent.

Aquarius Kind, charitable and humanitarian. Venus is unemotional in this sign, and often the trend is towards complete freedom in expression and friendship. Will do anything for anyone, but with a certain personal detachment. If married, freedom of expression and personal independence are considered important and must be respected by the partner. Unconventional in relationships. A certain glamour is likely, and while personal magnetism will attract, there is also a detachment which will repel. The financial attitude is usually sensible.

Pisces Totally ruled by the emotions in any relationship; at times over-sentimental, but with great ability to express genuine feeling. Will make considerable sacrifices for the loved one, to the point of self-abnegation. Desire to help the under-dog and identify with suffering. Will not find it easy to keep a rational outlook, unless practicability is shown elsewhere in the Chart. Generous to a fault; money will mean nothing and professional financial advice is recommended, if undue worry, especially by a partner, is not to upset the smooth tenor of life.

MARS

rules Aries and, by tradition, Scorpio (more recently attributed to Pluto); is exalted in Capricorn; detriment Libra; fall Cancer
Keywords: Energy, initiative

Mars is the first 'superior' planet. Its orbit falls outside that of Earth, and its position in the Birth Chart is not closely linked with that of the Sun – as happens with the 'inferior' planets, Mercury and Venus. Mars takes about two-and-a-half years to travel through all the signs, and remains in each sign for just over two months.

Associations
Mars is associated with the muscular and urogenital systems, gonads, adrenal glands, red blood corpuscles, the kidneys; cuts and burns; the masculine influence in both sexes; aggression, heat, action, weapons, sharp tools.

Positive Martian traits
Decisive, freedom-loving, a pioneer; direct in his approach, a strong leader especially in a crisis; a defender of the weak. Strongly sexed. A positive and lively response to all situations.

Negative Martian traits
Aggressive, irate, brutal, foolhardy, lacking forethought; selfish, quarrelsome, overhasty, indifferent to detail, rude, boisterous.

The Mars Factor *left*
An extremely potent Mars in Pisces, conjunct the Midheaven, appears in the Chart of **Vincent Van Gogh**. This placing of Mars strongly affected his artistic life; his paintings are rendered with power, and charged with high emotion.

The British Admiral **Lord Nelson** had Mars rising in Scorpio, giving him fantastic powers of endurance and an abundance of emotional energy. At sea he achieved remarkable success in his naval campaigns in the Mediterranean, despite the loss of an eye and an arm. On land his fervour was more than acceptable to Lady Hamilton, wife of the British Ambassador in Naples.

Mars Through the Houses

1 All Martian traits are strongly emphasized in the First House. If well aspected, the positive will dominate; if afflicted, the negative (but according to other planets involved). Accident-prone, may overtax his strength; headaches likely. Impatient and impulsive.

2 Ambitious to make money; a big spender. Could have a loud and powerful voice.

3 Keen at school; control needed to prevent energy, and anxiety to lead and be 'first', from becoming too aggressive. Will fight on behalf of brothers and sisters. A risk-taker.

4 A hard worker for the home. Energy needs plenty of outlet, perhaps through carpentry, metal-work, car maintenance. Under affliction, quarrelsome in the home.

5 Constantly falling in and out of love, and enjoying the experience. Keen on sport and able to do well in robust team games. Should work well with children.

6 Inflammatory complaints likely; particular disorders in health will depend on the Sign involved. A hard and conscientious worker, who will expect as much from subordinates.

7 An energetic and lively attitude towards marriage and partnerships; under affliction, quarrels and disappointments can occur.

8 Attracted to surgery, psychiatry, investigation, involvement with other people's money (perhaps through insurance, or death). Strongly sexed.

9 Desire for travel and adventure; a good placing for the sportsman. Intellectual energy provided there is sufficient enthusiasm for the subject.

10 Much energy will be put into the day's work. Ambitious to reach the top in chosen profession, but could be ruthless in the process.

11 Will gladly and energetically help friends, but may make and lose them rather quickly. The Martian spirit of enterprise will be expressed through objectives in life, towards friends, clubs and societies.

12 Deeply secretive; on the unconscious level a tendency towards masochism; but Martian energy directed positively from this House can contribute strength to help others, e.g. in various fields of social and welfare work.

Mars Through the Signs

Aries When Mars falls in Aries, it brings a powerful urge to take the initiative. The subject has great energy, often of an intellectual nature; he indulges in considerable mental activity and this may perhaps lead to strain. Love of independence, frankness; but prone to accidents through general haste. Impulsiveness and aggressiveness should be controlled: this could be difficult if Mars is afflicted and the negative traits associated with the planet are powerfully emphasized. Slight cuts and burns are almost inevitable. Strongly sexed.

Taurus This placing contributes firmness bordering on obstinacy. A hard, tenacious worker with considerable practical ability. The temper is slowly aroused but is seldom easy to control, and outbursts can be unpleasant for others; under affliction, violence can occur. Some danger of throat upsets. This position of Mars has a powerful financial influence, and although money may be well earned through hard work, spending could be equally heavy, and the more practical aspects of the position are needed to keep a balance. Sensuous and affectionate can be extremely possessive.

Gemini Intellectual energy is prominent, but restlessness and a tendency to fritter energy can occur. Powers of concentration must be carefully developed. Mentally and physically alert; also talkative. Sometimes writing ability is shown, or is admired in others. The latter feeling may be expressed through correspondence. Variety and changes of occupation are important; but patience may be lacking, and unfinished tasks may impede progress. If the subject has two or three different projects on hand, he must learn to complete them all in due course. It is important to learn this early in life. Under affliction, nervous tension can build up.

Cancer This placing tends to encourage a high emotional level, which needs conscious steadying. It is easy to become upset and bad-tempered, if Mars is afflicted. Tenacity and ambition are present, but sometimes there is a lack of straightforwardness. Tensions may be difficult to release and may cause slight stomach and nervous upsets. Originality, independence and sensuousness are strong traits. This position often gives a pronounced desire for home and

Mars and Earth Compared *above*
Mars is much smaller than the Earth; it has a diameter of 4,200 miles. It can approach us within 35,000,000 miles, closer than any other planet apart from Venus.

The Planet *right*
Much of the surface of Mars is reddish-ochre in hue. Associated with aggression and warfare, Mars varies more in brightness than any other planet and is regarded as the fount of man's sexual excesses.

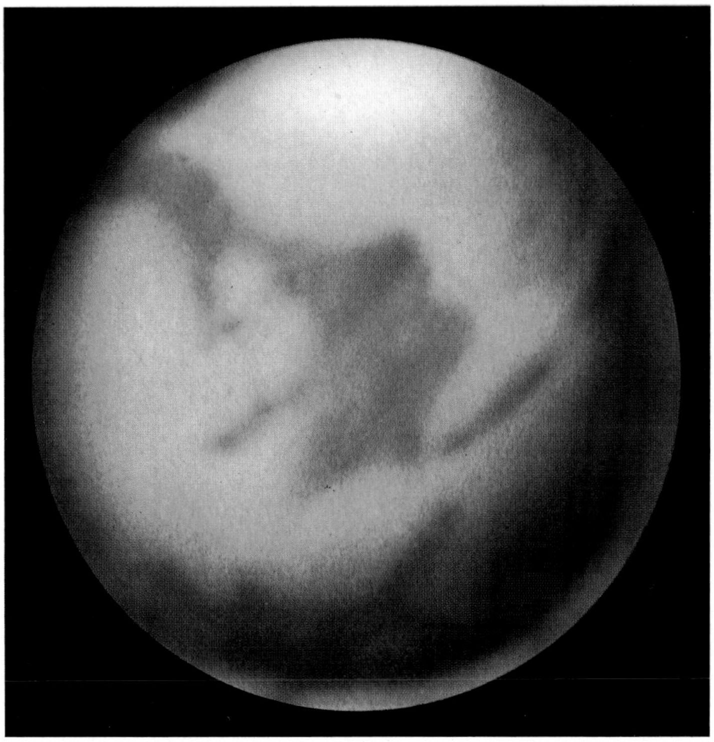

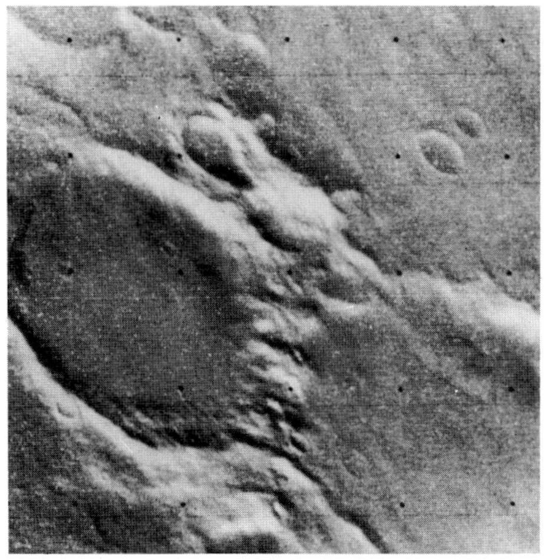

The Giant's Footprint *above*
The surface of Mars contains craters similar to those of the Moon; one such formation, nicknamed the Giant's Footprint, near the Martian pole, was photographed by Mariner 7. Most observers now doubt whether there is any life on Mars, although it remains the most Earthlike of the planets. Unlike Venus, our other near neighbour, Mars is receptive to most solar radiations, emphasizing its positive responses.

family – and makes energetic if tense mothers. Intuition is powerful and should be followed.

Leo Enthusiasm and a strong sense of purpose are the best qualities of Mars in Leo. A natural sense of drama can border on the melodramatic under affliction. There is ambition in plenty which, coupled with the inevitable enthusiasm, can be a powerful force. The negative indications are over-enthusiasm and bombastic tendencies. Generosity, affection and a genuine dislike of pettiness or small-mindedness are usual. The subject in this placing has a sociable nature and enjoys the company of others. Emotions are expressed through artistic creativity and a passionate love-life. Responsibility is well taken. A quick but easily appeased temper.

Virgo Good workers are born with Mars in Virgo, but are at their best under steady direction. They are often ambitious, but sometimes find responsibility hard to maintain. Worries may result, perhaps bringing stomach or skin troubles. Great trouble is taken, attention being paid to the smallest detail; though sometimes the over-all scheme is lost if the subject allows himself to become too involved with minutiae. Practical ability is abundant, coupled with ingenuity. Interfering, 'busy-body' tendencies occur, with tensions resulting from emotional frustration.

Libra There is a certain fluctuation of energy when Mars in this Sign: sometimes languid, sometimes passionate. No effort is spared in forming relationships, and all the persuasive powers are marshalled for 'getting the girl'. An inclination to quarrel may in fact motivate the subject's urge to persuade others. Falling in love hastily, and all too often – thus the subject learns the hard way, but sometimes fails to put the lessons into practice. Perceptiveness can be easily developed; intuitive.

Scorpio This placing contributes deep emotions; if these are allowed to flow positively there is real strength, but if (as indicated by other areas of the Chart) energy and emotion are blocked, the negative side can become dangerous, resulting in cruelty, jealousy and revenge; also secretiveness. A love of good food and drink, sometimes to excess, may be evident, perhaps in compensation for frustrated emotions, or some failure to find positive expression for them. Strength of character is required to realize the great potential of this position of Mars.

Sagittarius Boisterous, with schoolboyish energy and abundant mental activity; enthusiastic for new projects. Sometimes ideas seem outrageous, beyond the scope of other people. It is difficult to separate energy from enthusiasm, and these work hand-in-glove when Mars is in this Sign. Opinions are often removed from the conventional; scepticism, as well as moral courage, are common. Under affliction, the tendency to exaggerate is difficult to control.

Capricorn Energy is directed towards the achievement of objectives in life – which may be considerable. If other areas of the Chart show ambition, this will dominate – perhaps to the exclusion of all else. Success, both in the public eye and from a personal and financial point of view, will be all-important. Energy is carefully and constructively deployed. Waste and incompetence cannot be tolerated. There is a liking for authority and power, which can sometimes get out of hand. A cold, quick irritability.

Aquarius Although impulsive, the subject is usually determined to achieve his personal objectives. Freedom is important; intellectual ability leans towards the scientific. Unpredictable actions are strongly indicated, and these can cause difficulties with friends; In an emergency the reactions are quick and helpful. The pioneering spirit of Mars can be expressed through freedom-fighting for others. The emotional side of Mars is not conducive to Aquarian rationality or detachment, and some emotional discord is likely, which can lead to tension.

Pisces A strong emotional desire to work for other people, involving considerable self-sacrifice. At its best, the energy-force of Mars in Pisces can achieve splendid results in this direction, but practical ability in other areas of the Chart is necessary to get the best out of this placing; if real strength is lacking, energy will be lost in muddle and confusion. If Mars is afflicted, indolence and indecision can occur. Sometimes there is a tendency to be influenced by others.

JUPITER

rules Sagittarius and, by tradition, Pisces (now attributed to Neptune); is exalted in Cancer; detriment Gemini; fall Capricorn
Keyword: Expansion

Jupiter takes about 12 years to make its way through all the signs of the Zodiac; its orbit is somewhat eccentric and it spends a disproportionate amount of time in certain signs. The planet has always been associated with the idea of expansion: physically, its outer layers are composed of gas and it has a powerful magnetic field. Jupiter is also the largest planet in the Solar System.

Associations
Jupiter is associated with knowledge, advanced studies, a philosophical outlook, speculative thinking; religion; the liver, the pituitary gland; universities, further education, foreign countries, languages; book publication; good fortune.

Positive Jupiter traits
Optimistic, generous, loyal; jovial; a kind nature; a sense of justice and compassion, breadth of vision, well-directed mental powers; flair for languages; good at sport.

Negative Jupiter traits
Blindly optimistic; an extremist; wasteful, self-indulgent, a gambler, extravagant, lawless, conceited; unbalanced in beliefs.

The Jupiter Factor *left* In the Chart of **Albert Einstein** a well-placed Jupiter (in Aquarius in the Ninth House) contributed to his genius for abstract, scientific thought. His celebrated theory of relativity was the first work to break fundamentally with the Newtonian approach launched more than two hundred years before. As might be expected, the Jupiter influence acted differently in **Mata Hari's** Chart. Her exotic career as a spy seems relatively unaffected by her Jupiter rising in Scorpio, but it doubtless came to the fore when, faced by the firing squad, she thanked the officer in command of her execution.

Jupiter Through the Houses

1 A broad-minded and cheerful personality, often extremely fortunate in life; a stress on the positive Jupiter traits, if well aspected. Under affliction, a stress on negative traits; liver upsets then likely. The weight needs to be watched.

2 Fortunate from a material point of view; able to make money easily. Under affliction, financial carelessness.

3 Enjoyment of school, accompanied by success. Good relationships with brothers and sisters. Communications activities stressed, achievement in that field; possibly writing ability on a small scale.

4 Good relationships with parents; home conditions excellent and comfortable. Under affliction, parental relationships lack a proper perspective.

5 Pleasure and some ability in sport and the creative arts. Good at speculation; financial risks may be taken if Jupiter is well aspected and 'steadied'. Under affliction, a disastrous love of gambling.

6 A cheerful and contented worker. No lack of work, which should be particularly lucrative. Under affliction, Jupiter ailments likely.

7 Excellent for business partnerships and marriage. But in marriage special attention to the Aspects is necessary, as extreme tendencies may be present – over-optimism, extravagance, a liking for 'fun' outside marriage – these tendencies *not* being easy to control.

8 Strong possibility of inherited money or property. A healthy attitude towards death.

9 Ability for languages; possible work abroad or with foreigners. Success through publications; much enjoyment and profit from long-distance travel. Success in further education; good placing for lecturers.

10 A successful and lucrative career. Excellent for business or politics. Good opportunities. A devil-may-care attitude and outward 'show' if Jupiter afflicted. Acting ability.

11 Many good friends and acquaintances; is himself a good friend. Achieves objectives which are often of a high order.

12 Much good work of an intellectual nature done in seclusion. Success in matters concerning poetry, the psyche, dancing; also the sea and oil. A good placing for work in medicine.

Jupiter Through the Signs

Aries This placing gives generosity and enthusiasm. Often self-sufficient, bearing out the freedom-loving tendencies of both Jupiter and Aries. Risks should be carefully considered – whether Jupiter is afflicted or not. Under affliction, there is bullying, extravagance and over-optimism. At its best, Jupiter in Aries gives a genuine pioneering spirit, ambition and a positive outlook. A desire to develop the intellectual potential may bring benefits.

Taurus A love of good living, food and comfort. The judgment is usually sound; reliable and good-hearted. Emphasis on materialism and the accumulation of money, to be spent on creature comforts and luxuries. Acquired wealth is often generously distributed – though with sincerity and good humour, not for self-seeking aims. This placing may indicate a lack of inspiration, and under affliction can bring self-indulgence, liverishness (from over-eating) and a love of pleasure which can even lead to indolence.

Gemini This placing shows versatility and broadmindedness. A tendency to be superficial may impede potential progress in intellectual matters. Interests may tend to be scattered. Scepticism can alternate with credulity; generally there is all-round 'cleverness'. Jupiter in Gemini is excellent for teachers at high-school level. Under affliction, there may be craftiness and indiscretion, changeability and restlessness.

Cancer Much kindness, good humour and generosity. The charitable and protective instincts are strong, and will be fully expressed. Opinions on important matters – such as religious beliefs – may fluctuate. The emotional level is high. Under affliction there is a strong tendency or desire to hold on to those considered emotionally important. Intuition and imagination are powerful, and are worth conscious development. Enthusiasm for food, its preparation, and domesticity generally, may be present. A good business sense is likely (perhaps in antiques).

Leo Helpful, affectionate and generous; intelligent and ambitious. A taste for pomp; a love of display, power and dignity is combined with a sense of drama and the dramatic –

Jupiter and Earth Compared *above*
Jupiter is by far the most massive of the planets: the Great Red Spot, above, expands to a maximum length of 30,000 miles; Jupiter's total diameter is 88,700 miles; the planet is a major gravitational force.

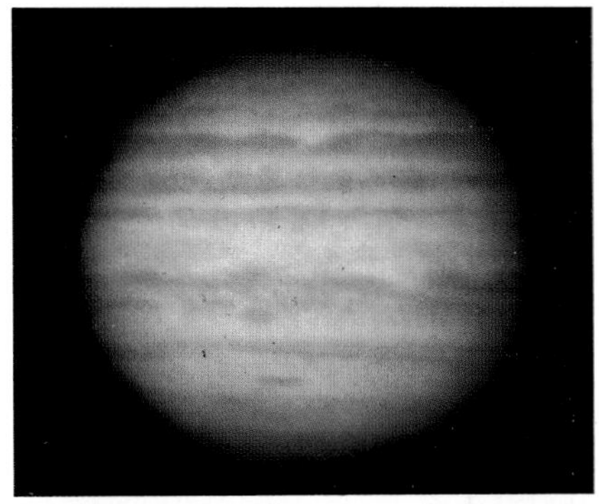

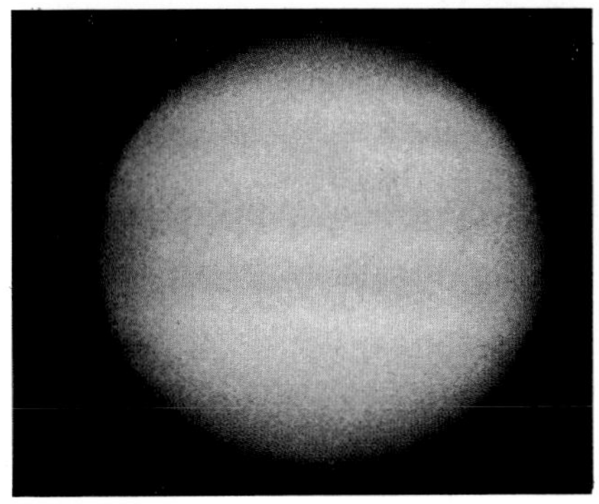

The Planet *right and far right*
Jupiter's surface is gaseous, recalling its astrological nature – expansive and emphasizing spiritual matters.

often shown in choice of clothes. Under affliction, often bumptious, intolerant, extravagant (for outward show), self-inflating and snobbish. Creative talent may be expressed through the theatre, in teaching or work with children and young people; qualities of leadership and organization are usual. Time spent in the development of intellectual/artistic interests proves beneficial.

Virgo This placing indicates critical, rather matter-of-fact outlook. Kind and conscientious, but also sceptical, sometimes in the extreme. Under affliction, practical ability may be offset by conceit and cynicism, absent-mindedness and carelessness. Jupiter in this Sign could cause difficulty with bowels, liver and digestion, especially if afflicted. A constructive approach needed to counteract narrow-mindedness and over-attention to detail. Technical and scientific ability is common.

Libra The positive and negative traits of Jupiter in this Sign are clear-cut: at its best (well aspected) there is sympathy, hospitality, charity and artistic ability: whereas under affliction there is laziness, self-indulgence, conceit and tractability. The subject is companionable and 'easily loved', but may abhor loneliness and need some form of partnership. In business too, those who have Jupiter in this Sign benefit from working in partnership. Expansion in life is most likely to occur under such conditions. Independence is not a strong characteristic, and should be consciously developed.

Scorpio This placing gives will-power, skill in analysis, and a capacity for deep emotion. There is an intense desire for life. The exaggerative powers of Jupiter can cause stress through excess of mental work, and self-indulgence: moderation must be consciously developed. When afflicted, pride, conceit and aggression can occur and there is a tendency to be suspicious. If writing ability is shown, this would be well developed in detective fiction and mystery. Generosity, perseverance, shrewdness (especially in financial matters) and determination are characteristic.

Sagittarius The positive traits of Jupiter are emphasized; intellectual capacity may be developed to the full. This placing is particularly favourable for literature, and residence overseas; for the study of philosophical or ancient subjects, languages and the law. There is optimism, a philosophical outlook and breadth of vision. A love of sport and animals, especially horses, is common. On the highest intellectual level there is the genuine sage: professor, philosopher, sometimes a churchman. If the planet is afflicted, the subject may be reckless, boastful, lawless, a devotee of gambling.

Capricorn Resourceful, a strong sense of responsibility. Success is often achieved gradually – the result of hard and conscientious work. Reticence and self-control sometimes border on rigidity. Conventional and orthodox in beliefs and outlook. Sometimes there is a lack of buoyancy and cheerfulness; the mind tends to be grave and negative. Thrift can border on stinginess. Steadfast and practical with excellent powers of concentration. While this placing makes for a thoughtful character, under affliction there is bigotry, pig-headedness and self-righteousness.

Aquarius Humanitarian, impartial, socially adept; no lack of imagination and originality – the two, combined, should be developed. A sense of justice and an attraction to causes will be expressed: the highest mental qualities are often positively expressed through philanthropy, science or music. Tolerance, sympathy and an independent spirit are to be found. Under affliction, tactless, intolerant, unpredictable in his opinions, uncertain of his objectives. Social life is usually extensive, with many useful friendships, but on a superficial level. Intuitions are strong.

Pisces An excellent planetary position for clerics, and those attracted to religion, also appearing frequently in the Charts of doctors, nurses and veterinary surgeons. Compassion, benevolence and good humour are dominant. There is a delightfully easy-going and friendly quality exuding through the whole personality; though restlessness and indecision may need counteracting. The imagination and emotions are powerful, and the mind impressionable. Under affliction, unreliability, extravagance, self-indulgence can occur. Generally there is identification with suffering; help and devotion will readily be given to the sick and oppressed. A definite tendency towards self-sacrifice.

SATURN

rules Capricorn and, by tradition, Aquarius (now attributed to Uranus) is exalted in Libra; detriment Cancer; fall Aries Keyword: Limitation

The keyword for Saturn is 'limitation'. In ancient times it was the outermost planet in the known universe; its rings, indicating bonds and restriction, were not discernible with the naked eye, and the idea that Saturn stood for limitation was part of accepted astrological knowledge long before telescopes were invented and the rings revealed.

Associations

Saturn is associated with the skin, teeth, bones, gall bladder, spleen, vagus nerve; crystallization and acid formation in the joints; also old age, perseverance, tenacity, cold; inevitable, slow change; inhibition, restriction, intolerance.

Positive Saturnian traits

Practical, cautious, constructive, responsible, patient, ambitious, thrifty; solid, reliable, trustworthy, with good endurance and self-discipline.

Negative Saturnian traits

Mean, selfish; despondent, narrow-minded, severe, aloof, acquisitive; dogmatic, heartless, cruel; suffers depressions, hardship, a life of sorrow or ill-health.

The Saturn Factor *left* There is a large stellium, or grouping of planets, in **Picasso's** Tenth House, the most dominant being Saturn (in Taurus). The planet's influence is most marked in Picasso's harsh works executed in the 1930s; *Guernica* is a typical example. The same planet may well have increased Picasso's talent for sculpture.

In the Chart of **George Gershwin,** Saturn was rising in Sagittarius in the First House; this can be an indication of weak health, and accounts for the great popular composer's relatively early death at the age of 39, two years after the completion of *Porgy and Bess*.

Saturn Through the Houses

1 Inhibition cramps the whole personality, and takes a long time to control. All Saturnian traits strongly emphasized: development must come through the cultivation of positive traits. Ill-health, or some burden in life is more than likely.

2 Money is earned only by hard work. Financial progress can be considerable, but not without struggle.

3 Limited education or a constructive and serious attitude to school life. Often made responsible early in life for brothers and sisters.

4 Unhappy or restricted home life; perhaps this may even mean psychological or physical deprivation as a child.

5 A domineering, strict or difficult father; may lack a sense of fun. This placing can cause infertility. Children may be a burden, through illness or physical handicap. Over-ambitious for children.

6 A good, careful, conscientious worker, though work may not be congenial. Saturnian ailments can occur.

7 Late marriage; age difference between partners most likely with this placing. Restriction, negation, frustration in marriage can occur, but only under serious affliction.

8 Responsibility likely in the financial affairs of others. Sexual inhibitions. Serious thoughts of death and the after-life.A careful attitude in business.

9 A serious, deep thinker, especially in questions of philosophy or faith. Good concentration, but mental exhaustion can occur. Contacts with elderly foreigners beneficial. Frustration and loss in long-distance travel.

10 Ambitious, demanding recognition. Positive traits of Saturn strongly emphasized. Under affliction, ruthless, even cruel in realizing ambitions. A lonely, responsible position likely.

11 A tendency to have elderly friends, who will be of help; but a shortage of real friends, as single-minded concentration on objectives will dominate.

12 A liking and psychological need for isolation. Sorrows and unhappiness will be withheld from others; there will be a general lack of exuberance, sometimes a tendency to be bogged down by cares and miseries, with only oneself to blame. An afflicted subconscious.

Saturn Through the Signs

Aries Strength and weakness alternate; initiative is often psychologically checked. This can be a source of conflict, and under affliction irresponsibility may take the place of caution. At its best, ambition is linked with ingenuity, self-reliance and persistence. A good placing for mechanics. Under affliction, a cruel streak may be in evidence; despite a destructive element, solid achievements are possible. Depression should be fought.

Taurus Long-suffering; patience, caution are prominent; a strong will borders on stubbornness. Methodical, matter-of-fact and practical; but under affliction the subject can be dour, avaricious, lacking in generosity. Emotions are steady and well controlled, but sometimes lack warmth of expression; beauty can mean little or nothing. Lethargy and thoughtlessness may accompany a lack of spontaneity. Kindness is a positive trait which can be easily expressed.

Gemini This placing gives intellectual ability, especially in scientific subjects. At its best the mind is steady, impartial and profound. However, the subject may be hard-headed or bitter; negative Saturnian traits often inhibit speech and expression. Some difficulty or illness in early life may cause late development. Under affliction, scepticism and coldness can occur. Good placing for work in education but teachers should cultivate warmth and a sense of fun; discipline should not be too harsh.

Cancer A desire for security may get out of proportion. Shrewdness, ambition and tenacity are present, but pessimism, suspicion, a self-pitying outlook and melancholia are negative traits that must be combated in favour of a more positive attitude. Unusually good at seeing tasks through to a satisfactory conclusion. Self-absorption, timidity and clannishness may inhibit the emotions and their expression. Although shrewd, care is needed in business, especially concerning valuable family interests.

Leo This placing gives powerful characteristics: strength of will, sense of honour, self-assurance, organizing ability, authority; but life can be short of

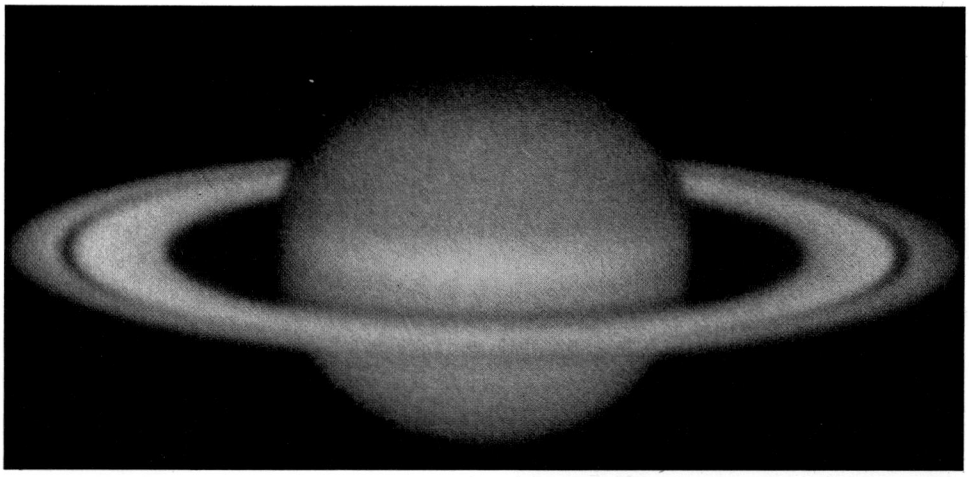

The Planet *above*
Saturn moves much more slowly against the stars than do the other naked-eye planets, and shines with a dull yellowish light which has been widely regarded as baleful. It is surrounded by a system of rings, made up of swarms of small particles, possibly icy, all moving round the planet in the manner of dwarf moons. Saturn itself is gaseous, and basically similar in constitution to Jupiter.

Satellites of Saturn *above*
Saturn has ten satellites. Of these the largest, Titan, is comparable in size with Mercury; the others are much smaller. The inner members of the system are shown here.

Rings of Saturn *left*
Saturn's rings shown almost edge-on to the Earth. Although the rings are extensive, they are very thin – no more than 10 miles wide at most.

fun. Of the negative traits, megalomania can occur under extreme affliction, and the subject needs to develop an awareness of limitations in others. Haughtiness is common, and there may be jealousy – though repressed envy can prove more harmful. The more pleasurable elements of life are suppressed; rigidity, even impotence (under serious affliction) can then subjugate the positive side of the personality, making it almost impossible for the subject to express pleasure or enjoyment.

Virgo Method, precision, prudence and practical ability are present when Saturn is in this Sign. Conscientiousness and devotion to duty have full expression in the working life. Tidiness is usual, and there is no fear of hard work; details are attended to with painstaking care. In a position of authority, severity to subordinates may stem from a high personal standard of workmanship. There is a fault-finding tendency. Sometimes obsession with detail and a dogmatic attitude to planning dominate. Intestinal trouble can occur.

Libra Kind, pleasant, lovable characteristics find outward expression. By tradition Saturn is well placed in Libra; patience, spirituality and a reasonable outlook are often prominent. There is good judgment, impartiality and enough flexibility to keep indecisiveness at bay. Under affliction, intolerance can occur, along with insincerity and impracticability. The desire for partnership, which is essential to happiness and full development, can be suppressed, and the resulting loneliness may bring considerable depression.

Scorpio The most positive indications of Saturn in Scorpio are executive ability and business sense. There is great sense of purpose, and strong reserves. A lack of flexibility, a tendency to brood, and secretiveness are very common. A certain grimness can melt into unexpected, dead-pan 'Saturnian' humour. Under affliction, ruthlessness and cruelty can be present. Emotions are deep, but suppressed. This placing gives strength and force to a personality, but unpopularity is sometimes notable. Sexuality may lack positive expression.

Sagittarius Application to long periods of study, and keeping to long-term plans are joined in this placing by dignity, gravity and a moralizing tendency, with an attraction to philosophical subjects. There is usually honesty, plain speech, often fearlessness. Sometimes popularity contrasts with a need for seclusion. The intellectual capacity is often considerable. Ostentatiousness, cynicism, tactlessness and insincerity are the most negative traits. The need to hang on to something well-established or safe conflicts with a tendency to accept more expansive challenges. This sometimes reveals itself as seemingly erratic and contradictory attitudes.

Capricorn Practical ability, perseverance, will to serve, a sense of discipline, patience and all positive Saturnian traits are usually prominent. Ambition can be over-important, and many personal sacrifices will be made for it. Under affliction, pessimism, hardness and selfishness are likely; economy can become miserliness, frugality reigning when circumstances would permit luxury. Self-inflicted melancholy may occur, also arrogance and rigidity. There is a love of power: responsibility can be carried well, but the extreme tendencies can dominate the positive traits.

Aquarius Saturn is well placed in Aquarius, as traditionally it ruled this Sign. Objectives in life are important; once determined, they are adhered to. An original mind; study presents no obstacles though inhibitions or frustration should be watched. Independence is favoured, but this may bring loneliness. There is a scientific inclination. Humanitarian ideals are prominent. Obstinacy, indifference to success and a cunning streak occur under affliction.

Pisces Though lacking a positive outlook, Saturn in Pisces gives excellent qualities: among them the ability to develop powers of intuition and imagination, and give them concrete form. There is also sympathy, flexibility and self-sacrifice. However, the subject is his own worst enemy; he may completely lack hope or courage. Self-reliance should be consciously developed. Moodiness and hypersensitivity are often present; untidiness and proneness to worry are almost inevitable. Existing conditions are too readily accepted. The necessary strength should be looked for in other areas of the Chart.

THE MODERN PLANETS

Uranus, Neptune and Pluto are the three 'modern' planets, discovered since the 18th century. Because of their distance from the Sun, they stay in one sign of the Zodiac for long periods of time: Uranus takes 7 years to pass through one sign; Neptune 14; and Pluto between 13 and 32 years. Their influences therefore are somewhat impersonal – unless one of them is sensitively placed in a chart. Astrologers tend to think of them more often as 'generation influences', that is to say bearing on a whole generation rather than an individual.

Uranus was discovered at the time of the industrial revolution in Europe, when drastic changes both in the mechanics and the social structure of life were being made. The Uranian influences are logically suited to the characteristics of Aquarius; it shared the rulership of this sign for many years with Saturn, but the younger generation of astrologers now thinks of Saturn as associated only with Capricorn, and Uranus as the rightful ruler of Aquarius.

Neptune was discovered in 1846, at a time when gas lighting was being introduced, when spiritualism and 'mesmerism' were popular, and anaesthetics were being introduced in surgical work. The planet is now attributed to Pisces, leaving Jupiter to rule Sagittarius. Neptune seems the most powerful and intense of the three 'generation influence' planets; recently its influence has been particularly notable.

Pluto was discovered in 1930, at a time when there was considerable criminal activity and upheaval in all spheres of life, particularly in the USA. Gradually, Pluto's influence became associated with these areas of life, and during the last few years it has been suspected that Pluto is the modern ruler of Scorpio, traditionally associated with Mars. Pluto is the least personal of the three modern planets; unless Scorpio is rising, the Sun is in Scorpio, or Pluto in the First House (heavily aspected) or within 8° of the Midheaven, its indications should not be given too much prominence.

The Uranus Factor *left above*
Franklin D. Roosevelt had Uranus rising in Virgo, contributing to that eminent politician's dynamic personality. Uranus, however, is also the planet associated with paralysis, from which Roosevelt suffered for many years. In the Birth Chart of **Karl Marx** the position of Uranus, conjunct the Midheaven in Sagittarius, gave him the radical, humanitarian instinct which drove him to seek a new social order.

The Neptune Factor
centre above
Marilyn Monroe broke away from her early reputation as a sex symbol to become one of Hollywood's best loved film comediennes. Her Birth Chart shows Neptune rising in Leo in the First House; the Chart as a whole shows many elements of strain, but the Neptune factor compounded the confusion in her personality, and eventually she tragically took her own life.

The Pluto Factor *right above*
Greta Garbo has Pluto in Gemini in the Twelfth House. This is a restrictive influence on whatever area of the life it affects, and in Garbo's case has no doubt emphasized the instinct for withdrawal both from career and public life. Although she made 24 films between 1926 and 1941, very little was known about the 'divine Garbo'. She disappeared completely from public life in 1941, after finishing *Two-Faced Woman.*
According to the famous German astrologer Reinhold Ebertin, Pluto conjunct the Midheaven indicates ability to maintain a position in life; fame is also likely. **Marlene Dietrich** has this conjunction in Gemini: Pluto falls in the 9th House and this placing could have a bearing on her great popularity outside her native Germany. One of the most fêted stars in cinema history, she has combined artistry with great strength of character.

URANUS

rules Aquarius; is exalted in Scorpio (recent); detriment Leo; fall Taurus.
Keyword: Change (disruptive or sudden)

Associations
Uranus is associated with the circulatory system, physical changes, sexual perversion and deviation; paralysis, cramp; sudden nervous breakdown; modern science – aeronautics, radio and television, space travel; science fiction.

Positive Uranian traits
Humanitarian, friendly, kind, independent, original, inventive, strong-willed, versatile, loathing restriction.

Negative Uranian traits
Cranky, eccentric, determined to be 'different', perverse, abnormal, rebellious.

Size and Nature of Uranus *left*
Uranus was discovered in 1781 by William Herschel; the planet is still referred to by some astrologers as Herschel, and the capital 'H' in the glyph commemorates his pioneering work. Uranus is a giant planet, 29,300 miles in diameter; its extraordinary axial inclination, more than a right angle, corresponds with the kind of cranky eccentricity for which the planet is noted in astrology. In physical terms first one pole of Uranus, then the other, has a 'night' lasting for 21 Earth-years. The surface of Uranus is made up of gas, and its temperature is very low. Its internal constitution has yet to be precisely established though in this respect it resembles Jupiter and Saturn more closely than Earth. So far five satellites of Uranus have been identified.

Uranus Through the Houses

1 Uranus' strong influence will be personal in this House, not merely a 'generation' influence.

2 Sudden financial breaks; if well aspected, these will be positive and lasting.

3 Changes in school life; inventive, original and lively during school years.

4 Will keep the rest of the family on its toes. Under affliction, a disruptive influence.

5 Sometimes sexual perversion; a changeable love life. Original, clever children likely.

6 An unpredictable worker. Uranian ailments likely. Crankiness in health and food.

7 Unusual conditions in marriage; an original partner. Changes in circumstances well received. Under affliction, a disruptive and rather cruel influence.

8 Money from unusual sources. Unconventional sexual ideas; unusual views about death. Under affliction, financial losses through big business; take no risks in this direction.

9 Exciting and unusual events while travelling abroad; accident-prone. Under affliction, difficulties while travelling. Erratic in study; may break down through sudden mental activity. Important to be methodical.

10 Far-sighted, a good leader, disliking routine work; unexpected career changes likely, easily adapted to.

11 Lively and interesting aims in life. Much pleasure from societies and clubs. Quick to make and lose acquaintances; favouring few emotional ties.

12 Secretive, attracted to the unusual. Under affliction, eccentricity; conflicts in the unconscious may be serious.

Uranus Through the Signs

Aries A lively imagination, spiced with originality (consideration of the rest of the Chart will show how this is expressed). Impulsiveness will if shown elsewhere, be strengthened by Uranus in Aries.

Taurus Fixed and immovable in opinions. A tendency to want new and different possessions. Perhaps obstinate and stubborn, if emphasized elsewhere in the Chart.

Gemini Inventive; flair for writing, perhaps scientific skill (if supported elsewhere in the Chart). An original and imaginative thinker, but nervous tension can occur under affliction, or if indicated elsewhere in the Chart.

Cancer May at times be eccentric, uncertain, unpredictable, especially if other areas of the Chart emphasize these characteristics.

Leo Splendid powers of leadership, sometimes misplaced. Eccentric, defiant, independent or arrogant. An additional emphasis if these qualities are shown in other areas of the Chart. This placing also adds originality if creative ability is shown elsewhere.

Virgo May be hypercritical; unusual ideas about food or health may lead to eccentric eating habits or 'quack' cures, especially if an interest in health and diet is shown elsewhere; the critical nature must be assessed from other areas of the Chart.

Libra Uranus entered this Sign in 1968, and will remain in it until 1974–5. This should contribute affection for children born in the late 60s and early-mid-70s. The solitary, independent nature of this planet will be softened; there should be greater consideration for the partner than usually occurs when either Uranus or its Sign, Aquarius, is emphasized, leading to easier relationships.

Scorpio Under affliction emotions are expressed with difficulty, perhaps even in an unconventional manner; emotional outlets could be blocked or negatively channelled; there may be a desire to take revenge. These tendencies will not be excessively marked unless a strong emotional level is indicated elsewhere.

Sagittarius The subject may be rebellious and reckless. It other areas of the Chart show restlessness and nervous tension, these tendencies will be increased making him difficult to live with; study, given the right inclination, will be approached in an original way and may lead to a career in research.

Capricorn Powers of leadership with good organizing ability. Thoughtful and serious if Uranus is free from affliction, but rebellious and domineering tendencies are emphasized if these are shown in other areas of the Chart.

Aquarius Original, ingenious and independent; possible interest in science. The positive Uranian traits are emphasized, and the planet should work well when in this, its own Sign. These traits will only be stressed if indicated elsewhere in the Chart. They are, for instance, at their most potent when the Sun is in Aquarius.

Pisces This can bring a waft of the true visionary, with idealism, religion and philosophical subjects assuming a more logical and real perspective; but Uranus needs to be prominently placed in the Chart, being perhaps at its best if Pisces is culminating, or the planet is in the Ninth House. The generation trend of this placing may provoke a fresh look at religion. Uranus was in this sign from 1919 to 1927. In 1928, Neptune entered Virgo. In that period orthodoxy and religious dogma were subjected to widespread scrutiny. A powerful generation influence seems to be present in those born at the time, within the overall influence of the three slow planets.

NEPTUNE

rules Pisces; is exalted in Leo (recent); detriment Virgo; fall Aquarius (recent) Keyword: Cloudiness

Associations

Neptune is associated with the spinal canal, the mental and nervous processes, the thalamus; drugs and poisons; gas, anaesthetics; maritime matters, prisons, institutions, hospitals; artistic and religious inspiration; mimicry, poetry, dancing.

Positive Neptunian traits

Idealistic, spiritual, imaginative, sensitive, subtle, artistically creative.

Negative Neptunian traits

Deceitful, careless, sentimental, diffuse, indecisive, self-deceiving; impractical, unwordly, a worrier.

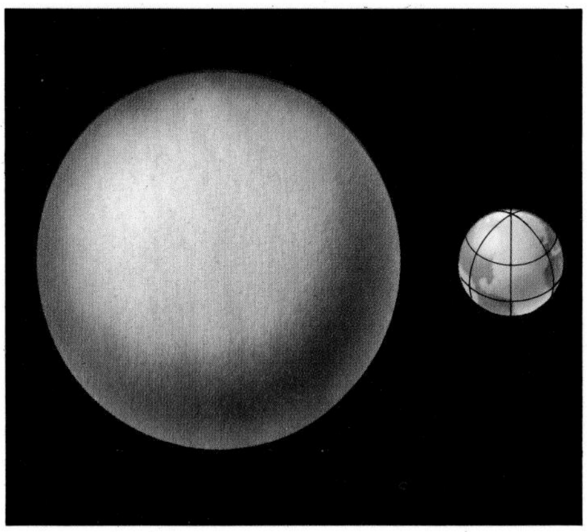

Size and Nature of Neptune *left*

Neptune, the second extra-Saturnian planet, was discovered in 1846 as a result of its gravitational effects on Uranus. Twelve years earlier an amateur astronomer, the Rev. T. J. Hussey, had suggested that the erratic motion of Uranus might be caused by the pull of an unknown planet; his theory was developed by J. C. Adams in England and Urbain Le Verrier in France; eventually Le Verrier's calculations were taken up by the Berlin Observatory and Neptune was located. It is slightly larger and more massive than Uranus, having a diameter of approximately 31,200 miles. Neptune has two satellites – Triton is larger than our Moon though Nereid is small and insignificant. Neptune's vast size, and its remoteness accord well with its astrological powers of strong if distant idealism.

Neptune Through the Houses

1 Whether afflicted or not, Neptune in this House weakens the personality, especially if the rising sign is Cancer or Libra. Strength is needed from other areas of the Chart. If unafflicted, the positive Neptune traits are present, but a practical attitude is required to get the best from them.

2 Uncertainty in financial affairs; over-free with money; an attraction to aesthetic objects and their acquisition.

3 Intuitive and imaginative; may tend to drift. Concentration and application should be consciously developed.

4 Untidy in the home. An imaginative parent; high ideals about home life. Under affliction, misunderstandings and confusion in family matters.

5 Much pleasure and inspiration from the cinema and the theatre. Loved ones seen through rose-coloured spectacles. Unusual, and often amusing, incidents concerning children.

6 Under affliction, a lack of concentration and laziness can mar working ability. The subject must be wary of drugs – even if medically prescribed, they can have adverse effects. Food poisoning is also a hazard.

7 An artistic or religious partner. Vagueness in relationships. Under affliction, unforeseen difficulties, confusion and disappointment in marriage.

8 Intuition and imagination very powerful. Confusion in financial matters. Professional financial advice should always be taken, especially if Neptune is in Leo or Libra.

9 If the Chart shows an interest in philosophical, religious or inspirational subjects, there is need for positive channelling; Neptune influences should be excellent here; especially when in Leo or Virgo.

10 Many changes of career or general direction in life. Strong idealism will give prestige if free from affliction. In the Tenth House Neptune is at its most controllable when in Virgo.

11 Idealistic, choosing inspired objectives; kind friends, but under affliction could be led astray by them.

12 Neptune's influence very strong, but if free from affliction and in a creative sign, much artistic ability. This is likely to be poetic if in Gemini, Cancer, Virgo or Sagittarius; directed towards ballet or the drama if in Leo.

Neptune Through the Signs

There is no one alive today with Neptune in Aries, Capricorn, Aquarius or Pisces. In the dates which appear below, more than two are sometimes given for a particular sign. This is because Neptune and Pluto were involved in retrograde motion, entering a new sign for a while, then returning to the previous one before they finally settled down to pass through the 'new' sign.

Gemini (1888/9–1902)
Intuition strong, but peevishness and worry can cloud main issues. Lack of breadth of vision, narrow-minded curiosity and gossip can become meddlesome under affliction.

Cancer (1901/2–1915)
The ability to escape from reality is apparent with this generation; also a certain dreaminess. Under affliction, this can turn to escapism. Neptune in Cancer gave great hope at the time (see p. 101 for aspects between Uranus and Neptune).

Leo (1915–1928/9)
Neptune is artistically creative in this sign, but ideas may be given inflated value. Self-approbation, and idealistic notions about one's own organizing ability are very common – extremely so if Neptune is rising in Leo. The generation influence in this sign relates to the rise of the cinema and its attendant glamour.

Virgo (1928/9–1942/3)
Highly critical of orthodox religion and accepted conventions. Analytical and discerning in these matters. Idealism and inspiration may be checked by the critical attitude.

Libra (1942/3–1956/7)
Easy-going, needing to relate to others. This is the hippy/flower-people generation in essence. Attraction to drugs, opting-out of society for an easier, lazier and less materialistic life are strongly pronounced. There is a marked streak of unworldly idealism. These characteristics are to the fore when Neptune is either rising in Libra, culminating, afflicted in the Twelfth House, or when Libra is the Sun-sign. Identification with one's own generation is inevitable; powers of leadership within that generation are emphasized if Neptune is strong.

Scorpio (1956/7–1970/1)
At its best, subtle; at its worst, cruel. Fascinated by revelations, exposing something previously hidden to the public view. Allied to a sense of social justice this trait can be harnessed to achieve much for the public good. If Neptune is rising or culminating and well aspected, influences could be particularly beneficial. But under affliction, children with Neptune in this sign need very careful direction, especially if cruel or underhand tendencies begin to emerge.

Sagittarius (1970/1–1984/5)
Those with Neptune in the Ninth and Tenth Houses, and free from affliction in this sign, should surely be a force to be reckoned with. Their minds should be of the highest calibre, and by the time they are old the world should have a generation of fine philosophers and sages. Utopian in outlook. A certain uplifting influence will be felt while Neptune is in this sign.

Capricorn (1984/5–1998)
Intuition and inspiration can be given concrete shape. Perhaps this generation will 'mould and solidify' the findings of the previous one, providing the practical drive their predecessors lacked; under affliction, scheming could occur on a more personal and petty level.

PLUTO

rules Scorpio; detriment Taurus;
the exaltation and fall have not yet been ascertained
Keyword: Elimination

Associations

Pluto is associated with the creative and regenerative forces of the body; the gonads, the unconscious; enforced change; also with the underworld, eruptions, volcanoes and earthquakes; big business; beginnings and ends of phases in life.

Positive Plutonic traits

Able to make a fresh start in unfavourable circumstances; flair for big business; financial security; analytical.

Negative Plutonic traits

An unhealthy unconscious, underhand, criminal tendencies; cruel, bestial, sadistic.

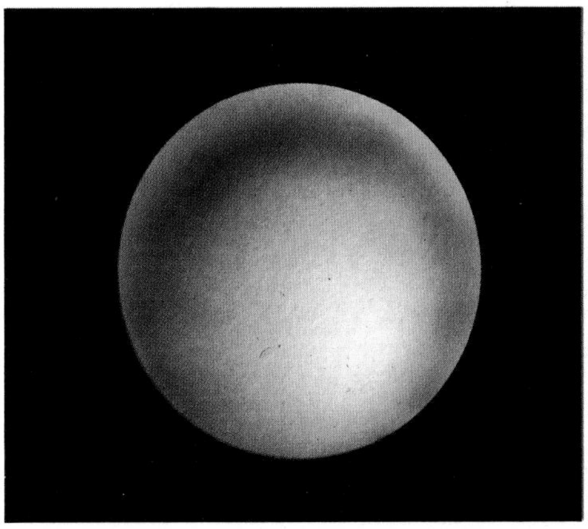

Size and Nature of Pluto *left*
In 1930, following irregularities in the motions of Uranus and Neptune, the third extra-Saturnian planet was discovered bringing the total of significant astrological planets to ten (including the Sun and Moon). Pluto is surprisingly small – perhaps no larger than Mars; its diameter is estimated to be in the region of 3,700 miles. Pluto may in fact be an ex-satellite of Neptune; certainly they share common astrological ground in the sphere of creative influence. However, the figures do not readily account for the strong pull which Pluto exerts on Uranus and Neptune; possibly it is considerably larger than calculations have suggested. It is 39½ times further away from the Sun than the Earth, but its orbit is so eccentric that at perihelion it is closer than Neptune.

Pluto Through the Houses

1 All Pluto traits will be emphasized, but special attention must be given to aspects. If negative (especially squares from Mars and Saturn), there will be areas of the personality which will not flow, and psychological problems of a deep-rooted nature may occur. This is more likely if Pluto is in Cancer or Virgo. If free from affliction, this pattern can add dynamism to a personality and the life will have distinct and clear-cut phases – necessary to the psychological well-being of the subject.

2 If free from affliction, possible grasp of business affairs and financial ability; perhaps covetousness if in Cancer. Probably at its best in Virgo in this House.

3 Obsessive powers of concentration if heavily aspected or in Virgo; or uneven and inconsistent flow of mental activity. In Leo, possibly domineering with brothers and sisters.

4 Intensity of feelings in family matters (especially in Cancer); liable to explosive domestic moods, needs careful handling if marriage is to last.

5 Excessive enjoyment of life; many love affairs, takes a rather exaggerated view of them, especially if in Leo or Libra.

6 Physical blockages can occur; constipation may be a source of worry, especially if in Virgo or Cancer. Ability to work to breaking point.

7 If well aspected, the imagination and cooperation prove excellent for business partnerships, especially if in Cancer, Virgo or Libra. Make the most of any such opportunities. Too autocratic if in Leo. Possibly an exhausting marriage partner.

8 Pluto is stronger in this, its own House. Can give great intuition, especially in Cancer. Good business acumen; analytical ability and keen sense of logic in Virgo or Gemini.

9 Mental strain can occur, perhaps over-forceful when dealing with foreigners.

10 A power complex is likely, especially in Leo. If close to the Midheaven in Leo, attraction to drugs; if under affliction, this can cause severe difficulty and great self-control is needed if severe addiction is to be avoided. In many latitudes Scorpio rises when Leo is culminating, bringing identification with Plutonic affairs. These powerful urges must have positive outlet, if possible through the pronounced flair for business, positive enjoyment of life, and the use of a dynamic and powerful energy to satisfactory ends.

11 Under affliction, obsessional about objectives, especially if in Virgo; otherwise, Pluto is not emphasized in this House.

12 Under severe affliction, deep-rooted psychological disorders. If free from affliction, a positive use of the unconscious.

Pluto Through the Signs

Taurus (1851/2–1883/4) Some very elderly people have Pluto in this Sign; its generation influence can be seen very clearly in the type of society so common in the late Victorian era – one of great and ever increasing inequality. It encouraged extremes – of wealth, of poverty, of ideals, of emotions. The rich received the beneficent qualities while the exploited working classes fared badly, often enduring, with little complaint, great hardship, poverty and squalor both at home and at work.

Gemini (1883/4–1912/13) The theme of change is strong during this overall period, and the sweeping away of old doctrines and ideas is particularly relevant. Much that had been unchallenged was attacked and many cherished customs and taboos were swept away. On a personal level, when strongly placed, Pluto in this Sign can contribute mental restlessness, but depth of character as well.

Cancer (1913/14–1937/8) The disruptive elements of Pluto in this Sign are shown through upheavals and changes in the general pattern of family life. This period is typified by the two World Wars from which many of this generation suffered with the loss of loved ones. On a personal level, if strongly placed, the planet in this Sign gives intuition; but sometimes resentfulness may also be apparent.

Leo (1937/8–1957) The long-term influence of Pluto in Leo is, at the time of writing, difficult to see in perspective. The Plutonic emphasis on the care and protection of mass interests could, at best, have a bearing on the development of the United Nations. In a more negative sense, the unrest, war and domineering influences of Leo show strongly. We need more time to take a longer view of Pluto in this Sign. On a personal level, good business ability and a sense of authority are shown, but a love of power and self-aggrandizement can also occur, combined with the more perverse pleasures associated with the negative Pluto traits.

Virgo (1958/9–1971) A long-term view of Pluto in this sign is impossible. The analytical and critical aspects of Virgo will work on a mass and personal level; self-criticism and the need to discover the source of world problems should emerge in those who were born with Pluto in this Sign. When sensitively placed in a Chart, Pluto will help these people to become good surgeons, psychiatrists and analysts, and successful and careful businessmen. (For information on the conjunction of Uranus and Pluto, see Aspects, p. 147.)

Libra (1971–1983/4) Perhaps a softening and more reasonable intellectual attitude will be shown towards matters associated with Pluto. This should be positive for big business, and there is a likelihood that underworld activities may decrease. If Pluto is ever going to work peacefully, it should do so while in Libra. On a personal level, a similar, more reasonable influence is likely to make itself felt.

THE SIGNS OF THE ZODIAC

The Signs and their Materials *right*
The attribution of flowers, colours, stones and other materials to the Signs is one of the lighter aspects of astrology: it is also an area in which there has been, and still is, considerable disagreement among astrologers. But it is of abiding interest: many people, for example, enjoy visiting the places attributed to signs prominent in their Birth Charts – especially the sign on the Midheaven, and the Sun-sign.

Masculine and Feminine Signs *left*
Keywords: Masculine, direct: Feminine, receptive. From very ancient times, the signs have been divided into groupings. The first is masculine and feminine, sometimes respectively known as positive and negative; here denoted by plus and minus symbols. The ancient theory was that a subject's extrovert or introvert tendencies could be gauged by the number of planets in masculine or feminine signs. This is an over-simplification, but such groupings can be a useful guide.

Triplicities (or Elements) *above left*
Keywords: Fire, enthusiastic; Earth, practical, stable; Air, intellectual, communicative; Water, emotional, intuitive.
This grouping is traditional. In interpretation, a Chart with, for example, more planets in 'Fire signs' will indicate lively enthusiasm.

Polarities *left*
Polarity is, in this context, a strong relationship between opposite signs of the Zodiac. The characteristics of one sign are related to its **polarity** – the characteristics of the opposite sign. Thus Aries, the first sign, is considered the most personal sign: people with this sign prominent tend to be self-centred, and to put themselves first in every way.

Those with strong Libran characteristics (Libra, the seventh sign, is directly opposite Aries) tend to be strongly geared to 'the other person'. To take another pairing, Taurus is concerned with money and possessions on a personal level; Scorpio has to do with inherited money or big business; and so on. Polarity is particularly relevant in matters of health.

Cardinal

Fixed

Mutable

Quadruplicities (or Qualities) *left*
Keywords: Cardinal, enterprising, outgoing; Fixed, resistant to change; Mutable (Common), adaptable, changing.
Each member of these groupings expresses its quality differently, because each falls into a different triplicity, e.g. Aries and Cancer are both Cardinal signs, but Aries is of the Fire triplicity and Cancer of the Water. Cancer and Aries both express enterprise; but Aries will show immediate enthusiasm, while Cancer will respond through the emotions and intuition.

As always, a prominent grouping must be considered in relation to the rest of the Chart.

If the reader turns to the page containing a description of the qualities of his Sun-sign, and expects to read a description of his own character, he will be disappointed. Many important factors will be missing. In essence, every man is the sum of the influences of his Sun-sign, his Ascending Sign and all the other astrological influences in his Birth Chart. If he was born near sunrise, the sign on the eastern horizon (the Ascendant) and the Sun-sign will be the same, giving additional force to the influence of that sign. Again, he may be born at sunrise *and* at the time of the new moon (which will then be 'in' the same sign); several planets may also be 'in' that sign. But, even so, only one part of the picture is seen in the placing of planets in a sign. It is for this reason that the Sun-signs are illustrated on the following pages by fictional characters: no real person could represent the characteristics of one sign and, even in fiction, the analogy is imperfect.

In general terms, the Sun-sign shows the personality the subject presents to the world – his 'image'; the Ascendant represents the true self. And while it is often possible to say 'how Geminian' or 'how Leonine' a person looks, if his Ascendant is neither of these but, for instance, Cancer, his real inner quality will be very different from his outward manner and appearance.

The descriptions of the signs should be used in several ways by the reader who wants to study astrology seriously. First, they should be read straight through, for a general idea of their characteristics; then in their polarity relationships, with regard to the triplicities and quadruplicities. The reader interested in how the various signs affect, for example, the mind, should read all these sub-sections together, and so on.

The *keywords* for each sign are important as a memory-guide, and it is always an advantage to know them by heart. For convenience, the attributes of the signs on the following pages are discussed in masculine terms, although they apply to both sexes. Sometimes a Chart may contain a group, or stellium, of three or more planets in one sign. Unless the Sun is one of the planets concerned, this does not mean that the characteristics of that sign will be emphasized. The *individual* positions of each planet should be considered, each in its own context. The *group* will combine to have a positive or negative effect, according to the general tenor of the Chart.

Aries

Astrologers have never doubted the Arian colour: accident-prone, possible war-like qualities . . . what else but red?

Body area: head * Colour: red * Metal: iron * Stone: diamond * Plants: geranium, thistle, honeysuckle, witch-hazel * Trees: all thorn-bearing trees and shrubs * Countries: England, France, Germany, Poland * Cities: Naples, Florence, Krakow.

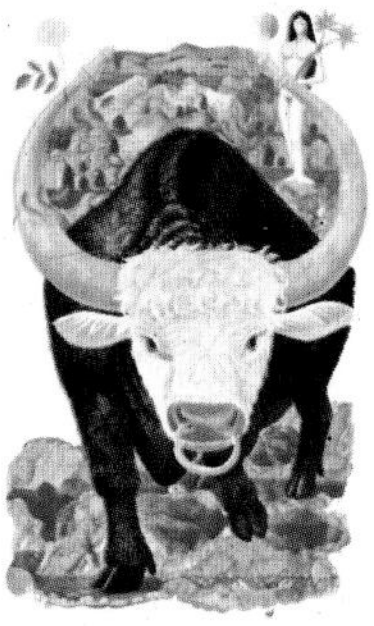

Taurus

The Taurean loves quiet countryside; yet, when roused, his temper is violent.

Body area: throat * Colours: pink and pale blue * Metal: copper (the metal of Venus) * Stone: sapphire * Plants: rose, poppy, violet, foxglove, vine * Trees: ash, cypress, apple * Countries: Ireland, Switzerland, Persia, Sweden * Cities: Dublin, Lucerne, Leipzig, St Louis.

Gemini

Ask a Geminian which colour he likes: he may say bright lemon-yellow, he may say all colours; Geminians enjoy being versatile.

Body area: ears, chest, arms, hands, lungs * Colours: all, especially yellow * Metal: mercury * Stone: agate * Plants: lily-of-the-valley, lavender * Trees: nut-trees * Countries: USA, Wales * Cities: London, Plymouth, Melbourne, San Francisco.

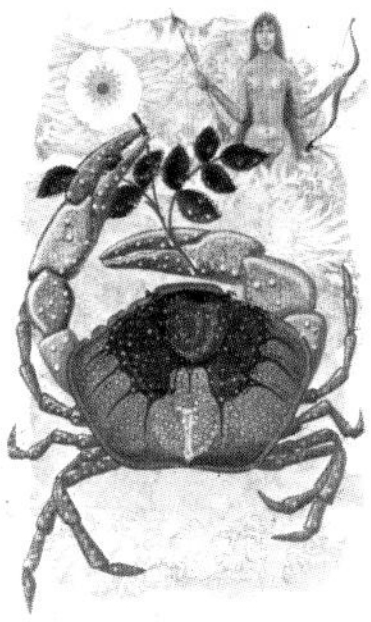

Cancer

Cancerians often collect antique silver: it is their favourite metal, and their collector's instinct draws them to it.

Body area: breasts * Colours: smoky greys, greens * Metal: silver * Stone: pearl * Plants: acanthus, wild-flowering plants * Trees: those rich in sap * Countries: Scotland, Holland, New Zealand * Cities: Amsterdam, New York, Venice, Manchester.

Leo

In Italy, the strong July-August sun is known as the 'lion sun' – when it is in Leo.

Body area: spine, heart, back * Colours: golden yellow, orange * Metal: gold * Stone: ruby * Plants: sunflower, marigold, rosemary * Trees: orange and all citrus trees, bay, palm * Countries: France, Italy, Rumania * Cities: Rome, Prague, Damascus, Los Angeles, Chicago, Philadelphia.

Virgo

Virgo was originally a pretty girl of 15 – far from the old-maidish spinster some characteristics of the sign suggest.

Body area: bowels, intestines * Colours: navy blue, dark greys, browns * Metal: mercury * Stone: sardonyx * Plants: small, brightly-coloured flowers * Trees: nut-trees * Countries: Greece, Turkey, the West Indies * Cities: Paris, Boston, Heidelberg.

Libra

The Libran's love of music and elegance makes the city of wine, women and song especially appropriate – Vienna.

Body area: kidneys * Colours: pale blue, pink * Metal: Copper * Stone: sapphire * Plants: with blue flowers, large opulent roses, vine * Trees: ash * Countries: Austria, Burma, Japan, Tibet * Cities: Vienna, Antwerp, Lisbon, Copenhagen, Frankfurt.

Scorpio

Originally Mars ruled Scorpio; but Pluto, associated with the underworld, has a particular application for Scorpians.

Body area: sexual organs * Colours: dark red, maroon * Metal: iron * Stone: opal * Plants: those with dark red flowers, e.g. rhododendron * Trees: bushy trees, blackthorn * Countries: Norway, Syria * Cities: Liverpool, New Orleans, Washington DC.

Sagittarius

The Sagittarian stone is topaz: correctly, it should come from Spain, a country under the Sagittarian influence.

Body area: hips, thighs * Colours: purple, dark regal blue * Metal: tin * Stone: topaz * Plants: asparagus, pinks, dandelion, tomato * Trees: lime, mulberry, ash, oak, birch * Countries: Spain, Australia, Hungary, Madagascar * Cities: Toledo, Budapest, Cologne.

Capricorn

Capricornians are often drawn to governmental work, and find the administrative areas of countries or cities congenial.

Body area: knees, shins * Colours: black, dark grey, very dark green, brown * Metal: lead * Stone: turquoise * Plants: pansies, onions, hemlock, ivy * Trees: pine, willow, elm, poplar * Countries: India, Mexico, Afghanistan * Cities: Oxford, Delhi, Brussels.

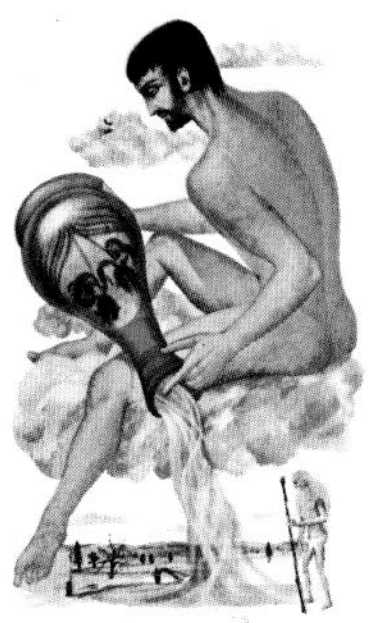

Aquarius

The Uranus myth is related to a man pouring out water; why, then, is Aquarius an Air sign? Perhaps the streams could represent air, even influences from outer space.

Body area: ankles * Colours: electric blue * Metal: uranium * Stone: amethyst * Plants: orchids, golden-rain * Trees: most fruit trees * Countries: USSR, Sweden * Cities: Hamburg, Bremen, Moscow.

Pisces

The Piscean metal is tin (the Jupiter metal). Its modern ruler is Neptune, but the explosive qualities of neptunium hardly suit the gentle Piscean.

Body area: feet * Colours: soft sea-green * Metal: tin * Stone: moonstone, bloodstone * Plants: water-lily * Trees: fig, willow, trees near water * Countries: Portugal, the Sahara * Cities: Alexandria, Seville.

ARIES

Masculine Fire Cardinal
Ruling planet: Mars
Keywords: Assertively, urgently

The Myth Phrixus, son of Nepele, falsely accused of ravishing Biadice, was condemned to death, but rescued by a golden ram, on whose back he escaped with his sister Helle. She became giddy and fell off; but Phrixus reached safety, and sacrificed the ram to Zeus, who placed its likeness in the heavens. Years later the ram's fleece became famous, when Jason captured it.

Positive Arian traits A pioneering and adventurous spirit; enterprising, courageous, direct in his approach; highly energetic, hating restriction, loving freedom.

Negative Arian traits Selfish, always putting himself first; unsubtle, impulsive, pugnacious; a satirist, quick-tempered, impatient – wanting everything *now*.

Character People with a strong Arian influence are enthusiastic, generous, lively. They rapidly grasp the essentials of a situation. This can also have its drawbacks, for in seeing the whole shape of a problem they may tend to overlook its details. They can be quick in other ways: quick, for instance, to give offence. They may be so eager to come to grips with an argument that they will speak brashly or aggressively – they're no diplomats.

They may be quick-tempered, and will at their worst be extremely selfish. This can take many forms: an Arian may be so keen to look after himself that he will forget to consider his friends; he may even tell quite blatant lies to avoid a minor inconvenience – though on the whole he will be such a bad liar that others can immediately see through him. But however selfish he may be, it is not hard to make him see sense; when his selfishness is pointed out to him, he will readily acknowledge the fact.

The Arian is a quick-witted, restless character, and finds it difficult to be patient in any situation he dislikes. He will put up with adverse conditions only so long as he is confident they will eventually bring him what *he* wants. It may well be this desire to achieve his own ends that drives him to take risks; Arian bravery and disregard for danger are legendary.

The Arian's tendency to take risks is not always confined to dangerous situations. He may win a medal for bravery, or merely a reputation for being the most careless and dangerous driver in the neighbourhood. The

Tarzan the Arian
With their reputation for energy and getting things done, the typical Arian face is clearcut and forceful, with high forehead and cheekbones, strong chin and firm mouth. The eyebrows are heavy, the eyes have a direct, piercing gaze and the nose is long. There could be no more typically Arian figure in fiction than the Tarzan of Edgar Rice Burrough's series of popular novels. A born fighter, equally adept with his hands or a weapon, Tarzan revels in the excitement of jungle life. Impatient and of uncertain temper, he nevertheless greets Jane, his mate, with childlike rapture.

Arian who feels spurred to drive fast might well take this compulsion to a logical conclusion – not by killing himself, but by becoming a really expert driver. On a less lethal level, the Arian tends to cut or burn himself without noticing. He has headaches more often than most people, although he does not mind noise; on occasion he likes it.

Mind The Arian may seem difficult and not be an easy friend. He has, however, an enormous fund of energy, lively as well as powerful, and does not take kindly to restrictions or monotony. Both at work and in personal relationships, he appears at his best when he is given enough freedom.

However trying the Arian may be, his quickness of wit, often satirical, will come to his rescue; he can almost always be relied upon to make his friends laugh, even at the most unlikely moments. But that quickness is also a danger, for his mind too often works erratically, his thoughts bounding from point to point, rather than following a logical progression (that would be *much* too boring). However, if he has to make a snap decision, he will tend to make the right one.

The positions of the planets in the Chart need study, for they can considerably modify the workings of the mind. For example, if Aries is the Sun-sign, Mercury often falls in Pisces: this may even reverse the Arian's advantage in speed of thought. He will still react quickly enough, but also become easily confused and forgetful, and sometimes just plain stupid. Mercury in Pisces will also injure his capacity for making snap decisions.

More sophisticated astrological types may tend to smile at the impulsive, erratic Arian: but his uncluttered, almost primaeval impulses are often refreshing to others, and at times they do give their owner certain advantages.

Emotional Relationships The Arian needs to express his sexuality more strongly than most, and in a positive fashion. If Aries is *rising*, the urgency will be tempered by a very real romantic streak; at the same time his selfishness will be emphasized. If the Sun is rising in Aries, this selfishness will present him with a deep-rooted psychological problem. He will probably have a rather childlike quality about him, especially when things go wrong.

Career Psychologist, psychiatrist, butcher, foundry worker, metal worker, explorer, engineer, engine-driver, fireman, arms-manufacturer, trade-unionist, mechanic, dentist, professional sportsman.

A slow, plodding, dull, safe job is precisely what the Arian does *not* need. He is at his best in competitive work – in a noisy, busy atmosphere, where preferably he is in charge, and can then use his initiative. In any event, he should not be trapped behind a desk. His high level of physical energy must find release if he is not to burst. Challenge is important to him, and may spur him towards a position of power.

The Arian has a pioneering spirit; he may well be an explorer, or like to feel himself one – finding his way over untried ground, trading in new areas, developing fresh lines of scientific research.

In his spare time, the Arian will find that robust sports such as hockey, football, boxing or wrestling, provide an extra channel for his energy. Carving will satisfy his talent for sharp instruments; rally-driving or motor-cycle racing his feelings for speed, danger – and noise.

Parent and Child 'Me first!' cries the Arian. Another version goes: 'My child first!' In his eagerness for a son or daughter to do well at school, the Arian may tend to be over-hard. Nor does his lack of patience help. This tendency to 'push' a child is the Arian parent's worst fault; mothers, especially, should watch for it. All the same, the out-going Arian qualities make a good parent, especially for the more extrovert child. But the child must be allowed to develop at his own rate.

The Arian child is full of energy, and a parent who does not organize his life accordingly will be in for considerable discomfort. Firm discipline is needed, though it must be remembered that the young Arian will smart under it, and may be driven to rebellion and wilfulness if it is too strict. At school, he may lack the patience to study Latin verbs or algebraic equations with proper attention; and rush onto the playing field with something like improper alacrity. His reports may contain allegations of laziness, carelessness, and lack of interest. He will indeed be lazy, careless and uninterested in the subjects he couldn't care less about. But this is true of most children, and once the Arian child has found his particular niche, his energy and application will be so frantic, there will be no holding him.

TAURUS

Feminine Earth Fixed
Ruling planet: Venus
Keywords: Possessively, permanently

The Myth Taurus was the white bull who courted Europa, bearing her on his back; he was in fact Zeus in disguise, and when the god changed back into his normal form, he placed the bull in the heavens.

Positive Taurean traits Practical, reliable, patient; adept in business, having strong powers of endurance; a firm sense of values, especially in relation to the arts; love of luxury and good food; persistent, solid, determined, strong-willed; affectionate, warm-hearted; trustworthy.

Negative Taurean traits Possessive, lazy, self-indulgent, a potential bore, static in his opinions, lacking flexibility and originality; greedy, stubborn, resentful; obsessed with routines.

Character Just as an oak tree becomes a permanent part of the landscape it is set in, so a Taurean will want to 'belong' to a permanent scene. To this end he will present a solid, steady, reliable front to the world. As the oak tree is rooted in the soil, so also the Taurean is rooted in his opinions, extremely stubborn and hating to be contradicted or crossed.

A feeling of security is important to him: he will demand it in his career, at home, and in his marriage – although he may himself undermine it by a sudden display of furious temper. He is slowly roused but then ferocious and difficult to cope with. Especially in marriage, his temper is most likely to be sparked off by jealousy; this in turn stems from what is probably his worst fault – possessiveness.

He can, however, be very patient, and will probably have plenty of charm, warmth and affection, even though he may tend to be a bit of a bore. He is not to be rushed – and will take no risks: his sense of self-preservation is far too well developed. Those around him may sometimes have to brave his dormant temper and shake him up a little, otherwise his plodding conservatism could drive them to distraction.

Taureans tend to have an excellent business sense – the ability to make money, and to hang on to it. If they are generous in entertaining their friends, it is generally because they enjoy an excuse for a good blow-out for themselves.

The Taurean will probably be happier living in the country than in town; he usually has flair for and finds psychological

Sun-sign period c 21 April to 21 May

Falstaff the Taurean
The overall effect of the Taurean face is one of bulk. Starting with a good head of hair, everything about the Taurean is full and earthy: the eyes are staring, intense and bulbous, the nose and jawline are fleshy and the neck is thick and bull-like. With all this heaviness, however, there is no hint of weakness, for the mouth and chin are firm. The fictional character that best sums up these qualities is Shakespeare's Sir John Falstaff, young Prince Hal's mentor and drinking companion. The lazy, greedy, stubborn old knight is the worst of Taurus personified. In him the positive Taurean qualities of patience, affection, persistence and practicability are all devoted to one end: himself.

contentment in tending his garden. If a dew-laden lawn gives him a chill, this is likely to centre around his throat.

Mind Ask a Taurean what he thinks, and he'll tell you. When he has told you, that will be the end of the matter; you need not expect him to change his opinion. Stubbornness is a main characteristic of the Sign; all too often it demonstrates the depth of the rut in which the Taurean's mind runs.

The mind itself will probably be slow and unoriginal, but constructive as well. No need to expect brilliant ideas from a Taurean; or original ones, or new angles on existing ideas. As usual, planetary positions can aggravate or mitigate the picture: if Mercury and the Sun are both in Taurus, the Taurean's attitude will be even more reactionary, and his ideas even more fixed. If the Sun-sign is Taurus and Mercury is in Gemini, his fixity of opinion may be a little less impervious to argument.

While the Taurean will undoubtedly work best along his own carefully-planned lines, he tends to be unduly upset by a tiny and unimportant deviation from the normal run of events. If he can be persuaded to encourage every tiny sprig of adaptability he can find in his own nature, he will not be quite so upset by changes when they do occur.

Emotional Relationships The passionate film star clutching his mistress and murmuring intensely, 'You're *mine*!' will undoubtedly be a Taurean, and will probably have Venus in Taurus to add to his passion. His possessiveness extends all too often to his girl-friend or wife, as though she were an acre of garden or a set of fish-knives. Not that he will not be charming and affectionate – indeed, an emotional relationship brings out these Taurean qualities delightfully – but his life does centre around his *possessions*. If and when he discovers that his wife or girl-friend does not belong utterly and completely to him, he will suffer considerably, and so, no doubt, will she.

Career Farmer, horticulturist, businessman, builder, architect, sculptor, singer, surveyor, jeweller, civil servant, accountant, auctioneer, property dealer, financier, model, art dealer, banker.

The bustle and movement of a city, and office life are not to the Taurean's liking. On the other hand, the security of a conventional office life will attract him, and he will work best when he knows that the end of each month will bring a guaranteed pay-cheque. He will very likely be successful in a career which has to do with finance, and he will look forward to security (with pension) in retirement.

There is another side to the Taurean which might seem a contradiction in terms: he has a distinct artistic leaning. This should obviously, given his temperament, be expressed against a conventional background – the commercial employee-artist rather than the speculative painter. Many successful sculptors and architects are Taureans. Often, too, singers are strongly influenced by this Sign; on a non-professional level, music and its appreciation will satisfy Taureans as a spare-time interest; so, too, will sculpture or women's craftwork. There is a tendency to lethargy, so Taureans will do well to involve themselves in some form of physical exercise during leisure time. Weight-lifting strongly suggests itself.

Parent and Child It is difficult for the Taurean, with his very conservative instincts, to bridge the generation gap with the young; and all too easy for him, with his liking for discipline, to ignore the fact that his children may not be in sympathy with his ideas. He will tend to be strict, and his discipline may be too rigid. He will invest generously in his children's education, wanting to give them the best that money can buy; and he will expect the results to show. In general terms he must also try hard not to be too dogmatic; and to curb possessiveness which, if unbridled, will make life a misery (especially for the Taurean mother) when the children want to leave home.

The Taurean child should be weaned from *his* possessiveness at an early age by being encouraged to share his toys and games. His inborn instinct for discipline will be at its happiest at school – he will enjoy obeying rules!

He should not be forced: he is a plodder, and his progress may well be slow; but what goes in stays in, and his movement upward will be sure and determined. His natural charm and good looks (Taurus has the reputation of being the most handsome or beautiful of the Signs) will no doubt combine with his natural sensuality to give his first dates an enviable, perhaps dangerous intensity – though his sense of convention will probably save him from premature social disaster.

GEMINI

Masculine Air Mutable
Ruling planet: Mercury
Keywords: Communicatively, adaptably, versatilely

The Myth There seems to be no particular myth associated with Gemini; in Egypt it was known as 'The Two Stars' – and took its name from the stars Castor and Pollux, the brightest of the constellation, also known as Hercules and Apollo, and Triptolemus and Iasion. The Egyptians illustrated Gemini by two kids rather than the two human figures commonly used.

Positive Geminian traits Adaptable, versatile, intellectual, witty and logical, busy, spontaneous, lively, talkative and amusing in conversation; having a flair for writing and for languages; always youthful and up-to-date in outlook and appearance.

Negative Geminian traits Changeable, restless; cunning; inquisitive, inconsistent and two-faced; unable to control nervous energy, lives 'on his nerves'; superficial, a gossip.

Character The Geminian is *always* right and *never* changes his mind – until the next time the argument comes round, when he will take a totally different stand, and deny ever having given vent to his earlier opinions. This is infuriating for his opponents in argument, especially as he has a considerable talent for dialogue – and a tendency to know a very little about a very great number of things, and to marshal this little knowledge so skilfully as to seem well informed. His ability to bluff his way out of tight corners is phenomenal!

There, then, are his worst faults – inconsistency and superficiality. Little wonder, perhaps, that the best popular journalists in newspapers, radio and television are Geminians. For, again, they have an insistent urge to communicate: women will spend hours gossiping on the telephone, the more intellectual Geminian will be constantly writing to the press, lecturing, appearing on TV 'chat' shows, addressing meetings . . . driven to desperation in his quest for someone to impress with his opinions, the Geminian will collar an old tramp on the street corner, and address *him*. His ideas must be spread about.

The Geminian will always be on the go, and generally speaking will be doing more than one thing at a time. This duality is an important part of his nature, and it would be unwise for anyone to attempt to hinder it; the Geminian needs plenty of variety and change. He can very easily become bored,

Sun-sign period c 22 May to 22 June

Don Juan – the Geminian lover
The Geminian face is intellectual and vivacious. A smooth oval in shape, it has few exaggerated features. The eyebrows are arched over inquiring eyes; the nose is thin, the cheekbones high. The jawline and chin are pointed. The mouth, though wide, is often not decisive. A typical example of the Geminian in literature is the Don Juan of Byron or Don Giovanni of Mozart. Expressing his Geminian versatility and restlessness by being all things to all women, Don Juan was fickle, inconsistent and two-faced, but his liveliness and wit were mitigating qualities.

and his answer is to drop whatever is boring him, and turn to the next job on hand. The phrase 'to live on one's nerves' seems to have been coined for Geminians; and they should be careful not to overstrain their sensitive and highly-strung nervous systems, which can break down under pressure. But they have their bodies on their side, for Gemini is considered the most youthful Sign.

Mind The Geminian will have many activities, and may even have several occupations during his life; he should try to find one or two major themes which will preoccupy him throughout his whole life-span. The other planets, once more, will help or hinder: if the Sun-sign is Gemini and Mercury is also in that Sign, restlessness will be emphasized. At university, for example, he may drop whatever he is reading in mid-term, and change to something else – not a tendency which endears him to his tutors, and which, although it may have advantages in journalism, will not gladden prospective employers. Mercury in Taurus may steady the restlessness, contributing a more practical outlook, an interesting depth to the character, and an ability to think less haphazardly and with greater coherence.

There is always a danger that if the Geminian mind is not properly stimulated, it may apply itself to cunning and fraud.

Emotional Relationships Geminians are not over-emotional; the rest of the Chart should be consulted for more precise information on their emotional level. Their ardour would be warmed, for instance, by Venus in Cancer. But, as may be expected, the Geminian expresses himself well in love, and his love-letters will be worth keeping. His tendency to flirt (strengthened if Venus is in Gemini) may well contribute liveliness to an affair or a marriage; so may his occasional real need for dual relationships – two mistresses or two lovers.

Career Journalist, broadcaster, commentator, teacher, lecturer, writer, linguist, secretary, travel agent, chauffeur, commercial traveller, shop assistant, light manual worker or craftsmen, telephone operator, postman, navigator.

Journalism (newspaper, radio or television) is an obvious career for the Geminian, suiting not only his instinct for language and his urge to communicate, but his need for variety and change. But there are other possible careers: his flair for talk and for travel make him a good commercial traveller, for instance. And he will make an excellent teacher, Gemini's reputation as the most up-to-date of the signs making it easy for him to keep abreast of the latest preoccupations of his pupils.

Obviously, the Geminian should try to steer clear of any job which means working in one environment, or in work that is tedious or monotonous. He should always be adding to his interests, always be studying new subjects (languages will appeal to him).

Physically, Geminians are generally light, wiry and quick-moving. Physical exercise should balance his intellectual side, but the sports he plays should be 'light' – fencing, skiing, archery, table-tennis and tennis. The most unliterary Geminian may find himself eventually writing something – even if it is just a limerick or a competition entry. But he should remember the disadvantages of speed: a Geminian starting a novel would be wise to plan every chapter in advance.

Parent and Child The Geminian can be a wonderful parent: his own wide interests will foster the waking interests of his child.

He will see to it that his child has plenty of books, and plenty of encouragement to read, from a very early age. His own love of argument and controversy may well stimulate a similar interest in his child.

The Geminian child needs plenty of intellectual stimulation, and will consume books and ideas as his friends eat sweets. The Geminian tendency to skim the surface should be watched, however: he should be encouraged to finish anything he starts (how exciting to start a new game, a new hobby; how dull to complete it). Restlessness or tension should be spotted early, and countered. Discipline is not greeted with rapture by Geminians, and the child will not enjoy the discipline of school, especially if his teachers have the temerity to attempt to stop him talking. Schools famous for their discipline should be avoided. The Geminian child will be reasonable, provided he is understood. Regimentation will stifle him; and while his mind may need taming and disciplining, it will always be lively, always susceptible to an intellectual appeal. A box of pencils and a large notebook will keep a Gemini child quiet for days; well, for hours; well, until he spots something else . . .

CANCER

Feminine Water Cardinal
Ruling planet: Moon
Keywords: Protectively, sensitively

The Myth As a crab, Cancer is Babylonian in origin; but in Egypt, the constellation was sometimes represented by two turtles, sometimes known as the Stars of the Water, and sometimes as Allul, an unidentified water-creature. Thus its association with water is ancient, but a more detailed mythological history is lacking.

Positive Cancerian traits Kind, sensitive, sympathetic; a powerful imagination; a strong maternal or paternal instinct, solicitous and protective; cautious, patriotic; tenacious, shrewd, thrifty; emotionally resourceful; an excellent home-maker.

Negative Cancerian traits Over-emotional, hyper-sensitive; touchy, a snappy temper; moody, changeable; a hard exterior hiding a weak character; an inclination to self-pity, unforgiving; unstable and too easily flattered; untidy.

Character There is little doubt that the Cancerian is not the easiest of characters either to understand or to bear with. At his best, kind, affable, helpful, thoughtful and understanding, he can also be – and for no good reason – bad-tempered and moody, short and snappy with anyone who speaks to him, or perhaps refusing to speak at all. Sometimes willing to listen with great sympathy to other people's problems, and to do what he can to help, at other times he will find it extremely difficult to listen patiently to any tale of woe but his own.

The Cancerian often seems hard as nails, and indeed in many ways *is* hard: he may be completely without magnanimity, for instance, forever harping, perhaps, on a tiny injustice done to him. Again, while he will quickly upset his friends by unthinking comments and hard words, he is himself over-sensitive to criticism. But, under this hard and perhaps unprepossessing exterior, is the soft inner flesh. Sometimes fearful or inhibited, he uses the exterior toughness as a form of protection – very like the crab his sign denotes.

That is the Cancerian's conflict: positive, kind, protective on the one hand – harsh, moody, bad-tempered on the other. It is not surprising that he will tend to swing, pendulum-like, between the two extremes. If the pendulum comes to rest, it will more than likely do so under the influence of a home and a family. He will love his home and cherish his marriage.

Sun-sign period
c 23 June to
23 July

Madame Butterfly – a true Cancerian
Cancerians are worriers and their faces show it; round, perhaps fleshy, with pronounced frown lines and mouths that turn down. There is an impression of patience, sympathy and motherliness in the heavyish neck and full jawline. The eyes are affectionate, the nose snub and the cheeks fairly flat. A fine example of the Cancerian is the Madame Butterfly of John L. Lang and later of Puccini's famous opera. Her tenacity and faithfulness reveal the true Cancerian, even to the touch of temper she shows with her servant.

The Cancerian has a sentimental streak: he is forever harking back to 'the good old days', and can very easily live in the past. (Mercury in Cancer will underline this trait.) But he also holds on to the present: there is more tenacity in Cancer than in any other Sign, and any project started by a Cancerian will be brought to its conclusion. He will also cling to a personal relationship until the bitter (or sweet) end.

Mind Cancerians are great worriers: they bring worry into the realm of art. They tend to hug their cares to themselves, rejecting the release of talking them over with friends; and the resultant tension all too often upsets their sensitive digestive systems, sometimes to the point of an ulcer.

Their imaginative powers are considerable, and while this can aggravate the tendency to worry, it can act as a release.

The positive elements of the Sign include an excellent memory: not only will Cancerians remember their early childhood, but facts, historical dates – anything. They will also be highly intuitive, and their basic instincts will usually be right. There is a tendency, though, for them not to think for themselves – simply to soak in the opinions of others, later venting them as original. If Mercury is in Gemini, Cancer is the Sun-sign, or Mercury in Aquarius (with Cancer rising), the situation is slightly eased.

Emotional Relationships Sensationalism can often colour the Cancerian's sex life; yet, in the home, the Cancerian woman is easily bogged down by domesticity, not allowing herself to enjoy life even when she has the chance. She will use her domestic activities to provide excuses for refusing invitations, when in fact her own natural reticence and timidity provide the real reasons. The Cancerian husband will be protective; but he, or the Cancerian wife, should be careful that moodiness does not mar their relationship.

Career Businessman, nurse, caterer, hotelier, fisherman, boat-builder, housewife, kindergarten teacher, domestic science specialist, sailor, antique dealer, museum curator, historian.

The Cancerian's natural urge to protect, and his excellent memory, will help him not only to look after his clients' interests, but to remember their names, faces and personal details; this, combined with shrewdness, makes him a formidable businessman. He may express these tendencies by looking after guests in an hotel or guest-house; a natural talent for cooking will not be unusual, and he may well become a top-grade chef. He will not be at his best, however, coping with double bookings or crises in the kitchens, for tension can lead to incessant worry, and then to digestive upsets. A calm working atmosphere is important.

Cancerians make out well as estate agents or market gardeners. The women are excellent nurses, especially working with babies or small children. This instinct will be valuable with their own families.

There are many Cancerian historians (exploiting their feeling for the past and their remarkable memories for dates and events). Museum work is a delight to the culture-conscious Cancerian – happy in the storeroom checking the collection. Any career involving the sea is also positive. Hobbies should include some form of collecting; sport may involve bodily contact, as in boxing, although swimming can also attract.

Parent and Child Cancer is traditionally the Sign of motherhood – but that charming convention can rebound on the poor children, for the Cancerian mother is all too likely to refuse to accept the fact that her children are growing up. 'Oh, no – you can't wear that, it makes you look far too old.' And when the child properly rebels, she will say, loftily: 'I didn't do that when *I* was young. Things were different *then* . . .'

The Cancerian parent's tenacious efforts to keep the family unit together can even provoke a split. Cancerians are not necessarily possessive, but they put the *family* first; any tentative move to step outside the magic circle fills them with horror and forboding. But the Cancerian's above-average orientation around his family is not to be despised; under the right conditions it can be marvellously rewarding.

The Cancerian child is best governed by an appeal to his home-loving instinct: rather than scolding him harshly, a parent will only have to say, 'It makes me sad to see you doing that', to provoke a stream of repentant tears. The child will be extremely affectionate, and easily hurt. At school he should put his excellent memory to good use, especially in history (probably his favourite subject). Dancing, swimming and some of the rougher sports can be attractive.

LEO

Masculine Fire Fixed
Ruling planet: Sun
Keywords: Creatively, impressively, powerfully

The Myth The lion commemorated in this constellation is traditionally the Nemean lion, its pelt proof against iron, bronze and stone, which Hercules killed (losing a finger to its teeth), and which commemorates his bravery.

Positive Leonine traits Magnanimous, generous; creative, enthusiastic, a good organizer; broadminded, expansive, having a sense of showmanship and drama.

Negative Leonine traits Dogmatic; bullying; pompous; snobbish, intolerant, fixed in his opinions; patronizing; power-mad; conceited.

Character There is nothing difficult or complicated about Leo; he is King – the boss, the leader. He knows he is far better at organizing everyone else's life than they are; and if they accept this, all will be well. The sign has obvious faults: the Leo can be interfering and intolerant, pompous and over-dogmatic; so he should make a habit of reassessing his opinion as often as possible, and make good use of the natural, spontaneous, warm-hearted charm which he undoubtedly possesses.

At their best, Leos are affectionate, enthusiastic, cheerful, optimistic people who, in the popular phrase, 'bring sunshine into other people's lives' – indeed in many ways this is their mission in life. It is a valuable quality, and they should not neglect it.

Rather surprisingly, Leos are often sensitive and easily hurt. Not that they will show it: if a Leo is treated unjustly he will show great magnanimity. But if he is really angered, he will put on the full regal act, at once 'mounting the throne' and making quite sure that the impertinent fool who has been stupid enough to consider himself an equal, steps back to his proper, lower, station! Whatever the Leo's background, he will have a kingdom of some sort.

Leos have a pronounced flair for drama: some make scenes in order to be the centre of attention. But their theatrical bent can be externalized in more positive and lively ways – in dressing splendidly, doing things in a big way, organizing outings, and altogether making sure they get the best of everything – as well as providing the best they can for others. Leos are extravagant; money slips through their fingers.

Leos are not only adept at organizing other people, they themselves are hard

Sun-sign period
c 24 July to
23 August

El Cid – a Leonine hero
The immediate impression of a Leonine face is one of strength. The eyes, the most striking feature, have a forceful, direct look. The forehead is open, the eyebrows arched and nose hooked; the jawline and chin are clear and definite, and the mouth is wide and firm – undoubtedly the face of a ruler, though he may be autocratic. There could be no better example of Leo than Le Cid, of Pierre Corneille's drama. The Cid is a hero on the grand scale. Magnanimous and brave, he offers himself to an honourable death, but then triumphs over the Moors and finally wins the promise of Chimène's hand in marriage.

workers, and can set a good example. This facet of the Leo personality is emphasized when Leo is the Sun-sign.

Mind The opinions a Leo forms in his youth will remain with him until he dies: there is a dangerous tendency to have a closed mind. His early opinions may be, for their time, advanced; but he will cling to them too stubbornly. He will have breadth of vision, and will at once see the general shape of a scheme or project; but sometimes he will lack an eye for detail (Mercury in Virgo will counteract this). He will have large-scale ideas, sometimes too large; but that is a vital element of his personality. He will not be the worrying kind; often involved by choice in intellectual discussion, he will appear perhaps better informed than he really is in intellectually more advanced company.

Although seldom depressed, he will really crumble when depression does hit him; but he has resilience, and his powers of recuperation are good. His own personal sun will soon shine again. If there is an artistic inclination he will be easily inspired and able to give shape to his ideas. His thought processes are constructive, and while he may not be a quick thinker, he will arrive steadily at firm conclusions, and will not commit himself until he is sure where he stands.

Emotional Relationships The Leo is traditionally said to find marriage difficult, particularly if Leo is rising; so those with a Leo Ascendant should be careful when embarking on a permanent emotional relationship. Leos need to be able to look up to and admire the object of their affections. They are extremely loyal and affectionate, and will express their love and loyalty in a positive fashion. Leo wives should check a tendency to take over the masculine role; both sexes share an appetite for cat-and-mouse games in sexual relationships.

Career Actor, dancer, teacher, youth worker, managing director, professional sportsman, astrologer, commissionaire, jeweller; any position carrying a promise of publicity and scope for showing off!

Ambitious but not ruthless, a Leo will be an enormously willing slave, provided that he can look up to and respect his master, and provided that his work is congenial – he will suffer enormously in work he finds dull or boring. If his superior is stupid, or small-minded, or a poor organizer, either he or the Leo will have to go! Leos need to express their natural exuberance and enthusiasm for life in their work, and often become deeply involved in it; work and leisure become indivisible, especially if the job is artistic or creative. The professional life may become so demanding that there is no time for hobbies or recreation. The Leo hates amateurism in all its forms, and will always want to work at the highest level – though his feeling for drama occasionally leads him to take an important role in an amateur dramatic society production. The Leo makes an excellent teacher, probably better with older children than with the very young. It is nevertheless good for him to spend some of his time working with the young, since he often has a happy knack of goading them into action; he will derive a great deal of satisfaction from such work.

Parent and Child A Leo expects as much from his child as he expects from himself, and tends to be unduly disappointed if the child does not measure up to his ideals. A Leo father (by tradition Leo is the sign of the father) can be over-dominating, but Leos do not generally make a burden of parenthood; they will embark on it with great enthusiasm – or not at all. Characteristically, Leos will spend more than they can afford on their children, sometimes for the wrong reasons. They will be enormously proud of them, and if the children themselves are lively and enthusiastic there will be a great deal of family happiness. However, if the child is timid and shy, the parents should be careful not to swamp the child with their own exuberance. On the whole, though, Leo parents should get a great deal of fun out of bringing up their children.

The Leo child needs careful handling. He may well be too full of himself, and although his spirit must never be curbed, he does need guidance. It should be made clear that, splendid though he no doubt is, he is not the only child in the world, nor even the cleverest. Criticism should be carefully expressed, for if his enthusiasm is dampened, he may not be too keen to try again. If he shows himself to be satisfied when he has not made a proper effort, it is better to *show* him how to improve than just to carp. He must also be taught not to be bossy, since too much freedom in this direction can lead to pomposity in the future.

VIRGO

Feminine Earth Mutable
Ruling planet: Mercury
Keywords: Critically, analytically

The Myth According to Hesiod, Virgo (also called Astraes) was the daughter of Jupiter and Themsis, and was goddess of Justice. When the Golden Age ended, and men defied her rule, she returned to the heavens in disgust.

Positive Virgoan traits Discriminating, analytical, meticulous; modest; tidy.

Negative Virgoan traits Fussy, a worrier, hypercritical, over-fastidious; abnormally conventional; finicky.

Character A hard worker, extremely practical and with a great appetite for detail, the Virgoan at his best is both careful and eager to help his fellows. He thrives on constant activity, and has a lot of nervous energy to burn. The trouble is that he finds it very difficult to let up; his ideas on relaxation seem like hard work to others. If Mercury, the ruling planet, is in Libra, there will be a greater ability to relax. Mercury, incidentally, also rules Gemini; but Virgoans are not so flighty.

The Virgoan's flair for detail can dominate him; in his quest for perfection in minutiae he can all too easily lose sight of the overall picture. Mercury will again have a powerful bearing on this tendency, and if Virgo is the Sun-sign and Mercury in Leo, there will be a better grasp of the total situation than otherwise.

The driving Virgoan motive is 'to serve' and, one way or another, he will gratify it. Precision and neatness are natural to him, and go with a purity which, as the sign's name suggests, is akin to virginity; in some cases this can build up a psychological barrier which is very difficult to break down, and which can make Virgoans seem particularly stand-offish. If they can work out a proper balance, their charitable, willing characteristics can make them very good friends; in such circumstances their natural reservation can be charming.

It is perhaps as a result of the 'purity' associated with the sign that Virgoans often take a considerable interest in health and hygiene; they often become vegetarians, or at least take a firm interest in diet.

Mind The Virgoan mind may not be of the highest intellectual order, if only because it lacks breadth of vision; but it is

Sun-sign period c 24 August to 23 September

Alice in the Land of Virgo
The Virgoan face is fastidious and intelligent, with a pleasant, kindly air, especially about the eyes. The forehead is high, nose thin and chin pointed. The mouth is well formed and the jawline broad. It is a face of fine distinction. All these qualities are summed up in the Alice of *Alice in Wonderland* by Lewis Caroll. Alice is neat, clean, meticulous with an eye for detail. At the same time she is critical and is extremely annoyed when she forgets her poems!

probably more capable than any other of analytical and detailed assimilation of facts. Confronted with a problem, the Virgoan's immediate instinct is to break it down and analyze it, missing no aspect or detail of the situation. To know how, why, when and where is enormously important to his well-being. He will thus be a wonderful researcher, and his shrewdness and logicality work well – though he must be careful not to clutter his work with fussy, irrelevant detail, clogging the main issue.

Virgo is a sign which brings worry. Virgoans often suffer inhibition and restriction, which surfaces in a tendency to be nervous or highly-strung. This can bring with it periods of considerable tension which in turn can affect the health, leading to intestinal upsets, skin eruptions and ulcers.

The Virgoan should try hard to allow the emotional levels of his personality positive freedom of expression. If he can turn his splendidly analytical attributes inward on himself, he may well find that his difficulties originate in an abnormal concern with small, unimportant details. Hypochondria is not uncommon.

Emotional Relationships The association of Virgo with chastity is so obvious it hardly needs restating; but it is a direct association, and can make emotional relationships difficult. It is not always easy for the Virgoan in love to express himself as fully or ardently as he really wants to. But the position of Venus has an important effect here: if Virgo is the Sun-sign and Venus occupies the same sign, the difficulties and inhibitions may be increased; but if Venus is in Libra, there will be a greater freedom of expression and warmth of feeling, making for easier relationships.

Career Secretary, analytical scientist, statistician, gardener, accountant, teacher; any career connected with health and hygiene; inspector, craftsman.

The ideal post for a Virgoan girl is a secretarial one: perhaps, indeed, she will make an ideal secretary – immaculate in a neat navy-blue-and-white dress, with an impossibly tidy desk, ready to perform precisely any task her boss may give her! This is a typical picture of the Virgoan. They like routine, and work which calls on their ability to cope with fine, tricky detail. They are at their best in supporting roles: they do not make very good heads of departments; their organizational abilities are not strong, and they are at their best working in the background, giving stability and practical help to those around them. At root the Virgoan needs security and a firm financial background to his work. Nursing is in many ways another ideal career, and they make excellent analysts of all kinds.

If Virgo is the rising sign, Gemini (the other Mercury sign) is often on the Midheaven, and a reference to Geminian careers is particularly relevant. With additional strength from Mercury, one might find for instance that the Virgoan would make an excellent literary critic, or, leaning still more towards Gemini, the need to communicate may be very powerful, and a career as a newspaper reporter or commentator would be successful.

The Virgoan will enjoy his hobbies, and will be constantly 'doing' or 'making' in his spare time. Gardening, walking or cycling are excellent for him.

Parent and Child The Virgoan love of neatness and tidiness can make him, and especially her, a difficult parent. The Virgoan mother, above all during periods of nervous tension, can be upset out of all proportion when her children come home from school dirty or untidy, and walk over her nice clean floor. But although there is a tendency to be over-critical, the Virgoan can happily encourage his children to spend their free time usefully and practically, and is particularly helpful with detailed work (homework, for example). He must watch the relationship closely, however, because he may be a little distant towards his children, and in extreme cases there may even be a lack of real warmth and affection. This is a tendency that should be carefully watched; where necessary, an effort should be made to develop a more positive attitude.

Teachers love Virgoan children: neat exercise books, always asking the right questions, excellent at tidying up after less careful children . . . all these qualities will appear once the child settles into the school routine. And he needs that routine, as well as the discipline of school. Not that he will accept discipline unquestioningly (his mind is too inquiring for that); but he will always be extremely reasonable if what is demanded of him is properly explained. Out of school, he should be encouraged to paint, to create, to make things. The girls will be good at dressmaking and boys will soon take an interest in bicycles and construction kits.

LIBRA

Masculine Air Cardinal
Ruling planet: Venus
Keywords: Harmoniously, together

The Myth There is no ancient myth involving Libra; but about 2000 BC the constellation was associated with the judgment of the living and dead in Babylonian religions, and Zibanitu, the Scales, weighed the souls. In Egypt, the harvest was weighed when the Moon was full in Libra.

Positive Libran traits Charming, prizing harmony and pleasant living conditions; an easy-going nature; romantic; diplomatic; idealistic; refined.

Negative Libran traits Indecisive, resentful; frivolous, changeable, flirtatious; easily influenced by others; gullible; oscillating between two extremes.

Character The Libran must, in all spheres of his life, express himself; and other people must accept that expression generously and fully. A favourite complaint of the Libran is: 'It's not fair that he should treat me like that *after all I've done for him!*' Of course, 'he' may simply be incapable of responding as fully as the Libran might wish; but the Libran will find this difficult to accept. In any event, a permanent emotional relationship in which the give and take are well balanced is an absolute pre-requisite for the Libran if he is to be happy, and is to develop properly as a person.

Hating quarrels, the Libran has great natural charm and a winning manner; the pretty Libran girl will easily wind her employer round her little finger in order to secure the extra salary she needs to buy that pretty hat or that new dress. In avoiding all forms of quarrels and upsets, the Libran reveals a characteristic tendency to try to be all things to all men. Certainly, too, there is indecision – the worst of Libran faults. 'We must just wait and see what happens,' he cries; and wait he will, putting off a decision, or a mildly unsavoury job, for as long as possible. Librans have a reputation for laziness, but often they are not as soft as they seem; they are usually fairly eager to get what they want, and may appear lazy simply because of their indecision. A Libran may adopt a *pose* of charming inactivity; but while in one case this may simply be a pause between one activity and the next, in another it may well be very consciously adopted and used. The Libran may be indecisive, but when he does decide that he wants something, he generally gets it, one way or another.

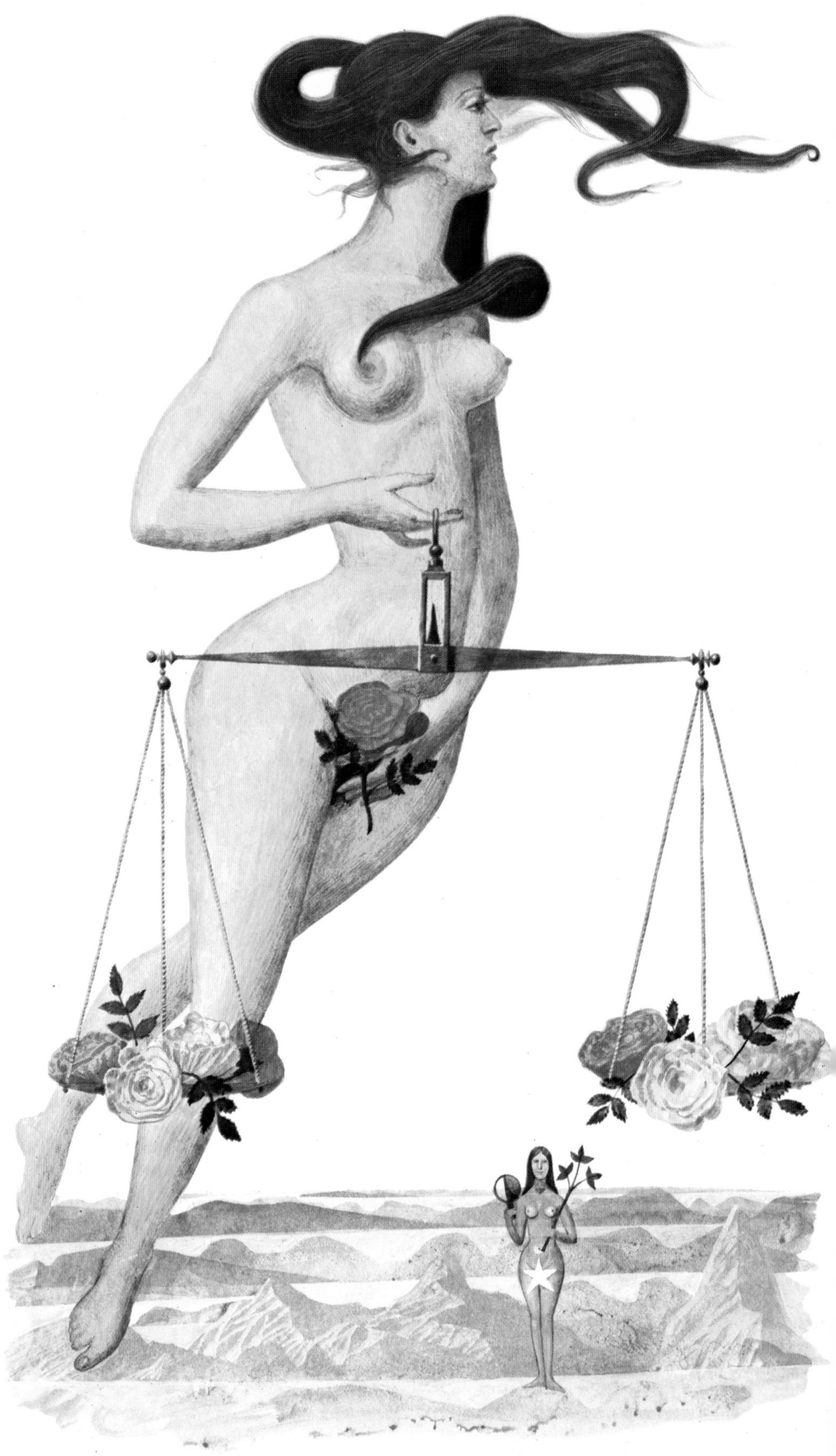

Sun-sign period
c 24 September to
23 October

Emma Bovary – a one-sided Libran
From the soft hair to the elegant neck the Libran face is one of refinement and poise. There are no coarse features; the eyes are calm, usually blue or brown, the nose slightly pointed and the mouth well-formed and wide. There is a definite sense of softness in the Libran Madame Bovary, the pathetic heroine of Gustave Flaubert's classic novel. She exhibits all negative aspects of Libra, gullible, frivolous and discontented and would have been a happier woman if Flaubert had given her some of the more positive traits of the Sign.

The Libran makes an excellent and thoughtful host: his home will be comfortable and 'pretty'. Guests will be greeted pleasantly, and will find the atmosphere restorative and relaxing.

Mind One of the reasons why the Libran is often indecisive is because he sees far too clearly all sides of every problem, and finds it extremely difficult to decide which side to take. He has a strong sense of justice, and will certainly do his best to see that justice is done (preferably without becoming personally involved). His instinct is usually right, and will help him to make decisions, by indicating a particular course of action.

He should always try to form his *own* opinions, for he will find himself very easily swayed by the views of others, and may even come to rely on a stronger personality to form his opinions for him. This can subsequently confuse him to the point where he seems incapable of thinking for himself. Mercury in Virgo will help to sharpen his mind; but in Libra, Mercury will make the problem of indecision even worse.

Cheerful, natural optimists, Librans cannot bear loneliness, and their lack of natural resistance to it can deflate their naturally positive spirits. This antipathy gives them a strong desire for partnership, not only in business or private life, but in their intellectual life also. The intellectual kinship they will feel for one person (or, perhaps, a writer or artist) will often be balanced by an equal and opposite antipathy for another – thus maintaining the theme so aptly expressed in the sign's very glyph – a symbol of 'scales' or 'balances'.

Emotional Relationships 'Falling in love with love' will be one problem for the Libran, so anxious to share his life that he may rush into an emotional relationship before he is ready for it. A difficult partner will find it all too easy to take advantage of his pleasantly casual qualities. The placing of Venus is crucial in this respect, and should be very carefully considered.

Career Beautician, dress designer, hairdresser, milliner; luxury trades generally; diplomat, welfare worker, receptionist, valuer, high-wire performer or juggler; but any work which is carried on in pleasant surroundings, and which is creative or appreciative of art.

The Libran is far better working in partnership than alone. If he thinks of going into business (and he will have a good business sense, even if he may be too kind to his rivals) he should always do so with a partner. Who should take the lead in the partnership is another matter; although his Chart should provide a fairly clear answer. In most cases, responsibilities will be fairly evenly shared, while the partner will have to learn to cope with the Libran's over-extravagance!

As to the kind of business most suited to him, it should certainly not involve difficult, dirty or unpleasant working conditions – he just will not be able to cope. He will have creative, artistic ability, and a flair for design, or at least for knowing what 'looks good' with what. Dress designing, dressmaking, hairdressing, millinery, are some obvious possibilities. Fashion, art dealing, or perhaps the recording business or a business concerned with musical instruments would also be suitable. The Libran's natural tact and diplomacy will make him an admirable 'front man', with the ability to make clients feel happy and at ease.

Parent and Child The affectionate Libran will like an affectionate child; and he will no doubt see to it that he is a polite child, too. Easy-going with their children, Librans also like them to look their best, and the Libran mother will spend an above-average amount of time and money in ensuring that they are well dressed; if they tend to be tomboyish or careless, she will be distressed. Libran parents will pretend to be disciplinarians, but their threats are rarely carried out. Over a period of time the crafty child will see this, and take advantage of it.

The Libran child's abundant charm will be used to his own advantage; but he will be extremely pleasant and friendly, with affable ways and manners, and he is not likely to need strong discipline. Chiefly, he should be encouraged to make his own decisions, and not to rely on parents or elder brothers and sisters for support. Encouragement to work steadily should also be given, because he may be all too quick to say that he doesn't feel like working. He should be encouraged to develop his artistic interests, and if possible should be allowed music and dancing lessons, and access to art materials. He will be adaptable enough to settle into most school routines, although he may suffer from the behaviour of rougher, uncouth children. He will not understand them and they, on their side, will probably be jealous of him because he will be instantly liked by the school staff.

SCORPIO

Feminine Water Fixed
Ruling planet: Pluto (traditionally, Mars)
Keywords: Intensively, passionately

The Myth At Juno's command the Scorpion rose from the earth to attack Orion. The Scorpion also caused the horses of the Sun to bolt when driven for a day by the boy Phaethon; Jove rebuked it with a thunderbolt.

Positive Scorpian traits Powerful feelings and emotions; a sense of purpose; highly imaginative, discerning, subtle; persistent, determined.

Negative Scorpian traits Jealous, resentful, stubborn; obstinate and intractable; secretive and suspicious.

Character Nearly every description of Scorpio emphasizes the depth of his passions, usually in sexual terms. But the Scorpian is passionate in other fields of his life: in his politics, in work, and in play. A peculiar intensity permeates his whole personality, giving him an extremely strong sense of purpose in life, and a determination to do nothing by halves. He must live his life to the full, and will usually over-indulge himself, not only in play, but in work, too.

He can be a very jealous person – again, not only in love. Whoever holds a position to which the Scorpio feels entitled will be disliked, and the Scorpio may even in extremity resort to some kind of victimization or even cruelty. His enormously powerful energy gives him hidden depths which are often unsuspected by less emotional people. When this force is properly channelled, it can give the Scorpio great qualities of endurance; he will battle against severe odds to win – sometimes to the point of trampling on others in the process.

The fact that the eagle was sometimes used as a symbol for this sign underlines not only this harsh tendency – the power to seize on an unsuspecting prey – but the power also to rise above worldly difficulties, to soar away from any earthbound antagonism. This side of his personality will make the Scorpio revolt from too pedestrian or dull an occupation – something he is able to do almost too easily, for he is quick to adapt to turning-points in his life: when he comes to such a point, he finds it easy to accept that one path has ended, and willingly turns to another. He may even force himself to leave one road and embark on another, working hard to build a career and then, for reasons obscure to others as they are profound in him, destroy what he has built, and start

Sun-sign period c 24 October to 22 November

James Bond – Scorpio Rampant
The Scorpio's face expresses his energetic, determined and passionate character. The general impression is dark and swarthy, with even a hint of the satanic about the penetrating eyes. The forehead and eyebrows are heavy, the cheekbones flat and fleshy. The mouth is firm and the chin determined, almost bulldog. James Bond, created by Ian Fleming, is the best example in fiction: the sex, violence and love of life that fill the Bond books, mark off their hero as more than typical of the Sign. His ruthless pursuit of women and readiness for any assignment that M gives him are further strong indications.

again. A masochistic instinct may contribute to this pattern of behaviour.

Scorpios have great personal magnetism: there is always something exciting, dynamic and fascinating about them, and a certain mystery. Others feel it in the Scorpio's company, as they may feel the tremors of a volcano about to erupt.

Mind Although the Scorpio does not lack reasoning power, has a strong sense of perception, and an analytical mind capable of penetrating to the root of any problem which faces him, he also has a high intuitive level. If he feels that a problem should be handled from a certain direction, he will more than likely be right.

His approach to problems is not easily determined, however, not because of the problems themselves, but because he finds it difficult to understand his own reactions to them. He tends to concentrate on analyzing his reactions rather than the problem itself, and in certain cases can – quite unnecessarily – turn in upon himself feelings of resentment and jealousy. Finally these will burst from him, perhaps in the form of an unwarranted quarrel. The more he tries to control this repressive tendency, the better he will be able to direct his high-powered emotions in a positive fashion.

Emotional Relationships The Scorpio's powerful emotional level finds a positive outlet through sex. This sphere of his life, too, can suffer from unwarranted jealousy which is definitely his worst trait. He loves intensely, passionately, ardently and enduringly; should his sex life be unsatisfactory, he will find it very difficult to fill this gap in his life and personality.

Career Psychiatrist, psychologist, detective, policeman, butcher undertaker, pathologist, sewage worker, pharmacist, psychic medium, spiritualist healer, criminal; work in insurance, big business or the armed forces. Anything that taxes his abilities to their fullest extent.

The Scorpio will be happiest when he is convinced that his work is really important; trivialities leave him cold. He will be at his best examining the roots of problems, personal or otherwise: as a psychologist discovers, analyzes and resolves his patients' problems, or as a detective brings light to what is hidden. From another angle, we find the criminal himself, working and planning in secret for his own ends, expressing to the full the Scorpio's clandestine leanings. These may stem from resentment of society at large, and more specifically of people occupying positions of power, privilege or wealth to which he feels himself entitled. He is a bad man to make an enemy of since his resentment is long lasting.

Study will not be difficult for the Scorpio if it involves research rather than speculation. A hard worker, he will gear his intensity happily to an academic career, readily undertaking long periods of study, often in specialist branches of medicine – (surgery or psychiatry, for instance). Scorpios make good soldiers or sailors: they like discipline and respond to it, perhaps with a view to inflicting it themselves in due time. In this they reveal a judicious smattering of the masochism and sadism which is, however faintly, part of their make-up.

Parent and Child As might be expected from his main characteristics, the Scorpio parent tends to be over-demanding in his role, and may be rather too strict. However, remembering his great talent for enjoying life, it is likely that he will enjoy the company of his children, and keep them busy with outings and visits. The Scorpio is generally speaking stubborn and fixed in his opinions; obviously these tendencies will not encourage him to give way easily when his children ask for favours. He must from time to time revise his opinions, especially in contemporary and controversial issues, otherwise he will not easily bridge that particular generation gap.

The Scorpio child must be kept busy, and be allowed plenty of outlet for his highly powered emotional energy. Toy forts, books about knights in shining armour, and detective stories will engross the boys; boys and girls alike should swim early in life, and will probably like robust sports. Aggression is likely to be considerable, and it is best if this is brought out in boxing.

The Scorpio's tendency to be secretive should be developed positively in the children. They should, for instance, be allowed to plan surprises for the rest of the family. The slightest tendency to jealousy, especially on the arrival of younger brothers and sisters, can be overcome by informing them thoroughly about such events. They should be encouraged to help their mother when a young baby is on the scene.

SAGITTARIUS

Masculine Fire Mutable
Ruling planet: Jupiter
Keywords: Widely, freely, exploratively

The Myth Sagittarius, with his two faces, animal and human, was the centaur Cheiron who raised Jason, Achilles and Aeneas. Famous as a prophet, doctor and scholar he was the son of Philyra by Cronus, also the father of Zeus, who, surprised in the act, turned himself into a stallion and galloped off, leaving Philyra; she, disgusted at her half-human, half-horse child, turned herself into a linden-tree.

Positive Sagittarian traits Jovial, optimistic; versatile, open-minded, adaptable, having good judgment and a philosophical, freedom-loving outlook; sincere and frank; dependable and scrupulous.

Negative Sagittarian traits Prone to exaggeration, extremism; tactless, restless, careless; blindly optimistic; boisterous; irresponsible, capricious.

Character Careless in his youth, given to driving fast cars with little regard for safety, over-pleased with the sense of excitement it provides him, the Sagittarian at least learns more from his mistakes than other signs. Although his delight in personal freedom never leaves him, he will eventually be able to make full use of formidable intellectual potential, studying serious, perhaps philosophical subjects.

His early years will be somewhat unconventional: he will turn up at a dinner-party in a sweater when everyone else is formally dressed, and he will give the impression of being more interested in sports and outdoor activities than in the intellectual exercise which he really needs.

He will particularly enjoy exploring subjects unknown to him – languages are a Sagittarian field – storing his knowledge and later putting it to good use. He will set his sights on an objective which seems beyond him; as it comes within reach, he will raise his sights still higher and be anxious to start on a new project almost before he has completed the old one.

The Sagittarian always needs to feel free: he cannot stand the slightest feeling of claustrophobia, either physical (the small room with a window facing a blank wall) or emotional (the marriage which, he feels, ties him down). The symbolism which gives the Sagittarian symbol a free-ranging, pointed arrow (aimed straight at his objective) and often the body of a horse, is significant. He will often be devoted to riding, as well as

Sun-sign period c 23 November to 22 December

Henry Higgins – the Sagittarian Teacher
Usually oval in shape, the Sagittarian face is aristocratic and refined. The hair is often fair and curly and the eyebrows arched. The nose is long, straight and Greek, according well with the almond-shaped, expressive eyes. The mouth is well-formed and the chin pointed; Sometimes the face can have rather a sharp look about it. Henry Higgins, the famous character from *Pygmalion* by Bernard Shaw, or the musical version, *My Fair Lady*, sums up the Sagittarian. The irascible professor has his idealistic side and was certainly adaptable and open-minded; but his exaggeration and tactlessness make him equally memorable as an example of the often infuriatingly unconventional Sagittarian mind.

to other sports which involve movement through open country. His exploration of the unknown may well be both physical and intellectual, and it is certainly true of him that 'to travel hopefully is better than to arrive'. His life must always contain some element of challenge.

The Sagittarian is versatile and, like the Geminian, needs to have more than one task on hand at a time. It is not unusual for him to hold down two jobs. As he needs a great deal of intellectual exercise, so he needs an above-average amount of physical exercise. If he feels tired, it usually means he is bored, and a change of occupation will be restorative. Every effort should be made to keep this restlessness under control, as otherwise it will cause considerable unhappiness to the subject and his marriage partner.

Mind The Sagittarian may overlook details, but his overall sense of planning is admirable. Once trained and disciplined, his mind is capable of a great deal. He is at his best dealing with old problems on new lines; each difficulty will be approached from several angles, perhaps unusual ones, and there will inevitably be a great deal of reassessment.

The challenge of a problem is a delight to a Sagittarian, for it caters to his pleasure in exploration, in pushing his mind ever outward – whether he is tracking down a mysterious noise beneath the bonnet of his car, or cracking the code of some ancient language. It is always the *challenge* – why *should* A plus B equal C – that grips him, rather than the problem itself, and its solution.

He will not be a worrying type – in fact there is some danger of blind optimism. He can have moralistic tendencies, particularly in old age, when he may too easily forget what it was like to be young.

Emotional Relationships Needing a lively, inventive sex life, the Sagittarian is not interested only in his partner's body; intellectually, she must be well equipped. It is not easy for the Sagittarian to settle into an emotional relationship in which he may have to make allowances for a difference of intellect. He needs, in addition, to feel that he retains some freedom. Jealousy or possessiveness in his partner will quickly shrivel his affection, and if his marriage suffers in this way, other spheres of his life will also suffer – and with this double burden he will more than likely break free.

Career Teacher, professor, lecturer, philosopher; lawyer, barrister; interpreter; veterinary surgeon, horse trainer; travel agent, explorer; sportsman, jockey; priest; publisher, writer, librarian, bookseller.

There must of course be many Sagittarians condemned to a lifetime of grindingly dull work in the office or on the factory floor. But they will not easily accept the situation, even if they have not initially had the opportunity of further education. They will identify with the intellect, and with study; there will be evening classes, perhaps, or advanced reading. Identification will occur in other ways – even on the level of working for a man whose intellect attracts and intrigues them sufficently.

The Sagittarian's need for challenge is at its height in the sphere of his career, and his ambitions must have positive expression. As a means of escape from dull conditions, he may take up physical exercise, sometimes in the form of extrovert sports.

With their need to feel free Sagittarians often love animals since they make no emotional demands, and will make good careers in veterinary work, or some other job concerning animals: jockeys and dog breeders are often Sagittarians.

Parent and Child Challenge, again, is the key-word: natural optimism bolsters the Sagittarian's faith in his children, and he will find the whole business of parenthood a constant challenge to him. He may expect too much on an intellectual level – so eager is he for his children to progress that he may, for example, weigh them down with books too advanced for their age. But he will have great fun with them, and they will often make just as much progress at home as at school, because of their wonderfully stimulating home background.

The Sagittarian child may tend to be a little wild, the girls somewhat tomboyish; but he will be good at games and athletics, and naturally intelligent. He will not like restrictive discipline, and will feel extremely inhibited if too tied; parents and teachers may occasionally have to meet to iron out difficulties. In their spare time, Sagittarian children like to ride, to study languages, and – being usually strong and well-built – to play games; sometimes dancing is a big attraction for both boys and girls who enjoy using their energy.

CAPRICORN

Feminine Earth Cardinal
Ruling planet: Saturn
Keywords: Prudently, aspiringly, calculatedly

The Myth The mythological associations of Capricorn are uncertain, though there is a faint reference to Pan – whose mother ran from him because of his ugliness, but whose success in seducing nymphs was notable. An ancient Babylonian god was Ea, known as the 'antelope of the subterranean ocean' – the fish-tailed goat also called *kusarikku*, the fish-ram.

Positive Capricornian traits Reliable, determined, ambitious; careful, prudent; a sense of humour; a sense of discipline; patient, persevering.

Negative Capricornian traits Rigid outlook; over-exacting; pessimistic; conventional; miserly, mean; a 'wet blanket'.

Character One astrological writer summed up the two types of Capricornian by describing the two types of goat: the giddy mountain goat, stepping neatly from crag to crag, always moving on to nibble greener grass further up the mountain; and the domestic goat restricted to the small patch of grass within the circle allowed him by a post and chain.

Generally speaking, Capricornians are ambitious, always looking out for promotion or a raise in salary. They do not have to keep up with the people next door; they either *are* the people next door, or are already ahead of them. They are splendid businessmen, and the positive Capricornian will surely make the grade if he sets out to do so. Capricornian wives will do their share of pushing their husbands (and themselves) up the social ladder.

So much for the mountain goat. The domestic goat, stuck in the valley, is sad indeed. He too has ambition: but try as he may – and he *will* try – the burdens of competition will simply be too much for him. If he is wise, he will find his own quiet, safe level in a simple job he can do quietly, unruffled, in his own way, in his own time.

One of the most delightful Capricornian traits is their sense of humour. Capricornians are basically people of few words; but their dry, somewhat dour comments can be extremely funny. Often their smile is a smile in reverse – a turning down of the corners of the mouth, sometimes accompanied by a deep grunt! Capricornians are reliable, patient, cautious – perhaps to a fault – and can bear considerable hardship if circumstances demand it. They tend to be conventional,

Sun-sign period c 23 December to 19 January

Old Grandet – the Capricornian Miser
The Capricornian face is formal and often grim. This effect is heightened by the deep frown lines on the forehead and beetle-browed, shrewd eyes. There is a serious, reserved cast to the mouth and jawline that expresses the ambitious, persevering character underneath. Old Grandet, the father of Eugénie Grandet by Honoré de Balzac typifies the Capricornian. He was harsh, a strong disciplinarian who tried to instil into his daughter his own avariciousness. Mean to the point of rationing his household to a single candle he was incapable of understanding Eugénie's generosity. As he was dying he grasped the cross from the priest administering the last rights: for the feel of gold.

and find it particularly difficult to identify with the emotional freedom and permissiveness of their young contemporaries.

Generally speaking, the Capricornian is a self-contained person, and because so much of his energy is geared towards his career interests and prestige, he may tend to miss some of the more human elements of life. His sense of discipline and purpose need not dehumanize him, though this can happen in extreme cases.

Mind The Capricornian's mind is extremely rational and serious. His thought-patterns are constructive, and he has great ability to plan ahead in detail. He will be able to cast aside anything which does not come up to his standards of propriety; and once he has made a move, he will not step back. The phrase 'cool and calculating' is perhaps the most apt way of summing up the Capricornian's mental outlook. He will not be quick to grasp situations, or to study: essentially, he must plod. But once something *is* fully understood or learned, he will not forget it. The Capricornian is a worrier, and is the most prone to depression of all the signs. If Mercury is in Scorpio, his mind will have greater depth and subtlety; but if it is in Aquarius there will be a more positive outlook, and overall the mind will be more forward-looking.

Emotional Relationships The Capricornian can find human relationships very difficult, above all in intimate circumstances. This may be a fault of communication due to shyness, or because he considers business more important. But, whatever the situation may be he tends to feel alone.

When Capricorn rises, these tendencies are rather lessened, and the Capricornian will make a cherishing and protective husband. But when Capricorn is the Sun-sign the position of Venus should be carefully assessed to guard against any possible bad influences.

Career Civil servant, mathematician, politician, osteopath, scientist, teacher, engineer, farmer, mineralogist, musician, builder, architect, surveyor, dentist; administrator of any kind.

The Capricornian needs security, and a regular pay-cheque, and this should be kept in mind when choosing a career. Any attempt to 'get rich quick' would not be likely to appeal; and should be discouraged if it does. The Capricornian should try to make steady progress; in the long term, the sky is the limit, and by hook or by crook he will reach the top of his profession. He likes fame, and being in the public eye; his career can be so important to him that all else is excluded. At some time during his life, he will more than likely be attracted to the potentially ruthless world of politics. The sign often gives musical ability, particularly so if Taurus and Libra are prominent in the Chart, or if Venus is sensitively placed.

If the Capricornian has no ambition – if he is a 'domestic goat' – he must find a career that is secure and not too demanding. He is a creature of habit, and satisfaction will come through small things, and through a sense of permanance and durability. Reading, listening to records, and rock-climbing are suitable recreations.

Parent and Child The Capricornian's pre-occupation with his child's success can get out of hand. He (or the Capricornian mother) may tend to dominate his children. His delightful sense of humour should certainly be brought into play, and he should always be ready with praise, encouraging his children to aspire, as he does, to better things. He should make a conscious effort to bring fun into his children's lives. The tendency to play the 'heavy father' can be in evidence; although sometimes the father is pre-occupied with business interests, and may quite genuinely be too busy. Too much responsibility may then fall on the mother. The Capricornian mother must be careful not to go back to work while her children are too young, even if she does find domesticity tedious – this may cause a lack of affection.

Young Capricornians should be encouraged to take an interest in music, natural history, archaeology, rock- and mountain-climbing. They can be good athletes, but may not find it easy to integrate with a team. They are voracious readers and, in order to ensure exercise, individual initiative in sport should be encouraged.

The slow Capricornian child may be spurred into action by some such comment as 'could do better if he tried'; and if he does try, and the next school report says 'steady improvement', it is even possible that he may tear himself free of his chain and transform himself from domestic to mountain goat. Unfortunately, this is rare.

AQUARIUS

Masculine Air Fixed
Ruling planet: Uranus (traditionally, Saturn)
Keywords: Independently, humanely

The Myth There are no strong myths associated with Aquarius. The god Hapi, watering from two jars, was an ancient symbol of the river Nile, and in Babylon the god Ea (see also for Capricorn) was sometimes called 'the god with streams'. The Babylonian name for Aquarius, GU.LA, was at first associated with the goddess of childbirth and healing.

Positive Aquarian traits Humanitarian, independent; friendly, willing; a progressive outlook, original, inventive; a reforming spirit; faithful, loyal; idealistic; intellectually inclined.

Negative Aquarian traits Unpredictable, eccentric; rebellious, contrary; tactless; fixed in his opinions; perverse, straining to be unconventional.

Character Kind, friendly, rather distant, and frequently unpredictable; one's first impression of an Aquarian is a sympathetic one, and indeed he will generally be a sympathetic character. But the feeling of distance is also important: the Aquarian will be ready to help others at a moment's notice, but will always remain personally detached. Often it is extremely difficult to feel really close to him.

Personal independence is of enormous importance to him, and he is capable of making great sacrifices for it – even to the point of rejecting intimate relationships. More conventional people will, for these reasons – and because of his unpredictability – find themselves at odds with him, particularly since his pursuit of 'causes' – anti-war protest, maybe, or devotion to a particular charity – will strike them as 'different', even unsympathetic. Their attitude will not worry him: he will shrug his shoulders, used to being 'out on a limb'. He will always have an original streak, and his application of this can range from finding new and original outlets for his artistic talent or scientific ability, to a passion for originality at all costs, leading to crankiness, pseudo-artiness, or wildly unconventional forms of absentmindedness.

Although he will be much in favour of reform and change, and the advancement of the human condition, he may equally be stubborn – modern in outlook, but fixed in his opinion. He is not easily persuaded that he is wrong. Some find this mixture of kind friendliness and obstinate insistence on the rightness of his own opinions very discon-

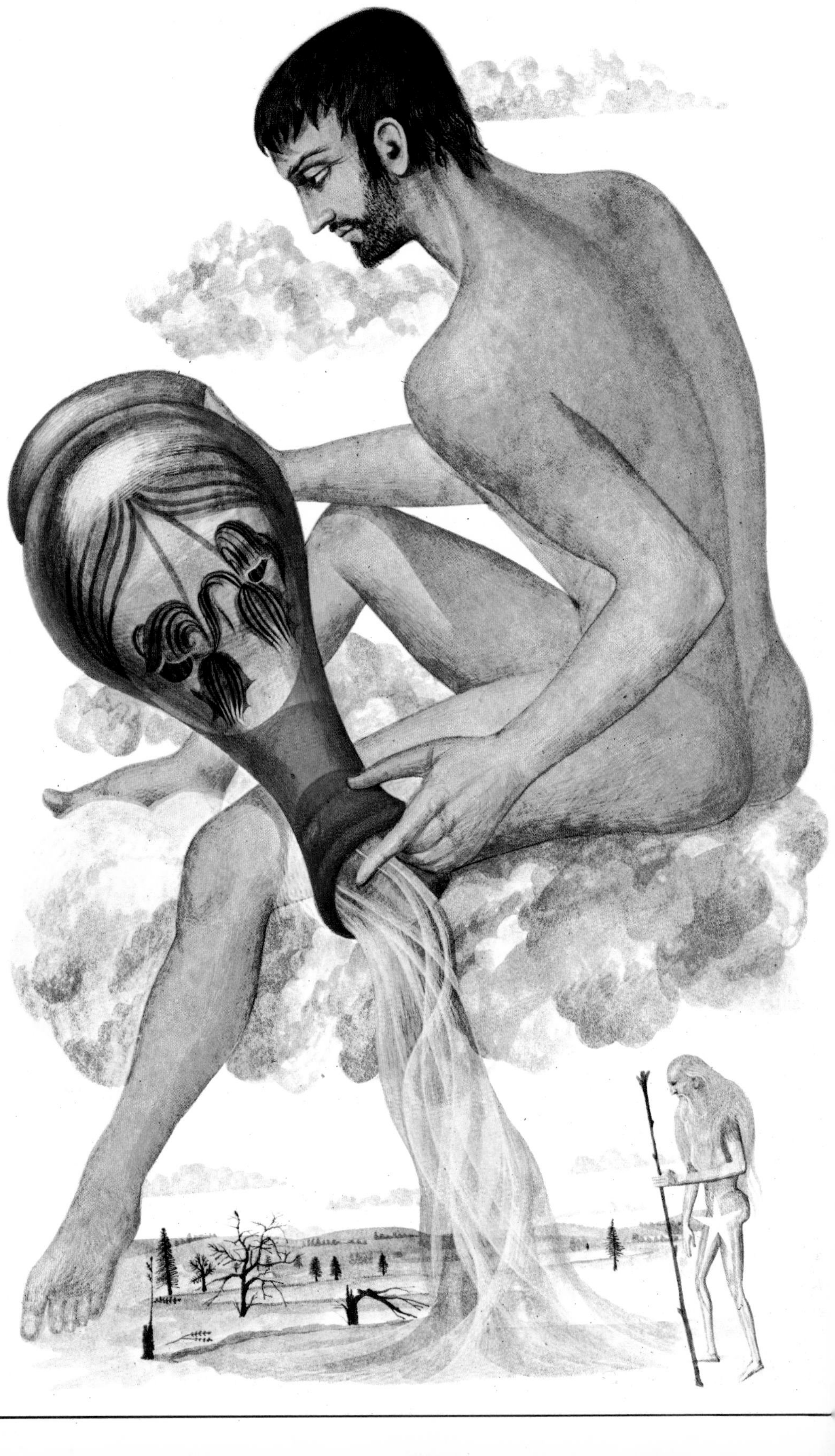

Sun-sign period
c 20 January to
19 February

Alyosha, the Aquarian Karamazov
The Aquarian face is handsome, but not very distinctive. The features are regular with lively eyes, strong nose and wide mouth – all of which lends an air of nobility. However, the jawline is fleshy and not very positive. Alyosha, one of the Brothers Karamazov by Fyodor Dostoyevsky, is a typical Aquarian. He has a strongly developed sense of humanity that sets him above the murder of his father. He does not have the Aquarian's lack of emotion, but certainly possesses the reforming spirit and aloof glamour of the type.

certing. The result is that the Aquarian has an aloof glamour that is fascinating and dynamic – but not warm or endearing.

Mind The Aquarian is not concerned with what other people think, and will often simply not bother to form an opinion of their behaviour. Not that he lacks imagination: his thinking is often ahead of its time, and clean-cut and clinical in style – rational, intelligent and intuitive. He will probably be broadminded, too; though often what one takes for broadmindedness is simply a display of indifference. Not having bothered to find out how other people really think, the Aquarian will let their opinions pass.

His mind is scientific in type: he approaches problems analytically. He may not be a scientist, however, although many Aquarians are. The placing of Mercury must be assessed for a guide to his mental balance. If Aquarius rises, the more unpredictable side of his nature will be stabilized if Mercury is in Taurus, Virgo or Capricorn. If Aquarius is the Sun-sign, there is a good chance of Mercury being in Capricorn; the stability this gives will be off-set somewhat because the Aquarian will also be a little harder and more brittle in character (these characteristics are already evident in the type).

Emotional Relationships The married Aquarian needs to retain a considerable degree of independence, even if there are young children in the family. This will demand a large measure of understanding and tolerance on his partner's side, for it is unwise to give an Aquarian the feeling of being trapped. All in all this does not make family life easy, and it is perhaps true that Aquarians feel most at ease when living alone, able to feel free in all respects. The good Aquarian marriage is extremely stable, however; he is very loyal and faithful, although his dispassionate nature can often prove a source of conflict.

Career Scientist, writer, sociologist, charity worker, astrologer, astronomer, archaeologist, industrial worker (particularly in television), radiographer, inventor; a career in the Air Force or work for the United Nations.

Independence, originality, and scope for inventiveness must be used by the Aquarian if he is to be happy in his work; a dull routine will bore him. These qualities are best used by him in humanitarian work, and one thinks immediately of the United Nations forces: he would be at his best working to raise the standard of living of remote people. He *can* do a dull job, of course; but will be wasted in it; given his head he will be capable of great invention, and will bring a fresh approach to any task he undertakes.

He is a born scientist, and is often involved either in something very new and modern – the space programme, biochemistry, or perhaps the latest astronomical techniques – or in something concerned with the deep past, such as ancient history, research into men's remote origins. Similarly, if he is an actor, he will probably be drawn to the most avant-garde aspects of the theatre.

The Aquarian can utilize his originality and scientific flair in spare-time activities; he may like to learn to fly, or to organize archaeological digs. He will feel strong revolutionary tendencies; whether he makes use of them is a matter for him.

Parent and Child The Aquarian will want his child to be as independent as himself, and he will support the most modern educational techniques. He may also attempt to force an old head onto young shoulders; he will freely discuss all controversial questions with his children, and should have no difficulty in maintaining close contact with them. He may not be eager to change his own opinions; but he will always want to know what is going on in the minds of his children; he will be friendly, rational and kind. If he sounds too ideal, one must remember that it is all too likely that *real* affection may be somewhat lacking; if other members of the family are more generous in showing their affection, the Aquarian parent may find that there is something missing between him and his children. He will not in any event create scenes; he is not made that way.

The Aquarian child should be clever, and ought to be encouraged to develop his natural inventiveness as early as possible. Chemistry sets will attract him, as will books on astronomy. He may be musical, and want to play some slightly unusual intrument – the flute, for instance. He will be quick to learn, and his school reports should be encouraging; but he may tend to be erratic, and should be helped to work evenly, if possible. Like his adult counterpart, he will have considerable charm, and may tend to be somewhat bossy.

PISCES

Feminine Water Mutable
Ruling planet: Neptune
Keywords: Nebulously, impressionably

The Myth Terrified by the giant Typhon, Venus and Cupid hurled themselves into the Euphrates and became fishes. Minerva commemorated the event by placing the fishes in the heavens. The Babylonians knew the constellation as KUN, or the Tails; it was also known as the Leash – upon which were tied the two fish-goddesses Anunitum and Simmah.

Positive Piscean traits Humble, compassionate, sympathetic; emotional; unworldly, sensitive; adaptable, impressionable; kind; intuitive; receptive.

Negative Piscean traits Vague, careless; secretive; easily confused; unable to cope with the practical running of their lives; weak-willed, indecisive.

Character Of all the signs, Pisces is the most susceptible to outside influence. The Piscean is very sensitive indeed, extremely unworldly and impractical, and always eager to try and escape from reality. Other areas of the Chart will show to what extent he is able to counteract these potentially negative tendencies.

On the positive side, the Piscean has great compassion and an ability to relieve the suffering of others: either practically, perhaps by nursing them, or in a more remote sense through prayer or meditation. But he cannot stand too much reality. If he is wise, he escapes 'positively', through the arts – by developing a flair, perhaps on a professional level, for poetry, acting, mime or dancing. If he is unwise, he may allow himself to escape through drugs, which will accentuate his natural weak will and indecisiveness. For this reason he will find it more than usually difficult to fight against their influence and must avoid ever starting to take them.

One can readily use 'watery' metaphors in speaking of Pisceans, for their characteristics are often those of the sea, with its hidden depths, sudden storms, and strong and shifting currents. The Piscean's torrent of emotion is so deep and strong that he himself may be confused and tormented by it. The more he can impose a creative shape on it, the greater chance he has of coming to terms with it psychologically. Some of the world's most inspired artists have this sign prominent in their Charts, and have been able to use their emotions through their art. Confusion, diffuseness and lack of purpose

Sun-sign period
c 20 February to
21 March

Cinderella Pisces
The sensitive, gentle and kind character of Pisceans is showed in the smooth oval of their face. The forehead is fine and the eyebrows are arched over large, round eyes. The almost etherial look is accentuated by the small nose, full cheeks, pointed chin and fine neck. The mouth is generous and can be sensual. Cinderella, from the book by Charles Perrault, is a typical Piscean. Her life of sacrifice, endurance and patience were out of the ordinary. However, it might well have been difficult for her to adjust to the rich living of a Queen.

can turn the Piscean's emotion in on himself – and all will be lost.

It is not easy for the Piscean to conform; he cannot cope with discipline or routine, and will not run his life in anything like a regimented or orderly way. His natural kindness, sympathy, charm and genuine 'softness' will inspire his friends, and because of his delightful manner they will probably not even notice the chaos which all too often abounds in the Piscean home.

Piscean sentimentality can sometimes annoy other, more practical, down-to-earth people; but to make up for this, his devotion and helpfulness to others is something from which more materialistic people can learn, revealing as it does an approach to life so very different to their own.

Mind When the Piscean does present his ideas or decisions in a coherent form, it will probably be without really knowing how they got into that state. He will not lack ideas, but sorting the wheat from the chaff will present great problems. Many of his ideas will indeed be quite impracticable, and someone will have, delicately, to point this out to him. 'Ha!' he will say blandly, 'I'd not thought of it in that way. Of course you are right.'

The Piscean needs a hero: if he is an artist, he will choose someone of the highest calibre in that field. He is likely to be more receptive to religion than those with other signs more prominent; yet his work can be his religion. He needs very strongly to *identify*; he needs to have a source of inspiration – his own god: perhaps a lover.

The Piscean is highly intuitive, and can develop psychic and mediumistic abilities. He should, however, approach these areas with some initial scepticism.

Emotional Relationships The Piscean must be careful in his approach to emotional relationships. He can easily be carried away and discover, when it is too late, that the marvellous attributes he saw in his mistress do not really exist. He will find it difficult to cope with the practical aspects of marriage. He makes a wonderful lover, and has a real flair for the romantic. If Pisces is rising there will be a surprisingly critical attitude towards the partner, which can steady his more nebulous attitudes. Romantic tendencies will be increased if Venus also occupies Pisces.

Career Actor, dancer, writer or poet, fishmonger, shoe trade, Navy, nurse (and the medical profession generally), hypnotist, illusionist, photographer, priest.

The Piscean should not in principle consider a career in which discipline or noise play too great a part. However, he would accept, for instance, the discipline of a life in the nursing profession, because the positive expression of his basic psyche would be so rewarding for him. And if he becomes a professional dancer, he will find himself able to become part of a company and work well within that discipline, because he has the capacity to mould himself to his work and become part of an overall set-up.

Generally speaking, the arts form the core of the Piscean's personality; he is not drawn to science. He may find some difficulty in rationalizing his artistic instincts – which may not come to the fore in his work at all, but in his spare-time activities. But if he can come to terms with his ideas and consciously make something of them, he will be a considerable artist.

Those who feel drawn to a religious life will find the Piscean influence helpful, adding much to their predisposition to healing the sick and lightening others' burdens.

Parent and Child Pisceans will find it difficult to insist on any form of correction – even verbal; and there is for that reason a strong tendency for the children of Pisceans to be spoilt. It is difficult to advise them how to combat this: but the position of the Moon in the Chart can help, if Pisces is the Sun-sign. If Pisces is rising, a slightly harsher critical element may balance over-indulgence.

The Piscean parent will give his children a splendid artistic background; but he must recognize his failings in practical matters – tidiness, punctuality, and so on – and make sure his children do not copy him.

The Piscean child will not be happy at a strict or over-academic school. He will dislike facts, except in the context of such subjects as history, which will stimulate his imagination. He may be good at languages, and should not find it difficult to acquire the necessary accent. He should be allowed to paint, and ballet classes or skating lessons are advisable. He will not like robust sports. The more artistic his interests, the more positive will be the satisfaction he gets.

INTERPRETATIONS

THE BIRTH CHART REVEALED

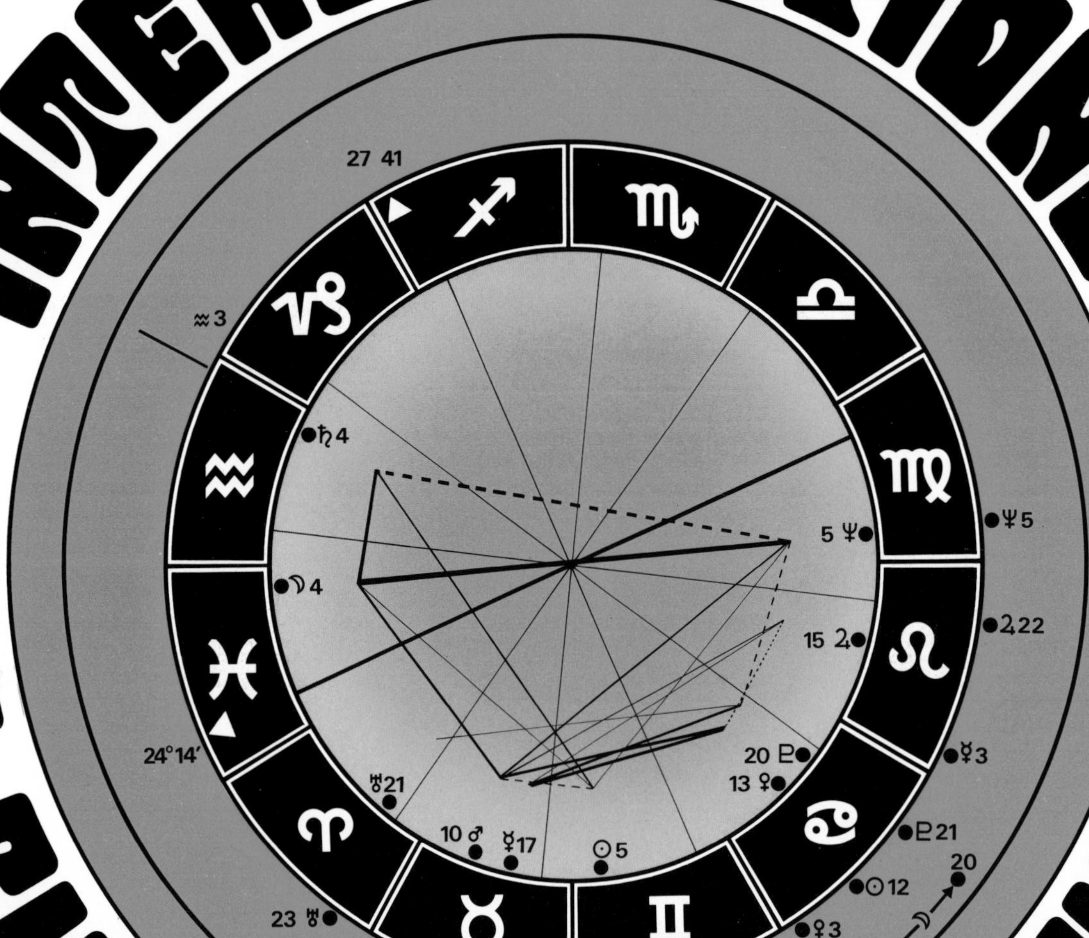

3

First ye haue many pleasant chosen rules for euer, to iudge the Coming Time by the Sunne, Moone, Planetes, with many Tokens extraordinarie: not omittinge the Coniunctions, Quadratures, and Oppositions of Planetes among themselves in the .12. Signes Celestiall. □ Here see a Prognostication general, for euer to take effect, how to tell what May Be. □ Here also diuers profitable collections shewing the iudgement of the Mappes of Children; of Manne and Woman ioined in Matrimonie or other Affection; of the Planetes and they Bodie's Health. □ Finally ye haue a conducible note of the most perfect Calculations Mathematical by which any Manne may make the most particular Discoveries: pleasauntly searched from Tables, new methods of shortening thy Labour may be found, in pages shewing forth the positions of each severall Planete between the yeares of Our Lorde AD 1900 & AD 1975, whose use is playnlye opened. □ With our final hope that the Reader, having been made Free of that which Manye struggled in the makying, may deale honestly in it.

THE ASPECTS

How to Discover and Interpret the Planetary Aspects in the Birth Chart

The Nature of Aspects

The next step in the process of calculating an individual Birth Chart is to work out which are the planets which form aspects to each other.

Planets are 'in aspect' when there are certain specific angular distances between them as they are placed along the ecliptic. The relationship between them reveals the areas of personality where the subject's characteristics can attain to full and positive expression, and other areas in which there may be some experience of psychological stresses and strains. In fact it will be obvious that the aspects are among the most important factors in a Chart.

Calculation

To calculate aspects is not a particularly difficult skill; but care is needed to ensure that none is overlooked – some of the aspects are less noticeable than others, but all are important. As will be seen from the table below, the aspects have their own set of symbols, and these form the third and last part of the astrologer's 'shorthand'.

If the birth time is known with reasonable accuracy, aspects that the planets make to the Ascendant and Midheaven should also be considered. But if the birth time is not known with any great precision, they are best left out.

Planets, then, are 'in aspect' when there are certain specific angular distances between them: an exact *conjunction*, for instance, occupies the same degree and minute of the ecliptic; and in an exact *square* aspect between two planets, they are separated by 90° (e.g. Sun Aries 15° : Moon Cancer 15°). An exact *trine* aspect is one of 120° (e.g. Venus Taurus 27° : Jupiter Capricorn 27°).

But we are permitted to allow what are known as orbs: a number of degrees and minutes which are either more or less than the exact aspect. The orb which is allowable varies in proportion to the strength of the aspect. Powerful aspects – conjunctions, oppositions and trines – can be allowed a greater orb than weaker aspects. For in-

Powerful Aspects
Conjunctions are a focal point in the Birth Chart. Their effect is to lay positive or negative stress according to the Sign and House positions of the planets concerned.
Oppositions accentuate the polarities in a Chart, and can also form a strong integrating link
Squares, depending on position, can indicate tension or give drive and strength to the character.
Trines are helpful to a strong character but may exercise a spoiling effect on shallow people.

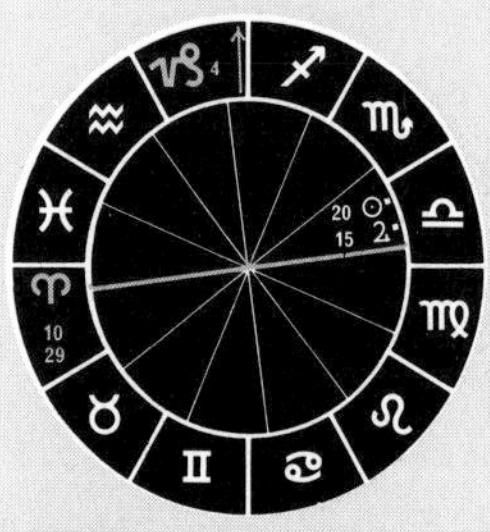

Conjunction
Exact aspect 0°
8° – 9° orb

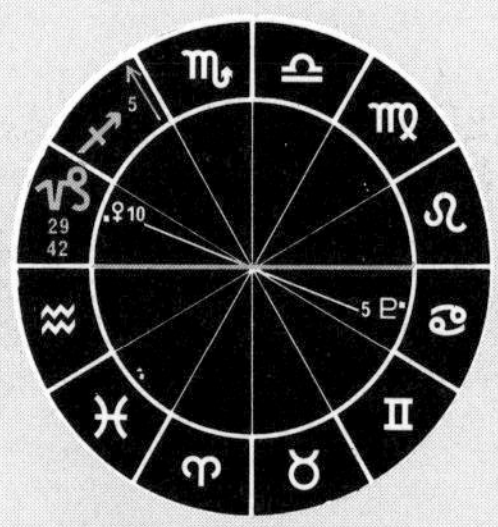

Opposition
Exact aspect 180°
8° – 9° orb

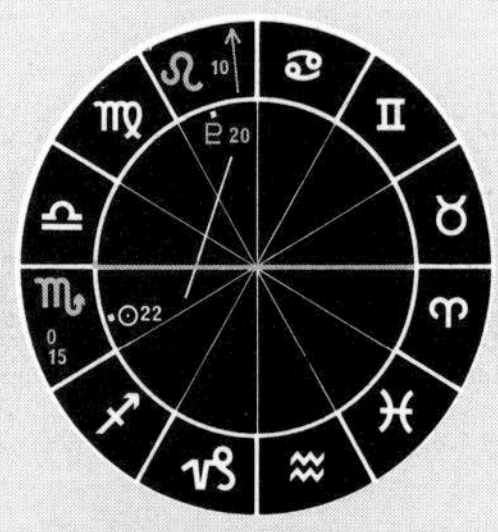

Square
Exact aspect 90°
8° – 9° orb

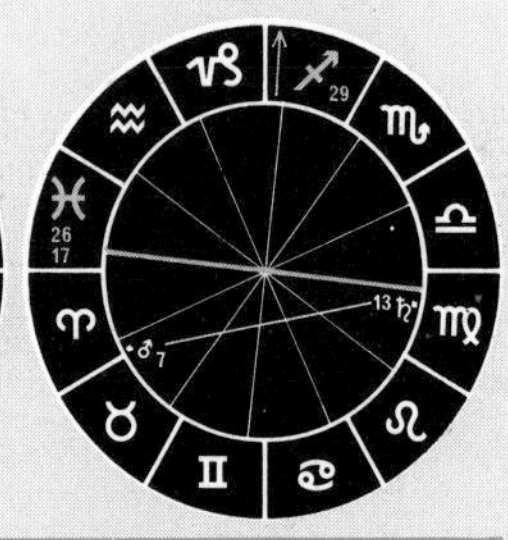

Trine
Exact aspect 120°
8° – 9° orb

Moderate Aspects
Sesquiquadrates indicate strain and should be carefully examined if they occur between two important planets.
Sextiles, like trines, can bring out the pleasant characteristics in a suitable subject though their capacity to influence is not so strong.
The *Quincunx* is an unpredictable aspect. Although it belongs properly in the 'moderate' category, its workings are to a certain extent unorthodox and variable; it may work with more than minor force and so should not be underestimated.

Sesquiquadrate
Exact aspect 135°
2° orb

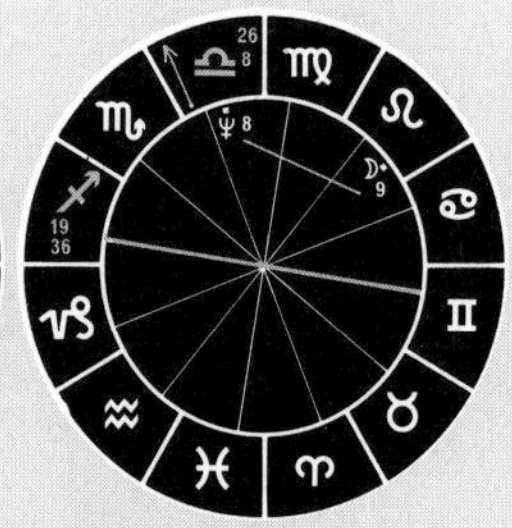

Sextile
Exact aspect 60°
5° – 6° orb

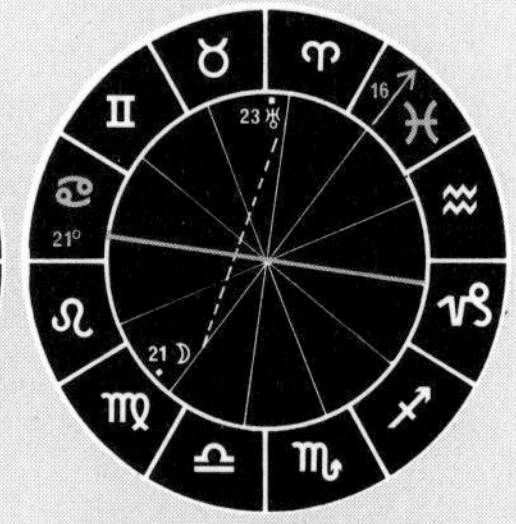

Quincunx
Exact aspect 150°
2° – 3° orb

Weak Aspects
Semi-squares and *Semi-sextiles* are less important but may suggest tension if major planets are involved; between two slow-moving planets unemphasized by a prominent House or Sign, their effect is merely slight, and need not enter into the astrologer's calculations when he is interpreting a Chart.
A range of still weaker aspects – semi-decile, decile, quintile, and bi-quintile – may be found in older text-books but these are seldom if ever used by modern astrologers since their effect is so slight as to be negligible.

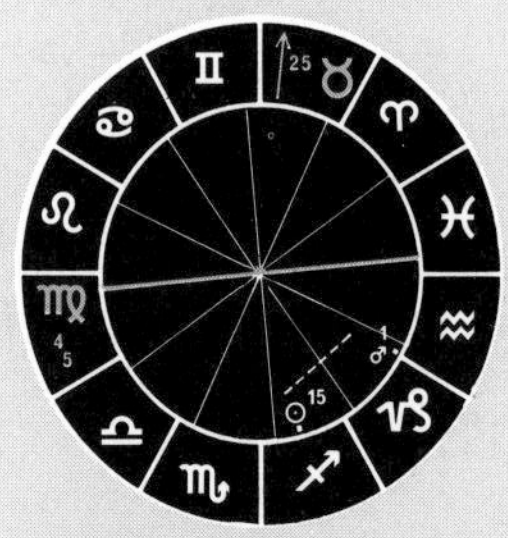

Semi-square
Exact aspect 45°
2° orb

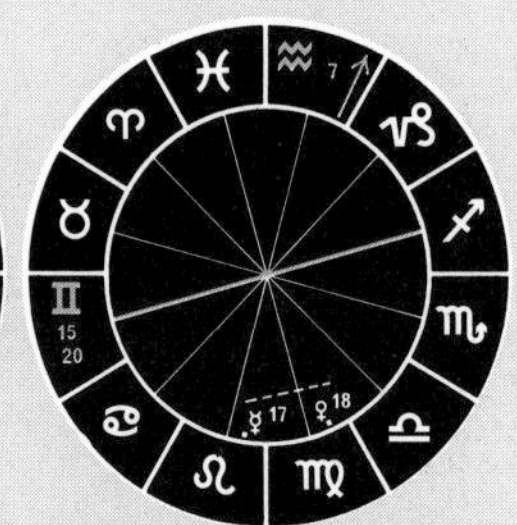

Semi-sextile
Exact aspect 30°
2° orb

Note
There are also strong aspects known as *parallels*. These work in much the same way as conjunctions or oppositions. Parallels are related to the positions of the planets in *declination* (north or south, as opposed to east or west). As it is quite often the case that planets forming parallels in declination are 'in aspect' along the ecliptic, the tables showing the declinations of planets have not been included here. An orb of $1\frac{1}{2}°$– 2° is usually allowed for these particular aspects.

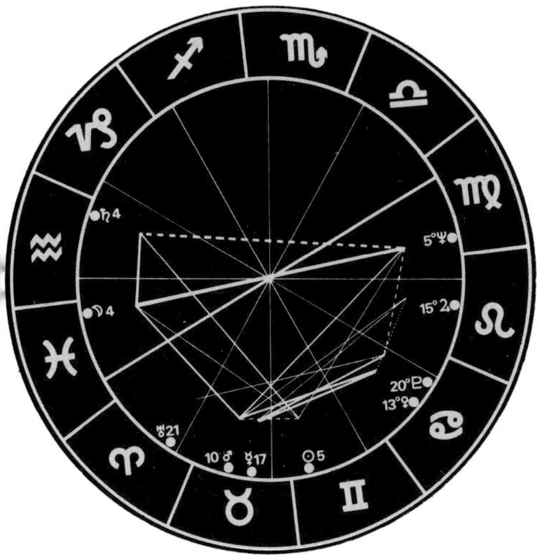

Plotting the Aspects *above*
Aspect lines are plotted on the Chart by placing a dot just inside and close to the planet's position. Oppositions and squares are conventionally indicated by solid black lines, trines and sextiles by solid red lines, and the minor aspects by broken black lines. Conjunctions are not marked as such, but the relatively close position of the planets, within 9° or even on the same degree, obviates the need for further indication.

Aspect Chart *right*
Box drawings such as this one are normally included on printed Birth Chart forms. Calculate the aspects for each planet in turn, beginning with the Sun and Moon and moving outward from Mercury to Pluto. Then place the symbol for the appropriate aspect in the relevant box; keep a check on your progress by placing a dot in the centre of boxes for which no aspect is discovered (A = Ascendant).

	☉	☽	☿	♀	♂	♃	♄	♅	♆	♇
☉		□	·	·	·	·	△	·	□	·
☽			·	·	✳	·	⚺	·	☍	⚼
☿				✳	☌	□	·	·	·	✳
♀					✳	⚺	·	□	·	☌
♂						□	□	·	△	·
♃							·	△	·	·
♄								·	⚻	·
♅									·	□
♆										∠
♇										
A	·	·	·	·	·	·	·	·	·	△
MC	·	·	·	·	·	·	·	△	·	·

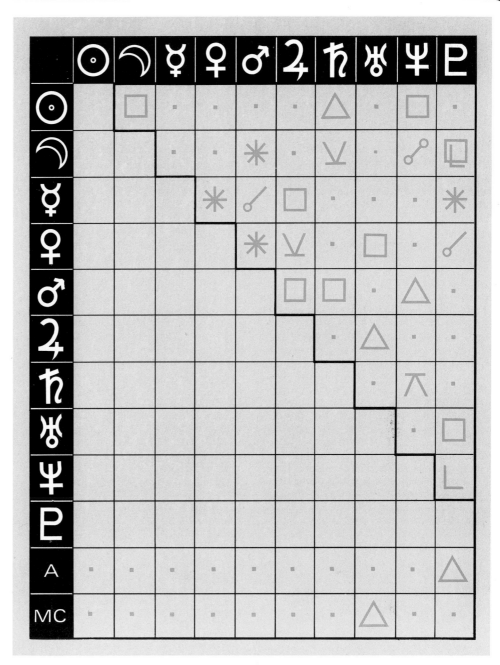

stance, a conjunction will still have to be taken into account if one planet occupies Gemini 13° and another planet Gemini 21°. The conjunction will not be exact, but it will be what is called 'within orb'. The square aspect mentioned above between the Sun and the Moon will still be an aspect if the Sun occupies Aries 15° and the Moon Cancer 22°; however, if the Moon were on Cancer 24°, the orb would be too great for it to feature in any interpretation of a subject's Birth Chart.

Sometimes it is necessary to take into consideration minutes of arc when calculating aspects; but basically, as far as orbs are concerned, the number of degrees allowed in our table represents the generally accepted margin.

So, to summarize the aspect diagrams on the facing page, planets are 'in aspect' when they are 0°, 30°, 45°, 60°, 90°, 120°, 135°, 150°, or 180° apart along the ecliptic; and an allowance either greater or smaller than these distances is allowed; the allowances are shown in the table

Method

Using a Chart for which the respective positions of the Ascendant, Midheaven and the planets have already been calculated, the method to be adopted runs as follows:

1 Begin with the Sun, its aspects being in general terms the most significant ones in the Birth Chart. Then relate position of Sun to Moon.
2 Relate position of Sun to Mercury.
3 Relate position of Sun to Venus.
4 Then to the positions of Mars, Jupiter, Saturn, Uranus, Neptune, Pluto, the Ascendant and the Midheaven.

Now apply the same technique to the Moon, again working outward from the Sun (the Moon-Sun position is already noted), taking Mercury first.

Now deal with Mercury likewise, and continue through Venus, Mars, Jupiter, Saturn, etc. Naturally, the more distant the planet concerned is from the Sun, the shorter the list of remaining planets with positions to be correlated to its own. When it comes to the most distant planet, Pluto, it is only necessary to relate it to the position of the Ascendant and Midheaven.

As each planet is considered, the symbol for the appropriate aspect is placed in the relevant box on the printed Birth Chart or drawn diagram (above right). Place a dot in the centre of the box if it should happen that an aspect has not been discovered.

Now draw aspect lines on the Chart itself. All aspects except conjunctions can be indicated in this way. Conjunctions are exceptional in that the planets either occupy the *same* degree of the ecliptic or are sufficiently close (within the 8–9° orb) to be automatically apparent.

The lines themselves are drawn by placing the point of a pair of compasses exactly in the middle of the centre circle, and then marking dots near the glyphs of the planets and the figures indicating their positions. Squares and oppositions are generally marked by a solid black line, the minor aspects in dotted black lines, while trines and sextiles are distinguished by being given in solid red lines.

INTERPRETING THE ASPECTS I

The Major Aspects

In the past, astrologers considered aspects either good or bad, or – in the case of conjunctions – neutral. Modern astrologers do not apply the rules in such a cut-and-dried manner.

In ancient astrology, the 'good' aspects were the trines and sextiles, the 'bad' aspects, oppositions and squares. This is still to some extent true, but modern thinking about aspects is constantly developing, and at present it is acknowledged that squares can give drive, push and strength to a personality, especially when they are well integrated with other planetary relationships in the Chart.

Oppositions accentuate polarities in a Chart, and can also form a strong integrating link; but these must be very carefully assessed. An opposition between the Sun and Saturn with the Sun in Leo and Saturn in Aquarius, in a Chart where extremely lively air and fire signs are emphasized, could easily be an anchorage for the person concerned, tying him down, quelling over-enthusiasm, and so on. Yet an opposition between the Moon and Uranus in a woman's Chart with water Signs emphasized could be extremely trying.

Conjunctions are a focal point. They lay stress on positivity or negativity according to Sign and House position. Sometimes planets are in conjunction, one at the end of one sign, and one at the beginning of the next. While the two will blend, it must not be forgotten that the positions should also be assessed by Sign and House.

Trines and *sextiles* are, as the ancients suspected, certainly helpful, and the really pleasant characteristics of a personality, indicated by the prominence in a Chart of well-placed planets, are often emphasized as a result. But do not be misled by a Chart which looks splendid! A whole bevy of trines and sextiles may show to all intents and purposes one of the pleasantest people on earth, but such a person may often find that things all too easily 'fall into his lap'. For the ancients a surfeit of trine aspects was a sign of evil. It is often those whose Charts show a veritable spider's web of squares and oppositions who have the greatest inner strength.

But it remains true that the whole Chart must be considered before we can assess whether a 'fighter' is going to overcome his stresses, or whether he will crumble under the whole burden.

The Minor Aspects

The most important minor aspect is the unpredictable quincunx. This can be very trying, especially when activated by adverse directions. It should not be underestimated.

Semi-squares, semi-sextiles and sesquiquadrates are also rather strenuous, and if they occur between two important planets, are worthy of serious consideration.

Semi-decile, decile, quintile and biquintile aspects are mentioned in some textbooks, but most astrologers do not use them.

Aspect Patterns

Sometimes aspects form one of three basic patterns – the Tee-Square, the Grand Trine, or the Grand Cross. These are formed because some planets are positioned in a Chart to form a group of relationships.

Unaspected Planets

Very rarely a planet will make no aspects to other planets in a Chart. The situation then needs extremely careful consideration, as the planet concerned will indicate (by its position in a particular Sign and House) an area of the subject's personality which is not well integrated. For instance, an unaspected Venus in the Seventh House may well mean that the person concerned wants desperately to form and maintain human relationships, but finds it difficult.

Interpretation

The aspects which follow are listed under three headings – Conjunctions, Positive Aspects, and Negative Aspects. This gives the student a good basis, but again it must be emphasized that often the negative aspects can be the 'makings' of a personality.

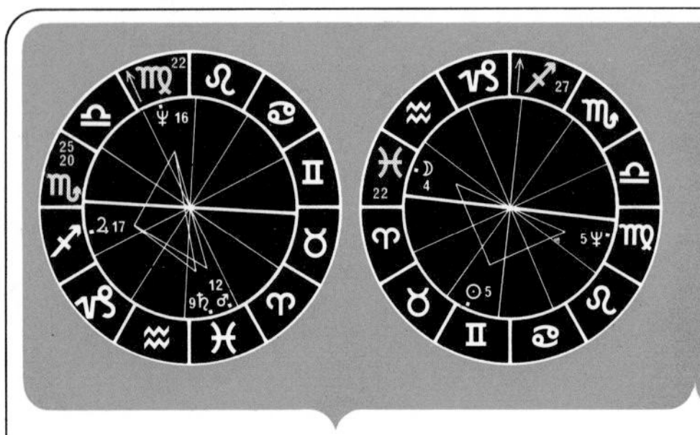

The Tee-Square
This is the most common of aspect-patterns, and is formed by an opposition aspect between two planets and a third planet halfway between them, and squaring them. As with all aspect-patterns, the Tee-Square is a mixed blessing. If other areas of the Chart counteract the obvious tension caused by these planets being at loggerheads, it can be a source of energy. However, it is often an obstructive feature – especially if the angles of the Chart are involved. Someone who has a Tee-Square in his Chart may well have to look to other areas of that Chart for a counter-balance to it, since a Tee-Square can block a normal flow of behaviour-patterns; and when the pattern is sensitively placed, it indicates a deviation from normal and accepted behaviour.

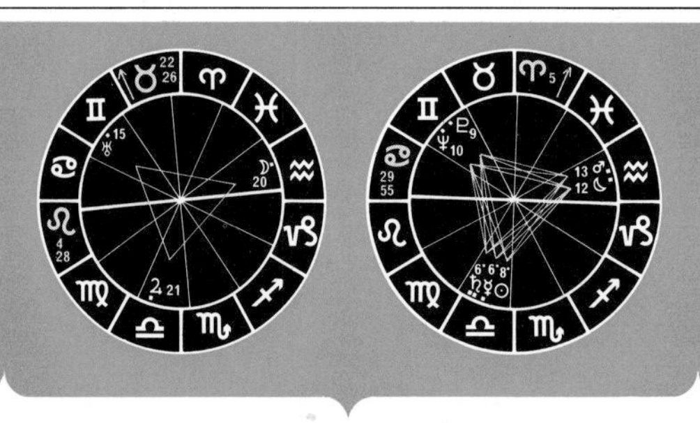

Grand Cross
The rarest of the aspect-patterns, this consists of two oppositions, the four planets involved forming square aspects to each other. This is often quoted as being the 'make-or-break' aspect pattern, and this seems indeed the best way of summing it up. Whether it makes or breaks depends on the position of the Grand Cross in the Chart, and on the planets involved. Success or failure, psychological problems or complete adjustment – all this apart, the subject with a Grand Cross in his Chart will have a cross to bear. The most obstructive Grand Crosses are those falling in fixed Signs; but it is generally true that the subject can more readily accept his difficulties with patience than is usually the case when this configuration falls in mutable or cardinal Signs.

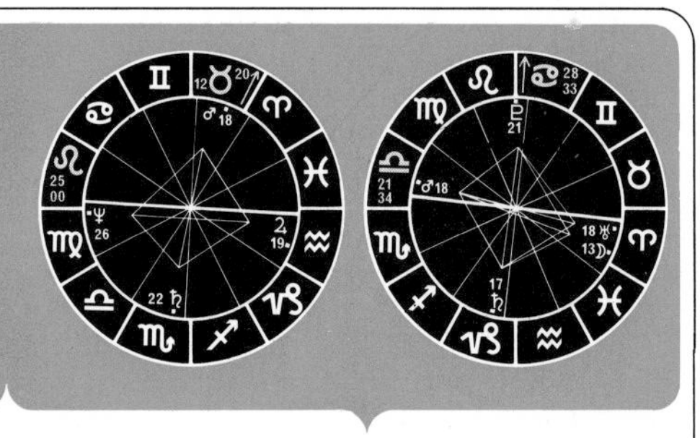

Grand Trine
A Grand Trine pattern is formed by three planets in trine aspect to each other. To all intents and purposes this shows someone who is 'well-adjusted'; but as will have been gathered from earlier comments, a predominance of trines can make life too easy for a weak personality, with the result that he will be unable to cope with any real adversity. If a Grand Trine is counteracted by a Tee-Square or by square and opposition aspects, they will help to correct the balance.

Note It may be found that more than the number of planets mentioned in the descriptions of the aspect-patterns may be involved in Tee-Squares, Grand Trines and Grand Crosses; if this is so, the effect is intensified.

THE SUN'S ASPECTS

The Sun influences the subject's conscious self, his active life, his vitality and self-expression.

SUN MOON

Conjunction
This gives an additional emphasis to the Sign containing the Sun. It is an extremely powerful focal point, and can tend to make the subject somewhat one-sided, perhaps contributing considerably to the formation of deep-rooted habits. This conjunction tends to narrow the outlook and there may be a lack of adaptability. Often Mercury and Venus are in the same Sign as the Sun, and if this is so, then there is a tendency towards imbalance because of too much stress on that particular Sign. Some degree of self-will and stubbornness is likely to manifest itself with this conjunction and the subject will have to look elsewhere in his Chart for mitigating influence. Particular attention must be paid to the Sign and House involved with this very important aspect. The more extreme tendencies will not manifest themselves so powerfully should the conjunction fall at the end of one Sign and the beginning of the next. This circumstance has the effect of diluting the properties of any one particular Sign.

Positive Aspects
These are excellent aspects to have in a Birth Chart, and unless both Sun and Moon are afflicted, they form a splendid integrating link between the conscious and unconscious. The trine especially shows a lack of inner conflict: the subject will possess tranquillity and often popularity, and will be a contented person but one who may lack a certain amount of ambition, since he is more likely to be motivated towards a life of peace and quiet than to participation in the competitive worlds of business or social activity. If this is too pronounced the subject may be exploited at work and used by his friends. General harmony in the character is extremely positively emphasized.

Negative Aspects
These aspects usually reveal a conflict in the personality – one which may be quite serious. Usually there is basically 'something wrong'. Perhaps the subject is tied to a career which he is not really interested in or there may be deep-rooted differences between parents and children. Even if all appears to be well, at least superficially, there will be an above-average 'generation gap' among members of the family. There will sometimes be a tendency towards arrogance, and those who have these negative aspects can be overbearing at times. The aspects can, however, be an incentive to achievement of objectives in life particularly in the context of the subject's career, perhaps as compensation for inner conflict.

Queen Juliana (*below*)
Queen Juliana of the Netherlands has a Sun/Moon trine in her Birth Chart; this encourages her well-integrated personality.

Emile Zola (*bottom*)
French writer Emile Zola's Sun, Moon, Mercury, Mars and Pluto all fall in Aries; many of his characters have Arian traits.

SUN MERCURY

Conjunction
The Sun and Mercury are never more than 28° apart along the ecliptic, Mercury being the planet closest to the Sun. Thus the only aspect they can make to each other is the conjunction. It is often said that if these planets are in close conjunction – less than 5° – this can lower the mental faculties. However, it seems more to the point to stress that *flexibility* of mind seems to suffer far more than simple ability or intelligence quotient. It is often the case that the person who has a 'combust' conjunction between the Sun and Mercury (i.e., a conjunction in which less than 5° of orb separates the planets) is likely to be stubborn, dogmatic and prejudiced. It may well be that the mind is not detached from personal feelings or self-expression. The tendency is eased, of course, if the conjunction 'crosses' Signs, that is, if it appears at the end of one Sign and the beginning of the next.

SUN VENUS

These planets can never be more than 48° apart along the ecliptic as seen from Earth. For this reason the contacts they can make with each other are limited to the conjunction, the semi-sextile and the semi-square.

Conjunction
This is a positively delightful planetary relationship and contributes warmheartedness, generosity and a charming disposition. People with this aspect in their Birth Charts often have an inclination towards the arts – most likely, perhaps, music. The subject's taste will be a refined and agreeable one inclining more to the traditional than the modern. It must be remembered, however, that some resentfulness can mar the pleasantness of the planetary relationship, and something of a persecution complex could emerge from time to time in those who have it sensitively placed in their Charts – i.e., in Libra, Taurus or the Seventh House.

Semi-Sextile
This seems to the writer to be only a much weaker edition of the conjunction; in other words, it is an indication to be considered, but not stressed, in interpretation.

Semi-Square
In women's Charts, there may be a tendency towards excitability, and the semi-square can contribute additional emotion. This aspect also has an artistic connotation with a special inclination toward music or dancing. But of all planetary relationships, the writer has found this aspect present in those who have broken marriages, or who are divorced. This seems to be its most notable effect. Those who have this relationship in their Charts need particular help and advice when the semi-square is activated by directions, as will be explained in the Progressions section of this book.

SUN MARS

There are some similarities between the effects of the Sun and Mars. Mars has a strong bearing on energy level, but is more aggressive, and more hasty in its action than the Sun. The two are linked by the traditional 'exaltation' of the Sun in Aries – the Sign ruled by Mars.

INTERPRETING THE ASPECTS 2

Conjunction
Contributes much to make the subject a hard worker; if placed in a 'gritty' Sign (such as Capricorn), it could mean a breaking-point through sheer physical exhaustion. But in a more emotional Sign, such as Pisces, the energy is likely to be more emotional than practical. Enthusiasm can run wild, with the unfortunate result that minor cuts, burns or head injuries can abound! If this additional energy can be well directed, it is an excellent aspect to have.

Positive Aspects
Usually an indication of strength and health. People who have them tend to be rather wiry in build. Energy can find an intellectual outlet, and there is an ability to reach quick decisions.

Negative Aspects
The more strenuous indications are likely to be emphasized. Energetic and injurious traits can develop into a positive joy in risk-taking, which must be controlled when the subject is driving or flying; though he may make a good driver or pilot. The tendency towards over-work is likely to be serious; quarrels will be above average. The subject can make an excellent debater, or be drawn towards a military career.

Dame Margot Fonteyn *above*
The Sun/Mars conjunction in Dame Margot Fonteyn's Chart gives her the necessary energy she needs to cope with a demanding career; her enigmatic glamour and concern for personal privacy are indicated by Venus conjunct Pluto.

SUN JUPITER

Conjunction
An extremely fortunate influence, with optimism and generosity present. When the conjunction is free from depressing affliction, the subject should have the best of many worlds: a well-developed and cultured mind and a sense of humour (with a tendency to satire if Mars is well-placed). The conjunction will relate helpfully to the House in which it falls.

Positive Aspects
The obvious way to interpret these aspects is to see them as bringing 'wealth, success and happiness'. This is not directly the case: happiness and contentment, perhaps – but the wealth can easily be intellectual wealth – a calm and benevolent disposition, unspoiled by materialistic cares. These aspects have direct links with such professions as publishing, the law and the church.

Negative Aspects
Restlessness is perhaps the most trying trait. Blind optimism and love of hazard (as in careless driving) may result. Pretentiousness can occur, and health can suffer as a result of a liking for good food. 'Get-rich-quick' and pseudo-religious schemes may attract. Negative Jupiter traits can be modified by the placings of Saturn in the Chart.

SUN SATURN

Of all aspects, these can give the necessary 'anchorage' and stability to a person, although limitation and frustration will undoubtedly be felt, the Sun and Saturn being naturally 'at loggerheads' – having little if anything in common.

Conjunction
Can mean considerable worldly but hard-won success – in short, it indicates the self-made man. But the life may lack 'fun', as sacrifices will have been made. A serious direction of energy and effort will be shown according to the House position.

Positive Aspects
Usually a capacity for a well-organized and moral life. Success likely through hard work and patience. As with all Sun/Saturn aspects, an above-average responsibility may well be in evidence. Positive aspects usually endow longevity, those who have them being indisposed to take risks.

Negative Aspects
The opposition between the Sun and Saturn is often less trying than the square, owing to their polarity. It is often present in successful people, with, again, an emphasis on self-discipline. The opposition or the square are 'crosses to be borne', and ambition can fail through incompetence or sheer ill-luck. Here we may invoke the key interpretation: limitation of self-expression. Self-consciousness and a sense of personal inadequacy are often accentuated. General health can suffer through lack of vitality.

Sir Winston Churchill *above*
Positive Sun/Saturn aspects can indicate longevity, as was the case with Sir Winston Churchill; his Chart shows a sextile between these planets.

Edward Heath *left*
The Sun/Saturn conjunction in Edward Heath's Chart reveals his worldly success; this, too, is the planetary aspect associated with self-made men and the drive needed to achieve their position.

SUN URANUS

Conjunction
This usually contributes a certain amount of stubbornness and perversity to a personality. There is often considerable originality; a need for independence and dramatic change will more than likely occur in those with Sun/Uranus contacts. Conventionality is not a characteristic of this conjunction, which may be a source of considerable talent, provided its unsettling nature can be controlled. More often than not there is a flair for the scientific and more 'modern' careers. If the tendency to self-will and obstinacy is not vigorously curbed, marriage partners will quickly lose patience.

Positive Aspects
Excellent powers of leadership, breadth of vision and originality are indicated (especially if Jupiter is well aspected). A lack of tact is sometimes in evidence; friendship and kindness are found and humanitarian principles. Emotional reserves are considerable

and a genuine sense of drama is positively expressed.

Negative Aspects
These are extremely trying, and can indicate considerable nervous strain, more likely in men than in women. Self-willed perversity can get out of hand, and even where there is real talent, the person concerned may, for reasons best known to himself, destroy the results of his own labours. There may well be a craving for something 'different', and eccentricity can also be present. Those who have these aspects may attempt to impose their moral and religious views on others, sometimes in extreme ways. Health can suffer, perhaps through an inability to release nervous tension.

SUN NEPTUNE

Often an indication of an individual's place in his generation, and his identification with that generation's thinking. For this reason the interpretation of these aspects takes on rather a different direction. It is nevertheless possible to draw conclusions from the point of view of the individual and these are outlined in the following paragraphs. The 'generation influence' of Neptune is discussed fully in the section of the book dealing with the planets and Signs. This planet will be especially emphasized, and its generation influences will be strong, if it falls near the angles of a Chart, or if it is strongly aspected by the Sun or the ruling planet.

Conjunction
Can be excellent for artistic creativity, especially in relation to ballet, poetry, theatre or cinema. This is particularly marked if the conjunction is strengthened by more 'concrete' and 'practical' aspects.

Positive Aspects
These need support from other planets in the Chart – especially positive aspects from Saturn – and then they show ability to bring ideas, inspiration and artistic potential to successful fruition.

Negative Aspects
In common with all the other slow-moving planets, these can be very trying, with an almost disproportionate amount of psychological confusion and perhaps weakness of character, especially where a high emotional content is also apparent.

SUN PLUTO

Pluto also has a 'generation influence', staying in a Sign for long periods of time. This influence is stressed where the Sun forms aspects to Pluto.

Conjunction
Those who have a Sun/Pluto conjunction may have a power complex; and if it falls in the Tenth House, exceptional stability is needed in other areas to counterbalance this trait. Those with the conjunction in Leo need to be cautious, since it can assume extremely 'meaty' proportions in the Birth Chart, and if they are not careful to bring calmer personality elements into play, they could find it a dangerously overwhelming planetary relationship to cope with. Upheaval and drastic changes will be likely when the conjunction is activated by directions.

Positive Aspects
To all intents and purposes these should act as a 'clearing-house' of the unconscious, although the writer has doubts whether this is always so. Considerable positive support from the placing of Pluto in the Chart (as regards House position) will have to be considered; for example, in its own House (the Eighth), with a trine or sextile from the Sun, these aspects will be well placed.

Negative Aspects
Additional strain and tension are present and extra positive sympathy from those in the subject's immediate circle can be a valuable aid. Important areas of the personality are often seriously blocked by these negative contacts. Positive expression is not, however, easy.

SUN ASCENDANT

Conjunction
Those with this aspect are born at or near sunrise. If the Sun falls in the First House, this could well indicate a tendency to concentrate overmuch on the self: if the Sun is over the horizon in the Twelfth House, there is a tendency to withdraw and concentrate on affairs connected with the Twelfth House – philanthropic organizations, hospitals and secret societies, for example. Characteristics of the Ascending Sign are strongly emphasized and will affect the subject on all levels of his personality.

Positive Aspects
Good integrating influences are felt, often accentuating the positive characteristics of the Sun and Ascending Signs.

Negative Aspects
Opposition: if the Sun is in the Sixth House, health indications associated with the Sun and Ascendant are emphasized. If it is in the Seventh, a strong polarity with the Ascendant will emphasize permanent relationships: marriage or business partnerships, for example, giving them stability and rapport. *Squares* accentuate possible strain, tension or drive, according to the House in which the Sun falls. In the Tenth, in the subject's career; in the Fourth, home and family.

SUN MIDHEAVEN

Conjunction
This aspect shows a basic psychological need to establish identity. At its best, it contributes to making a person who is completely at one with his occupation; in extreme cases, however, it may reveal a careerist.

Positive Aspects
Harmony between personality and objectives in life. With positive aspects between Sun and Midheaven, there will be a well-adjusted attitude towards social position and ambition; the subject will know his limitations. and live within them.

Negative Aspects
In extreme cases these can mean that the subject has difficulty in attaining his objectives; a deflated ego.

2 THE MOON'S ASPECTS

The subject's instincts and emotions will be influenced by the Moon which is the planet of fluctuation and response; in the context of lunar aspects it will be seen that the Moon 'receives' rather than 'gives'; that is, its effects will be coloured by those of another planet forming aspects to it, rather than the other way around.

Mahatma Ghandi *above*
Ghandi's Chart shows the Moon in Leo in the Tenth House, heavily aspected by seven other planets; this strongly indicates his immense popularity and exalted status among the people of India.

MOON MERCURY

Conjunction
This aspect is commonly found in the Charts of highly intelligent subjects, and of those who show a marked degree of sensitivity and imagination; whimsicality and eccentricity may be present. If the conjunction is well aspected, the nervous system should be strengthened.

Positive Aspects
Plenty of common sense and nervous energy are usually found. Shrewdness and intuition combine with honesty and logic. Affairs concerning the Third and Fourth Houses usually make positive progress, and are aspects excellent for health. Propensity to nervous tension should be minimal, unless strongly provoked elsewhere in the Chart.

Negative Aspects
Cunning and an astute intellect can tend to underhandedness and gossip. May be restless or excitable, nervous and inconsistent. But those with these negative aspects are enormously loyal and great defenders of their friends or others weaker than themselves. Often an interest in health.

INTERPRETING THE ASPECTS 3

MOON VENUS

Conjunction
Venusian traits being emphasized, there is a love of art and luxury. Emotions are calm and the outlook tranquil. On the whole, this conjunction seems more favourable for men than for women, especially in family life. Natural friendliness leads to popularity, which is eagerly sought, but too much self-love can occur. Excellent aspect for statesmen!

Positive Aspects
These give the subject excellent perception and a rational outlook. Family life and marriage will be helped, and women show an exceptional ability to support their husband's activities and interests. There is a genuine love of beauty; artistic talent may be expressed through such crafts as dressmaking or flower arrangement. Good for politicians and athletes.

Negative Aspects
Lack of ability to express emotion, leading to unhappiness and disappointments in emotional relationships, even considerable suffering. Moodiness and gullibility can be present, and judgment may be weak. Incompatability can occur in marriage. Subjects are likely to be popular, but sometimes an over-assertive manner conceals shyness.

MOON MARS

Conjunction
Great energy and a propensity to take risks. If the conjunction itself is afflicted (receiving, say, squares or oppositions from the Sun or Uranus), there will be physical and financial recklessness. There is courage but it may be marred by a tendency to rush headlong into action. Perhaps the subject will be moody, although generally he should be lively and healthy – especially if the other areas of the Chart are steadying and less prone to impulsiveness.

Positive Aspects
Usually indicate robust good health and an open manner. Honesty, sincerity and the inclination to do exactly as one wishes is usual. Positive Martian and Arian characteristics are common, their normal trait being acute appraisal of the self and others. A devil-may-care outlook with scant regard for the future.

Benito Mussolini *above*
Mussolini's Chart shows a double conjunction – Moon conjunct Mars and Saturn. The former provides will-power and energy, its more reckless tendencies being steadied by the grimmer characteristics of the Moon conjunct Saturn; this gave him a hard, selfish outlook, grudging in his praise of others.

Negative Aspects
Not good for health. The subject may be over-influenced by strong emotions, being irritable, impulsive and combative. There is a tendency to quarrel, and if this and excitability are not counterbalanced in other areas, they will cause trouble. Self-indulgence, alcoholism and promiscuity can occur; most likely if the planets are rising, or in Cancer or Pisces. Self-respect and self-control need to be cautiously developed.

MOON JUPITER

Conjunction
Apart from a tendency to self-importance and vanity, this is an excellent influence, bestowing generosity and a strong protective instinct. A liking for pleasure demands a high standard of living. An inner need for change is often satisfied by travel. There is enormous energy which is often harnessed to a flair for business.

Positive Aspects
A popular, pleasant temperament, sympathetic, with a love of animals. Business ability; a keen traveller, who can even be satisfied by imaginary journeys; perhaps benefiting from a period of living abroad, especially if the Ninth House or Sagittarius is emphasized.

Negative Aspects
While popularity and good humour are present, inner conflicts can centre around religious beliefs. Financial and general judgment may be weak. Sometimes a tendency to laziness. Health indications concern the liver, which can suffer from self-indulgence. These aspects are often found in the Birth Charts of successful people, but it is necessary to judge the strength of Saturn, which can steady the more lackadaisical tendencies.

MOON SATURN

Conjunction
A powerful conjunction, self-denial and thriftiness being common. There is an ability to work very hard, often with a craving for perfection. The sense of duty is extremely strong but discontent can show. Little praise is given to others, and there may be a hypercritical tendency. Although grim in essence, this conjunction can give stability in many cases.

Positive Aspects
An ability to organise, to take responsibility. Slight pomposity commonly combines with a liking for people. Somewhat limited, but conscientious.

Negative Aspects
Their effect is often depressive. The subject finds life hard. A difficult mother-child relationship usually leads to a lack of self-confidence. Marriage partners are often much older than the subject.

MOON URANUS

Conjunction
A high level of emotional tension is present in this powerful conjunction, with a hatred of conventionality or conformism. Subjects can be difficult to cope with; though at best they are particularly original, they need to develop less eccentric traits to keep more extreme tendencies under control. Sexual abnormality and perversion can occur. The desire for independence is marked and they are likely to make great sacrifices for it. They should not be thwarted.

Positive Aspects
Firmness and determination prominent, with a sense of duty and strong ambition. Sudden changes of mood are common, and the intuitive level is high. These aspects often appear in the Charts of astrologers; but if flair for astrology is present, the subject must learn to keep the more extreme tendencies under control: intuition is no substitute for understanding.

Negative Aspects
Stubbornness and fanaticism often combine with real talent and high intellectual ability. These positive traits need strength from other areas to combat inevitable restlessness, irritability and wilfulness. There is also a tendency to over-estimate problems and to ignore advice. Versatility is common.

MOON NEPTUNE

Conjunction
Sympathetic, warmhearted and kind – especially if the conjunction falls in Cancer or Leo; the subject tends to identify with people less fortunate than himself, often giving positive help. There may be a preference for seclusion bordering on escapism (if the conjunction falls in the Twelfth House). The emotional level is high: especially when in Cancer or Scorpio. To keep the emotions balanced may not be easy, but every effort must be made to achieve this. Other areas of the Chart will be helpful.

Positive Aspects
An overall tendency to want to do something rather special and unusual – taking bizarre forms in extreme cases. A desire to expand horizons is cramped by lack of ability; the subject finds it difficult to accept his own natural limitations. The imagination is powerful, and sometimes there is 'visionary inspiration'.

Negative Aspects
Much self-deception – the more practical areas must be brought into play to counterbalance this tendency. Complications can occur in emotional relationships. There is a predilection

for get-rich-quick methods, invariably disastrous in their outcome. Emotional tension can be high in women, with a negative Moon/Neptune aspect.

MOON PLUTO

Conjunction
An inclination towards impulsiveness is very strong, especially when the conjunction is in Cancer or Leo. A mood may change suddenly and explosively, with little regard for previous efforts; this is most likely if the conjunction falls on or near the Midheaven.

Positive Aspects
Emotions will probably be strong, with outbursts of an emotional nature, which may be a disruptive influence in relationships or marriage. The positive aspects should help to externalize this force. Business ability is likely, especially if Pluto is in Cancer or Virgo.

Negative Aspects
The flow of emotions is blocked, with a tendency towards unrest. Jealousy is common; business ability is present, but impulsiveness needs control. Life as a whole may be subject to new phases which are not of the subject's own choosing. These often involve his domestic and close family life.

Dr Albert Schweitzer *below*
In Dr Schweitzer's Chart the Moon conjunct Neptune in Aries in the Seventh House contributed to his kindness and sympathy.

The Duke of Windsor *above*
In the Duke of Windsor's Chart a Moon/Pluto square portends sudden change and fresh phases in life.

MOON ASCENDANT

Conjunction
In the First House, all Moon characteristics are powerfully emphasized, but according to the rising Sign. Mother-child relationships are particularly close. Perhaps a strong tendency to worry and restlessness. In the Twelfth House, a need is felt for seclusion with possible escapist tendencies.

Positive Aspects
Excellent for positive expression of the ways and habits of the Sign the Moon occupies.

Negative Aspects
Opposition: in the Sixth House, this weakens a child's health and may bring family upheaval; in the Seventh it bears particularly on marriage. These aspects all indicate emotional discord, according to the Sign the Moon is in.

MOON MIDHEAVEN

Conjunction
Considerable difficulty in settling into a career. At best (according to the Sign) possible flair for cooking, catering or hotel work. If the Chart shows medical ability, gynaecology may attract.

Positive Aspects
Outward expression of, and response to, lunar traits.

Negative Aspects
Opposition: brings emotional discord probably due to an unsettled family background or a lack of 'roots'. This may be connected with the House the Moon occupies – e.g. the Twelfth (solitude).

3 MERCURY'S ASPECTS

Mercury is usually regarded as a 'neutral' planet, having an influence neither for good nor evil; but, like the Moon, Mercury can be influenced by any planet with which it forms aspects. It affects mental ability and the nervous system, as well as the ability to communicate.

MERCURY VENUS

As Mercury and Venus can never be more than 76° apart, the only aspects they can make to each other are the conjunction, semi-sextile, semi-square and sextile. Both planets are harmless; the semi-sextile and semi-square, being the only negative aspects, are only mildly strenuous.

The Conjunction
This aspect usually gives charm of speech, with a calm mental outlook tinged with the balanced qualities of Venus. If there is an accent on Gemini and Virgo (the two Mercury Signs) or Taurus and Libra (the Venus Signs), the conjunction will assume greater beneficial strength. The sextile between these planets will operate much as the conjunction, but the Signs involved can strengthen or stifle its working, both planets being in themselves mild. If artistic ability is shown in other areas, this will be helped. These aspects are especially positive for those engaged in craft-work, dress design, hairdressing – any work where the expression of beauty is communicated through the hands. This could be extended to music.

INTERPRETING THE ASPECTS 4

The semi-sextile and semi-square are likely to give a certain amount of drive to Mercury and Venus, but they remain mild and not too much stress should be laid on them in interpretation. When Mercury is in Libra and Venus in Virgo, or when Venus is in Gemini and Mercury in Taurus, they are in mutual reception and are more important.

Mercury Mars

Conjunction
Gives mental energy and a lively mind. A rather sharp satirical element can be amusing. There is ability for hard intellectual work; if writing talent is shown, inspiration and flair can be exploited. If the conjunction is afflicted, bitter quarrels may result; or work to the point of mental breakdown. The more extreme elements should be pointed out in interpretation. The conjunction is at its best in Gemini or Virgo.

Positive Aspects
Mind-invigorating and particularly beneficial to the nervous system. Common sense is present, often with literary ability. Subjects are excellent in debate, make assertive drivers and like walking. There is bravery, but if Aries is prominent there may be rashness too and a disregard for personal safety. While subjects get on well with children, they may themselves remain childless. Eyesight and hearing are usually very good.

Edward Kennedy *above*
The Mercury/Mars conjunction in Edward Kennedy's Chart, being placed in Aquarius, gives him a lively and resilient mind though he is susceptible to impulse.

Negative Aspects
Irritability needs conscious control; a tendency to overwork can be dangerous. Fault-finding and self-importance are encouraged if mental energy fails to find a creative outlet. Other areas will show where this force can be most positively directed. Sometimes criminal tendencies.

Mercury Jupiter

Conjunction
This gives optimism and above-average intelligence; although real potential and ability are often developed through further education. Good natured, but may be conceited. There are philanthropic and philosophical qualities in this powerful conjunction. Success in art, literature, the law or religion is likely. Stubbornness may be in evidence.

Positive Aspects
An active mind, though it tends to lack ambition. Especially if Libra is strong, the subject may too easily be satisfied with his efforts. Controversial questions (especially concerning religion) are usually avoided. While these aspects are not indicative of great success (because the necessary drive is missing) they help to negate financial problems. An excellent sense of humour is often present.

Negative Aspects
The subject must be constantly on guard against indiscretion or taking too broad an outlook, but the aspects give an original and a fertile mind. He tends to be absent-minded (especially if Pisces is emphasized), but his worst trait is poor judgment, compensation for which must be sought in the more practical areas of the Chart. Artistic or literary ability is often stressed.

Mercury Saturn

Conjunction
If well aspected, in Capricorn or Virgo, and if other areas of the Chart show no lack of energy or initiative, this can give ability to work methodically and patiently. But, if afflicted, depression is common, and mental abilities will not be pronounced. Children with this conjunction must never be forced in their studies. Steady progress will occur with care. Obstinacy may show, especially if Taurus is strong, and endurance will feature.

Igor Stravinsky *above*
The unemotional elements in Stravinsky's music relate to the square aspect between Mercury and Saturn in his Birth Chart.

Positive Aspects
Depth of thought, good concentration, organizational ability, and directness of speech. There is no lack of ambition, and the outlook is serious and practical with a regard for honesty and morality.

Negative Aspects
Hard, abrupt, tending often to plot and scheme. A rigid routine is common. Fear, worry and loneliness can occur especially if Capricorn rises, or Cancer is prominent. Carefulness and reliability are not always lacking, but a bluntly harsh attitude covers shyness, and therefore few real friendships are formed.

Mercury Uranus

Conjunction
Wilfulness, independence and originality often combine with eccentricity and stubborness. But identification with new trends in scientific thought and a real talent bordering on genius can be shown. The subject must be allowed to live his life in his own way. Where the tendencies remain undeveloped, conceit or a lack of adaptability can too easily occur. Of all aspects, this conjunction and the trines and sextiles are most common in astrologers' Charts.

Positive Aspects
Inventive, mentally dextrous, having a sense of drama. Intuition and brilliance are commonly found, although at times the subject may appear stupid through his single-mindedness. There is usually a high degree of self-reliance; the memory is generally excellent.

Negative Aspects
A lack of tact is common, great talent may be undermined because the subject believes himself to be somehow special, to be 'chosen'. Eccentricity and brusqueness will be extremely tiresome to others. There is a tendency to expend energy wastefully, over a wide front, causing nervous tension and confusion.

Mercury Neptune

Conjunction
A powerful creative imagination, kind and gentle; but assessment must be related to the Sign involved. For instance, in Cancer the emphasis is on imagination, and perhaps on sensitivity; in Leo, on artistic ability; in Virgo, on writing; in Libra, on taking the easy way out (despite idealism). Whatever the Sign, the subject must be on the defensive against a tendency to delusion and uncontrollable impulses.

Positive Aspects
Imagination is of a high order, easily developed, perhaps through poetry, dancing, mime or acting (especially films). If creativity is shown in the Chart as a whole, it will greatly enhance the way intellectual sensitivity is applied. The subject will hate harsh conditions, and can be easily hurt by others; but without bearing resentment.

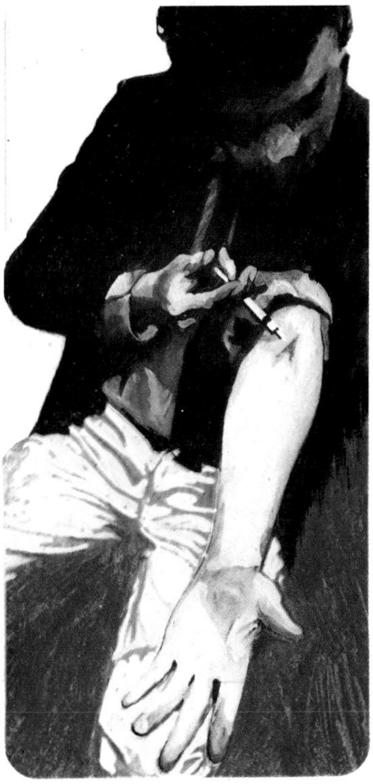

An afflicted conjunction between Mercury and Neptune in Libra in the Twelfth House, occurring in the Chart of a real-life drug addict, contributed to the introverted tendencies aggravating his condition.

Negative Aspects
Scheming and deceptive, especially if Cancer or Scorpio are prominent. Apparent deception may result from a circuitous approach. The imagination is fertile, the perception of a high order. But these are not always positively used. Worry, lack of self-confidence and gullibility are common.

MERCURY PLUTO

Conjunction
Something of a power complex may be present, especially if the conjunction falls in Leo. This can be expressed through writing – perhaps in inflammatory articles! If the conjunction is well aspected, there should be a natural ability to throw off worry, but consideration of the Sign involved is vital. In Cancer, worry may remain buried at the unconscious level. In Virgo, there is likely to be some psychological blockage, since this Sign is prone to worry. Health can be badly affected.

Positive Aspects
Restless thinking likely. Sudden changes of opinion and craftiness may occur; but nervous tension is usually easily released.

Negative Aspects
The subject often fails to consider a problem before committing himself verbally. He finds it hard to see matters in perspective, and the usual psychological 'lines of communication' can become easily blocked. Professional psychiatric help may be necessary to help release tensions, especially if tension is indicated elsewhere in the Chart.

MERCURY ASCENDANT

Conjunction
In the First House, there is much mental activity, and according to the rising Sign, restlessness should be controlled. Duality is likely, and should be accepted. Consistency must be developed, and Mercurial traits emphasized. In the Twelfth House, natural secrecy is common, which in children needs cautious direction, perhaps through letting them plan surprises for birthday's etc.

Positive Aspects
Excellent blending of intellect with the persona. Ability to get on with children, and enjoyment from intellectual pleasures. If Mercury is in the Ninth House, a possible flair for languages.

Negative Aspects
Opposition: in the Sixth House, worry can lead to health problems; hypochondria is common, with psychosomatic illnesses caused by over-concern. In the Seventh, critical but lively attitudes towards partners; the possibility of nervous disorders occurs with the opposition and with all other negative aspects from Mercury to the Ascendant.

MERCURY MIDHEAVEN

Conjunction
A career in journalism, communications, or other 'Mercurial' areas is likely. Changes in career are indicated. Sometimes the subject has difficulty in retaining a job. Much nervous energy, identifying with intellectual and educational affairs.

Positive Aspects
Contribute a beneficial attitude towards aspirations and ambitions.

Negative Aspects
Opposition: will perhaps contribute difficulties through lack of education. *Other negative aspects*: aspirations and ambitions may be blocked.

4 VENUS' ASPECTS

The effect of an aspect from Venus to any other planet will be to soften and sensitize. The ability to form lasting emotional and business relationships will be influenced.

VENUS MARS

Conjunction
It is important to decide whether Venus or Mars is the stronger planet. If Venus, feelings are sensitive and the subject easily hurt; but there is a strong sense of enjoyment. If Mars is stronger, anger may occur over minor matters and behaviour can be coarsened. Generally speaking, the sex-life is active, though not taken too seriously. There is a harmonious blending of male and female principles with the accent on Venusian charm and Martian energy. Drive is harmoniously expressed.

Positive Aspects
Much warmth and affection; feelings are fully expressed. Enthusiasm for love affairs is pronounced, and can tend to promiscuity. The subject needs freedom of expression. otherwise he may become highly-strung. In men's Charts, these aspects are excellent for relationships with women.

Negative Aspects
Hypersensitivity common, also strain in emotional and family relationships. Often discontent, the subject tends to expect too much, is then disappointed. Although the feelings are warm and affectionate, intense sexual relation-ships may often be marred by quarrels or capriciousness. Partnerships are likely to be very difficult and other areas must be examined to see where the strain can be counterbalanced.

Gloria Swanson *below*
The sexually orientated quincunx in Gloria Swanson's Chart – between Venus in Aquarius and Mars in Cancer – lent force to her memorable career as an exciting screen seductress.

INTERPRETING THE ASPECTS 5

VENUS JUPITER

Elizabeth Taylor *above*
Elizabeth Taylor's Chart has Venus in conjunction with Uranus, trine Jupiter; the first strongly indicates the glamour of her highly successful career, and financial success accompanies the trine to Jupiter.

Conjunction
Charm, generosity, and an abundance of feeling lead to popularity. Given control from other less outgoing areas, this helps to make the subject affectionate, artistic, a good host; but if Leo or Libra are prominent, he will tend to overdo the charm. Excellent for business partnerships, especially between opposite sexes.

Positive Aspects
Popularity in evidence, with much charm of expression. Excellent for those who have to deal with the public, putting people at their ease. There is a positive dislike of hazard; accident-proneness is minimized. Partnerships of all kinds are beneficial Extravagance is likely.

Negative Aspects
The subject follows an easy life; too many love affairs; an exaggerated sense of drama. There will also be extremes of feeling, and a craving for luxury. Other areas must be consulted in search of a controlling factor. Not good for business partnerships.

VENUS SATURN

Conjunction
All aspects between Venus and Saturn limit the affections, and indicate sacrifice. The conjunction shows a powerful drawback which provides a counter to the normal expression of love, preventing or delaying marriage. Sometimes inhibitive psychological factors are the reason – certainly likely if the Sun or Ascendant are in aspect to the conjunction. Sometimes the cause is not of the subject's making. A powerful sense of duty may well take pride of place over personal feelings, which will perhaps be sublimated for the sake of an elderly parent or relative.

Positive Aspects
Loneliness is commonly experienced; normal happiness through marriage is not often enjoyed. The Saturnian influence on Venus is chill and the elements of life that are ruled by Venus do not, in consequence, flow positively. At their best, they make the subject successful but over-practical. There is little or no happy social life, and partnerships lack fun. This could, however, be a constructive (if over-practical) influence in the conduct of business partnerships.

Mao Tse-tung *above*
A chill loneliness and restricted social life are characteristic of Venus/Saturn aspects; Mao Tse-tung, the Chinese leader, has a trine between these planets.

Negative Aspects
Sacrifices are made to ambitions or material progress. Disappointments, unhappiness and sometimes incompatibility in marriage or emotional relationships can occur. Selfishness and thoughtlessness can contribute to this. Small-mindedness, allowing minor faults to assume major importance is common. The theme of 'sacrifice for duty' remains strong. Often these aspects make for a considerable difference in age between the subject and the marriage partner.

VENUS URANUS

Conjunction
While there is a need for peace and harmony, excitable tension can be externalized through the arts. If this powerful force finds no positive outlet, emotionalism can occur, often with little regard for reputation. If artistic talent is shown in other areas, the conjunction will contribute much originality, especially through new and exciting artistic trends. Emotional freedom is necessary. Risks will be taken for sheer pleasure; self-will, lack of common sense and general wildness are in evidence.

Positive Aspects
Often involve artistic talent; musical ability popular, probably at his best working and enjoying himself as a member of societies or clubs. A very romantic and sensitive streak is likely and ties of friendship and acquaintance may well be above average.

Negative Aspects
A vein of emotional unconventionality often present. Regard for personal freedom is considerable, and restrictions in relationships will be fought against. Much kindness and goodness are often present, but so are stubbornness and rigidity of outlook. Care is needed in the choice of friends or business partners, as disastrous relationships can result. Sensitivity, nervous tension and uncontrolled emotions are common.

VENUS NEPTUNE

Conjunction
Kind, nervous and highly sensitive, often unrealistic; a lover of animals. Identification with suffering is often overruled by a lack of practical ability, unless other areas of the Chart provide a counterbalance. Where there is real strength and control, this conjunction can give great artistic ability. There is often strain, unhappiness or anxiety in emotional relationships, and health risks should be avoided at all costs.

Positive Aspects
Artistic potential is usually present, and should always be encouraged; otherwise it may be drained by a somewhat lackadaisical attitude. There is much that is ephemeral and unworldly in people with these aspects; but there is always sensitivity and refinement. A hatred of hard work or rigid routine is usual, leaving plenty of scope to exercise freedom of expression; work in a boutique, for example, rather than in a big store.

Negative Aspects
Dissatisfaction common; ideals are high, but a critical attitude must be adopted towards them. Decision-making is difficult. Disappointment often occurs in emotional relationships because of unreliability in the partner. Care is needed in the areas of business and finance. There is a tendency to be somewhat secretive about the love-life.

VENUS PLUTO

Conjunction
If well aspected, this conjunction can be good for financial ability – especially in Cancer, Virgo or the Eighth House. It can cause fanaticism in love, but the most common manifestation is a deep-rooted blockage of the normal flow of the affections. There is a tendency to fall suddenly, passionately but secretively in love. Sexual repression is more than likely to occur, if the conjunction is afflicted.

Positive Aspects
Financial ability, strengthened if Scorpio, Libra or Taurus is the Sign on the Midheaven. There is likely to be great, even exaggerated enjoyment of life, with self-indulgence leading to a weight problem. The subject is likely to be passionate, especially if Scorpio is prominent.

Negative Aspects
Lasciviousness and lust are present – though psychological inhibitions may curb the positive expression of strong sexual urges. Financial

difficulties can occur as a consequence of taking chances with over-investment. Moderation should be developed towards financial affairs.

VENUS ASCENDANT

Conjunction
In the First House this will give great charm, good looks, and an ability to influence others; but these graces can lead to the subject's undoing, as things may come too easily to him. His liking for an easy life may grow out of hand. Venusian traits will be strongly emphasized, influencing the subject according to the rising Sign. If Venus is afflicted, there may be kidney trouble. Children with this placing must be encouraged to work hard, but also to develop creative interests – piano lessons should be considered. In the Twelfth House there can be a tendency to take the easy way out. There may be a talent for poetry, which often proves attractive to the subject with this conjunction. Confusion and dreaminess can occur.

Positive Aspects
Venusian traits positively expressed to the full: in love affairs and a full social life – especially if Venus is in the Fifth House. Possible marriage to a foreigner if Venus is in the Ninth. The sextiles to the Ascendant will also bring out positive Venusian traits of charm and fluency.

Negative Traits
Opposition: in the Sixth House can provoke kidney upsets, and there may be an above-average number of headaches; on the whole, this aspect is a health hazard. In the Seventh, the opposition indicates a happy marriage, and positive business partnerships. *Other negative aspects:* show strain in the expression of feelings, and the need for care in business relationships.

VENUS MIDHEAVEN

Conjunction
Much depends on the Sign, but success is likely through business partnerships. Considerable artistic ability, success in fashion, hair-dressing, interior decoration, are all possible. The emphasis should be on Venusian activities and partnerships. This placing is not good for freelance workers on their own.

Positive Aspects
Easy expression of feelings, and identification and sympathy with the arts. A positive love life.

Negative Aspects
A possible difficulty in expressing feelings. A lack of affection as a child, if the aspect is in opposition.

Ringo Starr *above*
Ringo Starr has Venus opposition Midheaven and Neptune opposition Ascendant. His natural diffidence was overcome via the stronger Beatles, Lennon and McCartney.

5 MARS' ASPECTS

Mars is an energetic and self-assertive planet; when it is joined by aspect to another planet, Mars will have a strengthening effect. When forming a negative aspect, it can be exaggerative in its action.

MARS JUPITER

Conjunction
Open and frank, always able to concentrate on objectives in a positive, energetic way. The aspect is good for finance. Decision-making will present no problems, and there is a general ability to cope. The subject can often become involved in disputes. If Aries or Sagittarius are prominent, there may be a devil-may-care attitude and a raciness which need controlling.

Positive Aspects
Will-power, optimism, enthusiasm and the ability to enjoy life; the outlook is positive. A sense of freedom, organizational ability and, sometimes, creative talent can be present. A love of sport and physical exercise is common. The high energy level needs positive exploitation, in both physical and intellectual areas.

Negative Aspects
Hastiness and impulsiveness common; care and forethought should be developed, though this will not be easy. There is proneness to over-enthusiasm, perhaps to blind optimism. A form of exaggerated rebelliousness exists in those who have these aspects, which will emerge from time to time. The energy level is extremely high, but positive outlets for it can be hard to find. Serious restlessness and, perhaps, a lack of temperance can be indicated.

General de Gaulle *above*
Charles de Gaulle had the energetic, slightly belligerent conjunction of Mars and Jupiter rising in Aquarius. This accounts for his disputes but also his courage and daring.

MARS SATURN

U Thant *above*
U Thant's Mars trine Saturn helps him to survive difficult conditions, organize and cope with large, conflicting groups of people.

Conjunction
This very potent conjunction often indicates considerable suffering: sometimes this occurs as a result of physical handicap, or accident-proneness. A possible danger period is when Mars by transit conjuncts the natal conjunction (see under Progressions). Skin, teeth and bones may suffer. There is a conflict between inhibition and the urge for action which has to be conquered.

Positive Aspects
Endurance, an ability to live through harsh conditions – like those encountered by explorers. Hardship and discipline are easily accepted, even liked. Excellent aspects for the engineer and allied careers. Organizing ability is considerable; trade union involvement possible, or anything that involves control over large groups of men.

Negative Aspects
Those with negative Mars/Saturn aspects find it difficult to maintain an even flow of energy. At times they may be energetic, but inactive at others. The worst outcome is a lack of purpose and a tendency to drift. Enthusiasm and interest in new projects soon wears off.

INTERPRETING THE ASPECTS 6

MARS URANUS

Conjunction
This extremely powerful conjunction always contributes a high but tense energy level which can be near breaking-point for much of the time. Extremely wilful and sometimes intolerant and accident-prone. All potentialities shown will be developed to the full. The subject will be at his best in times of danger. If the conjunction is afflicted, nervous breakdown can occur.

Positive Aspects
An ability to make quick decisions, coupled with excellent energetic resources which can be called on at a moment's notice. The subject thrives on hard work, and should have no lack of physical strength. Much attention must be given to other areas to find if there is sufficient common sense to check energetic impulses. Nervous strain and tension can easily occur; discipline proves difficult to accept.

Negative Aspects
Argumentative, eccentric, tending to contradict; intolerance and accident-proneness are common. One positive outlet may be through militant causes, but self-control must be developed to combat the violence easily stirred in the subject. There will be no liking for routine. Nervous tension and erratic behaviour are common negative traits.

Rudolf Nureyev *below*
Nureyev's potent conjunction of Mars and Uranus provides him with daring energy, flowing intensity and the drive to realize his glorious potential as a dancer.

MARS NEPTUNE

Conjunction
A love of colour and romance will be married to the more emotional elements in the arts – as music, dancing and poetry. There is usually plenty of enthusiasm, but it may be rather carelessly directed. Vanity may occur, and sometimes aspirations aim too high. The energy store is not large, and disappointments are common according to the House position of the conjunction. The imagination is powerful.

Positive Aspects
Extremely powerful emotions, but self-control is well developed. At best, the aspects contribute charity and helpful traits. The subject can express these qualities fluently, for the good of others. The imagination is fertile, and there is a natural ability to keep a step ahead of others' thoughts and actions. Excellent aspects for those involved in sea telegraphy, marine instruments and shipping matters generally.

Negative Aspect
A tendency towards negative escapism through drugs or alcohol – more likely where one planet is in Cancer or the Twelfth House. Often the imagination is extremely sensitive, and subject to negative stimulation. A positive outlet – perhaps acting – may offset the negative traits. Worry can affect the health and there can be sensitivity to medicines, fish-poisoning and tainted water supplies.

MARS PLUTO

Conjunction
The emotional level is extremely high, and will need a great deal of positive outlet. If the conjunction is afflicted, then the normal emotional flow will be blocked and serious psychological upsets can develop; or emotional energy may be expressed in negative or even cruel and criminal ways. A quick, violent temper may be present which will take a great effort to control.

Positive Aspects
Emotional and physical energy will be positively utilized. There is an ability to make new beginnings and no lack of self-confidence or ambition. The subject is usually a passionately hard worker.

Negative Aspects
Objectives can become obsessions; despite the subject's efforts to conquer obstacles, they seem to loom still larger. But he will overcome them, if sometimes at the expense of others and without considering their feelings.

MARS ASCENDANT

Conjunction
If in the First House, all Martian traits will be emphasized: selfishness is likely as is impetuosity with accident-proneness (minor cuts and burns being prevalent). The physical energy level is high, and the subject will have an infectious freshness and zest. Energy is likely to be directed towards matters concerned with the rising Sign. In the Twelfth House, secretiveness is common, and needs conscious control. There may well be an inclination towards psychicism or mysticism, making for a less open and uncomplicated character than if the planet occupies the First House.

Positive Aspects
These will add a lively streak, blending the type of energy revealed by the Sign that Mars occupies with that of the Ascendant.

Negative Aspects
Opposition: in the Sixth House brings strain through overwork, the subject finding it difficult to know when to stop. In the Seventh House it will put an exceptional energy and enthusiasm into all partnerships; but a quarrelsome tendency must be controlled. *Other negative aspects* from Mars to the Ascendant will tend to show some negative stress on the Martian traits. Every effort must be made to combat this.

MARS MIDHEAVEN

Conjunction
An excellent placing for putting energy into the day's work. Hard tasks will be gladly undertaken, and the subject will find it easy to accomplish what many others cannot. Possible flair for engineering or the army; but the Sign on the Midheaven must be carefully considered.

Positive Aspects
Adding a lively Martian element to the expression of the self.

Negative Aspects
Opposition: will bring uncongenial work conditions. The subject's parents may force him into a career. *Other negative aspects:* these show possible strain through work.

6 Jupiter's Aspects

The aspects between Jupiter, Saturn, Uranus, Neptune and Pluto stay within orb for a long period. They must be assessed in relation to major aspects of the Sun, Moon or ruling planet. If any of the planets mentioned is on or near the Ascendant or Midheaven, its significance will be personal; if not, the influence will be more likely to be a generational working on the unconscious of all those born while any particular aspect is in orb.

Jupiter Saturn

Conjunction
This occurs every 21 years. There is considerable ability to achieve objectives through hard work; tenacity will always be present. This is a very potent planetary relationship, and there is great potential coupled with single-mindedness and physical endurance. The conjunction will be at its most powerful if it is on the Midheaven. Dissatisfaction can be countered by the urge for activity

Dr Konrad Adenauer *above*
A Jupiter/Saturn square brought restlessness to Dr Adenauer's life.

John Lennon *above*
An exact Jupiter/Saturn conjunction in Taurus shows Lennon's ambitious side, also a typical discontent, which led him to mysticism and the pursuit of personal publicity.

with the result that more often than not goals are eventually achieved in spite of all odds.

Positive Aspects
Excellent to have, progress in life coming through the steady use of constructive ability. They are most useful if either Jupiter or Saturn are joined by positive aspects from the Sun. Breadth of vision and recognition of limitations are always present. Success is likely, depending on the Signs prominent in the Chart.

Negative Aspects
Disappointments in life, the source of the trouble often being an inability to recognise limitations. Restlessness is usually present, especially if this trait appears in other areas. Personal restrictions are usually accepted with resignation. Negative Jupiter/Saturn aspects often occur in the Charts of military men, helping them to accept discipline.

Jupiter Uranus

Conjunction
This occurs every 14 years. Independence is important, and there will be much restlessness, resentfulness and often wilfulness if they feel tied down at all. Restrictions and conventionality are supportable if the conjunction is not sensitively placed; for those who have the conjunction on or near the Ascendant or Midheaven, or joined by the Sun, the need for unusual, unconventional, and progressive ideas and aspirations will be paramount. There is a tendency also to unusual physical appearance: extra height for example.

Positive Aspects
Originality, leadership and humanitarianism will be positively blended – probably at their strongest if Aquarius, Pisces or Cancer are prominent. There is a dislike of all forms of conventionality.

Negative Aspects
Restlessness can become serious, especially if shown in other areas. Outspokenness can become unbearable to others; wilfulness can mar relationships. Often there is a tendency to 'moan' over small matters. Pride and hypocrisy may also develop.

Jupiter Neptune

Conjunction
This occurs every 13 years. Idealism, perception and intuition are well-developed, and there is always affection for animals. Musical and artistic ability are common, with, sometimes, philosophical or religious tendencies. This conjunction's potentialities are excellent, but tenacity must appear in other areas for the potential to be fully realized.

Positive Aspects
Ability to help the under-privileged and involvement with charities (often animal ones) are common. There is a need periodically to retire from the world to recuperate – either to a religious retreat or somewhere with a calm background. It is sometimes difficult for the subject to keep to his own standards. An unusual or strange difficulty may be present – perhaps concerning the partner, who may call for a special kind of assistance.

Negative Aspects
If the Chart shows strength and practical ability, much positive help can come from these aspects. Hypersensitivity towards suffering can be directed towards assertive action. But religious difficulties and attraction to cults can be disastrous – especially if Libra is prominent. Financial affairs should be left to professional advisers.

Jupiter Pluto

Conjunction
This occurs every 13 years. There is considerable ability to break with the past and make fresh beginnings. This is perhaps least likely when the conjunction falls in Cancer, as there may be a tendency to cling to the past. Qualities of leadership are especially present when the conjunction falls in Leo (though there may be something of a power complex present in this Sign), or in the Tenth House, or the Midheaven.

Positive Aspects
Organizational skill is usual, with additional power for intellectual capabilities. There is an ability and desire to make new beginnings.

Negative Aspects
If sensitively placed, fanaticism and a desire to exploit people can occur. The tendency needs conscious control; though for it to be really strong Pluto would need to be near the Midheaven, perhaps forming a square to Jupiter in the First House. Wastefulness is a more common tendency. Personal inadequacy is often compensated for by destructiveness.

Richard Nixon *above*
Richard Nixon has Mercury, Mars and Jupiter opposition Pluto; these give political acumen, a psychological need for power and a certain ability to cope with the stresses and strains which mount up during a politician's tenure of high office.

INTERPRETING THE ASPECTS 7

JUPITER ASCENDANT

Conjunction
In the First House, if free from affliction, a cheerful happy-go-lucky person who will be generous and enthusiastic; but sometimes this placing can lead to over-optimism and hedonism. If there is indication of practical ability and control elsewhere, then the 'higher' side of Jupiter will be to the fore, giving the subject a splendid breadth of vision, an excellent mind and a flair for language and philosophy. All Jupiter traits will in fact be positively emphasized; there may also be a tendency to liverishness and a weight problem. In the Twelfth House the philosophical elements of Jupiter will be well developed, but there will be reclusive tendencies; there is a possibility that advanced work of an excellent quality will be done quietly. Indeed, the subject may develop into a sage. It is an excellent planetary relationship for the cleric. In some circumstances it can happen that the subject develops secretive inclinations: if Jupiter is afflicted, this could become a source of conflict, particularly in a marriage. Both partners will have to try to fight the unhealthy situation that could develop.

Positive Aspects
These will enliven the whole personality, especially if Capricorn, Cancer or Virgo rises. The ability to get on with children is present, and there may be speculative tendencies.

Negative Aspects
Opposition: in the Sixth House liverish upsets can mar health; a somewhat lackadaisical or over-optimistic attitude towards work and workmates may be in evidence. In the Seventh, marriage suffers. Freedom of expression is felt as a real need, and this may well include the desire for extra-marital fun. It is not easy to keep marriage problems in positive perspective. Divorce can occur. *Other negative aspects*: these also tend to over-optimism.

JUPITER MIDHEAVEN

Conjunction
This is an excellent aspect for success in life, giving the right positive attitudes towards both the career and general objectives in life. Jupiter professions, also the theatrical life may attract. Whatever the career chosen it will not dominate life to the exclusion of other interests.

Positive Aspects
Positive attitude to career, and an optimistic, expansive attitude to life.

Negative Aspects
Opposition: this will give big-headedness and an inflated ego; perhaps childhood bumptiousness was encouraged by parents, and not checked as it should have been. Certainly success at school can very easily be harmful to the subject's character. Achievements must always be seen in proportion. *Other negative aspects* also show an inflated ego, and possibly a tendency to behave in an exaggerated fashion.

7 SATURN'S ASPECTS

The aspects of Saturn will inhibit the action of the other planets, but they can show where caution, practical ability and anchorage lie and so often contribute stability.

SATURN URANUS

Conjunction
This occurs every 91 years; it is next due in the late 1980s. Ambitions and self-reliance are present, together with determination. Depression and nervous tension will alternate; if the conjunction is sensitively placed, these changes may be difficult to come to terms with and control.

Positive Aspects
Initiative and willpower will be revealed in the subject's attitude, together with the ability to show patience and caution. If powers of concentration are indicated elsewhere, they will be strengthened by these aspects. Administrative ability and scientific work are favoured.

Negative Aspects
Tensions and depression are common and likely to cause difficulty possibly long-term. The placing of the planets must be carefully considered, since they, like other Saturn/Uranus aspects, are wider, generation influences.

SATURN NEPTUNE

Conjunction
This occurs about every 36 years. In 1917 it fell in Leo, and in the early 1950's in Libra. The next conjunction, in the late 1980s, will fall in Capricorn. It is a splendid conjunction, and if the rest of the Chart shows artistic ability or high idealism, will contribute much to giving concrete form to inspiration. Planning ability is excellent, and the subject will work hard at chosen subjects. There can be some conflict, both materialism and idealism being much in evidence. Saturn, however, can stabilize the diffuseness of Neptune. Business ability and a flair for politics may be seen.

Positive Aspects
Common sense and hardworking ability usually present with powers of organization. Powerful intuition and imagination are controlled and put to good use. There is self-preservation, and usually an instinctive dislike of being overtaken by others in any field that the subject enters.

Negative Aspects
Emotional strain, tension and inhibition. Disappointments are above average. Paranoia can occur, sometimes with reclusive tendencies. Self-will is powerful, and there is often involvement with large, impractical projects. There is impatience with every-day affairs.

SATURN PLUTO

Conjunction
This occurs every 92 years. The most common outcome is frustration causing deep-rooted obsessional problems. But this would be most likely should the conjunction fall very near or bracket the Ascendant. Thus at times behaviour patterns could be extremely unpredictable. This is, however, a generation influence, and for these characteristics to apply to the individual it is the placing of the conjunction and the way in which it is aspected from other planets that is most relevant.

Positive Aspects
An ability to get the opposing factors and tendencies of the two planets into coherent perspective: frustration and limitation should thus be overcome.

Negative Aspects
As under conjunction, but negative indications may be more serious if one planet is also in conjunction with Sun, Moon or Ascendant.

SATURN ASCENDANT

Conjunction
In the First House other aspects to Saturn must be taken into account; if there is a trine between the Sun and Saturn, this can give the subject considerable common sense and a practical, if chill personality. There will be much ambition. There may well be dental difficulties, skin trouble and rheumatic complaints. If Saturn is afflicted, there will be inhibition, shyness and a general limitation on both the personality and the positive characteristics of the Ascending Sign. A burden of considerable importance is likely, which may take the form of physical limitation. In the Twelfth House shyness and strong tendencies to withdraw from others will be present; there will be a liking, and a need, for solitude which others, friends and family, must accept.

Positive Aspects
An excellent anchorage, contributing common sense and practical ability. Ambition will be strong, but should Saturn fall in the Fifth House there is possible difficulty with children, perhaps because the subject is over-ambitious for them.

Negative Aspects
Opposition: In the Sixth House illness may limit movement. In the Seventh – often indicative of an older marriage partner – partnerships could become dull and burdensome. *Other negative aspects*: these give a tendency to inhibit, contributing some self-consciousness.

SATURN MIDHEAVEN

Conjunction
If Saturn is in the Tenth House and free from affliction from other planets, this is an extremely powerful position: the subject will go all out for his ambitions, leaving little time for enjoyment or emotional relationships (though the nature of the Sign will mitigate this point). There will be coldness of manner, the eventual

Queen Elizabeth II *above*
Queen Elizabeth II's ruling planet, Saturn, conjuncts her Midheaven and squares a Mars/Jupiter conjunction in Aquarius, indicating responsibility and determination.

outcome often being a lonely, responsible position. In other Houses the same potentialities will be present, but slightly less potent, since Saturn is 'at home' in the Tenth. There will be possibly an adherence to discipline.

Positive Aspects
Will help provide ambition and a practical attitude towards career interests; while these are likely to assume exceptional importance, they will be kept in perspective.

Negative Aspects
Opposition: while ambition is likely, inhibition will prevent it from developing. The subject will plod, but without achieving his real wishes. This may perhaps be due to a difficult, unsympathetic father. *Other negative aspects* show frustration of career potential.

8 URANUS' ASPECTS

The aspects of Uranus will give a dynamism and magnetic attraction to the planet that contacts them.

URANUS NEPTUNE

This occurs every 171 years, the last time being during the 1820s. It has a remarkable influence; when operative it adds to the number of really great people being born. Self-will is extremely prominent and much originality; there is no lack of kindness.

Positive Aspects
These stay within orb for very long periods; where an aspect occurs one planet will have to be in contact with another major planet, the Ascendant or Midheaven, for its effects to be significantly felt. Kindness, intuition and sensitivity are usually present. These qualities will be strengthened if they are shown in more prominent areas of the Chart.

Negative Aspects
Usually contributing an intensely emotional level. The subject is easily upset and must guard against over-indulgence. If the aspect is strongly placed, or either planet is powerful, (because it is ruler of the Chart) then encouragement towards a positive emotional outlet is highly desirable. An interest in anything to do with the arts, dancing and poetry should be encouraged.

URANUS PLUTO

Conjunction
This occurs every 115 years. There was one in Virgo, within orb in 1963, which finally separated in the summer of 1969. Its potentialities are astounding: children having this aspect placed near the Midheaven will be leaders of their generation. A strong positive and negative potential gives children born during the 1963–9 period the power to rid the world of much evil, and create a dynamic, humanitarian and well-organized society. Equally, they have the negative power to blow everything and everybody to pieces. Let us hope the influence will be positive: it should be, as in many ways there is much in common with 'the Age of Aquarius'. On a personal level these children need a firm, steady and very careful upbringing. Independence will be of the utmost importance; they must be made aware of their obligations and responsibilities. This generation influence will be pronounced and the generation gap will be correspondingly far more strongly emphasized than it is at present.

Positive Aspects
An ability to direct powerful energy in a dynamic and impressive way.

Negative Aspects
These can cause a disruptive and destructive tendency: sudden emotional outbursts are likely to occur as a result of inner tensions.

URANUS ASCENDANT

Conjunction
In the First House originality, personal magnetism and independent behaviour will be present, with considerable nervous tension likely. Unpredictable, the subject will be prone to accidents and circulatory problems. In the Twelfth House there will be struggles and tensions on an unconscious level. There may be an addiction to 'secret' cults and unusual societies. Psychological conflict may appear.

Positive Aspects
Will add ingenuity and a liking for the unusual. If in the Fifth House, independence and originality of approach to children and the love life may even extend to pronounced sexual perversion.

Negative Aspects
Opposition: in the Sixth House this will provoke arthritic complaints and circulatory problems. The subject will be an erratic and unpredictable worker. In the Seventh House the unusual will be sought in emotional relationships: often disastrously. Overall, there will be sudden changes in private life. *Other negative aspects* will add nervous tension, hard to release.

URANUS MIDHEAVEN

Conjunction
Sudden changes of direction in career will be likely. Brilliance and much originality will be expressed, but eccentricity and rebelliousness can mar progress, especially when the subject consciously pursues the unconventional. Uranian interests will attract.

Positive Aspects
Strong liking for originality and independence, especially concerning the expression of the self through his career; though this will be kept in a happy perspective.

Negative Aspects
Opposition makes the subject nervous and apprehensive about his career and working life in general; he finds these tensions difficult to release. There will be sudden upheaval and uncertainty in childhood. *Other negative aspects* show a build-up of tension from external causes.

INTERPRETING THE ASPECTS 8

9 NEPTUNE'S ASPECTS

Any planet forming an aspect to Neptune will be softened and refined; but could be diffused by the intervention.

NEPTUNE PLUTO

These aspects are within orb for extremely long periods, and their action is concentrated on subtle, deep-rooted tendencies. For any of them to be felt personally, either planet must be rising or near the Midheaven, or both Scorpio and Pisces must be prominent. Fantasy, clairvoyance and second sight could well be present.

Conjunction
This fell in Gemini in the 1880s and 1890s. An intellectual approach and attitude towards the occult traits mentioned above is likely.

Positive Aspects
Positive use of occult traits.

Negative Aspects
Obsessional tendencies and a blocking of the normal flow of imagination. Negative involvement with clairvoyance, perhaps inclinations to black magic and sadism; but only if the aspect is sensitively placed.

Prince Charles *below*
Prince Charles' Neptune/Pluto sextile is emphasized because Pluto rises in his Chart, giving sympathetic powers of influence over his contemporaries.

NEPTUNE ASCENDANT

Conjunction
In the First House this weakens the personality and some confusion will cloud the subject's attitudes; it will often be difficult for others to know where they stand with him. In the Twelfth House, despite a tendency to escapism (especially if Neptune is in Libra and conjoined there by the Sun), there is often talent for poetry, and genuine artistic ability, though it may be difficult to develop this. Those with this conjunction in Libra are likely to be attracted to an occasional use of drugs; many with this generation influence have suffered considerably in this way and need to be warned of the potential weakness, which could be harmful.

Positive Aspects
Will add grace, delicacy and the sensitivity of Neptune; artistic ability or sympathies will be present.

Negative Aspects
Opposition: in the Sixth House this will make danger from medically administered drugs a real possibility. Additional care should be taken with household gas appliances. Troubles likely with the feet. Not a consistent or tidy worker. In the Seventh House the attitude to marriage is over-complacent, and if there are other negative aspects either to the Ascendant or to Neptune, disappointment in emotional relationships is likely. Not good for business partnerships. *Other negative aspects* tend to weaken the personality and cause deceptive trends.

NEPTUNE MIDHEAVEN

Conjunction
Many changes of direction in career; possibly a 'jack of all trades'. Ambitions and objectives may be rather woolly or too idealistic. Any change must be positive. Involvement in the arts is likely.

Positive Aspects
Will be much impressed by the artistic and glamorous, sympathies lying in art appreciation, cinema, theatre or ballet.

Negative Aspects
Opposition: worry, confusion over career interests, and no ability to see the wood for the trees; perhaps due to a lack of security and practicality in upbringing. *Other negative aspects* show a similar attitude with self-deceptive tendencies and a confused attitude towards career and professional interests.

10 PLUTO'S ASPECTS

Any planet forming an aspect to Pluto will be given depth, turbulence and power.

PLUTO ASCENDANT

Conjunction
In the First House this planet intensifies the characteristics of the rising sign. In Cancer it is likely to add stress to the propensity to worry and the subject will find it hard either to release or to come to terms with th When it conjuncts the Ascendant in Leo, it adds much that is dynamic

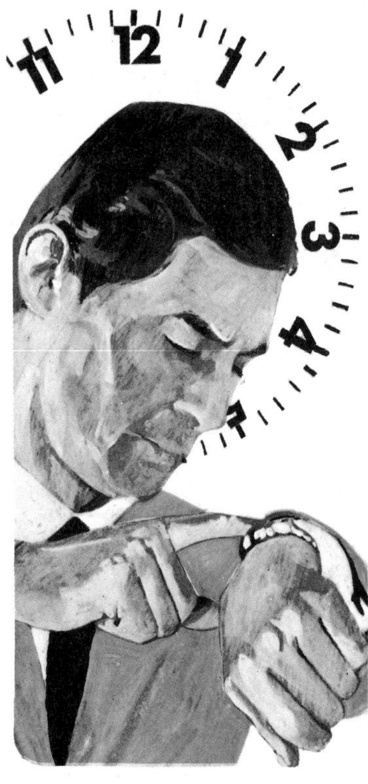

The Obsessional Type *above*
Deep-rooted obsessional features may be evident with the Pluto/Ascendant conjunction. At least one real-life subject found it a seriously disturbing force.

THE MOON'S NODES

(and often gives good looks, especially in men); but a somewhat domineering personality can also be present. In Virgo obsessional tendencies are likely, and the analytical traits will be emphasized, perhaps disproportionately. In all three signs, there will be intensity, directness and a tendency to destroy the life-pattern and start anew. In the Twelfth House these tendencies will remain unconscious, and deep-rooted psychological problems may occur regardless of the sign that Pluto is in.

Positive Aspects

Will help the subject to accept change and come to terms with new phases in life, which will be lived through with little difficulty.

Negative Aspects

Opposition: in the Sixth House, obscure illness may be related to negative psychological causes. In the Seventh House, the possibility of cruel behaviour in marriage occurs: a difficult marriage partner; dynamic and a hard bargainer in business. *Other negative aspects* lead to strain and difficulty in releasing and accepting obsessional tendencies.

PLUTO MIDHEAVEN

Conjunction

Those with this conjunction in Cancer or Virgo often perform brilliantly in business. And, if Leo is involved the subject may even qualify as a plutocrat! He will very likely have the ability to match his appetite for fame; and the strength to realize his ambitions, even if he is ruthless in the process.

Positive Aspects

Organizing ability; a good sense of vision; an ability to make clean breaks with the past and then to plan positively for a new future, often making a completely fresh start.

Negative Aspects

Opposition: this contributes foolhardiness and daring, an over-active sex life (perhaps the result of restrictive childhood conditions). *Other negative aspects* will show this to a lesser extent. In any case, however, strain is present; sudden setbacks, though not necessarily the subject's fault, will pose unforeseen difficulties and have a general effect of slowing progress. Ambitions in a chosen career or profession could be similarly checked.

As the Sun's apparent path around the earth crosses the celestial equator at the equinoxes, so the Moon's path crosses the ecliptic at its nodes. The North node marks the place where the Moon crosses from South to North; the South where it crosses from North to South.
The nodes' motion is *always retrograde*, so that they move backwards through the Zodiacal signs. This motion is the same as precession (see p. 68); but whereas a precession of the equinoxes takes about 25,800 years, a complete retrograde cycle of the nodes takes only 19 years.
The tables showing positions of the Moon's nodes from 1900–75 appear on p. 248. The positions given are for the days on which the North, or Ascending node, changes degree. The South, or Descending node, falls on the degree of the ecliptic opposite the North node (i.e. if the North node falls on 23° Aries, the South node will fall on 23° Libra).
Astrologically, the nodes mark sensitive areas.
In many respects the North node tends to be beneficial – its characteristics not unlike Jupiter's – while the South node is somewhat adverse, not unlike Saturn in effect. But the nodes are *by no means* as powerful an influence as the planets. Research has shown that a subject can derive advantage from the influence of the North node, or be somewhat drained by the South node. An influence of the South node may negate effort or even sacrifice.

If the nodal line (the astronomical term for the line joining the nodes) falls close to the line joining the Ascendant and Descendant, there can be something unusual about the subject's appearance – he might be very tall, for example.

Many astrologers feel that there is a relationship between social behaviour and the placing of the nodes: social or anti-social conduct, compatibility or incompatibility, may be shown by these points. The relationship is with the sign and House in which the nodes are found; but it must be remembered that two signs are involved – the sign of the North node, and its polarity or opposite sign, the one containing the South node. The nodes, however, only support other features.

The nodes are inserted in the relevant degree on the Birth Chart, within the band containing the glyphs of the signs. The North node glyph is not unlike the glyph for Leo, and beginners should be careful not to confuse them!

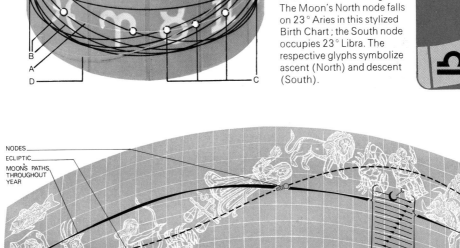

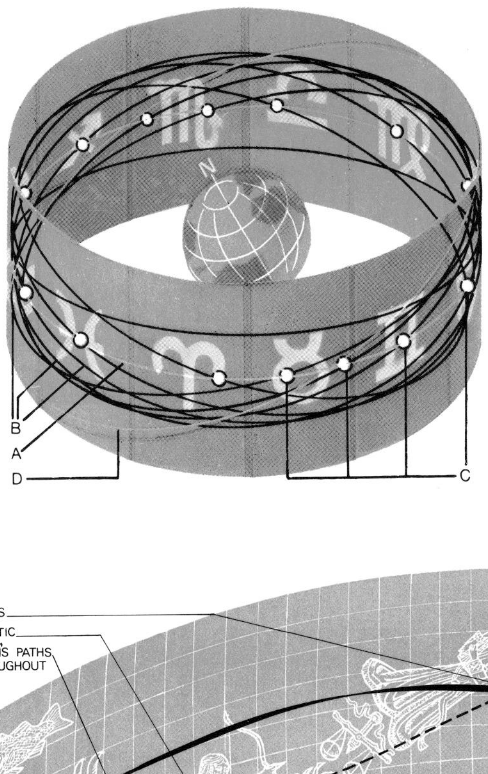

Precession of the Moon's Nodes *left*
The points of intersection of the ecliptic (A) and the Moon's orbit (B) move round the sky once every 19 years; these meeting points are called the Moon's nodes (C). The celestial equator appears at D.

The Moon's Nodes in the Birth Chart *right*
The Moon's North node falls on 23° Aries in this stylized Birth Chart; the South node occupies 23° Libra. The respective glyphs symbolize ascent (North) and descent (South).

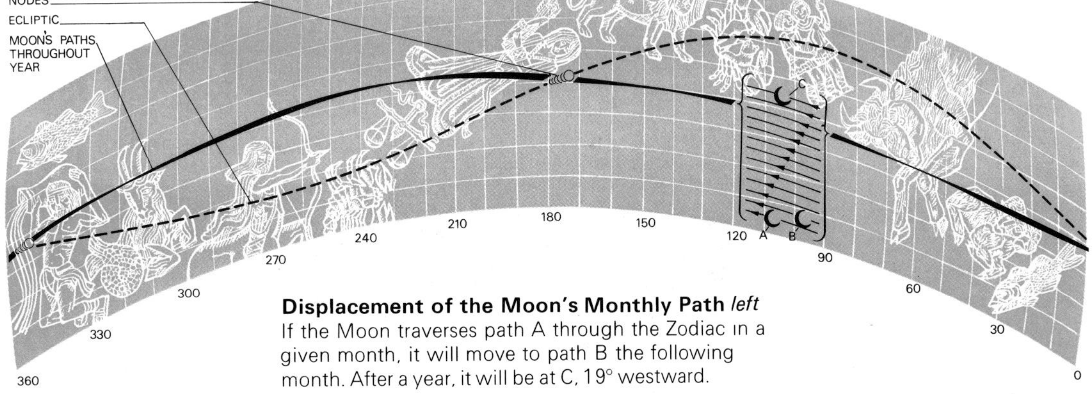

Displacement of the Moon's Monthly Path *left*
If the Moon traverses path A through the Zodiac in a given month, it will move to path B the following month. After a year, it will be at C, 19° westward.

PROGRESSIONS I

How to calculate and assess future trends in the Birth Chart

Progressions are used by astrologers to assess *trends* in the life of their subject, rather than to predict events.

There are various methods of 'progressing' a Birth Chart in order to discover the trends working in a life during future years. In this book, the 'day-for-a-year' method is used, by which the positions of the planets on the day after birth are taken to relate to conditions during the year after birth; the positions on the tenth day after birth, to the tenth year after birth, and so on.

Normally, one would have to recalculate the positions of all the planets for each day after birth. But this can be avoided by using the perpetual noon-date; this is a difficult conception to grasp, but in short it is a date directly related to the date and time of birth, peculiar to it alone and remaining the same throughout a person's life.

The positions of the planets at noon on the day for which calculations have to be made (i.e., the day related to the year) are taken to relate to noon on the perpetual noon-date, and to conditions in life for twelve months thereafter. The relationship between the perpetual noon-date and the date of birth is correlated to the interval of time between the birth-*time* and noon GMT on the birth-day.

How to Prepare a Progressed Chart

The following system of preparation is recommended. As with the natal Chart, care in calculation will avoid later errors of interpretation.

1

Copy the existing natal Birth Chart, in every detail onto a separate sheet of paper. Outside the Birth Chart, draw two additional circles, as shown in the diagram.

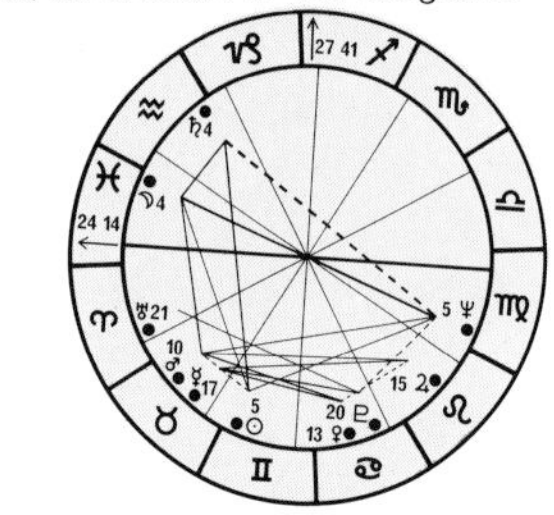

2

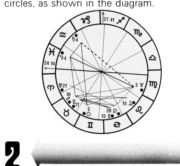

Draw the long-term aspect grid, and one for lunar progressions and transits.

3

Calculate the Perpetual Noon-Date: This is discovered by converting the interval of time between the birth-time and noon (in *am* births) or noon and the birth-time (in *pm* births) into days.

GMT is always used

There are two special pitfalls to watch for: but the process is often straightforward, as it is with our example birth-time, 1.50 am, GMT on 27 May 1932. The interval between the birth-time and noon is 10 hours 10 minutes.

Referring to the table on p. 251, ten hours represents 152.1 days; ten minutes represents 2.5 days. Add these together:

$$\begin{array}{r} 152.1 \\ +\ \ 2.5 \\ \hline 154.6 \end{array}$$

Rounding this up (or down) to the nearest whole figure we call it 155 days.

Using the same tables, discover the number of the birth day during the year (i.e., the days are counted from 1 to 365; since the relative effect is insignificant, we can ignore leap years), 27 May

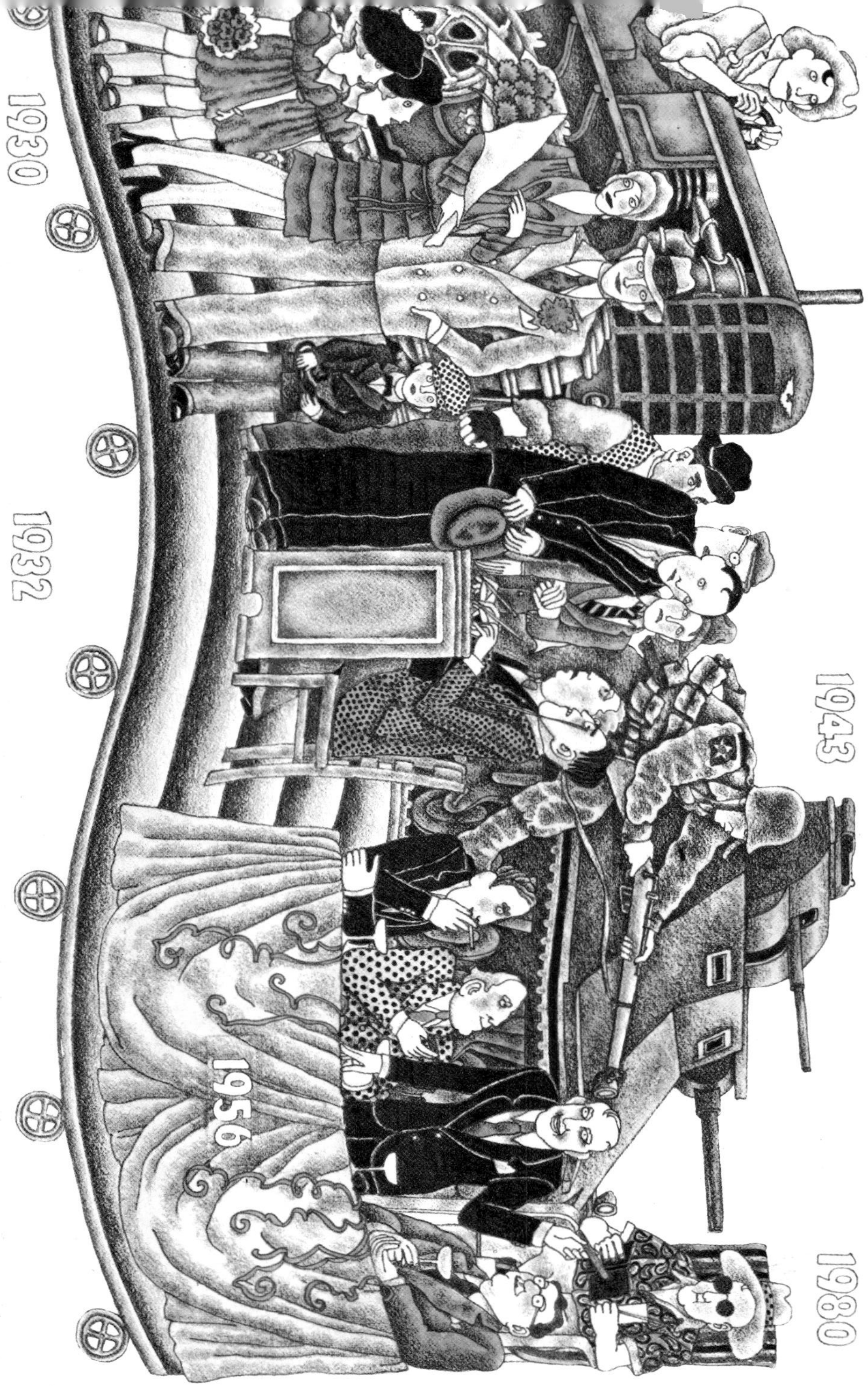

GMT, on 27 May.

For a birth at 1.50 *pm* GMT, the process is precisely the same, except that one subtracts the number of the day from the day in the year.

Interval from noon: 1 hour 50 minutes
1 hour 50 minutes = 15.2 days
+ 12.7 days
= 27.9 (Call this 28 days)

Subtract 28 from 147, to get 119. The 119th day of the year is 29 April, the perpetual noon-date for someone born at 1.50 pm GMT, on 27 May.

Gaining a Year

Suppose the birth-time is 11.50 pm, GMT, on 27 May 1932. The interval from noon is 11 hours 50 minutes.

11 hours = 167.3 days
50 mins = 12.7 days
180.0 days

Round this total up or down, where necessary, to the nearest whole number of days.
27 May is the 147th day of the year. But obviously one cannot subtract 180 from 147; so borrow a year, i.e. add 365 to 147. By this method we find that 27 May also represents 512. So, from 512 subtract 180; the result is 332, which equals 28 November. This is therefore the perpetual noon-date to be used throughout the calculations.

But because the process of calculation has involved crossing back into the previous year (1931), a day must be *added* when using the day-for-a-year method of progression; i.e., instead of the tenth day representing the tenth year of life, that year is represented by the *eleventh* day after birth; or in the example above, 7 June represents the tenth year of life – 1942.

Losing a Year

Suppose the birth-time to be 1.23 am, GMT, on 16 September 1932. The interval from noon is 10 hours 37 minutes.

10 hours = 152.1 days
37 mins = 9.3 days
161.4 days

Call this 161 days.
16 September is the 259th day of the year. 259 days plus 161 days gives a total of 420 days.
But since there are only 365 days in the year, subtract 365 from 420, which equals 55 days. The 55th day of the year is 24 February. This is the perpetual noon-date.

But because the process of calculation has involved crossing forward into the subsequent year (1933), a day must be *subtracted* when using the day-for-a-year method; i.e. instead of the tenth day representing the tenth year of life, that year is represented by the ninth day after birth; or in the example given above, 25 September represents the tenth year of life – 1942.

Sample Progressions

Let us assume that we wish to discover the trends in the life of a subject for the year 1970. The birth date is as for the Chart on p. 80: i.e. the subject was born at 1.50 am, GMT on 27 May 1932. First find the perpetual noon-date for 1.50 am, GMT, 27 May. The calculations are as in the first example given above: the perpetual noon-date is 29 October.

PROGRESSIONS 2

4

Calculate the Progressed Date

Take the ephemeris for 1932 (or use the Tables of Planetary Positions in this book beginning on p. 194). 1932 to 1970 = 38 years; so from 27 May, count forward 38 days. This gives us 4 July. Then take the planetary positions one by one and calculate their progressed positions on this basis (the Moon is progressed separately):

Sun 12° 6′ Cancer
Neptune 5° 50′ Virgo
Uranus 23° 9′ Aries
Saturn 2° 52′ R Aquarius
Jupiter 22° 15′ Leo
Mars 8° 34′ Gemini
Venus 3° 59′ R Cancer
Mercury 3° 34′ Leo.

Once the calculations have been made, the progressed planets are then inserted (see below) in their positions in the final progressed Chart.

5

Calculate the progressed Ascendant and Midheaven. If the birth-time is known then look up the sidereal time at noon, shown in the ephemeris opposite the progressed date (or in the tables on p. 234). In this case, 4 July gives us a sidereal time of 6 hrs 49 mins 8 secs. Calculate the Ascendant as you would for the natal Chart using the time of 6 hrs 49 mins 8 secs *instead of* the sidereal time at noon on the birth-day:

Sidereal time at noon GMT (Prog)	6	49	8
Interval to noon (am)	10	10	0
Subtract these	20	39	8
Acceleration on interval		1	40
Subtract	20	37	28
Longitude equivalent (W)		17	44
Subtract:	20	19	44

= Progressed Sidereal Time

The relevant Table of Houses gives a progressed Ascendant of 5° 6′ Gemini, a progressed Midheaven of 3° Aquarius.

6

In the wide band immediately outside the Birth Chart, mark the progressed Ascendant and Midheaven on their relevant degrees.

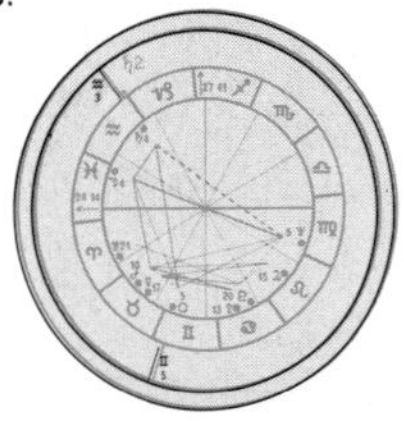

7

Mark the positions of the progressed planets (*except* the Moon which has still to be calculated) in the outer band.

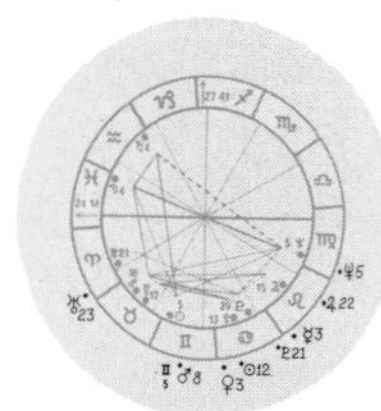

8

Using the accompanying grid as a guide, list the aspects made by the progressed planets, Ascendant and Midheaven. List also the aspects made by progressed planets to each other.

In each case, the aspects made by the Sun are of primary importance; these are listed separately, under 'Solar aspects'. But it must be borne in mind that solar aspects are not invariably present in a progressed Chart.

If the birth-time is only roughly known, the progressed Ascendant and Midheaven should not be used as they will not be accurate.

9

Now is the time to calculate the position of the progressed Moon. Because the Moon moves more rapidly than any other planet (at the rate of about 14° each day), we have to calculate its progressed position with greater accuracy. The noon position of another planet is adequate for a whole year; with the Moon, the *exact* position is needed for each month of the progressed year.

9

To progress the Moon for 1970 for the above example, begin with its position at noon on the progressed date, 4 July. This is 19° 1′ Cancer, representing the Moon's position on the perpetual noon-date, 29 October. To find the Moon's position for the other months of 1970, first discover the Moon's motion during the preceding months of the year, i.e., from January to October. The Moon's position on 3 July (representing 29 October 1969) was 6°14′ Cancer. Subtract this from 19° 1′ Cancer to obtain a result of 12° 47′ Cancer.

The Moon's motion between noon on 3 July and noon on 4 July was 12° 47′; this represents the Moon's motion in the progressed Chart between October 1969 and October 1970.

Next, discover the Moon's motion for each month, by dividing by twelve. We find that the Moon moved at a rate of almost 1° 04′ per month over the year; but in order to fill out the year's motion, one month must contain only a movement of 1° 03′. This difference of 1′ is so insignificant in astrological lunar progressions that we can safely place it in any month without affecting the accuracy of the Chart. So the Moon's motion over the year will be as follows:

Moon's longitude 1969

29 October	6° 14′
29 November	7° 17′
(adding 1° 03′ only)	
29 December	8° 21′
(adding 1° 04′ thereafter)	

Moon's longitude 1970

29 January	9° 25′
29 February	10° 29′
29 March	11° 33′
29 April	12° 37′
29 May	13° 41′
29 June	14° 45′
29 July	15° 49′
29 August	16° 53′
29 September	17° 57′
29 October	19° 01′

To complete the list to December, find the Moon's motion between noon on 4 July and noon on 5 July, representing October 1970 to October 1971.

9

Moon's position on 4 July (representing 29 October 1970) was 19° 01′ Cancer; on 5 July (representing 29 October 1971) was 2° 00′ Leo. Remembering that the Moon changes signs, the motion was 12° 59′. Divide by twelve = 1° 04′ with 11′ remaining. Motion for eleven months is therefore 1° 05′, with one month only 1° 04′.

Note: The remainder must be spread evenly over alternate months, ensuring the correct total over the year.

10

Mark in the outer circle of the progression Chart the scope of the Moon's positions within the year for which progressions are being made. These should then be listed carefully month by month in the relevant column of the grid. After that is done, list the aspects the Moon makes to the natal and progressed planets.

11

Examine the Shortened Ephemeris (p. 250) for the year for which progressions are to be made. Note whether any planet on any day of that year falls on the same degree occupied by any planet in the *original* Birth Chart. Note any such aspects in the transits grid. In the grid opposite, for instance, it will be seen that Uranus makes a trine to the Sun on 15 April which operates until 14 May; on 15 May, Uranus makes a quincunx to the Moon and a trine to Saturn, operative until 9 July. The next section shows how these may be interpreted.

12

Mark in the outer circle of the Chart the approximate positions of the slow-moving planets on the noon-date of the year for which progressions are being made. In the cases of Mars, Mercury and Venus only the conjunctions and oppositions are used, and need to be noted. In all cases, the semi-sextile and semi-square remain unused, and need not be listed as their influence is too small. The effects of the quincunx are weak, but worth noting.

Interpreting the Progressed Chart
Look up the progressed aspect and note the possible trends and influences that are indicated. Note also the progressed lunar aspects, and the possible outcome of the listed transits in the Chart.

Progressed aspects indicate general trends in a subject's life during the year in which they operate; lunar aspects affect the life for two to three months, and transits during a few weeks or a few days, according to the speed of movement of the planet concerned.

Detailed interpretations of the effects that the various combinations have are given on the following pages.

The One-Degree System of Progressions
The one-degree system can be integrated with the secondary system described earlier. It involves progressing a planet from its position at birth, one degree for each year of the life; and noting the aspects it makes to *natal* planets.

It will soon be realized that the progressed Sun shows very little difference in either system: for it moves only about one degree a day. But with the Moon, which moves very quickly, and with the major planets, which move slowly, this system can be helpful.
The writer does not advise singling out all the aspects that the one-degree system makes, but blending these with the more potent secondary progressions. This will give a more reliable and balanced interpretation of the subject's progressions.

Often the planets prominent in the secondary progressions seem to be echoed by the one-degree progressions, and this adds strength to the whole progressed Chart.

Roughly speaking, the one-degree progression lasts a year, fading rather slowly in and out for 12 months on either side. For instance, if natally Venus is on 23° Leo and Neptune on 0° Libra, when the subject is 37 years old, Venus progressed will be in conjunction with Neptune, and this conjunction will have its effect through the year preceding and the year following the 37th birthday.

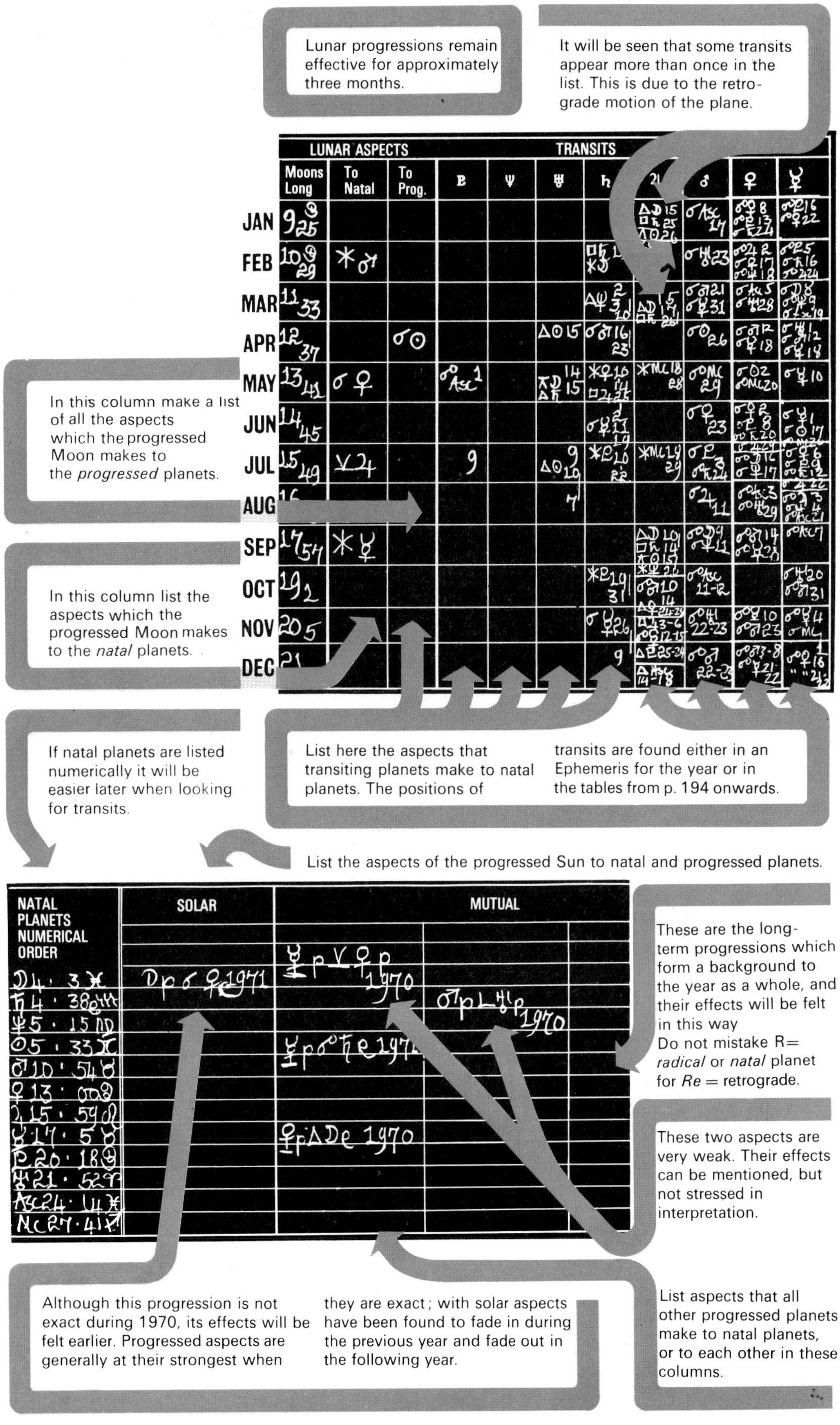

Lunar progressions remain effective for approximately three months.
It will be seen that some transits appear more than once in the list. This is due to the retrograde motion of the plane.
LUNAR ASPECTS
TRANSITS
Moons Long
To Natal
To Prog.
JAN
FEB
MAR
APR
MAY
JUN
JUL
AUG
SEP
OCT
NOV
DEC
In this column make a list of all the aspects which the progressed Moon makes to the *progressed* planets.
In this column list the aspects which the progressed Moon makes to the *natal* planets.
If natal planets are listed numerically it will be easier later when looking for transits.
List here the aspects that transiting planets make to natal planets. The positions of transits are found either in an Ephemeris for the year or in the tables from p. 194 onwards.
List the aspects of the progressed Sun to natal and progressed planets.
NATAL PLANETS NUMERICAL ORDER
SOLAR
MUTUAL
These are the long-term progressions which form a background to the year as a whole, and their effects will be felt in this way
Do not mistake R= *radical* or *natal* planet for *Re* = retrograde.
These two aspects are very weak. Their effects can be mentioned, but not stressed in interpretation.
Although this progression is not exact during 1970, its effects will be felt earlier. Progressed aspects are generally at their strongest when they are exact; with solar aspects have been found to fade in during the previous year and fade out in the following year.
List aspects that all other progressed planets make to natal planets, or to each other in these columns.

Listing the Transits *top*
Transits may be listed as shown in the grid above, and also as follows:

♃T △ ☽ = Jupiter transiting trine Moon

♂T ☌ A = Mars transiting conjunction Ascendant

Transits are normally used only in relation to the natal planets and not to progressed planets.

Listing the Progressions *above*
To deal with progressions the reader will need to learn a little more astrological shorthand (p. = progressed; R = radical). Two sample readings of the progression symbols are shown below, taken respectively from the columns headed 'Solar' and 'Mutual'.

☉p ☌ ♀R = Sun progressed conjunction Venus radical

☿p ⚺ ♀p = Mercury progressed semi-sextile Venus progressed

INTERPRETING PROGRESSIONS I

Serious astrologers do not 'predict' events; they assess trends. When mentioning potential hazards or beneficial periods, the astrologer must always remember to put these matters carefully to his client. He should never state: 'You will have an accident on the twenty-first of the month', but he can say that: 'On the twenty-first of the month you are likely to be somewhat prone to risks, so take additional care when handling hot dishes or sharp knives.'

Of course, in this way astrologers do lay themselves open to the criticism of using generalizations. It must be made clear to a client that progressions are rather like weather forecasts, and should be used in much the same way.

Progressions seem to work in layers. First, there are the secondary progressions (and the one-degree progressions described on p. 153),

Astrologers are not magicians. They do not deal in specific events and must always take care that no client is injured through taking their advice too literally.

led by the solar progressions, if present. Secondly, come the progressed mutual aspects, forming a general background over the year in question and remaining with the subject for the following year.

The Moon
Remember that, should the Moon make aspects to either natal or progressed planets activated by secondary progressions, this indicates the period when the conditions are most likely to occur. For instance, where a subject has Sun progressed square Saturn, should the progressed Moon make a square aspect to the natal (radical) or progressed Saturn, then it will be during those months that the effects of the Sun square Saturn will be most emphatic – here health or mental buoyancy may suffer as a result.

When lunar progressions highlight secondary progressions, it is highly probable that these months will be eventful. The same is true to a certain extent of the transits of the major planets; with the same Sun progressed square Saturn, the background conditions will be emphasized should Saturn by transit make an aspect to the natal Sun.

A Golden Rule
In interpreting any progression, there is a golden rule which should always be borne in mind: Aspects formed by progressed planets, whether positive, negative or a conjunction, will partake of the nature of the relationship between the same two planets in the Birth Chart so long as they appear in aspect there. So if two planets form aspect A in the natal Chart and aspect B in the progressed Chart, aspect B will be partly influenced by the nature of aspect A. If the two planets make no natal aspect, then aspect B must be considered alone.

If there is a badly afflicted planet in a Chart, not much 'good' will come from positive directions to it. Similarly, an afflicted natal planet will not 'do much' for any other planet to which it progresses.

Progressed minor aspects should not be overemphasized; the quincunx and semi-square are the most important, and should be used if they involve the Sun. Mutual minor aspects should not be stressed, but their influences noted.

Note
In astrological practice, aspects are listed from the Sun to Pluto, the Ascendant and Midheaven. Where, for example, the progressed Mars makes an aspect to the natal Sun, this is listed under Mars progressed (aspect made to) Sun. When referring to interpretation, it will therefore be necessary to look up the solar progressions to Mars. The effects are usually very similar, but the planet *making* the aspect will exert the greater influence; e.g., Venus progressed conjunction Mercury, see Mercury progressed conjunction Venus; Mercury progressed trine Moon see Moon's positive aspects to Mercury (but remember that the effect will be for a year, not the three months of the lunar progressions).

THE PROGRESSED SUN

Progressed solar aspects are the most important directions, though there are often quite long periods in a life when they are absent. If lacking strong transits, life is likely to be uneventful. It is vital to remember the Sun's natal position and its relationship – if any – to the planet it aspects in the Birth Chart. A year in which the Sun progresses from its natal sign into the next sign will be a milestone year.

SOLAR PROGRESSIONS TO THE MOON

Solar progressions to the Moon may produce a personal landmark in life, provided the planets appear well-aspected in the natal Chart.

Conjunction
An important period, possibly critical, and a time for changes. If planets are natally well aspected, very progressive, particularly for a man. Certainly a milestone period that will be long remembered.

Positive Aspects
A favourable period: a time of success in business or social life particularly in new projects and enterprises. Such a period should be used, e.g. in home-buying.

Negative Aspects
Possible domestic difficulties, and not a good period for health. There may be career upsets and disputes.

SOLAR PROGRESSIONS TO MERCURY

Natally, the Sun can only make a conjunction or a wide semi-sextile to Mercury; but by progression, the Sun can travel far enough to make a trine to the natal planet in old age. These aspects can, however, be covered under one heading, Mercury being a harmless planet. An emphasis on changes – in literary work, or perhaps a move from one district to another – might be expected. Should the aspect be semi-square or square, there is a possibility of strain, but overall a rather lively period may be anticipated.

SOLAR PROGRESSIONS TO VENUS

Conjunction
This should bolster finances, social and love life; other indications being reasonable, an extremely pleasant period. Marriage or, more usually, romance. But, should there be a semi-square between these planets, natally, extra-marital affairs may form a hazard for the married,

The Sun/Venus conjunction is a good sign for romance, except for the married. For them the dangers will be obvious.

particularly if Venus is conjunct with the natal Sun. The subject should be made aware that he will be particularly susceptible at this time.

Positive and Negative Aspects
Positive aspects make life pleasant, but negative ones lead to over-indulgence and extravagance.

SOLAR PROGRESSIONS TO MARS

Conjunction
Likely to indicate an exceptionally hardworking period. Abundant energy, not easily controlled, but health should be good. The subject may be more accident-prone than usual. Special care when Mars makes transiting conjunctions and oppositions to natal planets.

Positive Aspects
Much as the conjunction, but possibly more progressive. If the aspect is a trine, events could affect the course of a whole life and the period could be remembered for a long time to come.

Negative Aspects
Often a direct health hazard: inflammatory conditions, feverishness or physical exhaustion. The astrologer's advice should be emphasized, as the subject may be reluctant to listen.

SOLAR PROGRESSIONS TO JUPITER

Conjunction
Should prove extremely beneficial; a time of progress in finances and career. Guard against over-confidence.

Positive Aspects
The trine from the progressed Sun to Jupiter is the 'best in the book'. The subject should reach his full potential. Finances and social affairs will prosper if fostered.

Negative Aspects
Judgment will not be well tuned; health may suffer from liverishness caused by intemperance. Over-optimism may lead to minor troubles and disappointments. Not a good time to invest and there is a tendency to be deceitful.

While the Sun and Jupiter can carry you to the peak of your career, this aspect may also lead to disappointment and suffering from over-indulgence.

SOLAR PROGRESSIONS TO SATURN

Conjunction
Highly critical period with possible additional responsibilities. Difficulties will strengthen the personality, but life will certainly be no bed of roses. Circulation may suffer.

Positive Aspects
Often as critical as conjunction effects, but extra responsibilities may mean promotion, perhaps into an isolated position. Career, attitude and general way of life becomes more settled and permanent.

Negative Aspects
Domestic and health troubles likely. Keep to a steady, rather quiet routine; avoid change. Financial risks should not be taken.

SOLAR PROGRESSIONS TO URANUS

Conjunction
Dynamic and eventful period, with probable long-term changes in both career and inner life. Relationships may be emphasized – either their making or breaking, and perhaps both, through divorce.

Positive Aspects
Possible unexpected financial gains; increase in dynamism and outgoing interest. These positive aspects have long been considered excellent for studying astrology.

Negative Aspects
May bring a build-up of nervous tension; even breakdown if the Birth Chart also shows it. Not a good time for important changes.

SOLAR PROGRESSIONS TO NEPTUNE

Conjunction
Additional inspiration likely, which should help the artistic subject. But, with Neptune activated, the inspiration must be positively channelled to avoid diffuseness and escapism.

Positive Aspects
Similar to the conjunction, but better prospects of directing Neptunian influences. The creative sides of both the Sun and this planet should work extremely well when in a positive, progressed relationship, bringing happiness and good fortune.

Negative Aspects
If progressions occur in a Chart showing sensitivity but not much inner strength, there may be neurotic tendencies – especially if Neptune is afflicted at birth. If supported by more practical aspects, or if the Birth Chart shows these strongly emphasized, much inspiration and creativity may be present.

SOLAR PROGRESSIONS TO PLUTO

Conjunction
An eventful period likely, but let the progression pass before expecting benefits. Probable strong emphasis on finance, and the possibility of beginning a new phase, perhaps a complete change of direction, though not without difficulty.

Positive Aspects
Similar to the conjunction; but in theory there is less strain. Pluto's 'clearing-out' tendencies may be in evidence; important business projects may be started.

Negative Aspects
The subject should be prepared for a certain frustration of plans, with unexpected stumbling-blocks. A tough, strenuous, difficult period that will make his progress far from smooth; other areas may help to ease the situation.

The negative aspects of the Sun in Pluto may cause impediment to progress. Changes of direction will not be made easily.

SOLAR PROGRESSIONS TO THE ASCENDANT

Remember that these rely on complete accuracy of birth time. Four minutes out, either way, will represent a year out on the Chart, so the effects must be judged with care.

Conjunction
If the progressed Sun conjuncts the *natal* Ascendant, the period will not pass unnoticed; there will be a period of all-round psychological growth. Health likely to improve, and the progression is often an indication of marriage.

Positive Aspects
Similar to conjunction effects, but much less potent.

Negative Aspects
Possible period of psychological struggle; but the subject will learn from such experiences.

INTERPRETING PROGRESSIONS 2

SOLAR PROGRESSIONS TO THE MIDHEAVEN

These also rely totally on accuracy of birth-time calculation.

Conjunction
The peak year relating to career and public standing. Possibility of promotion, marriage or children.

Positive Aspects
Excellent, progressive career period.

Negative Aspects
Possible difficulties with career, children or domestic life.

Note Aspects of the Sun to its own place occur similarly for everyone. Thus, at 30 the semi-sextile falls; at 45, the semi-square; at 60, the sextile. These years may produce a slight emphasis of solar traits.

With the conjunction of Mercury and Mars, an excess of hasty impulsiveness may well lead to a tricky situation.

MERCURY'S PROGRESSIONS TO VENUS

In the Birth Chart, these aspects can never be more than 76° apart, so the largest possible aspect is the sextile. In the progressed Chart they can be separated by greater distances.
But both these planets remain so harmless that not even strenuous aspects will give much trouble. Generally, when there are progressed aspects, there is emphasis on everything they represent. If the subject is inclined to crafts and art work, he may under the sextile take up pottery, design, dressmaking. If he has literary leanings, the time is right for him to get his ideas on paper. Social life will be extremely pleasant, when progressions between Mercury and Venus are activated by lunar progressions and transits.

MERCURY'S PROGRESSIONS TO MARS

Conjunction
Gives additional mental energy. Inclination to write likely; perhaps a sudden flair for satire. Impulsiveness in speech and writing can make for over-assertiveness. But the progression gives a bright and optimistic outlook and opportunities for much good work provided that the inherent instability is countered.

Positive Aspects
Like the conjunction in effect, but more controllable. Extra ability to study and to put latent ideas and plans into action. Energetic, intellectual conditions very favourable to realization of dreams.

Negative Aspects
Likely to make the subject highly-strung; he may become unkind or over-sarcastic – trends he should try to control. Outside help should be sought where difficulties become a source of tension and worry. Advisable to delay signing documents or dealing with solicitors or house agents until the progressions have eased. Problems can cause mental stress.

MERCURY'S PROGRESSIONS TO JUPITER

Conjunction
An excellent progression. The mind will broaden and it is a good time for study, examinations and all Mercury/Jupiter pursuits (language, travel, writing, etc.). The nervous system will improve.

Positive Aspects
In effect the same as the conjunction, but probably less potent. Judgment and finance should be favourable; friendships long-lasting. Thoughts may turn to philosophy, and Mercury/Jupiter occupations and interests will prosper.

Negative Aspects
Lapses of judgment common, with possible serious mistakes. Not a good time for long-term planning or for extensive travel. Only too easy to make rash promises. Hypocrisy and anxiety may be in evidence.

MERCURY'S PROGRESSIONS TO SATURN

Conjunction
The subject will be put into a perhaps over-serious frame of mind, leading to periods of depression. But if he can combat this, his powers of concentration should be good and difficult problems constructively solved. Not much lively progress. Health may suffer, mostly through poor circulation and nervous strain.

Some sort of deception is likely to be encountered under the influence of the Mercury/Saturn negative aspects.

Positive Aspects
Constructive indications likely to be to the fore, but overall there will be increased responsibility. Prudence is advocated, and projects undertaken will make good progress. The influence will 'sober up' a rather boisterous character and help him to steady himself.

Negative Aspects
A possibility of the subject encountering some form of deception; and all round a rather depressing influence. The subject should muster all his resilience and try to bring any albeit sparse constructive elements into play. It will not be a good period for business which will add a further cause for despondency.

MERCURY'S PROGRESSIONS TO URANUS

Conjunction
Originality and a general intellectual brightness will be in evidence, though with 'edginess'. Exercise control and be ready for some uncharacteristic eccentricities. New and interesting people may be an influence, but he must ensure they are worthwhile and guard against cranks!

Positive Aspects
New thought-patterns will be a help in making plans for career or leisure interests. New friendships (spiced with dynamic attraction) often occur under this influence. The subject may well be more attractive to others while these aspects are operating.

Negative Aspects
A proneness to extremism; tensions can sometimes lead to nervous breakdown if the Birth Chart shows such tendencies. In this case the subject should be advised to live quietly. Behaviour patterns are sometimes influenced, and eccentricities like 'dropping-out' may occur.

MERCURY'S PROGRESSIONS TO NEPTUNE

Conjunction
A refining influence, possibly leading to a sudden liking for peace and quiet or poetry – the subject may even begin writing it. A heightening of aesthetic sensitivity probable.

Positive Aspects
Like the conjunction, but more difficult to shape. Inspiration might carry the subject away, losing good potential in the process.

The conjunction of Mercury to Neptune brings poetry into a life and leads to a rejection of the unaesthetic.

Negative Aspects
Unusual phobias and fears may occur; the subject can become the victim of deceit or self-confusion. He might need a strong arm to lean on at this time and should heed detached advice from others.

MERCURY'S PROGRESSIONS TO PLUTO

Inner battles are likely, whatever the aspect. New outlooks may have to be developed and old ideas discarded. This process should be less turbulent when the trine or sextile is formed. Conjunctions and negative aspects are likely to give the troubles increased prominence; to bring deep-rooted problems into perspective, the subject may be advised to consult an analyst. These aspects can lead to a complete change of attitude.

MERCURY'S PROGRESSIONS TO THE ASCENDANT

A positive period for study and all Mercurial concerns, spiced with a certain light-heartedness. If the aspect is negative, there should be little difficulty. But there may be some strain, and the subject should take extra time for relaxation.

MERCURY'S PROGRESSIONS TO THE MIDHEAVEN

A wish to communicate more with the general public is possible, e.g. the subject suddenly finding himself writing to newspapers. He may want to start new enterprises and will live through a busy, active and interesting period. The difficult aspects could contribute some mental strain through over-activity; but this is easily countered. Possible difficulty under the negative aspects.

When Mercury progresses to the Midheaven, a sudden urge to communicate may make itself felt.

MERCURY'S PROGRESSIONS TO ITS OWN PLACE

Enhancing for the qualities of the Sign and House occupied by Mercury at birth; and if they occur, they are best used in stressing the interpretation of Mercury in its own Sign and House, as found in Part 2 – Celestial Mechanics and Influences.

VENUS' PROGRESSIONS TO MARS

Conjunction
Love 'at first sight' can occur, with impulsiveness and hasty decisions. The period as a whole may be exciting, but feelings may come to dominate. This is less likely with Venus stronger, the tendency then being towards romanticism.

With Venus progressing to Mars the subject is liable to find himself suddenly swept off his feet; certainly in a romantic situation.

Positive Aspects
Similar to the conjunction but involving a greater desire for harmony in any relationship. Happiness in the emotional sphere is indicated.

Negative Aspects
These tend to over-sensitize the feelings and there may be difficulties in love-life, with thoughtlessness or indiscretion. The subject may be swept off his feet by a romantic attachment, but should allow the progression to ease before commitment.

VENUS' PROGRESSIONS TO JUPITER

The Conjunction
Indicative of great happiness. Financial and social success likely, with extra comfort. The progression is sensitive, bringing appreciation of beauty; the subject could 'advance' on an esoteric, possibly philosophical level. He will feel more at ease with himself.

Positive Aspects
Very positive; finances should improve and life become more enjoyable. The subject is likely to show increased generosity and sympathy. He should watch his weight as there may be a sudden liking for rich food.

Negative Aspects
Generally not too difficult, both planets being beneficial. But generosity could turn to over-extravagance, liking for good food to over-indulgence which may turn to liverishness. Even with stable natal indications, a rational approach to finance will be difficult.

VENUS' PROGRESSIONS TO SATURN

Conjunction
The most positive indication is a likely relationship with someone of a much greater age. It could be romantic, though not necessarily. Otherwise there may well be financial stress, perhaps leading to the subject becoming somewhat

Under the negative influences of Venus and Saturn, elderly relatives will tend to become an extra trial.

avaricious or too 'careful'.
Emotional expression is limited.

Positive Aspects
Tend to steady the emotions; there may be constructive financial gain. An excellent time to put financial affairs on a reliable basis. If lunar aspects are helpful, the period should be a good one.

Negative Aspects
Not a happy period for love; disappointments likely and permanent relationships may enter a depressing stage. The subject should watch for impositions. Elderly friends or relatives may become demanding in a rather unsatisfactory way. Positive, happier aspects from other areas of the Chart must lighten the period if life is to be at all easy.

VENUS' PROGRESSIONS TO URANUS

Conjunction
Possible unexpected and dynamic romantic relationships or the termination of one. Sudden general influence from others is likely, but the unexpected element will centre on love-life.

Positive Aspects
A period marked by a memorable social life and good all-round conditions; but in essence it is similar to the conjunction; the formation of interesting ties of affection is likely. The time is right for change; usually a very good period indeed.

Negative Aspects
Considerable trouble can occur, possibly centred on domestic life: difficulties, estrangements or break-ups. The subject could live through a critical period, and should avoid important changes like moving house. But the other progressions could ease the situation.

VENUS' PROGRESSIONS TO NEPTUNE

Conjunction
A splendidly romantic progression. Happiness of the most enduring kind is usual, and can bring platonic friendships with real depth, understanding and feeling. The influence refines the feelings and promotes emotional maturity, taking the subject to a more advanced level.

Positive Aspects
Indicative of a blissfully romantic period with stable emotional relationships. The subject will certainly always look back on such a period with nostalgia.

Negative Aspects
Possible tendency towards negative escapism, especially if the love-life goes wrong (as is likely under these influences). The subject may find it difficult to keep his feelings coherent; may well come under undesirable influences. It will not be easy for him to recognize deception while these aspects continue to be in operation. He must be careful.

VENUS' PROGRESSIONS TO PLUTO

Conjunction
Can be extremely difficult period, the subject being likely to fall suddenly and deeply in love, and the normal expression of feelings will be blocked in some way – by marital commitments, for instance. Often there is little or no release until passion eases as the aspect passes.

Positive Aspects
Should be financially positive; e.g. an excellent time to invest in long-term insurance. Sex life could assume more importance than usual. Even with the trine and sextile, there could be some blocking of a normal course of events.

Negative Aspects
Similar to the conjunction; but possibly with more prominent financial overtones. Sudden, unexpected obstacles will have to be coped with.

VENUS' PROGRESSIONS TO THE ASCENDANT

Conjunction
A very positive period. It will involve financial gain; the possible formation of a permanent relationship, or marriage. Sometimes the acquisition of property is indicated. The subject must make the best of the opportunities offered.

Positive Aspects
Like the conjunction, but with more accent on sheer enjoyment.

Negative Aspects
Not in themselves leading to any difficulties but extravagance may be the cause of financial setback. A display of possessiveness or a gust of sentimental emotion will prove unwelcome.

VENUS' PROGRESSIONS TO THE MIDHEAVEN

Conjunction
Excellent for financial advancement; a considerable raise in salary, perhaps. General popularity. Another indication of marriage. Prosperity, possibly not as a result of the subject's own efforts.

Positive Aspects
As the conjunction, with the good things of life coming with little or no effort.

Negative Aspects
Perhaps some disappointment or jealousy in relationships; extravagance by the partner may cause financial difficulties which will be a source of tension in the family.

With Venus on the Midheaven, some generous financial rewards are likely to be near.

MARS' PROGRESSIONS TO JUPITER

Conjunction
With this conjunction operative – its influence will last solidly for about three years – the subject can do much to further his worldly progress. Additional energy and enterprise are on his side; but he could also become over-extravagant. If there is constructiveness in his natal Chart, he should make splendid progress. If the Chart shows many lively and enthusiastic qualities, he could have difficulty controlling the more expansive, and rather impulsive traits.

Positive Aspects
A position for taking the initiative. Opportunities are likely to occur and should be seized. Energetic, hard-working but enjoyable.

Negative Aspects
The subject may go to extremes of action. Substantial losses may occur through gambling, over-investment or making loans. Such risks should be discouraged, but advice may not be heeded. Yet while this may be a difficult time, recuperative powers are good. Over-enthusiasm and an excess of feeling are likely.

MARS' PROGRESSIONS TO SATURN

Conjunction
Life will not be easy or pleasant under any Mars/Saturn progression, the subject being torn in two directions. If plans are put to him, he will want to go energetically ahead, and probably will – only to find his progress blocked. Health is likely to suffer to a certain extent; in sporting activities strength may be undermined or injury incurred. He must try to find a middle road.

Positive Aspects
Similar to the conjunction; but enterprise, enthusiasm and common sense will blend, and progress should be marked. But good results will still not come without some strain and hard work.

Negative Aspects
Strain likely, which could lead to rashness, impulsiveness and occasional depression. Outbursts of

Obstacles to smooth progress are likely to occur during the conjunction of Mars in Saturn.

temper may occur. Probably a very turbulent period, which the subject will find difficult to understand. He will need sympathy; but may neither deserve nor get it.

MARS' PROGRESSIONS TO URANUS

Conjunction
Likely to be an important and eventful period; a time for the unexpected and perhaps the exciting. Consequences likely to be long-lasting. Care necessary in making new friends and acquaintances; their influence may not be all it seems. Altogether a very interesting period.

Positive Aspects
Give extra enterprise, originality, and quick insight. Excellent if somewhat erratic progress may be made; personal magnetism is enormously increased.

Negative Aspects
A very difficult period, with extremely rash behaviour likely; the consequences may continue beyond the progression. The subject will be accident-prone, and should be cautious during the whole period, particularly when Mars is activated by transit. He should be warned against behaviour he may bitterly regret later.

MARS' PROGRESSIONS TO NEPTUNE

Conjunction
Makes the subject aware of all that is colourful and delicate. If he has artistic ability, and is not lacking in practical qualities, he will get a great deal from this very lively progression.

Positive Aspects
Much as the conjunction: but also enjoyable and beneficial for business enterprise. Social commitments should be fun.

Negative Aspects
Can be dangerous, especially if there is a tendency towards escapism through drink or drugs. Fulfilment through the arts should be advocated; their attraction will be activated. Sensuality can be emphasized.

The attraction of strange religious cults can prove strong under the negative upsets of Mars progressing to Neptune.

MARS' PROGRESSIONS TO PLUTO

Conjunction
These two planets are related through the rulership of Scorpio, and their influences somewhat balance. But the possibility of increased energy (Mars) and the blocking influence of Pluto can cause difficulties, which will be overcome only by sheer force. There may be a sudden ruthless striving for power, but the conjunction will certainly help push the subject up the ladder. Unpopularity may result.

Positive Aspects
Progress likely with the restricting influence of Pluto less marked. A new beginning may be made.

Negative Aspects
Difficult and strenuous, with a tendency to work to breaking-point. Success likely, but only after all-round strain.

MARS' PROGRESSIONS TO THE ASCENDANT

Conjunction
Improved health and heightened energy may contribute to a tendency to overwork. Some selfishness may emerge; headaches can be a health hazard. There will be a tendency to rush and to drive fast.

Positive Aspects
Energetic and healthy with perhaps an increased interest in active sport. According to the subject's age, this should be engaged in circumspectly. A good influence if controlled.

Negative Aspects
Accident-proneness and overwork likely; possible feverish complaints. The subject may become over-impulsive or easily angered. A quiet life advocated for the period.

MARS' PROGRESSIONS TO THE MIDHEAVEN

Conjunction
Likely to mark the subject's busiest and most hardworking period. Swimming with the tide, the subject should make good progress, but should be careful not to become over-anxious or impulsive.

Positive Aspects
As conjunction, but with less strain.

Negative Aspects
A strenuous, difficult career period. The subject should try not to force issues at this time.

PROGRESSED ASPECTS BETWEEN JUPITER, SATURN, URANUS, NEPTUNE AND PLUTO

These are extremely rare as the planets move so slowly. The natal aspects between those within orb may become more exact, or ease. Aspects of a slow-moving planet to an angle of the Chart will also be very slow to become exact, and their influence lasts for many years. The outcome of such a progression would depend on the nature of the planet involved.

The slow-moving planets can of course form all aspects when the one-degree system is used. When these occur, the nature and principles of the planets involved must be blended with the other progressions then operative.

THE PROGRESSED MOON

In interpreting the progressed Moon, it is important to remember that, while the aspect it makes to either the natal or progressed planets is exact for a month, the effect of the aspect will last overall for about three months, the month for which it is precise being central.

The effects of lunar progressions vary enormously: some people feel the effects of the tiniest semi-sextile, while others feel only quite potent squares and conjunctions. Astrologers are divided on their importance, and the truth seems to be that they are more important for some than for others. Lunar progressions are at their most potent if:
(a) Cancer is the Sun-sign or the Ascending sign, or the Moon conjuncts the Ascendant in the First House.
(b) The Moon is in Cancer.
(c) The Moon is in Taurus
and rather less important if the Moon is in the Fourth House. Bearing this in mind when writing an interpretation of lunar progressions is worth-while.

INTERPRETING PROGRESSIONS 4

The progressed Moon occupies a sign for about two and a half years. Those with Cancer prominent will be affected when the Moon by progression changes signs, and they may well be aware of their lives seeming to fall into thirty-month cycles, especially where psychological reactions, likes and dislikes, are concerned. Generally, it is only necessary to assess the aspects the progressed Moon makes, and not to lay stress on the progressed sign it occupies. But sometimes new interests, unusual ailments, and sudden feelings for places or things, can be traced to the sign the progressed Moon occupies, e.g. someone not prone to throat upsets may, while his progressed Moon occupies Taurus, become vulnerable to them; or he may suffer from wanderlust when his progressed Moon is in Sagittarius.

LUNAR PROGRESSIONS TO THE SUN

Conjunction
Possible change and social advancement. Ambitions and cherished dreams are often fulfilled when this conjunction occurs. Not always good for health, with a tendency towards feverishness. An important period sometimes accents domestic life.

Positive Aspects
A successful period with likely opportunities. Good for health, and the right time to seek help from others if needed. Social life will flourish and provide new chances for meeting people.

Negative Aspects
Not progressive period: vitality may be low. Plan a fairly quiet schedule. Disappointments can occur, with generally a rather trying period when there are negative or weak strenuous aspects between the Moon and Sun working in the progressed Chart.

LUNAR PROGRESSIONS TO ITS OWN PLACE

The Moon aspecting its own place brings to the fore the affairs of the House in which the Moon is natally situated. These will be affected according to the aspect the Moon makes: when it returns to its natal position (in other words when the progressed Moon makes a conjunction to the natal Moon) a new minor cycle is sometimes in evidence, and there is often an emphasis on family affairs, or perhaps a return to the area or country where the subject was born – either permanently or for a long visit. Nostalgia is evident.

LUNAR PROGRESSIONS TO MERCURY

Conjunction
An excellent time for beginning new studies, since the subject will be mentally alert. Also excellent for travel, or buying a new car. Concentration may have to be developed to make the most of new interests.

Positive Aspects
Much as for conjunction, but with positive periods for business and literary interests. Excellent for long-term work which will be of benefit in the future.

A domestic crisis can be the result of the negative aspects of a Moon/Mercury progression.

Negative Aspects
There may be some upset in domestic affairs with possibly family problems. Not a good time to plan a family holiday, or to push business. It is advisable to avoid signing important papers until this period is past.

LUNAR PROGRESSIONS TO VENUS

Conjunction
Usually indicates a good period for social life; for entertaining at home; or for love-life and emotions. Feelings are easily expressed, with 'cards put on the table'. This is a good aspect to be married under, other influences permitting; the possibility of forming long-lasting ties is there. All in all a period of good opportunities.

Positive Aspects
Like the conjunction, but often with a bearing on finance. Progress should be made in this direction.

Negative Aspects
A tendency for personal affairs to suffer. Not a good time for proposing marriage or forming permanent relationships as disappointments are likely. The subject may be easily hurt; social life may suffer.

The best way to deal with the negative aspects of the Moon and Mars is to live quietly and stay off the roads.

LUNAR PROGRESSIONS TO MARS

Conjunction
There will be a flow of additional physical and mental energy, and it is as well for the subject to plan some fairly demanding project on which he can work while the conjunction is operative. Without plenty to do, he may become restless; but impulsiveness is to be avoided, and there is some vulnerability to accidents and feverishness. While caution is necessary, positive good can come.

Positive Aspects
Tend to increase sexual desire, but also increasing enterprise, bringing ambitious tendencies to the surface. If the additional energy is properly controlled, it will remain a progressive period while it continues to operate.

Negative Aspects
A tendency to take risks; conscious care when driving is advisable. Extremes of action are likely, and it is not usually a positive period for romance. Considerable nervous strain and edginess can build up, with headaches occurring. A reasonably quiet schedule for the period should be arranged.

LUNAR PROGRESSIONS TO JUPITER

Conjunction
An extremely beneficial period; financial affairs should prosper. Every opportunity should be taken up. An excellent time for putting ideas or plans to others, or to ask for a raise in salary. Social life should be enjoyable. Travel will be pleasant now, and it is a good time for a long holiday as much as for business. The subject must use the period to the best advantage and good fortune will come his way.

Positive Aspects
Similar to the conjunction; but with less effort required to reach goals. Affairs often take a turn for the better; sometimes the mind turns towards religious or philosophical matters. A positive, constructive period.

Negative Aspects
Generally, not a good period for financial or social affairs. There is a tendency to go to extremes, and over-indulgence in food may make the subject liverish. Judgment can become very weak under the negative aspects of Jupiter, and important decisions should be temporarily shelved if possible.

LUNAR PROGRESSIONS TO SATURN

Conjunction
Generally, a depressing influence; but if Saturn is well aspected natally, with a trine between it and the Moon in the natal Chart, some steady, constructive progress may be made. It may not, however, be noticeable while the conjunction is operative. Not a good position for health, with vitality rather low. Advisable to plan a quiet period, if possible clearing up a back-log. Affairs should not be pushed or new projects put forward.

Positive Aspects
Give additional powers of concentration, sometimes with promotion or recognition of past hard work. An excellent time for long-term planning for the future. But the subject should not expect early results.

Negative Aspects
A vulnerability to chills and colds – inevitable if the aspect falls in winter. Depression may be experienced, and things may go wrong generally. There may be financial troubles, sometimes sadness. Not a time for ideas or plans.

LUNAR PROGRESSIONS TO URANUS

Conjunction
The subject should 'expect the unexpected'. Changes may seem exciting and dynamic – indeed perhaps they are – but the subject should be warned against undue haste. A new and interesting romantic relationship could be formed, but may lack permanence. He can be swept off his feet. Sudden splashes of inspiration occur, with inventive ideas. These will be fulfilled if supported by a more solid and practical transit (perhaps Saturn trine Sun, since this would slow down the impulsive lunar tendency). Sometimes a latent interest in astrology springs to life under this influence.

Positive Aspects
These have a 'reforming' side, with intuition and ingenuity to the fore. New and dynamic friendships, or new associations (i.e. with a club), can be formed; sometimes there is an unexpected financial gain. General all-round improvements may be made under this lively, dynamic influence.

Negative Aspects
Possible build-up of tension, and while excellent work may be done, the intensive flow of nervous energy can let the subject down at any time. Times for real relaxation must be set aside as the tendency to work to breaking-point will be strong, especially where a new project is concerned. Obstacles will occur, but if they can be taken in stride, much progress may be made, though not without nervous strain.

LUNAR PROGRESSIONS TO NEPTUNE

Conjunction
An extremely subtle influence, which many will live through without really noticing it. At best, it can give extra inspiration – for the artistic it will relate to a new line of creativity. But it needs a more dynamic influence to give inspiration concrete shape. Any tendency to negative escapism in the Birth Chart could be heightened by this influence, which could mean a relapse into old, bad habits like drug-taking.

The artist will need to get his aims properly organized to take full advantage of the subtle Moon/Neptune conjunction.

Positive Aspects
Very like the conjunction, but the subject must keep both feet firmly on the ground. Sometimes a memorable romantic experience occurs, and the period will be remembered nostalgically.

Negative Aspects
Will make the subject forgetful and woolly-minded; at worst, escapist. He may be easily deceived, and should be extremely careful in financial matters. Odd experiences occur, and if he is at all attracted to the psychic, he should be warned that 'wrong wavelengths' could be excited.

LUNAR PROGRESSIONS TO PLUTO

Conjunction
A strong possibility that the normal flow of events will become blocked. If a new plan or relationship comes up, something will interfere with its progress. With the lunar aspects to Pluto, a normal pattern of events is simply not possible. The influence must be allowed to pass.

Positive Aspects
Herald new beginnings and a positive period for business commitments. An excellent time for the housewife to start spring-cleaning her cupboards. A useful time to take out insurance policies. The 'clearing-out' effects of Pluto can work on a psychological level to make the subject feel more at ease, having been able to release former negative influences that were troubling.

Negative Aspects
Somewhat like the conjunction, with, again, the blocking of progress notable. Not a good time for new business projects; frustration and cramping in evidence.

LUNAR PROGRESSIONS TO THE ASCENDANT

Conjunction and Positive Aspects
Indicate a new phase, often involving a domestic change of some kind – the birth of a child, or perhaps a marriage. Traditionally, 'a long sea-voyage' might have been predicted; but this does not seem true today. An excellent time for looking for, or purchasing, a new house or other property.

Negative Aspects
Domestic difficulties could occur: sometimes, especially with the opposition, a break-up of marriage or of a personal relationship. Changes should be avoided if possible under these aspects.

LUNAR PROGRESSIONS TO THE MIDHEAVEN

Conjunction and Positive Aspects
A successful domestic period – possibly the birth of children. Sometimes an event will have long-term beneficial influences, often indicative of 'coming before the public' – like a TV appearance. The subject will tend to bolster his ego when he comes under these favourable conditions.

Negative Aspects
Forced changes in domestic life – or changes in career or between departments – may be detrimental. Allowances should be made for family troubles; parents could be extra demanding.

The subject experiencing a progression of the Moon to the Midheaven may well find himself putting in a public appearance.

INTERPRETING THE TRANSITS

Up to this point we have interpreted the secondary and one-degree progressions formed by the progressed Sun and planets to the natal planets and to each other. The progressed Moon's position and aspects have also been assessed. A picture of the conditions and trends working in the subject's life should therefore be emerging. It is useful to remember that if the progressed Moon makes aspects to the planets activated in the secondary progressions, it is during these months that the long-term aspects are most likely to be prominent.

The last stage in interpreting the progressed Chart is to consider the transits. These are made by the positions of the planets in the sky during the period to be assessed; and the tables at the back of the book (of planetary positions) or the ephemeris for the year in question have been used to calculate them exactly.

THE TRANSITS OF THE SLOW-MOVING PLANETS

Transits indicate trends. Transits from the slow-moving planets Saturn, Uranus, Neptune and Pluto hover for long periods – especially if the planet, by turning retrograde and then reverting to direct motion, passes over a degree which holds a *natal* planet; it will then affect this planet three times. In the case of Pluto, for instance, a recurring transit can be in evidence for as long as a year; while Jupiter may affect the life for about five months. Normal transits from Pluto and Neptune will be exact for about one month; from Uranus for about three weeks; from Saturn for about ten days; from Jupiter for four to five days.

The precise timing of transits is not easy, since their effects will in most cases (like the major progressions) fade in and out over a period. Saturn is the most difficult to time exactly, perhaps because of its general 'delaying' influence. The Birth Chart should be checked to see whether the two planets contacted by transit are in aspect natally. If several transits occur at the same time the subject's life will be unusually eventful (although in some case 'events' could mean non-events —such as a slowing down or frustration of plans). When interpreting all transits it must be remembered that the natal aspect and the planet's principles and associations are important.

THE TRANSITS OF JUPITER

These are beneficial and enjoyable, indicating a progressive period: usually a good time for action or travel.

Jupiter's transits to the Sun, Moon and Ascendant
Conjunction: Excellent for travel abroad (with family if the Moon is involved). Finances could improve; a time to go ahead with plans.
Positive aspects: As for conjunction: but tendency to over-indulgence and waste.
Negative aspects: Blind optimism, extravagance and over-indulgence. Possible over-commitment on hire-purchase. Judgment not sound; shelve important decisions. Strict dieting necessary.

Jupiter's transits to Mercury
Conjunction and positive aspects: Excellent for study, travel, Mercury/Jupiter pursuits.
Negative aspects: Forgetfulness, or unsound judgment – a bad time to change cars.

Jupiter's transits to Venus
Conjunction and positive aspects: Much enjoyment likely. Excellent for entertaining, investment and planning for the future.
Negative aspects: Over-extravagance; too much 'fun'.

Jupiter's transits to Mars
Conjunction and positive aspects: Positive and energetic. A time to take advantage of lively prevailing conditions.
Negative aspects: Restraint of impulsiveness necessary, as there is a tendency to extremes of action.

Jupiter's transits to its own place
Benefits according to the nature of the Sign and House in which Jupiter is natally placed. Generally, a good period.

Jupiter's transits to Saturn
Conjunction and positive aspects: A definite slowing-down of plans which will probably work for the subject's advantage.
Negative aspects: Possibly difficult period. Guard against over-commitment.

Jupiter's transits to Uranus
Conjunction and positive aspects: Events may take a lively turn; an interesting financial offer.
Negative aspects: Unexpected advantages not so sound as they first appear to be. Nervous tension in evidence.

Jupiter's transits to Neptune
Conjunction and positive aspects: A period of inspiration: the subject is likely to become dreamy and not quite himself, make mental journeys and be reluctant to come down to earth afterwards. Nevertheless enjoyable.
Negative aspects: Indecision, perhaps escapism. There may be a tendency to be carried away by enthusiasm.

Jupiter's transits to Pluto
Conjunction and positive aspects: Probably good for investments, but the natal planets must be carefully studied.
Negative aspects: *Not* a good time to invest; over-commitment could involve stocks and shares or even general insurance.

Jupiter's transits to the Midheaven
Conjunction and positive aspects: Promotion, more money – perhaps unexpectedly. All Jupiter associations strongly stressed.
Negative aspects: Progress may not come up to expectations; over optimism about career.

THE TRANSITS OF SATURN

Saturn's transits to the Sun, Moon and Ascendant
Conjunction: Hold back – make long-term plans, certainly, but without taking action. The health may be below par.
Positive aspects: As conjunction, but more constructive.
Negative aspects: Proneness to chills, influenza, possibly longer illnesses. A time to hold back and wait for easier times.

Saturn's transits to Mercury
Conjunction and positive aspects: Powers of concentration increased. Positively constructive.
Negative aspects: Depression – reasons obscure. Friends or relatives may be difficult.

Saturn's transits to Venus
Conjunction and positive aspects: Serious relationship with older person. A serious attitude to the love life.
Negative aspects: A relationship may be terminated. Not a good time to entertain.

Saturn's transits to Mars
Conjunction and positive aspects: A 'stop/go' influence; progress uneven, energy may suffer. With the initiative of Mars present, frustrating delays likely. At best these aspects curb the impulsive and give the unimpulsive a little more life.
Negative aspects: Avoid adventurous recreations, like rock-climbing and skiing, since sprains and injuries through falls may occur. The subject will work under pressure and not get much thanks for his efforts.

Saturn's transits to Jupiter
See Jupiter's transits to Saturn.

Saturn's transits to its own place
Will emphasize Saturn's Sign and House. Constructive progress if Saturn reasonably unafflicted.

Saturn's transits to Uranus
Conjunction and positive aspects: Can lead to new, better conditions. (Saturn and Uranus being 'related' through the rulership of Aquarius.) Take advantage of the unexpected.
Negative aspects: Strenuous, nerve-racking. Possible breakdown in extreme circumstances. Hard work and an uphill fight could be to long-term advantage.

Saturn's transits to Neptune
Conjunction and positive aspects: Excellent; ideas may take constructive shape, and any inspiration should be seriously considered.
Negative aspects: Inspiration with inner struggle, especially if the subject is artistically or scientifically inclined. Sometimes, on the other hand, it can be a time of indecision, confusion and worry.

Saturn's transits to Pluto
All aspects: Sharply restrictive. Investment inadvisable unless both planets really well placed, or form a trine aspect natally.

Saturn's transits to the Midheaven
Conjunction and positive aspects: At best, long-term promotion. Difficulties over which the subject has no control; authority in evidence.
Negative aspects: Unexpected setbacks; suppress initiative until the aspects pass.

THE TRANSITS OF URANUS

Uranus' transits to the Sun, Moon and Ascendant
Conjunction: Important, and possibly lively. Sudden drastic changes possible. Guard against impulsiveness.
Positive aspects: As conjunction but with less strain. An interesting and perhaps memorable period.
Negative aspects: Opposition can cause domestic or business unease. Strain will be hard to recognize. But all the same originality will not be lacking.

Uranus' transits to Mercury
Conjunction and positive aspects: Good ideas abound, but need steadying. A tendency to rush into action without considering the details.
Negative aspects: Strain, perhaps through too much mental application. Eccentricity may occur.

Uranus' transits to Venus
Conjunction and positive aspects: New, dynamic relationships can occur; life likely to be amusing and lively. Unexpected financial gains.
Negative aspects: Possible breaks in love or business.

Uranus' transits to Mars
Conjunction and positive aspects: Energy and originality; situations quickly grasped. Life more than usually eventful. Originality usually highlighted.
Negative aspects: Considerable strain with uncharacteristic behaviour likely.

Uranus' transits to Jupiter
See Jupiter's transits to Uranus.

Uranus' transits to Saturn
See Saturn's transits to Uranus.

Uranus' transits to Neptune
Conjunction and positive aspects: May well prove an extremely interesting period. A change of ideas or spiritual outlook is possible. A good time for new interests, especially if the new activity savours of Neptune (dancing, poetry) or Uranus (astronomy, astrology, archaeology).
Negative aspects: Confusion over religion or inspiration.

Uranus' transits to Pluto
Conjunction and positive aspects: Turbulence, with new beginnings imposed; not an easy period.
Negative aspects: As conjunction.

Uranus' transits to the Midheaven
Conjunction and positive aspects: Sudden, possibly drastic change of circumstance; but it could be possibly beneficial. It may be necessary to make rapid adjustments.
Negative aspects: Unexpected events may cause trouble. The strength of Uranus in the natal Chart is of great significance.

THE TRANSITS OF NEPTUNE

Neptune's transits to the Sun, Moon and Ascendant
Conjunction: A very subtle influence, with artistry and inspiration, given creativity in the Birth Chart. There may be a sudden craze for the cinema and romantic music or literature.
Positive aspects: As conjunction but more dreamy and poetic.
Negative aspects: Care needed against escapism through drugs, especially if Neptune is afflicted. Dangers from medically administered drugs unless care is taken.

Neptune's transits to Mercury
Conjunction and positive aspects: Excellent influence; inspiration and the sharper, more critical elements of Mercury combine and should be used to advantage.
Negative aspects: A subtle influence, causing absent-mindedness, but no serious difficulties.

Neptune's transits to Venus
Conjunction and positive aspects: The romantic and harmonious come together to produce a few happy and pleasant weeks.
Negative aspects: Romantic difficulties could occur but life can again be pleasant. Escapism may be a danger, especially if Neptune is in Libra.

Neptune's transits to Mars
Conjunction and positive aspects: Artistic, colourful things will attract. Romanticism and inspiration emphasized. A happy period.
Negative aspects: A vulnerability to poisoning. Fish, contaminated water, gas fumes, or medically administered drugs are dangers. The natal Chart will be all important in determining the seriousness. Emotionalism and indiscretion are more common outcomes.

Neptune's transits to Jupiter
See Jupiter's transits to Neptune.

Neptune's transits to Saturn
See Saturn's transits to Neptune.

Neptune's transits to Uranus
See Uranus' transits to Neptune.

Neptune's transits to Pluto
Sex life may be emotionally emphasized. Under negative aspects, feelings may be hard to express.

Neptune's transits to the Midheaven
Conjunction and positive aspects: Subtle change of direction likely.
Negative aspects: Vulnerability to deception. Trying and confusing time.

THE TRANSITS OF PLUTO

The transits of Pluto to the Sun, Moon and Ascendant
Conjunction: Dramatic change likely with a new outlook.
Positive aspects: Also upheaval, but less strain.
Negative aspects: An enforced upheaval not easily lived through.

Pluto's transits to Mercury
Conjunction and positive aspects: Pluto's effect will work on thought patterns and opinions. Dramatic change of mind likely.
Negative aspects: The subject could suffer psychologically if Pluto and Mercury are afflicted in the Chart.

Pluto's transits to Venus
Conjunction and positive aspects: Possibly a sudden falling in love, but with no chance of developing the relationship. Positive for finance.
Negative aspects: Tension in love, perhaps due to underhand behaviour.

Pluto's transits to Mars
Conjunction and positive aspects: Adding force and energy to Pluto's already somewhat explosive indications. Life can become uneven. Under severe affliction, violence can occur. Mars and Pluto are of a kind, and these transits are not really divisible into positive and negative.

Pluto's transits to Jupiter
See Jupiter's transits to Pluto.

Pluto's transits to Saturn
See Saturn's transits to Pluto.

Pluto's transits to Uranus
See Uranus' transits to Pluto.

Pluto's transits to Neptune
See Neptune's transits to Pluto.

Pluto's transits to the Midheaven
Conjunction and positive aspects: Indication of career change; perhaps redundancy and a golden handshake. Otherwise departmental reorganization or general upheaval.
Negative aspects: Similar.

THE TRANSITS OF MARS

Mars has a hastening effect.
The golden rule is to remember that Mars *energizes* another planet or the angles of the Chart. This can make the subject lively and energetic; but it will also make him prone to accidents. Be on guard when Mars conjuncts or opposes the Sun or Ascendant. Tension or quarrelsomeness follows when Mars makes a Moon transit.

THE TRANSITS OF VENUS

Transits of Venus last about two days, and usually indicate an enjoyable social or love life. Sometimes the influence is financial. Venus transits are useful: when the planet contacts an angle or another planet in the Chart (with the exception of Saturn), it is a good time for buying new clothes (Sun, Ascendant) or household goods (Moon): entertaining (Mercury, Jupiter); being entertained (its own place, or the Midheaven); going to the cinema or theatre (Neptune); or making a blind date (Uranus).

THE TRANSITS OF MERCURY

These transits only last a day or two, sometimes falling into groups during the year. Frequently several transits can occur in a month, encouraging a lively social round.
Mercury's short transits are admirable for helping with backlogs of correspondence, making short journeys or visits. The *communications* aspect should in short be used. Minor changes may be made when Mercury contacts the Sun and Ascendant – buying and selling, or exchanging things. Combined with Venus, entertaining can be indicated, or perhaps giving a talk or lecture.

PROBLEM ANALYSIS

Most people who consult an astrologer have a specific reason for doing so – although those reasons vary so widely that it would be difficult to tabulate them. Even if no specific reason is offered, the astrologer can very easily see from the progressed Chart whether his client is in difficulty or under stress; and if so, he should try to persuade him to be as frank as he would be with a doctor or psychiatrist.

It is possible for an astrologer to work 'blind' without any personal details other than the birth date. But this is no more desirable than a diagnosis without symptoms would be for a doctor; and if astrologers refuse to work without a 'case history' one must sympathize with them. To be properly effective, the astrologer needs the full birth data of all the people involved in any situation. If, say, the husband's and wife's birth data is complete, but there is no such data for the third party in a triangle, the astrologer's job becomes extremely difficult.

Care is the key word in all aspects of problem analysis. It is *not* for the astrologer to attempt to usurp the position of psychologist, analyst, priest, doctor or solicitor, although clients may expect him to be all of these – sometimes at one and the same time. While it is often a great temptation to give in to these pressures, it is nevertheless the astrologer's firm duty to keep within the bounds of his art by recognizing his own limitations as an adviser. He will serve the community best at times by referring clients to others with more appropriate qualifications.

It is especially helpful if the consultant astrologer can get to know a psychiatrist, a doctor, a marriage guidance official, and can build up a file of people whose professional business it is to be of help in all sorts of ways; he can then recommend clients personally to someone who can help them further – and at a time when, astrologically, they are likely to respond.

Basically, there are four types of problem an astrologer is likely to face: emotional or marriage problems; business or career problems; financial problems; or problems of health – sometimes allied to drug addiction, particularly among the young.

Addicts will approach an astrologer to help them reject drugs. The interpretation sections of this book refer to drugs: the Twelfth House is often prominently involved, also afflicted planets – perhaps the Sun and Neptune – especially in Libra. These have probably been activated by a progressed Venus, or by heavy transits. The astrologer may in fact assess when a period of negative escapism will end, and when for that reason the person concerned might respond best to psychiatric help.

A Marriage Endangered or The Astrologer's Remedy
Astrologers are often consulted over specific problems. When a marriage is threatened because the husband or wife suddenly goes off alone, or with someone new, the hurt partner turns to astrology for a solution.

In the astrologer's consulting room our unhappy wife tells her story. The astrologer takes down her birth time and that of her husband. 'But,' she explains, 'I do need the other woman's birth data if I am to give you a full report.' The wife agrees to provide this vital information.

Now the astrologer can go to work. A pattern is soon revealed: the wife's progressed Moon squares the husband's natal Mars (no wonder he was ready to walk out); his progressed Venus conjuncts the girl's Uranus (a sudden attraction!) But it will quickly wear off.

The astrologer makes her report. She tells the wife that all should soon be well – and that she, too, will be in a more receptive mood in a few days' time. The wife thinks over what she has learned – and in a short while begins to see her situation in a more hopeful light. She buys herself a new dress. That evening the husband comes home; the affair is over. He asks to be forgiven and she, relieved and thankful that the astrologer had forestalled any more drastic move she might have made, happily accepts him back.

The Unhappy Marriage

The astrologer begins by looking for factors in the Charts of both marriage partners which may be contributing to their unhappiness. For instance, progressed aspects might show that the wife simply feels restless, and places the blame for her feelings on her (dull?) husband. Or that the husband is simply feeling lazy, or that he suddenly feels a deep attraction to another woman. Will this be permanent or temporary? Again, the progressed Chart will be a guide.

Obviously, extreme tact and impartiality should be the astrologer's rule: intervention in the lives of other people must be taken very seriously, and great care should be taken not only in preparing and considering the Charts, but in giving any kind of advice. It is often true that in emotional problems the astrologer can be of the greatest help simply by being prepared to sit and listen to the problem. In any event, the people concerned must make their own decisions: what an astrologer *can* do is to put various solutions before them: and if the Chart shows very clearly that one line of action or inaction is likely to bear fruit, he should lay special emphasis upon it.

The Career Problem

Anyone consulting an astrologer about a business or career problem will usually be thinking of changing his job. Very often, in such cases, the progressed Ascendant will be on the point of changing its sign. If so, and assuming that the birth time is reasonably accurate, a change will usually be beneficial, provided that no seriously difficult progressions are due.

A change of Sun-sign can have the same effect: if a man has suddenly been offered a new job, without warning, it may well be that his progressed Midheaven is changing signs. Once more, if no adverse progressions are in the way, the time is probably ripe for a change and it should be made.

If difficult progressions are seen in the immediate future, the client should be told that there may be difficulties which could make a change somewhat strenuous: a difficult lunar progression, or a transiting Saturn in a negative position, could indicate delay, or perhaps a health hazard. On the other hand, there may be progress after a change: if, by transit, Jupiter crosses the natal Midheaven, then a change will be all to the good.

Astrology and Health

Clients will approach an astrologer to find out when they are going to die, or when an elderly relative is going to die. It would be quite unethical to tell them, even if it were not extremely difficult: for the astrological indications of death are equivocal. Sometimes there are indications of great calmness and even of joy; sometimes of great restriction or difficulty. But in any case, the astrologer is far less free than a doctor in this area, and in the writer's opinion should *never* attempt to answer the question, whatever happens.

He can be of great practical help, however, in pointing out to clients times when their health may not be markedly strong; or when, during the winter months, they may be particularly vulnerable to influenza. Then, if they wish, they can avoid crowds and not take on too many obligations until the difficulty passes.

Drug addiction forms one of the contemporary astrologer's most serious problems. Astrologers are consulted by young people in trouble and by parents wanting confirmation that their children are taking drugs, or are susceptible to them.

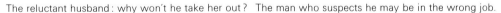

The reluctant husband: why won't he take her out?

The man who suspects he may be in the wrong job.

'When shall I die?' 'When will she die?'

THE CHILD'S CHART

Assessing a child's Birth Chart is a fascinating task. Professional astrologers find that work on children's Charts forms a large part of their regular business. Once again, the birth time, more precisely the moment of the first cry, is all important.

It is also important to take the birth data of parents, brothers and sisters fully into account; relationships between a child and various members of his family will nearly always differ. He may respond better to his father in some areas, to his mother in others.

The strongest aspect in a parent's Chart is sometimes repeated in the child's: where, for example, there is an opposition between two powerful planets in a parent's Chart, the same two planets will fall in conjunction in the Chart of the child.

Similarities will obviously be borne out in the personalities. The astrologer may perhaps have to make tactful allowance for a parent who has Virgo rising, and so will not be very affectionate.

Another source of conflict could arise from a parent's clinging Cancerian traits, or possessive Taurean behaviour.

A child with its Sun in Aquarius would simply not understand such parents (unless there were strong mitigating elements elsewhere) and it would be only fair to warn them of the child's need for independence.

Advice on the Future

An astrologer will often be able to advise on a suitable education, and suggest sympathetic hobbies or interests for the child.

Progressions can be particularly helpful to parents in the field of health. It is easy to see when a child may contract the usual childish illnesses; a school prize or scholarship should be clearly indicated, and here the aspects the progressed Sun makes will be revealing. The same applies to the progressed Moon: if, for example, the Moon is badly afflicted in the Birth Chart (say, by a square aspect to Saturn), then when the progressed Moon crosses the child's Ascendant his health may be weakened.

A time of change will be indicated through the progressed Sun-sign, or a change of Ascendant. Family changes may show in a child's progressed Midheaven changing signs. These and other pointers should be noted as possible 'milestone years', but their importance should not be over-dramatized.

There is no area of a child's potential that a competent astrologer cannot explore. The natal Chart will show his probable future behaviour.

Will he be happy at home? Parents are sometimes puzzled and hurt when a child seems to prefer a father or mother. The astrologer can point out where they should tread warily.

What will my child be? The child may choose any career; but he will be more suited to particular areas. The astrologer will point out the careers in which the child is more likely to be happy and successful.

What kind of hobbies? Parents with other interests might not think of encouraging their child to play the flute, or of giving him a set of paints. The astrologer can suggest hobbies likely to develop the child's abilities.

Who will his friends be? An astrologer will not only be able to tell a mother what kind of friends her child will be drawn to; but which friends will be best for him.

Which school should I send him to? The astrologer will be able to say whether strict discipline, or a more friendly approach, is most likely to result in a successful education.

The Child and His Parents

Aries
The Arian parent may push his child too hard; the Arian child's abundant energy needs to escape, but he should be firmly controlled.

Taurus
A Taurean parent will like discipline, but his child may not! Do not force a Taurean child: he will be naturally rather slow, but he is persistent.

Gemini
Geminian parents may be over-critical, but will stimulate their child's imagination. The Geminian child must be encouraged to stick at his tasks.

Cancer
Cancerians are natural worriers and may tend to cling to their children. The Cancerian child is very affectionate, but all too easily hurt.

Leo
Leos expect high standards from their children, and are too easily disappointed in them. Leo children's high spirits must not be broken.

Virgo
The neat Virgoan parent will be horrified by untidiness, and may fail to give real affection. Virgoan children can be distant – but flourish at school.

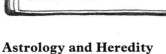

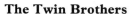

The Twin Brothers

Piers and Crispin are real-life twins, born ten minutes apart; even this short time makes a difference in some areas of their Birth Charts. The astrologer was able to tell their mother that Crispin tends to have more will-power and determination than his brother, who often lets him take the lead. But Piers is more inclined to worry than Crispin, while Crispin tends to suffer from minor nervous complaints.

As this case shows, the astrologer can find definite differences between the Charts of people born within a few minutes of each other. Sometimes, for instance, a planet near the angles in twin A may be even nearer in twin B, so the relationship between planet and angle will be much more powerful in effect on B than on A. Another indication to look for is the changing of Houses by planets between the births. Differences in appearance can sometimes be traced to the positions of rising planets.

Astrology and Heredity

The astrologer who is interested in his own family tree should do a little astrological research into it. (Cancerians, with their natural aptitude for history and their liking for the past, will be particularly attracted to this.)

He should begin with his own Chart and work backwards: if parents are alive, they may know their own birth times; grandparents may be more difficult to chart, but records of birth times can often be found in old family documents and albums.

Calculating the Birth Charts of whole families reveals the most interesting astrological links between generations. Sometimes a prominent sign will 'skip' a generation, to reappear in a grandchild's Chart, often very strongly indeed. It seems that in most families about five of the twelve signs crop up time and time again, sometimes their associations can be traced across as many as four generations.

Astrological Twins

You will be very lucky indeed to find an 'astrological twin'. It is extremely unlikely that another baby was born at precisely the same moment as yourself, and in the same house or hospital. But if you *can* find someone born within the same hour and in the same country, you will probably find that your lives are remarkably similar.

Julia Parker, one of the authors of this book, was born within half an hour and about 125 miles from the birthplace of David Blair, the internationally known ballet dancer. Both children studied ballet; at the same time – an unusually early age – they went to specialized schools. Both have taught ballet; they were married within six weeks of each other, and live within a mile of each other.

Comparisons of the lives of astrological twins is an absorbing field of study; several known cases reveal similarities in personal mannerisms, marriage partners – even the choice of a rug to decorate the home!

Libra
Libran parents love well-turned-out, polite children; they are extremely affectionate. Libran children should be encouraged to be decisive.

Scorpio
Scorpio parents tend to be too strict. Scorpio children may be secretive; they like 'rough' sports, and may be jealous of younger brothers or sisters.

Sagittarius
Parenthood is a challenge for Sagittarians; they will have fun with their children. Sagittarian children may not take to discipline.

Capricorn
Capricornian parents may be over-fond of success for their children. Young Capricornians will be good athletes. Praise will be needed.

Aquarius
An Aquarian will want independence for his child; he will be rational but perhaps cool. Aquarian children are clever, but erratic.

Pisces
Pisceans cannot bring themselves to inflict punishment. The Piscean child also hates discipline; he will be at his best studying artistic subjects.

SYNASTRY I

When clients arrive to consult an astrologer, one of the questions they most frequently ask is: 'Which signs of the Zodiac go together?' Members of the younger generation are also likely to say: 'I'm Aries. Who am I likely to fall in love with?'

For the astrologer, this is the thinnest of thin ice. Although many astrological books contain lists of the various signs which are traditionally said to harmonize with one another, these do represent a most dangerous form of generalization if the true circumstances of the individual, as shown by a close study of his Birth Chart, are not made the first priority of interpretation. The only revelation of compatibility will come with the detailed and sometimes complicated process of comparing fully calculated Birth Charts and progressed Charts; not with glib theories.

Marriage and Business Partners

High on the list of every practising astrologer are those clients who are thinking of marriage. Others are looking into the possible formation of a business partnership. Sometimes the problem is of more immediate strain on the emotions: perhaps there is an 'eternal triangle' to be resolved. But whether the astrologer needs to consult the Charts of two people or three, or still more in the case of large-scale business mergers, the principles of Chart comparison, or synastry – the technical term – remains much the same.

Synastry shows up the basic factors, the driving forces which provide the clues to the nature of relationships: whether they will succeed or how long they can be expected to last.

If two people are contemplating marriage and wish to determine their astrological compatibility, the first step – as with all forms of synastry – is to calculate their respective Birth Charts. As usual, the more complete the birth data, for both parties, the more the astrologer will be able to discover from the completed Charts. It often happens that one rather than both comes to consult the astrologer; he or she may bring a full list of personal information, but only the birth date of the partner. This is obviously a limiting factor, and the astrologer has then to do his best within this more restricted framework. The all-important Ascendant and the sign on the Midheaven will be missing from the other partner's Chart; only the positions of the planets on the day of birth can be brought into consideration. When this happens, the astrologer has to tell the client that his report cannot be as full as it might have been, before proceeding with the best information that can be mustered.

How Two Lovers Found Astrology

Pat and Paul were engaged to be married. Like most people they knew their Sun-signs: his was Aries and hers was Taurus. Then they found a book which said 'Aries and Taurus rarely get on well together, and in marriage would certainly be buying trouble.' Shocked and unhappy, they went to see an astrologer.

Fortunately they found a reputable, qualified astrologer. 'Nonsense,' she reassured them, 'that sort of view is absurdly over-simplified. What matters is the story of your Birth Charts as a whole!'

The astrologer drew up detailed Birth Charts for Pat and Paul. 'These popular astrologers are so unreliable,' she said to herself. 'It's quite obvious from their Charts that these two will get on perfectly well together if they marry.'

Pat and Paul were delighted with the astrologer's verdict. In the report the astrologer explained that, 'Of course there are certain areas where you can expect to disagree, but I have little doubt that if you make the necessary effort to play down these differences, you will be very happy.' The astrologer's separate analyses of Pat and Paul's Charts appears overleaf, together with her assessment of the combined Charts.

Major Indications
Having set up the two Charts, there are many points to be looked for; some are more important than others. Three questions that should be immediately asked are:

Is A's Sun-sign the same as B's Ascending Sign?

Is A's Sun-sign the sign also on the cusp of the Seventh House in B's Chart?

Is the girl's Sun in the same sign as the boy's Midheaven? – this would be splendid for both of them, since she will easily be able to identify with his aims and objectives in life, thus helping her to be a lively and positive 'power behind the throne'.

These three points are major ones, in that they are immediate indications that the partnership is likely to be successful. They are all parallels between the respective Suns and angles of the Charts; but the relationship can also be successful if opposite signs are involved: for instance, if A's Ascendant is Sagittarius, and B's Sun-sign is Gemini.

Other Considerations
After considering these three major points, the astrologer has to examine many other indications that arise from the joint Birth Charts. Six of the commonest that have a bearing on the compatibility of the couple are:

If the Sun and Ascendant are in the same sign: this indicates considerable similarity in personal behaviour and psychology and would help to soften other, less favourable alignments in the couple.

If the Sun and Ascendant are in opposition: this too is extremely positive, indicating considerable rapport between the subjects.

If the Sun and Ascendant are in square aspect: the relationship can be somewhat tense; but this aspect can give tremendous drive and push, providing there are other less harsh indications in the Charts which can combine to counteract any possible build-up of tension.

If the Sun and Ascendant are in trine or sextile aspect: the relationship is usually rather pleasant and easy-going, if perhaps slightly dull. It is likely to be, in fact, all that the relationship linked by a square aspect is *not*; which can, of course, be either splendid or aggravating, depending on the people concerned. It is at any rate a tendency that must be pointed out.

If the Sun and Ascendant are in semi-sextile aspect: this can be a negative indication. Signs next to each other are completely different, in every way, and common ground—even argumentative ground—between them is lacking. If this aspect is present, a great deal of close attention must be given to other planetary relationships, and to the sign containing the Midheaven, which could greatly ease the situation. For instance, if the Midheaven of A and the Ascendant of B fall in the same sign; or if important planets in A's Chart harmonize with the Midheaven of B's, the necessary mitigating factors would probably be present. But, on the whole, those who are linked by consecutive signs (unless there are very positive factors present elsewhere in the Chart) are most likely to get on each other's nerves, and to be completely incompatible. The subjects in this case will need to make a great effort of will to be realistic and accept that entering into a permanent relationship under these circumstances may not lead to happiness. Breaking it off now can be the best, if most difficult solution.

There is one notable *exception* to the semi-sextile rule: this is in the case of a relationship between Capricorn and Aquarius. Saturn rules Capricorn, and is also the traditional ruler of Aquarius; in many ways this could favour compatibility. The couple concerned might well be somewhat cold towards each other in some respects, since Capricorn is madly conventional, and might become quite disgusted with Aquarius' modern progressive outlook. Nevertheless, the couple would be quite strong enough to fight their own battles in their own rather aloof way. In any case, it is important in synastry that no generalization should be relied upon. There are many happy marriages between people with neighbouring Sun-signs—the mitigating factors in their Charts have come into their own, and eased the lack of compatibility between the Suns.

If the Sun and Ascendant are in quincunx aspect: this can contribute a negative factor: with some notable exceptions. Aries and Scorpio could share an unusually highly-keyed partnership, since Aries is ruled by Mars, which is also the traditional ruler of Scorpio. Their partnership would be highly emotional and stormy; and probably very highly sexed. The two people concerned would probably wallow in the pendulum ups and downs of their relationship! Another notable exception is in the case of the Venus signs, Taurus and Libra: the relationship here would be exactly the opposite of the Martian couple. Their relationship would be peaceful; they would share a love of good food, and of cushiony comfort. In consequence they would create round them a very pleasant environment, making excellent hosts their friends would be glad to visit.

A further marked exception to the strain imposed when signs are emphasised by quincunx aspects is in the case of Leo and Pisces. To all intents and purposes, the characteristics of these signs could not be more different, but basically they are 'creative', and it is quite often the case that those who have these signs prominent in their Charts are in general 'artistic'—often extremely so. It could be that Leo might give really constructive and sympathetic encouragement to Pisces, and be the making of his or her partner, since the fiery positivity of Leo can mould and pull into shape the less well-organized Pisces. There is often a shared love of the theatre, and although the signs are poles apart from a psychological point of view, they are both emotional and the combination is often marvellous.

Planetary Relationships
Having examined the relationship between the angles and the Suns in the two Birth Charts, the next stage is to consider the relationship between the planets, and to note how many strong aspects there are between them. This will provide further clues as to whether the relationship will be long lasting, or not, and what will be the finer points of the relationship. If the basic links (and the relationship between the Suns and angles) are weak or few, then there is little to show that a successful marriage or a permanent relationship will ensue. In this case the subjects would do well to consider their position carefully.

It is at this stage that we have to consider *orbs* in synastry, which we have not done in connection with the Sun and Ascendant. It is generally recommended that in this area of astrology five degrees of orb is sufficient between planets in the Birth Charts, and that only major aspects and the quincunx should be used.

It is important to remember that in synastry, as in all other kinds of astrology, the principles of the planets are the same and work in the same way; they must not be interpreted out of context: for instance, aspects between the two Moons in a pair of Charts will show how the couple will respond to each other's habits and moods. A conjunction, trine or sextile will show sympathy in this respect, although on the other hand there is quite a possibility that one will 'pick up' the other's mood—which can be a mixed blessing. Depression will quickly communicate itself and so be all the harder to get rid of. The Mars in the man's Chart in aspect to the Venus in the girl's will show sexual attraction. Aspects involving Mercury will show intellectual ties: but if there is an aspect between Mercury and Mars, the decision has to be made whether this indicates a lively rapport or a tendency to quarrel. In such a case it is advisable to look further to less harsh planets such as Jupiter, Venus or Neptune. If they are favourable then it could mean a happy relationship in store.

The Slow-Moving Planets
It is extremely important to remember that it is quite often the case that couples considering a liaison are of almost similar age. This can mean that their slow-moving planets (those from Saturn to Pluto) will be in the same sign. Saturn stays in a sign for roughly two-and-a-half years. But unless these slower planets are important in one of the Charts, care must be taken not to over-emphasize relationships between them. Conversely it is important not to ignore such aspects; the man's Sun squaring the girl's Saturn, for instance, could wet-blanket a relationship. On the other hand, should the girl have Capricorn rising, it may well mean that she could become a tower of strength to him, helping him through difficult periods.

If there are big differences in age between the couple, relationships between the slow-moving planets can be fascinating. In one case that the writer worked on recently where two people had instantly—and under the most unlikely circumstances—fallen deeply in love, the man, aged 40, was twelve years older than the girl. Their Charts had Jupiter in exactly the same degree of the Zodiac, and while Jupiter is not a planet that springs instantly to mind where sudden passionate affairs are concerned, it was felt that the way the couple could open up and broaden each other's lives would be something quite remarkable; and indeed this has proved to be the case.

SYNASTRY 2

This is a real case: Pat and Paul were married on 8 March 1970. During the first year of their married life, they travelled over 12,000 miles between London, Jamaica and the Far East, and the timing of their travels was often uncertain. At the time of writing, Paul is again en route for the East, leaving Pat to resume her nursing; they have dealt very well with the problems of parting for some months relatively soon after their marriage, and there are indications that the astrologer's assurance of a lasting, stable marriage will be fulfilled. Extracts from the astrologer's report for them follow below and on the facing page.

PAUL

Sun in Aries; Ascendant Leo; Mercury in Pisces; Sun in opposition to Neptune
'He is assertive, with organizational ability but in smaller matters minor weaknesses such as forgetfulness can cause chaos.'

Mars in Aquarius; MC Taurus
'He would hate to be restricted but at the same time he must have security.'

Ascendant Leo; Mars in Aquarius
'Although conventional he can enjoy unusual circumstances, in which his Arian pioneering spirit is at its best.'

Mars in Aquarius in 6th House; Moon in Virgo
'His career as a Radio Officer is clearly indicated satisfying the urge "to communicate".'

Moon conjunct Neptune; Sun in Aries in Opposition to Neptune
'His main fault is selfishness; but kindliness helps him to overcome this.'

Moon in Virgo; Sun in Opposition to Moon, Neptune; MC Taurus
'He tends to become easily confused about problems; so he must take time to analyze them.'

Venus in Aries; Aquarius on 7th House; Venus in 9th House
'In love and marriage he is passionate, likes unconventionality in relationships; he may marry a girl from overseas, and may live abroad.'

PAT

Sun and Ascendant in Taurus; Venus in Gemini
'Here is a practical, stable girl with a need for security; but also a bright creature with a light side to her personality.'

Venus in trine with Jupiter, Sun and Ascendant; Venus in 2nd House
'She likes to enjoy life; and she has a practical outlook on finance which will enable her to build a comfortable home and buy pretty clothes. She is sometimes extravagant.'

Sun and Ascendant in Taurus; Moon in Scorpio
'She must guard against possessiveness, which could become jealousy.'

Moon and Jupiter in 6th House; MC Aquarius; 'Bowl-shaped' Chart
'Her career in nursing is well-chosen, for she has strong humanitarian instincts. As she grows older, she will become more self-contained and dignified as she learns from experience.'

Mercury conjunct Ascendant; Mercury in Taurus; Moon in Scorpio
'She should allow her rational instincts to formulate her opinions; mental cobwebs must not be allowed to collect (they might, since she has a tendency to become opinionated).'

Moon in Scorpio; Venus in Gemini
'In love she is passionate. She may also develop a deep understanding of the other.'

Paul and Pat Together

His MC in conjunction with her Ascendant; his Leo Ascendant in square with her Moon; his Leo Ascendant in opposition to her MC; his Moon in trine with her Sun

'You can identify easily with each other's personality. Because of this strong potential, your relationship should have an excellent basis.'

His Mercury in square with her Venus; his Venus conjunct her Mercury

'Companionship and friendship will develop strongly; so you will be able to approach problems rationally.'

His Mars in opposition to her Mars, Pluto; his Venus conjunct her Mercury

'You share an excellent fighting spirit, and will work energetically for each other. Your lives are not likely to run on smoothly but I am confident that you will find the courage to change your whole life-pattern radically and suddenly, if you feel that it will be for your good.'

His Mars in opposition to her Mars; their Jupiters in square

'Like most married people, sparks will fly occasionally, but your Charts show a splendidly positive indication of an above-average sense of humour which will always hold you together. Arguments will end in laughter rather than tears.'

His Sun in Aries, her Sun and Ascendant in Taurus

'As I have suggested, your worst faults can be suggested by Paul's unspoken "Me first!" and Pat's muttered "He's *mine*!" You should both try rationally to keep these negative traits in their proper perspective.'

His Sun and Mercury in Aries; her Moon in Scorpio; her Sun and Ascendant in Taurus

'You are both passionate and emotional, and passion and emotion will find enjoyable release in your love for each other.'

The Planets and Synastry

This panel explains in general terms how the planets are applied to the problems of synastry.

Sun: self-expression.
Moon: habits, moods, ways and means.
Mercury: intellectual ties, opinions.
Venus: true affection, unity, consideration of partner and partnership.
Mars: sex life, and the more aggressive aspects, tiffs and quarrels.
Jupiter: sense of humour, shared fun.
Saturn: constructive progress, but also frustration, ambition, unhappiness; even misery, coldness and frigidity.
Uranus: originality, the dynamic aspects, the unexpected, general tension.
Neptune: inspiration, idealism, 'romance', escapism or deception, underhandedness.
Pluto: ability to make new beginnings, forget the past, 'start again'.

A planet in one Chart can form an aspect to the same planet in the companion Chart; but it is generally more revealing when a planet in one Chart aspects *another* in the other. Particularly positive planetary relationships between two Charts are:

The two Suns forming a close conjunction (i.e. both birthdays within a week)
Girl's Sun in conjunction with man's Moon.
Girl's Moon in conjunction with man's Sun.
Ruling planets making positive and strong aspects.
Ruling planets from one Chart making strong aspects to Sun and Moon in the other.

The positions of the planets in their Houses must not be forgotten and again basic interpretation and principles remain the same. For instance, the girl's Venus may be in Taurus, with the sign on the cusp of the man's Fourth House, showing that she would do much to make their home attractive and comfortable. Practical matters such as finance, children, career interests, should be assessed precisely as in straightforward character analysis, but *always* assessing the indications *between* the respective Charts.

Having calculated the two Birth Charts, found and assessed the relationships between the angles and the Sun-signs, and made a list of the joint aspects between the planets in the respective Charts, it is now necessary to calculate the *progressed* Charts. With these calculated, four lists of aspects must be made (these must be *exact*; no orb is allowed):

1 The man's progressed planets, to see if they form relationships with the girl's natal planets.
2 The man's progressed planets, to see if they form relationships with the girl's progressed planets.
3 The girl's progressed planets, to see if they form relationships with the man's natal planets.
4 The girl's progressed planets to see if they form relationships with the man's progressed planets.

The progressed angles of the Charts should also be considered as they can show important indications. If the man's progressed Ascendant has reached the same degree in the Zodiac as the girl's natal Ascendant, this is obviously splendid, since it forms an excellent integrating link, and the blending of personalities so essential to a happy marriage.

If the girl's Venus has progressed to the position of the man's natal Sun, *she* will probably have fallen for *him.* If the man's Mars forms an aspect to the girl's Venus, a lively sexual relationship will also be harmonious.

More dynamic and sudden attractions are often shown when Uranus is involved. For instance, if a progressed Mars makes a strong aspect to a natal Uranus, and there is Fifth House involvement, sparks will fly to say the least of it!— and if this is the case then other factors would show whether the relationship would be long-lasting or not.

Sometimes aspects will be found *only* between progressed planets—i.e., the girl's progressed Sun might conjunct the man's progressed Mars. If so, it is advisable to suggest a waiting period. The whole affair may cool off once the progression has passed and a permanent tie would have little chance of success.

Of all progressions, relationships between Venus and Pluto are perhaps the most highly-keyed as far as sudden affairs are concerned, and should be given special consideration. As explained elsewhere, these often block a natural course of events, and if they occur between Charts it may well be that there is some prevention of a normal, happy union.

The progressed Moon moving so quickly, should be considered somewhat differently from the other planets. If, for instance, the progressed Moon of one occupies the other's Sun-sign, this can be an interesting and positive indication; but it is so ephemeral that if these are the only aspects, the lovers will have parted within a few weeks!

Note
If it is felt desirable to assess future years, a list of aspects not yet exact should be drawn up. For instance, if the man's Sun is 4° away from the girl's natal Moon, this aspect will affect them in four years' time (possible outcome, children).

A Warning
It is vital to remember that it is not for an astrologer to say whether a couple should or should not marry. The final decision must rest with those concerned. Astrologers can only point out possible areas of compatibility or incompatibility between two people.

SEVEN ASTROLOGICAL TYPES

The American astrologer Marc Edmund Jones has evolved a theory which divides Birth Charts into seven distinct types, according to the distribution of planets within them. He claims that the 'shape' of this distribution indicates the nature of the individual concerned, and is therefore a useful guide for the astrologer.

Developing this idea further, it seems possible to link specific groupings with specific signs (though the theory itself is related by Mr Jones *solely* to the 'arrangement' of planets in the Chart). The planetary groupings appear capable of underlining certain sign-characteristics. For instance, a subject with Libra powerfully emphasized who also comes into the see-saw category, will be even more likely to see both sides of a question; the indecisiveness and inability to choose between conflicting paths will conversely be emphasized by the see-saw configuration.

The splay character – the individualist – is surely at his most potent when Aquarius is prominent; the bowl perhaps with Capricorn; the bundle with Cancer, and the locomotive with Aries. The splash needs a great deal of anchorage in the planetary positions, if it is present with Gemini or Pisces; as a grouping, though, it certainly seems related to both these signs.

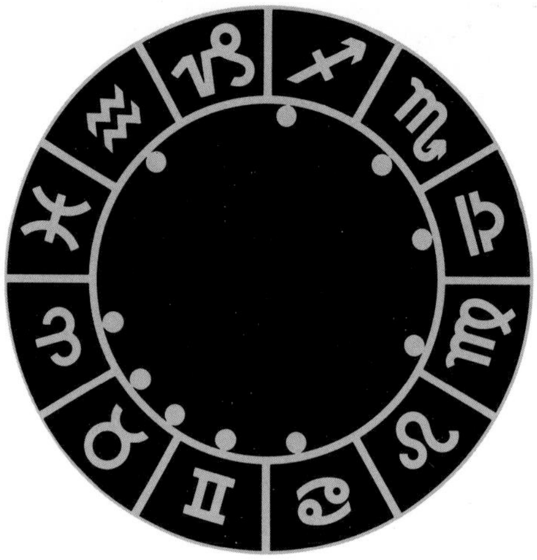

The Splash
This is a fairly easily recognized group. The principal Splash qualification is that the planets should occupy as many Signs as possible. The difference between it and the Splay is that the latter should have at least one stellium, or small group of planets. Splash people at their best show universal interests and an urge for broad knowledge. At worst, their behaviour reveals a scattering of energy.

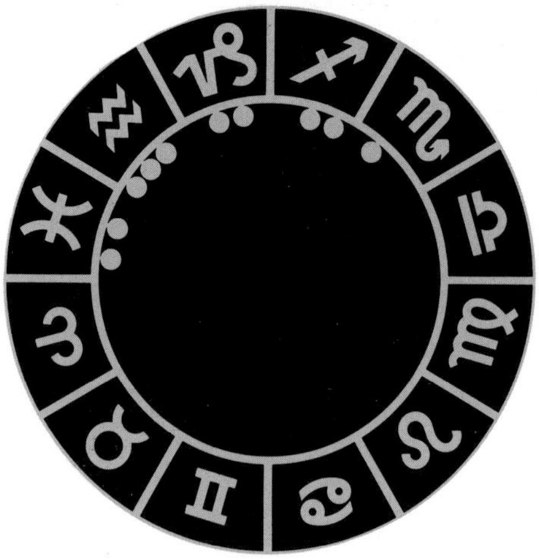

The Bundle
The Bundle is the rarest planetary grouping, so called because of the close grouping of the planets within a few consecutive divisions of the Zodiac. It shows a clear indication of a specialist: of someone – perhaps involved in an academic occupation – who tends very definitely to live and think within confines. People who show this type of grouping should cover one subject in depth.

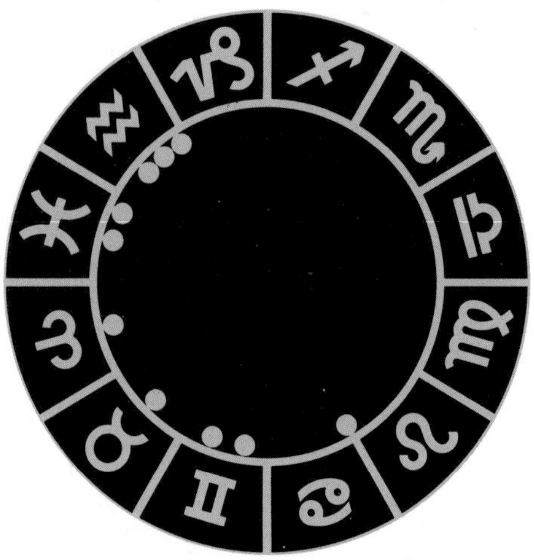

The Bowl
The Bowl type has particular force if the planets fall either entirely above or below the line of the Ascendant, or if they fall all in the eastern (left-hand) or western (right-hand) side. Bowl people are self-contained, tending to scoop up experience. The leading planet will be revealing in this area. Jupiter, for instance, will in a compatible Sign be helpful whereas an afflicted Saturn could be negative.

The Bucket
Nine planets fill one hemisphere of the Bucket Chart and one – called a Singleton – falls in the other, forming the 'handle'. Bucket people direct their efforts to a single purpose; often the Singleton planet indicates the nature of this purpose. What drives the Bucket type is the achievement of objectives. This is important to his psychological well-being. Bucket people are not usually concerned with self-preservation.

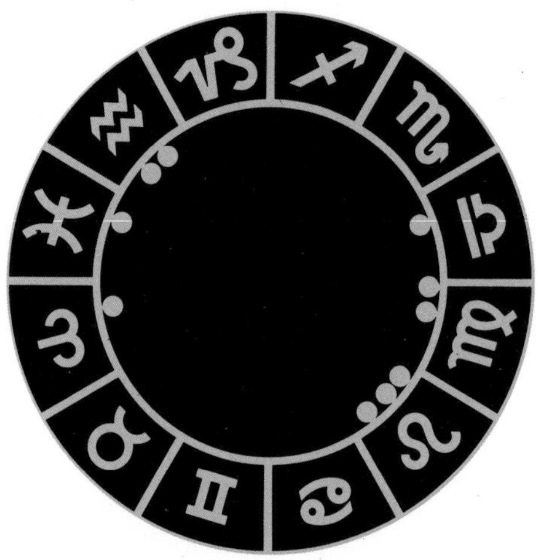

The See-saw
Ideally speaking, there should be five planets in each opposing group in a See-saw Chart. The numbers can vary as long as neither of the two empty sections of the Chart are less than a sextile aspect in span – in other words, the extent of two Signs or 60°. There is a tendency for those with this grouping always to consider opposing views and opinions and see life through a contrasting set of windows.

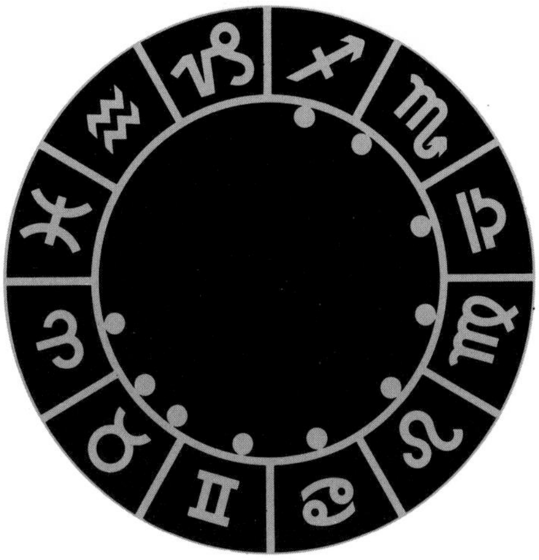

The Locomotive

The name Locomotive has an engineering origin and refers to the extra weight of metal necessary in a locomotive's driving wheel opposite the driving rod, which creates a balance. Locomotive people apply drive to problems and tasks and have an exceptional fund of energy at their disposal. The planet leading the others clockwise around the Chart is important; its House position may be particularly illuminating.

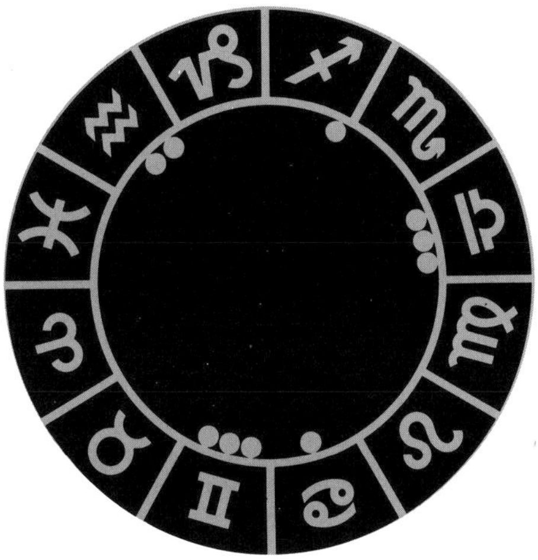

The Splay

The Splay type of Chart is not always easy to define, but there will sometimes be a grand trine present. It indicates an individualist, someone who has no wish for a regimented or highly organized life and who will avoid becoming trapped in any way within the bounds of strict routine. He will resent being pigeonholed and his temperament will 'jut out into experience, according to its own very special tastes'.

Fine Calculation of the Ascendant and Midheaven

The reader making a first attempt to set up a Birth Chart will find the methods given on pp. 78–81 adequate for most cases.
But it is possible to be more exact. Taking the same data as before, the local sidereal time was 17 hours 49 minutes 54 seconds. Referring to the Table of Houses for the appropriate latitude, we find the nearest sidereal time gives 17h 46h 55s. This gives the Ascendant 22° 32′ Pisces, and the Midheaven 27° Sagittarius.
This is a good working position for each; but the birth time is known accurately, so the positions can be made still more accurately.

1 First, we subtract the earlier of the sidereal times given from the later, *disregarding the hours:*

51m 17s
46m 55s
4m 22s

Convert the result to seconds:
4m 22s = 262s. Call this *A.*

2 Now find the difference between the local sidereal time and the earlier time (from the tables, again ignoring hours):

Local sidereal time 49m 54s
Earlier sidereal time 46m 55s
2m 59s

Convert to seconds:
2m 59s = 179s. Call this *B.*

3 Note the ascendant degree and minute which appears in the Table of Houses before and after the local sidereal time for the Chart:

Ascendant after = 25m 1s Pisces
Ascendant before = 22m 32s Pisces
2m 29s

Convert this to seconds:
2m 29s = 149s: Call this *C.*

4 Note the degree of the Midheaven which appears in the Table of Houses before and after the local sidereal time for the Chart:

Midheaven after = 28° Sagittarius
Midheaven before = 27° Sagittarius
1°

Convert this to minutes of arc (by multiplying by 60). 1° = 60′ Call this *D.*
NB: With the MC, the result is *always* 60.

5 Now multiply B by C and divide by A:

$$\frac{B \times C}{A}$$

179 × 149 = 26671 ÷ 262 = 102.
Call this 102′, and convert to 1°42′.
Add this to the earlier Ascendant time, thus:

Earlier Ascendant time 22° 32′ Pisces
1° 42′
Exact Ascendant = 24° 14′ Pisces

For the exact Midheaven, multiply B by D and divide by A:

$$\frac{B \times D}{A}$$

179 × 60 = 10740 ÷ 262 = 40.
Call this minutes of arc, and add it to the earlier Midheaven time:

27° 00′ Sagittarius
40′
Exact Midheaven = 27° 40′ Sagittarius

Rectification of Birth Time

People usually know their birthday or place of birth; quite often, however, many do not know their birth-time.
Citizens of the USA and certain European countries are at an advantage, for their birth-times are entered on birth certificates. Even where the birth-time is known, there is often an unfortunate tendency to round it off to the nearest quarter of an hour.
There are several important factors to take into consideration when 'rectifying' a Chart or correcting to actual birth-time.

1 If no birth time is given, it is unwise to attempt to find one. It is generally safer to calculate the planetary positions for noon, local time, with the proviso that the whole of the Chart cannot be calculated. The planets can be used in their signs (but no Houses are available); so can planetary aspects. Sometimes it will be impossible to assess the sign that contains the Moon as it is likely to change signs during the day. And the progressions are even more limited, as no noon-date, progressed Ascendant, Midheaven or lunar progressions can be calculated. The only reasonable accuracy would come from the transits. Solar and mutual progressions can only be assessed over a much longer period.

2 If the birth-time is said to be 'morning', 'late afternoon' or 'evening', this is a little help. But if the birth-time is known to within two hours, it is often possible to rectify a chart and so give a more accurate assessment of the subject.

3 If should be set up initially for the earliest possible birth-time, and for the latest. If a planet lies a few degrees from the Ascendant or Midheaven in either of these Charts, it is possible that when the progressed Ascendant or Midheaven reached that planet an event will have occurred which will be of the nature of the planet. For instance, if the Midheaven of the first Chart is on Scorpio 10°, and Saturn falls on 29° Scorpio, there would probably have been an event when the subject was 19 years old, characteristic of Saturn – perhaps his father died, or there was a bad turn of events in the family circle. In early life, a change of Midheaven can mean a family move or a change in the family's circumstances. A progressed Moon crossing the Ascendant can indicate the beginning of a new cycle in life, and so on.

4 Sometimes a Chart can be rectified by using one-degree progressions (see p. 153). Here it is the planet directed to the angle of the Chart that will matter; i.e. the Ascendant may be 15° Sagittarius, the Moon on 3° Gemini, and when the child was 12 there will have been a break-up between his parents. The Moon would then have progressed 12° to the Descendant, or to a position in opposition to the Ascendant.

5 Final rectification can often clarify a birth-time, adjusting it from, say, 3.15 to 3.12 or 3.09. You can then use the progressed Ascendant and Midheaven with a greater degree of confidence.

MIDPOINTS AND HOUSE DIVISIONS

The methods taught in this book for calculating, drawing, interpreting and progressing a Birth Chart, are basic; they have been proved sound by long practice. Astrologers can rely on them. The serious astrologer should, however, try to widen his knowledge by becoming familiar with as many other systems and theories as possible. Some will strike him as odd, but others may give him new insight.

Midpoints

Many contemporary astrologers are doing interesting work on *midpoints* – led by the German theorist Reinhold Ebertin (see p. 191). Midpoints were used as long ago as the 13th century. The theory holds basically that the degree of the ecliptic that falls halfway between any two planets, the Ascendant, or Midheaven, is a sensitive area of a Chart, being the point at which the magnetic influences of the two planets meet.

The midpoint can be activated by transits, lunar progressions or major progressions. If, for instance, there is a planet at 1° Leo, and another in opposition to it at 1° Aquarius, the midpoint between the two would fall on 1° Taurus. This is an ideal example, but the process of discovering midpoints is not unduly complicated. The true art lies in the interpretation of them.

In our example, a planet at the apex of a tee-square will be near the midpoint of the two planets in opposition. This point can be activated either by transits, lunar progressions or major progressions: for instance, by a transiting planet on the opposite degree across the Chart, appearing in this case at 1° Scorpio.

A large number of midpoints are to be found in a Chart: there is a midpoint between each planet and each other planet, and one between each planet and each angle, and between the angles. The beginner should nevertheless be selective in his search for significant midpoints. He might, for example, start by using the very sensitive midpoint which falls exactly between the Ascendant and Midheaven.

In the illustration at right, this position is arrived at by adding the degrees between Ascendant and Midheaven; divide the total of 87° by two and round off to a figure of 43°. Count on 43° from the Midheaven degree, and this gives Aquarius 10° – the 'half-sum' or midpoint. It is written: Asc/MC = Aquarius 10°. The midpoint is then assessed according to the planets; their basic influence exercised through the midpoint and modified by the influence of the transiting or progressed planet.

As with the Moon's Nodes, the midpoint should be considered as an axis, and its polarity is as important as the degree itself: so 10° Leo will be equally sensitive, and a transit or major direction to it will activate the Ascendant-Midheaven midpoint.

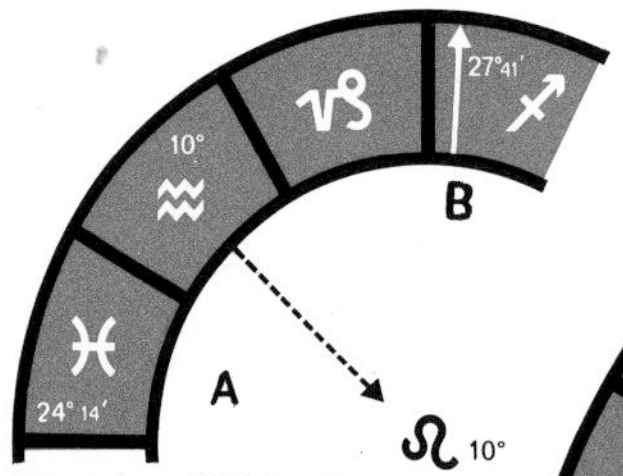

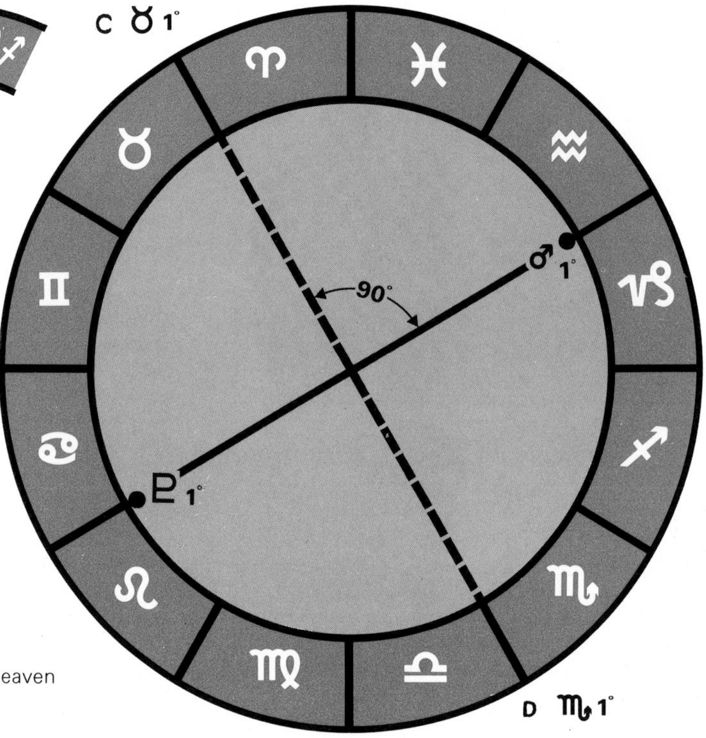

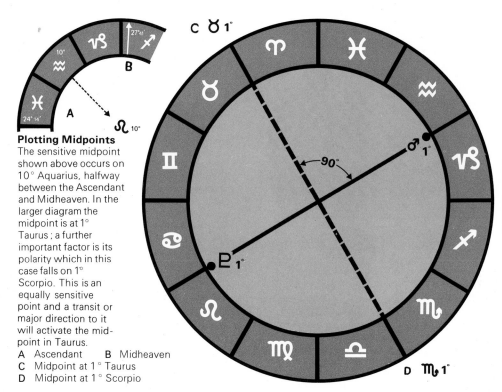

Plotting Midpoints
The sensitive midpoint shown above occurs on 10° Aquarius, halfway between the Ascendant and Midheaven. In the larger diagram the midpoint is at 1° Taurus; a further important factor is its polarity which in this case falls on 1° Scorpio. This is an equally sensitive point and a transit or major direction to it will activate the midpoint in Taurus.
A Ascendant B Midheaven
C Midpoint at 1° Taurus
D Midpoint at 1° Scorpio

Midpoints are often extremely revealing; sometimes unexpected and uncharted events will show themselves through the transit of a powerful planet over the midpoint. The midpoint concept is an area for extensive study. It has great depths and the beginner should make sure he has a thorough grasp of the basic theory of progressions and transits before exploring too far.

Horary Astrology

The student will be more than likely to encounter horary astrology. While there are astrologers who take this branch of the subject seriously, its effect is to trivialize astrology by its dangerous affinity to fortune-telling and divination.

In horary astrology the client asks a question, and the astrologer sets up a Chart for the moment it is asked, to obtain an answer. If the inquiry comes by post, the astrologer will use the time he opened the envelope or the time the question was written down. The theory that events take on the nature of the time at which they occur is basic to astrology. But the notion that the planetary positions can produce an 'answer' of this kind – usually to the most petty questions – seems too absurd for consideration and is the kind of activity that can only call serious astrology into disrepute.

Astrology by Question and Answer *above*
The kind of question the horary astrologer tends to be asked, is: 'Where did I lose my wallet last week?' or 'Which horse is going to win the 4.30?' His answer will depend on casting a horoscope for the moment of asking.

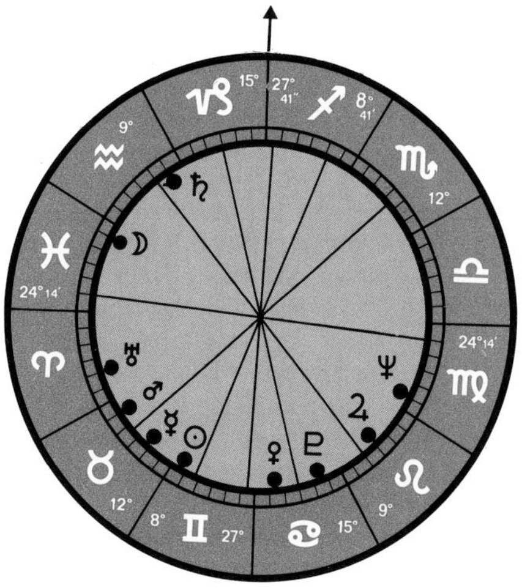

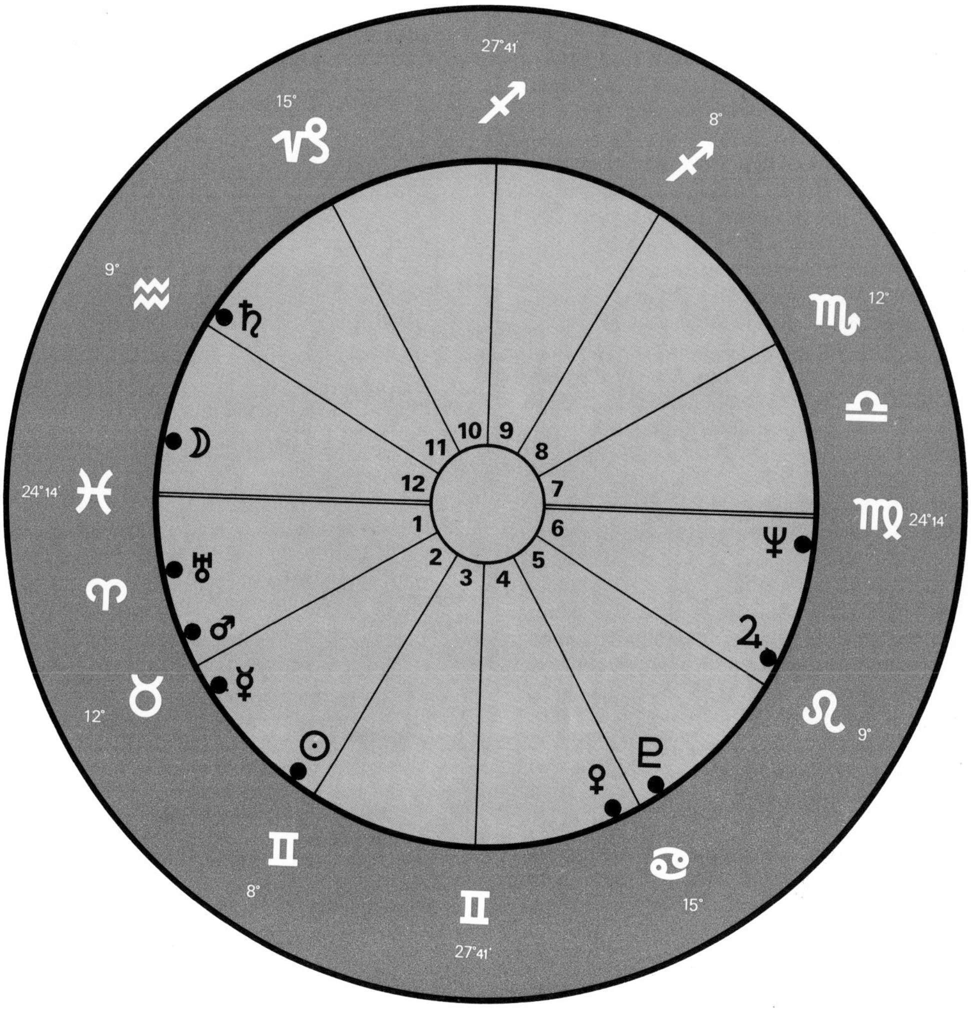

Placidean Charts *above and right*
The two Charts given here are for the same birth time and place which produced the Equal House Chart first shown on p. 78. Several planets change Houses – Mars from Second to First, the Sun from Third to Second, Pluto from Fourth to Fifth, Jupiter from Fifth to Sixth. (Aspect lines are never drawn on Placidean Charts.) The version of the Chart given at right is the style usually adopted in Britain and the U.S.

The continental method of drawing a Placidean Chart (above) is rather clearer than that used by British and American Placidean astrologers. It shows the unequal sizes of the Houses and the planets can be placed more accurately.

House Division

Of all astrological questions, probably the one most diligently debated concerns the systems of House division. This has always been a source of great controversy.

The system used throughout this book is the oldest and the simplest: the Equal House system. This fell into disuse for some years, but began to return to favour twenty or thirty years ago and is the system taught by the internationally known Faculty of Astrological Studies.

Whichever system is favoured, it remains true that the Houses are 'man-made'; they are an intricate intellectual system that has evolved over the centuries as a result of the various findings of mathematicians. The ecliptic, on the other hand – the apparent path of the Sun around the Earth, in whose plane the planets move and have their influence – is obviously not man-made. The Equal House system makes use of it. Astrologers who have an exaggerated notion of the Houses tend to favour other systems.

Of these, the most commonly used is that of Placidus. This system works well for southerly latitudes. The nearer to the equator the place of birth, the more equal the Houses in their number of degrees. But as we move into northerly latitudes, an increasing amount of distortion is introduced and in consequence it becomes less accurate.

Even for a birth in Scotland, the Houses become distorted in size; and when a Chart is set up for a birth within the Arctic Circle, the system becomes extremely difficult to operate. In general, for certain times of the day it is impossible to erect a Chart for extreme northern latitudes.

The Placidean system relies on the time taken for each degree of the ecliptic to rise on its parallel of declination, from the lower meridian to the horizon, and from the horizon to the upper meridian. The arcs made by the movements are trisected, and form the cusps of the Houses. But in northern latitudes, certain degrees are *circumpolar* (i.e. never touching the horizon) and planets falling on them cannot appear in the Birth Chart. Nor can the missing degrees form House cusps. So no complete Chart can be made. Followers of the Equal House system feel it is illogical to use a system with such obvious gaps in it.

Other systems of House division (also named after the men who instigated them) are Regiomontanus and Campanus. These use space rather than time: Campanus used the prime vertical of the celestial sphere as his basis; Regiomontanus the celestial equator as his.

Sometimes, when the Placidean or other House system is used, planets fall in different Houses than in the Equal House system. The interested reader who wants to experiment might begin by converting his own Chart from Equal to Placidean. Should a planet change House, both interpretations can be assessed, and he can decide which seems the most accurate and pertinent in his own case.

The Placidean system necessitates the use of a fuller Table of Houses than can be given here, but there are many sources from which it can be learned.

POLITICAL ASTROLOGY

Political or mundane astrology is astrological interpretation applied both to inanimate objects and collections of people – states, cities, governments, political parties and clubs, for example.

In considering the Birth Chart of a country, one has first to discern the proper time for which the Chart should be drawn up: in the case of England, most astrologers have used noon on Christmas Day, 1066 – the moment when the crown was set on the head of William the Conqueror. But others also use a Chart cast for midnight on 1 May 1707 (the time of the union of Great Britain and Scotland), and midnight on 1 January 1801 (the unification of Great Britain and Ireland). Which of these should be considered the more accurate is open to discussion.

The birth times of most countries are difficult to fix, although with more recent states the time is known with great exactness, and in some cases there are indications that astrologers have been at work: it has been conjectured that the People's Republic of China came into existence at a moment far too happy, astrologically, for its choice to have been an accident, even though, officially, astrology is frowned on.

As with countries, so with political parties or clubs or businesses: the Astrologers' Guild of America, for example was formed at noon, Eastern Standard Time, on 9 April 1927. But most other organizations were set up with less precision, which makes their birth times very difficult to ascertain.

A Car's Birth Date

The same problems face the astrologer drawing up the Birth Charts of inanimate objects – a car, a ship, a building. The difficulties are also considerable. An astrologer has to be able to answer the question, 'What is the "birth time" of a car?' The choice of times is wide. Is it the moment at which its wheels turn under power? The moment at which its first owner receives it? The moment at which he first starts its engine? A ship may be 'born' at the moment when it starts down the slipway at launching; but what of the keel-laying? Or the moment when the designer first sets pen to paper? (Perhaps the relationship between these times is similar to that between the moment of conception and the moment of birth of a human being.)

Once a Chart has been drawn up, it is considered in much the same way as a conventional 'human' Birth Chart, although astrologers use eclipses and conjunctions between 'heavy' planets in particular; and some, attempting to forecast events in a country's history, look at its Chart each month at the time of the new Moon. Examples of this forecasting are given opposite.

Celestial and Mundane Influences

The English astrologer, Charles E. O. Carter, correlated the results of his many years of study in *An Introduction to Political Astrology* (L. N. Fowler, 1951). In it he suggests specific areas of influence can be attributed to the planets, Houses and Signs.

The Planets

Sun: Supreme authority in the State: eclipses have their effect.
Moon: The population; also agriculture.
Mercury: The Press, literature, education; the post office and means of communication; political speeches.
Venus: Art, society; contributes to national happiness; victory in war.
Mars: The armed forces; violent crime; associated with Uranus, may cause explosions; with Neptune, treachery. Divisive elements in society.
Jupiter: Clergy and churches, judges, law; banking, insurance; 'upper classes'; philanthropic institutions (especially if associated with Neptune).
Saturn: Property.
Uranus: Administration; power in its physical sense – electrical and nuclear.
Neptune: Hospitals, charitable institutions; the Navy; under affliction associated with muddle, crime, scandal; brewing and alcohol; chemicals, oils, footwear, the arts.
Pluto: Mines and detection; under affliction, the underworld.

The Signs and Houses

The Signs and Houses, Mr Carter concluded, are very closely associated with political astrology.
First House: The nation as a whole.
Second House: The economy.
Third House: Education; periodical publications; the post office, radio and transport; communications in general.
Fourth House: Land and housing; agriculture. The Opposition in Parliament.
Fifth House: All forms of national pleasure and enjoyment; sport, general amusements. Society; children.
Sixth House: The 'Working classes', left-wing organizations. Public health. Armed forces, civil service.
Seventh House: Foreign affairs generally; war as well as treaties.
Eighth House: Financial relations with foreign countries; public safety.
Ninth House: The law; religion; philosophy; science (which is also associated with the Third House).
Tenth House: Heads of state; Government, national prestige.
Eleventh House: Parliament, especially the lower house. Local government.
Twelfth House: Prisons, hospitals, homes for the aged; philanthropic organizations; secret societies, monasteries and institutional religion.

Case One : the Titanic

The *Titanic*, belonging to the White Star Line, was the largest ship ever launched and reputed to be unsinkable. But on her maiden voyage she struck an iceberg and went down on April 15 1910 with the loss of 1,513 lives. Her astrological history is one of unrelieved gloom. At the moment when she started to leave the slipway, Mars was in opposition to the Ascendant (indicating 'bodily danger') and Mercury was in conjunction with Saturn, while both were in opposition to Jupiter. When she set sail at noon on 10 April, the Ascendant (representing the ship herself) was in opposition to Uranus (catastrophe) and the Moon (travellers); Neptune, the ruler of the sea, was in the Twelfth (misfortunes), square the Sun (a dangerous aspect). In the Birth Chart of the Captain,

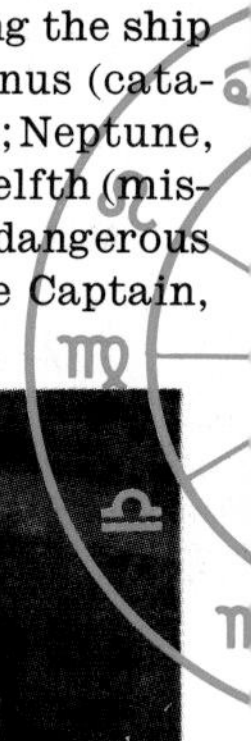

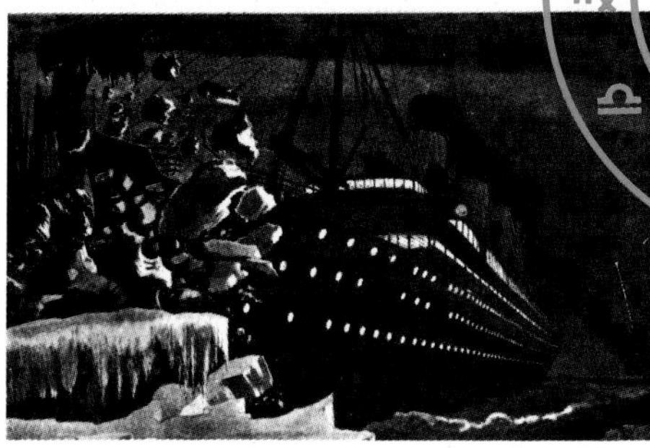

Neptune was in the House of Death, and Uranus (catastrophe) in the Ninth House (a House indicating long journeys). On the day of the sinking, Uranus was in exact opposition to the place where the Moon stood at the moment of the Captain's birth, and exactly in the position which the Sun held at that same moment. Captain Smith had the natal aspects Uranus opposition Moon, and Uranus conjunction Sun. The combination would be regarded by any astrologer as extremely dangerous.

The Unsinkable Titanic *left and above*
The fatal collision of the astrologically doomed liner is shown at left; over 1,500 lives were lost out of a total of 2,207 passengers and crew; above, one crowded lifeboat that got away.

John F. Kennedy in Dallas *below*
John F. Kennedy and his wife Jackie wave to supporters in Dallas moments before the President was shot – climax of a personal and national tragedy predicted by American astrologers.

France Mourns De Gaulle *above*
A crowd of 40,000 lines the funeral route of General de Gaulle. His death was a turning point in French history, the progressed Sun in the nation's astrological Chart forming a conjunction with Mercury which signalled a new era of flexibility in France's foreign affairs.

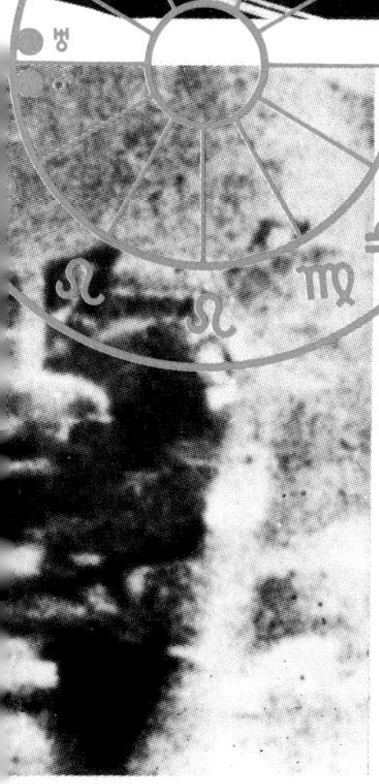

The President's Coffin *left*
Twelve young men of Colombey-les-Deux-Eglises carry General de Gaulle's coffin into the village cemetery; at the head of the cortège, his son, Philippe de Gaulle. This traumatic loss to France was heralded by a potent solar eclipse which occurred earlier the same year.

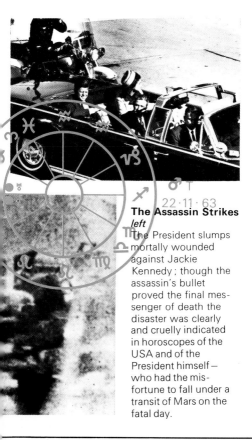

The Assassin Strikes *left*
The President slumps mortally wounded against Jackie Kennedy; though the assassin's bullet proved the final messenger of death the disaster was clearly and cruelly indicated in horoscopes of the USA and of the President himself – who had the misfortune to fall under a transit of Mars on the fatal day.

Case Two: John F. Kennedy

Six months before the assassination of President Kennedy in November 1963, Leslie McIntyre, an American astrologer, wrote in *American Astrology* that certain configurations in the progressed horoscope of the USA 'have coincided with personal danger to our head of State.' The tragedy that followed amply fulfilled his warning.

On his assassination the President's progressed Mars occupied 20° Gemini, forming a conjunction to both the Ascending degree and the degree of Mars in the USA's Chart. These were also activated by transits of Mars, which occupied Sagittarius 20°.

Case Three: France Under De Gaulle

Some astrologers believe that the solar eclipse in March 1970, which fell very near the ascending degree, cast its shadow forward to indicate the death of De Gaulle.

The Fourth Republic was astrologically 'born' at 2.40 pm on 10 October 1946 in Paris. In 1970–1 the progressed Sun in the Chart changed signs – from Scorpio into Sagittarius. Mercury fell on 0° Sagittarius; the progressed Sun at the end of 1970 formed a conjunction to that planet, indicating greater freedom to communicate with her neighbours. This has shown itself in easier Common Market negotiations.

ASTROLOGY AROUND THE WORLD

World-wide interest in astrology has increased enormously since 1900, but at different rates in various parts of the world. India, for instance, never suffered the virtual collapse of the astrological theory which, in Europe followed Newton's discoveries and the growth of science and scepticism that appeared with the Age of Reason in the 18th century. Beginning in England soon after the turn of the century, and greatly encouraged by the interest of such influential thinkers as the psychologist C. G. Jung, a newborn fascination with the subject has spread not only throughout Europe but also to the Americas, Asia and Australia. This map shows the extent of that interest at the beginning of the 1970', and names a few of the organizations which take astrology as a subject for serious study, not just as a topic of popular interest.

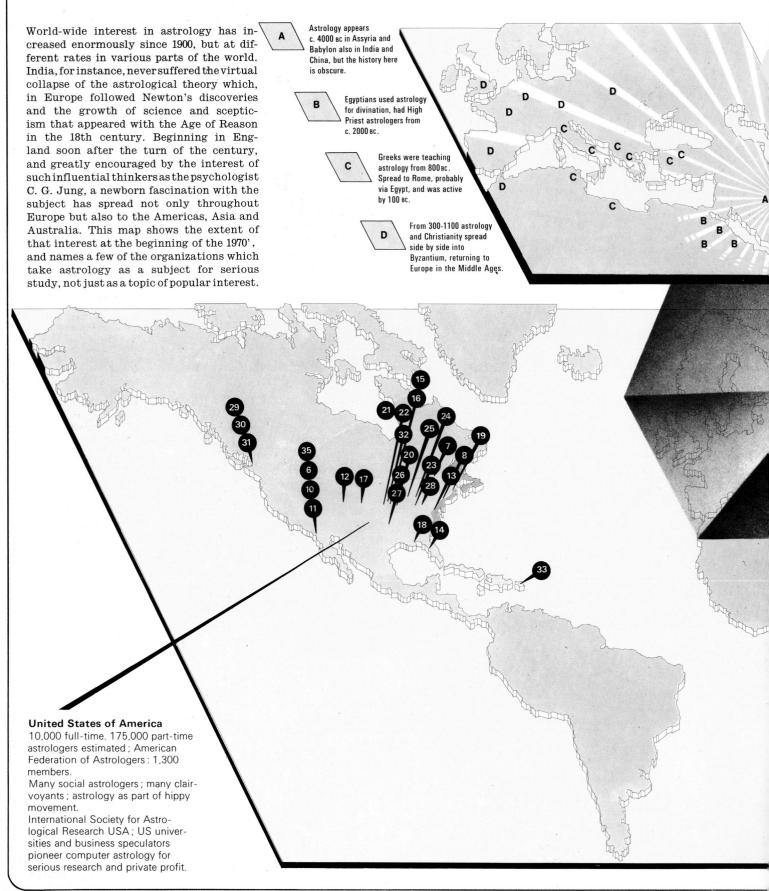

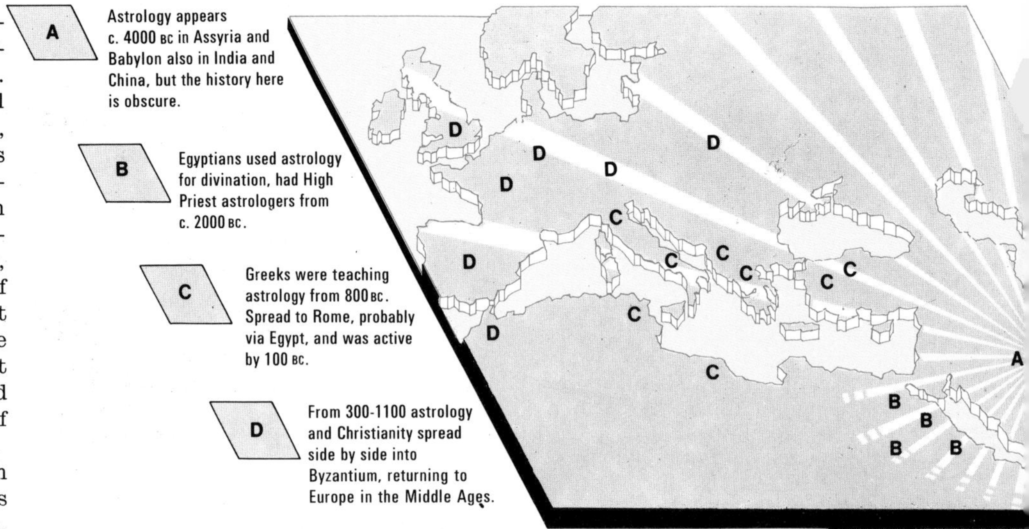

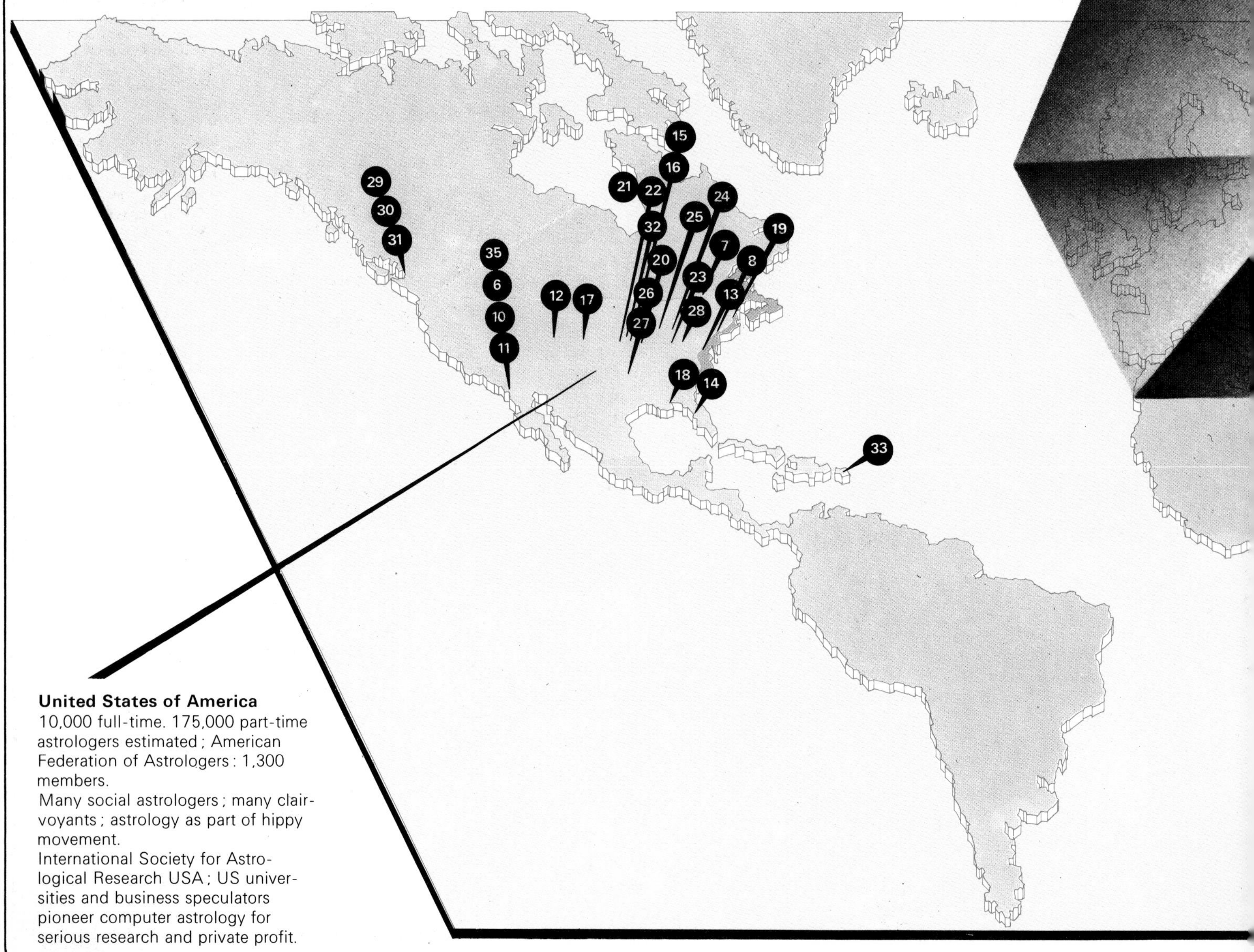

A Astrology appears c. 4000 BC in Assyria and Babylon also in India and China, but the history here is obscure.

C Greeks were teaching astrology from 800 BC. Spread to Rome, probably via Egypt, and was active by 100 BC.
D From 300-1100 astrology and Christianity spread side by side into Byzantium, returning to Europe in the Middle Ages.

United States of America
10,000 full-time. 175,000 part-time astrologers estimated; American Federation of Astrologers: 1,300 members.
Many social astrologers; many clairvoyants; astrology as part of hippy movement.
International Society for Astrological Research USA; US universities and business speculators pioneer computer astrology for serious research and private profit.

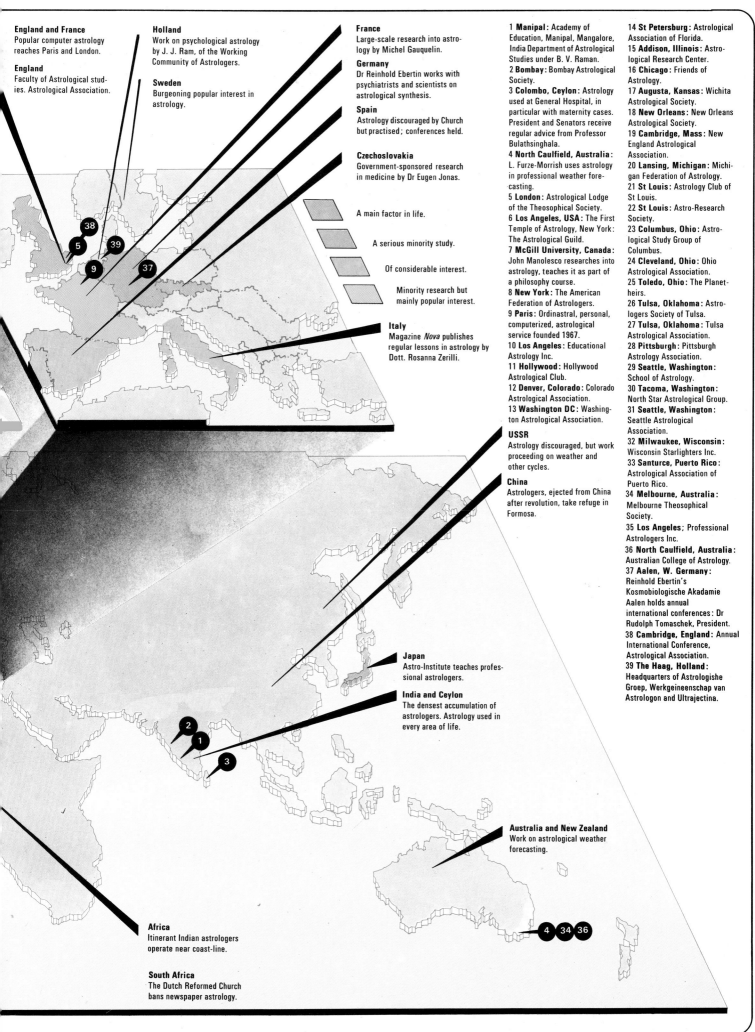

England and France
Popular computer astrology reaches Paris and London.

England
Faculty of Astrological studies. Astrological Association.

Holland
Work on psychological astrology by J. J. Ram, of the Working Community of Astrologers.

Sweden
Burgeoning popular interest in astrology.

France
Large-scale research into astrology by Michel Gauquelin.

Germany
Dr Reinhold Ebertin works with psychiatrists and scientists on astrological synthesis.

Spain
Astrology discouraged by Church but practised; conferences held.

Czechoslovakia
Government-sponsored research in medicine by Dr Eugen Jonas.

A main factor in life.

A serious minority study.

Of considerable interest.

Minority research but mainly popular interest.

Italy
Magazine *Nova* publishes regular lessons in astrology by Dott. Rosanna Zerilli.

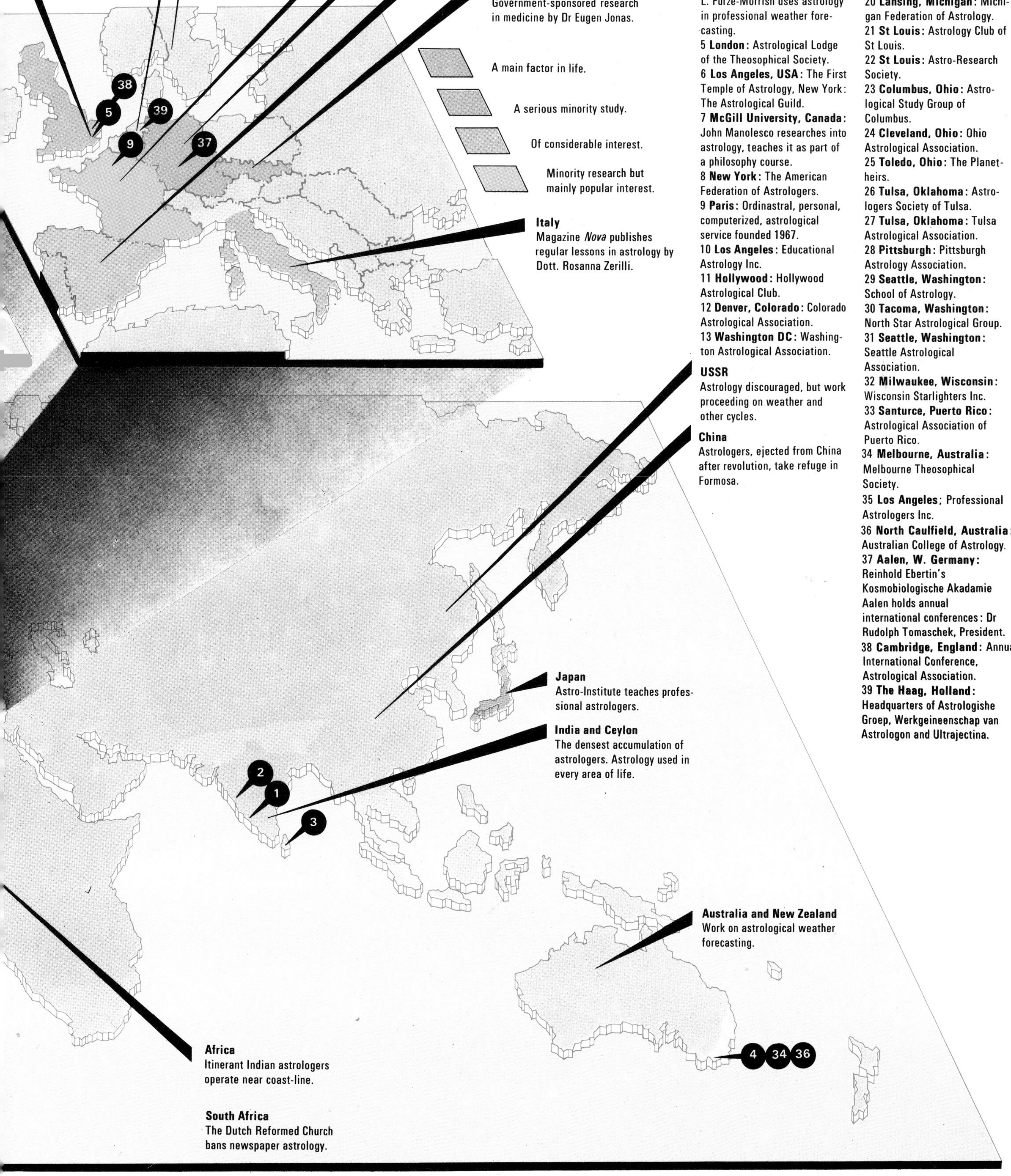

USSR
Astrology discouraged, but work proceeding on weather and other cycles.

China
Astrologers, ejected from China after revolution, take refuge in Formosa.

Japan
Astro-Institute teaches professional astrologers.

India and Ceylon
The densest accumulation of astrologers. Astrology used in every area of life.

Australia and New Zealand
Work on astrological weather forecasting.

Africa
Itinerant Indian astrologers operate near coast-line.

South Africa
The Dutch Reformed Church bans newspaper astrology.

1 **Manipal:** Academy of Education, Manipal, Mangalore, India Department of Astrological Studies under B. V. Raman.
2 **Bombay:** Bombay Astrological Society.
3 **Colombo, Ceylon:** Astrology used at General Hospital, in particular with maternity cases. President and Senators receive regular advice from Professor Bulathsinghala.
4 **North Caulfield, Australia:** L. Furze-Morrish uses astrology in professional weather forecasting.
5 **London:** Astrological Lodge of the Theosophical Society.
6 **Los Angeles, USA:** The First Temple of Astrology, New York: The Astrological Guild.
7 **McGill University, Canada:** John Manolesco researches into astrology, teaches it as part of a philosophy course.
8 **New York:** The American Federation of Astrologers.
9 **Paris:** Ordinastral, personal, computerized, astrological service founded 1967.
10 **Los Angeles:** Educational Astrology Inc.
11 **Hollywood:** Hollywood Astrological Club.
12 **Denver, Colorado:** Colorado Astrological Association.
13 **Washington DC:** Washington Astrological Association.
14 **St Petersburg:** Astrological Association of Florida.
15 **Addison, Illinois:** Astrological Research Center.
16 **Chicago:** Friends of Astrology.
17 **Augusta, Kansas:** Wichita Astrological Society.
18 **New Orleans:** New Orleans Astrological Society.
19 **Cambridge, Mass:** New England Astrological Association.
20 **Lansing, Michigan:** Michigan Federation of Astrology.
21 **St Louis:** Astrology Club of St Louis.
22 **St Louis:** Astro-Research Society.
23 **Columbus, Ohio:** Astrological Study Group of Columbus.
24 **Cleveland, Ohio:** Ohio Astrological Association.
25 **Toledo, Ohio:** The Planetheirs.
26 **Tulsa, Oklahoma:** Astrologers Society of Tulsa.
27 **Tulsa, Oklahoma:** Tulsa Astrological Association.
28 **Pittsburgh:** Pittsburgh Astrology Association.
29 **Seattle, Washington:** School of Astrology.
30 **Tacoma, Washington:** North Star Astrological Group.
31 **Seattle, Washington:** Seattle Astrological Association.
32 **Milwaukee, Wisconsin:** Wisconsin Starlighters Inc.
33 **Santurce, Puerto Rico:** Astrological Association of Puerto Rico.
34 **Melbourne, Australia:** Melbourne Theosophical Society.
35 **Los Angeles;** Professional Astrologers Inc.
36 **North Caulfield, Australia:** Australian College of Astrology.
37 **Aalen, W. Germany:** Reinhold Ebertin's Kosmobiologische Akadamie Aalen holds annual international conferences: Dr Rudolph Tomaschek, President.
38 **Cambridge, England:** Annual International Conference, Astrological Association.
39 **The Haag, Holland:** Headquarters of Astrologishe Groep, Werkgeineenschap van Astrologon and Ultrajectina.

BRIEF LIVES

A WHO'S WHO OF ASTROLOGY

4

Here, then, as they lived, finde brefe liues of those both willinge and able to performe the truth in like maters of which we haue discoursed. But just a fewe of these searchers, *viz.* Rameses II (Ozymandias, Kinge of Kinges) c. 1300-1236 BC ; Ptolemy, first singular good Astrologer, (AD 120-180) ; Regiomontanus, necessarie to the Pope (1436-76) ; Nostradamus, rude inuentor of prophesies (1503-66) ; Tycho Brahe, true mensurer of the sterres (1546-1601) ; Alar Leo, discursor of wonderfull unknowen pleasant profites of astrologi (1860-1917) ; Margaret Hone of diuers profitable collections authour (1892-1969) ; Dane Rudhyar, of the Americas a treasure to theoretick, (1895-) ; Reinhold Ebertin, of cosmobiologie the precursor (1901-) ; John Addey, commending the mathematicals and harmonicks (1920-). So peruse, Reader, recalling as Fr Bacon hath it, that 'certainely moderate prayse, not vulgar, is that whych doth the goode.'

THE ASTROLOGERS I

RAMESES II

Ozymandias, c. 1300 – 1236 BC, Pharaoh of Egypt

Rameses II, a man of immense personal courage and dedicated to astrological science, ruled Egypt for 67 years, and was the founder of the largest and most famous of early Egyptian libraries, at his new capital, Pi-Ramesse. The Pharoah of Exodus, he was responsible for fixing the cardinal astrological Signs – Aries, Libra, Cancer, Capricorn. At his bidding, the magnificent temple at Abu Simbel was carved out of the rock on astrological principles. Equally imposing was his grand hypostyle hall at the temple of Amon at Karnak, now known to have been engineered in relation to the fixed points on the Celestial Sphere. Works of such staggering dimensions were a measure of the economic prosperity which Rameses brought to Egypt during almost 50 years of peace after his decisive defeat of the Hittites at the battle of Kadesh.

ASSURBANIPAL

7th Century BC, King of Assyria

Assurbanipal succeeded to the throne of Assyria in 668 BC, and reigned until 625. He subdued his numerous enemies by a combination of political acumen and military force, and at the height of his power was so supreme that at least two kings (of Cicilia and Tabal) were honoured to offer their daughters for his harem. Astrologically, his importance lies in his foundation of a great library of cuneiform tablets at Nineveh, reflecting his preoccupation with astrology, history, mythology and the natural sciences. Although it seems unlikely to be true that, as was claimed, the library contained astrological manuscripts as early as 3800 BC, there were certainly copies of work of that time (the reign of Sargon, king of Agade). Assurbanipal's chief astrologers (who were of high rank and position) used the library to perfect their art, and some of them – Rammanu-sumausar, Nabu-musisi and Marduk-sakin-sumi, for instance – became so adept at deducing omens from daily planetary movements that a system of making periodical reports came into being, and Assurbanipal received (sometimes by swift messengers from far corners of his kingdom) details of 'all occurrences in heaven and earth', and the results of his astrologers' examinations of them. He used these as political weapons, and for the practical day-to-day conduct of the kingdom. After his death, Nineveh fell to the Medians and Chaldean Babylonians (in 612), and the library of 25,000 or so clay tablets was destroyed or dispersed.

Rameses II *above*
Wall painting from Rameses' rock temple at Beit El Wali showing defeat of enemies.

Assurbanipal *above*
The astrologer king enthroned at Nineveh; from an Assyrian relief of the 5th century BC.

Oxen *below*
A wooden model of oxen ploughing in Nile valley, from a tomb.

PTOLEMY

Claudius Ptolomaeus
120 – 180, First Celestial Scientist

Little is known about the life of this great astrologer, astronomer and geographer, other than the fact that he was observing the skies at Alexandria during the reigns of Hadrian and Antoninus Pius. For many centuries he was credited with the authorship of the first astrological textbook of any distinction, the *Tetrabiblos*. More recently, modern scholars claim that internal stylistic evidence suggests that perhaps the *Tetrabiblos* is based on early astrological documents, some Babylonian, some Egyptian, some Greek. However this may be, Ptolemy's astronomical observations (he described a spherical world in the centre of the universe, circled by the heavenly bodies, went on to discuss their dimensions – often very accurately – and to catalogue over 1,000 separate stars, 300 of them for the first time) is of the greatest importance in the development of both astronomical and astrological theories.

Ptolemy *left*
A medieval representation of the great Egyptian astrologer of the 2nd century, whose researches greatly influenced Renaissance astrological theory after their translation in the 15th century.

REGIOMONTANUS

Johann Müller
1436 – 76, Papal Astrologer

A German astronomer, Regiomontanus went in 1462 to Italy, in search of authentic Ptolemaic astrological manuscripts. In 1471 he settled in Nuremburg, and with his pupil and patron Bernhard Walther equipped the first European observatory, for which he made the instruments. He also established a printing press on which he printed much of his own work, including in 1474, a thirty-year ephemeris. He died of the plague in Rome, where he had been summoned by Pope Sixtus IV to help with the reformation of the calendar (but in all probability also to advise him on the astrological conduct of his war with Florence). His main astrological importance is as the inventor of one of the systems of house division still used by some modern astrologers.

The Celestial Sphere *above*
A woodcut by Erhard Schon, made at Nuremburg in 1515 as the title plate to Leonard Reymann's Birth Chart. It represents an example of the celestial sphere according to the astrology of Ptolemy. With Earth at the centre and all other heavenly bodies describing concentric circles around her, the Ptolemaic system was accepted for more than 1300 years after Ptolemy's time. On the right is Ptolemy taking a sighting. The figure of Astronomy is pointing at him.

THE ASTROLOGERS 2

COPERNICUS

1473 – 1543

Mathematical Revolutionary

Born in Poland, Copernicus studied first at Cracow University and then for ten years in the Italy of Leonardo da Vinci before returning home at the age of 33, learned in astronomy, mathematics, law, medicine and Greek; in the year of his death, he published *De revolutionibus orbium coelestium*, advancing the shattering theory – backed by observations – that the Earth was not the centre of the universe, but travelled round the Sun, as Aristarchus of Samos had suggested in about 270 BC. The work included an introduction written by his young colleague, Rhaeticus, dedicated to the astrology-conscious Pope Paul III, and addressed to the well-known contemporary astrologer Schoner. It contained a long astrological discourse, inserted in the middle of Copernicus' argument. Anti-astrologers who claim that Copernicus despised astrology fail to explain why he permitted this: for Rhaeticus wrote his part of the work in Copernicus' own house, and under the older man's direct supervision. It seems more likely that Copernicus, realizing that he had turned a system of astronomy upside down, also realized what astrologers have claimed ever since – that astrology itself is unaffected by the change in viewpoint; for it is the planetary positions which influence earthly events, and those positions remain constant in their relationship to Earth.

Copernicus *above*
The founder of an era, he began a scientific controversy which lasted over a hundred years. His great book remained on the Papal Index until 1835 !

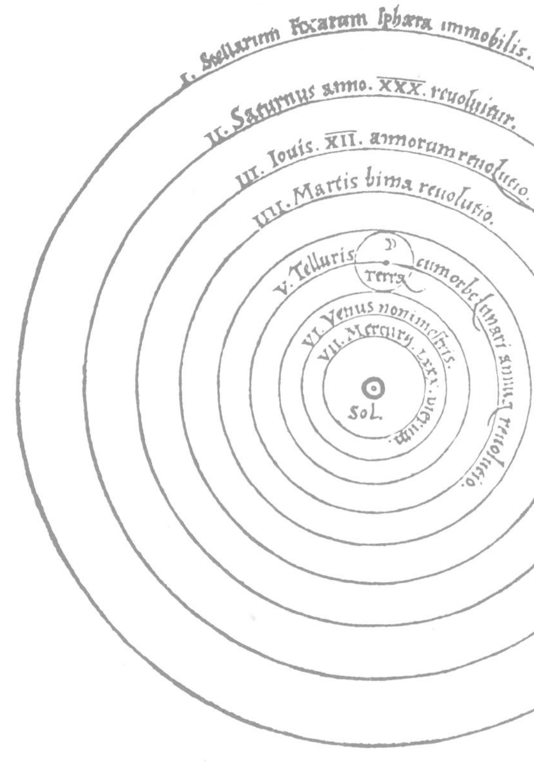

The Copernican Theory *right*
The heretical heliocentric system was wisely but vainly dedicated to Pope Paul III. Copernicus was later supported by Galileo.

PARACELSUS

Theophrastus Bombast von Hohenheim

1490 – 1541, Planetary Physician

Paracelsus was preoccupied throughout his life with the practice and philosophy of medicine. He coined the word 'laudanum', referring to a preparation of his own containing powdered gold and pearls, and not to be confused with the drug discovered much later by medical science. Paracelsus had an extremely noble view of his profession; his insistence on the study of alchemy, theology, theories of minerals, and of astrology, set him somewhat aside from the other medical men, and his place in the history of medicine is correspondingly obscure. He directed that if a man were deficient in blood, he should be given iron – for the deficiency would be replaced by the Martian activity of the metal. In his assessment of free will, a burning issue of the day, Paracelsus held that man and the planets were both free to act – 'The stars force nothing into us that we are not willing to take; they incline us to nothing we do not desire.'

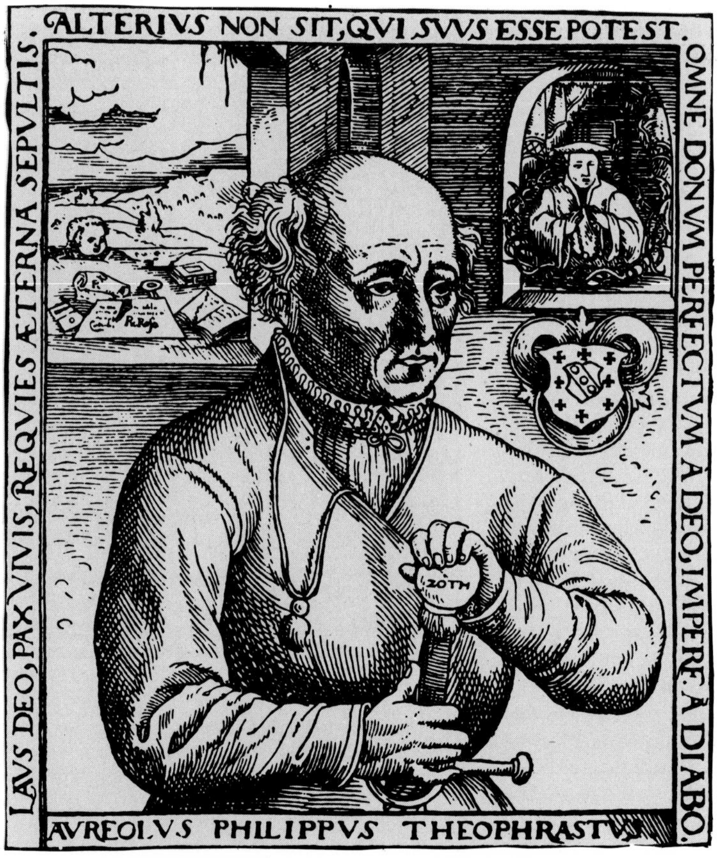

Paracelsus *left*
Paracelsus, the founder of medical chemistry, believed that 'all influences that come from the Sun, the planets and the stars, act invisibly on man, and if these are evil, they will produce evil effects.' Despite the astrological reasoning which he applied to his practice of medicine, he never became a professional astrologer: he did not calculate nativities or make horoscopes. Nevertheless, throughout his life he remained deeply interested in the interrelationships between man and the planets, finally concluding that the celestial bodies acted as free agents, but that man was not rigidly controlled by them: 'the stars are free for themselves, and we are free for ourselves.'

NOSTRADAMUS

Michel de Notre Dame
1503–66, Seer Extraordinary

Nostradamus began life as a conventional doctor near Aix-en-Provence, where he is supposed to have invented a cure for the plague; it may have been this that first brought him to the notice of his contemporaries, but in 1555 he consolidated his fame by publishing the first edition of his *Centuries* – a series of prophesies in verse so vague and obscure in their language that it is possible to read into them accurate predictions of various events in European history, including the French and English revolutions, and the Second World War.

In 1556, Nostradamus was summoned to the French court and commissioned by Catherine de Medici to draw up the horoscopes of the royal children. When Henri II fulfilled the prediction Nostradamus had made for him, and died at a tournament at the hands of a courtier, Nostradamus was suspected of witchcraft, and became extremely unpopular. Catherine, however, continued to patronize him until his death, when his wife erected a monument bearing the claim that he was 'the only one in the judgment of all mortals worthy to write with a pen almost divine under the influence of the stars of future events of the entire world'. A somewhat inflated claim!

The *Centuries*, however, while inspired by celestial events, are remembered chiefly for the extraordinary interpretations which Nostradamus gave them.

J'annonce vérité simplement et sans pompe.
Et mon présage vrai nullement ne me trompe.

Nostradamus *left*
'A true and remarkable portrait of the famous and celebrated astrologer Michel Nostradamus' – Paris, 16th century.

Tycho Brahe *below*
Portrait of Brahe (left) engraved by Gheya ; at right is a room at Brahe's observatory at Uraniborg, built for him by King Frederick II and incorporating Tycho's great quadrant. As an observer Brahe was supreme, and between 1575 and 1595 he compiled a star catalogue which was much more accurate than any previously drawn up. In addition he made excellent measurements of the positions of the planets and so introduced a far greater degree of exactitude into astrological science than had hitherto been possible. When he died, in 1601, his observations came into the hands of his last assistant, Kepler, who used them well. Both Kepler and Brahe were employed as astrologers at the Danish court. As a man Tycho was eccentric and often difficult. One curious feature of Tycho's observatory complex was a prison which he built for the incarceration of tenants who failed to pay their rents.

TYCHO BRAHE

1546–1601, Court Astrologer

In Brahe's time, scientific knowledge and traditional beliefs were still inextricably mixed. While Brahe disposed of the notion that the planets were fixed within crystalline spheres, he was unable to accept that Earth herself might be moving in space. He became the Danish court astrologer, and from the comet of 1577 predicted that a prince would be born in Finland who would lay German waste before vanishing in 1632. Gustavus Adolphus, the great Swedish king, known as the 'Lion of the North', perfectly fitted Tycho's vision.

Brahe was as convinced as Kepler that an empirical system of astrology would work. In a lecture of 1574 he said firmly that those who denied the influence of the planets 'violate clear evidence which for educated people of sane judgment it is not suitable to contradict. . . . We hold that the sky operates not only on the atmosphere but also directly upon man himself.'

THE ASTROLOGERS 3

FRANCIS BACON

1561 – 1626, The Astrological Philosopher

Philosopher, essayist and eventually Lord Chancellor of England under James I, Bacon had a distinguished career. (Although in 1620 he was convicted of bribery and sent to the Tower with a fine of £40,000 the king quashed the sentence immediately.)

The champion of the use of experiment, inductive reasoning and exact observation to verify theories, he represents the start of the modern scientific approach and reaction against Scholastic learning with its verbal and academic disputations. He held that the aim of knowledge was the improvement of man's lot.

Bacon, in his essay *Astrologia Sana*, agreed that Elizabethan astrology was full of superstition, but thought its assertions should be tested by thorough scientific research and, if verified, accepted. He was 'certain that the celestial bodies have in them certain influences besides heat and light', and believed that it was possible to predict not only heavenly events such as the appearance of comets and meteors, but earthly events such as floods, earthquakes, seditious schisms, revolutions and transmigrations of peoples.

In his essay *Of Prophesies*, he tells the story of how Nostradamus (q.v.) foretold the death of Henri II. 'When I was in France, I heard from one Dr Pena, that the queen mother, who was given to curious arts, caused the king her husband's nativity to be calculated under a false name, and the astrologer gave a judgment that he should be killed in a duel; at which the queen laughed, thinking her husband to be above challenges and duels; but he was slain upon a course at tilt, the splinters of the staff of Montgomery going in at his beaver.'

TOMMASO CAMPANELLA

1568 – 1639, The Astrologer-Priest

A Dominican priest and philosopher, Campanella offended his seniors by the uninhibited expression of his often very radical views and 'magical practices'. Finally sentenced to perpetual imprisonment for involvement in an attempt to stir up revolution against Spanish rule in Southern Italy, he was rescued by the intervention of Pope Urban VIII. Later, Richelieu and King Louis XIII recognized him as a great astrologer and scholar who had no difficulty in reconciling astrology with a brand of 'new Christianity'. In his *La città del sole* he advocated a theocratic form of government based on natural religion.

JOHN DEE

1527 – 1608, Astrologer Royal

John Dee, son of a minor courtier of King Henry VIII, was born in 1527, and had a brilliant career at Cambridge, where he became at the age of nineteen a Fellow of Trinity College, and Under-Reader in Greek. His passion for mechanical invention enabled him to construct a mechanical flying beetle for a production of Aristophanes' *Pax* so realistic that – for the first of many times – he was accused of sorcery.

Already Dee was interested in magic, alchemy and astrology. King Edward VI became his patron, and the young king's death was a severe disappointment; but the new queen, Mary, was sympathetic, and invited him to draw up a horoscope of her bridegroom, Philip of Spain, and herself. Dee did so – but with a shrewd political sense, was also in touch with the queen's younger sister, Princess Elizabeth, then in semi-captivity. He was unwise enough to discuss the queen's horoscope with her sister; the news leaked out, and Dee was arrested on charges of heresy and treason. Waiting to appear before the notorious Star Chamber, he saw a fellow-prisoner dragged out and burned at the stake; but his own thorough knowledge of the scriptures confounded his judges, and he was released.

When, in 1558, Elizabeth became queen, she sent for Dee, commanding him to predict a satisfactory date for her coronation. He did so, and for years enjoyed the queen's confidence and friendship. John Aubrey wrote of him at the time; 'He had a very faire, cleare, rosie complexion; a long beard as white as milke; he was tall and slender, a very handsome man . . . A mighty good man he was!'

The Queen insisted he should live within easy reach of her London palaces; when he was ill, sent her own doctors to care for him; and after riding in Richmond Park, would frequently call at his house to see his latest invention, or to discuss some new rare book he had acquired for his library.

She seems also to have trusted him with matters of state, for he travelled extensively abroad, sometimes for Elizabeth, sometimes for Sir Francis Walsingham, the head of the queen's secret intelligence service. But Dee's interest in the occult was growing: he now believed he could turn base metal into gold, that he would discover the Philosopher's Stone and the Elixir of Life. With his friend, Edward Kelley (a far from reliable, short-tempered eccentric who once insisted that the angels had instructed him that he and Dee should hold all property – including their wives – in common), he held long conversations with spirits; these may be regarded as early experiments in extrasensory perception.

He spent much of the rest of his life travelling in Europe – as, it was generally believed, one of Elizabeth's secret agents. If this is so, his reward was small, for on his return to England the queen seemed to have forgotten him, and he died in relative poverty. Historians still underestimate the importance of his early astrological advice to the queen; as for Dee himself, 'If I have done my dutiful service any way to her Majesties well liking, I am greatly bound to thank Allmighty God,' he wrote.

Astrology apart, among the many fruits of his fertile imagination he invented the paradoxical compass and predicted the development of the telescope.

John Dee *left*
A portrait of Dee, engaged in his astrological calculations which had such a profound influence on 16th-century politics in Europe.

The Virgin Queen *below*
Elizabeth I took Dee into her innermost confidence, and sought his guidance over matters of state as well as her personal problems.

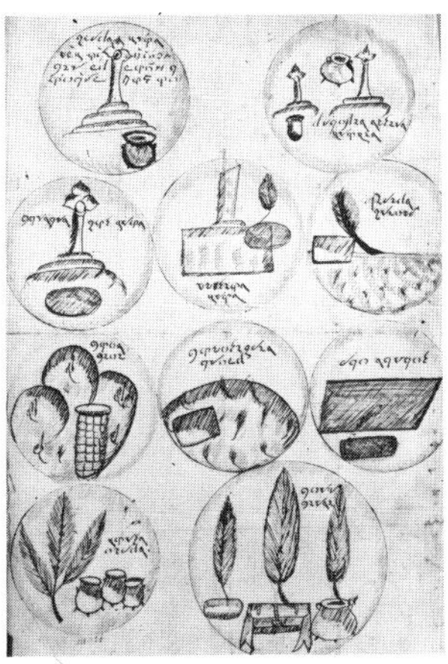

Raising a Ghost *above*
Dee and Kelley question a corpse to obtain insights into the future.

Angelic Devices *left*
Devices drawn by Dee on the instruction of the angels.

Angelic Geometry *right*
Dee's conference with the angels led to a multitude of calculations, of which this is by no means the most involved.

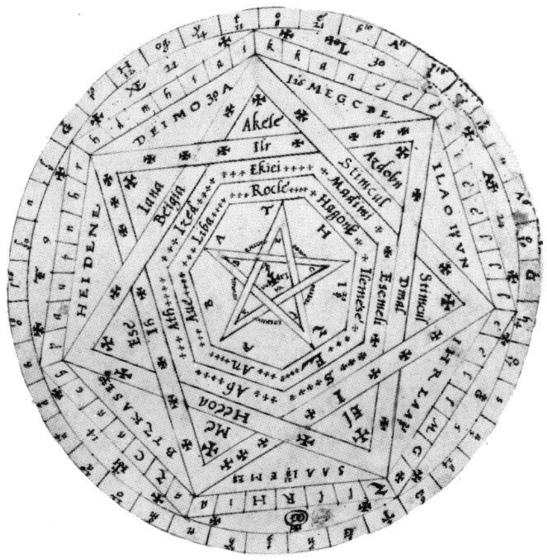

OTHER ELIZABETHANS

Shakespeare and Astrology

Born in Stratford-on-Avon on or about 23 April 1564, William Shakespeare moved to London c.1588 where he joined a troupe of actors, the 'Chamberlain's men'. The earliest of his 37 plays, Henry VI, was written in 1590–92.

The greatest Elizabethan writer naturally reflected in his plays and poems the age's interest in astrology: there are few of his plays in which some astrological reference is not found, and further evidence that Shakespeare himself believed in astrology, is adduced from the fact that when anything critical of the subject is to be said, it is always put into the mouths of the villains rather than the heroes of the plays. The most famous attack comes from the bastard Edmund, in *King Lear*.

'This is the excellent foppery of the world, that when we are sick in fortune – often the surfeit of our own behaviour – we make guilty of our disasters the sun, the moon, and the stars: as if we were villains by necessity, fools by heavenly compulsion; knaves, thieves and treachers by spherical predominance; drunkards, liars and adulturers by an enforced obedience of planetary influence. . . . My father compounded with my mother under Ursa major; so that it follows I am rough and lecherous. Tut, I should have been that I am, had the maidenliest star in the firmament twinkled on my bastardizing.'

And while his work is not so drenched in astrology as that of his great predecessor Chaucer, it shows at least how general was the interest in the subject during the sixteenth century, being considered by many statesmen as an indispensable aid for the furtherance of their schemes.

Dr Simon Forman
c. 1560 – 1620, Astrologer of Fortune

Dr Forman, the son of a chandler, went to Holland, a centre of astrological learning at the time, in 1580 to learn astrology. On return he set up as astrologer and physician in Lambeth. His practice soon flourished and both the poor and nobility beat a track to his door; the Countess of Essex, the Earl of Somerset and Sir Thomas Overbury, among others, all consulted him. His failures were happily recorded by his younger contemporary, William Lilly. Drawing up his own Birth Chart, Forman had confidently predicted that he would be a lord within two years; in the event by the end of the two years he found himself in Newgate prison. Forman died in 1620, leaving £1,200 – a not inconsiderable sum for a chandler's son.

THE ASTROLOGERS 4

Mr Evans, The Welsh Wizard

William Lilly's astrological master was a Welshman, Mr Evans, of Gunpowder Alley, a curate who had been forced to flee from his parish 'for some offences very scandalous'. Lilly described him as 'of a middle stature, broad forehead, beetle-browed, down-looked, black curling stiff hair, splay-footed . . . much addicted to debauchery, and then very abusive and quarrelsome, seldom without a black eye, or some mischief or other.' Lilly left him after realizing that Evans, while quite capable of properly interpreting an astrological Chart, usually told the client what he wanted to know rather than what the Chart indicated. He told Evans so: 'which when he had pondered, he called me boy, and must he be contradicted by such a novice? . . upon this we never came together after.'

JOHANNES KEPLER

1571–1630, Mystical Mathematician

Johannes Kepler was both mathematical genius and astrological mystic. Born of poor parents, he first worked as pot boy in his father's beer-house. However, he went to university at the age of 17 and was then appointed professor of astronomy in Graz. In 1600 he became Tycho Brahe's assistant at Prague, and in 1601 succeeded him as imperial mathematician and court astronomer. He recognized Tycho's error in regarding the Earth as the centre of the Solar System, but drew heavily on his former master's calculations when formulating his celebrated Laws of Planetary Motion – laws which explain the velocity of the planets and the nature of their orbits round the Sun. For some years, Kepler virtually kept himself by drawing and interpreting horoscopes, and no doubt considered this a relatively unimportant aspect of his work. Indeed, in a moment of exasperation, he called astrology 'the foolish and disreputable daughter of astronomy, without which the wise old mother would starve'.

He nevertheless believed that an empirical system of astrology could be devised. 'Nothing exists or happens in the visible sky', he wrote 'that is not sensed in some hidden manner by the faculties of Earth and Nature: these faculties of the spirit here on Earth are as much affected as the sky itself.' And his final conclusion on the subject, written when at the end of his life he was Court Astrologer to the Duke of Wallenstein, was that 'the belief in the effect of the constellations derives in the first place from experience, which is so convincing that it can be denied only by people who have not examined it.'

Mr Evans *left*
The ill-favoured astrologer of Wales, engraved in 1776 from an original drawing. This portrait accurately follows William Lilly's description of his master.

Johannes Kepler *left*
Portrait of the Graz professor; he wrote self-deprecatingly of the astrological influences on himself, saying that 'with me Saturn and the Sun work together, and so my body is knobbly and dry, not tall.'

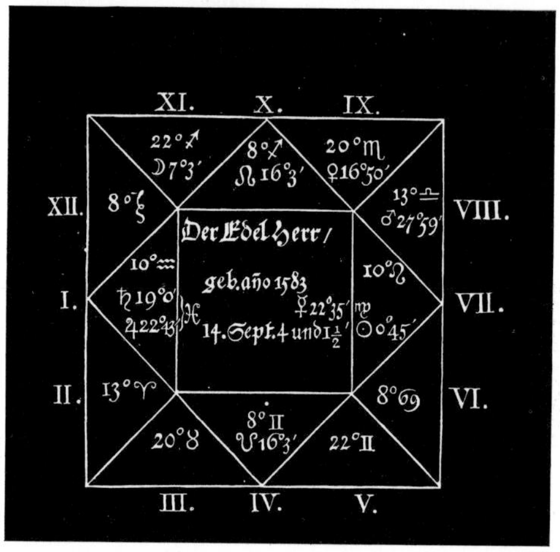

Kepler's Horoscope of Wallenstein *left*
The Birth Chart drawn up by Kepler in 1608 for Albrecht von Wallenstein, the German warrior from the Chart Kepler predicted 'fearful disorders over the land' in March 1634. Events proved him accurate to within days, even though Kepler's analysis was made 26 years earlier. Wallenstein was assassinated on 25 February 1634, his death causing severe political disruption.

Celestial Geometry *below*
Kepler was a mystic as well as a master mathematician; he believed that the planets emitted musical notes in their passage round the heavens. He also attempted to rationalize their orbital patterns in the construction shown here. The planets are linked in motion by means of five regular solids, each touching its neighbour within the celestial sphere.

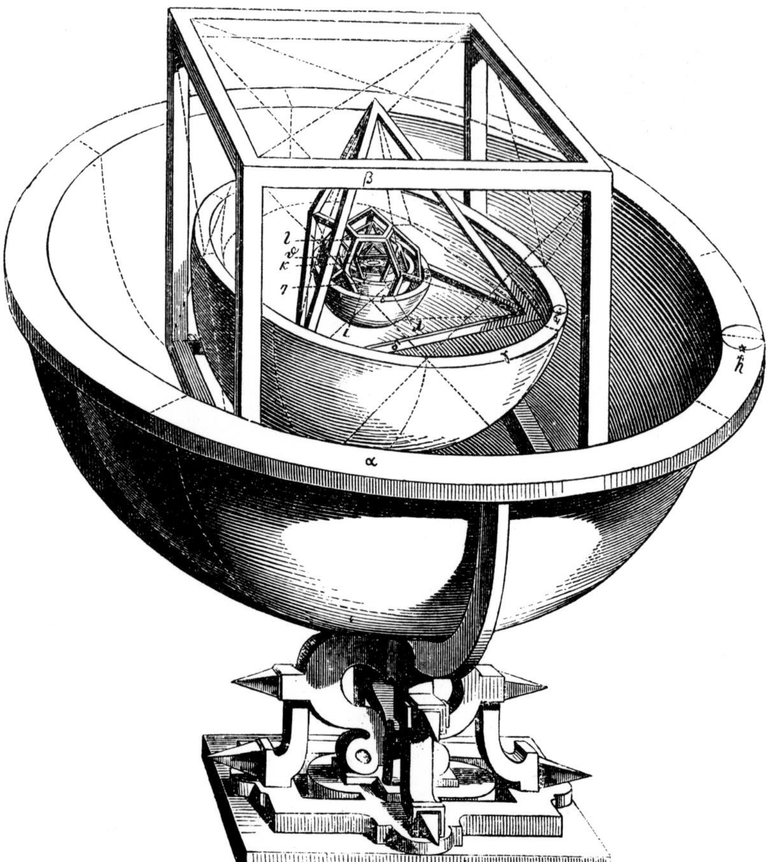

JEAN BAPTISTE MORIN

1591 – 1659, Court Astrologer

The most learned Catholic author of the seventeenth century, Morin is said to have studied astrology under a Scot named Davison. He made during his lifetime two excursions from France: one to accompany Henrietta Maria to England, another to Rome, where he was enthusiastically received by Pope Urban VIII, himself an extremely keen astrologer. His well-argued theological works did not save Morin from general condemnation on the publication of his *Astrologica Gallica*; his criticism of various aspects of the administration of the Church completed a record which led directly to the suppression of most of his voluminous writings. He was Cardinal Richelieu's private astrologer, and predicted exactly the deaths of King Louis XIII and several notable contemporaries. With these successes to his credit, he is generally believed to have been the astrologer concealed by Richelieu behind the curtains of the bedchamber during the birth of Louis XIV, in order that the heir's horoscope might be set up with perfect accuracy.

WILLIAM LILLY

1602 – 81, Master Astrologer

William Lilly was born in 1602, the last year of Elizabeth I's reign, and one year after the death of the great astronomer Tycho Brahe. The son of a yeoman farmer he found he 'could not work, drive the plough, or endure any country labour'. In 1620 he went to London to seek his fortune. He became secretary and general servant to an illiterate but wealthy gentleman, Gilbert Wright, who died seven years later leaving Lilly an annuity of £20 a year. Lilly had ingratiated himself with Mrs Wright, who had already been married twice, to husbands considerably older than herself. The 25-year-old servant proposed and was accepted.

Rescued from the pots and pans, he became interested in astrology, and had the money to pay for his lessons from Mr Evans. After they parted company, Lilly bought up a large astrological library with his wife's considerable fortune.

In 1633, Lilly found comparatively few rivals in London, and certainly none with his gift of language. He began publishing books of predictions, some of which landed him in trouble. Lilly seems to have been by nature litigious, and had several law-suits over his steadily growing property, as well as being continually called to account by disgruntled clients, suspicious Members of Parliament and magistrates.

Pope Urban VIII *left*
Pope Urban VIII (1568–44) was one of the most sympathetic popes to astrologers; he welcomed J.-B. Morin in Rome, and rescued Campanella from prison to help him draw up horoscopes and generally plan future moves in his running battle with the Borgias.

William Lilly *left*
William Lilly portrayed at his desk with astrological equipment; a Birth Chart hovers above the background landscape.

The Great Fire *below*
Lilly's hieroglyphic of 1651 accurately predicted the Great Fire of London in 1666.

THE ASTROLOGERS 5

When in 1642 the Civil War broke out, Lilly managed dextrously to take both sides at once: he 'loved and approved of Monarchy', but 'engaged body and soul in the cause of Parliament'. He attended the execution of Charles I, having a few months before supplied the file which the King had used in a fruitless attempt to escape from prison on the Isle of Wight.

After the Great Fire of London in 1666, he was summoned to Parliament, to appear before a committee examining the cause of the conflagration. Lilly had successfully forecast the Fire, publishing a picture of the Geminian twins (who rule London) falling into a city in flames, but he managed to persuade the committee that he had not been personally responsible either for the fire or for the plague which preceded it and was allowed to go home.

Lilly cared seriously for his art but he was able to recognize its shortcomings. His advice to a young astrologer is still sane and wise – and is presented to each graduate of the English Faculty of Astrological Studies, as a kind of Hippocratic Oath. It begins:

'As thou daily conversest with the heavens, so instruct and form thy mind according to the image of the Divinity: learn all the ornaments of virtue, be sufficiently instructed therein: be humane, curtius, familiar to all, easie of accesse: afflict not the miserable with terror of a harsh judgment; direct such to call on God to divert his judgments impending over them: be civil, sober, covet not an estate; give freely to the poor, both money and judgment; let no wordly wealth procure an erroneous judgment from thee, or such as may dishonour the art.'

Eccentrics

Lilly, in his autobiography, described some of the astrologers practising in London in the first half of the seventeenth century. Making allowances for professional jealousy, they were still a poor lot. There was Alexander Hart, an ex-soldier, whose speciality was telling young men the time when they might expect to win at dice. Hauled before the magistrates at the Old Bailey for failing to raise a spirit, which he had promised to do, he escaped to Holland while on bail, and died there.

In Lambeth at the same time, Captain Bubb appeared in the pillory for persuading his servant to impersonate the ghost of a robber he had promised to raise.

There were one or two sounder astrologers: John Booker, from Manchester, an ex-haberdasher, who became clerk to a city Alderman, and who apparently was a very successful predictor; and Nicholas Fiske, a university man and a doctor, who also was an astronomer and mathematician.

ALAN LEO

1860 – 1917, Victorian Revivalist

The most successful professional astrologer of his time, Leo was born W. F. Allen. Like many astrologers of the day, he took his ascending sign as a pseudonym. He became interested in astrology around the age of 25, and shortly after moving to London met Walter Richard Old (who later became well-known as 'Seraphial'). Old was a member of the Theosophist movement, and an intimate of Madame Blavatsky, its impressive leader. He introduced Leo to the Theosophists; and with another astrologer, F. W. Lacey, Leo started the influential periodical, *The Astrologer's Magazine*.

Hard work and the offer of free horoscopes to new readers made the magazine a quick success; it became *Modern Astrology*, and after his marriage to a rich divorcee and palmist, he became a full-time astrologer. He wrote a number of astrological textbooks still in use today. His prosecution for 'fortune-telling' in 1914 (case dismissed on a technicality) and again in 1917 (fined £25) remain the only test-cases of their kind in British law.

EVANGELINE ADAMS

1865 – 1932, First American Astrologer

The first really popular American astrologer Mrs George E. Jordan – or Evangeline Adams, as she called herself – at the peak of her fame was consulted by most well-known Americans and visiting Europeans. Her career started when, on her first visit to New York, she informed her hotelier that he was 'under the worst possible combination of planets, bringing conditions terrifying in their unfriendliness.' That night his hotel burned to the ground, and his wife and several relatives perished. The resulting publicity given to this accurate prediction meant that Miss Adams' reputation was made. She never looked back.

For the next thirty years she flourished, her business increasing as a result of her prosecution for fortune-telling in 1914. During the trial she was given an anonymous horoscope to interpret. The Judge announced that the horoscope was that of his son, that Miss Adams had been totally accurate, and that in his opinion she had 'raised astrology to the dignity of an exact science'. The case was dismissed.

In 1930, two years before her death (which she correctly predicted) she ran a regular and extremely popular radio programme; thousands of her clients attended her lying-in-state, and the *New York Times* threw up its hands in wonder at 'radio and astrology dancing to victory hand in hand.'

Alan Leo *left*
Alan Leo, one of the first to repopularize astrology at the turn of the century. Leo built up *The Astrologer's Magazine*, and helped to prepare astrology for its 20th-century rebirth.

Evangeline Adams *above*
Evangeline Adams, greatly adored by an enormous clientele of rich and famous Americans, created a nation-wide interest in astrology with a series of radio programmes.

CHARLES CARTER

1887 – 1968, Empirical Astrologer

Charles Carter was perhaps the most distinguished British astrologer of the first half of this century. He learned the rudiments of astrology from Alan Leo's shilling manuals, and became preoccupied by its deeper implications for the rest of his life. He carried on the work of Leo within the Theosophical Society (becoming its President in 1922), founded the magazine *Astrology*, and was the first Principal of the Faculty of Astrological Studies, sponsored by the London Lodge of the Society in 1948.

Carter was the outstanding technical writer of his generation, interpreting and expanding older textbooks from his own empirical observations. In 1955 he wrote to a colleague and friend suggesting that he was unlikely to see the first men reach the Moon, since for various astrological reasons he seemed likely to die in 1968. He was correct in this personal prophesy.

MARGARET HONE

1892–1969, Author and Interpreter

Margaret Hone joined the London Lodge of the Theosophical Society in her early forties. She became involved in the foundation of the Faculty of Astrological Studies, for which she wrote two textbooks – *The Modern Textbook of Astrology* and *Applied Astrology*, still the basis of the Faculty's teaching system. She was for many years Principal of the Faculty, which after the war rapidly expanded until it now has pupils in over 80 countries. Her death in 1969 was a great loss to modern astrology.

DANE RUDHYAR

1895– , Celebrated American Practitioner

Dane Rudhyar began a musical career in Paris in the early years of the century, publishing some works for piano, and a book about Debussy. In America, aged 21, he joined the avant-garde of musical theorists and composers. His preoccupation with astrology came about through his interest in oriental music and philosophy. His purpose is to bring astrology 'to a level of thinking at which it can be fully accepted by the college-trained minds of our day, presenting it mainly as a symbolic language'. He believes that 'by using this language – an algebra of life – man can discover the pattern of order which reveals both his individuality and his destiny underneath or within the often seemingly chaotic and bewildering events of his personal daily existence.' In *The Planetarization of Consciousness* (1970) he sums up his whole philosophy of life, and sets out a foundation on which he intends to erect a series of new volumes dealing with the crucial problems of contemporary western society.

KARL ERNST KRAFFT

1900–45, 'Gestapo' Astrologer

Krafft, a Swiss astrologer in sympathy with the Nazis, successfully predicted the attack on Hitler's life which took place in the Munich beer-cellar; he was arrested by the Gestapo and accused of complicity in the plot, but was released and later employed by Goebbels to translate some of the prophesies of Nostradamus, which Frau Goebbels had suggested as useful propaganda.

After Hess's defection to England, in 1941, Krafft was one of the many astrologers arrested by the Gestapo as scapegoats. (Hess, it was suggested, had been 'crazed by astrologers'.) He worked for a while on astrological propaganda material, and eventually died of typhus on a train which was taking him to Buchenwald.

REINHOLD EBERTIN

1901– , Cosmobiologist

Reinhold Ebertin, the son of a well-known pre-war German astrologer, Elspeth Ebertin, started a specialist publishing firm producing advanced astrological textbooks. In 1928 he founded the German astrological magazine *Kosmobiologie*, and in 1932 organized a congress of 'astrological pioneers'.

Ebertin's theories have been published in a number of books, perhaps the most important of which is *Komination der Gestirneinflüsse* (The Combination of Stellar Influences) (1940). He works with his son, Dr Baldur Ebertin, and a group of doctors, neurologists, physicists, theoretical physicists, mathematicians and chemists, examining brain-patterns and the indications of diseases among other factors, in his pursuit of a firm methodology.

LOUIS DE WOHL

1903–61, Astrologer to the British War Cabinet

Ludwig von Wohl, born in Berlin, settled in Britain in 1935. During the war, de Wohl persuaded the British Government that Karl Ernst Krafft was working for Hitler, and that it would be wise to employ him (de Wohl) to work out what Hitler's astrologer was telling him. De Wohl held an honorary commission in the Army for the rest of the war, and was partly responsible for forging copies of German astrological magazines, smuggled into Germany by British agents, in an attempt to spread alarm and despondency by false astrological predictions. As a result both sides believed that the other was using astrology as a war weapon.

JOHN ADDEY

1920– , Philosopher and Experimentalist

John Addey's interest in astrology has preoccupied him since, in 1946, he first visited the Astrological Lodge of the Theosophical Society, and met the late Charles Carter. He took the Diploma of the Faculty of Astrological Studies and served for a time as a tutor and member of the Council; from 1951 until 1958 he was a Vice-President of the Astrological Lodge, and in 1958 founded the Astrological Association (with Brig. Roy Firebrace and Joan Rodgers), was its secretary until 1961, and then became its President, a post he still holds. He edits its periodical, *The Astrological Journal*.

His interest in astrology is philosophical and he has become increasingly certain that 'all astrology is based on the harmonics of cosmic periods'.

Margaret Hone *left*
Margaret Hone, one of the best-known teachers of modern astrological practice, and a former Principal of the Faculty of Astrological Studies, whose textbooks are standard works among students of astrological technique.

Hitler's Escape *above and left*
The ruined beer cellar in Munich after the failed attempt on the life of Hitler (left), predicted by Karl Ernst Krafft who was accused of complicity in the plot.

Louis de Wohl *above*
De Wohl was employed to predict Hitler's movements.

John Addey *left*
John Addey, the British astrologer respected for his experimental theories of cosmic rhythms.

ASTROLOGICAL TABLES 1910-1984

The tables on the following pages provide a complete planetary information service for subjects born anywhere in the world between 1 January 1910 and 31 December 1984 that will be invaluable for the accurate drawing up of the Birth Chart. A further table, the Shortened Ephemeris, shows the future positions of the outer planets, Mars to Pluto, on the first day of each month from January 1976 to December 2000.

How to Use the Tables

1 Planetary Positions 1910-1984

This table charts the daily positions to the nearest degree of all the known planets. To find their positions on a given birth-date, first look up the year of birth. Then locate the data panel for the month of birth. Each month from January to December is respectively numbered 1–12 in the top left-hand corner.

The column for the day of birth is found by referring to the boxes numbered 1–31 at the head of the page. Having located the correct column for the birth-date under consideration, read off in vertical order the respective positions of the Sun, Moon, Mercury, Venus and Mars.

The retrograde or apparent backward motion of a planet is indicated by the symbol 'R' on the day retrograding begins; when the planet resumes direct motion this is indicated, on the first day it occurs, by the symbol 'D'.

To discover the positions of the slower-moving planets – Jupiter, Saturn, Uranus, Neptune and Pluto – refer to the bottom line of the data panel for the month of birth. The positions of the slower-moving planets are noted only for those days when the planet *changes* degree.

Example Find the position of the planets for someone born on 11 May 1936. By following the instructions above (locating the year, month and day of birth) you should arrive at this reading: Sun in 21° Taurus; Moon, 16° Capricorn; Mercury, 11° Gemini; Venus, 7° Taurus; Mars, 29° Taurus; Jupiter, 22° Sagittarius Retrograde; Saturn, 20° Pisces; Uranus, 6° Taurus; Neptune, 14° Virgo Retrograde; Pluto, 25° Cancer.

Note When the Sun changes Sign during a particular day, a double reading is given. To find out which of the two possible Signs is correct for the birth-time under consideration refer to Table 1a.

1a Sun-sign Changes 1910-1984

Once a month the Sun moves from one sign of the Zodiac to the next sign. This table gives the time to the nearest minute when the change takes place, and notes the glyph of the *new* sign.

Example On 21 May 1936 the Sun moved into Gemini (the glyph shown) at 6.08 hours by the 24-hour clock. The correct Sun-sign reading for birth-times *before* 6.08 hours on that date is 29° Taurus; *after* 6.08 hours the correct reading is 0° Gemini.

2 Sidereal Times 1910-1984

To find the sidereal time for noon at Greenwich on any birth-date between 1900 and 1975, refer in the tables to the year of birth and then locate the month of birth (1–12, January–December) at the head of the yearly table. The days of the month are listed 1–31 down the left-hand margin. Readings are given in hours, minutes and seconds.

Example The sidereal time corresponding to 11 May 1936 is 3 hours 16 minutes 22 seconds.

3 Houses for Northern Latitudes

A = Sidereal time
10 = Midheaven (10th House)
B = Ascendant

This table is used to find a subject's Ascendant and Midheaven Signs to the nearest degree *and minute* of a Sign. First find the nearest sidereal time in the column headed 'A'. Then refer to the column headed 'B' and select the nearest latitude to the birth-place. These latitudes may be used to within 1° to either side of the exact figure. Then read off the Ascending Sign. For full instructions on calculating the Ascending Sign refer to p. 78–81. The Sign on the Midheaven is found in the column headed '10'. For birth-places in the Southern Hemisphere, 12 hours must be added to the local sidereal time at birth, and the opposite Signs used (see p. 79).

Example (*Northern Hemisphere*) A person born in New York (latitude 40°45′N) and whose correct sidereal time is 3 hours 14 minutes 15 seconds will have as his Ascendant 27°17′ Leo: the Sign on the Midheaven will be 21° Taurus.

Example (*Southern Hemisphere*) A person born within 1° of latitude 40°45′S and whose correct sidereal time is 3 hours 14 minutes 15 seconds will have as his Ascendant 27°17′ Aquarius: the Sign on the Midheaven will be 21° Scorpio.

4 The Moon's Nodes 1910-1984

The Moon's North Node is charted for the first day of the month and for those days of the month when it occupies a new degree of the ecliptic. In the tables, the day of the degree-change is noted first, followed by the new degree. (The Moon's South Node appears at the opposite or polarity point on the ecliptic.)

5 Shortened Ephemeris 1980-2000

The purpose of this shortened ephemeris is to provide a brief guide to future positions of the outer planets: Mars, Jupiter, Saturn, Uranus, Neptune and Pluto. The planets are recorded as they will appear on the first day of each month between the years 1976 and 2000.

6 Proportional Logarithms

Proportional logarithms are used to calculate the precise position of a planet. The actual position is expressed as a proportion of the motion between noon and the birth-time on the previous or subsequent day.

7 Noon Date Card

This calculates Noon Dates when preparing the progressed Chart. The interval between the birth-time and noon is translated from hours to days by reference to the lower table. This is then added (for am births) to, or subtracted (for pm) from, the code number appearing against the day in the right-hand table.

Example If the birth-time is 9.25 am GMT, the interval from noon is 2 hours 35 minutes. The table value for 2 hours is 30.4 days; the value for 35 minutes is 8.9 days, equaling a total of 39.3 days. The noon date will be 39 days forward from the birth-date. If the birth-date is 11 May which is the 131st day of the year, 39 is added to 131 to obtain a total of 170. The 170th day is 19 June. This is the Noon Date required. When a large figure has apparently to be subtracted from a smaller figure, or when the birth-date figure is in excess of 365, add or subtract 365, as necessary.

8 Zone Standard Times

These lists show how the standard time of a locality may be converted to GMT. List 1 includes places fast on GMT; the times should be subtracted from Standard Time. List 2 details places normally keeping GMT. List 3 includes places slow on GMT; the times should be added to Standard Time.

I PLANETARY POSITIONS 1910–1984

1910

1

	1	2	3	4	5	6	7	8	9	10	11	12	13	14	15	16	17	18	19	20	21	22	23	24	25	26	27	28	29	30	31
☉	10	11	12	13	14	15	16	17	18	19	20	21	22	23	24	25	26	27	28	29	0	1	2	3	4	5	6	7	8	9	10
☽	17	29	11	23	5	17	29	11	24	7	20	4	18	2	16	0	14	28	12	26	10	24	8	21	5	18	0	13	25	7	19
☿	26	28	0	1	2	3	5	6	7	8	9	10	11	11	12	12	12	12	12	11	10	10	9	8	6	5	4	3	1	0	29
♀	23	24	24	25	25	26	27	27	27	28	28	29	29	29	0	0	0	1	1	1	1	1	1	1	1	0	0	29	29	29	
♂	18	18	19	20	21	21	22	22	23	24	24	25	25	26	27	27	28	28	29	0	0	1	1	2	2	3	4	4	5		

♃ 1 10 ♎13 14 — ♄ 1 15 31 ♈16 17 18 — ♅ 1 10 25 ♑20 21 22 — ♆ 1R 25 ♋18 17 — ♇ 1 ♊25

2

	1	2	3	4	5	6	7	8	9	10	11	12	13	14	15	16	17	18	19	20	21	22	23	24	25	26	27	28
☉	11	12	13	14	15	16	17	18	19	20	21	22	23	24	25	26	27	28	29	0	1	2	3	4	5	6	7	8
☽	1	13	25	7	19	2	15	29	12	27	11	26	10	25	9	23	7	21	4	18	1	14	26	9	21	3	15	27
☿	28	28	27	27	27	26	26	26	26	27	27	27	28	28	29	0	1	2	3	4	5	6	8	9	10	11	12	13
♀	29	28	28	27	27	26	26	25	24	24	23	23	22	21	21	20	20	19	19	18	18	17	17	16	16	16	16	15
♂	5	6	6	7	7	8	9	9	10	11	11	12	12	13	13	14	15	15	16	17	17	18	18	19	19	20	21	21

♃ 1R 25 ♎14 13 — ♄ 1 15 25 ♈18 19 20 — ♅ 1 10 ♑22 23 — ♆ 1R ♋17 — ♇ 1 ♊25

3

	1	2	3	4	5	6	7	8	9	10	11	12	13	14	15	16	17	18	19	20	21	22	23	24	25	26	27	28	29	30	31
☉	10	11	12	13	14	15	16	17	18	19	20	21	22	23	24	25	26	27	28	29	0	1	2	3	4	5	6	7	8	9	10
☽	9	21	3	15	27	10	23	6	21	5	20	5	20	5	19	4	18	1	15	28	10	23	6	18	0	12	24	6	17	29	11
☿	15	16	18	19	20	22	23	25	26	28	0	1	2	4	6	7	9	10	12	14	16	17	19	21	23	25	26	28	0	2	4
♀	15	15	15	15	15	15	15	15	15	16	16	16	17	17	17	18	18	19	19	20	20	21	21	21	22	22	23	24	24	25	26
♂	22	23	23	24	24	25	26	26	27	27	28	29	29	0	0	1	2	3	3	3	4	5	5	6	7	7	8	9	9	10	10

♃ 1R 10 15 25 31 ♎13 12 11 10 9 — ♄ 1 5 15 25 31 ♈20 21 22 23 24 — ♅ 1 5 31 ♑23 24 25 — ♆ 1R ♋16 — ♇ 1 ♊25

4

	1	2	3	4	5	6	7	8	9	10	11	12	13	14	15	16	17	18	19	20	21	22	23	24	25	26	27	28	29	30
☉	11	12	13	14	15	16	17	18	19	20	21	22	23	24	25	26	27	28	29	0	1	2	3	4	5	6	7	8	9	10
☽	23	6	18	1	15	29	13	28	13	28	13	27	11	24	7	20	3	15	27	9	21	3	14	26	8	20	2	15		
☿	6	8	10	12	14	16	18	20	22	25	27	29	1	3	5	7	9	11	13	15	16	18	20	21	23	24	26	27	28	29
♀	27	27	28	29	0	1	2	2	3	4	5	6	7	8	9	10	10	11	12	13	14	15	16	17	18	19	20	21	22	23
♂	11	11	12	13	14	14	15	15	16	17	17	18	18	19	20	20	21	22	22	23	23	24	25	25	26	27	27	28	28	29

♃ 1R 10 20 26 ♎9 8 7 6 — ♄ 1 10 15 25 30 ♈24 25 26 27 28 — ♅ 1 5 ♑24 25 — ♆ 1 ♋16 — ♇ 1 ♊25

5

	1	2	3	4	5	6	7	8	9	10	11	12	13	14	15	16	17	18	19	20	21	22	23	24	25	26	27	28	29	30	31
☉	10	11	12	13	14	15	16	17	18	19	20	21	22	23	24	25	26	27	28	29	0	1	2	3	4	5	6	7	8	9	
☽	27	10	24	7	22	6	21	6	22	7	21	6	20	3	17	29	12	24	6	18	29	11	23	5	17	29	12	24	7	20	3
☿	1	2	3	4	5	5	6	6	7	7	7	8	8	8	7	7	7	7	6	6	5	4	4	4	3	3	2	2	1	1	0
♀	24	25	26	27	28	29	0	1	2	3	4	5	6	7	8	9	10	11	12	13	14	15	16	17	18	20	21	22	23	24	25	26
♂	29	0	1	1	2	3	3	4	4	5	6	6	7	7	8	9	9	10	10	11	11	12	12	13	14	14	15	15	16	17	17	18

♃ 1R 10 25 ♎6 5 4 — ♄ 1 10 17 25 ♈28 29 ♉0 1 — ♅ 1R ♑25 — ♆ 1 10 ♋16 17 — ♇ 1 31 ♊25 26

6

	1	2	3	4	5	6	7	8	9	10	11	12	13	14	15	16	17	18	19	20	21	22	23	24	25	26	27	28	29	30
☉	10	11	12	13	14	15	16	17	18	19	19	20	21	22	23	24	25	26	27	28	29	0	1	2	3	4	5	6	7	8
☽	17	1	16	0	15	0	15	29	14	28	12	25	8	20	3	14	26	8	20	2	14	26	9	21	4	17	0	14	28	12
☿	0	29	29	29	29	29	29	29	29	29	29	0	0	1	2	2	3	4	5	5	6	7	9	10	11	12	14	15	17	18
♀	27	28	0	1	2	3	4	5	6	7	9	10	11	12	13	14	16	17	18	19	20	21	22	24	25	26	27	28	0	0
♂	19	19	20	21	21	22	23	23	24	24	25	25	26	26	27	27	28	29	29	0	0	1	2	2	3	3	4	5	5	6

♃ 1 15 ♎4 5 — ♄ 1 5 15 25 ♉1 2 3 4 — ♅ 1R ♑24 — ♆ 1 10 ♋17 18 — ♇ 1 ♊26

7

	1	2	3	4	5	6	7	8	9	10	11	12	13	14	15	16	17	18	19	20	21	22	23	24	25	26	27	28	29	30	31
☉	9	10	10	11	12	13	14	15	16	17	18	19	20	21	22	23	24	25	26	27	28	29	0	1	2	3	4	5	6	7	
☽	26	10	25	9	24	8	22	6	20	3	16	28	11	23	4	16	28	10	22	5	17	0	14	28	11	25	8	23	7	21	5
☿	20	21	23	25	27	28	0	2	4	6	8	9	11	13	15	17	19	21	23	25	28	29	2	4	6	8	10	12	14	16	18	20
♀	2	3	4	5	6	7	9	10	11	12	13	15	16	17	18	19	20	22	23	24	25	27	28	29	0	2	3	4	5	6	7
♂	7	7	8	8	9	9	10	11	11	12	12	13	13	14	15	15	16	17	17	18	18	19	20	21	21	22	22	23	24	24	25	26

♃ 1 15 20 31 ♎6 7 8 9 — ♄ 1 5 25 ♉4 5 6 — ♅ 1R 31 ♑23 22 — ♆ 1 5 ♋18 19 — ♇ 1 31 ♊26 27

8

	1	2	3	4	5	6	7	8	9	10	11	12	13	14	15	16	17	18	19	20	21	22	23	24	25	26	27	28	29	30	31
☉	8	9	10	11	12	13	14	15	16	17	18	15	20	21	22	23	24	25	26	27	28	28	29	0	1	2	3	4	5	6	7
☽	19	3	17	1	15	28	11	24	6	19	1	12	24	6	18	0	13	26	9	23	6	21	5	19	3	18	2	16	29	13	27
☿	21	23	25	27	29	0	2	4	5	7	8	10	12	13	15	16	17	19	20	21	22	23	24	25	26	27	28	29	0	1	2	3	4
♀	8	9	11	12	13	14	15	17	18	19	20	22	23	24	25	26	28	29	0	1	3	4	5	6	7	9	10	11	12	13	15
♂	27	27	28	29	29	0	0	1	1	2	3	3	4	4	5	6	6	7	8	8	9	10	10	11	11	12	13	13	14	15	16

♃ 1 5 10 15 25 31 ♎9 10 11 12 13 14 — ♄ 1 20R ♉6 6 — ♅ 1R 25 ♑22 21 — ♆ 1 5 ♋19 20 — ♇ 1 ♊27

9

	1	2	3	4	5	6	7	8	9	10	11	12	13	14	15	16	17	18	19	20	21	22	23	24	25	26	27	28	29	30
☉	8	9	10	11	12	13	13	14	15	16	17	18	19	20	21	22	23	24	25	26	27	28	29	0	1	2	3	4	5	6
☽	11	24	6	20	2	15	27	9	20	2	14	26	8	21	4	17	1	15	29	14	28	12	27	10	24	7	20	3		
☿	5	6	7	8	9	9	10	10	11	11	11	11	11	10	10	9	9	8	7	6	5	4	3	2	1	29	29	28		
♀	16	17	18	20	21	22	23	24	26	27	28	29	0	1	3	4	6	7	8	9	11	12	13	14	15	17	18	19	20	21
♂	17	17	18	19	19	20	21	21	22	22	23	24	24	25	26	26	27	28	28	29	29	0	1	1	2	3	3	4	4	5

♃ 1 5 11 16 21 25 30 ♎15 16 17 18 19 20 21 — ♄ 1R 25 ♉6 5 — ♅ 1R ♑21 — ♆ 1 5 ♋20 21 — ♇ 1 ♊27

10

	1	2	3	4	5	6	7	8	9	10	11	12	13	14	15	16	17	18	19	20	21	22	23	24	25	26	27	28	29	30	31
☉	7	8	9	10	11	12	13	14	15	16	17	18	19	20	21	22	23	24	25	26	27	28	29	0	1	2	3	4	5	6	7
☽	16	29	11	23	5	17	29	10	22	4	16	29	12	25	9	23	8	23	8	23	8	22	7	21	4	18	0	13	25	8	20
☿	27	27	26	26	26	26	26	26	27	27	28	28	29	0	1	2	4	5	7	8	10	11	13	14	16	18	19	21	23	24	26
♀	23	24	26	27	28	29	0	2	3	4	5	7	8	9	10	11	13	14	15	16	17	19	20	21	22	24	25	26	27	29	0
♂	6	7	7	8	9	9	10	11	11	12	13	14	14	15	15	16	17	17	18	18	19	20	21	22	22	23	24	24	25	26	

♃ 1 5 10 15 20 25 31 ♎21 22 23 24 25 26 27 — ♄ 1R 10 20 ♉5 4 3 — ♅ 1 ♑21 — ♆ 1 26R ♋21 21 — ♇ 1 ♊27

11

	1	2	3	4	5	6	7	8	9	10	11	12	13	14	15	16	17	18	19	20	21	22	23	24	25	26	27	28	29	30
☉	8	9	10	11	12	13	14	15	16	17	18	19	20	21	22	23	24	25	26	27	28	29	0	1	2	3	4	5	6	7
☽	2	14	26	7	19	1	13	25	8	20	3	17	1	16	1	16	1	16	0	16	0	14	27	10	23	5	17	29	11	22
☿	1	3	4	6	8	9	11	12	14	15	17	18	20	21	23	24	26	27	29	0	2	3	5	6	8	9	11	13	14	16	17
♀	2	3	4	5	7	8	9	11	12	13	14	15	17	18	19	21	22	23	24	26	27	28	0	1	2	3	5	6	7	8
♂	26	27	28	28	29	0	0	1	2	2	3	4	5	5	6	7	7	8	9	9	10	11	12	12	13	14	14	15	15	16

♃ 1 5 10 11 20 25 30 ♎27 28 29 ♏0 1 2 3 — ♄ 1R 15 30 ♉2 1 0 — ♅ 1 5 ♑21 22 — ♆ 1R ♋21 — ♇ 1 ♊27

12

	1	2	3	4	5	6	7	8	9	10	11	12	13	14	15	16	17	18	19	20	21	22	23	24	25	26	27	28	29	30	31
☉	8	9	10	11	12	13	14	15	16	17	18	19	20	21	22	23	24	25	26	27	28	29	0	1	2	3	4	5	6	7	8
☽	4	16	28	10	22	4	17	29	13	26	10	24	9	24	9	24	8	22	6	19	1	14	26	7	19	1	13	25	7		
☿	18	20	22	23	25	26	28	0	1	2	4	5	7	8	10	11	12	14	15	17	18	19	20	21	22	23	24	25	25	26	26
♀	9	11	12	13	15	16	17	18	20	21	22	23	25	26	27	28	0	1	2	3	5	6	7	8	10	11	12	13	15	16	17
♂	17	17	18	19	19	20	21	22	22	23	24	24	25	26	26	27	28	28	29	0	1	1	2	3	4	4	5	6	6	7	8

♃ 1 5 10 15 25 31 ♏4 5 6 7 8 9 — ♄ 1R 15 ♉0 ♈29 — ♅ 1 5 25 ♑22 23 24 — ♆ 1R 25 ♋21 20 — ♇ 1R 31 ♊27 26

1911

1

	1	2	3	4	5	6	7	8	9	10	11	12	13	14	15	16	17	18	19	20	21	22	23	24	25	26	27	28
☉	10	11	12	13	14	15	16	17	18	19	20	21	22	23	24	25	26	27	28	29	0	1	2	3	4	5	6	7
☽	19	1	14	27	10	23	6	20	4	18	3	17	2	17	2	16	0	14	27	9	22	4	16	27	9	21	3	15
☿	26	26	26	25	25	24	23	21	20	19	17	16	15	14	13	12	11	11	10	10	10	10	10	11	11	11	12	13
♀	18	20	21	22	23	25	26	27	28	29	1	2	3	5	6	7	9	10	11	12	13	15	16	17	18	20	21	22
♂	8	9	10	11	12	12	13	14	15	15	16	17	17	18	19	20	20	21	22	22	23	23	24	24	25	26	27	27

♃ 1 5 10 20 25 ♏9 10 11 12 13 — ♄ 1 20 ♈29 ♉0 — ♅ 1 10 31 ♑24 25 26 — ♆ 1R 25 ♋20 19 — ♇ 1R ♊26

2

	1	2	3	4	5	6	7	8	9	10	11	12	13	14	15	16	17	18	19	20	21	22	23	24	25	26	27	28
☉	11	12	13	14	15	16	17	18	19	20	21	22	23	24	25	26	27	28	29	0	1	2	3	4	5	6	7	8
☽	6	20	3	17	1	15	29	13	27	12	26	10	24	8	21	4	17	29	12	23	5	17	29	11	23	6	19	2
☿	16	17	18	19	20	21	23	24	25	26	28	29	0	1	3	4	6	7	9	10	12	13	15	16	18	19	21	22
♀	27	28	29	1	2	4	5	6	7	9	10	11	12	14	15	16	17	19	20	21	22	23	25	26	27	28	29	0
♂	0	1	1	2	3	4	4	5	6	7	7	8	9	10	10	11	12	13	13	14	15	15	16	17	18	18	19	20

♃ 1 10 ♏13 14 — ♄ 1 10 25 ♉0 1 2 — ♅ 1 15 ♑26 27 — ♆ 1R ♋19 — ♇ 1R ♊25

3

	1	2	3	4	5	6	7	8	9	10	11	12	13	14	15	16	17	18	19	20	21	22	23	24	25	26	27	28
☉	9	10	11	12	13	14	15	16	17	18	19	20	21	22	23	24	25	26	27	28	29	0	1	2	3	4	5	6
☽	16	29	13	27	11	25	10	24	8	22	6	20	3	17	29	12	25	7	19	1	13	25	7	19	1	14	27	10
☿	24	26	28	0	1	3	4	6	8	10	11	13	15	17	19	21	23	25	27	29	0	2	5	7	9	11	14	16
♀	2	3	5	6	7	8	10	11	12	13	14	16	17	18	19	21	22	23	24	25	27	28	29	0	2	3	4	5
♂	20	21	22	23	23	24	25	26	27	27	28	29	29	0	1	2	2	3	4	5	5	6	7	8	8	9	10	11

♃ 1R 31 ♏14 13 — ♄ 1 5 15 25 31 ♉2 3 4 5 6 — ♅ 1 10 ♑27 28 — ♆ 1R 31D ♋19 19 — ♇ 1 ♊25

4

	1	2	3	4	5	6	7	8	9	10	11	12	13	14	15	16	17	18	19	20	21	22	23	24	25	26	27	28
☉	10	11	12	13	14	15	16	17	18	19	20	21	22	23	24	25	26	27	28	29	0	1	2	3	4	5	6	7
☽	7	21	6	20	5	19	3	16	29	13	26	9	21	3	15	27	9	21	3	15	27	9	22	5	18	2	16	1
☿	23	25	26	28	0	2	3	5	6	8	9	11	12	13	14	15	16	17	17	18	18	18	18	18	18	18	18	18
♀	11	12	13	14	15	16	17	18	19	20	21	22	23	25	26	27	28	29	0	1	2	3	4	5	6	8	9	10
♂	13	14	15	16	16	17	18	19	19	20	21	22	23	24	25	26	27	28	28	29	0	1	2	3	3	4	5	6

♃ 1R 10 15 25 ♏13 12 11 10 — ♄ 1 10 20 25 ♉6 7 8 9 — ♅ 1 5 ♑28 29 — ♆ 1 15 ♋18 19 — ♇ 1 ♊25

5

	1	2	3	4	5	6	7	8	9	10	11	12	13	14	15	16	17	18	19	20	21	22	23	24	25	26	27	28
☉	10	11	12	13	14	15	16	17	18	19	20	21	22	23	24	25	26	27	28	29	0	1	2	3	4	5	6	7
☽	16	0	15	29	13	27	10	23	5	18	0	18	0	12	24	6	18	29	6	18	0	13	27	10	25	9	24	9
☿	16	16	15	15	14	13	13	12	12	11	11	10	10	10	9	9	9	9	9	9	9	9	10	10	10	11	11	12
♀	16	17	18	19	21	22	23	24	25	27	28	29	0	1	2	3	5	6	7	8	9	10	11	12	13	14	15	16
♂	6	7	8	9	10	11	12	13	13	14	15	16	17	18	18	19	20	21	22	23	24	25	26	27	28	29	0	1

♃ 1R 10 20 31 ♏9 8 7 6 — ♄ 1 10 20 25 ♉10 11 12 13 — ♅ 1 5R ♑29 29 — ♆ 1 ♋19 — ♇ 1 ♊26

6

	1	2	3	4	5	6	7	8	9	10	11	12	13	14	15	16	17	18	19	20	21	22	23	24	25	26	27	28
☉	10	11	12	13	14	15	16	17	18	19	20	21	22	23	24	25	26	27	28	29	0	1	2	3	4	5	6	7
☽	23	6	20	2	15	27	9	21	3	15	27	9	20	2	15	27	10	22	6	19	3	18	2	18	3	18	3	18
☿	15	16	17	18	19	21	22	23	25	26	28	29	0	2	4	5	7	9	11	13	14	16	18	20	22	25	26	29
♀	22	23	24	25	26	27	28	29	0	1	2	3	4	5	6	7	8	9	10	11	12	13	14	15	16	17	18	19
♂	29	0	0	1	2	2	3	4	5	6	7	8	9	10	11	12	13	13	14	15	15	16	17	18	19	20	21	22

♃ 1R 5 25 ♏6 5 4 — ♄ 1 5 15 20 30 ♉13 14 15 16 17 — ♅ 1R 15 ♑29 28 — ♆ 1 5 ♋19 20 — ♇ 1 ♊26

7

	1	2	3	4	5	6	7	8	9	10	11	12	13	14	15	16	17	18	19	20	21	22	23	24	25	26	27	28
☉	8	9	10	11	12	13	14	15	16	17	18	19	20	21	22	23	24	25	26	27	28	29	0	1	2	3	4	5
☽	16	29	12	24	6	18	0	12	24	6	17	29	12	24	7	19	2	15	29	13	27	12	26	11	26	11	26	10
☿	5	7	9	12	14	16	18	20	22	25	27	29	1	3	4	6	8	10	12	14	15	17	18	20	22	24	25	27
♀	24	25	26	27	28	29	0	0	1	2	3	4	5	5	6	7	8	9	10	10	11	12	13	14	14	15	16	17
♂	20	21	22	22	23	24	25	26	26	27	28	28	29	0	0	1	2	2	3	4	4	5	5	6	7	7	8	9

♃ 1 3D 5 31 ♏4 4 5 6 — ♄ 1 10 26 ♉17 18 19 — ♅ 1R 15 ♑28 27 — ♆ 1 5 31 ♋20 21 22 — ♇ 1 31 ♊26 2[illegible]

8

	1	2	3	4	5	6	7	8	9	10	11	12	13	14	15	16	17	18	19	20	21	22	23	24	25	26	27	28
☉	8	9	10	11	11	12	13	14	15	16	17	18	19	20	21	22	23	24	25	26	27	28	29	0	1	2	3	4
☽	3	15	27	9	20	2	14	26	9	21	4	16	29	12	26	9	23	7	22	6	21	5	20	4	18	2	15	28
☿	3	4	5	7	8	9	10	12	13	14	15	16	17	18	19	20	21	22	22	23	23	24	24	24	24	24	24	24
♀	20	21	22	22	23	23	24	24	25	25	26	26	26	27	27	28	28	28	28	29	29	29	29	29	29	29	29	29
♂	10	11	12	12	13	14	14	15	15	16	17	17	18	19	19	20	20	21	22	22	23	23	24	24	25	25	26	26

♃ 1 10 20 31 ♏6 7 8 9 — ♄ 1 15 ♉19 20 — ♅ 1R ♑26 — ♆ 1 31 ♋22 23 — ♇ 1 ♊2[illegible]

9

	1	2	3	4	5	6	7	8	9	10	11	12	13	14	15	16	17	18	19	20	21	22	23	24	25	26	27	28
☉	8	9	10	11	12	13	14	15	16	17	17	18	19	20	21	22	23	24	25	26	27	28	29	0	1	2	3	4
☽	17	29	10	22	4	17	29	13	26	9	23	6	20	4	18	2	17	1	15	29	13	27	10	23	6	18	1	13
☿	22	22	21	20	20	19	18	17	16	15	14	13	12	11	11	10	10	10	10	10	10	11	11	12	13	14	15	16
♀	28	28	27	27	27	26	26	25	25	24	24	23	23	22	22	21	21	20	20	19	19	18	18	17	17	16	16	15
♂	28	28	29	29	0	0	1	1	2	2	3	3	4	4	5	5	5	6	6	6	7	7	7	8	8	8	8	8

♃ 1 5 10 15 20 25 30 ♏9 10 11 12 13 14 15 — ♄ 1 3R 30 ♉20 20 19 — ♅ 1 ♑25 — ♆ 1 ♋23 — ♇ 1 ♊2[illegible]

10

	1	2	3	4	5	6	7	8	9	10	11	12	13	14	15	16	17	18	19	20	21	22	23	24	25	26	27	28
☉	7	8	9	10	11	12	13	14	15	16	17	18	19	20	21	22	23	24	25	26	27	28	29	0	1	2	3	4
☽	18	0	13	25	8	21	4	18	2	16	0	15	29	13	28	12	26	9	23	6	19	2	14	27	9	21	3	14
☿	21	23	24	26	27	29	0	2	4	6	8	10	11	13	15	17	18	20	22	24	25	27	29	0	2	3	5	7
♀	13	13	13	13	13	13	13	13	13	13	14	14	14	14	15	15	15	16	16	17	17	18	18	19	19	20	20	21
♂	9	9	9	9	10	10	10	10	10	10	10	11	11	11	11	11	11	11	11	11	11	11	11	10	10	10	10	10

♃ 1 5 10 15 20 25 31 ♏15 16 17 18 19 20 21 — ♄ 1R 15 31 ♉19 18 17 — ♅ 1R 6D ♑25 25 — ♆ 1 28R ♋23 23 — ♇ 1 ♊2[illegible]

11

	1	2	3	4	5	6	7	8	9	10	11	12	13	14	15	16	17	18	19	20	21	22	23	24	25	26	27	28
☉	8	9	10	11	12	13	14	15	16	17	18	19	20	21	22	23	24	25	26	27	28	29	0	1	2	3	4	5
☽	3	16	29	12	26	11	25	10	25	10	24	8	22	6	19	3	15	28	10	23	5	17	29	11	23	4	16	29
☿	13	15	16	18	19	21	23	24	26	27	29	0	2	3	5	6	8	9	11	12	14	15	17	18	20	21	22	24
♀	24	25	25	26	27	28	28	29	0	1	2	3	4	5	6	7	8	9	10	11	12	13	14	15	16	17	18	19
♂	9	9	9	8	8	8	8	7	7	7	6	6	6	5	5	5	4	4	4	3	3	2	2	2	1	1	0	0

♃ 1 5 10 15 20 25 30 ♏21 22 23 24 25 26 27 — ♄ 1R 10 25 ♉17 16 15 — ♅ 1 10 ♑25 26 — ♆ 1R ♋23 — ♇ 1 ♊2[illegible]

12

	1	2	3	4	5	6	7	8	9	10	11	12	13	14	15	16	17	18	19	20	21	22	23	24	25	26	27	28
☉	8	9	10	11	12	13	14	15	16	17	18	19	20	21	22	23	24	25	26	27	28	29	0	1	2	3	4	5
☽	7	20	4	19	3	18	4	19	4	18	2	16	29	12	25	7	20	2	14	26	8	19	1	13	25	7	20	2
☿	28	29	0	2	3	4	5	6	7	8	9	10	10	10	10	10	9	9	8	7	5	4	3	2	0	29	29	27
♀	21	22	23	25	26	27	28	29	0	1	2	3	5	6	7	8	9	10	11	12	14	15	16	17	18	19	20	21
♂	29	29	28	28	27	27	27	27	26	26	26	26	26	26	25	25	25	25	25	25	24	24	24	24	24	24	24	24

♃ 1 5 10 15 20 25 31 ♏28 29 ♐0 1 2 3 4 — ♄ 1R 5 25 ♉15 14 13 — ♅ 1 5 25 ♑26 27 28 — ♆ 1R ♋23 — ♇ 1 ♊[illegible]

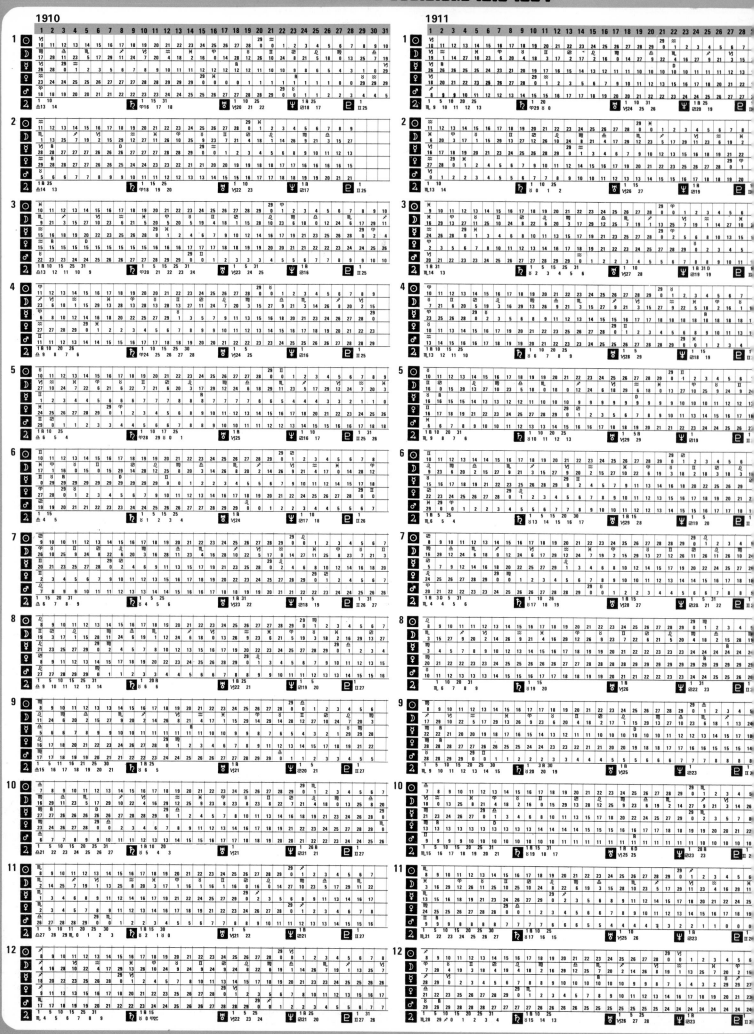

1912

1 2 3 4 5 6 7 8 9 10 11 12 13 14 15 16 17 18 19 20 21 22 23 24 25 26 27 28 29 30 31

1
☉ ♑ 10 11 12 13 14 15 16 17 18 19 20 21 22 23 24 25 26 27 28 29 0 1 2 3 4 5 6 7 8 9 10
☽ 27 11 26 12 27 12 27 12 25 9 22 4 17 29 11 23 5 16 28 10 22 4 17 29 12 24 8 21 5 20 5
☿ ♐ 25 24 24 24 24 24 24 25 25 26 27 27 28 29 0 1 2 3 4 5 7 8 9 11 12 13 14 16 17 19 20
♀ ♏ 26 27 28 0 1 2 3 4 5 7 8 9 10 11 13 14 15 16 17 18 20 21 22 23 24 26 27 28 0 1 2
♂ ♉ 24 24 24 24 24 24 25 25 25 25 25 25 25 26 26 26 26 26 26 27 27 27 27 28 28 28 28 29 29 29 0
♃ 1 5 10 15 20 25 31 ♐4 5 6 7 8 9 10 — ♄ 1 R 16 D 13 13 — ♅ 1 15 30 29 31 ♑28 29 0 ♒ 0 — ♆ 1 ♋22 — ♇ 1 15 ♊28 27

2
☉ 11 12 13 14 15 16 17 18 19 20 21 22 23 24 25 26 27 28 29 0 1 2 3 4 5 6 7 8 9
☽ 20 5 20 5 20 4 17 0 13 25 8 20 1 13 25 7 19 1 14 26 9 23 7 21 5 18 1 15 29
☿ 21 23 24 26 27 29 0 2 4 5 7 8 10 11 13 15 16 18 20 21 23 25 27 29 0 2 4 6 8
♀ ♑ 3 4 5 7 8 9 10 11 13 14 15 16 17 19 20 21 22 24 25 26 27 28 0 1 2 3 5 6 7
♂ ♊ 0 0 1 1 2 2 2 3 3 3 4 4 5 5 5 6 6 7 7 7 8 8 9 9 9 10 10 11 11 11
♃ 1 5 15 20 29 ♐10 11 12 13 14 — ♄ 1 10 29 ♉13 14 15 — ♅ 1 15 ♒0 1 — ♆ 1 R 20 ♋22 21 — ♇ 1 ♊27

3
☉ ♓ 10 11 12 13 14 15 16 17 18 19 20 21 22 23 24 25 26 27 28 29 0 1 2 3 4 5 6 7 8 9 10
☽ 14 28 13 28 12 25 8 21 4 16 28 10 22 3 15 28 10 22 5 18 1 15 28 12 26 10 25 9 23 8 22
☿ 9 11 13 15 17 19 21 23 25 27 29 0 2 5 6 8 10 12 14 15 17 19 20 21 23 24 25 26 27 28 28
♀ 8 9 11 12 13 14 16 17 18 19 20 22 23 24 25 27 28 29 0 1 3 4 5 6 8 9 10 11 13 14 15
♂ ♊ 12 13 13 14 14 14 15 15 16 16 17 17 18 18 19 19 20 20 21 21 22 22 23 23 24 25 25 26 26 27 27
♃ 1 15 ♐14 15 — ♄ 1 10 20 31 ♉15 16 17 18 — ♅ 1 ♒1 2 3 — ♆ 1 R ♋21 — ♇ 1 ♊27

4
☉ ♈ 11 12 13 14 15 16 17 18 19 20 21 22 23 24 25 26 27 28 29 0 1 2 3 4 5 6 7 8 9 10
☽ 6 20 3 16 29 11 24 6 18 29 11 23 6 18 1 14 27 11 25 9 23 7 21 6 20 4 18 1 15 28
☿ 29 29 29 29 29 29 29 29 29 28 28 27 27 26 26 25 25 24 23 23 22 22 21 20 20 20 19 19 19 19
♀ 16 17 19 20 21 22 24 25 26 27 28 0 1 2 3 5 6 7 8 10 11 12 13 14 16 17 18 19 21 22
♂ ♊ 28 28 29 29 0 1 1 2 2 3 4 4 5 5 6 7 7 8 8 9 10 10 11 11 12 12 13 13 14 15
♃ 1 R 25 ♐15 14 — ♄ 1 10 29 ♉18 19 21 — ♅ 1 ♒3 — ♆ 1 20 ♋21 21 — ♇ 1 ♊27

5
☉ ♉ 11 12 13 14 15 16 17 18 19 20 21 22 23 24 25 26 27 28 29 0 1 2 3 4 5 6 7 8 9 10
☽ 12 24 7 19 2 14 25 7 19 1 13 26 9 22 5 19 3 18 3 18 2 16 1 15 28 12 25 8 20 3 15
☿ 19 19 20 20 21 22 23 24 24 25 26 27 28 0 0 1 2 3 4 6 7 8 10 11 13 14 16 18 19 21 22
♀ 23 24 25 27 28 29 0 1 3 4 5 6 8 9 10 11 13 14 15 16 18 19 20 21 22 24 25 26 27 28 0
♂ 14 15 15 16 17 17 18 18 19 20 21 21 22 22 23 23 24 25 25 26 27 28 28 29 29 0 1 1 2
♃ 1 R 10 15 25 31 ♐14 13 12 11 10 — ♄ 1 10 20 25 ♉22 23 24 25 — ♅ 1 8 R ♒3 3 — ♆ 1 25 ♋21 22 — ♇ 1 31 ♊27 28

6
☉ ♊ 10 11 12 13 14 15 16 17 18 19 20 21 22 23 24 25 26 27 28 29 0 1 2 3 4 5 6 7 8
☽ 28 10 22 4 16 27 9 22 4 17 0 14 28 12 27 12 27 11 25 8 22 5 17 0 12 24 6 18
☿ 23 25 27 28 0 2 4 6 8 10 13 15 17 19 21 23 26 28 0 2 4 7 9 11 13 15 17 19 21 23
♀ 1 2 3 5 6 7 8 10 11 12 13 15 16 17 18 19 20 22 23 24 26 27 28 29 0 2 3 4 5 7
♂ ♋ 3 4 5 5 6 7 8 8 9 10 11 11 12 13 13 14 15 15 16 17 17 18 19 20 21 21 22 23
♃ 1 R 10 20 25 ♐10 9 8 7 — ♄ 1 10 20 30 ♉26 27 28 29 — ♅ 1 R 20 ♒3 2 — ♆ 1 30 ♋22 23 — ♇ 1 ♊28

7
☉ ♋ 9 10 11 12 13 14 15 16 17 18 19 20 21 22 23 24 25 26 27 28 29 0 1 2 3 4 5 6 7 8
☽ 0 12 24 6 18 0 12 25 8 22 6 21 6 21 6 21 5 18 2 14 27 9 21 3 15 27 9 21 3
☿ 25 26 28 0 2 4 5 7 8 10 12 13 14 16 17 19 20 21 22 24 25 26 27 28 29 0 1 1 2 3 4
♀ 8 9 10 12 13 14 15 16 17 19 20 21 22 24 25 26 27 29 0 1 2 4 5 6 7 9 10 11 12 14 15
♂ 20 21 22 22 23 24 25 25 26 27 28 28 29 29 0 1 1 2 3 4 4 5 6 7 8 8 9
♃ 1 R 10 25 ♐7 6 5 — ♄ 1 7 29 10 15 31 ♉29 0 ♊ 0 1 2 — ♅ 1 R 20 ♒2 1 — ♆ 1 25 ♋23 24 — ♇ 1 15 ♊28 29

8
☉ ♌ 8 9 10 11 12 13 14 15 16 17 18 19 20 21 22 23 24 25 26 27 28 29 0 1 2 3 4 5 6 7
☽ 15 27 9 22 4 17 1 15 29 14 29 15 29 14 27 11 24 6 18 0 12 24 6 18 0 12 24 6 19
☿ ♍ 4 5 5 6 6 6 6 6 6 6 5 5 5 4 4 3 2 1 0 29 28 28 27 26 25 25 24 24 23 23 23
♀ ♑ 16 17 18 20 21 22 23 25 26 27 28 0 1 2 3 4 6 7 8 9 11 12 13 14 16 17 18 19 21 22 23
♂ ♍ 9 10 11 11 12 13 13 14 14 15 16 16 17 18 18 19 19 20 21 21 22 22 23 24 24 25 25 26 27 27 28
♃ 1 R 30 20 31 ♐5 5 6 7 — ♄ 1 10 31 ♊1 2 3 4 — ♅ 1 R 10 ♒1 0 — ♆ 1 25 ♋24 25 — ♇ 1 ♊29

9
☉ ♍ 8 9 10 11 12 13 14 15 16 17 18 19 20 21 22 23 24 25 26 27 28 29 0 1 2 3 4 5 6 7
☽ 1 14 27 11 25 9 23 8 23 8 23 8 22 6 19 2 15 27 9 21 3 15 27 9 21 4 16 28 11 24
☿ 23 23 23 24 24 25 26 27 28 0 1 3 5 7 9 10 12 14 16 17 19 21 23 25 27 28 0 2 4
♀ 24 25 27 28 29 0 1 3 4 5 7 8 9 10 12 13 14 15 16 18 19 20 21 23 24 25 26 28 29 0
♂ 29 0 1 2 2 3 3 4 5 6 6 7 8 8 9 10 10 11 12 12 13 14 14 15 16 16 17 17 18
♃ 1 10 20 25 ♐7 8 9 10 — ♄ 1 17 R ♊4 4 — ♅ 1 R 5 ♒0 ♑29 — ♆ 1 ♋25 — ♇ 1 23 ♊29 ♋0

10
☉ ♎ 7 8 9 10 11 12 13 14 15 16 17 18 19 20 21 22 23 24 25 26 27 28 29 0 1 2 3 4 5 6 7
☽ 8 21 5 19 3 18 2 17 1 16 29 14 27 10 23 5 17 29 11 23 5 17 29 11 24 7 21 4 18 2 16
☿ 7 9 11 12 14 16 17 19 21 22 24 25 27 28 0 1 3 4 6 7 9 10 12 13 15 16 17 19 20 21 22
♀ 1 2 4 5 6 7 8 10 11 12 14 15 16 17 19 20 21 22 24 25 26 27 29 0 1 2 4 5 6 7 8
♂ 19 19 20 21 21 22 22 23 24 25 25 26 27 28 28 29 29 0 1 2 2 3 4 5 5 6 6 7 8 8 9
♃ 1 5 10 15 20 25 31 ♐10 11 12 13 14 15 16 — ♄ 1 R 5 31 ♊4 3 2 — ♅ 1 R 10 D ♑29 29 — ♆ 1 15 30 R ♋25 26 26 — ♇ 1 ♋0 0 ♊29

11
☉ ♏ 8 9 10 11 12 13 14 15 16 17 18 19 20 21 22 23 24 25 26 27 28 29 0 1 2 3 4 5 6 7
☽ 0 14 28 12 27 11 25 8 22 5 18 0 13 25 7 19 1 13 25 7 19 1 13 25 8 20 3 16 0 14
☿ 23 24 25 26 27 28 29 0 0 0 0 0 29 29 28 27 26 25 24 22 21 20 19 18 18 17 17 17 17 17
♀ 10 11 12 13 14 16 17 18 19 21 22 23 24 26 27 28 29 1 2 3 4 6 7 8 9 11 12 13 14 16
♂ 10 10 11 12 12 13 14 14 15 15 16 17 17 18 19 19 20 21 21 22 23 24 24 25 26 26 27 28 28 29
♃ 1 5 10 15 20 25 30 ♐16 17 18 19 20 21 22 — ♄ 1 10 20 ♊2 1 0 — ♅ 1 R 29 D ♑29 ♒0 — ♆ 1 R 30 ♋26 25 — ♇ 1 ♋29

12
☉ ♐ 9 10 11 12 13 14 15 16 17 18 19 20 21 22 23 24 25 26 27 28 29 0 1 2 3 4 5 6 7 8 9
☽ 28 12 27 11 25 9 23 7 20 4 17 0 13 26 9 21 3 15 27 9 20 2 14 26 8 21 3 16 29 12 26
☿ 17 17 18 18 19 20 21 22 23 24 25 26 27 28 29 0 1 3 4 5 7 8 9 11 12 14 15 17 18 20 21
♀ 17 18 19 21 22 23 24 26 27 28 29 1 2 3 4 6 7 8 9 11 12 13 14 16 17 18 19 21 22 23
♂ 0 1 1 2 3 3 4 5 5 6 7 8 8 9 10 10 11 12 13 14 14 15 16 17 17 18 19 19 20 21 22
♃ 1 5 11 16 20 25 31 ♐22 23 24 25 26 27 28 29 — ♄ 1 R 20 ♉29 28 — ♅ 1 10 25 ♒0 1 2 — ♆ 1 R ♋25 — ♇ 1 15 ♊29 28

1913

1 2 3 4 5 6 7 8 9 10 11 12 13 14 15 16 17 18 19 20 21 22 23 24 25 26 27 28 29 30 31

1
☉ ♑ 10 11 12 13 14 15 16 17 18 19 20 21 22 23 24 25 26 27 28 29 0 1 2 3 4 5 6 7 8 9 10 11
☽ ♏ 1 14 27 10 22 5 17 29 11 23 5 17 29 11 23 5 18 1 15 29 14 29 15 0 15 29 14 28 11 24 7
☿ ♐ 18 19 21 22 23 25 26 27 29 0 2 3 5 6 7 9 10 12 13 15 16 18 19 21 23 24 26 27 29 0 2
♀ ♒ 23 24 25 27 28 29 0 1 2 4 5 6 7 8 9 10 12 13 14 15 16 17 18 19 21 22 23 24 25 26 27
♂ ♑ 23 24 24 25 26 27 27 28 29 0 0 1 2 3 4 4 5 6 7 7 8 9 9 10 11 12 12 13 14 15 15
♃ 1 3 29 5 10 15 20 26 31 ♐29 0 ♑0 1 3 4 5 6 — ♄ 1 R 29 D ♉27 27 — ♅ 1 15 31 ♒2 3 4 — ♆ 1 R 10 ♋25 24 — ♇ 1 ♊28

2
☉ ♒ 12 13 14 15 16 17 18 19 20 21 22 23 24 25 26 27 28 29 0 1 2 3 4 5 6 7 8 9
☽ 20 2 14 26 8 20 2 14 25 7 19 1 14 27 10 24 8 23 8 23 8 23 7 20 4 16
☿ ♒ 4 5 7 9 10 12 14 16 17 19 21 23 24 26 28 0 2 4 6 7 9 11 13 15 17 18 20 21 22
♀ ♓ 28 29 0 1 3 4 5 5 7 8 9 10 11 12 13 14 15 16 17 18 19 19 20 21 22 23 24 25
♂ ♑ 16 17 18 19 19 20 21 21 22 23 24 25 25 26 27 28 28 29 0 1 2 3 4 4 5 6 7
♃ 1 5 10 15 20 25 ♑6 7 8 9 10 11 — ♄ 1 25 ♉27 28 — ♅ 1 20 ♒4 5 — ♆ 1 R 15 ♋24 23 — ♇ 1 ♋1 ♊28

3
☉ ♓ 10 11 12 13 14 15 16 17 18 19 20 21 22 23 24 25 26 27 28 29 0 1 2 3 4 5 6 7 8 9 10
☽ 29 11 23 5 17 29 11 22 4 16 29 11 23 6 20 3 17 1 16 1 16 1 16 11 15 29 12 25 8 20 2
☿ 24 26 27 29 0 2 3 5 6 7 8 9 10 11 12 12 12 12 12 11 11 10 9 9 8 7 7 6 6 5 4
♀ 25 26 27 28 29 0 1 2 3 3 4 5 5 6 7 7 8 8 9 9 10 10 10 10 11 11 11 11 12 12 12
♂ ♒ 7 8 9 10 11 11 12 13 14 14 15 16 17 18 18 19 20 21 22 22 23 24 25 25 26 27 28 28 29 0 1
♃ 1 5 10 15 20 31 ♑11 12 13 14 15 16 — ♄ 1 15 26 ♉28 29 ♊0 — ♅ 1 10 31 ♒5 6 7 — ♆ 1 R ♋23 — ♇ 1 ♊28

4
☉ ♈ 11 12 13 14 15 16 17 18 19 20 21 22 23 24 25 26 27 28 29 0 1 2 3 4 5 6 7 8 9
☽ 14 26 7 19 1 13 25 8 20 3 16 29 13 27 11 26 10 25 10 24 9 23 7 20 3 16 28 10 22 4
☿ 3 2 2 1 0 0 29 29 29 29 29 29 29 0 0 1 1 2 2 3 4 5 6 6 7 8 9 11 12 13
♀ 12 12 12 12 12 12 12 12 12 11 11 11 10 10 10 9 9 8 8 7 6 6 5 5 4 4 3 3 2 1 1
♂ 1 2 3 4 5 5 6 7 8 8 9 10 11 11 12 13 13 14 15 16 17 18 18 19 20 21 22 22 23 24
♃ 1 10 ♑16 17 — ♄ 1 5 15 25 30 ♊0 1 2 3 4 — ♅ 1 ♒7 — ♆ 1 R ♋23 — ♇ 1 ♊28

5
☉ ♉ 10 11 12 13 14 15 16 17 18 19 20 21 22 23 24 25 26 27 28 29 0 1 2 3 4 5 6 7 8 9
☽ 16 28 10 22 4 17 0 13 27 10 24 8 22 6 20 5 19 3 17 1 15 28 11 24 6 18 0 12 24 6 18
☿ 14 15 17 18 20 21 22 24 25 27 28 0 2 4 5 7 9 11 13 14 16 18 20 22 24 26 28 0 2 5 7
♀ 0 29 29 29 28 28 27 27 27 26 26 26 26 26 26 26 26 26 26 26 26 26 27 27 27 28 28 28 29 29 0
♂ 25 25 26 27 28 28 29 0 1 2 2 3 4 5 5 6 7 8 8 9 10 10 11 11 12 13 14 14 15 16 17 18
♃ 1 6 R 31 ♑17 17 16 — ♄ 1 10 20 25 ♊4 5 6 7 — ♅ 1 13 R ♒7 7 — ♆ 1 25 ♋23 24 — ♇ 1 ♊28

6
☉ ♊ 10 11 12 13 14 15 16 17 18 19 20 21 22 23 24 25 26 27 28 29 0 1 2 3 4 5 6 7 8
☽ 0 13 26 9 23 6 20 5 19 3 17 1 15 29 13 27 10 23 6 19 2 14 26 8 20 2 13 26 8 21
☿ 10 12 14 16 18 21 23 25 27 0 1 3 5 7 9 11 12 14 16 18 19 21 23 24 26 27 29 0 1 3
♀ 0 1 1 2 3 3 4 5 5 6 6 7 8 9 10 11 12 13 14 14 15 16 17 18 19 20 21 22
♂ 18 19 20 21 21 22 23 23 24 25 26 26 27 28 29 29 0 1 1 2 3 4 5 5 6 7 7 8 9 9
♃ 1 R 15 25 30 ♑16 15 14 13 — ♄ 1 10 20 25 ♊8 9 10 11 — ♅ 1 R 30 ♒7 6 — ♆ 1 25 ♋24 25 — ♇ 1 ♊29

7
☉ ♋ 9 10 11 12 13 14 14 15 16 17 18 19 20 21 22 23 24 25 26 27 28 29 0 1 2 3 4 5 6 7
☽ 4 17 1 16 0 15 29 14 28 12 26 10 23 7 20 3 15 28 10 22 4 16 28 10 22 4 16 29 12 26 10
☿ 4 5 6 7 9 10 11 12 12 13 14 14 15 16 16 17 17 18 18 18 18 18 18 17 17 17 16 16 15 15 14
♀ 23 24 25 26 27 28 29 0 1 2 3 4 5 6 7 8 9 10 11 12 13 14 15 16 17 18 19 21 22 23 24
♂ 10 11 12 12 13 14 14 15 16 17 17 18 19 19 20 21 22 22 23 24 24 25 26 26 27 28 28 29 0 0 1
♃ 1 R 10 15 25 ♑13 12 11 10 — ♄ 1 10 20 31 ♊12 13 14 15 — ♅ 1 R 31 ♒6 5 — ♆ 1 25 ♋25 26 — ♇ 1 10 ♊29 ♋0

8
☉ ♌ 8 9 10 11 12 13 14 15 16 17 18 19 20 21 22 23 24 25 26 27 28 29 0 1 2 3 4 5 6 7
☽ 24 9 24 9 24 8 23 7 20 4 17 29 12 25 7 19 1 13 25 6 18 0 12 25 7 20 4 18 2 17 2
☿ 13 13 12 11 11 10 9 9 8 8 7 7 7 7 6 6 7 7 7 7 8 8 9 10 11 12 13 15 16 18 19 21 23
♀ 25 26 27 28 29 0 1 2 4 5 6 7 8 9 10 11 13 14 15 16 17 18 19 20 21 22 23 24 25 26 27 29
♂ ♊ 2 2 3 4 5 5 6 7 7 8 8 9 10 10 11 12 12 13 14 14 15 15 16 17 17 18 19 19 20 20 21
♃ 1 R 15 ♑9 8 — ♄ 1 10 25 ♊15 16 17 — ♅ 1 R 20 ♒5 4 — ♆ 1 20 ♋26 27 — ♇ 1 ♋0

9
☉ ♍ 8 9 10 11 12 13 14 15 16 17 18 19 20 21 22 23 24 25 26 27 28 29 0 1 2 3 4 5 6
☽ 17 2 17 2 16 0 14 27 9 22 4 16 28 10 22 3 15 27 9 21 4 16 29 13 27 11 25 10 26 11
☿ 24 26 28 0 2 4 6 8 9 11 13 15 17 19 20 22 24 26 28 29 1 2 3 5 7 9 10 12 14 15 17
♀ 0 1 2 3 5 6 7 8 9 11 12 13 14 15 16 18 19 20 21 22 24 25 26 27 28 29 1 2 3 4
♂ 21 22 23 23 24 24 25 26 26 27 27 28 28 29 0 0 1 1 2 3 3 4 5 5 6 6 7
♃ 1 R 4 D 30 ♑8 8 9 — ♄ 1 15 ♊17 18 — ♅ 1 R 25 ♒4 3 — ♆ 1 30 ♋27 28 — ♇ 1 15 ♋0 1

10
☉ ♎ 7 8 9 10 11 12 13 14 15 16 17 18 19 20 21 22 23 24 25 26 27 28 29 0 1 2 3 4 5 6 7
☽ 25 11 25 9 23 6 18 1 13 25 7 19 1 13 25 7 19 1 12 24 6 18 1 13 26 9 23 6 20 5 19 4 19 4
☿ 19 20 22 23 25 27 28 0 1 3 4 5 7 9 10 11 13 14 16 17 18 20 21 22 24 25 26 27 28 29 0
♀ 6 7 8 9 11 12 13 14 15 17 18 19 20 21 23 24 25 26 28 29 0 1 3 4 5 6 8 9 10 11 13
♂ 8 8 9 9 10 10 11 11 12 12 13 13 14 14 14 15 15 16 16 17 17 18 18 18 19 19 19 20 20 20
♃ 1 10 20 25 ♑9 10 11 12 — ♄ 1 R 20 ♊18 17 — ♅ 1 R 14 D ♒3 3 — ♆ 1 ♋28 — ♇ 1 ♋1

11
☉ ♏ 8 9 10 11 12 13 14 15 16 17 18 19 20 21 22 23 24 25 26 27 28 29 0 1 2 3 4 5 6 7
☽ 17 1 14 27 9 21 3 15 27 9 21 3 15 28 10 23 6 20 3 17 1 15 29 13 27 11 25 9
☿ 2 3 4 5 6 6 7 7 7 8 8 8 8 8 7 7 7 6 5 4 3 2 0 29 28 27 26 25 24 23
♀ 14 15 16 17 19 20 21 22 24 25 26 27 29 0 1 2 4 5 6 7 9 10 11 12 14 15 16 17 19 20
♂ 20 21 21 21 21 22 22 22 22 22 23 23 23 23 23 23 23 24 24 24 24 24 24 24 24 24 24 24 24 24
♃ 1 10 15 20 25 30 ♑13 14 15 16 17 18 — ♄ 1 R 15 25 ♊17 16 15 — ♅ 1 10 ♒3 4 — ♆ 1 ♋28 — ♇ 1 15 ♋1 0

12
☉ ♐ 8 9 10 11 12 13 14 15 16 17 18 19 20 21 22 23 24 25 26 27 28 29 0 1 2 3 4 5 6 7 8 9
☽ 22 6 17 29 11 23 5 17 29 11 23 5 18 0 13 26 9 23 6 19 3 16 29 14 28 12 26 10 24 8 22
☿ 22 22 22 22 22 23 23 24 25 26 26 27 28 29 0 1 2 4 5 6 7 9 10 12 13 15 16 18 19 20 22
♀ 22 23 24 25 26 27 28 29 0 1 2 4 5 6 8 9 10 11 12 14 15 16 17 19 20 21 22 24 25 26 27
♂ 24 24 24 24 24 24 23 23 23 23 23 23 22 22 22 22 21 21 21 21 20 20 20 20 19 19 18 18 18 17 17 16
♃ 1 5 10 15 20 25 31 ♑18 19 20 21 22 24 25 — ♄ 1 R 10 20 ♊15 14 13 — ♅ 1 10 25 ♒4 5 6 — ♆ 1 R 20 ♋28 27 — ♇ 1 25 ♋0 ♊29

1914

1

	1	2	3	4	5	6	7	8	9	10	11	12	13	14	15	16	17	18	19	20	21	22	23	24	25	26	27	28	29	30	31
☉	♑ 10	11	12	13	14	15	16	17	18	19	20	21	22	23	24	25	26	27	28	29	♒ 0	1	2	3	4	5	6	7	8	9	10
☽	7	19	1	13	24	7	19	1	14	27	11	25	9	23	8	22	6	21	5	19	2	16	29	12	25	8	21	3	15	27	9
☿	♐ 26	28	0	1	2	4	6	7	9	10	12	13	15	17	18	20	21	23	25	26	28	0	1	3	5	6	8	10	11	13	15
♀	♒ 0	1	3	4	5	6	8	9	10	12	13	14	15	17	18	19	20	21	23	24	25	26	28	29	0	1	3	4	5	7	8
♂	♋ R 16	16	15	15	15	14	14	13	13	13	12	12	11	11	11	11	10	10	10	9	9	9	9	8	8	8	8	7	7	7	6

♃ 1 5 10 15 21 29 25 31 / ♑25 26 27 28 0 ♒1 2 — ♄ 1 R 20 / ♊12 11 — ♅ 1 15 / ♒6 7 — ♆ 1 R / ♋27 26 — ♇ 1 / ♊29

2

	1	2	3	4	5	6	7	8	9	10	11	12	13	14	15	16	17	18	19	20	21	22	23	24	25	26	27	28
☉	♒ 11	12	13	14	15	16	17	18	19	20	21	22	23	24	25	26	27	28	29	♓ 0	1	2	3	4	5	6	7	8	9
☽	21	2	14	27	9	22	5	19	3	18	2	17	2	17	1	15	29	13	26	9	22	5	17	29	11	23	5	17
☿	♒ 17	19	20	22	24	26	28	29	♓ 0	1	3	5	6	8	10	11	13	15	16	17	19	20	21	22	23	23	24	24
♀	♒ 9	10	12	13	14	15	17	18	19	20	22	23	24	25	27	28	29	♓ 0	2	3	4	5	7	8	9	10	12	13
♂	♋ R 6	6	6	6	6	6	6	6	6	6	6	D 6	6	6	6	6	6	6	6	6	6	6	6	6	6	6	7	7

♃ 1 5 10 15 20 25 / ♒2 3 4 5 7 8 — ♄ 1 R 12 D / ♊11 11 — ♅ 1 20 / ♒8 9 — ♆ 1 R / ♋26 — ♇ 1 / ♊29

3

	1	2	3	4	5	6	7	8	9	10	11	12	13	14	15	16	17	18	19	20	21	22	23	24	25	26	27	28	29	30	31
☉	♓ 10	11	12	13	14	15	16	17	18	19	20	21	22	23	24	25	26	27	28	29	♈ 0	1	2	3	4	5	6	7	8	9	10
☽	29	11	23	5	17	0	13	27	11	26	10	25	11	26	11	25	9	23	6	19	2	14	26	8	20	2	14	26	8	19	2
☿	♓ R 24	24	24	24	23	23	22	21	20	19	18	17	16	15	14	13	12	12	11	11	11	D 11	11	11	11	11	11	11	12	12	13
♀	♓ 14	15	17	18	19	20	22	23	24	25	27	28	29	♈ 0	2	3	4	5	7	8	9	10	12	13	14	15	17	18	19	20	22
♂	♋ 7	7	7	7	8	8	8	9	9	9	9	10	10	10	11	11	11	12	12	12	13	13	13	14	14	14	14	15	15	16	16

♃ 1 6 10 15 20 25 31 / ♒9 10 11 12 13 14 15 — ♄ 1 10 25 / ♊11 12 13 — ♅ 1 10 / ♒9 10 — ♆ 1 R / ♋25 — ♇ 1 / ♊29

4

	1	2	3	4	5	6	7	8	9	10	11	12	13	14	15	16	17	18	19	20	21	22	23	24	25	26	27	28	29	30
☉	♈ 11	12	13	14	15	16	17	18	19	20	21	22	23	24	25	26	27	28	29	♉ 0	1	2	3	4	5	6	7	8	9	10
☽	14	26	9	22	5	19	4	18	4	19	4	19	4	18	2	16	29	11	23	5	17	29	11	23	5	17	29	11	23	6
☿	♓ 14	15	15	16	17	18	19	20	21	22	23	24	26	27	28	29	♈ 0	1	2	4	5	7	8	10	11	13	15	16	18	20
♀	♈ 23	24	25	27	28	29	♉ 0	1	3	4	5	6	8	9	10	11	13	14	15	16	17	19	20	21	22	24	25	26	27	28
♂	♋ 16	17	17	17	18	18	19	19	19	20	20	20	21	21	22	22	22	23	23	24	24	24	25	25	25	26	26	27	27	28

♃ 1 5 10 20 25 / ♒15 16 17 18 19 — ♄ 1 10 20 30 / ♊13 14 15 16 — ♅ 1 5 / ♒10 11 — ♆ 1 R / ♋25 — ♇ 1 / ♊29

5

	1	2	3	4	5	6	7	8	9	10	11	12	13	14	15	16	17	18	19	20	21	22	23	24	25	26	27	28	29	30	31
☉	♉ 10	11	12	13	14	15	16	17	18	19	20	21	22	23	24	25	26	27	28	29	♊ 0	1	2	3	4	5	6	7	8	9	10
☽	18	2	15	29	13	27	12	27	12	27	12	27	11	24	7	20	2	14	26	8	20	2	14	26	8	20	3	16	29	12	25
☿	♈ 23	25	27	29	♉ 0	1	3	5	6	8	10	12	15	17	19	21	23	26	28	29	♊ 0	2	4	7	9	11	13	15	17	19	21	23	25
♀	♉ 29	♊ 0	1	2	3	5	6	7	8	10	11	12	13	14	16	17	18	19	20	22	23	24	25	27	28	29	♋ 0	1	3	4	5	6
♂	♋ 29	♌ 0	0	1	1	2	2	3	3	4	4	5	5	6	6	7	7	8	8	9	9	10	10	11	11	12	12	13	13	14	14	15	15

♃ 1 5 10 25 / ♒19 20 21 22 — ♄ 1 5 15 25 31 / ♊16 17 18 19 20 — ♅ 1 18 R / ♒11 11 — ♆ 1 15 / ♋25 26 — ♇ 1 25 / ♊29 ♋0

6

	1	2	3	4	5	6	7	8	9	10	11	12	13	14	15	16	17	18	19	20	21	22	23	24	25	26	27	28	29	30
☉	♊ 10	11	12	13	14	15	16	17	18	19	20	21	22	23	24	25	26	27	28	29	♋ 0	1	2	3	4	5	6	7	8
☽	9	23	7	22	6	21	6	20	5	19	2	15	28	10	22	4	16	28	10	22	4	17	29	12	25	9	22	6	20	4
☿	♊ 27	28	29	♋ 0	2	4	5	7	8	10	11	13	14	15	17	18	19	20	21	22	23	24	25	25	26	27	27	28	28	28
♀	♋ 7	9	10	11	12	13	15	16	17	18	19	21	22	23	24	25	27	28	29	♌ 0	1	3	4	5	6	7	9	10	11	12
♂	♌ 16	16	17	18	18	19	19	20	20	21	21	22	23	23	24	24	25	25	26	27	27	28	28	29	29	♍ 0	0	1	1	2

♃ 1 12 R 30 / ♒22 22 21 — ♄ 1 10 15 25 30 / ♊20 21 22 23 24 — ♅ 1 R / ♒11 — ♆ 1 20 / ♋26 27 — ♇ 1 / ♋0

7

	1	2	3	4	5	6	7	8	9	10	11	12	13	14	15	16	17	18	19	20	21	22	23	24	25	26	27	28	29	30	31
☉	♋ 8	9	10	11	12	13	14	15	16	17	18	19	20	21	22	23	24	25	26	27	28	29	♌ 0	1	2	3	4	5	6	7	8
☽	18	2	16	1	15	29	13	27	10	23	6	18	0	12	24	6	18	0	12	25	8	21	5	18	2	16	0	15	29	13	27
☿	♋ 29	29	29	R 29	29	29	28	28	28	27	27	26	25	24	24	23	23	22	21	21	20	20	19	19	19	D 19	19	19	19	19	19
♀	♌ 13	14	16	17	18	19	20	22	23	24	25	26	27	28	29	♍ 0	1	2	3	4	5	7	8	9	10	11	12	14	15	16	17	18
♂	♍ 3	4	4	5	5	6	6	7	8	8	9	10	10	11	11	12	12	13	14	14	15	16	16	17	17	18	19	19	20	20	21

♃ 1 R 15 25 31 / ♒21 20 19 18 — ♄ 1 10 15 25 / ♊24 25 26 27 — ♅ 1 R 10 31 / ♒11 10 9 — ♆ 1 20 / ♋27 28 — ♇ 1 10 / ♋0 1

8

	1	2	3	4	5	6	7	8	9	10	11	12	13	14	15	16	17	18	19	20	21	22	23	24	25	26	27	28	29	30	31
☉	♌ 8	9	10	11	12	13	14	15	16	17	18	19	20	21	22	23	24	25	26	27	28	29	♍ 0	1	2	3	4	5	6	7
☽	11	25	9	22	6	19	1	14	26	8	20	2	14	26	8	20	3	16	29	13	27	12	26	11	25	10	24	8	22	6	19
☿	♋ 20	21	21	22	23	24	25	26	27	29	♌ 0	2	3	5	7	8	10	12	14	16	18	20	22	24	26	28	29	♍ 0	2	4	6	8
♀	♍ 19	21	21	22	23	24	25	26	27	28	29	♎ 0	1	2	3	4	5	6	7	8	9	11	12	13	14	15	16	17	18	19	20	21	23
♂	♍ 21	22	23	24	24	25	25	26	27	27	28	28	29	♎ 0	0	1	2	2	3	3	4	5	5	6	7	7	8	9	9	10	11

♃ 1 R 10 15 25 31 / ♒18 17 16 15 14 — ♄ 1 5 10 24 29 25 / ♊27 28 29 ♋0 0 — ♅ 1 R 31 / ♒9 8 — ♆ 1 15 / ♋28 29 — ♇ 1 31 / ♋1 2

9

	1	2	3	4	5	6	7	8	9	10	11	12	13	14	15	16	17	18	19	20	21	22	23	24	25	26	27	28	29	30
☉	♍ 8	9	10	11	12	13	14	15	16	17	18	19	20	21	22	22	23	24	25	26	27	28	29	♎ 0	1	2	3	4	5	6
☽	2	15	28	10	22	4	16	28	10	22	4	16	28	11	24	7	21	5	20	5	20	5	20	4	19	2	16	29	12	24
☿	♍ 10	11	13	15	17	19	21	23	24	26	28	29	♎ 0	1	3	5	6	8	9	11	13	14	16	17	19	20	22	23	25	26	27
♀	♎ 23	25	26	27	28	29	♏ 0	1	2	3	4	5	6	7	8	9	10	11	12	13	14	15	16	17	18	19	20	21	22	23
♂	♎ 11	12	13	13	14	15	15	16	17	17	18	19	19	20	21	21	22	23	23	24	25	25	26	27	27	28	29	29	♏ 0	0

♃ 1 R 10 30 / ♒14 13 12 — ♄ 1 5 20 / ♋0 1 2 — ♅ 1 R 30 / ♒8 7 — ♆ 1 23 / ♋29 ♌0 — ♇ 1 / ♋2

10

	1	2	3	4	5	6	7	8	9	10	11	12	13	14	15	16	17	18	19	20	21	22	23	24	25	26	27	28	29	30	31
☉	♎ 7	8	9	10	11	12	13	14	15	16	17	18	19	20	21	22	23	24	25	26	27	28	29	♏ 0	1	2	3	4	5	6	7
☽	7	19	1	13	25	7	19	0	12	25	7	19	2	16	29	13	28	13	28	14	29	14	28	12	26	9	21	4	16	28	10
☿	♎ 29	♏ 0	1	3	4	5	7	8	9	10	12	13	14	15	16	17	18	19	19	20	21	22	22	23	23	23	23	23	22	22	22
♀	♏ 23	24	25	25	26	27	28	29	29	♐ 0	1	2	2	3	3	4	4	5	5	6	6	6	7	7	7	8	8	8	8	8	8
♂	♏ 1	2	2	3	4	4	5	6	7	7	8	9	9	10	11	11	12	13	13	14	15	15	16	17	18	18	19	20	20	21	22

♃ 1 R 10 D 25 / ♒12 12 13 — ♄ 1 16 R / ♋2 2 — ♅ 1 R 19 D 31 / ♒7 7 7 — ♆ 1 / ♌0 — ♇ 1 / ♋2

11

	1	2	3	4	5	6	7	8	9	10	11	12	13	14	15	16	17	18	19	20	21	22	23	24	25	26	27	28	29	30
☉	♏ 8	9	10	11	12	13	14	15	16	17	18	19	20	21	22	23	24	25	26	27	28	29	♐ 0	1	2	3	4	5	6	7
☽	22	4	16	27	9	21	4	16	28	11	24	8	22	6	21	6	22	7	22	7	21	5	18	0	13	25	7	19	1	13
☿	♏ 21	20	19	18	17	15	14	13	11	10	9	8	8	7	D 7	7	7	8	8	9	10	10	11	13	14	15	16	17	19
♀	♐ 11	12	12	12	12	12	12	R 12	12	12	12	11	11	11	11	10	10	10	9	9	9	8	8	7	6	6	5	5	4	3
♂	♏ 23	23	24	25	26	26	27	28	28	29	♐ 0	1	1	2	3	3	4	5	5	6	7	8	8	9	10	11	11	12	13	14

♃ 1 10 20 25 / ♒13 14 15 16 — ♄ 1 R 15 30 / ♋2 1 0 — ♅ 1 5 / ♒7 8 — ♆ 1 4 R / ♌0 — ♇ 1 25 / ♋2 1

12

	1	2	3	4	5	6	7	8	9	10	11	12	13	14	15	16	17	18	19	20	21	22	23	24	25	26	27	28	29	30	31
☉	♐ 8	9	10	11	12	13	14	15	16	17	18	19	20	21	22	23	24	25	26	27	28	29	♑ 0	1	2	3	4	5	6	7	8	9
☽	24	6	18	1	13	26	8	21	4	18	2	16	0	15	0	15	29	13	26	9	21	3	15	27	9	21	3	15	27
☿	♐ 20	22	23	24	26	27	29	♑ 0	2	3	5	6	8	9	11	12	14	15	17	19	20	22	23	25	26	28	29	♑ 0	2	3	5	6
♀	♐ R 2	1	0	0	29	29	29	28	28	28	27	27	27	27	27	27	D 27	27	27	27	27	27	28	28	28	28	29	29	29	♐ 0
♂	♐ 14	15	16	17	17	18	19	19	20	21	22	22	23	24	25	25	26	27	28	28	29	♑ 0	1	2	2	3	4	5	5	6	7

♃ 1 10 15 25 31 / ♒17 18 19 20 21 22 — ♄ 1 R 7 0 10 25 / ♋0 29 ♊29 28 — ♅ 1 10 31 / ♒8 9 10 — ♆ 1 R 15 / ♌0 ♋29 — ♇ 1 / ♋1

1915

1

	1	2	3	4	5	6	7	8	9	10	11	12	13	14	15	16	17	18	19	20	21	22	23	24	25	26	27	28	29
☉	♑ 10	11	12	13	14	15	16	17	18	19	20	21	22	23	24	25	26	27	28	29	♒ 0	1	2	3	4	5	6	7	8
☽	10	22	5	18	1	15	28	12	26	10	25	9	24	8	23	7	20	4	16	29	11	23	5	17	29	11	23	5	18
☿	♑ 9	11	12	14	15	17	19	20	22	24	25	27	29	♒ 0	2	4	5	7	9	11	12	14	16	17	19	21	22	24
♀	♐ 0	1	2	2	3	3	4	5	6	7	7	8	9	10	11	12	13	13	14	15	16	17	18	19	20	21	22
♂	♑ 8	9	10	11	12	12	13	14	15	16	16	17	18	19	19	20	21	22	23	23	24	25	25	26	27	28	29

♃ 1 5 10 15 17 22 26 31 / ♒22 23 24 25 26 27 28 29 — ♄ 1 R 20 / ♊27 26 — ♅ 1 20 / ♒10 11 — ♆ 1 R / ♋29 — ♇ …

2

	1	2	3	4	5	6	7	8	9	10	11	12	13	14	15	16	17	18	19	20	21	22	23	24	25	26	27	28
☉	♒ 11	12	13	14	15	16	17	18	19	20	21	22	23	24	25	26	27	28	29	♓ 0	1	2	3	4	5	6	7	8	9
☽	27	11	25	9	23	7	21	5	20	4	18	1	15	28	11	24	7	19	1	13	25	7	19	1	13	26	9	22
☿	♒ 28	29	♓ 0	1	2	3	4	5	6	7	8	8	R 8	8	7	7	6	5	4	3	2	1	29	29	28	27	26	26
♀	♑ 25	26	27	28	29	♒ 0	1	2	3	4	5	6	7	8	9	10	11	12	13	14	15	16	17	18	19	20	21	22	23
♂	♒ 1	2	3	4	5	5	6	7	8	9	9	10	11	12	13	14	15	16	16	17	18	19	20	21	21	22	23

♃ 1 4 10 15 20 25 28 / ♒29 ♓0 1 3 4 5 6 — ♄ 1 R 27 D / ♊25 25 — ♅ 1 15 / ♒11 12 13 — ♆ 1 R / ♋28 — ♇ …

3

	1	2	3	4	5	6	7	8	9	10	11	12	13	14	15	16	17	18	19	20	21	22	23	24	25	26	27	28	29
☉	♓ 9	10	11	12	13	14	15	16	17	18	19	20	21	22	23	24	25	26	27	28	29	♈ 0	1	2	3	4	5	6	7
☽	6	20	4	19	3	18	2	16	0	14	28	11	24	7	20	2	15	27	9	21	3	15	27	9	21	4	17	0	14
☿	♒ 24	24	24	23	D 23	23	23	23	24	24	24	25	25	26	27	27	28	29	♓ 0	1	2	3	4	5	6	8	9	10	11
♀	♒ 24	25	26	27	28	29	♓ 0	1	3	4	5	6	8	9	10	11	12	13	15	16	17	18	19	20	21	23	24	25	26
♂	♒ 23	24	25	26	27	27	28	29	♓ 0	1	2	3	4	5	5	6	7	8	9	10	10	11	12	12	13	14	15	16

♃ 1 5 10 15 17 22 26 31 / ♓6 7 8 9 10 11 12 13 — ♄ 1 20 / ♊25 26 — ♅ 1 15 / ♒13 14 — ♆ 1 R 15 / ♋28 27 — ♇ …

4

	1	2	3	4	5	6	7	8	9	10	11	12	13	14	15	16	17	18	19	20	21	22	23	24	25	26	27	28	29	30
☉	♈ 10	11	12	13	14	15	16	17	18	19	20	21	22	23	24	25	26	27	28	29	♉ 0	1	2	3	4	5	6	7	8
☽	28	13	28	13	27	11	25	8	21	4	17	29	11	23	6	17	29	11	23	5	17	29	12	25	8	22	7	21	7
☿	♓ 16	17	18	20	21	23	25	26	28	♈ 0	1	3	4	6	8	10	11	13	15	17	19	21	23	25	27	♉ 0	1	3	5
♀	♓ 29	♈ 0	1	2	3	4	6	7	8	9	10	11	13	14	15	16	17	19	20	21	22	23	24	26	27	28	29	♈ 0	1	3
♂	♓ 18	18	19	20	21	22	22	23	24	25	26	26	27	28	29	♈ 0	1	2	3	4	4	5	6	7	8	9	10

♃ 1 5 10 15 20 25 30 / ♓13 14 15 16 17 18 19 — ♄ 1 10 20 / ♊26 27 28 — ♅ 1 5 / ♒14 15 — ♆ 1 10 D / ♋27 27 — ♇ …

5

	1	2	3	4	5	6	7	8	9	10	11	12	13	14	15	16	17	18	19	20	21	22	23	24	25	26	27	28	29	30
☉	♉ 10	11	12	13	14	15	16	17	18	19	19	20	21	22	23	24	25	26	27	28	29	♊ 0	1	2	3	4	5	6	7
☽	7	22	7	21	5	18	1	14	26	8	20	2	14	26	8	20	2	14	26	8	21	4	17	1	15	29	15	0	16
☿	♉ 10	12	14	16	18	20	23	25	27	29	♊ 1	3	5	7	9	11	12	14	16	18	19	21	22	24	25	26	27	29
♀	♈ 5	6	7	9	10	11	12	14	15	16	17	18	19	21	22	23	24	25	27	28	29	♉ 0	1	3	4	5	6	8
♂	♈ 11	12	13	13	14	15	16	17	18	19	19	20	21	22	23	24	24	25	26	27	28	28	29	♉ 0	1	1	2

♃ 1 10 15 20 25 31 / ♓20 21 22 23 24 25 — ♄ 1 11 29 15 20 31 / ♊29 ♋0 0 1 2 — ♅ 1 21 R / ♒15 15 — ♆ 1 15 / ♋27 28 — ♇ …

6

	1	2	3	4	5	6	7	8	9	10	11	12	13	14	15	16	17	18	19	20	21	22	23	24	25	26	27	28	29	30
☉	♊ 10	10	11	12	13	14	15	16	17	18	19	20	21	22	23	24	25	26	27	28	29	♋ 0	1	2	3	4	5
☽	0	14	27	10	23	5	18	29	11	23	5	17	29	11	23	5	18	0	13	27	10	24	9	24	9	24	8
☿	♋ 3	4	5	5	6	7	7	8	8	8	9	9	9	R 9	9	9	9	9	8	8	7	7	6	6	5	5	4	3
♀	♉ 12	14	15	16	17	18	20	21	22	23	24	26	27	28	29	♊ 0	1	3	4	5	6	8	9	10	11	13	14	15
♂	♉ 4	5	6	7	8	9	10	11	11	12	13	13	14	15	16	17	17	18	19	20	21	21	22	23	24	25

♃ 1 10 15 30 / ♓25 26 27 28 — ♄ 1 5 15 20 30 / ♋2 3 4 5 6 — ♅ 1 R / ♒15 — ♆ 1 20 / ♋28 29 — ♇ …

7

	1	2	3	4	5	6	7	8	9	10	11	12	13	14	15	16	17	18	19	20	21	22	23	24	25	26	27	28	29	30	31
☉	♋ 8	9	10	11	12	13	14	15	16	17	18	19	20	21	22	23	24	25	26	27	28	29	♌ 0	1	2	3	4
☽	6	19	2	14	26	8	20	2	14	26	8	20	2	15	28	10	24	7	21	5	19	3	18	3	18	2	16	0
☿	♋ R 2	1	1	1	0	0	0	D 0	0	0	0	1	1	1	2	2	3	4	5	6	7	9	10	11	13	14	16	17	19
♀	♊ 19	20	21	22	23	25	26	27	28	29	♋ 0	1	2	3	4	6	7	8	9	11	12	13	14	15	17	18	19	20	22
♂	♉ 26	27	28	28	29	♊ 0	1	2	3	4	4	5	6	7	8	9	10	10	11	12	12	13	14	15	15	16

♃ 1 20 R / ♓28 28 — ♄ 1 5 15 20 31 / ♋6 7 8 9 10 — ♅ 1 R 15 / ♒15 14 — ♆ 1 19 / ♋29 ♌0 — ♇ …

8

	1	2	3	4	5	6	7	8	9	10	11	12	13	14	15	16	17	18	19	20	21	22	23	24	25	26	27	28	29	30	31
☉	♌ 8	9	10	11	12	13	14	15	16	17	17	18	19	20	21	22	23	24	25	26	27	28	29	♍ 0	1	2	3	4
☽	22	5	17	28	10	22	4	16	29	11	24	7	20	4	18	1	15	29	14	28	13	27	11	25	9	22	5	18	1
☿	♌ 24	26	28	29	♍ 0	2	4	6	8	10	12	14	16	18	21	23	25	27	28	29	♍ 0	2	4	6	8	10	12	13	15	17
♀	♋ 26	28	29	♌ 0	1	3	4	5	6	8	9	10	11	12	14	15	16	17	19	20	21	22	24	25	26	27	28	29
♂	♊ 18	19	19	20	21	22	23	23	24	25	25	26	27	27	28	29	29	♋ 0	1	2	3	3	4	4	5	6

♃ 1 R 10 25 / ♓28 27 26 — ♄ 1 10 15 25 / ♋10 11 12 13 — ♅ 1 R / ♒13 — ♆ 1 15 / ♌0 1 — ♇ …

9

	1	2	3	4	5	6	7	8	9	10	11	12	13	14	15	16	17	18	19	20	21	22	23	24	25	26	27	28	29	30
☉	♍ 8	9	10	11	12	13	14	14	15	16	17	18	19	20	21	22	23	24	25	26	27	28	29	♎ 0	1	2	3	4
☽	6	18	0	12	24	7	20	3	16	29	14	28	12	26	11	25	9	23	7	21	4	17	0	13	26	8	20	2	14
☿	♍ 24	25	27	28	♎ 0	1	3	5	6	8	9	10	12	13	15	16	17	19	20	21	22	24	25	26	27	28	29	♏ 0
♀	♍ 5	6	7	8	10	11	12	13	15	16	17	18	20	21	22	23	25	26	27	28	29	♎ 0	1	3	5	6	7
♂	♋ 8	9	9	10	11	11	12	13	14	14	15	16	16	17	17	18	19	19	20	20	21	21	22	23	24	25

♃ 1 R 10 20 30 / ♓25 24 23 22 21 — ♄ 1 5 15 / ♋13 14 15 — ♅ 1 R / ♒12 — ♆ 1 15 / ♌1 2 — ♇ …

10

	1	2	3	4	5	6	7	8	9	10	11	12	13	14	15	16	17	18	19	20	21	22	23	24	25	26	27	28	29	30
☉	♎ 7	8	9	10	11	12	13	14	15	16	17	18	19	20	21	22	23	24	25	26	27	28	29	♏ 0	1	2	3	4
☽	8	20	2	15	28	11	25	9	23	8	22	7	22	6	20	4	17	1	14	27	9	22	4	17	29	11	23	4
☿	♏ 2	3	4	5	5	6	6	7	7	R 7	7	7	7	6	6	5	5	4	3	2	1	29	28	27	26	24	24	22	22
♀	♎ 12	13	15	16	17	18	20	21	22	23	25	26	27	28	29	♏ 0	1	2	3	5	6	7	8	9	11	12	13	15	16
♂	♋ 26	27	27	28	29	29	♌ 0	0	1	1	2	2	3	3	4	5	5	6	7	7	8	8	9	9	10	10	11

♃ 1 R 10 25 / ♓21 20 19 — ♄ 1 5 30 R / ♋15 16 16 — ♅ 1 R 23 D / ♒11 11 — ♆ 1 / ♌2 — ♇ …

11

	1	2	3	4	5	6	7	8	9	10	11	12	13	14	15	16	17	18	19	20	21	22	23	24	25	26	27	28	29	30
☉	♏ 8	9	10	11	12	13	14	15	16	17	18	19	20	21	22	23	24	25	26	27	28	29	♐ 0	1	2	3	4
☽	23	5	19	2	17	1	16	1	16	1	16	0	14	28	11	24	6	19	1	13	25	7	19	1	13	25	7
☿	♎ 21	20	19	18	17	16	15	14	14	14	D 14	14	15	15	16	17	18	19	21	22	23	25	26	28	29	♏ 0	2	3	5
♀	♏ 21	22	23	24	25	26	28	29	♐ 0	1	2	3	5	6	7	8	10	11	12	13	14	16	17	18	19	21	22	23
♂	♌ 13	13	14	14	14	15	15	16	16	16	16	17	17	17	18	18	18	18	19	19	19	20	20	20	21	21

♃ 1 R 15 30 / ♓18 18 19 — ♄ 1 2 R 30 / ♋16 16 15 — ♅ 1 15 / ♒11 12 — ♆ 1 6 R / ♌2 2 — ♇ …

12

	1	2	3	4	5	6	7	8	9	10	11	12	13	14	15	16	17	18	19	20	21	22	23	24	25	26	27	28	29	30
☉	♐ 8	9	10	11	12	13	14	15	16	17	18	19	20	21	22	23	24	25	26	27	28	29	♑ 0	1	2	3	4
☽	27	11	25	9	24	10	25	10	25	9	24	7	20	3	16	28	10	22	4	16	28	10	22	4	16	28	10	23
☿	♏ 29	♐ 0	1	3	5	6	8	9	11	13	14	16	17	19	20	22	24	25	27	28	♑ 0	1	3	5	6	8	9	11	13
♀	♐ 28	29	♑ 0	1	2	3	4	6	7	8	9	11	12	13	14	16	17	18	19	21	22	23	24	26	27	28	29	♒ 0	1	2
♂	♌ 24	25	25	25	26	26	26	26	27	27	27	27	27	27	27	28	28	28	28	28	28	29	29	29	29	29	29

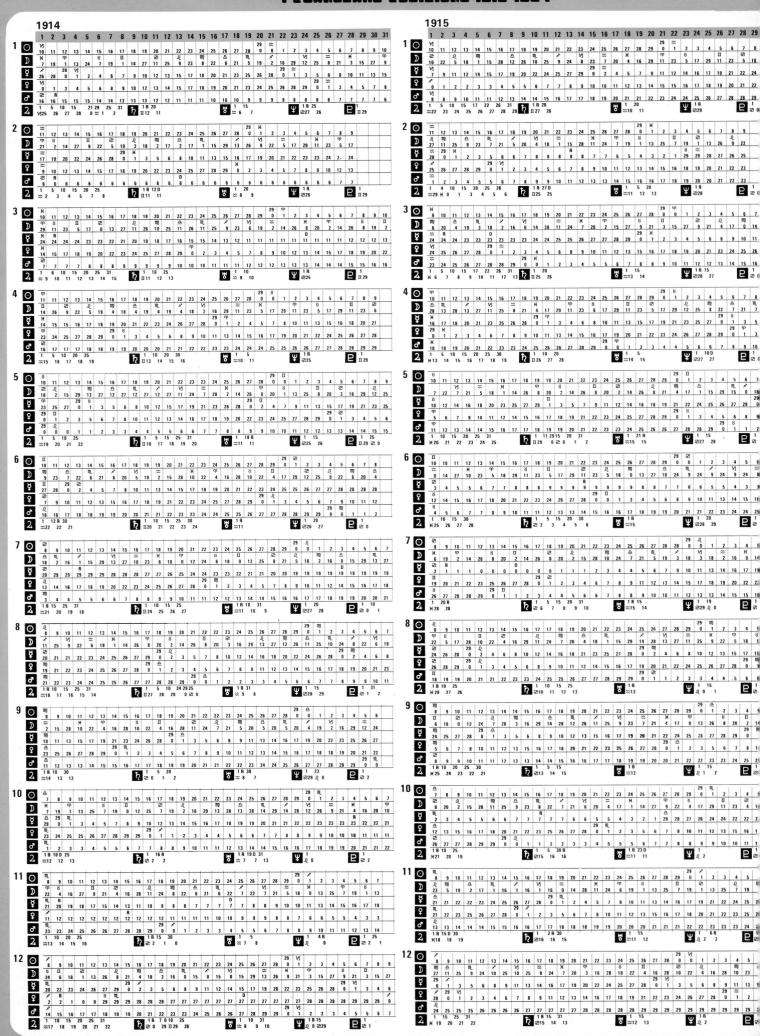

♃ 1 15 25 31 / ♓19 20 21 22 — ♄ 1 R 15 31 / ♋15 14 13 — ♅ 1 15 / ♒12 13 — ♆ 1 R / ♌2 — ♇ …

1916

1	2	3	4	5	6	7	8	9	10	11	12	13	14	15	16	17	18	19	20	21	22	23	24	25	26	27	28	29	30	31
♑ 10	11	12	13	14	15	16	17	18	19	20	21	22	23	24	25	26	27	28	29	29 0	♒ 1	2	3	4	5	6	7	8	9	10
♏ 18	♐ 2	18	♑ 3	18	♒ 3	18	♓ 2	16	29	♈ 12	25	♉ 7	19	♊ 1	13	25	♋ 7	19	♌ 1	13	25	♍ 7	20	♎ 3	16	29	♏ 13	27	♐ 12	26
♑ 19	21	22	24	26	27	29	29 0	♒ 2	4	5	7	8	10	11	13	14	15	17	18	19	19	20	21	21	22	R 22	22	21	21	20
♒ 7	8	9	11	12	13	14	16	17	18	19	21	22	23	24	25	27	28	29	29 0	♓ 2	3	4	5	7	8	9	10	11	13	14
♌ 29	R 29	29	29	29	29	29	29	29	29	29	29	29	28	28	28	28	28	27	27	27	27	26	26	26	25	25	25	24	24	24

1 5 10 20 25 31 — ♓22 23 24 25 26 27 · ♄ 1 R 10 25 — ♋13 12 11 · ♅ 1 20 — ♒14 15 · ♆ 1 R 10 — ♌ 2 1 · ♇ 1 31 — ♋ 2 1

1	2	3	4	5	6	7	8	9	10	11	12	13	14	15	16	17	18	19	20	21	22	23	24	25	26	27	28	29	30	31
♒ 11	12	13	14	15	16	17	18	19	20	21	22	23	24	25	26	27	28	29 0	♓ 0	1	2	3	4	5	6	7	8	9		
♑ 11	26	♒ 11	25	♓ 10	24	♈ 7	20	♉ 3	15	28	♊ 10	21	♋ 3	15	27	♌ 9	21	♍ 4	17	29	♎ 13	26	♏ 10	24	♐ 8	22	♑ 6	21		
♒ 19	R 18	17	16	15	14	12	11	10	9	8	8	7	7	6	6	6	D 6	6	6	7	7	8	8	9	10	11	11	12		
♓ 15	16	18	19	20	21	22	24	25	26	27	28	29 0	♈ 1	2	3	4	6	7	8	9	10	12	13	14	15	16	18	19		
♌ 23	R 23	22	22	21	21	21	21	20	20	19	19	19	18	18	17	17	17	16	16	16	15	15	15	14	14	14	13	13		

1 10 12 15 20 25 29 — ♓28 29 ♈0 1 2 3 4 · ♄ 1 R 5 29 — ♋11 10 9 · ♅ 1 5 25 — ♒15 16 17 · ♆ 1 R 15 — ♌ 1 0 · ♇ 1 — ♋ 1

1	2	3	4	5	6	7	8	9	10	11	12	13	14	15	16	17	18	19	20	21	22	23	24	25	26	27	28	29	30	31
♓ 10	11	12	13	14	15	16	17	18	19	20	21	22	23	24	25	26	27	28	29 0	♈ 0	1	2	3	4	5	6	7	8	9	10
♒ 5	19	♓ 4	18	♈ 2	15	28	♉ 11	23	♊ 5	17	29	♋ 11	23	♌ 5	17	29	♍ 13	26	♎ 9	23	♏ 7	21	♐ 5	19	♑ 3	17	♒ 1	15	29	♓ 13
♒ 13	14	15	16	18	19	20	21	22	24	25	26	28	29 0	♓ 1	2	3	5	6	8	10	11	13	14	16	18	19	21	23	25	26
♈ 20	21	22	24	25	26	27	28	29 0	♉ 1	2	3	4	5	6	7	9	10	11	12	13	14	15	17	18	19	20	21	22	23	24
♌ 13	R 13	12	12	12	12	11	11	11	11	11	11	11	10	10	10	10	10	10	10	10	D 10	10	10	10	10	10	10	11	11	11

1 5 10 15 20 25 31 — ♈4 5 6 7 8 10 11 · ♄ 1 R 12 D 25 — ♋ 9 9 10 · ♅ 1 15 — ♒17 18 · ♆ 1 R 20 — ♌ 0 ♋29 · ♇ 1 — ♋ 1

1	2	3	4	5	6	7	8	9	10	11	12	13	14	15	16	17	18	19	20	21	22	23	24	25	26	27	28	29	30	31
♈ 11	12	13	14	15	16	17	18	19	20	21	22	23	24	25	26	27	28	29	29 0	♉ 1	2	3	4	5	6	7	8	9	10	
♓ 27	♈ 10	23	♉ 6	19	♊ 1	13	25	♋ 7	19	♌ 1	13	25	♍ 8	21	♎ 4	18	♏ 2	16	♐ 1	15	29	♑ 14	28	♒ 12	26	♓ 9	23	♈ 6	19	
♓ 28	29 0	♈ 2	4	6	7	9	11	13	15	17	19	22	24	26	28	29 0	♉ 2	4	6	8	11	13	15	17	19	21	22	24	26	
♉ 25	27	28	29	29 0	♊ 1	2	3	4	5	6	7	8	9	10	11	12	13	14	15	16	17	18	19	20	21	22	23	24	25	
♌ 11	11	11	11	12	12	12	12	12	13	13	13	13	14	14	14	14	15	15	15	15	16	16	16	16	17	17	17	18	18	

1 5 10 15 20 25 30 — ♈11 12 14 15 16 17 18 · ♄ 1 20 30 — ♋10 11 12 · ♅ 1 5 — ♒18 19 · ♆ 1 R 10 D — ♋29 29 · ♇ 1 — ♋ 1

1	2	3	4	5	6	7	8	9	10	11	12	13	14	15	16	17	18	19	20	21	22	23	24	25	26	27	28	29	30	31
♉ 11	12	13	14	14	15	16	17	18	19	20	21	22	23	24	25	26	27	28	29	29 0	♊ 1	2	3	4	5	6	7	8	9	10
♉ 2	15	27	♊ 9	21	♋ 3	15	27	♌ 9	21	♍ 3	16	29	♎ 12	26	♏ 10	25	♐ 10	25	♑ 9	24	♒ 8	23	♓ 6	20	♈ 3	16	29	♉ 11	24	♊ 6
♉ 28	29 0	♊ 1	3	4	6	7	8	10	11	12	13	14	15	15	16	17	17	18	18	19	19	19	19	R 19	19	19	19	18	18	18
♊ 26	27	28	29	29 0	♋ 0	1	2	3	4	5	5	6	7	8	8	9	10	10	11	12	12	13	14	14	15	15	16	16	17	17
♌ 18	19	19	20	20	20	21	21	21	22	22	23	23	23	24	24	25	25	26	26	27	27	27	28	28	29	29	29 0	♍ 0	1	1

1 10 15 20 25 31 — ♈19 21 22 23 24 25 · ♄ 1 15 25 31 — ♋12 13 14 15 · ♅ 1 15 25 R — ♒19 20 20 · ♆ 1 2 — ♋29 ♌ 0 · ♇ 1 20 — ♋ 1 2

1	2	3	4	5	6	7	8	9	10	11	12	13	14	15	16	17	18	19	20	21	22	23	24	25	26	27	28	29	30	31
♊ 10	11	12	13	14	15	16	17	18	19	20	21	22	23	24	25	26	27	28	29	29 0	♋ 1	1	2	3	4	5	6	7	8	
♊ 18	♋ 0	12	24	♌ 5	17	29	♍ 11	24	♎ 7	20	♏ 4	18	♐ 3	18	♑ 3	18	♒ 3	18	♓ 2	16	♈ 0	13	26	♉ 8	21	♊ 3	15	27	♋ 9	
♊ 17	R 17	16	16	15	15	14	13	13	12	12	12	11	11	11	11	11	D 11	11	11	11	11	12	12	13	13	14	15	16	17	
♋ 17	18	18	18	19	19	19	19	19	20	20	R 20	20	19	19	19	19	19	19	18	18	18	17	17	16	16	15	15	14	13	
♍ 2	2	3	3	4	4	5	5	6	6	7	7	8	8	9	9	10	10	11	11	12	12	13	13	14	15	15	16	16	17	

1 5 10 15 20 26 — ♈25 26 27 28 29 ♉ 0 · ♄ 1 10 20 25 — ♋15 16 17 18 · ♅ 1 R 5 — ♒20 19 · ♆ 1 10 — ♌ 0 1 · ♇ 1 30 — ♋ 2 ♋ 3

1	2	3	4	5	6	7	8	9	10	11	12	13	14	15	16	17	18	19	20	21	22	23	24	25	26	27	28	29	30	31
♋ 9	10	11	12	13	14	15	16	17	18	19	20	21	22	22	23	24	25	26	27	28	29	29 0	♌ 1	2	3	4	5	6	7	8
♋ 21	♌ 2	14	26	♍ 8	20	♎ 3	16	29	♏ 13	27	♐ 12	26	♑ 12	27	♒ 12	27	♓ 11	25	♈ 9	22	♉ 5	18	♊ 0	12	24	♋ 6	18	29	♌ 11	23
♊ 18	19	20	21	22	23	25	26	28	29 0	♋ 1	3	5	6	8	10	12	14	16	18	20	22	24	27	29	♌ 0	3	5	7	9	11
♋ 13	R 12	12	11	10	10	9	8	8	7	7	6	6	5	5	5	4	4	4	4	3	3	3	3	D 3	3	3	3	3	4	4
♍ 17	18	18	19	20	20	21	21	22	22	23	24	24	25	25	26	26	27	28	28	29	29	29 0	♎ 1	1	2	2	3	4	4	5

1 10 15 25 — ♉ 1 2 3 4 · ♄ 1 5 10 20 25 — ♋18 19 20 21 22 · ♅ 1 R 20 — ♒19 18 · ♆ 1 10 — ♌ 1 2 · ♇ 1 — ♋ 3

1	2	3	4	5	6	7	8	9	10	11	12	13	14	15	16	17	18	19	20	21	22	23	24	25	26	27	28	29	30	31
♌ 9	10	11	12	13	13	14	15	16	17	18	19	20	21	22	23	24	25	26	27	28	29	29 0	♍ 1	2	3	4	5	6	7	8
♍ 5	17	♎ 0	13	25	♏ 9	22	♐ 6	21	♑ 5	20	♒ 5	20	♓ 5	20	♈ 4	18	♉ 1	14	27	♊ 9	21	♋ 3	14	26	♌ 8	20	♍ 2	14	27	♎ 10
♌ 13	15	17	19	21	23	25	27	29	29 0	♍ 2	4	6	7	9	11	12	14	16	17	19	20	22	23	25	26	28	29	29 0	♎ 2	3
♋ 4	4	5	5	5	6	6	6	7	7	8	8	9	10	10	11	12	12	13	14	14	15	16	17	17	18	19	20	21	21	22
♎ 5	6	7	7	8	9	9	10	10	11	12	12	13	14	14	15	15	16	17	17	18	19	19	20	21	21	22	22	23	24	24

1 5 25 R — ♉ 4 5 5 · ♄ 1 5 10 20 31 — ♋22 23 24 25 26 · ♅ 1 R 15 — ♒18 17 · ♆ 1 5 31 — ♌ 2 3 4 · ♇ 1 25 — ♋ 3 4

1	2	3	4	5	6	7	8	9	10	11	12	13	14	15	16	17	18	19	20	21	22	23	24	25	26	27	28	29	30	31
♍ 9	9	10	11	12	13	14	15	16	17	18	19	20	21	22	23	24	25	26	27	28	29	29 0	♎ 1	2	3	4	5	6	7	
♎ 23	♏ 6	19	♐ 3	16	♑ 1	15	29	♒ 14	29	♓ 13	28	♈ 12	26	♉ 9	22	♊ 5	17	29	♋ 11	23	♌ 4	16	28	♍ 11	23	♎ 6	19	♏ 2	16	
♎ 4	5	7	8	9	10	11	12	13	14	15	16	17	17	18	19	19	20	20	20	20	21	R 21	20	20	20	19	19	18	17	
♋ 23	24	25	26	27	28	29	29 0	♌ 0	1	2	3	4	5	6	7	8	9	10	11	12	13	14	15	16	17	19	20	21	22	
♎ 25	26	26	27	28	28	29	29 0	♏ 0	1	2	2	3	4	4	5	6	6	7	8	8	9	10	10	11	12	13	13	14	15	

1 R 20 30 — ♉ 5 4 3 · ♄ 1 5 15 30 — ♋26 27 28 29 · ♅ 1 R 10 — ♒17 16 · ♆ 1 — ♌ 4 · ♇ 1 — ♋ 4

1	2	3	4	5	6	7	8	9	10	11	12	13	14	15	16	17	18	19	20	21	22	23	24	25	26	27	28	29	30	31
♎ 8	9	10	11	12	13	14	15	16	17	18	19	20	21	22	23	24	25	26	27	28	29	29 0	♏ 1	2	3	4	5	6	7	8
♏ 29	♐ 13	27	♑ 11	25	♒ 10	24	♓ 8	22	♈ 6	20	♉ 4	17	♊ 0	13	25	♋ 7	19	♌ 0	12	24	♍ 6	19	♎ 2	15	28	♏ 12	26	♐ 10	24	♑ 8
♎ 16	R 15	14	13	12	10	9	8	7	7	6	6	5	D 5	5	6	6	7	8	8	9	11	12	13	14	16	17	19	20	22	24
♌ 23	24	25	26	27	28	29 0	♍ 0	2	3	4	5	6	7	8	9	11	12	13	14	15	16	18	19	20	21	22	23	25	26	27
♏ 15	16	17	17	18	19	19	20	21	22	22	23	24	24	25	26	27	27	28	29	29	29 0	♐ 1	2	2	3	4	4	5	6	7

1 R 10 15 25 26 0 27 — ♉ 3 2 1 0 29 ♈29 · ♄ 1 17 — ♋29 ♌ 0 · ♅ 1 R 26 D — ♒16 16 · ♆ 1 10 — ♌ 4 5 · ♇ 1 — ♋ 4

1	2	3	4	5	6	7	8	9	10	11	12	13	14	15	16	17	18	19	20	21	22	23	24	25	26	27	28	29	30	31
♏ 9	10	11	12	13	14	15	16	17	18	19	20	21	22	23	24	25	26	27	28	29 0	♐ 0	1	2	3	4	5	6	7	8	
♑ 22	♒ 6	20	♓ 4	18	♈ 2	16	29	♉ 12	25	♊ 8	21	♋ 3	15	27	♌ 8	20	♍ 2	14	27	♎ 9	23	♏ 6	20	♐ 5	19	♑ 4	18	♒ 3	17	
♎ 25	27	28	29 0	♏ 1	3	5	6	8	10	11	13	14	16	18	19	21	22	24	26	27	29	29 0	♐ 2	4	5	7	8	10	11	
♍ 28	29	29 0	♎ 2	3	4	5	6	8	9	10	11	12	14	15	16	17	18	20	21	22	23	24	26	27	28	29	29 0	♏ 2	3	
♐ 7	8	9	10	10	11	12	12	13	14	15	15	16	17	18	18	19	20	21	21	22	23	24	24	25	26	27	27	28	29	

1 R 10 15 25 — ♈29 28 27 26 · ♄ 1 12 R — ♌ 0 0 · ♅ 1 — ♒16 · ♆ 1 7 R — ♌ 5 5 · ♇ 1 — ♋ 4

1	2	3	4	5	6	7	8	9	10	11	12	13	14	15	16	17	18	19	20	21	22	23	24	25	26	27	28	29	30	31
♐ 9	10	11	12	13	14	15	16	17	18	19	20	21	22	23	24	25	26	27	28	29	29 0	♑ 1	2	3	4	5	6	7	8	9
♓ 1	15	29	♈ 12	26	♉ 9	22	♊ 4	17	29	♋ 11	23	♌ 5	16	28	♍ 10	22	♎ 5	17	♏ 0	14	28	♐ 13	27	♑ 12	27	♒ 12	27	♓ 11	26	♈ 9
♐ 13	15	16	18	19	21	22	24	25	27	29	29 0	♑ 2	3	5	6	8	10	11	13	14	16	17	19	20	22	23	24	26	27	28
♏ 4	5	7	8	9	10	12	13	14	15	16	18	19	20	21	23	24	25	26	28	29	29 0	♐ 1	3	4	5	6	8	9	10	11
29 0	♑ 0	1	2	3	3	4	5	6	7	7	8	9	10	10	11	12	13	13	14	15	16	17	17	18	19	20	20	21	22	23

1 R 10 21 D — ♈26 25 25 · ♄ 1 R 7 0 10 31 — ♌ 0 29 ♋29 28 · ♅ 1 15 — ♒16 17 · ♆ 1 R 10 — ♌ 5 4 · ♇ 1 20 — ♋ 4 3

1917

	1	2	3	4	5	6	7	8	9	10	11	12	13	14	15	16	17	18	19	20	21	22	23	24	25	26	27	28	29	30	31
1 ☉	♑ 10	11	12	13	14	15	16	17	18	19	20	21	22	23	24	25	26	27	28	29 0	♒ 1	2	3	4	5	6	7	8	9	10	11
☽	♈ 23	♉ 6	19	♊ 1	13	26	♋ 8	19	♌ 1	13	25	♍ 7	19	♎ 1	13	26	♏ 9	22	♐ 6	20	♑ 5	20	♒ 5	21	♓ 6	20	♈ 5	19	♉ 2	15	28
☿	29 0	♒ 1	2	3	4	4	5	5	5	R 5	5	5	4	4	3	2	0	♑ 29	♑ 28	27	26	24	23	22	21	21	20	20	20	19	20
♀	♐ 12	14	15	16	17	19	20	21	22	24	25	26	27	29	29 0	♑ 1	2	4	5	6	7	9	10	11	12	14	15	16	17	19	20
♂	♑ 24	24	25	26	27	27	28	29	29 0	♒ 1	1	2	3	4	5	5	6	7	8	8	9	10	11	12	12	13	14	15	16	16	17

♃ 1 5 20 31 — ♈25 26 27 28 · ♄ 1 R 15 25 — ♋28 27 26 · ♅ 1 5 25 — ♒17 18 19 · ♆ 1 R 20 — ♌ 4 3 · ♇ 1 31 — ♋ 3 2

	1	2	3	4	5	6	7	8	9	10	11	12	13	14	15	16	17	18	19	20	21	22	23	24	25	26	27	28	29	30	31
2 ☉	♒ 12	13	14	15	16	17	18	19	20	21	22	23	24	25	26	27	28	29	29 0	♓ 1	2	3	4	5	6	7	8	9			
☽	♊ 10	23	♋ 5	16	28	♌ 10	22	♍ 4	16	28	♎ 10	22	♏ 5	18	♐ 1	15	29	♑ 13	28	♒ 13	29	♓ 14	29	♈ 13	27	♉ 11	24	♊ 7			
☿	♑ 20	20	20	21	21	22	23	23	24	25	26	27	28	29	29 0	♒ 1	3	4	5	6	8	9	10	12	13	14	16	17			
♀	♑ 21	22	24	25	26	27	29	29 0	♒ 1	2	4	5	6	7	9	10	11	12	14	15	16	17	19	20	21	22	24	25			
♂	♒ 18	19	20	20	21	22	23	23	24	25	26	27	27	28	29	29 0	♓ 1	1	2	3	4	5	5	6	7	8	8	9			

♃ 1 5 12 29 15 20 25 28 — ♈28 29 0 ♉ 0 1 2 3 · ♄ 1 R 5 20 — ♋26 25 24 · ♅ 1 10 28 — ♒19 20 21 · ♆ 1 R 25 — ♌ 3 2 · ♇ 1 — ♋ 2

	1	2	3	4	5	6	7	8	9	10	11	12	13	14	15	16	17	18	19	20	21	22	23	24	25	26	27	28	29	30	31
3 ☉	♓ 10	11	12	13	14	15	16	17	18	19	20	21	22	23	24	25	26	27	28	29	29 0	♈ 1	2	3	4	5	6	7	8	9	10
☽	♊ 19	♋ 1	13	25	♌ 7	19	♍ 1	13	25	♎ 7	19	♏ 2	15	28	♐ 11	25	♑ 9	23	♒ 7	22	♓ 7	22	♈ 7	21	♉ 5	19	♊ 2	15	28	♋ 10	22
☿	♒ 19	20	22	23	25	26	28	29 0	♓ 1	3	5	6	8	10	11	13	15	17	19	20	22	24	26	28	29 0	♈ 2	4	6	8	10	12
♀	♒ 26	27	29	29 0	♓ 1	2	4	5	6	7	9	10	11	12	13	15	16	17	18	20	21	22	23	25	26	27	28	29 0	♈ 1	2	3
♂	♓ 10	11	12	12	13	14	15	16	16	17	18	19	20	20	21	22	23	23	24	25	26	27	27	28	29	29 0	♈ 0	1	2	3	4

♃ 1 5 10 15 20 25 31 — ♉ 3 4 5 6 7 8 9 · ♄ 1 R 25 D 31 — ♋24 23 24 · ♅ 1 20 — ♒21 22 · ♆ 1 R — ♌ 2 · ♇ 1 — ♋ 2

	1	2	3	4	5	6	7	8	9	10	11	12	13	14	15	16	17	18	19	20	21	22	23	24	25	26	27	28	29	30	31
4 ☉	♈ 11	12	13	14	15	16	17	18	19	20	21	22	23	24	25	26	27	28	29	29 0	♉ 1	2	3	4	5	6	6	7	8	9	
☽	♌ 3	15	27	♍ 9	21	♎ 4	16	29	♏ 12	25	♐ 8	22	♑ 5	19	♒ 3	18	♓ 2	16	♈ 1	15	29	♉ 13	27	♊ 10	23	♋ 5	18	29	♌ 11	23	
☿	♈ 14	16	18	20	22	24	26	28	29 0	♉ 2	4	6	8	10	11	13	15	16	18	19	20	22	23	24	25	26	26	27	28	28	
♀	♈ 5	6	7	8	10	11	12	13	15	16	17	18	19	21	22	23	24	26	27	28	29 0	♉ 1	2	3	4	6	7	8	9	10	
♂	♈ 4	5	6	7	7	8	9	10	11	11	12	13	14	14	15	16	17	17	18	19	20	20	21	22	23	23	24	25	26	27	

♃ 1 5 10 15 20 25 30 — ♉ 9 10 11 12 14 15 16 · ♄ 1 30 — ♋24 25 · ♅ 1 10 — ♒22 23 · ♆ 1 R 13 D — ♌ 2 2 · ♇ 1 — ♋ 2

	1	2	3	4	5	6	7	8	9	10	11	12	13	14	15	16	17	18	19	20	21	22	23	24	25	26	27	28	29	30	31
5 ☉	♉ 10	11	12	13	14	15	16	17	18	19	20	21	22	23	24	25	26	27	28	29	29 0	♊ 1	2	3	4	4	5	6	7	8	9
☽	♍ 5	17	29	♎ 12	25	♏ 8	21	♐ 5	18	♑ 2	16	♒ 0	14	29	♓ 13	27	♈ 11	25	♉ 9	22	♊ 5	18	♋ 1	13	25	♌ 7	19	♍ 1	13	25	♎ 7
☿	♉ 29	29	29	29	29	R 29	29	29	29	28	28	28	27	27	26	25	25	24	24	23	23	22	22	21	21	21	21	20	20	D 20	21
♀	♉ 12	13	14	15	17	18	19	20	22	23	24	25	27	28	29	29 0	♊ 1	3	4	5	6	8	9	10	11	13	14	15	16	17	19
♂	♈ 27	28	29	29 0	♉ 0	1	2	3	3	4	5	6	6	7	8	8	9	10	11	11	12	13	14	14	15	16	17	17	18	19	19

♃ 1 5 10 12 15 20 25 31 — ♉16 17 18 19 20 21 22 23 · ♄ 1 15 25 — ♋25 26 27 · ♅ 1 20 29 R — ♒23 24 24 · ♆ 1 31 — ♌ 2 3 · ♇ 1 — ♋ 3

	1	2	3	4	5	6	7	8	9	10	11	12	13	14	15	16	17	18	19	20	21	22	23	24	25	26	27	28	29	30	31
6 ☉	♊ 10	11	12	13	14	15	16	17	18	19	20	21	22	23	24	25	26	26	27	28	29	29 0	♋ 1	2	3	4	5	6	7	8	
☽	♎ 20	♏ 3	16	29	♐ 13	28	♑ 12	26	♒ 11	25	♓ 10	24	♈ 8	21	♉ 5	18	♊ 1	14	27	♋ 9	22	♌ 4	16	27	♍ 9	21	♎ 3	15	28	♏ 11	
☿	♉ 21	21	21	22	22	23	23	24	25	26	27	27	28	29 0	♊ 1	2	3	4	6	7	9	10	12	13	15	17	18	20	22	24	
♀	♊ 20	21	22	24	25	26	27	28	29 0	♋ 1	2	3	5	6	7	8	9	11	12	13	14	16	17	18	19	21	22	23	24	25	
♂	♉ 20	21	22	22	23	24	25	25	26	27	27	28	29	29 0	♊ 0	1	2	2	3	4	5	5	6	7	7	8	9	9	10	11	

♃ 1 7 10 15 20 25 29 29 30 — ♉24 25 26 27 28 29 0 ♊ 0 · ♄ 1 5 15 24 30 — ♋27 28 29 ♌ 0 1 · ♅ 1 R 10 — ♒24 23 · ♆ 1 — ♌ 3 · ♇ 1 20 — ♋ 3 4

	1	2	3	4	5	6	7	8	9	10	11	12	13	14	15	16	17	18	19	20	21	22	23	24	25	26	27	28	29	30	31
7 ☉	♋ 9	10	11	12	13	14	15	16	17	17	18	19	20	21	22	23	24	25	26	27	28	29	29 0	♌ 1	2	3	4	5	6	7	8
☽	♏ 24	♐ 8	22	♑ 6	21	♒ 6	21	♓ 5	20	♈ 4	18	♉ 2	15	28	♊ 11	24	♋ 6	18	♌ 0	12	24	♍ 6	18	29	♎ 12	24	♏ 6	19	♐ 2	16	♑ 0
☿	♊ 26	28	29 0	♋ 2	4	6	8	11	13	15	17	19	21	23	26	28	29 0	♌ 2	4	6	8	10	12	14	15	17	19	21	23	24	26
♀	♋ 27	28	29	29 0	♌ 2	3	4	5	6	8	9	10	11	13	14	15	16	17	19	20	21	22	23	25	26	27	28	29 0	♍ 1	2	3
♂	♊ 12	12	13	14	14	15	16	16	17	18	19	19	20	21	21	22	23	23	24	25	25	26	27	27	28	29	29	29 0	♋ 1	1	2

♃ 1 5 10 15 20 25 31 — ♊ 0 1 2 3 4 5 6 · ♄ 1 10 20 25 31 — ♌ 1 2 3 4 5 · ♅ 1 R 25 — ♒23 22 · ♆ 1 5 31 — ♌ 3 4 5 · ♇ 1 — ♋ 4

	1	2	3	4	5	6	7	8	9	10	11	12	13	14	15	16	17	18	19	20	21	22	23	24	25	26	27	28	29	30	31
8 ☉	♌ 8	9	10	11	12	13	14	15	16	17	18	19	20	21	22	23	24	25	26	27	28	29	29 0	♍ 1	2	2	3	4	5	6	7
☽	♑ 14	29	♒ 14	29	♓ 15	29	♈ 14	28	♉ 12	25	♊ 8	21	♋ 3	15	27	♌ 9	21	♍ 3	15	27	♎ 8	21	♏ 3	15	28	♐ 11	25	♑ 8	23	♒ 8	23
☿	♌ 28	29 0	♍ 1	3	4	6	7	9	10	11	13	14	16	17	18	19	21	22	23	24	25	26	27	28	29	29 0	♎ 0	1	2	2	3
♀	♍ 4	6	7	8	9	10	12	13	14	15	17	18	19	20	21	23	24	25	26	27	29	29 0	♎ 1	2	3	5	6	7	8	9	11
♂	♋ 3	3	4	5	5	6	7	7	8	9	9	10	11	11	12	13	13	14	15	15	16	17	17	18	18	19	20	20	21	22	22

♃ 1 5 10 15 20 31 — ♊ 6 7 7 8 9 10 · ♄ 1 10 20 25 — ♌ 5 6 7 8 · ♅ 1 R 20 — ♒22 21 · ♆ 1 31 — ♌ 5 6 · ♇ 1 5 — ♋ 4 5

	1	2	3	4	5	6	7	8	9	10	11	12	13	14	15	16	17	18	19	20	21	22	23	24	25	26	27	28	29	30	31
9 ☉	♍ 8	9	10	11	12	13	14	15	16	17	18	19	20	21	22	23	24	25	26	27	28	29	29 0	♎ 1	2	3	4	5	6	7	
☽	♓ 8	23	♈ 8	23	♉ 7	21	♊ 5	17	♋ 0	12	24	♌ 6	18	29	♍ 12	24	♎ 6	18	♏ 0	12	25	♐ 8	21	♑ 4	18	♒ 2	16	♓ 1	16	♈ 2	
☿	♎ 3	3	4	4	4	R 4	4	4	3	3	2	1	1	♍ 29	♍ 29	28	27	26	25	24	23	22	21	20	20	20	19	D 19	20	20	
♀	♎ 12	13	14	15	17	18	19	20	21	23	24	25	26	27	29	29 0	♏ 1	2	3	5	6	7	8	9	10	12	13	14	15	16	
♂	♋ 23	24	24	25	25	26	27	27	28	29	29	29 0	♌ 1	1	2	2	3	4	4	5	5	6	7	7	8	8	9	10	10	11	

♃ 1 10 — ♊10 11 · ♄ 1 10 20 30 — ♌ 9 10 11 12 · ♅ 1 R 15 — ♒21 20 · ♆ 1 30 — ♌ 6 7 · ♇ 1 — ♋ 5

	1	2	3	4	5	6	7	8	9	10	11	12	13	14	15	16	17	18	19	20	21	22	23	24	25	26	27	28	29	30	31
10 ☉	♎ 8	9	10	11	12	12	13	14	15	16	17	18	19	20	21	22	23	24	25	26	27	28	29 0	♏ 0	1	2	3	4	5	6	7
☽	♈ 17	♉ 1	16	29	♊ 13	26	♋ 9	21	♌ 3	15	27	♍ 8	20	♎ 2	14	27	♏ 9	22	♐ 5	18	♑ 1	14	28	♒ 12	26	♓ 11	25	♈ 10	25	♉ 10	24
☿	♍ 20	21	22	23	24	25	26	27	29	29 0	♎ 2	3	5	7	8	10	12	13	15	17	18	20	22	24	25	27	29	29 0	♏ 2	4	5
♀	♏ 18	19	20	21	22	23	25	26	27	28	29	♐ 0	2	3	4	5	6	7	9	10	11	12	13	14	15	17	18	19	20	21	22
♂	♌ 11	12	13	13	14	14	15	16	16	17	17	18	19	19	20	20	21	21	22	23	23	24	24	25	25	26	27	27	28	28	29

♃ 1 R 25 — ♊11 10 · ♄ 1 15 31 — ♌12 13 14 · ♅ 1 R 30 D — ♒20 20 · ♆ 1 — ♌ 7 · ♇ 1 — ♋ 5

	1	2	3	4	5	6	7	8	9	10	11	12	13	14	15	16	17	18	19	20	21	22	23	24	25	26	27	28	29	30	31
11 ☉	♏ 8	9	10	11	12	13	14	15	16	17	18	19	20	21	22	23	24	25	26	27	28	29 0	♐ 0	1	2	3	4	5	6	7	
☽	♊ 8	21	♋ 4	17	29	♌ 11	23	♍ 5	17	29	♎ 11	23	♏ 5	18	♐ 1	14	28	♑ 11	25	♒ 9	23	♓ 7	21	♈ 5	20	♉ 4	18	♊ 2	16	29	
☿	♏ 7	9	10	12	13	15	17	18	20	21	23	25	26	28	29 0	♐ 1	2	4	5	7	9	10	12	13	15	16	18	19	21	22	
♀	♐ 23	25	26	27	28	29	29 0	♑ 1	2	4	5	6	7	8	9	10	11	12	13	14	15	17	18	19	20	21	22	23	24	25	
♂	♌ 29	29 0	♍ 0	1	1	2	3	3	4	4	5	5	6	6	7	7	8	8	9	9	10	10	11	11	12	12	13	13	14	14	

♃ 1 R 5 15 20 30 — ♊10 9 8 7 6 · ♄ 1 26 R — ♌14 14 · ♅ 1 — ♒20 · ♆ 1 10 R — ♌ 7 7 · ♇ 1 — ♋ 5

	1	2	3	4	5	6	7	8	9	10	11	12	13	14	15	16	17	18	19	20	21	22	23	24	25	26	27	28	29	30	31
12 ☉	♐ 9	10	11	12	13	14	15	16	17	18	19	20	21	22	23	24	25	26	27	28	29 0	♑ 0	1	2	3	4	5	6	7	8	9
☽	♋ 12	24	♌ 7	19	♍ 1	13	25	♎ 6	19	♏ 1	14	26	♐ 10	23	♑ 7	21	♒ 5	19	♓ 4	18	♈ 2	16	♉ 0	14	28	♊ 11	24	♋ 7	20	♌ 2	15
☿	♐ 24	25	27	28	29 0	♑ 1	2	4	5	7	8	9	11	12	13	14	15	16	17	18	18	19	19	20	R 20	19	19	18	18	17	16
♀	♑ 26	27	28	29	29 0	♒ 1	2	3	4	5	6	6	7	8	9	10	11	12	13	13	14	15	16	17	17	18	19	19	20	21	21
♂	♍ 15	15	16	16	17	17	18	18	19	19	20	20	20	21	21	22	22	22	23	23	24	24	24	24	25	25	25	26	26	26	27

♃ 1 R 5 15 25 31 — ♊ 6 5 4 3 2 · ♄ 1 R 31 — ♌14 13 · ♅ 1 15 — ♒20 21 · ♆ 1 R 25 — ♌ 7 6 · ♇ 1 20 — ♋ 5 4

I PLANETARY POSITIONS 1910-1984

1918

1

	1	2	3	4	5	6	7	8	9	10	11	12	13	14	15	16	17	18	19	20	21	22	23	24	25	26	27	28	29	30	31
☉	♑ 10	11	12	13	14	15	16	17	18	19	20	21	22	23	24	25	26	27	28	29 0	♒ 0	1	2	3	4	5	6	7	8	9	10
☽	♌ 27	♍ 9	20	♎ 2	14	26	♏ 9	21	♐ 4	18	♑ 1	15	♒ 0	15	29	♓ 14	29	♈ 13	27	♉ 11	24	♊ 8	21	♋ 3	16	28	♌ 11	23	♍ 5	17	29
☿	♑ 14	R 13	12	11	9	8	7	6	5	4	4	4	3	D 3	3	4	4	4	5	6	6	7	8	9	10	11	12	13	14	15	17
♀	♒ 22	23	23	24	24	25	25	26	26	26	27	27	27	28	28	28	28	28	28	28	R 28	28	28	28	28	28	27	27	27	26	26
♂	♊ 27	R 27	28	28	29	29	29	29	29	29	29 0	♎ 0	0	1	1	1	1	1	2	2	2	2	2	2	2	2	3	3	3	3	3

♃ 1 R 20 28 D / ♊ 2 1 1 — ♄ 1 R 15 25 / ♌13 12 11 — ♅ 1 10 31 / ♒21 22 23 — ♆ 1 R 31 / ♌ 6 5 — ♇ 1 / ♋ 4

2

	1	2	3	4	5	6	7	8	9	10	11	12	13	14	15	16	17	18	19	20	21	22	23	24	25	26	27	28
☉	♒ 12	13	14	15	16	17	18	19	20	21	22	23	24	25	26	27	28	29	29 0	♓ 1	2	3	4	5	6	7	8	9
☽	♎ 10	22	♏ 4	17	29	♐ 12	25	♑ 9	23	♒ 8	23	♓ 8	23	♈ 8	23	♉ 7	21	♊ 5	18	♋ 0	13	25	♌ 7	20	♍ 2	13	25	♎ 7
☿	♑ 18	19	20	22	23	24	26	27	29	29 0	♒ 1	3	4	6	7	9	10	12	13	15	17	18	20	22	23	25	27	28
♀	♒ 25	R 25	24	24	23	23	22	21	21	20	19	19	18	18	17	17	16	16	15	15	14	14	13	13	13	13	13	13
♂	♎ 3	3	3	R 3	3	3	3	3	3	3	2	2	2	2	2	2	2	2	1	1	1	1	0	0	♉ 29	♍ 29	29	29

♃ 1 10 25 / ♊ 1 2 3 — ♄ 1 R 10 20 / ♌11 10 9 — ♅ 1 15 / ♒23 24 — ♆ 1 R / ♌ 5 — ♇ 1 15 / ♋ 4 3

3

	1	2	3	4	5	6	7	8	9	10	11	12	13	14	15	16	17	18	19	20	21	22	23	24	25	26	27	28	29	30	31
☉	♓ 10	11	12	13	14	15	16	17	18	19	20	21	22	23	24	25	26	27	28	29	29 0	♈ 1	2	3	4	5	6	7	8	9	10
☽	♎ 19	♏ 1	13	25	♐ 8	21	♑ 4	17	♒ 1	16	♓ 1	16	♈ 2	17	♉ 2	16	♊ 0	14	27	♋ 10	22	♌ 5	17	29	♍ 10	22	♎ 4	16	28	♏ 10	22
☿	♓ 0	2	4	5	7	9	11	13	15	17	18	20	22	24	26	28	29 0	♈ 2	4	6	8	10	12	14	16	18	20	22	23	25	27
♀	♒ 13	R 13	D 13	13	13	13	13	13	13	14	14	14	15	15	16	16	17	17	18	18	19	19	20	21	21	22	23	23	24	25	26
♂	♍ 29	R 28	28	28	27	27	27	26	26	26	25	25	24	24	24	23	23	22	22	22	21	21	21	20	20	19	19	19	18	18	18

♃ 1 5 15 20 31 / ♊ 3 4 5 6 7 — ♄ 1 R 10 / ♌ 9 8 — ♅ 1 5 20 / ♒24 25 26 — ♆ 1 R 10 / ♌ 5 4 — ♇ 1 / ♋ 3

4

	1	2	3	4	5	6	7	8	9	10	11	12	13	14	15	16	17	18	19	20	21	22	23	24	25	26	27	28	29	30
☉	♈ 11	12	13	14	15	16	17	18	19	20	21	22	23	24	25	26	26	27	28	29 0	♉ 0	1	2	3	4	5	6	7	8	9
☽	♐ 5	17	♑ 0	13	26	♒ 10	25	♓ 9	25	♈ 10	25	♉ 10	25	♊ 9	23	♋ 6	19	♌ 1	13	25	♍ 7	19	♎ 1	13	25	♏ 7	19	♐ 2	14	27
☿	♈ 28	29 0	♉ 1	2	4	5	6	7	8	8	9	9	10	10	10	10	R 10	10	10	10	9	9	8	8	7	6	6	5	4	4
♀	♒ 26	27	28	29	29 0	♓ 0	1	2	3	4	5	6	7	8	8	9	10	11	12	13	14	15	16	17	18	19	20	21	22	23
♂	♍ 17	R 17	17	17	16	16	16	16	15	15	15	15	15	14	14	14	14	14	14	14	14	14	14	14	D 14	14	14	14	14	14

♃ 1 10 15 20 25 30 / ♊ 8 9 10 11 12 13 — ♄ 1 R 5 9 D 20 / ♌ 8 7 7 8 — ♅ 1 15 / ♒26 27 — ♆ 1 R 15 D / ♌ 4 4 — ♇ 1 20 / ♋ 3 4

5

	1	2	3	4	5	6	7	8	9	10	11	12	13	14	15	16	17	18	19	20	21	22	23	24	25	26	27	28	29	30	31
☉	♉ 10	11	12	13	14	15	16	17	18	19	20	21	22	23	24	25	26	27	28	29	29 0	♊ 0	1	2	3	4	5	6	7	8	9
☽	♑ 10	23	♒ 7	20	♓ 5	19	♈ 4	19	♉ 3	18	♊ 3	17	♋ 1	14	27	♌ 9	22	♍ 4	16	28	♎ 10	21	♏ 4	16	28	♐ 11	24	♑ 7	20	♒ 3	17
☿	♉ 3	R 3	2	2	1	1	1	0	0	D 0	0	0	1	1	1	2	2	3	3	4	5	6	6	7	8	9	10	12	13	14	15
♀	♓ 24	25	26	27	28	29 0	♈ 1	2	3	4	5	6	7	8	9	10	11	12	13	15	16	17	18	19	20	21	22	23	25	26	27
♂	♍ 14	14	14	14	14	14	15	15	15	15	15	15	16	16	16	16	16	17	17	17	17	18	18	18	18	19	19	19	20	20	20

♃ 1 5 10 15 20 25 31 / ♊13 14 15 16 18 19 20 — ♄ 1 15 31 / ♌ 8 9 10 — ♅ 1 25 / ♒27 28 — ♆ 1 25 / ♌ 4 5 — ♇ 1 / ♋ 4

6

	1	2	3	4	5	6	7	8	9	10	11	12	13	14	15	16	17	18	19	20	21	22	23	24	25	26	27	28	29	30
☉	♊ 10	11	12	13	14	15	16	17	18	19	20	21	21	22	23	24	25	26	27	28	29	29 0	♋ 1	2	3	4	5	6	7	8
☽	♓ 1	15	29	♈ 14	28	♉ 13	27	♊ 11	25	♋ 9	22	♌ 5	17	29	♍ 12	24	♎ 6	18	29	♏ 12	24	♐ 7	20	♑ 3	16	29	♒ 14	28	♓ 12	26
☿	♉ 17	18	19	21	22	24	26	27	29 0	♊ 1	2	4	6	8	10	12	14	16	18	20	22	24	27	29	♋ 1	3	5	8	10	12
♀	♈ 28	29	29 0	♉ 1	2	4	5	6	7	8	9	10	12	13	14	15	16	17	18	20	21	22	23	24	25	27	28	29	29 0	1
♂	♍ 21	21	21	22	22	23	23	23	24	24	24	25	25	26	26	27	27	27	28	28	29	29	29 0	♎ 0	1	1	2	2	3	3

♃ 1 5 10 15 20 25 30 / ♊20 21 22 24 25 26 27 — ♄ 1 10 20 30 / ♌10 11 12 13 — ♅ 1 R 15 / ♒28 27 — ♆ 1 30 / ♌ 5 6 — ♇ 1 20 / ♋ 4 5

7

	1	2	3	4	5	6	7	8	9	10	11	12	13	14	15	16	17	18	19	20	21	22	23	24	25	26	27	28	29	30	31
☉	♋ 9	10	11	12	13	13	14	15	16	17	18	19	20	21	22	23	24	25	26	27	28	29	29 0	♌ 0	1	2	3	4	5	6	7
☽	♈ 10	25	♉ 9	23	♊ 7	20	♋ 4	17	♌ 0	13	25	♍ 8	20	♎ 2	14	26	♏ 7	20	♐ 2	15	28	♑ 11	25	♒ 9	23	♓ 8	23	♈ 7	21	♉ 6	20
☿	♋ 14	16	18	20	22	24	26	28	29 0	♌ 2	4	6	7	9	11	13	14	16	18	19	21	22	24	25	26	28	29	29 0	♍ 2	3	4
♀	♊ 2	4	5	6	7	8	9	11	12	13	14	15	16	18	19	20	21	22	24	25	26	27	28	29 0	♋ 1	2	3	4	5	7	8
♂	♎ 4	4	5	5	6	6	7	7	8	8	9	9	10	10	11	11	12	12	12	14	14	15	15	16	16	17	17	18	19	19	20

♃ 1 5 10 13 29 15 20 25 31 / ♊27 28 29 0 ♋ 0 1 3 4 — ♄ 1 10 15 25 31 / ♌13 14 15 16 — ♅ 1 R 31 / ♒27 26 — ♆ 1 31 / ♌ 6 7 — ♇ 1 / ♋ 5

8

	1	2	3	4	5	6	7	8	9	10	11	12	13	14	15	16	17	18	19	20	21	22	23	24	25	26	27	28	29	30	31
☉	♌ 8	9	10	11	12	13	14	15	16	17	18	19	20	21	22	23	24	25	26	26	27	28	29 0	♍ 0	1	2	3	4	5	6	7
☽	♊ 3	17	♋ 0	13	26	♌ 9	21	♍ 4	16	28	♎ 10	22	♏ 4	16	28	♐ 10	23	♑ 6	19	♒ 3	18	♓ 2	17	♈ 2	17	♉ 2	16	♊ 0	14	27	♋ 10
☿	♍ 5	6	7	8	9	10	11	12	13	14	14	15	15	16	16	16	17	17	R 17	17	17	16	16	15	15	14	14	13	12	11	10
♀	♋ 9	10	11	13	14	15	16	17	19	20	21	22	24	25	26	27	28	29 0	♌ 1	2	3	4	6	7	8	9	11	12	13	14	15
♂	♎ 20	21	22	22	23	23	24	25	25	26	26	27	28	28	29	29	29 0	♏ 1	1	2	3	3	4	4	5	6	6	7	8	8	9

♃ 1 5 10 15 20 25 31 / ♋ 4 5 6 7 8 9 10 — ♄ 1 10 20 25 / ♌17 18 19 20 — ♅ 1 R 25 / ♒26 25 — ♆ 1 25 / 7 8 — ♇ 1 / ♋ 6

9

	1	2	3	4	5	6	7	8	9	10	11	12	13	14	15	16	17	18	19	20	21	22	23	24	25	26	27	28	29	30
☉	♍ 8	9	10	11	12	13	14	15	16	17	18	19	20	21	22	23	24	25	26	27	28	28	29 0	♎ 0	1	2	3	4	5	6
☽	♋ 23	♌ 6	18	♍ 0	13	25	♎ 6	18	♏ 0	12	24	♐ 6	18	♑ 1	14	27	♒ 11	26	♓ 11	26	♈ 11	26	♉ 11	26	♊ 10	24	♋ 7	20	♌ 3	15
☿	♍ 9	R 8	7	6	6	5	4	4	3	3	3	D 3	3	4	4	5	6	7	8	9	10	12	13	15	16	18	20	21	23	25
♀	♌ 17	18	19	20	22	23	24	25	26	28	29	29 0	♍ 1	3	4	5	6	8	9	10	11	13	14	15	16	18	19	20	21	22
♂	♏ 10	10	11	12	12	13	14	14	15	16	16	17	18	18	19	20	20	21	22	22	23	24	24	25	26	26	27	28	28	29

♃ 1 5 15 20 30 / ♋10 11 12 13 14 — ♄ 1 10 20 30 / ♌21 22 23 24 — ♅ 1 R 20 / ♒25 24 — ♆ 1 25 / ♌ 8 9 — ♇ 1 / ♋ 6

10

	1	2	3	4	5	6	7	8	9	10	11	12	13	14	15	16	17	18	19	20	21	22	23	24	25	26	27	28	29	30	31
☉	♎ 7	8	9	10	11	12	13	14	15	16	17	18	19	20	21	22	23	24	25	26	27	28	29	29 0	♏ 1	2	3	4	5	6	7
☽	♌ 27	♍ 10	22	♎ 3	15	27	♏ 9	21	♐ 3	15	27	♑ 10	23	♒ 6	20	♓ 4	19	♈ 4	19	♉ 5	20	♊ 5	19	♋ 3	16	29	♌ 12	24	♍ 7	19	♎ 0
☿	♍ 27	28	29 0	♎ 2	4	5	7	9	11	13	14	16	18	19	21	23	25	26	28	29 0	♏ 1	3	4	6	8	9	11	12	14	16	17
♀	♍ 24	25	26	27	28	29 0	♎ 1	2	4	5	6	7	9	10	11	12	14	15	16	17	19	20	21	23	24	25	26	27	28	29 0	1
♂	29 0	♐ 0	1	2	3	4	4	5	6	6	7	8	9	9	10	11	11	12	13	14	14	15	16	17	17	18	19	19	20	21	22

♃ 1 10 25 / ♋14 15 16 — ♄ 1 10 20 31 / ♌24 25 26 27 — ♅ 1 R / ♒24 — ♆ 1 / ♌ 9 — ♇ 1 / ♋ 6

11

	1	2	3	4	5	6	7	8	9	10	11	12	13	14	15	16	17	18	19	20	21	22	23	24	25	26	27	28	29	30
☉	♏ 8	9	10	11	12	13	14	15	16	17	18	19	20	21	22	23	24	25	26	27	28	29	29 0	♐ 1	2	3	4	5	6	7
☽	♎ 12	24	♏ 6	18	♐ 0	12	24	♑ 7	19	♒ 2	16	29	♓ 13	28	♈ 13	28	♉ 13	28	♊ 13	27	♋ 11	25	♌ 8	21	♍ 3	15	27	♎ 9	21	♏ 3
☿	♏ 19	20	22	23	25	26	28	29 0	♐ 1	2	4	5	7	8	9	11	12	14	15	16	18	19	20	22	23	24	25	27	28	29
♀	♏ 2	4	5	6	8	9	10	11	13	14	15	16	18	19	20	21	23	24	25	26	28	29	29 0	♐ 1	3	4	5	6	8	9
♂	♐ 22	23	24	25	25	26	27	28	28	29	29 0	♑ 1	1	2	3	4	4	5	6	7	7	8	9	10	11	11	12	13	14	14

♃ 1 4 R 15 30 / ♋16 16 15 14 — ♄ 1 15 / ♌27 28 — ♅ 1 R 4 D / ♒24 24 — ♆ 1 12 R / ♌ 9 9 — ♇ 1 / ♋ 6

12

	1	2	3	4	5	6	7	8	9	10	11	12	13	14	15	16	17	18	19	20	21	22	23	24	25	26	27	28	29	30	31
☉	♐ 8	9	10	11	12	13	14	15	16	17	18	19	20	21	22	23	24	25	26	27	28	29 0	♑ 1	2	3	4	5	6	7	8	9
☽	♏ 15	27	♐ 9	21	♑ 4	16	29	♒ 13	26	♓ 10	24	♈ 8	22	♉ 7	21	♊ 6	21	♋ 5	19	♌ 2	16	28	♍ 11	23	♎ 5	17	29	♏ 11	23	♐ 5	17
☿	29 0	♑ 1	1	2	3	3	3	3	R 3	3	3	3	2	1	♉ 29	♐ 29	27	26	25	23	22	21	20	19	18	18	18	17	D 17	18	18
♀	♐ 10	11	13	14	15	16	18	19	20	21	23	24	25	27	28	29	29 0	♑ 2	3	4	5	7	8	9	10	12	13	14	15	17	18
♂	♑ 15	16	17	17	18	19	20	21	21	22	23	24	24	25	26	27	28	28	29	29 0	♒ 1	2	2	3	4	5	5	6	7	8	9

♃ 1 R 10 20 31 / ♋14 13 12 11 — ♄ 1 10 R / ♌28 28 — ♅ 1 20 / ♒24 25 — ♆ 1 R / 9 — ♇ 1 15 / ♋ 6 5

1919

1

	1	2	3	4	5	6	7	8	9	10	11	12	13	14	15	16	17	18	19	20	21	22	23	24	25	26	27	28
☉	♑ 10	11	12	13	14	15	16	17	18	19	20	21	22	23	24	25	26	27	28	29	29 0	♒ 1	2	3	4	5	6	7
☽	♐ 29	♑ 13	26	♒ 9	23	♓ 7	20	♈ 5	19	♉ 3	17	♊ 1	15	29	♋ 13	27	♌ 10	23	♍ 6	19	♎ 1	13	25	♏ 7	19	♐ 1	13	25
☿	♐ 18	19	19	20	21	22	23	24	25	26	27	28	29 0	♑ 1	2	3	5	6	7	9	10	11	13	14	16	17	19	20
♀	♑ 19	20	22	23	24	25	27	28	29	♒ 0	2	3	4	5	7	8	9	10	12	13	14	16	17	18	19	21	22	23
♂	♒ 9	10	11	12	13	13	14	15	16	16	17	18	19	20	20	21	22	23	24	24	25	26	27	28	28	29	29 0	♓ 1

♃ 1 R 5 10 20 31 / ♋11 10 9 8 7 — ♄ 1 R 5 25 / ♌28 27 26 — ♅ 1 15 31 / ♒25 26 27 — ♆ 1 R 5 / ♌ 9 8 — ♇

2

	1	2	3	4	5	6	7	8	9	10	11	12	13	14	15	16	17	18	19	20	21	22	23	24	25	26	27	28
☉	♒ 11	12	13	14	15	16	17	18	19	20	21	22	23	24	25	26	27	28	29 0	♓ 1	2	3	4	5	6	7	8	9
☽	♒ 18	♓ 2	17	♈ 1	15	29	♉ 14	28	♊ 12	25	♋ 9	22	♌ 6	19	♍ 2	14	27	♎ 9	21	♏ 3	15	26	♐ 8	20	♑ 3	16	29	♒ 13
☿	♑ 26	28	29 0	♒ 1	3	4	6	7	9	11	12	14	16	17	19	21	23	24	26	28	29 0	♓ 2	3	5	7	9	11	13
♀	♒ 28	29 0	♓ 1	2	3	4	6	7	8	9	11	12	13	14	15	17	18	19	20	22	23	24	25	27	28	29	29 0	♈ 2
♂	♓ 4	5	5	6	7	8	9	9	10	11	12	12	13	14	15	16	16	17	18	19	20	20	21	22	23	23	24	25

♃ 1 R 10 / ♋ 7 6 — ♄ 1 R 5 20 / ♌26 25 24 — ♅ 1 20 / ♒27 28 — ♆ 1 R 10 / ♌ 8 7 — ♇

3

	1	2	3	4	5	6	7	8	9	10	11	12	13	14	15	16	17	18	19	20	21	22	23	24	25	26	27	28
☉	♓ 10	11	12	13	14	15	16	17	18	19	20	21	22	23	24	25	26	27	28	29	29 0	♈ 1	2	3	4	5	6	7
☽	♒ 27	♓ 11	26	♈ 11	25	♉ 10	24	♊ 9	22	♋ 6	19	♌ 2	15	28	♍ 11	23	♎ 5	17	29	♏ 11	23	♐ 5	16	29	♑ 11	24	♒ 7	21
☿	♓ 15	17	19	20	22	24	26	28	29 0	♈ 2	4	5	7	9	10	12	13	15	16	17	18	19	20	21	21	22	22	22
♀	♈ 3	4	5	7	8	9	10	12	13	14	15	16	18	19	20	21	23	24	25	26	27	29	29 0	♉ 1	2	4	5	6
♂	♓ 26	27	27	28	29	29 0	♈ 0	1	2	3	3	4	5	6	7	7	8	9	10	10	11	12	13	14	14	15	16	17

♃ 1 R 3 D 31 / ♋ 6 6 7 — ♄ 1 R 20 / ♌23 22 — ♅ 1 10 / ♒28 29 — ♆ 1 R 31 / ♌ 7 6 — ♇

4

	1	2	3	4	5	6	7	8	9	10	11	12	13	14	15	16	17	18	19	20	21	22	23	24	25	26	27	28
☉	♈ 11	12	13	14	15	15	16	17	18	19	20	21	22	23	24	25	26	27	28	29	29 0	♉ 1	2	3	4	5	6	7
☽	♈ 19	♉ 4	19	♊ 4	19	♋ 2	16	29	♌ 12	25	♍ 8	20	♎ 2	14	26	♏ 8	20	♐ 1	13	25	♑ 7	20	♒ 2	16	29	♓ 13	28	♈ 12
☿	♈ 21	R 21	21	20	19	19	18	17	16	16	15	14	13	13	12	12	11	11	11	11	10	D 10	11	11	11	11	12	12
♀	♉ 11	12	13	14	16	17	18	19	21	22	23	24	25	27	28	29	29 0	♊ 1	2	4	5	6	7	8	10	11	12	13
♂	♈ 20	20	21	22	23	23	24	25	26	26	27	28	29	29	29 0	♉ 1	2	2	3	4	5	5	6	7	7	8	9	10

♃ 1 10 15 25 30 / ♋ 7 8 9 10 11 — ♄ 1 R 5 24 D / ♌22 21 21 — ♅ 1 20 / ♓ 0 1 — ♆ 1 R / ♌ 6 — ♇

5

	1	2	3	4	5	6	7	8	9	10	11	12	13	14	15	16	17	18	19	20	21	22	23	24	25	26	27	28
☉	♉ 10	11	12	13	14	15	16	17	18	19	20	21	22	22	23	24	25	26	27	28	29	29 0	♊ 1	2	3	4	5	6
☽	♉ 28	♊ 13	28	♋ 12	26	♌ 9	22	♍ 5	17	29	♎ 11	23	♏ 5	17	28	♐ 10	22	♑ 4	17	29	♒ 12	25	♓ 8	22	♈ 7	21	♉ 6	21
☿	♈ 14	15	16	16	17	18	19	20	21	23	24	25	26	28	29	29 0	♉ 2	3	5	6	8	10	11	13	15	16	18	20
♀	♊ 17	18	19	20	21	23	24	25	26	27	28	29 0	♋ 1	2	3	4	5	6	8	9	10	11	12	13	14	15	17	18
♂	♉ 12	13	13	14	15	16	16	17	18	18	19	20	21	21	22	23	23	24	25	26	26	27	28	28	29	29 0	♊ 1	1

♃ 1 10 15 20 25 31 / ♋11 12 13 14 15 16 — ♄ 1 15 / ♌21 22 — ♅ 1 / ♓ 1 — ♆ 1 10 / ♌ 6 7 — ♇

6

	1	2	3	4	5	6	7	8	9	10	11	12	13	14	15	16	17	18	19	20	21	22	23	24	25	26	27	28
☉	♊ 10	11	12	13	14	15	16	16	17	18	19	20	21	22	23	24	25	26	27	28	29	29 0	♋ 1	2	3	4	5	6
☽	♋ 20	♌ 4	18	♍ 1	13	26	♎ 8	20	♏ 2	13	25	♐ 7	19	♑ 1	14	26	♒ 9	22	♓ 5	19	♈ 2	16	♉ 1	15	♊ 0	15	29	♋ 14
☿	♉ 28	29 0	♊ 2	4	6	8	10	13	15	17	19	21	24	26	28	29 0	♋ 2	4	6	9	11	13	15	16	18	20	22	24
♀	♋ 22	23	24	26	27	28	29	29 0	♌ 1	2	3	4	5	6	7	9	10	11	12	13	14	15	16	17	18	19	20	21
♂	♊ 4	5	6	6	7	8	8	9	10	10	11	12	13	13	14	15	15	16	17	17	18	19	19	20	21	22	22	23

♃ 1 5 10 15 20 25 30 / ♋16 17 18 19 20 21 22 — ♄ 1 5 15 30 / ♌22 23 24 25 — ♅ 1 7 R / ♓ 1 1 — ♆ 1 25 / ♌ 7 8 — ♇

7

	1	2	3	4	5	6	7	8	9	10	11	12	13	14	15	16	17	18	19	20	21	22	23	24	25	26	27	28
☉	♋ 8	9	10	11	12	13	14	15	16	17	18	19	20	21	22	23	24	25	26	27	28	28	29 0	♌ 0	1	2	3	4
☽	♌ 26	♍ 9	22	♎ 4	16	28	♏ 10	22	♐ 4	16	28	♑ 10	23	♒ 6	19	♓ 2	16	29	♈ 13	27	♉ 11	25	♊ 10	24	♋ 9	23	♌ 7	21
☿	♋ 29	29 0	♌ 2	4	5	7	8	10	11	12	14	15	16	17	18	19	20	21	22	23	24	25	26	26	27	27	28	28
♀	♌ 24	25	26	27	28	29	29 0	♍ 1	1	2	3	4	5	6	7	8	9	9	10	11	12	13	13	14	15	16	16	17
♂	♊ 25	26	26	27	28	28	29	29 0	♋ 0	1	2	2	3	4	4	5	6	6	7	8	8	9	10	10	11	12	12	13

♃ 1 5 10 15 20 25 31 / ♋23 24 25 26 27 28 29 — ♄ 1 10 20 25 / ♌25 26 27 28 — ♅ 1 R 31 / ♓ 1 0 — ♆ 1 25 / ♌ 8 9 — ♇

8

	1	2	3	4	5	6	7	8	9	10	11	12	13	14	15	16	17	18	19	20	21	22	23	24	25	26	27	28
☉	♌ 8	9	10	11	12	13	14	15	16	17	18	19	20	20	21	22	23	24	25	26	27	28	29	29 0	♍ 1	2	3	4
☽	♎ 12	24	♏ 6	18	♐ 0	12	24	♑ 6	19	♒ 1	15	28	♓ 12	26	♈ 10	24	8	22	♊ 6	20	♋ 4	18	♌ 2	16	29	♍ 12	25	♎ 8
☿	♌ 29	R 29	29	28	28	28	27	27	26	26	25	24	23	22	22	21	20	19	18	18	17	17	17	16	D 16	16	17	17
♀	♍ 20	20	21	21	22	23	23	24	24	24	25	25	25	26	26	26	27	27	27	27	27	27	R 27	27	27	27	27	26
♂	♋ 16	16	17	18	18	19	20	20	21	22	22	23	24	24	25	25	26	27	27	28	29	29	29 0	♌ 1	1	2	3	3

♃ 1 2 29 3 5 10 15 20 25 / ♋29 0 ♌ 0 1 2 3 4 5 — ♄ 1 5 12 29 13 20 31 / ♌28 29 0 ♍ 0 1 2 — ♅ 1 R 16 0 / ♓ 0 ♒29 — ♆ 1 20 / ♌ 9 10 — ♇ 1 / ♋ 7

9

	1	2	3	4	5	6	7	8	9	10	11	12	13	14	15	16	17	18	19	20	21	22	23	24	25	26	27	28
☉	♍ 8	9	10	11	12	13	14	15	16	17	18	18	19	20	21	22	23	24	25	26	27	28	29	29 0	♎ 1	2	3	4
☽	♏ 26	♐ 8	20	♑ 2	14	27	♒ 10	23	♓ 7	21	♈ 5	20	♉ 4	19	♊ 3	17	♋ 1	15	29	♌ 12	25	♍ 8	21	♎ 4	16	28	♏ 10	22
☿	♌ 20	21	22	23	24	26	27	29	29 0	♍ 2	4	6	7	9	11	13	15	17	19	20	22	24	26	28	29 0	♎ 1	3	5
♀	♍ 25	R 25	24	24	24	23	22	22	21	21	20	19	19	18	18	17	16	16	15	15	14	14	13	13	13	12	12	12
♂	♌ 6	6	7	8	8	9	10	10	11	11	12	13	13	14	15	15	16	16	17	18	18	19	20	20	21	21	22	23

♃ 1 5 10 15 20 25 30 / ♌ 6 7 8 9 10 11 12 — ♄ 1 5 10 20 30 / ♍ 2 3 4 5 6 — ♅ 1 R 25 / ♒29 28 — ♆ 1 20 / ♌10 11 — ♇ 1 / ♋ 7

10

	1	2	3	4	5	6	7	8	9	10	11	12	13	14	15	16	17	18	19	20	21	22	23	24	25	26	27	28
☉	♎ 7	8	9	10	11	12	13	14	15	16	17	18	19	20	21	22	23	24	25	26	27	28	29	29 0	♏ 1	2	3	4
☽	♐ 28	♑ 10	22	♒ 5	18	♓ 1	15	29	♈ 14	29	♉ 14	29	♊ 13	28	♋ 12	26	♌ 9	22	♍ 5	18	♎ 0	13	25	♏ 7	19	♐ 1	12	24
☿	♎ 10	12	14	15	17	19	20	22	24	25	27	28	29 0	♏ 2	3	5	6	8	9	11	12	14	15	17	18	20	21	23
♀	♍ 11	R 11	11	D 11	11	11	11	11	11	12	12	12	12	13	13	14	14	15	15	16	16	17	17	18	18	19	20	20
♂	♌ 25	25	26	26	27	28	28	29	29	29 0	♍ 1	1	2	2	3	4	4	5	6	6	7	7	8	8	9	10	10	11

♃ 1 5 15 20 31 / ♌12 13 14 15 16 — ♄ 1 10 15 25 / ♍ 6 7 8 9 — ♅ 1 R / ♒28 — ♆ 1 / ♌11 — ♇ 1 / ♋ 7

11

	1	2	3	4	5	6	7	8	9	10	11	12	13	14	15	16	17	18	19	20	21	22	23	24	25	26	27	28
☉	♏ 8	9	10	11	12	13	14	15	16	17	18	19	20	21	22	23	24	25	26	27	28	29	29 0	♐ 1	2	3	4	5
☽	♒ 13	26	♓ 9	23	♈ 7	22	♉ 7	22	♊ 7	22	♋ 7	22	♌ 5	19	♍ 2	15	27	♎ 10	22	♏ 4	16	27	♐ 9	21	♑ 3	15	27	♒ 9
☿	♏ 28	29 0	♐ 1	2	3	5	6	7	8	9	10	12	13	13	14	15	16	17	17	17	18	18	R 18	18	17	17	16	15
♀	♍ 23	24	25	26	27	27	28	29	29 0	♎ 1	2	3	4	5	5	6	7	8	9	10	11	12	13	14	15	16	17	18
♂	♍ 13	14	14	15	16	16	17	17	18	18	19	20	20	21	21	22	23	23	24	24	25	25	26	26	27	28	28	29

♃ 1 5 20 / ♌16 17 18 — ♄ 1 5 20 / ♍ 9 10 11 — ♅ 1 R 8 D / ♒28 28 — ♆ 1 15 R / ♌11 11 — ♇ 1 / ♋ 7

12

	1	2	3	4	5	6	7	8	9	10	11	12	13	14	15	16	17	18	19	20	21	22	23	24	25	26	27	28
☉	♐ 8	9	10	11	12	13	14	15	16	17	18	19	20	21	22	23	24	25	26	27	28	29 0	♑ 0	1	2	3	4	5
☽	♓ 18	♈ 2	16	♉ 0	15	♊ 0	15	♋ 1	16	♌ 0	14	28	♍ 11	24	♎ 7	19	♏ 1	13	24	♐ 6	18	♑ 0	12	24	♒ 6	19	♓ 1	14
☿	♐ 11	R 10	9	7	6	5	4	3	3	2	2	2	D 2	2	2	3	3	4	5	6	7	8	9	10	11	12	14	15
♀	♎ 22	23	24	25	26	27	28	29	29 0	♏ 1	2	4	5	6	7	8	9	10	11	13	14	15	16	17	18	19	21	22
♂	♎ 0	1	1	2	3	3	4	4	5	5	6	6	7	7	8	8	9	10	10	11	11	12	12	13	13	14	14	15

♃ 1 5 R 25 / ♌18 18 17 — ♄ 1 23 R / ♍11 11 — ♅ 1 25 / ♒28 29 — ♆ 1 R / ♌11 — ♇ 1 / ♋ 7

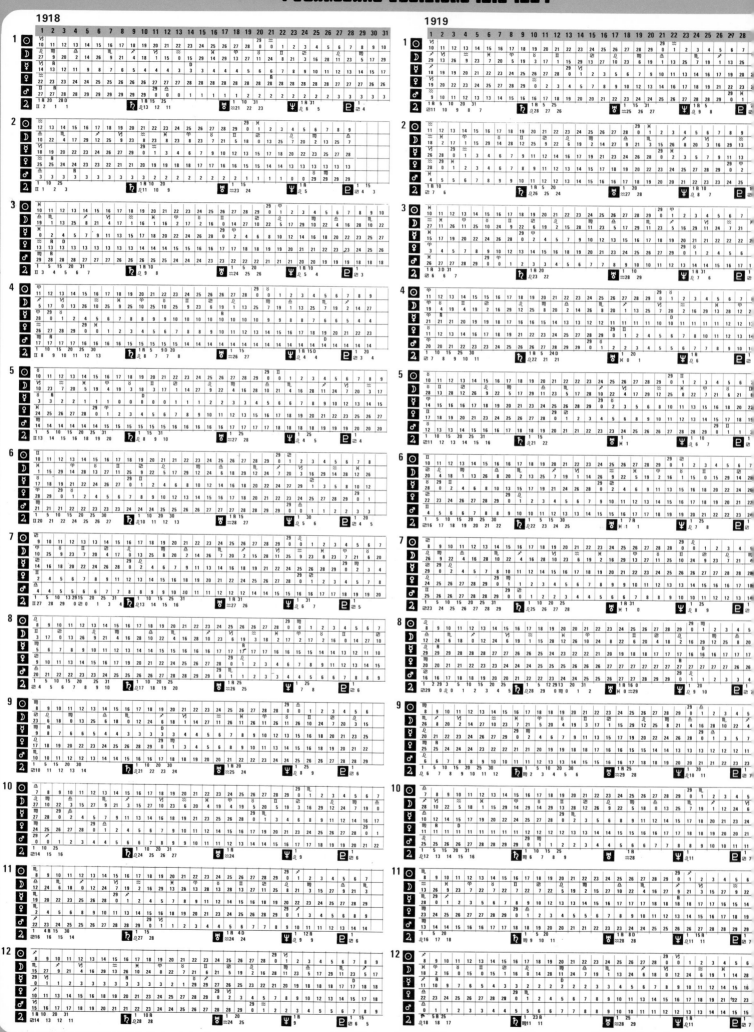

1920

1

1	2	3	4	5	6	7	8	9	10	11	12	13	14	15	16	17	18	19	20	21	22	23	24	25	26	27	28	29	30	31
♑ 10	11	12	13	14	15	16	17	18	19	20	21	22	23	24	25	26	27	28	29	29 0	♒ 1	2	3	4	5	6	7	8	9	10
♉ 9	24	♊ 8	23	♋ 8	23	♌ 8	22	♍ 6	20	♎ 3	15	27	♏ 9	21	♐ 3	15	27	♑ 9	21	♒ 3	16	28	♓ 11	25	♈ 8	21	♉ 5	19	♊ 3	18
♐ 20	22	23	24	26	27	29	29 0	♑ 2	3	5	6	8	9	11	12	14	15	17	18	20	22	23	25	26	28	29 0	♒ 1	3	5	6
♏ 26	28	29	29 0	♐ 1	2	4	5	6	7	8	9	11	12	13	14	15	17	18	19	20	21	23	24	25	26	27	29	29 0	♑ 1	2
♎ 17	17	18	18	19	19	19	20	20	21	21	22	22	23	23	24	24	24	25	25	26	26	27	27	27	28	28	29	29	29	29

1 B 5 15 25 31 — ♌17 16 15 14 13 | ♄ 1 B 31 — ♍11 10 | ♅ 1 22 — ♒29 ♓ 0 | ♆ 1 B 15 — ♌11 10 | ♇ 1 — ♋ 6

2

1	2	3	4	5	6	7	8	9	10	11	12	13	14	15	16	17	18	19	20	21	22	23	24	25	26	27	28	29	30	31
♒ 11	12	13	14	15	16	17	18	19	20	21	22	23	24	25	26	27	28	29 0	♓ 0	1	2	3	4	5	6	7	8	9		
♋ 2	17	♌ 2	16	♍ 0	14	27	♎ 10	23	♏ 5	17	29	♐ 11	23	♑ 5	17	29	♒ 12	25	♓ 8	21	♈ 5	18	♉ 2	16	♊ 0	14	28	♋ 12		
♒ 8	10	12	13	15	17	19	20	22	24	26	28	29 0	♓ 1	3	5	7	9	10	12	14	16	18	19	21	23	24	26	27		
♑ 3	5	6	7	8	10	11	12	13	14	16	17	18	19	21	22	23	24	25	27	28	29	29 0	♒ 1	3	4	5	6	8		
♏ 0	0	1	1	1	2	2	2	3	3	3	4	4	4	4	5	5	5	6	6	6	6	7	7	7	7	7	8	8		

1 B 10 15 25 — ♌13 12 11 10 | ♄ 1 B 15 25 — ♍10 9 8 | ♅ 1 10 25 — ♓ 0 1 2 | ♆ 1 B 20 — ♌10 9 | ♇ 1 — ♋ 6

3

1	2	3	4	5	6	7	8	9	10	11	12	13	14	15	16	17	18	19	20	21	22	23	24	25	26	27	28	29	30	31
♓ 10	11	12	13	14	15	16	17	18	19	20	21	22	23	24	25	26	27	28	29 0	♈ 0	1	2	3	4	5	6	7	8	9	10
♋ 27	♌ 11	25	♍ 9	22	♎ 5	18	♏ 1	13	25	♐ 7	19	♑ 1	13	25	♒ 7	20	♓ 3	16	♈ 0	14	28	♉ 12	27	♊ 11	25	♋ 9	23	♌ 7	21	♍ 4
♓ 28	29 0	♈ 1	2	2	3	4	4	4	5	B 4	4	4	4	3	2	1	1	♉ 29	♓ 29	28	27	26	26	25	24	23	23	22	22	22
♒ 9	10	11	13	14	15	16	17	19	20	21	22	24	24	26	27	28	29 0	♓ 1	2	3	5	6	7	8	9	11	12	13	14	16
♏ 8	8	8	8	8	9	9	9	9	9	9	9	9	9	B 9	9	9	9	9	9	9	9	8	8	8	8	8	8	8	7	7

1 B 5 20 — ♌10 9 8 | ♄ 1 B 10 20 — ♍ 8 7 6 | ♅ 1 10 31 — ♓ 2 3 4 | ♆ 1 B — ♌ 9 | ♇ 1 — ♋ 6

4

1	2	3	4	5	6	7	8	9	10	11	12	13	14	15	16	17	18	19	20	21	22	23	24	25	26	27	28	29	30	31
♈ 11	12	13	14	15	16	17	18	19	20	21	22	23	24	25	26	27	28	29	29 0	♉ 1	2	3	4	5	6	7	8	9	10	
♍ 18	♎ 1	14	26	♏ 9	21	♐ 3	15	27	♑ 9	20	♒ 3	15	28	♓ 11	24	♈ 8	23	♉ 7	22	♊ 6	21	♋ 6	20	♌ 4	18	♍ 1	15	28	♎ 10	
♓ 22	B 22	D 22	22	22	22	22	23	23	24	25	25	26	27	28	29	29 0	♈ 1	2	3	4	5	6	8	9	10	12	13	15	16	
♓ 17	18	19	21	22	23	24	25	27	28	29	29 0	♈ 2	3	4	5	6	8	9	10	11	13	14	15	16	18	19	20	21	22	
♏ 7	B 7	7	6	6	6	6	5	5	5	4	4	4	3	3	3	2	2	1	1	1	0	♉ 29	♎ 29	29	29	28	28	28	27	

1 B 4 D 25 — ♌ 8 8 9 | ♄ 1 B 5 — ♍ 6 5 | ♅ 1 20 — ♓ 4 5 | ♆ 1 B 19 D — ♌ 9 9 | ♇ 1 — ♋ 6

5

1	2	3	4	5	6	7	8	9	10	11	12	13	14	15	16	17	18	19	20	21	22	23	24	25	26	27	28	29	30	31
♉ 11	12	13	14	15	15	16	17	18	19	20	21	22	23	24	25	26	27	28	29	29 0	♊ 1	2	3	4	5	6	7	8	9	10
♎ 23	♏ 5	17	29	♐ 11	23	♑ 5	17	29	♒ 11	23	♓ 6	19	♈ 2	16	♉ 1	15	♊ 0	15	♋ 0	15	♌ 0	14	28	♍ 11	25	♎ 7	20	♏ 2	14	26
♈ 18	19	21	22	24	26	27	29	♉ 1	3	4	6	8	10	12	14	16	18	20	22	24	27	29	♊ 1	3	5	7	10	12	14	16
♈ 24	25	26	27	29	29 0	♉ 1	2	3	5	6	7	8	10	11	12	13	15	16	17	18	19	21	22	23	24	26	27	28	29	0
♎ 27	B 27	26	26	26	25	25	25	24	24	24	24	23	23	23	23	22	22	22	22	22	22	22	21	21	21	21	21	21	21	21

1 10 20 25 31 — ♌ 9 10 11 12 13 | ♄ 1 B 7 D — ♍ 5 5 | ♅ 1 — ♓ 5 | ♆ 1 — ♌ 9 | ♇ 1 — ♋ 6

6

1	2	3	4	5	6	7	8	9	10	11	12	13	14	15	16	17	18	19	20	21	22	23	24	25	26	27	28	29	30	31
♊ 10	11	12	13	14	15	16	17	18	19	20	21	22	23	24	25	26	27	28	29	29 0	♋ 0	1	2	3	4	5	6	7	8	
♐ 8	20	♑ 2	14	26	♒ 8	20	♓ 2	15	28	♈ 11	25	♉ 9	24	♊ 9	24	♋ 9	24	♌ 9	24	♍ 8	21	♎ 4	17	29	♏ 11	23	♐ 5	17	29	
♊ 18	20	23	25	27	29	29 0	♋ 2	4	6	8	10	11	13	15	16	18	19	21	22	24	25	26	27	29	29 0	♌ 1	2	3	4	
♊ 2	3	4	5	7	8	9	10	11	13	14	15	16	18	19	20	21	23	24	25	26	27	29	29 0	♋ 1	2	4	5	6	7	
♎ 21	21	21	21	21	21	21	21	22	22	22	22	22	22	22	23	23	23	23	23	24	24	24	24	25	25	25	26	26	26	

1 10 15 20 25 30 — ♌13 14 15 16 17 18 | ♄ 1 10 25 — ♍ 5 6 7 | ♅ 1 10 B — ♓ 5 5 | ♆ 1 20 — ♌ 9 10 | ♇ 1 15 — ♋ 6 7

7

1	2	3	4	5	6	7	8	9	10	11	12	13	14	15	16	17	18	19	20	21	22	23	24	25	26	27	28	29	30	31
♋ 9	10	11	12	13	14	15	16	17	18	19	20	21	22	22	23	24	25	26	27	28	29	29 0	♌ 1	2	3	4	5	6	7	8
♑ 11	23	♒ 5	17	29	♓ 11	24	♈ 7	20	♉ 4	18	♊ 2	17	♋ 2	18	♌ 3	18	♍ 2	16	29	♎ 13	26	♏ 8	20	♐ 2	14	26	♑ 8	19	♒ 2	14
♌ 5	6	6	7	8	8	9	9	9	10	10	10	10	B 10	10	10	10	9	9	8	8	7	6	6	5	4	4	3	2	2	1
♋ 9	10	11	12	13	15	16	17	18	20	21	22	23	24	26	27	28	29 0	♌ 1	2	3	4	6	7	8	9	11	12	13	14	15
♎ 26	27	27	28	28	28	29	29	29	29 0	♏ 0	1	1	1	2	2	3	3	4	4	4	5	5	6	6	7	7	8	8	9	9

1 5 10 15 20 25 31 — ♌18 19 20 21 22 23 24 | ♄ 1 5 20 25 — ♍ 7 8 9 10 | ♅ 1 B — ♓ 5 | ♆ 1 20 — ♌10 11 | ♇ 1 15 — ♋ 7 8

8

1	2	3	4	5	6	7	8	9	10	11	12	13	14	15	16	17	18	19	20	21	22	23	24	25	26	27	28	29	30	31
♌ 9	10	11	12	13	14	15	15	16	17	18	19	20	21	22	23	24	25	26	27	28	29	29 0	♍ 1	2	3	4	5	6	7	8
♒ 26	♓ 9	21	♈ 4	17	♉ 0	14	28	♊ 12	27	♋ 11	26	♌ 11	26	♍ 10	24	♎ 8	21	♏ 4	16	28	♐ 10	22	♑ 4	16	28	♒ 10	23	♓ 5	18	♈ 1
B 0	♉ 29	♋ 29	29	29	29	D 29	29	29	29 0	♌ 0	1	2	3	3	4	6	7	8	10	11	13	14	16	18	20	22	24	25	27	29
♌ 17	18	19	20	22	23	24	25	27	28	29	29 0	♍ 1	3	4	5	6	8	9	10	11	13	14	15	16	18	19	20	21	22	24
♏ 10	10	11	11	12	12	13	14	14	15	15	16	16	17	17	18	19	19	20	20	21	22	22	23	23	24	25	25	26	26	27

1 5 10 15 20 25 27 29 31 — ♌24 25 26 27 28 29 0 ♍ 1 | ♄ 1 5 15 20 31 — ♍10 11 12 13 14 | ♅ 1 B 31 — ♓ 4 3 | ♆ 1 15 — ♌11 12 | ♇ 1 — ♋ 8

9

1	2	3	4	5	6	7	8	9	10	11	12	13	14	15	16	17	18	19	20	21	22	23	24	25	26	27	28	29	30	31
♍ 9	10	10	11	12	13	14	15	16	17	18	19	20	21	22	23	24	25	26	27	28	29	29 0	♎ 1	2	3	4	5	6	7	
♈ 14	27	♉ 11	25	♊ 9	23	♋ 7	21	♌ 6	20	♍ 5	19	♎ 3	16	29	♏ 12	24	♐ 6	18	♑ 0	12	24	♒ 6	18	♓ 1	14	27	♈ 10	24	♉ 7	
♍ 1	3	5	7	9	11	13	15	17	19	20	22	24	26	28	29 0	♎ 1	3	5	6	8	10	11	13	15	16	18	19	21	22	
♍ 25	26	27	29	29 0	♎ 1	2	4	5	6	7	8	10	11	12	13	15	16	17	18	20	21	22	23	25	26	27	28	29 0	♏ 1	
♏ 28	28	29	29 0	♐ 0	1	2	2	3	3	4	5	5	6	7	7	8	9	9	10	11	11	12	13	14	14	15	16	16	17	

1 5 10 15 20 25 30 — ♍ 1 2 3 4 5 6 7 | ♄ 1 5 15 25 30 — ♍14 15 16 17 18 | ♅ 1 B 25 — ♓ 3 2 | ♆ 1 15 — ♌12 13 | ♇ 1 — ♋ 8

10

1	2	3	4	5	6	7	8	9	10	11	12	13	14	15	16	17	18	19	20	21	22	23	24	25	26	27	28	29	30	31
♎ 8	9	10	11	12	13	14	15	16	17	18	19	20	21	22	23	24	25	26	27	28	29	29 0	♏ 1	2	3	4	5	6	7	8
♉ 21	♊ 5	20	♋ 4	18	♌ 2	16	♍ 0	14	28	♎ 11	24	♏ 7	20	♐ 2	14	26	♑ 8	20	♒ 2	14	26	♓ 9	22	♈ 5	19	♉ 2	17	♊ 1	16	♋ 0
♎ 24	26	27	29	29 0	♏ 1	3	4	6	7	9	10	11	13	14	15	16	18	19	20	21	22	24	25	26	27	27	28	29	29 0	♐ 0
♏ 2	3	4	6	7	8	9	11	12	13	14	15	17	18	19	20	22	23	24	25	27	28	29	29 0	♐ 1	3	4	5	6	8	9
♐ 18	18	19	20	20	21	22	23	23	24	25	25	26	27	28	28	29	29 0	♑ 1	1	2	3	4	4	5	6	6	7	8	9	9

1 5 10 15 20 25 31 — ♍ 7 8 9 10 11 12 13 | ♄ 1 10 20 25 — ♍18 19 20 21 | ♅ 1 B — ♓ 2 | ♆ 1 — ♌13 | ♇ 1 — ♋ 8

11

1	2	3	4	5	6	7	8	9	10	11	12	13	14	15	16	17	18	19	20	21	22	23	24	25	26	27	28	29	30	31
♏ 9	10	11	12	13	14	15	16	17	18	19	20	21	22	23	24	25	26	27	28	29	29 0	♐ 1	2	3	4	5	6	7	8	
♋ 15	29	♌ 13	27	♍ 11	24	♎ 7	20	♏ 3	16	28	♐ 10	22	♑ 4	16	28	♒ 10	22	♓ 4	17	29	♈ 13	26	♉ 10	25	♊ 10	25	♋ 10	25	♌ 9	
♐ 1	1	2	2	2	B 2	2	1	1	0 29	♏ 29	28	27	26	24	23	22	21	19	18	17	17	16	16	16	D 16	16	17	17	18	
♐ 10	11	12	14	15	16	17	19	20	21	22	23	25	26	27	28	29 0	♑ 1	2	3	4	6	7	8	9	11	12	13	14	15	
♑ 10	11	12	12	13	14	15	15	16	17	18	18	19	20	21	21	22	23	24	24	25	26	27	27	28	29	29 0	♒ 1	1	2	

1 5 15 20 30 — ♍13 14 15 16 17 | ♄ 1 5 20 30 — ♍21 22 23 24 | ♅ 1 B 11 D — ♓ 2 2 | ♆ 1 16 B — ♌13 13 | ♇ 1 — ♋ 8

12

1	2	3	4	5	6	7	8	9	10	11	12	13	14	15	16	17	18	19	20	21	22	23	24	25	26	27	28	29	30	31
♐ 9	10	11	12	13	14	15	16	17	18	19	20	21	22	23	24	25	26	27	28	29	29 0	♑ 1	2	3	4	5	6	7	8	9
♌ 24	♍ 7	21	♎ 4	17	♏ 0	12	25	♐ 7	19	♑ 1	13	25	♒ 6	18	♓ 0	12	25	♈ 8	21	♉ 4	18	♊ 3	18	♋ 3	18	♌ 3	18	♍ 3	17	♎ 1
♏ 19	20	21	22	23	24	25	26	28	29	29 0	♐ 2	3	4	6	7	9	10	12	13	15	16	18	19	21	22	24	25	27	28	29 0
♑ 17	18	19	20	21	23	24	25	26	27	29	29 0	♒ 1	2	3	5	6	7	8	9	11	12	13	14	15	17	18	19	20	21	22
♒ 3	4	4	5	6	7	7	8	9	10	11	11	12	13	14	14	15	16	17	18	18	19	20	21	21	22	23	24	25	25	26

1 10 25 — ♍17 18 19 | ♄ 1 25 — ♍24 25 | ♅ 1 31 — ♓ 2 3 | ♆ 1 B — ♌13 | ♇ 1 — ♋ 8

1921

1

	1	2	3	4	5	6	7	8	9	10	11	12	13	14	15	16	17	18	19	20	21	22	23	24	25	26	27	28	29	30	31
☉	♑ 10	11	12	13	14	15	16	17	19	20	21	22	23	24	25	26	27	28	29	29 0	♒ 1	2	3	4	5	6	7	8	9	10	11
☽	♎ 14	27	♏ 9	22	♐ 4	16	28	♑ 10	22	♒ 3	15	27	♓ 9	21	♈ 4	16	29	♉ 13	27	♊ 14	26	♋ 11	26	♌ 11	27	♍ 11	26	♎ 10	23	♏ 6	19
☿	♑ 1	3	5	6	8	9	11	12	14	16	17	19	21	22	24	26	27	29	29 0	♒ 2	4	6	7	9	11	13	14	16	18	20	21
♀	♒ 24	25	26	27	28	29 0	♓ 1	2	3	4	5	6	7	9	10	11	12	13	14	15	17	18	19	20	21	22	23	24	25	26	27
♂	♒ 27	28	28	29	29 0	♓ 1	2	2	3	4	5	5	6	7	8	9	9	10	11	12	12	13	14	15	15	16	17	18	19	19	20

♃ ♍19 19 18 | ♄ 1 4 B 17 — ♍25 25 24 | ♅ 1 26 — ♓ 3 4 | ♆ 1 B 23 — ♌13 12 | ♇ 1 B 31 — ♋ 8 7

2

	1	2	3	4	5	6	7	8	9	10	11	12	13	14	15	16	17	18	19	20	21	22	23	24	25	26	27	28	29	30	31
☉	♒ 12	13	14	15	16	17	18	19	20	21	22	23	24	25	26	27	28	29	29 0	♓ 1	2	3	4	5	6	7	8	9			
☽	♐ 1	13	25	♑ 7	18	♒ 0	12	24	♓ 6	19	♈ 1	13	26	♉ 9	23	♊ 6	20	♋ 5	19	♌ 4	20	♍ 5	19	♎ 4	18	♏ 1	14	27			
☿	♒ 23	25	27	28	29 0	♓ 2	3	5	6	8	9	11	12	13	14	15	16	17	17	17	17	B 17	17	17	17	16	15	14			
♀	♓ 28	29 0	♈ 1	2	3	4	5	6	7	8	9	10	11	12	13	14	15	16	17	17	18	19	20	21	22	23	24	25			
♂	♓ 21	22	22	23	24	25	25	26	27	28	29	29	29 0	♈ 1	2	2	3	4	5	5	6	7	8	8	9	10	11	11			

♃ 1 B 16 25 28 — ♍17 16 15 14 | ♄ 1 B 10 25 — ♍24 23 22 | ♅ 1 13 25 — ♓ 4 5 6 | ♆ 1 — ♌12 | ♇ 1 — ♋ 7

3

	1	2	3	4	5	6	7	8	9	10	11	12	13	14	15	16	17	18	19	20	21	22	23	24	25	26	27	28	29	30	31
☉	♓ 10	11	12	13	14	15	16	17	18	19	20	21	22	23	24	25	26	27	28	29	29 0	♈ 1	2	3	4	5	6	7	8	9	10
☽	♐ 9	21	♑ 3	15	27	♒ 9	21	♓ 3	15	28	♈ 10	23	♉ 6	19	♊ 3	17	♋ 1	15	29	♌ 14	29	♍ 13	28	♎ 12	26	♏ 9	22	♐ 5	17	29	♑ 11
☿	♓ 13	B 12	11	10	9	8	7	7	6	5	5	4	4	3	3	D 3	3	4	4	4	5	5	6	6	7	8	9	9	10	11	12
♀	♈ 25	26	27	28	28	29	29 0	♉ 1	1	2	3	3	4	4	5	6	6	7	7	7	8	8	9	9	9	9	10	10	10	10	10
♂	♈ 12	13	14	14	15	16	17	17	18	19	20	20	21	22	23	23	24	25	26	26	27	28	29	29	29 0	♉ 1	1	2	3	4	4

♃ 1 B 8 15 24 — ♍14 13 12 11 | ♄ 1 B 10 22 — ♍22 21 20 | ♅ 1 15 — ♓ 6 7 | ♆ 1 B — ♌11 | ♇ 1 — ♋ 7

4

	1	2	3	4	5	6	7	8	9	10	11	12	13	14	15	16	17	18	19	20	21	22	23	24	25	26	27	28	29	30	31
☉	♈ 11	12	13	14	15	16	17	18	19	20	21	22	23	24	25	26	27	28	29	29 0	♉ 1	2	3	4	5	6	7	7	8	9	
☽	♑ 23	♒ 5	17	29	♓ 11	24	♈ 6	19	♉ 3	16	29	♊ 14	28	♋ 12	26	♌ 10	24	♍ 8	23	♎ 7	20	♏ 4	17	♐ 0	13	25	♑ 7	19	♒ 1	13	
☿	♓ 13	14	16	17	18	19	21	22	23	25	26	27	29	29 0	♈ 2	4	5	7	8	10	12	13	15	17	19	21	23	24	26	28	
♀	♉ 10	B 10	10	10	10	10	9	9	9	8	8	8	7	7	6	6	5	5	4	3	3	2	1	1	♉ 29	♈ 29	29	28	28	27	
♂	♉ 5	6	7	7	8	9	9	10	11	12	12	13	14	15	15	16	17	17	18	19	20	20	21	22	22	23	24	25	25	26	

♃ 1 B 9 29 — ♍11 10 9 | ♄ 1 B 5 22 — ♍20 19 18 | ♅ 1 9 25 — ♓ 7 8 9 | ♆ 1 B 22 D — ♌11 11 | ♇ 1 — ♋ 7

5

	1	2	3	4	5	6	7	8	9	10	11	12	13	14	15	16	17	18	19	20	21	22	23	24	25	26	27	28	29	30	31
☉	♉ 10	11	12	13	14	15	16	17	18	19	20	21	22	23	24	25	26	27	28	29	29 0	♊ 1	2	3	4	5	6	6	7	8	9
☽	♒ 25	♓ 7	19	♈ 2	15	28	♉ 11	25	♊ 9	24	♋ 8	22	♌ 7	21	♍ 5	19	♎ 3	16	29	♏ 13	26	♐ 8	21	♑ 3	15	27	♒ 9	21	♓ 3	15	27
☿	♈ 29 ♉ 0	♉ 2	4	6	8	11	13	15	17	19	21	24	26	28	29 0	♊ 2	4	6	8	11	13	15	16	18	20	22	24	25	27	29	29 ♋ 0
♀	♈ 27	B 26	26	26	25	25	25	24	24	24	24	24	24	D 24	24	24	24	24	24	24	25	25	25	26	26	26	27	27	28	28	29
♂	♉ 27	27	28	29	29	29 0	♊ 1	2	2	3	4	4	5	6	6	7	8	9	9	10	11	11	12	13	13	14	15	15	16	17	17

♃ 1 B 6 D 31 — ♍ 9 9 10 | ♄ 1 B 21 D — ♍18 18 | ♅ 1 — ♓ 9 | ♆ 1 — ♌11 | ♇ 1 — ♋ 7

6

	1	2	3	4	5	6	7	8	9	10	11	12	13	14	15	16	17	18	19	20	21	22	23	24	25	26	27	28	29	30	31
☉	♊ 10	11	12	13	14	15	16	17	18	19	20	21	22	23	24	25	26	27	27	28	29 0	♋ 0	1	2	3	4	5	6	7	8	
☽	♈ 10	23	♉ 6	20	♊ 4	18	♋ 3	18	♌ 3	17	♍ 2	16	29	♎ 13	26	♏ 9	22	♐ 5	17	29	♑ 12	24	♒ 6	17	29	♓ 11	23	♈ 5	18	♉ 1	
☿	♋ 2	3	5	6	7	9	10	11	12	13	14	15	16	17	17	18	19	19	20	20	20	20	21	21	B 21	21	20	20	20	20	
♀	♈ 29	29 0	♉ 1	1	2	3	3	4	5	5	6	7	8	8	9	10	11	12	12	13	14	15	16	17	18	19	20	20	21	22	
♂	♊ 18	19	19	20	21	22	22	23	24	24	25	26	26	27	28	28	29	29 0	♋ 0	1	2	2	3	4	4	5	6	6	7	8	

♃ 1 12 21 29 — ♍10 11 12 13 | ♄ 1 24 — ♍18 19 | ♅ 1 14 B — ♓ 9 9 | ♆ 1 12 — ♌11 12 | ♇ 1 — ♋ 8

7

	1	2	3	4	5	6	7	8	9	10	11	12	13	14	15	16	17	18	19	20	21	22	23	24	25	26	27	28	29	30	31
☉	♋ 9	10	11	12	13	14	15	16	17	17	18	19	20	21	22	23	24	25	26	27	28	29	29 0	♌ 1	2	3	4	5	6	7	8
☽	♉ 14	28	♊ 12	27	♋ 12	27	♌ 12	27	♍ 12	26	♎ 10	23	♏ 7	19	♐ 2	14	26	♑ 9	21	♒ 2	14	26	♓ 8	20	♈ 2	14	27	♉ 9	23	♊ 6	21
☿	♋ 19	B 19	18	18	17	16	16	15	15	14	13	13	12	12	12	11	11	11	D 11	11	11	11	12	12	13	14	14	15	16	17	18
♀	♉ 23	24	25	26	27	28	29 29	♊ 0	1	2	3	4	5	6	7	8	9	10	11	12	13	15	16	17	18	19	20	21	22	23	24
♂	♋ 8	9	10	10	11	12	12	13	14	14	15	16	16	17	18	18	19	20	20	21	21	22	23	23	24	25	25	26	27	27	28

♃ 1 5 10 17 23 28 — ♍13 14 15 16 17 18 | ♄ 1 9 21 — ♍19 20 21 | ♅ 1 B — ♓ 9 | ♆ 1 23 — ♌12 13 | ♇ 1 15 — ♋ 8 9

8

	1	2	3	4	5	6	7	8	9	10	11	12	13	14	15	16	17	18	19	20	21	22	23	24	25	26	27	28	29	30	31
☉	♌ 8	9	10	11	12	13	14	15	16	17	18	19	20	21	22	23	24	25	26	27	28	29	29 0	♍ 1	2	3	3	4	5	6	7
☽	♋ 5	20	♌ 5	20	♍ 6	21	♎ 5	19	♏ 3	16	29	♐ 11	24	♑ 6	18	29	♒ 11	23	♓ 5	17	29	♈ 11	24	♉ 6	19	♊ 2	16	29	♋ 14	29	♌ 14
☿	♋ 19	21	22	24	25	27	28	29 0	♌ 2	4	6	8	10	12	14	16	18	20	22	24	26	28	29 0	♍ 2	4	6	7	9	11	13	15
♀	♊ 25	26	28	29	29 0	♋ 1	2	3	4	5	6	8	9	10	11	12	13	14	15	17	18	19	20	21	22	24	25	26	27	28	29 0
♂	♋ 29	29	29 0	♌ 1	1	2	2	3	4	4	5	5	6	7	8	8	9	10	10	11	11	12	13	14	14	15	15	16	17	17	18

♃ 1 4 9 13 18 23 28 — ♍18 19 20 21 22 23 24 | ♄ 1 10 19 27 — ♍22 23 24 25 | ♅ 1 B 5 31 — ♓ 9 8 7 | ♆ 1 20 — ♌13 14 | ♇ 1 — ♋ 9

9

	1	2	3	4	5	6	7	8	9	10	11	12	13	14	15	16	17	18	19	20	21	22	23	24	25	26	27	28	29	30	31
☉	♍ 8	9	10	11	12	13	14	15	16	17	18	19	20	21	22	23	24	25	26	27	28	29	29 0	♎ 1	2	3	4	5	6	7	
☽	♌ 29	♍ 14	29	♎ 14	28	♏ 12	25	♐ 8	20	♑ 2	♒ 14	26	8	20	♓ 2	14	26	♈ 8	21	♉ 3	16	29	♊ 12	26	♋ 10	24	♌ 8	23	♍ 8	23	
☿	♍ 17	19	20	22	24	25	27	29	29 0	♎ 2	4	5	7	8	10	12	13	15	16	17	19	20	22	23	24	26	27	28	29 0	♏ 1	
♀	♌ 1	2	3	4	5	6	8	9	10	11	12	13	15	16	17	18	19	21	22	23	24	25	27	28	29	29 0	♍ 1	3	4	5	
♂	♌ 18	19	20	20	21	22	22	23	24	24	25	25	26	27	27	28	29	29	29 0	♍ 0	1	2	2	3	4	4	5	6	6	7	

♃ 1 6 12 15 20 25 29 30 — ♍25 26 27 28 29 ♎ 0 1 | ♄ 1 5 13 20 30 — ♍25 26 27 28 29 | ♅ 1 B 30 — ♓ 7 6 | ♆ 1 18 — ♌14 15 | ♇ 1 — ♋10

10

	1	2	3	4	5	6	7	8	9	10	11	12	13	14	15	16	17	18	19	20	21	22	23	24	25	26	27	28	29	30	31
☉	♎ 8	9	10	11	12	13	14	14	15	16	17	18	19	20	21	22	23	24	25	26	27	28	29 0	♏ 0	1	2	3	4	5	6	7
☽	♎ 7	22	♏ 6	20	♐ 3	16	28	♑ 11	23	♒ 5	17	28	♓ 10	22	♈ 5	17	29	♉ 13	26	♊ 9	23	♋ 6	20	♌ 4	19	♍ 3	17	♎ 2	16	♏ 0	14
☿	♏ 2	3	4	6	7	8	9	10	11	12	12	13	14	14	15	15	16	16	16	B 16	16	16	15	15	14	13	12	11	10	9	7
♀	♍ 6	8	9	10	11	12	14	15	16	17	19	20	21	22	23	25	26	27	28	29 0	♎ 1	2	3	5	6	7	8	9	11	12	13
♂	♍ 7	8	9	9	10	11	11	12	12	13	14	14	15	16	16	17	17	18	19	19	20	20	21	22	22	23	24	24	25	25	26

♃ 1 5 10 15 20 25 31 — ♎ 1 2 3 4 5 6 7 | ♄ 1 7 15 25 31 — ♍29 ♎ 0 1 2 3 | ♅ 1 B — ♓ 6 | ♆ 1 31 — ♌15 16 | ♇ 1 — ♋10

11

	1	2	3	4	5	6	7	8	9	10	11	12	13	14	15	16	17	18	19	20	21	22	23	24	25	26	27	28	29	30	31
☉	♏ 8	9	10	11	12	13	14	15	16	17	18	19	20	21	22	23	24	25	26	27	28	29 0	♐ 1	2	3	4	5	6	7	8	
☽	♏ 28	♐ 11	24	♑ 6	19	♒ 1	13	24	♓ 6	18	♈ 0	13	25	♉ 8	22	♊ 5	19	♋ 3	17	♌ 1	15	29	♍ 14	28	♎ 12	25	♏ 9	23	♐ 6	19	
☿	♏ B 6	5	4	3	2	1	1	0	D 0	0	1	1	2	2	3	4	5	6	7	9	10	11	13	14	16	17	18	20	21	23	
♀	♎ 14	16	17	18	19	21	22	23	24	26	27	28	29 0	♏ 1	2	3	4	6	7	8	9	11	12	13	14	16	17	18	19	21	
♂	♍ 27	27	28	29	29	29 0	♎ 0	1	2	2	3	3	4	5	5	6	6	7	8	8	9	10	10	11	11	12	13	13	14	14	

♃ 1 8 13 18 24 30 — ♎ 8 9 10 11 12 13 | ♄ 1 12 22 — ♎ 3 4 5 | ♅ 1 B 15 D — ♓ 6 6 | ♆ 1 19 B — ♌16 16 | ♇ 1 30 — ♋10 9

12

	1	2	3	4	5	6	7	8	9	10	11	12	13	14	15	16	17	18	19	20	21	22	23	24	25	26	27	28	29	30	31
☉	♐ 9	10	11	12	13	14	15	16	17	18	19	20	21	22	23	24	25	26	27	28	29	29 0	♑ 1	2	3	4	5	6	7	8	9
☽	♑ 2	14	26	♒ 9	20	♓ 2	14	26	♈ 8	20	♉ 3	16	29	♊ 14	28	♋ 12	27	♌ 12	26	♍ 11	25	♎ 9	22	♏ 6	19	♐ 2	15	28	♑ 10	22	♒ 5
☿	♏ 24	26	28	29	♐ 0	2	4	5	7	8	10	11	13	15	16	18	19	21	22	24	25	27	29	29 0	♑ 2	3	5	7	8	10	11
♀	♏ 22	23	24	26	27	28	29 0	♐ 1	2	3	4	6	7	8	9	11	12	13	15	16	17	18	20	21	22	23	25	26	27	28	29 ♑ 0
♂	♎ 15	16	16	17	17	18	19	19	20	20	21	22	22	23	23	24	25	25	26	26	27	28	28	29	29	29 0	♏ 0	1	2	2	3

♃ 1 6 13 20 29 — ♎13 14 15 16 17 | ♄ 1 22 — ♎ 6 7 | ♅ 1 — ♓ 6 | ♆ 1 B 31 — ♌16 15 | ♇ 1 — ♋ 9

I PLANETARY POSITIONS 1910-1984

1922

1
	1	2	3	4	5	6	7	8	9	10	11	12	13	14	15	16	17	18	19	20	21	22	23	24	25	26	27	28	29	30	31
☉	♑10	11	12	13	14	15	16	17	18	19	20	21	22	23	24	25	26	27	28	29 ♒0	1	2	3	4	5	6	7	8	9	10	11
☽	♒17	28	♓10	22	♈4	16	28	♉11	24	♊8	22	♋6	21	♌6	21	♍6	21	♎5	19	♏3	16	29	♐12	24	♑7	19	♒1	13	25	♓7	19
☿	♑13	15	16	18	20	21	23	25	26	28	29 ♒0	1	3	5	6	8	10	11	13	14	16	18	19	21	22	23	25	26	27	28	29
♀	♑1	2	3	5	6	7	8	10	11	12	13	15	16	17	18	20	21	22	24	25	26	27	29	29 ♒0	1	2	4	5	6	7	9
♂	♏3	4	5	5	6	6	7	7	8	9	9	10	10	11	11	12	13	13	14	14	15	15	16	16	17	18	18	19	19	20	20

♃ 1 10 ♎17 18 · ♄ 1 17R ♎7 7 · ♅ 1 10 31 ♓6 7 8 · ♆ 1R ♌15 · ♇ 1 31 ♋9 8

2
	1	2	3	4	5	6	7	8	9	10	11	12	13	14	15	16	17	18	19	20	21	22	23	24	25	26	27	28
☉	♒12	13	14	15	16	17	18	19	20	21	22	23	24	25	26	27	28	29	♓0	1	2	3	4	5	6	7	8	9
☽	♈1	12	24	7	19	2	16	29	14	29	14	29	14	28	12	26	9	21	4	16	28	10	22	4	16	28		
☿	♒29 ♓0	0	1	1	1	1R	1	0	29	29	28	27	26	25	24	22	21	20	19	18	18	17	17	16	16	16	16D	16
♀	♒10	11	12	14	15	16	17	19	20	21	22	24	25	26	27	29	♓0	1	2	4	5	6	7	9	10	11	12	14
♂	♏21	21	22	22	23	24	24	25	25	26	26	27	27	28	28	29	29	♐0	0	1	1	2	2	3	3	4	4	5

♃ 1 3R ♎18 18 · ♄ 1R 28 ♎7 6 · ♅ 1 18 ♓8 9 · ♆ 1R 25 ♌15 14 · ♇ 1 ♋8

3
	1	2	3	4	5	6	7	8	9	10	11	12	13	14	15	16	17	18	19	20	21	22	23	24	25	26	27	28	29	30	31
☉	♓10	11	12	13	14	15	16	17	18	19	20	21	22	23	24	25	26	27	28	29	29 ♈0	1	2	3	4	5	6	7	8	9	10
☽	♈9	21	3	16	28	11	25	8	22	7	22	7	22	8	22	7	21	5	18	1	13	25	7	19	1	13	24	6	18	1	13
☿	♒16	16	17	17	18	18	19	20	21	22	23	24	26	27	28	29	♓0	1	3	4	5	7	8	9	11	12	14	15	17	18	
♀	♓15	16	17	19	20	21	22	24	25	26	27	29	♈0	1	2	4	5	6	7	9	10	11	12	14	15	16	17	19	20	21	22
♂	♐5	6	6	7	7	8	8	8	9	9	10	10	11	11	12	12	13	13	14	14	14	15	15	16	16	16	17	17	17	18	18

♃ 1R 10 19 27 31 ♎18 17 16 15 14 · ♄ 1R 16 28 ♎6 5 4 · ♅ 1 8 25 ♓9 10 11 · ♆ 1R 31 ♌14 13 · ♇ 1 ♋8

4
	1	2	3	4	5	6	7	8	9	10	11	12	13	14	15	16	17	18	19	20	21	22	23	24	25	26	27	28	29	30
☉	♈11	12	13	14	15	16	17	18	19	20	21	22	23	24	25	26	27	28	28	29 ♉0	1	2	3	4	5	6	7	8	9	
☽	♉25	8	21	4	18	2	16	1	16	1	16	0	15	29	13	26	9	21	4	16	28	9	21	3	15	27	10	22	5	18
☿	♓20	22	23	25	27	28	29 ♈0	2	4	5	7	9	11	13	15	17	19	21	23	25	27	29 ♉0	1	3	5	7	10	12	14	16
♀	♈23	25	26	27	28	29 ♉0	1	2	3	5	6	7	8	10	11	12	13	14	16	17	18	19	21	22	23	24	25	27	28	29
♂	♐18	18	19	19	19	20	20	20	21	21	21	21	22	22	22	23	23	23	23	24	24	24	24	24	24	25	25	25	25	25

♃ 1R 12 20 29 ♎14 13 12 11 · ♄ 1R 11 26 ♎4 3 2 · ♅ 1 14 ♓11 12 · ♆ 1R 24D ♌13 13 · ♇ 1 ♋8

5
	1	2	3	4	5	6	7	8	9	10	11	12	13	14	15	16	17	18	19	20	21	22	23	24	25	26	27	28	29	30	31
☉	♉10	11	12	13	14	15	16	17	18	19	20	21	22	23	24	25	26	27	28	29	29 ♊0	1	2	3	4	5	6	7	8	9	
☽	♋1	15	29	13	27	11	25	10	24	9	23	7	21	4	17	29	12	24	6	17	29	11	23	6	18	1	14	28	12	25	9
☿	♉18	20	22	24	26	28	♊0	2	4	6	8	9	11	12	14	15	17	18	19	21	22	23	24	25	26	27	27	28	28	29	29
♀	♊0	2	3	4	5	7	8	9	10	11	13	14	15	16	17	19	20	21	22	24	25	26	27	28	29 ♋0	1	2	3	4	6	7
♂	♐25	25	25	25	25	25	25R	25	25	25	25	25	25	25	25	25	25	25	24	24	24	24	24	24	23	23	23	23	22	22	22

♃ 1R 10 31 ♎11 10 9 · ♄ 1R 19 ♎2 1 · ♅ 1 10 ♓12 13 · ♆ 1 ♌13 · ♇ 1 31 ♋8 9

6
	1	2	3	4	5	6	7	8	9	10	11	12	13	14	15	16	17	18	19	20	21	22	23	24	25	26	27	28	29	30
☉	♊10	11	12	13	14	15	16	17	18	19	20	21	22	23	24	25	26	27	28	29	29 ♋0	1	2	3	4	5	6	7	8	
☽	♍23	8	22	6	20	4	18	2	16	29	12	25	7	20	2	13	25	7	19	1	14	27	10	23	7	21	6	20	4	19
☿	♋0	0	1	1	1	1	1	0	0	29	29	29	29	28	28	27	27	26	26	25	24	24	23	23	22	22	22	22	22	22D
♀	♋8	9	10	12	13	14	15	16	18	19	20	21	22	24	25	26	27	28	29 ♌0	1	2	3	4	5	6	7	8	9	10	11
♂	♐21	21	21	20	20	20	19	19	19	19	18	18	18	17	17	17	16	16	16	15	15	15	14	14	14	14	13	13	13	13

♃ 1R 6D 10 30 ♎9 9 10 · ♄ 1R 3D 18 ♎1 1 · ♅ 1 19R ♓13 13 · ♆ 1 19 ♌13 14 · ♇ 1 ♋9

7
	1	2	3	4	5	6	7	8	9	10	11	12	13	14	15	16	17	18	19	20	21	22	23	24	25	26	27	28	29	30	31
☉	♋9	10	11	12	13	13	14	15	16	17	18	19	20	21	22	23	24	25	26	27	28	29	29 ♌0	1	2	3	4	5	5	6	7
☽	♎3	17	1	14	28	12	25	8	21	3	16	28	10	21	3	15	27	9	22	5	18	2	16	0	15	29	14	29	13	28	11
☿	♊22	22	22	23	23	24	24	25	26	27	27	28	29 ♋0	1	2	3	4	6	7	9	11	12	14	16	18	20	22	24	26	28	29 ♌0
♀	♌14	15	16	17	19	20	21	22	23	24	26	27	28	29 ♍0	1	3	4	5	6	7	8	10	11	12	13	14	15	16	17	18	19
♂	♐13	12	12	12	12	12	12	12	11	11	11	11	11	11	11	11D	11	11	11	11	11	11	11	11	11	12	12	12	12	12	12

♃ 1 13 22 30 ♎10 11 12 12 · ♄ 1 11 25 ♎1 2 3 · ♅ 1R ♓13 · ♆ 1 20 ♌14 15 · ♇ 1 31 ♋9 10

8
	1	2	3	4	5	6	7	8	9	10	11	12	13	14	15	16	17	18	19	20	21	22	23	24	25	26	27	28	29	30	31
☉	♌8	9	10	11	12	13	14	15	16	17	18	19	20	21	22	23	24	25	26	27	27	28	29 ♍0	0	1	2	3	4	5	6	7
☽	♏25	8	22	4	17	29	12	24	6	18	29	12	23	5	18	0	13	26	10	24	9	23	8	24	8	23	8	22	5	19	1
☿	♌2	4	6	8	10	12	14	16	18	20	22	24	26	28	29 ♍0	2	4	6	7	9	11	12	14	16	17	19	20	22	23	24	26
♀	♍20	21	22	23	24	25	27	27	29	29 ♎0	1	2	3	4	6	7	8	9	10	11	12	13	14	15	16	17	18	19	20	21	22
♂	♐13	13	13	13	13	14	14	14	15	15	15	15	16	16	16	17	17	18	18	18	19	20	20	20	21	21	22	22	22	23	23

♃ 1 6 12 18 24 29 ♎13 14 15 16 17 18 · ♄ 1 6 16 26 ♎3 4 5 6 · ♅ 1R 26 ♓13 12 · ♆ 1 17 ♌15 16 · ♇ 1 ♋10 11

9
	1	2	3	4	5	6	7	8	9	10	11	12	13	14	15	16	17	18	19	20	21	22	23	24	25	26	27	28	29	30
☉	♍8	9	10	11	12	13	14	15	16	17	18	19	20	21	22	23	24	25	26	27	28	29	29 ♎0	1	2	3	4	5	6	
☽	♑14	27	9	21	3	15	27	8	20	2	14	26	9	22	5	18	2	17	2	17	2	17	1	15	28	11	24	6	18	
☿	♍29	29 ♎0	2	3	5	6	7	9	10	11	13	14	15	16	18	19	20	21	22	23	24	25	26	27	28	29	29	29	29	
♀	♎24	25	26	27	28	29	29 ♏0	1	2	3	4	5	6	7	8	9	10	11	12	13	14	15	16	17	18	19	20	21	22	
♂	♐24	24	25	25	26	26	27	27	28	28	29	29	29 ♑0	0	1	1	2	3	3	4	4	5	6	7	7	8	9	9	10	

♃ 1 4 9 14 19 24 29 ♎18 19 20 21 22 23 24 · ♄ 1 4 12 20 29 ♎6 7 8 9 10 · ♅ 1R 28 30 ♓12 11 10 · ♆ 1 ♌16 17 · ♇ 1 ♋11

10
	1	2	3	4	5	6	7	8	9	10	11	12	13	14	15	16	17	18	19	20	21	22	23	24	25	26	27	28	29	30	31
☉	♎7	8	9	10	11	12	13	14	15	16	17	18	19	20	21	22	23	24	25	26	27	28	29	29 ♏0	1	2	3	4	5	6	7
☽	♒18	0	12	24	5	17	29	11	23	6	18	1	14	28	11	26	10	25	10	25	10	25	9	23	7	20	2	15	27	9	20
☿	♎29	0	0	29	29	29	28	28	27	26	25	23	22	21	20	19	18	17	16	16	15	15D	15	15	15	16	16	17	18	18	19
♀	♏23	23	24	15	26	27	27	28	29	29 ♐0	0	1	2	2	3	3	4	5	5	6	6	7	7	7	8	8	8	9	9	9	9
♂	♑10	11	12	12	13	14	14	15	16	17	17	18	19	19	20	21	22	22	23	23	24	25	26	26	27	28	28	29	29 ♒0		

♃ 1 3 8 13 17 22 26 29 31 ♎24 25 26 27 28 29 ♏0 1 · ♄ 1 7 15 23 31 ♎10 11 12 13 14 · ♅ 1R ♓10 · ♆ 1 20 ♌17 18 · ♇ 1 ♋11

11
	1	2	3	4	5	6	7	8	9	10	11	12	13	14	15	16	17	18	19	20	21	22	23	24	25	26	27	28	29	30
☉	♏8	9	10	11	12	13	14	15	16	17	18	19	20	21	22	23	24	25	26	27	28	29	29 ♐0	1	2	3	4	5	6	7
☽	♓2	14	26	8	20	3	15	28	11	24	8	22	6	20	5	20	4	19	3	17	1	15	28	11	23	5	17	29	10	22
☿	♎20	21	22	23	25	26	28	29 ♏0	1	2	4	5	7	8	10	12	13	15	16	18	20	21	23	24	26	28	29 ♐0	1	2	4
♀	♐9	10	10	10	10	10	10	10	10	9	9	9	9	8	8	8	7	7	6	6	5	5	4	4	3	2	2	1	0	29 ♏29
♂	♒1	2	2	3	4	5	5	6	7	7	8	9	10	10	11	12	12	13	14	15	15	16	17	17	18	19	19	20	21	22

♃ 1 5 9 14 19 23 28 ♏1 2 3 4 5 6 7 · ♄ 1 9 19 29 ♎14 15 16 17 · ♅ 1R 20 D ♓10 10 · ♆ 1 21 ♌18 18R · ♇ 1 ♋11

12
	1	2	3	4	5	6	7	8	9	10	11	12	13	14	15	16	17	18	19	20	21	22	23	24	25	26	27	28	29	30	31
☉	♐8	9	10	11	12	13	14	15	16	17	18	19	20	21	22	23	24	25	26	27	28	29 ♑0	1	2	3	4	5	6	7	8	9
☽	♈4	17	29	12	25	8	21	5	18	2	16	0	14	28	13	27	11	25	9	23	6	18	1	13	25	7	18	0	12	25	7
☿	♐5	7	9	10	12	13	15	16	18	20	21	23	24	26	27	29	29 ♑0	2	4	5	7	9	10	12	13	15	17	18	20	21	23
♀	♏28	28	27	27	26	26	26	25	25	25	25	24	24	24	24	24D	24	24	24	24	24	24	25	25	25	25	26	26	26	27	27
♂	♒23	23	24	25	25	26	27	27	28	29	29 ♓0	1	1	2	3	4	4	5	6	6	7	8	8	9	10	10	11	12	13	14	15

♃ 1 3 8 13 19 24 30 ♏7 8 9 10 11 12 13 · ♄ 1 11 25 ♎17 18 19 · ♅ 1 ♓10 · ♆ 1R ♌18 · ♇ 1R ♋10

1923

1
	1	2	3	4	5	6	7	8	9	10	11	12	13	14	15	16	17	18	19	20	21	22	23	24	25	26	27	28	29	30	31
☉	♑10	11	12	13	14	15	16	17	18	19	20	21	22	23	24	25	26	27	28	29	29 ♒0	1	2	3	4	5	6	7	8	9	10
☽	♊20	3	17	1	15	29	13	27	11	25	9	23	7	21	4	18	1	14	26	9	21	2	14	26	8	20	2	14	28	10	22
☿	♑24	26	28	29 ♒0	1	2	4	5	6	7	8	9	10	11	12	13	14	14	15	15	15	15R	14	14	13	12	11	10	9	8	6
♀	♏29	29 ♐0	1	1	2	3	4	5	5	6	7	8	8	9	10	11	12	12	13	14	15	16	17	17	18	19	20	21	22	22	23
♂	♓15	16	17	17	18	19	19	20	20	21	22	22	23	24	24	25	26	26	27	28	28	29 ♈0	0	1	2	2	3	4	4	5	6

♃ 1 5 12 20 28 ♏13 14 15 16 17 · ♄ 1 18 30R ♎19 20 20 · ♅ 1 15 ♓10 11 · ♆ 1R 31 ♌18 17 · ♇ 1 ♋10

2
	1	2	3	4	5	6	7	8	9	10	11	12	13	14	15	16	17	18	19	20	21	22	23	24	25	26	27	28
☉	♒11	12	13	14	15	16	17	18	19	20	21	22	23	24	25	26	27	28	29 ♓0	1	2	3	4	5	6	7	8	9
☽	♌9	24	8	23	7	22	6	20	4	17	1	14	27	10	22	5	17	29	11	22	4	16	28	10	23	6	19	3
☿	♒4	3	2	1	0	29	29	29	29	29	29D	29	29	29	29 ♒0	1	1	2	3	3	4	5	6	7	8	9	10	11
♀	♐25	26	27	28	29	29 ♑0	1	2	3	4	5	6	7	8	9	10	11	12	13	15	16	17	18	19	20	21	22	23
♂	♈8	9	9	10	11	12	12	13	14	14	15	16	16	17	17	18	19	19	20	21	21	22	22	23	24	24	25	26

♃ 1 9 ♏17 18 · ♄ 1R 28 ♎20 19 · ♅ 1 12 ♓11 12 13 · ♆ 1R ♌17 16 · ♇ 1 ♋9

3
	1	2	3	4	5	6	7	8	9	10	11	12	13	14	15	16	17	18	19	20	21	22	23	24	25	26	27	28	29	30	31
☉	♓10	11	12	13	14	15	16	17	18	19	20	21	22	23	24	25	26	27	28	29	29 ♈0	1	2	3	4	5	6	7	8	9	10
☽	♌17	2	17	2	17	2	16	0	14	28	11	24	7	19	1	13	25	7	19	1	13	25	7	19	1	14	27	11	25		
☿	♒14	15	16	18	19	20	22	23	25	26	27	29 ♓0	2	4	5	7	8	10	12	13	15	17	18	20	22	24	26	27	29		
♀	♑25	26	27	28	29	29 ♒0	1	2	4	5	6	7	8	9	10	12	13	14	15	16	17	19	20	21	22	23	24	25	26	27	
♂	♈28	29	29 ♉0	1	2	2	3	4	4	5	6	6	7	7	8	9	9	10	10	11	11	12	13	13	14	14	15	15	16	16	17	18

♃ 1 6R ♏18 18 · ♄ 1R 22 31 ♎19 18 17 · ♅ 1 13 31 ♓13 14 15 · ♆ 1R ♌16 15 · ♇ 1 ♋9

4
	1	2	3	4	5	6	7	8	9	10	11	12	13	14	15	16	17	18	19	20	21	22	23	24	25	26	27	28	29	30
☉	♈11	12	13	14	15	16	17	18	19	20	20	21	22	23	24	25	26	27	28	29	29 ♉0	1	2	3	4	5	6	7	8	
☽	♎10	25	10	25	10	24	8	21	4	16	28	10	22	4	16	28	10	22	4	16	28	11	23	7	20	4	18	3	18	
☿	♓3	5	7	9	11	13	15	17	19	21	23	26	28	29 ♈0	2	4	6	8	10	12	14	16	18	19	21	23	24	26	27	
♀	♒29 ♓0	1	3	4	5	6	7	8	10	11	12	13	14	15	17	18	19	20	21	22	24	25	26	27	29	29 ♈0	1	2	3	
♂	♉20	20	21	22	23	23	24	24	25	25	26	27	27	28	28	29	29	29 ♊0	1	1	2	3	3	4	5	5	6	6	7	8

♃ 1R 10 20 28 ♏18 17 16 15 · ♄ 1R 17 30 ♎17 16 15 · ♅ 1 20 ♓15 16 · ♆ 1R 27D ♌15 15 · ♇ 1 ♋9

5
	1	2	3	4	5	6	7	8	9	10	11	12	13	14	15	16	17	18	19	20	21	22	23	24	25	26	27	28	29	30	31
☉	♉10	11	12	13	14	15	16	17	18	19	20	21	22	23	24	25	26	27	28	29	29 ♊0	1	2	3	4	5	6	7			
☽	♏19	4	18	3	16	29	13	25	7	19	1	13	25	7	19	1	13	25	8	20	3	16	0	14	28	12	27	12			
☿	♉29 ♊0	1	3	4	5	6	7	7	8	9	10	10	11	11	11	11	11	11R	11	11	10	10	9	9	8	8	7	7	6		
♀	♈6	7	8	9	11	12	13	14	16	17	18	19	20	22	23	24	25	26	28	29 ♉0	1	2	4	5	6	7	8	9			
♂	♊10	11	12	12	13	14	14	15	16	16	17	18	18	19	19	20	21	21	22	23	23	24	25	25	26	26	27	28	28	29	29

♃ 1R 14 22 31 ♏13 12 11 · ♄ 1R 9 31 ♎15 14 13 · ♅ 1 16 ♓16 17 · ♆ 1 ♌15 · ♇ 1 ♋9

6
	1	2	3	4	5	6	7	8	9	10	11	12	13	14	15	16	17	18	19	20	21	22	23	24	25	26	27	28	29	30
☉	♊10	11	12	13	14	15	16	17	18	19	20	21	22	23	24	25	26	27	28	29	29 ♋0	1	2	3	4	5	6	7		
☽	♑11	25	8	21	4	16	28	10	21	3	15	27	9	22	4	17	0	13	27	10	24	8	22	7	21	6	21	5	19	
☿	♊5	4	4	3	3	3	2	2	2	2D	2	2	2	2	3	3	3	4	4	5	5	6	7	8	9	10	11	12	13	14
♀	♉13	14	15	17	18	19	20	21	23	24	25	26	27	29	29 ♊0	1	2	3	5	6	7	8	10	11	12	13	14	16	17	18
♂	♋0	1	2	3	4	4	5	6	6	7	7	8	9	9	10	11	11	12	13	13	14	15	15	16	17	17	18	18	19	19

♃ 1R 12 30 ♏11 10 9 · ♄ 1R 17D ♎13 13 · ♅ 1 23R ♓17 17 · ♆ 1 14 ♌15 16 · ♇ 1 ♋10

7
	1	2	3	4	5	6	7	8	9	10	11	12	13	14	15	16	17	18	19	20	21	22	23	24	25	26	27	28	29	30	31
☉	♋8	9	10	11	12	13	14	15	16	17	18	19	20	21	22	23	24	25	26	27	28	28	29 ♌0	1	2	3	4	5			
☽	♒16	29	12	24	6	18	29	11	23	6	18	1	13	27	10	23	7	21	5	19	3	18	2	16	0	14	28	11	24		
☿	♊18	20	21	23	24	26	28	29 ♋0	2	4	6	8	10	12	14	16	18	20	22	24	26	29	29 ♌0	3	5	7	9	11			
♀	♊19	20	22	23	24	25	27	28	29 ♋0	1	3	4	5	6	8	9	10	11	12	14	15	16	17	19	20	21	22	23			
♂	♋20	21	22	22	23	24	24	25	25	26	27	27	28	29	29 ♌0	1	1	2	3	3	4	5	5	6	7	7	8				

♃ 1R 7D 31 ♏9 9 10 · ♄ 1 14 31 ♎13 14 15 · ♅ 1R ♓17 · ♆ 1 17 ♌16 17 · ♇ 1 ♋10

8
	1	2	3	4	5	6	7	8	9	10	11	12	13	14	15	16	17	18	19	20	21	22	23	24	25	26	27	28	29	30	31
☉	♌8	9	10	11	12	13	14	15	16	17	18	19	20	21	22	23	24	25	26	27	28	29	29 ♍0	1	2	3	4	5			
☽	♓2	14	26	8	19	1	14	26	9	22	5	19	3	17	1	16	0	14	29	13	26	10	24	7	20	3	15	28	10		
☿	♌19	21	23	24	26	28	29 ♍0	1	3	5	6	8	10	12	14	16	17	19	20	22	23	24	26	27	29 ♎0	1	2				
♀	♋27	28	29 ♌0	1	3	5	6	7	8	9	11	12	13	14	16	17	18	19	20	21	22	23	24	26	27	28	29 ♍0				
♂	♌10	11	11	12	13	13	14	14	15	15	16	17	17	18	18	19	19	20	21	21	22	23	23	24	25	25	26	27	28	28	

♃ 1 13 21 29 31 ♏10 11 12 13 13 · ♄ 1 14 25 31 ♎15 16 17 17 · ♅ 1R 29 31 ♓17 16 16 · ♆ 1 14 31 ♌17 18 18 · ♇ 1 ♋11

9
	1	2	3	4	5	6	7	8	9	10	11	12	13	14	15	16	17	18	19	20	21	22	23	24	25	26	27	28	29	30
☉	♍8	9	10	11	12	13	14	15	16	17	18	19	20	21	22	23	24	25	26	27	28	29	29 ♎0	1	2	3	4	5		
☽	♈16	27	9	22	4	17	0	13	27	12	26	11	26	10	25	9	23	7	21	4	17	29	12	24	6	18	0	12	24	
☿	♎5	6	7	8	9	9	10	11	11	12	12	13	13	13	13	13R	13	13	12	12	11	10	9	8	7	6	4			
♀	♍5	7	8	9	10	12	13	14	15	17	18	19	20	22	23	24	25	27	28	29 ♎0	1	2	3	5	6	7	9	10	11	
♂	♍29 ♍0	1	1	2	3	3	4	5	5	6	7	7	8	9	9	10	11	11	12	13	13	14	15	15	16	16	17	18		

♃ 1 5 11 17 23 28 ♏13 14 15 16 17 18 · ♄ 1 4 13 21 30 ♎17 18 19 20 21 · ♅ 1R ♓16 15 · ♆ 1 11 ♌18 19 · ♇ 1 ♋12

10
	1	2	3	4	5	6	7	8	9	10	11	12	13	14	15	16	17	18	19	20	21	22	23	24	25	26	27	28	29	30	31
☉	♎7	8	9	10	11	12	13	14	15	16	17	18	19	20	21	22	23	24	25	26	27	28	29	29 ♏0	1	2	3	4	5		
☽	♊18	0	12	25	8	21	5	20	4	19	5	20	5	19	4	17	1	14	26	9	21	3	15	27	9	21	3	15	27		
☿	♎2	1	29	29	29	29	29	29	29	29	29D	29 ♎0	1	2	3	5	6	7	9	10	12	14	15	17	19	20	22	24	25	27	
♀	♎13	14	15	16	18	19	20	21	23	24	25	26	27	29	29 ♏0	1	3	4	5	6	8	9	10	11	13	14	15	16	18	19	
♂	♎19	20	20	21	22	22	23	24	24	25	26	26	27	28	28	29	29 ♏0	1	1	2	3	3	4	5	5	6	7				

♃ 1 4 9 14 19 23 28 ♏18 19 20 21 22 23 24 · ♄ 1 8 17 25 ♎21 22 23 24 · ♅ 1R 25 ♓15 14 · ♆ 1 19 ♌19 20 · ♇ 1 ♋12

11
	1	2	3	4	5	6	7	8	9	10	11	12	13	14	15	16	17	18	19	20	21	22	23	24	25	26	27	28	29	30
☉	♏8	9	10	11	12	13	14	15	16	17	18	19	20	21	22	23	24	25	26	27	28	29	29 ♐0	1	2	3	4	5	6	
☽	♋4	16	29	14	28	12	27	12	28	13	28	13	27	11	24	7	19	1	13	25	7	19	1	14	26	8	21	4	17	0
☿	♏29	29 ♐0	2	4	5	7	9	10	12	14	15	17	18	20	22	23	25	26	28	29	29 ♑0	2	3	5	6	7	9	10	11	12
♀	♏21	23	24	25	26	26	27	28	29	29 ♐0	1	3	4	5	6	8	9	10	11	13	14	15	16	18	19	20	21	23	24	25
♂	♏9	10	10	11	12	12	13	14	15	15	16	17	17	18	19	19	20	20	21	22	23	23	24	24	25	26	26	27	27	

♃ 1 7 11 15 20 24 29 29 ♏25 26 27 28 29 ♐0 1 · ♄ 1 10 19 29 ♎25 26 27 28 · ♅ 1R 24D ♓14 14 · ♆ 1 24R ♌20 20 · ♇ 1 ♋12

12
	1	2	3	4	5	6	7	8	9	10	11	12	13	14	15	16	17	18	19	20	21	22	23	24	25	26	27	28	29	30	31
☉	♐8	9	10	11	12	13	14	15	16	17	18	19	20	21	22	23	24	25	26	27	28	29	29 ♑0	0	1	2	3	4	5	6	
☽	♍9	23	7	21	6	21	6	21	6	21	5	19	2	14	27	9	21	3	14	26	8	20	3	15	27	10	23	6	19	3	
☿	♑17	18	19	20	21	23	24	26	28	29 ♒0	2	4	5	7	8	10	11	13	14	15	17	18	20	21	22	23	24	25	25	26	
♀	♑28	29	29 ♑0	1	3	4	5	6	8	9	10	11	13	14	15	16	18	19	20	21	23	24	25	26	28	29	29 ♒0	1	3	4	
♂	♐29 ♐0	1	1	2	3	3	4	5	5	6	7	7	8	9	9	10	11	11	12	13	13	14	14	15	16						

♃ 1 3 8 12 17 22 26 31 ♐1 2 3 4 5 6 7 8 · ♄ 1 9 20 31 ♎28 29 ♏0 1 · ♅ 1 ♓14 · ♆ 1R ♌20 · ♇ 1R ♋11

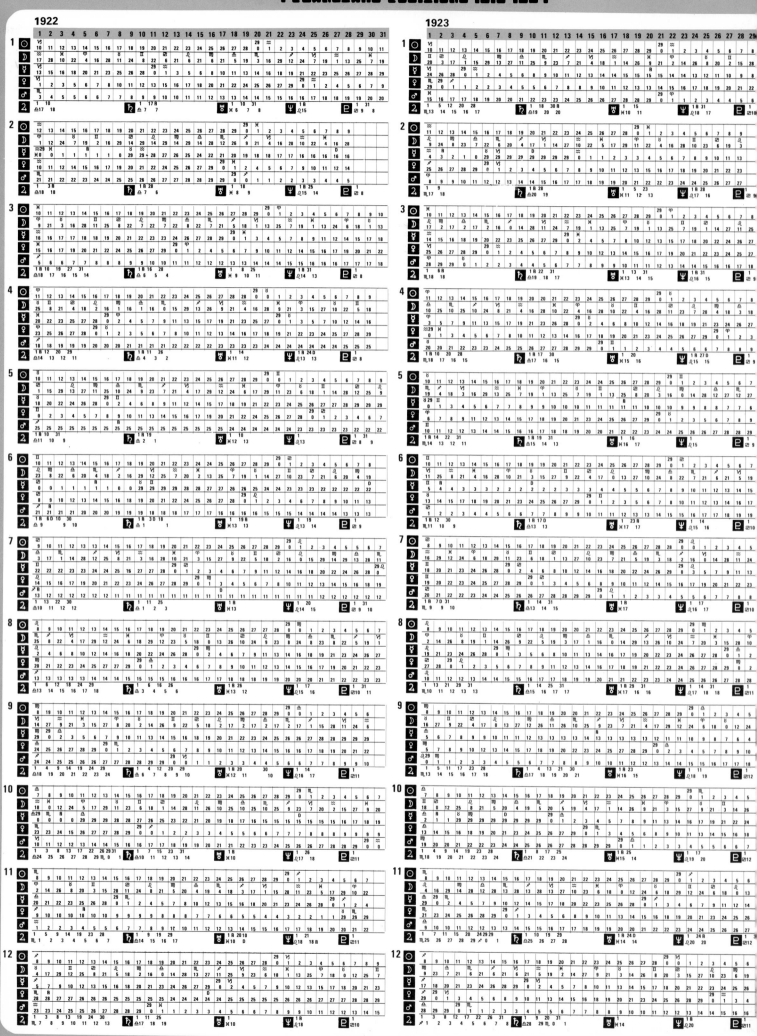

1924

	1	2	3	4	5	6	7	8	9	10	11	12	13	14	15	16	17	18	19	20	21	22	23	24	25	26	27	28	29	30	31
	♑10	11	12	13	14	15	16	17	18	19	20	21	22	23	24	25	26	27	28	29	29/0	♒1	2	3	4	5	6	7	8	9	10
	♏1	15	♐0	15	29	♑14	29	♒13	26	♓10	22	♈5	17	29	♉11	23	♊5	17	29	♋11	24	♌6	19	♍3	16	29	♎13	27	♏12	26	♐10
	♑28	29	29	℞29	29	28	28	27	26	25	24	22	21	20	19	17	16	15	14	13	13	13	13	D13	13	13	13	14	14	15	15
	♒8	9	10	11	12	14	15	16	17	19	20	21	22	24	25	26	27	29	29/0	♓1	2	3	5	6	7	8	10	11	12	13	14
	♏18	19	19	20	21	21	22	23	23	24	25	25	26	26	27	28	28	29	29/0	♐0	1	2	2	3	4	4	5	5	6	7	7

1 5 10 15 20 26 31 / ♐8 9 10 11 12 13 14 — ♄ 1 22 / ♏1 2 — ♅ 1 21 / ♓14 15 — ♆ 1 ℞ 31 / ♌20 19 — ♇ 1 / ♋11

	1	2	3	4	5	6	7	8	9	10	11	12	13	14	15	16	17	18	19	20	21	22	23	24	25	26	27	28	29	30	31
	♒11	12	13	14	15	16	17	18	19	20	21	22	23	24	25	26	27	28	29/0	♓0	1	2	3	4	5	6	7	8	9		
	♐24	♑9	23	♒7	21	♓4	17	♈0	13	25	♉7	19	♊1	12	24	♋7	19	♌2	15	28	♍12	26	♎10	24	♏8	23	♐7	21	♑5		
	♑16	17	18	19	20	21	22	23	24	25	27	28	29	29/0	♒2	3	4	6	7	9	10	11	13	14	16	17	19	21	22		
	♓16	17	18	19	21	22	23	24	25	27	28	29	29/0	♈1	3	4	5	6	7	9	10	11	12	13	15	16	17	18	19		
	♐8	9	9	10	11	11	12	12	13	14	14	15	16	16	17	18	18	19	20	20	21	21	22	23	23	24	25	25	26		

1 7 14 21 29 / ♐14 15 16 17 18 — ♄ 1 11℞ / ♏2 2 — ♅ 1 10 28 / ♓15 16 17 — ♆ 1 ℞ 29 / ♌19 18 — ♇ 1 / ♋10

	1	2	3	4	5	6	7	8	9	10	11	12	13	14	15	16	17	18	19	20	21	22	23	24	25	26	27	28	29	30	31
	♓10	11	12	13	14	15	16	17	18	19	20	21	22	23	24	25	26	27	28	29/0	♈0	1	2	3	4	5	6	7	8	9	10
	♑19	♒3	16	29	♓13	25	♈8	20	♉3	15	27	♊8	20	♋2	14	27	♌10	23	♍6	20	♎5	19	♏4	19	♐3	18	♑2	16	29	♒13	26
	♒24	25	27	29	29/0	♓2	4	5	7	9	11	12	14	16	18	20	22	24	26	28	29/0	♈2	4	6	8	10	12	14	16	18	20
	♈21	22	23	24	25	26	28	29	29/0	♉1	2	3	4	6	7	8	9	10	11	12	13	15	16	17	18	19	20	21	22	24	25
	♐26	27	28	28	29	29/0	♑0	1	2	2	3	3	4	5	5	6	7	7	8	8	9	10	10	11	12	12	13	13	14	15	15

1 12 / ♐18 19 — ♄ 1 ℞ 22 31 / ♏2 1 0 — ♅ 1 17 / ♓17 18 — ♆ 1 ℞ 31 / ♌18 17 — ♇ 1 / ♋10

	1	2	3	4	5	6	7	8	9	10	11	12	13	14	15	16	17	18	19	20	21	22	23	24	25	26	27	28	29	30	31
	♈11	12	13	14	15	16	17	18	19	20	21	22	23	24	25	26	27	28	29	29/0	♉1	2	3	4	5	6	7	8	9	10	
	♓9	22	♈4	17	29	♉11	23	♊5	17	28	♋10	23	♌5	18	♍1	14	28	♎13	28	♏13	28	♐13	28	♑12	26	♒10	23	♓6	19	♈1	
	♈22	24	26	28	29/0	♉1	3	5	6	8	10	11	12	14	15	16	17	18	18	19	20	20	21	21	21	21	℞21	21	21	21	
	♉26	27	28	29	29/0	♊1	2	3	4	5	6	7	8	10	11	12	13	14	15	16	17	17	18	19	20	21	22	23	24	25	
	♑16	17	17	18	18	19	20	20	21	21	22	23	23	24	24	25	26	26	27	27	28	29	29	29/0	♒0	1	2	2	3	3	

1 6℞ / ♐19 19 — ♄ 1 ℞ 6D 30 / ♏0 ♎29 28 — ♅ 1 4 24 / ♓18 19 20 — ♆ 1 ℞ 28D / ♌17 17 — ♇ 1 / ♋10

	1	2	3	4	5	6	7	8	9	10	11	12	13	14	15	16	17	18	19	20	21	22	23	24	25	26	27	28	29	30	31
	♉11	12	13	14	15	16	17	17	18	19	20	21	22	23	24	25	26	27	28	29	29/0	♊1	2	3	4	5	6	7	8	9	10
	♈13	25	♉8	20	♊1	13	25	♋7	19	♌1	13	26	♍9	23	♎7	21	♏6	21	♐7	22	♑7	21	♒6	19	♓3	16	28	♈10	23	♉5	17
	♉20	℞20	20	19	19	18	17	17	16	16	15	14	14	14	13	13	12	12	12	12	D12	12	12	12	13	13	13	14	15	15	16
	♊26	27	28	29	29	29/0	♋1	2	3	3	4	5	6	6	7	8	9	9	10	10	11	12	12	13	13	14	14	15	15	15	16
	♒4	4	5	6	6	7	7	8	8	9	9	10	11	11	12	12	13	13	14	14	15	15	16	16	17	17	18	18	19	19	20

1 ℞ 11 21 29 / ♐19 18 17 16 — ♄ 1 ℞ 17 31 / ♎28 27 26 — ♅ 1 21 / ♓20 21 — ♆ 1 31 / ♌17 18 — ♇ 1 31 / ♋10 11

	1	2	3	4	5	6	7	8	9	10	11	12	13	14	15	16	17	18	19	20	21	22	23	24	25	26	27	28	29	30	31
	♊10	11	12	13	14	15	16	17	18	19	20	21	22	23	24	25	26	27	28	29	29/0	♋0	1	2	3	4	5	6	7	8	
	♉28	♊10	22	♋4	16	28	♌10	23	♍5	18	♎2	16	♏0	15	29	♐10	♑0	15	♒0	14	28	♓12	25	♈7	20	♉2	14	25	♊7	19	
	♉17	18	18	19	20	21	23	24	25	26	28	29	29/0	♊2	3	5	7	8	10	12	14	16	17	19	21	23	26	28	29/0	♋2	
	♋16	16	17	17	17	17	17	17	17	℞17	17	17	17	17	17	17	16	16	16	15	15	14	14	13	13	12	12	11	10	10	
	♒20	21	21	22	22	23	23	24	24	24	25	25	26	26	26	27	27	28	28	28	29	29	29	29/0	♓0	0	1	1	1	2	

1 ℞ 14 22 30 / ♐15 14 13 12 — ♄ 1 ℞ 29D / ♎26 25 — ♅ 1 26℞ / ♓21 21 — ♆ 1 / ♌18 — ♇ 1 / ♋11

	1	2	3	4	5	6	7	8	9	10	11	12	13	14	15	16	17	18	19	20	21	22	23	24	25	26	27	28	29	30	31
	♋9	10	11	12	13	14	15	16	17	18	19	20	21	22	23	23	24	25	26	27	28	29	29/0	♌1	2	3	4	5	6	7	8
	♋1	13	25	♌7	20	♍2	15	28	♎12	25	♏10	24	♐9	24	♑9	24	♒8	23	♓6	20	♈3	16	28	♉10	22	♊4	16	28	♋10	22	♌4
	♋4	6	8	11	13	15	17	19	21	23	25	28	29/0	♌2	4	5	7	9	11	13	15	17	18	20	22	23	25	26	28	29/0	♍1
	♋9	℞9	8	7	7	6	6	5	5	4	4	3	3	2	2	2	2	1	1	1	1	1	D1	1	1	1	1	1	2	2	2
	♓2	2	2	3	3	3	3	4	4	4	4	4	4	5	5	5	5	5	5	5	5	5	5	℞5	5	5	5	5	5	5	5

1 ℞ 13 31 / ♐12 11 10 — ♄ 1 20 / ♎25 26 — ♅ 1 ℞ / ♓21 — ♆ 1 13 / ♌18 19 — ♇ 1 / ♋12

	1	2	3	4	5	6	7	8	9	10	11	12	13	14	15	16	17	18	19	20	21	22	23	24	25	26	27	28	29	30	31
	♌9	10	11	12	13	14	15	15	16	17	18	19	20	21	22	23	24	25	26	27	28	29	29/0	♍1	2	3	4	5	6	7	8
	♌17	29	♍12	25	♎9	22	♏6	20	♐4	19	♑3	18	♒2	17	♓1	14	28	♈11	24	♉6	18	♊0	12	24	♋6	18	♌0	13	25	♍8	22
	♍3	4	5	7	8	9	11	12	13	14	15	17	18	19	20	20	21	22	23	24	24	25	25	26	26	26	27	27	℞27	27	26
	♋2	3	3	4	4	4	5	5	6	7	7	8	8	9	10	10	11	12	12	13	14	15	15	16	17	18	19	19	20	21	22
	♓5	℞5	4	4	4	4	4	4	4	3	3	3	3	2	2	2	2	1	1	1	1	9	0	♉29	♒29	29	29	29	28	28	28

1 ℞ 7D 31 / ♐10 10 11 — ♄ 1 9 23 / ♎26 27 28 — ♅ 1 ℞ 31 / ♓21 20 — ♆ 1 10 / ♌19 20 — ♇ 1 31 / ♋12 13

	1	2	3	4	5	6	7	8	9	10	11	12	13	14	15	16	17	18	19	20	21	22	23	24	25	26	27	28	29	30	31
	♍8	9	10	11	12	13	14	15	16	17	18	19	20	21	22	23	24	25	26	27	28	29	29/0	♎1	2	3	4	5	6	7	
	♎5	19	♏3	17	♐1	15	29	♑14	28	♒12	26	♓9	23	♈6	19	♉2	14	26	♊8	20	♋2	14	26	♌8	21	♍4	17	♎0	14	29	
	♍26	℞26	25	25	24	23	22	21	20	19	18	17	16	16	15	14	13	13	13	13	D13	13	13	14	14	15	16	17	18	20	
	♋23	24	25	26	27	28	29	29/0	♌0	1	2	3	4	5	6	7	8	9	10	11	12	14	15	16	17	18	19	20	21	22	
	♒28	℞28	27	27	27	27	27	26	26	26	26	26	26	26	25	25	25	25	25	25	25	D25	25	25	25	25	25	25	26	26	

1 12 21 28 / ♐11 12 13 14 — ♄ 1 3 13 29 23 30 / ♎28 29 ♏0 1 2 — ♅ 1 ℞ 26 / ♓20 19 — ♆ 1 6 / ♌20 21 — ♇ 1 / ♋13

	1	2	3	4	5	6	7	8	9	10	11	12	13	14	15	16	17	18	19	20	21	22	23	24	25	26	27	28	29	30	31
	♎8	9	10	11	12	13	14	15	16	17	18	19	20	21	22	23	24	25	26	27	28	29	29/0	♏1	2	3	4	5	6	7	8
	♏13	27	♐12	26	♑10	24	♒8	22	♓5	19	♈2	15	27	♉10	22	♊4	16	28	♋10	22	♌4	16	28	♍11	25	♎9	23	♏8	22	♐7	22
	♍21	22	24	25	27	29	29/0	♎2	4	6	7	9	11	12	14	16	18	19	21	23	25	26	28	29/0	♏1	3	5	6	8	9	11
	♌23	24	25	26	28	29	29/0	♍1	2	3	4	5	6	8	9	10	11	12	13	14	16	17	18	19	20	21	23	24	25	26	27
	♒26	26	26	26	26	26	27	27	27	27	28	28	28	28	29	29	29	29	29/0	♓0	0	1	1	1	2	2	2	3	3	4	4

1 5 11 17 22 28 / ♐14 15 16 17 18 19 — ♄ 1 10 19 27 / ♏2 3 4 5 — ♅ 1 ℞ 26 / ♓19 18 — ♆ 1 9 / ♌21 22 — ♇ 1 / ♋13

	1	2	3	4	5	6	7	8	9	10	11	12	13	14	15	16	17	18	19	20	21	22	23	24	25	26	27	28	29	30	31
	♏9	10	11	12	13	14	15	16	17	18	19	20	21	22	23	24	25	26	27	28	29	29/0	♐1	2	3	4	5	6	7	8	
	♑7	21	♒5	19	♓2	15	28	♈11	24	♉6	18	♊1	13	24	♋6	18	♌0	12	24	♍7	19	♎3	17	♏1	16	♐1	16	♑1	16	♒1	
	♏13	14	16	17	19	21	22	24	25	27	28	29/0	♐1	3	4	6	7	9	10	12	13	15	16	18	19	21	22	23	25	26	
	♍20	29/0	♎1	2	3	4	6	7	8	9	10	12	13	14	15	16	18	19	20	21	23	24	25	26	27	29	29/0	♏1	2	4	
	♓5	5	5	6	6	7	7	8	8	9	9	10	10	11	11	11	12	13	13	14	14	15	15	16	16	17	17	18	18	19	

1 7 12 16 21 26 30 / ♐20 21 22 23 24 25 26 — ♄ 1 4 13 21 30 / ♏5 6 7 8 9 — ♅ 1 ℞ 27D / ♓17 17 — ♆ 1 25℞ / ♌22 22 — ♇ 1 / ♋13

	1	2	3	4	5	6	7	8	9	10	11	12	13	14	15	16	17	18	19	20	21	22	23	24	25	26	27	28	29	30	31
	♐9	10	11	12	13	14	15	16	17	18	19	20	21	22	23	24	25	26	27	28	29	29/0	♑1	2	3	4	5	6	7	8	9
	♒15	29	♓12	25	♈8	21	♉3	15	27	♊9	21	♋3	15	27	♌9	21	♍3	15	28	♎11	25	♏9	24	♐9	24	♑9	24	♒9	24	♓8	22
	♐28	29/0	♑1	2	3	4	6	7	8	9	10	11	11	12	12	13	13	℞13	13	12	12	11	10	9	8	6	5	4	2	1	0
	♏5	6	7	8	10	11	12	13	15	16	17	18	20	21	22	23	24	26	27	28	29/0	♐1	2	3	4	6	7	8	9	11	12
	♓19	20	21	21	22	22	23	23	24	25	25	26	26	27	27	28	29	29	29/0	♈0	1	2	2	3	3	4	5	5	6	7	7

1 5 9 13 18 29 22 26 31 / ♐26 27 28 29 ♑0 1 2 3 — ♄ 1 9 19 31 / ♏9 10 11 12 — ♅ 1 27 / ♓17 18 — ♆ 1 ℞ / ♌22 — ♇ 1 31 / ♋13 12

1925

	1	2	3	4	5	6	7	8	9	10	11	12	13	14	15	16	17	18	19	20	21	22	23	24	25	26	27	28	29	30	31
1 ☉	♑10	11	12	13	14	15	16	17	18	19	20	21	22	23	24	25	26	27	28	29/0	♒1	2	3	4	5	6	7	8	9	10	11
☽	♈5	18	♉0	12	24	♊6	18	♋0	12	24	♌6	18	♍0	12	25	♎8	21	♏4	18	♐3	17	♑2	17	♒2	17	♓2	16	♈0	13	26	♉9
☿	♐29	℞28	28	27	27	27	D27	27	27	27	28	29	29	29/0	♑1	2	3	4	5	6	7	8	9	11	12	13	14	16	17	19	20
♀	♐13	14	16	17	18	19	21	22	23	24	26	27	28	29	29/0	♑2	3	4	6	7	8	9	11	12	13	14	16	17	18	19	21
♂	♈8	8	9	10	10	11	12	12	13	13	14	15	15	16	17	17	18	18	19	20	20	21	22	22	23	23	24	25	25	26	26

♃ 1 4 9 13 18 22 27 31 / ♑3 4 5 6 7 8 9 10 — ♄ 1 13 31 / ♏12 13 14 — ♅ 1 25 / ♓18 19 — ♆ 1 ℞ 31 / ♌22 21 — ♇ 1 / ♋12

	1	2	3	4	5	6	7	8	9	10	11	12	13	14	15	16	17	18	19	20	21	22	23	24	25	26	27	28	29	30	31
2 ☉	♒12	13	14	15	16	17	18	19	20	21	22	23	24	25	26	27	28	29	29/0	♓1	2	3	4	5	6	7	8	9			
☽	♉21	♊3	15	27	♋9	20	♌2	14	27	♍9	22	♎5	18	♏1	15	28	♐12	27	♑11	26	♒11	25	♓10	24	♈8	21	♉4	17			
☿	♑21	23	24	26	27	29	29/0	♒2	3	5	6	8	9	11	13	14	16	17	19	21	23	24	26	28	29/0	♓1	3	5			
♀	♑22	23	24	26	27	28	29/0	♒1	2	3	4	6	7	8	9	11	12	13	14	15	17	18	19	20	22	23	24	25			
♂	♈27	28	29	29	29/0	♉1	1	2	2	3	4	4	5	6	6	7	8	8	9	10	10	11	11	12	13	13	14	15			

♃ 1 5 10 15 20 25 / ♑10 11 12 13 14 15 — ♄ 1 22℞ / ♏14 14 — ♅ 1 14 / ♓19 20 — ♆ 1 ℞ / ♌21 — ♇ 1 28 / ♋12 11

	1	2	3	4	5	6	7	8	9	10	11	12	13	14	15	16	17	18	19	20	21	22	23	24	25	26	27	28	29	30	31
3 ☉	♓10	11	12	13	14	15	16	17	18	19	20	21	22	23	24	25	26	27	28	29	29/0	♈1	2	3	4	5	6	7	8	9	10
☽	♉29	♊11	23	♋5	17	29	♌11	23	♍5	18	♎1	14	28	♏11	25	♐9	23	♑7	22	♒6	20	♓4	18	♈2	16	29	♉12	25	♊7	19	♋1
☿	♓7	9	10	12	14	16	18	20	22	24	26	28	29/0	♈2	4	6	8	10	11	13	15	17	18	20	22	23	24	26	27	28	29
♀	♒27	28	29	♓0	2	3	4	5	7	8	9	10	12	13	14	15	17	18	19	20	22	23	24	25	27	28	29	29/0	♈2	3	4
♂	♉15	16	17	17	18	19	19	20	20	21	22	22	23	24	24	25	26	26	27	28	28	29	29	29/0	♊1	1	2	3	3	4	5

♃ 1 3 9 15 22 30 / ♑15 16 17 18 19 20 — ♄ 1 ℞ 31 / ♏14 13 — ♅ 1 4 21 / ♓20 21 22 — ♆ 1 ℞ 31 / ♌21 20 — ♇ 1 / ♋11

	1	2	3	4	5	6	7	8	9	10	11	12	13	14	15	16	17	18	19	20	21	22	23	24	25	26	27	28	29	30	31
4 ☉	♈11	12	13	14	15	16	17	18	19	20	21	22	23	24	25	26	27	28	29	29/0	♉1	2	3	4	5	5	6	7	8	9	
☽	♋13	25	♌7	19	♍1	14	26	♎10	23	♏7	21	♐6	20	♑4	18	♒3	17	♓0	14	28	♈11	24	♉7	20	♊3	15	27	♋9	21	♌2	
☿	♈29/0	♉0	1	2	2	2	2	℞2	2	2	2	2	1	1	♉29	♈29	29	28	27	27	26	25	25	24	24	23	23	22	22	22	
♀	♈5	7	8	9	10	11	13	14	15	16	18	19	20	21	23	24	25	26	28	29	29/0	♉1	3	4	5	6	8	9	10	11	
♂	♊5	6	7	7	8	9	9	10	10	11	12	12	13	14	14	15	16	16	17	17	18	19	19	20	21	21	22	23	23	24	

♃ 1 9 22 / ♑20 21 22 — ♄ 1 ℞ 18 30 / ♏13 12 11 — ♅ 1 9 29 / ♓22 23 24 — ♆ 1 ℞ / ♌20 — ♇ 1 / ♋11

	1	2	3	4	5	6	7	8	9	10	11	12	13	14	15	16	17	18	19	20	21	22	23	24	25	26	27	28	29	30	31
5 ☉	♉10	11	12	13	14	15	16	17	18	19	20	21	22	23	24	25	26	27	28	29	29/0	♊1	2	3	4	5	5	6	7	8	9
☽	♌14	26	♍9	21	♎5	18	♏2	16	♐1	15	♑0	15	29	♒13	27	♓11	25	♈8	21	♉4	16	11	♊23	5	♋5	17	29	♌11	23	♍5	17
☿	♈22	℞22	D22	22	22	23	23	23	24	25	25	26	27	27	28	29	29/0	♉1	2	4	5	6	7	9	10	11	13	14	16	17	19
♀	♉12	14	15	16	17	19	20	21	22	23	25	26	27	28	29/0	♊1	2	3	5	6	7	8	9	11	12	13	14	16	17	18	19
♂	♊24	25	26	26	27	28	28	29	29/0	♋0	1	1	2	3	3	4	5	5	6	7	7	8	8	9	10	10	11	12	12	13	14

♃ 1 11℞ / ♑22 22 — ♄ 1 ℞ 15 30 / ♏11 10 9 — ♅ 1 27 / ♓24 25 — ♆ 1 ℞ / ♌20 — ♇ 1 / ♋12

	1	2	3	4	5	6	7	8	9	10	11	12	13	14	15	16	17	18	19	20	21	22	23	24	25	26	27	28	29	30	31
6 ☉	♊10	11	12	13	14	15	16	17	18	19	20	21	22	23	24	25	26	27	28	29	29/0	♋0	1	2	3	4	5	6	7	8	
☽	♍29	♎13	26	♏10	25	♐9	24	♑9	24	♒9	24	♓8	21	♈5	18	♉1	13	26	♊8	20	♋2	14	26	♌7	19	♍1	13	26	♎8	21	
☿	♉21	22	24	26	28	29/0	♊1	3	5	7	9	12	14	16	18	20	22	24	27	29/0	♋1	3	5	8	10	12	14	16	18	20	
♀	♊21	22	23	24	25	27	28	29	29/0	♋2	3	4	5	6	8	9	10	11	13	14	15	16	17	19	20	21	22	24	25	26	
♂	♋14	15	15	16	17	17	18	19	19	20	20	21	22	22	23	24	24	25	26	26	27	27	28	29	29	29/0	♌1	1	2	2	

♃ 1 ℞ 11 21 29 / ♑22 21 20 19 — ♄ 1 ℞ 20 / ♏9 8 — ♅ 1 / ♓25 — ♆ 1 / ♌20 — ♇ 1 30 / ♋12 13

	1	2	3	4	5	6	7	8	9	10	11	12	13	14	15	16	17	18	19	20	21	22	23	24	25	26	27	28	29	30	31
7 ☉	♋9	10	11	12	13	14	15	16	17	18	18	19	20	21	22	23	24	25	26	27	28	29	29/0	♌1	2	3	4	5	6	7	8
☽	♏5	19	♐3	18	♑3	18	♒3	18	♓3	17	♈1	15	28	♉10	23	♊5	17	29	♋11	23	♌4	16	28	♍10	22	♎5	17	♏0	14	28	♐12
☿	♋22	24	26	28	29/0	♌1	3	5	6	8	10	11	13	14	16	17	19	20	21	23	24	25	27	28	29	29/0	♍1	2	3	4	5
♀	♋27	29	29/0	♌1	2	3	5	6	7	8	9	11	12	13	14	16	17	18	19	20	22	23	24	25	27	28	29	29/0	♍1	3	4
♂	♌3	4	4	5	6	6	7	7	8	9	9	10	11	11	12	13	13	14	14	15	16	16	17	18	18	19	19	20	21	21	22

♃ 1 ℞ 7 15 23 31 / ♑19 18 17 16 15 — ♄ 1 ℞ 12D / ♏8 8 — ♅ 1 ℞ / ♓25 — ♆ 1 9 31 / ♌20 21 22 — ♇ 1 / ♋13

	1	2	3	4	5	6	7	8	9	10	11	12	13	14	15	16	17	18	19	20	21	22	23	24	25	26	27	28	29	30	31
8 ☉	♌8	9	10	11	12	13	14	15	16	17	18	19	20	21	22	23	24	25	26	27	28	29	29/0	♍0	1	2	3	4	5	6	7
☽	♐26	♑11	26	♒11	26	♓11	26	♈10	24	♉7	19	♊2	14	26	♋8	20	♌1	13	25	♍7	19	♎2	14	27	♏10	24	♐7	21	♑6	20	♒5
☿	♍5	6	7	7	8	8	9	9	9	9	9	℞9	9	9	9	8	8	7	6	6	5	4	3	2	1	0	♉29	♌29	28	28	27
♀	♍5	6	7	9	10	11	12	14	15	16	17	18	20	21	22	23	24	26	27	28	29/0	♎0	2	3	4	5	6	8	9	10	11
♂	♌23	23	24	25	25	26	26	27	28	28	29	29/0	♍0	1	2	2	3	3	4	5	5	6	7	7	8	9	9	10	10	11	12

♃ 1 ℞ 11 26 / ♑15 14 13 — ♄ 1 22 / ♏8 9 — ♅ 1 ℞ 31 / ♓25 24 — ♆ 1 31 / ♌22 23 — ♇ 1 / ♋14

	1	2	3	4	5	6	7	8	9	10	11	12	13	14	15	16	17	18	19	20	21	22	23	24	25	26	27	28	29	30	31
9 ☉	♍8	9	10	11	12	13	14	15	16	17	18	19	20	21	22	23	24	25	26	27	28	29	29/0	♎1	2	3	4	5	6	7	
☽	♒20	♓5	20	♈4	18	♉2	15	28	♊10	23	♋5	16	28	♌10	22	♍4	16	29	♎11	24	♏7	21	♐4	18	♑2	16	♒0	15	29	♓14	
☿	♌27	℞26	26	D26	26	27	27	28	28	29	29/0	♍1	2	4	5	7	8	10	11	13	15	17	18	20	22	24	26	28	29/0	♎1	
♀	♎12	14	15	16	17	18	20	22	23	24	25	27	28	29	29/0	♏0	2	3	4	5	6	7	9	10	11	12	13	15	16	17	
♂	♍12	13	14	14	15	16	16	17	17	18	19	19	20	21	21	22	23	23	24	25	25	26	26	27	28	28	29	29/0	♎0	1	

♃ 1 ℞ 9D / ♑13 13 — ♄ 1 5 16 26 / ♏9 10 11 12 — ♅ 1 ℞ 29 / ♓24 23 — ♆ 1 30 / ♌23 24 — ♇ 1 / ♋14

	1	2	3	4	5	6	7	8	9	10	11	12	13	14	15	16	17	18	19	20	21	22	23	24	25	26	27	28	29	30	31
10 ☉	♎8	9	10	11	12	12	13	14	15	16	17	18	19	20	21	22	23	24	25	26	27	28	29/0	♏0	1	2	3	4	5	6	7
☽	♓28	♈12	26	♉10	23	♊6	18	♋1	13	24	♌6	18	♍0	12	25	♎7	20	♏4	17	♐1	15	29	♑13	27	♒11	25	♓9	23	♈7	21	♉5
☿	♎3	5	7	8	10	12	14	15	17	19	20	22	24	26	27	29	29/0	♏2	4	5	7	8	10	11	13	15	16	18	19	21	22
♀	♏18	19	20	22	23	24	25	26	27	29	29/0	♐1	2	3	4	6	7	8	9	10	11	12	14	15	16	17	18	19	20	22	23
♂	♎2	2	3	4	4	5	5	6	7	7	8	9	9	10	11	11	12	13	13	14	15	15	16	17	17	18	19	19	20	21	21

♃ 1 8 18 26 / ♑13 14 15 16 — ♄ 1 6 15 23 31 / ♏12 13 14 15 16 — ♅ 1 ℞ 29 / ♓23 22 — ♆ 1 / ♌24 — ♇ 1 / ♋14

	1	2	3	4	5	6	7	8	9	10	11	12	13	14	15	16	17	18	19	20	21	22	23	24	25	26	27	28	29	30	31
11 ☉	♏8	9	10	11	12	13	14	15	16	17	18	19	20	21	22	23	24	25	26	27	28	29/0	♐1	2	3	4	5	6	7	8	
☽	♉18	♊1	14	26	♋8	20	♌2	14	26	♍8	20	♎3	15	29	♏12	26	♐10	25	♑9	23	♒8	22	♓6	20	♈4	17	♉1	14	27	♊9	
☿	♏24	25	27	28	29/0	♐1	2	4	5	7	8	9	11	12	13	14	16	17	18	19	20	21	22	23	24	25	26	26	27	27	
♀	♐24	25	26	27	28	29/0	♑0	2	3	4	5	6	7	8	9	10	11	12	13	15	16	17	18	19	20	21	22	23	24	25	
♂	♎22	23	23	24	24	25	26	26	27	28	28	29	29/0	♏0	1	2	2	3	4	4	5	6	6	7	8	8	9	10	10	11	

♃ 1 8 14 19 25 30 / ♑17 18 19 20 21 22 — ♄ 1 9 18 26 / ♏16 17 18 19 — ♅ 1 ℞ 30 / ♓22 21 — ♆ 1 27℞ / ♌24 24 — ♇ 1 / ♋14

	1	2	3	4	5	6	7	8	9	10	11	12	13	14	15	16	17	18	19	20	21	22	23	24	25	26	27	28	29	30	31
12 ☉	♐9	10	11	12	13	14	15	16	17	18	19	20	21	22	23	24	25	26	27	28	29	29/0	♑1	2	3	4	5	6	7	8	9
☽	♊22	♋4	16	28	♌10	22	♍4	16	28	♎10	23	♏7	20	♐4	19	♑4	18	♒3	18	♓2	17	♈0	14	27	♉10	23	♊6	18	♋1	13	25
☿	♐27	℞27	27	26	26	25	24	23	22	21	19	18	16	15	14	13	12	12	11	11	11	D11	11	11	12	12	13	14	15	16	17
♀	♑26	27	28	29	29/0	♒1	2	3	3	4	5	6	7	8	9	10	11	11	12	13	14	14	15	16	17	17	18	19	19	20	20
♂	♏12	13	13	14	15	15	16	17	17	18	19	19	20	21	21	22	23	23	24	25	25	26	27	27	28	29	29	♐0	1	2	2

♃ 1 5 10 14 19 23 28 31 / ♑22 23 24 25 26 27 28 29 — ♄ 1 5 14 23 31 / ♏19 20 21 22 23 — ♅ 1D 31 / ♓21 22 — ♆ 1 ℞ / ♌24 — ♇ 1 / ♋14

1926

1
☉ 10 11 12 13 14 15 16 17 18 19 20 21 22 23 24 25 26 27 28 29 0 1 2 3 4 5 6 7 8 9 10 11
☽ 7 18 0 12 24 6 19 1 14 28 12 27 12 27 12 27 11 26 10 24 7 20 3 15 28 10 22 3 15 27 9
☿ 18 19 20 21 22 24 25 26 27 29 0 1 3 4 6 7 9 10 12 13 14 16 17 19 21 22 24 25 26 28 29 0
♀ 21 22 22 23 23 23 24 24 25 25 25 25 26 26 26 26 26 26 26 26 26 25 25 25 25 24 24 24 23 23 22 22
♂ 3 4 4 5 6 6 7 8 8 9 10 11 11 12 13 13 14 15 15 16 17 17 18 19 20 20 21 22 22 23 24
♃ 1 6 10 14 18 23 27 31 — ♑29 ♒0 1 2 3 4 5 6 | ♄ 1 14 29 — ♏23 24 25 | ♅ 1 31 — ♓22 23 | ♆ 1 R — ♌26 | ♇ 1 — ♋13

2
☉ 12 13 14 15 16 17 18 19 20 21 22 23 24 25 26 27 28 29 0 1 2 3 4 5 6 7 8 9
☽ 21 3 15 27 10 23 7 20 5 19 4 20 5 20 5 19 3 17 29 12 25 7 19 0 12 24 6 18
☿ 2 3 5 7 8 10 12 13 15 17 18 20 22 24 25 27 29 0 1 3 5 7 8 10 12 14 16 18 20
♀ 22 21 20 20 19 19 18 17 17 16 16 15 14 14 13 13 13 12 12 11 11 11 11 10 10 10 10 10
♂ 24 25 26 27 27 28 29 29 29 0 1 2 3 4 4 5 6 6 7 8 9 10 11 11 12 13 14
♃ 1 4 9 13 17 21 26 — ♒6 7 8 9 10 11 12 | ♄ 1 24 — ♏25 26 | ♅ 1 19 — ♓23 24 | ♆ 1 R 28 — ♌24 23 | ♇ 1 — ♋13

3
☉ 10 11 12 13 14 15 16 17 18 19 20 21 22 23 24 25 26 27 28 29 0 1 2 3 4 5 6 7 8 9 10
☽ 29 12 24 7 20 3 16 29 14 28 13 28 13 28 13 27 11 25 8 21 3 15 27 9 21 3 15 27 9 21 4
☿ 22 23 25 27 29 0 2 4 5 7 8 9 10 11 12 13 13 14 14 15 15 15 15 14 14 13 13 12 11 10 9
♀ 10 10 10 11 11 11 11 11 12 12 13 13 13 14 14 15 15 16 17 17 18 18 19 20 20 21 21 22 23 24 25
♂ 14 15 16 16 17 18 19 19 20 21 21 22 23 24 24 25 26 26 27 28 29 29 0 1 2 2 3 4 4 5 6
♃ 1 2 7 12 16 21 26 31 — ♒12 13 14 15 16 17 18 19 | ♄ 1 6 R 31 — ♏26 26 25 | ♅ 1 9 26 — ♓24 25 26 | ♆ 1 R 31 — ♌23 22 | ♇ 1 31 — ♋13 12

4
☉ 11 12 13 14 15 16 17 18 19 20 21 22 23 24 25 26 27 28 29 0 1 2 3 4 5 6 7 8 9 10
☽ 17 29 13 26 10 24 8 23 7 22 7 21 5 19 3 16 29 11 23 5 17 29 11 23 5 17 0 13 26 10
☿ 9 8 7 6 5 5 4 4 3 3 3 2 2 2 2 3 3 3 3 4 4 5 5 6 7 8 9 10 11 12
♀ 26 27 28 28 29 0 1 2 3 4 5 6 7 8 9 10 11 12 13 14 15 16 17 18 19 20 21 22 23
♂ 7 8 9 9 10 11 12 12 13 14 15 15 16 17 17 18 19 20 20 21 22 22 23 24 25 25 26 27 28
♃ 1 6 11 17 24 30 — ♒19 20 21 22 23 24 | ♄ 1 R 27 — ♏25 24 | ♅ 1 14 — ♓26 27 | ♆ 1 R — ♌22 | ♇ 1 — ♋12

5
☉ 10 11 12 13 14 15 16 17 18 19 20 21 22 23 24 25 26 27 28 29 0 1 2 3 4 5 6 7 8 9
☽ 23 7 21 5 19 3 17 2 16 0 14 28 11 25 7 19 1 13 25 7 19 1 13 26 9 22 5 19 3 17 1
☿ 14 15 16 17 18 20 21 22 24 25 27 28 0 2 3 5 7 8 10 12 14 16 18 19 21 23 26 28 0 2 4
♀ 24 25 27 28 29 0 1 2 3 4 5 6 7 8 9 11 12 13 14 15 16 17 18 19 20 22 23 24 25 26 27
♂ 28 29 0 0 1 2 3 3 4 5 5 6 7 8 8 9 10 11 11 12 13 13 14 15 16 16 17 18 18 19 20
♃ 1 9 20 — ♒24 25 26 | ♄ 1 R 11 24 31 — ♏24 23 22 21 | ♅ 1 31 — ♓28 29 | ♆ 1 R 3 D — ♌22 22 | ♇ 1 — ♋13

6
☉ 10 11 12 13 14 15 16 17 18 19 20 21 22 22 23 24 25 26 27 28 29 0 1 2 3 4 5 6 7 8
☽ 16 0 14 28 12 26 10 23 7 20 2 15 27 9 21 3 15 27 9 21 4 17 0 14 28 12 27 12 26 11
☿ 6 8 11 13 15 17 19 21 24 26 28 0 2 4 6 8 10 12 14 16 17 19 21 23 24 26 27 29 0 2
♀ 28 0 1 2 3 4 5 6 7 9 10 11 12 13 14 15 17 18 19 20 21 22 24 25 26 27 28 29 0 1 2
♂ 20 21 22 22 23 24 25 25 26 27 27 28 29 29 0 1 1 2 3 4 4 5 6 6 7 8 9 9 10 10
♃ 1 6 16 R 26 — ♒26 27 27 | ♄ 1 R 27 — ♏21 20 | ♅ 1 — ♓29 | ♆ 1 — ♌22 | ♇ 1 30 — ♋13 14

7
☉ 9 10 11 12 13 13 14 15 16 17 18 19 20 21 22 23 24 25 26 27 28 29 0 1 2 3 4 5 6 7
☽ 25 9 23 7 20 3 16 29 11 23 5 17 29 11 23 5 17 29 12 25 8 22 6 21 6 21 5 19 3
☿ 3 4 6 7 8 9 10 11 12 13 14 15 16 17 18 19 20 20 21 21 21 21 21 21 21 21 20 20 20 19
♀ 3 4 5 6 8 9 10 11 12 13 15 16 17 18 19 21 22 23 24 25 27 28 29 0 1 3 4 5 6 7 8
♂ 11 11 12 13 13 14 14 15 15 16 17 17 18 19 19 20 21 21 22 22 23 24 24 25 25 26 27 27 28 28 29
♃ 1 R 13 24 31 — ♒27 26 25 24 | ♄ 1 R 24 D 31 — ♏20 20 19 | ♅ 1 5 R — ♓29 29 | ♆ 1 5 — ♌22 23 | ♇ 1 31 — ♋14 15

8
☉ 9 10 11 12 13 14 15 16 17 18 19 20 21 22 23 24 25 26 27 28 28 29 0 1 2 3 4 5 6 7
☽ 17 0 13 26 8 20 2 14 26 8 20 2 14 26 8 20 3 17 0 14 29 14 29 14 29 13 27 10 23
☿ 19 18 17 17 16 15 14 14 13 13 12 11 11 10 10 9 9 9 10 10 11 11 12 13 14 15 16 18 19 21
♀ 10 11 12 13 15 16 17 18 19 21 22 23 24 25 27 28 29 0 1 3 4 5 6 8 9 10 11 12 14 15 16
♂ 0 0 1 2 2 3 3 4 4 5 5 6 6 7 7 8 8 9 9 9 10 10 11 11 12 12 13 13 13 14
♃ 1 R 9 17 25 31 — ♒24 23 22 21 20 | ♄ 1 20 — ♏19 20 | ♅ 1 R 31 — ♓29 28 | ♆ 1 31 — ♌24 25 | ♇ 1 — ♋15

9
☉ 8 9 10 11 12 13 14 15 16 17 18 19 20 21 22 23 24 25 26 27 28 29 0 1 2 3 4 5 6 7
☽ 5 17 29 11 23 5 17 29 11 23 5 17 29 12 26 9 23 7 22 8 23 8 22 6 20 3 16 29
☿ 22 24 26 27 0 1 3 5 7 9 10 12 14 16 18 20 22 24 26 27 29 1 3 5 6 8 10 11 13 15
♀ 19 20 21 22 24 25 26 27 28 0 1 2 3 5 6 7 8 10 11 12 13 14 16 17 18 19 21 22 23 25
♂ 14 15 15 15 15 16 16 16 17 17 17 18 18 18 18 18 19 19 19 19 19 19 19 19 19 19 19 19 19 19
♃ 1 R 11 23 30 — ♒20 19 18 17 | ♄ 1 7 20 30 — ♏20 21 22 23 | ♅ 1 R 30 — ♓28 27 | ♆ 1 30 — ♌25 26 | ♇ 1 — ♋15

10
☉ 7 8 9 10 11 12 13 14 15 16 17 18 19 20 21 22 23 24 25 26 27 28 29 0 1 2 3 4 5 6 7
☽ 8 20 2 14 26 8 20 2 14 27 9 22 5 19 3 17 1 16 1 16 0 14 27 10 22 5 17 28 10
☿ 16 18 20 21 23 25 26 28 29 0 1 2 4 5 7 8 9 11 12 13 14 15 16 17 18 19 20 21 22 23 29 0
♀ 24 26 27 28 0 1 2 3 4 6 7 8 9 11 12 13 14 15 17 18 19 20 21 23 24 25 26 28 29 0 1 2
♂ 19 19 19 19 19 19 19 19 19 18 18 18 18 18 18 18 17 17 17 17 16 16 16 15 15 15 14 14 14 13 13
♃ 1 R 14 D — ♒17 17 | ♄ 1 11 21 29 — ♏23 24 25 26 | ♅ 1 R 31 — ♓27 26 | ♆ 1 — ♌26 | ♇ 1 — ♋15

11
☉ 8 9 10 11 12 13 14 15 16 17 18 19 20 21 22 23 24 25 26 27 28 29 0 1 2 3 4 5 6 7
☽ 22 4 16 28 11 24 6 19 2 16 29 13 27 11 26 10 25 10 24 8 22 5 18 0 13 25 6 18 0 12
☿ 1 2 3 4 5 6 7 8 9 10 11 11 12 12 12 11 11 11 10 9 8 7 6 5 3 2 1 29 28 27
♀ 3 4 6 7 8 9 11 12 13 14 16 17 18 19 20 22 23 24 25 27 28 29 0 2 3 4 5 7 8 9 10
♂ 12 12 12 11 11 11 10 10 10 9 9 9 8 8 8 8 7 7 7 7 6 6 6 6 5 5 5 5 5 5
♃ 1 15 24 30 — ♒18 19 20 21 | ♄ 1 7 16 24 — ♏26 27 28 29 | ♅ 1 R 30 — ♓26 25 | ♆ 1 30 R — ♌27 27 | ♇ 1 — ♋15

12
☉ 8 9 10 11 12 13 14 15 16 17 18 19 20 21 22 23 24 25 26 27 28 29 0 1 2 3 4 5 6 7 8 9
☽ 24 7 19 2 15 29 12 26 10 24 8 22 7 21 5 19 3 16 29 12 25 8 20 2 14 26 8 20 2 15 27
☿ 26 26 25 25 25 25 25 26 26 27 28 29 0 2 3 4 5 6 8 9 10 12 13 14 16 17 19 20 22 23
♀ 12 13 15 16 17 18 20 21 22 23 25 26 27 28 0 1 2 3 5 6 7 9 10 11 12 13 15 16 17 19
♂ 5 4 4 4 4 4 4 4 4 4 5 5 5 5 5 5 5 5 6 6 6 6 6 6 7 7 7 7 7 8 8
♃ 1 8 14 19 25 30 — ♒21 22 23 24 25 26 | ♄ 1 2 29 11 20 29 — ♏29 0 ♐1 2 3 | ♅ 1 R 6 D — ♓25 25 | ♆ 1 R — ♌27 | ♇ 1 — ♋15

1927

1
☉ 10 11 12 13 14 15 16 17 18 19 20 21 22 23 24 25 26 27 28 29 0 1 2 3 4 5 6 7
☽ 10 24 7 21 6 20 5 19 3 18 2 15 29 12 26 8 21 4 16 28 10 22 4 16 28 10 22 5
☿ 24 26 27 29 0 2 4 5 7 8 10 11 13 14 16 18 19 21 22 24 26 27 29 0 2 4 6 7
♀ 20 21 22 24 25 26 27 29 0 1 2 4 5 6 7 9 10 11 12 14 15 16 17 19 20 21 22 24 25
♂ 8 8 9 9 10 10 10 11 11 11 12 12 12 13 13 14 14 14 15 15 16 16 16 17 17 18 18 19
♃ 1 4 9 13 18 22 27 31 — ♒26 27 28 29 0 ♓1 2 3 | ♄ 1 8 19 31 — ♐3 4 5 6 | ♅ 1 — ♓26 | ♆ 1 R — ♌26 | ♇ 1 — ♋1…

2
☉ 11 12 13 14 15 16 17 18 19 20 21 22 23 24 25 26 27 28 29 0 1 2 3 4 5 6 7 8 9
☽ 29 14 29 14 29 14 28 12 26 9 22 5 18 0 12 25 7 19 1 13 25 7 19 1 13 26 9 23
☿ 14 16 18 20 21 23 25 27 29 0 2 4 6 8 9 11 13 14 16 17 19 20 22 24 25 26
♀ 29 0 1 2 4 5 6 7 9 10 11 12 13 15 16 17 19 20 21 22 24 25 26 27 29 0 1
♂ 20 20 21 21 22 22 23 23 24 24 25 25 25 26 26 27 27 28 28 29 29 29 0 1 1 2 2 3 3
♃ 1 4 9 13 17 21 25 — ♓3 4 5 6 7 8 9 | ♄ 1 17 — ♐6 7 | ♅ 1 24 — ♓27 28 | ♆ 1 R 28 — ♌26 25 | ♇ 1 — ♋1…

3
☉ 10 11 12 13 14 15 16 17 18 19 20 21 22 23 24 25 26 27 28 29 0 1 2 3 4 5 6 7
☽ 8 22 7 23 8 23 8 22 6 19 2 15 27 10 22 4 16 28 8 21 3 15 27 10 22 5 18 2
☿ 27 27 27 27 27 27 26 26 25 25 24 24 23 22 21 20 19 19 18 18 17 17 16 15 15 14 14 14 14
♀ 3 5 6 7 8 10 11 12 13 15 16 17 18 20 21 22 23 25 26 27 28 0 1 2 3 5 6 7
♂ 4 4 5 5 6 6 7 7 8 8 9 9 10 10 11 11 12 12 13 13 14 14 15 15 16 16 17 17 18 19
♃ 1 6 10 14 18 22 27 31 — ♓10 11 12 13 14 15 16 17 | ♄ 1 18 R — ♐7 7 | ♅ 1 14 31 — ♓28 29 ♈0 | ♆ 1 R 31 — ♌25 24 | ♇ 1 — ♋1…

4
☉ 11 12 13 14 15 16 17 18 19 20 21 22 23 24 25 26 27 28 29 0 1 2 3 4 5 6 7 8
☽ 1 16 1 16 1 15 28 11 24 7 19 1 13 24 6 18 0 12 24 7 19 2 15 28 11 25 10 24
☿ 15 16 16 17 17 18 19 20 21 21 22 23 24 25 26 27 29 0 1 2 4 5 7 8 10 11 13 14
♀ 11 13 14 15 16 17 19 20 21 22 23 24 25 26 27 28 0 1 2 3 4 5 7 8 9 10 11 13
♂ 21 21 22 22 23 23 24 24 25 25 26 26 27 27 28 28 29 29 0 1 1 2 2 3 3 4 4 5 6
♃ 1 4 9 13 18 22 27 — ♓17 18 19 20 21 22 23 | ♄ 1 R 30 — ♐7 6 | ♅ 1 18 — ♈0 1 | ♆ 1 R — ♌24 | ♇ 1 — ♋1…

5
☉ 10 11 12 13 14 15 16 17 18 19 20 21 22 23 24 25 26 27 28 29 0 1 2 3 4 5 6
☽ 10 24 9 23 7 20 3 15 27 9 21 3 15 27 9 21 3 16 29 12 25 8 22 6 20 4 19
☿ 21 23 24 26 28 0 2 4 6 8 10 12 14 16 18 20 22 24 27 29 1 3 5 8 10 12 14 16
♀ 17 18 20 21 22 23 24 25 27 28 29 0 1 2 3 5 6 7 8 9 10 11 13 14 15 16 17 19
♂ 8 9 9 10 11 11 12 12 13 13 14 14 15 15 16 16 17 17 18 18 19 19 20 20 21 21 22 23 23 24 25
♃ 1 7 12 18 24 30 — ♓24 25 26 27 28 29 | ♄ 1 R 17 31 — ♐6 5 4 | ♅ 1 9 — ♈1 2 | ♆ 1 R 6 D — ♌24 24 | ♇ 1 — ♋1…

6
☉ 10 11 12 13 14 14 15 16 17 18 19 20 21 22 23 24 25 26 27 28 29 0 1 2 3 4 5 6 7
☽ 1 15 28 11 23 5 17 29 11 23 5 17 29 12 24 7 20 3 17 1 15 29 14 28 12 26 9
☿ 24 26 28 0 2 3 5 7 8 10 11 13 14 16 17 18 19 20 21 22 23 24 25 26 27 28 28 29 0
♀ 23 24 25 26 27 28 29 0 1 2 3 5 6 7 8 9 10 11 12 13 14 15 16 17 18 19 20 21
♂ 27 27 28 28 29 29 0 0 1 2 2 3 3 4 5 5 6 6 7 7 8 8 9 9 10 10 11 11 12 12 13 13 14
♃ 1 6 29 14 23 — ♓29 0 ♈1 2 | ♄ 1 R 14 30 — ♐4 3 2 | ♅ 1 — ♈3 | ♆ 1 30 — ♌24 25 | ♇ 1 — ♋1…

7
☉ 8 9 10 11 12 13 14 15 16 17 18 19 20 21 22 23 24 25 26 27 28 29 0 1 2 3 4 5
☽ 6 19 1 13 25 7 19 1 13 25 8 21 4 17 1 15 29 13 27 12 26 10 24 8 22 5 18 1
☿ 1 1 2 2 2 2 2 2 2 1 1 1 0 29 29 29 28 28 27 26 26 25 25 24 24 23 23 22 22 22
♀ 24 25 26 27 28 29 0 1 2 3 4 5 6 7 8 9 10 11 12 13 14 14 15 16 17 17 18
♂ 15 16 16 17 18 18 19 19 20 21 21 22 22 23 24 24 25 25 26 27 27 28 28 29 0 1 1 2
♃ 1 6 25 R — ♈2 3 3 | ♄ 1 R 31 — ♐2 1 | ♅ 1 9 R — ♈3 3 | ♆ 1 — ♌25 26 | ♇ 1 — ♋1…

8
☉ 8 9 10 11 12 13 14 15 16 17 18 19 20 21 22 23 24 25 26 27 28 29 0 1 2 3 4 5
☽ 21 3 15 27 9 21 3 16 29 12 25 9 24 8 23 8 22 7 21 5 19 2 15 28 11 23 5 18 29
☿ 22 22 22 23 23 24 25 26 27 28 29 0 2 3 5 6 8 10 11 13 15 17 19 21 23 25 27 29 0 1
♀ 19 19 20 20 21 21 22 22 22 23 23 23 23 23 23 24 24 24 24 24 24 24 24 24 24 23 23 23
♂ 4 5 6 6 7 7 8 9 9 10 11 11 12 13 13 14 14 15 16 16 17 17 18 18 19 20 20 21 21 22 22
♃ 1 R 24 31 — ♈3 2 1 | ♄ 1 R 6 D — ♐1 1 | ♅ 1 R 31 — ♈3 2 | ♆ 1 28 — ♌26 27 | ♇ 1 — ♋1…

9
☉ 8 9 10 11 12 13 14 15 16 17 18 19 20 21 22 23 24 25 26 27 28 29 0 1 2 3 4
☽ 5 19 29 11 24 7 20 3 18 2 17 2 17 2 17 1 15 29 12 25 8 20 2 15 27 9 20
☿ 7 9 11 13 14 16 18 20 22 24 25 27 29 0 2 4 6 7 9 11 12 14 15 17 18 20 21 23 24
♀ 22 21 21 21 20 19 19 18 17 17 16 16 15 15 14 14 13 13 12 12 11 11 10 10 9 9 9 9 9
♂ 24 25 25 26 27 27 28 28 29 0 0 1 2 2 3 3 4 4 5 6 6 7 7 8 9 9 10 11 11 12
♃ 1 R 11 0 26 30 — ♈1 29 ♓28 27 | ♄ 1 9 25 — ♐1 2 3 | ♅ 1 R 30 — ♈2 1 | ♆ 1 26 — ♌27 28 | ♇ 1 — ♋1…

10
☉ 7 8 9 10 11 12 13 14 15 16 17 18 19 20 21 22 23 24 25 26 27 28 29 0 1 2 3 4
☽ 8 20 2 15 28 12 26 10 25 10 26 11 26 10 25 8 22 5 17 29 12 24 6 17 29 11 23 5
☿ 27 29 0 1 3 4 5 7 8 9 11 12 13 14 16 17 18 19 20 21 22 23 24 25 26 26 27 28
♀ 9 9 9 9 9 9 9 9 10 10 10 11 11 11 12 12 13 13 14 14 15 15 16 16 17 17 18 19
♂ 13 14 14 15 15 16 17 17 18 19 19 20 21 21 22 22 23 24 24 25 25 26 27 27 28 28 29 0 1 2
♃ 1 R 12 21 31 — ♓27 26 25 24 | ♄ 1 7 17 27 — ♐3 4 5 6 | ♅ 1 R 31 — ♈1 0 | ♆ 1 31 — ♌28 29 | ♇ 1 — ♋1…

11
☉ 8 9 10 11 12 13 14 15 16 17 18 19 20 21 22 23 24 25 26 27 28 29 0 1 2 3 4 5 6
☽ 24 7 21 5 19 4 19 4 19 3 17 0 14 26 8 20 2 14 26 8 20 2 14 26 9 21 4 18 2
☿ 25 24 23 22 21 20 19 18 17 16 15 14 13 12 11 10 9 9 10 11 12 12 13 14 15 16 17 19
♀ 23 24 25 25 26 27 28 29 0 1 2 3 4 5 6 7 8 9 10 11 12 13 14 15 16 17 18 20
♂ 4 5 6 7 7 8 9 9 10 11 11 12 13 13 14 15 15 16 16 17 18 18 19 20 20 21 22 22 23 24
♃ 1 R 20 D — ♓24 24 | ♄ 1 6 14 23 30 — ♐6 7 8 9 10 | ♅ 1 R 5 — ♈0 ♓29 | ♆ 1 — ♌29 | ♇ 1 — ♋1…

12
☉ 8 9 10 11 12 13 14 15 16 17 18 19 20 21 22 23 24 25 26 27 28 29 0 1 2 3 4 5 6 7
☽ 1 14 28 13 28 12 27 12 27 11 25 9 22 4 17 29 11 23 5 17 29 11 23 5 18 1 14 28 11
☿ 20 22 23 24 26 27 29 0 1 3 4 6 7 9 10 12 13 15 17 18 20 21 23 24 26 27 29
♀ 23 24 25 26 27 28 29 0 1 2 3 5 6 7 8 10 11 12 13 14 16 17 18 19 20 21 23
♂ 26 26 27 28 28 29 0 1 1 2 3 3 4 5 5 6 7 7 8 9 9 10 11 11 12 13 13 14 15
♃ 1 18 27 — ♓24 25 26 | ♄ 1 10 18 27 — ♐10 11 12 13 | ♅ 1 6 18 D — ♓29 29 | ♆ 1 R — ♌29 | ♇ 1 — ♋1…

1928

1

	1	2	3	4	5	6	7	8	9	10	11	12	13	14	15	16	17	18	19	20	21	22	23	24	25	26	27	28	29	30	31
☉	♑10	11	12	13	14	15	16	17	18	19	20	21	22	23	24	25	26	27	28	29	29/0	♒1	2	3	4	5	6	7	8	9	10
☽	♈23	♉7	22	♊6	21	♋5	19	♌3	16	29	♍12	25	♎7	19	♏1	12	24	♐6	19	♑1	14	27	♒10	24	♓8	22	♈6	20	♉4	18	♊2
☿	♑5	7	8	10	12	13	15	16	18	20	21	23	25	26	28	29/0	♒1	3	5	7	8	10	12	14	15	17	19	20	22	24	25
♀	♏27	28	29	♐0	2	3	4	5	6	8	9	10	11	12	14	15	16	17	18	20	21	22	23	24	26	26	28	29	29/0	♑2	3
♂	♐17	18	18	19	20	21	21	22	23	24	24	25	26	26	27	28	29	29	29/0	♑1	2	2	3	4	5	5	6	7	8	8	9

♃ 1 4 11 17 23 28 — ♓26 27 28 29 ♈0 1 ♄ 1 5 15 25 — ♐13 14 15 16 ♅ 1 13 — ♓29 ♈0 ♆ 1 R — ♌28 ♇ 1 31 — ♋16 15

2

	1	2	3	4	5	6	7	8	9	10	11	12	13	14	15	16	17	18	19	20	21	22	23	24	25	26	27	28	29	30	31
☉	♒11	12	13	14	15	16	17	18	19	20	21	22	23	24	25	26	27	28	29/0	♓0	1	2	3	4	5	6	7	8	9		
☽	♊16	♋0	14	28	♌11	24	♍7	20	♎2	15	27	♏8	20	♐2	14	26	♑9	22	♒5	19	♓3	17	♈2	16	♉1	15	29	♊13	17		
☿	♒27	28	29/0	♓1	3	4	5	7	8	8	9	10	10	11	11	R 11	10	10	9	9	8	7	6	5	4	3	2	1	0/29♒		
♀	♑4	5	6	8	9	10	11	13	14	15	16	17	19	20	21	22	24	25	26	27	28	29/0	♒1	2	3	5	6	7	8		
♂	♑10	11	11	12	13	13	14	15	16	16	17	18	19	19	20	21	22	22	23	24	25	25	26	27	28	29	29	29/0	♒1		

♃ 1 7 12 17 21 26 29 — ♈2 3 4 5 6 7 8 ♄ 1 6 20 — ♐16 17 18 ♅ 1 8 28 — ♈0 1 2 ♆ 1 R 29 — ♌28 27 ♇ 1 — ♋15

3

	1	2	3	4	5	6	7	8	9	10	11	12	13	14	15	16	17	18	19	20	21	22	23	24	25	26	27	28	29	30	31
☉	♓10	11	12	13	14	15	16	17	18	19	20	21	22	23	24	25	26	27	28	29/0	♈0	1	2	3	4	5	6	7	8	9	10
☽	♋11	24	♌7	20	♍3	16	28	♎11	23	♏5	16	28	♐10	22	♑4	17	29	♒13	27	♓11	26	♈10	25	♉10	25	♊10	24	♋7	21	♌4	17
☿	♒29	R 28	27	27	26	26	26	26	D 26	26	26	27	27	28	28	29	29	29/0	♓1	2	3	4	5	6	7	8	9	10	12	13	14
♀	♒9	11	12	13	14	16	17	18	19	20	22	23	24	25	27	28	29	29/0	♓2	3	4	5	6	8	9	10	11	13	14	15	16
♂	♒2	2	3	4	5	5	6	7	8	8	9	10	11	11	12	13	14	14	15	16	17	18	18	19	20	21	21	22	23	24	24

♃ 1 5 10 14 18 22 27 31 — ♈8 9 10 11 12 13 14 15 ♄ 1 16 29 R — ♐18 19 19 ♅ 1 17 — ♈2 3 ♆ 1 R — ♌27 ♇ 1 — ♋15

4

	1	2	3	4	5	6	7	8	9	10	11	12	13	14	15	16	17	18	19	20	21	22	23	24	25	26	27	28	29	30	31
☉	♈11	12	13	14	15	16	17	18	19	20	21	22	23	24	25	26	27	28	29	29/0	♉1	2	3	4	5	6	7	8	9	10	
☽	♍0	12	25	♎7	19	♏1	13	25	♐7	18	♑0	13	25	♒8	21	♓5	19	♈4	19	♉4	19	♊4	19	♋3	17	♌1	14	27	♍10	22	
☿	♓16	17	18	20	21	23	24	26	27	29	29/0	♈2	4	6	7	9	11	13	14	16	18	20	22	24	26	28	29/0	♉2	4	6	
♀	♓17	19	20	21	22	24	25	26	27	29	29/0	♈1	2	3	5	6	7	8	10	11	12	13	15	16	17	18	19	21	22	23	
♂	♒25	26	27	27	28	29	29/0	♓1	1	2	3	4	4	5	6	7	7	8	9	10	10	11	12	13	14	14	15	16	17	17	

♃ 1 4 8 12 16 20 25 29 — ♈15 16 17 18 19 20 21 22 ♄ 1 R 30 — ♐19 18 ♅ 1 22 — ♈4 5 ♆ 1 R — ♌26 ♇ 1 — ♋15

5

	1	2	3	4	5	6	7	8	9	10	11	12	13	14	15	16	17	18	19	20	21	22	23	24	25	26	27	28	29	30	31
☉	♉11	12	13	14	15	15	16	17	18	19	20	21	22	23	24	25	26	27	28	29	29/0	♊1	2	3	4	5	6	7	8	9	10
☽	♎4	16	28	♏10	22	♐4	15	27	♑9	22	♒4	17	♓0	14	28	♈12	27	♉12	27	♊12	27	♋12	26	♌10	23	♍6	19	♎1	13	25	♏7
☿	♉8	10	13	15	17	19	21	23	26	28	29/0	♊2	4	6	8	10	12	14	15	17	19	21	22	24	25	27	28	29/0	♋1	2	3
♀	♈24	26	27	28	29	♉0	2	3	4	5	7	8	9	10	12	13	14	15	16	18	19	20	21	23	24	25	26	27	29	29/0	♊1
♂	♓18	19	20	20	21	22	23	23	24	25	26	27	27	28	29	29/0	♈0	1	2	3	3	4	5	6	6	7	8	9	9	10	11

♃ 1 3 7 12 16 21 25 30 — ♈22 23 24 25 26 27 28 28 ♄ 1 R 21 31 — ♐18 17 16 ♅ 1 13 — ♈5 6 ♆ 1 R — ♌26 ♇ 1 — ♋15

6

	1	2	3	4	5	6	7	8	9	10	11	12	13	14	15	16	17	18	19	20	21	22	23	24	25	26	27	28	29	30	31
☉	♊10	11	12	13	14	15	16	17	18	19	20	21	22	23	24	25	26	27	28	29	29/0	♋0	1	2	3	4	5	6	7	8	
☽	♏19	♐1	12	24	♑6	19	♒1	14	27	♓10	23	♈7	22	♉6	21	♊6	21	♋6	20	♌5	18	♍2	15	27	♎10	22	♏4	15	27	♐9	
☿	♋4	5	6	7	8	8	9	10	10	11	11	12	12	12	12	12	R 12	12	12	12	11	11	11	10	10	9	9	8	7	7	
♀	♊2	4	5	6	7	8	10	11	12	13	15	16	17	18	20	20	22	23	24	26	27	28	29/0	♋1	2	3	4	5	7	8	
♂	♈12	12	13	14	15	15	16	17	18	18	19	20	20	21	22	23	23	24	25	26	26	27	28	28	29	29/0	♉1	1	2	3	

♃ 1 4 29 9 14 19 25 30 — ♈29 0 ♉1 2 3 4 5 ♄ 1 R 18 30 — ♐16 15 14 ♅ 1 11 — ♈6 7 ♆ 1 24 — ♌26 27 ♇ 1 30 — ♋15 16

7

	1	2	3	4	5	6	7	8	9	10	11	12	13	14	15	16	17	18	19	20	21	22	23	24	25	26	27	28	29	30	31
☉	♋9	10	11	12	13	14	15	16	17	18	19	20	21	22	22	23	24	25	26	27	28	29	29/0	♌1	2	3	4	5	6	7	8
☽	♐21	♑3	15	28	♒11	24	♓7	20	♈4	18	♉2	16	♊0	15	29	♋14	29	♌13	27	♍10	23	♎6	18	♏0	12	24	♐5	17	29	♑12	24
☿	♋6	R 6	5	5	4	4	4	3	3	3	D 3	3	3	4	4	5	5	6	6	7	8	9	10	11	13	14	15	17	19	20	22
♀	♋9	10	12	13	14	15	17	18	19	20	21	23	24	25	26	28	29	29/0	♌1	3	4	5	6	7	9	10	11	12	14	15	16
♂	♉4	4	5	6	6	7	8	8	9	10	11	11	12	13	13	14	15	15	16	17	17	18	19	20	20	21	22	22	23	24	24

♃ 1 7 14 22 31 — ♉5 6 7 8 9 ♄ 1 R 22 — ♐14 13 ♅ 1 13 R — ♈7 7 ♆ 1 28 — ♌27 28 ♇ 1 31 — ♋16 17

8

	1	2	3	4	5	6	7	8	9	10	11	12	13	14	15	16	17	18	19	20	21	22	23	24	25	26	27	28	29	30	31
☉	♌9	10	11	12	13	14	15	16	17	18	18	19	20	21	22	23	24	25	26	27	28	29	29/0	♍1	2	3	4	5	6	7	8
☽	♒7	20	♓3	17	♈1	15	28	♉13	27	♊11	25	♋9	23	♌7	21	♍5	18	♎1	14	26	♏8	20	♐2	13	25	♑7	20	♒3	16	29	♓13
☿	♋24	25	27	29/0	♌1	3	5	7	9	11	13	16	17	20	21	24	26	27	29/0	♍1	3	5	7	9	11	13	14	16	18	20	21
♀	♌17	19	20	21	22	24	25	26	27	28	29/0	♍1	2	3	5	6	7	8	10	11	12	13	14	16	17	18	19	21	22	23	24
♂	♉25	26	26	27	27	28	29	29	29/0	♊1	1	2	3	3	4	4	5	6	6	7	8	8	9	9	10	11	11	12	12	13	13

♃ 1 14 30 R — ♉9 10 10 ♄ 1 R 17 D — ♐13 13 ♅ 1 R 31 — ♈7 6 ♆ 1 24 — ♌28 29 ♇ 1 31 — ♋17 18

9

	1	2	3	4	5	6	7	8	9	10	11	12	13	14	15	16	17	18	19	20	21	22	23	24	25	26	27	28	29	30	31
☉	♍9	10	11	12	13	13	14	15	16	17	18	19	20	21	22	23	24	25	26	27	28	29	29/0	♎1	2	3	4	5	6	7	
☽	♓27	♈11	25	♉9	23	♊8	22	♋6	20	♌3	17	♍0	14	27	♎9	22	♏4	16	28	♐9	21	♑3	15	28	♒10	24	♓7	21	♈6	20	
☿	♍23	25	26	28	29/0	♎1	3	4	6	7	9	10	12	13	15	16	17	19	20	21	23	24	25	26	27	28	29/0	♏1	2	3	
♀	♍26	27	28	29/0	♎1	2	3	4	5	7	8	9	10	12	13	14	15	17	18	19	20	21	23	24	25	26	28	29	29/0	♏1	
♂	♊14	15	15	16	16	17	17	18	18	19	20	20	21	21	22	22	23	23	24	24	25	25	26	26	26	27	27	28	28	29	

♃ 1 R 28 — ♉10 9 ♄ 1 29 — ♐13 14 ♅ 1 R 30 — ♈6 5 ♆ 1 21 — ♌29 ♍0 ♇ 1 — ♋18

10

	1	2	3	4	5	6	7	8	9	10	11	12	13	14	15	16	17	18	19	20	21	22	23	24	25	26	27	28	29	30	31
☉	♎8	9	10	11	12	13	14	15	16	17	18	19	20	21	22	23	24	25	26	27	28	29	29/0	♏1	2	3	4	5	6	7	8
☽	♉5	19	♊4	18	♋3	17	♌0	14	27	♍10	23	♎5	18	♏0	12	24	♐6	18	29	♑11	23	♒6	18	♓2	15	29	♈14	28	♉13	28	♊13
☿	♏4	4	5	6	7	7	8	8	9	9	9	9	R 9	9	9	8	8	7	6	5	4	3	2	0	♉29	♎28	27	26	25	24	24
♀	♏3	4	5	6	7	9	10	11	12	14	15	16	17	19	20	21	22	23	25	26	27	28	29/0	♐1	2	3	4	6	7	8	9
♂	♊29	29	29/0	♋0	1	1	2	2	2	3	3	3	4	4	4	5	5	5	6	6	6	6	7	7	7	7	8	8	8	8	8

♃ 1 R 8 16 24 31 — ♉9 8 7 6 5 ♄ 1 13 24 — ♐14 15 16 ♅ 1 R 31 — ♈5 4 ♆ 1 27 — ♍0 1 ♇ 1 — ♋18

11

	1	2	3	4	5	6	7	8	9	10	11	12	13	14	15	16	17	18	19	20	21	22	23	24	25	26	27	28	29	30	31
☉	♏9	10	11	12	13	14	15	16	17	18	19	20	21	22	23	24	25	26	27	28	29	29/0	♐1	2	3	4	5	6	7	8	
☽	♊28	♋13	27	♌11	24	♍7	20	♎2	15	27	♏9	21	♐3	14	26	♑8	20	♒2	14	27	♓10	23	♈7	22	♉6	21	♊7	22	♋7	22	
☿	♎24	D 24	24	24	25	25	26	27	28	29	29/0	♏1	2	4	5	7	8	10	11	13	14	16	17	19	20	22	23	25	26	28	
♀	♐11	12	13	14	16	17	18	19	20	22	23	24	25	26	28	29	29/0	♑1	3	4	5	6	7	9	10	11	12	14	15	16	
♂	♋8	8	9	9	9	9	9	9	9	9	9	R 9	9	9	9	9	9	9	9	9	9	8	8	8	8	8	7	7	7	7	

♃ 1 R 8 16 25 30 — ♉5 4 3 2 1 ♄ 1 12 21 30 — ♐17 18 19 20 ♅ 1 R 30 — ♈4 3 ♆ 1 — ♍1 ♇ 1 — ♋18

12

	1	2	3	4	5	6	7	8	9	10	11	12	13	14	15	16	17	18	19	20	21	22	23	24	25	26	27	28	29	30	31
☉	♐9	10	11	12	13	14	15	16	17	18	19	20	21	22	23	24	25	26	27	28	29	29/0	♑1	2	3	4	5	6	7	8	9
☽	♌6	20	♍4	17	29	♎12	24	♏6	18	29	♐11	23	♑5	17	29	♒11	24	♓6	19	♈2	16	♉0	15	29	♊14	29	♋15	29	♌14	29	♍12
☿	♏29/0	♐1	3	4	6	7	9	10	12	14	15	17	18	20	21	23	25	26	28	29/0	♑1	3	4	6	7	9	11	12	14	15	17
♀	♑17	18	20	21	22	23	24	26	27	28	29	29/0	♒2	3	4	5	6	8	9	10	11	12	13	15	16	17	18	19	21	22	23
♂	♋6	R 6	6	6	5	5	5	4	4	4	3	3	2	2	2	1	1	1	0	♉29	♊29	29	29	28	28	27	27	27	26	26	26

♃ 1 R 26 D — ♉1 1 0 ♄ 1 9 17 26 — ♐20 21 22 23 ♅ 1 R 13 D — ♈3 3 ♆ 1 4 R — ♍1 1 ♇ 1 31 — ♋18 17

1929

1

	1	2	3	4	5	6	7	8	9	10	11	12	13	14	15	16	17	18	19	20	21	22	23	24	25	26	27	28	29	30	31
☉	♑10	11	12	13	14	15	16	17	18	19	20	21	22	23	24	25	26	27	28	29/0	♒1	2	3	4	5	6	7	8	9	10	11
☽	♍25	♎8	21	♏3	15	26	♐8	20	♑2	14	26	♒8	21	♓3	16	29	♈13	26	♉10	24	♊8	23	♋8	23	♌8	22	♍6	20	♎3	16	29
☿	♑19	20	22	24	25	27	28	29/0	♒2	3	5	7	8	10	11	13	14	16	17	18	19	20	21	22	23	24	24	24	R 24	24	24
♀	♒24	25	26	28	29	29/0	♓1	2	3	4	6	7	8	9	10	11	12	13	15	16	17	18	19	20	21	22	23	24	26	27	28
♂	♊25	R 25	25	24	24	24	23	23	23	23	23	22	22	22	22	22	21	21	21	21	21	21	21	21	21	21	D 21	21	21	21	21

♃ 1 13 25 — ♉0 1 2 ♄ 1 12 21 31 — ♐24 25 26 27 ♅ 1 17 — ♈3 4 ♆ 1 R 31 — ♍1 0 ♇ 1 — ♋17

2

	1	2	3	4	5	6	7	8	9	10	11	12	13	14	15	16	17	18	19	20	21	22	23	24	25	26	27	28	29	30	31
☉	♒12	13	14	15	16	17	18	19	20	21	22	23	24	25	26	27	28	29	29/0	♓1	2	3	4	5	6	7	8	9			
☽	♏11	23	♐5	17	28	♑10	22	♒5	17	♓0	13	26	♈9	23	♉7	21	♊5	19	♋3	17	♌2	16	♍0	14	28	♎11	24	♏7			
☿	♒23	R 23	22	21	20	19	17	16	15	14	13	12	11	10	10	9	9	9	9	D 9	9	9	10	10	11	11	12	13			
♀	♓29	29/0	♈1	2	3	4	5	6	7	8	9	10	11	12	13	14	15	16	16	17	18	19	20	21	22	23	23	24			
♂	♊21	21	21	21	21	21	22	22	22	22	22	22	23	23	23	23	23	24	24	24	24	24	25	25	25	26	26	26			

♃ 1 10 17 23 28 — ♉3 4 5 6 7 ♄ 1 12 25 — ♐27 28 29 ♅ 1 12 — ♈4 5 ♆ 1 R 20 — ♍0 29♌ ♇ 1 — ♋16

3

	1	2	3	4	5	6	7	8	9	10	11	12	13	14	15	16	17	18	19	20	21	22	23	24	25	26	27	28	29	30	31
☉	♓10	11	12	13	14	15	16	17	18	19	20	21	22	23	24	25	26	27	28	29	29/0	♈1	2	3	4	5	6	7	8	9	10
☽	♏19	♐1	13	24	♑6	18	♒0	13	26	♓9	22	♈6	19	♉3	17	♊1	15	29	♋14	28	♌12	26	♍10	23	♎6	19	♏2	14	27	♐9	20
☿	♒13	14	15	16	17	18	19	20	21	23	24	25	26	28	29	29/0	♓2	3	5	6	8	9	11	12	14	15	17	19	20	22	24
♀	♈25	26	26	27	28	29	29	29/0	♉1	1	2	2	3	4	4	4	5	5	6	6	6	7	7	7	7	8	8	8	R 8	8	8
♂	♊27	27	27	28	28	28	29	29	29	29/0	♋0	0	1	1	2	2	2	3	3	3	4	4	5	5	6	6	7	7	7	8	8

♃ 1 6 12 17 21 26 31 — ♉7 8 9 10 11 12 13 ♄ 1 15 — ♐29 ♑0 ♅ 1 22 — ♈6 7 ♆ 1 R — ♌29 ♇ 1 — ♋16

4

	1	2	3	4	5	6	7	8	9	10	11	12	13	14	15	16	17	18	19	20	21	22	23	24	25	26	27	28	29	30	31
☉	♈11	12	13	14	15	16	17	18	19	20	21	22	23	24	25	26	27	28	29	29/0	♉1	2	3	4	5	6	6	7	8	9	
☽	♑2	14	26	♒8	21	♓4	17	♈0	14	28	♉13	27	♊12	26	♋11	25	♌9	22	♍6	19	♎2	15	28	♏10	23	♐5	17	28	♑10	22	
☿	♓26	27	29/0	♈1	3	5	7	8	10	12	14	16	18	20	22	25	27	29	♉1	3	5	7	9	12	14	16	18	20	22	24	
♀	♉8	R 8	7	7	7	7	6	6	6	5	5	4	4	3	3	2	1	1	0	♉29	♈29	28	28	27	27	26	25	25	24	24	
♂	♋9	9	10	10	11	11	12	12	13	13	14	14	14	15	15	16	16	17	17	18	18	19	19	20	21	21	22	22	23	23	

♃ 1 4 9 13 18 22 26 30 — ♉13 14 15 16 17 18 19 20 ♄ 1 10 R — ♑0 0 ♅ 1 8 27 — ♈7 8 9 ♆ 1 R 30 — ♌29 28 ♇ 1 — ♋16

5

	1	2	3	4	5	6	7	8	9	10	11	12	13	14	15	16	17	18	19	20	21	22	23	24	25	26	27	28	29	30	31
☉	♉10	11	12	13	14	15	16	17	18	19	20	21	22	23	24	25	26	27	28	29	29/0	♊1	2	3	4	4	5	6	7	8	9
☽	♒4	16	29	♓12	25	♈8	23	♉7	22	♊6	21	♋6	21	♌5	19	♍3	16	29	♎12	25	♏7	19	♐1	13	25	♑7	19	♒1	13	25	♓7
☿	♉26	27	29/0	♊1	3	4	6	7	9	10	11	13	14	15	16	17	18	18	19	20	20	21	21	22	22	22	22	R 22	22	22	22
♀	♈24	R 23	23	23	22	22	22	22	22	22	21	D 21	22	22	22	22	22	22	23	23	23	24	24	24	25	25	26	26	27	27	28
♂	♋24	24	25	25	26	26	27	27	28	28	29	29	29/0	♌1	1	2	2	3	3	4	4	5	6	6	7	7	8	8	9	10	10

♃ 1 5 9 13 17 22 26 30 — ♉20 21 22 23 24 25 26 27 ♄ 1 R 5 31 — ♑0 ♐29 28 ♅ 1 18 — ♈9 10 ♆ 1 R 10 D — ♌28 28 ♇ 1 31 — ♋16 17

6

	1	2	3	4	5	6	7	8	9	10	11	12	13	14	15	16	17	18	19	20	21	22	23	24	25	26	27	28	29	30	31
☉	♊10	11	12	13	14	15	16	17	18	19	20	21	22	23	24	25	26	27	28	28	29/0	♋0	1	2	3	4	5	6	7	8	
☽	♓20	♈3	17	♉1	15	♊0	15	♋0	15	♌0	15	29	♍13	26	♎9	22	♏4	16	28	♐10	22	♑4	16	28	♒10	22	♓4	16	29	♈12	
☿	♊22	R 21	21	21	20	20	19	18	18	17	17	16	16	15	15	15	14	14	14	14	D 14	14	14	14	14	15	15	16	16	17	
♀	♈29	29	29/0	♉1	1	2	3	3	4	5	6	6	7	8	9	10	11	11	12	13	14	15	16	17	18	19	20	20	21	22	
♂	♌11	11	12	12	13	13	14	15	15	16	16	17	18	18	19	19	20	20	21	22	22	23	23	24	25	25	26	26	27	28	

♃ 1 3 8 12 16 21 25 30 — ♉27 28 29 ♊0 1 2 3 4 ♄ 1 R 22 30 — ♐28 27 26 ♅ 1 16 — ♈10 11 ♆ 1 18 — ♌28 29 ♇ 1 — ♋17

7

	1	2	3	4	5	6	7	8	9	10	11	12	13	14	15	16	17	18	19	20	21	22	23	24	25	26	27	28	29	30	31
☉	♋9	10	11	12	13	14	15	16	17	18	18	19	20	21	22	23	24	25	26	27	28	29	29/0	♌1	2	3	4	5	6	7	8
☽	♈26	♉9	24	♊8	23	♋9	24	♌9	24	♍8	22	♎5	18	♏1	13	25	♐7	19	♑1	13	25	♒7	19	♓1	13	26	♈9	22	♉5	19	♊3
☿	♊18	19	19	20	22	23	24	25	26	28	29/0	♋1	2	4	6	8	9	11	13	15	17	19	21	23	25	27	29/0	♌2	4	6	8
♀	♉23	24	25	26	27	28	29	29/0	♊1	2	3	4	5	6	7	8	10	11	12	13	14	15	16	17	18	19	20	21	22	24	25
♂	♌28	29	29	29/0	♍0	1	2	2	3	4	4	5	5	6	7	7	8	8	9	10	10	11	11	12	13	13	14	15	15	16	16

♃ 1 5 10 15 20 25 31 — ♊4 5 6 7 8 9 10 ♄ 1 R 21 31 — ♐26 25 24 ♅ 1 17 R — ♈11 11 ♆ 1 24 — ♌29 ♍0 ♇ 1 — ♋18

8

	1	2	3	4	5	6	7	8	9	10	11	12	13	14	15	16	17	18	19	20	21	22	23	24	25	26	27	28	29	30	31
☉	♌8	9	10	11	12	13	14	15	16	17	18	19	20	21	22	23	24	25	26	27	28	29	29/0	♍0	1	2	3	4	5	6	7
☽	♊18	♋2	17	♌2	17	♍2	16	♎0	14	27	♏10	22	♐4	16	28	♑10	21	♒3	16	28	♓10	23	♈6	19	♉2	16	29	♊13	27	♋12	26
☿	♌10	12	14	16	18	20	22	24	26	28	29/0	♍1	3	5	7	9	10	12	14	15	17	18	20	21	23	24	26	27	29	29/0	♎2
♀	♊26	27	28	29	29/0	♋1	2	3	5	6	7	8	9	10	11	13	14	15	16	17	18	19	21	22	23	24	25	26	28	29	29♌/0
♂	♍17	18	18	19	19	20	21	21	22	23	23	24	25	25	26	26	27	28	28	29	29/0	♎0	1	2	2	3	3	4	5	5	6

♃ 1 6 12 19 27 — ♊10 11 12 13 14 ♄ 1 R 29 D — ♐24 24 ♅ 1 R 31 — ♈11 10 ♆ 1 21 — ♍0 1 ♇ 1 31 — ♋18 19

9

	1	2	3	4	5	6	7	8	9	10	11	12	13	14	15	16	17	18	19	20	21	22	23	24	25	26	27	28	29	30	31
☉	♍8	9	10	11	12	13	14	15	16	17	18	19	20	21	22	23	24	25	26	27	28	29	29/0	♎1	2	3	4	5	6	7	
☽	♌11	26	♍10	25	♎9	22	♏5	18	♐0	12	24	♑6	18	29	♒12	24	♓7	19	♈2	15	29	♉12	26	♊10	24	♋8	22	♌7	21	♍5	
☿	♎3	4	6	7	8	9	10	12	13	14	15	16	17	18	18	19	20	21	21	22	22	23	23	23	23	R 23	23	23	22	22	
♀	♌1	2	3	5	6	7	8	9	10	12	13	14	15	16	18	19	20	21	22	24	25	26	27	28	29/0	♍1	2	3	4	6	
♂	♎7	7	8	9	9	10	11	11	12	13	13	14	14	15	16	16	17	18	18	19	20	20	21	22	22	23	24	24	25	26	

♃ 1 5 19 — ♊14 15 16 ♄ 1 — ♐24 ♅ 1 R 30 — ♈10 9 ♆ 1 17 — ♍1 2 ♇ 1 — ♋19

10

	1	2	3	4	5	6	7	8	9	10	11	12	13	14	15	16	17	18	19	20	21	22	23	24	25	26	27	28	29	30	31
☉	♎8	9	10	11	12	13	14	15	16	17	18	19	20	20	21	22	23	24	25	26	27	28	29/0	♏0	1	2	3	4	5	6	7
☽	♍19	♎3	17	♏0	13	26	♐8	20	♑2	14	26	♒8	20	♓2	15	28	♈11	24	♉8	22	♊6	21	♋5	19	♌3	18	♍1	15	29	♎12	25
☿	♎21	R 20	20	19	18	16	15	14	13	12	11	10	9	9	8	8	D 8	8	8	9	9	10	11	12	13	15	16	17	19	20	22
♀	♍7	8	9	11	12	13	14	15	17	18	19	20	22	23	24	25	27	28	29	29/0	♎1	3	4	5	6	8	9	10	11	13	14
♂	♎26	27	28	28	29	29/0	♏1	1	2	3	3	4	5	5	6	7	7	8	9	9	10	11	11	12	13	14	14	15	16	16	17

♃ 1 5 R 31 — ♊16 16 15 ♄ 1 5 20 31 — ♐24 25 26 27 ♅ 1 R 31 — ♈9 8 ♆ 1 21 — ♍2 3 ♇ 1 — ♋19

11

	1	2	3	4	5	6	7	8	9	10	11	12	13	14	15	16	17	18	19	20	21	22	23	24	25	26	27	28	29	30	31
☉	♏8	9	10	11	12	13	14	15	16	17	18	19	20	21	22	23	24	25	26	27	28	29/0	♐0	1	2	3	4	5	6	7	
☽	♏8	21	♐4	16	28	♑10	22	♒4	15	28	♓10	22	♈5	19	♉3	17	♊1	16	♋1	15	♌0	14	28	♍12	26	♎9	22	♏5	17	29	
☿	♎23	25	26	28	29/0	♏1	3	4	6	7	9	11	12	14	15	17	19	20	22	24	25	27	28	29/0	♐1	3	5	6	8	9	
♀	♎15	16	18	19	20	21	23	24	25	26	28	29	29/0	♏1	3	4	5	6	8	9	10	11	13	14	15	16	18	19	20	21	
♂	♏18	18	19	20	21	21	22	23	23	24	25	26	26	27	28	28	29	29/0	♐1	1	2	3	3	4	5	6	6	7	8	8	

♃ 1 R 13 21 29 30 — ♊15 14 13 12 12 ♄ 1 11 21 30 — ♐27 28 29 ♑0 ♅ 1 R 30 — ♈8 7 ♆ 1 — ♍3 ♇ 1 — ♋19

12

	1	2	3	4	5	6	7	8	9	10	11	12	13	14	15	16	17	18	19	20	21	22	23	24	25	26	27	28	29	30	31
☉	♐8	9	10	11	12	13	14	15	16	17	18	20	21	22	23	24	25	26	27	28	29	29/0	♑1	2	3	4	5	6	7	8	9
☽	♐12	24	♑6	18	♒0	12	24	♓6	18	♈0	13	27	♉10	25	♊9	24	♋9	24	♌9	24	♍9	22	♎6	19	♏2	14	27	♐9	21	♑3	15
☿	♐11	12	14	16	17	19	20	22	23	25	27	28	29/0	♑1	3	4	6	8	9	11	12	14	15	17	18	20	21	23	24	26	27
♀	♏23	24	25	26	28	29	29/0	♐1	3	4	5	6	8	9	10	11	13	14	15	16	18	19	20	21	23	24	25	27	28	29	29♑/0
♂	♐9	10	11	11	12	13	14	14	15	16	17	17	18	19	19	20	21	22	22	23	24	25	25	26	27	28	28	29	29/0	♑1	1

♃ 1 R 13 21 30 — ♊11 10 9 8 ♄ 1 8 17 26 — ♑0 1 2 3 ♅ 1 R 17 D — ♈7 7 ♆ 1 6 R — ♍3 3 ♇ 1 — ♋19

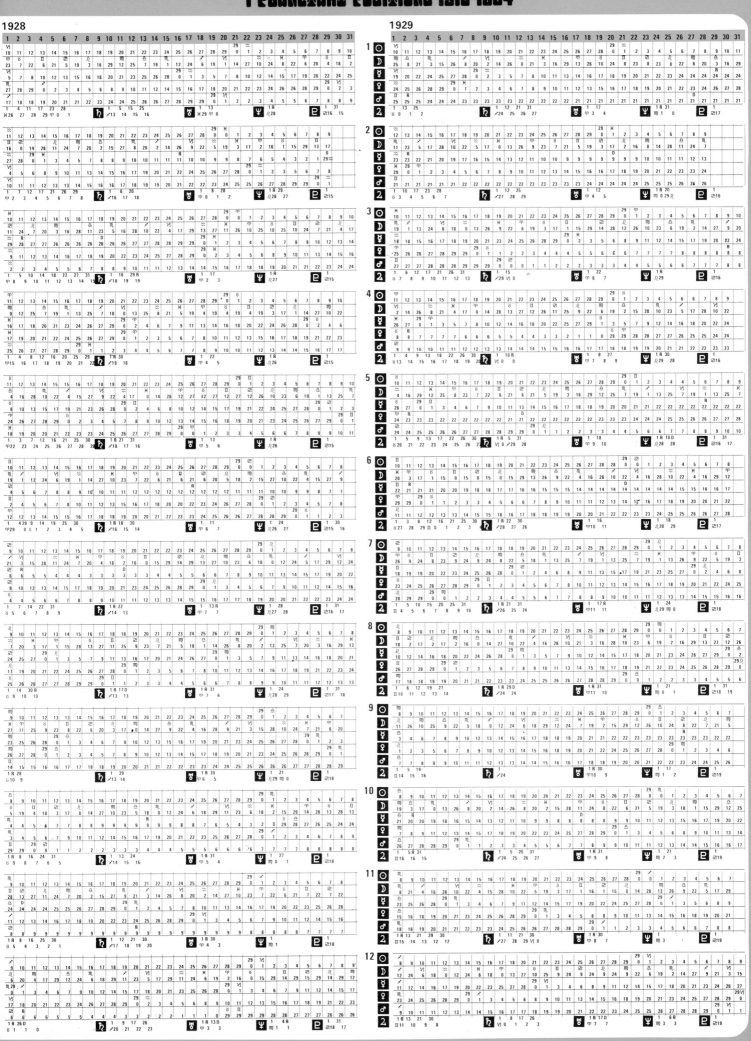

1930

1
☉ 10 11 12 13 14 15 16 17 18 19 20 21 22 23 24 25 26 27 28 29 0 1 2 3 4 5 6 7 8 9 10 11
☽ 27 20 2 14 27 9 22 5 18 2 17 2 17 3 18 3 18 2 15 29 11 24 6 18 0 12 24 5 17 29
☿ 29 0 1 2 4 5 6 7 7 8 8 8 8 8 7 6 5 4 3 2 1 29 28 27 26 25 24 23 23 22
♀ 1 3 4 5 7 8 9 10 12 13 14 15 17 18 19 20 22 23 24 25 27 28 29 0 2 3 4 5 7 8 9
♂ 2 3 4 4 5 6 7 7 8 9 10 11 11 12 13 14 14 15 16 17 17 18 19 20 20 21 22 23 23 24 25
♃ 1 R 11 31 D — ♊ 8 7 6 | ♄ 1 12 20 30 — ♑ 4 5 6 7 | ♅ 1 21 — ♈ 7 8 | ♆ 1 R 31 — ♍ 3 2 | ♇ ♋18

2
☉ 12 13 14 15 16 17 18 19 20 21 22 23 24 25 26 27 28 29 0 1 2 3 4 5 6 7 8 9
☽ 11 24 6 18 1 14 27 11 26 10 25 11 26 11 26 10 24 7 20 3 15 27 9 20 2 14 26 8
☿ 22 22 22 22 23 23 23 24 25 25 26 27 28 29 0 1 2 3 4 5 6 8 9 10 12 13 14 16
♀ 11 12 13 14 16 17 18 19 21 22 23 24 26 27 28 29 0 1 2 3 4 6 7 8 9 11 12 13 14
♂ 26 27 27 28 29 29 0 0 1 2 3 4 4 5 6 7 7 8 9 10 11 11 12 13 14 14 15 16 17
♃ 1 20 — ♊ 6 7 | ♄ 1 8 19 — ♑ 7 8 9 | ♅ 1 17 — ♈ 8 9 | ♆ 1 R — ♍ 2 | ♇ 1 28 — ♋ 18 17

3
☉ 10 11 12 13 14 15 16 17 18 19 20 21 22 23 24 25 26 27 28 29 0 1 2 3 4 5 6 7 8 9 10
☽ 21 3 15 28 11 24 8 21 5 20 4 19 4 19 4 18 2 15 28 11 23 5 17 29 11 23 5 17 29 12 25
☿ 17 19 20 21 23 24 26 28 29 0 2 4 6 7 9 11 12 14 16 18 20 21 23 25 27 29 0 1 3 5 7 9
♀ 16 17 18 19 21 22 23 24 26 27 28 29 0 1 2 3 4 6 7 8 9 10 12 13 14 15 17 18 19 20 22 23
♂ 18 18 19 20 21 21 22 23 24 25 25 26 27 28 28 29 0 1 2 2 3 4 5 6 6 7 8 9 9 10 11
♃ 1 13 20 27 — ♊ 8 9 10 11 | ♄ 1 19 — ♑ 10 11 | ♅ 1 8 26 — ♈ 9 10 11 | ♆ 1 R 31 — ♍ 2 1 | ♇ 1 — ♋17

4
☉ 11 12 13 14 15 16 17 18 19 20 21 22 23 24 25 26 27 28 29 0 1 2 3 4 5 6 7 8 9
☽ 8 21 5 18 2 16 0 15 29 14 28 12 26 10 23 6 18 1 13 25 7 19 1 13 25 8 20 4 17 1
☿ 11 13 15 17 19 21 23 25 27 29 0 1 3 5 7 9 11 13 15 16 18 19 21 22 23 25 26 27 28 28 29
♀ 24 25 27 28 29 0 1 3 4 5 6 8 9 10 11 13 14 15 16 18 19 20 21 22 24 25 26 27 29 0
♂ 12 13 14 15 15 16 17 18 19 20 20 21 22 23 23 24 25 26 27 27 28 29 0 0 1 2 3 4
♃ 1 3 8 14 19 24 29 — ♊ 11 12 13 14 15 16 17 | ♄ 1 22 R — ♑ 11 11 | ♅ 1 13 30 — ♈ 11 12 13 | ♆ 1 R — ♍ 1 | ♇ 1 — ♋17

5
☉ 10 11 12 13 14 15 16 17 18 19 20 21 22 23 24 25 26 27 28 29 0 1 2 3 4 5 6 7 8 9
☽ 15 29 13 27 11 26 10 24 8 21 5 18 1 14 26 9 21 3 15 27 9 21 3 16 29 12 26 10 24 9 23
☿ 29 0 1 1 2 2 2 2 2 2 2 2 2 1 1 0 29 29 29 28 27 26 26 25 25 25 24 24 24 24 24
♀ 1 2 3 5 6 7 8 10 11 12 13 14 16 17 18 19 21 22 23 24 25 27 28 29 0 1 3 4 5 6 7
♂ 5 6 7 7 8 9 10 10 11 12 13 14 14 15 16 17 17 18 19 20 20 21 22 23 23 24 25 26 26 27 28
♃ 1 4 9 13 18 22 27 31 — ♊ 17 18 19 20 21 22 23 24 | ♄ 1 R — ♑11 | ♅ 1 22 — ♈ 13 14 | ♆ 1 R 12 D 31 — ♍ 0 0 1 | ♇ 1 31 — ♋ 17 18

6
☉ 10 11 12 13 14 15 16 17 18 19 20 21 22 23 24 24 25 26 27 28 29 0 1 2 3 4 5 6 7 8
☽ 8 22 7 21 4 18 1 14 27 10 22 5 17 29 11 23 5 17 29 11 24 7 20 4 18 3 18 3 18 3
☿ 24 24 24 24 24 24 25 25 26 26 27 28 29 0 1 3 4 5 6 7 9 10 12 13 15 16 18 20 21
♀ 9 10 11 12 13 15 16 17 18 19 21 22 23 24 25 27 28 29 0 1 3 4 5 6 7 9 10 11 12
♂ 29 29 0 1 2 2 3 4 5 5 6 7 8 8 9 10 10 11 12 13 13 14 15 16 16 17 18 19 20
♃ 1 5 9 13 18 22 27 30 — ♊ 24 25 26 27 28 29 ♋ 0 1 | ♄ 1 R 25 30 — ♑ 10 9 8 | ♅ 1 20 — ♈ 14 15 | ♆ 1 — ♍ 1 | ♇ 1 30 — ♋ 18 19

7
☉ 9 10 11 12 13 14 14 15 16 17 18 19 20 21 22 23 24 25 26 27 28 29 0 1 2 3 4 5 6 7
☽ 17 1 15 28 11 24 7 19 1 14 26 8 19 1 13 25 7 19 2 15 28 12 27 11 26 12 27 11 26 10 24
☿ 23 25 27 29 0 1 3 5 7 9 11 14 16 18 20 22 24 26 29 0 3 5 7 9 10 12 13 15 16 18 20 21 22 24
♀ 14 16 17 18 19 20 21 23 24 25 26 27 28 0 1 2 3 4 5 7 8 9 10 11 12 13 15 16 17 18 19
♂ 21 21 22 23 23 24 25 26 26 27 28 28 29 0 1 1 2 3 3 4 5 5 6 7 7 8 9 10 10 11 12
♃ 1 5 10 14 19 23 28 — ♋ 1 2 3 4 5 6 7 | ♄ 1 R 23 31 — ♑ 8 7 6 | ♅ 1 22 R — ♈ 15 15 | ♆ 1 20 — ♍ 1 2 | ♇ 1 — ♋19

8
☉ 8 9 10 11 12 13 14 15 16 17 18 19 20 21 22 23 24 25 26 27 28 29 0 1 2 3 4 5 6 7
☽ 8 21 4 16 29 11 23 5 16 28 10 22 4 16 28 11 24 7 21 5 20 5 20 5 21 5 20 4 17 0 13
☿ 25 27 29 0 2 4 5 7 8 10 11 13 14 15 16 17 18 20 21 22 23 24 25 26 27 28 28 29 0 1 2 3 4
♀ 20 21 22 23 24 25 26 27 28 29 0 1 3 4 5 6 7 8 9 10 11 12 13 15 16 17 18 19 20 21 22 23
♂ 12 13 14 14 15 16 16 17 18 18 19 20 20 21 22 22 23 23 24 25 25 26 27 27 28 29 29 0 0 1 2
♃ 1 6 11 16 21 27 — ♋ 8 9 10 11 12 13 | ♄ 1 R 31 — ♑ 6 5 | ♅ 1 R — ♈15 | ♆ 1 18 — ♍ 2 3 | ♇ 1 31 — ♋ 19 20

9
☉ 8 9 10 11 12 13 14 15 16 17 18 19 20 21 22 23 24 25 26 27 28 29 0 1 2 3 4 5 6
☽ 25 8 20 2 13 25 7 19 1 13 26 8 21 4 17 1 15 29 14 28 12 26 9 22 4 16
☿ 4 5 5 6 6 6 7 7 7 7 7 6 6 5 5 4 3 2 1 0 29 29 27 26 25 24 23 22 22 22
♀ 24 25 26 27 28 29 0 1 2 3 4 5 6 7 8 9 10 11 12 13 14 15 16 17 18 19 20 21 21
♂ 2 3 3 4 5 5 6 7 7 8 8 9 10 10 11 12 12 13 13 14 15 15 16 16 17 17 18 19 19
♃ 1 7 14 21 28 — ♋ 14 15 16 17 18 | ♄ 1 R 10 D — ♑ 5 5 | ♅ 1 R 30 — ♈ 14 13 | ♆ 1 14 — ♍ 3 4 | ♇ 1 — ♋20

10
☉ 7 8 9 10 11 12 13 14 15 16 17 18 19 20 21 22 23 24 25 26 27 28 29 0 1 2 3 4 5 6 7
☽ 28 10 22 4 16 28 10 22 5 18 1 14 27 11 25 9 24 8 23 7 22 6 20 4 17 29 12 24 6 18 0
☿ 22 22 22 23 24 24 25 26 28 29 0 2 3 5 6 8 9 11 13 14 16 18 20 21 23 25 26 28 0 1 3
♀ 22 23 24 25 25 26 27 27 28 28 29 29 0 0 1 1 2 2 3 3 4 4 5 5 5 6 6 6 7 7 7
♂ 20 21 21 22 22 23 23 24 24 25 25 26 26 27 27 28 28 29 29 0 0 1 1 2 2 3 3 3 4 4 5
♃ 1 8 21 — ♋ 18 19 20 | ♄ 1 10 26 — ♑ 5 6 7 | ♅ 1 R 31 — ♈ 13 12 | ♆ 1 15 — ♍ 4 5 | ♇ 1 — ♋20

11
☉ 8 9 10 11 12 13 14 15 16 17 18 19 20 21 22 23 24 25 26 27 28 29 0 1 2 3 4 5 6 7
☽ 12 24 6 18 1 14 27 10 24 8 22 6 20 4 18 3 17 1 14 28 12 25 7 20 2 14 26 8 20 2
☿ 5 6 8 10 11 13 14 16 17 19 21 22 24 25 27 28 29 0 2 3 5 6 8 9 10 11 13 14 16 17 19 20
♀ 7 7 7 7 7 7 7 6 6 6 6 5 5 5 4 4 3 3 2 1 1 0 29 29 28 27 27 26 26 25
♂ 5 5 6 6 6 7 7 7 8 8 8 9 9 9 10 10 10 11 11 11 12 12 12 12 13 13 14 14 14 14 15
♃ 1 8 R — ♋ 20 20 | ♄ 1 8 19 29 — ♑ 7 8 9 10 | ♅ 1 R 30 — ♈ 12 11 | ♆ 1 — ♍5 | ♇ 1 — ♋20

12
☉ 8 9 10 11 12 13 14 15 16 17 18 19 20 21 22 23 24 25 26 27 28 29 0 1 2 3 4 5 6 7 8 9
☽ 14 26 9 22 6 20 4 18 2 17 1 15 29 13 27 10 24 7 20 3 16 28 10 22 4 16 28 10 22 4 17
☿ 22 23 25 26 28 0 1 3 4 6 7 9 10 11 13 15 16 17 18 19 20 21 22 22 22 22 22 21 20 19 18 17
♀ 25 24 24 23 23 23 23 22 22 22 22 22 22 22 22 22 23 23 23 23 23 24 24 25 25 26 26 27 27
♂ 15 15 15 15 16 16 16 16 16 16 16 17 17 17 17 17 17 17 17 17 17 17 17 16 16 16 16 16 16 16 16
♃ 1 R 18 26 31 — ♋ 19 18 17 16 | ♄ 1 8 17 26 — ♑ 10 11 12 13 | ♅ 1 R 21 D — ♈ 11 11 | ♆ 1 9 R 31 — ♍ 5 5 5 | ♇ 1 — ♋20

1931

1
☉ 10 11 12 13 14 15 16 17 18 19 20 21 22 23 24 25 26 27 28 29 0 1 2 3 4 5 6 7
☽ 0 14 28 12 27 12 27 11 26 10 24 7 21 4 17 29 12 24 6 18 0 12 24 6 18 29 12 25
☿ 20 19 18 17 16 14 13 12 10 9 8 8 7 6 6 6 6 6 6 7 7 7 8 8 9 10 11 12 13
♀ 28 29 0 0 1 2 2 3 4 5 6 7 8 9 10 10 11 12 13 14 15 16 17 18 19 20 21
♂ 15 15 15 14 14 14 13 13 13 12 12 12 11 11 11 10 10 10 9 9 8 8 7 7 6
♃ 1 R 10 17 25 — ♋ 16 15 14 13 | ♄ 1 11 20 29 — ♑ 14 15 16 17 | ♅ 1 26 — ♈ 11 12 | ♆ 1 R — ♍5

2
☉ 11 12 13 14 15 16 17 18 19 20 21 22 23 24 25 26 27 28 29 0 1 2 3 4 5 6 7 8 9
☽ 20 5 20 6 21 5 20 4 17 1 14 26 9 21 3 15 27 9 21 3 14 26 8 21 3 16 0 14
☿ 17 18 19 21 22 23 24 26 27 28 29 0 1 3 4 6 7 9 10 12 13 15 16 18 19 21 23 24 26
♀ 25 26 27 28 29 0 1 2 3 4 5 6 7 8 9 10 12 13 14 15 16 17 18 19 20 21 23 24
♂ 5 4 4 4 4 3 3 2 2 2 1 1 1 0 0 29 29 29 29 29 29 28 28 28 28 28
♃ 1 R 16 28 — ♋ 12 11 10 | ♄ 1 7 16 26 — ♑ 17 18 19 20 | ♅ 1 — ♈ 12 13 | ♆ 1 R 28 — ♍ 5 4

3
☉ 10 11 12 13 14 15 16 17 18 19 20 21 22 23 24 25 26 27 28 29 0 1 2 3 4 5 6 7
☽ 28 13 28 14 29 14 29 13 27 10 23 6 18 0 12 24 6 18 29 11 23 5 18 0 13 26 9 23 7 21
☿ 28 29 1 3 5 6 8 10 12 14 16 18 19 21 23 25 27 0 1 3 5 7 9 11 13 15 17 19
♀ 25 26 27 28 29 0 2 3 4 5 6 7 9 10 11 12 13 15 16 17 18 19 20 22 23 24 25 26
♂ 28 27 27 27 27 27 27 27 27 27 27 27 27 28 28 28 28 28 28 28 28 29 29 29 29 29
♃ 1 R 7 D 25 — ♋ 10 10 11 | ♄ 1 10 24 — ♑ 20 21 22 | ♅ 1 13 31 — ♈ 13 14 15 | ♆ 1 R 31 — ♍ 4 3

4
☉ 10 11 12 13 14 15 16 17 18 19 20 21 22 23 24 25 26 27 28 29 0 1 2 3 4 5 6 7
☽ 22 7 22 7 21 5 19 2 15 27 9 21 3 15 26 8 20 2 15 27 10 23 6 20 3 17 2 16
☿ 26 28 0 1 3 4 5 7 8 9 10 11 12 12 13 13 13 13 13 13 13 13 13 12 12 11 11 10
♀ 1 2 3 4 5 7 8 9 10 11 12 14 15 16 17 18 20 21 22 23 24 26 27 28 29 0 2 3
♂ 0 1 1 1 1 1 2 2 2 3 3 3 3 4 4 4 5 5 5 6 6 6 7 7 7 8 8 9 9 9
♃ 1 7 17 25 — ♋ 11 12 13 14 | ♄ 1 15 — ♑ 22 23 | ♅ 1 17 — ♈ 15 16 | ♆ 1 R — ♍3

5
☉ 10 11 12 13 14 15 16 17 18 19 20 21 22 23 24 24 25 26 27 28 29 0 1 2 3 4 5 6
☽ 0 15 29 13 27 10 23 5 17 29 11 23 5 17 29 11 24 7 20 3 16 0 14 28 12 26 11 25
☿ 8 8 7 6 6 5 5 4 4 4 4 3 3 3 4 4 4 4 5 5 6 6 7 7 8 9 10 11
♀ 6 8 9 10 11 12 13 15 16 17 18 19 21 22 23 24 26 27 28 29 0 1 3 4 5 6 8 9
♂ 11 11 11 12 12 13 13 14 14 14 15 15 16 16 17 17 18 18 19 19 20 21 21 22 22 23 23
♃ 1 8 14 20 25 31 — ♋ 15 16 17 18 19 20 | ♄ 1 4 R 31 — ♑ 23 23 22 | ♅ 1 6 26 — ♈ 16 17 18 | ♆ 1 R 15 D — ♍ 3 3

6
☉ 10 11 12 13 14 15 16 17 18 19 20 21 22 23 24 25 26 27 28 29 0 1 2 3 4 5 6
☽ 21 5 18 1 13 25 7 19 1 13 25 7 20 2 15 29 13 27 11 25 9 23 7 21 5 19 3 17
☿ 16 17 18 20 21 22 24 25 27 29 0 2 4 5 7 9 11 13 15 17 19 21 23 25 28 0 2 4
♀ 14 15 16 17 18 20 21 22 23 24 26 27 28 29 0 1 2 3 4 5 7 8 9 10 11 13 14 15 16
♂ 25 26 26 27 27 28 28 29 29 0 0 1 1 2 2 3 3 4 4 5 5 6 6 7 7 8 9 9 10
♃ 1 5 10 14 19 24 29 — ♋ 20 21 22 23 24 25 26 | ♄ 1 R 29 — ♑ 22 21 | ♅ 1 — ♈ 18 19 | ♆ 1 — ♍3

7
☉ 8 9 10 11 12 13 14 15 16 17 18 19 20 21 22 23 24 25 26 27 28 29 0 1 2 3 4
☽ 9 21 3 15 27 9 21 3 15 28 11 24 8 22 6 21 5 20 4 18 2 16 29 13 26 9 22
☿ 11 13 15 17 19 21 23 25 27 29 0 1 3 5 7 9 10 12 14 15 17 19 20 22 23 25 26 28 29
♀ 20 21 22 24 25 26 27 28 29 0 1 2 3 5 6 7 8 9 11 12 13 14 16 17 18 19 20 22 23
♂ 11 12 12 13 13 14 14 15 15 16 16 17 17 18 18 19 19 20 21 21 22 22 23 23 24 24 25 25 26 27 27
♃ 1 3 8 12 17 29 21 26 31 — ♋ 26 27 28 29 0 1 2 3 | ♄ 1 R 12 26 31 — ♑ 21 20 19 18 | ♅ 1 26 R — ♈ 19 19 | ♆ 1 16 — ♍ 3 4

8
☉ 8 9 10 11 12 13 14 15 16 17 18 19 20 21 22 23 24 25 26 27 28 29 0 1 2 3 4
☽ 11 23 5 17 29 11 23 6 19 2 16 0 15 29 14 29 13 27 10 24 7 20 2 14 26 8 19
☿ 4 6 7 8 9 10 11 12 13 14 15 16 16 17 17 18 18 18 18 19 19 19 19 19 19 18 18 17
♀ 28 29 0 2 3 4 5 6 8 9 10 11 13 14 15 16 17 19 20 21 22 24 25 26 27 29 0 1
♂ 0 0 1 2 2 3 3 4 5 5 6 7 7 8 8 9 10 10 11 11 12 12 13 14 14 15 15 16 17
♃ 1 4 8 13 18 22 27 31 — ♌ 3 4 5 6 7 8 9 10 | ♄ 1 R 31 — ♑ 18 17 | ♅ 1 R — ♈19 | ♆ 1 15 — ♍ 4 5

9
☉ 8 9 10 11 12 13 14 15 16 17 18 19 20 21 22 23 24 25 26 27 28 29 0 1 2 3 4
☽ 25 7 19 2 14 27 10 24 8 23 8 23 8 23 8 22 6 20 3 16 29 11 23 5 17 29 11 22
☿ 15 14 13 12 11 10 9 8 7 7 6 6 6 6 6 7 7 8 9 10 11 12 13 15 16 18 19
♀ 6 7 9 10 11 12 13 15 16 17 18 20 21 22 23 25 26 27 28 29 0 1 2 3 5 6 7 8
♂ 19 20 20 21 21 22 23 23 24 25 25 26 26 27 28 28 29 29 0 1 1 2 3 3 4 5 5 6 7
♃ 1 5 10 16 21 26 30 — ♌ 10 11 12 13 14 15 16 | ♄ 1 R 22 D — ♑ 17 17 | ♅ 1 R 25 — ♈ 19 18 | ♆ 1 11 — ♍ 5 6

10
☉ 7 8 9 10 11 12 13 14 15 16 17 18 19 20 21 22 23 24 25 26 27 28 29 0 1 2 3 4
☽ 28 11 23 6 19 3 17 1 16 1 16 2 16 1 15 29 12 25 8 20 2 14 26 8 19 1 13
☿ 24 26 28 29 1 3 5 6 8 10 12 14 15 17 19 20 22 24 25 27 28 29 0 2 4 5 7 9 10
♀ 13 15 16 17 18 20 21 22 23 25 26 27 28 29 1 2 3 4 6 7 8 9 11 12 13 14 16 17
♂ 9 10 11 11 12 13 13 14 15 15 16 17 17 18 18 19 20 20 21 22 22 23 24 24 25 26 26 27 28
♃ 1 8 14 21 29 — ♌ 16 17 18 19 20 | ♄ 1 31 — ♑ 17 18 | ♅ 1 R 20 31 — ♈ 18 17 16 | ♆ 1 11 — ♍ 6 7

11
☉ 8 9 10 11 12 13 14 15 16 17 18 19 20 21 22 23 24 25 26 27 28 29 0 1 2 3 4 5
☽ 16 29 12 26 10 25 10 25 10 25 9 23 7 21 4 16 29 11 22 4 16 28 10 22 4 17 29 13
☿ 17 18 20 21 23 24 26 27 29 0 2 3 5 6 8 9 11 12 14 15 16 18 19 21 22 23 24 26
♀ 22 23 25 26 27 28 29 0 1 2 3 5 6 7 8 10 11 12 13 15 16 17 18 20 21 22 23 25 26
♂ 1 2 3 3 4 5 6 6 7 8 9 9 10 11 12 12 13 14 14 15 16 17 17 18 19 20 20 21
♃ 1 7 19 — ♌ 20 21 22 | ♄ 1 15 27 — ♑ 18 19 20 | ♅ 1 R — ♈16 | ♆ 1 30 — ♍ 7 8

12
☉ 8 9 10 11 12 13 14 15 16 17 18 19 20 21 22 23 24 25 26 27 28 29 0 1 2 3 4 5 6
☽ 7 21 5 19 4 18 3 17 1 15 29 12 24 6 18 0 12 24 6 18 0 13 26 9 22 6 20
☿ 29 0 1 2 3 4 5 5 6 6 6 6 6 5 4 3 2 1 0 29 28 27 26 24 23 22 22 21 21
♀ 29 0 1 2 3 5 6 7 8 10 11 12 13 15 16 17 18 20 21 22 23 25 26 27 28 29 0 1 2 3 4
♂ 23 24 25 26 26 27 28 29 29 0 1 2 3 3 4 5 6 7 7 8 9 10 11 11 12 12 13 14 1
♃ 1 10 R — ♌ 22 22 | ♄ 1 7 16 25 — ♑ 20 21 22 23 | ♅ 1 R 26 D — ♈ 16 15 | ♆ 1 11 R — ♍ 8 8

1932

1

	1	2	3	4	5	6	7	8	9	10	11	12	13	14	15	16	17	18	19	20	21	22	23	24	25	26	27	28	29	30	31
☉	♑ 10	11	12	13	14	15	16	17	18	19	20	21	22	23	24	25	26	27	28	29	29 0	♒ 1	2	3	4	5	6	7	8	9	10
☽	♎ 15	29	♏ 14	28	♐ 12	26	♑ 10	23	♒ 7	19	♓ 2	14	26	♈ 8	20	♉ 2	14	26	♊ 8	21	♋ 4	17	♌ 1	15	29	♍ 14	28	♎ 12	26	♏ 11	25
☿	♐ 20	D 20	20	21	21	22	23	24	25	26	27	28	29	29 0	♑ 1	2	3	5	6	7	9	10	11	13	14	16	17	18	20	21	23
♀	♒ 8	9	11	12	13	14	16	17	18	19	21	22	23	24	25	27	28	29	29 0	♓ 2	3	4	5	7	8	9	10	11	13	14	15
♂	♑ 17	18	19	19	20	21	22	22	23	24	25	26	26	27	28	29	29 0	♒ 0	1	2	3	3	4	5	6	6	7	8	9	10	10

♃ 1 R 20 28 31 — ♌21 20 19 18 · ♄ 1 11 20 28 — ♑24 25 26 27 · ♅ 1 31 — ♈15 16 · ♆ 1 R 31 — ♍ 8 7 · ♇ 1 31 — ♋21 20

2

	1	2	3	4	5	6	7	8	9	10	11	12	13	14	15	16	17	18	19	20	21	22	23	24	25	26	27	28	29	30	31
☉	♒ 11	12	13	14	15	16	17	18	19	20	21	22	23	24	25	26	27	28	29 0	♓ 0	1	2	3	4	5	6	7	8	9		
☽	♐ 8	22	♑ 6	19	♒ 2	15	28	♓ 10	22	♈ 4	16	28	♉ 10	22	♊ 4	16	29	♋ 12	25	♌ 9	24	♍ 8	23	♎ 8	22	♏ 7	21	♐ 5	19		
☿	♑ 24	26	27	29	29 0	♒ 2	4	5	7	8	10	12	13	15	17	18	20	22	24	25	27	29	29 0	♓ 3	4	6	8	10	12		
♀	♓ 16	17	19	20	21	22	24	25	26	27	28	29 0	♈ 1	2	3	4	6	7	8	9	10	12	13	14	15	16	17	19	20		
♂	♒ 11	12	13	14	14	15	16	17	18	18	19	20	21	21	22	23	24	25	25	26	27	28	28	29	29 0	♓ 1	2	3	3		

♃ 1 R 12 20 28 — ♌18 17 16 15 · ♄ 1 6 14 24 — ♑27 28 29 ♒ 0 · ♅ 1 25 — ♈16 17 · ♆ 1 R 29 — ♍ 7 6 · ♇ 1 — ♋20

3

	1	2	3	4	5	6	7	8	9	10	11	12	13	14	15	16	17	18	19	20	21	22	23	24	25	26	27	28	29	30	31
☉	♓ 11	12	13	14	15	16	17	18	19	20	21	22	23	24	25	26	27	28	29	29 0	♈ 0	1	2	3	4	5	6	7	8	9	10
☽	♑ 3	16	29	♒ 12	24	♓ 6	19	♈ 1	12	24	♉ 6	18	29	♊ 12	24	♋ 7	20	♌ 3	17	♍ 1	16	♎ 1	16	♏ 1	16	♐ 1	15	29	♑ 13	26	♒ 9
☿	♓ 14	16	18	20	21	23	25	27	29 0	♈ 1	3	5	7	8	10	12	13	15	16	18	19	20	21	22	23	23	24	24	25	25	R 25
♀	♈ 21	22	23	25	26	27	28	29	29 0	♉ 1	3	4	5	6	7	8	9	11	12	13	14	15	16	17	18	20	21	22	23	24	25
♂	♓ 4	5	6	6	7	8	9	10	10	11	12	13	13	14	15	16	17	18	18	19	20	21	21	22	23	24	25	25	26	27	28

♃ 1 R 9 23 — ♌15 14 13 · ♄ 1 16 28 — ♒ 1 2 3 · ♅ 1 16 31 — ♈17 18 19 · ♆ 1 R — ♍ 6 · ♇ 1 — ♋20

4

	1	2	3	4	5	6	7	8	9	10	11	12	13	14	15	16	17	18	19	20	21	22	23	24	25	26	27	28	29	30	31
☉	♈ 11	12	13	14	15	16	17	18	19	20	21	22	23	24	25	26	27	28	29	29 0	♉ 1	2	3	4	5	6	7	8	9	10	
☽	♒ 21	♓ 3	15	27	♈ 9	21	♉ 3	15	27	♊ 9	21	♋ 3	16	29	♌ 12	26	♍ 10	24	♎ 9	24	♏ 10	25	♐ 10	24	♑ 8	22	♒ 5	18	♓ 0	13	
☿	♈ 25	R 25	24	24	23	23	22	22	21	20	19	19	18	17	17	16	15	15	14	14	14	14	14	D 14	14	14	14	14	15	15	
♀	♉ 26	27	28	29	♊ 0	1	2	4	5	6	7	8	9	10	11	12	13	14	15	16	17	17	18	19	20	21	22	23	24	25	
♂	♓ 28	29	29 0	♈ 1	2	2	3	4	5	5	6	7	8	9	9	10	11	12	12	13	14	15	15	16	17	18	19	19	20	21	

♃ 1 R 9 24 — ♌12 D 13 · ♄ 1 14 — ♒ 3 4 · ♅ 1 21 — ♈19 20 · ♆ 1 R 30 — ♍ 6 5 · ♇ 1 — ♋20

5

	1	2	3	4	5	6	7	8	9	10	11	12	13	14	15	16	17	18	19	20	21	22	23	24	25	26	27	28	29	30	31
☉	♉ 11	12	13	14	15	16	17	18	19	19	20	21	22	23	24	25	26	27	28	29	29 0	♊ 1	2	3	4	5	6	7	8	9	10
☽	♓ 25	♈ 6	18	♉ 0	12	24	♊ 6	18	♋ 0	12	25	♌ 8	21	♍ 5	19	♎ 3	18	♏ 3	18	♐ 3	18	♑ 3	17	♒ 1	14	27	♓ 9	21	♈ 3	15	27
☿	♈ 16	16	17	18	19	19	20	21	22	23	24	26	27	28	29 0	♉ 1	2	3	5	6	8	9	11	13	14	16	18	19	21	23	25
♀	♊ 26	27	27	28	29	29 0	♋ 1	2	2	3	4	5	5	6	7	7	8	9	9	10	10	11	11	12	12	13	13	13	14	14	14
♂	♈ 21	22	23	24	25	25	26	27	28	28	29	29 0	♉ 1	1	2	3	4	4	5	6	7	7	8	9	10	10	11	12	13	13	14

♃ 1 9 19 27 — ♌13 14 15 16 · ♄ 1 15 R — ♒ 4 4 · ♅ 1 9 30 — ♈20 21 22 · ♆ 1 R 16 D — ♍ 5 5 · ♇ 1 — ♋20

6

	1	2	3	4	5	6	7	8	9	10	11	12	13	14	15	16	17	18	19	20	21	22	23	24	25	26	27	28	29	30	31
☉	♊ 10	11	12	13	14	15	16	17	18	19	20	21	22	23	24	25	26	27	28	29	29 0	♋ 0	1	2	3	4	5	6	7	8	
☽	♉ 9	21	♊ 3	15	27	♋ 10	22	♌ 5	18	♍ 1	15	29	♎ 13	27	♏ 12	27	♐ 12	26	♑ 11	25	♒ 9	22	♓ 5	17	29	♈ 12	23	♉ 5	17	29	
☿	♉ 27	29 0	♊ 1	3	5	7	9	11	14	16	18	20	21	24	27	29 0	♋ 1	3	5	7	10	12	14	16	17	19	21	23	25	27	
♀	♋ 15	15	15	15	15	15	15	R 15	15	15	15	15	15	14	14	14	13	13	13	12	12	11	10	10	9	9	8	7	7	6	
♂	♉ 15	15	16	17	18	18	19	20	21	21	22	23	23	24	25	26	26	27	28	29	29	29 0	♊ 1	1	2	3	3	4	5	6	

♃ 1 3 10 16 22 27 — ♌16 17 18 19 20 21 · ♄ 1 R 30 — ♒ 4 3 · ♅ 1 28 — ♈22 23 · ♆ 1 — ♍ 5 · ♇ 1 30 — ♋20 21

7

	1	2	3	4	5	6	7	8	9	10	11	12	13	14	15	16	17	18	19	20	21	22	23	24	25	26	27	28	29	30	31
☉	♋ 9	10	11	12	13	14	15	16	17	18	19	20	21	22	23	23	24	25	26	27	28	29	29 0	♌ 1	2	3	4	5	6	7	8
☽	♊ 11	24	♋ 6	19	♌ 2	15	28	♍ 12	26	♎ 10	24	♏ 8	22	♐ 7	21	♑ 5	20	♒ 3	17	♓ 0	13	25	♈ 7	19	♉ 1	13	25	♊ 7	19	♋ 2	15
☿	♋ 28	29 0	♌ 2	3	5	7	8	10	11	12	14	15	16	18	19	20	21	22	23	24	25	26	27	28	28	29	29 0	♍ 0	1	1	1
♀	♋ 6	R 5	4	4	3	3	2	2	1	1	0	0	0 29	♊ 29	29	29	29	29	29	29	D 29	29	29	29	29	29	29	29 0	♋ 0	0	1
♂	♊ 6	7	8	8	9	10	11	11	12	13	13	14	15	15	16	17	17	18	19	19	20	21	22	22	23	24	24	25	26	26	27

♃ 1 8 13 18 23 28 31 — ♌22 23 24 25 26 27 28 · ♄ 1 R 16 30 — ♒ 3 2 1 · ♅ 1 29 R — ♈23 23 · ♆ 1 11 — ♍ 5 6 · ♇ 1 31 — ♋21 22

8

	1	2	3	4	5	6	7	8	9	10	11	12	13	14	15	16	17	18	19	20	21	22	23	24	25	26	27	28	29	30	31
☉	♌ 9	10	11	12	13	14	14	15	16	17	18	19	20	21	22	23	24	25	26	27	28	29	29 0	♍ 1	2	3	4	5	6	7	8
☽	♋ 28	♌ 11	25	♍ 8	22	♎ 6	20	♏ 5	19	♐ 3	17	♑ 1	15	29	♒ 12	25	♓ 8	21	♈ 3	15	27	♉ 9	21	♊ 3	15	27	♋ 10	23	♌ 6	19	♍ 3
☿	♍ 2	2	2	R 2	2	1	1	1	0	0 29	♌ 29	28	28	27	26	25	24	24	23	22	21	21	20	20	19	19	D 19	19	19	20	20
♀	♋ 1	2	2	2	3	3	4	5	5	6	6	7	8	8	9	10	10	11	12	13	13	14	15	16	17	18	18	19	20	21	22
♂	♊ 28	28	29	29 0	♋ 0	1	2	2	3	4	4	5	6	6	7	8	8	9	10	10	11	11	12	13	13	14	15	15	16	17	17

♃ 1 6 11 16 20 25 29 — ♌28 29 ♍ 0 1 2 3 4 · ♄ 1 R 14 — ♒ 0 ♑29 · ♅ 1 R — ♈23 · ♆ 1 11 — ♍ 6 7 · ♇ 1 31 — ♋22 23

9

	1	2	3	4	5	6	7	8	9	10	11	12	13	14	15	16	17	18	19	20	21	22	23	24	25	26	27	28	29	30	31
☉	♍ 8	9	10	11	12	13	14	15	16	17	18	19	20	21	22	23	24	25	26	27	28	29	29 0	♎ 1	2	3	4	5	6	7	
☽	♍ 18	♎ 2	16	♏ 1	15	♐ 0	14	28	♑ 12	25	♒ 9	22	♓ 4	17	29	♈ 12	24	♉ 6	17	29	♊ 11	23	♋ 5	18	♌ 1	14	27	♍ 12	26	♎ 11	
☿	♌ 21	22	23	24	25	26	27	29	29 0	♍ 2	3	5	7	9	10	12	14	16	18	20	21	23	25	27	29	29 0	♎ 2	4	6	8	
♀	♋ 23	24	25	26	27	28	29	29 0	♌ 1	1	2	3	4	5	6	8	9	10	11	12	13	14	15	16	17	18	19	20	21	22	
♂	♋ 18	18	19	20	20	21	22	22	23	24	24	25	25	26	27	27	28	28	29	29 0	♌ 0	1	1	2	3	3	4	4	5	6	

♃ 1 3 7 12 17 21 26 30 — ♍ 4 5 6 7 8 9 10 11 · ♄ 1 R 30 — ♑29 28 · ♅ 1 R 30 — ♈23 22 · ♆ 1 7 — ♍ 7 8 · ♇ 1 — ♋23

10

	1	2	3	4	5	6	7	8	9	10	11	12	13	14	15	16	17	18	19	20	21	22	23	24	25	26	27	28	29	30	31
☉	♎ 8	9	10	11	12	13	14	15	16	17	18	19	20	21	22	23	24	25	26	27	28	29	29 0	♏ 1	2	3	4	5	6	7	8
☽	♎ 26	♏ 11	26	♐ 11	25	♑ 9	22	♒ 5	18	♓ 1	14	26	♈ 8	20	♉ 2	14	26	♊ 8	20	♋ 2	14	26	♌ 9	22	♍ 5	19	♎ 4	19	♏ 4	19	♐ 4
☿	♎ 10	11	13	15	16	18	20	21	23	25	26	28	29 0	♏ 1	3	4	6	7	9	10	12	14	15	16	18	19	21	22	24	25	27
♀	♌ 23	25	26	27	28	29	29 0	♍ 1	2	4	5	6	7	8	9	10	12	13	14	15	16	17	18	20	21	22	23	24	26	27	28
♂	♌ 6	7	7	8	9	9	10	10	11	11	12	13	13	14	14	15	15	16	17	17	18	18	19	19	20	20	21	21	22	23	23

♃ 1 6 11 16 22 27 — ♍11 12 13 14 15 16 · ♄ 1 R — ♑28 · ♅ 1 R 24 — ♈22 21 · ♆ 1 — ♍ 9 · ♇ 1 — ♋23

11

	1	2	3	4	5	6	7	8	9	10	11	12	13	14	15	16	17	18	19	20	21	22	23	24	25	26	27	28	29	30	31
☉	♏ 9	10	11	12	13	14	15	16	17	18	19	20	21	22	23	24	25	26	27	28	29	29 0	♐ 1	2	3	4	5	6	7	8	
☽	♐ 19	♑ 4	18	♒ 2	15	28	♓ 11	23	♈ 5	17	29	♉ 11	23	♊ 5	17	29	♋ 11	23	♌ 5	18	♍ 1	14	28	♎ 12	27	♏ 12	27	♐ 13	28	♑ 13	
☿	♏ 28	29 0	♐ 1	2	3	5	6	7	9	10	11	12	13	14	15	16	17	18	19	19	20	20	20	20	R 20	20	20	19	18	17	
♀	♍ 29	29 0	♎ 1	3	4	5	6	7	9	10	11	12	13	15	16	17	18	19	21	22	23	24	26	27	28	29	♏ 0	2	3	4	
♂	♌ 24	24	25	25	26	26	27	27	28	28	29	29	29 0	♍ 0	1	1	2	2	3	3	3	4	4	5	5	6	6	7	7	7	

♃ 1 8 15 22 30 — ♍17 18 19 20 21 · ♄ 1 20 30 — ♑29 ♒ 0 1 · ♅ 1 R 21 — ♈21 20 · ♆ 1 16 — ♍ 9 10 · ♇ 1 — ♋23

12

	1	2	3	4	5	6	7	8	9	10	11	12	13	14	15	16	17	18	19	20	21	22	23	24	25	26	27	28	29	30	31
☉	♐ 9	10	11	12	13	14	15	16	17	18	19	20	21	22	23	24	25	26	27	28	29	29 0	♑ 1	2	3	4	5	6	7	8	9
☽	♑ 27	♒ 11	24	♓ 7	20	♈ 2	14	26	♉ 8	20	♊ 2	14	26	♋ 8	20	♌ 2	15	28	♍ 11	24	♎ 8	22	♏ 6	21	♐ 6	21	♑ 6	21	♒ 5	19	♓ 2
☿	♐ 16	R 15	14	12	11	10	8	7	6	6	5	4	4	D 4	4	4	5	5	6	7	8	8	9	10	12	13	14	15	16	18	19
♀	♏ 5	7	8	9	10	12	13	14	15	16	18	19	20	21	23	24	25	26	28	29	29 0	♐ 1	3	4	5	6	8	9	10	11	13
♂	♍ 8	8	9	9	9	10	10	11	11	11	12	12	12	13	13	14	14	14	14	15	15	15	16	16	16	17	17	17	17	18	18

♃ 1 10 26 — ♍21 22 23 · ♄ 1 12 22 31 — ♒ 1 2 3 4 · ♅ 1 R 31 — ♈20 19 · ♆ 1 12 R — ♍10 10 · ♇ 1 31 — ♋23 22

1933

1

	1	2	3	4	5	6	7	8	9	10	11	12	13	14	15	16	17	18	19	20	21	22	23	24	25	26	27	28	29	30	31
☉	♑ 10	11	12	13	14	15	16	17	18	19	20	21	22	23	24	25	26	27	28	29 0	♒ 1	2	3	4	5	6	7	8	9	10	11
☽	♓ 16	28	♈ 10	23	♉ 4	16	28	♊ 10	22	♋ 4	17	29	♌ 12	25	♍ 8	21	♎ 4	18	♏ 2	16	♐ 0	15	29	♑ 14	29	♒ 13	27	♓ 10	23	♈ 6	18
☿	♐ 20	22	23	24	26	27	29	29 0	♑ 1	3	4	6	7	9	10	12	13	15	16	18	20	21	23	24	26	28	29 0	♒ 1	2	4	6
♀	♐ 14	15	16	17	19	20	21	22	24	25	26	27	29	29 0	♑ 1	2	4	5	6	7	9	10	11	12	14	15	16	17	19	20	21
♂	♍ 18	18	18	19	19	19	19	19	19	19	20	20	20	20	20	20	20	20	20	20	R 20	20	20	20	20	20	20	20	20	20	19

♃ 1 8 R 31 — ♍23 23 22 · ♄ 1 9 17 26 — ♒ 4 5 6 7 · ♅ 1 31 — ♈19 20 · ♆ 1 R 31 — ♍10 9 · ♇ 1 — ♋22

2

	1	2	3	4	5	6	7	8	9	10	11	12	13	14	15	16	17	18	19	20	21	22	23	24	25	26	27	28	29	30	31
☉	♒ 12	13	14	15	16	17	18	19	20	21	22	23	24	25	26	27	28	29	29 0	♓ 1	2	3	4	5	6	7	8	9			
☽	♉ 1	12	24	♊ 6	18	♋ 0	12	25	♌ 8	21	♍ 4	17	♎ 1	15	29	♏ 13	27	♐ 11	25	♑ 10	24	♒ 8	21	♓ 5	18	♈ 1	14	26			
☿	♒ 7	9	11	13	14	16	18	20	21	23	25	27	29	29 0	♓ 2	4	6	8	10	11	13	15	17	19	21	22	24	26			
♀	♑ 22	24	25	26	27	29	29 0	♒ 1	2	4	5	6	7	9	10	11	12	14	15	16	17	19	20	21	22	24	25	26			
♂	♍ 19	R 19	19	19	19	18	18	18	18	17	17	17	17	16	16	16	15	15	15	14	14	14	13	13	12	12	12	11			

♃ 1 R 15 24 28 — ♍22 21 20 19 · ♄ 1 12 20 28 — ♒ 8 9 10 11 · ♅ 1 28 — ♈20 21 · ♆ 1 R — ♍ 9 · ♇ 1 28 — ♋22 21

3

	1	2	3	4	5	6	7	8	9	10	11	12	13	14	15	16	17	18	19	20	21	22	23	24	25	26	27	28	29	30	31
☉	♓ 10	11	12	13	14	15	16	17	18	19	20	21	22	23	24	25	26	27	28	29	29 0	♈ 1	2	3	4	5	6	7	8	9	10
☽	♉ 8	20	♊ 2	14	26	♋ 8	20	♌ 3	16	29	♍ 12	26	♎ 10	25	♏ 9	24	♐ 8	22	♑ 6	20	♒ 4	18	♓ 1	14	27	♈ 9	22	♉ 4	16	28	♊ 10
☿	♓ 27	29	29 0	♈ 1	2	3	4	5	6	6	7	7	7	R 7	7	7	6	6	5	4	4	3	2	1	0 29	♓ 29	29	28	27	26	26
♀	♒ 27	29	29 0	♓ 1	2	4	5	6	7	9	10	11	12	14	15	16	17	19	20	21	22	24	25	26	27	29	29 0	♈ 1	2	3	5
♂	♍ 11	R 10	10	10	9	9	8	8	8	7	7	7	6	6	6	5	5	5	4	4	4	3	3	3	3	2	2	2	2	2	2

♃ 1 R 11 19 28 31 — ♍19 18 17 16 15 · ♄ 1 11 21 31 — ♒11 12 13 14 · ♅ 1 20 — ♈21 22 · ♆ 1 R 31 — ♍ 9 8 · ♇ 1 — ♋21

4

	1	2	3	4	5	6	7	8	9	10	11	12	13	14	15	16	17	18	19	20	21	22	23	24	25	26	27	28	29	30	31
☉	♈ 11	12	13	14	15	16	17	18	19	20	21	22	23	24	25	26	27	28	29	29 0	♉ 1	2	3	4	5	6	7	8	9	10	
☽	♊ 22	♋ 4	16	28	♌ 11	24	♍ 7	20	♎ 5	19	♏ 4	19	♐ 4	18	♑ 3	17	♒ 1	14	28	♓ 11	23	♈ 6	18	♉ 1	13	25	♊ 7	18	♋ 0	12	
☿	♓ 25	R 25	25	25	24	D 24	25	25	25	25	26	26	27	27	28	29	29 0	♈ 1	2	2	3	5	6	7	8	9	11	12	13	15	
♀	♈ 6	7	8	10	11	12	13	15	16	17	18	20	21	22	23	25	26	27	28	29 0	♉ 1	2	3	4	6	7	8	9	11	12	
♂	♍ 1	R 1	1	1	1	1	1	1	1	1	1	D 1	1	1	1	1	1	1	1	1	1	1	1	1	2	2	2	2	2	3	

♃ 1 R 18 30 — ♍15 14 13 · ♄ 1 15 30 — ♒14 15 16 · ♅ 1 7 25 — ♈22 23 24 · ♆ 1 R 30 — ♍ 8 7 · ♇ 1 — ♋21

5

	1	2	3	4	5	6	7	8	9	10	11	12	13	14	15	16	17	18	19	20	21	22	23	24	25	26	27	28	29	30	31
☉	♉ 10	11	12	13	14	15	16	17	18	19	20	21	22	23	24	25	26	27	28	29	29 0	♊ 1	2	3	4	5	6	7	7	8	9
☽	♋ 24	♌ 6	19	♍ 2	15	29	♎ 13	27	♏ 12	27	♐ 13	28	♑ 13	27	♒ 11	25	♓ 8	21	♈ 3	15	28	♉ 10	22	♊ 4	15	27	♋ 9	21	♌ 3	15	28
☿	♈ 16	17	19	20	22	24	25	27	28	29 0	♉ 2	4	5	7	9	11	13	15	17	19	21	23	25	27	29 0	♊ 2	4	6	8	11	13
♀	♉ 13	14	16	17	18	19	20	22	23	24	25	26	28	29	29 0	♊ 2	3	4	5	6	8	9	10	11	13	14	15	16	18	19	20
♂	♍ 3	3	3	3	4	4	4	4	5	5	5	6	6	6	7	7	7	8	8	8	9	9	9	10	10	10	11	11	12	12	12

♃ 1 R 10 D 31 — ♍13 13 14 · ♄ 1 27 R — ♒16 16 · ♅ 1 13 31 — ♈24 25 26 · ♆ 1 R 19 D — ♍ 7 7 · ♇ 1 31 — ♋21 22

6

	1	2	3	4	5	6	7	8	9	10	11	12	13	14	15	16	17	18	19	20	21	22	23	24	25	26	27	28	29	30	31
☉	♊ 10	11	12	13	14	15	16	17	18	19	20	21	22	23	24	25	26	27	28	29	29 0	♋ 0	1	2	3	4	5	6	7	8	
☽	♍ 10	24	♎ 7	21	♏ 6	21	♐ 6	21	♑ 6	21	♒ 6	20	♓ 4	17	♈ 0	12	25	♉ 7	19	♊ 1	12	24	♋ 6	18	♌ 0	12	25	♍ 7	20	♎ 3	
☿	♊ 15	17	19	21	24	26	28	29 0	♋ 2	4	5	7	9	11	13	14	16	18	19	21	22	24	25	27	28	29	29 0	♌ 2	3	4	
♀	♊ 21	22	24	25	26	27	29	29 0	♋ 1	2	3	5	6	7	8	10	11	12	13	14	16	17	18	19	21	22	23	24	26	27	
♂	♍ 13	13	14	14	14	15	15	16	16	17	17	18	18	19	19	19	20	20	21	21	22	22	23	23	24	24	25	25	26	26	

♃ 1 13 23 30 — ♍14 15 16 17 · ♄ 1 R 30 — ♒16 15 · ♅ 1 30 — ♈26 27 · ♆ 1 30 — ♍ 7 8 · ♇ 1 — ♋22

7

	1	2	3	4	5	6	7	8	9	10	11	12	13	14	15	16	17	18	19	20	21	22	23	24	25	26	27	28	29	30	31
☉	♋ 9	10	11	12	13	14	15	16	17	18	18	19	20	21	22	23	24	25	26	27	28	29	29 0	♌ 1	2	3	4	5	6	7	8
☽	♎ 17	♏ 0	15	29	♐ 15	29	♑ 15	29	♒ 14	29	♓ 12	26	♈ 9	21	♉ 3	16	27	♊ 9	21	♋ 3	15	27	♌ 9	22	♍ 4	17	♎ 0	13	27	♏ 11	25
☿	♌ 5	6	7	8	8	9	10	11	11	12	12	12	13	13	13	13	R 13	13	13	13	12	12	11	11	10	10	9	8	7	7	6
♀	♋ 28	29	♌ 0	2	3	4	5	6	8	9	10	11	13	14	15	16	17	19	20	21	22	24	25	26	27	28	29 0	♍ 1	2	3	4
♂	♍ 27	27	28	29	29	29 0	♎ 0	1	1	2	2	3	3	4	5	5	6	6	7	7	8	9	9	10	10	11	11	12	13	13	14

♃ 1 8 14 20 26 31 — ♍17 18 19 20 21 22 · ♄ 1 R 23 31 — ♒15 14 13 · ♅ 1 — ♈27 · ♆ 1 — ♍ 8 · ♇ 1 31 — ♋22 23

8

	1	2	3	4	5	6	7	8	9	10	11	12	13	14	15	16	17	18	19	20	21	22	23	24	25	26	27	28	29	30	31
☉	♌ 8	9	10	11	12	13	14	15	16	17	18	19	20	21	22	23	24	25	26	27	28	29	29 0	♍ 0	1	2	3	4	5	6	7
☽	♐ 9	24	♑ 9	23	♒ 8	23	♓ 7	21	♈ 4	17	29	♉ 12	24	♊ 6	18	29	♋ 12	24	♌ 6	18	♍ 1	14	27	♎ 10	24	♏ 7	21	♐ 6	20	♑ 4	18
☿	♌ 5	R 5	4	3	3	3	2	2	2	D 2	2	2	3	3	4	5	5	6	7	9	10	11	13	14	16	17	19	21	23	25	27
♀	♍ 6	7	8	9	11	12	13	14	15	17	18	19	20	21	23	24	25	26	27	29	29 0	♎ 1	2	3	5	6	7	8	9	11	12
♂	♎ 14	15	16	16	17	17	18	19	19	20	21	21	22	22	23	24	24	25	26	26	27	27	28	29	29	29 0	♏ 1	1	2	3	3

♃ 1 6 11 17 22 26 31 — ♍22 23 24 25 26 27 28 · ♄ 1 R 20 31 — ♒13 12 11 · ♅ 1 3 R — ♈27 27 · ♆ 1 8 31 — ♍ 8 9 10 · ♇ 1 31 — ♋23 24

9

	1	2	3	4	5	6	7	8	9	10	11	12	13	14	15	16	17	18	19	20	21	22	23	24	25	26	27	28	29	30	31
☉	♍ 8	9	10	11	12	13	14	15	16	17	18	19	20	21	22	23	24	25	26	27	28	29	29 0	♎ 1	2	3	4	5	6	7	
☽	♒ 3	17	♓ 1	15	29	♈ 12	25	♉ 7	20	♊ 2	14	26	♋ 8	20	♌ 2	14	27	♍ 9	23	♎ 6	20	♏ 4	18	♐ 2	17	♑ 1	15	29	♒ 13	27	
☿	♌ 28	29 0	♍ 2	4	6	8	10	12	14	16	18	20	21	23	25	27	29	29 0	♎ 2	4	6	7	9	11	12	14	16	17	19	20	
♀	♎ 13	14	15	17	18	19	20	21	23	24	25	26	27	29	29 0	♏ 1	2	3	4	6	7	8	9	10	12	13	14	15	16	17	
♂	♏ 4	5	5	6	7	7	8	9	9	10	11	11	12	13	13	14	15	15	16	17	17	18	19	19	20	21	21	22	23	24	

♃ 1 5 10 29 14 19 24 28 — ♍28 29 ♎ 0 1 2 3 4 · ♄ 1 R 26 — ♒11 10 · ♅ 1 R 30 — ♈27 26 · ♆ 1 30 — ♍10 11 · ♇ 1 30 — ♋24 23

10

	1	2	3	4	5	6	7	8	9	10	11	12	13	14	15	16	17	18	19	20	21	22	23	24	25	26	27	28	29	30	31
☉	♎ 8	9	10	11	12	13	14	15	16	17	18	19	20	21	22	22	23	24	25	26	27	28	29 0	♏ 0	1	2	3	4	5	6	7
☽	♓ 10	24	♈ 7	20	♉ 3	15	28	♊ 10	22	♋ 4	15	27	♌ 9	22	♍ 4	17	♎ 1	15	29	♏ 13	28	♐ 13	27	♑ 12	26	♒ 10	23	♓ 7	20	♈ 3	16
☿	♎ 22	24	25	27	28	29 0	♏ 1	3	4	6	7	8	10	11	13	14	15	17	18	19	20	22	23	24	25	26	27	28	29	29 0	♐ 1
♀	♏ 19	20	21	22	23	24	26	27	28	29	29 0	♐ 1	3	4	5	6	7	8	9	11	12	13	14	15	16	17	19	20	21	22	23
♂	♏ 24	25	26	26	27	28	28	29	29 0	♐ 1	1	2	3	3	4	5	6	6	7	8	8	9	10	11	11	12	13	14	14	15	16

♃ 1 3 8 12 17 22 26 31 — ♎ 4 5 6 7 8 9 10 11 · ♄ 1 R 15 D — ♒10 10 · ♅ 1 R 29 — ♈26 25 · ♆ 1 31 — ♍11 12 · ♇ 1 31 — ♋23 24

11

	1	2	3	4	5	6	7	8	9	10	11	12	13	14	15	16	17	18	19	20	21	22	23	24	25	26	27	28	29	30	31
☉	♏ 8	9	10	11	12	13	14	15	16	17	18	19	20	21	22	23	24	25	26	27	28	29 0	♐ 1	2	3	4	5	6	7	8	
☽	♈ 29	♉ 11	24	♊ 6	18	29	♋ 12	23	♌ 5	17	29	♍ 12	25	♎ 9	23	♏ 7	22	♐ 7	22	♑ 7	22	♒ 6	20	♓ 4	17	♈ 0	13	26	♉ 8	20	
☿	♐ 2	2	3	4	4	4	5	R 5	5	4	4	3	3	2	1	0 29	♏ 28	27	25	24	23	22	21	20	19	19	19	D 18	19	19	
♀	♐ 24	25	26	27	29	29 0	♑ 1	2	3	4	5	6	7	8	9	10	12	13	14	15	16	17	18	19	20	21	22	23	24	25	
♂	♐ 17	17	18	19	19	20	21	22	22	23	24	25	25	26	27	28	28	29	29 0	♑ 1	2	2	3	4	5	5	6	7	8	8	

♃ 1 5 10 15 21 26 — ♎11 12 13 14 15 16 · ♄ 1 23 — ♒10 11 · ♅ 1 R 26 — ♈25 24 · ♆ 1 — ♍12 · ♇ 1 — ♋24

12

	1	2	3	4	5	6	7	8	9	10	11	12	13	14	15	16	17	18	19	20	21	22	23	24	25	26	27	28	29	30	31
☉	♐ 9	10	11	12	13	14	15	16	17	18	19	20	21	22	23	24	25	26	27	28	29	29 0	♑ 1	2	3	4	5	6	7	8	9
☽	♊ 2	15	26	♋ 8	20	♌ 2	14	26	♍ 8	21	♎ 3	17	♏ 1	15	♐ 0	15	♑ 0	16	♒ 1	15	29	♓ 14	27	♈ 10	23	♉ 5	17	29	♊ 11	23	♋ 5
☿	♏ 19	20	21	21	22	23	24	25	27	28	29	29 0	♐ 2	3	4	6	7	9	10	11	13	14	16	17	19	20	22	23	25	26	28
♀	♑ 26	27	28	29	29 0	♒ 1	1	2	3	4	5	6	7	8	8	9	10	11	12	12	13	14	15	15	16	17	17	18	18	19	19
♂	♑ 9	10	11	11	12	13	14	15	15	16	17	18	18	19	20	21	22	22	23	24	25	25	26	27	28	29	29	29 0	♒ 1	2	2

♃ 1 8 15 22 31 — ♎17 18 19 20 21 · ♄ 1 6 18 28 — ♒11 12 13 14 · ♅ 1 R 31 — ♈24 23 · ♆ 1 15 R — ♍12 12 · ♇ 1 — ♋24

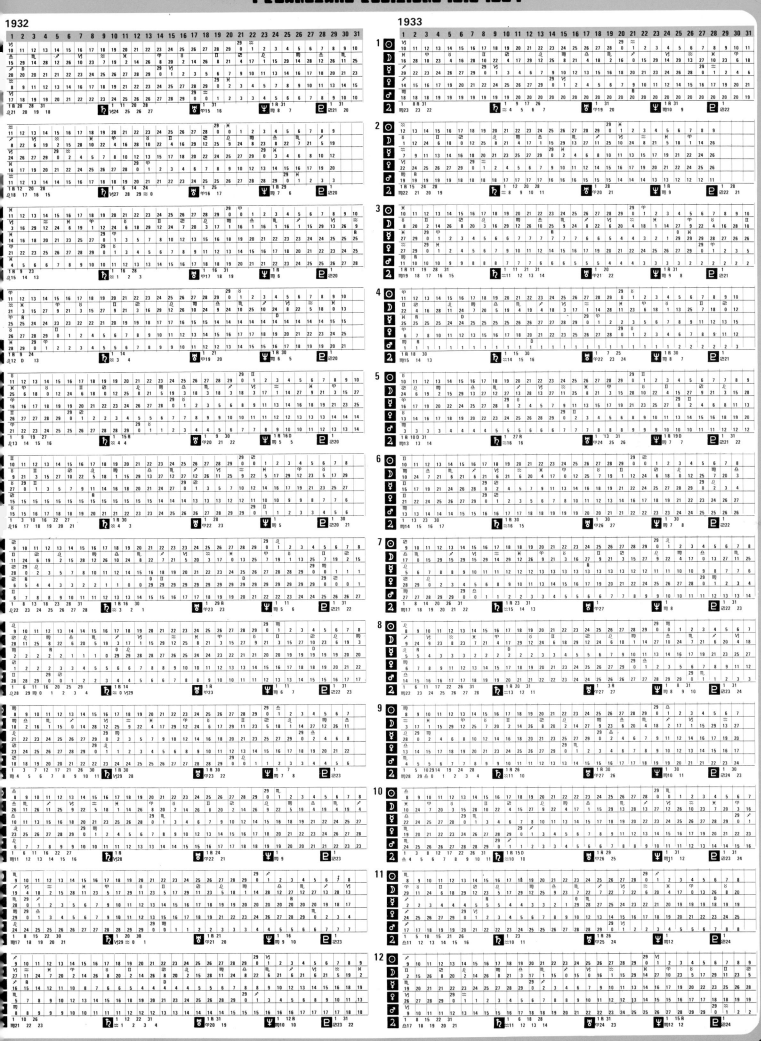

1934

	1	2	3	4	5	6	7	8	9	10	11	12	13	14	15	16	17	18	19	20	21	22	23	24	25	26	27	28	29	30	31
1 ☉	♑ 10	11	12	13	14	15	16	17	18	19	20	21	22	23	24	25	26	27	28	29 0	♒ 1	2	3	4	5	6	7	8	9	10	11
☽	♋ 17	29	♌ 11	23	♍ 5	17	29	♎ 13	26	♏ 9	24	♐ 8	23	♑ 8	24	♒ 9	24	♓ 8	22	♈ 6	19	♉ 2	14	26	♊ 8	20	♋ 2	14	26	♌ 8	20
☿	♐29 0	♑ 1	3	4	6	7	9	10	12	14	15	17	18	20	22	23	25	27	28	29 0	♒ 2	3	5	7	8	10	12	14	15	17	19
♀	♒ 20	20	21	21	22	22	22	23	23	23	23	23	23	23	R 23	23	23	23	23	23	23	22	22	22	21	21	21	20	20	19	18
♂	♒ 3	4	5	6	6	7	8	9	10	10	11	12	13	14	14	15	16	17	17	18	19	20	21	21	22	23	24	25	25	26	27

♃ 1 10 27 / ♎21 22 23 — ♄ 1 6 15 24 31 / ♒14 15 16 17 18 — ♅ 1 R 3 D 31 / ♈23 23 24 — ♆ 1 R / ♍12 — ♇ 1 31 / ♋24 23

	1	2	3	4	5	6	7	8	9	10	11	12	13	14	15	16	17	18	19	20	21	22	23	24	25	26	27	28
2 ☉	♒ 12	13	14	15	16	17	18	19	20	21	22	23	24	25	26	27	28	29	29 0	♓ 1	2	3	4	5	6	7	8	9
☽	♍ 2	14	27	♎ 9	22	♏ 6	19	♐ 3	17	♑ 2	17	♒ 2	17	♓ 1	16	♈ 0	14	27	♉ 10	23	♊ 5	17	29	♋ 10	22	♌ 4	16	28
☿	♒ 21	22	24	26	28	29 0	♓ 1	3	5	6	8	9	11	12	14	15	16	17	18	19	19	20	20	20	R 20	20	20	19
♀	♒ 18	R 17	17	16	15	15	14	13	13	12	12	11	11	10	10	10	9	9	9	8	8	8	8	8	8	D 8	8	8
♂	♒ 28	29	29	29 0	♓ 1	2	2	3	4	5	6	6	7	8	9	10	10	11	12	13	14	14	15	16	17	17	18	19

♃ 1 7 R 28 / ♎23 23 22 — ♄ 1 9 18 26 / ♒18 19 20 21 — ♅ 1 / ♈24 — ♆ 1 R 28 / ♍12 11 — ♇ 1 / ♋23

	1	2	3	4	5	6	7	8	9	10	11	12	13	14	15	16	17	18	19	20	21	22	23	24	25	26	27	28	29	30	31
3 ☉	♓ 10	11	12	13	14	15	16	17	18	19	20	21	22	23	24	25	26	27	28	29	29 0	♈ 1	2	3	4	5	6	7	8	9	10
☽	♍ 11	23	♎ 6	19	♏ 3	16	♐ 0	14	28	♑ 12	26	♒ 11	25	♓ 10	24	♈ 8	22	♉ 5	18	♊ 0	13	25	♋ 7	18	♌ 0	12	24	♍ 7	19	♎ 2	15
☿	♓ 19	R 18	17	16	15	14	13	12	11	10	9	9	8	7	7	7	6	6	D 6	6	6	7	7	7	8	8	9	10	11	11	12
♀	♒ 8	8	8	9	9	9	10	10	10	11	11	12	12	13	13	14	14	15	16	16	17	18	18	19	20	21	21	22	23	24	25
♂	♓ 20	21	21	22	23	24	24	25	26	27	28	28	29	29 0	♈ 1	1	2	3	4	5	5	6	7	8	8	9	10	11	12	12	13

♃ 1 R 17 26 31 / ♎22 21 20 19 — ♄ 1 7 16 25 / ♒21 22 23 24 — ♅ 1 24 / ♈25 26 — ♆ 1 R 31 / ♍11 10 — ♇ 1 31 / ♋23 22

	1	2	3	4	5	6	7	8	9	10	11	12	13	14	15	16	17	18	19	20	21	22	23	24	25	26	27	28	29	30
4 ☉	♈ 11	12	13	14	15	16	17	18	19	20	21	22	23	24	25	25	26	27	28	29 0	♉ 0	1	2	3	4	5	6	7	8	9
☽	♎ 29	♏ 13	27	♐ 11	25	♑ 9	23	♒ 7	21	♓ 5	19	♈ 3	16	♉ 0	13	26	♊ 8	21	♋ 3	14	26	♌ 8	20	♍ 2	15	27	♎ 11	24	♏ 8	22
☿	♓ 13	14	15	16	17	18	20	21	22	23	25	26	27	29	29 0	♈ 2	3	5	6	8	10	11	13	15	16	18	20	22	24	25
♀	♒ 26	26	27	28	29	29 0	♓ 1	2	3	4	5	6	6	7	8	9	10	11	12	13	14	15	17	17	18	19	20	22	23	24
♂	♈ 14	15	15	16	17	18	18	19	20	21	21	22	23	24	24	25	26	27	27	28	29	29 0	♉ 0	1	2	3	3	4	5	6

♃ 1 R 11 19 27 / ♎19 18 17 16 — ♄ 1 5 17 30 / ♒24 25 26 27 — ♅ 1 11 28 / ♈26 27 28 — ♆ 1 R / ♍10 — ♇ 1 / ♋22

	1	2	3	4	5	6	7	8	9	10	11	12	13	14	15	16	17	18	19	20	21	22	23	24	25	26	27	28	29	30	31
5 ☉	♉ 10	11	12	13	14	15	16	17	18	19	20	21	22	23	24	25	26	27	28	29	29 0	♊ 0	1	2	3	4	5	6	7	8	9
☽	♐ 6	21	♑ 5	20	♒ 4	18	♓ 2	16	29	♈ 13	26	♉ 9	22	♊ 4	17	29	♋ 11	23	♌ 4	16	28	♍ 10	23	♎ 5	19	♏ 2	16	♐ 1	15	♑ 0	15
☿	♈ 27	29 0	♉ 1	3	5	7	9	11	14	16	18	20	22	24	27	29	♊ 1	3	5	7	10	12	14	16	18	19	21	23	25	27	28
♀	♓ 25	26	27	28	29	29 0	♈ 1	2	3	4	5	6	8	9	10	11	12	13	14	15	16	18	19	20	21	22	23	24	25	27	28
♂	♉ 6	7	8	9	9	10	11	12	12	13	14	15	15	16	17	17	18	19	20	20	21	22	23	23	24	25	25	26	27	28	28

♃ 1 R 19 31 / ♎15 14 13 — ♄ 1 24 / ♒27 28 — ♅ 1 17 / ♈28 29 — ♆ 1 R 21 D / ♍10 10 — ♇ 1 31 / ♋22 23

	1	2	3	4	5	6	7	8	9	10	11	12	13	14	15	16	17	18	19	20	21	22	23	24	25	26	27	28	29	30
6 ☉	♊ 10	11	12	13	14	15	16	17	18	19	20	21	22	23	24	24	25	26	27	28	29	29 0	♋ 1	2	3	4	5	6	7	8
☽	♒ 0	14	29	♓ 13	26	♈ 10	23	♉ 6	18	♊ 1	13	25	♋ 7	19	♌ 1	13	24	♍ 6	18	♎ 1	14	27	♏ 10	25	♐ 9	24	♑ 9	24	♒ 9	24
☿	♊29 0	♋ 2	3	5	6	8	9	10	12	13	14	15	16	17	18	19	20	20	21	22	22	23	23	23	24	24	24	R 24	24	24
♀	♈ 29	29 0	♉ 1	2	3	4	6	7	8	9	10	11	13	14	15	16	17	18	19	21	22	23	24	25	26	28	29	29 0	♊ 1	2
♂	♉ 29	29 0	♊ 1	1	2	3	3	4	5	5	6	7	8	8	9	10	10	11	12	12	13	14	15	15	16	17	17	18	19	19

♃ 1 R 11 D / ♎13 13 — ♄ 1 9 R / ♒28 28 — ♅ 1 6 30 / ♈29 ♉ 0 1 — ♆ 1 29 / ♍ 9 10 — ♇ 1 30 / ♋23 24

	1	2	3	4	5	6	7	8	9	10	11	12	13	14	15	16	17	18	19	20	21	22	23	24	25	26	27	28	29	30	31
7 ☉	♋ 9	10	11	12	13	14	14	15	16	17	18	19	20	21	22	23	24	25	26	27	28	29	29 0	♌ 0	1	2	3	4	5	6	7
☽	♓ 8	23	♈ 6	20	♉ 3	15	28	♊ 10	22	♋ 4	16	28	♌ 10	21	♍ 3	15	27	♎ 10	23	♏ 6	19	♐ 3	18	♑ 2	17	♒ 3	18	♓ 3	17	♈ 2	16
☿	♋ 23	R 23	23	22	22	21	21	20	20	19	18	18	17	16	16	15	15	15	14	14	14	D 14	14	14	14	15	15	16	16	17	18
♀	♊ 3	5	6	7	8	9	11	12	13	14	15	16	18	19	20	21	22	24	25	26	27	28	29 0	♋ 1	2	3	4	6	7	8	9
♂	♊ 20	21	21	22	23	23	24	25	26	26	27	28	28	29	29 0	♋ 0	1	2	2	3	4	4	5	6	6	7	8	8	9	10	10

♃ 1 15 24 31 / ♎14 15 16 17 — ♄ 1 R 17 31 / ♒28 27 26 — ♅ 1 / ♉ 1 — ♆ 1 31 / ♍10 11 — ♇ 1 / ♋24

	1	2	3	4	5	6	7	8	9	10	11	12	13	14	15	16	17	18	19	20	21	22	23	24	25	26	27	28	29	30	31
8 ☉	♌ 8	9	10	11	12	13	14	15	16	17	18	19	20	21	22	23	24	25	26	27	28	29	29 0	♍ 0	1	2	3	4	5	6	7
☽	♈ 29	♉ 12	25	♊ 7	19	♋ 1	13	25	♌ 7	18	♍ 0	12	24	♎ 7	19	♏ 2	15	29	♐ 12	27	♑ 11	26	♒ 11	26	♓ 11	26	♈ 10	24	♉ 8	21	♊ 4
☿	♋ 19	20	21	22	24	25	27	28	29 0	♌ 1	3	5	7	9	11	13	15	17	19	21	23	25	27	29	29 0	♍ 3	5	7	8	10	12
♀	♋ 10	12	13	14	15	16	18	19	20	21	22	24	25	26	27	28	29 0	♌ 1	2	3	5	6	7	8	9	11	12	13	14	16	17
♂	♋ 11	12	12	13	14	14	15	16	16	17	18	18	19	19	20	21	21	22	23	23	24	25	25	26	27	27	28	29	29	29 0	♌ 0

♃ 1 8 15 21 27 31 / ♎17 18 19 20 21 22 — ♄ 1 R 15 29 / ♒26 25 24 — ♅ 1 7 R / ♉ 1 1 — ♆ 1 31 / ♍11 12 — ♇ 1 31 / ♋24 25

	1	2	3	4	5	6	7	8	9	10	11	12	13	14	15	16	17	18	19	20	21	22	23	24	25	26	27	28	29	30
9 ☉	♍ 8	9	10	11	12	13	14	15	16	17	18	19	20	21	22	23	24	25	26	27	28	29	29 0	♎ 0	1	2	3	4	5	6
☽	♊ 16	28	♋ 10	22	♌ 3	15	27	♍ 9	21	♎ 4	16	29	♏ 12	25	♐ 9	23	♑ 7	21	♒ 5	20	♓ 5	19	♈ 4	18	♉ 2	16	29	♊ 12	24	♋ 6
☿	♍ 14	16	18	20	21	23	25	27	28	29 0	♎ 2	3	5	6	8	10	11	13	14	16	17	19	20	22	23	24	26	27	28	29♏ 0
♀	♌ 18	19	20	22	23	24	25	27	28	29	29 0	♍ 2	3	4	5	6	8	9	10	11	13	14	15	16	18	19	20	21	23	24
♂	♌ 1	2	2	3	4	4	5	6	6	7	7	8	9	9	10	11	11	12	12	13	14	14	15	15	16	17	17	18	19	19

♃ 1 7 12 17 22 27 / ♎22 23 24 25 26 27 — ♄ 1 R 12 30 / ♒24 23 22 — ♅ 1 R 30 / ♉ 1 0 — ♆ 1 29 / ♍12 13 — ♇ 1 30 / ♋25 26

	1	2	3	4	5	6	7	8	9	10	11	12	13	14	15	16	17	18	19	20	21	22	23	24	25	26	27	28	29	30	31
10 ☉	♎ 7	8	9	10	11	12	13	14	15	16	17	18	19	20	21	22	23	24	25	26	27	28	29	29 0	♏ 1	2	3	4	5	6	7
☽	♋ 18	♌ 0	12	24	♍ 6	18	♎ 0	13	26	♏ 9	22	♐ 6	19	♑ 3	17	♒ 1	15	29	♓ 14	28	♈ 13	27	♉ 10	24	♊ 7	20	♋ 2	14	26	♌ 8	20
☿	♏ 1	2	4	5	6	7	8	9	10	11	12	13	14	15	16	16	17	18	18	18	19	19	R 19	19	18	18	17	16	16	14	13
♀	♍ 25	26	28	29	29 0	♎ 1	3	4	5	6	8	9	10	11	13	14	15	16	18	19	20	21	23	24	25	26	28	29	29 0	♏ 1	3
♂	♌ 20	20	21	22	22	23	23	24	25	25	26	26	27	28	28	29	29	29 0	♍ 1	1	2	2	3	4	4	5	5	6	6	7	8

♃ 1 6 11 15 20 25 29 / ♎28 29 ♏ 0 1 2 3 4 — ♄ 1 R 27 D 31 / ♒22 22 21 — ♅ 1 R 10 / ♉ 0 ♈29 — ♆ 1 31 / ♍13 14 — ♇ 1 / ♋26

	1	2	3	4	5	6	7	8	9	10	11	12	13	14	15	16	17	18	19	20	21	22	23	24	25	26	27	28	29	30
11 ☉	♏ 8	9	10	11	12	13	14	15	16	17	18	19	20	21	22	23	24	25	26	27	28	29 0	♐ 0	1	2	3	4	5	6	7
☽	♍ 2	14	26	♎ 8	21	♏ 5	18	♐ 2	16	♑ 0	14	28	♒ 12	26	♓ 10	24	♈ 8	22	♉ 6	19	♊ 2	15	28	♋ 10	22	♌ 4	16	27	♍ 9	21
☿	♏ 12	R 11	10	8	7	6	5	4	4	3	3	D 3	3	3	4	4	5	6	7	8	9	10	11	13	14	15	17	18	20	21
♀	♏ 4	5	6	8	9	10	11	13	14	15	16	18	19	20	21	23	24	25	26	28	29	29 0	♐ 1	3	4	5	7	8	9	10
♂	♍ 8	9	9	10	10	11	12	12	13	13	14	14	15	16	16	17	17	18	18	19	19	20	21	21	22	22	23	23	24	24

♃ 1 3 7 12 17 21 26 30 / ♏ 4 5 6 7 8 9 10 11 — ♄ 1 20 / ♒21 22 — ♅ 1 R 30 / ♈29 28 — ♆ 1 / ♍14 — ♇ 1 / ♋26

	1	2	3	4	5	6	7	8	9	10	11	12	13	14	15	16	17	18	19	20	21	22	23	24	25	26	27	28	29	30	31
12 ☉	♐ 8	9	10	11	12	13	14	15	16	17	18	19	20	21	22	23	24	25	26	27	28	29 0	♑ 1	2	3	4	5	6	7	8	9
☽	♎ 4	16	29	♏ 13	26	♐ 11	25	♑ 9	24	♒ 9	23	♓ 7	21	♈ 5	19	♉ 2	15	28	♊ 11	24	♋ 6	18	♌ 0	12	24	♍ 5	17	29	♎ 12	24	♏ 7
☿	♏ 23	24	26	27	29	29 0	♐ 2	3	5	6	8	9	11	12	14	16	17	19	20	22	23	25	27	28	29 0	♑ 1	3	4	6	8	9
♀	♐ 12	13	14	15	17	18	19	20	22	23	24	25	27	28	29	29 0	♑ 2	3	4	5	7	8	9	10	12	13	14	15	17	18	19
♂	♍ 25	25	26	26	27	27	28	28	29	29	29 0	♎ 0	1	1	2	2	3	3	4	4	5	5	6	6	7	7	8	8	8	9	9

♃ 1 6 11 16 21 27 31 / ♏11 12 13 14 15 16 17 — ♄ 1 8 21 31 / ♒22 23 24 25 — ♅ 1 R 31 / ♈28 27 — ♆ 1 17 R / ♍14 14 — ♇ 1 31 / ♋26 25

1935

	1	2	3	4	5	6	7	8	9	10	11	12	13	14	15	16	17	18	19	20	21	22	23	24	25	26	27	28	29
1 ☉	♑ 10	11	12	13	14	15	16	17	18	19	20	21	22	23	24	25	26	27	28	29 0	♒ 0	1	2	3	4	5	6	7	8
☽	♏ 20	♐ 4	18	♑ 3	18	♒ 3	18	♓ 3	17	♈ 2	15	29	♉ 12	25	♊ 8	20	♋ 3	15	27	♌ 9	20	♍ 2	14	26	♎ 8	20	♏ 3	15	29
☿	♑ 11	12	14	16	17	19	21	22	24	26	27	29	29 0	♒ 2	4	6	7	9	11	12	14	16	17	19	20	22	23	25	26
♀	♑ 21	22	23	24	26	27	28	29 0	♒ 1	2	3	4	6	7	8	9	11	12	13	14	16	17	18	19	21	22	23	24	26
♂	♎ 10	10	11	11	11	12	12	13	13	13	14	15	15	15	16	16	16	17	17	18	18	18	19	19	19	19	19	20	20

♃ 1 8 14 21 30 / ♏17 18 19 20 21 — ♄ 1 10 20 28 / ♒25 26 27 28 — ♅ 1 / ♈27 — ♆ 1 R / ♍14 — ♇ 1 / ♋25

	1	2	3	4	5	6	7	8	9	10	11	12	13	14	15	16	17	18	19	20	21	22	23	24	25	26	27	28
2 ☉	♒ 11	12	13	14	15	16	17	18	19	20	21	22	23	24	25	26	27	28	29 0	♓ 1	2	3	4	5	6	7	8	9
☽	♑ 11	26	♒ 11	26	♓ 11	26	♈ 11	25	♉ 9	22	♊ 5	17	29	♋ 12	24	♌ 5	17	29	♍ 11	23	♎ 5	17	29	♏ 12	25	♐ 8	21	♑ 5
☿	♒29 0	♓ 1	2	2	3	3	4	R 4	4	3	3	2	1	0	0 29	♒ 28	27	26	25	24	23	22	21	20	20	19	19	19
♀	♒29 0	♓ 1	2	3	4	6	7	8	9	11	12	13	14	16	17	18	19	21	22	23	24	25	27	28	29	♈ 0	2	3
♂	♎ 21	21	21	22	22	22	22	22	23	23	23	23	23	24	24	24	24	24	24	24	24	24	24	24	24	24	R 24	24

♃ 1 9 24 / ♏21 22 23 — ♄ 1 14 29 22 28 / ♒28 ♓ 0 1 2 — ♅ 1 9 / ♈27 28 — ♆ 1 R 28 / ♍14 13 — ♇ 1 / ♋24

	1	2	3	4	5	6	7	8	9	10	11	12	13	14	15	16	17	18	19	20	21	22	23	24	25	26	27	28	29
3 ☉	♓ 10	11	12	13	14	15	16	17	18	19	20	21	22	23	24	25	26	27	28	29	29 0	♈ 1	2	3	4	5	6	7	8
☽	♑ 19	♒ 4	19	♓ 4	19	♈ 4	19	♉ 4	17	♊ 1	14	26	♋ 9	21	♌ 2	14	26	♍ 8	20	♎ 2	14	26	♏ 9	22	♐ 4	18	♑ 1	15	29
☿	♒ 19	D 19	19	19	19	20	20	21	21	22	23	23	24	25	26	27	28	29 0	♓ 1	2	3	4	5	7	8	9	11	12	14
♀	♈ 4	5	7	8	9	10	12	13	14	15	16	18	19	20	21	23	24	25	26	27	29	29 0	♉ 1	2	4	5	6	7	8
♂	♎ 24	R 24	24	24	24	24	24	24	24	24	24	23	23	23	23	23	22	22	22	22	21	21	21	21	20	20	20	19	19

♃ 1 10 R / ♏23 22 — ♄ 1 11 20 29 / ♓ 2 3 4 5 — ♅ 1 8 27 28 / ♈28 29 29 ♉ 0 — ♆ 1 R 31 / ♍13 12 — ♇ 1 / ♋24

	1	2	3	4	5	6	7	8	9	10	11	12	13	14	15	16	17	18	19	20	21	22	23	24	25	26	27	28	29
4 ☉	♈ 11	12	13	14	15	16	17	18	19	20	21	22	22	23	24	25	26	27	28	29	29 0	♉ 1	2	3	4	5	6	7	8
☽	♓ 13	28	♈ 13	27	♉ 12	26	♊ 9	22	♋ 5	17	29	♌ 11	23	♍ 4	16	28	♎ 11	23	♏ 6	18	♐ 1	15	28	♑ 12	25	♒ 9	23	♓ 8	22
☿	♓ 18	20	21	23	24	26	28	29 0	♈ 1	3	5	6	8	10	12	14	16	18	20	22	24	26	28	29 0	♉ 2	4	6	8	10
♀	♉ 12	13	14	16	17	18	19	20	22	23	24	25	26	28	29	29 0	♊ 1	2	4	5	6	7	8	10	11	12	13	14	15
♂	♎ 18	R 17	17	17	16	16	16	15	15	14	14	15	13	13	12	12	12	11	11	11	10	10	10	9	9	9	9	8	8

♃ 1 R 18 27 30 / ♏22 21 20 19 — ♄ 1 7 17 29 / ♓ 5 6 7 8 — ♅ 1 15 30 / ♉ 0 1 2 — ♆ 1 R / ♍12 — ♇ 1 / ♋24

	1	2	3	4	5	6	7	8	9	10	11	12	13	14	15	16	17	18	19	20	21	22	23	24	25	26	27	28	29
5 ☉	♉ 10	11	12	13	14	15	16	17	18	19	20	21	22	23	24	25	25	26	27	28	29	29 0	♊ 1	2	3	4	5	6	7
☽	♈ 21	♉ 6	20	♊ 4	17	♋ 0	13	25	♌ 7	19	♍ 1	12	24	♎ 7	19	♏ 1	14	27	♐ 11	24	♑ 8	22	♒ 6	20	♓ 4	19	♈ 3	17	♉ 1
☿	♉ 15	17	19	21	23	25	27	29 0	♊ 1	3	5	7	9	11	12	14	15	17	18	20	21	22	23	25	26	27	28	29	29 0
♀	♊ 18	19	20	21	22	24	25	26	27	28	29 0	♋ 1	2	3	4	5	6	7	9	10	11	12	13	14	15	16	17	19	20
♂	♎ 8	R 7	7	7	7	7	7	6	6	6	6	6	6	6	6	6	6	D 6	6	6	6	6	6	6	6	6	6	7	7

♃ 1 R 13 21 29 / ♏19 18 17 16 — ♄ 1 13 31 / ♓ 8 9 10 — ♅ 1 20 / ♉ 2 3 — ♆ 1 R 24 D 31 / ♍12 12 12 — ♇ 1 / ♋24

	1	2	3	4	5	6	7	8	9	10	11	12	13	14	15	16	17	18	19	20	21	22	23	24	25	26	27	28	29
6 ☉	♊ 10	11	12	13	14	15	16	17	18	19	19	20	21	22	23	24	25	26	27	28	29	29 0	♋ 1	2	3	4	5	6	7
☽	♊ 12	25	♋ 8	20	♌ 3	15	27	♍ 9	20	♎ 2	14	27	♏ 10	23	♐ 6	20	♑ 4	18	♒ 2	17	♓ 1	15	29	♈ 14	28	♉ 11	25	♊ 8	21
☿	♋ 2	2	3	3	3	3	4	4	R 4	4	4	4	3	3	3	2	2	1	0	0 29	♊ 29	29	28	28	27	27	26	26	26
♀	♋ 23	24	25	26	27	28	29 0	♌ 1	2	3	4	5	6	7	8	9	10	11	12	13	14	15	16	17	18	19	20	21	22
♂	♎ 7	7	8	8	8	8	8	9	9	9	9	10	10	10	11	11	11	11	12	12	12	13	13	14	14	14	15	15	15

♃ 1 R 8 22 30 / ♏16 15 14 13 — ♄ 1 22 R / ♓10 10 — ♅ 1 9 30 / ♉ 3 4 5 — ♆ 1 / ♍12 — ♇ 1 / ♋24

	1	2	3	4	5	6	7	8	9	10	11	12	13	14	15	16	17	18	19	20	21	22	23	24	25	26	27	28	29
7 ☉	♋ 8	9	10	11	12	13	14	15	16	17	18	19	20	21	22	23	24	25	26	27	28	29	29 0	♌ 0	1	2	3	4	5
☽	♋ 16	29	♌ 11	23	♍ 5	17	28	♎ 10	23	♏ 5	18	♐ 1	14	28	♑ 12	27	♒ 12	26	♓ 11	26	♈ 10	24	♉ 8	22	♊ 5	18	♋ 1	13	25
☿	♊ 25	R 25	D 25	25	25	26	26	26	27	27	28	29	29 0	♋ 0	1	2	4	5	6	7	9	10	12	14	15	17	19	21	23
♀	♌ 24	25	26	27	28	29	29 0	♍ 0	1	2	3	4	5	6	6	7	8	9	10	10	11	12	12	13	14	14	15	16	16
♂	♎ 16	17	17	18	18	18	19	19	20	20	21	21	22	22	23	23	24	24	25	25	26	26	27	27	28	28	29	29	29 0

♃ 1 R 12 D 31 / ♏13 13 14 — ♄ 1 R 31 / ♓10 9 — ♅ 1 / ♉ 5 — ♆ 1 31 / ♍12 13 — ♇ 1 / ♋25

	1	2	3	4	5	6	7	8	9	10	11	12	13	14	15	16	17	18	19	20	21	22	23	24	25	26	27	28	29
8 ☉	♌ 8	9	10	11	12	13	14	15	16	17	18	19	20	21	22	22	23	24	25	26	27	28	29	29 0	♍ 1	2	3	4	5
☽	♍ 1	13	25	♎ 7	19	♏ 1	13	26	♐ 9	22	♑ 6	20	♒ 5	20	♓ 5	20	♈ 5	20	♉ 4	18	♊ 2	15	28	♋ 10	22	♌ 4	16	28	♍ 10
☿	♋ 29	29 0	♌ 3	5	7	9	11	13	15	17	19	21	23	25	27	29 0	♍ 1	3	5	7	8	10	12	14	15	17	19	21	22
♀	♍ 18	18	19	19	20	20	21	21	21	22	22	22	22	22	22	23	23	R 23	23	22	22	22	22	22	22	21	21	20	20
♂	♏ 1	2	3	3	4	4	5	5	6	6	7	8	8	9	9	10	11	11	12	12	13	14	14	15	16	16	17	17	18

♃ 1 13 23 31 / ♏14 15 16 17 — ♄ 1 R 15 29 / ♓ 9 8 7 — ♅ 1 12 R / ♉ 5 5 — ♆ 1 29 / ♍13 14 — ♇ 1 / ♋26

	1	2	3	4	5	6	7	8	9	10	11	12	13	14	15	16	17	18	19	20	21	22	23	24	25	26	27	28	29
9 ☉	♍ 8	9	10	11	12	13	14	15	16	17	18	19	20	21	22	23	23	24	25	26	27	28	29 0	♎ 0	1	2	3	4	5
☽	♎ 16	28	♏ 10	22	♐ 5	18	♑ 1	15	29	♒ 13	28	♓ 14	29	♈ 14	29	♉ 14	28	♊ 11	24	♋ 7	19	♌ 1	13	25	♍ 7	19	♎ 1	13	25
☿	♍ 27	28	29 0	♎ 2	3	4	6	7	9	10	11	13	14	15	17	18	19	20	21	22	24	25	26	26	27	28	29	29 0	♏ 0
♀	♍ 19	R 18	18	17	16	16	15	15	14	13	13	12	12	11	10	10	9	9	9	8	8	7	7	7	7	7	7	6	6
♂	♏ 20	21	21	22	23	23	24	24	25	26	26	27	28	28	29	29 0	♐ 0	1	2	3	3	4	5	5	6	7	7	8	9

♃ 1 7 13 19 25 30 / ♏17 18 19 20 21 22 — ♄ 1 R 11 25 / ♓ 7 6 5 — ♅ 1 R 30 / ♉ 5 4 — ♆ 1 26 / ♍14 15 — ♇ 1 / ♋27

	1	2	3	4	5	6	7	8	9	10	11	12	13	14	15	16	17	18	19	20	21	22	23	24	25	26	27	28	29
10 ☉	♎ 7	8	9	10	11	12	13	14	15	16	17	18	19	20	21	22	23	24	25	26	27	28	29	29 0	♏ 1	2	3	4	5
☽	♏ 19	♐ 2	14	27	♑ 10	24	♒ 8	22	♓ 7	22	♈ 7	22	♉ 7	22	♊ 6	20	♋ 3	16	28	♌ 10	22	♍ 4	15	28	♎ 10	22	♏ 4	16	29
☿	♏ 1	2	2	2	2	R 2	2	2	2	1	1	0 29	♎ 29	28	27	26	25	23	22	21	20	19	18	18	17	17	D 17	17	18
♀	♍ 7	7	7	7	7	7	8	8	8	9	9	9	10	10	11	11	12	12	13	14	14	15	16	16	17	18	19	19	20
♂	♐ 10	11	12	12	13	14	14	15	16	17	17	18	19	19	20	21	22	22	23	24	24	25	26	27	27	28	29	29 0	♑ 0

♃ 1 6 11 16 21 26 31 / ♏22 23 24 25 26 27 28 — ♄ 1 R 31 / ♓ 4 3 — ♅ 1 R 31 / ♉ 4 3 — ♆ 1 27 / ♍15 16 — ♇ 1 / ♋27

	1	2	3	4	5	6	7	8	9	10	11	12	13	14	15	16	17	18	19	20	21	22	23	24	25	26	27	28	29
11 ☉	♏ 8	9	10	11	12	13	14	15	16	17	18	19	20	21	22	23	24	25	26	27	28	29	29 0	♐ 1	2	3	4	5	6
☽	♑ 7	20	♒ 4	18	♓ 2	16	♈ 1	16	♉ 1	15	♊ 0	14	28	♋ 11	24	♌ 6	18	♍ 0	12	24	♎ 6	18	♏ 0	12	25	♐ 8	21	♑ 4	17
☿	♎ 19	20	21	22	24	25	26	28	29	29 0	♏ 2	3	5	7	8	10	11	13	14	16	18	19	21	22	24	25	27	29	29 0
♀	♍ 23	23	24	25	26	27	28	29	29 0	♎ 1	2	2	3	4	5	6	7	8	9	10	11	12	14	15	16	17	18	19	20
♂	♑ 3	3	4	5	6	6	7	8	9	9	10	11	12	12	13	14	15	15	16	17	18	19	19	20	21	22	22	23	24

♃ 1 4 9 29 13 18 22 27 30 / ♏28 29 ♐ 0 1 2 3 4 5 — ♄ 1 R 8 D 30 / ♓ 3 3 4 — ♅ 1 R 30 / ♉ 3 2 — ♆ 1 / ♍16 — ♇ 1 / ♋27

	1	2	3	4	5	6	7	8	9	10	11	12	13	14	15	16	17	18	19	20	21	22	23	24	25	26	27	28	29
12 ☉	♐ 8	9	10	11	12	13	14	15	16	17	18	19	20	21	22	23	24	25	26	27	28	29 0	♑ 1	2	3	4	5	6	7
☽	♒ 15	29	♓ 13	27	♈ 11	26	♉ 10	24	♊ 8	22	♋ 5	19	♌ 1	14	26	♍ 8	20	♎ 2	14	26	♏ 8	20	♐ 3	16	29	♑ 13	27	♒ 11	25
☿	♐ 3	5	6	8	10	11	13	14	16	17	19	21	22	24	25	27	29	29 0	♑ 2	3	5	6	8	10	11	13	14	16	18
♀	♎ 22	23	24	25	26	27	29	29 0	♏ 1	2	3	4	5	6	8	9	20	11	12	13	15	16	17	18	19	20	21	23	24
♂	♑ 25	26	27	28	29	29	29 0	♒ 1	2	2	3	4	5	6	6	7	8	9	9	10	11	12	13	13	14	15	16	16	17

♃ 1 6 10 15 19 24 29 / ♐ 5 6 7 8 9 10 11 — ♄ 1 19 31 / ♓ 4 5 6 — ♅ 1 R 31 / ♉ 2 1 — ♆ 1 20 R 31 / ♍16 16 16 — ♇ 1 3 / ♋27

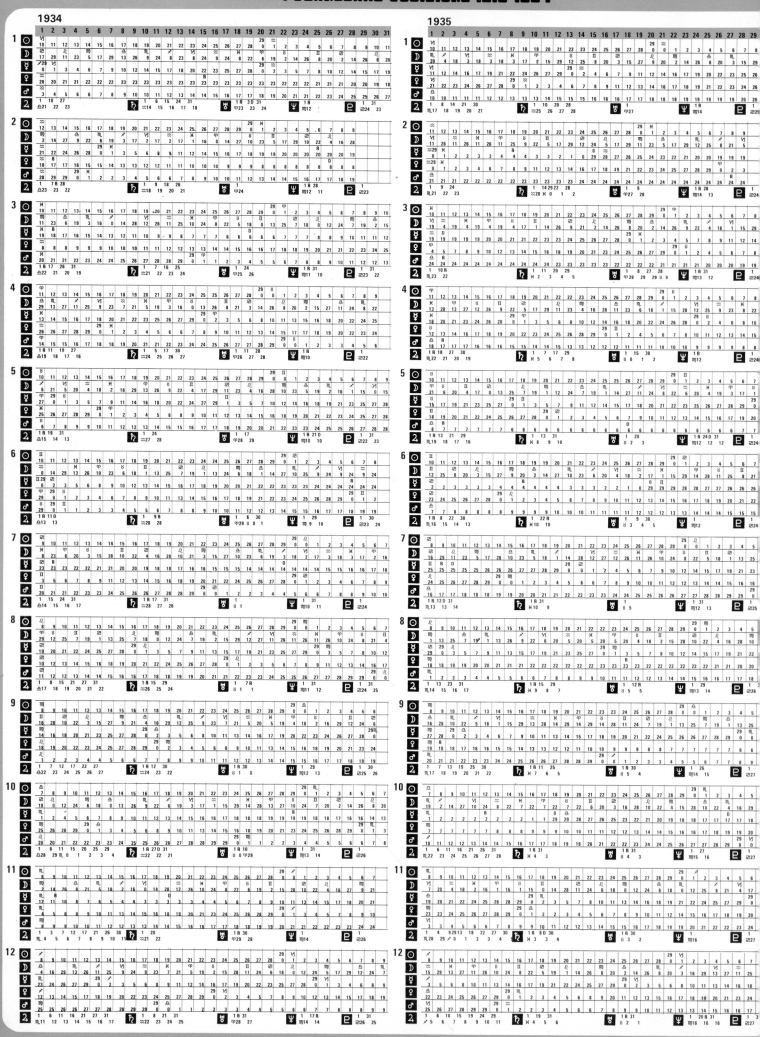

1936

	1	2	3	4	5	6	7	8	9	10	11	12	13	14	15	16	17	18	19	20	21	22	23	24	25	26	27	28	29	30	31
Jan ☉	♑10	11	12	13	14	15	16	17	18	19	20	21	22	23	24	25	26	27	28	29	29♒0	1	2	3	4	5	6	7	8	9	10
☽	♈8	22	6	20	4	17	1	14	27	9	22	4	16	28	10	22	4	16	28	11	24	8	22	6	20	5	20	4	19	3	17
☿	♑22	24	26	27	29	29♒0	2	3	5	6	7	8	9	10	12	13	14	15	16	17	17	17	℞17	17	16	15	14	13	12	10	
♀	♏27	29	0	1	2	3	4	6	7	8	9	10	12	13	14	15	16	18	19	20	21	22	23	25	26	27	29	0	1	2	3
♂	♒20	20	21	22	23	24	25	26	27	27	28	29	0	1	1	2	3	4	4	5	6	7	8	8	9	10	11	11	12	13	

♃ 1 2 7 11 17 22 28 ♐11 12 13 14 15 16 17 — ♄ 1 12 22 31 ♓6 7 8 9 — ♅ 1 ♉1 — ♆ 1 ♍16 — ♇ 1℞18 ♋26 25

	1	2	3	4	5	6	7	8	9	10	11	12	13	14	15	16	17	18	19	20	21	22	23	24	25	26	27	28	29
Feb ☉	♒11	12	13	14	15	16	17	18	19	20	21	22	23	24	25	26	27	29	29♓0	1	2	3	4	5	6	7	8	9	10
☽	♊1	14	27	10	23	5	18	0	12	24	6	18	0	12	24	6	19	2	15	29	14	29	14	29	14	29	13	27	11
☿	♒10	8	7	6	5	4	3	2	2	2	1	1	1	D1	1	2	2	3	3	4	5	5	6	7	8	9	10	11	12 13
♀	♑5	6	7	8	9	11	12	13	14	16	17	18	19	20	22	23	24	25	27	28	29	29♒0	1	3	4	5	6	8	9
♂	♓14	15	15	16	17	18	19	19	20	21	22	23	23	24	25	25	26	26	27	28	29	29	29♈0	1	2	2	3	4	5

♃ 1 2 8 15 22 ♐17 18 19 20 21 — ♄ 1 9 17 25 ♓9 10 11 12 — ♅ 1 11 ♉1 2 — ♆ 1℞12 ♍16 15 — ♇ 1℞ ♋25

	1	2	3	4	5	6	7	8	9	10	11	12	13	14	15	16	17	18	19	20	21	22	23	24	25	26	27	28	29	30	31
Mar ☉	♓11	12	13	14	15	16	17	18	19	20	21	22	23	24	25	26	27	28	29	29♈0	1	2	3	4	5	6	7	8	9	10	11
☽	♋24	7	20	2	15	27	9	21	3	14	26	8	20	2	15	27	10	24	7	22	7	22	7	22	8	22	7	20	4	17	29
☿	♒14	15	17	18	19	20	22	23	24	26	27	28	29♓0	2	3	5	6	8	9	11	12	14	16	18	20	21	23	25	27	29	0
♀	♒10	11	13	14	15	16	17	19	20	21	22	25	26	27	28	28	29♓0	1	2	3	5	6	7	8	10	11	12	13	14	16	17
♂	♈6	7	8	9	9	10	11	12	12	13	14	15	15	16	17	17	18	19	19	20	21	22	23	24	25	26	27	27	28	29	

♃ 1 10 24 ♐22 23 24 — ♄ 1 4 12 21 29 ♓12 13 14 15 16 — ♅ 1 10 30 ♉2 3 4 — ♆ 1℞20 ♍15 14 — ♇ 1℞ ♋25

	1	2	3	4	5	6	7	8	9	10	11	12	13	14	15	16	17	18	19	20	21	22	23	24	25	26	27	28	29	30
Apr ☉	♈11	12	13	14	15	16	17	18	19	20	21	22	23	24	25	26	27	28	29	29♉0	1	2	3	4	5	6	7	8	9	10
☽	♌12	24	6	18	0	11	23	5	17	29	12	24	7	19	3	16	1	15	0	15	1	16	1	15	29	13	26	8	21	3
☿	♈2	4	6	8	10	12	14	16	18	20	22	24	27	29	29♉1	3	5	7	9	11	13	15	17	19	21	23	24	26	27	29
♀	♓18	19	21	22	23	24	26	27	28	29	29♈0	2	3	4	5	7	8	9	10	11	13	14	15	16	18	19	20	21	23	24
♂	♈29	29♉0	1	2	3	3	4	5	6	7	7	8	9	10	10	11	12	13	13	14	15	16	16	17	18	19	19	20	21	

♃ 1 11℞27 ♐24 24 23 — ♄ 1 7 16 26 ♓16 17 18 19 — ♅ 1 17 ♉4 5 — ♆ 1 ♍14 — ♇ 1℞ ♋25

	1	2	3	4	5	6	7	8	9	10	11	12	13	14	15	16	17	18	19	20	21	22	23	24	25	26	27	28	29	30	31
May ☉	♉11	12	13	14	15	16	17	18	19	20	21	22	23	24	25	26	27	28	29	29♊0	1	2	3	4	5	6	7	8	9	10	
☽	♍15	27	8	20	2	14	26	9	21	3	16	29	13	26	10	25	9	24	9	24	9	23	7	21	4	17	29	11	23	5	17
☿	♉29	♊0	2	3	4	6	7	8	9	10	11	12	12	13	13	13	14	℞14	13	13	13	13	12	12	11	11	10	10	9		
♀	♈25	26	27	29	29♉0	1	2	4	5	6	7	9	10	11	12	13	15	16	17	18	20	21	22	23	25	26	27	28	29♊0	1	2
♂	♉21	22	23	23	24	24	25	26	27	28	28	29	29♊0	1	2	3	3	4	5	5	6	7	8	8	9	10	11	12	13		

♃ 1℞11 21 30 ♐23 22 21 20 — ♄ 1 8 21 ♓19 20 21 — ♅ 1 4 22 ♉5 6 7 — ♆ 1℞21 25D 29 ♍14 13 13 14 — ♇ 1 ♋25

	1	2	3	4	5	6	7	8	9	10	11	12	13	14	15	16	17	18	19	20	21	22	23	24	25	26	27	28	29	30
Jun ☉	♊11	12	13	14	15	16	17	17	18	19	20	21	22	23	24	25	26	27	28	29♋0	1	2	3	4	5	6	7	8	9	
☽	♎29	11	23	5	18	0	13	26	10	23	7	21	5	20	4	19	3	17	1	15	29	12	24	7	19	1	13	25	7	19
☿	♊℞9	8	7	7	6	6	5	5	5	5	D5	5	5	6	6	7	7	8	9	9	10	11	12	14	15	16	17			
♀	♊3	4	5	7	8	9	10	12	13	14	15	17	18	19	20	21	23	24	25	26	28	29♋0	1	2	4	5	6	7	9	
♂	♊13	14	15	16	16	17	17	18	19	19	20	21	22	22	23	24	25	25	26	27	27	28	29	29♋0	1	2	3	3		

♃ 1℞7 15 23 ♐20 19 18 17 — ♄ 1 8 ♓21 22 — ♅ 1 11 ♉7 8 — ♆ 1 ♍14 — ♇ 1 10 ♋25 26

	1	2	3	4	5	6	7	8	9	10	11	12	13	14	15	16	17	18	19	20	21	22	23	24	25	26	27	28	29	30	31
Jul ☉	♋9	10	11	12	13	14	15	16	17	18	19	20	21	22	23	24	25	26	27	28	28	29♌0	1	2	3	4	5	6	7	8	
☽	♐1	14	26	9	23	6	20	4	18	2	16	1	15	29	13	27	10	24	7	20	2	15	27	9	21	3	15	27	9	22	4
☿	♊18	20	21	23	24	26	27	29♋0	1	3	5	7	9	11	13	15	17	19	21	23	25	27	29♌0	2	4	6	8	10	12	14	16
♀	♋10	11	12	14	15	16	17	18	20	21	22	23	25	26	27	28	29♌0	1	2	3	4	6	7	8	9	11	12	13	14	16	17
♂	♋4	4	5	6	6	7	8	8	9	10	10	11	12	13	14	14	15	16	16	17	18	18	19	20	20	21	22	22	23	23	

♃ 1℞11 26 ♐16 15 14 — ♄ 1 4℞29 ♓22 22 21 — ♅ 1 7 ♉8 9 — ♆ 1 27 ♍14 15 — ♇ 1 10 ♋26 27

	1	2	3	4	5	6	7	8	9	10	11	12	13	14	15	16	17	18	19	20	21	22	23	24	25	26	27	28	29	30	31
Aug ☉	♌9	10	11	12	13	14	15	16	17	18	19	20	21	21	22	23	24	25	26	27	28	29	29♍0	1	2	3	4	5	6	7	8
☽	♑17	1	15	29	14	28	13	27	12	26	10	23	7	20	3	16	28	11	23	5	17	29	11	23	5	17	0	12	26	10	24
☿	♌18	20	22	24	25	27	29♍0	1	3	4	6	8	9	10	12	13	14	16	17	19	20	21	23	24	26	27	28	29♎0	1	2	3	4
♀	♌18	19	20	22	23	24	25	27	28	29♍0	2	3	4	5	7	8	9	10	12	13	14	15	17	18	19	20	22	23	24	25	
♂	♋24	25	25	26	27	27	28	29	29♌0	0	1	1	2	3	3	4	5	5	6	7	7	8	9	9	10	10	11	11	12	13	13

♃ 1℞12D 27 ♐14 14 15 — ♄ 1℞17 ♓21 20 — ♅ 1 15℞ ♉9 9 — ♆ 1 26 ♍15 16 — ♇ 1 12 ♋27 28

	1	2	3	4	5	6	7	8	9	10	11	12	13	14	15	16	17	18	19	20	21	22	23	24	25	26	27	28	29	30
Sep ☉	♍9	10	11	12	13	14	15	16	17	18	19	20	21	22	23	24	25	26	27	28	29	29♎0	1	2	3	4	5	6	7	
☽	♓8	23	8	23	8	22	6	20	4	17	0	12	25	7	20	2	14	26	8	20	2	14	26	8	21	4	18	2	17	2
☿	♎5	7	8	9	9	10	11	12	13	14	15	15	16	16	16	16	℞16	16	16	15	15	14	13	12	11	10	9	8		
♀	♍26	27	29	29♎0	1	2	4	5	6	7	9	10	11	12	14	15	16	17	19	20	21	22	23	25	26	27	28	29♏0	1	2
♂	♌14	15	15	16	17	17	18	18	19	20	20	21	22	22	23	24	24	25	26	26	27	28	28	29	29♍0	1	1	2		

♃ 1 11 20 28 ♐15 16 17 18 — ♄ 1℞13 26 ♓19 18 17 — ♅ 1℞22 ♉9 8 — ♆ 1 26 ♍16 17 — ♇ 1 ♋28

	1	2	3	4	5	6	7	8	9	10	11	12	13	14	15	16	17	18	19	20	21	22	23	24	25	26	27	28	29	30	31
Oct ☉	♎8	9	10	11	12	13	14	15	16	17	18	19	20	21	22	23	24	25	26	27	28	29	29♏0	1	2	3	4	5	6	7	8
☽	♈17	2	17	2	16	0	14	27	10	22	5	17	29	11	23	5	17	29	11	23	6	18	1	15	29	12	26	10	25	9	24
☿	♎6	5	4	3	2	2	1	1	1	D1	1	2	3	4	5	6	7	9	10	11	13	14	16	17	19	20	22	23	25	27	
♀	♏3	4	5	7	8	9	11	12	13	14	16	17	18	19	20	22	23	24	25	27	28	29♐0	1	3	4	5	6	8	9	10	
♂	♍3	3	4	5	5	6	6	7	8	8	9	10	10	11	12	12	13	13	14	15	15	16	16	17	18	18	19	20	20	21	

♃ 1 6 12 18 24 29 ♐18 19 20 21 22 23 — ♄ 1℞11 ♓17 16 — ♅ 1℞20 ♉8 7 — ♆ 1 21 ♍17 18 — ♇ 1℞ ♋28

	1	2	3	4	5	6	7	8	9	10	11	12	13	14	15	16	17	18	19	20	21	22	23	24	25	26	27	28	29	30
Nov ☉	♏9	10	11	12	13	14	15	16	17	18	19	20	21	22	23	24	25	26	27	28	29	29♐0	1	2	3	4	5	6	7	8
☽	♉11	25	9	23	6	19	1	14	26	8	20	1	13	25	7	19	1	14	26	9	22	5	19	4	18	3	18	3	18	3
☿	♏29	0	2	3	5	7	8	10	11	13	15	16	18	19	21	23	24	26	27	29♐0	2	4	5	7	8	10	11	12	14	15
♀	♐11	12	14	15	16	17	19	20	21	22	23	25	26	27	28	29♑0	1	2	3	5	6	7	8	9	10	11	12	13	15	16
♂	♍22	22	23	23	24	24	25	26	26	27	27	28	28	29	29♎0	0	1	2	3	3	4	4	5	6	6	7	7	8	9	

♃ 1 3 8 13 18 23 27 ♑23 24 25 26 27 28 29 — ♄ 1℞3 19D ♓16 15 15 — ♅ 1℞14 ♉7 6 — ♆ 1 ♍18 — ♇ 1 ♋28

	1	2	3	4	5	6	7	8	9	10	11	12	13	14	15	16	17	18	19	20	21	22	23	24	25	26	27	28	29	30	31
Dec ☉	♐9	10	11	12	13	14	15	16	17	18	19	20	21	22	23	24	25	26	27	28	29	29♑0	1	2	3	4	5	6	7	8	9
☽	♋17	1	14	27	10	22	4	16	28	10	22	4	16	28	10	23	6	19	2	16	0	14	28	12	26	11	25	9	22		
☿	♐16	18	19	21	22	24	26	27	29	29♑0	2	3	5	6	8	9	11	12	14	15	17	18	20	21	22	24	25	26	27	28	29
♀	♑18	19	20	21	22	24	25	26	27	29	29♒0	1	3	4	6	7	8	9	10	12	13	14	15	17	18	19	20	21	22	23	
♂	♎10	10	11	11	12	12	13	14	14	15	16	16	17	18	18	19	20	20	21	22	22	23	24	24	25	25	26	26	27		

♃ 1 2 29 3 6 11 15 19 24 ♑29 0 ♑0 1 2 3 4 5 — ♄ 1 4 26 ♓15 16 17 — ♅ 1℞14 ♉6 5 — ♆ 1 21℞ ♍18 18 — ♇ 1℞ ♋28

1937

day of Birth

	1	2	3	4	5	6	7	8	9	10	11	12	13	14	15	16	17	18	19	20	21	22	23	24	25	26	27	28	29	30	31
1 ☉	♑11	12	13	14	15	16	17	18	19	20	21	22	23	24	25	26	27	28	29	29♒0	1	2	3	4	5	6	7	8	9	10	11
☽	♍5	18	0	12	24	6	18	0	12	24	7	19	2	16	29	13	26	10	24	9	23	7	21	5	19	3	17	0	13	26	8
☿	♑29	0	0	1	1	1	1	1	0	29	29	28	26	25	24	22	21	20	19	18	17	16	16	15	15	15	D15	15	15	16	17
♀	♒24	26	27	28	29	29♓0	1	3	4	5	6	7	8	9	10	12	13	14	15	16	17	18	19	20	21	23	24	25	26	27	28
♂	♎27	28	29	29♏0	1	1	2	2	3	3	4	4	5	5	6	6	7	7	8	8	9	9	10	10	10	11	11	12	12	13	13

♃ 1 2 6 10 15 19 23 28 ♑6 7 8 9 10 11 12 13 — ♄ 1 9 20 30 ♓17 18 19 20 — ♅ 1℞14D ♉5 5 — ♆ 1℞ ♍18 — ♇ 1℞15 ♋28 27

	1	2	3	4	5	6	7	8	9	10	11	12	13	14	15	16	17	18	19	20	21	22	23	24	25	26	27	28
2 ☉	♒12	13	14	15	16	17	18	19	20	21	22	23	24	25	26	27	28	29	29♓0	1	2	3	4	5	6	7	8	9
☽	♎20	2	14	26	8	20	2	15	28	11	25	8	23	7	21	5	20	4	18	2	15	29	12	25	8	21	4	16
☿	♑17	18	19	20	21	21	22	24	25	26	27	28	29	29♒0	2	3	4	6	7	8	10	11	13	14	16	17	19	20
♀	♓29	♈0	0	1	2	3	4	5	6	7	8	9	10	11	12	13	14	15	15	16	17	18	19	20	21	21	22	23 24
♂	♏14	14	15	15	16	16	16	17	17	18	18	18	19	19	19	20	20	21	21	22	22	23	23	23	24	24	25	25

♃ 1 2 6 11 16 21 26 ♑13 14 15 16 17 18 19 — ♄ 1 8 17 25 ♓20 21 22 23 — ♅ 1 12 ♉5 6 — ♆ 1℞21 ♍18 17 — ♇ 1℞13 ♋27 26

	1	2	3	4	5	6	7	8	9	10	11	12	13	14	15	16	17	18	19	20	21	22	23	24	25	26	27	28	29	30	31
3 ☉	♓10	11	12	13	14	15	16	17	18	19	20	21	22	23	24	25	26	27	28	29	29♈0	1	2	3	4	5	6	7	8	9	10
☽	♏28	10	22	4	16	28	10	23	6	19	3	17	2	16	1	16	0	14	28	12	26	9	22	5	17	0	12	24	6	18	0
☿	♒22	23	25	26	28	29♓0	1	3	5	6	8	10	12	14	15	17	19	21	23	25	27	29	29♈1	3	5	7	9	11	13	15	17
♀	♈24	25	26	27	27	28	28	29	29	29♉0	0	1	1	2	2	3	3	4	4	4	5	5	5	5	5	5	5	5	℞5	5	5
♂	♏26	26	27	27	27	28	28	28	29	29	29	29	29	29♐0	0	0	1	1	1	1	2	2	2	2	3	3	3	3	4	4	

♃ 1 3 9 15 22 29 ♑19 20 21 22 23 24 — ♄ 1 6 14 22 30 ♓23 24 25 26 27 — ♅ 1 ♉6 7 — ♆ 1℞30 ♍17 16 — ♇ 1℞ ♋26

	1	2	3	4	5	6	7	8	9	10	11	12	13	14	15	16	17	18	19	20	21	22	23	24	25	26	27	28	29	30
4 ☉	♈11	12	13	14	15	16	17	18	19	20	21	22	23	24	25	26	27	28	29	29♉0	1	2	3	4	5	6	7	8	9	10
☽	♐12	24	6	18	1	14	27	11	25	10	25	10	24	9	22	6	19	2	14	27	9	21	3	15	27	8	20	2		
☿	♈19	21	23	25	27	29♉1	3	4	6	8	9	11	12	14	15	16	17	18	19	20	21	22	22	23	23	24	24	24	℞24	
♀	♉℞5	5	4	4	4	3	3	3	2	2	1	1	0	0	29♈29	28	27	27	26	26	25	25	24	23	23	22	22	21	21	20
♂	♐4	4	4	4	5	5	5	5	5	5	5	5	5	5	℞5	5	5	5	5	5	5	5	5	5	4	4	4	4	4	3

♃ 1 6 16 ♑24 25 26 — ♄ 1 7 16 25 29 26 ♓27 28 29 ♈0 ♈0 — ♅ 1 2 20 ♉7 8 9 — ♆ 1 ♍16 — ♇ 1℞13D ♋26 26

	1	2	3	4	5	6	7	8	9	10	11	12	13	14	15	16	17	18	19	20	21	22	23	24	25	26	27	28	29	30	31
5 ☉	♉11	12	13	14	15	16	17	18	19	20	21	22	23	24	25	26	27	28	29	29♊0	1	2	3	4	5	6	7	8	9	10	
☽	♑14	27	9	22	5	19	4	18	3	18	4	19	3	18	2	15	29	11	24	6	18	0	12	24	6	17	29	11	24	6	19
☿	♉24	24	23	23	23	22	22	21	21	20	20	19	19	18	18	17	17	16	16	16	15	15	15	15	D15	15	15	15	16	16	17
♀	♈℞20	20	19	19	19	19	19	19	19	D19	19	19	19	19	19	19	20	20	20	20	21	21	21	22	22	23	23	24	25	25	26 27
♂	♐℞3	3	3	2	2	2	1	1	1	0	0	0	29♏29	29	29	28	28	28	27	27	27	26	26	26	25	25	25	25	24	24	

♃ 1 16℞29 ♑27 27 26 — ♄ 1 4 14 26 ♈0 1 2 3 — ♅ 1 7 25 ♉9 10 11 — ♆ 1℞29D ♍16 16 — ♇ 1 14 ♋26 27

	1	2	3	4	5	6	7	8	9	10	11	12	13	14	15	16	17	18	19	20	21	22	23	24	25	26	27	28	29	30
6 ☉	♊11	11	12	13	14	15	16	17	18	19	20	21	22	23	24	25	26	27	28	29	29♋0	1	2	3	3	4	5	6	7	8
☽	♓1	15	28	13	27	12	27	12	27	12	26	11	24	8	20	3	15	27	9	21	3	14	26	8	21	3	16	28	11	25
☿	♉18	18	19	20	21	22	23	24	26	27	28	29♊0	1	2	3	5	6	8	10	11	13	15	17	19	21	23	25	27	29	
♀	♈28	29	29♉0	1	1	2	3	4	5	6	7	8	9	10	10	11	12	13	14	15	16	17	18	19	20	21	22	23		
♂	♏℞23	23	23	22	22	22	22	21	21	21	21	21	20	20	20	20	20	20	19	19	19	19	19	19	19	19	D19	19	19	

♃ 1℞13 24 ♑26 25 24 — ♄ 1 10 ♈3 4 — ♅ 1 14 ♉11 12 — ♆ 1 ♍16 — ♇ 1 ♋27

	1	2	3	4	5	6	7	8	9	10	11	12	13	14	15	16	17	18	19	20	21	22	23	24	25	26	27	28	29	30	31
7 ☉	♋9	10	11	12	13	14	15	16	17	18	19	20	21	22	23	24	25	26	27	28	29	29♌0	1	2	3	4	5	6	7	8	
☽	♈8	22	7	21	6	21	5	20	5	19	3	16	29	11	24	6	17	29	11	23	5	17	0	12	25	8	22	5	19	3	17
☿	♋1	3	5	7	9	11	14	16	18	20	22	24	26	28	29♌0	2	3	5	6	8	10	12	14	16	18	19	21	23	24	26	28 29
♀	♉23	24	25	26	27	28	29	29♊0	1	3	4	5	6	7	8	9	10	11	12	13	14	15	16	17	18	19	20	21	22	23	24 25
♂	♏19	19	19	19	20	20	20	20	20	20	20	21	21	21	21	21	21	22	22	22	22	23	23	23	24	24	24	25	25	26	26

♃ 1℞2 10 18 26 ♑24 23 22 21 20 — ♄ 1 4 17℞28 ♈4 5 5 4 — ♅ 1 8 ♉12 13 — ♆ 1 23 ♍16 17 — ♇ 1 15 ♋27 28

	1	2	3	4	5	6	7	8	9	10	11	12	13	14	15	16	17	18	19	20	21	22	23	24	25	26	27	28	29	30	31
8 ☉	♌9	10	11	12	13	14	15	15	16	17	18	19	20	21	22	23	24	25	26	27	28	29	29♍0	1	2	3	4	5	6	7	8
☽	♊1	16	0	15	29	13	27	11	24	7	19	2	14	25	7	19	1	13	26	8	21	4	18	2	16	0	14	28	12	26	10
☿	♍1	2	4	5	7	8	9	11	12	13	15	16	17	18	19	19	20	21	22	23	24	25	25	26	26	27	28	28	29	29	29
♀	♊26	27	28	29♋0	1	2	3	4	5	6	7	8	10	11	12	13	14	15	16	17	19	20	21	22	23	25	26	27	28	29♌0	1
♂	♏27	27	28	28	28	29	29	29♐0	0	1	1	1	2	2	3	3	3	4	4	5	5	6	6	7	7	8	9	9	10	10	11

♃ 1℞3 13 26 ♑20 19 18 17 — ♄ 1℞23 ♈4 3 — ♅ 1 19℞ ♉13 13 — ♆ 1 23 ♍17 18 — ♇ 1 17 ♋28 29

	1	2	3	4	5	6	7	8	9	10	11	12	13	14	15	16	17	18	19	20	21	22	23	24	25	26	27	28	29	30
9 ☉	♍9	10	11	12	13	14	15	16	17	18	19	20	21	22	23	24	25	26	27	28	29	29♎0	1	2	3	4	5	6	7	
☽	♋24	8	22	6	19	2	15	27	9	21	3	15	27	9	21	4	16	0	13	27	11	26	10	25	9	23	7	21	5	18
☿	♍℞29	29	29	28	28	27	27	26	25	24	23	22	21	20	19	18	17	16	16	15	15	15	15	D15	15	16	16	17	18	19
♀	♌2	3	4	5	6	8	9	10	11	12	13	15	16	17	18	19	21	22	23	24	25	27	28	29♍0	1	2	3	4	5	
♂	♐12	12	13	14	14	15	16	16	17	18	18	19	20	21	21	22	23	24	24	25	26	27	27	28	29	29♑0	1	2	3	

♃ 1℞14D ♑17 17 — ♄ 1℞7 21 ♈3 2 1 — ♅ 1℞30 ♉13 12 — ♆ 1 19 ♍18 19 — ♇ 1 ♋29

	1	2	3	4	5	6	7	8	9	10	11	12	13	14	15	16	17	18	19	20	21	22	23	24	25	26	27	28	29	30	31
10 ☉	♎8	9	10	11	12	13	14	15	16	17	18	19	20	21	22	23	24	25	26	27	28	29	29♏0	1	2	3	4	5	6	7	8
☽	♍2	15	28	11	23	5	18	29	11	23	5	17	29	11	24	7	20	4	19	3	18	4	19	5	20	4	19	2	15	29	12
☿	♍20	21	22	24	25	27	28	29♎0	2	3	5	7	8	10	12	14	15	17	19	20	22	24	25	27	29	29♏0	2	4	5	7	
♀	♍6	7	8	9	10	11	12	13	15	16	17	19	20	21	22	23	25	26	27	28	29♎0	1	3	4	5	6	7	8	10	11	12 13 14
♂	♑1	1	2	3	3	4	5	5	6	7	7	8	9	9	10	11	12	13	14	14	15	16	17	17	18	19	20	21	21	22	

♃ 1 2 15 24 ♑17 18 19 20 — ♄ 1℞4 17 0 18 ♈1 0 29 ♓29 — ♅ 1℞27 ♉12 11 — ♆ 1 18 ♍19 20 — ♇ 1 ♋29

	1	2	3	4	5	6	7	8	9	10	11	12	13	14	15	16	17	18	19	20	21	22	23	24	25	26	27	28	29	30
11 ☉	♏9	10	11	12	13	14	15	16	17	18	19	20	21	22	23	24	25	26	27	28	29	29♐0	1	2	3	4	5	6	7	8
☽	♏20	2	14	26	8	20	2	14	26	8	20	2	14	26	8	20	3	16	29	13	27	12	27	12	27	12	25	9	22	4
☿	♏11	12	14	15	17	18	20	21	22	24	25	27	28	29♐0	1	2	4	6	7	9	10	11	12	13	14	15	16	17	18	
♀	♎16	17	18	19	21	22	23	24	25	27	28	29♏0	1	3	4	5	6	7	8	10	11	12	13	15	16	17	18	19	20	21 22
♂	♑22	23	24	25	25	26	27	27	28	29	29♒0	1	2	3	3	4	5	6	6	7	8	8	9	10	11	11	12	13	14	

♃ 1 7 14 20 25 30 ♑21 22 23 24 25 26 — ♄ 1℞4 ♓29 28 — ♅ 1℞21 ♉11 10 — ♆ 1 30 ♍20 21 — ♇ 3℞14 0 ♋0 29

	1	2	3	4	5	6	7	8	9	10	11	12	13	14	15	16	17	18	19	20	21	22	23	24	25	26	27	28	29	30	31
12 ☉	♐9	10	11	12	13	14	15	16	17	18	19	20	21	22	23	24	25	26	27	28	29	29♑0	1	2	3	4	5	6	7	8	9
☽	♑23	5	17	28	10	22	4	16	29	11	24	8	22	6	21	6	21	6	21	6	21	4	18	1	14	26	8	20	2	13	25
☿	♐26	28	0	1	2	3	5	6	7	8	9	10	11	12	13	14	15	15	15	15	℞15	15	14	13	13	12	10	9	8	6	5
♀	♏23	25	26	27	28	29♐0	1	2	3	5	6	7	8	9	10	12	13	14	15	16	17	18	20	21	22	23	25	26	27	28	29
♂	♒15	15	16	17	17	18	18	19	20	21	21	22	23	24	24	25	26	27	28	28	29♓0	1	1	2	3	4	4	5	6	7	

♃ 1 5 10 15 20 29 21 24 29 ♑26 27 28 29 ♒0 0 1 2 — ♄ 1℞8 20 D 28 ♓28 28 28 29 — ♅ 1℞23 ♉10 9 — ♆ 1 24℞ ♍21 21 — ♇ 1℞ ♋29

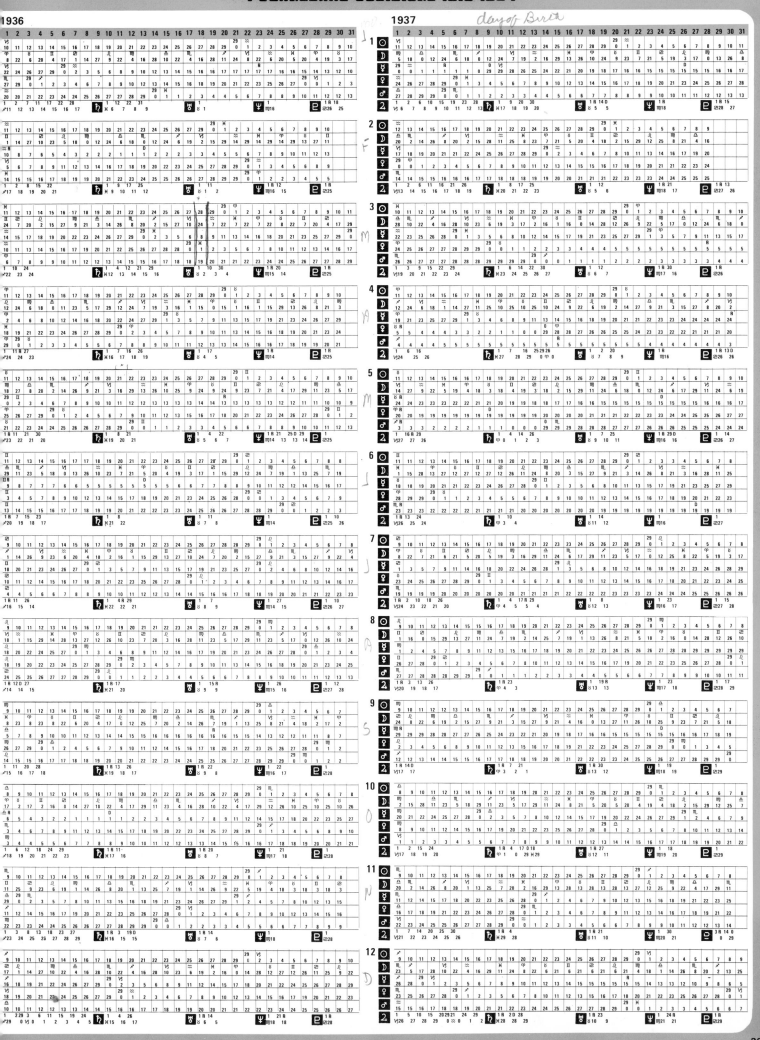

1938

	1	2	3	4	5	6	7	8	9	10	11	12	13	14	15	16	17	18	19	20	21	22	23	24	25	26	27	28	29	30	31
1 ☉	10	11	12	13	14	15	16	17	18	19	20	21	22	23	24	25	26	27	28	29	29 0	1	2	3	4	5	6	7	8	9	10 11
☽	7	19	1	13	26	8	21	4	17	1	15	29	14	29	14	29	14	29	12	26	9	22	4	17	28	10	22	4	16	28	10
☿	5	3	2	1	0	29	29	29	29	29	29	0	0	1	1	2	3	4	5	6	7	8	9	10	11	12	13	15	16	17	18
♀	2	4	5	6	7	9	10	11	12	14	15	16	17	19	20	21	22	24	25	26	27	29	0	1	2	4	5	6	7	9	10
♂	8	9	10	10	11	12	13	13	14	15	16	16	17	18	19	19	20	21	22	22	23	24	25	25	26	27	28	28	29	0	1

♃ 1 2 6 11 15 19 23 28 / ♒ 2 3 4 5 6 7 8 9 — ♄ 1 4 14 15 26 / ♓29 0 ♈0 1 — ♅ 1 ℞ 18 D / ♉ 9 9 — ♆ 1 ℞ 16 / ♍21 20 — ♇ 1 ℞ 16 / ♋29 28

	1	2	3	4	5	6	7	8	9	10	11	12	13	14	15	16	17	18	19	20	21	22	23	24	25	26	27	28
2 ☉	12	13	14	15	16	17	18	19	20	21	22	23	24	25	26	27	28	29	29 0	1	2	3	4	5	6	7	8	9
☽	23	5	18	1	14	28	11	25	9	24	8	23	7	22	6	20	4	17	0	12	25	6	18	0	12	24	6	19
☿	20	21	23	24	25	27	28	29 0	1	3	4	6	7	9	10	12	14	15	17	19	20	22	24	25	27	29	1	2
♀	11	12	14	15	16	17	19	20	21	22	24	25	26	28	29	0	1	3	4	5	6	8	9	10	11	13	14	15
♂	1	2	3	4	4	5	6	7	7	8	9	10	11	11	12	12	13	14	15	15	15	16	17	18	18	19	20	21

♃ 1 5 9 14 18 22 26 / ♒10 11 12 13 14 15 16 — ♄ 1 6 15 24 / ♈1 2 3 4 — ♅ 1 12 / ♉10 11 — ♆ 1 ℞ / ♍20 — ♇ 1 ℞ / ♋28

	1	2	3	4	5	6	7	8	9	10	11	12	13	14	15	16	17	18	19	20	21	22	23	24	25	26	27	28	29	30	31
3 ☉	10	11	12	13	14	15	16	17	18	19	20	21	22	23	24	25	26	27	28	29	29 0	1	2	3	4	5	6	7	8	9	10
☽	1	14	27	11	24	8	22	6	20	4	18	3	17	1	15	29	12	25	8	20	2	14	26	8	20	2	14	27	10	23	6
☿	4	6	8	10	11	13	15	17	19	21	23	25	27	29 0	1	3	5	7	9	11	13	14	16	18	20	21	23	25	26	27	29
♀	16	18	19	20	21	23	24	25	26	28	29 0	1	2	3	4	4	5	5	6	7	8	9	9	10	11	11	11	12	13	14	14
♂	22	23	23	24	25	26	26	27	28	29	29 0	1	1	2	3	4	4	5	6	7	8	8	9	9	10	11	11	12	13	14	14

♃ 1 3 7 12 16 21 26 31 / ♒16 17 18 19 20 21 22 23 — ♄ 1 5 13 21 29 / ♈4 5 6 7 8 — ♅ 1 14 / ♉10 11 — ♆ 1 ℞ 3 / ♍20 19 — ♇ 1 ℞ 19 / ♋28 27

	1	2	3	4	5	6	7	8	9	10	11	12	13	14	15	16	17	18	19	20	21	22	23	24	25	26	27	28	29	30
4 ☉	11	12	13	14	15	16	17	18	19	20	21	22	23	24	25	26	27	28	29	29 0	1	2	3	4	5	6	7	8	9	9
☽	20	4	18	2	17	1	15	29	13	27	11	24	8	21	3	16	28	10	22	4	16	28	10	22	5	18	1	15	29	13
☿	0	1	2	3	3	4	5	5	5	5	5	5	5	4	4	4	3	3	2	1	1	0	29	29	28	28	27	27	26	25
♀	25	26	27	28	29 0	1	3	5	6	7	8	10	11	12	13	15	16	17	18	19	21	22	23	24	26	27	28	29 0	1	1
♂	15	15	16	17	17	18	19	19	20	21	21	22	23	23	24	25	25	26	27	27	28	28	29 0	1	1	2	2	3	4	4

♃ 1 5 10 16 22 29 / ♒23 24 25 26 27 28 — ♄ 1 6 14 22 / ♈8 9 10 11 — ♅ 1 4 22 / ♉11 12 13 — ♆ 1 ℞ 3 / ♍19 18 — ♇ 1 ℞ 27 D / ♋27 27

	1	2	3	4	5	6	7	8	9	10	11	12	13	14	15	16	17	18	19	20	21	22	23	24	25	26	27	28	29	30	31
5 ☉	10	11	12	13	14	15	16	17	18	19	20	21	22	23	24	25	26	27	28	29	29 0	1	2	3	4	5	6	7	8	9	9
☽	28	12	27	11	26	10	24	8	21	4	17	0	12	24	7	19	0	12	24	6	18	0	13	26	9	23	7	21	6	21	6
☿	25	25	25	25	25	25	25	25	26	26	26	27	27	28	28	29	29 0	0	1	2	3	4	5	7	8	9	10	12	13	14	16 17
♀	2	3	4	5	7	8	9	10	11	13	14	15	16	18	19	20	21	22	24	25	26	27	28	29 0	1	2	3	4	6	7	8
♂	5	6	7	7	8	9	9	10	11	11	12	13	13	14	15	15	16	17	17	18	19	20	20	21	21	22	23	23	24	25	25

♃ 1 6 14 29 15 24 / ♒28 29 0 ♓0 1 — ♄ 1 10 19 30 / ♈12 13 14 15 — ♅ 1 9 27 / ♉13 14 15 — ♆ 1 ℞ 30 D / ♍18 18 — ♇ 1 25 / ♋27 28

	1	2	3	4	5	6	7	8	9	10	11	12	13	14	15	16	17	18	19	20	21	22	23	24	25	26	27	28	29	30
6 ☉	10	11	12	13	14	15	16	17	18	19	20	21	22	23	24	25	26	27	28	28	29	29 0	1	2	3	4	5	6	7	8
☽	21	6	20	4	18	1	14	27	9	21	3	15	27	9	21	3	15	27	9	22	4	17	1	15	0	14	0	15	0	15
☿	19	20	22	24	25	27	29	1	3	5	6	8	10	13	15	17	19	21	23	25	28	0	2	4	6	8	11	13	15	17
♀	9	11	12	13	14	15	17	18	19	20	21	22	24	25	26	27	28	29 0	1	2	3	4	6	7	8	9	10	11	13	14
♂	26	27	27	28	29	29 0	1	1	2	3	3	4	5	5	6	7	7	8	9	9	10	11	11	12	13	13	14	14	15	15

♃ 1 8 22 ℞ / ♓1 2 2 — ♄ 1 10 25 / ♈15 16 17 — ♅ 1 16 / ♉15 16 — ♆ 1 / ♍18 — ♇ 1 17 / ♋28 29

	1	2	3	4	5	6	7	8	9	10	11	12	13	14	15	16	17	18	19	20	21	22	23	24	25	26	27	28	29	30	31
7 ☉	9	10	11	12	13	14	15	16	17	18	18	19	20	21	22	23	24	25	26	27	28	29	29 0	1	2	3	4	5	6	7	8
☽	0	14	28	11	24	6	18	0	12	24	6	18	0	12	24	6	18	1	14	27	10	24	8	23	8	23	8	23	8	23	6
☿	19	21	23	25	27	29	1	2	4	6	8	9	11	13	14	16	17	19	20	22	23	24	26	27	28	29 0	1	2	3	4	5
♀	15	16	17	19	20	21	22	23	24	26	27	28	29 0	1	2	4	5	6	7	8	9	11	12	13	14	15	16	17	18	20	20
♂	16	17	17	18	19	19	20	21	21	22	22	23	24	24	25	25	26	27	28	28	29	29 0	1	1	2	2	3	3	4	5	5

♃ 1 ℞ 3 19 30 0 31 / ♓2 1 0 29 ♒29 — ♄ 1 23 31 ℞ / ♈17 18 18 — ♅ 1 9 / ♉16 17 — ♆ 1 18 / ♍18 19 — ♇ 1 / ♋29

	1	2	3	4	5	6	7	8	9	10	11	12	13	14	15	16	17	18	19	20	21	22	23	24	25	26	27	28	29	30	31
8 ☉	9	10	10	11	12	13	14	15	16	17	18	19	20	21	22	23	24	25	26	27	28	29	29 0	1	2	3	4	4	5	6	7
☽	20	3	15	27	9	21	3	15	27	9	21	3	15	28	11	24	7	20	4	18	2	17	2	17	2	16	1	15	28	11	23
☿	6	7	8	9	9	10	11	11	11	12	12	12	12	12	12	12	11	11	10	10	9	9	8	7	6	5	4	3	2	2	1
♀	21	22	23	24	25	26	27	29	29 0	1	2	3	4	5	6	7	8	9	11	12	13	14	15	16	17	18	19	20	21	22	23
♂	6	7	7	8	9	9	10	10	11	12	12	13	14	14	15	15	16	17	17	18	19	19	20	21	21	22	23	23	24	25	25

♃ 1 ℞ 7 15 23 30 / ♒29 28 27 26 25 — ♄ 1 ℞ 7 / ♈18 17 — ♅ 1 24 ℞ / ♉17 17 — ♆ 1 / ♍19 — ♇ 1 3 29 4 / ♋29 0 ♌0

	1	2	3	4	5	6	7	8	9	10	11	12	13	14	15	16	17	18	19	20	21	22	23	24	25	26	27	28	29	30
9 ☉	8	9	10	11	12	13	14	15	16	17	18	19	20	21	22	23	24	25	26	27	28	29	29 0	1	2	3	4	5	6	7
☽	6	18	0	11	23	5	17	0	12	25	8	21	4	17	1	15	29	13	27	12	26	11	25	9	23	6	19	1	14	26
☿	0	0	29	29	29	29	29	29	29	29 0	0	1	2	3	4	5	7	8	10	11	13	14	16	18	20	21	23	25	27	29
♀	24	25	26	27	27	28	29	29 0	1	2	3	4	5	6	7	8	9	10	11	12	13	14	15	15	16	17	18	19	19	20
♂	26	26	27	28	28	29	29 0	1	1	2	3	3	4	5	5	6	7	7	8	9	9	10	10	11	12	12	13	14	14	15

♃ 1 ℞ 8 17 29 / ♒25 24 23 22 — ♄ 1 ℞ 4 20 / ♈17 16 15 — ♅ 1 ℞ / ♉17 — ♆ 1 17 / ♍20 21 — ♇ 1 8 / ♌0 1

	1	2	3	4	5	6	7	8	9	10	11	12	13	14	15	16	17	18	19	20	21	22	23	24	25	26	27	28	29	30	31
10 ☉	8	9	10	11	12	13	14	15	16	17	18	19	20	21	22	23	24	25	26	27	28	29	29 0	1	2	3	4	5	6	7	7
☽	8	19	1	13	26	8	21	3	17	0	14	27	11	25	10	24	8	22	6	20	4	18	1	14	27	9	21	4	15	27	9
☿	0	2	4	6	8	9	11	13	15	16	18	20	22	23	25	27	28	29 0	1	3	5	6	8	9	11	12	14	15	16	17	18 19 20
♀	22	22	23	24	25	25	26	27	27	28	28	29	29 0	0	1	1	2	2	2	3	3	3	4	4	4	4	4	4	4	4	4
♂	15	15	16	17	17	18	19	19	20	21	21	22	22	23	24	24	25	26	26	27	28	28	29	29 0	1	1	2	3	3	3	4

♃ 1 ℞ 19 D / ♒22 22 — ♄ 1 ℞ 3 16 29 / ♈15 14 13 12 — ♅ 1 ℞ 8 / ♉17 16 — ♆ 1 15 / ♍21 22 — ♇ 1 / ♌1

	1	2	3	4	5	6	7	8	9	10	11	12	13	14	15	16	17	18	19	20	21	22	23	24	25	26	27	28	29	30
11 ☉	8	9	10	11	12	13	14	15	16	17	18	19	20	21	22	23	24	25	26	27	28	29 0	1	2	3	4	5	6	7	8
☽	21	23	16	28	11	25	9	23	7	21	6	20	5	19	3	17	0	14	27	10	23	5	17	0	12	23	5	17	19	11
☿	22	23	25	26	28	29 0	1	3	4	5	6	8	9	11	12	13	15	16	17	19	20	22	23	24	25	26	27	28	28	28
♀	4	4	4	4	4	3	3	3	3	2	2	1	1	1	0	0	29	29	28	28	27	26	26	25	25	24	23	23	22	21
♂	4	5	6	6	7	8	8	9	9	10	11	11	12	13	13	14	15	15	16	16	17	18	18	19	20	20	21	22	22	23

♃ 1 7 19 28 / ♒22 23 24 25 — ♄ 1 ℞ 15 / ♈12 11 — ♅ 1 ℞ 3 28 / ♉16 15 14 — ♆ 1 21 / ♍22 23 — ♇ 1 / ♌1

	1	2	3	4	5	6	7	8	9	10	11	12	13	14	15	16	17	18	19	20	21	22	23	24	25	26	27	28	29	30	31
12 ☉	9	10	11	12	13	14	15	16	17	18	19	20	21	22	23	24	25	26	27	28	29	29 0	1	2	3	4	5	6	7	8	9
☽	24	6	19	3	17	1	16	0	15	0	15	29	14	27	11	24	7	19	2	14	26	8	20	2	14	26	7	20	2	14	27
☿	29	29	29	29	29	29	28	28	27	26	25	24	23	22	20	19	18	17	16	15	14	14	13	13	13	13	13	14	15	16	17
♀	21	20	20	20	20	19	19	19	19	19	19	19	19	19	19	19	20	20	20	21	21	21	22	22	23	23	23	24	25	26	27
♂	23	24	25	25	26	26	27	28	28	29	29 0	0	1	2	3	4	4	5	5	6	6	7	8	8	9	10	10	11	11	12	12

♃ 1 5 12 18 24 29 29 30 / ♒25 26 27 28 29 0 ♓0 — ♄ 1 ℞ 15 D / ♈11 11 — ♅ 1 ℞ / ♉14 — ♆ 1 26 ℞ / ♍23 23 — ♇ 1 ℞ / ♌1

1939

	1	2	3	4	5	6	7	8	9	10	11	12	13	14	15	16	17	18	19	20	21	22	23	24	25	26	27	28	29
1 ☉	10	11	12	13	14	15	16	17	18	19	20	21	22	23	24	25	26	28	29	29 0	1	2	3	4	5	6	7	8	9
☽	11	24	9	23	8	24	9	24	9	23	7	21	4	16	29	11	23	5	17	29	11	22	4	16	28	11	23	6	19
☿	17	18	19	20	21	23	24	25	26	27	29	0	1	3	4	6	7	8	10	11	13	14	16	17	19	20	22	23	25
♀	27	28	29	29 0	1	2	3	3	4	5	6	7	8	9	10	11	12	13	14	15	16	16	17	18	19	20	21	22	22
♂	13	13	14	15	15	16	16	17	18	18	19	19	20	21	21	22	22	23	24	24	25	25	26	27	27	28	28	29	29 0

♃ 1 3 8 13 18 22 27 31 / ♓0 1 2 3 4 5 6 7 — ♄ 1 13 28 / ♈11 12 13 — ♅ 1 ℞ 2 22 D / ♉14 13 13 — ♆ 1 ℞ 30 / ♍23 22 — ♇ 1 ℞ / ♌0

	1	2	3	4	5	6	7	8	9	10	11	12	13	14	15	16	17	18	19	20	21	22	23	24	25	26	27	28
2 ☉	12	13	14	15	16	17	18	19	20	21	22	23	24	25	26	27	28	29	29 0	1	2	3	4	5	6	7	8	9
☽	1	16	2	17	2	17	2	16	0	13	25	8	20	2	14	26	7	19	1	13	26	8	20	3	16	29	12	26
☿	29	1	3	4	6	8	9	11	13	14	16	18	20	21	23	25	27	28	29 0	2	4	6	8	9	11	13	15	17
♀	25	26	27	28	29	29 0	1	2	3	4	5	6	7	8	9	10	11	12	13	14	15	16	17	18	20	21	22	23 24
♂	2	2	3	4	4	5	5	6	7	7	8	8	9	10	10	11	11	12	12	13	13	14	14	15	16	16	17	17 18

♃ 1 4 9 13 17 21 26 / ♓7 8 9 10 11 12 13 — ♄ 1 9 19 / ♈13 14 15 — ♅ 1 10 / ♉13 14 — ♆ 1 ℞ / ♍22 — ♇ 1 ℞ / ♌0

	1	2	3	4	5	6	7	8	9	10	11	12	13	14	15	16	17	18	19	20	21	22	23	24	25	26	27	28	29
3 ☉	10	11	12	13	14	15	16	17	18	19	20	21	22	23	24	25	26	27	28	29	29 0	1	2	3	4	5	6	7	8
☽	11	25	10	25	10	25	10	24	8	21	4	16	29	11	22	4	16	28	10	22	5	17	0	13	26	9	23	7	21
☿	19	21	23	25	26	28	29 0	2	3	5	7	8	10	11	12	13	14	15	16	16	17	17	17	17	17	17	17	16	16
♀	25	26	27	29	29 0	1	2	3	4	6	7	8	9	10	11	12	14	15	16	17	18	19	21	22	23	24	25	26	28
♂	18	19	20	20	21	22	22	23	23	24	25	25	26	26	27	27	28	28	29	29 0	0	1	1	2	2	3	3	4	4

♃ 1 2 6 10 14 18 22 27 / ♓13 14 15 16 17 18 19 20 — ♄ 1 10 18 26 / ♈16 17 18 19 — ♅ 1 16 / ♉14 15 — ♆ 1 ℞ 11 / ♍22 21 — ♇ 1 ℞ / ♋29

	1	2	3	4	5	6	7	8	9	10	11	12	13	14	15	16	17	18	19	20	21	22	23	24	25	26	27	28	29
4 ☉	11	12	13	14	15	16	17	18	19	20	21	22	23	24	25	26	27	28	29	29 0	1	2	3	4	5	6	7	8	9
☽	4	19	4	18	2	16	29	12	24	7	19	1	12	24	6	18	1	13	26	9	22	6	20	3	18	2	16	0	14
☿	13	12	11	10	9	9	8	7	7	6	6	6	5	5	5	5	5	6	6	6	7	7	8	8	9	9	10	11	11
♀	1	2	4	5	6	7	8	10	11	12	13	14	15	16	17	18	19	20	21	23	24	25	26	27	29	29 0	1	3	5
♂	6	7	7	8	8	9	9	10	10	11	11	12	12	13	13	14	14	15	15	16	16	17	17	18	18	19	19	20	21

♃ 1 4 8 13 17 22 26 / ♓21 22 23 24 25 26 27 — ♄ 1 3 11 19 27 / ♈19 20 21 22 23 — ♅ 1 6 24 / ♉15 16 17 — ♆ 1 ℞ 20 / ♍21 20 — ♇ 1 ℞ / ♋29

	1	2	3	4	5	6	7	8	9	10	11	12	13	14	15	16	17	18	19	20	21	22	23	24	25	26	27	28	29
5 ☉	10	11	12	13	14	15	16	17	18	19	20	21	22	23	24	25	26	27	28	29	29 0	0	1	2	3	4	5	6	7
☽	13	27	10	24	7	20	2	14	26	8	20	2	14	26	9	21	4	18	1	15	0	14	28	13	27	11	25	9	23
☿	13	14	15	16	18	19	20	21	23	24	25	27	28	0	1	3	4	6	8	9	11	13	15	17	19	21	22	24	27
♀	7	8	9	11	12	13	14	15	17	18	19	20	21	23	24	25	26	28	29	29 0	1	2	3	5	6	7	8	9	11
♂	21	21	22	22	23	23	24	24	25	25	25	26	26	27	27	27	28	28	28	29	29	29	29	29	29 0	0	0	0	1

♃ 1 6 11 29 12 16 22 27 / ♓28 29 0 ♈0 1 2 3 — ♄ 1 5 14 22 / ♈23 24 25 26 — ♅ 1 12 29 / ♉17 18 19 — ♆ 1 ℞ / ♍20 — ♇ 1 12 / ♋29

	1	2	3	4	5	6	7	8	9	10	11	12	13	14	15	16	17	18	19	20	21	22	23	24	25	26	27	28	29
6 ☉	10	11	12	13	14	15	16	17	18	19	20	21	22	23	23	24	25	26	27	28	29	29 0	1	2	3	4	5	6	7
☽	2	15	28	10	22	5	16	28	10	22	4	17	29	13	26	10	24	9	24	8	23	8	22	6	20	3	16	29	12
☿	3	5	7	9	11	14	16	18	20	22	25	27	29	1	3	5	7	9	11	13	15	17	19	20	22	24	25	27	29
♀	14	15	17	18	19	20	21	23	24	25	26	28	29 0	1	2	4	5	6	7	8	10	11	12	13	15	16	17	18	18
♂	2	2	2	2	3	3	3	3	3	3	3	3	4	4	4	4	4	4	4	4	4	4	4	4	4	4	4	4	4

♃ 1 3 9 17 26 / ♈3 4 5 6 7 — ♄ 1 11 22 / ♈27 28 29 — ♅ 1 17 / ♉19 20 — ♆ 1 ℞ 2 D / ♍20 20 — ♇ 1 / ♌0

	1	2	3	4	5	6	7	8	9	10	11	12	13	14	15	16	17	18	19	20	21	22	23	24	25	26	27	28	29
7 ☉	9	10	11	12	13	14	15	16	17	18	19	20	21	22	23	24	25	26	27	28	29	29 0	1	2	3	4	4	5	6
☽	7	19	1	13	25	7	18	0	13	25	8	21	4	18	3	18	3	18	2	16	0	13	26	9	21	3	16	28	10
☿	2	3	5	6	7	9	10	11	12	13	14	15	16	17	17	18	19	20	21	21	22	22	23	24	24	24	24	24	24
♀	21	22	23	24	25	27	28	29	29 0	2	3	4	5	6	8	9	10	11	13	14	15	16	17	19	20	21	22	23	25
♂	4	3	3	3	3	2	2	2	2	2	1	1	1	1	0	0	0	29	29	29	29	29	28	28	28	28	28	28	27

♃ 1 8 30 ℞ / ♈7 8 8 — ♄ 1 5 29 6 27 / ♈29 0 ♉0 1 — ♅ 1 10 / ♉20 21 — ♆ 1 13 / ♍20 21 — ♇ 1 / ♌1

	1	2	3	4	5	6	7	8	9	10	11	12	13	14	15	16	17	18	19	20	21	22	23	24	25	26	27	28	29
8 ☉	8	9	10	11	12	13	14	15	16	17	18	19	20	21	22	23	24	25	26	27	28	28	29	29 0	1	2	3	4	5
☽	22	3	15	27	9	21	4	16	29	13	27	11	26	11	26	12	27	11	26	9	23	6	18	1	13	25	7	19	0
☿	23	22	22	21	20	20	19	18	17	16	16	15	15	14	14	13	12	12	12	12	12	12	12	12	13	13	14	15	16
♀	29	29 0	1	2	3	5	6	7	8	10	11	12	13	15	16	17	18	19	21	22	23	24	26	27	28	29	29 0	1	2
♂	26	26	26	26	26	25	25	25	25	25	25	25	25	24	24	24	24	24	24	24	24	23	23	23	23	23	23	23	24

♃ 1 ℞ 20 / ♈8 7 — ♄ 1 14 ℞ 31 / ♉1 1 0 — ♅ 1 29 ℞ / ♉21 21 — ♆ 1 17 / ♍21 22 — ♇ 1 / ♌1

	1	2	3	4	5	6	7	8	9	10	11	12	13	14	15	16	17	18	19	20	21	22	23	24	25	26	27	28	29
9 ☉	8	9	10	11	12	13	14	15	16	17	18	19	20	21	22	23	24	25	26	27	28	29	29 0	1	2	2	3	4	5
☽	6	18	0	13	26	9	22	6	20	5	20	5	20	5	20	4	18	1	14	27	10	22	4	16	27	9	21	3	15
☿	21	22	24	25	27	29	29 0	2	4	6	8	10	12	13	15	17	19	21	23	25	27	28	29 0	2	4	6	7	9	11
♀	7	8	9	11	12	13	14	15	17	18	19	20	22	23	24	25	27	28	29	29 0	2	3	4	5	7	8	9	10	12
♂	24	24	24	24	25	25	25	25	25	26	26	26	26	26	26	27	27	27	28	28	28	29	29	29 0	0	0	1	1	2

♃ 1 ℞ 10 18 25 / ♈6 5 4 3 — ♄ 1 ℞ 22 0 23 0 / ♉0 0 29 ♈29 — ♅ 1 ℞ / ♉21 — ♆ 1 14 / ♍22 23 — ♇ 1 / ♌2

	1	2	3	4	5	6	7	8	9	10	11	12	13	14	15	16	17	18	19	20	21	22	23	24	25	26	27	28	29
10 ☉	7	8	9	10	11	12	13	14	15	16	17	18	19	20	21	22	23	24	25	26	27	28	29	29 0	1	2	3	4	5
☽	10	23	5	19	2	16	0	14	29	14	28	13	28	12	26	10	23	5	18	0	12	24	6	18	0	12	24	7	19
☿	14	16	17	19	21	22	24	26	27	29	29 0	2	3	5	6	8	9	11	12	14	15	16	18	19	21	22	24	25	26
♀	14	15	16	17	18	19	20	22	23	24	25	27	28	29	29 0	2	3	4	5	7	8	9	10	12	13	14	15	17	18
♂	3	3	4	4	4	5	5	6	6	7	7	8	8	9	9	10	10	11	11	12	12	13	14	14	15	15	16	16	17

♃ 1 ℞ 10 19 24 30 0 31 / ♈3 2 1 0 29 ♓29 — ♄ 1 ℞ 6 19 / ♈29 28 27 — ♅ 1 ℞ 17 / ♉21 20 — ♆ 1 12 / ♍23 24 — ♇ 1 / ♌1

	1	2	3	4	5	6	7	8	9	10	11	12	13	14	15	16	17	18	19	20	21	22	23	24	25	26	27	28	29
11 ☉	8	9	10	11	12	13	14	15	16	17	18	19	20	21	22	23	24	25	26	27	28	29	29 0	1	2	3	4	5	6
☽	29	13	26	10	25	9	23	8	22	6	20	4	17	1	13	26	8	20	2	14	26	8	20	2	15	28	11	25	8
♀	0	1	3	4	5	6	7	8	9	10	11	12	12	13	13	14	14	14	14	13	13	12	12	11	10	9	7	6	5
♀	23	24	25	27	28	29	29 0	1	2	4	5	6	7	8	10	11	12	13	15	16	17	18	20	21	22	23	24	26	27
♂	19	19	20	21	21	22	22	23	23	24	25	25	26	27	27	28	29	29 0	0	1	1	2	2	3	4	4	5	5	6

♃ 1 16 25 D / ♓29 28 28 — ♄ 1 ℞ 14 / ♈26 25 — ♅ 1 ℞ 11 / ♉20 19 — ♆ 1 15 / ♍24 25 — ♇ 1 / ♌1

	1	2	3	4	5	6	7	8	9	10	11	12	13	14	15	16	17	18	19	20	21	22	23	24	25	26	27	28	29
12 ☉	8	9	10	11	12	13	14	16	17	18	19	20	21	22	23	24	25	26	27	28	29	29 0	1	2	3	4	5	6	7
☽	7	21	6	20	4	18	2	15	29	12	26	9	21	4	16	28	10	21	3	15	27	10	22	5	19	3	17	2	16
☿	1	0	29	28	27	27	27	27	27	28	28	29	29 0	0	1	2	3	4	5	7	8	9	10	12	13	14	16	17	19
♀	29	0	1	3	4	5	6	8	9	10	11	13	14	15	16	18	19	20	21	23	24	25	26	28	29	29 0	1	3	4
♂	7	8	8	9	10	10	11	12	12	13	14	14	15	15	16	17	17	18	19	19	20	21	21	22	23	23	24	25	25

♃ 1 3 20 29 21 30 / ♓28 29 0 ♈0 1 — ♄ 1 ℞ 2 28 D / ♈25 24 24 — ♅ 1 ℞ 6 / ♉19 18 — ♆ 1 28 ℞ / ♍25 25 — ♇ 1 / ♌1

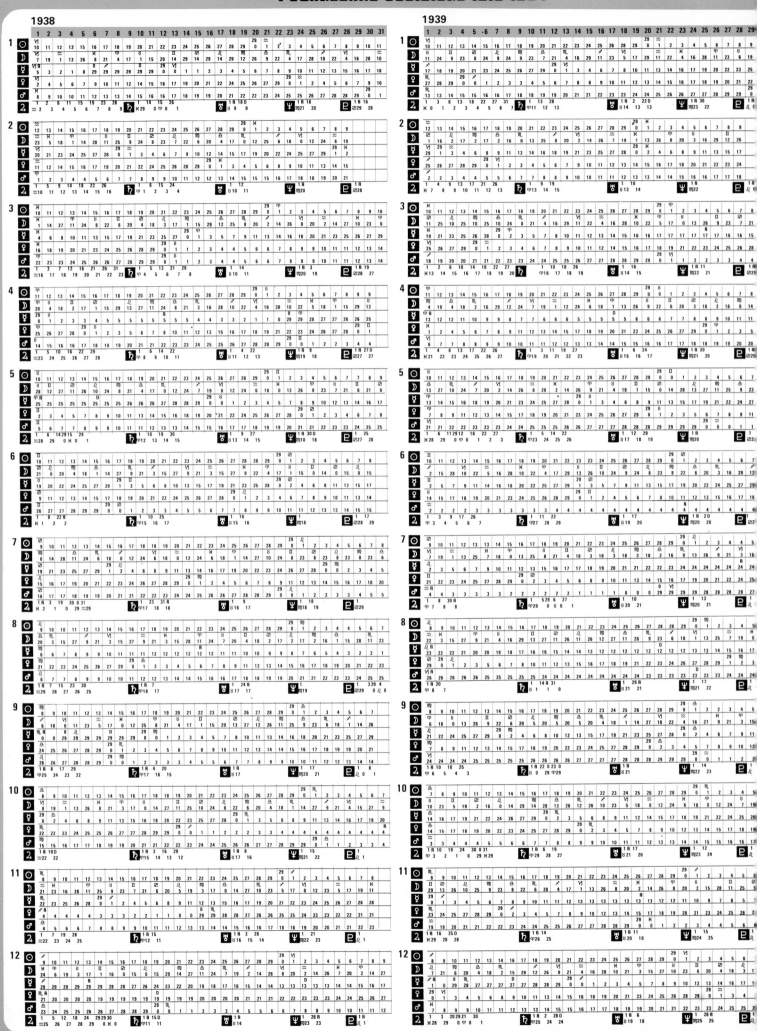

1940

1

1	2	3	4	5	6	7	8	9	10	11	12	13	14	15	16	17	18	19	20	21	22	23	24	25	26	27	28	29	30	31
♑ 10	11	12	13	14	15	16	17	18	19	20	21	22	23	24	25	26	27	28	29	29 0	♒ 1	2	3	4	5	6	7	8	9	10
♎ 1	15	28	♏ 12	25	♐ 9	22	♑ 4	17	29	♒ 12	24	♓ 6	18	29	♈ 11	23	♉ 5	18	♊ 1	14	28	♋ 12	27	♌ 12	27	♍ 12	26	♎ 11	25	♏ 9
♐ 23	24	26	27	28	29 0	♑ 2	3	5	6	8	9	11	12	14	15	17	19	20	22	23	25	27	28	29 0	♒ 2	3	5	7	8	10
♒ 9	10	11	12	14	15	16	17	19	20	21	22	24	25	26	27	29	29 0	♓ 1	2	3	5	6	7	8	10	11	12	13	14	16
♓ 28	29	29 0	♈ 0	1	2	2	3	4	4	5	6	6	7	8	8	9	10	10	11	12	12	13	14	14	15	16	17	17	18	19

1 7 14 20 26 / ♈1 2 3 4 5
♄ 1 22 / ♈24 25
♅ 1 R 20 27 D / ♉18 17 17
♆ 1 R / ♍25
♇ 1 R 13 / ♌2 1

2

1	2	3	4	5	6	7	8	9	10	11	12	13	14	15	16	17	18	19	20	21	22	23	24	25	26	27	28	29	30	31
♒ 11	13	14	15	16	17	18	19	20	21	22	23	24	25	26	27	28	29	29 0	♓ 1	2	3	4	5	6	7	8	9	10		
♏ 22	♐ 6	18	♑ 1	14	26	♒ 8	20	♓ 2	14	26	♈ 8	20	♉ 2	14	26	♊ 9	22	♋ 6	20	♌ 5	20	♍ 5	20	♎ 4	19	♏	19	♐ 2		
♒ 12	14	15	17	19	21	22	24	26	28	29 0	♓ 2	3	5	7	9	11	12	14	16	17	19	20	22	23	24	26	27	28		
♓ 17	18	19	21	22	23	24	25	27	28	29	29 0	♈ 1	3	4	5	6	7	9	10	11	12	13	14	16	17	18	19	20		
♈ 19	20	21	21	22	23	23	24	25	25	26	27	27	28	29	29	29 0	♉ 1	1	2	3	4	4	5	6	6	7	8	8		

1 6 11 16 21 25 / ♈6 7 8 9 10 11
♄ 1 8 20 / ♈25 26 27
♅ 1 / ♉18
♆ 1 R 10 / ♍25 24
♇ 1 R 29 / ♌1 0

3

1	2	3	4	5	6	7	8	9	10	11	12	13	14	15	16	17	18	19	20	21	22	23	24	25	26	27	28	29	30	31
♓ 11	12	13	14	15	16	17	18	19	20	21	22	23	24	25	26	27	28	29	29 0	♈ 1	2	3	4	5	6	7	8	9	10	11
♐ 15	28	♑ 11	23	♒ 5	17	29	♓ 11	23	♈ 5	17	28	♉ 10	23	♊ 5	18	♋ 1	15	28	♌ 13	28	♍ 13	28	♎ 13	28	♏ 13	27	♐ 11	24	♑ 7	20
♓ 28	29	29	29 0	♈ 0	R 0	0	0 29	♓ 29	28	27	27	26	25	24	23	22	21	20	20	19	18	18	17	17	17	16	16	D 16	17	17
♈ 22	23	24	25	26	27	28	29 0	♉ 1	2	3	4	5	7	8	9	10	11	12	13	14	15	17	18	19	20	21	22	23	24	25
♉ 9	10	10	11	12	12	13	14	14	15	16	16	17	18	18	19	20	20	21	22	22	23	24	24	25	26	26	27	28	28	29

1 5 9 14 18 22 26 31 / ♈12 13 14 15 16 17 18 19
♄ 1 2 11 20 29 21 28 / ♈27 28 29 0 ♉ 0 1
♅ 1 15 / ♉18 19
♆ 1 R 19 / ♍24 23
♇ 1 R / ♌0

4

1	2	3	4	5	6	7	8	9	10	11	12	13	14	15	16	17	18	19	20	21	22	23	24	25	26	27	28	29	30	31
♈ 12	13	14	15	16	17	18	18	19	20	21	22	23	24	25	26	27	28	29	29 0	♉ 1	2	3	4	5	6	7	8	9	10	
♒ 2	14	26	♓ 8	20	♈ 2	14	26	♉ 8	20	♊ 2	15	28	♋ 11	24	♌ 8	22	♍ 7	22	♎ 6	21	♏ 6	21	♐ 5	19	♑ 3	16	28	♒ 11	23	
♓ 17	18	18	18	19	20	20	21	22	23	24	25	26	27	28	29	29 0	♈ 1	3	4	5	7	8	10	11	12	14	16	17	19	
♉ 26	27	29	29 0	♊ 1	2	3	4	5	6	7	8	9	10	11	12	13	14	15	16	17	18	19	20	20	21	22	23	24	25	
29 0	♊ 0	1	2	2	3	4	4	5	6	6	7	8	8	9	10	10	11	12	12	13	14	14	15	15	16	17	17	18	19	

1 4 8 12 16 20 24 29 / ♈19 20 21 22 23 24 25 26
♄ 1 5 13 21 29 / ♉1 2 3 4 5
♅ 1 6 25 / ♉19 20 21
♆ 1 R / ♍23
♇ 1 R 13 D / ♌0 0

5

1	2	3	4	5	6	7	8	9	10	11	12	13	14	15	16	17	18	19	20	21	22	23	24	25	26	27	28	29	30	31
♉ 11	12	13	14	15	16	17	18	19	20	21	22	23	24	25	25	26	27	28	29	29 0	♊ 1	2	3	4	5	6	7	8	9	10
♓ 5	17	28	♈ 10	22	♉ 4	17	29	♊ 12	25	♋ 8	21	♌ 5	19	♍ 3	17	♎ 1	16	♏ 0	15	29	♐ 13	27	♑ 11	24	♒ 7	19	♓ 1	13	25	♈ 7
♈ 20	22	24	26	27	29 1	♉ 3	5	7	9	11	13	15	17	19	21	23	25	27	28	29 0	♊ 2	4	6	8	11	13	15	17	19	21
♊ 26	26	27	28	29	29 0	♋ 0	1	2	3	3	4	5	5	6	7	7	8	8	9	9	10	10	11	11	11	12	12	12	12	13
♊ 19	20	21	21	22	23	23	24	25	25	26	27	27	28	28	29	29 0	♋ 0	1	2	2	3	4	4	5	6	6	7	8	8	9

1 3 7 11 16 29 17 20 25 / ♈26 27 28 29 0 ♉ 0 1 2
♄ 1 7 15 23 / ♉5 6 7 8
♅ 1 12 30 / ♉21 22 23
♆ 1 R 2 / ♍23 22
♇ 1 25 / ♌0 1

6

1	2	3	4	5	6	7	8	9	10	11	12	13	14	15	16	17	18	19	20	21	22	23	24	25	26	27	28	29	30	31
♊ 11	12	13	14	15	16	17	18	18	19	20	21	22	23	24	25	26	27	28	29	29 0	♋ 1	2	3	4	5	6	7	8	9	
♈ 18	♉ 0	13	25	♊ 8	21	♋ 4	18	♌ 2	15	29	♍ 14	28	♎ 12	26	♏ 10	24	♐ 8	22	♑ 6	19	♒ 2	14	27	♓ 9	21	♈ 3	14	26	♉ 8	
♊ 23	25	27	29 0	♋ 1	3	5	6	8	10	11	13	14	16	17	19	20	21	22	24	25	26	27	28	29	29 0	♌ 1	1	2	3	
♋ 13	13	13	13	R 13	13	13	13	12	12	12	12	11	11	11	10	10	9	9	8	8	7	6	6	5	5	4	3	3	2	
♋ 9	10	11	11	12	13	13	14	15	15	16	16	17	18	18	19	20	20	21	22	22	23	24	24	25	25	26	27	27	28	

1 3 8 12 18 23 28 / ♉3 4 5 6 7 8 9
♄ 1 9 19 30 / ♉9 10 11 12
♅ 1 17 / ♉23 24
♆ 1 R / ♍22
♇ 1 / ♌1

7

1	2	3	4	5	6	7	8	9	10	11	12	13	14	15	16	17	18	19	20	21	22	23	24	25	26	27	28	29	30	31
♋ 9	10	11	12	13	14	15	16	17	18	19	20	21	22	23	24	25	26	27	28	29	29	29 0	♌ 1	2	3	4	5	6	7	8
♉ 21	♊ 3	16	♋ 0	13	27	♌ 12	26	♍ 10	24	♎ 9	23	♏ 7	21	♐ 4	18	♑ 1	15	28	♒ 10	23	♓ 5	17	29	♈ 11	22	♉ 4	16	29	♊ 11	25
♌ 3	4	4	4	5	5	5	5	R 5	5	4	4	4	3	3	2	2	1	0	0	0 29	♋ 28	27	27	26	26	25	24	24	24	24
♋ R 1	1	0	0	0 29	♊ 29	28	28	28	27	27	27	27	27	26	26	26	26	D 26	26	26	27	27	27	27	28	28	28	29	29	29
♋ 29	29	29 0	♌ 1	1	2	2	3	4	4	5	6	6	7	8	8	9	9	10	11	11	12	13	13	14	15	15	16	16	17	18

1 4 10 17 25 / ♉9 10 11 12 13
♄ 1 12 28 / ♉12 13 14
♅ 1 9 / ♉24 25
♆ 1 5 / ♍22 23
♇ 1 8 / ♌1 2

8

1	2	3	4	5	6	7	8	9	10	11	12	13	14	15	16	17	18	19	20	21	22	23	24	25	26	27	28	29	30	31
♌ 9	10	11	12	13	14	15	16	17	18	19	20	21	22	22	23	24	25	26	27	28	29	29 0	♍ 1	2	3	4	5	6	7	8
♋ 8	22	♌ 6	21	♍ 5	20	♎ 5	19	♏ 4	18	♐ 1	15	28	♑ 11	24	♒ 7	19	♓ 1	13	25	♈ 7	19	♉ 1	13	25	♊ 7	20	♋ 3	16	♌ 0	15
♋ 24	D 24	24	25	25	26	26	27	28	29	29 0	♌ 1	2	3	5	6	8	9	11	13	14	16	18	20	22	24	26	28	29 0	♍ 2	4
29 0	♋ 0	1	1	2	3	3	4	4	5	6	6	7	8	9	9	10	11	12	12	13	14	15	16	17	17	18	19	20	21	22
♌ 18	19	20	20	21	21	22	23	23	24	25	25	26	27	27	28	28	29	29 0	♍ 0	1	2	2	3	4	4	5	5	6	7	7

1 3 14 / ♉13 14 15
♄ 1 28 R / ♉14 14
♅ 1 13 / ♉25 26
♆ 1 13 / ♍23 24
♇ 1 13 / ♌2 3

9

1	2	3	4	5	6	7	8	9	10	11	12	13	14	15	16	17	18	19	20	21	22	23	24	25	26	27	28	29	30	31
♍ 9	10	11	12	13	14	15	16	17	18	19	20	21	21	22	23	24	25	26	27	28	29	29 0	♎ 1	2	3	4	5	6	7	
♌ 29	♍ 14	29	♎ 14	29	♏ 14	28	♐ 12	25	♑ 8	21	♒ 4	16	28	♓ 10	22	♈ 4	16	27	♉ 9	21	♊ 3	16	28	♋ 11	25	♌ 8	23	♍ 7	22	
♍ 6	8	10	12	14	16	17	19	21	23	25	26	28	29 0	♎ 2	3	5	7	8	10	12	13	15	16	18	19	21	23	24	25	
♋ 23	24	25	26	27	28	29	29 0	♌ 1	2	3	4	5	6	7	8	9	10	11	12	13	14	15	16	17	18	19	21	22	23	
♍ 8	9	9	10	11	11	12	12	13	14	14	15	16	16	17	18	18	19	20	20	21	21	22	23	23	24	25	25	26	27	

1 5 R 24 / ♉15 15 14
♄ 1 R 26 / ♉14 13
♅ 1 R 19 / ♉26 25
♆ 1 11 / ♍24 25
♇ 1 26 / ♌3 4

10

1	2	3	4	5	6	7	8	9	10	11	12	13	14	15	16	17	18	19	20	21	22	23	24	25	26	27	28	29	30	31
♎ 8	9	10	11	12	13	14	15	16	17	18	19	20	21	22	23	24	25	26	27	28	29	29 0	♏ 1	2	3	4	5	6	7	8
♎ 8	23	♏ 8	23	♐ 7	21	♑ 5	18	♒ 1	13	25	♓ 7	19	♈ 1	13	24	♉ 6	18	♊ 0	13	25	♋ 8	21	♌ 4	17	♍ 2	16	♎ 1	16	♏ 1	16
♎ 27	28	29 0	♏ 1	3	4	5	7	8	9	11	12	13	14	16	17	18	19	20	21	22	23	24	25	25	26	27	27	28	28	28
♌ 24	25	26	27	28	29 0	♍ 1	2	3	4	5	6	7	9	10	11	12	13	14	15	17	18	19	20	21	22	24	25	26	27	28
♍ 27	28	29	29	29 0	♎ 0	1	2	2	3	4	4	5	6	6	7	8	8	9	9	10	11	11	12	13	13	14	15	15	16	17

1 R 6 15 23 31 / ♉14 13 12 11 10
♄ 1 R 12 26 / ♉13 12 11
♅ 1 R 25 / ♉25 24
♆ 1 8 / ♍25 26
♇ 1 / ♌4

11

1	2	3	4	5	6	7	8	9	10	11	12	13	14	15	16	17	18	19	20	21	22	23	24	25	26	27	28	29	30	31
♏ 9	10	11	12	13	14	15	16	17	18	19	20	21	22	23	24	25	26	27	28	29	29 0	♐ 1	2	3	4	5	6	7	8	
♐ 1	15	♑ 0	13	27	♒ 9	22	♓ 4	16	28	♈ 10	21	♉ 3	15	27	♊ 10	22	♋ 5	18	♌ 1	14	27	♍ 11	25	♎ 10	24	♏ 9	24	♐ 9	23	
♏ R 28	27	27	26	26	25	24	23	22	21	19	18	17	16	14	13	13	12	12	12	D 12	12	12	13	13	14	15	16	17	18	
29 0	♎ 1	2	3	4	6	7	8	9	10	12	13	14	15	16	18	19	20	21	22	24	25	26	27	29	29 0	♏ 1	2	4	5	
♎ 17	18	19	19	20	21	21	22	22	23	24	24	25	26	26	27	28	28	29	29 0	♏ 0	1	2	2	3	4	4	5	6	6	

1 R 7 15 23 / ♉10 9 8 7
♄ 1 R 7 20 / ♉11 10 9
♅ 1 R 19 / ♉24 23
♆ 1 9 / ♍26 27
♇ 1 6 R / ♌4 4

12

1	2	3	4	5	6	7	8	9	10	11	12	13	14	15	16	17	18	19	20	21	22	23	24	25	26	27	28	29	30	31
♐ 9	10	11	12	13	14	15	16	17	18	19	20	21	22	23	24	25	26	27	28	29 0	♑ 1	2	3	4	5	6	7	8	9	10
♑ 8	21	♒ 5	18	♓ 0	12	24	♈ 6	18	♉ 0	12	24	♊ 6	18	♋ 1	14	27	♌ 11	24	♍ 8	22	♎ 6	20	♏ 4	19	♐ 3	17	♑ 2	16	29	♒ 12
♏ 19	20	22	23	24	26	27	28	29 0	♐ 1	3	4	6	7	9	10	12	13	15	16	18	19	21	22	24	25	27	28	29 0	♑ 2	3
♏ 6	7	8	10	11	12	13	15	16	17	18	20	21	22	23	24	26	27	28	29 0	♐ 1	2	3	4	6	7	8	9	11	12	13
♏ 7	8	8	9	10	10	11	12	12	13	14	14	15	16	16	17	18	18	19	20	20	21	22	22	23	24	24	25	26	26	27

1 R 3 17 31 D / ♉7 6 5 5
♄ 1 R 5 29 / ♉9 8 7
♅ 1 R 15 / ♉23 22
♆ 1 30 R / ♍27 27
♇ 1 R 16 / ♌4 3

1941

1

	1	2	3	4	5	6	7	8	9	10	11	12	13	14	15	16	17	18	19	20	21	22	23	24	25	26	27	28	29	30	31
☉	♑ 11	12	13	14	15	16	17	18	19	20	21	22	23	24	25	26	27	28	29	29 0	♒ 1	2	3	4	5	6	7	8	9	10	11
☽	♒ 25	♓ 8	20	♈ 2	14	26	♉ 8	19	♊ 2	14	27	♋ 10	23	♌ 7	21	♍ 5	19	♎ 3	17	♏ 1	15	29	♐ 13	27	♑ 11	24	♒ 7	21	♓ 3	16	28
☿	♑ 5	6	8	9	11	13	14	16	18	19	21	22	24	26	27	29 0	♒ 1	2	4	6	8	9	11	13	15	16	18	20	21	23	25
♀	♐ 14	16	17	18	19	21	22	23	24	26	27	28	29 0	♑ 1	2	3	4	6	7	8	9	11	12	13	14	16	17	18	19	21	22
♂	♏ 28	28	29	29 0	♐ 0	1	2	2	3	4	4	5	6	6	7	8	8	9	10	10	11	12	12	13	14	15	15	16	17	17	18

♃ 1 13 28 / ♉5 6 7
♄ 1 R 9 D 20 / ♉7 7 8
♅ 1 R 30 D / ♉22 22
♆ 1 R / ♍27
♇ 1 R / ♌3

2

	1	2	3	4	5	6	7	8	9	10	11	12	13	14	15	16	17	18	19	20	21	22	23	24	25	26	27	28	29	30	31
☉	♒ 12	13	14	15	16	17	18	19	20	21	22	23	24	25	26	27	28	29	29 0	♓ 1	2	3	4	6	7	8	9	10			
☽	♈ 10	22	♉ 3	15	27	♊ 9	22	♋ 5	18	♌ 1	15	♍ 0	14	29	♎ 13	28	♏ 12	26	♐ 10	24	♑ 7	21	♒ 4	16	29	♓ 12	24	♈ 6			
☿	♒ 27	28	29 0	♓ 1	3	4	6	7	8	9	10	11	12	13	13	13	R 13	13	12	12	11	10	10	9	8	7	5	4			
♀	♑ 23	24	26	27	28	29 0	♒ 1	2	3	4	6	7	8	9	11	12	13	14	16	17	18	19	21	22	23	24	26	27			
♂	♐ 19	19	20	21	21	22	23	23	24	25	25	26	27	27	28	29	29 0	♑ 0	1	2	2	3	4	4	5	6	6	7			

♃ 1 6 14 21 27 / ♉7 8 9 10 11
♄ 1 13 27 / ♉8 9 10
♅ 1 / ♉22
♆ 1 R 19 / ♍27 26
♇ 1 R 2 / ♌3 2

3

	1	2	3	4	5	6	7	8	9	10	11	12	13	14	15	16	17	18	19	20	21	22	23	24	25	26	27	28	29	30	31
☉	♓ 11	12	13	14	15	16	17	18	19	20	21	22	23	24	25	26	27	27	28	29	29 0	♈ 1	2	3	4	5	6	7	8	9	10
☽	♈ 18	♉ 0	11	23	♊ 5	17	♋ 0	13	26	♌ 9	23	♍ 8	22	♎ 7	22	♏ 7	22	♐ 6	20	♑ 4	18	♒ 1	13	26	♓ 8	20	♈ 2	14	26	♉ 8	20
☿	♓ R 4	3	2	1	0	0	0 29	♒ 29	29	28	28	D 28	29	29	29	29 0	♓ 0	1	2	2	3	4	5	6	7	8	9	10	11	12	13
♀	♒ 28	29 0	♓ 1	2	3	4	6	7	8	9	11	12	13	14	16	17	18	19	20	22	23	24	26	27	28	29	29 0	♈ 1	2	3	4
♂	♑ 8	8	9	10	11	11	12	13	13	14	15	15	16	17	17	18	19	19	20	21	22	22	23	24	24	25	26	26	27	28	28

♃ 1 5 10 16 21 26 30 / ♉11 12 13 14 15 16 17
♄ 1 10 20 29 / ♉10 11 12 13
♅ 1 15 / ♉22 23
♆ 1 R 28 / ♍26 25
♇ 1 R / ♌2

4

	1	2	3	4	5	6	7	8	9	10	11	12	13	14	15	16	17	18	19	20	21	22	23	24	25	26	27	28	29	30	31
☉	♈ 11	12	13	14	15	16	17	18	19	20	21	22	23	24	25	26	27	28	29	29 0	♉ 1	2	3	4	5	6	7	8	9	10	
☽	♊ 2	14	26	♋ 8	21	♌ 4	17	♍ 1	16	♎ 1	16	♏ 1	16	♐ 1	16	♑ 0	14	27	♒ 10	23	♓ 5	18	♈ 0	11	23	♉ 5	17	29	♊ 11	23	
☿	♓ 14	16	17	18	20	21	23	24	26	27	29	29 0	♈ 2	3	5	7	8	10	12	14	15	17	19	21	23	25	27	29 0	♉ 1	3	
♀	♈ 7	8	9	10	12	13	14	15	17	18	19	20	22	23	24	25	26	28	29	29 0	♉ 1	3	4	5	6	8	9	10	11	13	
♂	♑ 29	29 0	♒ 1	1	2	3	3	4	5	5	6	7	7	8	9	10	10	11	12	12	13	14	14	15	16	16	17	18	18	19	

♃ 1 4 9 13 17 22 26 / ♉17 18 19 20 21 22 23
♄ 1 6 15 23 30 / ♉13 14 15 16 17
♅ 1 7 26 / ♉23 24 25
♆ 1 R / ♍25
♇ 1 R 21 D / ♌2 2

5

	1	2	3	4	5	6	7	8	9	10	11	12	13	14	15	16	17	18	19	20	21	22	23	24	25	26	27	28	29	30	31
☉	♉ 11	12	13	14	15	16	17	17	18	19	20	21	22	23	24	25	26	27	28	29	29 0	♊ 1	2	3	4	5	6	7	8	9	10
☽	♋ 5	17	♌ 0	13	26	♍ 10	24	♎ 9	24	♏ 9	24	♐ 9	24	♑ 9	23	♒ 6	19	♓ 2	14	27	♈ 8	20	♉ 2	14	26	♊ 8	20	♋ 2	14	27	♌ 10
☿	♉ 5	7	9	11	14	16	18	20	22	24	27	29	29 1	♊ 3	5	7	9	11	13	15	17	18	20	22	23	25	27	28	29 0	♋ 1	2
♀	♉ 14	15	16	17	19	20	21	22	24	25	26	27	29	29 0	♊ 1	2	3	5	6	7	8	10	11	12	13	15	16	17	18	19	21
♂	♒ 20	21	21	22	23	23	24	25	25	26	27	27	28	29	29	29 0	♓ 1	1	2	3	3	4	5	5	6	7	7	8	9	9	10

♃ 1 5 9 13 17 22 26 29 27 / ♉24 25 26 27 28 29 0 ♊ 0
♄ 1 8 16 24 / ♉17 18 19 20
♅ 1 14 31 / ♉25 26 27
♆ 1 R 18 / ♍25 24
♇ 1 R / ♌2

6

	1	2	3	4	5	6	7	8	9	10	11	12	13	14	15	16	17	18	19	20	21	22	23	24	25	26	27	28	29	30	31
☉	♊ 11	12	13	13	14	15	16	17	18	19	20	21	22	23	24	25	26	27	28	29	29 0	♋ 1	2	3	3	4	5	6	7	8	
☽	♌ 23	♍ 6	20	♎ 4	18	♏ 3	18	♐ 3	18	♑ 3	17	♒ 1	15	28	♓ 11	23	♈ 5	17	29	♉ 11	22	♊ 4	17	29	♋ 11	24	♌ 7	20	♍ 3	17	
☿	♋ 3	5	6	7	8	9	10	11	12	12	13	14	14	14	15	15	15	15	15	R 15	15	15	15	14	14	13	13	12	12	11	
♀	♊ 22	23	24	26	27	28	29	29 1	♋ 2	3	4	5	7	8	9	10	11	13	14	15	16	18	19	20	21	22	24	25	26	27	
♂	♓ 11	11	12	13	13	14	15	15	16	17	17	18	18	19	20	20	21	22	22	23	23	24	25	25	26	26	27	28	28	29	

♃ 1 3 8 12 17 21 25 30 / ♊1 2 3 4 5 6 7 8
♄ 1 9 18 27 / ♉21 22 23 24
♅ 1 18 / ♉27 28
♆ 1 D 23 / ♍24 25
♇ 1 23 / ♌2 3

7

	1	2	3	4	5	6	7	8	9	10	11	12	13	14	15	16	17	18	19	20	21	22	23	24	25	26	27	28	29	30	31
☉	♋ 9	10	11	12	13	14	15	16	17	18	19	20	21	22	23	24	24	25	26	27	28	29	29 0	♌ 1	2	3	4	5	6	7	8
☽	♎ 0	14	28	♏ 13	27	♐ 12	27	♑ 11	25	♒ 9	23	♓ 6	19	♈ 1	13	25	♉ 7	19	♊ 1	13	25	♋ 8	20	♌ 3	16	♍ 0	13	27	♎ 11	25	♏ 9
☿	♋ R 11	10	9	9	8	8	7	6	6	6	6	6	6	D 6	6	6	6	7	7	8	9	9	10	11	12	13	14	16	17	18	20
♀	♋ 29	29 0	♌ 1	2	3	5	6	7	8	10	11	12	13	14	16	17	18	19	21	22	23	24	25	27	28	29	29 0	♍ 1	3	4	5
♂	♓ 29	29 0	♈ 1	1	2	2	3	3	4	5	5	6	6	7	7	8	8	9	9	10	10	11	11	12	12	13	13	14	14	14	15

♃ 1 5 9 14 19 24 30 / ♊8 9 10 11 12 13 14
♄ 1 6 17 30 / ♉24 25 26 27
♅ 1 9 / ♉28 29
♆ 1 / ♍25
♇ 1 30 / ♌3 4

8

	1	2	3	4	5	6	7	8	9	10	11	12	13	14	15	16	17	18	19	20	21	22	23	24	25	26	27	28	29	30	31
☉	♌ 9	10	11	12	13	14	15	16	16	17	18	19	20	21	22	23	24	25	26	27	28	29	29 0	♍ 1	2	3	4	5	6	7	8
☽	♏ 23	♐ 8	22	♑ 6	20	♒ 4	18	♓ 1	14	27	♈ 9	21	♉ 3	15	27	♊ 9	21	♋ 3	16	29	♌ 12	25	♍ 9	23	♎ 7	22	♏ 6	20	♐ 4	19	♑ 3
☿	♋ 22	23	25	27	28	29 0	♌ 2	4	6	8	10	12	14	16	18	20	22	24	26	28	29 0	♍ 2	4	6	8	10	12	14	15	17	19
♀	♍ 6	8	9	10	11	12	14	15	16	17	18	20	21	22	23	24	26	27	28	29	29 0	♎ 2	3	4	5	6	8	9	10	11	12
♂	♈ 15	16	16	16	17	17	18	18	18	18	19	19	19	20	20	20	21	21	21	21	22	22	22	22	22	22	23	23	23	23	23

♃ 1 4 10 17 23 31 / ♊14 15 16 17 18 19
♄ 1 16 / ♉27 28
♅ 1 7 29 8 / ♉29 0 ♊ 0
♆ 1 10 / ♍25 26
♇ 1 / ♌4

9

	1	2	3	4	5	6	7	8	9	10	11	12	13	14	15	16	17	18	19	20	21	22	23	24	25	26	27	28	29	30	31
☉	♍ 9	10	11	12	13	13	14	15	16	17	18	19	20	21	22	23	24	25	26	27	28	29	29 0	♎ 1	2	3	4	5	6	7	
☽	♑ 16	♒ 0	13	27	♓ 10	22	♈ 5	17	29	♉ 11	23	♊ 5	17	29	♋ 11	24	♌ 7	20	♍ 4	18	♎ 2	17	♏ 1	16	♐ 1	15	29	♑ 13	27	♒ 10	
☿	♍ 21	22	24	26	27	29	29 1	♎ 2	4	5	7	8	10	11	13	14	16	17	19	20	21	23	24	25	26	28	29	29 0	♏ 1	2	
♀	♎ 14	15	16	17	18	20	21	22	23	24	26	27	28	29	29 0	♏ 1	3	4	5	6	7	9	10	11	12	13	14	16	17	18	
♂	♈ 23	23	23	23	23	23	R 23	23	23	23	23	23	23	23	23	22	22	22	22	22	22	21	21	21	21	20	20	20	20	19	

♃ 1 10 23 / ♊19 20 21
♄ 1 12 R / ♉28 28
♅ 1 6 R / ♊0 0
♆ 1 8 / ♍26 27
♇ 1 5 / ♌4 5

10

	1	2	3	4	5	6	7	8	9	10	11	12	13	14	15	16	17	18	19	20	21	22	23	24	25	26	27	28	29	30	31
☉	♎ 8	9	10	11	12	13	14	15	16	17	18	19	20	21	22	23	24	25	26	27	28	29	29 0	♏ 1	2	3	4	5	6	7	8
☽	♒ 23	♓ 6	19	♈ 1	13	25	♉ 7	19	♊ 1	13	25	♋ 7	19	♌ 2	15	28	♍ 12	26	♎ 10	25	♏ 10	25	♐ 10	25	♑ 10	24	♒ 7	20	♓ 3	16	28
☿	♏ 3	4	5	6	7	8	9	9	10	11	11	12	12	12	R 12	12	11	11	10	10	9	8	7	5	4	3	2	0	0 29	♎ 28	27
♀	♏ 19	20	21	23	24	25	26	27	28	29 0	♐ 1	2	3	4	5	6	8	9	10	11	12	13	14	15	17	18	19	20	21	22	23
♂	♈ R 19	19	18	18	18	17	17	17	16	16	16	16	15	15	15	14	14	14	14	13	13	13	13	12	12	12	12	12	11	11	11

♃ 1 10 R 26 / ♊21 21 20
♄ 1 R 5 23 / ♉28 27 26
♅ 1 R 4 0 5 / ♊0 29 ♉29
♆ 1 5 / ♍27 28
♇ 1 / ♌5

11

	1	2	3	4	5	6	7	8	9	10	11	12	13	14	15	16	17	18	19	20	21	22	23	24	25	26	27	28	29	30	31
☉	♏ 9	10	11	12	13	14	15	16	17	18	19	20	21	22	23	24	25	26	27	28	29	29 0	♐ 1	2	3	4	5	6	7	8	
☽	♈ 10	22	♉ 4	16	28	♊ 10	22	♋ 4	16	28	♌ 10	23	♍ 6	20	♎ 4	18	♏ 3	18	♐ 4	19	♑ 4	19	♒ 3	17	♓ 0	13	25	♈ 7	19	♉ 1	
☿	♎ R 27	26	26	26	D 26	26	27	27	28	29	29 0	♏ 1	2	3	4	5	7	8	9	11	12	14	15	17	18	20	21	23	24	26	
♀	♐ 24	26	27	28	29	29 0	♑ 1	2	3	4	5	6	7	9	10	11	12	13	14	15	16	17	18	19	20	21	22	23	24	25	
♂	♈ R 11	11	11	11	11	11	11	11	11	D 11	11	11	11	11	11	11	11	11	11	11	11	12	12	12	12	12	13	13	13	13	

♃ 1 R 8 18 26 / ♊20 19 18 17
♄ 1 R 6 18 30 / ♉26 25 24 23
♅ 1 R 4 28 / ♉29 28 27
♆ 1 5 / ♍28 29
♇ 1 7 R / ♌5 5

12

	1	2	3	4	5	6	7	8	9	10	11	12	13	14	15	16	17	18	19	20	21	22	23	24	25	26	27	28	29	30	31
☉	♐ 9	10	11	12	13	14	15	16	17	18	19	20	21	22	23	24	25	26	27	28	29	29 0	♑ 1	2	3	4	5	6	7	8	9
☽	♉ 13	25	♊ 7	19	♋ 1	13	25	♌ 7	20	♍ 2	15	29	♎ 13	27	♏ 12	27	♐ 12	27	♑ 12	27	♒ 11	25	♓ 8	21	♈ 4	16	28	♉ 10	22	♊ 4	15
☿	♏ 28	29	29 1	♐ 2	4	5	7	8	10	12	13	15	16	18	19	21	22	24	26	27	29	29 0	♑ 2	4	5	7	8	10	12	13	15
♀	♑ 26	27	28	29	29 0	♒ 0	1	2	3	4	5	6	6	7	8	9	10	10	11	12	12	13	14	14	15	16	16	17	17	18	18
♂	♈ 13	14	14	14	15	15	15	15	16	16	16	17	17	17	18	18	19	19	19	20	20	20	21	21	22	22	23	23	23	24	24

♃ 1 R 4 11 18 26 / ♊17 16 15 14 13
♄ 1 R 14 / ♉23 22
♅ 1 R 25 / ♉27 26
♆ 1 / ♍29
♇ 1 R / ♌5

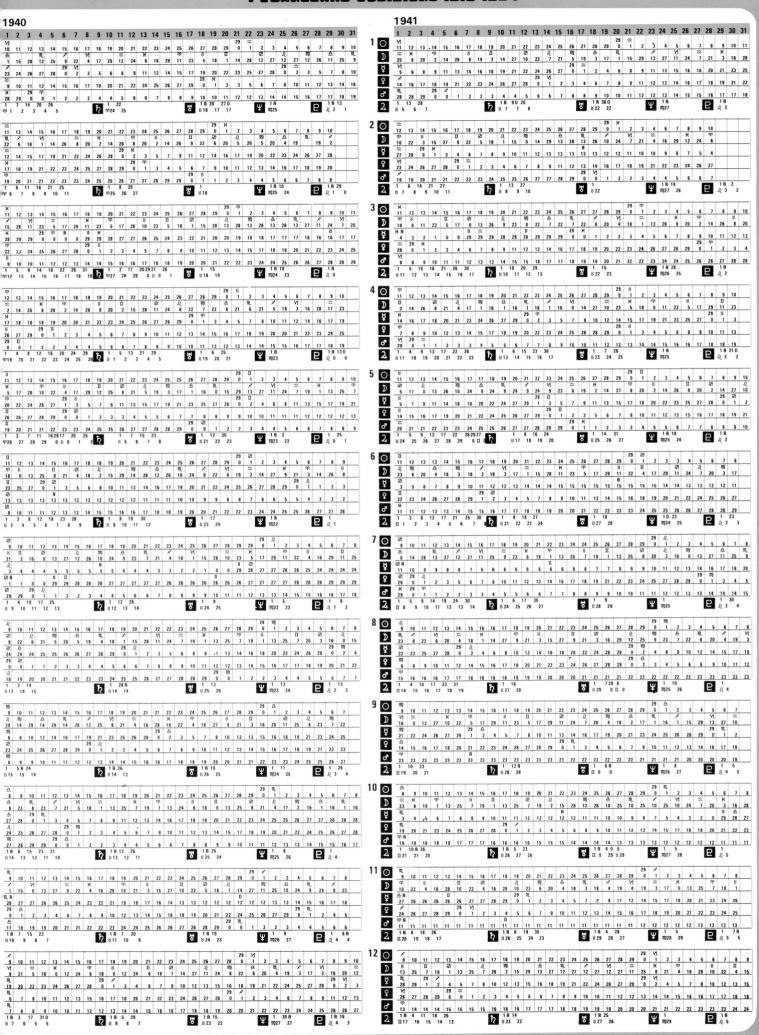

1942

1

	1	2	3	4	5	6	7	8	9	10	11	12	13	14	15	16	17	18	19	20	21	22	23	24	25	26	27	28	29	30	31
☉	♑ 10	11	13	14	15	16	17	18	19	20	21	22	23	24	25	26	27	28	29	29/0	♒ 1	2	3	4	5	6	7	8	9	10	11
☽	♊ 27	♋ 10	22	♌ 4	17	29	♍ 12	26	♎ 9	23	♏ 7	21	♐ 6	20	♑ 5	20	♒ 5	19	♓ 3	16	29	♈ 12	24	♉ 6	18	♊ 0	12	24	♋ 6	18	♌ 1
☿	♑ 17	18	20	21	23	25	26	28	29/0	♒ 1	3	5	6	8	9	11	13	14	16	17	18	20	21	22	23	24	25	26	26	27	27
♀	♒ 18	19	19	19	20	20	20	20	20	21	21	21	℞ 21	21	21	20	20	20	20	19	19	19	18	18	17	17	16	16	15	14	14
♂	♈ 25	25	26	26	27	27	28	28	29	29	29/0	♉ 0	1	1	2	2	3	3	4	4	5	5	6	6	7	7	8	8	9	9	10

♃ 1℞ 5 17 / ♊13 12 11 · ♄ 1℞ 3 23D / ♉22 21 21 · ♅ 1℞ / ♉26 · ♆ 1℞ / ♍29 · ♇ 1℞ 9 / ♌5 4

2

	1	2	3	4	5	6	7	8	9	10	11	12	13	14	15	16	17	18	19	20	21	22	23	24	25	26	27	28
☉	♒ 12	13	14	15	16	17	18	19	20	21	22	23	24	25	26	27	28	29	29/0	♓ 1	2	3	4	5	6	7	8	9
☽	♌ 13	26	♍ 9	22	♎ 6	20	♏ 3	17	♐ 2	16	♑ 0	15	29	♒ 13	27	♓ 11	24	♈ 7	20	♉ 2	14	26	♊ 8	20	♋ 2	14	26	♌ 9
☿	♒℞ 26	26	26	25	24	23	22	21	20	19	18	17	16	15	14	13	12	12	11	11	11	11	D 11	11	12	12	13	13
♀	♒℞ 13	13	12	11	11	10	10	9	9	8	8	7	7	6	6	6	6	5	5	5	5	5	D 5	5	5	5	5	6
♂	♉ 10	11	12	12	13	13	14	14	15	16	16	17	17	18	18	19	20	20	21	21	22	22	23	24	24	25	25	26

♃ 1℞ 5D 24 / ♊11 11 12 · ♄ 1 11 / ♉21 22 · ♅ 1℞ 4D / ♉26 26 · ♆ 1℞ / ♍29 · ♇ 1℞ 25 / ♌4 3

3

	1	2	3	4	5	6	7	8	9	10	11	12	13	14	15	16	17	18	19	20	21	22	23	24	25	26	27	28	29	30	31
☉	♓ 10	11	12	13	14	15	16	17	18	19	20	21	22	23	24	25	26	27	28	29	29/0	♈ 1	2	3	4	5	6	7	8	9	10
☽	♌ 22	♍ 5	18	♎ 2	16	♏ 0	14	28	♐ 13	27	♑ 11	25	♒ 9	22	♓ 6	19	♈ 2	15	27	♉ 10	22	♊ 4	16	28	♋ 10	22	♌ 4	17	29	♍ 13	27
☿	♒ 14	15	15	16	17	18	19	20	21	22	23	24	25	27	28	29/0	♓ 1	2	3	4	6	7	9	10	12	13	15	17	18	20	22
♀	♒ 6	6	6	7	7	8	8	8	9	9	10	11	11	12	12	13	14	14	15	16	16	17	18	19	19	20	21	22	23	24	24
♂	♉ 26	27	28	28	29	29	29/0	♊ 0	1	2	2	3	3	4	5	5	6	6	7	8	8	9	9	10	11	11	12	12	13	14	14

♃ 1 8 17 25 / ♊12 13 14 15 · ♄ 1 3 15 26 / ♉22 23 24 25 · ♅ 1 14 / ♉26 27 · ♆ 1℞ / ♍28 · ♇ 1℞ / ♌3

4

	1	2	3	4	5	6	7	8	9	10	11	12	13	14	15	16	17	18	19	20	21	22	23	24	25	26	27	28	29	30
☉	♈ 11	12	13	14	15	16	17	18	19	20	21	22	23	24	25	26	27	28	29	29/0	♉ 1	2	3	4	5	6	7	8	9	10
☽	♎ 11	25	♏ 10	24	♐ 9	23	♑ 8	22	♒ 6	19	♓ 2	15	28	♈ 11	23	♉ 6	18	♊ 0	12	24	♋ 6	18	♌ 0	12	25	♍ 7	21	♎ 5	19	♏ 4
☿	♓ 23	25	27	28	29/0	♈ 2	4	6	8	9	11	13	15	17	19	21	23	26	28	29/0	♉ 2	4	6	8	10	12	15	17	19	21
♀	♒ 25	26	27	28	29	29/0	♓ 1	2	3	4	5	6	7	8	9	10	11	12	13	14	15	16	17	18	19	20	21	22	23	24
♂	♊ 15	15	16	17	17	18	18	19	20	20	21	21	22	23	23	24	25	25	26	26	27	28	28	29	29	29/0	♋ 1	1	2	2

♃ 1 7 13 19 24 29 / ♊16 17 18 19 20 21 · ♄ 1 5 14 22 30 / ♉25 26 27 28 29 · ♅ 1 8 27 / ♉27 28 29 · ♆ 1℞ 7 / ♍28 27 · ♇ 1℞ 16D / ♌3 3

5

	1	2	3	4	5	6	7	8	9	10	11	12	13	14	15	16	17	18	19	20	21	22	23	24	25	26	27	28	29	30	31
☉	♉ 10	11	12	13	14	15	16	17	18	19	20	21	22	23	24	25	26	27	28	29	29/0	♊ 1	2	3	4	5	6	6	7	8	9
☽	♏ 18	♐ 4	19	♑ 3	18	♒ 2	16	29	♓ 12	25	♈ 8	20	♉ 2	15	27	♊ 9	21	♋ 2	14	26	♌ 8	20	♍ 3	16	29	♎ 13	27	♏ 12	27	♐ 12	27
☿	♉ 23	25	27	29	29/0	♊ 2	4	6	7	9	10	12	13	14	16	17	18	19	20	21	21	22	23	23	24	24	25	25	25	25	25
♀	♓ 25	26	27	28	29	29/0	♈ 1	2	4	5	6	7	8	9	10	11	12	13	15	16	17	18	19	20	21	22	24	25	26	27	28
♂	♋ 3	4	4	5	5	6	7	7	8	9	9	10	10	11	12	12	13	13	14	15	15	16	17	17	18	18	19	20	20	21	21

♃ 1 4 9 14 18 23 28 / ♊21 22 23 24 25 26 27 · ♄ 1 8 29 9 16 24 31 / ♉29 0 ♊ 0 1 2 3 · ♅ 1 15 29 16 / ♉29 0 ♊ 0 · ♆ 1℞ / ♍27 · ♇ 1 / ♌3

6

	1	2	3	4	5	6	7	8	9	10	11	12	13	14	15	16	17	18	19	20	21	22	23	24	25	26	27	28	29	30
☉	♊ 10	11	12	13	14	15	16	17	18	19	20	21	22	23	24	25	26	27	28	28	29	29/0	♋ 1	2	3	4	5	6	7	8
☽	♑ 13	27	♒ 12	26	♓ 9	22	♈ 5	17	♉ 0	12	24	♊ 6	18	♋ 0	11	23	♌ 5	17	♍ 0	12	25	♎ 8	22	♏ 6	20	♐ 5	21	♑ 6	21	♒ 6
☿	♊℞ 25	25	25	24	24	24	23	23	22	22	21	21	20	20	19	19	18	18	17	17	17	17	17	17	D 17	17	17	17	18	18
♀	♈ 29	29/0	♉ 2	3	4	5	6	7	8	10	11	12	13	14	15	17	18	19	20	21	22	23	25	26	27	28	29/0	♊ 1	2	3
♂	♋ 22	23	23	24	25	25	26	26	27	28	28	29	29	29/0	♌ 1	1	2	2	3	4	4	5	6	6	7	7	8	9	9	10

♃ 1 5 10 29 11 14 19 23 27 / ♊28 29 0 ♋ 0 1 2 3 4 · ♄ 1 8 16 24 / ♊3 4 5 6 · ♅ 1 18 / ♊1 2 · ♆ 1℞ 8D / ♍27 27 · ♇ 1 7 / ♌3 4

7

	1	2	3	4	5	6	7	8	9	10	11	12	13	14	15	16	17	18	19	20	21	22	23	24	25	26	27	28	29	30	31
☉	♋ 9	10	11	12	13	14	15	16	17	18	19	19	20	21	22	23	24	25	26	27	28	29	29/0	♌ 1	2	3	4	5	6	7	8
☽	♒ 21	♓ 5	18	♈ 1	14	27	♉ 9	21	♊ 3	15	26	♋ 8	20	♌ 2	14	27	♍ 9	22	♎ 5	18	♏ 2	16	♐ 0	15	29	♑ 14	29	♒ 14	29	♓ 13	27
☿	♊ 19	19	20	21	22	22	23	24	26	27	28	29/0	♋ 1	2	4	5	7	9	11	12	14	16	18	20	22	24	26	28	29/1	♌ 3	5
♀	♊ 4	5	6	8	9	10	11	12	13	15	16	17	18	19	21	22	23	24	25	27	28	29	29/0	♋ 1	3	4	5	6	7	9	10
♂	♌ 11	11	12	12	13	14	14	15	16	16	17	17	18	19	19	20	21	21	22	22	23	24	24	25	26	26	27	27	28	29	29

♃ 1 2 6 11 15 20 24 29 / ♋4 5 6 7 8 9 10 11 · ♄ 1 3 12 21 / ♊6 7 8 9 · ♅ 1 8 / ♊2 3 · ♆ 1 / ♍27 · ♇ 1 7 / ♌4 5

8

	1	2	3	4	5	6	7	8	9	10	11	12	13	14	15	16	17	18	19	20	21	22	23	24	25	26	27	28	29	30	31
☉	♌ 9	10	10	11	12	13	14	15	16	17	18	19	20	21	22	23	24	25	26	27	28	29	29/0	♍ 1	2	3	4	5	5	6	7
☽	♈ 10	23	♉ 5	17	29	♊ 11	23	♋ 5	17	29	♌ 11	24	♍ 6	19	♎ 2	15	28	♏ 12	26	♐ 10	25	♑ 9	24	♒ 8	23	♓ 7	21	♈ 5	18	♉ 1	13
☿	♌ 7	9	11	13	15	17	19	21	23	25	27	29	29/1	♍ 3	4	6	8	10	11	13	15	16	18	20	21	23	24	26	27	29	29/0
♀	♋ 11	12	13	15	16	17	18	19	21	22	23	24	25	27	28	29	29/0	♌ 2	3	4	5	6	8	9	10	11	13	14	15	16	17
♂	29/0	♍ 1	1	2	2	3	4	4	5	6	6	7	8	8	9	9	10	11	11	12	13	13	14	14	15	16	16	17	18	18	19

♃ 1 2 7 12 17 22 27 / ♋11 12 13 14 15 16 17 · ♄ 1 14 / ♊10 11 · ♅ 1 3 / ♊3 4 · ♆ 1 6 / ♍27 28 · ♇ 1 21 / ♌5 6

9

	1	2	3	4	5	6	7	8	9	10	11	12	13	14	15	16	17	18	19	20	21	22	23	24	25	26	27	28	29	30
☉	♍ 8	9	10	11	12	13	14	15	16	17	18	19	20	21	22	23	24	25	26	27	28	29	29/0	♎ 1	2	3	4	5	6	7
☽	♉ 25	♊ 8	19	♋ 1	13	25	♌ 7	20	♍ 2	15	28	♎ 11	25	♏ 9	23	♐ 7	21	♑ 5	20	♒ 4	18	♓ 2	16	29	♈ 13	26	♉ 9	21	♊ 3	15
☿	♎ 1	3	4	6	7	8	9	11	12	13	14	15	16	17	18	19	20	21	22	23	23	24	24	25	25	26	26	℞ 26	25	25
♀	♌ 19	20	21	22	24	25	26	27	28	29/0	♍ 1	2	3	5	6	7	8	10	11	12	13	15	16	17	18	20	21	22	23	25
♂	♍ 20	20	21	22	22	23	23	24	25	25	26	27	27	28	29	29	29/0	♎ 1	1	2	2	3	4	4	5	6	6	7	8	8

♃ 1 2 7 13 20 27 / ♋17 18 19 20 21 22 · ♄ 1 25℞ / ♊12 12 · ♅ 1 10℞ / ♊4 4 · ♆ 1 6 / ♍28 29 · ♇ 1 / ♌6

10

	1	2	3	4	5	6	7	8	9	10	11	12	13	14	15	16	17	18	19	20	21	22	23	24	25	26	27	28	29	30	31
☉	♎ 8	9	10	11	12	13	14	15	16	17	18	19	20	21	22	22	23	24	25	26	27	28	29/0	♏ 0	1	2	3	4	5	6	7
☽	♊ 27	♋ 9	21	♌ 3	15	28	♍ 10	23	♎ 7	21	♏ 5	19	♐ 3	18	♑ 2	16	♒ 0	14	28	♓ 12	25	♈ 8	21	♉ 4	17	29	♊ 11	23	♋ 5	17	29
☿	♎℞ 25	24	24	23	22	21	20	19	18	17	16	14	13	12	12	11	11	10	D 10	10	10	11	12	12	13	14	15	16	17	19	20
♀	♍ 26	27	28	29	29/1	♎ 2	3	4	6	7	8	9	11	12	13	14	16	17	18	19	21	22	23	24	26	27	28	29/0	♏ 1	2	3
♂	♎ 9	10	10	11	12	12	13	14	14	15	16	16	17	18	18	19	20	20	21	22	22	23	24	24	25	26	26	27	28	28	29

♃ 1 5 15 31 / ♋22 23 24 25 · ♄ 1℞ 19 / ♊12 11 · ♅ 1℞ 18 / ♊4 3 · ♆ 1 3 29 4 31 / ♍29 0 ♎ 0 1 · ♇ 1 6 / ♌6 7

11

	1	2	3	4	5	6	7	8	9	10	11	12	13	14	15	16	17	18	19	20	21	22	23	24	25	26	27	28	29	30
☉	♏ 8	9	10	11	12	13	14	15	16	17	18	19	20	21	22	24	25	26	27	28	29	29/0	♐ 1	2	3	4	5	6	7	8
☽	♌ 11	23	♍ 5	18	♎ 1	15	29	♏ 13	28	♐ 13	28	♑ 13	27	♒ 11	25	♓ 9	22	♈ 5	18	♉ 1	13	25	♊ 8	20	♋ 2	14	25	♌ 7	19	♍ 1
☿	♎ 21	23	24	26	27	29	29/1	♏ 2	4	5	7	9	10	12	13	15	17	18	20	21	23	25	26	28	29/0	♐ 1	2	4	6	7
♀	♏ 5	6	7	8	10	11	12	13	15	16	17	18	20	21	22	23	25	26	27	28	29/0	♐ 1	2	3	5	6	7	8	10	11
♂	29/0	♏ 0	1	2	2	3	4	4	5	6	6	7	8	8	9	10	10	11	12	12	13	14	14	15	16	17	17	18	19	19

♃ 1 13℞ 24 / ♋25 25 24 · ♄ 1℞ 6 19 / ♊11 10 9 · ♅ 1℞ 14 / ♊3 2 · ♆ 1 / ♎1 · ♇ 1 8℞ / ♌7 7

12

	1	2	3	4	5	6	7	8	9	10	11	12	13	14	15	16	17	18	19	20	21	22	23	24	25	26	27	28	29	30	31
☉	♐ 9	10	11	12	13	14	15	16	17	18	19	20	21	22	23	24	25	26	27	28	29	29/0	♑ 1	2	3	4	5	6	7	8	9
☽	♍ 13	26	♎ 9	23	♏ 7	21	♐ 6	22	♑ 7	22	♒ 7	21	♓ 5	19	♈ 2	15	28	♉ 10	22	♊ 4	17	28	♋ 10	22	♌ 4	16	28	♍ 10	22	♎ 5	18
☿	♐ 9	10	12	13	15	17	18	20	21	23	24	26	28	29/0	♑ 1	2	4	5	7	9	10	12	13	15	17	18	20	21	23	24	26
♀	♐ 12	13	15	16	17	18	20	21	22	24	25	26	27	29	29/0	♑ 1	2	4	5	6	7	9	10	11	12	14	15	16	17	19	20
♂	♏ 20	21	21	22	23	23	24	25	26	26	27	28	28	29	29/0	♐ 0	1	2	3	3	4	5	5	6	7	7	8	9	10	10	11

♃ 1℞ 10 20 28 / ♋24 23 22 21 · ♄ 1℞ 2 14 28 / ♊9 8 7 6 · ♅ 1℞ 8 / ♊2 1 · ♆ 1 19 / ♎1 2 · ♇ 1℞ 11 / ♌7 6

1943

1

	1	2	3	4	5	6	7	8	9	10	11	12	13	14	15	16	17	18	19	20	21	22	23	24	25	26	27	28
☉	♑ 10	11	12	13	14	15	16	17	18	19	20	21	22	23	24	26	27	28	29	29/0	♒ 1	2	3	4	5	6	7	8
☽	♏ 1	15	29	♐ 14	29	♑ 15	♒ 0	15	♓ 0	14	28	♈ 11	24	♉ 7	19	♊ 2	14	25	♋ 7	19	♌ 1	13	25	♍ 7	19	♎ 2	14	27
☿	♑ 27	29	29/0	♒ 1	3	4	5	6	7	8	9	10	10	10	℞ 11	10	10	9	9	8	7	6	5	3	2	1	0	0/29
♀	♑ 21	22	24	25	26	27	29	29/0	♒ 1	2	4	5	6	7	9	10	11	12	14	15	16	18	19	20	21	23	24	25
♂	♐ 12	12	13	14	15	15	16	17	17	18	19	20	20	21	22	22	23	24	25	25	26	27	27	28	29	29/0	♑ 0	1

♃ 1℞ 5 12 20 28 / ♋21 20 19 18 17 · ♄ 1℞ 16 / ♊6 5 · ♅ 1℞ 7 / ♊1 0 · ♆ 1 5℞ 19 / ♎2 2 1 · ♇ 1 / ♌

2

	1	2	3	4	5	6	7	8	9	10	11	12	13	14	15	16	17	18	19	20	21	22	23	24	25	26	27	28
☉	♒ 12	13	14	15	16	17	18	19	20	21	22	23	24	25	26	27	28	29	29/0	♓ 1	2	3	4	5	6	7	8	9
☽	♐ 23	♑ 8	23	♒ 8	23	♓ 8	22	♈ 6	20	♉ 3	16	28	♊ 10	22	♋ 4	16	28	♌ 10	22	♍ 4	16	29	♎ 11	24	♏ 7	21	♐ 4	18
☿	♑℞ 25	25	25	24	24	D 25	25	25	26	26	27	27	28	29	29/0	♒ 0	1	2	3	5	6	7	8	9	10	12	13	14
♀	29/0	♓ 1	3	4	5	6	7	9	10	11	12	14	15	16	17	19	20	21	22	24	25	26	27	29	29/0	♈ 1	2	4
♂	♑ 4	5	5	6	7	8	8	9	10	11	11	12	13	14	14	15	16	16	17	18	19	19	20	21	22	22	23	24

♃ 1℞ 6 17 / ♋17 16 15 · ♄ 1℞ 8D 27 / ♊5 5 6 · ♅ 1℞ 8D / ♊0 0 · ♆ 1℞ / ♎1 · ♇ 1℞ / ♌

3

	1	2	3	4	5	6	7	8	9	10	11	12	13	14	15	16	17	18	19	20	21	22	23	24	25	26	27	28
☉	♓ 10	11	12	13	14	15	16	17	18	19	20	21	22	23	24	25	26	27	28	29	29/0	♈ 1	2	3	4	5	6	7
☽	♑ 3	17	♒ 2	16	♓ 1	16	♈ 0	14	28	♉ 11	24	♊ 6	18	♋ 0	12	24	♌ 6	18	♍ 0	12	25	♎ 8	21	♏ 4	18	♐ 1	15	29
☿	♒ 16	17	18	20	21	23	24	26	27	29	29/0	♓ 2	3	5	7	8	10	12	13	15	17	19	21	22	24	26	28	29/0
♀	♈ 5	6	7	8	10	11	12	13	15	16	17	18	20	21	22	23	24	26	27	28	29/0	♉ 1	2	3	4	5	7	8
♂	♑ 25	25	26	27	28	28	29	29/0	♒ 1	1	2	3	4	4	5	6	7	7	8	9	10	10	11	12	13	13	14	15

♃ 1℞ 12D / ♋15 15 · ♄ 1 17 30 / ♊6 7 8 · ♅ 1 11 / ♊0 1 · ♆ 1℞ 10 / ♎1 0 · ♇ 1 / ♌

4

	1	2	3	4	5	6	7	8	9	10	11	12	13	14	15	16	17	18	19	20	21	22	23	24	25	26	27	28
☉	♈ 11	12	13	14	15	16	17	18	19	20	21	22	23	24	25	26	27	28	29	29/0	♉ 0	1	2	3	4	5	6	7
☽	♒ 26	♓ 10	24	♈ 8	22	♉ 6	19	♊ 2	14	26	♋ 8	20	♌ 2	14	26	♍ 8	20	♎ 3	16	♏ 0	14	28	♐ 12	26	♑ 10	24	♒ 8	22
☿	♈ 8	10	12	14	16	18	20	22	24	26	28	29/0	♉ 3	5	7	8	10	12	14	16	18	19	21	22	24	25	26	28
♀	♉ 13	14	15	16	17	19	20	21	22	23	25	26	27	28	29/0	♊ 1	2	3	4	5	7	8	9	10	11	12	14	15
♂	♒ 18	19	19	20	21	22	22	23	24	25	25	26	27	28	28	29	29/0	♓ 1	1	2	3	4	4	5	6	7	7	8

♃ 1 3 15 24 / ♋15 16 17 18 · ♄ 1 10 19 28 / ♊8 9 10 11 · ♅ 1 7 27 / ♊1 2 3 · ♆ 1℞ 17 0 18 / ♎0 29 ♍29 · ♇ 1 / ♌

5

	1	2	3	4	5	6	7	8	9	10	11	12	13	14	15	16	17	18	19	20	21	22	23	24	25	26	27	28
☉	♉ 10	11	12	13	14	15	16	17	18	19	20	21	22	23	24	25	26	27	28	29	29/0	♊ 0	1	2	3	4	5	6
☽	♈ 4	18	♉ 1	14	27	♊ 10	22	♋ 4	16	28	♌ 10	22	♍ 4	16	28	♎ 11	25	♏ 8	22	♐ 7	21	♑ 6	21	♒ 5	19	♓ 3	17	♈ 1
☿	♊ 1	2	2	3	4	4	4	5	5	5	5	5	℞ 5	5	5	4	4	4	3	3	2	1	1	0	0	0/29	♉ 29	28
♀	♊ 18	20	21	22	23	24	25	26	28	29	29/0	♋ 1	2	3	4	6	7	8	9	10	11	12	14	15	16	17	18	19
♂	♓ 10	11	12	13	13	14	15	16	16	17	18	19	19	20	21	22	22	23	24	25	25	26	27	28	28	29	29/0	♈ 1

♃ 1 8 15 21 26 / ♋19 20 21 22 23 · ♄ 1 7 15 23 30 / ♊11 12 13 14 15 · ♅ 1 15 31 / ♊3 4 5 · ♆ 1℞ / ♍29 · ♇ 1 / ♌

6

	1	2	3	4	5	6	7	8	9	10	11	12	13	14	15	16	17	18	19	20	21	22	23	24	25	26	27	28
☉	♊ 10	11	12	13	14	15	16	17	18	19	20	21	22	23	23	24	25	26	27	28	29	29/0	♋ 1	2	3	4	5	6
☽	♉ 23	♊ 6	18	♋ 0	12	24	♌ 6	18	♍ 0	12	24	♎ 6	19	♏ 3	16	♐ 1	15	♑ 0	15	♒ 0	15	29	♓ 14	28	♈ 11	24	♉ 7	20
☿	♉℞ 27	27	27	27	D 27	27	27	27	27	28	28	29	29	29/0	♊ 1	2	3	4	5	6	7	8	9	10	12	13	15	16
♀	♋ 23	24	26	27	28	29	29/0	♌ 1	2	3	4	5	6	7	8	9	10	11	12	13	14	15	16	17	18	19	20	21
♂	♈ 4	4	5	6	7	7	8	9	10	10	11	12	12	13	14	15	15	16	17	17	18	19	20	20	21	22	22	23

♃ 1 6 11 16 21 26 30 29 / ♋24 25 26 27 28 29 0 · ♄ 1 7 15 23 30 / ♊15 16 17 18 19 · ♅ 1 19 / ♊5 6 · ♆ 1℞ 11D / ♍29 29 · ♇ 1 / ♌

7

	1	2	3	4	5	6	7	8	9	10	11	12	13	14	15	16	17	18	19	20	21	22	23	24	25	26	27	28
☉	♋ 9	10	11	12	13	14	14	15	16	17	18	19	20	21	22	23	24	25	26	27	28	29	29/0	♌ 1	2	3	4	5
☽	♊ 27	♋ 9	21	♌ 3	15	27	♍ 8	20	♎ 3	15	28	♏ 11	25	♐ 9	24	♑ 9	24	♒ 9	24	♓ 9	23	♈ 7	21	♉ 4	17	♊ 0	12	24
☿	♊ 21	23	24	26	28	29/0	♋ 2	4	6	8	10	12	15	17	19	21	23	25	27	29/0	♌ 2	4	6	8	10	12	14	16
♀	♌ 24	25	26	27	28	29	29/0	♍ 0	1	2	3	4	4	5	6	7	8	8	9	10	10	11	12	12	13	14	14	15
♂	♈ 25	26	27	27	28	29	29/0	♉ 0	1	2	2	3	4	4	5	6	6	7	8	8	9	10	10	11	12	12	13	14

♃ 1 5 10 14 19 23 28 / ♌0 1 2 3 4 5 6 · ♄ 1 9 17 26 / ♊19 20 21 22 · ♅ 1 8 31 / ♊6 7 8 · ♆ 1 / ♍29 · ♇ 1 / ♌

8

	1	2	3	4	5	6	7	8	9	10	11	12	13	14	15	16	17	18	19	20	21	22	23	24	25	26	27	28
☉	♌ 8	9	10	11	12	13	14	15	16	17	18	19	20	21	22	23	24	25	26	27	28	28	29	29/0	♍ 1	2	3	4
☽	♌ 12	24	♍ 5	17	29	♎ 12	24	♏ 7	20	♐ 4	18	♑ 2	17	♒ 2	17	♓ 2	17	♈ 2	16	♉ 0	13	26	♊ 9	21	♋ 3	15	27	♌ 9
☿	♌ 23	25	27	28	29/0	♍ 2	3	5	6	8	10	11	13	14	15	17	18	20	21	22	23	25	26	27	28	29	29/0	♎ 1
♀	♍ 17	17	18	18	18	19	19	19	19	20	20	20	20	20	20	℞ 20	20	20	20	19	19	19	19	18	18	18	17	17
♂	♉ 16	17	18	18	19	19	20	21	21	22	22	23	24	24	25	25	26	27	27	28	28	29	29/0	♊ 0	1	1	2	2

♃ 1 6 10 15 20 24 29 / ♌7 8 9 10 11 12 13 · ♄ 1 4 15 27 / ♊22 23 24 25 · ♅ 1 / ♊8 · ♆ 1 2 29 3 / ♍29 0 ♎ 0 · ♇ 1 / ♌

9

	1	2	3	4	5	6	7	8	9	10	11	12	13	14	15	16	17	18	19	20	21	22	23	24	25	26	27	28
☉	♍ 8	9	10	11	12	13	14	15	16	17	18	19	20	21	22	23	24	25	26	27	28	29	29/0	♎ 1	2	3	3	4
☽	♍ 27	♎ 9	21	♏ 4	17	♐ 0	14	27	♑ 12	26	♒ 11	26	♓ 11	25	♈ 10	24	♉ 8	22	♊ 5	17	♋ 0	11	24	♌ 5	17	29	♍ 11	23
☿	♎ 5	6	6	7	8	8	8	9	9	9	9	℞ 9	9	8	8	7	7	6	5	4	3	2	1	0	0/29	♍ 28	27	26
♀	♍℞ 15	14	13	13	12	11	11	10	10	9	8	8	7	7	6	6	6	5	5	5	4	4	4	4	4	4	D 4	4
♂	♊ 4	5	5	6	6	7	7	8	8	9	9	10	10	11	11	12	12	12	13	13	14	14	14	15	15	16	16	16

♃ 1 3 7 12 17 23 28 / ♌13 14 15 16 17 18 19 · ♄ 1 13 / ♊25 26 · ♅ 1 15℞ / ♊8 8 · ♆ 1 3 30 / ♎0 1 2 · ♇ 1 / ♌

10

	1	2	3	4	5	6	7	8	9	10	11	12	13	14	15	16	17	18	19	20	21	22	23	24	25	26	27	28
☉	♎ 7	8	9	10	11	12	13	14	15	16	17	18	19	20	21	22	23	24	25	26	27	28	29	29/0	♏ 1	2	3	4
☽	♏ 1	14	27	♐ 10	24	♑ 8	22	♒ 6	20	♓ 5	19	♈ 4	18	♉ 3	16	♊ 0	13	25	♋ 8	20	♌ 2	14	25	♍ 7	19	♎ 2	14	27
☿	♍℞ 25	24	24	D 24	25	25	26	26	27	28	29/0	♎ 1	2	3	5	6	8	9	11	12	14	16	17	19	21	22	24	26
♀	♍ 4	4	5	5	5	6	6	6	7	7	8	8	9	9	10	10	11	12	12	13	14	14	15	16	17	17	18	19
♂	♊ 17	18	18	18	19	19	19	19	20	20	20	20	20	20	21	21	21	21	21	21	21	22	22	22	22	22	22	℞ 22

♃ 1 3 9 15 22 29 / ♌19 20 21 22 23 24 · ♄ 1 10℞ / ♊26 26 · ♅ 1℞ 30 / ♊8 7 · ♆ 1 29 / ♎2 3 · ♇ 1 / ♌

11

	1	2	3	4	5	6	7	8	9	10	11	12	13	14	15	16	17	18	19	20	21	22	23	24	25	26	27	28
☉	♏ 8	9	10	11	12	13	14	15	16	17	18	19	20	21	22	23	24	25	26	27	28	29	29/0	♐ 1	2	3	4	5
☽	♐ 21	♑ 5	19	♒ 3	17	♓ 1	15	29	♈ 13	27	♉ 11	25	♊ 8	21	♋ 3	16	28	♌ 9	21	♍ 3	15	27	♎ 9	22	♏ 5	19	♐ 2	16
☿	♏ 2	4	6	7	9	11	12	14	15	17	19	20	22	23	25	27	28	29/0	♐ 1	3	4	6	8	9	11	12	14	15
♀	♍ 22	23	24	25	26	27	28	29	29/0	♎ 1	2	3	4	5	6	7	8	9	10	11	12	13	14	15	16	17	18	19
♂	♊℞ 22	21	21	21	21	21	21	21	21	20	20	20	20	19	19	19	19	18	18	18	17	17	17	16	16	16	15	15

♃ 1 7 17 / ♌24 25 26 · ♄ 1℞ 5 22 / ♊26 25 24 · ♅ 1℞ 25 / ♊7 6 · ♆ 1 / ♎3 · ♇ ♌

12

	1	2	3	4	5	6	7	8	9	10	11	12	13	14	15	16	17	18	19	20	21	22	23	24	25	26	27	28
☉	♐ 8	9	10	11	12	14	15	16	17	18	19	20	21	22	23	24	25	26	27	28	29	29/0	♑ 1	2	3	4	5	6
☽	♑ 29	♒ 14	28	♓ 12	26	♈ 10	23	♉ 7	20	♊ 3	16	29	♋ 11	24	♌ 6	17	29	♍ 11	23	♎ 5	17	♏ 0	13	27	♐ 10	25	♑ 9	24
☿	♐ 20	21	23	24	26	27	29	29/0	♑ 2	3	5	6	8	9	11	12	13	15	16	17	18	20	21	22	22	23	24	24
♀	♎ 22	23	24	26	27	28	29	29/0	♏ 1	2	3	5	6	7	8	9	10	11	13	14	15	16	17	18	20	21	22	23
♂	♊℞ 14	13	13	13	12	12	11	11	11	10	10	10	9	9	9	8	8	8	7	7	7	7	6	6	6	6	6	5

♃ 1 7 14℞ 20 / ♌26 27 27 26 · ♄ 1℞ 5 17 30 / ♊24 23 22 21 · ♅ 1℞ 19 / ♊6 5 · ♆ 1 7 / ♎3 4 · ♇ 1 / ♌

1944

1

1	2	3	4	5	6	7	8	9	10	11	12	13	14	15	16	17	18	19	20	21	22	23	24	25	26	27	28	29	30	31
♑ 10	11	12	13	14	15	16	17	18	19	20	21	22	23	24	25	26	27	28	29	29 0	♒ 1	2	3	4	5	6	7	8	9	11
♓ 22	♈ 6	20	♉ 4	17	♊ 0	13	25	♋ 8	20	♌ 2	14	26	♍ 7	19	♎ 1	13	25	♏ 8	21	♐ 4	18	♑ 3	17	♒ 2	17	♓ 2	17	♈ 2	16	♉ 0
♑R 24	23	23	22	21	19	18	17	15	14	13	12	11	10	9	9	8	8	8	D 8	8	9	9	10	10	11	12	13	13	14	15
♏ 28	29	29 0	♐ 1	3	4	5	6	7	9	10	11	12	13	15	16	17	18	19	21	22	23	24	25	27	28	29	29 0	♑ 2	3	4
♊R 5	5	5	5	4	4	4	4	4	D 4	4	4	4	4	5	5	5	5	5	5	5	5	6	6	6	6	6	6	7	7	7

1R 9 19 / ♌26 25 24 — ♄ 1R 12 / ♊21 20 — ♅ 1R 23 / ♊5 4 — ♆ 1 7R / ♎4 4 — ♇ 1R 10 / ♌8 7

2

1	2	3	4	5	6	7	8	9	10	11	12	13	14	15	16	17	18	19	20	21	22	23	24	25	26	27	28	29	30	31
♒ 12	13	14	15	16	17	18	19	20	21	22	23	24	25	26	27	28	29	29 0	♓ 1	2	3	4	5	6	7	8	9	10		
♉ 14	27	♊ 10	22	♋ 5	17	29	♌ 11	22	♍ 4	16	28	♎ 10	22	♏ 4	17	♐ 0	13	27	♑ 11	25	♒ 10	25	♓ 11	26	♈ 11	25	♉ 9	23		
♑ 16	17	18	20	21	22	23	24	26	27	28	29 0	♒ 1	2	4	5	7	8	10	11	13	14	16	17	19	21	22	24	25		
♑ 5	6	8	9	10	11	12	14	15	16	17	19	20	21	22	23	25	26	27	28	29 0	♒ 1	2	3	5	6	7	8	9		
♊ 7	8	8	8	8	9	9	9	10	10	10	11	11	11	12	12	12	13	13	13	14	14	14	15	15	16	16	16	17		

1R 4 12 20 28 / ♌23 22 21 20 19 — ♄ 1R 2 21D / ♊20 19 19 — ♅ 1R 13D / ♊4 4 — ♆ 1R 5 / ♎4 3 — ♇ 1R 24 / ♌7 6

3

1	2	3	4	5	6	7	8	9	10	11	12	13	14	15	16	17	18	19	20	21	22	23	24	25	26	27	28	29	30	31
♓ 11	12	13	14	15	16	17	18	19	20	21	22	23	24	25	26	27	28	29	29 0	♈ 1	2	3	4	5	6	7	8	9	10	11
♊ 6	19	♋ 2	14	26	♌ 8	19	♍ 1	13	25	♎ 7	19	♏ 1	14	26	♐ 9	22	♑ 6	20	♒ 4	19	♓ 4	19	♈ 4	19	♉ 4	18	♊ 2	15	28	♋ 10
♒ 27	29	29 0	♓ 2	4	6	7	9	11	13	15	17	19	20	22	24	26	28	29 0	♈ 2	4	6	8	10	12	14	16	18	20	22	24
♒ 11	12	13	14	16	17	18	19	20	22	23	24	25	27	28	29	29 0	♓ 2	3	4	5	6	8	9	10	11	13	14	15	16	18
♊ 17	18	18	19	19	19	20	20	21	21	22	22	23	23	24	24	24	25	25	26	26	27	27	28	28	29	29	29 0	♋ 0	1	1

1R 7 19 / ♌19 18 17 — ♄ 1 9 29 / ♊19 20 21 — ♅ 1 3 / ♊4 5 — ♆ 1R 19 / ♎3 2 — ♇ 1R / ♌6

4

1	2	3	4	5	6	7	8	9	10	11	12	13	14	15	16	17	18	19	20	21	22	23	24	25	26	27	28	29	30	31
♈ 12	13	14	15	16	17	18	19	19	20	21	22	23	24	25	26	27	28	29	29 0	♉ 1	2	3	4	5	6	7	8	9	10	
♋ 22	♌ 4	16	28	♍ 10	22	♎ 4	16	28	♏ 11	23	♐ 6	19	♑ 3	16	♒ 0	14	28	♓ 13	28	♈ 12	27	♉ 12	26	♊ 10	23	♋ 6	18	♌ 1	13	
♈ 26	28	29 0	♉ 1	3	4	6	7	8	10	11	12	13	13	14	15	15	16	16	16	16	R 16	16	16	15	15	14	14	13	13	
♓ 19	20	21	22	24	25	26	27	29	29 0	♈ 1	2	4	5	6	7	8	10	11	12	13	15	16	17	18	20	21	22	23	24	
♋ 2	2	3	3	4	4	5	5	6	6	7	8	8	9	9	10	10	11	11	12	12	13	13	14	15	15	16	16	17	17	

1R 13D / ♌17 17 — ♄ 1 11 22 / ♊21 22 23 — ♅ 1 5 26 / ♊5 6 7 — ♆ 1R 26 / ♎2 1 — ♇ 1R 20D / ♌6 6

5

1	2	3	4	5	6	7	8	9	10	11	12	13	14	15	16	17	18	19	20	21	22	23	24	25	26	27	28	29	30	31
♉ 11	12	13	14	15	16	17	18	19	20	21	22	23	24	24	25	26	27	28	29	29 0	♊ 1	2	3	4	5	6	7	8	9	10
♌ 24	♍ 6	18	♎ 0	12	24	♏ 7	20	♐ 3	16	♑ 0	13	27	♒ 11	25	♓ 9	23	♈ 8	22	♉ 6	20	♊ 4	18	♋ 1	14	26	♌ 8	20	♍ 2	14	26
♉R 12	11	11	10	10	9	9	8	8	7	7	6	6	6	6	D 6	6	7	7	7	8	8	9	9	10	11	12	12	13	14	15
♈ 26	27	28	29 0	♉ 1	2	3	4	5	7	8	9	10	12	13	14	15	17	18	19	20	21	23	24	25	26	28	29	29 0	♊ 1	2
♋ 18	18	19	20	20	21	21	22	22	23	23	24	25	25	26	26	27	28	28	29	29	29 0	♌ 0	1	1	2	3	3	4	4	5

1 8 19 28 / ♌17 18 19 20 — ♄ 1 11 19 27 / ♊24 25 26 27 — ♅ 1 14 31 / ♊7 8 9 — ♆ 1R / ♎1 — ♇ 1 / ♌6

6

1	2	3	4	5	6	7	8	9	10	11	12	13	14	15	16	17	18	19	20	21	22	23	24	25	26	27	28	29	30	31
♊ 11	12	13	14	15	16	17	18	18	19	20	21	22	23	24	25	26	27	28	29	29 0	♋ 1	2	3	4	5	6	7	8	9	
♎ 8	20	♏ 3	15	28	♐ 12	25	♑ 9	23	♒ 7	22	♓ 6	20	♈ 4	18	♉ 2	16	♊ 0	13	26	♋ 9	22	♌ 4	16	28	♍ 10	22	♎ 4	16	28	
♉ 16	18	19	20	21	23	24	25	27	28	29 0	♊ 1	3	5	7	8	10	12	14	16	18	20	22	24	26	29	29 1	♋ 3	5	7	
♊ 4	5	6	7	9	10	11	12	14	15	16	17	18	20	21	22	23	25	26	27	28	29 0	♋ 1	2	3	4	6	7	8	9	
♌ 6	6	7	7	8	8	9	10	10	11	11	12	13	13	14	14	15	16	16	17	17	18	19	19	20	20	21	22	22	23	

1 4 11 18 24 30 / ♌20 21 22 23 24 25 — ♄ 1 4 12 20 29 21 27 / ♊27 28 29 0 ♋0 1 — ♅ 1 17 / ♊9 10 — ♆ 1R 13D / ♎1 1 — ♇ 1 11 / ♌6 7

7

1	2	3	4	5	6	7	8	9	10	11	12	13	14	15	16	17	18	19	20	21	22	23	24	25	26	27	28	29	30	31
♋ 9	10	11	12	13	14	15	16	17	18	19	20	21	22	23	24	25	26	27	28	29	29 0	♌ 0	1	2	3	4	5	6	7	8
♏ 11	23	♐ 7	20	♑ 4	18	♒ 3	17	♓ 2	16	♈ 1	15	29	♉ 13	26	♊ 10	23	♋ 5	18	♌ 0	13	25	♍ 7	18	♎ 0	12	24	♏ 6	19	♐ 2	15
♋ 9	11	14	16	18	20	22	24	26	28	29 0	♌ 2	4	6	8	10	11	13	15	17	18	20	22	23	25	26	28	29	29 1	♍ 2	3
♋ 11	12	13	14	15	17	18	19	20	22	23	24	25	27	28	29	29 0	♌ 1	3	4	5	6	8	9	10	11	13	14	15	16	17
♌ 23	24	25	25	26	26	27	28	28	29	29	29 0	♍ 1	1	2	3	3	4	4	5	6	6	7	7	8	9	9	10	11	11	12

1 5 10 15 21 25 29 26 30 / ♌25 26 27 28 29 0 ♍0 1 — ♄ 1 5 13 21 29 / ♋1 2 3 4 5 — ♅ 1 6 27 / ♊10 11 12 — ♆ 1 27 / ♎1 2 — ♇ 1 20 / ♌7 8

8

1	2	3	4	5	6	7	8	9	10	11	12	13	14	15	16	17	18	19	20	21	22	23	24	25	26	27	28	29	30	31
♌ 9	10	11	12	13	14	15	16	17	18	19	20	21	22	22	23	24	25	26	27	28	29	29 0	♍ 1	2	3	4	5	6	7	8
♐ 28	♑ 12	27	♒ 11	26	♓ 11	26	♈ 11	25	♉ 10	23	♊ 7	20	♋ 2	15	27	♌ 9	21	♍ 3	15	27	♎ 9	21	♏ 3	15	27	♐ 10	23	♑ 7	20	♒ 5
♍ 5	6	7	8	10	11	12	13	14	15	16	17	18	18	19	20	20	21	21	22	22	22	22	R 22	22	22	21	21	20	20	19
♌ 19	20	21	22	24	25	26	27	29	29 0	♍ 1	2	3	5	6	7	8	10	11	12	13	15	16	17	18	20	21	22	23	24	26
♍ 12	13	14	14	15	16	16	17	17	18	19	19	20	21	21	22	22	23	24	24	25	26	26	27	28	28	29	29 0	♎ 0	1	1

1 4 9 14 18 23 27 / ♍1 2 3 4 5 6 7 — ♄ 1 7 16 27 / ♋5 6 7 8 — ♅ 1 31 / ♊12 13 — ♆ 1 30 / ♎2 3 — ♇ 1 24 / ♌8 9

9

1	2	3	4	5	6	7	8	9	10	11	12	13	14	15	16	17	18	19	20	21	22	23	24	25	26	27	28	29	30	31
♍ 9	10	11	12	13	14	15	16	17	18	19	20	21	22	22	23	24	25	26	27	28	29	29 0	♎ 1	2	3	4	5	6	7	
♒ 20	♓ 5	20	♈ 5	20	♉ 5	19	♊ 3	16	♋ 0	12	♌ 24	6	18	♍ 0	12	24	♎ 6	18	♏ 0	12	24	♐ 6	19	♑ 2	15	29	♒ 13	28	♓ 13	
♍R 18	17	17	16	15	14	13	12	11	10	9	9	8	8	8	D 8	8	9	9	10	10	11	12	13	15	16	17	19	20	22	
♍ 27	28	29 0	♎ 1	2	3	4	6	7	8	9	11	12	13	14	16	17	18	19	20	22	23	24	25	27	28	29	29 0	♏ 2	3	
♎ 2	3	3	4	5	5	6	7	7	8	9	9	10	11	11	12	13	13	14	14	15	16	16	17	18	18	19	20	20	21	

1 6 10 15 20 24 29 / ♍8 9 10 11 12 13 14 — ♄ 1 8 23 / ♋8 9 10 — ♅ 1 19R / ♊13 13 — ♆ 1 27 / ♎3 4 — ♇ 1 / ♌9

10

1	2	3	4	5	6	7	8	9	10	11	12	13	14	15	16	17	18	19	20	21	22	23	24	25	26	27	28	29	30	31
♎ 8	9	10	11	12	13	14	15	16	17	18	19	20	21	22	23	24	25	26	27	28	29	29 0	♏ 1	2	3	4	5	6	7	8
♓ 28	♈ 14	29	♉ 14	28	♊ 12	25	♋ 8	21	♌ 3	15	27	♍ 9	21	♎ 3	15	27	♏ 9	21	♐ 4	16	29	♑ 12	25	♒ 9	23	♓ 7	22	♈ 7	22	♉ 7
♍ 24	25	27	29	29 1	♎ 2	4	6	8	9	11	13	15	16	18	20	21	23	25	27	28	29 0	♏ 2	3	5	6	8	10	11	13	14
♏ 4	5	6	8	9	10	11	12	14	15	16	17	19	20	21	22	23	25	26	27	28	29 0	♐ 1	2	3	4	6	7	8	9	11
♎ 22	22	23	24	24	25	26	26	27	28	28	29	29 0	♏ 1	1	2	3	3	4	5	5	6	7	7	8	9	9	10	11	11	12

1 4 9 14 19 24 30 / ♍14 15 16 17 18 19 20 — ♄ 1 23R / ♋10 10 — ♅ 1R 6 / ♊13 12 — ♆ 1 24 / ♎4 5 — ♇ 1 8 / ♌9 10

11

1	2	3	4	5	6	7	8	9	10	11	12	13	14	15	16	17	18	19	20	21	22	23	24	25	26	27	28	29	30	31
♏ 9	10	11	12	13	14	15	16	17	18	19	20	21	22	23	24	25	26	27	28	29	29 0	♐ 1	2	3	4	5	6	7	8	
♉ 2	♊ 6	20	♋ 4	17	29	♌ 12	24	♍ 6	18	29	♎ 11	23	♏ 6	18	♐ 0	13	26	♑ 9	22	♒ 6	19	♓ 3	17	♈ 2	16	♉ 1	15	♊ 0	14	
♏ 16	18	19	21	22	24	25	27	28	29 0	♐ 1	3	4	6	7	9	10	12	13	15	16	18	19	20	22	23	25	26	27	28	
♐ 12	13	14	15	17	18	19	20	22	23	24	25	26	28	29	29 0	♑ 1	3	4	5	6	7	9	10	11	12	13	15	16	17	
♏ 13	14	14	15	16	16	17	18	18	19	20	21	21	22	23	23	24	25	25	26	27	28	28	29	29 0	♐ 0	1	2	3	3	

1 4 11 17 24 / ♍20 21 22 23 24 — ♄ 1R 21 / ♋10 9 — ♅ 1R 11 / ♊12 11 — ♆ 1 29 / ♎5 6 — ♇ 1 10R / ♌10 10

12

1	2	3	4	5	6	7	8	9	10	11	12	13	14	15	16	17	18	19	20	21	22	23	24	25	26	27	28	29	30	31
♐ 9	10	11	12	13	14	15	16	17	18	19	20	21	22	23	24	25	26	27	29	29 0	♑ 1	2	3	4	5	6	7	8	9	10
♊ 28	♋ 11	25	♌ 7	20	♍ 2	14	26	♎ 8	19	♏ 2	14	26	♐ 9	22	♑ 5	19	♒ 2	16	♓ 0	14	28	♈ 12	27	♉ 11	25	♊ 9	23	♋ 6	19	♌ 2
29 0	♑ 1	2	3	4	5	6	7	7	8	8	8	8	R 8	8	7	7	6	5	4	2	1	0	0 29	♐ 27	26	25	24	23	23	22
♑ 18	19	21	22	23	24	25	27	28	29	29 0	♒ 1	3	4	5	6	7	9	10	11	12	13	14	16	17	18	19	20	21	23	24
♐ 4	5	5	6	7	8	8	9	10	11	11	12	13	13	14	15	16	16	17	18	19	19	20	21	21	22	23	24	24	25	26

2 11 25 / ♍24 25 26 27 — ♄ 1R 7 20 / ♋9 8 7 — ♅ 1R 5 30 / ♊11 10 9 — ♆ 1 / ♎6 — ♇ 1R 15 / ♌10 9

1945

1

	1	2	3	4	5	6	7	8	9	10	11	12	13	14	15	16	17	18	19	20	21	22	23	24	25	26	27	28	29	30	31
☉	♑ 11	12	13	14	15	16	17	18	19	20	21	22	23	24	25	26	27	28	29	29 0	♒ 1	2	3	4	5	6	7	8	9	10	11
☽	♌ 15	27	♍ 10	22	♎ 3	15	27	♏ 9	22	♐ 4	17	♑ 0	14	28	♒ 12	26	10	25	♈ 9	23	♉ 8	21	♊ 5	19	♋ 2	15	28	♌ 11	23	♍ 5	17
☿	♐R 22	22	D 22	23	23	24	24	25	26	26	27	28	29	29 0	♑ 1	2	4	5	6	7	9	10	11	13	14	15	17	18	20	21	23
♀	♒ 25	26	27	29	29 0	♓ 1	2	3	4	5	6	8	9	10	11	12	13	14	15	16	18	19	20	21	22	23	24	25	26	27	28
♂	♐ 27	27	28	29	29 0	♑ 0	1	2	3	3	4	5	6	6	7	8	9	9	10	11	12	12	13	14	15	15	16	17	18	18	19

♃ 1 12R 29 / ♍27 27 26 — ♄ 1R 14 28 / ♋6 5 4 — ♅ 1R / ♊9 — ♆ 1 8R / ♎6 6 — ♇ 1R / ♌9

2

	1	2	3	4	5	6	7	8	9	10	11	12	13	14	15	16	17	18	19	20	21	22	23	24	25	26	27	28	29	30	31
☉	♒ 12	13	14	15	16	17	18	19	20	21	22	23	24	25	26	27	28	29	29 0	♓ 2	3	4	5	6	7	8	9	10			
☽	♍ 29	♎ 11	23	♏ 5	17	29	♐ 12	25	♑ 8	22	♒ 6	20	♓ 5	20	♈ 5	19	♉ 4	18	♊ 2	16	29	♋ 12	25	♌ 7	20	♍ 2	14	26			
☿	♑ 24	25	27	28	29 0	♒ 2	3	5	6	8	9	11	13	14	16	18	19	21	23	25	26	28	29 0	♓ 2	4	5	7	9			
♀	♓ 29	29 0	♈ 1	2	3	4	5	6	7	8	9	10	11	12	13	14	14	15	16	17	18	19	20	20	21	22	22	23			
♂	♑ 20	21	21	22	23	24	25	25	26	27	28	28	29	29 0	♒ 1	1	2	3	4	5	5	6	7	8	8	9	10	11			

♃ 1R 12 21 / ♍26 25 24 — ♄ 1R 20 / ♋4 3 — ♅ 1R 16D / ♊9 9 — ♆ 1R 16 / ♎6 5 — ♇ 1R 2 / ♌9 8

3

	1	2	3	4	5	6	7	8	9	10	11	12	13	14	15	16	17	18	19	20	21	22	23	24	25	26	27	28	29	30	31
☉	♓ 11	12	13	14	15	16	17	18	19	20	21	22	23	24	25	26	27	28	29	29 0	♈ 1	1	2	3	4	5	6	7	8	9	10
☽	♎ 8	20	♏ 2	13	25	♐ 8	20	♑ 3	16	29	♒ 14	28	♓ 13	28	♈ 13	29	♉ 14	28	♊ 12	26	♋ 9	22	♌ 4	17	29	♍ 11	23	♎ 5	17	28	♏ 10
☿	♓ 11	13	15	17	19	21	23	24	26	28	29 0	♈ 2	4	6	8	10	11	13	15	16	18	19	21	22	23	24	25	26	26	27	27
♀	♈ 24	25	25	26	27	27	28	28	29	29	29 0	♉ 0	1	1	1	2	2	2	2	3	3	3	3	3	R 3	3	3	3	3	2	2
♂	♒ 12	12	13	14	15	15	16	17	18	19	19	20	21	22	22	23	24	25	25	26	27	28	29	29	29 0	♓ 1	2	2	3	4	5

♃ 1R 2 10 17 25 / ♍24 23 22 21 20 — ♄ 1R 6D 19 / ♋3 3 4 — ♅ 1 / ♊9 — ♆ 1R 28 / ♎5 4 — ♇ 1R 29 / ♌8 7

4

	1	2	3	4	5	6	7	8	9	10	11	12	13	14	15	16	17	18	19	20	21	22	23	24	25	26	27	28	29	30	31
☉	♈ 11	12	13	14	15	16	17	18	19	20	21	22	23	24	25	26	27	28	29	29 0	♉ 1	2	3	4	5	6	7	8	9	10	
☽	♏ 22	♐ 4	16	29	♑ 12	25	♒ 8	22	♓ 6	21	♈ 6	22	♉ 7	22	♊ 7	21	♋ 5	18	♌ 1	13	26	♍ 8	20	♎ 2	14	25	♏ 7	19	♐ 1	14	
☿	♈ 27	27	27	R 27	27	27	26	26	25	25	24	23	23	22	21	20	19	19	18	18	17	17	17	17	16	16	D 16	17	17	17	
♀	♉R 2	2	1	1	0	0	0 29	♈ 29	28	28	27	27	26	25	25	24	23	23	22	22	21	21	20	20	19	19	18	18	18	18	
♂	♓ 6	6	7	8	9	9	10	11	12	13	13	14	15	16	16	17	18	19	20	20	21	22	23	23	24	25	26	26	27	28	

♃ 1R 3 13 26 / ♍20 19 18 17 — ♄ 1 10 24 / ♋4 5 6 — ♅ 1 2 25 / ♊9 10 11 — ♆ 1R / ♎4 — ♇ 1R 20D / ♌7 7

5

	1	2	3	4	5	6	7	8	9	10	11	12	13	14	15	16	17	18	19	20	21	22	23	24	25	26	27	28	29	30	31
☉	♉ 11	12	13	14	15	16	17	17	18	19	20	21	22	23	24	25	26	27	28	28	29	29 0	♊ 1	2	3	4	6	7	8	9	10
☽	♐ 26	♑ 8	21	♒ 4	18	♓ 1	16	♈ 0	15	♉ 0	15	♊ 0	15	29	♋ 13	27	♌ 10	22	♍ 4	17	28	♎ 10	22	♏ 4	16	28	♐ 11	23	♑ 5	18	♒ 1
☿	♈ 17	18	18	19	19	20	21	22	22	23	24	25	26	27	29	29 0	♉ 1	2	3	5	6	8	9	11	12	14	15	17	19	21	22
♀	♈R 17	17	17	17	17	17	D 17	17	17	17	17	17	18	18	18	19	19	19	20	20	21	21	22	22	23	23	24	25	25	26	27
♂	♓ 29	29 0	♈ 0	1	2	3	3	4	5	6	6	7	8	9	10	10	11	12	13	13	14	15	16	16	17	18	19	19	20	21	22

♃ 1R 15D / ♍17 17 — ♄ 1 5 15 24 / ♋6 7 8 9 — ♅ 1 13 31 / ♊11 12 13 — ♆ 1R 8 / ♎4 3 — ♇ 1 11 / ♌7 8

6

	1	2	3	4	5	6	7	8	9	10	11	12	13	14	15	16	17	18	19	20	21	22	23	24	25	26	27	28	29	30	31
☉	♊ 11	12	13	13	14	15	16	17	18	19	20	21	22	23	24	25	26	27	28	29	29 0	♋ 1	2	3	4	4	5	6	7	8	
☽	♒ 14	28	♓ 12	26	♈ 10	25	♉ 9	24	♊ 9	23	♋ 7	21	♌ 5	18	♍ 0	13	25	♎ 7	19	♏ 1	12	25	♐ 7	19	♑ 2	15	28	♒ 11	25	♓ 9	
☿	♉ 24	26	28	29 0	♊ 2	4	6	8	10	12	14	17	19	21	23	25	28	29 0	♋ 2	4	6	8	10	13	15	17	19	20	22	24	
♀	♈ 27	28	29	29	29 0	♉ 1	2	3	3	4	5	6	7	8	9	9	10	11	12	13	14	15	16	17	18	19	20	21	22	23	
♂	♈ 22	23	24	25	25	26	27	28	28	29	29 0	♉ 1	1	2	3	4	4	5	6	6	7	8	9	9	10	11	12	12	13	14	

♃ 1 15 25 / ♍18 19 20 — ♄ 1 2 10 18 26 / ♋9 10 11 12 13 — ♅ 1 17 / ♊13 14 — ♆ 1R 15D / ♎3 3 — ♇ 1 / ♌8

7

	1	2	3	4	5	6	7	8	9	10	11	12	13	14	15	16	17	18	19	20	21	22	23	24	25	26	27	28	29	30	31
☉	♋ 9	10	11	12	13	14	15	16	17	18	19	20	21	22	23	24	24	25	26	27	28	29	29 0	♌ 1	2	3	4	5	6	7	8
☽	♓ 23	♈ 7	21	♉ 5	19	♊ 4	18	♋ 2	16	29	♌ 13	26	♍ 8	21	♎ 3	15	27	♏ 9	20	♐ 3	15	27	♑ 10	24	♒ 7	21	♓ 5	19	♈ 3	18	♉ 2
☿	♋ 26	28	29 0	♌ 1	3	5	6	8	9	11	12	14	15	17	18	19	20	22	23	24	25	26	27	28	29	29 0	♍ 1	1	2	3	3
♀	♉ 24	25	26	27	28	29	29 0	♊ 1	2	3	4	5	6	7	8	9	10	11	12	13	14	16	17	18	19	20	21	22	23	24	25
♂	♉ 14	15	16	17	17	18	19	19	20	21	22	22	23	24	24	25	26	26	27	28	29	29	29 0	♊ 1	1	2	3	3	4	5	5

♃ 1 3 10 17 23 29 / ♍20 21 22 23 24 25 — ♄ 1 3 11 19 27 / ♋13 14 15 16 17 — ♅ 1 4 25 / ♊14 15 16 — ♆ 1 20 / ♎3 4 — ♇ 1 3 / ♌8 9

8

	1	2	3	4	5	6	7	8	9	10	11	12	13	14	15	16	17	18	19	20	21	22	23	24	25	26	27	28	29	30	31
☉	♌ 9	10	11	12	13	14	15	16	16	17	18	19	20	21	22	23	24	25	26	27	28	29	29 0	♍ 1	2	3	4	5	6	7	8
☽	♉ 16	♊ 0	14	28	♋ 12	25	♌ 8	21	♍ 4	16	29	♎ 11	23	♏ 5	16	28	♐ 11	23	♑ 5	18	♒ 2	16	♓ 0	14	29	♈ 14	28	♉ 13	27	♊ 11	25
☿	♍ 3	4	4	4	4	4	R 4	4	4	3	3	3	2	1	1	0	0 29	♌ 28	27	26	25	25	24	23	23	22	22	22	22	D 21	22
♀	♊ 27	28	29	29 0	♋ 1	2	3	4	6	7	8	9	10	11	12	14	15	16	17	18	19	20	22	23	24	25	26	28	29	29 0	♌ 1
♂	♊ 6	7	7	8	9	9	10	11	11	12	13	13	14	15	15	16	17	17	18	18	19	20	20	21	22	22	23	24	24	25	25

♃ 1 4 9 15 20 25 29 26 30 / ♍25 26 27 28 29 0 ♎0 1 — ♄ 1 4 12 21 30 / ♋17 18 19 20 21 — ♅ 1 21 / ♊16 17 — ♆ 1 27 / ♎4 5 — ♇ 1 7 / ♌9 10

9

	1	2	3	4	5	6	7	8	9	10	11	12	13	14	15	16	17	18	19	20	21	22	23	24	25	26	27	28	29	30	31
☉	♍ 9	10	11	12	13	14	14	15	16	17	18	19	20	21	22	23	24	25	26	27	28	29	29 0	♎ 1	2	3	4	5	6	7	
☽	♋ 8	21	♌ 5	17	♍ 0	13	25	♎ 7	19	♏ 1	13	25	♐ 6	19	♑ 1	13	26	♒ 10	24	♓ 8	23	♈ 8	23	♉ 8	23	♊ 7	21	♋ 5	19	♌ 2	
☿	♌ 22	22	23	24	24	25	26	28	29	29 0	♍ 2	3	5	6	8	10	12	13	15	17	19	21	22	24	26	28	29 0	♎ 2	3	5	
♀	♌ 2	3	5	6	7	8	9	10	12	13	14	15	16	18	19	20	21	22	24	25	26	27	28	29 0	♍ 1	2	3	4	6	7	
♂	♊ 26	27	27	28	28	29	29 0	♋ 0	1	1	2	3	3	4	4	5	5	6	7	7	8	8	9	9	10	10	11	11	12	12	

♃ 1 3 8 13 18 22 27 / ♎1 2 3 4 5 6 7 — ♄ 1 9 21 / ♋21 22 23 — ♅ 1 23R / ♊17 17 — ♆ 1 24 / ♎5 6 — ♇ 1 12 / ♌10 11

10

	1	2	3	4	5	6	7	8	9	10	11	12	13	14	15	16	17	18	19	20	21	22	23	24	25	26	27	28	29	30	31
☉	♎ 8	9	10	11	12	13	14	15	16	17	18	19	20	21	22	23	24	25	26	27	28	29	29 0	♏ 1	2	3	4	5	6	7	8
☽	♌ 14	27	♍ 9	22	♎ 4	16	28	♏ 10	21	♐ 3	15	27	♑ 9	22	♒ 5	18	♓ 2	16	♈ 1	16	♉ 1	17	♊ 2	17	♋ 1	15	28	♌ 11	24	♍ 6	19
☿	♎ 7	9	11	12	14	16	17	19	21	23	24	26	27	29	29 1	♏ 2	4	5	7	9	10	12	13	15	16	18	19	21	22	23	25
♀	♍ 8	9	11	12	13	14	15	17	18	19	20	22	23	24	25	27	28	29	29 0	♎ 1	3	4	5	6	8	9	10	11	13	14	15
♂	♋ 13	14	14	15	15	15	16	16	17	17	18	18	19	19	20	20	21	21	22	22	22	23	23	24	24	24	25	25	25	26	26

♃ 1 2 6 11 15 20 25 30 / ♎7 8 9 10 11 12 13 14 — ♄ 1 6 / ♋23 24 — ♅ 1R 25 / 17 16 — ♆ 1 21 / ♎6 7 — ♇ 1 / ♌11

11

	1	2	3	4	5	6	7	8	9	10	11	12	13	14	15	16	17	18	19	20	21	22	23	24	25	26	27	28	29	30	31
☉	♏ 9	10	11	12	13	14	15	16	17	18	19	20	21	22	23	24	25	26	27	28	29	29 0	♐ 1	2	3	4	5	6	7	8	
☽	♎ 1	13	25	♏ 7	18	♐ 0	11	24	♑ 6	18	♒ 1	14	27	♓ 11	25	♈ 9	24	♉ 9	25	♊ 10	25	♋ 9	23	♌ 7	20	♍ 3	15	28	♎ 10	22	
☿	♏ 26	28	29 0	♐ 1	2	3	5	6	7	9	10	11	12	14	15	16	17	18	19	20	21	21	22	22	23	23	R 23	22	22	22	
♀	♎ 16	18	19	20	21	23	24	25	26	28	29	29 0	♏ 1	3	4	5	6	8	9	10	11	13	14	15	16	18	19	20	21	23	
♂	♋ 26	27	27	27	28	28	28	29	29	29	29 0	♌ 0	0	0	0	1	1	1	1	1	2	2	2	2	2	2	2	2	3	3	

♃ 1 3 8 13 19 24 29 / ♎14 15 16 17 18 19 20 — ♄ 1 7R / ♋24 24 — ♅ 1R 23 / ♊16 15 — ♆ 1 23 / ♎7 8 — ♇ 1 12R / ♌11 11

12

	1	2	3	4	5	6	7	8	9	10	11	12	13	14	15	16	17	18	19	20	21	22	23	24	25	26	27	28	29	30	31
☉	♐ 9	10	11	12	13	14	15	16	17	18	19	20	21	22	23	24	25	26	27	28	29	29 0	♑ 1	2	3	4	5	6	7	8	9
☽	♏ 3	15	27	♐ 9	21	♑ 3	15	28	♒ 11	24	♓ 7	20	♈ 4	19	♉ 3	18	♊ 3	18	♋ 3	17	♌ 1	15	28	♍ 11	24	♎ 6	18	♏ 0	12	24	♐ 6
☿	♐R 21	20	19	18	17	16	15	13	12	10	9	8	7	6	6	6	D 6	7	7	7	8	9	9	10	11	12	13	14	15	17	18
♀	♏ 24	25	26	28	29	29 0	♐ 1	3	4	5	6	8	9	10	12	13	14	15	17	18	19	20	22	23	24	25	27	28	29	29 0	♑ 2
♂	♌ 3	3	3	3	R 3	3	3	3	3	2	2	2	2	2	2	2	2	1	1	1	1	0	0	0	0	0 29	♋ 29	28	28	28	28

♃ 1 5 11 18 25 / ♎20 21 22 23 24 — ♄ 1R 7 23 / ♋24 23 22 — ♅ 1R 17 / ♊15 14 — ♆ 1 / ♎8 — ♇ 1 / ♌11

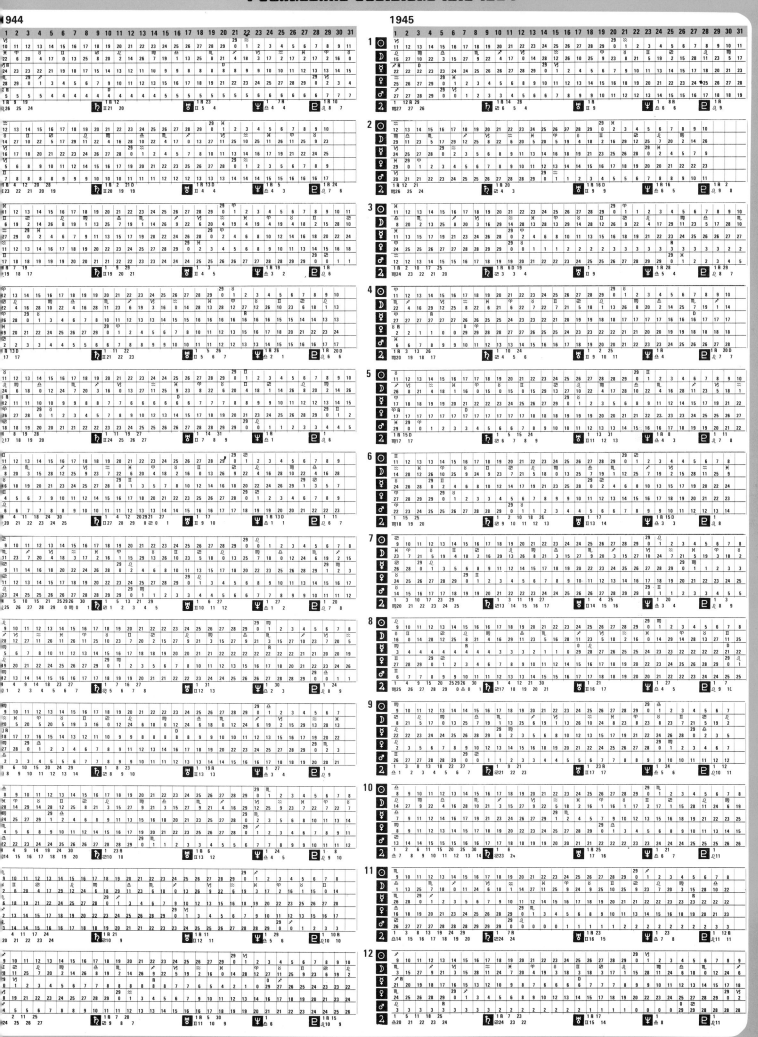

1946

1

	1	2	3	4	5	6	7	8	9	10	11	12	13	14	15	16	17	18	19	20	21	22	23	24	25	26	27	28	29	30	31
☉	♑ 10	12	13	14	15	16	17	18	19	20	21	22	23	24	25	26	27	28	29	29 0	♒ 1	2	3	4	5	6	7	8	9	10	11
☽	♐ 18	♑ 0	12	25	♒ 8	21	♓ 4	17	♈ 1	15	29	♉ 13	28	♊ 12	27	♋ 11	25	♌ 9	23	♍ 6	19	♎ 2	14	26	♏ 8	20	♐ 2	14	26	♑ 8	21
☿	♐ 19	20	22	23	24	26	27	28	29 0	♑ 1	3	4	5	7	8	10	11	13	14	16	18	19	21	22	24	25	27	29	29 0	♒ 2	3
♀	♑ 3	4	5	7	8	9	10	12	13	14	15	17	18	19	21	22	23	24	26	27	28	29 0	♒ 1	2	3	4	6	7	8	9	11
♂	♋R 27	27	27	26	26	26	25	25	24	24	24	23	23	22	22	22	21	21	20	20	20	19	19	19	18	18	18	17	17	17	16

♃ 1, 2, 12, 26: ♎24, 25, 26, 27 — ♄ 1R, 5, 17, 30: ♋22, 21, 20, 19 — ♅ 1R, 13: ♊14, 14 — ♆ 1, 10R: ♎8, 8 — ♇ 1R, 15: ♌11, 10

2

	1	2	3	4	5	6	7	8	9	10	11	12	13	14	15	16	17	18	19	20	21	22	23	24	25	26	27	28
☉	♒ 12	13	14	15	16	17	18	19	20	21	22	23	24	25	26	27	28	29	29 0	♓ 1	2	3	4	5	6	7	8	9
☽	♒ 3	17	♓ 0	14	28	♈ 12	26	♉ 10	24	♊ 8	22	♋ 6	20	♌ 4	18	♍ 1	14	27	♎ 9	22	♏ 4	16	28	♐ 9	21	♑ 3	16	28
☿	♒ 5	7	8	10	12	14	15	17	19	21	22	24	26	28	29 0	♓ 1	3	5	7	9	11	13	14	16	18	20	22	23
♀	♒ 12	13	14	16	17	18	19	21	22	23	24	26	27	28	29 0	♓ 1	2	3	4	6	7	8	9	11	12	13	14	16
♂	♋R 16	16	16	15	15	15	15	15	15	14	14	14	14	14	14	14	14	14	14	14	14	D 14	14	14	14	14	14	14

♃ 1, 11R, 26: ♎27, 27, 26 — ♄ 1R, 13: ♋19, 18 — ♅ 1R, 20D: ♊13, 13 — ♆ 1R, 28: ♎8, 7 — ♇ 1R, 28: ♌10, 9

3

	1	2	3	4	5	6	7	8	9	10	11	12	13	14	15	16	17	18	19	20	21	22	23	24	25	26	27	28	29	30	31
☉	♓ 10	11	12	13	14	15	16	17	18	19	20	21	22	23	24	25	26	27	28	29	29 0	♈ 1	2	3	4	5	6	7	8	9	10
☽	♒ 12	25	♓ 9	23	♈ 7	22	♉ 6	21	♊ 5	19	♋ 3	17	♌ 0	14	27	♍ 10	23	♎ 5	18	♏ 0	12	24	♐ 5	17	29	♑ 11	24	♒ 6	19	♓ 3	17
☿	♓ 25	27	28	29 0	♈ 1	3	4	5	6	7	8	9	9	9	10	10	R 10	9	9	9	8	7	7	6	5	4	3	2	2	1	0
♀	♓ 17	18	19	21	22	23	24	26	27	28	29 0	♈ 1	2	3	4	6	7	8	9	11	12	13	14	16	17	18	19	21	22	23	24
♂	♋ 14	14	14	14	14	15	15	15	15	15	15	16	16	16	16	17	17	17	17	18	18	18	18	19	19	19	20	20	20	21	21

♃ 1R, 13, 23, 31: ♎26, 25, 24, 23 — ♄ 1, 12, 20D, 27: ♋18, 17, 17, 18 — ♅ 1, 28: ♊13, 14 — ♆ 1R: ♎7 — ♇ 1R: ♌9

4

	1	2	3	4	5	6	7	8	9	10	11	12	13	14	15	16	17	18	19	20	21	22	23	24	25	26	27	28	29	30
☉	♈ 11	12	13	14	15	16	17	18	19	20	21	22	23	24	25	26	27	28	29	29 0	♉ 1	2	3	4	5	6	7	8	9	10
☽	♈ 1	16	♉ 1	16	♊ 1	15	♋ 0	14	27	♌ 11	24	♍ 7	19	♎ 2	14	26	♏ 8	20	♐ 2	14	26	♑ 8	20	♒ 2	15	28	♓ 11	25	♈ 10	25
☿	♉R 29	♓ 29	28	28	28	27	27	27	D 27	27	28	28	28	29	29	29 0	♈ 0	1	2	3	3	4	5	6	7	9	10	11	12	13
♀	♈ 25	27	28	29	29 0	♉ 2	3	4	5	7	8	9	10	12	13	14	15	17	18	19	20	21	23	24	25	26	27	29	29 0	♊ 1
♂	♋ 21	22	22	22	23	23	23	24	24	25	25	25	26	26	27	27	27	28	28	29	29	29 0	♏ 0	0	1	1	2	2	3	3

♃ 1R, 8, 17, 24: ♎23, 22, 21, 20 — ♄ 1, 23: ♋18, 19 — ♅ 1, 23: ♊14, 15 — ♆ 1R, 6: ♎7, 6 — ♇ 1R, 22D: ♌9, 9

5

	1	2	3	4	5	6	7	8	9	10	11	12	13	14	15	16	17	18	19	20	21	22	23	24	25	26	27	28	29	30	31
☉	♉ 10	11	12	13	14	15	16	17	18	19	20	21	22	23	24	25	26	27	28	29	29 0	♊ 1	2	3	4	5	6	7	7	8	9
☽	♉ 10	25	♊ 10	25	♋ 9	23	♌ 7	21	♍ 4	16	29	♎ 11	23	♏ 5	17	29	♐ 11	23	♑ 4	16	29	♒ 11	24	♓ 7	20	♈ 4	18	♉ 3	18	♊ 3	18
☿	♈ 15	16	17	19	20	22	23	25	26	28	29 0	♉ 1	3	5	7	8	10	12	14	16	18	20	22	24	26	29	29 1	♊ 3	5	7	9
♀	♊ 2	4	5	6	7	8	10	11	12	13	15	16	17	18	19	21	22	23	24	25	27	28	29	29 0	♋ 1	3	4	5	6	7	9
♂	♌ 4	4	5	5	6	6	7	7	8	8	9	9	9	10	10	11	12	12	13	13	14	14	15	15	16	16	17	17	18	18	19

♃ 1R, 3, 13, 26: ♎20, 19, 18, 17 — ♄ 1, 7, 19, 29: ♋19, 20, 21, 22 — ♅ 1, 12, 30: ♊15, 16, 17 — ♆ 1R, 23: ♎6, 5 — ♇ 1: ♌9

6

	1	2	3	4	5	6	7	8	9	10	11	12	13	14	15	16	17	18	19	20	21	22	23	24	25	26	27	28	29	30
☉	♊ 10	11	12	13	14	15	16	17	18	19	20	21	22	23	24	25	26	27	28	29	29	29 0	♋ 1	2	3	4	5	6	7	8
☽	♋ 3	18	♌ 2	16	♍ 0	13	26	♎ 8	20	♏ 2	14	26	♐ 8	20	♑ 1	13	26	♒ 8	20	♓ 3	16	♈ 0	13	27	♉ 12	27	♊ 12	27	♋ 12	26
☿	♊ 11	14	16	18	20	22	24	27	29	29 1	♋ 3	5	7	8	10	12	14	16	17	19	21	22	24	25	27	28	29 0	♌ 1	2	3
♀	♋ 10	11	12	14	15	16	17	18	19	21	22	23	24	26	27	28	29	29 0	♌ 1	3	4	5	6	7	8	10	11	12	13	14
♂	♌ 19	20	21	21	22	22	23	23	24	24	25	25	26	27	27	28	28	29	29	29 0	♍ 0	1	2	2	3	3	4	4	5	6

♃ 1R, 15D: ♎17, 17 — ♄ 1, 7, 16, 24: ♋22, 23, 24, 25 — ♅ 1, 16: ♊17, 18 — ♆ 1R, 17D: ♎5, 5 — ♇ 1, 13: ♌9, 10

7

	1	2	3	4	5	6	7	8	9	10	11	12	13	14	15	16	17	18	19	20	21	22	23	24	25	26	27	28	29	30	31
☉	♋ 9	10	11	12	13	14	15	16	17	18	19	19	20	21	22	23	24	25	26	27	28	29	29 0	♌ 1	2	3	4	5	6	7	8
☽	♌ 11	25	♍ 8	22	♎ 4	17	29	♏ 11	23	♐ 5	16	28	♑ 10	22	♒ 5	17	♓ 0	13	26	♈ 10	24	♉ 8	22	♊ 6	21	♋ 6	20	♌ 5	19	♍ 3	17
☿	♌ 4	6	7	8	9	10	11	11	12	13	14	14	15	15	15	15	16	16	16	R 16	16	15	15	15	15	14	13	13	12	11	11
♀	♌ 16	17	18	19	20	21	23	24	25	26	27	29	29 0	♍ 1	2	3	4	5	7	8	9	10	11	12	13	15	16	17	18	19	20
♂	♍ 6	7	7	8	9	9	10	10	11	12	12	13	13	14	14	15	16	16	17	17	18	19	11	12	13	14	15	17	18	19	20

♃ 1, 3, 17, 27: ♎17, 18, 19, 20 — ♄ 1, 2, 10, 18, 25: ♋25, 26, 27, 28, 29 — ♅ 1, 3, 22: ♊18, 19, 20 — ♆ 1, 11: ♎5, 6 — ♇ 1, 22: ♌10, 11

8

	1	2	3	4	5	6	7	8	9	10	11	12	13	14	15	16	17	18	19	20	21	22	23	24	25	26	27	28	29	30	31
☉	♌ 9	10	11	11	12	13	14	15	16	17	18	19	20	21	22	23	24	25	26	27	28	29	29 0	♍ 1	2	3	4	5	6	6	7
☽	♎ 0	13	25	♏ 7	19	♐ 1	13	25	♑ 7	19	♒ 1	14	27	♓ 10	23	♈ 7	21	♉ 4	18	♊ 3	17	♋ 1	15	29	♌ 14	28	♍ 11	25	♎ 8	21	♏ 3
☿	♌R 10	10	8	7	7	6	6	5	5	5	4	4	D 4	5	5	5	6	7	7	8	9	10	12	13	14	16	17	19	20	22	24
♀	♍ 21	22	23	25	26	27	28	29	29 0	♎ 1	2	3	5	6	7	8	9	10	11	12	13	14	15	16	17	18	19	20	21	22	23
♂	♍ 25	25	26	27	27	28	29	29	29 0	♎ 0	1	2	2	3	4	4	5	5	6	7	7	8	9	9	10	11	11	12	13	13	14

♃ 1, 4, 11, 18, 24, 30: ♎20, 21, 22, 23, 24, 25 — ♄ 1, 2, 29, 3, 10, 18, 26: ♋29, 0 ♌ 0, 1, 2, 3 — ♅ 1, 15: ♊20, 21 — ♆ 1, 24: ♎6, 7 — ♇ 1, 25: ♌11, 12

9

	1	2	3	4	5	6	7	8	9	10	11	12	13	14	15	16	17	18	19	20	21	22	23	24	25	26	27	28	29	30
☉	♍ 8	9	10	11	12	13	14	15	16	17	18	19	20	21	22	23	24	25	26	27	28	29	29 0	♎ 1	2	3	4	5	6	7
☽	♏ 15	27	♐ 9	21	♑ 3	15	27	♒ 9	22	♓ 6	19	♈ 3	17	♉ 1	15	29	♊ 14	28	♋ 12	26	♌ 10	23	♍ 7	20	♎ 3	16	29	♏ 11	23	♐ 5
☿	♌ 26	28	29 0	♍ 1	3	5	7	9	11	13	15	17	19	21	22	24	26	28	29 0	♎ 1	3	5	7	8	10	12	13	15	17	18
♀	♎ 25	26	27	28	29	29 0	♏ 0	1	2	3	4	5	6	7	8	9	10	11	12	12	13	14	15	16	17	17	18	19	20	20
♂	♎ 14	15	16	16	17	18	18	19	20	20	21	22	22	23	24	24	25	26	26	27	28	28	29	29 0	♏ 0	1	2	3	3	4

♃ 1, 4, 10, 15, 20, 25, 29, 26, 30: ♎25, 26, 27, 28, 29, 0 ♏ 0, 1 — ♄ 1, 4, 13, 23: ♌3, 4, 5, 6 — ♅ 1, 28R: ♊21, 21 — ♆ 1, 22: ♎7, 8 — ♇ 1: ♌12

10

	1	2	3	4	5	6	7	8	9	10	11	12	13	14	15	16	17	18	19	20	21	22	23	24	25	26	27	28	29	30	31
☉	♎ 8	9	10	11	12	13	14	15	16	17	18	19	20	21	22	23	24	24	25	26	27	28	29	29 0	♏ 1	2	3	4	5	6	7
☽	♐ 17	29	♑ 10	22	♒ 5	17	♓ 0	14	27	♈ 12	26	♉ 11	25	♊ 10	24	♋ 8	23	♌ 6	20	♍ 3	17	♎ 0	12	25	♏ 7	19	♐ 1	13	25	♑ 7	19
☿	♎ 20	22	23	25	26	28	29 0	♏ 1	2	4	5	7	8	10	11	12	14	15	17	18	19	21	22	23	24	25	27	28	29	29 0	♐ 1
♀	♏ 21	22	23	23	24	25	25	26	26	27	27	28	28	29	29	29 0	♐ 0	0	1	1	1	1	2	2	2	2	2	R 2	2	2	2
♂	♏ 4	5	6	7	7	8	9	9	10	11	11	12	13	13	14	15	16	16	17	18	18	19	20	20	21	22	23	23	24	25	25

♃ 1, 5, 9, 14, 19, 23, 28: ♏1, 2, 3, 4, 5, 6, 7 — ♄ 1, 5, 20: ♌6, 7, 8 — ♅ 1R: ♊21 — ♆ 1, 19: ♎8, 9 — ♇ 1, 5: ♌12, 13

11

	1	2	3	4	5	6	7	8	9	10	11	12	13	14	15	16	17	18	19	20	21	22	23	24	25	26	27	28	29	30
☉	♏ 8	9	10	11	12	13	14	15	16	17	18	20	21	22	23	24	25	26	27	28	29	29 0	♐ 1	2	3	4	5	6	7	8
☽	♒ 1	13	25	♓ 8	22	♈ 5	20	♉ 4	19	♊ 4	19	♋ 4	19	♌ 3	17	♍ 0	14	27	♎ 9	22	♏ 4	16	28	♐ 10	22	♑ 3	15	27	♒ 9	21
☿	♐ 2	3	4	4	5	6	6	6	7	7	R 7	7	6	6	5	4	3	2	1	0 29	♏ 28	27	25	24	23	22	22	21	21	21
♀	♐R 2	1	1	1	0	0	0	0 29	♏ 29	28	28	27	27	26	25	25	24	23	23	22	22	21	21	20	20	19	19	18	18	18
♂	♏ 26	27	28	28	29	29 0	♐ 0	1	2	3	3	4	5	5	6	7	8	8	9	10	11	11	12	13	13	14	15	16	16	17

♃ 1, 6, 10, 15, 20, 24, 29: ♏8, 9, 10, 11, 12, 13, 14 — ♄ 1, 21R: ♌8, [illegible] — ♅ 1, 10: ♊21, 20 — ♆ 1, 18: ♎9, 10 — ♇ 1, 14R: ♌13, 13

12

	1	2	3	4	5	6	7	8	9	10	11	12	13	14	15	16	17	18	19	20	21	22	23	24	25	26	27	28	29	30	31
☉	♐ 9	10	11	12	13	14	15	16	17	18	19	20	21	22	23	24	25	26	27	28	29	29 0	♑ 1	2	3	4	5	6	7	8	9
☽	♓ 4	17	♈ 0	13	28	♉ 12	27	♊ 12	27	♋ 13	28	♌ 12	26	♍ 10	23	♎ 6	19	♏ 1	13	25	♐ 7	19	♑ 0	12	24	♒ 6	18	♓ 0	13	26	♈ 9
☿	♏ 21	21	21	22	23	23	24	25	26	27	28	29 0	♐ 1	2	3	4	6	7	8	10	11	13	14	16	17	19	20	21	23	24	26
♀	♏R 17	17	17	17	17	17	17	D 17	17	17	17	17	17	17	18	18	18	19	19	20	20	21	21	22	22	23	23	24	25	25	26
♂	♐ 18	19	19	20	21	22	22	23	24	25	25	26	27	28	28	29	29 0	♑ 1	1	2	3	4	4	5	6	7	8	8	9	10	11

♃ 1, 4, 9, 14, 19, 24, 29: ♏14, 15, 16, 17, 18, 19, 20 — ♄ 1R, 21: ♌8, 7 — ♅ 1R, 6, 30: ♊20, 19, 18 — ♆ 1: ♎10 — ♇ 1R, 25: ♌13, 12

1947

1

	1	2	3	4	5	6	7	8	9	10	11	12	13	14	15	16	17	18	19	20	21	22	23	24	25	26	27	28
☉	♑ 10	11	12	13	14	15	16	17	18	19	20	21	22	23	25	26	27	28	29	29 0	♒ 1	2	3	4	5	6	7	8
☽	♈ 22	♉ 6	20	♊ 5	20	♋ 5	20	♌ 6	20	♍ 5	19	♎ 2	15	28	♏ 10	22	♐ 4	16	27	♑ 9	21	♒ 3	15	28	♓ 10	23	♈ 6	19
☿	♐ 27	29	29 1	♑ 2	4	5	7	8	10	11	13	15	16	18	19	21	23	24	26	28	29 0	♒ 1	3	4	6	8	9	11
♀	♏ 27	27	28	29	29 0	♐ 0	1	2	3	4	5	5	6	7	8	9	10	11	12	13	14	15	16	17	18	19	20	21
♂	♑ 11	12	13	14	14	15	16	17	17	18	19	20	21	21	22	23	24	24	25	26	27	28	28	29	29 0	♒ 1	1	2

♃ 1, 4, 10, 17, 23, 31: ♏20, 21, 22, 23, 24, 25 — ♄ 1R, 6, 19, 31: ♏7, 6, 5, 4 — ♅ 1R, 31: ♊18, 17 — ♆ 1, 13R: ♎10, 10 — ♇

2

	1	2	3	4	5	6	7	8	9	10	11	12	13	14	15	16	17	18	19	20	21	22	23	24	25	26	27	28
☉	♒ 12	13	14	15	16	17	18	19	20	21	22	23	24	25	26	27	28	29	29 0	♓ 1	2	3	4	5	6	7	8	9
☽	♊ 14	29	♋ 14	29	♌ 13	28	♍ 13	27	♎ 10	23	♏ 6	18	♐ 0	12	24	♑ 6	18	♒ 0	12	24	♓ 7	20	♈ 3	16	29	♉ 13	26	♊ 10
☿	♒ 18	20	22	24	25	27	29	29 1	♓ 2	4	6	8	9	11	12	14	15	17	18	19	20	21	22	22	23	23	23	R 23
♀	♐ 25	26	27	28	29	29 0	♑ 1	2	3	4	6	7	8	9	10	11	12	13	14	15	17	18	19	20	21	22	23	24
♂	♒ 5	6	7	8	8	9	10	11	12	12	13	14	15	16	16	17	18	19	20	20	21	22	23	23	24	25	26	27

♃ 1, 10, 23: ♏25, 26, 27 — ♄ 1R, 13, 28: ♌4, 3, 2 — ♅ 1R, 25D: ♊17, 17 — ♆ 1R: ♎10 — ♇

3

	1	2	3	4	5	6	7	8	9	10	11	12	13	14	15	16	17	18	19	20	21	22	23	24	25	26	27	28
☉	♓ 10	11	12	13	14	15	16	17	18	19	20	21	22	23	24	25	26	27	28	29	29 0	♈ 1	2	3	4	5	6	7
☽	♊ 25	♋ 9	23	♌ 8	22	♍ 7	21	♎ 4	18	♏ 1	14	26	♐ 8	20	♑ 2	14	26	♒ 8	20	♓ 2	15	29	♈ 12	26	♉ 9	23	♊ 7	21
☿	♓R 22	22	21	21	20	19	18	17	16	15	14	13	12	11	11	10	10	9	9	9	9	D 9	9	9	9	10	10	11
♀	♑ 26	27	28	29	29 0	♒ 1	2	4	5	6	7	8	9	11	12	13	14	15	16	18	19	20	21	22	23	25	26	27
♂	♒ 27	28	29	29 0	♓ 1	1	2	3	4	4	5	6	7	8	8	9	10	11	12	12	13	14	15	15	16	17	18	19

♃ 1, 14R: ♏27, 27 — ♄ 1R, 27: ♌2, 1 — ♅ 1, 20: ♊17, 18 — ♆ 1R, 9: ♎10, 9 — ♇

4

	1	2	3	4	5	6	7	8	9	10	11	12	13	14	15	16	17	18	19	20	21	22	23	24	25	26	27	28
☉	♈ 11	12	13	14	15	16	17	18	19	20	21	22	23	24	25	26	27	28	29	29 0	♉ 1	2	2	3	4	5	6	7
☽	♌ 18	♍ 2	16	29	♎ 13	26	♏ 9	22	♐ 4	16	28	♑ 10	21	3	♒ 16	28	♓ 11	24	♈ 7	21	♉ 5	19	♊ 3	18	♋ 2	16	♌ 1	15
☿	♓ 13	14	15	16	17	18	19	20	21	22	24	25	26	28	29	29 0	♈ 2	3	5	6	8	9	11	12	14	16	18	19
♀	♓ 2	3	4	5	6	8	9	10	11	12	14	15	16	17	18	20	21	22	23	24	26	27	28	29	29 0	♈ 1	3	4
♂	♓ 22	22	23	24	25	26	26	27	28	29	29 0	♈ 0	1	2	3	3	4	5	6	6	7	8	9	10	10	11	12	13

♃ 1R, 2, 15, 25: ♏27, 26, 25, 24 — ♄ 1R, 4D, 10: ♌1, 1, 2 — ♅ 1, 20: ♊18, 19 — ♆ 1R, 16: ♎9, 8 — ♇

5

	1	2	3	4	5	6	7	8	9	10	11	12	13	14	15	16	17	18	19	20	21	22	23	24	25	26	27	28
☉	♉ 10	11	12	13	14	15	16	17	18	19	20	21	22	23	24	26	26	27	28	29	29	29 0	♊ 1	2	3	4	5	6
☽	♍ 26	♎ 9	22	♏ 5	17	♐ 0	12	24	♑ 6	18	29	♒ 11	24	♓ 6	19	♈ 2	15	29	♉ 13	27	♊ 12	27	♋ 12	27	♌ 11	25	♍ 9	23
☿	♈ 25	27	28	29 0	♉ 2	4	6	8	10	12	15	17	19	21	23	25	28	29 0	♊ 2	4	6	8	11	13	15	17	19	21
♀	♈ 7	9	10	11	12	13	15	16	17	18	20	21	22	23	24	26	27	28	29	29 0	♉ 2	3	4	5	6	8	9	10
♂	♈ 15	16	16	17	18	19	20	20	21	22	23	23	24	25	26	26	27	28	29	29	29 0	♉ 1	2	2	3	4	5	5

♃ 1R, 3, 11, 19, 27: ♏24, 23, 22, 21, 20 — ♄ 1, 7, 22: ♌2, 3, 4 — ♅ 1, 11, 28: ♊19, 20, 21 — ♆ 1R: ♎8 — ♇

6

	1	2	3	4	5	6	7	8	9	10	11	12	13	14	15	16	17	18	19	20	21	22	23	24	25	26	27	28
☉	♊ 10	11	12	13	14	15	16	17	18	19	20	21	22	23	24	24	25	26	27	28	29	29 0	♋ 1	2	3	4	5	6
☽	♏ 14	26	♐ 8	20	♑ 2	14	26	♒ 8	20	♓ 2	14	27	♈ 10	23	♉ 7	21	♊ 6	21	♋ 6	21	♌ 6	21	♍ 5	19	♎ 3	16	29	♏ 11
☿	♊ 28	29 0	♋ 1	3	5	6	8	9	11	12	13	14	16	17	18	19	20	21	22	23	23	24	25	25	26	26	26	26
♀	♉ 15	16	17	19	20	21	22	23	25	26	27	28	29 0	♊ 1	2	3	4	5	7	8	9	10	12	13	14	15	16	18
♂	♉ 8	9	10	11	11	12	13	13	14	15	16	16	17	18	19	19	20	21	21	22	23	24	24	25	26	27	27	28

♃ 1R, 5, 16: ♏20, 19, 18 — ♄ 1, 3, 13, 22: ♌4, 5, 6, 7 — ♅ 1, 14: ♊21, 22 — ♆ 1R, 20D: ♎8, 8 — ♇

7

	1	2	3	4	5	6	7	8	9	10	11	12	13	14	15	16	17	18	19	20	21	22	23	24	25	26	27	28
☉	♋ 9	10	11	12	13	14	15	16	17	18	19	20	21	22	23	24	25	26	27	28	29	29 0	♌ 1	2	3	4	5	5
☽	♐ 17	29	♑ 11	23	♒ 5	17	29	♓ 11	23	♈ 6	19	♉ 2	16	♊ 0	14	29	♋ 14	29	♌ 15	♍ 0	14	28	♎ 12	25	♏ 8	20	♐ 3	14
☿	♋R 27	27	26	26	26	25	25	25	24	23	23	22	21	21	20	20	19	18	18	18	17	17	17	17	17	D 17	17	17
♀	♊ 21	23	24	25	26	27	29	29 0	♋ 1	2	3	5	6	7	8	10	11	12	13	14	16	17	18	19	21	22	23	24
♂	29 0	♊ 1	2	2	3	4	4	5	6	6	7	8	9	9	10	11	11	12	13	13	14	15	15	16	17	18	18	19

♃ 1R, 16D, 30: ♏17, 17, 18 — ♄ 1, 9, 17, 25: ♌8, 9, 10, 11 — ♅ 1, 20: ♊23, 24 — ♆ 1: ♎8 — ♇

8

	1	2	3	4	5	6	7	8	9	10	11	12	13	14	15	16	17	18	19	20	21	22	23	24	25	26	27	28
☉	♌ 8	9	10	11	12	13	14	15	16	17	18	19	20	21	22	23	24	25	26	27	28	29	29	29 0	♍ 1	2	3	4
☽	♒ 2	14	26	♓ 8	20	♈ 3	15	28	♉ 12	25	♊ 9	23	♋ 8	23	♌ 8	23	♍ 8	23	♎ 7	21	♏ 4	17	29	♐ 11	23	♑ 5	17	29
☿	♋ 19	20	21	22	23	24	25	27	28	29 0	♌ 1	3	4	6	8	10	12	14	16	18	20	22	24	26	28	29 0	♍ 2	4
♀	♋ 29	29 1	♌ 2	3	4	5	7	8	9	10	12	13	14	15	16	18	19	20	21	23	24	25	26	28	29	29 0	♍ 1	3
♂	♊ 22	22	23	24	24	25	26	26	27	28	28	29	29 0	♋ 0	1	2	2	3	4	4	5	5	6	7	7	8	9	9

♃ 1, 14, 24: ♏18, 19, 20 — ♄ 1, 2, 10, 17, 25: ♌11, 12, 13, 14, 15 — ♅ 1, 10: ♊24, 25 — ♆ 1, 20: ♎8, 9 — ♇

9

	1	2	3	4	5	6	7	8	9	10	11	12	13	14	15	16	17	18	19	20	21	22	23	24	25	26	27	28
☉	♍ 8	9	10	11	12	13	14	15	16	17	18	19	20	21	22	23	24	25	26	27	28	29	29 0	♎ 1	2	3	4	5
☽	♓ 17	♈ 0	13	25	♉ 8	22	♊ 5	19	♋ 3	18	♌ 2	17	♍ 2	16	♎ 1	15	29	♏ 12	25	♐ 7	19	♑ 1	13	25	♒ 7	19	♓ 1	14
☿	♍ 11	13	15	17	19	21	22	24	26	28	29 0	♎ 1	3	4	6	7	9	11	12	14	15	17	18	20	21	23	24	26
♀	♍ 7	9	10	11	12	14	15	16	17	19	20	21	22	24	25	26	27	29	29 0	♎ 1	2	4	5	6	7	9	10	11
♂	♋ 12	12	13	14	14	15	16	16	17	17	18	19	19	20	21	21	22	22	23	24	24	25	25	26	27	27	28	28

♃ 1, 2, 9, 16, 22, 28: ♏20, 21, 22, 23, 24, 25 — ♄ 1, 2, 11, 20, 29: ♌15, 16, 17, 18, 19 — ♅ 1, 12: ♊25, 26 — ♆ 1, 19: ♎9, 10 — ♇

10

	1	2	3	4	5	6	7	8	9	10	11	12	13	14	15	16	17	18	19	20	21	22	23	24	25	26	27	28
☉	♎ 7	8	9	10	11	12	13	14	15	16	17	18	19	20	21	22	23	24	25	26	27	28	29	29 0	♏ 1	2	3	4
☽	♈ 22	♉ 5	19	♊ 2	16	♋ 0	14	28	♌ 13	27	♍ 11	25	♎ 9	23	♏ 7	20	♐ 3	15	27	♑ 9	21	♒ 3	15	27	♓ 9	22	♈ 4	17
☿	29 0	♏ 1	2	3	5	6	7	9	10	11	12	13	14	15	16	17	18	18	19	20	20	20	21	21	21	R 21	21	20
♀	♎ 15	16	17	19	20	21	22	24	25	26	27	29	29 0	♏ 1	2	4	5	6	7	8	10	11	12	13	15	16	17	18
♂	29 0	♌ 1	1	2	2	3	3	4	5	5	6	6	7	7	8	8	9	10	10	11	11	12	12	13	13	14	14	15

♃ 1, 3, 9, 14, 19, 24, 29, 25, 28: ♏25, 26, 27, 28, 29, 0 ♐ 0, 1 — ♄ 1, 9, 22: ♌19, 20, 21 — ♅ 1, 3R, 22: ♊26, 26, 25 — ♆ 1, 16: ♎10, 11 — ♇

11

	1	2	3	4	5	6	7	8	9	10	11	12	13	14	15	16	17	18	19	20	21	22	23	24	25	26	27	28
☉	♏ 8	9	10	11	12	13	14	15	16	17	18	19	20	21	22	23	24	25	26	27	28	29	29 0	♐ 1	2	3	4	5
☽	♊ 12	27	♋ 11	25	♌ 9	23	♍ 7	21	♎ 5	19	♏ 2	15	28	♐ 11	23	♑ 5	17	29	♒ 11	23	♓ 5	17	29	♈ 12	25	♉ 9	23	♊ 7
☿	♏R 17	16	15	13	13	11	10	8	7	7	6	5	5	5	D 5	5	6	6	7	8	9	10	11	12	13	14	16	17
♀	♏ 23	25	26	27	28	29 0	♐ 1	2	3	5	6	7	8	10	11	12	13	15	16	17	18	20	21	22	23	25	26	27
♂	♌ 17	17	18	18	19	19	20	20	21	21	22	22	23	23	23	24	24	25	25	25	26	26	27	27	27	28	28	29

♃ 1, 2, 7, 11, 16, 20, 25, 29: ♐1, 2, 3, 4, 5, 6, 7, 8 — ♄ 1, 7: ♌21, 22 — ♅ 1R, 25: ♊25, 24 — ♆ 1, 14: ♎11, 12 — ♇

12

	1	2	3	4	5	6	7	8	9	10	11	12	13	14	15	16	17	18	19	20	21	22	23	24	25	26	27	28
☉	♐ 8	9	10	11	13	14	15	16	17	18	19	20	21	22	23	24	25	26	27	28	29	29 0	♑ 1	2	3	4	5	6
☽	♋ 21	♌ 6	28	♍ 4	18	♎ 2	15	29	♏ 11	24	♐ 7	19	♑ 1	13	25	♒ 7	19	♓ 1	13	25	♈ 7	20	♉ 3	17	♊ 1	15	♋ 0	15
☿	♏ 21	22	24	25	27	28	29 0	♐ 1	3	4	6	7	9	10	12	14	15	17	18	20	21	23	24	26	28	29 0	♑ 1	2
♀	♑ 1	2	3	5	6	7	8	10	11	12	13	15	16	17	18	20	21	22	23	25	26	27	28	29 0	♒ 1	2	3	4
♂	29 0	♍ 0	0	1	1	1	2	2	2	3	3	3	3	4	4	4	4	5	5	5	5	5	6	6	6	6	6	6

♃ 1, 4, 8, 13, 17, 22, 26, 31: ♐8, 9, 10, 11, 12, 13, 14, 15 — ♄ 1, 4R, 31: ♌22, 22, 21 — ♅ 1R, 20: ♊24, 23 — ♆ 1: ♎12 — ♇

1948

1

	1	2	3	4	5	6	7	8	9	10	11	12	13	14	15	16	17	18	19	20	21	22	23	24	25	26	27	28	29	30	31
☉	♑10	11	12	13	14	15	16	17	18	19	20	21	22	23	24	25	26	27	28	29	♒0	1	2	3	4	5	6	7	9	10	11
☽	♍14	♎29	12	♏26	9	♐21	4	16	♑28	10	♒22	4	16	♓28	9	21	♈4	16	28	♉11	25	♊9	23	♋8	23	♌8	24	♍9	24	♎8	22
☿	♑9	10	12	13	15	17	18	20	22	23	25	27	28	♒0	2	3	5	7	8	10	12	14	15	17	19	20	22	23	25	26	28
♀	♒9	11	12	13	14	16	17	18	19	21	22	23	24	25	27	28	29	♓0	2	3	4	5	6	8	9	10	11	13	14	15	16
♂	♍7	7	7	7	7	7	7	7	7R	7	7	7	7	7	7	7	7	6	6	6	6	6	6	5	5	5	5	4	4	4	4

♃ 1 4 9 14 19 24 30 — ♐15 16 17 18 19 20 21; ♄ 1R 17 30 — ♌21 20 19; ♅ 1R 13 — ♊23 22; ♆ 1 11 15R 18 — ♎12 13 13 12; ♇ 1R 24 — ♌14 13

2

	1	2	3	4	5	6	7	8	9	10	11	12	13	14	15	16	17	18	19	20	21	22	23	24	25	26	27	28	29
☉	♒12	13	14	15	16	17	18	19	20	21	22	23	24	25	26	27	28	29	♓0	1	2	3	4	5	6	7	8	9	10
☽	♏5	♐18	1	♑13	25	♒7	19	♓1	13	25	♈6	18	♉1	13	25	♊8	21	♋4	17	♌2	16	♍1	16	♎2	17	♏2	16	0	14
☿	♒29	♓0	2	3	4	5	5	6	6	6	6	6R	6	5	5	4	3	2	1	0	♒29	28	27	26	25	24	23	22	22
♀	♓18	19	20	21	22	23	25	26	27	28	29	♈0	1	2	3	4	5	7	8	9	10	11	13	14	15	16	17	19	20
♂	♍R3	3	3	2	2	2	1	1	1	0	0	0	♌29	29	28	28	28	27	27	27	26	26	25	25	25	24	24	23	23

♃ 1 4 10 16 23 — ♐21 22 23 24 25; ♄ 1R 12 24 — ♌19 18 17; ♅ 1R — ♊22; ♆ 1R — ♎12; ♇ 1R — ♌13

3

	1	2	3	4	5	6	7	8	9	10	11	12	13	14	15	16	17	18	19	20	21	22	23	24	25	26	27	28	29	30	31
☉	♓11	12	13	14	15	16	17	18	19	20	21	22	23	24	25	26	27	28	29	♈0	1	2	3	4	5	6	7	8	9	10	11
☽	♏27	♐9	22	♑4	16	28	♒10	21	♓3	15	28	♈10	22	♉5	18	♊1	14	27	♋11	26	♌10	25	♍10	25	♎10	24	♏8	22	♐5	18	♑0
☿	♒R21	21	21	21D	21	22	22	22	23	23	23	24	25	26	26	27	28	29	♓0	1	3	4	6	7	8	10	11	13	14	15	16
♀	♈22	23	24	25	27	28	29	♉0	1	2	4	5	6	7	8	9	10	11	13	14	15	16	17	18	19	20	21	22	24	25	26
♂	♌R22	22	22	21	21	21	21	20	20	20	20	19	19	19	19	19	18	18	18	18	18	18	18	18	18	18	18	18	18	18D	18

♃ 1 10 21 — ♐26 27 28; ♄ 1R 9 31 — ♌17 16 15; ♅ 1R 2D — ♊22 22; ♆ 1R — ♎12 11; ♇ 1R 8 — ♌13 12

4

	1	2	3	4	5	6	7	8	9	10	11	12	13	14	15	16	17	18	19	20	21	22	23	24	25	26	27	28	29	30
☉	♈12	13	14	15	16	17	18	19	20	21	22	23	24	25	26	27	28	29	♉0	1	2	3	4	5	6	7	8	9	10	
☽	♑12	24	♒6	18	♓0	12	24	♈6	19	♉1	14	27	♊11	24	♋8	22	♌6	21	♍5	19	♎4	18	♏2	16	♐0	13	25	♑8	20	♒2
☿	♓18	19	21	22	24	26	27	29	♈1	2	4	6	7	9	11	13	15	17	19	21	23	25	27	29	♉1	3	5	7	9	11
♀	♉27	28	29	♊0	1	2	3	4	5	6	7	8	9	10	11	12	13	14	15	16	17	18	19	20	21	22	23	24	25	
♂	♌18	18	18	18	18	18	18	18	18	18	18	19	19	19	19	19	20	20	20	20	21	21	21	21	22	22	22	22	23	23

♃ 1 15R — ♐28 28; ♄ 1R 17D — ♌15 15; ♅ 1 14 — ♊22 23; ♆ 1R — ♎11 10; ♇ 1R 25D — ♌12 12

5

	1	2	3	4	5	6	7	8	9	10	11	12	13	14	15	16	17	18	19	20	21	22	23	24	25	26	27	28	29	30	31
☉	♉11	12	13	14	15	16	17	18	19	20	21	22	23	24	25	25	26	27	28	29	♊0	1	2	3	4	5	6	7	8	9	10
☽	♒14	26	♓8	20	♈2	15	27	♉10	23	♊7	21	♋5	19	♌3	17	♍1	16	♎0	14	28	♏11	25	♐8	21	♑3	16	28	♒10	22	♓4	16
☿	♉14	16	18	20	22	24	26	28	♊0	2	4	6	8	10	12	14	16	18	20	21	23	24	25	27	28	29	♋0	1	2	3	
♀	♊25	26	27	28	28	29	♋0	1	1	2	3	3	4	5	5	6	6	7	7	8	8	9	9	9	10	10	10	10	10	11	11
♂	♌23	24	24	24	25	25	25	26	26	26	27	27	28	28	28	29	29	♍0	0	1	1	2	2	2	3	3	3	4	4	5	

♃ 1R 10 21 30 — ♐28 27 26 25; ♄ 1 3 24 — ♌15 16 17; ♅ 1 7 26 — ♊23 24 25; ♆ 1R — ♎10; ♇ 1 — ♌12

6

	1	2	3	4	5	6	7	8	9	10	11	12	13	14	15	16	17	18	19	20	21	22	23	24	25	26	27	28	29	30
☉	♊11	12	13	14	15	16	17	18	19	19	20	21	22	23	24	25	26	27	28	29	♋0	1	2	3	4	5	6	7	8	9
☽	♓28	♈10	23	♉5	19	♊2	16	♋0	15	29	♌14	28	♍12	27	♎10	24	♏8	21	♐4	17	♑29	♒12	24	♓6	18	♈0	12	24	♉6	18
☿	♋3	4	5	5	6	6	7	7	7	7	7	7R	7	6	6	6	6	5	5	4	3	3	2	1	1	0	0	♊29	29	29
♀	♋11	11	11	11	10R	10	10	10	10	9	9	9	8	8	8	7	7	7	6	6	5	5	4	3	3	2	2	1	0	♊29
♂	♍6	7	7	8	8	9	9	9	10	10	11	11	12	12	13	13	14	14	15	15	16	16	17	17	18	18	19	19	20	20

♃ 1R 7 15 23 — ♐25 24 23 22; ♄ 1 7 18 28 — ♌17 18 19 20; ♅ 1 12 29 — ♊25 26 27; ♆ 1R 21D — ♎10 10; ♇ 1 9 — ♌12 13

7

	1	2	3	4	5	6	7	8	9	10	11	12	13	14	15	16	17	18	19	20	21	22	23	24	25	26	27	28	29	30	31
☉	♋10	10	11	12	13	14	15	16	17	18	19	20	21	22	23	24	25	26	27	28	29	♌0	1	2	3	4	5	6	7	8	
☽	♈1	♉13	27	♊10	24	♋9	24	♌9	24	♍8	23	7	♎21	5	♏18	1	14	♐26	8	♑21	3	♒15	27	♓9	21	♈3	15	27	♉9	22	♊5
☿	♊R28	28	28	28	28	28	28	28	28D	28	29	29	♋0	0	1	2	3	5	6	8	9	10	12	13	15	17	18	20	22	24	26
♀	♊R28	28	27	27	26	26	25	25	25	25	24	24	24	24D	24	24	24	24	24	24	24	25	25	26	26	26	27	27	28	28	
♂	♍21	21	22	23	23	24	24	25	25	26	27	27	28	28	29	29	♎0	1	1	2	2	3	3	4	5	5	6	6	7	7	

♃ 1R 11 21 — ♐21 20 19; ♄ 1 8 16 25 — ♌20 21 22 23; ♅ 1 16 — ♊27 28; ♆ 1 — ♎10; ♇ 1 19 — ♌13 14

8

	1	2	3	4	5	6	7	8	9	10	11	12	13	14	15	16	17	18	19	20	21	22	23	24	25	26	27	28	29	30	31
☉	♌9	10	11	12	13	14	15	16	17	18	19	20	21	22	23	24	25	26	27	28	29	♍0	1	2	3	4	5	6	7	8	
☽	♊18	♋3	17	♌2	17	♍3	18	♎3	17	♏1	15	28	♐11	23	♑6	18	♒0	12	24	♓6	17	29	♈11	23	♉5	18	♊1	14	27	♋11	26
☿	♌28	♍0	2	4	6	8	10	12	14	16	18	20	22	24	26	28	♎0	2	4	6	8	9	11	13	15	16	18	20	21	23	25
♀	♊29	♋0	1	1	2	2	3	4	4	5	6	7	8	8	9	10	11	12	13	14	15	16	17	18	19	20	21	22	23	24	25
♂	♎9	9	10	11	11	12	13	13	14	14	15	16	16	17	18	18	19	20	20	21	22	22	23	23	24	25	25	26	27	27	28

♃ 1R 16D — ♐19 19; ♄ 1 5 10 18 25 — ♌23 24 25 26 27; ♅ 1 5 30 29 31 — ♊28 29 0 ♋0; ♆ 1 15 — ♎10 11; ♇ 1 21 — ♌14 15

9

	1	2	3	4	5	6	7	8	9	10	11	12	13	14	15	16	17	18	19	20	21	22	23	24	25	26	27	28	29	30
☉	♍9	10	11	12	13	14	15	16	17	18	19	20	21	22	23	24	25	26	27	28	29	♎0	1	2	3	4	5	6	7	
☽	♌11	26	♍11	26	♎11	26	♏10	24	♐7	20	♑2	15	27	♒9	21	♓3	14	26	♈8	20	♉2	15	28	♊11	24	♋8	22	♌6	20	♍4
☿	♎26	28	♏0	1	3	4	6	7	9	10	11	13	14	15	17	18	19	20	21	22	23	24	25	26	27	28	29	29	0	1
♀	♋23	24	25	26	27	28	29	♌0	1	2	3	4	5	6	7	8	9	10	11	12	13	14	15	16	17	18	19	21	22	23
♂	♎28	29	♏0	0	1	2	2	3	4	5	5	6	7	7	8	9	10	10	11	12	12	13	14	15	15	16	17	17	18	18

♃ 1 9 20 29 — ♐19 20 21 22; ♄ 1 2 10 19 29 20 27 — ♌27 28 29 0 ♍0 1; ♅ 1 — ♋0; ♆ 1 15 — ♎11 12; ♇ 1 29 — ♌15 16

10

	1	2	3	4	5	6	7	8	9	10	11	12	13	14	15	16	17	18	19	20	21	22	23	24	25	26	27	28	29	30	31
☉	♎8	9	10	11	12	13	14	15	16	17	18	19	20	21	22	23	24	25	26	27	28	29	♏0	1	2	3	4	5	6	7	8
☽	♏19	♐5	19	♑4	18	♒2	16	28	♓11	23	♈6	17	29	♉11	23	♊5	17	29	♋12	24	♌7	20	♍4	17	♎1	15	29	♏14	28	♐13	28
☿	♏3	4	4	4	5	5	5	5R	5	4	4	4	3	3	2	1	0	♎29	28	26	25	24	23	22	21	21	20	19	20D	20	
♀	♍24	25	26	28	29	♎0	1	2	3	4	6	7	8	9	10	12	13	14	15	16	18	19	20	21	22	24	25	26	27	28	29
♂	♏19	19	20	21	21	22	23	24	24	25	26	26	27	28	29	29	♐0	1	2	3	3	4	5	6	6	7	8	8	9	10	11

♃ 1 6 13 19 25 31 — ♐22 23 24 25 26 27; ♄ 1 6 16 27 — ♍1 2 3 4; ♅ 1 6R — ♋0 0; ♆ 1 12 — ♎12 13; ♇ 1 — ♌16

11

	1	2	3	4	5	6	7	8	9	10	11	12	13	14	15	16	17	18	19	20	21	22	23	24	25	26	27	28	29	30
☉	♏9	10	11	12	13	14	15	16	17	18	19	20	21	22	23	24	25	26	27	28	29	♐0	1	2	3	4	5	6	7	8
☽	♐12	26	♑10	23	♒6	19	♓2	14	26	♈7	19	♉1	13	26	♊8	21	♋4	17	♌0	14	28	♍12	26	♎10	24	♏8	23	♐7	21	♑4
☿	♎21	22	23	24	25	26	28	29	♏1	3	4	6	7	9	11	12	14	15	17	19	20	22	23	25	27	28	♐0	1	3	
♀	♎0	1	3	4	5	6	7	9	10	11	12	13	15	16	17	18	19	21	22	23	24	26	27	28	29	♐1	2	3	5	
♂	♐11	12	13	14	15	15	16	17	18	18	19	20	21	21	22	23	24	24	25	26	27	27	28	29	29	♑0	1	2	3	

♃ 1 5 10 15 29 16 20 24 29 — ♐27 28 29 0 ♑0 1 2 3; ♄ 1 10 — ♍4 5; ♅ 1R 12 0 13 — ♋0 29 ♊29; ♆ 1 10 — ♎13 14; ♇ 1 18R — ♌16 16

12

	1	2	3	4	5	6	7	8	9	10	11	12	13	14	15	16	17	18	19	20	21	22	23	24	25	26	27	28	29	30	31
☉	♐9	10	11	12	13	14	15	16	17	18	19	20	21	22	23	24	25	27	28	29	♑0	1	2	3	4	5	6	7	8	9	10
☽	♑18	♒1	14	27	♓9	21	♈3	15	27	♉9	21	♊3	16	29	♋12	26	♌10	24	♍8	22	♎6	20	♏5	19	♐3	17	♑0	13	27	♒10	22
☿	♐3	4	6	8	9	11	12	14	15	17	18	20	22	23	25	26	28	♑0	1	3	4	6	7	9	10	12	14	16	17	19	20
♀	♐7	8	9	10	12	13	14	15	16	17	18	20	21	22	23	24	25	26	27	29	♑0	1	2	3	4	5	6	7	9	10	11
♂	♑3	4	5	6	7	7	8	8	9	10	11	12	13	13	14	15	16	16	17	18	19	20	20	21	22	23	24	25	25	26	27

♃ 1 4 8 12 17 21 26 30 — ♑3 4 5 6 7 8 9 10; ♄ 1R 17R 31 — ♍6 6 5; ♅ 1R 9 — ♊29 28; ♆ 1 15 — ♎14 15; ♇ 1R — ♌16

1949

1

	1	2	3	4	5	6	7	8	9	10	11	12	13	14	15	16	17	18	19	20	21	22	23	24	25	26	27	28	29	30	31
☉	♑11	12	13	14	15	16	17	18	19	20	21	22	23	24	25	26	27	28	29	♒0	1	2	3	4	5	6	7	8	9	10	11
☽	♒5	17	♓29	11	♈23	5	♉17	29	♊11	24	♋7	20	♌4	18	♍3	18	♎2	17	♏2	16	♐0	14	27	♑10	23	♒6	19	♓1	13	26	♈8
☿	♑22	24	25	27	29	♒0	2	3	5	6	8	9	11	12	14	15	16	17	18	18	19	20	20	20	20R	19	19	18	17	16	15
♀	♐15	16	18	19	20	21	23	24	25	26	28	29	♑0	1	3	4	5	6	8	9	10	11	13	14	15	16	18	19	20	21	23
♂	♑27	28	29	♒0	1	2	3	4	5	6	7	8	9	10	11	12	13	13	14	15	16	17	18	19	20	21					

♃ 1 3 7 12 16 21 25 29 — ♑10 11 12 13 14 15 16 17; ♄ 1R 22 — ♍5 4; ♅ 1R 2 30 — ♊28 27 26; ♆ 1 16R — ♎15 15; ♇ 1R 6 — ♌16 15

2

	1	2	3	4	5	6	7	8	9	10	11	12	13	14	15	16	17	18	19	20	21	22	23	24	25	26	27	28
☉	♒12	13	14	15	16	17	18	19	20	21	22	23	24	25	26	27	28	29	♓0	1	2	3	4	5	6	7	8	9
☽	♈19	♉1	13	25	♊7	19	♋2	15	28	♌12	26	♍11	26	♎11	26	♏10	24	♐7	20	♑3	16	28	♒10	22	♓4	16		
☿	♒R15	13	12	10	9	8	7	6	6	5	5	4	4	4	4	4D	4	5	5	5	6	7	7	8	9	10	11	12
♀	♑24	25	26	28	29	♒0	1	3	4	5	6	8	9	10	11	13	14	15	16	17	19	20	21	22	24	25	26	27
♂	♒22	23	23	24	25	26	27	28	29	♓0	1	2	3	4	4	5	6	7	8	8	9	10	11	11	12	13		

♃ 1 3 7 12 17 22 27 — ♑17 18 19 20 21 22 23; ♄ 1R 6 19 — ♍4 3 2; ♅ 1R — ♊26; ♆ 1R 19 — ♎15 14; ♇ 1R 19 — ♌15 14

3

	1	2	3	4	5	6	7	8	9	10	11	12	13	14	15	16	17	18	19	20	21	22	23	24	25	26	27	28	29	30	31
☉	♓11	12	13	14	15	16	17	18	19	20	21	22	23	24	25	26	27	28	29	♈0	1	2	3	4	5	6	7	8	9	10	
☽	♈28	♉10	22	♊4	16	28	♋10	23	♌6	20	♍4	19	♎4	19	♏4	19	♐4	18	♑3	17	♒0	13	25	♓7	19	♈1	13	25	♉7	19	♊1
☿	♒14	15	16	17	18	19	20	22	23	24	26	27	29	♓0	1	3	4	6	7	9	11	12	14	16	17	19	21	22	24	26	28
♀	♒29	♓0	1	2	4	5	6	7	9	10	11	12	14	15	16	17	19	20	21	22	24	25	26	27	29	♈0	1	2	4	5	6
♂	♓14	15	15	16	17	18	19	19	20	21	22	22	23	24	25	26	26	27	28	29	♈0	0	1	2	3	3	4	5	6	7	7

♃ 1 4 9 15 21 26 — ♑23 24 25 26 27 28; ♄ 1R 3 16 — ♍2 1 0; ♅ 1R 5D — ♊26 26; ♆ 1R 27 — ♎14 13; ♇ 1R — ♌14

4

	1	2	3	4	5	6	7	8	9	10	11	12	13	14	15	16	17	18	19	20	21	22	23	24	25	26	27	28	29	30
☉	♈11	12	13	14	15	16	17	18	19	20	21	22	23	24	25	26	27	28	29	♉0	1	2	3	4	5	6	7	8	9	10
☽	♉13	25	♊7	20	♋2	16	29	♌13	28	♍12	27	♎13	28	♏13	28	♐11	25	♑9	21	♒4	16	28	♓10	22	♈4	16	27	♉10	22	♊4
☿	♈0	1	3	5	7	9	11	13	15	17	19	21	23	25	27	♉0	2	4	6	8	10	12	14	16	18	20	22	24	26	27
♀	♈7	9	10	11	12	14	15	16	17	18	20	21	22	23	25	26	27	28	♉0	1	2	3	5	6	7	8	9	11	12	13
♂	♈8	9	10	10	11	12	13	13	14	15	16	17	17	18	19	20	20	21	22	23	23	24	25	26	26	27	28	29	29	♉0

♃ 1 4 12 29 13 23 — ♑29 ♒0 0 1; ♄ 1R 3 0 4 — ♍0 29 ♌29; ♅ 1 7 — ♊26 27; ♆ 1R — ♎13; ♇ 1R 26D — ♌14 14

5

	1	2	3	4	5	6	7	8	9	10	11	12	13	14	15	16	17	18	19	20	21	22	23	24	25	26	27	28	29	30	31
☉	♉11	12	13	14	15	16	17	18	19	20	21	22	23	24	25	26	27	28	29	♊0	1	2	3	4	5	6	7	8	9	10	
☽	♊17	♋29	12	26	♌9	23	♍7	22	♎6	21	♏6	21	♐5	19	♑3	17	♒0	12	25	♓7	19	♈1	12	24	♉6	18	♊1	13	26	♋9	23
☿	♉29	♊0	2	3	5	6	7	9	10	11	12	13	14	15	15	16	16	17	17	17	17	17	17	16R	16	16	15	15	15	14	
♀	♉14	16	17	18	19	21	22	23	24	25	27	28	29	♊0	2	3	4	5	7	8	9	10	12	13	14	15	16	18	19	20	21
♂	♉1	2	2	3	4	5	5	6	7	8	8	9	10	11	12	13	13	14	15	16	16	17	18	19	20	21	21	22	23		

♃ 1 9 21R 30 — ♒1 2 2 1; ♄ 1R 2D 29 29 30 — ♌29 29 0 ♍0; ♅ 1 3 23 — ♊27 28 29; ♆ 1R 5 — ♎13 12; ♇ 1 — ♌14

6

	1	2	3	4	5	6	7	8	9	10	11	12	13	14	15	16	17	18	19	20	21	22	23	24	25	26	27	28	29	30
☉	♊11	12	13	13	14	15	16	17	18	19	20	21	22	23	24	25	26	27	28	29	♋0	1	2	3	4	5	6	7	8	9
☽	♌6	20	♍4	18	♎2	17	♏1	15	♐0	14	28	♑11	25	♒8	20	♓3	15	27	♈8	20	♉2	14	27	♊9	22	♋5	19	♌3	17	♍1
☿	♊R14	13	12	12	11	11	10	10	9	9	9	9	8	8	8	8D	9	9	9	9	10	10	11	11	12	13	14	14	15	16
♀	♊23	24	25	26	27	29	♋0	1	2	4	5	6	7	8	10	11	12	13	15	16	17	18	19	21	22	23	24	26	27	28
♂	♉24	24	25	26	26	27	27	28	29	29	♊0	1	2	2	3	4	4	5	6	7	7	8	9	10	10	11	12	13	13	14

♃ 1R 17 27 0 28 — ♒1 0 29 ♑29; ♄ 1 14 27 — ♍0 1 2; ♅ 1 9 29 10 26 — ♊29 0 ♋0 1; ♆ 1R 24D — ♎12 12; ♇ 1 29 — ♌14 15

7

	1	2	3	4	5	6	7	8	9	10	11	12	13	14	15	16	17	18	19	20	21	22	23	24	25	26	27	28	29	30	31
☉	♋9	10	11	12	13	14	15	16	17	18	19	20	21	22	23	24	25	25	26	27	28	29	♌0	1	2	3	4	5	6	7	8
☽	♍15	29	♎13	27	♏11	25	♐9	23	♑7	20	♒3	16	28	♓11	23	♈4	16	28	♉10	22	♊5	17	♋0	14	28	♌12	26	♍11	25	♎10	24
☿	♊18	19	20	21	23	24	26	27	29	♋0	2	4	6	8	10	12	14	16	18	20	22	24	26	28	♌0	3	5	7	9	11	13
♀	♌0	1	2	3	4	5	7	8	10	11	13	14	15	16	18	19	20	21	22	24	25	26	27	28	♍0	1	2	3	5	6	
♂	♊15	16	16	17	18	18	19	20	20	21	22	22	23	24	24	25	26	26	27	28	28	29	♋0	0	1	2	2	3	4	4	5

♃ 1R 6 14 22 30 — ♑29 28 27 26 25; ♄ 1 8 17 26 — ♍2 3 4 5; ♅ 1 13 — ♋1 2; ♆ 1 — ♎12; ♇ 1 — ♌15

8

	1	2	3	4	5	6	7	8	9	10	11	12	13	14	15	16	17	18	19	20	21	22	23	24	25	26	27	28	29	30	31
☉	♌9	10	11	12	13	14	15	16	17	17	18	19	20	21	22	23	24	25	26	27	28	29	♍0	1	2	3	4	5	6	7	8
☽	♏8	22	♐6	19	♑3	16	29	♒12	24	♓7	19	♈1	12	24	♉6	18	♊0	13	25	♋8	21	♌5	20	♍5	20	♎4	19	♏3	16		
☿	♌15	17	19	21	23	25	26	28	♍0	2	4	5	7	9	10	12	14	15	17	18	20	21	23	24	26	27	28	♎0	1	2	3
♀	♍7	8	9	11	12	13	14	15	17	18	19	20	22	23	24	25	26	28	29	♎0	1	2	4	5	6	7	9	10	11	12	13
♂	♋6	7	7	8	9	9	10	11	11	12	13	13	14	15	16	16	17	17	18	19	19	20	21	22	22	23	24	24	25	26	

♃ 1R 7 16 29 — ♑25 24 23 22; ♄ 1 4 12 20 28 — ♍5 6 7 8 9; ♅ 1 22 — ♋3 4; ♆ 1 10 — ♎12 13; ♇ 1 3 — ♌15 16

9

	1	2	3	4	5	6	7	8	9	10	11	12	13	14	15	16	17	18	19	20	21	22	23	24	25	26	27	28	29	30
☉	♍9	10	11	12	13	14	15	15	16	17	18	19	20	21	22	23	24	25	26	27	28	29	♎0	1	2	3	4	5	6	7
☽	♑0	13	26	♒8	21	♓3	15	27	♈9	21	♉3	15	27	♊9	21	♋4	17	♌0	14	29	♍14	29	♎14	29	♏13	28	♐13	26	♑10	23
☿	♎5	6	7	8	9	10	11	12	13	14	15	15	16	16	17	17	18	18	18	18	18R	18	17	17	16	16	15	14	13	
♀	♎14	15	17	18	19	20	21	22	24	25	26	27	28	♏0	1	2	3	4	5	7	8	9	10	11	13	14	15	16	17	18
♂	♋26	27	27	28	29	29	♌0	1	2	3	3	4	5	5	6	7	7	8	9	9	10	10	11	11	12	13	13	14	14	

♃ 1R 19D — ♑22 22; ♄ 1 5 13 21 29 — ♍9 10 11 12 13; ♅ 1 — ♋4; ♆ 1 13 — ♎13 14; ♇ 1 5 — ♌16 17

10

	1	2	3	4	5	6	7	8	9	10	11	12	13	14	15	16	17	18	19	20	21	22	23	24	25	26	27	28	29	30	31
☉	♎8	9	10	11	12	13	14	15	16	17	18	19	20	21	22	23	24	25	26	27	28	29	♏0	1	2	3	4	5	6	7	8
☽	♒6	18	♓0	12	24	♈6	18	♉0	11	23	♊5	18	♋0	13	26	♌9	23	♍7	22	♎7	22	♏7	22	♐7	22	♑6	19	♒2	15	27	♓9
☿	♎R12	11	10	9	7	6	5	5	4	4	4D	4	5	5	6	7	8	9	10	11	12	14	15	16	17	19	20	21	23	24	
♀	♏20	21	22	23	24	25	26	28	29	♐0	1	2	3	4	5	6	7	8	9	10	11	12	13	14	15	16	17	18	19	20	21
♂	♌15	15	16	17	17	18	18	19	19	20	20	21	21	22	23	23	24	24	25	25	26	26	27	27	28	28	29	♍0	0	1	2

♃ 1 8 21 30 — ♑22 23 24 25; ♄ 1 8 17 27 — ♍13 14 15 16; ♅ 1 3 11R 18 — ♋4 5 5 4; ♆ 1 10 — ♎14 15; ♇ 1 22 — ♌17 18

11

	1	2	3	4	5	6	7	8	9	10	11	12	13	14	15	16	17	18	19	20	21	22	23	24	25	26	27	28	29	30
☉	♏9	10	11	12	13	14	15	16	17	18	19	20	21	22	23	24	25	26	27	28	29	♐0	1	2	3	4	5	6	7	8
☽	♓21	♈3	15	27	♉8	20	♊2	15	27	♋9	22	♌5	19	♍2	16	♎1	15	♏0	15	♐0	15	29	♑14	27	♒11	23	♓6	18	♈0	
☿	♏26	28	♐0	1	3	4	6	8	9	11	12	14	16	17	19	20	22	23	25	26	28	♑0	1	3	4	6	7	9	11	13
♀	♐25	26	27	28	29	♑0	1	2	3	4	5	6	7	8	9	10	11	12	13	14	15	16	17	18	19	20	21	22	23	24
♂	♍3	3	4	5	5	6	6	7	7	8	8	9	10	10	11	11	12	12	13	13	14	14	15	15	16	16	17	17	18	18

♃ 1 6 13 19 25 30 29 — ♑25 26 27 28 29 0 ♒0; ♄ 1 17 19 — ♍16 17 18; ♅ 1R 29 — ♋4 3; ♆ 1 7 — ♎15 16; ♇ 1 19R — ♌18 18

12

	1	2	3	4	5	6	7	8	9	10	11	12	13	14	15	16	17	18	19	20	21	22	23	24	25	26	27	28	29	30	31
☉	♐9	10	11	12	13	14	15	16	17	18	19	20	21	22	23	24	25	26	27	28	29	♑0	1	2	3	4	5	6	7	8	10
☽	♈23	♉5	17	29	♊11	24	♋6	19	♌2	16	29	♍13	26	♎11	25	♏9	24	♐9	24	♑8	22	♒5	18	♓1	14	26	♈8	20	♉1	13	25
☿	♐14	16	17	19	20	22	24	25	27	28	♑0	1	3	4	6	8	9	11	12	14	15	17	18	20	21	22	24	25	26	28	29
♀	♑26	26	27	28	29	♒0	1	2	3	4	5	6	7	8	9	10	10	11	12	13	14	14	15	15	16	16	17	17			
♂	♍19	19	20	20	21	21	22	22	23	23	24	24	25	25	26	26	27	27	27	28	28	28	29	29	29	♎0	0	0	1	1	2

♃ 1 5 10 15 20 25 29 — ♒0 1 2 3 4 5 6; ♄ 1 8 — ♍18 19; ♅ 1R 24 — ♋3 2; ♆ 1 13 — ♎16 17; ♇ 1R 18 — ♌18 17

1950

Month	Planet	1	2	3	4	5	6	7	8	9	10	11	12	13	14	15	16	17	18	19	20	21	22	23	24	25	26	27	28	29	30	31
1	☉	11	12	13	14	15	16	17	18	19	20	21	22	23	24	25	26	27	28	29	0	1	2	3	4	5	6	7	8	9	10	11
	☽	7	20	3	16	29	12	26	10	23	7	21	5	20	4	18	2	16	0	13	26	9	21	4	15	27	9	21	3	15	28	11
	☿	0	1	2	2	3	3	4	4	3	3	3	2	1	1	29	27	26	25	24	23	22	21	20	19	18	18	18	18	18	18	18
	♀	17	17	17	18	18	18	18	18	18	18	18	18	18	18	17	17	17	17	16	16	16	15	15	14	14	13	12	12	11	11	10
	♂	2	3	3	3	3	4	4	4	5	5	5	5	6	6	6	7	7	7	7	8	8	8	8	9	9	9	9	10	10	10	10

♃ 1 3 7 11 16 20 24 28 / ≈6 7 8 9 10 11 12 13 — ♄ 1 ℞ 21 ♍19 18 — ♅ 1 ℞ 17 ♋2 1 — ♆ 1 18℞ ♎17 17 — ♇ 1 ℞ ♌17

Month	Planet	1	2	3	4	5	6	7	8	9	10	11	12	13	14	15	16	17	18	19	20	21	22	23	24	25	26	27	28
2	☉	12	13	14	15	16	17	18	19	20	21	22	23	24	25	26	27	28	29	0	1	2	3	4	5	6	7	8	9
	☽	24	7	21	5	20	4	18	2	16	1	14	28	12	25	9	22	5	17	29	11	23	5	17	29	11	23	6	18
	☿	18	19	19	20	21	22	22	23	24	25	26	27	29	0	1	2	3	5	6	7	8	10	11	12	14	15	17	18
	♀	10	9	8	7	7	6	6	5	5	4	4	4	4	3	3	3	3	3	3	3	3	3	3	3	3	3	4	4
	♂	10	10	10	10	10	10	10	10	11	11	11	11	11	11	10	10	10	10	10	10	10	10	10	10	10	9	9	9

♃ 1 2 6 10 14 18 23 27 / ≈13 14 15 16 17 18 19 20 — ♄ 1 ℞ 9 23 ♍18 17 16 — ♅ 1 ℞ 27 ♋1 0 — ♆ 1 ℞ 24 ♎17 16 — ♇ 1 ℞ 6 ♌7 6

Month	Planet	1	2	3	4	5	6	7	8	9	10	11	12	13	14	15	16	17	18	19	20	21	22	23	24	25	26	27	28	29	30	31
3	☉	10	11	12	13	14	15	16	17	18	19	20	21	22	23	24	25	26	27	28	29	0	1	2	3	4	5	6	7	8	9	10
	☽	2	16	0	14	29	13	28	13	27	11	25	9	22	5	18	1	13	26	8	20	2	13	25	7	19	1	14	27	10	23	8
	☿	20	21	23	24	26	28	29	1	2	4	6	8	9	11	13	15	16	18	20	22	24	26	28	0	1	3	5	8	10	12	14
	♀	4	5	5	5	6	6	7	7	8	8	9	10	10	11	12	12	13	14	14	15	16	17	17	18	19	20	21	21	22	23	24
	♂	9	8	8	8	7	7	7	6	6	6	5	5	5	4	4	4	3	3	2	2	2	1	1	0	0	0	29	29	29	29	28

♃ 1 3 7 12 16 21 26 30 / ≈20 21 22 23 24 25 26 27 — ♄ 1 ℞ 7 20 ♍16 15 14 — ♅ 1 ℞ 9D 21 ♋0 0 1 — ♆ 1 ℞ ♎16 — ♇ 1 ℞ 27 ♌16 15

Month	Planet	1	2	3	4	5	6	7	8	9	10	11	12	13	14	15	16	17	18	19	20	21	22	23	24	25	26	27	28	29	30
4	☉	11	12	13	14	15	16	17	18	19	20	21	22	23	24	25	26	27	28	29	0	1	2	3	4	5	6	7	8	9	10
	☽	22	7	22	7	22	7	21	5	19	2	15	28	10	23	5	17	28	10	22	4	16	28	10	22	5	18	2	16	0	15
	☿	16	18	20	22	24	26	28	0	2	4	6	7	9	11	12	14	15	17	18	20	21	22	23	24	24	25	26	26	26	27
	♀	25	26	27	28	29	0	1	2	3	4	5	6	7	8	9	10	11	12	13	14	15	16	17	18	19	20	21	22	23	24
	♂	28	27	27	27	26	26	26	25	25	25	25	24	24	24	24	23	23	23	23	23	22	22	22	22	22	22	22	22	22	22

♃ 1 4 10 15 29 16 20 26 / ≈27 28 29 0 ♓0 1 2 — ♄ 1 ℞ 3 23 ♍14 13 12 — ♅ 1 ℞ 2 ♋1 2 — ♆ 1 ℞ 5 ♎16 15 — ♇ 1 ℞ 28D ♌15 15

Month	Planet	1	2	3	4	5	6	7	8	9	10	11	12	13	14	15	16	17	18	19	20	21	22	23	24	25	26	27	28	29	30	31
5	☉	11	11	12	13	14	15	16	17	18	19	20	21	22	23	24	25	26	27	28	29	0	1	2	3	4	5	6	7	8	9	9
	☽	0	15	1	16	0	15	28	12	25	7	20	2	14	25	7	19	1	13	25	7	19	2	15	28	11	25	9	24	9	24	9
	☿	27	27	27	27	27	26	26	25	25	24	24	23	23	22	22	22	21	21	20	20	19	19	19	18	18	18	18	18	18	18	18
	♀	25	26	27	28	0	1	2	3	4	5	6	7	8	9	11	12	13	14	15	16	17	18	20	21	22	23	24	25	26	28	29
	♂	22	22	22	22	22	22	22	22	22	22	22	22	22	23	23	23	23	23	23	23	24	24	24	24	25	25	25	25	26	26	26

♃ 1 3 10 17 27 / ♓2 3 4 5 6 — ♄ 1 ℞ 15D ♍12 12 — ♅ 1 20 ♋2 3 — ♆ 1 ℞ 16 ♎15 14 — ♇ 1 29 ♌15 16

Month	Planet	1	2	3	4	5	6	7	8	9	10	11	12	13	14	15	16	17	18	19	20	21	22	23	24	25	26	27	28	29	30
6	☉	10	11	12	13	14	15	16	17	18	19	20	21	22	23	24	25	26	27	28	29	0	1	2	3	4	5	6	7	8	9
	☽	24	9	23	7	21	4	16	28	10	22	4	16	28	10	22	4	16	29	12	25	8	21	5	19	3	18	3	18	2	17
	☿	19	20	20	21	21	22	23	24	24	25	27	28	29	0	1	2	4	5	6	8	9	11	13	15	16	18	20	22	24	26
	♀	0	1	2	3	4	6	7	8	9	10	11	13	14	15	16	17	18	20	21	22	23	24	25	27	28	29	0	1	2	3
	♂	26	27	27	27	27	28	28	28	29	29	29	29	0	0	1	1	1	1	2	2	2	3	3	3	4	4	5	5	6	6

♃ 1 10 26℞ / ♓6 7 7 — ♄ 1 6 25 ♍12 13 14 — ♅ 1 7 24 ♋3 4 5 — ♆ 1 ℞ 26D ♎14 14 — ♇ 1 ♌16

Month	Planet	1	2	3	4	5	6	7	8	9	10	11	12	13	14	15	16	17	18	19	20	21	22	23	24	25	26	27	28	29	30	31
7	☉	9	10	11	12	13	14	15	16	17	18	19	20	21	22	23	24	25	26	27	28	29	0	1	2	3	4	5	6	7	8	8
	☽	1	15	29	12	24	7	19	1	13	24	6	18	1	13	26	8	22	5	18	2	16	0	14	28	12	26	11	26	10	24	8
	☿	28	0	2	4	6	8	10	12	14	17	19	21	23	25	27	29	1	3	5	7	9	11	13	15	17	19	20	22	24	26	27
	♀	5	6	7	8	9	11	12	13	14	15	17	18	19	20	21	22	24	25	26	27	28	29	1	2	3	4	6	7	8	9	10
	♂	8	8	9	9	10	10	11	11	12	12	13	13	14	14	15	15	16	17	17	18	18	19	19	20	20	21	22	22	23	23	24

♃ 1℞ 13 27 / ♓7 6 5 — ♄ 1 8 19 29 ♍14 15 16 17 — ♅ 1 10 28 ♋5 6 7 — ♆ 1 ♎14 — ♇ 1 14 ♌16 17

Month	Planet	1	2	3	4	5	6	7	8	9	10	11	12	13	14	15	16	17	18	19	20	21	22	23	24	25	26	27	28	29	30	31
8	☉	9	10	11	12	12	13	14	15	16	17	18	19	20	21	22	23	24	25	26	27	28	29	0	1	2	3	4	5	6	7	7
	☽	20	2	15	27	9	21	2	14	27	9	21	4	18	1	15	28	12	27	11	25	9	23	7	21	5	19	2	15	28	10	23
	☿	29	0	2	4	5	7	8	9	11	12	14	15	16	17	19	20	21	22	23	24	25	26	27	27	28	28	29	0	0	1	2
	♀	12	13	14	15	16	18	19	20	21	23	24	25	26	27	29	0	1	2	3	5	6	7	8	10	11	12	13	14	16	17	18
	♂	24	25	26	26	27	27	28	28	29	0	0	1	1	2	3	3	4	5	5	6	7	7	8	8	9	10	10	11	12	12	13

♃ 1℞ 6 15 22 29 / ♓5 4 3 2 1 — ♄ 1 8 16 25 ♍17 18 19 20 — ♅ 1 6 ♋7 8 — ♆ 1 5 ♎14 15 — ♇ 1 16 ♌17 18

Month	Planet	1	2	3	4	5	6	7	8	9	10	11	12	13	14	15	16	17	18	19	20	21	22	23	24	25	26	27	28	29	30
9	☉	8	9	10	11	12	13	14	15	16	17	18	19	20	21	22	23	24	25	26	27	28	29	0	1	2	3	4	5	6	7
	☽	5	17	28	10	22	4	17	0	13	26	10	24	8	22	7	21	6	20	4	18	2	16	0	13	26	9	21	4	16	28
	☿	2	2	2	2	2	1	1	1	0	29	29	28	27	26	25	24	23	22	21	20	19	18	17	17	17	18	18	18	18	19
	♀	19	21	22	23	24	26	27	28	29	1	2	3	4	5	7	8	9	10	12	13	14	15	16	18	19	20	21	22	24	25
	♂	13	14	15	15	16	17	17	18	19	19	20	21	21	22	23	23	24	25	25	26	27	27	28	29	29	0	1	1	2	3

♃ 1℞ 6 15 0 16 24 / ♓1 0 29 ≈29 28 — ♄ 1 2 10 18 26 ♍20 21 22 23 24 — ♅ 1 12 ♋8 9 — ♆ 1 ♎15 16 — ♇ 1 20 ♌18 19

Month	Planet	1	2	3	4	5	6	7	8	9	10	11	12	13	14	15	16	17	18	19	20	21	22	23	24	25	26	27	28	29	30	31
10	☉	8	9	10	11	12	13	14	15	16	17	18	19	20	21	22	23	24	25	26	27	28	29	0	1	2	3	4	5	6	7	8
	☽	7	18	0	12	25	7	20	4	18	2	17	1	16	0	15	29	13	27	11	24	8	21	3	15	27	9	21	3	15	27	9
	☿	20	21	22	23	24	25	27	28	0	1	3	4	6	8	10	11	13	15	16	18	20	21	23	25	27	28	0	2	3	5	7
	♀	26	28	29	0	1	3	4	5	6	8	9	10	11	13	14	15	16	18	19	20	21	23	24	25	26	28	29	0	2	3	4
	♂	4	5	5	6	7	7	8	9	9	10	11	11	12	13	14	14	15	16	17	17	18	19	20	20	21	22	22	23	24	25	26

♃ 1℞ 8 24D / ≈28 27 27 — ♄ 1 4 13 21 30 ♍24 25 26 27 28 — ♅ 1 15℞ ♋9 9 — ♆ 1 ♎16 17 — ♇ 1 ♌19

Month	Planet	1	2	3	4	5	6	7	8	9	10	11	12	13	14	15	16	17	18	19	20	21	22	23	24	25	26	27	28	29	30
11	☉	8	9	10	11	12	13	14	15	16	17	18	19	20	21	22	23	24	25	26	27	28	29	0	1	2	3	4	5	6	7
	☽	21	3	16	29	12	26	10	25	10	25	10	25	10	24	8	22	5	18	1	14	26	8	20	2	14	26	8	20	2	14
	☿	8	10	11	13	15	16	18	20	21	23	24	26	27	29	0	2	4	5	7	8	10	11	13	14	16	17	19	20	22	23
	♀	5	7	8	9	10	11	13	14	15	16	18	19	20	21	23	24	25	27	28	29	0	1	3	4	5	7	8	9	10	12
	♂	26	27	28	29	0	1	2	3	3	4	5	5	6	7	8	8	9	10	11	11	12	13	14	14	15	16	17	17	18	19

♃ 1 8 22 / ≈27 28 29 — ♄ 1 9 20 29 21 ♍28 29 0 ♎0 — ♅ 1 ℞ 18 ♋9 8 — ♆ 1 4 ♎17 18 — ♇ 1 21℞ ♌19 19

Month	Planet	1	2	3	4	5	6	7	8	9	10	11	12	13	14	15	16	17	18	19	20	21	22	23	24	25	26	27	28	29	30	31
12	☉	9	10	11	12	13	14	15	16	17	18	19	20	21	22	23	24	25	26	27	28	29	0	1	2	3	4	5	6	7	8	9
	☽	25	7	21	4	18	3	18	3	18	3	18	3	17	1	14	27	9	21	3	15	27	9	21	3	15	27	9	22	4	17	0
	☿	25	26	28	29	1	2	3	5	6	7	9	10	11	12	13	14	15	16	17	17	18	18	18	17	17	16	16	15	14	13	12
	♀	13	14	16	17	18	19	21	22	23	24	26	27	28	0	1	2	3	4	6	7	8	9	11	12	13	14	16	17	18	19	21
	♂	19	20	21	21	22	23	24	25	25	26	27	28	28	29	0	1	2	3	4	4	5	6	7	7	8	9	9	10	11	12	13

♃ 1 29 2 9 16 22 28 / ♓0 ♓0 1 2 3 4 — ♄ 1 3 22 ♎0 1 2 — ♅ 1 ℞ 16 ♋8 7 — ♆ 1 8 ♎18 19 — ♇ 1 ℞ ♌19

1951

Month	Planet	1	2	3	4	5	6	7	8	9	10	11	12	13	14	15	16	17	18	19	20	21	22	23	24	25	26	27	28
1	☉	10	11	12	13	14	15	16	17	18	19	20	21	22	23	24	25	26	27	28	29	0	1	2	3	4	5	6	7
	☽	14	28	12	26	11	26	11	26	11	25	9	22	5	18	0	12	24	5	17	29	11	24	6	18	1	14	27	11
	☿	22	9	7	6	5	4	3	2	2	2	1	1	2	2	2	3	3	4	5	5	6	7	8	9	10	11	13	14
	♀	22	23	24	26	27	28	0	1	2	3	5	6	7	8	9	11	12	13	15	16	17	18	20	21	22	23	25	26
	♂	13	14	15	16	16	17	18	19	19	20	21	21	22	23	24	24	25	26	27	28	28	29	0	1	2	3	4	5

♃ 1 2 7 12 17 22 26 31 / ♓4 5 6 7 8 9 10 11 — ♄ 1 11℞ ♎2 2 — ♅ 1 ℞ 9 ♋7 6 — ♆ 1 20℞ ♎19 19 — ♇ ♌

Month	Planet	1	2	3	4	5	6	7	8	9	10	11	12	13	14	15	16	17	18	19	20	21	22	23	24	25	26	27	28
2	☉	12	13	14	15	16	17	18	19	20	21	22	23	24	25	26	27	28	29	0	1	2	3	4	5	6	7	8	9
	☽	6	21	5	20	5	19	3	17	0	13	25	8	20	2	14	25	7	20	2	14	27	10	24	7	21	5	19	3
	☿	18	20	21	22	24	25	27	28	29	0	2	4	5	7	8	10	12	13	15	16	18	20	21	23	25	26	28	29
	♀	1	2	3	4	6	7	8	10	11	12	13	15	16	17	18	20	21	22	23	25	26	27	28	29	1	2	3	4
	♂	8	9	9	10	11	12	12	13	14	15	15	16	17	18	18	19	20	21	21	22	23	23	24	25	26	27	27	28

♃ 1 4 8 13 17 21 25 / ♓11 12 13 14 15 16 17 — ♄ 1 ℞ 21 ♎1 0 — ♅ 1 ℞ 4 ♋6 5 — ♆ 1 ℞ ♎19 — ♇ ♌

Month	Planet	1	2	3	4	5	6	7	8	9	10	11	12	13	14	15	16	17	18	19	20	21	22	23	24	25	26	27	28
3	☉	10	11	12	13	14	15	16	17	18	19	20	21	22	23	24	25	26	27	28	29	0	1	2	3	4	5	6	7
	☽	17	1	16	0	14	28	11	25	8	21	3	15	28	9	21	3	15	27	10	22	5	19	3	16	1	15	29	14
	☿	2	3	5	7	9	11	12	14	16	18	20	22	24	26	28	0	2	4	6	8	10	12	14	16	17	19	21	22
	♀	5	7	8	9	10	12	13	14	15	17	18	19	20	22	23	24	25	26	28	29	0	1	3	4	5	6	7	9
	♂	0	0	1	2	3	3	4	5	6	6	7	8	9	9	10	11	12	12	13	13	14	15	15	16	17	18	19	19

♃ 1 2 6 10 14 18 22 26 / ♓17 18 19 20 21 22 23 24 — ♄ 1 ℞ 7 0 8 20 ♎0 29 ♍29 28 — ♅ 1 ℞ 13D ♋5 5 — ♆ 1 ℞ 7 ♎19 18 — ♇ ♌

Month	Planet	1	2	3	4	5	6	7	8	9	10	11	12	13	14	15	16	17	18	19	20	21	22	23	24	25	26	27	28
4	☉	11	12	13	14	15	16	17	18	19	20	21	22	23	24	25	26	27	28	29	0	1	2	3	4	5	6	7	8
	☽	10	24	7	20	3	16	29	11	23	6	17	29	11	23	5	18	0	13	27	11	25	10	24	9	24	9	23	7
	☿	29	0	2	3	4	5	6	7	7	8	8	8	8	8	8	8	7	7	6	6	5	4	4	3	2	2	1	1
	♀	13	15	16	17	18	20	21	22	23	24	26	27	28	29	1	2	3	4	5	7	8	9	10	11	12	13	14	16
	♂	23	24	25	25	26	27	27	28	28	29	0	1	1	2	3	4	4	5	6	7	7	8	9	10	11	11	12	12

♃ 1 4 8 12 17 21 29 22 26 / ♓25 26 27 28 29 ♈0 ♈0 1 — ♄ 1 ℞ 2 16 ♍28 27 26 — ♅ 1 20 ♋5 6 — ♆ 1 ℞ 14 ♎18 17 — ♇ ♌

Month	Planet	1	2	3	4	5	6	7	8	9	10	11	12	13	14	15	16	17	18	19	20	21	22	23	24	25	26	27	28
5	☉	10	11	12	13	14	15	16	17	18	19	20	21	22	23	24	25	26	27	28	29	0	1	2	3	4	5	6	7
	☽	17	0	13	25	8	20	2	14	26	8	19	1	14	26	8	21	5	19	3	18	3	18	4	18	3	17	1	14
	☿	0℞	29	29	29	28	28	28	28	28	28	28	28	29	29	29	0	0	1	1	2	3	3	4	5	6	7	8	9
	♀	19	20	21	22	24	25	26	27	28	29	1	2	3	4	5	6	7	9	10	11	12	13	14	15	16	17	19	20
	♂	15	16	17	18	18	19	20	20	21	22	22	23	24	25	25	26	27	27	28	29	29	0	1	2	2	3	3	4

♃ 1 5 10 15 20 25 31 / ♈2 3 4 5 6 7 8 — ♄ 1 ℞ 5 28D ♍26 25 25 — ♅ 1 15 ♋6 7 — ♆ 1 ℞ 29 ♎17 16 — ♇ ♌

Month	Planet	1	2	3	4	5	6	7	8	9	10	11	12	13	14	15	16	17	18	19	20	21	22	23	24	25	26	27	28
6	☉	10	11	12	13	14	15	16	17	18	19	20	21	22	23	24	25	26	27	28	29	0	1	2	3	4	5	6	7
	☽	5	17	29	11	23	5	16	28	10	22	5	17	0	13	27	12	26	12	27	12	27	12	26	10	24	7	19	2
	☿	17	19	20	22	23	25	27	28	0	2	4	6	8	10	12	14	16	18	20	22	24	26	28	0	3	5	7	9
	♀	24	25	26	27	28	29	0	1	2	3	5	6	7	8	9	10	11	12	13	14	15	16	16	17	18	18	19	20
	♂	8	9	9	10	11	11	12	13	13	14	14	15	16	16	17	18	18	19	20	20	21	22	22	23	24	24	25	26

♃ 1 6 12 19 27 / ♈8 9 10 11 12 — ♄ 1 21 ♍25 26 — ♅ 1 3 20 ♋7 8 9 — ♆ 1 ℞ 28D ♎16 16 — ♇ ♌

Month	Planet	1	2	3	4	5	6	7	8	9	10	11	12	13	14	15	16	17	18	19	20	21	22	23	24	25	26	27	28
7	☉	9	10	11	12	13	14	15	15	16	17	18	19	20	21	22	23	24	25	26	27	28	29	0	1	2	3	4	5
	☽	8	20	2	13	15	7	19	2	14	27	10	23	7	21	5	20	5	21	6	20	5	19	2	16	28	11	23	5
	☿	16	18	20	22	24	26	28	29	0	2	3	5	7	9	10	12	14	15	17	19	20	22	24	26	27	28	29	0
	♀	24	25	26	27	28	28	29	0	1	2	3	3	4	5	6	7	8	9	9	10	11	11	12	12	13	13	14	14
	♂	28	29	0	0	1	2	2	3	4	5	5	6	6	7	7	8	9	10	10	11	12	12	13	14	14	15	16	16

♃ 1 8 24 / ♈12 13 14 — ♄ 1 10 23 ♍26 27 28 — ♅ 1 7 24 ♋9 10 11 — ♆ 1 28 ♎16 17 — ♇ ♌

Month	Planet	1	2	3	4	5	6	7	8	9	10	11	12	13	14	15	16	17	18	19	20	21	22	23	24	25	26	27	28
8	☉	8	9	10	11	12	13	14	15	16	17	18	19	20	21	22	23	24	25	26	27	28	29	0	1	2	3	4	5
	☽	22	4	16	29	11	24	7	20	3	17	1	15	0	14	29	14	29	13	27	11	24	6	19	1	13	25	7	19
	☿	6	7	8	9	10	11	12	12	13	13	14	14	15	15	15	15	15	15	14	14	13	13	12	12	11	11	10	9
	♀	16	16	16	17	17	17	17	17	17	17	17	17	17	17	17	17	17	17	17	17	17	16	16	16	15	15	15	14
	♂	19	19	20	21	21	22	22	23	24	25	25	26	27	27	28	29	29	0	0	1	2	2	3	3	4	5	5	6

♃ 1 3℞ 14 31 / ♈14 14 13 12 — ♄ 1 3 13 29 14 22 31 ♍28 29 0 ♎0 1 2 — ♅ 1 11 ♋11 12 — ♆ 1 ♎17 — ♇ ♌

Month	Planet	1	2	3	4	5	6	7	8	9	10	11	12	13	14	15	16	17	18	19	20	21	22	23	24	25	26	27	28
9	☉	8	9	10	11	12	13	14	15	16	17	18	19	20	21	22	23	24	25	26	27	28	29	0	1	2	3	4	5
	☽	8	20	3	17	0	14	27	11	26	10	24	9	23	7	21	5	19	2	14	27	9	21	3	15	27	9	21	3
	☿	5	4	3	2	2	2	1	1	1	1	1	2	2	3	4	5	5	7	8	10	11	12	14	15	17	19	21	21
	♀	11	10	10	9	8	8	7	7	6	5	5	4	4	3	3	3	2	2	2	2	2	2	2	2	2	2	2	2
	♂	9	9	10	10	11	11	12	13	13	14	15	15	16	16	17	18	18	19	19	20	20	21	22	22	23	24	24	25

♃ 1℞ 10 18 26 / ♈12 11 10 9 — ♄ 1 9 17 25 ♎2 3 4 5 — ♅ 1 2 ♋12 13 — ♆ 1 ♎17 18 — ♇ ♌

Month	Planet	1	2	3	4	5	6	7	8	9	10	11	12	13	14	15	16	17	18	19	20	21	22	23	24	25	26	27	28
10	☉	7	8	9	10	11	12	13	14	15	16	17	18	19	20	21	22	23	24	25	26	27	28	29	0	1	2	3	4
	☽	13	26	10	24	8	22	7	21	5	19	3	17	0	14	27	10	22	5	17	29	11	23	5	17	29	11	24	6
	☿	28	0	2	4	5	7	9	10	12	13	15	17	18	20	21	23	25	26	28	29	1	2	4	5	7	8	10	11
	♀	3	3	3	4	4	5	5	6	6	7	7	8	8	9	10	10	11	12	12	13	14	14	15	16	17	17	18	19
	♂	28	28	29	0	0	1	1	2	3	3	4	4	5	6	6	7	8	8	9	9	10	11	11	12	12	13	13	14

♃ 1℞ 4 12 20 29 / ♈8 7 6 5 — ♄ 1 3 11 20 28 ♎5 6 7 8 9 — ♅ 1 18 20℞ 23 ♋13 14 14 13 — ♆ 1 5 ♎18 19 — ♇ ♌

Month	Planet	1	2	3	4	5	6	7	8	9	10	11	12	13	14	15	16	17	18	19	20	21	22	23	24	25	26	27	28
11	☉	8	9	10	11	12	13	14	15	16	17	18	19	20	21	22	23	24	25	26	27	28	29	0	1	2	3	4	5
	☽	4	18	3	18	2	16	0	13	27	10	23	6	18	1	13	25	7	19	1	13	25	7	19	2	15	29	12	26
	☿	20	21	23	24	26	27	29	0	2	3	5	6	8	9	10	12	13	14	16	17	18	19	20	21	22	23	24	24
	♀	22	23	24	25	26	27	28	29	0	1	2	3	4	5	6	7	8	9	10	11	12	13	14	15	16	17	18	19
	♂	17	17	18	18	19	19	20	20	21	22	22	23	23	24	24	25	25	26	26	27	28	28	29	29	0	0	1	1

♃ 1℞ 9 29D / ♓5 4 4 — ♄ 1 6 15 25 ♎9 10 11 12 — ♅ 1℞ ♋13 — ♆ 1 2 ♎19 20 — ♇ ♌

Month	Planet	1	2	3	4	5	6	7	8	9	10	11	12	13	14	15	16	17	18	19	20	21	22	23	24	25	26	27	28
12	☉	8	10	11	12	13	14	15	16	17	18	19	20	21	22	23	24	25	26	27	28	29	0	1	2	3	4	5	6
	☽	13	28	12	26	10	24	7	20	2	15	27	10	22	4	16	27	9	21	3	15	27	10	23	7	21	6	21	6
	☿	0	0	1	1	1	1	2	2	1	1	0	29	28	27	25	24	23	22	21	18	17	17	16	16	16	16	16	16
	♀	23	24	25	26	27	28	29	0	2	3	4	5	6	7	8	10	11	12	13	14	15	17	18	19	20	21	23	24
	♂	4	5	5	6	6	7	7	8	9	9	10	11	11	12	12	13	13	14	14	15	15	16	16	17	17	18	18	19

♃ 1 21 / ♈4 5 — ♄ 1 7 22 ♎12 13 14 — ♅ 1℞ 8 ♋13 12 — ♆ 1 3 ♎20 21 — ♇ ♌21

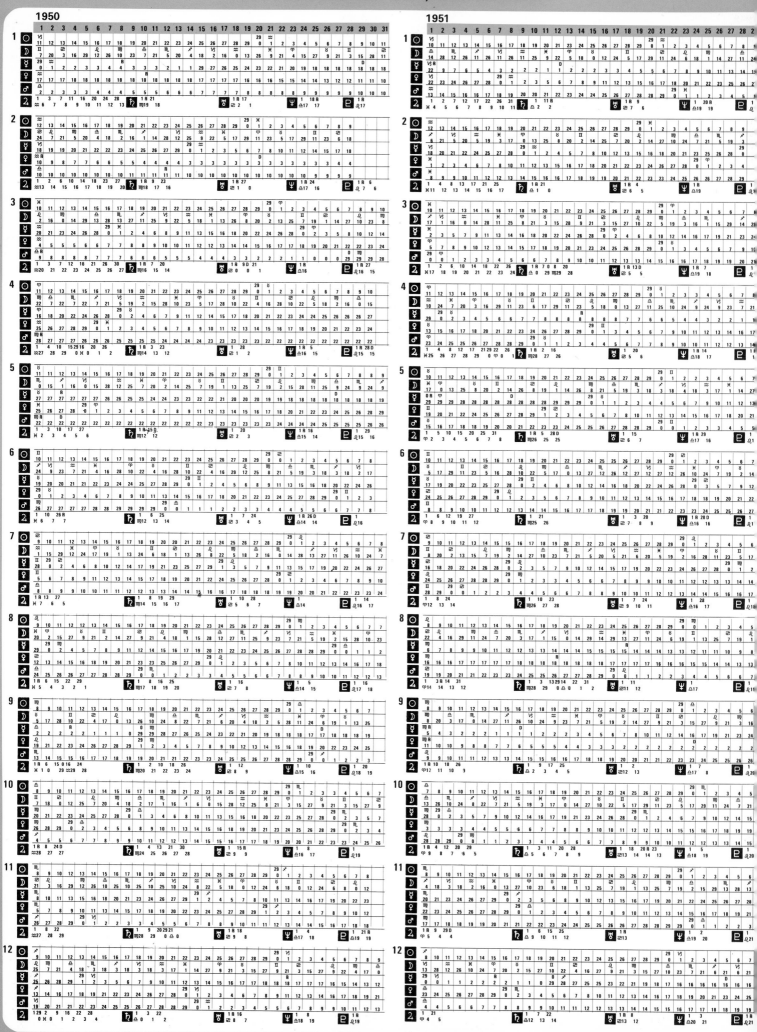

1952

1	2	3	4	5	6	7	8	9	10	11	12	13	14	15	16	17	18	19	20	21	22	23	24	25	26	27	28	29	30	31
♑ 10	11	12	13	14	15	16	17	18	19	20	21	22	23	24	25	26	27	28	29	29 0	♒ 1	2	3	4	5	7	8	9	10	11
♓ 6	20	♈ 3	17	29	♉ 12	24	♊ 7	19	♋ 1	12	24	♌ 6	18	♍ 0	12	24	♎ 6	19	♏ 2	16	♐ 0	14	29	♑ 14	29	♒ 14	29	♓ 14	28	♈ 12
♐ 18	18	19	20	21	22	23	24	25	27	28	29	29 0	♑ 1	3	4	5	7	8	10	11	13	14	15	17	18	20	21	23	24	26
♏ 20	29 0	♐ 1	2	3	4	5	7	8	9	10	11	13	14	15	16	18	19	20	21	22	24	25	26	27	29	29 0	♑ 1	2	3	5
♎ 21	21	22	22	23	23	24	24	25	25	26	26	27	27	28	28	29	29	29	29 0	♏ 0	1	1	2	2	3	3	4	4	4	5

♃ 1 9 17 23 29 / ♈6 7 8 9 10 — ♄ 1 25R / ♎14 14 — ♅ 1R 2 26 / ♋12 11 10 — ♆ 1 24R / ♎21 21 — ♇ 1R 12 / ♌21 20

1	2	3	4	5	6	7	8	9	10	11	12	13	14	15	16	17	18	19	20	21	22	23	24	25	26	27	28	29	30	31
♒ 12	13	14	15	16	17	18	19	20	21	22	23	24	25	26	27	28	29	29 0	♓ 1	2	3	4	5	6	7	8	9	10		
♈ 26	♉ 9	21	♊ 3	16	27	♋ 9	21	♌ 3	15	27	♍ 9	21	♎ 3	16	29	♏ 12	25	♐ 9	23	♑ 8	23	♒ 7	22	♓ 7	22	♈ 6	20	♉ 4		
♑ 27	29	29 1	♒ 2	4	5	7	9	10	12	14	15	17	19	20	22	24	26	28	29 0	♓ 1	3	5	7	9	10	12	14	16		
♑ 6	7	8	9	11	12	13	14	16	17	18	19	20	22	23	24	25	27	28	29	29 0	♒ 1	3	4	5	6	8	9	10		
♏ 5	6	6	6	7	7	8	8	8	9	9	9	10	10	11	11	11	12	12	12	12	13	13	13	14	14	14	14	15		

♃ 1 4 9 14 19 24 29 / ♈10 11 12 13 14 15 16 — ♄ 1R 27 / ♎14 13 — ♅ 1R / ♋10 — ♆ 1R / ♎21 — ♇ 1R 23 / ♌20 19

1	2	3	4	5	6	7	8	9	10	11	12	13	14	15	16	17	18	19	20	21	22	23	24	25	26	27	28	29	30	31
♓ 11	12	13	14	15	16	17	18	19	20	21	22	23	24	25	26	27	28	29	29 0	♈ 1	2	3	4	5	6	7	8	9	10	11
♉ 17	♊ 0	12	24	♋ 6	18	♌ 0	11	23	♍ 5	18	♎ 0	13	26	♏ 9	22	♐ 6	20	♑ 4	18	♒ 2	17	♓ 1	16	♈ 0	14	28	♉ 12	25	♊ 7	20
♓ 18	20	22	24	26	28	29 0	♈ 1	3	5	6	8	10	11	13	14	15	16	17	18	19	19	19	20	20	20	R 20	20	19	19	18
♒ 11	13	14	15	16	17	19	20	21	22	24	25	26	27	29	29 0	♓ 1	2	3	5	6	7	8	10	11	12	13	15	16	17	18
♏ 15	15	15	16	16	16	16	16	17	17	17	17	17	17	17	18	18	18	18	18	18	18	18	18	R 18	18	18	18	18	18	18

♃ 1 4 9 13 17 22 26 30 / ♈16 17 18 19 20 21 22 23 — ♄ 1R 14 28 / ♎13 12 11 — ♅ 1R 3 18D / ♋10 9 9 — ♆ 1R 16 / ♎21 20 — ♇ 1R / ♌19

1	2	3	4	5	6	7	8	9	10	11	12	13	14	15	16	17	18	19	20	21	22	23	24	25	26	27	28	29	30	31
♈ 12	13	14	15	16	17	18	19	20	21	22	23	23	24	25	26	27	28	29	29 0	♉ 1	2	3	4	5	6	7	8	9	10	
♋ 2	14	26	♌ 8	20	♍ 2	14	26	♎ 9	22	♏ 5	19	♐ 3	17	♑ 1	15	29	♒ 13	27	♓ 11	25	♈ 9	23	♉ 6	20	♊ 3	15	28	♋ 10	22	
♈R 18	17	16	16	15	14	13	12	12	11	10	10	9	9	9	8	8	8	D 8	8	9	9	9	10	10	11	11	12	13	14	
♓ 20	21	22	23	24	26	27	28	29 0	♈ 1	2	3	4	5	7	8	9	10	12	13	14	15	16	18	19	20	21	23	24	25	
♏R 18	18	17	17	17	17	17	17	16	16	16	16	16	15	15	15	15	14	14	14	13	13	13	12	12	12	11	11	11	10	

♃ 1 3 8 12 16 20 24 28 29 / ♈23 24 25 26 27 28 29 0 — ♄ 1R 9 23 / ♎11 10 9 — ♅ 1 / ♋10 — ♆ 1R 22 / ♎20 19 — ♇ 1R / ♌19

1	2	3	4	5	6	7	8	9	10	11	12	13	14	15	16	17	18	19	20	21	22	23	24	25	26	27	28	29	30	31
♉ 11	12	13	14	15	16	17	18	19	20	21	22	23	24	25	26	26	27	28	29	29 0	♊ 1	2	3	4	5	6	7	8	9	10
♌ 4	15	27	♍ 9	22	♎ 14	17	♏ 1	14	28	♐ 12	27	♑ 11	26	♒ 10	24	♓ 8	22	♈ 5	19	♉ 2	15	28	♊ 11	24	♋ 6	18	♌ 0	12	23	♍ 5
♈ 14	15	16	17	18	20	21	22	23	24	26	27	28	29 0	♉ 1	3	4	6	7	9	11	13	14	16	18	20	22	24	26	28	29 0
♈ 26	28	29	29 0	♉ 1	2	4	5	6	7	9	10	11	12	14	15	16	17	18	20	21	22	23	25	26	27	28	29 0	♊ 1	2	3
♏R 10	9	9	9	8	8	8	7	7	7	6	6	5	5	5	5	4	4	4	3	3	3	3	2	2	2	2	2	2	1	1

♃ 1 2 7 11 15 20 24 28 / ♉0 1 2 3 4 5 6 7 — ♄ 1R 10 / ♎9 8 — ♅ 1 7 29 / ♋10 11 12 — ♆ 1R / ♎19 — ♇ 1 / ♎19

1	2	3	4	5	6	7	8	9	10	11	12	13	14	15	16	17	18	19	20	21	22	23	24	25	26	27	28	29	30	31
♊ 11	12	13	14	15	16	17	18	19	20	20	21	22	23	24	25	26	27	28	29	29 0	♋ 1	2	3	4	5	6	7	8	9	
♍ 17	♎ 0	12	25	♏ 9	23	♐ 7	21	♑ 6	21	♒ 6	20	♓ 5	19	♈ 2	16	29	♉ 12	25	♊ 8	20	♋ 2	14	26	♌ 8	20	♍ 2	14	26	♎ 8	
♊ 2	4	6	8	10	12	15	17	19	21	23	26	28	29 0	♋ 2	4	6	8	10	12	14	16	18	20	22	23	25	27	29	29 0	
♊ 4	6	7	8	9	11	12	13	14	15	17	18	19	20	22	23	24	25	26	28	29	29 0	♋ 1	3	4	5	6	8	9	10	
♏R 1	1	1	1	1	1	1	1	1	D 1	1	1	1	1	1	1	1	1	1	1	2	2	2	2	2	2	3	3	3	3	

♃ 1 2 7 11 16 21 26 / ♉7 8 9 10 11 12 13 — ♄ 1R 11D / ♎8 8 — ♅ 1 15 / ♋12 13 — ♆ 1R 14 30D / ♎19 18 18 — ♇ 1 / ♌19

1	2	3	4	5	6	7	8	9	10	11	12	13	14	15	16	17	18	19	20	21	22	23	24	25	26	27	28	29	30	31
♋ 10	10	11	12	13	14	15	16	17	18	19	20	21	22	23	24	25	26	27	28	29	29 0	♌ 1	2	3	4	5	6	7	8	8
♎ 20	♏ 3	17	♐ 1	15	♑ 0	15	♒ 0	15	♓ 0	14	29	♈ 13	26	♉ 9	22	♊ 5	17	29	♋ 11	23	♌ 5	17	29	♍ 10	22	♎ 4	17	29	♏ 12	26
♌ 2	3	5	6	7	9	10	12	13	14	15	16	18	19	20	20	21	22	23	24	24	25	25	26	26	26	27	27	27	R 27	26
♋ 11	13	14	15	16	17	19	20	21	22	24	25	26	27	28	29 0	♌ 1	2	3	5	6	7	8	10	11	12	13	14	16	17	18
♏ 4	4	4	5	5	5	5	6	6	6	7	7	7	8	8	8	9	9	10	10	10	11	11	12	12	13	13	14	14	15	15

♃ 1 2 7 14 20 27 / ♉13 14 15 16 17 18 — ♄ 1 11 27 / ♎8 9 10 — ♅ 1 2 19 / ♋13 14 15 — ♆ 1 15 / ♎18 19 — ♇ 1 4 / ♌19 20

1	2	3	4	5	6	7	8	9	10	11	12	13	14	15	16	17	18	19	20	21	22	23	24	25	26	27	28	29	30	31
♌ 9	10	11	12	13	14	15	16	17	18	19	20	21	22	23	24	24	25	26	27	28	29	29 0	♍ 1	2	3	4	5	6	7	8
♐ 9	24	♑ 8	23	♒ 8	23	♓ 9	23	♈ 8	22	♉ 6	19	♊ 2	14	26	♋ 8	20	♌ 2	14	26	♍ 8	19	♎ 2	14	26	♏ 9	22	♐ 5	19	♑ 3	17
♌R 26	26	26	25	24	24	23	22	22	21	20	19	18	18	17	16	16	15	15	15	14	14	D 14	15	15	16	16	17	18	19	20
♌ 20	21	22	23	24	26	27	28	29 0	♍ 1	2	3	4	5	7	8	9	10	12	13	14	15	16	18	19	20	21	23	24	25	26
♏ 15	16	16	17	17	18	18	19	20	20	21	21	22	22	23	23	24	24	25	26	26	27	27	28	28	29	29 0	♐ 0	1	1	2

♃ 1 5 16 / ♉18 19 20 — ♄ 1 9 20 29 / ♎10 11 12 13 — ♅ 1 5 25 / ♋15 16 17 — ♆ 1 / ♎19 — ♇ 1 7 / ♌20 21

1	2	3	4	5	6	7	8	9	10	11	12	13	14	15	16	17	18	19	20	21	22	23	24	25	26	27	28	29	30	31
♍ 9	10	11	12	13	14	15	16	17	18	19	20	21	22	23	24	25	25	26	27	28	29	29 0	♎ 1	2	3	4	5	6	7	
♒ 2	17	♓ 2	17	♈ 2	16	♉ 1	14	28	♊ 10	23	♋ 5	17	29	♌ 11	23	♍ 4	16	28	♎ 11	23	♏ 6	19	♐ 2	15	29	♑ 12	27	♒ 11	26	
♌ 21	22	24	25	27	28	29 0	♍ 2	3	5	7	9	11	13	14	16	18	20	22	24	26	28	29 0	♎ 3	3	5	7	8	10	12	
♍ 28	29	29 0	♎ 1	3	4	5	6	8	9	10	11	12	14	15	16	17	19	20	21	22	24	25	26	27	28	29 0	♏ 1	2	3	
♐ 3	3	4	5	5	6	6	7	8	8	9	10	10	11	12	12	13	14	14	15	16	16	17	18	18	19	20	20	21	22	

♃ 1 10R / ♉20 20 — ♄ 1 8 16 25 / ♎13 14 15 16 — ♅ 1 19 / ♋17 18 — ♆ 1 3 / ♎19 20 — ♇ 1 9 / ♌21 22

1	2	3	4	5	6	7	8	9	10	11	12	13	14	15	16	17	18	19	20	21	22	23	24	25	26	27	28	29	30	31
♎ 8	9	10	11	12	13	14	15	16	17	18	19	20	21	22	23	24	25	26	27	28	29	29 0	♏ 1	2	3	4	5	6	7	8
♓ 10	25	♈ 10	24	♉ 9	22	♊ 6	19	♋ 1	13	25	♌ 7	19	♍ 1	13	25	♎ 7	20	♏ 2	16	29	♐ 12	26	♑ 9	23	♒ 7	21	♓ 6	20	♈ 4	19
♎ 13	15	17	18	20	22	23	25	27	28	29 0	♏ 1	3	4	6	7	9	11	12	13	15	16	18	19	21	22	23	25	26	28	29 0
♏ 4	6	7	8	9	11	12	13	14	16	17	18	19	20	22	23	24	25	27	28	29	29 0	♐ 1	3	4	5	6	8	9	10	11
♐ 22	23	24	24	25	26	27	27	28	29	29	29 0	♑ 1	1	2	3	4	4	5	6	7	7	8	9	9	10	11	12	12	13	14

♃ 1R 4 14 23 31 / ♉20 19 18 17 16 — ♄ 1 3 11 19 28 / ♎16 17 18 19 20 — ♅ 1 25R / ♋18 18 — ♆ 1 2 29 / ♎20 21 22 — ♇ 1 22 / ♌22 23

1	2	3	4	5	6	7	8	9	10	11	12	13	14	15	16	17	18	19	20	21	22	23	24	25	26	27	28	29	30	31
♏ 9	10	11	12	13	14	15	16	17	18	19	20	21	22	23	24	25	26	27	28	29	29 0	♐ 1	2	3	4	5	6	7	8	
♉ 3	17	♊ 0	14	27	♋ 9	21	♌ 3	15	27	♍ 9	21	♎ 3	15	28	♏ 11	24	♐ 8	22	♑ 6	20	♒ 4	18	♓ 2	16	♈ 0	14	28	♉ 12	25	
♐ 0	1	3	4	5	7	8	9	10	11	12	13	13	14	15	15	16	16	R 16	16	16	15	15	14	13	12	11	10	9	7	
♐ 13	14	15	16	17	19	20	21	22	23	25	26	27	28	29 0	♑ 1	2	3	4	6	7	8	9	11	12	13	14	15	17	18	
♑ 15	15	16	17	18	18	19	20	21	21	22	23	24	24	25	26	27	27	28	29	29 0	♒ 0	1	2	3	3	4	5	6	7	

♃ 1R 7 15 22 / ♉16 15 14 13 — ♄ 1 5 14 23 / ♎20 21 22 23 — ♅ 1R 28 / ♋18 17 — ♆ 1 28 / ♎22 23 — ♇ 1 24R / ♌23 23

1	2	3	4	5	6	7	8	9	10	11	12	13	14	15	16	17	18	19	20	21	22	23	24	25	26	27	28	29	30	31
♐ 9	10	11	12	13	14	15	16	17	18	19	20	21	22	23	25	26	27	28	29	29 0	♑ 1	2	3	4	5	6	7	8	9	10
♊ 9	22	♋ 5	17	29	♌ 11	23	♍ 5	17	29	♎ 11	23	♏ 6	19	♐ 3	17	♑ 1	15	♒ 0	14	29	♓ 13	27	♈ 11	25	♉ 8	22	♊ 5	18	♋ 0	13
♐R 6	5	3	2	1	1	0	0	0	D 0	0	0	1	2	2	3	4	5	6	7	8	9	11	12	13	14	16	17	18	20	21
♑ 19	20	21	22	24	25	26	27	29	29 0	♒ 1	2	3	4	6	7	8	9	10	12	13	14	15	16	17	19	20	21	22	23	24
♒ 7	8	9	10	10	11	12	13	13	14	15	16	16	17	18	19	20	20	21	22	23	23	24	25	26	26	27	28	29	29 0	♓ 0

♃ 1R 11 / ♉12 11 — ♄ 1 3 14 28 / ♎23 24 25 26 — ♅ 1R 26 / ♋17 16 — ♆ 1 / ♋23 — ♇ 1 29 / ♌23 22

1953

	1	2	3	4	5	6	7	8	9	10	11	12	13	14	15	16	17	18	19	20	21	22	23	24	25	26	27	28	29	30	31
1 ☉	♑ 11	12	13	14	15	16	17	18	19	20	21	22	23	24	25	26	27	28	29	29 0	♒ 1	2	3	4	5	6	7	8	9	10	11
☽	♋ 25	♌ 7	19	♍ 1	13	25	♎ 7	19	♏ 1	14	27	♐ 10	25	♑ 9	24	♒ 9	24	♓ 8	23	♈ 8	22	♉ 5	19	♊ 2	15	27	♋ 10	22	♌ 4	16	28
☿	♐ 23	24	25	27	28	29 0	♑ 1	3	4	6	7	9	10	12	13	15	17	18	20	21	23	24	26	28	29 0	♒ 1	3	4	6	8	9
♀	♒ 25	26	28	29	29 0	♓ 1	2	3	5	6	7	8	9	10	11	12	13	15	16	17	18	19	20	21	22	23	24	25	26	27	28
♂	♓ 1	2	3	3	4	5	6	6	7	8	9	10	10	11	12	13	13	14	15	16	16	17	18	19	20	20	21	22	23	23	24

♃ 1R 2 4D 8 29 / ♉11 10 10 11 12 — ♄ 1 17 / ♎26 27 — ♅ 1R 18 / ♋16 15 — ♆ 1 25R / ♎23 23 — ♇ 1R / ♌22

	1	2	3	4	5	6	7	8	9	10	11	12	13	14	15	16	17	18	19	20	21	22	23	24	25	26	27	28	29	30	31
2 ☉	♒ 12	13	14	15	16	17	18	19	20	21	22	23	25	26	27	28	29	29 0	♓ 1	2	3	4	5	6	7	8	9	10			
☽	♍ 9	21	♎ 3	15	27	♏ 9	22	♐ 5	19	♑ 2	17	♒ 2	17	♓ 2	17	♈ 2	17	♉ 1	15	28	♊ 12	24	♋ 7	19	♌ 1	13	24	♍ 6			
☿	♒ 11	13	15	16	18	20	22	24	25	27	29 0	♓ 1	3	4	6	8	10	12	13	15	17	19	20	22	23	25	26	27			
♀	29	29 0	♈ 1	2	3	4	5	6	7	8	9	10	11	11	12	13	14	15	16	17	17	18	19	20	20	21	22	23			
♂	♓ 25	26	26	27	28	29	29	29 0	♈ 1	2	2	3	4	5	5	6	7	8	9	9	10	11	12	12	13	14	14	15			

♃ 1 9 17 24 / ♉12 13 14 15 — ♄ 1 5R 23 / ♎27 27 26 — ♅ 1R 14 / ♋15 14 — ♆ 1R / ♎23 — ♇ 1R 13 / ♌22 21

	1	2	3	4	5	6	7	8	9	10	11	12	13	14	15	16	17	18	19	20	21	22	23	24	25	26	27	28	29	30	31
3 ☉	♓ 11	12	13	14	15	16	17	18	19	20	21	22	23	24	25	26	27	28	29	29 0	♈ 1	2	3	4	5	6	7	8	8	9	10
☽	♍ 18	♎ 0	12	24	♏ 6	19	♐ 1	14	27	♑ 11	25	♒ 10	25	♓ 10	25	♈ 10	25	♉ 10	24	♊ 7	21	♋ 3	16	28	♌ 10	21	♍ 3	15	27	♎ 9	21
☿	♓ 29	29 0	♈ 0	1	2	2	2	2	R 2	2	2	1	1	0	0 29	♓ 28	27	26	25	25	24	23	22	22	21	21	20	20	20	19	19
♀	♈ 23	24	24	25	26	26	27	27	28	28	29	29	29	29 0	♉ 0	0	0	1	1	1	1	1	R 1	1	1	1	0	0	0	0	0 29
♂	♈ 16	17	17	18	19	20	20	21	22	23	23	24	25	26	26	27	28	29	29	29 0	♉ 1	1	2	3	4	4	5	6	7	7	8

♃ 1 3 8 14 19 25 30 / ♉15 16 17 18 19 20 21 — ♄ 1R 16 31 / ♎26 25 24 — ♅ 1R 23D / ♋14 14 — ♆ 1R 25 / ♎23 22 — ♇ 1R / ♌21

	1	2	3	4	5	6	7	8	9	10	11	12	13	14	15	16	17	18	19	20	21	22	23	24	25	26	27	28	29	30	31
4 ☉	♈ 11	12	13	14	15	16	17	18	19	20	21	22	23	24	25	26	27	28	29	29 0	♉ 1	2	3	4	5	6	7	8	9	10	
☽	♏ 3	16	28	♐ 11	24	♑ 7	21	♒ 5	19	♓ 4	18	♈ 3	18	♉ 3	18	♊ 2	16	29	♋ 12	24	♌ 6	18	♍ 0	12	24	♎ 5	18	♏ 0	12	25	
☿	♓R 19	D 19	20	20	20	21	21	22	23	23	24	25	26	27	28	29	29 0	♈ 1	2	3	4	6	7	8	10	11	12	14	15	17	
♀	♈R 29	28	28	27	27	26	26	25	25	24	23	22	22	21	21	20	20	19	19	18	18	17	17	16	16	16	15	15	15	15	
♂	♉ 9	9	10	11	12	12	13	14	14	15	16	17	17	18	19	19	20	21	22	22	23	24	24	25	26	27	27	28	29	29	

♃ 1 3 8 13 17 22 26 30 / ♉21 22 23 24 25 26 27 28 — ♄ 1R 13 26 / ♎24 23 22 — ♅ 1 27 / ♋14 15 — ♆ 1R / ♎22 — ♇ 1R 3 / ♌21 20

	1	2	3	4	5	6	7	8	9	10	11	12	13	14	15	16	17	18	19	20	21	22	23	24	25	26	27	28	29	30	31
5 ☉	♉ 11	12	13	14	15	16	17	18	19	20	20	21	22	23	24	25	26	27	28	29	29 0	♊ 1	2	3	4	5	6	7	8	9	10
☽	♐ 8	21	♑ 4	18	♒ 1	15	29	♓ 14	28	♈ 13	27	♉ 12	26	♊ 10	24	♋ 7	20	♌ 2	14	26	♍ 8	20	♎ 2	14	26	♏ 8	21	♐ 4	17	♑ 1	14
☿	♈ 18	20	22	23	25	27	28	29 0	♉ 2	4	6	8	10	12	14	16	18	20	22	24	26	28	29 1	♊ 3	5	7	9	12	14	16	18
♀	♈R 15	15	14	D 14	15	15	15	15	15	15	16	16	16	16	17	17	18	18	19	19	20	20	21	21	22	23	23	24	25	25	26
♂	29 0	♊ 1	1	2	3	4	4	5	6	6	7	8	8	9	10	10	11	12	12	13	14	15	15	16	17	17	18	19	19	20	21

♃ 1 5 9 29 10 13 18 22 26 / ♉28 29 0 ♊ 0 1 2 3 4 — ♄ 1R 11 31 / ♎22 21 20 — ♅ 1 23 / ♋15 16 — ♆ 1R 2 / ♎22 21 — ♇ 1R 2D / ♌20 20

	1	2	3	4	5	6	7	8	9	10	11	12	13	14	15	16	17	18	19	20	21	22	23	24	25	26	27	28	29	30	31
6 ☉	♊ 11	12	13	14	14	15	16	17	18	19	20	21	22	23	24	25	26	27	28	29	29 0	♋ 1	2	3	4	5	6	7	8	8	
☽	♑ 28	♒ 12	26	♓ 10	24	♈ 9	23	♉ 7	21	♊ 5	19	♋ 2	15	28	♌ 10	22	♍ 4	16	28	♎ 10	22	♏ 4	17	29	♐ 13	26	♑ 10	24	♒ 8	23	
☿	♊ 20	22	24	26	28	29 0	♋ 2	4	6	7	9	11	13	14	16	17	19	20	22	23	24	26	27	28	29	29 0	♌ 1	2	3	4	
♀	♈ 27	28	28	29	29 0	♉ 1	2	2	3	4	5	6	7	8	8	9	10	11	12	13	14	15	16	17	18	19	20	21	22	23	
♂	♊ 21	22	23	23	24	25	25	26	27	27	28	29	29	29 0	♋ 1	1	2	3	3	4	5	6	6	7	7	8	9	9	10	11	

♃ 1 4 8 12 17 21 25 30 / ♊5 6 7 8 9 10 11 12 — ♄ 1R 24D / ♎20 20 — ♅ 1 11 28 / ♋16 17 18 — ♆ 1R / ♎21 — ♇ 1 / ♌21

	1	2	3	4	5	6	7	8	9	10	11	12	13	14	15	16	17	18	19	20	21	22	23	24	25	26	27	28	29	30	31
7 ☉	♋ 9	10	11	12	13	14	15	16	17	18	19	20	21	22	23	24	25	26	26	27	28	29	29 0	♌ 1	2	3	4	5	6	7	8
☽	♓ 7	21	♈ 6	20	♉ 4	18	♊ 1	15	28	♋ 11	23	♌ 6	18	♍ 0	12	24	♎ 6	18	♏ 0	12	25	♐ 7	21	♑ 4	18	♒ 3	17	♓ 2	17	♈ 2	16
☿	♌ 4	5	6	6	7	7	7	8	8	8	R 8	8	8	7	7	7	6	6	5	5	4	3	3	2	1	1	0	0 29	♋ 29	28	28
♀	♉ 24	25	26	27	28	29	29 0	♊ 1	2	3	4	5	6	7	8	10	11	12	13	14	15	16	17	18	19	20	22	23	24	25	26
♂	♋ 11	12	13	13	14	15	15	16	17	17	18	19	19	20	21	21	22	23	23	24	24	25	26	26	27	28	28	29	29 0	♌ 0	1

♃ 1 5 9 14 19 24 29 / ♊12 13 14 15 16 17 18 — ♄ 1 16 / ♎20 21 — ♅ 1 14 31 / ♋18 19 20 — ♆ 1R 3D / ♎21 21 — ♇ 1 17 / ♌21 22

	1	2	3	4	5	6	7	8	9	10	11	12	13	14	15	16	17	18	19	20	21	22	23	24	25	26	27	28	29	30	31
8 ☉	♌ 9	10	11	12	13	14	15	16	17	18	18	19	20	21	22	23	24	25	26	27	28	29	29 0	♍ 1	2	3	4	5	6	7	8
☽	♉ 0	14	28	♊ 11	24	♋ 7	20	♌ 2	14	27	♍ 9	20	♎ 2	14	26	♏ 8	20	♐ 3	16	29	♑ 12	27	♒ 11	26	♓ 11	26	♈ 11	26	♉ 11	25	♊ 8
☿	♋R 27	27	27	27	D 27	27	28	28	28	29	29 0	♌ 1	2	3	4	5	6	8	9	11	12	14	16	17	19	21	23	25	27	29 0	♍ 1
♀	♊ 27	28	29	29 0	♋ 2	3	4	5	6	7	8	10	11	12	13	14	15	16	18	19	20	21	22	23	25	26	27	28	29	29 0	♌ 2
♂	♌ 2	2	3	4	4	5	5	6	7	7	8	9	9	10	11	11	12	13	13	14	14	15	16	16	17	18	18	19	20	20	21

♃ 1 3 9 15 21 28 / ♊18 19 20 21 22 23 — ♄ 1 5 18 29 / ♎21 22 23 24 — ♅ 1 18 / ♋20 21 — ♆ 1 30 / ♎21 22 — ♇ 1 17 / ♌22 23

	1	2	3	4	5	6	7	8	9	10	11	12	13	14	15	16	17	18	19	20	21	22	23	24	25	26	27	28	29	30	31
9 ☉	♍ 9	10	11	12	13	14	15	16	16	17	18	19	20	21	22	23	24	25	26	27	28	29	29 0	♎ 1	2	3	4	5	6	7	
☽	♊ 21	♋ 4	17	29	♌ 11	23	♍ 5	17	29	♎ 11	23	♏ 5	17	29	♐ 11	24	♑ 7	21	♒ 5	19	♓ 4	19	♈ 5	20	♉ 5	20	♊ 4	18	♋ 1	14	
☿	♍ 3	5	7	9	11	13	15	16	18	20	22	24	26	28	29 0	♎ 1	3	5	6	8	9	11	13	14	16	17	19	21	22	24	
♀	♌ 3	4	5	6	7	9	10	11	12	13	15	16	17	18	19	21	22	23	24	25	27	28	29	29 0	♍ 2	3	4	5	6	8	
♂	♌ 21	22	23	23	24	25	25	26	27	27	28	28	29	29 0	♍ 0	1	2	2	3	3	4	5	5	6	7	7	8	9	9	10	

♃ 1 5 14 28 / ♊23 24 25 26 — ♄ 1 9 18 27 / ♎24 25 26 27 — ♅ 1 8 / ♋21 22 — ♆ 1 30 / ♎22 23 — ♇ 1 20 / ♌23 24

	1	2	3	4	5	6	7	8	9	10	11	12	13	14	15	16	17	18	19	20	21	22	23	24	25	26	27	28	29	30	31
10 ☉	♎ 8	9	10	11	12	13	14	15	16	17	18	19	20	21	22	23	24	25	26	27	28	29	29 0	♏ 1	2	3	4	5	6	7	8
☽	♋ 26	♌ 9	21	♍ 2	14	26	♎ 8	20	♏ 2	14	26	♐ 8	21	♑ 4	17	♒ 0	14	28	♓ 13	28	♈ 13	28	♉ 13	28	♊ 12	26	♋ 10	23	♌ 5	17	29
☿	♎ 25	27	28	29 0	♏ 1	2	4	5	7	8	9	11	12	13	15	16	17	18	20	21	22	23	24	25	26	27	27	28	29	29	29 0
♀	♍ 9	10	11	12	14	15	16	18	19	20	21	22	24	25	26	27	28	29 0	♎ 1	2	4	5	6	7	8	10	11	12	13	15	16
♂	♍ 10	11	12	12	13	14	14	15	15	16	17	17	18	19	19	20	20	21	22	22	23	24	24	25	25	26	27	27	28	29	29

♃ 1 15R 31 / ♊26 26 25 — ♄ 1 5 14 22 29 23 30 / ♎27 28 29 0 ♏ 0 1 — ♅ 1 13 29R / ♋22 23 23 — ♆ 1 27 / ♎23 24 — ♇ 1 / ♌24

	1	2	3	4	5	6	7	8	9	10	11	12	13	14	15	16	17	18	19	20	21	22	23	24	25	26	27	28	29	30	31
11 ☉	♏ 9	10	11	12	13	14	15	16	17	18	19	20	21	22	23	24	25	26	27	28	29	29 0	♐ 1	2	3	4	5	6	7	8	
☽	♍ 11	23	♎ 5	17	29	♏ 11	23	♐ 5	18	♑ 1	14	27	♒ 10	24	♓ 8	22	♈ 7	22	♉ 7	21	♊ 6	20	♋ 4	18	♌ 1	13	25	♍ 8	19	♎ 1	
☿	♐ 0	0	R 0	0	0	0 29	♏ 29	28	27	26	25	24	23	21	20	19	18	17	16	15	14	14	D 14	14	14	15	15	16	17	18	
♀	♎ 17	18	20	21	22	23	25	26	27	28	29 0	♏ 1	2	3	5	6	7	8	10	11	12	13	15	16	17	18	20	21	22	23	
♂	29 0	♎ 0	1	2	2	3	4	4	5	5	6	7	7	8	8	9	10	10	11	12	12	13	13	14	15	15	16	16	17	18	

♃ 1R 14 23 / ♊25 24 23 — ♄ 1 8 16 25 / ♏1 2 3 4 — ♅ 1R 14 / ♋23 22 — ♆ 1 24 / ♊24 25 — ♇ 1 17 27R / ♌24 25 25

	1	2	3	4	5	6	7	8	9	10	11	12	13	14	15	16	17	18	19	20	21	22	23	24	25	26	27	28	29	30	31
12 ☉	♐ 9	10	11	12	13	14	15	16	17	18	19	20	21	22	23	24	25	26	27	28	29	29 0	♑ 1	2	3	4	5	6	8	9	10
☽	♎ 13	25	♏ 7	19	♐ 2	15	27	♑ 10	24	♒ 7	21	♓ 5	19	♈ 3	17	♉ 1	16	♊ 0	14	28	♋ 12	25	♌ 8	21	♍ 3	15	27	♎ 9	21	♏ 3	15
☿	♏ 19	20	21	22	23	24	26	27	28	29 0	♐ 1	3	4	6	7	8	10	11	13	14	16	17	19	20	22	23	25	26	28	29 0	♑ 1
♀	♏ 25	26	27	28	29 0	♐ 1	2	4	5	6	7	9	10	11	12	14	15	16	17	18	20	21	22	24	25	26	27	29	29 0	♑ 1	2
♂	♎ 18	19	19	20	21	21	22	23	23	24	24	25	26	26	27	27	28	29	29	29 0	♏ 0	1	2	2	3	3	4	5	5	6	6

♃ 1R 9 16 24 / ♊22 21 20 19 — ♄ 1 4 14 25 / ♏4 5 6 7 — ♅ 1R 20 / ♋22 21 — ♆ 1 / ♎25 — ♇ 1R 2 / ♌25 24

1949

1

	1	2	3	4	5	6	7	8	9	10	11	12	13	14	15	16	17	18	19	20	21	22	23	24	25	26	27	28	29	30	31
☉	♑ 11	12	13	14	15	16	17	18	19	20	21	22	23	24	25	26	27	28	29	29 0	♒ 1	2	3	4	5	6	7	8	9	10	11
☽	♒ 5	17	29	♓ 11	23	♈ 5	17	29	♉ 11	24	♊ 7	20	♋ 4	18	♌ 3	18	♍ 2	17	♎ 2	16	♏ 0	14	27	♐ 10	23	♑ 6	19	♒ 1	13	26	♓ 8
☿	♑ 22	24	25	27	29	29 0	♒ 2	3	5	6	8	9	11	12	13	14	16	17	18	18	19	20	20	20	R 20	19	19	18	17	16	15
♀	♐ 15	16	18	19	20	21	23	24	25	26	28	29	29 0	♑ 1	3	4	5	6	8	9	10	11	13	14	15	16	18	19	20	21	23
♂	♑ 27	28	29	29 0	♒ 0	1	2	3	4	4	5	6	7	8	8	9	10	11	11	12	13	14	15	15	16	17	18	19	19	20	21

♃ 1 3 7 12 16 21 25 29 / ♑10 11 12 13 14 15 16 17 — ♄ 1 R 22 / ♍5 4 — ♅ 1 R 2 30 / ♊28 27 26 — ♆ 1 16 R / ♎15 15 — ♇ 1 R 6 / ♌16 15

2

	1	2	3	4	5	6	7	8	9	10	11	12	13	14	15	16	17	18	19	20	21	22	23	24	25	26	27	28
☉	♒ 12	13	14	15	16	17	18	19	20	21	22	23	24	25	26	27	29	29 0	♓ 1	2	3	4	5	6	7	8	9	10
☽	♓ 19	♈ 1	13	25	♉ 7	19	♊ 2	15	28	♋ 12	26	♌ 11	26	♍ 11	26	♎ 11	26	♏ 10	24	♐ 7	20	♑ 3	16	28	♒ 10	22	♓ 4	16
☿	♒ R 15	13	12	10	9	8	7	6	6	5	5	4	4	4	D 4	4	5	5	5	6	7	7	8	9	10	10	11	12
♀	♑ 24	25	26	28	29	29 0	♒ 1	3	4	5	6	8	9	10	11	13	14	15	16	17	19	20	21	22	24	25	26	27
♂	♒ 22	23	23	24	25	26	26	27	28	29	29 0	♓ 0	1	2	3	4	4	5	6	7	8	8	9	10	11	11	12	13

♃ 1 3 7 12 17 22 27 / ♑17 18 19 20 21 22 23 — ♄ 1 R 6 19 / ♍4 3 2 — ♅ 1 R / ♊26 — ♆ 1 R 10 / ♎15 14 — ♇ 1 R 19 / ♌15 14

3

	1	2	3	4	5	6	7	8	9	10	11	12	13	14	15	16	17	18	19	20	21	22	23	24	25	26	27	28	29	30	31
☉	♓ 11	12	13	14	15	16	17	18	19	20	21	22	23	24	25	26	27	28	29	29 0	♈ 1	2	3	4	5	5	6	7	8	9	10
☽	♓ 28	♈ 10	22	♉ 4	16	28	♊ 10	23	♋ 6	20	♌ 4	19	♍ 4	19	♎ 4	20	♏ 4	19	♐ 3	17	♑ 0	13	25	♒ 7	19	♓ 1	13	25	♈ 7	19	♉ 1
☿	♒ 14	15	16	17	18	19	20	22	23	24	26	27	29	29 0	♓ 1	3	4	6	7	9	11	12	14	16	17	19	21	22	24	26	28
♀	♒ 29	29 0	♓ 1	2	4	5	6	7	9	10	11	12	14	15	16	17	19	20	21	22	24	25	26	27	29	29 0	♈ 1	2	4	5	6
♂	♓ 14	15	15	16	17	18	19	19	20	21	22	22	23	24	25	26	26	27	28	29	29 0	♈ 0	1	2	3	3	4	5	6	7	7

♃ 1 4 9 15 21 28 / ♑23 24 25 26 27 28 — ♄ 1 R 3 16 / ♍2 1 0 — ♅ 1 R 5 D / ♊26 26 — ♆ 1 R 27 / ♎14 13 — ♇ 1 R / ♌14

4

	1	2	3	4	5	6	7	8	9	10	11	12	13	14	15	16	17	18	19	20	21	22	23	24	25	26	27	28	29	30
☉	♈ 11	12	13	14	15	16	17	18	19	20	21	22	23	24	25	26	27	28	29	29 0	♉ 1	2	3	4	5	6	7	8	9	10
☽	♉ 13	25	♊ 7	20	♋ 2	16	29	♌ 13	28	♍ 12	27	♎ 13	28	♏ 13	27	♐ 11	25	♑ 9	21	♒ 4	16	28	♓ 10	22	♈ 4	16	27	♉ 10	22	♊ 4
☿	29 0	♈ 1	3	5	7	9	11	13	15	17	19	21	23	25	27	29 0	♉ 2	4	6	8	10	12	14	16	18	20	22	24	26	27
♀	♈ 7	9	10	11	12	14	15	16	17	18	20	21	22	23	25	26	27	28	29 0	♉ 1	2	3	5	6	7	8	9	11	12	13
♂	♈ 8	9	10	10	11	12	13	13	14	15	16	17	17	18	19	20	20	21	22	23	23	24	25	26	26	27	28	29	29	29 0

♃ 1 4 12 29 13 23 / ♑28 29 0 ♒ 0 1 — ♄ 1 R 3 0 4 / ♍0 29 ♌29 — ♅ 1 7 / ♊26 27 — ♆ 1 R / ♎13 — ♇ 1 R 26 D / ♌14 14

5

	1	2	3	4	5	6	7	8	9	10	11	12	13	14	15	16	17	18	19	20	21	22	23	24	25	26	27	28	29	30	31
☉	♉ 11	12	13	14	15	16	17	18	19	19	20	21	22	23	24	25	26	27	28	29	29 0	♊ 1	2	3	4	5	6	7	8	9	10
☽	♊ 17	29	♋ 12	26	♌ 9	23	♍ 7	22	♎ 6	21	♏ 6	21	♐ 5	19	♑ 3	17	♒ 0	12	25	♓ 7	19	♈ 0	12	24	♉ 6	18	♊ 1	13	26	♋ 9	23
☿	♉ 29	29 0	♊ 2	3	5	6	7	9	10	11	12	13	13	14	15	15	16	16	16	17	17	17	R 17	17	16	16	16	15	15	15	14
♀	♉ 14	16	17	18	19	21	22	23	24	26	27	28	29	29 0	♊ 2	3	4	5	7	8	9	10	12	13	14	15	16	18	19	20	21
♂	♉ 1	2	2	3	4	5	5	6	7	8	8	9	10	11	11	12	13	14	14	15	16	16	17	18	19	19	20	21	22	22	23

♃ 1 9 21 R 30 / ♒1 2 2 1 — ♄ 1 R 2 D 29 29 30 / ♌29 29 0 ♍0 — ♅ 1 3 23 / ♊27 28 29 — ♆ 1 R 5 / ♎13 12 — ♇ 1 / ♌14

6

	1	2	3	4	5	6	7	8	9	10	11	12	13	14	15	16	17	18	19	20	21	22	23	24	25	26	27	28	29	30
☉	♊ 11	12	13	13	14	15	16	17	18	19	20	21	22	23	24	25	26	27	28	29	29 0	♋ 1	2	3	4	5	5	6	7	8
☽	♌ 6	20	♍ 4	18	♎ 2	17	♏ 1	15	♐ 0	14	28	♑ 11	25	♒ 8	20	♓ 3	15	27	♈ 8	20	♉ 2	14	27	♊ 9	22	♋ 5	19	♌ 3	17	♍ 1
☿	♊ R 14	13	12	12	11	11	10	10	9	9	9	9	8	8	8	D 8	8	9	9	9	10	10	11	11	12	13	14	14	15	16
♀	♊ 23	24	25	26	27	29	29 0	♋ 1	2	4	5	6	7	8	10	11	12	13	15	16	17	18	19	21	22	23	24	26	27	28
♂	♉ 24	24	25	26	27	27	28	29	29	29 0	♊ 1	2	2	3	4	4	5	6	7	7	8	9	9	10	11	11	12	13	14	14

♃ 1 R 17 27 0 28 / ♒1 0 29 ♑29 — ♄ 1 14 27 / ♍0 1 2 — ♅ 1 9 29 10 26 / ♊29 0 ♋ 0 1 — ♆ 1 R 24 D / ♎12 12 — ♇ 1 29 / ♌14 15

7

	1	2	3	4	5	6	7	8	9	10	11	12	13	14	15	16	17	18	19	20	21	22	23	24	25	26	27	28	29	30	31
☉	♋ 9	10	11	12	13	14	15	16	17	18	19	20	21	22	23	24	25	25	26	27	28	29	29 0	♌ 1	2	3	4	5	6	7	8
☽	♍ 15	29	♎ 13	27	♏ 11	25	♐ 9	23	♑ 7	20	♒ 3	16	28	♓ 11	23	♈ 4	16	28	♉ 10	22	♊ 5	17	♋ 0	14	28	♌ 12	26	♍ 11	25	♎ 10	24
☿	♊ 18	19	20	21	23	24	26	27	29	29 0	♋ 2	4	6	8	10	12	14	16	18	20	22	24	26	28	29 0	♌ 3	5	7	9	11	13
♀	29 0	♌ 1	2	3	4	5	7	8	9	10	11	13	14	15	16	18	19	20	21	22	24	25	26	27	28	29 0	♍ 1	2	3	5	6
♂	♊ 15	16	16	17	18	18	19	20	20	21	22	23	23	24	25	25	26	27	27	28	29	29	29 0	♋ 1	1	2	3	3	4	5	5

♃ 1 R 6 14 22 30 / ♑29 28 27 26 25 — ♄ 1 8 17 26 / ♍2 3 4 5 — ♅ 1 13 / ♋1 2 — ♆ 1 / ♎12 — ♇ 1 / ♌15

8

	1	2	3	4	5	6	7	8	9	10	11	12	13	14	15	16	17	18	19	20	21	22	23	24	25	26	27	28	29	30	31
☉	♌ 9	10	11	12	13	14	15	16	17	17	18	19	20	21	22	23	24	25	26	27	28	29	29 0	♍ 1	2	3	4	5	6	7	8
☽	♏ 8	22	♐ 6	19	♑ 3	16	29	12	24	♓ 7	19	♈ 1	12	24	♉ 6	18	♊ 0	13	25	♋ 9	22	♌ 6	21	♍ 5	20	♎ 5	20	♏ 4	19	♐ 3	16
☿	♌ 15	17	19	21	23	25	26	28	29 0	♍ 2	4	5	7	9	10	12	14	15	17	18	20	21	23	24	26	27	28	29 0	♎ 1	2	3
♀	♍ 7	8	9	11	12	13	14	15	17	18	19	20	21	23	24	25	26	28	29	29 0	♎ 1	2	4	5	6	7	8	9	11	12	13
♂	♋ 6	7	7	8	9	9	10	11	11	12	13	13	14	15	15	16	17	17	18	19	19	20	20	21	22	22	23	24	24	25	26

♃ 1 R 7 16 29 / ♑25 24 23 22 — ♄ 1 4 12 20 28 / ♍5 6 7 8 9 — ♅ 1 22 / ♋3 4 — ♆ 1 10 / ♎12 13 — ♇ 1 3 / ♌15 16

9

	1	2	3	4	5	6	7	8	9	10	11	12	13	14	15	16	17	18	19	20	21	22	23	24	25	26	27	28	29	30
☉	♍ 9	10	11	12	13	14	15	15	16	17	18	19	20	21	22	23	24	25	26	27	28	29	29 0	♎ 1	2	3	4	5	6	7
☽	♑ 0	13	26	♒ 8	21	♓ 3	15	27	♈ 9	21	♉ 3	15	26	♊ 9	21	♋ 4	17	♌ 0	14	29	♍ 14	29	♎ 14	29	♏ 14	28	♐ 13	26	♑ 10	23
☿	♎ 5	6	7	8	9	10	11	12	13	14	15	16	16	17	17	18	18	18	19	19	R 19	18	18	18	17	17	16	15	14	13
♀	♎ 14	15	17	18	19	20	21	22	24	25	26	27	28	29 0	♏ 1	2	3	4	5	7	8	9	10	11	13	14	15	16	17	18
♂	♋ 26	27	27	28	29	29	29 0	♌ 1	1	2	3	3	4	4	5	6	6	7	7	8	9	9	10	11	11	12	12	13	14	14

♃ 1 R 19 D / ♑22 22 — ♄ 1 5 13 21 29 / ♍9 10 11 12 13 — ♅ 1 / ♋4 — ♆ 1 13 / ♎13 14 — ♇ 1 5 / ♌16 17

10

	1	2	3	4	5	6	7	8	9	10	11	12	13	14	15	16	17	18	19	20	21	22	23	24	25	26	27	28	29	30	31
☉	♎ 8	9	10	11	12	13	14	15	16	17	18	19	20	21	22	23	24	25	26	27	28	29	29 0	♏ 1	2	3	4	5	6	7	8
☽	♒ 6	18	♓ 0	12	24	♈ 6	18	♉ 0	11	23	♊ 5	18	♋ 0	13	26	♌ 9	23	♍ 7	22	♎ 7	22	♏ 7	22	♐ 7	22	♑ 5	19	♒ 2	15	27	♓ 9
☿	♎ R 12	11	10	9	7	6	5	5	4	4	4	D 3	4	4	4	5	6	7	8	9	10	11	12	14	15	17	18	20	21	23	24
♀	♏ 20	21	22	23	24	25	26	28	29	29 0	♐ 1	2	3	5	6	7	8	9	10	11	13	14	15	16	17	18	19	20	21	23	24
♂	♌ 15	15	16	17	17	18	18	19	20	20	21	21	22	23	23	24	24	25	25	26	27	27	28	28	29	29 0	♍ 0	1	1	2	2

♃ 1 8 21 30 / ♑22 23 24 25 — ♄ 1 8 17 27 / ♍13 14 15 16 — ♅ 1 3 11 R 18 / ♋4 5 5 4 — ♆ 1 10 / ♎14 15 — ♇ 1 22 / ♌17 18

11

	1	2	3	4	5	6	7	8	9	10	11	12	13	14	15	16	17	18	19	20	21	22	23	24	25	26	27	28	29	30
☉	♏ 9	10	11	12	13	14	15	16	17	18	19	20	21	22	23	24	25	26	27	28	29	29 0	♐ 1	2	3	4	5	6	7	8
☽	♓ 21	♈ 3	15	27	♉ 8	20	♊ 2	15	27	♋ 9	22	♌ 5	19	♍ 2	16	♎ 1	15	♏ 0	15	♐ 0	15	♑ 0	14	27	♒ 11	23	♓ 6	18	♈ 0	11
☿	♎ 26	28	29 0	♏ 1	3	4	6	8	9	11	12	14	16	17	19	21	22	24	25	27	28	29 0	♐ 2	3	5	6	8	9	11	13
♀	♐ 25	26	27	28	29	29 0	♑ 1	2	3	4	6	7	8	9	10	11	12	13	14	15	16	17	18	19	20	21	22	23	24	25
♂	♍ 3	3	4	5	5	6	6	7	7	8	8	9	9	10	11	11	12	12	13	13	14	14	15	15	16	16	17	17	18	18

♃ 1 6 13 19 25 30 29 / ♑25 26 27 28 29 0 — ♄ 17 19 / ♍16 17 18 — ♅ 1 R 29 / ♋4 3 — ♆ 1 7 / ♎15 16 — ♇ 1 19 R / ♌18 18

12

	1	2	3	4	5	6	7	8	9	10	11	12	13	14	15	16	17	18	19	20	21	22	23	24	25	26	27	28	29	30	31
☉	♐ 9	10	11	12	13	14	15	16	17	18	19	20	21	22	23	24	25	26	27	28	29	29 0	♑ 1	2	3	4	5	6	7	8	10
☽	♈ 23	♉ 5	17	29	♊ 11	24	♋ 6	19	♌ 2	16	29	♍ 13	26	♎ 11	25	♏ 9	24	♐ 9	23	♑ 8	22	♒ 5	18	♓ 1	14	26	♈ 8	20	♉ 1	13	25
☿	♐ 14	16	17	19	20	22	24	25	27	28	29 0	♑ 1	3	4	6	8	9	11	12	14	15	17	18	20	21	22	24	25	26	28	29
♀	♑ 26	26	27	28	29	29 0	♒ 1	2	3	3	4	5	6	7	7	8	9	10	10	11	12	12	13	13	14	14	15	15	16	16	17
♂	♍ 19	19	20	20	21	21	22	22	22	23	23	24	24	25	25	26	26	27	27	27	28	28	29	29	29	29 0	♎ 0	1	1	1	2

♃ 1 5 10 15 20 25 29 / ♒0 1 2 3 4 5 6 — ♄ 1 8 / ♍18 19 — ♅ 1 R 24 / ♋3 2 — ♆ 1 13 / ♎16 17 — ♇ 1 R 18 / ♌18 17

1950

1

	1	2	3	4	5	6	7	8	9	10	11	12	13	14	15	16	17	18	19	20	21	22	23	24	25	26	27	28	29
☉	♑ 11	12	13	14	15	16	17	18	19	20	21	22	23	24	25	26	27	28	29	29 0	♒ 1	2	3	4	5	6	7	8	9
☽	♊ 7	20	♋ 3	16	29	♌ 12	26	♍ 10	23	♎ 7	21	♏ 5	20	♐ 4	18	♑ 2	16	♒ 0	13	26	♓ 9	21	♈ 4	15	27	♉ 9	21	♊ 3	15
☿	29 0	♒ 1	2	2	3	3	4	R 4	3	3	3	2	1	1	29	27	26	25	24	23	22	21	20	19	18	18	18	18	D 18
♀	♒ 17	17	17	18	18	18	18	18	18	R 18	18	18	18	18	17	17	17	17	16	16	16	15	15	14	14	13	12	12	11
♂	♎ 2	2	3	3	3	4	4	4	5	5	5	6	6	6	7	7	7	7	8	8	8	8	8	9	9	9	9	9	10

♃ 1 3 7 11 16 20 24 28 / ♒6 7 8 9 10 11 12 13 — ♄ 1 R 21 / ♍19 18 — ♅ 1 R 17 / ♋2 1 — ♆ 1 18 R / ♎17 17 — ♇ 1 R / ♌17

2

	1	2	3	4	5	6	7	8	9	10	11	12	13	14	15	16	17	18	19	20	21	22	23	24	25	26	27	28
☉	♒ 12	13	14	15	16	17	18	19	20	21	22	23	24	25	26	27	28	29	29 0	♓ 1	2	3	4	5	6	7	8	9
☽	♋ 24	♌ 7	21	♍ 5	20	♎ 4	18	♏ 2	16	♐ 1	14	28	♑ 12	25	♒ 9	22	♓ 5	17	29	♈ 11	23	♉ 5	17	29	♊ 11	23	♋ 6	18
☿	♑ 18	19	19	20	21	22	22	23	24	25	26	27	29	29 0	♒ 1	2	3	5	6	7	8	10	11	12	14	15	17	18
♀	♒ R 10	9	8	7	7	6	6	5	5	4	4	4	4	3	3	3	3	3	3	D 3	3	3	3	3	3	3	4	4
♂	♎ 10	10	10	10	10	10	10	10	11	11	11	R 11	11	10	10	10	10	10	10	10	10	10	10	10	9	9	9	9

♃ 1 2 6 10 14 18 23 27 / ♒13 14 15 16 17 18 19 20 — ♄ 1 R 9 23 / ♍18 17 16 — ♅ 1 R 27 / ♋1 0 — ♆ 1 R 24 / ♎17 16 — ♇ 1 R / ♌

3

	1	2	3	4	5	6	7	8	9	10	11	12	13	14	15	16	17	18	19	20	21	22	23	24	25	26	27	28	29
☉	♓ 10	11	12	13	14	15	16	17	18	19	20	21	22	23	24	25	26	27	28	29	29 0	♈ 1	2	3	4	5	6	7	8
☽	♌ 2	16	♍ 0	14	29	♎ 13	28	♏ 13	27	♐ 11	25	♑ 9	22	♒ 5	18	♓ 1	13	26	♈ 8	20	♉ 2	13	25	♊ 7	19	♋ 1	14	27	♌ 10
☿	♒ 20	21	23	24	26	28	29 0	♓ 1	2	4	6	8	9	11	13	15	16	18	20	22	24	26	28	29 0	♈ 2	3	5	8	10
♀	♒ 4	5	5	5	6	6	7	7	8	8	9	10	10	11	12	12	13	14	14	15	16	17	17	18	19	20	21	22	22
♂	♎ R 9	8	8	8	8	7	7	7	6	6	6	5	5	5	4	4	4	3	3	2	2	2	1	1	0	0	0	0 29	♍ 29

♃ 1 3 7 12 16 21 26 30 / ♒20 21 22 23 24 25 26 27 — ♄ 1 R 7 20 / ♍16 15 14 — ♅ 1 R 9 D 21 / ♋0 0 1 — ♆ 1 R / ♎16 — ♇ 1 R / ♌16

4

	1	2	3	4	5	6	7	8	9	10	11	12	13	14	15	16	17	18	19	20	21	22	23	24	25	26	27	28	29
☉	♈ 11	12	13	14	15	16	17	18	19	20	21	22	23	24	25	26	27	28	29	29 0	♉ 1	2	3	4	5	6	7	8	9
☽	♍ 22	♎ 7	22	♏ 7	22	♐ 7	21	♑ 5	19	♒ 2	15	28	♓ 10	23	♈ 5	17	28	♉ 10	22	♊ 4	16	28	♋ 10	22	♌ 5	18	♍ 2	16	♎ 0
☿	♈ 16	18	20	22	24	26	28	29 0	♉ 2	4	6	7	9	11	12	14	15	17	18	20	21	22	23	24	24	25	26	26	26
♀	♒ 25	26	27	28	29	29 0	♓ 1	2	3	4	5	6	7	8	9	10	11	12	13	14	15	16	17	18	19	20	21	22	23
♂	♍ R 28	27	27	27	26	26	26	25	25	25	25	24	24	24	24	23	23	23	23	23	22	22	22	22	22	22	22	22	22

♃ 1 4 10 15 29 16 20 26 / ♒27 28 29 0 ♓ 0 1 2 — ♄ 1 R 3 23 / ♍14 13 12 — ♅ 1 28 / ♋1 2 — ♆ 1 R 5 / ♎16 15 — ♇ 1 R / ♌15

5

	1	2	3	4	5	6	7	8	9	10	11	12	13	14	15	16	17	18	19	20	21	22	23	24	25	26	27	28	29
☉	♉ 11	11	12	13	14	15	16	17	18	19	20	21	22	23	24	25	26	27	28	29	29 0	♊ 1	2	3	4	5	6	7	8
☽	♏ 0	15	♐ 1	16	♑ 0	15	28	♒ 12	25	♓ 7	20	♈ 2	14	25	♉ 7	19	♊ 1	13	25	♋ 7	19	♌ 2	15	28	♍ 11	25	♎ 9	24	♏ 9
☿	♉ 27	27	R 27	27	27	27	26	26	25	25	24	24	23	23	22	22	21	20	20	20	19	19	18	18	18	18	D 18	18	18
♀	♓ 25	26	27	28	29 0	♈ 1	2	3	4	5	6	7	8	9	11	12	13	14	15	16	17	18	20	21	22	23	24	25	26
♂	♍ R 22	22	D 22	22	22	22	22	22	22	22	22	22	22	22	22	23	23	23	23	23	23	24	24	24	24	25	25	25	25

♃ 1 3 10 17 27 / ♓2 3 4 5 6 — ♄ 1 R 15 D / ♍12 12 — ♅ 1 20 / ♋2 3 — ♆ 1 R 16 / ♎15 14 — ♇ 1 / ♌15

6

	1	2	3	4	5	6	7	8	9	10	11	12	13	14	15	16	17	18	19	20	21	22	23	24	25	26	27	28	29
☉	♊ 10	11	12	13	14	15	16	17	18	19	20	21	22	23	24	25	26	27	28	29	29 0	♋ 0	1	2	3	4	5	6	7
☽	♐ 24	♑ 9	23	♒ 7	21	♓ 4	16	28	♈ 10	22	♉ 4	16	28	♊ 10	22	♋ 4	16	29	♌ 12	25	♍ 8	21	♎ 5	19	♏ 3	18	♐ 3	18	♑ 2
☿	♉ 19	20	20	21	21	22	23	24	24	25	27	28	29	29 0	♊ 1	2	4	5	6	8	9	11	13	15	16	18	20	22	24
♀	29 0	♉ 1	2	3	4	6	7	8	9	10	11	13	14	15	16	17	18	20	21	22	23	24	25	27	28	29	29 0	♊ 1	2
♂	♍ 26	27	27	27	27	28	28	29	29	29	29	29 0	♎ 0	1	1	1	2	2	3	3	4	4	4	5	5	6	6	7	7

♃ 1 10 26 R / ♓6 7 7 — ♄ 1 6 25 / ♍12 13 14 — ♅ 1 7 24 / ♋3 4 5 — ♆ 1 R 26 D / ♎14 14 — ♇ 1 / ♌16

7

	1	2	3	4	5	6	7	8	9	10	11	12	13	14	15	16	17	18	19	20	21	22	23	24	25	26	27	28	29
☉	♋ 9	10	11	12	13	14	15	16	17	18	19	20	20	21	22	23	24	25	26	27	28	29	29 0	♌ 1	2	3	4	5	6
☽	♒ 1	15	29	♓ 12	24	♈ 17	19	♉ 1	13	24	♊ 6	18	♋ 1	13	26	♌ 8	22	♍ 5	18	♎ 2	16	♏ 0	14	28	♐ 13	27	♑ 11	26	♒ 10
☿	♊ 28	29 0	♋ 2	4	6	8	10	12	14	17	19	21	23	25	27	29	29 1	♌ 3	5	7	9	11	13	15	17	19	20	22	24
♀	♊ 5	6	7	8	9	11	12	13	14	15	17	18	19	20	21	22	24	25	26	27	28	29 0	♋ 1	2	3	4	6	7	8
♂	♎ 8	8	9	9	10	10	11	11	12	12	13	13	14	14	15	16	16	17	18	18	18	19	19	20	20	21	22	22	23

♃ 1 R 13 27 / ♓7 6 5 — ♄ 1 8 19 29 / ♍14 15 16 17 — ♅ 1 10 28 / ♋5 6 7 — ♆ 1 / ♎14 — ♇ 1 / ♌16

8

	1	2	3	4	5	6	7	8	9	10	11	12	13	14	15	16	17	18	19	20	21	22	23	24	25	26	27	28	29
☉	♌ 9	10	11	12	12	13	14	15	16	17	18	19	20	21	22	23	24	25	26	27	28	29	29 0	♍ 1	2	3	4	5	6
☽	♓ 20	♈ 2	15	27	♉ 9	21	♊ 2	14	27	♋ 9	21	♌ 4	18	♍ 1	15	28	♎ 12	27	♏ 11	25	♐ 9	23	♑ 7	21	♒ 5	19	♓ 2	15	28
☿	29	29 0	♍ 2	4	5	7	8	9	11	12	14	15	16	17	19	20	21	22	23	24	25	26	27	28	28	29	29 0	♎ 0	1
♀	♋ 12	13	14	15	16	18	19	20	21	23	23	25	26	27	29	29 0	♌ 1	2	3	5	6	7	8	10	11	12	13	14	16
♂	♎ 24	25	26	26	27	27	28	28	29	29 0	♏ 0	1	2	2	3	3	4	5	5	6	6	7	8	8	9	10	10	11	12

♃ 1 R 6 15 22 29 / ♓5 4 3 2 1 — ♄ 1 8 16 25 / ♍17 18 19 20 — ♅ 1 16 / ♋7 8 — ♆ 1 5 / ♎14 15 — ♇ 1 / ♌17

9

	1	2	3	4	5	6	7	8	9	10	11	12	13	14	15	16	17	18	19	20	21	22	23	24	25	26	27	28	29
☉	♍ 8	9	10	11	12	13	14	15	16	17	18	19	20	21	22	23	24	25	26	27	28	29	29 0	♎ 1	2	3	4	5	6
☽	♉ 5	17	28	♊ 10	22	♋ 4	17	♌ 0	13	26	♍ 10	24	♎ 8	22	♏ 7	21	♐ 6	20	♑ 4	18	♒ 2	5	28	♓ 11	24	♈ 6	19	♉ 1	13
☿	♎ 2	2	2	R 2	2	1	1	1	0	0 29	♍ 29	28	27	26	25	24	23	22	21	20	19	18	18	18	17	D 17	18	18	18
♀	♌ 19	21	22	23	24	26	27	28	29	29 1	♍ 2	3	4	5	7	8	9	10	12	13	14	15	16	18	19	20	22	23	24
♂	♏ 13	14	15	15	16	17	17	18	19	19	20	21	21	22	23	23	24	25	25	26	27	28	28	29	29 0	♐ 0	1	2	2

♃ 1 R 6 15 0 16 24 / ♓1 0 29 ♒29 28 — ♄ 1 2 10 18 26 / ♍20 21 22 23 24 — ♅ 1 12 / ♋8 9 — ♆ 1 10 / ♎15 16 — ♇ 1 / ♌18

10

	1	2	3	4	5	6	7	8	9	10	11	12	13	14	15	16	17	18	19	20	21	22	23	24	25	26	27	28	29
☉	♎ 8	9	10	11	12	13	14	15	16	17	18	19	20	21	22	23	24	25	26	27	28	29	29 0	♏ 1	2	3	3	4	5
☽	♊ 7	18	♋ 0	12	25	♌ 7	20	♍ 4	18	♎ 2	17	♏ 1	16	♐ 1	6	♑ 0	15	28	♒ 12	25	♓ 8	21	♈ 3	15	27	♉ 9	21	♊ 3	15
☿	♍ 20	21	22	23	24	25	27	28	29 0	♎ 1	3	4	6	8	10	11	13	15	16	18	20	22	23	25	27	28	29 0	♏ 2	3
♀	♍ 26	28	29	29 0	♎ 2	3	4	5	6	8	9	10	11	13	14	15	16	18	19	20	21	23	24	25	26	28	29	29 0	♏ 2
♂	♐ 4	5	5	6	7	7	8	9	9	10	11	12	12	13	14	15	15	16	17	17	18	19	20	20	21	22	23	23	24

♃ 1 R 8 24 D / ♒28 27 27 — ♄ 1 4 13 21 30 / ♍24 25 26 27 28 — ♅ 1 15 R / ♋9 9 — ♆ 1 8 / ♎16 17 — ♇ 1 / ♌19

11

	1	2	3	4	5	6	7	8	9	10	11	12	13	14	15	16	17	18	19	20	21	22	23	24	25	26	27	28	29
☉	♏ 8	9	10	12	13	14	15	16	17	18	19	20	21	22	23	24	25	26	27	28	29	29 0	♐ 1	2	3	4	5	6	7
☽	♋ 21	♌ 3	16	29	♍ 12	26	♎ 10	25	♏ 10	25	♐ 10	25	♑ 10	24	♒ 8	22	♓ 5	18	♈ 0	12	24	♉ 6	18	♊ 0	12	24	♋ 6	8	♌ 0
☿	♏ 8	10	11	13	15	16	18	20	21	23	24	26	27	29	29 1	♐ 2	4	5	7	8	10	11	13	14	16	17	19	20	22
♀	♏ 5	7	8	9	10	11	13	14	15	17	18	19	20	22	23	24	25	27	28	29	29 1	♐ 2	3	4	5	7	8	9	10
♂	♐ 26	27	28	29	29 0	♑ 1	2	2	3	3	4	5	5	6	7	8	8	9	10	11	11	12	13	14	14	15	16	17	18

♃ 1 8 22 / ♒27 28 29 — ♄ 1 9 20 29 21 / ♍28 29 0 ♎ 0 — ♅ 1 R 18 / ♋9 8 — ♆ 1 4 / ♎17 18 — ♇ 1 / ♌19

12

	1	2	3	4	5	6	7	8	9	10	11	12	13	14	15	16	17	18	19	20	21	22	23	24	25	26	27	28	29
☉	♐ 9	10	11	12	13	14	15	16	17	18	19	20	21	22	23	24	25	26	27	28	29	29 0	♑ 1	2	3	4	5	6	7
☽	♌ 25	♍ 7	21	♎ 4	18	♏ 3	18	♐ 3	18	♑ 3	18	♒ 3	17	♓ 1	14	27	♈ 9	21	♉ 3	15	27	♊ 9	21	♋ 3	15	27	♌ 9	22	♍ 4
☿	♐ 25	26	28	29	29 1	♑ 2	3	5	6	7	9	10	11	12	13	14	15	16	17	17	18	18	R 18	17	17	17	16	15	14
♀	♐ 13	14	16	17	18	19	21	22	23	24	26	27	28	29 0	♑ 1	2	3	4	6	7	8	9	11	12	13	14	16	17	18
♂	♑ 19	20	21	21	22	23	24	25	25	26	27	28	28	29	29 0	♒ 1	2	2	3	4	5	5	6	7	8	9	9	10	11

♃ 1 29 2 9 16 22 28 / 0 ♓ 0 1 2 3 4 — ♄ 1 3 22 / ♎0 1 2 — ♅ 1 R 16 / ♋8 7 — ♆ 1 8 / ♎18 19 — ♇ 1 R / ♌19

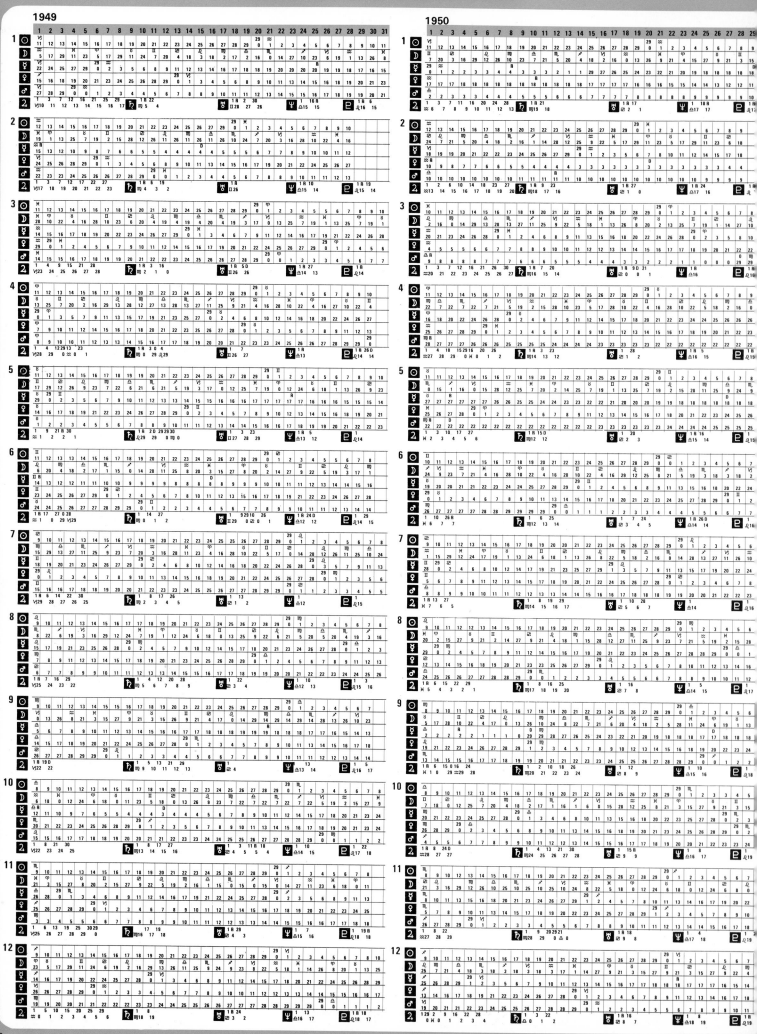

1951

	2	3	4	5	6	7	8	9	10	11	12	13	14	15	16	17	18	19	20	21	22	23	24	25	26	27	28	29	30	31
	11	12	13	14	15	16	17	18	19	20	21	23	24	25	26	27	28	29	29 0	♒ 1	2	3	4	5	6	7	8	9	10	11
	28	♏ 12	26	♐ 11	26	♑ 11	26	♒ 11	25	♓ 9	22	♈ 5	18	♉ 0	12	24	♊ 5	17	29	♋ 11	24	♌ 6	18	♍ 1	14	27	♎ 11	24	♏ 8	22
	9	7	6	5	4	3	2	2	2	1	D 1	2	2	2	3	3	4	5	5	6	7	8	9	10	11	13	14	15	16	17
	23	24	26	27	28	29 0	♒ 1	2	3	5	6	7	8	9	11	12	13	15	16	17	18	20	21	22	23	25	26	27	28	29 0
	14	15	16	16	17	18	19	20	20	21	22	23	24	24	25	26	27	28	28	29	29 0	♓ 1	1	2	3	4	5	5	6	7

♃ 2 7 12 17 22 26 31 / 4 5 6 7 8 9 10 11 — ♄ 1 11 R / ♎ 2 2 — ♅ 1 R 9 / ♋ 7 6 — ♆ 1 20 R / ♎19 19 — ♇ 1 R 25 / ♌19 18

	2	3	4	5	6	7	8	9	10	11	12	13	14	15	16	17	18	19	20	21	22	23	24	25	26	27	28	29	30	31
	13	14	15	16	17	18	19	20	21	22	23	24	25	26	27	28	29	29 0	♓ 1	2	3	4	5	6	7	8	9			
	21	♑ 5	20	♒ 5	19	♓ 3	17	♈ 0	13	25	♉ 8	20	♊ 2	14	25	♋ 7	20	♌ 2	14	27	♍ 10	24	♎ 7	21	♏ 5	19	♐ 3			
	20	21	22	24	25	27	28	29 0	♒ 1	2	4	5	7	8	10	12	13	15	16	18	20	21	23	25	26	28	29 0			
	2	3	4	6	7	8	10	11	12	13	15	16	17	18	20	21	22	23	24	26	27	28	29 0	♈ 1	2	3	4			
	9	9	10	11	12	12	13	14	15	16	16	17	18	19	19	20	21	22	23	23	24	25	26	26	27	28	29			

♃ 4 8 13 17 21 25 / 12 13 14 15 16 17 — ♄ 1 R 21 / ♎ 1 0 — ♅ 1 R 4 / ♋ 6 5 — ♆ 1 R / ♎19 — ♇ 1 R / ♌18

	2	3	4	5	6	7	8	9	10	11	12	13	14	15	16	17	18	19	20	21	22	23	24	25	26	27	28	29	30	31
	11	12	13	14	15	16	17	18	19	20	21	22	23	24	25	26	27	28	29	29 0	♈ 1	2	3	4	5	6	7	8	9	10
	♑ 1	16	♒ 0	14	28	♓ 11	25	♈ 8	21	♉ 3	15	28	♊ 9	21	♋ 3	15	27	♌ 10	22	♍ 5	19	♎ 3	16	♏ 1	15	29	♐ 14	28	♑ 12	26
	3	5	7	9	11	13	14	16	18	20	22	24	26	28	29 0	♈ 2	4	6	8	10	12	14	16	17	19	21	23	24	26	28
	7	8	9	10	12	13	14	15	17	18	19	20	21	23	24	25	26	28	29	29 0	♉ 1	3	4	5	6	7	9	10	11	12
	♈ 0	1	2	3	3	4	5	6	6	7	8	9	10	10	11	12	13	13	14	15	16	16	17	18	19	19	20	21	22	22

♃ 2 6 10 14 18 22 26 / 7 18 19 20 21 22 23 24 — ♄ 1 R 7 0 8 20 / ♎ 0 29 ♍29 28 — ♅ 1 R 13 D / ♋ 5 5 — ♆ 1 R 7 / ♎19 18 — ♇ 1 R 8 / ♌18 17

	2	3	4	5	6	7	8	9	10	11	12	13	14	15	16	17	18	19	20	21	22	23	24	25	26	27	28	29	30	31
	12	13	14	15	16	17	18	19	20	21	22	23	24	25	26	27	28	29	29 0	♉ 1	2	3	3	4	5	6	7	8	9	
	24	♓ 7	20	♈ 3	16	29	♉ 11	23	♊ 6	17	29	♋ 11	23	♌ 5	18	♍ 0	13	27	♎ 11	25	♏ 10	24	♐ 9	24	♑ 9	23	♒ 7	21	♓ 4	
	29 0	♉ 2	3	4	5	6	6	7	7	8	8	8	R 8	8	8	8	7	7	6	6	5	4	4	3	2	2	1	1	0	
	15	16	17	18	20	21	22	23	24	26	27	28	29	29 0	♊ 1	3	4	5	6	7	9	10	11	12	13	14	16	17	18	
	24	25	25	26	27	28	28	29	29 0	♉ 1	1	2	3	4	4	5	6	7	7	8	9	10	10	11	12	12	13	14	15	

♃ 4 8 12 17 21 29 22 26 / 5 26 27 28 29 0 ♈ 0 1 — ♄ 1 R 2 16 / ♍28 27 26 — ♅ 1 20 / ♋ 5 6 — ♆ 1 R 14 / ♎18 17 — ♇ 1 R 30 D / 17 17

	2	3	4	5	6	7	8	9	10	11	12	13	14	15	16	17	18	19	20	21	22	23	24	25	26	27	28	29	30	31
	11	12	13	14	15	16	17	18	19	20	21	22	23	24	25	26	27	28	29	29 0	♊ 1	2	2	3	4	5	6	7	8	9
	♈ 0	13	25	♉ 8	20	♊ 2	14	26	♋ 8	19	♌ 1	14	26	♍ 8	21	♎ 5	19	♏ 3	18	♐ 3	18	♑ 4	18	♒ 3	17	♓ 1	14	27	♈ 10	22
	♈ 29	29	28	28	28	28	D 28	28	28	28	29	29	29	29 0	♉ 1	1	2	3	4	4	5	6	7	9	10	11	12	13	14	16
	20	21	22	24	25	26	27	28	29	29 1	♋ 2	3	4	5	6	7	8	10	11	12	13	14	15	16	17	18	20	21	22	23
	16	17	18	18	19	20	20	21	22	23	23	24	25	25	26	27	28	28	29	29 0	♊ 0	1	2	3	3	4	5	5	6	7

♃ 5 10 15 20 25 31 / 2 3 4 5 6 7 8 — ♄ 1 R 5 28 D / ♍26 25 25 — ♅ 1 15 / ♋ 6 7 — ♆ 1 R 29 / ♎17 16 — ♇ 1 / ♌17

	2	3	4	5	6	7	8	9	10	11	12	13	14	15	16	17	18	19	20	21	22	23	24	25	26	27	28	29	30	31
	11	12	13	14	15	16	17	18	19	20	21	22	23	24	25	25	26	27	28	29	29 0	♋ 1	2	3	4	5	6	7	8	
	17	29	♊ 11	23	♋ 5	16	28	♌ 10	22	♍ 5	17	♎ 0	13	27	♏ 12	26	♐ 12	27	♑ 12	27	♒ 12	26	♓ 10	24	♈ 7	19	♉ 2	14	26	
	19	20	22	23	25	27	28	29 0	♊ 2	4	6	8	10	12	14	16	18	20	22	24	26	28	29 0	♋ 3	5	7	9	12	14	
	25	26	27	28	29	29 0	♌ 1	2	3	5	6	7	8	9	10	11	12	13	14	15	16	17	18	18	19	20	21	22	23	
	8	9	10	10	11	12	12	13	14	14	15	16	17	17	18	19	19	20	21	21	22	23	23	24	25	25	26	27	27	

♃ 6 12 19 27 / 8 9 10 11 12 — ♄ 1 21 / ♍25 26 — ♅ 1 3 20 / ♋ 7 8 9 — ♆ 1 R 28 D / ♎16 16 — ♇ 1 20 / ♌17 18

	2	3	4	5	6	7	8	9	10	11	12	13	14	15	16	17	18	19	20	21	22	23	24	25	26	27	28	29	30	31
	10	11	12	13	14	15	15	16	17	18	19	20	21	22	23	24	25	26	27	28	29	29 0	♌ 1	2	3	4	5	6	6	7
	20	♋ 2	13	15	♌ 7	19	♍ 2	14	27	♎ 10	23	♏ 7	21	♐ 5	20	♑ 5	21	♒ 6	20	♓ 5	19	♈ 2	16	28	♉ 11	23	♊ 5	17	28	♋ 10
	18	20	22	24	26	28	29 0	♌ 2	3	5	7	9	10	12	14	15	17	19	20	22	23	24	26	27	28	29 0	♍ 1	2	3	4
	25	26	27	28	28	29	29 0	♍ 1	2	3	3	4	5	6	6	7	8	9	9	10	10	11	12	12	13	13	14	14	15	15
	29	29 0	♋ 0	1	2	2	3	4	4	5	6	6	7	8	8	9	10	10	11	12	12	13	14	14	15	16	16	17	17	18

♃ 8 24 / 2 13 14 — ♄ 1 10 23 / ♍26 27 28 — ♅ 1 7 24 / ♋ 9 10 11 — ♆ 1 28 / ♎16 17 — ♇ 1 26 / ♌18 19

	2	3	4	5	6	7	8	9	10	11	12	13	14	15	16	17	18	19	20	21	22	23	24	25	26	27	28	29	30	31
	9	10	11	12	13	14	15	16	17	18	19	20	21	22	23	24	25	26	27	28	29	29 0	♍ 0	1	2	3	4	5	6	7
	♌ 4	16	29	♍ 11	24	♎ 7	20	♏ 3	17	♐ 1	15	♑ 0	14	29	♒ 14	29	♓ 13	27	♈ 11	24	♉ 6	19	♊ 1	13	25	♋ 7	19	♌ 1	13	25
	7	8	9	9	10	11	12	12	13	13	14	14	14	15	15	15	R 15	14	14	14	13	13	12	11	11	10	9	8	7	6
	16	16	17	17	17	17	17	18	18	18	R 18	18	18	18	18	17	17	17	17	16	16	16	15	15	14	14	13	13	12	11
	19	20	21	21	22	23	23	24	25	25	26	27	27	28	29	29 0	♌ 0	1	1	2	2	3	4	4	5	6	6	7	8	8

♃ 3 R 14 31 / 4 14 13 12 — ♄ 1 3 13 29 14 22 31 / ♍28 29 0 ♎ 0 1 2 — ♅ 1 11 / ♋11 12 — ♆ 1 / ♎17 — ♇ 1 29 / ♌19 20

	2	3	4	5	6	7	8	9	10	11	12	13	14	15	16	17	18	19	20	21	22	23	24	25	26	27	28	29	30	31
	9	10	11	12	13	14	15	16	17	18	19	20	21	22	23	24	25	26	27	28	29	29 0	♎ 1	2	3	4	5	6	7	
	20	♎ 3	17	♏ 0	14	27	♐ 11	26	♑ 10	24	♒ 9	23	♓ 7	21	♈ 5	19	♉ 2	14	27	♊ 9	21	♋ 3	15	27	♌ 9	21	♍ 3	16	29	
	4	3	2	2	2	1	1	D 1	1	2	2	2	3	4	5	6	7	8	10	11	12	14	16	17	19	21	23	24	26	
	10	10	9	8	8	7	7	6	5	5	5	4	4	3	3	3	2	2	2	2	2	2	D 2	2	2	2	2	2	2	
	9	10	11	11	12	13	13	14	15	15	16	16	17	18	18	19	20	20	21	21	22	23	23	24	25	25	26	26	27	

♃ R 10 18 26 / 2 11 10 9 — ♄ 1 9 17 25 / ♎ 2 3 4 5 — ♅ 1 2 / ♋12 13 — ♆ 1 7 / ♎17 8 — ♇ 1 / ♌20

	2	3	4	5	6	7	8	9	10	11	12	13	14	15	16	17	18	19	20	21	22	23	24	25	26	27	28	29	30	31
	8	9	10	11	12	13	14	15	16	17	18	19	20	21	22	23	24	25	26	27	28	29	29 0	♏ 1	2	3	4	5	6	7
	26	♏ 10	24	♐ 8	22	♑ 7	21	♒ 5	19	♓ 3	17	♈ 0	14	27	♉ 10	22	♊ 5	17	29	♋ 11	23	♌ 5	17	29	♍ 11	24	♎ 7	21	♏ 5	19
	29 0	♎ 2	3	5	7	9	10	12	14	16	17	19	21	23	24	26	28	29 0	♏ 1	2	4	6	7	9	10	12	14	15	17	18
	3	3	3	4	4	5	5	6	6	7	7	8	8	9	10	10	11	12	12	13	14	15	15	16	17	18	19	19	20	21
	28	29	29 0	♍ 0	1	1	2	3	3	4	4	5	6	6	7	7	8	9	9	10	10	11	12	12	13	13	14	15	15	16

♃ R 4 12 20 29 / 9 8 7 6 5 — ♄ 1 3 11 20 28 / ♎ 5 6 7 8 9 — ♅ 1 18 20 R 23 / ♋13 14 14 13 — ♆ 1 5 / ♎18 19 — ♇ 1 6 / ♌20 21

	2	3	4	5	6	7	8	9	10	11	12	13	14	15	16	17	18	19	20	21	22	23	24	25	26	27	28	29	30	31
	9	10	11	12	13	14	15	16	17	18	19	20	21	22	23	24	25	26	27	28	29	29 0	♐ 1	2	3	4	5	6	7	
	18	♑ 3	18	♒ 2	16	♓ 0	13	27	♈ 10	23	♉ 6	18	♊ 1	13	25	♋ 7	19	♌ 1	13	25	♍ 7	19	♎ 2	15	29	♏ 13	28	♐ 13	28	
	21	23	24	26	27	29	29 0	♐ 2	3	5	6	8	9	10	12	13	15	16	17	19	20	21	22	24	25	26	27	28	29	
	23	24	25	26	27	28	29	29 0	♎ 1	2	3	4	5	6	7	8	9	10	11	12	13	14	15	16	17	18	19	21	22	
	17	18	18	19	19	20	21	21	22	22	23	24	24	25	25	26	26	27	28	28	29	29	29 0	♎ 1	1	2	2	3	3	

♃ R 9 29 D / 5 4 4 — ♄ 1 6 15 25 / ♎ 9 10 11 12 — ♅ 1 R / ♋13 — ♆ 1 2 / ♎19 20 — ♇ 1 23 R / ♌21 21

	2	3	4	5	6	7	8	9	10	11	12	13	14	15	16	17	18	19	20	21	22	23	24	25	26	27	28	29	30	31
	10	11	12	13	14	15	16	17	18	19	20	21	22	23	24	25	26	27	28	29	29 0	♑ 1	2	3	4	5	6	7	8	9
	28	♒ 12	26	♓ 10	24	♈ 7	20	♉ 2	15	27	♊ 10	22	♋ 4	16	27	♌ 9	21	♍ 3	15	27	♎ 10	23	♏ 7	21	♐ 6	21	♑ 6	21	♒ 6	21
	♑ 0	1	1	2	2	R 2	2	1	1	0	0 29	♐ 28	27	25	25	23	22	21	19	18	17	16	16	16	16	D 16	16	16	17	17
	24	25	26	27	28	29	29 0	♏ 2	3	4	5	6	7	8	10	11	12	13	14	16	17	18	19	20	21	23	24	25	26	27
	4	5	6	6	7	7	8	8	9	9	10	11	11	12	12	13	13	14	14	15	15	16	17	17	18	18	19	19	20	20

♃ 21 / 4 5 — ♄ 1 7 22 / ♎12 13 14 — ♅ 1 R 8 / ♋13 12 — ♆ 1 3 / ♎20 21 — ♇ 1 R / ♌21

1952

1

	1	2	3	4	5	6	7	8	9	10	11	12	13	14	15	16	17	18	19	20	21	22	23	24	25	26	27	28	29	30	31
☉	♑ 10	11	12	13	14	15	16	17	18	19	20	21	22	23	24	25	26	27	28	29	29 0	♒ 1	2	3	4	5	7	8	9	10	11
☽	♓ 6	20	♈ 3	17	29	♉ 12	24	♊ 7	19	♋ 1	12	24	♌ 6	18	♍ 0	12	24	♎ 6	19	♏ 2	16	♐ 0	14	29	♑ 14	29	♒ 14	29	♓ 14	28	♈ 12
☿	♐ 18	18	19	20	21	22	23	24	25	27	28	29	29 0	♑ 1	3	4	5	7	8	10	11	13	14	15	17	18	20	21	23	24	26
♀	♏ 20	29 0	♐ 1	2	3	4	5	7	8	9	10	11	13	14	15	16	18	19	20	21	22	24	25	26	27	29	29 0	♑ 1	2	3	5
♂	♎ 21	21	22	22	23	23	24	24	25	25	26	26	27	27	28	28	29	29	29	29 0	♏ 0	1	1	2	2	3	3	4	4	4	5

♃ 1 9 17 23 29 / ♈ 6 7 8 9 10 — ♄ 1 25 R / ♎14 14 — ♅ 1 R 2 26 / ♋12 11 10 — ♆ 1 24 R / ♎21 21 — ♇ 1 R 12 / ♌21 20

2

	1	2	3	4	5	6	7	8	9	10	11	12	13	14	15	16	17	18	19	20	21	22	23	24	25	26	27	28	29	30	31
☉	♒ 12	13	14	15	16	17	18	19	20	21	22	23	24	25	26	27	28	29	29 0	♓ 1	2	3	4	5	6	7	8	9	10		
☽	♈ 26	♉ 9	21	♊ 3	16	27	♋ 9	21	♌ 3	15	27	♍ 9	21	♎ 3	16	29	♏ 12	25	♐ 9	23	♑ 8	23	♒ 7	22	♓ 7	22	♈ 6	20	♉ 4		
☿	♑ 27	29	29 1	♒ 2	4	5	7	9	10	12	14	15	17	19	20	22	24	26	28	29 0	♓ 1	3	5	7	9	10	12	14	16		
♀	♑ 6	7	8	9	11	12	13	14	16	17	18	19	20	22	23	24	25	27	28	29	29 0	♒ 1	3	4	5	6	8	9	10		
♂	♏ 5	6	6	6	7	7	8	8	8	9	9	9	10	10	11	11	11	12	12	12	12	13	13	13	14	14	14	14	15		

♃ 1 4 9 14 19 24 29 / ♈10 11 12 13 14 15 16 — ♄ 1 R 27 / ♎14 13 — ♅ 1 R / ♋10 — ♆ 1 R / ♎21 — ♇ 1 R 23 / ♌20 19

3

	1	2	3	4	5	6	7	8	9	10	11	12	13	14	15	16	17	18	19	20	21	22	23	24	25	26	27	28	29	30	31
☉	♓ 11	12	13	14	15	16	17	18	19	20	21	22	23	24	25	26	27	28	29	29 0	♈ 1	2	3	4	5	6	7	8	9	10	11
☽	♉ 17	♊ 0	12	24	♋ 6	18	♌ 0	11	23	♍ 5	18	♎ 0	13	26	♏ 9	22	♐ 6	20	♑ 4	18	♒ 2	17	♓ 1	16	♈ 0	14	28	♉ 12	25	♊ 7	20
☿	♓ 18	20	22	24	26	28	29 0	♈ 1	3	5	6	8	10	11	13	14	15	16	17	18	19	19	19	20	20	20	R 20	20	19	19	18
♀	♒ 11	13	14	15	16	17	19	20	21	22	24	25	26	27	29	29 0	♓ 1	2	3	5	6	7	8	10	11	12	13	15	16	17	18
♂	♏ 15	15	15	16	16	16	16	16	17	17	17	17	17	17	17	18	18	18	18	18	18	18	18	18	R 18	18	18	18	18	18	18

♃ 1 4 9 13 17 22 26 30 / ♈16 17 18 19 20 21 22 23 — ♄ 1 R 14 28 / ♎13 12 11 — ♅ 1 R 3 18 D / ♋10 9 9 — ♆ 1 R 16 / ♎21 20 — ♇ 1 R / ♌19

4

	1	2	3	4	5	6	7	8	9	10	11	12	13	14	15	16	17	18	19	20	21	22	23	24	25	26	27	28	29	30	31
☉	♈ 12	13	14	15	16	17	18	19	20	21	22	23	23	24	25	26	27	28	29	29 0	♉ 1	2	3	4	5	6	7	8	9	10	
☽	♋ 2	14	26	♌ 8	20	♍ 2	14	26	♎ 9	22	♏ 5	19	♐ 3	17	♑ 1	15	29	♒ 13	27	♓ 11	25	♈ 9	23	♉ 6	20	♊ 3	15	28	♋ 10	22	
☿	♈ R 18	17	16	16	15	14	13	12	12	11	10	10	9	9	9	8	8	8	D 8	8	9	9	9	10	10	11	11	12	13	14	
♀	♓ 20	21	22	23	24	26	27	28	29 0	♈ 1	2	3	4	5	7	8	9	10	12	13	14	15	16	18	19	20	21	23	24	25	
♂	♏ R 18	18	17	17	17	17	17	17	16	16	16	16	16	15	15	15	15	14	14	14	13	13	13	12	12	12	11	11	11	10	

♃ 1 3 8 12 16 20 24 28 29 / ♈23 24 25 26 27 28 29 0 — ♄ 1 R 9 23 / ♎11 10 9 — ♅ 1 / ♋10 — ♆ 1 R 22 / ♎20 19 — ♇ 1 R / ♌19

5

	1	2	3	4	5	6	7	8	9	10	11	12	13	14	15	16	17	18	19	20	21	22	23	24	25	26	27	28	29	30	31
☉	♉ 11	12	13	14	15	16	17	18	19	20	21	22	23	24	25	26	26	27	28	29	29 0	♊ 1	2	3	4	5	6	7	8	9	10
☽	♌ 4	15	27	♍ 9	22	♎ 14	17	♏ 1	14	28	♐ 12	27	♑ 11	26	♒ 10	24	♓ 8	22	♈ 5	19	♉ 2	15	28	♊ 11	24	♋ 6	18	♌ 0	12	23	♍ 5
☿	♈ 14	15	16	17	18	20	21	22	23	24	26	27	28	29 0	♉ 1	3	4	6	7	9	11	13	14	16	18	20	22	24	26	28	29 0
♀	♈ 26	28	29	29 0	♉ 1	2	4	5	6	7	9	10	11	12	14	15	16	17	18	20	21	22	23	25	26	27	28	29 0	♊ 1	2	3
♂	♏ R 10	9	9	9	8	8	8	7	7	7	6	6	5	5	5	5	4	4	4	3	3	3	3	2	2	2	2	2	2	1	1

♃ 1 2 7 11 15 20 24 28 / ♉ 0 1 2 3 4 5 6 7 — ♄ 1 R 10 / ♎ 9 8 — ♅ 1 7 29 / ♋10 11 12 — ♆ 1 R / ♎19 — ♇ 1 / ♌19

6

	1	2	3	4	5	6	7	8	9	10	11	12	13	14	15	16	17	18	19	20	21	22	23	24	25	26	27	28	29	30	31
☉	♊ 11	12	13	14	15	16	17	18	19	20	20	21	22	23	24	25	26	27	28	29	29 0	♋ 1	2	3	4	5	6	7	8	9	
☽	♍ 17	♎ 0	12	25	♏ 9	23	♐ 7	21	♑ 6	21	♒ 6	20	♓ 5	19	♈ 2	16	29	♉ 12	25	♊ 8	20	♋ 2	14	26	♌ 8	20	♍ 2	14	26	♎ 8	
☿	♊ 2	4	6	8	10	12	15	17	19	21	23	26	28	29 0	♋ 2	4	6	8	10	12	14	16	18	20	22	23	25	27	29	29 0	
♀	♊ 4	6	7	8	9	11	12	13	14	15	17	18	19	20	22	23	24	25	26	28	29	29 0	♋ 1	3	4	5	6	8	9	10	
♂	♏ R 1	1	1	1	1	1	1	1	1	D 1	1	1	1	1	1	1	1	1	1	1	2	2	2	2	2	2	3	3	3	3	

♃ 1 2 7 11 16 21 26 / ♉ 7 8 9 10 11 12 13 — ♄ 1 R 11 D / ♎ 8 8 — ♅ 1 15 / ♋12 13 — ♆ 1 R 14 30 D / ♎19 18 18 — ♇ 1 / ♌19

7

	1	2	3	4	5	6	7	8	9	10	11	12	13	14	15	16	17	18	19	20	21	22	23	24	25	26	27	28	29	30	31
☉	♋ 10	10	11	12	13	14	15	16	17	18	19	20	21	22	23	24	25	26	27	28	29	29 0	♌ 1	2	3	4	5	6	7	8	8
☽	♎ 20	♏ 3	17	♐ 1	15	♑ 0	15	♒ 0	15	♓ 0	14	29	♈ 13	26	♉ 9	22	♊ 5	17	29	♋ 11	23	♌ 5	17	29	♍ 10	22	♎ 4	17	29	♏ 12	26
☿	♌ 2	3	5	6	7	9	10	12	13	14	15	16	18	19	20	20	21	22	23	24	24	25	25	26	26	26	27	27	27	R 27	26
♀	♋ 11	13	14	15	16	17	19	20	21	22	24	25	26	27	28	29 0	♌ 1	2	3	5	6	7	8	10	11	12	13	14	16	17	18
♂	♏ 4	4	4	5	5	5	5	6	6	6	7	7	7	8	8	8	9	9	10	10	10	11	11	12	12	13	13	14	14	15	15

♃ 1 2 7 14 20 27 / ♉13 14 15 16 17 18 — ♄ 1 11 27 / ♎ 8 9 10 — ♅ 1 2 19 / ♋13 14 15 — ♆ 1 15 / ♎18 19 — ♇ 1 4 / ♌19 20

8

	1	2	3	4	5	6	7	8	9	10	11	12	13	14	15	16	17	18	19	20	21	22	23	24	25	26	27	28	29	30	31
☉	♌ 9	10	11	12	13	14	15	16	17	18	19	20	21	22	23	24	24	25	26	27	28	29	29 0	♍ 1	2	3	4	5	6	7	8
☽	♐ 9	24	♑ 8	23	♒ 8	23	♓ 9	23	♈ 8	22	♉ 6	19	♊ 2	14	26	♋ 8	20	♌ 2	14	26	♍ 8	19	♎ 2	14	26	♏ 9	22	♐ 5	19	♑ 3	17
☿	♌ R 26	26	26	25	24	24	23	22	22	21	20	19	18	18	17	16	16	15	15	15	14	14	D 14	15	15	16	16	17	18	19	20
♀	♌ 20	21	22	23	24	26	27	28	29 0	♍ 1	2	3	4	5	7	8	9	10	12	13	14	15	16	18	19	20	21	23	24	25	26
♂	♏ 15	16	16	17	17	18	18	19	20	20	21	21	22	22	23	23	24	24	25	26	26	27	27	28	28	29	29 0	♐ 0	1	1	2

♃ 1 5 16 / ♉18 19 20 — ♄ 1 9 20 29 / ♎10 11 12 13 — ♅ 1 5 25 / ♋15 16 17 — ♆ 1 / ♎19 — ♇ 1 7 / ♌20 21

9

	1	2	3	4	5	6	7	8	9	10	11	12	13	14	15	16	17	18	19	20	21	22	23	24	25	26	27	28	29	30	31
☉	♍ 9	10	11	12	13	14	15	16	17	18	19	20	21	22	23	24	25	25	26	27	28	29	29 0	♎ 1	2	3	4	5	6	7	
☽	♒ 2	17	♓ 2	17	♈ 2	16	♉ 1	14	28	♊ 10	23	♋ 5	17	29	♌ 11	23	♍ 4	16	28	♎ 11	23	♏ 6	19	♐ 2	15	29	♑ 12	27	♒ 11	26	
☿	♌ 21	22	24	25	27	28	29 0	♍ 2	3	5	7	9	11	13	14	16	18	20	22	24	26	28	29 0	♎ 3	3	5	7	8	10	12	
♀	♍ 28	29	29 0	♎ 1	3	4	5	6	8	9	10	11	12	14	15	16	17	19	20	21	22	24	25	26	27	28	29 0	♏ 1	2	3	
♂	♐ 3	3	4	5	5	6	6	7	8	8	9	10	10	11	12	12	13	14	14	15	16	16	17	18	18	19	20	20	21	22	

♃ 1 10 R / ♉20 20 — ♄ 1 8 16 25 / ♎13 14 15 16 — ♅ 1 19 / ♋17 18 — ♆ 1 3 / ♎19 20 — ♇ 1 9 / ♌21 22

10

	1	2	3	4	5	6	7	8	9	10	11	12	13	14	15	16	17	18	19	20	21	22	23	24	25	26	27	28	29	30	31
☉	♎ 8	9	10	11	12	13	14	15	16	17	18	19	20	21	22	23	24	25	26	27	28	29	29 0	♏ 1	2	3	4	5	6	7	8
☽	♓ 10	25	♈ 10	24	♉ 9	22	♊ 6	19	♋ 1	13	25	♌ 7	19	♍ 1	13	25	♎ 7	20	♏ 2	16	29	♐ 12	26	♑ 9	23	♒ 7	21	♓ 6	20	♈ 4	19
☿	♎ 13	15	17	18	20	22	23	25	27	28	29 0	♏ 1	3	4	6	7	9	11	12	13	15	16	18	19	21	22	23	25	26	28	29 0
♀	♏ 4	6	7	8	9	11	12	13	14	16	17	18	19	20	22	23	24	25	27	28	29	29 0	♐ 1	3	4	5	6	8	9	10	11
♂	♐ 22	23	24	24	25	26	27	27	28	29	29	29 0	♑ 1	1	2	3	4	4	5	6	7	7	8	9	9	10	11	12	12	13	14

♃ 1 R 4 14 23 31 / ♉20 19 18 17 16 — ♄ 1 3 11 19 28 / ♎16 17 18 19 20 — ♅ 1 25 R / ♋18 18 — ♆ 1 2 29 / ♎20 21 22 — ♇ 1 22 / ♌22 23

11

	1	2	3	4	5	6	7	8	9	10	11	12	13	14	15	16	17	18	19	20	21	22	23	24	25	26	27	28	29	30	31
☉	♏ 9	10	11	12	13	14	15	16	17	18	19	20	21	22	23	24	25	26	27	28	29	29 0	♐ 1	2	3	4	5	6	7	8	
☽	♉ 3	17	♊ 0	14	27	♋ 9	21	♌ 3	15	27	♍ 9	21	♎ 3	15	28	♏ 11	24	♐ 8	22	♑ 6	20	♒ 4	18	♓ 2	16	♈ 0	14	28	♉ 12	25	
☿	♐ 0	1	3	4	5	7	8	9	10	11	12	13	13	14	15	15	16	16	R 16	16	16	15	15	14	13	12	11	10	9	7	
♀	♐ 13	14	15	16	17	19	20	21	22	23	25	26	27	28	29 0	♑ 1	2	3	4	6	7	8	9	11	12	13	14	15	17	18	
♂	♑ 15	15	16	17	18	18	19	20	21	21	22	23	24	24	25	26	27	27	28	29	29 0	♒ 0	1	2	3	3	4	5	6	7	

♃ 1 R 7 15 22 / ♉16 15 14 13 — ♄ 1 5 14 23 / ♎20 21 22 23 — ♅ 1 R 28 / ♋18 17 — ♆ 1 28 / ♎22 23 — ♇ 1 24 R / ♌23 23

12

	1	2	3	4	5	6	7	8	9	10	11	12	13	14	15	16	17	18	19	20	21	22	23	24	25	26	27	28	29	30	31
☉	♐ 9	10	11	12	13	14	15	16	17	18	19	20	21	22	23	25	26	27	28	29	29 0	♑ 1	2	3	4	5	6	7	8	9	10
☽	♊ 9	22	♋ 5	17	29	♌ 11	23	♍ 5	17	29	♎ 11	23	♏ 6	19	♐ 3	17	♑ 1	15	♒ 0	14	29	♓ 13	27	♈ 11	25	♉ 8	22	♊ 5	18	♋ 0	13
☿	♐ R 6	5	3	2	1	1	0	0	0	D 0	0	0	1	2	2	3	4	5	6	7	8	9	11	12	13	14	16	17	18	20	21
♀	♑ 19	20	21	22	24	25	26	27	29	29 0	♒ 1	2	3	4	6	7	8	9	10	12	13	14	15	16	17	19	20	21	22	23	24
♂	♒ 7	8	9	10	10	11	12	13	13	14	15	16	16	17	18	19	20	20	21	22	23	23	24	25	26	26	27	28	29	29 0	♊ 0

♃ 1 R 11 / ♉12 11 — ♄ 1 3 14 28 / ♎23 24 25 26 — ♅ 1 R 26 / ♋17 16 — ♆ 1 / ♎23 — ♇ 1 29 / ♌23 22

1953

Columns are days 1–31. Rows: ☉ Sun, ☽ Moon, ☿ Mercury, ♀ Venus, ♂ Mars; last line: ♃ Jupiter, ♄ Saturn, ♅ Uranus, ♆ Neptune, ♇ Pluto.

1
☉ 11 12 13 14 15 16 17 18 19 20 21 22 23 24 25 26 27 28 29 0 1 2 3 4 5 6 7 8 9 10 11
☽ 25 7 19 1 13 25 7 19 1 14 27 10 25 9 24 9 24 8 23 8 22 5 19 2 15 27 10 22 4 16 28
☿ 23 24 25 27 28 0 1 3 4 6 7 9 10 12 13 15 17 18 20 21 23 24 26 28 0 1 3 4 6 8 9
♀ 25 26 28 29 0 1 2 3 5 6 7 8 9 10 11 12 13 15 16 17 18 19 20 21 22 23 24 25 26 27 28
♂ 1 2 3 3 4 5 6 6 7 8 9 10 10 11 12 13 13 14 15 16 17 18 19 20 20 21 22 23 23 24
♃ 1R 2 4D 8 29 — 11 10 10 11 12; ♄ 1 17 — 26 27; ♅ 1R 18 — 16 15; ♆ 1 25R — 23 23; ♇ 1R — 22

2
☉ 12 13 14 15 16 17 18 19 20 21 22 23 25 26 27 28 29 0 1 2 3 4 5 6 7 8 9 10
☽ 9 21 3 15 27 9 22 5 19 2 17 2 17 2 17 1 15 28 12 24 7 19 1 13 24 6
☿ 11 13 15 16 18 20 22 24 25 27 0 1 3 4 6 8 10 12 13 15 17 19 20 22 23 25 26 27
♀ 29 0 1 2 3 4 5 6 7 8 9 10 11 12 13 14 15 16 17 18 19 20 20 21 22 23
♂ 25 26 26 27 28 29 29 0 1 2 2 3 4 5 5 6 7 8 9 9 10 11 12 12 13 14 14 15
♃ 1 9 17 24 — 12 13 14 15; ♄ 1 5R 23 — 27 27 26; ♅ 1R 14 — 15 14; ♆ 1R — 23; ♇ 1R 13 — 22 21

3
☉ 11 12 13 14 15 16 17 18 19 20 21 22 23 24 25 26 27 28 29 0 1 2 3 4 5 6 7 8 9 10
☽ 18 0 12 24 6 19 1 14 27 11 25 10 25 10 25 10 24 7 21 3 16 28 10 21 3 15 27 9 21
☿ 29 0 0 1 2 2 2 2 2 2 2 2 1 1 0 0 29 28 27 26 25 25 24 23 22 22 21 21 20 20 20 19 19
♀ 23 24 24 25 26 26 27 27 28 28 28 29 29 29 0 0 0 0 1 1 1 1 1 1 1 1 0 0 0 0 29
♂ 16 17 17 18 19 20 20 21 22 23 23 24 25 26 27 27 28 29 29 0 1 2 3 4 4 5 6 7 8
♃ 1 3 8 14 19 25 30 — 15 16 17 18 19 20 21; ♄ 1R 16 31 — 26 25 24; ♅ 1R 23D — 14 14; ♆ 1R 25 — 23 22; ♇ 1R — 21

4
☉ 11 12 13 14 15 16 17 18 19 20 21 22 23 24 25 26 27 28 29 0 1 2 3 4 5 6 7 8 9 10
☽ 3 16 28 11 24 7 21 5 19 4 18 3 18 2 16 29 12 24 6 18 0 12 24 6 18 0 12 25
☿ 19 19 20 20 20 21 21 22 23 23 24 25 26 27 28 29 0 1 2 3 4 6 7 8 10 11 12 14 15 17
♀ 29 28 28 27 27 26 26 25 25 24 23 22 22 21 21 20 20 19 19 18 18 17 17 16 16 16 15 15 15
♂ 9 10 11 12 12 13 14 14 15 16 17 17 18 19 19 20 21 22 22 23 24 25 25 26 27 27 28 29 29
♃ 1 3 8 13 17 22 26 30 — 21 22 23 24 25 26 27 28; ♄ 1R 13 26 — 24 23 22; ♅ 1 27 — 14 15; ♆ 1R — 22; ♇ 1R 3 — 21 20

5
☉ 11 12 13 14 15 16 17 18 19 20 20 21 22 23 24 25 26 27 28 29 0 1 2 3 4 5 6 7 8 9 10
☽ 8 21 4 18 1 15 29 14 28 13 27 12 26 10 24 7 20 2 14 26 8 20 2 14 26 8 21 4 17 1 14
☿ 18 20 22 23 25 27 28 0 2 4 6 8 10 12 14 16 18 20 22 24 26 28 1 3 5 7 9 12 14 16 18
♀ 15 14 14 15 15 15 15 15 15 16 16 16 16 17 17 18 18 19 19 20 21 21 22 23 23 24 25 25 26
♂ 0 1 1 2 3 4 4 5 6 6 7 8 8 9 10 10 11 12 12 13 14 15 15 16 17 17 18 19 19 20 21
♃ 1 5 9 29 10 13 18 22 26 — 28 29 0 0 1 2 3 4; ♄ 1R 11 31 — 22 21 20; ♅ 1 23 — 15 16; ♆ 1R 2 — 22 21; ♇ 1R 2D — 20 20

6
☉ 11 12 13 14 14 15 16 17 18 19 20 21 22 23 24 25 26 27 28 29 0 1 2 3 4 5 6 7 8
☽ 12 26 10 24 9 23 7 21 5 19 2 15 28 10 22 4 16 28 10 22 4 17 29 13 26 10 24 8 23
☿ 20 22 24 26 28 0 2 4 6 7 9 11 13 14 16 17 19 20 22 23 24 26 27 28 29 0 1 2 3 4
♀ 27 28 28 29 0 1 2 2 3 4 5 6 7 8 9 10 11 12 13 14 15 16 17 18 19 20 21 22 23
♂ 21 22 23 23 24 25 25 26 27 27 28 29 29 0 1 1 2 3 3 4 5 5 6 7 7 8 9 10 11
♃ 1 4 8 12 17 21 25 30 — 5 6 7 8 9 10 11 12; ♄ 1R 24D — 20 20; ♅ 1 11 28 — 16 17 18; ♆ 1R — 21; ♇ 1R — 21

7
☉ 9 10 11 12 13 14 15 16 17 18 19 20 21 22 23 24 25 26 27 28 29 0 1 2 3 4 5 6 7 8
☽ 7 21 5 20 4 18 1 15 28 11 23 6 18 0 12 24 6 18 0 12 25 7 21 4 18 3 17 2 17 2 16
☿ 4 5 6 6 7 7 7 8 8 8 8 8 8 7 7 7 6 6 5 5 4 3 3 2 1 1 0 29 29 28 28
♀ 24 25 26 27 28 29 0 1 2 3 4 5 6 7 8 10 11 12 13 14 15 16 17 18 19 20 22 23 24 25 26
♂ 11 12 13 13 14 15 15 16 17 17 18 19 19 20 21 21 22 23 23 24 25 25 26 26 27 28 28 29 0 0 1
♃ 1 5 9 14 19 24 29 — 12 13 14 15 16 17 18; ♄ 1 16 — 20 21; ♅ 1 14 31 — 18 19 20; ♆ 1 18 3D — 21 21; ♇ 1 17 — 21 22

8
☉ 9 10 11 12 13 14 15 16 17 18 18 19 20 21 22 23 24 25 26 27 28 29 0 1 2 3 4 5 6 7 8
☽ 0 14 28 11 24 7 20 2 14 27 9 20 2 14 26 8 20 3 16 29 12 27 11 26 11 26 11 25 9 23
☿ 27 27 27 27 27 28 28 28 28 29 0 1 2 3 4 5 6 8 9 11 12 14 16 17 19 21 23 25 27 0 1
♀ 27 28 29 0 2 3 4 5 6 7 8 10 11 12 13 14 15 16 18 19 20 21 22 23 25 26 27 28 29 0 2
♂ 2 3 4 4 5 5 6 7 7 8 9 9 10 10 11 12 12 13 13 14 15 15 16 16 17 18 18 19 20 20 21
♃ 1 3 9 15 21 28 — 18 19 20 21 22 23; ♄ 1 5 18 29 — 21 22 23 24; ♅ 1 — 20 21; ♆ 1 30 — 21 22; ♇ 1 17 — 22 23

9
☉ 9 10 11 12 13 14 15 16 16 17 18 19 20 21 22 23 24 25 26 27 28 29 0 1 2 3 4 5 6 7
☽ 21 4 17 29 11 23 5 17 29 11 23 5 17 29 11 24 7 21 5 19 4 19 5 20 5 20 4 18 1 14
☿ 3 5 7 9 11 13 15 16 18 20 22 24 26 28 0 1 3 5 6 8 9 11 13 14 16 17 19 21 22 24
♀ 3 4 5 6 7 9 10 11 12 13 15 16 17 18 19 20 22 23 24 25 27 28 29 0 1 3 4 5 6 8
♂ 21 22 22 23 24 24 25 25 26 27 27 28 28 29 0 0 1 2 2 3 3 4 5 5 6 7 7 8 9 10
♃ 1 5 14 28 — 23 24 25 26; ♄ 1 9 18 27 — 24 25 26 27; ♅ 1 8 — 21 22; ♆ 1 30 — 22 23; ♇ 1 20 — 23 24

10
☉ 8 9 10 11 12 13 14 15 16 17 18 19 20 21 22 23 24 25 26 27 28 29 0 1 2 3 4 5 6 7 8
☽ 26 9 21 2 14 26 8 20 2 14 26 8 21 4 17 0 14 28 13 28 13 28 12 26 10 23 5 17 29
☿ 25 27 28 29 1 2 4 5 7 8 9 11 12 13 15 16 17 18 20 21 22 23 24 25 26 27 27 28 29 29 29
♀ 9 10 11 12 14 15 16 17 19 20 21 22 24 25 26 27 28 0 1 2 4 5 6 7 8 10 11 12 13 15 16
♂ 10 11 11 12 12 13 14 14 15 16 16 17 17 18 19 19 20 20 21 22 22 23 23 24 25 25 26 27 27 28 29
♃ 1 15R 31 — 26 26 25; ♄ 1 5 14 22 29 23 30 — 27 28 29 0 0 1; ♅ 1 13 29R — 22 23 23; ♆ 1 27 — 23 24; ♇ 1 — 24

11
☉ 9 10 11 12 13 14 15 16 17 18 19 20 21 22 23 24 25 26 27 28 29 0 1 2 3 4 5 6 7 8
☽ 11 23 5 17 29 11 23 5 18 1 14 27 10 24 8 22 7 22 7 21 6 20 4 18 1 13 25 8 19 1
☿ 0 0 0 0 0 29 29 28 27 26 25 24 23 21 20 19 18 17 16 15 15 14 14 14 15 15 16 16 17 18
♀ 17 18 20 21 22 23 25 26 27 28 29 1 2 3 4 6 7 8 10 11 12 13 15 16 17 18 20 21 22 23
♂ 0 0 1 2 2 3 4 4 5 6 6 7 7 8 9 9 10 10 11 12 12 13 13 14 15 15 16 16 17 18
♃ 1R 14 23 — 25 24 23; ♄ 1 8 16 25 — 1 2 3 4; ♅ 1R 14 — 23 22; ♆ 1 24 — 24 25; ♇ 1 17 27R — 24 25 25

12
☉ 9 10 11 12 13 14 15 16 17 18 19 20 21 22 23 24 25 26 27 28 29 0 1 2 3 4 5 6 7 8 9 10
☽ 13 25 7 19 2 15 27 10 24 7 21 5 19 3 17 1 16 0 14 28 12 25 8 21 3 15 27 9 21 3 15
☿ 19 20 21 22 23 24 26 27 28 29 1 2 3 5 6 8 9 11 12 14 15 17 18 20 21 23 24 26 28 29 1
♀ 25 26 27 28 0 1 2 3 4 6 7 8 9 11 12 13 14 16 17 18 19 21 22 23 24 26 27 28 29 1 2
♂ 18 19 19 20 21 21 22 22 23 23 24 24 25 25 26 26 27 27 28 28 29 29 0 1 1 2 2 3 4 5 6 6
♃ 1R 9 16 24 — 22 21 20 19; ♄ 1 4 14 25 — 4 5 6 7; ♅ 1R 21 30 — 22 21; ♆ 1 — 25; ♇ 1R 25 — 25 24

1954

1
☉ 11 12 13 14 15 16 17 18 19 20 21 22 23 24 25 26 27 28 29 0 1 2 3 4 5 6 7 8 9
☽ 27 10 23 6 19 3 17 1 15 0 14 28 12 26 10 24 7 20 3 16 29 11 23 5 17 29 11 23 5
☿ 3 4 6 7 9 11 12 14 15 17 19 20 22 23 25 27 28 0 2 4 5 7 9 10 12 14 16 17 19
♀ 4 5 6 7 9 10 11 12 14 15 16 17 19 20 21 22 24 25 26 27 29 0 1 3 4 5 6 8 9
♂ 7 8 8 9 9 10 11 11 12 12 13 14 14 15 15 16 16 17 18 18 19 19 20 21 21 22 22 23 23
♃ 1R 10 22 — 18 17 16; ♄ 1 8 27 — 7 8 9; ♅ 1R 13 — 21 20; ♆ 1 11 28R — 25 26 26; ♇ 1R — 24

2
☉ 12 13 14 15 16 17 18 19 20 21 22 23 24 25 26 27 28 29 0 1 2 3 4 5 6 7 8 9
☽ 14 28 12 26 11 25 10 25 9 23 7 20 4 17 0 12 25 7 19 1 13 25 7 19 1 13 26 8
☿ 24 27 28 0 1 3 4 6 7 9 10 11 12 13 14 15 15 16 16 16 15 15 14 14 13 12 11
♀ 13 14 15 16 18 19 20 21 23 24 25 26 28 29 0 1 3 4 5 6 8 9 10 12 13 14 15 16
♂ 25 26 26 27 27 28 28 29 29 0 0 1 1 2 2 3 3 4 5 5 6 6 7 7 8 8 9 10
♃ 1R 10D — 16 16; ♄ 1 17R — 9 9; ♅ 1R — 20 19; ♆ 1R — 26 25; ♇ 1R — 24

3
☉ 10 11 12 13 14 15 16 17 18 19 20 21 22 23 24 25 26 27 28 29 0 1 2 3 4 5 6 7 8
☽ 22 6 20 4 19 4 19 3 17 1 14 27 9 21 4 16 28 10 22 44 15 27 9 22 4 17 0
☿ 9 8 7 6 5 4 4 3 2 2 2 2 1 1 1 1 2 2 2 3 3 4 4 5 6 7 8 9 10 11
♀ 18 19 20 21 23 24 25 27 28 29 0 2 3 4 5 7 8 9 10 11 13 14 15 16 18 19 20 21 23
♂ 10 11 11 12 12 13 13 14 15 15 16 16 17 17 18 18 19 19 20 20 21 21 22 22 23 23 24
♃ 1 13 22 30 — 17 18 19 20; ♄ 1R 9 30 — 9 8 7; ♅ 1R 27D — 19 19; ♆ 1R — 25; ♇ 1R — 23

4
☉ 11 12 13 14 15 16 17 18 19 20 21 22 23 24 25 26 27 28 29 0 1 2 3 4 5 6 7 8 9
☽ 12 28 13 28 13 27 10 23 6 19 1 13 25 7 19 1 12 24 6 18 1 13 26 9 23 7 21
☿ 14 15 16 17 19 20 21 23 24 25 27 28 0 2 3 5 6 8 10 11 13 15 17 18 20 22 24 26 28 0
♀ 26 27 29 0 1 2 4 5 6 7 8 10 11 12 13 15 16 17 18 20 21 22 23 24 26 27 28 0 1
♂ 25 26 26 26 27 27 27 28 28 28 29 29 29 0 0 1 1 1 1 2 2 3 3 3 4 4 4 5
♃ 1 6 12 18 24 29 — 20 21 22 23 24 25; ♄ 1R 13 27 — 7 6 5; ♅ 1 — 19; ♆ 1R 4 — 25 24; ♇ 1R — 22

5
☉ 11 12 13 14 15 16 17 18 19 20 21 22 23 24 25 26 27 28 29 0 1 2 3 4 5 6 7 8
☽ 21 6 22 7 21 5 19 2 15 28 10 22 4 16 28 9 21 3 16 28 10 23 6 19 3 16 1 15 0
☿ 2 4 6 8 10 12 15 17 19 21 23 25 28 0 2 4 6 8 10 12 14 16 18 20 21 23 25 26 28
♀ 3 4 6 7 8 9 10 12 13 14 15 16 18 19 20 21 23 24 25 26 27 28 0 1 2 3 5 6 7
♂ 5 6 6 6 7 7 7 7 7 7 7 8 8 8 8 8 8 8 8 8 8 8 8 8 8 8 8 8 8
♃ 1 4 9 14 19 24 29 25 28 — 25 26 27 28 29 0 0 1; ♄ 1R 10 25 — 5 4 3; ♅ 1 14 — 19 20; ♆ 1R 11 — 24 23; ♇ 1R — 22

6
☉ 10 11 12 13 14 15 16 17 18 19 20 21 22 23 24 25 26 27 28 29 0 1 2 3 4 5 6 7
☽ 15 29 14 27 11 23 6 18 0 12 24 6 18 0 12 25 7 20 3 16 29 13 27 11 26 10 25 9 24
☿ 2 4 5 6 8 9 10 11 12 13 14 15 15 16 16 17 17 18 18 18 18 18 18 18 17 17
♀ 11 12 13 14 15 17 18 19 20 21 23 24 25 26 27 29 0 1 2 3 5 6 7 8 9 10 12 13 14
♂ 7 7 7 7 7 7 7 6 6 6 6 5 5 5 5 5 4 4 4 3 3 3 2 2 2 1 1 1 1
♃ 1 2 6 11 15 20 24 28 — 1 2 3 4 5 6 7 8; ♄ 1R 15 — 3 2; ♅ 1 5 23 — 20 21 22; ♆ 1R — 23; ♇ 1R — 22

7
☉ 9 10 11 12 13 14 15 16 17 18 19 20 21 22 23 24 25 26 27 28 29 0 1 2 3 4 5 6
☽ 5 19 1 14 26 8 20 2 14 26 8 21 3 16 29 12 26 10 24 8 22 6 21 5 19 3 17 0
☿ 16 15 14 14 13 12 11 11 10 10 10 9 9 9 9 9 9 9 9 9 10 10 11 11 12 13 14 15 16 17 18
♀ 16 17 19 20 21 22 23 24 26 27 28 29 0 1 3 4 5 6 7 8 10 11 12 13 14 15 16 17 18
♂ 0 0 29 29 29 28 28 28 28 27 27 27 27 27 26 26 26 26 25 25 25 25 25 25 25 25 25 25 25
♃ 1 3 7 12 16 21 25 30 — 8 9 10 11 12 13 14 15; ♄ 1R 6D 27 — 2 2 3; ♅ 1 10 26 — 22 23 24; ♆ 1R 5D — 23 23; ♇ 1 — 23

8
☉ 9 10 11 12 13 14 15 16 17 18 19 20 21 22 23 24 25 26 27 28 29 0 1 2 3 4 5 6
☽ 9 22 4 16 28 10 22 4 16 28 11 24 8 22 6 20 4 19 3 17 2 16 0 13 26 10 22 5 18
☿ 20 21 23 25 26 28 0 2 4 5 7 9 11 13 15 17 19 21 23 25 27 0 1 3 5 7 9 11 13
♀ 22 23 24 25 26 27 28 29 0 2 3 4 5 6 7 8 9 10 11 12 13 14 15 16 17 18 19 20 21 22
♂ 25 25 25 25 25 26 26 26 26 26 26 27 27 27 27 27 28 28 28 28 28 29 29 29 29 0 0 0 1 1
♃ 1 3 8 13 18 23 28 — 15 16 17 18 19 20 21; ♄ 1 16 30 — 3 4 5; ♅ 1 12 31 — 24 25 26; ♆ 1 26 — 23 24; ♇ 1 — 24

9
☉ 9 10 11 12 13 14 15 16 17 18 19 20 21 22 23 24 25 26 27 28 29 0 1 2 3 4 5 6
☽ 24 6 18 0 12 24 6 19 2 16 0 14 29 14 28 12 26 10 23 6 19 2 14 27 9 21 3
☿ 18 20 22 24 25 27 28 0 2 3 5 7 8 10 11 13 14 16 17 19 20 21 23 24 25 27 28 29
♀ 24 26 27 28 29 0 0 1 2 3 4 5 6 7 8 9 10 11 12 13 14 15 15 16 17 18 18
♂ 3 3 3 4 4 5 5 6 6 7 7 8 8 9 9 10 10 11 11 12 12 13 13 14 14 14 15 15 16 16
♃ 1 2 8 14 20 26 — 21 22 23 24 25 26; ♄ 1 11 21 30 — 5 6 7 8; ♅ 1 24 — 26 27; ♆ 1 27 — 24 25; ♇ 1 — 25

10
☉ 8 9 10 11 12 13 14 15 16 17 18 19 20 21 22 23 24 25 26 27 28 29 0 1 2 3 4 5
☽ 27 8 20 2 15 27 10 24 8 22 7 23 8 23 8 22 6 20 3 16 29 11 24 6 18 0 12 23
☿ 3 4 5 6 7 8 9 10 11 12 13 13 14 14 14 14 14 14 13 13 12 11 10 9 8 7
♀ 21 21 22 22 23 23 24 24 24 25 26 26 27 27 27 28 28 29 29 29 29 29 0 0 0 29 29 29
♂ 18 18 19 19 20 20 21 21 22 22 23 23 24 24 25 25 26 26 27 27 28 28 29 29 0 0 1 1 2 2 3
♃ 1 4 12 23 — 26 27 28 29; ♄ 1 9 18 26 — 8 9 10 11; ♅ 1 — 27; ♆ 1 24 — 25 26; ♇ 1 — 26

11
☉ 9 10 11 12 13 14 15 16 17 18 19 20 21 22 23 24 25 26 27 28 29 0 1 2 3 4 5 6 7
☽ 11 26 6 19 2 16 0 15 1 16 1 16 1 15 29 13 26 8 21 3 15 27 9 20 2 14 26 8
☿ 2 1 0 29 29 29 29 29 0 1 1 2 3 4 6 7 8 10 11 12 14 15 17 18 20 21
♀ 29 28 28 27 27 26 26 25 25 24 24 23 23 22 21 21 20 20 19 19 18 18 17 17 16 16 15 15
♂ 7 8 9 10 10 11 12 12 13 14 14 15 16 17 17 18 19 19 20 21 22 22 23 24 24 25 26 26
♃ 1 17R — 29 29; ♄ 1 4 12 21 29 — 11 12 13 14 15; ♅ 1 3R — 27 27; ♆ 1 21 — 26 27; ♇ 1 — 26

12
☉ 9 10 11 12 13 14 15 16 17 18 19 20 21 22 23 24 25 26 27 28 29 0 1 2 3 4 5 6 7
☽ 15 28 12 25 9 24 9 24 9 23 7 21 4 17 29 12 24 6 17 29 11 23 5 17 0 13 26
☿ 26 27 29 0 2 3 5 6 8 9 11 13 14 16 17 19 20 22 24 25 27 28 0 1 3 5 7 8 9
♀ 14 14 14 14 14 14 14 14 14 15 15 15 16 16 17 17 18 18 19 19 20 21 21 22 23 23 24
♂ 28 29 29 0 1 1 2 3 4 4 5 6 6 7 8 9 9 10 11 12 12 13 14 14 15 16 17 18
♃ 1R 11 21 — 29 28 27 26; ♄ 1 11 30 — 15 16 17 18; ♅ 1R 13 — 27 26; ♆ 1 31 — 27 28; ♇ 1 — 26

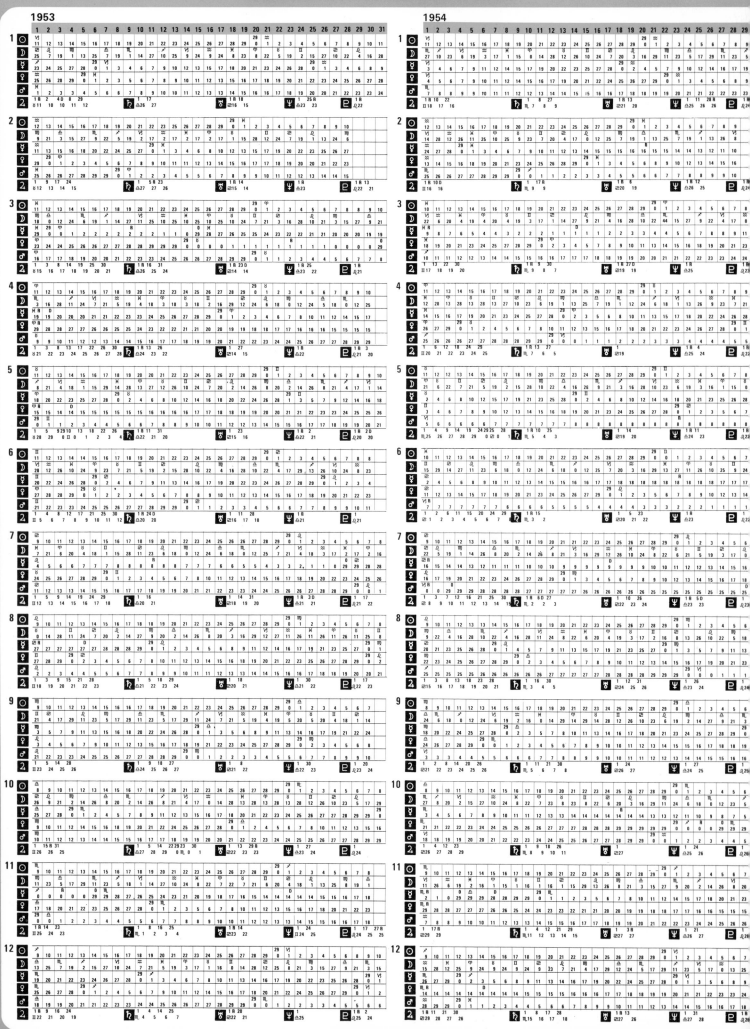

1960

1

	1	2	3	4	5	6	7	8	9	10	11	12	13	14	15	16	17	18	19	20	21	22	23	24	25	26	27	28	29	30	31
☉	10	11	12	13	14	15	16	17	18	19	20	21	22	23	24	25	26	27	28	29	0	1	2	3	4	5	6	7	8	9	10
☽	17	1	15	28	11	23	5	17	29	11	23	5	17	29	11	24	6	19	2	15	29	13	27	11	26	11	26	11	25	9	23
☿	26	27	29	0	2	3	5	6	8	9	11	12	14	16	17	19	20	22	24	25	27	29	0	2	4	5	7	9	10	12	14
♀	29	0	1	2	4	5	6	7	8	10	11	12	13	14	16	17	18	19	20	22	23	24	25	27	28	29	0	1	3	4	5
♂	21	21	22	23	23	24	25	26	26	27	28	29	29	0	1	2	2	3	4	5	5	6	7	7	8	9	10	10	11	12	13

♃ 1 2 6 11 16 17 26 31 — ♐18 19 20 21 22 23 24 25 · ♄ 1 4 9 13 14 22 31 — ♑9 10 11 12 13 · ♅ 1 R 16 — ♌20 19 · ♆ 1 18 — ♏8 9 · ♇ 1 R 5 — ♍6 5

2

	1	2	3	4	5	6	7	8	9	10	11	12	13	14	15	16	17	18	19	20	21	22	23	24	25	26	27	28	29
☉	11	12	13	14	15	16	17	18	19	20	21	22	23	24	25	26	27	28	29	0	1	2	3	4	5	6	7	8	9
☽	6	19	1	13	25	7	19	1	13	25	7	20	3	16	29	12	26	9	23	7	22	6	20	5	19	3	17	1	14
☿	16	17	19	21	23	25	26	28	0	2	4	5	7	9	10	12	14	15	17	18	19	21	22	23	24	24	25	25	26
♀	6	8	9	10	11	12	14	15	16	17	19	20	21	22	23	25	26	27	28	0	1	2	3	5	6	7	8	9	11
♂	13	14	15	15	16	17	18	19	19	20	21	22	23	23	24	25	26	26	27	28	28	29	0	1	2	2	3	4	5

♃ 1 5 11 17 23 — ♐25 26 27 28 29 · ♄ 1 10 20 — ♑13 14 15 · ♅ 1 R 8 — ♌19 18 · ♆ 1 10 R — ♏9 9 · ♇ 1 R 21 — ♍5 4

3

	1	2	3	4	5	6	7	8	9	10	11	12	13	14	15	16	17	18	19	20	21	22	23	24	25	26	27	28	29	30	31
☉	10	11	12	13	14	15	16	17	18	19	20	21	22	23	24	25	26	27	28	29	0	1	2	3	4	5	6	7	8	9	10
☽	27	9	21	3	15	27	9	21	3	16	28	11	25	8	22	6	20	4	18	3	17	1	15	29	12	26	9	22	4	17	29
☿	25	25	25	24	24	23	22	22	21	20	19	18	17	16	15	14	13	13	13	12	12	12	12	12	12	12	13	13	13	14	14
♀	12	13	14	16	17	18	19	21	22	23	24	25	27	28	29	0	2	3	4	5	7	8	9	10	11	13	14	15	16	18	19
♂	5	6	7	8	8	9	10	11	12	12	13	14	15	15	16	17	18	18	19	20	21	22	22	23	24	25	25	26	27	28	28

♃ 1 29 2 9 18 31 — ♐29 ♑0 1 2 3 · ♄ 1 2 16 — ♑15 16 17 · ♅ 1 R 4 — ♌18 17 · ♆ 1 R 4 — ♏9 8 · ♇ 1 R — ♍4

4

	1	2	3	4	5	6	7	8	9	10	11	12	13	14	15	16	17	18	19	20	21	22	23	24	25	26	27	28	29	30
☉	11	12	13	14	15	16	17	18	19	20	21	22	23	24	25	26	27	28	29	0	1	2	3	4	5	6	7	8	9	10
☽	23	5	17	29	11	23	6	19	3	17	1	15	0	15	29	14	28	12	25	9	22	5	18	0	13	25	7	19	1	
☿	15	16	16	17	18	19	20	21	22	23	24	25	27	28	29	0	2	3	5	6	7	9	11	12	14	15	17	19	20	22
♀	20	21	23	24	25	26	27	29	0	1	2	4	5	6	7	9	10	11	12	13	15	16	17	18	20	21	22	23	25	26
♂	20	0	0	2	2	3	4	5	5	6	7	8	8	9	10	11	11	12	13	14	15	15	16	17	18	19	19	20	21	22

♃ 1 20 R — ♑3 3 · ♄ 1 4 28 R — ♑17 18 18 · ♅ 1 R 12 25 D — ♌17 16 16 · ♆ 1 R 19 — ♏8 7 · ♇ 1 R 2 — ♍4 3

5

	1	2	3	4	5	6	7	8	9	10	11	12	13	14	15	16	17	18	19	20	21	22	23	24	25	26	27	28	29	30	31
☉	11	12	13	14	14	15	16	17	18	19	20	21	22	23	24	25	26	27	28	29	0	1	2	3	4	5	6	7	8	9	10
☽	13	25	7	19	1	14	27	11	25	9	24	9	24	9	24	8	24	6	19	2	15	27	9	22	4	16	28	10	22	3	15
☿	24	26	28	0	1	3	5	7	9	11	13	15	18	20	22	24	26	28	0	3	5	7	9	11	14	16	18	20	22	24	26
♀	27	28	0	1	2	3	4	6	7	8	9	11	12	13	14	15	17	18	19	20	22	23	24	25	26	28	29	0	1	3	4
♂	22	23	24	25	25	26	27	28	28	29	0	1	1	2	3	4	4	5	6	7	8	8	9	10	11	11	12	13	13	14	15

♃ 1 R 10 22 — ♑3 2 1 · ♄ 1 R 20 — ♑18 17 · ♅ 1 6 — ♌16 17 · ♆ 1 R 27 — ♏7 6 · ♇ 1 R 14 D — ♍3 3

6

	1	2	3	4	5	6	7	8	9	10	11	12	13	14	15	16	17	18	19	20	21	22	23	24	25	26	27	28	29	30
☉	10	11	12	13	14	15	16	17	18	19	20	21	22	23	24	25	26	27	28	29	0	1	1	2	3	4	5	6	7	8
☽	10	23	6	19	3	18	3	18	3	18	2	16	29	12	24	7	19	1	13	25	7	19	0	12	24	7	19			
☿	27	0	1	3	4	6	8	9	11	11	14	16	17	19	20	21	22	23	24	25	26	26	27	28	28	28	29	29	29	29
♀	5	6	8	9	10	11	12	14	15	16	17	19	20	21	22	23	25	26	27	28	29	0	2	3	5	6	8	9	11	
♂	16	17	17	18	19	20	20	21	22	23	23	24	25	26	26	27	27	28	28	29	0	1	2	3	4	4	5	6	7	

♃ 1 R 10 0 11 17 25 — ♑0 ♐29 29 28 27 · ♄ 1 R 10 20 — ♑17 16 15 · ♅ 1 12 — ♌17 18 · ♆ 1 R — ♏6 · ♇ 1 25 — ♍3 4

7

	1	2	3	4	5	6	7	8	9	10	11	12	13	14	15	16	17	18	19	20	21	22	23	24	25	26	27	28	29	30	31
☉	9	10	11	12	13	14	15	16	17	18	19	20	21	22	23	24	25	26	27	28	29	0	1	2	3	4	5	6	7	8	
☽	15	28	12	26	11	26	12	27	11	25	8	21	4	16	28	10	22	4	16	27	9	21	4	16	28	11	24	8	21	6	
☿	0	0	0	0	0	29	29	29	29	28	28	27	27	26	25	25	24	23	23	22	21	21	20	20	20	19	20	20	20		
♀	12	13	14	16	17	18	19	21	22	23	24	25	27	28	29	0	2	3	4	5	7	8	9	10	11	13	14	15	16	18	19
♂	8	8	9	10	11	11	12	13	14	14	15	16	16	17	18	19	19	20	21	21	22	23	23	24	25	25	26	27	27	28	29

♃ 1 R 3 12 23 — ♐27 26 25 24 · ♄ 1 R 8 22 — ♑15 14 13 · ♅ 1 4 21 — ♌18 19 20 · ♆ 1 R 18 D — ♏6 6 · ♇ 1 — ♍4

8

	1	2	3	4	5	6	7	8	9	10	11	12	13	14	15	16	17	18	19	20	21	22	23	24	25	26	27	28	29	30	31
☉	9	10	11	12	13	14	15	16	17	18	19	20	21	22	23	24	25	26	27	28	29	0	1	2	3	4	5	6	7	8	
☽	22	6	20	5	20	5	20	5	19	3	16	0	12	25	7	19	1	13	25	7	19	1	13	26	8	21	5	18	2	16	0
☿	21	21	21	22	23	24	25	26	27	28	0	1	3	5	7	9	11	13	15	17	19	21	23	25	27	29	1	3	5	6	8
♀	20	21	23	24	25	26	27	29	0	1	2	4	5	6	7	9	10	11	12	13	15	16	17	18	20	21	22	23	25	26	27
♂	29	0	1	1	2	3	3	4	5	5	6	7	7	8	9	9	10	11	11	12	12	13	14	14	15	15	16	17	17	18	18

♃ 1 R 8 20 D — ♐24 23 23 · ♄ 1 R 7 — ♑13 12 · ♅ 1 7 23 — ♌20 21 22 · ♆ 1 — ♏6 · ♇ 1 2 — ♍4 5

9

	1	2	3	4	5	6	7	8	9	10	11	12	13	14	15	16	17	18	19	20	21	22	23	24	25	26	27	28	29	30
☉	9	10	10	11	12	13	14	15	16	17	18	19	20	21	22	23	24	25	26	27	28	29	0	1	2	3	4	5	6	7
☽	15	29	14	29	13	27	11	24	8	20	3	15	27	9	21	2	14	27	9	22	5	18	1	15	29	13	27	11	25	10
☿	10	12	14	16	18	20	21	23	25	27	29	0	2	4	5	7	9	10	12	13	15	16	18	19	21	22	24	25	27	28
♀	28	0	1	2	3	4	6	7	8	9	11	12	13	14	15	17	18	19	20	22	23	24	25	27	28	29	0	1	3	4
♂	19	20	20	21	21	22	22	23	24	24	25	25	26	26	27	27	28	28	29	29	0	0	1	1	2	2	3	3	4	4

♃ 1 17 28 — ♐24 25 26 · ♄ 1 R 16 D 30 — ♑11 11 12 · ♅ 1 9 27 — ♌22 23 24 · ♆ 1 5 — ♏6 7 · ♇ 1 2 — ♍5 6

10

	1	2	3	4	5	6	7	8	9	10	11	12	13	14	15	16	17	18	19	20	21	22	23	24	25	26	27	28	29	30	31
☉	8	9	10	11	12	13	14	15	16	17	18	19	20	21	22	23	24	25	26	27	28	29	0	1	2	3	4	5	6	7	8
☽	24	8	22	6	19	2	15	28	11	23	5	17	29	11	23	5	17	0	13	27	11	25	9	24	8	22	6	20	4	18	1
☿	29	0	1	2	4	5	6	7	9	10	11	12	13	15	16	17	18	19	19	20	21	21	22	22	23	23	23	23	23	23	22
♀	5	6	8	9	10	11	12	14	15	16	17	19	20	21	22	24	25	26	27	28	0	1	2	3	5	6	7	8	10	11	12
♂	5	5	6	6	7	7	7	8	8	8	9	9	10	10	10	11	11	12	12	13	13	13	14	14	14	15	15	15	16	16	16

♃ 1 6 13 20 26 29 27 31 — ♐26 27 28 29 ♑0 0 1 · ♄ 1 24 — ♑12 13 · ♅ 1 19 — ♌24 25 · ♆ 1 8 — ♏7 8 · ♇ 1 3 — ♍6 7

11

	1	2	3	4	5	6	7	8	9	10	11	12	13	14	15	16	17	18	19	20	21	22	23	24	25	26	27	28	29	30
☉	9	10	11	12	13	14	15	16	17	18	19	20	21	22	23	24	25	26	27	28	29	0	1	2	3	4	5	6	7	8
☽	15	28	11	24	6	19	1	13	24	6	18	0	12	24	7	20	3	17	1	16	1	16	1	16	0	15	28	11	24	7
☿	21	20	19	18	17	16	15	13	12	11	10	9	8	8	8	8	8	9	9	10	11	12	13	14	15	16	17	18	20	
♀	13	14	15	17	18	19	20	22	23	24	25	26	28	29	0	2	3	4	5	7	8	10	11	12	13	14	16	17	18	
♂	16	16	16	17	17	17	17	17	17	17	18	18	18	18	18	18	18	18	18	18	18	18	18	18	18	18	18	18	18	17

♃ 1 6 11 16 21 26 30 — ♑1 2 3 4 5 6 7 · ♄ 1 7 19 29 — ♑13 14 15 16 · ♅ 1 — ♌25 · ♆ 1 9 — ♏8 9 · ♇ 1 17 — ♍7 8

12

	1	2	3	4	5	6	7	8	9	10	11	12	13	14	15	16	17	18	19	20	21	22	23	24	25	26	27	28	29	30	31
☉	9	10	11	12	13	14	15	16	17	18	19	20	21	22	23	24	25	26	27	28	29	0	1	2	3	4	5	6	7	8	9
☽	20	2	15	27	9	21	3	14	26	8	20	3	16	29	13	27	12	27	12	27	11	25	8	22	4	17	29	12	24		
☿	21	22	24	25	27	28	0	1	3	4	6	7	9	10	12	13	15	16	18	19	21	22	24	25	27	29	0	2	3	5	6
♀	19	20	22	23	24	25	26	28	29	0	1	2	4	5	6	7	9	10	11	12	13	15	16	17	18	19	20	21	22	23	25
♂	17	17	17	17	17	16	16	16	16	15	15	15	15	14	14	14	13	13	12	12	12	11	11	10	10	10	9	9	8	8	

♃ 1 5 9 14 18 22 27 31 — ♑7 8 9 10 11 12 13 14 · ♄ 1 6 17 28 — ♑16 17 18 19 · ♅ 1 R — ♌25 · ♆ 1 9 — ♏9 10 · ♇ 1 10 R — ♍8 8

1961

1

	1	2	3	4	5	6	7	8	9	10	11	12	13	14	15	16	17	18	19	20	21	22	23	24	25	26	27	28	29	30	31
☉	11	12	13	14	15	16	17	18	19	20	21	22	23	24	25	26	27	28	29	0	1	2	3	4	5	6	7	8	9	10	11
☽	6	18	29	11	23	5	17	29	11	24	8	21	5	20	5	20	6	21	6	20	4	18	1	14	26	9	21	3	15	26	8
☿	8	10	11	13	15	16	18	19	21	23	24	26	28	0	1	3	4	6	8	10	11	13	15	16	18	20	21	23	25	26	28
♀	26	27	28	29	0	1	2	4	5	6	7	8	9	10	11	12	14	15	16	17	18	19	20	21	22	23	24	25	26	27	28
♂	7	7	6	6	6	5	5	5	4	4	4	3	3	3	3	2	2	2	2	1	1	1	1	0	0	0	0	0	0	0	0

♃ 1 4 8 13 18 22 26 30 — ♑14 15 16 17 18 19 20 21 · ♄ 1 4 12 21 29 — ♑19 20 21 22 23 · ♅ 1 R 12 — ♌25 24 · ♆ 1 8 — ♏10 11 · ♇ 1 R 2 — ♍18 7

2

	1	2	3	4	5	6	7	8	9	10	11	12	13	14	15	16	17	18	19	20	21	22	23	24	25	26	27	28
☉	12	13	14	15	16	17	18	19	20	21	22	23	24	25	26	27	28	29	0	1	2	3	4	5	6	7	8	9
☽	20	2	14	26	8	21	4	17	0	14	29	13	28	14	29	14	28	12	26	10	23	5	17	29	11	23	5	17
☿	0	1	2	3	4	6	6	7	8	8	9	9	9	9	8	7	6	6	5	4	3	2	1	0	29	28	27	26
♀	29	0	1	2	3	4	5	6	7	8	9	10	10	11	12	13	14	15	15	16	17	18	18	19	20	21	21	22
♂	0	0	0	0	0	0	0	0	0	0	0	0	0	0	0	0	0	0	0	0	1	1	1	1	1	2	2	2

♃ 1 4 8 13 18 22 27 — ♑21 22 23 24 25 26 27 · ♄ 1 7 16 26 — ♑23 24 25 26 · ♅ 1 R 6 — ♌24 23 · ♆ 1 11 R — ♏11 11 · ♇ 1 R 19 — ♍7 6

3

	1	2	3	4	5	6	7	8	9	10	11	12	13	14	15	16	17	18	19	20	21	22	23	24	25	26	27	28	29	30	31
☉	11	12	13	14	15	16	17	18	19	20	21	22	23	24	25	26	27	28	29	0	1	2	3	4	5	6	7	8	9	10	11
☽	29	11	23	5	18	1	14	27	11	24	8	22	7	22	7	22	6	20	4	18	1	13	26	8	20	1	13	25	7	19	2
☿	25	25	24	24	24	24	24	24	24	25	25	26	26	27	27	28	28	29	0	1	3	4	5	6	8	10	11	12	14	15	
♀	22	23	24	24	25	25	26	26	27	27	27	28	28	28	28	28	29	29	29	29	29	29	29	28	28	28	28	28	27	27	26
♂	3	3	3	3	4	4	4	5	5	5	6	6	6	7	7	8	8	8	9	9	10	10	11	11	11	11	12	12	13	13	

♃ 1 4 9 15 29 16 20 27 — ♑27 28 29 0 ♒0 1 2 · ♄ 1 9 21 — ♑26 27 28 · ♅ 1 R 2 — ♌23 22 · ♆ 1 R 17 — ♏11 10 · ♇ 1 R — ♍6

4

	1	2	3	4	5	6	7	8	9	10	11	12	13	14	15	16	17	18	19	20	21	22	23	24	25	26	27	28	29	30
☉	12	13	14	15	16	17	18	19	20	21	22	23	24	25	26	27	28	29	0	1	2	3	4	5	6	7	8	9	10	
☽	14	27	10	24	7	21	5	19	3	18	2	16	0	15	29	12	26	8	21	3	16	28	9	21	3	15	27	10	23	6
☿	16	18	19	21	22	24	25	27	28	0	2	3	5	7	9	10	12	14	16	18	20	22	24	26	28	0	2	4	6	8
♀	26	25	25	24	23	23	22	22	21	20	20	19	19	18	18	17	17	16	16	15	15	14	14	14	13	13	13	13	12	12
♂	13	14	14	15	15	15	16	17	17	17	18	18	18	19	19	20	20	21	21	21	22	22	23	23	24	24	25	25	26	27

♃ 1 2 9 18 28 — ♒2 3 4 5 6 · ♄ 1 7 — ♑28 29 · ♅ 1 R 29 D — ♌21 21 · ♆ 1 R 28 — ♏10 9 · ♇ 1 R 3 — ♍6 5

5

	1	2	3	4	5	6	7	8	9	10	11	12	13	14	15	16	17	18	19	20	21	22	23	24	25	26	27	28	29	30	31
☉	11	12	13	14	15	16	17	18	19	20	21	22	23	24	25	26	27	28	29	0	1	2	3	4	5	6	7	8	9	10	
☽	20	4	18	2	16	0	14	28	12	26	10	24	7	21	4	17	29	11	23	5	17	29	11	23	5	18	1	15	29	13	27
☿	10	12	14	17	19	21	23	25	27	0	2	4	6	7	9	11	13	15	17	18	20	21	23	24	26	27	28	0	1	2	3
♀	12	12	12	12	12	13	13	13	13	14	14	14	15	15	15	16	16	17	17	18	18	19	19	20	21	21	22	23	23	24	25
♂	28	28	29	29	29	0	0	1	1	2	2	3	3	4	4	5	5	6	6	7	7	8	8	9	9	10	10	11	11	12	12

♃ 1 16 26 R — ♒6 7 7 · ♄ 1 10 R — ♑29 29 · ♅ 1 29 D — ♌21 21 · ♆ 1 R — ♏9 · ♇ 1 R 17 D — ♍5 5

6

	1	2	3	4	5	6	7	8	9	10	11	12	13	14	15	16	17	18	19	20	21	22	23	24	25	26	27	28	29	30
☉	11	12	13	14	15	16	16	17	18	19	20	21	22	23	24	25	26	27	28	29	0	1	2	3	4	5	6	7	8	
☽	12	26	11	25	9	23	7	21	4	17	0	13	25	8	20	2	14	25	7	19	1	13	26	9	23	7	21	6	21	6
☿	4	5	6	6	7	8	8	9	9	10	10	10	10	10	10	10	10	10	9	9	9	8	8	7	7	6	5	5	4	4
♀	26	27	28	29	0	0	1	2	3	4	5	6	7	7	8	9	10	11	12	13	14	15	16	17	18	19	20	21	22	23
♂	14	15	15	16	16	17	17	18	18	19	19	20	20	21	21	22	22	23	23	24	24	25	26	26	27	27	28	28	29	0

♃ 1 R 4 22 — ♒7 6 5 · ♄ 1 R 11 28 — ♑29 28 27 · ♅ 1 24 — ♌22 23 · ♆ 1 R 7 — ♏9 8 · ♇ 1 28 — ♍5 6

7

	1	2	3	4	5	6	7	8	9	10	11	12	13	14	15	16	17	18	19	20	21	22	23	24	25	26	27	28	29	30	31
☉	9	10	11	12	13	14	15	16	17	18	19	20	21	22	23	24	25	26	27	28	29	0	1	2	3	4	5	6	7	8	
☽	21	5	20	4	18	1	14	27	10	22	4	16	28	10	22	4	16	28	10	22	5	18	1	15	0	14	29	15	0	15	29
☿	3	2	2	1	1	1	1	1	1	1	1	1	1	2	2	3	3	4	4	5	6	7	8	9	11	12	13	15	16	18	20
♀	24	25	26	27	28	29	0	1	2	3	4	5	7	8	9	10	11	12	13	14	15	16	17	19	20	21	22	23	24	25	26
♂	1	2	3	3	4	4	5	6	6	7	7	8	8	9	10	10	11	11	12	12	13	13	14	15	15	16	16	17	17	18	18

♃ 1 R 2 11 19 27 — ♒5 4 3 2 1 · ♄ 1 R 13 26 — ♑27 26 25 · ♅ 1 14 31 — ♌23 24 25 · ♆ 1 R 21 D — ♏8 8 · ♇ 1 — ♍6

8

	1	2	3	4	5	6	7	8	9	10	11	12	13	14	15	16	17	18	19	20	21	22	23	24	25	26	27	28	29	30	31
☉	9	10	11	12	13	14	15	16	17	18	19	20	20	21	22	23	24	25	26	27	28	29	0	1	2	3	4	5	6	7	8
☽	14	27	11	24	7	19	1	13	25	7	19	1	13	24	6	19	1	14	27	10	24	8	23	8	23	8	23	8	22	6	20
☿	25	27	29	1	3	5	7	9	11	13	15	17	19	21	23	25	27	0	1	3	5	7	9	10	12	14	16	18	19	21	23
♀	27	29	0	1	2	3	4	5	7	8	9	10	11	12	13	15	16	17	18	19	20	22	23	24	25	26	27	29	0	1	2
♂	20	21	21	22	23	23	24	24	25	26	26	27	27	28	28	29	0	0	1	1	2	3	3	4	5	5	6	7	7	8	9

♃ 1 R 4 12 0 13 21 — ♒1 0 ♑29 29 28 · ♄ 1 R 9 27 — ♑25 24 23 · ♅ 1 16 — ♌25 26 · ♆ 1 31 — ♏8 9 · ♇ 1 5 — ♍6 7

9

	1	2	3	4	5	6	7	8	9	10	11	12	13	14	15	16	17	18	19	20	21	22	23	24	25	26	27	28	29	30
☉	9	10	11	12	13	14	15	16	17	18	19	20	21	22	23	24	25	26	27	28	29	0	1	2	3	4	5	6	7	
☽	3	16	28	10	22	4	16	28	10	22	4	16	28	11	23	6	20	3	17	2	16	1	16	1	16	1	15	28	12	24
☿	24	26	28	0	1	2	4	5	7	8	10	11	13	14	15	17	18	19	21	22	23	24	25	26	27	28	29	0	1	2
♀	3	4	6	7	8	9	10	12	13	14	15	16	18	19	20	21	22	24	25	26	27	28	0	1	2	3	5	6	7	8
♂	10	10	11	12	12	13	14	14	15	16	16	17	18	18	19	20	20	21	22	22	23	24	24	25	26	26	27	28	28	29

♃ 1 R 3 24 D — ♑28 27 27 · ♄ 1 R 28 D — ♑23 23 · ♅ 1 2 — ♌26 27 · ♆ 1 — ♏9 · ♇ 1 4 — ♍7 8

10

	1	2	3	4	5	6	7	8	9	10	11	12	13	14	15	16	17	18	19	20	21	22	23	24	25	26	27	28	29	30	31
☉	8	9	10	11	12	13	14	15	16	17	18	19	20	21	22	23	24	25	26	27	28	29	0	1	2	3	4	5	6	7	8
☽	7	19	1	13	25	6	18	0	13	25	8	20	3	17	0	14	28	13	28	12	27	11	25	9	23	6	20	2	15	27	9
☿	4	4	5	6	6	7	7	8	8	8	8	8	8	8	7	7	6	5	4	3	2	2	0	29	27	26	26	24	24	23	22
♀	9	11	12	13	14	16	17	18	19	20	22	23	24	25	27	28	29	0	2	3	4	5	6	8	9	10	11	12	14	15	16
♂	0	1	2	2	3	4	4	5	6	7	7	8	9	9	10	11	11	12	13	14	14	15	16	16	17	18	18	19	20	20	21

♃ 1 14 26 — ♑27 28 29 · ♄ 1 28 — ♑23 24 · ♅ 1 7 — ♌28 29 · ♆ 1 5 — ♏9 10 · ♇ 1 4 — ♍8 9

11

	1	2	3	4	5	6	7	8	9	10	11	12	13	14	15	16	17	18	19	20	21	22	23	24	25	26	27	28	29	30
☉	9	10	11	12	13	14	15	16	17	18	19	20	21	22	23	24	25	26	27	28	29	0	1	2	3	4	5	6	7	8
☽	21	3	14	26	9	21	4	17	0	13	27	11	25	9	23	7	21	5	19	3	17	1	14	27	10	23	5	17	29	10
☿	22	22	23	23	24	25	26	27	28	0	2	3	5	7	9	10	12	14	15	17	18	20	21	23	24	26	28	29	1	2
♀	18	19	20	21	23	24	25	26	28	29	0	1	3	4	5	6	8	9	10	11	13	14	15	16	18	19	20	21	23	24
♂	21	22	22	23	24	24	25	26	27	27	28	29	29	0	1	2	2	3	4	5	6	6	7	8	8	9	10	10	11	12

♃ 1 4 29 5 11 18 24 30 — ♑29 0 ♒0 1 2 3 4 · ♄ 1 13 26 — ♑24 25 26 · ♅ 1 29 2 — ♌29 ♍0 · ♆ 1 2 29 — ♏10 11 12 · ♇ 1 20 — ♍9 10

12

	1	2	3	4	5	6	7	8	9	10	11	12	13	14	15	16	17	18	19	20	21	22	23	24	25	26	27	28	29	30	31
☉	9	10	11	12	13	14	15	16	17	18	19	20	21	22	23	24	25	26	27	28	29	0	1	2	3	4	6	7	8	9	10
☽	22	4	17	29	12	25	9	23	7	21	5	19	4	18	2	16	29	13	27	11	23	6	18	1	13	25	6	18	0	12	24
☿	1	2	4	5	7	9	10	12	13	15	16	18	20	21	23	24	26	27	29	1	2	4	5	7	9	10	12	13	15	17	18
♀	25	27	28	29	0	2	3	4	5	7	8	9	10	12	13	14	15	17	18	19	20	22	23	24	25	27	28	29	0	2	3
♂	13	14	15	16	16	17	18	18	19	20	21	21	22	23	24	24	25	26	27	28	28	29	0	0	1	2	3	3	4	5	

♃ 1 5 10 15 20 25 29 — ♒4 5 6 7 8 9 10 · ♄ 1 7 16 25 — ♑26 27 28 29 · ♅ 1 6 R — ♍0 0 · ♆ 1 — ♏12 · ♇ 1 12 R — ♍10 10

1962

1	1	2	3	4	5	6	7	8	9	10	11	12	13	14	15	16	17	18	19	20	21	22	23	24	25	26	27	28	29	30	31
☉	11	12	13	14	15	16	17	18	19	20	21	22	23	24	25	26	27	28	29	0	1	2	3	4	5	6	7	8	9	10	11
☽	7	20	3	17	1	15	0	15	29	14	28	12	26	10	23	7	19	2	15	27	9	21	3	15	26	8	20	2	15	28	11
☿	20	22	23	25	26	28	0	1	3	4	6	8	9	11	12	13	15	16	17	18	19	20	21	22	22	22	22	22	22	22	21
♀	4	6	7	8	9	11	12	13	14	16	17	18	19	21	22	23	24	26	27	28	29	0	1	2	3	4	6	7	8	9	11	12
♂	6	6	7	8	9	10	10	11	12	13	13	14	15	16	16	17	18	19	19	20	21	22	23	23	24	25	26	26	27	28	29

♃ 1 3 7 11 16 20 24 29 / ≈10 11 12 13 14 15 16 17 — ♄ 1 3 29 4 12 20 29 / ♑29 0 ≈0 1 2 3 — ♅ 1 R 10 0 11 / ♍0 29 ♌29 — ♆ 1 2 / ♏12 13 — ♇ 1 R 3 / ♍10 9

2	1	2	3	4	5	6	7	8	9	10	11	12	13	14	15	16	17	18	19	20	21	22	23	24	25	26	27	28
☉	12	13	14	15	16	17	18	19	20	21	22	23	24	25	26	27	28	29	0	1	2	3	4	5	6	7	8	9
☽	25	9	23	8	23	8	23	8	22	6	20	4	16	29	12	24	6	18	0	11	23	5	17	29	11	24	6	19
☿	20	19	18	17	15	14	13	12	11	10	9	8	8	7	7	7	7	7	7	7	8	8	9	9	10	11	11	12
♀	13	14	16	17	18	20	21	22	23	25	26	27	28	0	1	2	3	5	6	7	8	10	11	12	13	15	16	17
♂	0	0	1	2	3	3	4	5	6	6	7	8	9	10	10	11	12	13	14	14	15	16	17	17	18	19	20	21

♃ 1 6 10 14 19 23 27 / ≈18 19 20 21 22 23 24 — ♄ 1 6 15 24 / ≈3 4 5 6 — ♅ 1 R 6 28 / ♌29 28 27 — ♆ 1 13 R / ♏13 13 — ♇ 1 R 23 / ♍9 8

3	1	2	3	4	5	6	7	8	9	10	11	12	13	14	15	16	17	18	19	20	21	22	23	24	25	26	27	28	29	30	31
☉	10	11	12	13	14	15	16	17	18	19	20	21	22	23	24	25	26	27	28	29	0	1	2	3	4	5	6	7	8	9	10
☽	3	17	1	16	1	16	1	16	1	16	29	13	26	8	21	3	15	27	8	20	2	14	26	8	21	3	16	29	12	26	10
☿	13	14	15	16	17	18	20	21	22	23	24	26	27	28	0	1	3	4	6	7	9	10	12	13	15	17	18	20	22	23	25
♀	18	20	21	22	23	25	26	27	28	0	1	2	3	5	6	7	8	9	11	12	13	14	16	17	18	19	21	22	23	24	26
♂	21	22	23	24	24	25	26	27	28	28	29	0	1	2	3	3	4	5	5	6	7	8	8	9	10	11	11	12	13	14	15

♃ 1 3 8 12 16 21 25 29 26 / ≈24 25 26 27 28 29 0 ♓0 1 — ♄ 1 5 15 27 / ≈6 7 8 9 — ♅ 1 R 27 / ♌27 26 — ♆ 1 R 29 / ♏13 12 — ♇ 1 R / ♍8

4	1	2	3	4	5	6	7	8	9	10	11	12	13	14	15	16	17	18	19	20	21	22	23	24	25	26	27	28	29	30
☉	11	12	13	14	15	16	17	18	19	20	21	22	23	24	25	26	27	28	29	0	1	2	3	4	5	6	7	8	9	10
☽	24	9	24	9	25	9	24	8	22	5	17	0	12	23	5	17	29	11	23	5	18	0	13	26	9	22	6	20	4	19
☿	27	29	1	2	4	6	8	10	12	14	16	18	20	22	24	26	28	0	3	5	7	9	11	13	15	17	19	21	23	25
♀	27	28	0	1	2	3	4	5	7	8	9	10	12	13	14	15	17	18	19	20	21	23	24	25	26	28	29	0	1	2
♂	16	16	17	18	19	20	20	21	22	23	23	24	25	26	27	27	28	29	0	0	1	2	3	3	4	5	6	7	7	8

♃ 1 4 9 14 19 25 30 30 / ♓1 2 3 4 5 6 7 1 — ♄ 1 10 29 / ≈9 10 11 — ♅ 1 R / ♌26 — ♆ 1 R / ♏12 — ♇ 1 R 4 / ♍8 7

5	1	2	3	4	5	6	7	8	9	10	11	12	13	14	15	16	17	18	19	20	21	22	23	24	25	26	27	28	29	30	31
☉	11	12	13	14	15	16	17	18	19	20	21	22	23	24	25	26	27	28	29	0	1	2	3	4	5	6	7	8	9	10
☽	3	18	3	18	2	16	0	13	25	8	20	2	14	25	7	19	2	14	27	9	23	6	19	3	17	1	15	29	13	28	12
☿	27	29	0	2	3	5	6	8	9	10	12	13	14	15	16	16	17	18	18	19	19	20	20	20	20	20	20	20	19	19	19
♀	4	5	6	7	9	10	11	12	13	15	16	17	18	19	21	22	23	24	25	27	28	29	0	2	3	4	5	6	8	9	10
♂	9	10	11	11	12	13	14	14	15	16	17	17	18	19	20	20	21	22	23	23	24	25	26	26	27	28	29	29	0	1	2

♃ 1 7 13 21 30 / ♓7 8 9 10 11 — ♄ 1 22 R / ≈11 11 — ♅ 1 R 4 D / ♌26 26 — ♆ 1 R 7 / ♏12 11 — ♇ 1 R 19 D / ♍7 7

6	1	2	3	4	5	6	7	8	9	10	11	12	13	14	15	16	17	18	19	20	21	22	23	24	25	26	27	28	29	30
☉	11	11	12	13	14	15	16	17	18	19	20	21	22	23	24	25	26	27	28	29	0	1	2	3	4	5	6	7	8
☽	26	11	24	8	21	3	16	28	10	22	3	15	27	10	22	5	18	2	15	29	13	27	12	26	10	24	8	22	6	20
☿	18	18	17	16	16	15	15	14	14	14	13	13	12	12	12	12	11	11	11	11	11	12	12	12	13	13	14	15	16	17
♀	11	12	14	15	16	17	18	19	21	22	23	24	25	27	28	29	0	1	3	4	5	6	7	8	10	11	12	13	14	15
♂	2	3	4	5	5	6	7	8	8	9	10	11	11	12	13	14	14	15	16	16	17	18	19	19	20	21	22	22	23	24

♃ 1 11 / ♓11 12 — ♄ 1 R 13 / ≈11 10 — ♅ 1 10 / ♌26 27 — ♆ 1 R 13 R / ♏11 10 — ♇ 1 / ♍7

7	1	2	3	4	5	6	7	8	9	10	11	12	13	14	15	16	17	18	19	20	21	22	23	24	25	26	27	28	29	30	31
☉	9	10	11	12	13	14	15	16	17	18	19	20	21	22	23	24	25	26	27	28	29	0	1	2	3	4	5	6	7	8
☽	3	16	29	11	24	6	18	29	11	23	5	18	0	13	27	10	24	9	23	8	22	7	21	5	19	3	16	29	12	25	7
☿	17	18	19	21	22	23	24	26	27	29	0	2	3	5	7	9	11	13	15	17	19	21	23	25	27	29	1	3	6	8	10
♀	17	18	19	20	21	22	24	25	26	27	28	29	0	2	3	4	5	6	7	8	10	11	12	13	14	15	16	18	19	20	21
♂	24	25	26	27	27	28	29	29	0	1	1	2	3	4	4	5	6	7	7	8	9	10	10	11	11	12	13	14	14	15

♃ 1 R 22 / ♓12 11 — ♄ 1 R 4 18 / ≈10 9 8 — ♅ 1 5 24 / ♌27 28 29 — ♆ 1 R 22 D / ♏10 10 — ♇ 1 2 / ♍7 8

8	1	2	3	4	5	6	7	8	9	10	11	12	13	14	15	16	17	18	19	20	21	22	23	24	25	26	27	28	29	30	31
☉	9	10	11	12	13	14	14	15	16	17	18	19	20	21	22	23	24	25	26	27	28	29	0	1	2	3	4	5	6	7	8
☽	20	2	14	26	8	19	1	13	26	8	21	5	19	3	17	2	17	2	17	1	16	0	13	26	9	22	4	16	29	11	22
☿	12	14	16	18	20	22	24	26	28	0	1	3	5	6	8	10	11	13	15	16	18	19	21	22	24	25	27	28	29	1	2
♀	22	23	24	25	26	27	29	0	1	2	3	4	5	6	7	8	9	10	11	12	13	14	16	17	18	19	20	21	22	23	24
♂	16	17	17	18	19	19	20	21	21	22	23	23	24	25	26	27	27	28	29	29	0	1	1	2	3	3	4	5	6

♃ 1 R 4 13 21 29 / ♓11 10 9 8 7 — ♄ 1 R 15 30 / ≈7 6 5 — ♅ 1 9 29 10 26 / ♌29 0 ♍0 0 1 — ♆ 1 24 / ♏10 11 — ♇ 1 7 / ♍8 9

9	1	2	3	4	5	6	7	8	9	10	11	12	13	14	15	16	17	18	19	20	21	22	23	24	25	26	27	28	29	30
☉	9	10	11	11	12	13	14	15	16	17	18	19	20	21	22	23	24	25	26	27	28	29	0	1	2	3	4	5	6	7
☽	4	16	28	10	22	4	17	0	13	27	11	25	10	26	11	26	11	26	11	25	9	23	6	19	1	14	26	8	19	1	13	25
☿	4	5	6	7	9	10	11	12	13	14	15	16	17	18	19	19	20	20	21	21	21	21	21	21	21	20	20	19	19	19
♀	25	26	26	27	28	29	0	1	2	3	4	5	6	7	8	9	10	11	12	12	13	14	15	15	16	17	17	18	19
♂	6	7	7	8	9	9	10	11	11	12	12	13	14	14	15	16	16	17	17	18	19	19	20	21	21	22	22	23	24

♃ 1 R 6 13 22 / ♓7 6 5 4 — ♄ 1 R 22 / ≈5 4 — ♅ 1 11 28 / ♍1 2 3 — ♆ 1 / ♏11 — ♇ 1 6 / ♍9 10

10	1	2	3	4	5	6	7	8	9	10	11	12	13	14	15	16	17	18	19	20	21	22	23	24	25	26	27	28	29	30	31
☉	8	9	10	11	12	13	14	15	16	17	18	19	20	21	22	23	24	25	26	27	28	29	0	1	2	3	4	5	6	7	8
☽	7	19	1	13	26	9	22	5	19	4	19	4	19	4	19	4	18	2	16	29	12	25	7	19	1	13	25	7	19	1	13
☿	18	17	16	15	13	12	11	10	9	8	7	7	6	6	6	6	6	7	7	8	9	10	11	12	13	14	15	17	18	19	21
♀	20	20	21	22	22	23	23	24	24	25	25	25	26	26	26	27	27	27	27	27	27	27	27	27	27	27	27	26	26	26	26
♂	24	25	25	26	26	27	28	28	29	0	0	1	1	2	3	3	4	4	5	5	6	6	7	7	8	8	8	9	9	10

♃ 1 R 2 18 29 D / ♓4 3 2 2 — ♄ 1 R 9 D 26 / ≈4 4 5 — ♅ 1 17 / ♍3 4 — ♆ 1 3 31 / ♏11 12 13 — ♇ 1 6 / ♍10 11

11	1	2	3	4	5	6	7	8	9	10	11	12	13	14	15	16	17	18	19	20	21	22	23	24	25	26	27	28	29	30
☉	9	10	11	12	13	14	15	16	17	18	19	20	21	22	23	24	25	26	27	28	29	0	1	2	3	4	5	6	7	8
☽	23	5	18	1	15	29	13	28	12	27	13	28	12	26	10	24	7	20	3	15	27	9	21	3	14	26	8	20	2	15
☿	24	26	27	0	1	2	4	5	7	9	10	12	13	15	16	18	19	21	22	24	25	27	28	0	1	3	4	6	7	9	11
♀	25	25	24	24	23	23	22	22	21	21	20	20	19	18	18	17	17	16	16	16	15	15	15	15	15	15	15	15	15	15
♂	10	10	11	11	12	12	12	13	13	14	14	15	15	15	16	16	16	17	17	18	18	18	19	19	19	20	20	20	21

♃ 1 8 25 / ♓2 3 4 — ♄ 1 17 / ≈5 6 — ♅ 1 / ♍4 5 — ♆ 1 27 / ♏13 14 — ♇ 1 20 / ♍11 12

12	1	2	3	4	5	6	7	8	9	10	11	12	13	14	15	16	17	18	19	20	21	22	23	24	25	26	27	28	29	30	31
☉	9	10	11	12	13	14	15	16	17	18	19	20	21	22	23	24	25	26	27	28	29	0	1	2	3	4	5	6	7	8	9
☽	28	12	25	9	23	7	22	7	21	6	20	4	18	1	14	27	9	21	3	15	27	9	21	3	16	29	12	25	8	22	6
☿	12	14	15	17	18	20	21	23	25	26	28	0	1	3	4	6	7	9	10	12	13	15	16	18	19	21	22	24	25	27	28
♀	12	12	12	12	12	12	12	13	13	13	14	14	14	15	15	16	16	17	17	18	18	19	20	20	21	22	22	23	24	25
♂	21	21	21	22	22	22	22	23	23	23	23	23	23	24	24	24	24	24	24	24	24	24	24	24	24	24	24	24	24	24	24

♃ 1 4 12 19 26 31 / ♓4 5 6 7 8 9 — ♄ 1 12 23 / ≈7 8 9 — ♅ 1 11 R / ♍5 5 — ♆ 1 24 / ♏14 15 — ♇ 1 14 R / ♍12 12

1963

1	1	2	3	4	5	6	7	8	9	10	11	12	13	14	15	16	17	18	19	20	21	22	23	24	25	26	27	28	29
☉	10	11	12	13	14	15	16	17	18	19	20	21	22	23	24	25	26	27	28	29	0	1	2	3	4	5	6	7	8
☽	20	4	18	2	17	1	15	29	13	26	9	22	4	17	29	11	23	4	16	29	11	24	7	20	4	18	2	16	1
☿	28	0	2	3	4	5	6	6	6	6	6	6	6	5	4	3	2	1	0	29	29	27	26	25	24	24	22	21	21
♀	25	26	27	29	29	0	1	2	3	4	5	6	7	8	9	10	11	12	13	14	15	16	17	18	19	20	21	22
♂	24	24	24	24	24	23	23	23	23	23	23	22	22	22	22	22	21	21	21	20	20	20	19	19	19	18	18	17	17

♃ 1 6 11 16 21 26 30 / ♓9 10 11 12 13 14 15 — ♄ 1 10 19 27 / ≈10 11 12 13 — ♅ 1 R 5 / ♍5 4 — ♆ 1 / ♏15 — ♇ 1 R / ♍12

2	1	2	3	4	5	6	7	8	9	10	11	12	13	14	15	16	17	18	19	20	21	22	23	24	25	26	27	28
☉	12	13	14	15	16	17	18	19	20	21	22	23	24	25	26	27	28	29	0	1	2	3	4	5	6	7	8	9
☽	13	27	11	25	8	22	5	17	0	12	25	7	19	1	12	24	6	19	1	14	28	12	26	11	25	10	25	10
☿	20	21	21	21	22	22	22	23	23	24	25	26	27	28	29	0	1	2	3	5	6	7	8	10	11	13	14	15	17
♀	25	26	27	28	0	1	2	3	4	5	6	7	8	9	10	11	12	13	14	15	16	17	18	20	21	22	23	24	25
♂	15	15	14	14	14	13	13	13	12	12	12	11	11	10	10	10	9	9	9	8	8	8	7	7	7	6

♃ 1 4 8 13 17 21 25 / ♓15 16 17 18 19 20 21 — ♄ 1 4 13 21 / ≈13 14 15 16 — ♅ 1 R 5 18 / ♍4 3 2 — ♆ 1 16 R / ♏15 15 — ♇ 1 R / ♍11

3	1	2	3	4	5	6	7	8	9	10	11	12	13	14	15	16	17	18	19	20	21	22	23	24	25	26	27	28	29
☉	10	11	12	13	14	15	16	17	18	19	20	21	22	23	24	25	26	27	28	29	0	1	2	3	4	5	6	7	8
☽	24	8	22	5	18	1	14	26	9	21	3	15	27	9	21	3	15	27	10	22	6	20	4	19	4	19	4	19	4
☿	18	19	21	22	24	26	27	29	0	2	4	5	7	9	10	12	14	16	17	19	21	23	25	27	29	1	2	4	6
♀	26	28	29	0	1	2	3	5	6	7	8	9	10	12	13	14	15	16	17	19	20	21	22	23	24	26	27	28	29
♂	6	6	6	6	5	5	5	5	5	5	5	5	5	5	5	5	5	5	5	5	5	5	5	5	5	5	6	6

♃ 1 2 6 10 14 18 22 26 / ♓21 22 23 24 25 26 27 28 — ♄ 1 2 11 21 31 / ≈16 17 18 19 20 — ♅ 1 R 24 / ♍2 1 — ♆ 1 R / ♏15 — ♇ 1 R / ♍10

4	1	2	3	4	5	6	7	8	9	10	11	12	13	14	15	16	17	18	19	20	21	22	23	24	25	26	27	28	29
☉	11	12	13	14	15	16	17	18	19	20	21	22	23	24	25	26	27	28	29	0	1	2	3	4	5	6	7	8
☽	15	28	11	23	6	18	0	12	24	6	18	29	11	23	5	18	1	14	28	12	27	12	27	12	28	13	27	11	25
☿	13	15	17	19	21	23	25	27	0	1	3	5	7	9	10	12	14	15	17	18	20	21	22	24	25	26	27	28
♀	3	4	5	6	8	9	10	11	12	13	15	16	17	18	19	21	22	23	24	25	27	28	29	0	1	3	4	5	6
♂	6	7	7	7	7	8	8	8	9	9	9	10	10	11	11	11	12	12	12	13	13	14	14

♃ 1 4 29 5 8 12 16 21 25 / ♓29 0 ♈0 1 2 3 4 5 — ♄ 1 12 27 / ≈20 21 22 — ♅ 1 R / ♍1 — ♆ 1 R 8 / ♏15 14 — ♇ 1 R / ♍10

5	1	2	3	4	5	6	7	8	9	10	11	12	13	14	15	16	17	18	19	20	21	22	23	24	25	26	27	28	29
☉	10	11	12	13	14	15	16	17	18	19	20	21	22	23	24	25	26	27	28	29	0	1	2	3	4	5	6	7
☽	20	3	15	27	9	21	3	15	26	8	21	3	15	28	11	24	8	22	6	21	6	21	6	21	6	20	3	16	29
☿	29	29	0	0	0	0	0	0	0	0	29	29	29	28	28	27	27	26	25	25	24	23	23	22	22	22	22	22	22
♀	9	10	11	12	14	15	16	17	18	20	21	22	23	25	26	27	28	29	0	2	3	4	5	6	8	9	10	11	12
♂	15	15	16	16	17	17	17	18	18	19	19	19	20	20	21	21	22	22	23	23	23	24	24	25	25	26	26	27	27

♃ 1 4 9 13 18 23 29 / ♈6 7 8 9 10 11 12 — ♄ 1 22 / ≈22 23 — ♅ 1 R 9 D / ♍1 1 — ♆ 1 R 16 / ♏14 13 — ♇ 1 R / ♍9

6	1	2	3	4	5	6	7	8	9	10	11	12	13	14	15	16	17	18	19	20	21	22	23	24	25	26	27	28	29
☉	10	11	12	13	14	15	16	17	18	19	20	21	22	23	24	25	26	27	27	28	29	0	1	2	3	4	5	6	7
☽	6	18	0	11	23	5	17	0	12	25	8	21	4	18	2	16	0	15	0	15	29	14	28	11	24	7	20	2	14
☿	21	22	22	22	23	23	24	24	25	26	27	27	28	29	0	1	2	3	4	5	7	8	9	11	12	14	16	17	19	21
♀	16	17	19	20	21	22	23	25	26	27	28	0	1	2	3	4	6	7	8	9	10	12	13	14	15	16	18	19	20
♂	29	29	0	0	1	1	2	2	3	4	4	5	5	6	6	7	8	8	9	9	10	10	11	11	12	12	13	13	14

♃ 1 3 9 16 22 30 / ♈12 13 14 15 16 17 — ♄ 1 3 R 14 / ≈23 23 22 — ♅ 1 22 / ♍1 2 — ♆ 1 R / ♏13 — ♇ 1 R / ♍9

7	1	2	3	4	5	6	7	8	9	10	11	12	13	14	15	16	17	18	19	20	21	22	23	24	25	26	27	28	29
☉	9	10	11	12	13	14	15	16	17	18	18	19	20	21	22	23	24	25	26	27	28	29	0	1	2	3	4	5	6
☽	8	20	2	14	26	9	21	4	18	1	15	29	13	27	11	25	10	24	8	22	6	19	2	15	28	10	22	4	16
☿	25	27	29	1	3	5	7	9	11	13	15	18	20	22	24	26	28	0	2	4	6	8	10	12	14	16	18	20	21
♀	23	24	25	26	28	29	0	1	2	4	5	6	7	8	10	11	12	13	15	16	17	18	19	21	22	23	24	26	27
♂	15	15	16	17	17	18	18	19	19	20	21	21	22	22	23	24	24	25	25	26	27	27	28	28	29	0	0	1

♃ 1 10 23 / ♈17 18 19 — ♄ 1 R 11 27 / ≈22 21 20 — ♅ 1 15 / ♍2 3 — ♆ 1 R 6 26 D / ♏13 12 12 — ♇ 1 / ♍9

8	1	2	3	4	5	6	7	8	9	10	11	12	13	14	15	16	17	18	19	20	21	22	23	24	25	26	27	28	29
☉	9	9	10	11	12	13	14	15	16	17	18	19	20	21	22	23	24	25	26	27	28	29	0	1	2	3	4
☽	22	4	17	0	13	27	11	25	9	24	8	22	6	20	4	18	1	15	28	11	23	6	18	0	12	24	6	18	0
☿	27	28	0	1	3	5	6	8	9	11	12	13	14	15	16	18	19	20	21	22	23	24	25	26	26	27	28	28	29	0
♀	1	2	3	4	5	7	8	9	10	12	13	14	15	17	18	19	20	21	23	24	25	26	27	29	0	1	3	4
♂	3	4	4	5	6	7	7	8	8	9	10	10	11	12	13	13	14	14	15	16	16	17	17	18	19	19	20	20	21

♃ 1 10 R 26 / ♈19 19 18 — ♄ 1 R 9 23 / ≈20 19 18 — ♅ 1 2 18 / ♍3 4 5 — ♆ 1 14 / ♏12 13 — ♇ 1 / ♍10

9	1	2	3	4	5	6	7	8	9	10	11	12	13	14	15	16	17	18	19	20	21	22	23	24	25	26	27	28	29
☉	8	9	10	11	12	13	14	15	16	17	18	19	20	21	22	23	24	25	26	27	28	29	0	1	2	3	4
☽	8	22	6	20	5	19	4	18	3	17	1	15	28	11	24	7	19	2	14	26	8	20	2	14	26	8	20	3	16
☿	3	4	4	4	5	5	5	4	4	4	3	3	2	1	0	29	29	28	27	26	25	24	23	22	22	21	21	20	20
♀	9	10	11	13	14	15	16	18	19	20	21	23	24	25	26	28	29	0	1	3	4	5	6	7	9	10	11	12	14
♂	23	23	24	25	25	26	27	27	28	28	29	0	0	1	2	2	3	3	4	5	5	6	7	7	8	9	10	11

♃ 1 R 8 18 26 / ♈18 17 16 15 — ♄ 1 R 6 25 / ≈18 17 16 — ♅ 1 3 20 / ♍5 6 7 — ♆ 1 29 / ♏13 14 — ♇ 1 / ♍11

10	1	2	3	4	5	6	7	8	9	10	11	12	13	14	15	16	17	18	19	20	21	22	23	24	25	26	27	28	29
☉	8	9	10	11	12	13	14	15	16	17	18	19	20	21	22	23	24	25	26	27	28	29	0	1	2	3	4
☽	14	29	14	29	14	29	13	27	11	25	8	21	4	16	29	11	23	5	17	29	10	22	4	16	29	11	24	7	20
☿	21	21	22	23	23	24	26	27	28	0	1	3	4	6	7	9	11	12	14	16	17	19	21	23	24	26	28	29	1
♀	16	17	19	20	21	22	24	25	26	27	29	0	1	2	4	5	6	7	9	10	11	12	14	15	16	17	19	20	21
♂	13	13	14	15	16	16	17	18	18	19	20	21	21	22	23	24	24	25	26	26	27	28	29	29	0	1	2	2	3

♃ 1 R 4 11 19 27 / ♈15 14 13 12 11 — ♄ 1 R 22 D / ≈16 16 — ♅ 1 7 28 / ♍7 8 9 — ♆ 1 28 / ♏14 15 — ♇ 1 / ♍12

11	1	2	3	4	5	6	7	8	9	10	11	12	13	14	15	16	17	18	19	20	21	22	23	24	25	26	27	28	29
☉	8	9	10	11	12	13	14	15	16	17	18	19	20	21	22	23	24	25	26	27	28	29	0	1	2	3	4	5	6
☽	7	22	8	22	7	25	5	18	1	13	26	8	20	2	14	26	7	19	1	14	26	9	23	6	20	4	18	2	16
☿	6	8	9	11	12	14	15	17	18	19	20	22	23	24	25	26	27	28	29	0	0	1	1	1	1	0	29	29	28
♀	25	26	27	29	0	1	2	4	5	6	7	9	10	11	12	13	15	16	17	18	20	21	22	23	25	26	27	28	0
♂	5	5	6	7	8	8	9	10	11	11	12	13	14	14	15	16	16	17	18	19	19	20	21	22	22	23	24	25	25

♃ 1 R 15 / ♈11 10 9 — ♄ 1 16 / ≈16 17 — ♅ 1 / ♍9 — ♆ 1 24 / ♏15 16 — ♇ 1 / ♍13

12	1	2	3	4	5	6	7	8	9	10	11	12	13	14	15	16	17	18	19	20	21	22	23	24	25	26	27	28	29
☉	9	10	11	12	13	14	15	16	17	18	19	20	21	22	23	24	25	26	27	28	29	0	1	2	3	4	5	6	7
☽	16	1	15	0	13	27	10	22	5	17	29	11	23	4	16	28	10	22	5	17	0	13	27	10	24	9	24	9	24
☿	23	24	26	27	29	0	2	3	5	6	7	9	10	11	13	15	16	17	18	19	20	20	20	20	19	18	17	16
♀	2	3	5	6	7	8	10	11	12	13	15	16	17	18	20	21	22	23	25	26	27	28	29	0	1	3	4	5	6
♂	27	28	28	29	0	1	1	2	3	4	5	5	6	7	8	9	9	10	11	11	12	12	13	14	14	15	16	17	18

♃ 1 R 5 D 21 / ♈9 9 10 — ♄ 1 3 16 27 / ≈17 18 19 20 — ♅ 1 3 16 R 28 / ♍9 10 10 10 9 — ♆ 1 24 / ♏16 17 — ♇ 1 / ♍14

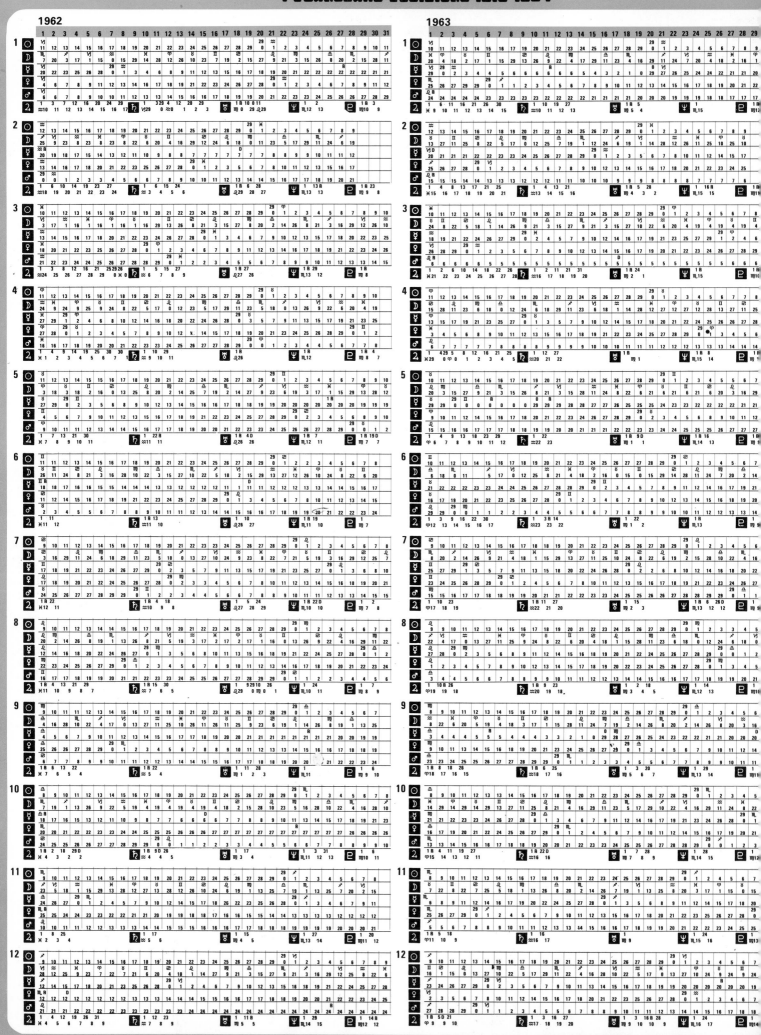

1964

1 (January)

Planet	Days 1–31
☉	10 11 12 13 14 15 16 17 18 19 20 21 22 23 24 25 26 27 28 29 0 1 2 3 4 5 6 7 8 9 10
☽	7 21 5 18 1 13 25 7 19 1 13 25 7 19 2 14 27 10 24 7 21 5 19 3 18 2 17 1 15 29 13
☿	16 15 14 12 11 10 8 7 6 5 4 4 4 4 D 4 4 5 5 6 7 7 8 9 10 11 12 13 14 15 16
♀	11 12 13 14 16 17 18 19 20 22 23 24 25 27 28 29 0 2 3 4 5 6 8 9 10 11 13 14 15 16 17
♂	21 21 22 23 24 25 25 26 27 28 28 29 0 1 2 2 3 4 5 6 6 7 8 9 9 10 11 12 13 13 14

♃ 1 3 12 20 27 / ♈10 11 12 13 14 — ♄ 1 6 15 24 / ≈20 21 22 23 — ♅ 1 R / ♍9 — ♆ 1 / ♏17 — ♇ 1 R / ♍14 13

2 (February)

Planet	Days
☉	12 13 14 15 16 17 18 19 20 21 22 23 24 25 26 27 28 29 0 1 2 3 4 5 6 7 8 9 10
☽	26 9 21 3 15 27 9 21 3 15 27 10 23 6 20 4 18 2 16 0 14 28 12 26 10 24 7 21 4
☿	18 19 20 21 22 24 25 26 28 0 1 2 4 5 7 8 10 11 13 14 16 17 19 21 22 24 26 27 0
♀	19 20 21 22 23 25 26 27 28 0 1 2 3 4 5 7 8 9 10 11 12 14 15 16 17 18 19 21 22
♂	15 16 17 17 18 19 20 21 21 22 23 24 24 25 26 27 28 28 29 0 1 2 2 3 4 5 6 6 7

♃ 1 2 8 13 18 23 28 / ♈14 15 16 17 18 19 20 — ♄ 1 4 10 18 26 / ≈23 24 25 26 27 — ♅ 1 R / ♍9 8 7 — ♆ 1 18 R / ♏17 17 — ♇ 1 R / ♍13

3 (March)

Planet	Days
☉	11 12 13 14 15 16 17 18 19 20 21 22 23 24 25 26 27 28 29 0 1 2 3 4 5 6 7 8 9 10 11
☽	16 29 11 23 5 17 29 11 23 5 18 1 15 29 13 28 12 27 11 25 9 23 6 20 3 16 29 12 25 7 19
☿	1 3 4 6 8 10 12 13 15 17 19 21 23 25 27 0 1 3 5 7 9 11 13 15 17 19 21 22 24 26 27
♀	23 24 25 26 28 29 0 1 2 3 4 5 7 8 9 10 11 12 13 14 15 16 17 18 20 21 22 23 24 25 26
♂	8 9 10 11 12 12 13 14 15 16 17 17 18 19 20 20 21 22 23 24 24 25 26 27 28 28 29 0 1 1

♃ 1 4 8 13 17 22 26 30 / ♈20 21 22 23 24 25 26 27 — ♄ 1 6 15 24 29 25 / ≈27 28 29 0 ♓0 — ♅ 1 R 22 / ♍7 6 — ♆ 1 / ♏17 — ♇ 1 R / ♍12

4 (April)

Planet	Days
☉	12 13 14 15 16 17 18 19 20 21 22 23 24 25 26 27 28 29 0 1 2 3 4 5 6 7 8 9 10
☽	1 13 25 6 18 1 13 26 9 23 8 22 7 22 7 21 7 20 3 17 0 13 26 9 21 3 15 27 9 21
☿	29 1 2 3 5 6 7 8 9 10 10 11 11 11 11 11 11 11 11 10 10 9 9 8 8 7 6 6 5 4
♀	27 28 29 0 1 2 3 4 5 6 7 8 9 10 11 12 13 14 15 16 16 17 18 19 19 20 21 22 22 23 24
♂	2 3 4 5 5 6 7 8 8 9 10 11 11 12 13 14 15 15 16 17 18 18 19 20 21 21 22 23 24

♃ 1 3 8 12 29 13 16 20 24 / ♈27 28 29 0 ♉0 1 2 3 — ♄ 1 2 3 25 / ♓0 1 2 3 — ♅ 1 R 29 / ♍6 5 — ♆ 1 R 16 / ♏17 16 — ♇ 1 R 12 / ♍12 11

5 (May)

Planet	Days
☉	11 12 13 14 15 16 17 18 19 20 21 22 23 24 25 26 27 28 29 0 1 2 3 4 5 6 7 8 9 10
☽	3 15 27 9 21 4 18 1 16 0 15 0 16 1 15 0 13 27 10 23 6 18 0 12 24 6 18 0 12 24 6
☿	3 3 2 2 2 1 1 1 1 D 1 1 1 1 2 2 3 3 4 4 5 6 7 8 9 10 11 12 14 15 16
♀	25 25 26 27 27 28 29 29 0 0 1 2 2 3 3 4 4 4 5 5 5 6 6 6 6 6 6 6 6 6 6
♂	25 26 27 28 28 29 0 1 2 3 4 5 6 7 7 8 9 10 10 11 12 13 14 15 15 16 17 18

♃ 1 3 7 11 15 20 24 28 / ♉4 5 6 7 8 9 10 11 — ♄ 1 10 / ♓3 4 — ♅ 1 R 13 D 26 / ♍5 5 6 — ♆ 1 R 24 / ♏16 15 — ♇ 1 R 22 D / ♍11 11

6 (June)

Planet	Days
☉	11 12 13 14 15 16 17 18 19 20 21 22 23 24 25 26 27 28 29 0 1 2 3 4 5 6 7 8 9
☽	18 0 13 26 10 24 9 24 9 24 9 23 6 20 3 15 27 9 21 3 15 27 9 21 3 15 27 10
☿	17 19 20 22 23 25 27 28 0 1 3 5 7 9 11 13 15 17 19 21 23 25 27 0 2 4 6 8 10 12
♀	6 6 6 5 5 5 4 4 3 3 2 2 1 1 0 29 28 28 27 27 26 26 25 24 24 23 23 23 22 22
♂	18 19 20 20 21 22 23 24 24 25 26 27 28 28 29 0 1 1 2 3 4 4 5 6 7 7 8 9

♃ 1 2 6 11 16 20 25 / ♉11 12 13 14 15 16 17 — ♄ 1 8 15 R 22 / ♓4 5 5 4 — ♅ 1 / ♍6 — ♆ 1 R / ♏15 — ♇ 1 / ♍11

7 (July)

Planet	Days
☉	10 11 12 13 14 15 16 17 18 19 20 21 22 23 24 25 26 27 28 29 0 1 2 3 4 4 5 6 7 8
☽	23 6 20 4 18 2 17 2 17 1 15 28 11 24 6 18 0 12 24 6 17 0 12 24 7 20 3 16 0
☿	15 17 19 21 23 25 27 29 1 3 5 6 8 10 11 13 15 17 18 20 21 23 24 26 27 29 0 1 2 4 5
♀	22 21 21 21 20 20 20 20 20 20 D 20 20 20 20 20 20 20 21 21 21 22 23 23 24 24 25 25 26 27
♂	10 10 11 12 13 13 14 15 16 17 18 19 20 21 21 22 23 24 24 25 26 27 28 28 29 0

♃ 1 6 12 18 24 31 / ♉18 19 20 21 22 23 — ♄ 1 R 21 / ♓4 3 — ♅ 1 2 23 / ♍6 7 8 — ♆ 1 R 23 D / ♏15 15 — ♇ 1 2 / ♍11 12

8 (August)

Planet	Days
☉	9 10 11 12 13 14 15 16 17 18 19 20 21 22 23 24 25 26 27 28 29 0 1 2 3 4 5 6 7 8
☽	14 28 12 27 11 26 11 25 9 23 7 20 2 14 26 8 20 2 14 26 8 21 3 16 0 13 27 11 24 8 23
☿	6 7 8 9 10 11 12 13 14 15 16 17 17 17 17 17 17 17 17 17 17 17 17 16 16 15 14 13 12 12 11
♀	27 28 29 29 0 1 2 3 4 5 6 7 8 9 10 11 12 13 14 15 16 17 18 19 20 21 22
♂	1 2 2 3 4 5 6 7 7 8 9 10 11 12 12 13 14 14 15 15 16 17 17 18 18 19 20 21

♃ 1 9 19 / ♉23 24 25 — ♄ 1 R 6 20 / ♓3 2 1 — ♅ 1 / ♍8 9 10 — ♆ 1 / ♏15 — ♇ 1 8 / ♍12 13

9 (September)

Planet	Days
☉	9 10 11 12 13 14 15 16 17 18 19 20 21 22 23 24 25 26 27 28 29 0 1 2 3 4 5 6 7
☽	7 21 5 20 4 18 1 15 28 10 22 4 16 28 10 22 4 16 29 12 25 9 23 7 21 5 19 4 18 2
☿	10 9 8 7 6 5 5 4 4 4 4 4 4 5 5 6 7 8 9 10 11 12 13 14 15 17 19 20 22 24 25
♀	23 24 25 26 27 28 29 0 1 2 3 4 5 6 7 8 9 10 11 12 13 14 15 16 17 18 19 20 21 22 23 24
♂	21 22 23 23 24 25 26 26 27 28 28 29 0 0 1 1 2 3 4 5 6 6 7 8 8 9

♃ 1 5 15 R 23 / ♉25 26 26 25 — ♄ 1 R 2 16 0 17 / ♓1 0 29 ≈29 — ♅ 1 11 27 / ♍10 11 12 — ♆ 1 25 / ♏15 16 — ♇ 1 6 / ♍13 14

10 (October)

Planet	Days
☉	8 9 10 11 12 13 14 15 16 17 18 19 20 21 22 23 24 25 26 27 28 29 0 1 2 3 4 5 6 7 8
☽	16 29 13 27 10 23 5 18 0 12 24 6 18 0 12 24 7 20 4 18 2 16 1 16 0 14 28 12 26 10 23
☿	27 29 1 3 4 6 8 10 11 13 15 17 18 20 22 24 25 27 29 0 2 3 5 7 8 10 11 13 15 16 18
♀	25 26 27 28 0 1 2 3 4 5 6 8 9 10 11 12 13 15 16 17 18 19 20 22 23 24 25 26 27 29 0
♂	9 10 11 12 12 13 14 14 15 16 16 17 17 18 19 19 20 20 21 21 22 22 23 23 24 24 25 25 26 26 27

♃ 1 R 10 21 29 / ♉25 24 23 22 — ♄ 1 R 4 / ≈29 28 — ♅ 1 15 / ♍12 13 — ♆ 1 25 / ♏16 17 — ♇ 1 5 / ♍14 15

11 (November)

Planet	Days
☉	9 10 11 12 13 14 15 16 17 18 19 20 21 22 23 24 25 26 27 28 29 0 1 2 3 4 5 6 7 8
☽	6 19 2 14 26 9 20 2 14 26 8 20 2 14 26 8 20 2 15 28 12 26 10 24 9 23 7 21 5 19
☿	19 21 22 24 25 27 28 0 1 3 4 6 7 9 10 12 13 14 16 17 19 20 22 23 25 26 27 28 0
♀	1 2 4 5 6 7 8 10 11 12 13 14 16 17 18 19 21 22 23 24 25 27 28 29 0 2 3 4 5 7
♂	27 28 28 29 29 0 1 1 2 3 3 4 5 6 6 7 7 8 8 9 9 10 10 11 12

♃ 1 R 6 13 21 28 / ♉22 21 20 19 18 — ♄ 1 D 29 / ≈28 29 — ♅ 1 6 / ♍13 14 — ♆ 1 21 / ♏17 18 — ♇ 1 13 / ♍15 16

12 (December)

Planet	Days
☉	9 10 11 12 13 14 15 16 17 18 19 20 21 22 23 24 25 26 27 28 29 0 1 2 3 4 5 6 7 8 9 10
☽	11 23 5 17 29 11 22 4 16 28 11 23 6 19 4 18 3 18 3 18 2 16 0 13 26 8 20 2 14
☿	1 1 2 3 4 4 4 4 4 4 4 3 3 2 1 0 29 28 26 25 24 22 21 20 19 19 19 18 18 18
♀	8 9 10 11 12 13 14 16 17 18 19 20 21 22 23 25 26 27 28 29 1 2 3 4 6 7 8 9 10 11 12 13 14 15
♂	12 13 13 14 14 14 15 15 16 16 16 17 17 17 18 18 18 19 19 19 20 20 21 21 21 22 22 22 22 23 24

♃ 1 R 7 18 / ♉18 17 16 — ♄ 1 16 29 17 28 / ≈29 0 ♓0 1 — ♅ 1 20 R / ♍14 14 — ♆ 1 20 / ♏18 19 — ♇ 1 18 R / ♍16 16

1965

1 (January)

Planet	Days 1–31
☉	11 12 13 14 15 16 17 18 19 20 21 22 23 24 25 26 27 28 29 0 1 2 3 4 5 6 7 8 9 10 11
☽	26 8 19 1 13 25 7 20 2 15 29 12 26 11 26 11 26 11 26 11 25 9 22 5 17 29 11 23 5 16 28
☿	19 20 20 21 22 23 24 25 26 27 28 29 0 2 3 4 5 7 8 9 11 12 14 15 16 18 19 21 22 24 25
♀	16 18 19 20 21 23 24 25 26 28 29 0 1 3 4 5 6 8 9 10 11 13 14 15 16 18 19 20 21 23 24
♂	24 24 24 24 25 25 25 25 26 26 26 26 26 26 26 27 27 27 27 27 27 27 27 27 28 28 28 R 28 28 27

♃ 1 R 10 D / ♉16 16 — ♄ 1 8 18 27 / ♓1 2 3 4 — ♅ 1 R / ♍14 — ♆ 1 / ♏19 — ♇ 1 R 23 / ♍16 15

2 (February)

Planet	Days
☉	12 13 14 15 16 18 19 20 21 22 23 24 25 26 27 28 29 0 1 2 3 4 5 6 7 8 9 10
☽	10 22 4 17 29 12 25 8 22 6 20 4 19 4 19 4 19 3 17 0 13 25 7 19 1 13 25 7
☿	27 28 0 2 3 5 6 8 10 11 13 15 16 18 20 21 23 25 27 29 0 2 4 6 8 10 11 13
♀	25 26 28 29 0 1 3 4 5 6 8 9 10 11 13 14 15 16 18 19 20 21 23 24 25 26 28 29
♂	27 27 27 27 27 27 27 27 27 27 26 26 26 26 26 25 25 25 25 24 24 24 23 23 23 22 22 21

♃ 1 2 13 21 28 / ♉16 17 18 19 20 — ♄ 1 4 13 21 / ♓4 5 6 7 — ♅ 1 R 2 28 / ♍14 13 12 — ♆ 1 12 20 R 27 / ♏19 20 20 19 — ♇ 1 / ♍15

3 (March)

Planet	Days
☉	11 12 13 14 15 16 17 18 19 20 21 22 23 24 25 26 27 28 29 0 1 2 3 4 5 6 7 8 9 10 11
☽	19 1 14 26 9 22 5 19 3 16 0 15 29 14 28 13 27 11 25 8 21 3 15 27 9 21 3 15 27 9 22
☿	15 17 19 21 23 25 27 29 1 2 4 6 8 9 11 13 14 15 17 18 19 20 21 22 22 23 23 R 22 22
♀	0 1 3 4 5 6 8 9 10 11 13 14 15 16 18 19 20 21 23 24 25 26 27 29 0 1 2 4 5 6 7
♂	21 20 20 20 19 19 18 18 18 17 17 17 16 16 15 15 14 14 14 13 13 13 12 12 12 11 11 10

♃ 1 7 13 19 24 29 / ♉20 21 22 23 24 25 — ♄ 1 9 18 26 / ♓8 9 10 11 — ♅ 1 R 22 / ♍12 11 — ♆ 1 R / ♏19 — ♇ 1 R 7 / ♍15 14

4 (April)

Planet	Days
☉	12 13 14 15 16 17 18 19 20 21 22 23 24 25 26 27 28 29 0 1 2 3 4 5 6 7 8 9 10
☽	5 18 2 15 29 13 27 11 25 10 24 8 22 6 19 3 16 29 11 23 5 17 29 11 23 5 17 0 13 27
☿	22 22 21 21 20 19 18 18 17 16 15 15 14 13 13 12 12 12 11 11 11 11 11 11 12 12 12 13 13 14 14
♀	9 10 11 12 14 15 16 17 19 20 21 22 24 25 26 27 28 0 1 2 3 5 6 7 8 10 11 12 13 15
♂	10 10 10 10 10 9 9 9 9 9 9 9 9 9 8 8 8 8 8 8 8 8 8 8 8 8 8 9 9 9 9

♃ 1 3 8 13 17 22 29 23 27 / ♉25 26 27 28 29 0 ♊0 1 — ♄ 1 4 14 24 / ♓11 12 13 14 — ♅ 1 R 21 / ♍11 10 — ♆ 1 R 26 / ♏19 18 — ♇ 1 R 18 / ♍14 13

5 (May)

Planet	Days
☉	11 12 13 14 15 16 17 18 19 20 21 22 23 24 25 26 27 28 29 0 1 2 3 4 5 6 7 8 9 10
☽	11 25 9 23 8 23 6 21 5 18 2 15 29 12 24 7 19 1 13 25 7 19 1 13 25 8 21 5 19 3 18
☿	15 16 16 17 18 19 20 21 22 23 25 26 27 28 0 1 3 4 6 7 9 10 12 14 15 17 19 21 23 25 27
♀	16 17 18 19 21 22 23 24 26 27 28 0 1 2 3 4 5 7 8 9 10 12 13 14 15 17 18 19 20 21 23
♂	9 9 9 9 9 10 10 10 10 10 11 11 11 11 12 12 12 12 13 13 13 14 14 14 15 15 15 16 16 16 17 17

♃ 1 5 10 14 18 23 27 31 / ♊2 3 4 5 6 7 8 9 — ♄ 1 6 20 / ♓14 15 16 — ♅ 1 R 18 D / ♍10 10 — ♆ 1 / ♏18 — ♇ 1 R 25 D / ♍13 13

6 (June)

Planet	Days
☉	11 12 13 14 15 16 17 17 18 19 20 21 22 23 24 25 26 27 28 29 0 1 2 3 4 5 6 7 8
☽	3 18 2 17 1 15 29 12 25 8 21 3 16 28 10 22 4 16 28 11 23 6 19 3 17 2 17 2 17 2
☿	29 1 3 5 7 9 11 13 15 18 20 22 24 26 29 3 5 7 9 11 13 15 17 19 21 23 24 26 28
♀	24 25 26 28 29 0 1 2 4 5 6 7 9 10 11 12 14 15 16 17 18 20 21 22 23 24 26 27 28 0
♂	18 18 18 19 19 19 20 20 20 21 21 21 22 22 22 23 23 23 24 24 25 25 25 26 26 26 27 27 28 28 29 29 0 0 1

♃ 1 4 9 13 17 22 26 / ♊9 10 11 12 13 14 15 — ♄ 1 12 28 R / ♓16 17 17 — ♅ 1 13 / ♍10 11 — ♆ 1 R 2 / ♏18 17 — ♇ 1 28 / ♍13 14

7 (July)

Planet	Days
☉	9 10 11 12 13 14 15 16 17 18 19 20 21 22 23 24 25 26 27 28 29 0 1 2 3 4 5 6 7 8
☽	12 27 11 25 9 22 5 18 0 13 25 7 18 0 12 24 6 18 0 13 25 8 22 6 20 5 20 5 20 6 20
☿	0 1 3 4 6 7 9 10 12 13 14 16 17 18 19 20 21 22 23 24 25 26 26 27 28 28 29 29 29 29 0
♀	1 2 3 4 5 7 8 9 10 12 13 14 15 16 18 19 20 21 22 24 25 26 27 28 0 1 2 3 5 6 7
♂	1 1 2 2 3 3 4 4 5 6 6 7 7 8 8 9 10 10 11 11 12 12 13 14 14 15 15 16 17 18

♃ 1 5 10 14 19 24 29 / ♊16 17 18 19 20 21 22 — ♄ 1 R 14 / ♓17 16 — ♅ 1 13 / ♍11 12 — ♆ 1 R 30 D / ♏17 17 — ♇ 1 / ♍14

8 (August)

Planet	Days
☉	9 10 11 12 13 14 15 16 17 18 19 20 21 22 23 24 25 26 27 28 29 0 1 2 3 4 5 6 7 8
☽	5 18 2 15 27 10 22 4 15 27 9 21 3 15 27 10 22 5 18 1 15 29 14 29 14 29 13 27 10
☿	0 0 29 29 28 28 27 27 26 25 25 24 23 22 22 21 20 20 19 18 18 17 17 17 17 17 17 D 17 18 18 19 20
♀	8 9 11 12 13 14 15 17 18 19 20 21 23 24 25 26 27 29 0 1 2 4 5 6 7 8 9 11 12
♂	18 19 19 20 21 21 22 22 23 24 24 25 25 26 27 27 28 29 29 0 0 1 2 2 3 4 4 5 6 7

♃ 1 3 9 14 20 27 / ♊22 23 24 25 26 27 — ♄ 1 R 6 21 / ♓16 15 14 — ♅ 1 / ♍12 13 14 — ♆ 1 / ♏17 — ♇ 1 7 / ♍14 15

9 (September)

Planet	Days
☉	9 10 11 12 13 14 15 16 17 18 19 20 21 22 23 24 25 26 27 28 29 0 1 2 3 4 5 6 7
☽	23 6 18 0 12 24 6 18 0 12 24 7 19 2 16 29 13 28 13 28 13 27 11 25 8 22 4 17
☿	21 22 23 24 25 26 28 29 1 2 4 6 8 10 11 13 15 17 19 21 23 25 27 29 0 2 4 6 7 9
♀	15 16 18 19 20 21 22 24 25 26 27 28 0 1 2 3 4 6 7 8 9 10 11 13 14 15 16 17 18 19
♂	8 9 10 11 12 12 13 14 14 15 16 16 17 18 18 19 20 21 22 22 23 24 25 26 26 27

♃ 1 3 11 21 29 12 / ♊27 28 29 0 ♋0 — ♄ 1 R 4 17 / ♓14 13 12 — ♅ 1 4 20 / ♍14 15 16 — ♆ 1 22 / ♏17 18 — ♇ 1 6 / ♍15 16

10 (October)

Planet	Days
☉	8 9 10 11 12 13 14 15 16 17 18 19 20 21 22 23 24 25 26 27 28 29 0 1 2 3 4 5 6 7 8
☽	27 9 21 2 14 26 8 21 3 16 29 13 26 9 24 9 23 8 22 6 20 4 18 1 16 0 13 26
☿	11 13 14 16 18 19 21 22 24 26 27 29 0 2 3 5 6 8 9 11 12 14 15 16 18 19 20 21 22 24 25
♀	20 22 23 24 25 26 27 28 29 1 2 3 4 5 6 7 8 9 10 11 12 13 14 15 16 17 18 19 20 21 22 23 24
♂	28 28 29 0 0 1 2 3 4 4 5 6 7 7 8 9 10 11 11 12 13 14 15 15 16 17 18 19 20

♃ 1 5 19 R / ♋0 1 1 — ♄ 1 R 20 / ♓11 10 — ♅ 1 6 25 / ♍16 17 18 — ♆ 1 23 / ♏18 19 — ♇ 1 4 / ♍16 17

11 (November)

Planet	Days
☉	9 10 11 12 13 14 15 16 17 18 19 20 21 22 23 24 25 26 27 28 29 0 1 2 3 4 5 6 7 8
☽	10 22 4 16 29 11 24 7 21 4 18 2 17 1 15 29 13 27 11 25 8 22 5 17 0 12 24 6 18 0
☿	29 0 2 3 4 5 7 8 9 10 11 12 13 14 15 15 16 17 17 18 18 18 18 17 17 16 16 15 14
♀	25 26 27 28 0 1 2 3 4 5 6 7 8 9 10 11 12 13 14 15 16 17 18 19 20 21 22 23 24
♂	20 21 22 23 23 24 25 26 27 28 29 0 1 2 2 3 4 5 6 7 7 8 9 10 11 12 12

♃ 1 R 2 17 0 18 26 / ♋1 0 29 ♊29 28 — ♄ 1 R 14 D / ♓10 10 — ♅ 1 17 / ♍18 19 — ♆ 1 19 / ♏19 20 — ♇ 1 9 / ♍17 18

12 (December)

Planet	Days
☉	9 10 11 12 13 14 15 16 17 18 19 20 21 22 23 24 25 26 27 28 29 0 1 2 3 5 6 7 8 9 10
☽	12 24 6 19 2 15 29 13 27 12 27 11 26 10 24 8 22 5 18 1 14 26 8 20 2 14 26 8 20 2 14
☿	12 11 9 8 7 5 4 4 3 3 2 2 2 D 2 3 3 4 4 5 5 6 7 8 9 10 11 12 13 14 15 16 17 18 20
♀	25 26 27 28 29 29 0 1 2 3 4 5 6 7 8 9 10 10 11 11 12 12 12 13 13 13 13 14 14 14 14
♂	13 14 15 15 16 17 18 18 19 20 21 21 22 23 24 25 25 26 27 28 29 0 0 1 2 3 3 4 5 6

♃ 1 R 5 12 20 27 / ♊28 27 26 25 24 — ♄ 1 8 25 / ♓10 11 12 — ♅ 1 25 R / ♍19 19 — ♆ 1 17 / ♏20 21 — ♇ 1 21 R / ♍18 18

1966

1

	1	2	3	4	5	6	7	8	9	10	11	12	13	14	15	16	17	18	19	20	21	22	23	24	25	26	27	28	29	30	31
☉	♑ 11	12	13	14	15	16	17	18	19	20	21	22	23	24	25	26	27	28	29	29 0	♒ 1	2	3	4	5	6	7	8	9	10	11
☽	♈ 27	♉ 10	23	♊ 7	21	♋ 6	21	♌ 6	21	♍ 6	20	♎ 5	18	♏ 2	15	28	♐ 10	23	♑ 5	17	29	♒ 11	23	♓ 5	17	29	♈ 11	23	♉ 5	18	♊ 1
☿	♐ 21	22	24	25	27	28	29 0	♑ 1	2	4	5	7	8	10	11	13	14	16	18	19	21	22	24	26	27	29	29 0	♒ 2	4	5	7
♀	♒ 13	13	13	13	℞ 13	13	13	13	13	13	12	12	12	12	11	11	10	10	9	9	8	7	7	6	6	5	4	4	3	3	2
♂	♒ 7	8	9	9	10	11	12	13	13	14	15	16	17	17	18	19	20	21	21	22	23	24	24	25	26	27	28	28	29	29 0	♓ 1

♃ 1℞ 4 13 24 / ♊24 23 22 21 — ♄ 1 7 18 28 / ♓12 13 14 15 — ♅ 1℞ / ♍19 — ♆ 1 27 / ♏21 22 — ♇ 1℞ / ♍18

2

	1	2	3	4	5	6	7	8	9	10	11	12	13	14	15	16	17	18	19	20	21	22	23	24	25	26	27	28
☉	♒ 12	13	14	15	16	17	18	19	20	21	22	23	24	25	26	27	28	29	29 0	♓ 1	2	3	4	5	6	7	8	9
☽	♊ 15	29	♋ 13	28	♌ 14	29	♍ 14	29	♎ 14	28	♏ 12	25	♐ 7	20	♑ 2	14	26	♒ 8	20	♓ 2	14	26	♈ 8	20	♉ 2	14	27	♊ 10
☿	♒ 9	10	12	14	16	17	19	21	23	25	26	28	29 0	♓ 2	4	6	7	9	11	13	15	16	18	20	22	23	25	26
♀	♒℞ 2	1	1	0	0	0 29	♑ 29	29	28	28	28	28	28	28	D 28	28	28	27	28	28	29	29	29	29	29 0	♒ 0	0	1
♂	♓ 2	2	3	4	5	6	6	7	8	9	9	10	11	12	13	13	14	15	16	17	17	18	19	20	20	21	22	23

♃ 1℞ 15D / ♊21 21 — ♄ 1 6 15 23 / ♓15 16 17 18 — ♅ 1℞ 27 / ♍18 17 — ♆ 1 22℞ / ♏22 22 — ♇ 1℞ 2 / ♍18 17

3

	1	2	3	4	5	6	7	8	9	10	11	12	13	14	15	16	17	18	19	20	21	22	23	24	25	26	27	28	29	30	31
☉	♓ 10	11	12	13	14	15	16	17	18	19	20	21	22	23	24	25	26	27	28	29	29 0	♈ 1	2	3	4	5	6	7	8	9	10
☽	♊ 24	♋ 8	22	♌ 7	22	♍ 7	22	♎ 7	22	♏ 6	20	♐ 3	16	29	♑ 11	23	♒ 5	17	29	♓ 11	23	♈ 5	17	29	♉ 11	24	♊ 7	20	♋ 4	17	♌ 1
☿	♓ 28	29	29 0	♈ 1	2	3	4	5	5	5	5	℞ 5	5	5	4	4	3	2	1	1	0	0 29	♓ 29	28	26	25	25	24	24	23	23
♀	♒ 1	2	2	3	4	4	5	5	6	7	7	8	9	9	10	11	12	13	13	14	15	16	17	18	18	19	20	21	22	23	24
♂	♓ 24	24	25	26	27	27	28	29	29 0	♈ 1	1	2	3	4	4	5	6	7	8	8	9	10	11	11	12	13	14	14	15	16	17

♃ 1 8 20 29 / ♊21 22 23 24 — ♄ 1 3 11 19 28 / ♓18 19 20 21 22 — ♅ 1℞ 22 / ♍17 16 — ♆ 1℞ 20 / ♏22 21 — ♇ 1℞ 14 / ♍17 16

4

	1	2	3	4	5	6	7	8	9	10	11	12	13	14	15	16	17	18	19	20	21	22	23	24	25	26	27	28	29	30
☉	♈ 11	12	13	14	15	16	17	18	19	20	21	22	23	24	25	26	27	28	29	29 0	♉ 1	2	3	4	5	6	7	8	9	10
☽	♌ 16	♍ 1	16	♎ 1	16	♏ 0	14	28	♐ 12	25	♑ 7	19	♒ 1	13	25	♓ 7	19	♈ 1	13	26	♉ 8	21	♊ 4	17	♋ 1	14	28	♌ 12	26	♍ 11
☿	♓℞ 22	22	22	D 22	22	23	23	23	24	24	25	25	26	27	28	29	29 0	♈ 0	1	2	4	5	6	7	9	10	11	12	14	15
♀	♒ 25	26	27	28	29	29 0	♓ 1	2	3	4	5	6	7	8	9	10	11	12	13	14	15	16	17	18	19	20	21	23	24	25
♂	♈ 18	18	19	20	21	21	22	23	24	24	25	26	27	27	28	29	29 0	♉ 0	1	2	3	3	4	5	6	6	7	8	9	9

♃ 1 5 12 18 24 30 / ♊24 25 26 27 28 29 — ♄ 1 5 14 23 / ♓22 23 24 25 — ♅ 1℞ 19 / ♍16 15 — ♆ 1℞ / ♏21 — ♇ 1℞ 29 / ♍16 15

5

	1	2	3	4	5	6	7	8	9	10	11	12	13	14	15	16	17	18	19	20	21	22	23	24	25	26	27	28	29	30	31
☉	♉ 11	12	13	14	15	16	16	17	18	19	20	21	22	23	24	25	26	27	28	29	29 0	♊ 1	2	3	4	5	6	7	8	9	10
☽	♍ 25	♎ 10	24	♏ 8	22	♐ 6	19	♑ 2	15	27	♒ 9	21	♓ 3	15	27	♈ 9	21	♉ 4	17	♊ 0	13	27	♋ 11	25	♌ 9	23	♍ 7	22	♎ 6	20	♏ 4
☿	♈ 17	18	20	21	23	25	26	28	29 0	♉ 1	3	5	7	9	11	13	15	17	19	21	23	25	27	29 0	♊ 1	4	6	8	10	12	15
♀	♓ 26	27	28	29	29 0	♈ 1	2	4	5	6	7	8	9	10	11	12	14	15	16	17	18	19	20	22	23	24	25	26	27	28	29 0
♂	♉ 10	11	11	12	13	14	14	15	16	17	17	18	19	19	20	21	22	22	23	24	25	25	26	27	27	28	29	29 0	♊ 0	1	2

♃ 1 5 29 6 10 15 20 25 30 / ♊29 0 ♋0 1 2 3 4 5 — ♄ 1 3 14 26 / ♓25 26 27 28 — ♅ 1℞ 24D / ♍15 15 — ♆ 1℞ 5 / ♏21 20 — ♇ 1℞ 27D / ♍15 15

6

	1	2	3	4	5	6	7	8	9	10	11	12	13	14	15	16	17	18	19	20	21	22	23	24	25	26	27	28	29	30
☉	♊ 11	11	12	13	14	15	16	17	18	19	20	21	22	23	24	25	26	27	28	29	29 0	♋ 1	2	3	3	4	5	6	7	8
☽	♏ 18	♐ 1	14	28	♑ 10	23	♒ 5	17	29	♓ 11	23	♈ 5	17	♉ 0	12	25	♊ 9	22	♋ 6	21	♌ 5	19	♍ 4	18	♎ 3	17	♏ 0	14	27	♐ 11
☿	♊ 17	19	21	23	25	27	29 0	♋ 1	3	5	7	9	10	12	14	15	17	19	20	22	23	24	26	27	28	29 0	♌ 1	2	3	4
♀	♉ 1	2	3	4	5	6	8	9	10	11	12	13	15	16	17	18	19	20	22	23	24	25	26	28	29	29 0	♊ 1	2	3	5
♂	♊ 2	3	4	5	5	6	7	7	8	9	9	10	11	12	12	13	14	14	15	16	16	17	18	18	19	20	21	21	22	23

♃ 1 3 8 12 17 21 26 30 / ♋5 6 7 8 9 10 11 12 — ♄ 1 12 / ♓28 29 — ♅ 1 26 / ♍15 16 — ♆ 1℞ 12 / ♏20 19 — ♇ 1 23 / ♍15 16

7

	1	2	3	4	5	6	7	8	9	10	11	12	13	14	15	16	17	18	19	20	21	22	23	24	25	26	27	28	29	30	31
☉	♋ 9	10	11	12	13	14	15	16	17	18	19	20	21	22	23	23	24	25	26	27	28	29	29 0	♌ 1	2	3	4	5	6	7	8
☽	♐ 23	♑ 6	19	♒ 1	13	26	♓ 7	19	♈ 1	13	25	♉ 8	20	♊ 3	17	♋ 1	15	♌ 0	14	29	♍ 14	29	♎ 13	27	♏ 11	24	♐ 7	20	♑ 3	15	28
☿	♌ 5	6	6	7	8	9	9	10	10	10	11	11	11	℞ 11	11	11	11	10	10	9	9	8	8	7	6	6	5	4	4	3	2
♀	♊ 6	7	8	9	11	12	13	14	15	16	18	19	20	21	22	24	25	26	27	29	29 0	♋ 1	2	3	4	6	7	8	9	10	12
♂	♊ 23	24	25	25	26	27	27	28	29	29	29 0	♋ 1	1	2	3	3	4	5	5	6	7	7	8	9	9	10	11	11	12	13	13

♃ 1 5 9 13 18 22 27 31 / ♋12 13 14 15 16 17 18 19 — ♄ 1 11℞ / ♓29 29 — ♅ 1 22 / ♍16 17 — ♆ 1℞ / ♏19 — ♇ 1 / ♍16

8

	1	2	3	4	5	6	7	8	9	10	11	12	13	14	15	16	17	18	19	20	21	22	23	24	25	26	27	28	29	30	31
☉	♌ 9	10	11	12	13	14	15	15	16	17	18	19	20	21	22	23	24	25	26	27	28	29	29 0	♍ 1	2	3	4	5	6	7	8
☽	♒ 10	22	♓ 4	16	28	♈ 10	21	♉ 4	16	28	♊ 11	25	♋ 9	23	♌ 8	23	♍ 8	24	♎ 8	23	♏ 7	21	♐ 4	17	♑ 0	13	25	♒ 7	19	♓ 1	13
☿	♌℞ 2	1	1	0	0	0	D 0	0	0	0	1	1	2	3	3	4	5	6	8	9	10	12	14	15	17	19	20	22	24	26	28
♀	♋ 13	14	15	16	18	19	20	21	23	24	25	26	27	29	29 0	♌ 1	2	3	5	6	7	8	10	11	12	13	14	16	17	18	19
♂	♋ 14	15	15	16	17	17	18	19	19	20	21	21	22	23	23	24	25	25	26	27	27	28	28	29	29 0	♌ 0	1	2	2	3	4

♃ 1 5 10 14 19 24 29 / ♋19 20 21 22 23 24 25 — ♄ 1℞ 9 26 / ♓29 28 27 — ♅ 1 10 27 / ♍17 18 19 — ♆ 1D / ♏19 — ♇ 1 5 / ♍16 17

9

	1	2	3	4	5	6	7	8	9	10	11	12	13	14	15	16	17	18	19	20	21	22	23	24	25	26	27	28	29	30
☉	♍ 9	10	11	12	12	13	14	15	16	17	18	19	20	21	22	23	24	25	26	27	28	29	29 0	♎ 1	2	3	4	5	6	7
☽	♓ 25	♈ 7	18	♉ 0	12	25	♊ 7	20	♋ 4	17	♌ 2	16	♍ 1	17	♎ 2	17	♏ 2	16	♐ 0	14	27	♑ 9	22	♒ 4	16	28	♓ 10	22	♈ 4	15
☿	29 0	♍ 2	4	6	8	10	12	14	16	17	19	21	23	25	27	29	29 0	♎ 2	4	5	7	9	10	12	14	15	17	18	20	22
♀	♌ 21	22	23	24	26	27	28	29	29 0	♍ 2	3	4	5	7	8	9	10	12	13	14	15	17	18	19	20	22	23	24	25	27
♂	♌ 4	5	5	6	7	7	8	9	9	10	11	11	12	12	13	14	14	15	16	16	17	17	18	19	19	20	21	21	22	22

♃ 1 4 9 15 21 27 29 28 / ♋25 26 27 28 29 0 ♌0 — ♄ 1℞ 10 22 / ♓27 26 25 — ♅ 1 12 28 / ♍19 20 21 — ♆ 1 17 / ♏19 20 — ♇ 1 4 / ♍17 18

10

	1	2	3	4	5	6	7	8	9	10	11	12	13	14	15	16	17	18	19	20	21	22	23	24	25	26	27	28	29	30	31
☉	♎ 8	9	10	11	12	13	14	15	16	17	18	19	20	21	22	23	24	25	26	27	28	29	29 0	♏ 1	2	3	4	5	6	7	8
☽	♈ 27	♉ 10	22	♊ 4	17	♋ 0	13	27	♌ 11	25	♍ 10	25	♎ 10	25	♏ 10	25	♐ 9	22	♑ 5	18	♒ 1	13	25	♓ 7	18	♈ 0	12	24	♉ 6	19	♊ 1
☿	♎ 23	25	26	28	29 0	♏ 1	2	4	5	6	8	9	11	12	13	15	16	17	18	20	21	22	23	24	25	26	27	28	29	29 0	♐ 1
♀	♍ 28	29	29 0	♎ 2	3	4	5	7	8	9	10	12	13	14	15	17	18	19	20	22	23	24	25	27	28	29	29 0	♏ 2	3	4	5
♂	♌ 23	24	24	25	25	26	27	27	28	28	29	29 0	♍ 0	1	1	2	3	3	4	4	5	6	6	7	7	8	9	9	10	10	11

♃ 1 4 12 21 / ♌0 1 2 3 — ♄ 1℞ 6 21 / ♓25 24 23 — ♅ 1 15 / ♍21 22 — ♆ 1 20 / ♏20 21 — ♇ 1 2 / ♍18 19

11

	1	2	3	4	5	6	7	8	9	10	11	12	13	14	15	16	17	18	19	20	21	22	23	24	25	26	27	28	29	30
☉	♏ 9	10	11	12	13	14	15	16	17	18	19	20	21	22	23	24	25	26	27	28	29	29 0	♐ 1	2	3	4	5	6	7	8
☽	♊ 14	27	♋ 10	23	♌ 7	21	♍ 5	20	♎ 4	19	♏ 4	18	♐ 2	16	♑ 0	13	26	♒ 9	21	♓ 3	15	27	♈ 8	20	♉ 3	15	27	♊ 10	23	♋ 7
☿	♐ 1	2	2	3	3	℞ 3	3	2	2	1	1	0	0 29	♏ 27	26	25	24	22	21	20	19	18	17	17	17	D 17	17	17	18	18
♀	♏ 7	8	9	10	12	13	14	15	17	18	19	20	22	23	24	25	27	28	29	29 1	♐ 2	3	4	5	7	8	9	10	12	13
♂	♍ 12	12	13	13	14	14	15	16	16	17	17	18	18	19	20	20	21	21	22	22	23	24	24	25	25	26	26	27	27	28

♃ 1 4 21℞ / ♌3 4 4 — ♄ 1℞ 16 26D / ♓23 22 22 — ♅ 1 3 29 / ♍22 23 24 — ♆ 1 16 / ♏21 22 — ♇ 1 4 / ♍19 20

12

	1	2	3	4	5	6	7	8	9	10	11	12	13	14	15	16	17	18	19	20	21	22	23	24	25	26	27	28	29	30	31
☉	♐ 9	10	11	12	13	14	15	16	17	18	19	20	21	22	23	24	25	26	27	28	29	29 0	♑ 1	2	3	4	5	6	7	8	9
☽	♋ 20	♌ 4	18	♍ 1	16	♎ 0	14	28	♏ 13	27	♐ 11	24	♑ 8	21	♒ 4	16	29	♓ 11	23	♈ 4	16	28	♉ 10	23	♊ 6	19	♋ 2	16	♌ 0	14	28
☿	♏ 19	20	20	21	22	23	25	26	27	28	29 0	♐ 1	2	4	5	7	8	9	11	12	14	15	17	18	20	21	23	24	26	27	29
♀	♐ 14	16	17	18	19	21	22	23	24	26	27	28	29 0	♑ 1	2	3	4	6	7	8	9	11	12	13	14	16	17	18	19	21	22
♂	♍ 28	29	29 0	♎ 1	1	1	2	2	3	3	4	4	5	5	6	6	7	7	8	8	9	9	10	10	11	11	12	12	13	13	14

♃ 1℞ 8 21 31 / ♌4 3 2 1 — ♄ 1 6 31 / ♓22 23 24 — ♅ 1 30℞ / ♍24 24 — ♆ 1 14 / ♏22 23 — ♇ 1 23℞ / ♍20 20

1967

1

	1	2	3	4	5	6	7	8	9	10	11	12	13	14	15	16	17	18	19	20	21	22	23	24	25	26	27	28	29
☉	♑ 10	11	12	13	14	15	16	18	19	20	21	22	23	24	25	26	27	28	29	29 0	♒ 1	2	3	4	5	6	7	8	9
☽	♍ 13	27	♎ 11	25	♏ 9	23	♐ 6	20	♑ 3	16	29	♒ 12	24	♓ 7	19	♈ 0	12	24	♉ 6	18	♊ 1	13	27	♋ 10	24	♌ 9	23	♍ 8	23
☿	29 1	♑ 2	4	5	7	8	10	12	13	15	16	18	20	21	23	25	26	28	29 0	♒ 1	3	5	6	8	10	11	13	15	17
♀	♑ 23	24	26	27	28	29 0	♒ 1	2	3	4	6	7	8	9	11	12	13	14	16	17	18	20	21	22	23	25	26	27	28
♂	♎ 14	15	15	16	16	16	17	17	18	18	19	19	20	20	20	21	21	22	22	22	23	23	24	24	24	25	25	25	26

♃ 1℞ 8 16 0 17 23 31 / ♌1 0 29 ♋29 28 27 — ♄ 1 14 26 / ♓24 25 26 — ♅ 1℞ 29 / ♍24 23 — ♆ 1 20 / ♏23 24 — ♇ 1℞ / ♍20

2

	1	2	3	4	5	6	7	8	9	10	11	12	13	14	15	16	17	18	19	20	21	22	23	24	25	26	27	28
☉	♒ 12	13	14	15	16	17	18	19	20	21	22	23	24	25	26	27	28	29	29 0	♓ 1	2	3	4	5	6	7	8	9
☽	♏ 6	20	♐ 3	17	♑ 0	13	25	♒ 8	20	♓ 3	15	27	♈ 9	20	♉ 2	14	26	♊ 8	21	♋ 4	18	♌ 2	17	♍ 2	17	♎ 2	17	♏ 2
☿	♒ 22	24	25	27	29	29 1	♓ 2	4	6	7	9	10	12	13	14	15	16	17	18	18	18	18	℞ 18	18	18	17	16	16
♀	♓ 2	3	4	6	7	8	9	11	12	13	14	16	17	18	20	21	22	23	24	26	27	28	29 0	♈ 1	2	3	4	5
♂	♎ 27	27	27	27	28	28	28	28	29	29	29	29 0	♏ 0	0	0	1	1	1	1	1	1	2	2	2	2	2	2	3

♃ 1℞ 8 17 / ♋27 26 25 — ♄ 1 5 14 23 / ♓26 27 28 29 — ♅ 1℞ 27 / ♍23 22 — ♆ 1 24℞ / ♏24 24 — ♇ 1℞ / ♍20

3

	1	2	3	4	5	6	7	8	9	10	11	12	13	14	15	16	17	18	19	20	21	22	23	24	25	26	27	28	29
☉	♓ 10	11	12	13	14	15	16	17	18	19	20	21	22	23	24	25	26	27	28	29	29 0	♈ 1	2	3	4	5	6	7	8
☽	♏ 16	♐ 0	14	27	♑ 10	22	♒ 5	17	29	♓ 12	23	♈ 5	17	29	♉ 11	23	♊ 5	17	♋ 0	13	26	♌ 10	25	♍ 10	25	♎ 10	25	♏ 10	25
☿	♓℞ 15	14	13	12	11	10	9	8	7	6	6	5	5	4	4	4	D 4	4	4	5	5	5	6	7	7	8	9	9	10
♀	♈ 7	8	9	10	12	13	14	15	17	18	19	20	21	23	24	25	26	28	29	29 0	♉ 1	2	4	5	6	7	8	10	11
♂	♏ 2	2	3	3	3	3	3	℞ 3	3	3	3	3	3	2	2	2	2	2	2	2	2	1	1	1	1	1	0	0	0

♃ 1℞ 2 21D / ♋25 24 24 — ♄ 1 3 29 4 11 20 28 / ♓29 0 ♈0 1 2 3 — ♅ 1℞ 22 / ♍22 21 — ♆ 1℞ / ♏24 — ♇ 1℞ / ♍19

4

	1	2	3	4	5	6	7	8	9	10	11	12	13	14	15	16	17	18	19	20	21	22	23	24	25	26	27	28	29
☉	♈ 11	12	13	14	15	16	17	18	19	20	21	22	23	24	25	26	27	28	29	29 0	♉ 1	2	3	4	5	6	7	8	8
☽	♑ 6	19	♒ 2	14	27	♓ 9	20	♈ 2	14	26	♉ 8	20	♊ 2	14	26	♋ 9	22	♌ 6	19	♍ 4	18	♎ 3	18	♏ 3	18	♐ 3	18	♑ 2	15
☿	♓ 13	14	15	16	18	19	20	21	23	24	25	27	28	29 0	♈ 1	3	4	6	7	9	11	12	14	16	18	19	21	23	25
♀	♉ 14	16	17	18	19	20	22	23	24	25	26	28	29	29 0	♊ 1	2	3	5	6	7	8	9	11	12	13	14	15	16	18
♂	♎℞ 29	29	28	28	28	27	27	27	26	26	26	25	25	25	24	24	23	23	23	22	22	21	21	21	20	20	20	19	19

♃ 1 9 22 / ♋24 25 26 — ♄ 1 5 13 21 30 / ♈3 4 5 6 7 — ♅ 1℞ 17 / ♍21 20 — ♆ 1℞ 2 / ♏24 23 — ♇ 1℞ / ♍18

5

	1	2	3	4	5	6	7	8	9	10	11	12	13	14	15	16	17	18	19	20	21	22	23	24	25	26	27	28	29
☉	♉ 10	11	12	13	14	15	16	17	18	19	20	21	22	23	24	25	26	27	28	29	29 0	♊ 1	2	3	4	5	6	6	7
☽	♒ 11	23	♓ 5	17	29	♈ 11	23	♉ 5	17	29	♊ 11	23	♋ 6	19	♌ 2	16	29	♍ 13	28	♎ 12	27	♏ 12	27	♐ 11	26	♑ 10	23	♒ 7	19
☿	29 0	♉ 1	3	5	7	9	11	13	15	18	20	22	24	26	29	29 1	♊ 3	5	7	9	11	13	15	17	19	21	23	24	26
♀	♊ 20	21	22	23	24	26	27	28	29	29 0	♋ 1	2	4	5	6	7	8	9	10	11	12	14	15	16	17	18	19	20	21
♂	♎℞ 18	18	18	17	17	17	17	16	16	16	16	16	15	15	15	15	15	15	15	15	15	15	15	14	14	D 14	15	15	15

♃ 1 9 16 23 29 24 29 / ♋27 28 29 0 ♌0 1 — ♄ 1 9 19 30 / ♈7 8 9 10 — ♅ 1℞ 28D / ♍20 20 — ♆ 1℞ 13 / ♏23 22 — ♇ 1℞ / ♍18

6

	1	2	3	4	5	6	7	8	9	10	11	12	13	14	15	16	17	18	19	20	21	22	23	24	25	26	27	28	29
☉	♊ 10	11	12	13	14	15	16	17	18	19	20	21	22	23	24	25	26	27	28	28	29	29 0	♋ 1	2	3	4	5	6	7
☽	♓ 26	♈ 8	19	♉ 1	13	25	♊ 8	20	♋ 3	16	29	♌ 13	26	♍ 10	24	♎ 8	22	♏ 7	21	♐ 6	20	♑ 4	18	♒ 1	15	27	♓ 10	22	♈ 4
☿	♋ 1	3	4	5	7	8	9	11	12	13	14	15	16	17	18	18	19	20	20	21	21	21	21	21	21	℞ 21	21	21	21
♀	♋ 24	25	26	28	29	29 0	♌ 1	2	3	4	5	6	7	8	9	10	11	12	13	14	15	16	17	17	18	19	20	21	22
♂	♎ 15	15	15	15	15	15	15	16	16	16	16	16	17	17	17	17	18	18	18	18	19	19	19	20	20	20	20	21	21

♃ 1 4 9 14 20 25 30 / ♌1 2 3 4 5 6 7 — ♄ 1 13 / ♈10 11 — ♅ 1 / ♍20 — ♆ 1℞ 23 / ♏22 21 — ♇ 1 / ♍17

7

	1	2	3	4	5	6	7	8	9	10	11	12	13	14	15	16	17	18	19	20	21	22	23	24	25	26	27	28	29
☉	♋ 9	10	11	12	13	14	15	16	17	18	19	19	20	21	22	23	24	25	26	27	28	29	29 0	♌ 1	2	3	4	5	6
☽	♈ 28	♉ 9	21	♊ 4	16	29	♋ 12	25	♌ 9	23	♍ 7	21	♎ 5	19	♏ 3	17	♐ 1	15	29	♑ 13	26	♒ 10	23	♓ 5	18	♈ 0	12	24	♉ 5
☿	♋℞ 20	20	19	19	18	18	17	16	16	15	15	14	14	13	13	12	12	12	12	D 12	12	12	12	13	13	14	14	15	16
♀	♌ 24	25	25	26	27	28	29	29 0	♍ 0	1	2	3	3	4	5	5	6	7	7	8	8	9	9	10	10	11	11	12	12
♂	♎ 22	22	23	23	24	24	24	25	25	26	26	26	27	27	28	28	29	29	29 0	♏ 0	1	1	2	2	3	3	4	4	5

♃ 1 4 9 14 19 23 28 / ♌7 8 9 10 11 12 13 — ♄ 1 25℞ / ♈12 12 — ♅ 1 8 / ♍20 21 — ♆ 1℞ / ♍21 — ♇ 1 / ♍18

8

	1	2	3	4	5	6	7	8	9	10	11	12	13	14	15	16	17	18	19	20	21	22	23	24	25	26	27	28	29
☉	♌ 9	10	10	11	12	13	14	15	16	17	18	19	20	21	22	23	24	25	26	27	28	29	29 0	♍ 1	2	3	4	4	5
☽	♊ 12	24	♋ 7	20	♌ 4	18	♍ 2	17	♎ 1	16	♏ 0	14	28	♐ 12	26	♑ 9	23	♒ 6	19	♓ 1	14	26	♈ 8	20	♉ 2	13	25	♊ 7	20
☿	♋ 19	20	22	23	24	26	27	29 0	♌ 1	3	4	6	8	10	12	14	16	18	20	22	24	26	28	29 0	♍ 2	4	6	8	10
♀	♍ 13	13	13	13	13	13	13	℞ 13	13	13	13	13	13	13	12	12	12	11	11	10	10	9	9	8	8	7	7	6	5
♂	♏ 6	7	7	8	8	9	9	10	10	11	12	12	13	13	14	15	15	16	16	17	18	18	19	19	20	21	21	22	22

♃ 1 6 10 15 20 24 29 / ♌14 15 16 17 18 19 20 — ♄ 1℞ 17 / ♈12 11 — ♅ 1 19 / ♍22 23 — ♆ 1℞ 3D / ♏21 21 — ♇ 1 / ♍18

9

	1	2	3	4	5	6	7	8	9	10	11	12	13	14	15	16	17	18	19	20	21	22	23	24	25	26	27	28	29
☉	♍ 8	9	10	11	12	13	14	15	16	17	18	19	20	21	22	23	24	25	26	27	28	29	29 0	♎ 1	2	3	4	5	6
☽	♋ 29	♌ 12	27	♍ 11	26	♎ 11	26	♏ 10	25	♐ 9	23	♑ 6	19	♒ 2	15	28	♓ 10	22	♈ 4	16	28	♉ 10	22	♊ 4	16	28	♋ 10	23	♌ 7
☿	♍ 16	17	19	21	23	24	26	28	29 0	♎ 1	3	4	6	8	9	11	12	14	15	17	18	20	21	22	24	25	27	28	29
♀	♍℞ 3	3	2	2	1	1	0	0	0 29	♌ 29	29	28	28	28	28	27	27	27	27	D 27	27	27	27	28	28	28	28	29	29
♂	♏ 24	25	26	26	27	28	28	29	29	29 0	♐ 1	1	2	3	3	4	5	5	6	7	7	8	9	10	10	11	12	12	13

♃ 1 2 7 12 17 22 27 / ♌20 21 22 23 24 25 26 — ♄ 1℞ 6 20 / ♈11 10 9 — ♅ 1 5 21 / ♍23 24 25 — ♆ 1 12 / ♏21 22 — ♇ 1 / ♍19

10

	1	2	3	4	5	6	7	8	9	10	11	12	13	14	15	16	17	18	19	20	21	22	23	24	25	26	27	28	29
☉	♎ 8	9	10	11	12	13	14	15	16	16	17	18	19	20	21	22	23	24	25	26	27	28	29	29 0	♏ 1	2	3	4	5
☽	♍ 5	20	♎ 4	20	♏ 5	20	♐ 4	19	♑ 3	16	29	♒ 12	25	♓ 7	19	♈ 1	13	25	♉ 7	19	♊ 1	12	25	♋ 7	19	♌ 2	15	29	♍ 13
☿	♏ 2	3	4	5	6	7	9	10	11	11	12	13	14	15	15	16	16	17	17	17	℞ 17	17	16	16	15	14	14	13	11
♀	29 0	♍ 0	1	1	1	2	3	3	4	4	5	6	6	7	8	8	9	10	11	11	12	13	14	15	16	16	17	18	19
♂	♐ 14	15	16	16	17	18	19	19	20	21	21	22	23	24	24	25	26	26	27	28	29	29	29 0	♑ 1	2	2	3	4	5

♃ 1 2 7 13 19 29 20 25 / ♌26 27 28 29 0 ♍0 1 — ♄ 1℞ 3 15 30 / ♈9 8 7 6 — ♅ 1 7 24 / ♍25 26 27 — ♆ 1 18 / ♏22 23 — ♇ 1 / ♍21

11

	1	2	3	4	5	6	7	8	9	10	11	12	13	14	15	16	17	18	19	20	21	22	23	24	25	26	27	28	29
☉	♏ 8	9	10	11	12	13	14	15	16	17	18	19	20	21	22	23	24	25	26	27	28	29	29 1	♐ 2	3	4	5	6	7
☽	♎ 28	♏ 13	28	♐ 13	28	♑ 12	25	♒ 9	22	♓ 4	16	28	♈ 10	22	♉ 4	16	28	♊ 9	22	♋ 4	16	29	♌ 12	25	♍ 8	22	♎ 7	21	♏ 6
☿	♏℞ 8	6	5	4	3	2	2	1	1	D 1	1	1	2	3	3	4	5	6	7	8	9	11	12	13	15	16	18	19	21
♀	♍ 22	23	24	25	26	27	28	29	29 0	♎ 1	2	3	4	5	6	7	8	9	10	11	12	13	14	15	17	18	19	20	21
♂	♑ 7	8	8	9	10	11	11	12	13	14	14	15	16	17	17	18	19	20	20	21	22	23	23	24	25	26	27	27	28

♃ 1 9 17 29 / ♍2 3 4 5 — ♄ 1℞ 19 / ♈6 5 — ♅ 1 13 / ♍27 28 — ♆ 1 14 / ♏23 24 — ♇ 1 / ♍22

12

	1	2	3	4	5	6	7	8	9	10	11	12	13	14	15	16	17	18	19	20	21	22	23	24	25	26	27	28	29
☉	♐ 9	10	11	12	13	14	15	16	17	18	19	20	21	22	23	24	25	26	27	28	29	29 0	♑ 1	2	3	4	5	6	7
☽	♐ 6	21	♑ 6	20	♒ 4	17	♓ 0	13	25	♈ 7	19	♉ 1	12	24	♊ 6	18	♋ 1	13	26	♌ 9	22	♍ 5	19	♎ 2	16	♏ 1	15	♐ 0	14
☿	♏ 24	25	27	28	29 0	♐ 1	3	4	6	7	9	11	12	14	15	17	18	20	21	23	25	26	28	29 0	♑ 1	2	4	6	7
♀	♎ 23	24	25	27	28	29	29 0	♏ 1	2	3	5	6	7	8	9	10	12	13	14	15	16	17	19	20	21	22	23	25	26
♂	29 0	♒ 0	1	2	3	3	4	5	6	7	7	8	9	10	10	11	12	13	14	14	15	16	17	17	18	19	20	21	21

♃ 1 22℞ / ♍5 5 — ♄ 1℞ 9D 28 / ♈5 5 6 — ♅ 1 13 / ♍28 29 — ♆ 1 11 / ♏24 25 — ♇ 1 / ♍22

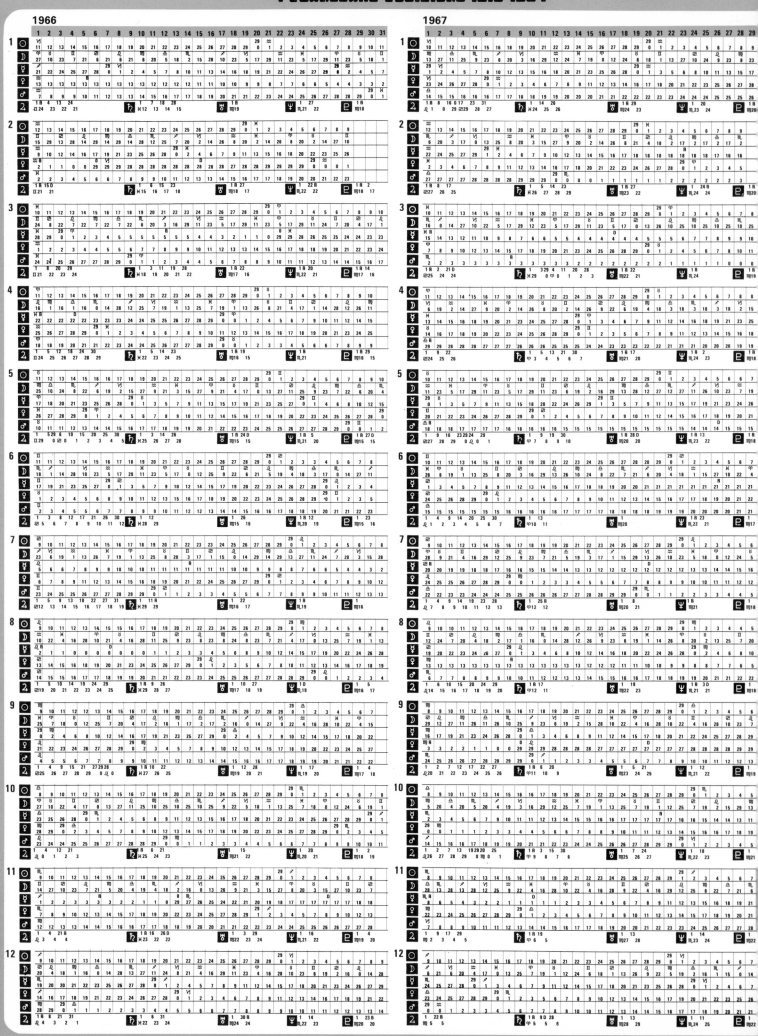

1968

1

	1	2	3	4	5	6	7	8	9	10	11	12	13	14	15	16	17	18	19	20	21	22	23	24	25	26	27	28	29	30	31
☉	♑ 10	11	12	13	14	15	16	17	18	19	20	21	22	23	24	25	26	27	28	29	29 1	♒ 2	3	4	5	6	7	8	9	10	11
☽	♑ 28	♒ 12	25	♓ 8	21	♈ 3	15	27	♉ 9	20	♊ 2	14	27	♋ 9	22	♌ 5	19	♍ 2	16	29	♎ 13	27	♏ 11	25	♐ 10	24	♑ 8	22	♒ 6	20	♓ 3
☿	♑ 12	14	15	17	19	20	22	24	25	27	29	29 0	♒ 2	4	5	7	9	10	12	13	15	17	18	20	21	23	24	25	27	28	29
♀	29 0	♐ 1	2	3	4	5	7	8	9	10	11	13	14	15	16	17	19	20	21	22	23	25	26	27	28	29 0	♑ 1	2	3	4	6
♂	♒ 24	24	25	26	27	28	28	29	29 0	♓ 1	1	2	3	4	5	5	6	7	8	8	9	10	11	12	12	13	14	15	15	16	17

♃	♄	♅	♆	♇
1 R 14 25 ♍ 5 4 3	1 17 30 ♈ 6 7 8	1 4 R 25 ♍ 29 29 28	1 14 ♏ 25 26	1 R ♍ 22

2

	1	2	3	4	5	6	7	8	9	10	11	12	13	14	15	16	17	18	19	20	21	22	23	24	25	26	27	28	29	30	31
☉	♒ 12	13	14	15	16	17	18	19	20	21	22	23	24	25	26	27	28	29	29 0	♓ 1	2	3	4	5	6	7	8	9	10		
☽	♓ 16	28	♈ 11	23	♉ 5	16	28	♊ 10	22	♋ 5	17	♌ 0	14	28	♍ 11	25	♎ 10	24	♏ 8	22	♐ 6	20	♑ 4	18	♒ 2	15	28	♓ 11	24		
☿	29 0	♓ 1	1	2	2	R 2	2	1	1	0	0 29	♒ 28	27	26	25	24	23	22	21	20	19	18	18	17	17	17	17	D 17	17		
♀	♑ 7	8	9	11	12	13	14	15	17	18	19	20	22	23	24	25	27	28	29	29 0	♒ 1	3	4	5	6	8	9	10	11		
♂	♓ 18	19	19	20	21	22	22	23	24	25	26	26	27	28	29	29	29 0	♈ 1	2	2	3	4	5	5	6	7	8	9	9		

♃	♄	♅	♆	♇
1 R 3 11 19 27 0 28 ♍ 3 2 1 0 29 ♌ 29	1 10 20 29 ♈ 8 9 10 11	1 R 27 ♍ 28 27	1 27 R ♏ 26 26	1 R 23 ♍ 22 21

3

	1	2	3	4	5	6	7	8	9	10	11	12	13	14	15	16	17	18	19	20	21	22	23	24	25	26	27	28	29	30	31
☉	♓ 11	12	13	14	15	16	17	18	19	20	21	22	23	24	25	26	27	28	29	29 0	♈ 1	2	3	4	5	6	7	8	9	10	11
☽	♈ 6	19	♉ 1	12	24	♊ 6	18	♋ 0	13	25	♌ 8	22	♍ 6	20	♎ 4	19	♏ 4	18	♐ 3	17	♑ 1	15	29	♒ 12	25	♓ 8	20	♈ 3	15	27	♉ 9
☿	♒ 17	17	18	18	19	19	20	21	22	22	23	24	25	26	27	29	29 0	♓ 1	2	3	5	6	7	9	10	12	13	14	16	18	19
♀	♒ 13	14	15	16	17	19	20	21	22	24	25	26	27	29	29 0	♓ 1	2	3	5	6	7	8	10	11	12	13	15	16	17	18	19
♂	♈ 10	11	12	12	13	14	15	15	16	17	18	18	19	20	21	21	22	23	24	24	25	26	27	27	28	29	29 0	♉ 0	1	2	2

♃	♄	♅	♆	♇
1 R 6 14 25 ♌ 29 28 27 26	1 8 17 25 ♈ 11 12 13 14	1 R 21 ♍ 27 26	1 R ♏ 26	1 R ♍ 21

4

	1	2	3	4	5	6	7	8	9	10	11	12	13	14	15	16	17	18	19	20	21	22	23	24	25	26	27	28	29	30	31
☉	♈ 12	13	14	15	16	17	18	19	20	21	22	23	24	25	26	27	28	29	29	29 0	♉ 1	2	3	4	5	6	7	8	9	10	
☽	♉ 21	♊ 2	14	26	♋ 8	21	♌ 3	16	♍ 0	14	28	♎ 13	28	♏ 13	28	♐ 13	27	♑ 11	25	♒ 9	22	♓ 5	17	♈ 0	12	24	♉ 6	17	29	♊ 11	
☿	♓ 21	22	24	26	27	29	29 1	♈ 2	4	6	8	10	12	13	15	17	19	21	23	25	27	29 0	♉ 2	4	6	8	10	12	14	17	
♀	♓ 21	22	23	24	26	27	28	29 0	♈ 1	2	3	4	6	7	8	9	10	12	13	14	15	17	18	19	20	22	23	24	25	26	
♂	♉ 3	4	5	5	6	7	8	8	9	10	10	11	12	13	13	14	15	16	16	17	18	18	19	20	21	21	22	23	23	24	

♃	♄	♅	♆	♇
1 R 11 22 D ♌ 26 25 25	1 2 10 18 26 ♈ 14 15 16 17 18	1 R 15 ♍ 26 25	1 R 12 ♏ 26 25	1 R 2 ♍ 21 20

5

	1	2	3	4	5	6	7	8	9	10	11	12	13	14	15	16	17	18	19	20	21	22	23	24	25	26	27	28	29	30	31
☉	♉ 11	12	13	14	15	16	17	18	19	20	21	22	23	24	25	26	27	28	29	29 0	♊ 0	1	2	3	4	5	6	7	8	9	10
☽	♊ 23	♋ 5	17	29	♌ 12	25	♍ 8	22	♎ 6	21	♏ 6	21	♐ 6	21	♑ 6	21	♒ 5	18	♓ 2	14	27	♈ 9	21	♉ 3	14	26	♊ 8	20	♋ 2	14	26
☿	♉ 19	21	23	25	27	29 0	♊ 1	3	5	6	8	10	12	13	15	16	18	19	20	21	23	24	25	26	27	28	28	29	29 0	♋ 0	1
♀	♈ 28	29	29 0	♉ 1	3	4	5	6	7	9	10	11	12	14	15	16	17	19	20	21	22	23	25	26	27	28	29 0	♊ 1	2	3	5
♂	♉ 25	26	26	27	28	28	29	29 0	♊ 0	1	2	3	3	4	5	5	6	7	7	8	9	10	10	11	12	12	13	14	14	15	16

♃	♄	♅	♆	♇
1 2 19 30 ♌ 25 26 27 28	1 4 13 22 ♈ 18 19 20 21	1 R ♍ 25	1 R 21 ♏ 25 24	1 R 31 D ♍ 20 20

6

	1	2	3	4	5	6	7	8	9	10	11	12	13	14	15	16	17	18	19	20	21	22	23	24	25	26	27	28	29	30	31
☉	♊ 11	12	13	14	15	16	17	18	19	20	21	22	23	23	24	25	26	27	28	29	29 0	♋ 1	2	3	4	5	6	7	8	9	
☽	♌ 9	21	♍ 4	17	♎ 1	15	♏ 0	14	29	♐ 15	♑ 0	15	29	♒ 14	27	♓ 10	23	♈ 6	18	♉ 0	11	23	♊ 5	17	29	♋ 11	23	♌ 6	18	♍ 1	
☿	♋ 1	1	1	1	2	R 2	1	1	1	1	0	0	0 29	♊ 29	28	28	27	27	26	26	25	25	24	24	23	23	23	23	23	D 23	
♀	♊ 6	7	8	9	11	12	13	14	16	17	18	19	20	22	23	24	25	27	28	29	29 0	♋ 2	3	4	5	6	8	9	10	11	
♂	♊ 16	17	18	19	19	20	21	21	22	23	23	24	25	25	26	27	27	28	29	29	29 0	♋ 1	1	2	3	3	4	5	5	6	

♃	♄	♅	♆	♇
1 8 15 29 16 22 28 ♌ 28 29 0 ♍ 0 1 2	1 12 24 ♈ 22 23 24	1 R 2 D ♍ 25 25	1 R ♏ 24	1 ♍ 20

7

	1	2	3	4	5	6	7	8	9	10	11	12	13	14	15	16	17	18	19	20	21	22	23	24	25	26	27	28	29	30	31
☉	♋ 10	11	12	13	14	14	15	16	17	18	19	20	21	22	23	24	25	26	27	28	29	29 0	♌ 1	2	3	4	4	5	6	7	8
☽	♍ 14	27	♎ 11	25	♏ 9	24	♐ 8	23	♑ 8	23	♒ 8	22	♓ 5	19	♈ 1	14	26	♉ 8	20	♊ 2	14	26	♋ 8	20	♌ 2	15	28	♍ 11	24	♎ 8	22
☿	♊ 23	23	24	24	24	25	25	26	27	27	28	29	29 0	♋ 1	3	4	5	7	8	10	11	13	15	17	18	20	22	24	26	28	29 0
♀	13	14	15	16	18	19	20	21	22	24	25	26	27	29	29 0	♌ 1	2	3	5	6	7	8	10	11	12	13	15	16	17	18	19
♂	♋ 7	7	8	9	9	10	11	11	12	13	13	14	15	15	16	17	17	18	19	19	20	21	21	22	23	23	24	25	25	26	26

♃	♄	♅	♆	♇
1 4 10 15 21 26 31 ♍ 2 3 4 5 6 7 8	1 12 ♈ 24 25	1 18 ♍ 25 26	1 R 5 ♏ 24 23	1 27 ♍ 20 21

8

	1	2	3	4	5	6	7	8	9	10	11	12	13	14	15	16	17	18	19	20	21	22	23	24	25	26	27	28	29	30	31
☉	♌ 9	10	11	12	13	14	15	16	17	18	19	20	21	22	23	24	25	26	27	28	28	29	29 0	♍ 1	2	3	4	5	6	7	8
☽	♏ 6	20	♐ 4	18	♑ 3	17	♒ 2	16	♓ 0	14	27	♈ 9	22	♉ 4	16	28	♊ 10	22	♋ 4	16	28	♌ 11	24	♍ 7	21	♎ 5	18	♏ 2	16	♐ 1	15
☿	♌ 2	5	7	9	11	13	15	17	19	21	23	25	27	29	29 1	♍ 3	4	6	8	10	12	13	15	17	18	20	22	23	25	26	28
♀	♌ 21	22	23	24	26	27	28	29 0	♍ 10	2	3	4	6	7	8	9	10	12	13	14	15	17	18	19	20	22	23	24	25	26	28
♂	♋ 27	28	28	29	29 0	♌ 0	1	2	2	3	4	4	5	6	6	7	7	8	9	9	10	11	11	12	13	13	14	14	15	16	16

♃	♄	♅	♆	♇
1 5 10 14 19 24 28 ♍ 8 9 10 11 12 13 14	1 6 R ♈ 25 25	1 9 27 ♍ 26 27 28	1 R 5 D ♏ 23 23	1 27 ♍ 21 22

9

	1	2	3	4	5	6	7	8	9	10	11	12	13	14	15	16	17	18	19	20	21	22	23	24	25	26	27	28	29	30	31
☉	♍ 9	10	11	12	13	14	15	16	17	18	19	20	21	22	23	24	25	26	27	28	29	29 0	♎ 1	1	2	3	4	5	6	7	
☽	♐ 29	♑ 13	27	♒ 11	25	♓ 9	22	♈ 5	17	♉ 0	12	24	♊ 6	18	♋ 0	12	24	♌ 6	19	♍ 2	16	♎ 0	14	28	♏ 12	27	♐ 12	26	♑ 10	24	
☿	29 0	♎ 1	3	4	5	7	8	10	11	12	13	15	16	17	18	19	21	22	23	24	25	26	26	27	28	29	29	29 0	♏ 0	1	
♀	♍ 29	♎ 0	1	3	4	5	6	8	9	10	11	12	14	15	16	17	19	20	21	22	23	25	26	27	28	29 0	♏ 1	2	3	5	
♂	♌ 17	18	19	20	20	20	21	21	22	23	23	24	25	25	26	27	27	28	28	29	29 0	♍ 0	1	2	2	3	3	4	5	5	

♃	♄	♅	♆	♇
1 2 7 11 16 21 25 30 ♍ 14 15 16 17 18 19 20 21	1 R 19 ♈ 24 23	1 12 28 29 29 ♍ 28 29 0 ♎ 0	1 3 ♏ 23 24	1 24 ♍ 22 23

10

	1	2	3	4	5	6	7	8	9	10	11	12	13	14	15	16	17	18	19	20	21	22	23	24	25	26	27	28	29	30	31
☉	♎ 8	9	10	11	12	13	14	15	16	17	18	19	20	21	22	23	24	25	26	27	28	29	29 0	♏ 1	2	3	4	5	6	7	8
☽	♒ 8	21	♓ 5	18	♈ 1	13	26	♉ 8	20	♊ 2	14	26	♋ 8	20	♌ 2	14	27	♍ 10	24	♎ 8	22	♏ 7	22	♐ 7	22	♑ 6	21	♒ 5	18	♓ 2	15
☿	♏ 1	1	R 1	1	1	0	0	0 29	♎ 28	27	26	25	24	23	22	20	19	18	17	16	16	15	15	D 15	15	16	16	17	18	18	19
♀	♏ 6	7	8	9	11	12	13	14	16	17	18	19	20	22	23	24	25	27	28	29	29 0	♐ 1	3	4	5	6	8	9	10	11	12
♂	♍ 6	7	7	8	8	9	10	10	11	12	12	13	13	14	15	15	16	17	17	18	18	19	20	20	21	21	22	23	23	24	25

♃	♄	♅	♆	♇
1 5 9 14 19 24 30 ♍ 21 22 23 24 25 26 27	1 R 3 16 29 ♈ 23 22 21 20	1 14 ♎ 0 1	1 13 ♏ 24 25	1 23 ♍ 23 24

11

	1	2	3	4	5	6	7	8	9	10	11	12	13	14	15	16	17	18	19	20	21	22	23	24	25	26	27	28	29	30	31
☉	♏ 9	10	11	12	13	14	15	16	17	18	19	20	21	22	23	24	25	26	27	28	29	29 0	♐ 1	2	3	4	5	6	7	8	
☽	♓ 27	♈ 10	22	♉ 4	16	28	♊ 10	22	♋ 4	16	28	♌ 10	23	♍ 5	18	♎ 2	16	♏ 0	15	♐ 0	16	♑ 1	16	♒ 0	15	28	♓ 11	24	♈ 7	19	
☿	♎ 21	22	23	24	26	27	28	29 0	♏ 1	3	4	6	8	9	11	12	14	16	17	19	20	22	23	25	27	28	29 0	♐ 1	3	5	
♀	♐ 14	15	16	17	18	20	21	22	23	25	26	27	28	29 0	♑ 1	2	3	4	5	7	8	9	10	11	13	14	15	16	17	19	
♂	♍ 25	26	26	27	28	28	29	29	29 0	♎ 1	1	2	2	3	4	4	5	5	6	7	7	8	8	9	10	10	11	11	12	13	

♃	♄	♅	♆	♇
1 4 10 15 29 16 22 28 ♍ 27 28 29 0 ♎ 0 1 2	1 R 12 ♈ 20 19	1 22 ♎ 2 3	1 11 ♏ 25 26	1 ♍ 24

12

	1	2	3	4	5	6	7	8	9	10	11	12	13	14	15	16	17	18	19	20	21	22	23	24	25	26	27	28	29	30	31
☉	♐ 9	10	11	12	13	14	15	16	17	19	20	21	22	23	24	25	26	27	28	29	29 0	♑ 1	2	3	4	5	6	7	8	9	10
☽	♉ 1	13	25	♊ 7	19	♋ 1	13	25	♌ 7	19	♍ 1	14	27	♎ 10	24	♏ 9	23	♐ 8	24	♑ 9	24	♒ 9	23	♓ 7	21	♈ 4	16	28	♉ 10	22	♊ 4
☿	♐ 6	8	9	11	12	14	16	17	19	20	22	23	25	27	28	29 0	♑ 1	3	4	6	8	9	11	12	14	16	17	18	20	22	24
♀	♑ 20	21	22	23	25	26	27	28	29 0	♒ 1	2	3	4	5	6	8	9	10	11	12	13	15	16	17	18	19	20	22	23	24	25
♂	♎ 13	14	14	15	16	16	17	17	18	19	19	20	20	21	22	22	23	23	24	24	25	26	26	27	27	28	28	29	29 0	♏ 0	1

♃	♄	♅	♆	♇
1 6 14 25 ♎ 2 3 4 5	1 R 3 21 D ♈ 19 18 18	1 ♎ 3	1 8 ♏ 26 27	1 7 27 R ♍ 24 25 25

1969

1

	1	2	3	4	5	6	7	8	9	10	11	12	13	14	15	16	17	18	19	20	21	22	23	24	25	26	27	28	29	30	31
☉	♑ 11	12	13	14	15	16	17	18	19	20	21	22	23	24	25	26	27	28	29	29 0	♒ 1	2	3	4	5	6	7	8	9	10	11
☽	♊ 16	28	♋ 10	22	♌ 4	16	28	♍ 11	24	♎ 7	20	♏ 4	18	♐ 2	17	♑ 2	17	♒ 2	17	♓ 1	15	29	♈ 12	25	♉ 7	19	♊ 1	13	25	♋ 6	18
☿	♑ 25	27	28	29 0	♒ 1	3	4	6	7	8	10	11	12	13	14	14	15	15	15	R 16	15	15	14	14	13	12	11	9	8	7	6
♀	♒ 26	27	28	29 0	♓ 1	2	3	4	5	6	7	8	9	11	12	13	14	15	16	17	18	19	20	21	22	23	24	25	26	27	28
♂	♏ 1	2	2	3	4	4	5	5	6	6	7	7	8	9	9	10	10	11	11	12	12	13	13	14	15	15	16	16	17	17	18

♃	♄	♅	♆	♇
1 14 20 R 26 ♎ 5 6 6 5	1 8 28 ♈ 18 19 20	1 2 8 R 13 ♎ 3 4 4 3	1 8 ♏ 27 28	1 R 16 ♍ 25 24

2

	1	2	3	4	5	6	7	8	9	10	11	12	13	14	15	16	17	18	19	20	21	22	23	24	25	26	27	28	29	30	31
☉	♒ 12	13	14	16	17	18	19	20	21	22	23	24	25	26	27	28	29	29 0	♓ 1	2	3	4	5	6	7	8	9	10			
☽	♌ 1	13	25	♍ 8	21	♎ 4	17	♏ 0	14	28	♐ 12	27	♑ 11	26	♒ 11	25	♓ 9	23	♈ 7	20	♉ 2	15	27	♊ 9	21	♋ 3	15	27			
☿	♒ R 5	3	3	2	1	1	0	0	0	D 0	0	0	0	1	1	2	3	3	4	5	6	7	8	9	10	11	12	13			
♀	♓ 29	29 0	♈ 1	2	3	4	5	6	7	8	8	9	10	11	12	13	13	14	15	16	16	17	18	19	19	20	20	21			
♂	♏ 18	19	19	20	20	21	21	22	22	23	23	24	24	25	25	26	26	27	27	28	28	29	29	29	29 0	♐ 0	1	1			

♃	♄	♅	♆	♇
1 R 15 26 ♎ 5 4 3	1 10 22 ♈ 20 21 22	1 R 26 ♎ 3 2	1 28 R ♏ 28 28	1 R ♍ 24

3

	1	2	3	4	5	6	7	8	9	10	11	12	13	14	15	16	17	18	19	20	21	22	23	24	25	26	27	28	29	30	31
☉	♓ 11	12	13	14	15	16	17	18	19	20	21	22	23	24	25	26	27	28	29	29 0	♈ 1	2	3	4	5	6	7	8	9	10	11
☽	♌ 9	21	♍ 4	17	♎ 0	13	27	♏ 11	25	♐ 9	23	♑ 7	21	♒ 6	20	♓ 4	18	♈ 1	15	28	♉ 10	23	♊ 5	17	29	♋ 11	23	♌ 5	17	29	♍ 12
☿	♒ 15	16	17	18	20	21	22	24	25	27	28	29 0	♓ 1	3	4	6	7	9	11	12	14	16	17	19	21	23	24	26	28	29 0	♈ 2
♀	♈ 22	22	23	23	24	24	24	25	25	25	26	26	26	26	26	26	26	R 26	26	26	26	26	26	25	25	25	25	24	24	23	23
♂	♐ 2	2	3	3	3	4	4	5	5	5	6	6	7	7	7	8	8	9	9	9	10	10	10	11	11	11	11	12	12	12	13

♃	♄	♅	♆	♇
1 R 7 15 23 30 0 31 ♎ 3 2 1 0 29 ♍ 29	1 3 12 21 29 ♈ 22 23 24 25 26	1 R 22 ♎ 2 1	1 R ♏ 28	1 R 6 ♍ 24 23

4

	1	2	3	4	5	6	7	8	9	10	11	12	13	14	15	16	17	18	19	20	21	22	23	24	25	26	27	28	29	30	31
☉	♈ 12	13	14	15	16	17	17	18	19	20	21	22	23	24	25	26	27	28	29	29 0	♉ 1	2	3	4	5	6	7	8	9	10	
☽	♍ 25	♎ 9	23	♏ 7	21	♐ 5	20	♑ 4	18	♒ 2	16	♓ 0	14	27	♈ 10	23	♉ 6	18	♊ 1	13	25	♋ 7	18	♌ 0	12	25	♍ 7	20	♎ 3	17	
☿	♈ 4	6	8	10	12	14	16	18	20	22	24	26	28	29 0	♉ 2	5	7	9	11	13	15	17	18	20	22	24	25	27	28	29 0	
♀	♈ R 22	22	21	20	20	19	19	18	17	17	16	15	15	14	14	13	13	12	12	12	11	11	11	10	10	10	10	10	10	D 10	
♂	♐ 13	13	13	13	14	14	14	14	15	15	15	15	15	15	16	16	16	16	16	16	16	16	16	16	16	16	R 16	16	16	16	

♃	♄	♅	♆	♇
1 R 8 17 29 ♍ 29 28 27 26	1 6 14 21 29 29 30 ♈ 26 27 28 29 0 ♉ 0	1 R 15 ♎ 1 0	1 R 23 ♏ 28 27	1 R 15 ♍ 23 22

5

	1	2	3	4	5	6	7	8	9	10	11	12	13	14	15	16	17	18	19	20	21	22	23	24	25	26	27	28	29	30	31
☉	♉ 11	12	13	14	15	16	17	18	19	20	21	22	23	24	24	25	26	27	28	29	29 0	♊ 1	2	3	4	5	6	7	8	9	10
☽	♏ 1	16	♐ 0	15	♑ 0	15	29	♒ 13	27	♓ 10	24	♈ 7	20	♉ 2	15	27	♊ 9	21	♋ 3	15	27	♌ 9	21	♍ 3	15	28	♎ 11	25	♏ 9	24	♐ 9
☿	♊ 1	2	4	5	6	7	7	8	9	10	10	11	11	11	11	11	R 12	11	11	11	11	11	10	10	9	9	8	8	7	6	6
♀	♈ 10	10	10	11	11	11	11	12	12	12	13	13	14	14	15	15	16	16	17	17	18	19	19	20	21	21	22	23	24	24	25
♂	♐ R 16	16	16	16	16	16	16	15	15	15	15	15	15	14	14	14	14	13	13	13	13	12	12	12	11	11	11	10	10	10	9

♃	♄	♅	♆	♇
1 R 23 D ♍ 26 26	1 7 16 24 ♉ 0 1 2 3	1 R 20 0 21 ♎ 0 29 ♍ 29	1 R 30 ♏ 27 26	1 R ♍ 22

6

	1	2	3	4	5	6	7	8	9	10	11	12	13	14	15	16	17	18	19	20	21	22	23	24	25	26	27	28	29	30	31
☉	♊ 11	12	13	14	15	16	17	18	18	19	20	21	22	23	24	25	26	27	28	29	29 0	♋ 1	2	3	4	5	6	7	8	9	
☽	♐ 24	♑ 9	24	♒ 9	23	♓ 7	21	♈ 4	17	29	♉ 12	24	♊ 6	18	♋ 0	12	24	♌ 5	17	29	♍ 12	24	♎ 7	20	♏ 4	18	♐ 2	17	♑ 3	18	
☿	♊ R 5	5	4	4	4	3	3	3	3	D 3	3	3	3	4	4	4	5	6	6	7	8	9	9	10	12	13	14	15	16	18	
♀	♈ 26	27	28	29	29	29 0	♉ 1	2	3	4	5	6	6	7	8	9	10	11	12	13	14	15	16	17	18	19	20	21	22	23	
♂	♐ R 9	9	8	8	8	7	7	7	6	6	6	5	5	5	5	4	4	4	3	3	3	3	3	2	2	2	2	2	2	2	

♃	♄	♅	♆	♇
1 17 28 ♍ 26 27 28	1 2 11 22 ♉ 3 4 5 6	1 R 7 D 24 29 25 ♍ 29 29 0 ♎ 0	1 R ♏ 26	1 R 2 D ♍ 22 22

7

	1	2	3	4	5	6	7	8	9	10	11	12	13	14	15	16	17	18	19	20	21	22	23	24	25	26	27	28	29	30	31
☉	♋ 9	10	11	12	13	14	15	16	17	18	19	20	21	22	23	24	25	26	27	28	29	29	29 0	♌ 1	2	3	4	5	6	7	8
☽	♒ 3	18	♓ 3	17	♈ 0	13	26	♉ 9	21	♊ 3	15	27	♋ 9	21	♌ 3	14	26	♍ 9	21	♎ 3	16	29	♏ 13	27	♐ 11	26	♑ 11	26	♒ 11	26	♓ 11
☿	♊ 19	20	22	24	25	27	29	29 1	♋ 2	4	6	8	10	12	14	16	19	21	23	25	27	29	29 1	♌ 3	6	8	10	12	14	16	18
♀	♉ 24	25	26	27	28	29	29 0	♊ 2	3	4	5	6	7	8	9	10	11	12	13	15	16	17	18	19	20	21	22	23	25	26	27
♂	♐ R 1	1	1	1	1	1	1	D 1	1	1	1	1	1	2	2	2	2	2	2	2	2	3	3	3	3	4	4	4	4	5	5

♃	♄	♅	♆	♇
1 7 15 29 16 22 29 ♍ 28 29 0 ♎ 0 1 2	1 4 19 ♉ 6 7 8	1 28 ♎ 0 1	1 R 24 ♏ 26 25	1 20 22 23

8

	1	2	3	4	5	6	7	8	9	10	11	12	13	14	15	16	17	18	19	20	21	22	23	24	25	26	27	28	29	30	31
☉	♌ 9	10	11	12	13	14	15	16	17	18	19	20	21	22	22	23	24	25	26	27	28	29	29 0	♍ 1	2	3	4	5	6	7	8
☽	♓ 25	♈ 9	22	♉ 5	18	♊ 0	12	24	♋ 6	18	♌ 0	11	23	♍ 6	18	♎ 0	13	26	♏ 9	23	♐ 7	21	♑ 5	20	♒ 5	20	♓ 5	19	♈ 3	17	♉ 0
☿	♌ 19	21	23	25	27	29	29 0	♍ 2	4	6	7	9	10	12	14	15	17	18	19	21	22	24	25	26	28	29	29 0	♎ 1	2	4	5
♀	♊ 28	29	29 0	♋ 1	2	4	5	6	7	8	9	10	12	13	14	15	16	17	19	20	21	22	23	24	26	27	28	29	29 0	♌ 1	3
♂	♐ 5	6	6	6	7	7	7	8	8	8	9	9	10	10	10	11	11	12	12	13	13	14	14	14	15	15	16	16	17	17	18

♃	♄	♅	♆	♇
1 4 9 15 20 25 30 ♎ 2 3 4 5 6 7 8	1 21 R ♉ 8 8	1 18 ♎ 1 2	1 R 7 D 21 ♏ 25 25 26	1 23 ♍ 23 24

9

	1	2	3	4	5	6	7	8	9	10	11	12	13	14	15	16	17	18	19	20	21	22	23	24	25	26	27	28	29	30	31
☉	♍ 9	10	11	12	13	14	15	16	17	18	19	20	21	21	22	23	24	25	26	27	28	29	29 0	♎ 1	2	3	4	5	6	7	
☽	♉ 13	26	♊ 8	20	♋ 2	14	26	♌ 8	20	♍ 2	15	27	♎ 10	23	♏ 6	20	♐ 3	17	♑ 1	16	♒ 0	15	29	♓ 13	28	♈ 11	25	♉ 8	21	♊ 4	
☿	♎ 6	7	8	9	9	10	11	12	12	13	13	14	14	14	14	R 14	14	14	14	13	13	12	11	10	9	8	7	6	5	4	
♀	♌ 4	5	6	7	9	10	11	12	13	15	16	17	18	19	21	22	23	24	25	27	28	29	29 0	♍ 2	3	4	5	6	8	9	
♂	♐ 18	19	20	20	21	21	22	22	23	23	24	25	25	26	26	27	28	28	29	29	29 0	♑ 1	1	2	2	3	4	4	5	6	

♃	♄	♅	♆	♇
1 4 9 14 19 24 28 ♎ 8 9 10 11 12 13 14	1 R 23 ♉ 8 7	1 5 21 ♎ 2 3 4	1 ♏ 26	1 19 ♍ 24 25

10

	1	2	3	4	5	6	7	8	9	10	11	12	13	14	15	16	17	18	19	20	21	22	23	24	25	26	27	28	29	30	31
☉	♎ 8	9	10	11	12	13	14	15	16	17	18	19	20	21	22	23	24	25	26	27	28	29	29 0	♏ 1	2	3	4	5	6	7	8
☽	♊ 16	28	♋ 10	22	♌ 4	16	28	♍ 10	23	♎ 6	19	♏ 2	16	♐ 0	14	28	♑ 12	27	♒ 11	25	♓ 9	23	♈ 7	20	♉ 3	16	29	♊ 12	24	♋ 6	18
☿	♎ R 3	2	1	0	0	0	0 29	♍ D 29	29 0	♎ 0	1	1	2	3	4	5	6	7	9	10	12	13	15	16	18	20	21	23	25	26	28
♀	♍ 10	11	12	14	15	16	17	19	20	21	22	24	25	26	27	28	29 0	♎ 1	2	3	5	6	7	8	10	11	12	13	15	16	17
♂	♑ 6	7	8	8	9	10	10	11	12	12	13	14	14	15	16	16	17	18	18	19	20	20	21	22	23	23	24	25	25	26	27

♃	♄	♅	♆	♇
1 3 7 12 17 21 26 31 ♎ 14 15 16 17 18 19 20 21	1 R 9 22 ♉ 7 6 5	1 7 23 ♎ 4 5 6	1 11 ♏ 26 27	1 17 ♍ 25 26

11

	1	2	3	4	5	6	7	8	9	10	11	12	13	14	15	16	17	18	19	20	21	22	23	24	25	26	27	28	29	30	31
☉	♏ 9	10	11	12	13	14	15	16	17	18	19	20	21	22	23	24	25	26	27	28	29	29 0	♐ 1	2	3	4	5	6	7	8	
☽	♌ 0	12	24	♍ 6	18	♎ 1	14	27	♏ 11	25	♐ 10	24	♑ 9	23	♒ 8	22	♓ 6	19	♈ 3	16	29	♉ 12	25	♊ 8	20	♋ 2	14	26	♌ 8	20	
☿	29 0	♏ 1	3	4	6	8	9	11	13	14	16	18	19	21	22	24	26	27	29	29 0	♐ 2	3	5	7	8	10	11	13	14	16	
♀	♎ 18	20	21	22	23	25	26	27	28	29 0	♏ 1	2	3	5	6	7	8	10	11	12	13	15	16	17	18	20	21	22	23	25	
♂	♑ 27	28	29	29 0	♒ 0	1	2	3	3	4	5	5	6	7	8	8	9	10	11	11	12	13	13	14	15	16	16	17	18	19	

♃	♄	♅	♆	♇
1 4 9 14 19 24 29 ♎ 21 22 23 24 25 26 27	1 R 3 16 ♉ 5 4 3	1 10 ♎ 6 7	1 9 ♏ 27 28	1 22 ♍ 26 27

12

	1	2	3	4	5	6	7	8	9	10	11	12	13	14	15	16	17	18	19	20	21	22	23	24	25	26	27	28	29	30	31
☉	♐ 9	10	11	12	13	14	15	16	17	18	19	20	21	22	23	24	25	26	27	28	29	29 0	♑ 1	3	4	5	6	7	8	9	10
☽	♍ 2	14	26	♎ 9	22	♏ 5	19	♐ 4	18	♑ 3	18	♒ 3	18	♓ 2	16	♈ 0	13	26	♉ 9	22	♊ 4	17	29	♋ 11	23	♌ 5	16	28	♍ 10	22	♎ 4
☿	♐ 17	19	21	22	24	25	27	28	29 0	♑ 1	3	4	6	7	9	10	12	13	15	16	18	19	20	22	23	24	25	26	27	28	29
♀	♏ 26	27	28	29 0	♐ 1	2	3	5	6	7	9	10	11	12	14	15	16	17	19	20	21	22	24	25	26	27	29	29 0	♑ 1	2	4
♂	♒ 19	20	21	22	22	23	24	25	25	26	27	28	28	29	29 0	♓ 1	1	2	3	4	4	5	6	6	7	8	9	9	10	11	12

♃	♄	♅	♆	♇
1 5 10 16 29 17 22 29 ♎ 27 28 29 0 ♏ 0 1 2	1 R 2 ♉ 3 2	1 3 ♎ 7 8	1 5 ♏ 28 29	1 29 R ♍ 27 27

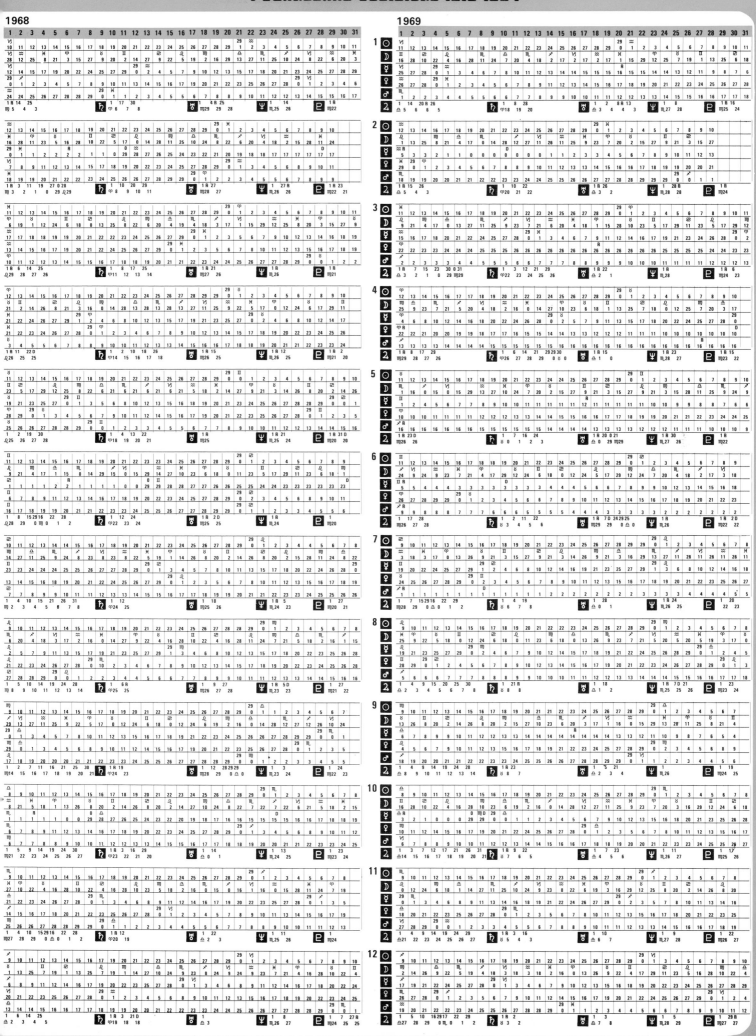

1970

1

	1	2	3	4	5	6	7	8	9	10	11	12	13	14	15	16	17	18	19	20	21	22	23	24	25	26	27	28	29	30	31
☉	♑ 11	12	13	14	15	16	17	18	19	20	21	22	23	24	25	26	27	28	29	29 0	♒ 1	2	3	4	5	6	7	8	9	10	11
☽	♎ 17	♏ 0	13	27	♐ 12	26	♑ 12	27	♒ 12	27	♓ 12	26	♈ 10	23	♉ 6	19	♊ 1	14	26	♋ 8	20	♌ 1	13	25	♍ 7	19	♎ 1	13	26	♏ 9	22
☿	♑ 29	29 0	♒ 0	R 0	0	0	0 29	♑ 27	26	25	24	23	22	20	19	18	17	16	15	14	14	14	13	D 13	14	14	14	14	15	16	16
♀	♑ 5	6	7	9	10	11	12	14	15	16	18	19	20	21	23	24	25	26	28	29	29 0	♒ 1	3	4	5	6	8	9	10	11	13
♂	♓ 12	13	14	15	15	16	17	18	18	19	20	21	21	22	23	24	24	25	26	27	27	28	29	29 0	♈ 0	1	2	3	3	4	5

♃ 1 6 14 25 / ♏2 3 4 5 — ♄ 1R / ♉2 — ♅ 1 13R / ♎8 8 — ♆ 1 4 29 5 / ♏29 0 ♐0 — ♇ 1R / ♍27

2

	1	2	3	4	5	6	7	8	9	10	11	12	13	14	15	16	17	18	19	20	21	22	23	24	25	26	27	28
☉	♒ 12	13	14	15	16	17	18	19	20	21	22	23	24	25	26	27	28	29	29 0	♓ 1	2	3	4	5	6	7	8	9
☽	♐ 6	20	♑ 5	20	♒ 5	20	♓ 5	20	♈ 4	18	♉ 2	15	28	♊ 10	23	♋ 5	17	28	♌ 10	22	♍ 4	16	28	♎ 10	23	♏ 5	18	♐ 2
☿	♑ 17	18	19	20	21	22	23	24	25	26	27	29	29 0	♒ 1	2	4	5	6	8	9	11	12	14	15	17	18	20	21
♀	♒ 14	15	16	18	19	20	21	23	24	25	26	28	29	29 0	♓ 1	3	4	5	6	8	9	10	11	13	14	15	16	18
♂	♈ 5	6	7	8	8	9	10	11	11	12	13	14	14	15	16	16	17	18	19	19	20	21	22	22	23	24	24	25

♃ 1 19R / ♏5 5 — ♄ 1 4 19 / ♉2 3 4 — ♅ 1R 24 / ♎8 7 — ♆ 1 / ♐0 — ♇ 1R 5 / ♍27 26

3

	1	2	3	4	5	6	7	8	9	10	11	12	13	14	15	16	17	18	19	20	21	22	23	24	25	26	27	28	29	30	31
☉	♓ 10	11	12	13	14	16	17	18	19	20	21	21	22	23	24	25	26	27	28	29	29 0	♈ 1	2	3	4	5	6	7	8	9	10
☽	♐ 15	29	♑ 14	28	♒ 13	28	♓ 13	28	♈ 12	27	♉ 10	24	♊ 6	19	♋ 1	13	25	♌ 7	19	♍ 1	13	25	♎ 7	20	♏ 2	15	29	♐ 12	26	♑ 10	24
☿	♒ 23	24	26	28	29 0	♓ 1	3	4	6	8	10	11	13	15	17	19	21	22	24	26	28	29 0	♈ 2	4	6	8	10	12	14	16	18
♀	♓ 19	20	21	23	24	25	26	28	29	29 0	♈ 1	3	4	5	6	8	9	10	11	13	14	15	16	17	19	20	21	23	24	25	26
♂	♈ 26	27	27	28	29	29	29 0	♉ 1	2	2	3	4	4	5	6	7	7	8	9	9	10	11	12	12	13	14	14	15	16	16	17

♃ 1R 16 28 / ♏5 4 3 — ♄ 1 3 13 22 30 / ♉4 5 6 7 8 — ♅ 1R 22 / ♎7 6 — ♆ 1 3R / ♐0 0 — ♇ 1R 19 / ♍26 25

4

	1	2	3	4	5	6	7	8	9	10	11	12	13	14	15	16	17	18	19	20	21	22	23	24	25	26	27	28	29	30
☉	♈ 11	12	13	14	15	16	17	18	19	20	21	22	23	24	25	26	27	28	29	29 0	♉ 1	2	3	4	5	6	7	8	9	10
☽	♒ 8	23	♓ 7	22	♈ 6	20	♉ 4	18	♊ 1	14	27	♋ 9	21	♌ 3	15	27	♍ 9	21	♎ 3	16	29	♏ 12	25	♐ 9	23	♑ 7	21	♒ 5	19	♓ 3
☿	♈ 20	22	24	26	28	29 0	♉ 2	4	6	7	9	10	12	13	14	16	17	18	19	19	20	21	21	22	22	22	22	R 22	22	22
♀	♈ 28	29	29 0	♉ 1	3	4	5	6	7	9	10	11	12	13	15	16	17	18	20	21	22	23	25	26	27	28	29 0	♊ 1	2	3
♂	♉ 18	19	19	20	21	21	22	23	23	24	25	26	26	27	28	28	29	29 0	♊ 0	1	2	2	3	4	4	5	6	6	7	8

♃ 1R 6 14 22 29 0 30 / ♏3 2 1 0 29 ♎29 — ♄ 1 8 16 24 / ♉8 9 10 11 — ♅ 1R 14 / ♎6 5 — ♆ 1R / ♐0 — ♇ 1R 30 / ♍25 24

5

	1	2	3	4	5	6	7	8	9	10	11	12	13	14	15	16	17	18	19	20	21	22	23	24	25	26	27	28	29	30	31
☉	♉ 11	12	13	14	15	16	17	17	18	19	20	21	22	23	24	25	26	27	28	29	29 0	♊ 1	2	3	4	5	6	7	8	9	10
☽	♓ 17	♈ 1	15	29	♉ 13	26	♊ 10	22	♋ 5	17	29	♌ 11	23	♍ 5	17	29	♎ 11	24	♏ 7	21	♐ 4	18	♑ 3	17	♒ 1	16	♓ 0	14	28	♈ 12	25
☿	♉R 21	21	21	20	20	19	19	18	18	17	16	16	15	15	14	14	13	13	13	13	13	D 13	13	13	13	14	14	14	15	15	16
♀	♊ 4	6	7	8	9	10	12	13	14	15	16	18	19	20	21	22	24	25	26	27	29	29 0	♋ 1	2	3	5	6	7	8	9	11
♂	♊ 9	9	10	11	11	12	13	13	14	15	15	16	17	17	18	19	19	20	21	21	22	23	23	24	25	25	26	27	27	28	29

♃ 1R 8 17 29 / ♎29 28 27 26 — ♄ 1 2 9 17 25 / ♉11 12 13 14 15 — ♅ 1R 15 / ♎5 4 — ♆ 1R 3 0 4 / ♐0 29 ♏29 — ♇ 1R / ♍24

6

	1	2	3	4	5	6	7	8	9	10	11	12	13	14	15	16	17	18	19	20	21	22	23	24	25	26	27	28	29	30
☉	♊ 11	12	12	13	14	15	16	17	18	19	20	21	22	23	24	25	26	27	28	29	29 0	♋ 1	2	3	4	4	5	6	7	8
☽	♉ 9	22	♊ 5	18	♋ 1	13	25	♌ 7	19	♍ 1	13	25	♎ 7	19	♏ 2	15	29	♐ 13	27	♑ 12	27	♒ 11	26	♓ 10	25	♈ 9	22	♉ 6	19	♊ 2
☿	♉ 17	18	18	19	20	21	22	23	25	26	27	28	29 0	♊ 1	3	4	6	8	9	11	13	14	16	18	20	22	24	26	28	29 0
♀	♋ 12	13	14	15	17	18	19	20	21	22	24	25	26	27	28	29 0	♌ 1	2	3	4	5	7	8	9	10	11	12	14	15	16
♂	♊ 29	29 0	♋ 1	1	2	3	3	4	5	5	6	7	7	8	9	9	10	11	11	12	12	13	14	14	15	16	16	17	18	18

♃ 1R 23D / ♎26 26 — ♄ 1 2 11 20 29 / ♉15 16 17 18 19 — ♅ 1R 2D / ♎4 4 — ♆ 1R 9 / ♏29 28 — ♇ 1R 5D / ♍24 24

7

	1	2	3	4	5	6	7	8	9	10	11	12	13	14	15	16	17	18	19	20	21	22	23	24	25	26	27	28	29	30	31
☉	♋ 9	10	11	12	13	14	15	16	17	18	19	20	21	22	23	24	24	25	26	27	28	29	29 0	♌ 1	2	3	4	5	6	7	8
☽	♊ 15	27	♋ 9	22	♌ 4	15	27	♍ 9	21	♎ 3	15	27	♏ 10	23	♐ 7	21	♑ 6	21	♒ 6	21	♓ 6	20	♈ 5	19	♉ 2	16	29	♊ 12	24	♋ 6	18
☿	♋ 2	5	7	9	11	13	15	18	20	22	24	26	28	29 0	♌ 2	4	6	8	10	12	14	15	17	19	21	22	24	26	27	29	29 0
♀	♌ 17	18	19	21	22	23	24	25	26	28	29	29 0	♍ 1	2	3	4	6	7	8	9	10	11	12	13	15	16	17	18	19	20	21
♂	♋ 19	20	20	21	22	22	23	24	24	25	25	26	27	27	28	29	29	29 0	♌ 0	1	2	3	3	4	4	5	6	6	7	8	8

♃ 1 18 29 / ♎26 27 28 — ♄ 1 10 22 / ♉19 20 21 — ♅ 1 10 / ♎4 5 — ♆ 1R / ♏28 — ♇ 1 8 / ♍24 25

8

	1	2	3	4	5	6	7	8	9	10	11	12	13	14	15	16	17	18	19	20	21	22	23	24	25	26	27	28	29	30	31
☉	♌ 9	10	11	12	13	14	15	16	16	17	18	19	20	21	22	23	24	25	26	27	28	29	29 0	♍ 1	2	3	4	5	6	7	8
☽	♌ 0	12	24	♍ 6	18	♎ 0	12	24	♏ 6	19	♐ 2	16	♑ 0	14	29	♒ 14	29	♓ 14	29	♈ 14	28	♉ 12	25	♊ 8	21	♋ 3	16	28	♌ 9	21	♍ 3
☿	♍ 2	3	5	6	7	9	10	11	13	14	15	16	17	18	19	20	21	22	23	24	25	25	26	26	27	27	27	27	27	R 27	27
♀	♍ 22	23	25	26	27	28	29	29 0	♎ 1	2	3	4	5	6	7	8	9	11	12	13	14	15	16	17	18	19	20	21	22	23	24
♂	♌ 9	10	10	11	12	12	13	13	14	15	15	16	17	17	18	19	19	20	20	21	22	22	23	24	24	25	26	26	27	27	28

♃ 1 7 15 29 16 22 29 / ♎28 29 0 ♏0 1 2 — ♄ 1 8 / ♉21 22 — ♅ 1 7 27 / ♎5 6 7 — ♆ 1R 10 / ♏28 28 — ♇ 1 17 / ♍25 26

9

	1	2	3	4	5	6	7	8	9	10	11	12	13	14	15	16	17	18	19	20	21	22	23	24	25	26	27	28	29	30
☉	♍ 9	10	11	12	13	13	14	15	16	17	18	19	20	21	22	23	24	25	26	27	28	29	29 0	♎ 1	2	3	4	5	6	7
☽	♍ 15	27	♎ 9	21	♏ 3	15	28	♐ 11	25	♑ 9	23	♒ 7	22	♓ 7	23	♈ 8	22	♉ 7	21	♊ 4	17	♋ 0	12	24	♌ 6	18	♍ 0	12	24	♎ 6
☿	♍R 27	27	26	26	25	24	24	23	22	21	20	19	18	17	16	15	15	14	14	13	13	D 13	14	14	15	15	16	17	18	19
♀	♎ 25	26	26	27	28	29	29 0	♏ 1	2	3	4	5	6	6	7	8	9	10	11	11	12	13	14	14	15	16	16	17	18	18
♂	♌ 29	29	29 0	♍ 1	1	2	3	3	4	4	5	6	6	7	8	8	9	10	10	11	11	12	13	13	14	15	15	16	17	17

♃ 1 4 9 15 20 25 30 / ♏2 3 4 5 6 7 8 — ♄ 1 4R / ♉22 22 — ♅ 1 13 29 / ♎7 8 9 — ♆ 1 / ♏28 — ♇ 1 14 / ♍26 27

10

	1	2	3	4	5	6	7	8	9	10	11	12	13	14	15	16	17	18	19	20	21	22	23	24	25	26	27	28	29	30	31
☉	♎ 8	9	10	11	12	13	14	15	16	17	18	19	20	21	22	23	24	25	26	27	28	29	29 0	♏ 1	2	3	4	5	6	7	8
☽	♎ 18	♏ 0	13	25	♐ 8	21	♑ 5	19	♒ 3	17	♓ 1	16	♈ 1	16	♉ 0	15	29	♊ 12	26	♋ 8	21	♌ 3	15	26	♍ 8	20	♎ 2	14	27	♏ 9	22
☿	♍ 20	22	23	25	26	28	29 0	♎ 1	3	4	6	8	10	11	13	15	17	18	20	22	24	25	27	29	29 0	♏ 2	4	5	7	8	10
♀	♏ 19	19	20	21	21	22	22	22	23	23	24	24	24	24	25	25	25	25	25	R 25	25	25	24	24	24	24	24	23	23	23	22
♂	♍ 18	18	19	20	20	21	22	22	23	24	24	25	25	26	27	27	28	29	29	29 0	♎ 1	1	2	2	3	4	4	5	6	6	7

♃ 1 5 10 15 19 24 28 / ♏8 9 10 11 12 13 14 — ♄ 1R 18 / ♉21 20 — ♅ 1 15 / ♎9 10 — ♆ 1 7 / ♏28 29 — ♇ 1 12 / ♍27 28

11

	1	2	3	4	5	6	7	8	9	10	11	12	13	14	15	16	17	18	19	20	21	22	23	24	25	26	27	28	29	30
☉	♏ 9	10	11	12	13	14	15	16	17	18	19	20	21	22	23	24	25	26	27	28	29	29 0	♐ 1	2	3	4	5	6	7	8
☽	♐ 5	18	♑ 2	15	29	♒ 13	27	♓ 11	26	♈ 10	25	♉ 9	23	♊ 7	20	♋ 3	16	29	♌ 11	23	♍ 4	16	28	♎ 10	22	♏ 5	18	♐ 1	14	28
☿	♏ 12	13	15	17	18	20	21	23	24	26	27	29	29 1	♐ 2	4	5	7	8	10	11	13	14	16	17	19	20	22	23	24	26
♀	♏R 22	21	21	20	20	19	18	18	17	17	16	15	15	14	14	13	13	12	12	11	11	11	10	10	10	10	9	9	9	9
♂	♎ 7	8	9	9	10	11	11	12	13	13	14	14	15	16	16	17	18	18	19	20	20	21	21	22	23	23	24	25	25	26

♃ 1 2 7 11 16 20 25 29 / ♏14 15 16 17 18 19 20 21 — ♄ 1R 13 25 / ♉19 18 17 — ♅ 1 19 / ♎11 12 — ♆ 1 6 29 7 / ♏29 0 ♐0 — ♇ 1 12 / ♍28 29

12

	1	2	3	4	5	6	7	8	9	10	11	12	13	14	15	16	17	18	19	20	21	22	23	24	25	26	27	28	29	30	31
☉	♐ 9	10	11	12	13	14	15	16	17	18	19	20	21	22	23	24	25	26	27	28	29	29 0	♑ 1	2	3	4	5	6	7	8	9
☽	♑ 12	26	♒ 10	24	♓ 8	22	♈ 6	20	♉ 4	18	♊ 2	15	28	♋ 11	24	♌ 6	18	♍ 0	12	24	♎ 6	18	♏ 0	13	26	♐ 9	23	♑ 7	21	♒ 6	20
☿	♐ 27	29	29 0	♑ 1	3	4	5	6	7	9	10	11	11	12	13	13	14	14	R 14	13	13	12	11	10	9	8	7	6	4	3	2
♀	♏D 9	9	9	10	10	10	10	11	11	11	12	12	12	13	13	14	15	15	16	16	17	18	18	19	20	20	21	22	23	23	24
♂	♎ 27	27	28	28	29	29 0	♏ 0	1	2	2	3	4	4	5	5	6	7	7	8	9	9	10	11	11	12	12	13	14	14	15	16

♃ 1 4 9 13 18 23 28 / ♏21 22 23 24 25 26 27 — ♄ 1R 9 30 / ♉17 16 15 — ♅ 1 14 / ♎12 13 — ♆ 1 3 / ♐0 1 — ♇ 1 29R / ♍29 29

1971

1

	1	2	3	4	5	6	7	8	9	10	11	12	13	14	15	16	17	18	19	20	21	22	23	24	25	26	27	28	29
☉	♑ 10	11	12	13	15	16	17	18	19	20	21	22	23	24	25	26	27	28	29	29 0	♒ 1	2	3	4	5	6	7	8	9
☽	♓ 5	19	♈ 3	17	♉ 1	15	28	♊ 11	24	♋ 7	20	♌ 2	14	26	♍ 8	20	♎ 2	14	26	♏ 8	21	♐ 4	17	♑ 1	15	29	♒ 14	29	♓ 14
☿	♑R 1	0	0 29	♐ 28	28	27	27	D 27	28	28	28	29	29	29 0	♑ 1	2	3	4	5	6	7	8	9	10	12	13	14	15	17
♀	♏ 25	26	27	28	28	29	29 0	♐ 1	2	3	4	5	6	7	8	9	10	11	12	13	14	15	16	17	18	19	20	21	22
♂	♏ 16	17	17	18	19	19	20	21	21	22	23	23	24	24	25	26	26	27	28	28	29	29	29 0	♐ 1	1	2	3	3	4

♃ 1 3 8 14 29 15 20 26 / ♏27 28 29 0 ♐0 1 2 — ♄ 1R 17D / ♉15 15 — ♅ 1 18R / ♎13 13 — ♆ 1 / ♐2 — ♇ 1R / ♍29

2

	1	2	3	4	5	6	7	8	9	10	11	12	13	14	15	16	17	18	19	20	21	22	23	24	25	26	27	28
☉	♒ 12	13	14	15	16	17	18	19	20	21	22	23	24	25	26	27	28	29	29 0	♓ 1	2	3	4	5	6	7	8	9
☽	♈ 28	♉ 11	25	♊ 8	21	♋ 4	16	29	♌ 11	23	♍ 5	17	28	♎ 10	22	♏ 4	16	29	♐ 12	25	♑ 9	23	♒ 7	22	♓ 7	23	♈ 8	23
☿	♑ 21	22	23	25	26	28	29 0	♒ 1	2	4	5	7	8	10	12	13	15	16	18	20	21	23	25	27	28	29 0	♓ 2	4
♀	♐ 25	26	28	29	29 0	♑ 1	2	3	4	5	6	7	9	10	11	12	13	14	15	16	18	19	20	21	22	23	25	26
♂	♐ 6	6	7	8	8	9	10	10	11	11	12	13	13	14	15	15	16	16	17	18	18	19	19	20	21	21	22	23

♃ 1 2 10 20 / ♐2 3 4 5 — ♄ 1 4 24 / ♉15 16 17 — ♅ 1R 22 / ♎13 12 — ♆ 1 16 / ♐2 3 — ♇ 1 / ♍29

3

	1	2	3	4	5	6	7	8	9	10	11	12	13	14	15	16	17	18	19	20	21	22	23	24	25	26	27	28	29
☉	♓ 10	11	12	13	14	15	16	17	18	19	20	21	22	23	24	25	26	27	28	29	29 0	♈ 1	2	3	4	5	6	7	8
☽	♉ 7	21	♊ 5	18	♋ 1	14	26	♌ 8	20	♍ 2	14	25	♎ 7	19	♏ 1	13	25	♐ 8	21	♑ 4	17	♒ 1	16	♓ 0	15	♈ 1	16	♉ 1	16
☿	♓ 6	7	9	11	13	15	17	19	21	23	25	26	28	29 0	♈ 2	4	6	8	10	12	14	16	17	19	21	22	24	25	26
♀	♑ 27	28	29	29 0	♒ 1	3	4	5	6	7	8	10	11	12	13	14	16	17	18	19	20	21	23	24	25	26	27	29	29 0
♂	♐ 23	24	24	25	26	26	27	27	28	29	29	29 0	♑ 0	1	2	2	3	4	4	5	5	6	7	7	8	8	9	9	10

♃ 1 6 24R / ♐5 6 6 — ♄ 1 9 20 30 / ♉17 18 19 20 — ♅ 1R 21 / ♎12 11 — ♆ 1 5R 22 / ♐3 3 2 — ♇ 1 / ♍28

4

	1	2	3	4	5	6	7	8	9	10	11	12	13	14	15	16	17	18	19	20	21	22	23	24	25	26	27	28	29
☉	♈ 11	12	13	14	15	16	17	18	19	20	21	22	23	24	25	26	27	28	29	29 0	♉ 1	2	3	4	5	6	7	8	9
☽	♊ 27	♋ 10	23	♌ 5	17	29	♍ 11	22	♎ 4	16	28	♏ 10	23	♐ 5	18	♑ 1	14	27	♒ 11	25	♓ 9	24	♈ 9	24	♉ 9	24	♊ 8	22	♋ 6
☿	29 0	♉ 1	1	2	3	3	3	3	3	R 3	3	3	2	2	2	1	0	0 29	♈ 29	28	27	27	26	25	25	24	24	23	23
♀	♓ 3	5	6	7	8	9	10	12	13	14	15	16	18	19	20	21	22	24	25	26	27	28	29 0	♈ 1	2	3	4	6	7
♂	♑ 12	12	13	14	14	15	15	16	16	17	18	18	19	19	20	20	21	22	22	23	23	24	24	25	25	26	26	27	28

♃ 1R 9 23 / ♐6 5 4 — ♄ 1 7 16 24 / ♉20 21 22 23 — ♅ 1R 14 / ♎11 10 — ♆ 1R / ♐2 — ♇ 1R / ♍28

5

	1	2	3	4	5	6	7	8	9	10	11	12	13	14	15	16	17	18	19	20	21	22	23	24	25	26	27	28	29
☉	♉ 10	11	12	13	14	15	16	17	18	19	20	21	22	23	24	25	26	27	28	29	29 0	♊ 1	2	3	4	5	6	7	7
☽	♌ 1	13	25	♍ 7	19	♎ 1	13	25	♏ 7	19	♐ 2	15	28	♑ 11	24	♒ 8	21	♓ 5	20	♈ 4	19	♉ 3	18	♊ 2	16	♋ 0	14	27	♌ 9
☿	♈R 23	23	23	D 23	23	23	24	24	24	25	25	26	27	28	28	29	29 0	♉ 1	2	3	4	6	7	8	9	11	12	14	15
♀	♈ 9	10	12	13	14	15	17	18	19	20	21	23	24	25	26	27	29	29 0	♉ 1	2	3	5	6	7	8	9	11	12	13
♂	♑ 29	29	29 0	♒ 0	1	1	2	2	3	3	4	4	5	5	6	6	7	7	8	8	8	9	9	10	10	11	11	11	12

♃ 1R 3 12 20 27 / ♐4 3 2 1 0 — ♄ 1 2 10 17 25 / ♉23 24 25 26 27 — ♅ 1R 11 / ♎10 9 — ♆ 1R 13 / ♐2 1 — ♇ 1R / ♍27

6

	1	2	3	4	5	6	7	8	9	10	11	12	13	14	15	16	17	18	19	20	21	22	23	24	25	26	27	28	29
☉	♊ 10	11	12	13	14	15	16	17	18	19	20	21	22	23	24	25	26	27	28	29	29	29 0	♋ 1	2	3	4	5	6	7
☽	♍ 15	27	♎ 9	21	♏ 3	15	28	♐ 11	24	♑ 7	21	♒ 4	18	♓ 2	16	♈ 0	15	29	♉ 13	27	♊ 11	25	♋ 9	22	♌ 4	17	29	♍ 11	23
☿	♉ 20	21	23	25	27	28	29 0	♊ 2	4	6	8	10	12	14	16	19	21	23	25	27	29 0	♋ 2	4	6	8	10	12	14	17
♀	♉ 17	18	19	20	22	23	24	25	26	28	29	29 0	♊ 1	3	4	5	6	7	9	10	11	12	13	15	16	17	18	20	21
♂	♒ 13	13	14	14	14	15	15	16	16	16	17	17	17	18	18	18	18	19	19	19	19	20	20	20	20	20	21	21	21

♃ 1R 5 0 6 13 23 / ♐0 29 ♏29 28 27 — ♄ 1 2 10 18 29 19 27 / ♉27 28 29 0 ♊0 1 — ♅ 1R 17D / ♎9 9 — ♆ 1R 19 / ♐1 0 — ♇ 1R / ♍26

7

	1	2	3	4	5	6	7	8	9	10	11	12	13	14	15	16	17	18	19	20	21	22	23	24	25	26	27	28	29
☉	♋ 9	10	11	12	13	14	15	16	17	18	19	19	20	21	22	23	24	25	26	27	28	29	29 0	♌ 1	2	3	4	5	6
☽	♎ 17	29	♏ 11	24	♐ 6	19	♑ 3	16	♒ 0	14	28	♓ 13	27	♈ 11	26	♉ 10	24	♊ 7	21	♋ 4	17	♌ 0	13	25	♍ 7	19	♎ 1	13	25
☿	♋ 21	23	24	26	28	29 0	♌ 2	4	5	7	9	10	12	14	15	17	18	19	21	22	24	25	26	27	28	29 0	♍ 1	2	3
♀	♊ 23	24	26	27	28	29 0	♋ 1	2	3	4	5	7	8	9	10	12	13	14	15	16	18	19	20	21	23	24	25	26	28
♂	♒ 21	21	21	21	21	21	21	21	21	21	R 21	21	21	21	21	21	21	21	21	21	21	21	20	20	20	20	20	20	19

♃ 1R 8 24D / ♏27 26 26 — ♄ 1 6 15 26 / ♊1 2 3 4 — ♅ 1 23 / ♎9 10 — ♆ 1R / ♐0 — ♇ 1 / ♍27

8

	1	2	3	4	5	6	7	8	9	10	11	12	13	14	15	16	17	18	19	20	21	22	23	24	25	26	27	28	29
☉	♌ 9	10	11	11	12	13	14	15	16	17	18	19	20	21	22	23	24	25	26	27	28	29	29 0	♍ 1	2	3	4	5	5
☽	♐ 1	14	27	♑ 11	25	♒ 9	23	♓ 8	23	♈ 8	22	♉ 6	20	♊ 4	18	♋ 1	14	27	♌ 9	22	♍ 4	16	28	♎ 10	21	♏ 3	15	27	♐ 10
☿	♍ 5	6	7	8	8	9	9	10	10	10	10	10	R 10	10	10	9	9	8	7	7	6	5	5	4	3	2	1	0	0 29
♀	♌ 1	2	4	5	6	7	9	10	11	12	14	15	16	17	18	20	21	22	23	25	26	27	28	29 0	♍ 1	2	3	5	6
♂	♒R 19	18	18	18	18	17	17	17	17	16	16	16	16	15	15	15	15	14	14	14	14	13	13	13	13	13	12	12	12

♃ 1 10 24 / ♏26 27 28 — ♄ 1 8 25 / ♊4 5 6 — ♅ 1 17 / ♎10 11 — ♆ 1 / ♐0 — ♇ 1 / ♍27

9

	1	2	3	4	5	6	7	8	9	10	11	12	13	14	15	16	17	18	19	20	21	22	23	24	25	26	27	28	29
☉	♍ 8	9	10	11	12	13	14	15	16	17	18	19	20	21	22	23	24	25	26	27	28	29	29 0	♎ 1	2	3	4	5	6
☽	♑ 19	♒ 3	17	♓ 2	17	♈ 2	17	♉ 2	17	♊ 1	15	28	♋ 11	24	♌ 6	18	♍ 1	13	24	♎ 6	18	♏ 0	12	24	♐ 6	18	♑ 1	14	27
☿	♌R 28	27	27	27	D 27	27	27	28	28	29	29 0	♍ 1	2	3	5	6	7	9	11	12	14	16	17	19	21	23	25	26	28
♀	♍ 10	11	12	13	14	16	17	18	19	21	22	23	24	26	27	28	29 0	♎ 1	2	3	4	6	7	8	9	11	12	13	14
♂	♒R 12	12	12	12	11	11	11	11	11	D 11	11	11	12	12	12	12	12	12	12	12	12	13	13	13	13	13	14	14	14

♃ 1 3 11 29 12 18 25 / ♏28 29 0 ♐0 1 2 — ♄ 1 19R / ♊6 6 — ♅ 1 5 22 / ♎11 12 13 — ♆ 1 / ♐0 — ♇ 1 / ♍28

10

	1	2	3	4	5	6	7	8	9	10	11	12	13	14	15	16	17	18	19	20	21	22	23	24	25	26	27	28	29
☉	♎ 8	9	10	11	12	13	14	15	16	17	18	19	19	20	21	22	23	24	25	26	27	28	29	29 0	♏ 1	2	3	4	5
☽	♒ 25	♓ 10	25	♈ 10	26	♉ 11	26	♊ 10	24	♋ 8	21	♌ 3	16	28	♍ 10	22	♎ 3	15	27	♏ 9	21	♐ 3	15	28	♑ 10	23	♒ 6	20	♓ 4
☿	♎ 2	4	5	7	9	11	13	14	16	18	19	21	23	25	26	28	29 0	♏ 1	3	4	6	7	9	11	12	14	15	17	18
♀	♎ 17	18	19	21	22	23	24	26	27	28	29 0	♏ 1	2	3	4	6	7	8	9	11	12	13	14	15	17	18	19	20	22
♂	♒ 15	15	15	16	16	16	17	17	17	18	18	18	19	19	19	20	20	21	21	22	22	23	23	23	24	24	25	25	25

♃ 1 7 12 17 23 28 / ♐3 4 5 6 7 8 — ♄ 1R 13 31 / ♊6 5 4 — ♅ 1 8 24 / ♎13 14 15 — ♆ 1 3 / ♐0 1 — ♇ 1 / ♍29

11

	1	2	3	4	5	6	7	8	9	10	11	12	13	14	15	16	17	18	19	20	21	22	23	24	25	26	27	28	29
☉	♏ 8	9	10	11	12	13	14	15	16	17	18	19	20	21	22	23	24	25	26	28	29	29 0	♐ 1	2	3	4	5	6	7
☽	♈ 18	♉ 4	19	♊ 4	18	♋ 3	16	29	♌ 12	24	♍ 6	18	♎ 0	12	24	♏ 6	18	♐ 0	12	25	♑ 7	20	♒ 3	16	♓ 0	14	28	♈ 13	27
☿	♏ 23	24	26	27	29	29 0	♐ 2	3	4	6	7	9	10	11	13	14	15	17	18	19	20	21	22	23	24	25	26	27	27
♀	♏ 25	27	28	29	29 0	♐ 2	3	4	5	7	8	9	10	12	13	14	15	17	18	19	20	22	23	24	25	27	28	29	29 0
♂	♒ 27	28	28	29	29	29 0	♓ 0	1	1	2	3	3	4	4	5	5	6	6	7	8	8	9	9	10	10	11	12	12	13

♃ 1 2 6 11 15 20 24 29 / ♐8 9 10 11 12 13 14 15 — ♄ 1R 13 26 / ♊4 3 2 — ♅ 1 10 29 / ♎15 16 17 — ♆ 1 4 30 / ♐1 2 3 — ♇ 1 / ♎0

12

	1	2	3	4	5	6	7	8	9	10	11	12	13	14	15	16	17	18	19	20	21	22	23	24	25	26	27	28	29
☉	♐ 9	10	11	12	13	14	15	16	17	18	19	20	21	22	23	24	25	26	27	28	29	29 0	♑ 1	2	3	4	5	6	7
☽	♉ 27	♊ 12	26	♋ 10	24	♌ 7	20	♍ 3	15	27	♎ 9	20	♏ 2	14	26	♐ 9	21	♑ 4	17	♒ 0	13	27	♓ 11	24	♈ 9	23	♉ 7	22	♊ 6
☿	♐ 28	28	R 28	28	27	26	26	25	24	22	21	20	18	17	16	14	13	13	12	12	12	D 11	12	12	12	13	13	14	15
♀	♑ 3	4	5	7	8	9	10	12	13	14	15	16	18	19	20	21	23	24	25	26	28	29	29 0	♒ 1	3	4	5	6	8
♂	♓ 14	15	15	16	16	17	18	18	19	20	20	21	21	22	23	23	24	24	25	26	26	27	28	28	29	29 0	♈ 0	1	2

♃ 1 3 8 12 17 21 25 30 / ♐15 16 17 18 19 20 21 22 — ♄ 1R 8 22 / ♊2 1 0 — ♅ 1 28 / ♎17 18 — ♆ 1 29 / ♐3 4 — ♇ 1 / ♎1

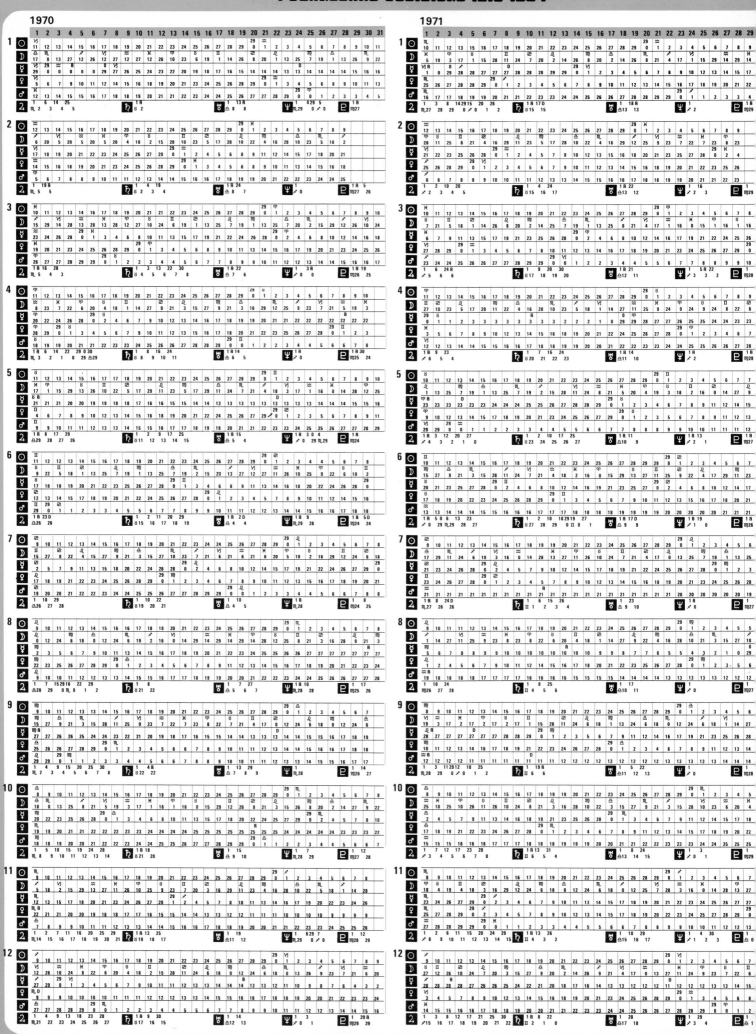

1972

1

	1	2	3	4	5	6	7	8	9	10	11	12	13	14	15	16	17	18	19	20	21	22	23	24	25	26	27	28	29	30	31
☉	♑ 10	11	12	13	14	15	16	17	18	19	20	21	22	23	24	25	26	27	28	29/0	♒ 0	1	2	3	4	5	6	7	8	9	10
☽	♋ 18	♌ 2	15	28	♍ 10	22	♎ 5	17	28	♏ 10	22	♐ 4	17	29	♑ 13	26	♒ 9	23	♓ 7	21	♈ 5	20	♉ 4	18	♊ 2	16	29	♋ 13	27	♌ 10	23
☿	♐ 17	18	19	20	21	22	24	25	26	28	29/0	♑ 1	2	3	5	6	8	9	11	12	13	15	17	18	20	21	22	24	26	27	29
♀	♒ 11	12	14	15	16	17	19	20	21	22	24	25	26	27	28	29/0	♓ 1	2	3	5	6	7	8	9	11	12	13	14	15	17	18
♂	♈ 3	4	4	5	6	7	7	8	9	9	10	11	11	12	13	13	14	15	15	16	17	17	18	19	19	20	21	21	22	23	23

♃ 4 9 13 18 23 28 / ♐22 23 24 25 26 27 28 — ♄ 1 2 R 10 31 D / ♊0 0 0 29 ♉29 — ♅ 1 23 R / ♎18 18 — ♆ 1 / ♐4 — ♇ 1 5 R 31 / ♎2 2 1

2

	1	2	3	4	5	6	7	8	9	10	11	12	13	14	15	16	17	18	19	20	21	22	23	24	25	26	27	28	29
☉	♒ 11	12	13	14	15	16	17	18	19	20	21	22	23	24	25	26	27	28	29/0	♓ 1	2	3	4	5	6	7	8	9	10
☽	♍ 6	18	♎ 0	12	24	♏ 6	18	♐ 0	12	25	♑ 8	22	♒ 4	18	♓ 2	17	♈ 1	16	♉ 0	15	29	♊ 13	26	♋ 10	23	♌ 6	19	♍ 2	14
☿	♑ 9 0	♒ 2	4	6	7	9	10	12	14	15	17	19	21	22	24	26	28	29/0	♓ 1	3	5	7	9	11	13	15	17	18	20
♀	♓ 19	20	22	23	24	25	26	28	29	29/0	♈ 1	2	3	5	6	7	8	9	11	12	13	14	15	16	18	19	20	21	22
♂	♈ 24	24	25	26	26	27	28	28	29	29/0	♉ 0	1	2	2	3	4	4	5	6	6	7	8	8	9	10	10	11	12	12

♃ 7 12 18 24 / ♐29 29 0 ♑ 1 2 3 — ♄ 1 21 29 / ♉29 29 0 ♊ 0 — ♅ 1 R 29 / ♎18 17 — ♆ 1 / ♐5 — ♇ 1 R / ♎1

3

	1	2	3	4	5	6	7	8	9	10	11	12	13	14	15	16	17	18	19	20	21	22	23	24	25	26	27	28	29	30	31
☉	♓ 11	12	13	14	15	16	17	18	19	20	21	22	23	24	25	26	27	28	29	29/0	♈ 1	2	3	4	5	6	7	8	9	10	11
☽	♍ 26	♎ 8	20	♏ 2	14	26	♐ 8	20	♑ 3	15	28	♒ 12	26	♓ 10	25	♈ 10	25	♉ 10	25	♊ 9	23	♋ 7	20	♌ 3	16	28	♍ 11	23	♎ 5	18	29
☿	♓ 22	24	26	28	29/0	♈ 1	3	4	6	7	9	10	11	12	13	14	14	15	15	15	15	R 15	15	15	15	14	14	13	12	11	11
♀	♈ 23	25	26	27	28	29	29/0	♉ 1	2	4	5	6	7	8	9	10	11	12	14	15	16	17	18	19	20	21	22	23	24	25	26
♂	♉ 13	14	14	15	16	16	17	18	18	19	20	20	21	22	22	23	23	24	25	25	26	27	28	29	29	29	29/0	♊ 1	1	2	3

♃ 1 8 16 26 / ♑4 5 6 7 — ♄ 1 11 24 / ♊0 1 2 — ♅ 1 R 31 / ♎17 16 — ♆ 1 7 R / ♐5 5 — ♇ 1 R 31 / ♎1 0

4

	1	2	3	4	5	6	7	8	9	10	11	12	13	14	15	16	17	18	19	20	21	22	23	24	25	26	27	28	29	30
☉	♈ 12	13	14	15	16	17	18	19	20	21	22	23	23	24	25	26	27	28	29/0	♉ 0	1	2	3	4	5	6	7	8	9	10
☽	♏ 11	23	♐ 5	17	29	♑ 11	24	♒ 7	20	♓ 4	18	♈ 3	18	♉ 4	19	♊ 4	18	♋ 3	16	♌ 0	13	25	♍ 8	20	♎ 2	14	26	♏ 8	20	♐ 2
☿	♈ 10	R 9	8	7	7	6	5	5	4	4	3	3	3	D 3	3	4	4	5	5	5	6	6	7	8	8	9	10	11	12	13
♀	♉ 27	28	29/0	♊ 0	1	2	3	4	5	6	7	8	9	10	11	12	13	14	15	16	16	17	18	19	20	20	21	22	23	23
♂	♊ 3	4	5	5	6	7	8	8	9	9	10	10	11	12	12	13	14	14	15	15	16	16	17	18	19	20	20	21	22	22

♃ 1 11 25 R / ♑7 8 8 — ♄ 1 3 13 22 30 / ♊2 3 4 5 6 — ♅ 1 R 30 / ♎16 15 — ♆ 1 R 30 / ♐5 4 — ♇ 1 R 17 / ♎0 ♍29

5

	1	2	3	4	5	6	7	8	9	10	11	12	13	14	15	16	17	18	19	20	21	22	23	24	25	26	27	28	29	30	31
☉	♉ 11	12	13	14	15	16	17	18	19	20	21	22	23	24	25	26	27	27	28	29/0	♊ 0	1	2	3	4	5	6	7	8	9	10
☽	♐ 14	26	♑ 8	20	♒ 3	16	29	♓ 13	27	♈ 11	27	♉ 12	27	♊ 12	27	♋ 12	25	♌ 9	22	♍ 5	17	29	♎ 11	22	♏ 5	17	29	♐ 11	23	♑ 5	17
☿	♈ 14	15	16	18	19	20	21	23	25	26	27	29	♉ 0	2	4	5	7	9	11	12	14	16	18	20	22	24	26	28	29/0	♊ 2	4
♀	♊ 24	25	26	26	27	27	28	28	29	29/0	♋ 1	1	2	2	2	3	3	3	3	4	4	4	4	4	4	4	R 4	4	4	4	4
♂	♊ 23	23	24	25	25	26	26	27	28	29	29	29/0	♋ 0	1	2	2	3	3	4	5	5	6	7	7	8	8	9	10	10	11	12

♃ 1 R 24 31 / ♑8 7 6 — ♄ 1 8 16 24 31 / ♊6 7 8 9 10 — ♅ 1 R 31 / ♎15 14 — ♆ 1 R / ♐4 — ♇ 1 / ♍29

6

	1	2	3	4	5	6	7	8	9	10	11	12	13	14	15	16	17	18	19	20	21	22	23	24	25	26	27	28	29	30
☉	♊ 11	12	13	14	15	16	17	18	19	20	21	21	22	23	24	25	26	27	28	29	29/0	♋ 1	2	3	4	5	6	7	8	9
☽	♑ 29	♒ 12	25	♓ 9	23	♈ 6	21	♉ 6	21	♊ 6	21	♋ 5	19	♌ 4	17	♍ 0	13	25	♎ 8	20	♏ 2	13	25	♐ 7	19	♑ 1	14	27	♒ 10	22
☿	♊ 6	9	11	13	15	18	20	22	24	26	28	29/0	♋ 2	5	7	9	11	13	15	16	18	20	22	24	25	26	28	29/0	♌ 1	2
♀	♋ 4	R 4	4	3	3	3	2	2	1	1	0/29	♊ 29	29	28	28	27	27	26	26	25	24	24	23	23	22	21	21	21	20	20
♂	♋ 13	13	14	14	15	16	17	17	18	19	19	20	20	21	21	22	23	23	24	25	25	26	26	27	28	28	29	29/0	♌ 0	1

♃ 1 R 12 20 28 / ♑6 5 4 3 — ♄ 1 8 16 24 / ♊10 11 12 13 — ♅ 1 R 22 D / ♎14 14 — ♆ 1 R 29 / ♐4 3 — ♇ 1 9 D / ♍29 29

7

	1	2	3	4	5	6	7	8	9	10	11	12	13	14	15	16	17	18	19	20	21	22	23	24	25	26	27	28	29	30	31
☉	♋ 10	11	12	13	14	14	15	16	17	18	19	20	21	22	23	24	25	26	27	28	29	29/0	♌ 1	2	3	4	5	6	7	8	9
☽	♓ 6	19	♈ 3	17	♉ 1	16	♊ 0	15	29	♋ 14	28	♌ 11	25	♍ 9	21	♎ 3	16	28	♏ 10	22	♐ 3	15	28	♑ 10	23	♒ 6	18	♓ 3	16	♈ 0	14
☿	♌ 4	5	6	7	8	10	12	13	13	14	15	16	17	18	19	19	20	20	20	21	22	22	22	22	R 22	22	22	21	21	21	21
♀	♊ 19	R 19	19	19	18	18	18	18	18	D 18	18	18	18	18	19	19	19	19	20	20	21	21	21	22	22	23	23	24	24	25	26
♂	♌ 2	2	3	4	4	5	6	6	7	7	8	8	9	10	10	11	12	12	13	13	14	15	15	16	17	17	18	18	19	20	21

♃ 1 R 15 24 31 / ♑2 1 0 29 ♐ 29 — ♄ 1 10 19 29 / ♊14 15 16 17 — ♅ 1 31 / ♎14 15 — ♆ 1 R 31 / ♐3 2 — ♇ 1 30 31 / ♍29 29 0 ♎ 0

8

	1	2	3	4	5	6	7	8	9	10	11	12	13	14	15	16	17	18	19	20	21	22	23	24	25	26	27	28	29	30	31
☉	♌ 9	10	11	12	13	14	15	16	17	18	19	20	21	22	23	24	25	26	26	27	28	29	29/0	♍ 1	2	3	4	5	6	7	8
☽	♈ 28	♉ 12	27	♊ 11	25	♋ 9	23	♌ 6	20	♍ 3	16	29	♎ 11	24	♏ 6	18	29	♐ 11	23	♑ 6	18	♒ 1	14	28	♓ 12	26	♈ 10	25	♉ 9	23	♊ 8
☿	♌ 20	R 19	19	18	17	16	16	15	14	14	13	12	12	11	11	11	10	D 10	10	11	11	12	12	13	14	15	16	17	18	20	21
♀	♊ 27	27	28	29	29	29/0	♋ 1	2	2	3	4	5	5	6	7	8	9	10	11	12	13	13	15	16	16	17	18	19	20	21	22
♂	♌ 21	22	23	24	24	24	25	26	26	27	28	28	29	29	29/0	♍ 1	1	2	3	3	4	5	5	6	6	7	8	8	9	10	10

♃ 1 R 26 D 31 / ♐29 29 28 — ♄ 1 8 21 / ♊17 18 19 — ♅ 1 27 / ♎15 16 — ♆ 1 R 14 D 31 / ♐2 2 2 — ♇ 1 31 / ♎0 1

9

	1	2	3	4	5	6	7	8	9	10	11	12	13	14	15	16	17	18	19	20	21	22	23	24	25	26	27	28	29	30
☉	♍ 9	10	11	12	13	14	15	16	17	18	19	20	21	22	23	24	25	25	26	27	28	29/0	♎ 0	1	2	3	4	5	6	7
☽	♊ 22	♋ 6	19	♌ 3	16	29	♍ 12	25	♎ 7	19	♏ 2	14	26	♐ 7	19	♑ 1	14	26	♒ 9	22	♓ 6	20	♈ 5	19	♉ 4	19	♊ 4	18	♋ 2	16
☿	♌ 23	24	26	28	29/0	♍ 1	3	5	7	9	11	13	15	16	18	20	22	24	26	28	29/0	♎ 1	3	5	6	8	10	12	13	15
♀	♋ 23	24	25	26	27	28	29/0	♌ 0	1	2	3	4	5	6	7	8	9	11	12	13	14	15	16	17	18	19	20	22	23	24
♂	♍ 11	12	12	13	14	14	15	15	16	17	17	18	18	19	20	21	21	22	22	23	24	24	25	26	26	27	28	28	29	29

♃ 1 12 25 30 / ♐28 29 29 0 ♑ 0 — ♄ 1 7 / ♊19 20 — ♅ 1 14 30 / ♎16 17 18 — ♆ 1 27 / ♐2 3 — ♇ 1 27 / ♎1 2

10

	1	2	3	4	5	6	7	8	9	10	11	12	13	14	15	16	17	18	19	20	21	22	23	24	25	26	27	28	29	30	31
☉	♎ 8	9	10	11	12	13	14	15	16	17	18	19	20	21	22	23	24	25	26	27	28	29	29/0	♏ 1	2	3	4	5	6	7	8
☽	♋ 29	♌ 13	26	♍ 8	21	♎ 4	16	28	♏ 10	22	♐ 4	16	28	♑ 10	22	♒ 4	17	♓ 0	14	28	♈ 13	28	♉ 13	28	♊ 13	28	♋ 12	26	♌ 10	23	♍ 5
☿	♎ 17	18	20	22	23	25	26	28	29/0	♏ 1	3	4	5	7	8	10	12	13	14	16	17	18	20	21	22	24	25	26	28	29/0	♐ 1
♀	♌ 25	26	27	29	29/0	♍ 1	2	3	4	6	7	8	9	10	11	12	14	15	16	17	18	19	20	22	23	25	26	27	28	29/0	♎ 0
♂	♎ 0	1	2	2	3	4	4	5	5	6	7	7	8	9	9	10	11	11	12	13	13	14	14	15	16	16	17	18	18	19	19

♃ 5 13 20 26 31 / ♑0 1 2 3 4 5 — ♄ 1 3 R / ♊20 20 — ♅ 1 17 31 / ♎18 19 20 — ♆ 1 31 / ♐3 4 — ♇ 1 24 / ♎3 3

11

	1	2	3	4	5	6	7	8	9	10	11	12	13	14	15	16	17	18	19	20	21	22	23	24	25	26	27	28	29	30
☉	♏ 9	10	11	12	13	14	15	16	17	18	19	20	21	22	23	24	25	26	27	28	29	29/0	♐ 1	2	3	4	5	6	7	8
☽	♍ 19	♎ 1	13	25	♏ 7	19	♐ 1	13	25	♑ 6	18	♒ 0	13	26	♓ 9	22	♈ 7	21	♉ 6	21	♊ 6	22	♋ 7	22	♌ 6	20	♍ 2	15	28	♎ 10
☿	♐ 2	3	4	5	6	7	8	9	10	10	11	11	12	12	12	R 12	12	12	11	11	10	9	8	7	5	4	3	1	0/29	♏ 29
♀	♎ 2	3	4	5	7	8	9	10	11	12	13	15	16	17	19	20	21	22	24	25	26	27	29	29/0	♏ 1	2	3	4	6	7
♂	♎ 20	21	22	22	23	24	24	25	26	26	27	28	28	29	29/0	♏ 0	1	1	2	3	3	4	5	5	6	7	8	8	9	9

♃ 6 12 17 22 27 / ♑5 6 7 8 9 10 — ♄ 1 R 14 28 / ♊20 19 18 — ♅ 1 19 / ♎20 21 — ♆ 1 27 / ♐4 5 — ♇ 1 28 / ♎3 4

12

	1	2	3	4	5	6	7	8	9	10	11	12	13	14	15	16	17	18	19	20	21	22	23	24	25	26	27	28	29	30	31
☉	♐ 9	10	11	12	13	14	15	16	17	18	19	20	21	22	23	24	25	26	27	28	29/0	♑ 1	2	3	4	5	6	7	8	9	10
☽	♎ 22	♏ 4	16	28	♐ 10	22	♑ 3	15	27	♒ 10	22	♓ 5	18	♈ 2	16	♉ 0	14	29	♊ 15	♋ 0	15	29	♌ 14	28	♍ 11	24	♎ 6	19	♏ 1	13	25
☿	♏ 28	R 27	26	26	26	D 26	26	27	27	28	28	29	♐ 0	1	2	3	4	5	7	8	9	11	12	14	15	16	18	19	21	22	24
♀	♏ 8	10	11	12	13	15	16	17	18	19	21	22	23	25	26	27	28	29/0	♐ 1	2	3	4	6	7	8	9	11	12	13	15	16
♂	♏ 10	11	12	12	13	13	14	15	16	16	17	18	18	19	20	20	21	22	23	23	24	24	25	25	26	27	28	28	29	29/0	♐ 0

♃ 6 11 15 19 24 28 / ♑11 12 13 14 15 16 17 — ♄ 1 R 22 31 / ♊17 16 15 — ♅ 1 10 / ♎21 22 — ♆ 1 25 / ♐5 6 — ♇ 1 / ♎4

1973

1

	1	2	3	4	5	6	7	8	9	10	11	12	13	14	15	16	17	18	19	20	21	22	23	24	25	26	27	28	29	30	31
☉	♑ 11	12	13	14	15	16	17	18	19	20	21	22	23	24	25	26	27	28	29	29/0	♒ 1	2	3	4	5	6	7	8	9	10	11
☽	♐ 6	18	♑ 0	12	24	♒ 7	20	♓ 2	15	28	♈ 11	26	♉ 10	24	♊ 8	23	♋ 8	23	♌ 7	21	♍ 5	19	♎ 2	14	27	♏ 9	21	♐ 3	15	26	♑ 8
☿	♐ 25	27	28	29/0	♑ 1	3	4	5	7	9	10	12	14	15	17	19	20	21	23	24	26	28	29/0	♒ 1	3	4	6	8	10	11	13
♀	♐ 17	18	19	20	22	23	24	25	27	28	29/0	♑ 1	2	3	4	5	7	8	9	11	12	13	14	16	17	18	19	21	22	23	24
♂	♐ 1	2	2	3	4	4	5	6	6	7	8	8	9	10	10	11	12	13	13	14	15	15	16	17	17	18	19	19	20	21	22

♃ 1 6 10 14 19 23 27 31 / ♑18 19 20 21 22 23 24 25 — ♄ 1 R 24 / ♊15 14 — ♅ 1 15 27 R / ♎22 23 23 — ♆ 1 29 / ♐6 7 — ♇ 1 6 R / ♎4 4

2

	1	2	3	4	5	6	7	8	9	10	11	12	13	14	15	16	17	18	19	20	21	22	23	24	25	26	27	28
☉	♒ 12	13	14	15	16	17	18	19	20	21	22	23	24	25	26	27	28	29/0	♓ 1	2	3	4	5	6	7	8	9	10
☽	♑ 21	♒ 3	16	29	♓ 12	25	♈ 9	22	♉ 6	20	♊ 4	18	♋ 3	17	♌ 1	16	29	♍ 12	26	♎ 10	22	♏ 5	17	29	♐ 11	22	♑ 4	16
☿	♒ 15	17	18	20	22	24	25	27	29/0	♓ 1	3	4	6	8	10	12	13	15	16	18	20	21	22	23	25	26	27	27
♀	♑ 26	27	28	29/0	♒ 1	2	3	4	5	6	8	9	10	12	13	14	16	17	18	19	20	22	23	24	25	27	28	29/0 ♓
♂	♐ 22	23	24	24	25	26	26	27	28	29	29	29/0	♑ 1	1	2	3	3	4	5	5	6	7	8	8	9	9	10	11

♃ 1 5 9 14 18 23 28 / ♑25 26 27 28 29 29 0 ♒ 1 — ♄ 1 R 14 D / ♊14 14 — ♅ 1 R 28 / ♎23 22 — ♆ 1 / ♐7 — ♇ 1 R / ♎4

3

	1	2	3	4	5	6	7	8	9	10	11	12	13	14	15	16	17	18	19	20	21	22	23	24	25	26	27	28	29	30	31
☉	♓ 11	12	13	14	15	16	17	18	19	20	21	22	23	24	25	26	27	28	29	29/0	♈ 1	2	3	4	5	6	7	8	9	10	11
☽	♑ 29	♒ 11	24	♓ 7	21	♈ 5	19	♉ 3	17	♊ 1	16	29	♋ 14	28	♌ 11	25	♍ 8	22	♎ 5	18	♏ 0	13	25	♐ 7	18	♑ 0	12	24	♒ 6	19	♓ 2
☿	♓ 28	28	28	28	R 28	28	28	27	27	26	25	24	23	22	22	21	20	19	18	17	17	16	16	15	15	15	15	D 15	15	15	16
♀	♓ 1	2	3	4	5	7	8	9	11	12	13	14	16	17	18	19	21	22	23	24	26	27	28	29/0	♈ 1	2	3	4	5	7	8
♂	♑ 12	13	13	14	14	15	16	17	18	18	19	20	20	21	22	22	23	24	25	25	26	27	27	28	29	29/0	♒ 0	1	2	2	3

♃ 1 5 10 15 20 26 31 / ♒1 2 3 4 5 6 7 — ♄ 1 24 / ♊14 15 — ♅ 1 R / ♎22 — ♆ 1 9 R 31 / ♐7 7 7 — ♇ 1 R / ♎3

4

	1	2	3	4	5	6	7	8	9	10	11	12	13	14	15	16	17	18	19	20	21	22	23	24	25	26	27	28	29	30
☉	♈ 11	12	13	14	15	16	17	18	19	20	21	22	23	24	25	26	27	28	29	29/0	♉ 1	2	3	4	5	6	7	8	9	10
☽	♓ 16	29	♈ 14	28	♉ 13	27	♊ 12	26	♋ 10	24	♌ 7	21	♍ 5	18	♎ 1	14	26	♏ 9	21	♐ 3	15	27	♑ 8	20	♒ 2	15	27	♓ 10	24	♈ 7
☿	♓ 16	16	17	18	19	19	20	21	22	23	24	25	26	27	28	29/0	♈ 1	2	3	4	5	6	8	10	12	13	15	16	18	20
♀	♈ 9	11	12	13	14	15	17	18	19	20	21	23	24	25	27	28	29	29/0	♉ 2	3	4	5	7	8	9	10	11	13	14	15
♂	♒ 4	4	5	6	6	7	8	9	9	10	11	12	12	13	14	14	15	16	17	17	18	19	19	20	21	22	22	23	24	24

♃ 1 8 15 23 / ♒7 8 9 10 — ♄ 1 6 17 26 / ♊15 16 17 18 — ♅ 1 R 30 / ♎21 20 — ♆ 1 R / ♐7 — ♇ 1 R 30 / ♎3 2

5

	1	2	3	4	5	6	7	8	9	10	11	12	13	14	15	16	17	18	19	20	21	22	23	24	25	26	27	28	29	30	31
☉	♉ 11	12	13	14	15	16	17	18	19	20	21	22	22	23	24	25	26	27	28	29	29/0	♊ 1	2	3	4	5	6	7	8	9	10
☽	♈ 22	♉ 7	22	♊ 7	21	♋ 6	21	♌ 5	18	♍ 2	15	28	♎ 11	23	♏ 5	17	29	♐ 11	23	♑ 5	17	29	♒ 11	23	♓ 6	19	♈ 2	16	♉ 0	15	♊ 0
☿	♈ 21	23	25	27	28	29/0	♉ 2	4	6	8	10	12	14	16	18	20	22	24	27	29/0	♊ 1	4	6	8	10	12	14	17	19	21	22
♀	♉ 17	18	19	20	21	23	24	25	26	28	29	29/0	♊ 1	2	3	5	6	7	9	10	11	12	13	15	16	17	18	20	21	22	23
♂	♒ 25	26	27	27	28	28	29	29/0	♓ 1	1	2	3	4	4	5	6	6	7	8	9	9	10	11	11	12	13	13	14	15	15	16

♃ 1 4 21 31 R / ♒10 11 12 12 — ♄ 1 5 14 22 30 / ♊18 19 20 21 22 — ♅ 1 R 31 / ♎20 19 — ♆ 1 R 31 / ♐7 6 — ♇ 1 R / ♎2

6

	1	2	3	4	5	6	7	8	9	10	11	12	13	14	15	16	17	18	19	20	21	22	23	24	25	26	27	28	29	30
☉	♊ 11	12	13	14	15	16	16	17	18	19	20	21	22	23	24	25	26	27	28	29	29/0	♋ 1	2	3	4	5	6	7	8	9
☽	♊ 15	♋ 0	15	♌ 0	14	28	♍ 11	25	♎ 8	20	♏ 2	15	27	♐ 8	20	♑ 2	14	26	♒ 7	20	♓ 2	15	28	♈ 11	24	♉ 9	22	♊ 8	23	♋ 8
☿	♊ 24	26	28	29/0	♋ 2	4	5	7	9	10	12	14	15	16	17	19	20	21	23	24	25	26	27	28	29	29	29/0	♌ 1	1	2
♀	♊ 25	26	27	28	29/0	♋ 1	2	3	4	5	7	8	9	10	11	13	14	15	17	18	19	20	22	23	24	25	26	27	29	29/0 ♌
♂	♓ 17	17	18	19	19	20	21	22	22	23	24	24	25	26	26	27	28	28	29	29/0	♈ 0	1	2	2	3	4	4	5	6	6

♃ 1 R 27 / ♒12 11 — ♄ 1 6 14 22 30 / ♊22 23 24 25 26 — ♅ 1 R 27 D / ♎19 19 — ♆ 1 R 30 / ♐6 5 — ♇ 1 R 12 D / ♎2 2

7

	1	2	3	4	5	6	7	8	9	10	11	12	13	14	15	16	17	18	19	20	21	22	23	24	25	26	27	28	29	30	31
☉	♋ 9	10	11	12	13	14	15	16	17	18	19	20	21	22	23	24	25	26	27	27	28	29	♌ 0	1	2	3	4	5	6	7	8
☽	♋ 24	♌ 9	23	♍ 7	20	♎ 4	17	29	♏ 11	24	♐ 5	17	29	♑ 11	23	♒ 5	17	29	♓ 12	25	♈ 8	21	♉ 5	19	♊ 3	17	♋ 2	17	♌ 2	17	♍ 1
☿	♌ 2	3	3	3	3	3	R 3	3	3	3	2	2	2	1	0	0/29	♋ 29	28	28	28	27	26	25	25	24	24	23	23	22	22	D 22
♀	♌ 1	2	3	5	6	7	8	9	11	12	13	14	16	17	18	19	20	22	23	24	25	26	28	29	29/0	♍ 1	3	4	5	6	7
♂	♈ 7	7	8	8	9	10	10	11	12	12	13	13	14	15	15	16	16	17	17	18	18	19	20	20	21	21	22	22	23	23	24

♃ 1 R 16 24 31 / ♒10 9 8 7 — ♄ 1 7 16 24 / ♊26 27 28 29 — ♅ 1 / ♎19 — ♆ 1 R / ♐5 — ♇ 1 / ♎2

8

	1	2	3	4	5	6	7	8	9	10	11	12	13	14	15	16	17	18	19	20	21	22	23	24	25	26	27	28	29	30	31
☉	♌ 9	10	11	12	13	14	15	16	17	18	19	19	20	21	22	23	24	25	26	27	28	29	29/0	♍ 1	2	3	4	5	6	7	8
☽	♍ 15	29	♎ 12	25	♏ 8	20	♐ 2	14	25	♑ 8	19	♒ 1	13	26	♓ 9	22	♈ 5	18	♉ 1	15	29	♊ 13	27	♋ 11	26	♌ 11	25	♍ 9	24	♎ 7	20
☿	♋ 23	23	23	24	24	25	26	27	28	29	29/0	♌ 1	2	3	5	7	8	10	12	14	15	17	19	21	23	25	27	29/0	♍ 1	3	5
♀	♍ 9	10	11	12	13	15	16	17	18	20	21	22	23	24	26	27	28	29	29/0	♎ 1	3	4	5	6	7	8	10	11	12	13	14
♂	♈ 24	25	26	26	27	27	27	28	28	29	29	29/0	♉ 0	1	1	1	2	2	3	3	3	4	4	5	5	5	5	6	6	6	7

♃ 1 R 9 17 26 31 / ♒7 6 5 4 3 — ♄ 1 2 11 21 31 / ♊29 ♋ 0 1 2 3 — ♅ 1 16 / ♎19 20 — ♆ 1 R 16 D 31 / ♐4 4 5 — ♇ 1 23 / ♎2 3

9

	1	2	3	4	5	6	7	8	9	10	11	12	13	14	15	16	17	18	19	20	21	22	23	24	25	26	27	28	29	30
☉	♍ 9	10	11	12	13	14	15	16	16	17	18	19	20	21	22	23	24	25	26	27	28	29	29/0	♎ 1	2	3	4	5	6	7
☽	♏ 3	16	28	♐ 10	22	♑ 4	16	28	♒ 10	22	♓ 5	18	♈ 1	15	28	♉ 12	26	♊ 10	24	♋ 8	22	♌ 6	20	♍ 5	18	♎ 2	15	29	♏ 11	24
☿	♍ 7	9	11	13	15	17	19	21	22	24	26	28	29/0	♎ 1	3	4	6	8	9	11	13	14	16	17	19	20	22	23	25	26
♀	♎ 16	17	18	19	20	22	23	24	25	26	28	29	29/0	♏ 1	2	3	5	6	7	8	9	10	12	13	14	15	16	17	19	20
♂	♉ 7	7	7	8	8	8	8	8	8	9	9	9	9	9	9	9	9	9	9	R 9	9	9	9	9	9	9	9	9	8	8

♃ 1 R 29 D 30 / ♒3 3 2 — ♄ 1 18 / ♋3 4 — ♅ 1 6 23 / ♎20 21 22 — ♆ 1 21 / ♐4 5 — ♇ 1 20 / ♎3 4

10

	1	2	3	4	5	6	7	8	9	10	11	12	13	14	15	16	17	18	19	20	21	22	23	24	25	26	27	28	29	30	31
☉	♎ 8	9	10	11	12	13	14	15	16	17	18	19	20	21	22	23	24	25	26	27	28	29	29/0	♏ 1	2	3	4	5	6'	7	8
☽	♐ 6	18	♑ 0	12	24	♒ 6	18	♓ 0	13	26	♈ 10	24	♉ 8	22	♊ 6	21	♋ 5	19	♌ 3	16	♍ 1	14	28	♎ 11	24	♏ 7	20	♐ 3	14	26	♑ 8
☿	♎ 28	29/0	♏ 1	2	3	5	6	7	9	10	11	12	14	15	16	18	19	20	21	21	22	23	24	25	25	25	26	26	26	26	R 26
♀	♏ 21	22	23	24	25	27	28	29	29/0	♐ 1	2	3	5	6	7	8	9	10	11	12	13	15	16	17	18	19	20	21	22	23	24
♂	♉ 8	R 8	8	8	8	7	7	7	7	6	6	6	5	5	5	4	4	4	3	3	3	2	2	2	2	1	1	0	0	♈ 29	29

♃ 1 19 31 / ♒2 3 4 — ♄ 1 17 R / ♋4 4 — ♅ 1 10 31 / ♎22 23 24 — ♆ 1 28 / ♐5 6 — ♇ 1 16 / ♎4 5

11

	1	2	3	4	5	6	7	8	9	10	11	12	13	14	15	16	17	18	19	20	21	22	23	24	25	26	27	28	29	30
☉	♏ 9	10	11	12	13	14	15	16	17	18	19	20	21	22	23	24	25	26	27	28	29	29/0	♐ 1	2	3	4	5	6	7	8
☽	♑ 20	♒ 1	13	25	♓ 8	21	♈ 4	18	♉ 2	17	♊ 1	16	♋ 1	15	29	♌ 14	28	♍ 11	25	♎ 7	21	♏ 4	16	28	♐ 10	22	♑ 4	16	28	♒ 10
☿	♏ 26	R 26	25	25	24	23	22	21	20	18	17	16	14	13	12	11	11	11	11	D 11	11	11	12	12	13	14	15	16	17	18
♀	♐ 25	26	28	29	29/0	♑ 1	2	3	4	5	6	7	8	9	10	11	12	13	14	15	16	17	18	19	20	21	22	23	23	24
♂	♈ 29	R 29	29	28	28	28	27	27	27	27	27	26	26	26	26	26	26	25	25	25	25	25	25	25	25	D 25	25	25	25	25

♃ 1 9 16 23 29 / ♒4 5 6 7 8 — ♄ 1 R 30 / ♋4 3 — ♅ 1 11 29 / ♎24 25 26 — ♆ 1 25 / ♐6 7 — ♇ 1 15 / ♎5 6

12

	1	2	3	4	5	6	7	8	9	10	11	12	13	14	15	16	17	18	19	20	21	22	23	24	25	26	27	28	29	30	31
☉	♐ 9	10	11	12	13	14	15	16	17	18	19	20	21	22	23	24	25	26	27	28	29	29/0	♑ 1	2	3	4	5	6	7	8	9
☽	♒ 22	♓ 4	16	29	♈ 12	26	♉ 10	24	♊ 9	24	♋ 9	24	♌ 9	24	♍ 8	22	♎ 5	18	♏ 0	13	25	♐ 7	19	♑ 1	13	25	♒ 6	18	♓ 0	12	25
☿	♏ 20	21	22	24	25	26	28	29/0	♐ 1	2	4	5	7	8	9	11	13	14	16	7	19	20	22	23	25	26	28	29/0	♑ 1	2	4
♀	♑ 25	26	26	27	28	29	29/0	♒ 0	1	2	2	3	4	5	5	6	6	7	7	8	8	9	9	9	10	10	10	10	11	11	11
♂	♈ 25	25	25	26	26	26	26	26	26	27	27	27	27	27	27	28	28	28	28	29	29	29	29	29/0	♉ 0	0	1	1	1	2	2

♃ 1 5 10 15 20 25 30 / ♒8 9 10 11 12 13 14 — ♄ 1 R 14 26 31 / ♋3 2 1 0 — ♅ 1 22 / ♎26 27 — ♆ 1 22 / ♐7 8 — ♇ 1 31 / ♎6 7

1974

1 (January)
Planet	Days 1–31
☉	♑ 11 12 13 14 15 16 17 18 19 20 21 22 23 24 25 26 27 28 29 ♒ 0 1 2 3 4 5 6 7 8 9 10 11
☽	8 21 4 18 2 17 2 17 2 18 3 17 1 14 27 10 22 4 16 28 10 22 3 15 27 10 23 4 17 0 13
☿	6 8 9 11 12 14 15 17 19 20 22 24 25 27 29 0 2 4 5 7 9 10 12 14 16 17 19 21 22 24 26
♀	11 11 11 11 11 11 11 11 11 10 10 10 9 9 8 8 7 7 6 6 5 5 4 3 3 2 1 1 29 29 29
♂	2 3 3 4 4 5 5 5 6 6 6 7 7 8 8 8 9 9 10 10 11 11 12 12 13 13 14 14 15 15 15

♃ 1 3 8 12 17 21 25 29 ♒14 15 16 17 18 19 20 21 — ♄ 1℞ 8 31 ♋0 II29 28 — ♅ 1 ♎27 — ♆ 1 23 ♐8 9 — ♇ 1 10℞ ♎7 7

2 (February)
Planet	Days
☉	12 13 14 15 16 17 18 19 20 21 22 23 24 25 26 27 28 29 0 1 2 3 4 5 6 7 8 9
☽	27 11 25 9 25 10 26 11 25 9 23 6 19 1 13 25 7 19 0 12 24 7 19 1 14 27 10 23
☿	27 29 0 1 2 3 5 6 7 8 9 10 11 12 12 12 11 11 11 10 9 8 7 6 4 3 2
♀	28 28 28 27 27 27 26 26 26 26 26 26 26 26 26 26 26 26 26 27 27 27 27 28 28 29 29 0
♂	16 17 17 18 18 19 19 20 20 21 21 22 22 23 23 24 24 25 25 26 26 27 27 28 28 29 29 0

♃ 1 3 7 11 15 19 24 28 ♒21 22 23 24 25 26 27 28 — ♄ 1℞ 28 D II28 28 — ♅ 1℞ ♎27 — ♆ 1 ♐9 — ♇ 1℞ 28 ♎7 6

3 (March)
Planet	Days
☉	10 11 12 13 14 15 16 17 18 19 20 21 22 23 24 25 26 27 28 29 0 1 2 3 4 5 6 7 8 9 10
☽	7 21 5 19 4 19 4 18 3 17 0 14 27 9 21 3 15 27 8 20 3 15 28 11 24 7 21 4 18 2 16
☿	1 29 29 29 28 28 27 27 27 27 27 27 27 28 28 28 29 0 0 1 2 3 4 5 6 7 8 9 11 12 13
♀	0 1 1 2 2 3 4 4 5 6 6 7 8 8 9 9 10 11 12 13 13 14 15 16 17 18 19 20 21 22 23
♂	1 2 2 3 4 4 5 5 6 6 7 8 8 9 9 10 10 11 12 12 13 13 14 14 15 16 16 17 17 18

♃ 1 4 8 12 17 21 26 30 ♒28 29 0 ♓1 2 3 4 5 — ♄ 1 II28 — ♅ 1℞ 31 ♎27 26 — ♆ 1 12℞ ♐9 9 — ♇ 1℞ 31 ♎6 5

4 (April)
Planet	Days
☉	11 12 13 14 15 16 17 18 19 20 21 22 23 24 25 26 27 28 29 0 1 2 3 4 5 6 7 8 9 10
☽	0 14 29 13 27 11 25 8 22 4 17 29 11 23 5 16 28 11 23 6 20 3 17 0 14 28 13 27 11 25
☿	15 16 17 19 20 22 23 24 26 28 29 1 3 4 6 8 9 11 13 15 17 19 21 22 24 26 28 0 2 4
♀	25 26 27 28 29 0 1 2 3 4 5 6 7 8 9 10 11 12 13 14 15 16 17 18 19 20 21 22 23 24
♂	19 19 20 20 21 21 22 23 23 24 24 25 25 26 27 27 28 28 29 0 0 1 1 2 3 3 4 4 5 6

♃ 1 4 9 13 18 24 29 ♓5 6 7 8 9 10 11 — ♄ 1 15 19 30 II28 29 ♋0 1 — ♅ 1℞ 30 ♎26 25 — ♆ 1℞ ♐9 — ♇ 1℞ 30 ♎5 4

5 (May)
Planet	Days
☉	11 12 13 14 14 15 16 17 18 19 20 21 22 23 24 25 26 27 28 29 0 1 2 3 4 5 6 7 8 9 10
☽	9 23 7 21 4 17 0 12 25 7 19 1 13 24 6 19 1 14 28 11 25 9 24 9 23 8 22 6 20 4 17
☿	7 9 11 13 15 17 19 22 24 26 28 0 2 5 7 9 11 13 14 16 18 19 21 22 23 24 25 27 29 0 2
♀	26 27 28 0 1 2 3 4 5 6 7 8 9 10 11 13 14 15 16 17 18 19 20 21 22 23 24 25 27 28 29
♂	7 7 8 9 9 10 10 11 12 12 13 14 14 15 16 16 17 17 18 19 19 20 20 21 22 22 23 23 24 24 25

♃ 1 5 11 18 25 ♓11 12 13 14 15 — ♄ 1 9 18 27 ♋1 2 3 4 — ♅ 1℞ 31 ♎25 24 — ♆ 1℞ 31 ♐9 8 — ♇ 1℞ ♎4

6 (June)
Planet	Days
☉	10 11 12 13 14 15 16 17 18 19 20 21 22 23 24 25 26 27 28 29 0 1 2 3 4 5 6 7 8
☽	0 13 26 8 21 3 15 27 9 21 2 15 27 9 23 7 19 4 18 3 18 3 18 2 16 0 14 27 10 23
☿	4 5 6 7 8 9 9 10 11 11 12 12 13 13 13 13 13 13 13 13 13 13 13 12 12 11 11 10 10 9
♀	1 2 3 5 6 7 8 9 10 12 13 14 15 16 18 19 20 21 23 24 25 26 27 29 0 1 3 4 5
♂	25 26 26 27 28 28 29 29 0 1 1 2 2 3 4 4 5 5 6 7 7 8 8 9 10 10 11 11 12 12

♃ 1 14 ♓16 17 — ♄ 1 4 12 20 28 ♋4 5 6 7 8 — ♅ 1℞ ♎24 — ♆ 1℞ 30 ♐8 7 — ♇ 1℞ 15 D ♎4 4

7 (July)
Planet	Days
☉	9 10 11 12 13 14 15 16 17 18 19 20 21 22 23 24 25 26 27 28 29 0 1 2 3 4 5 6 7 8
☽	5 18 29 12 24 5 17 29 11 23 5 18 1 14 28 12 26 11 26 11 27 11 26 10 24 7 21 2 15 27 9
☿	8 8 7 7 6 6 5 5 5 4 4 4 4 4 4 4 5 5 5 6 6 7 7 8 9 10 11 12 14 16 17 18 20
♀	6 7 8 9 11 12 13 14 16 17 18 19 21 22 23 24 25 27 28 29 0 1 3 4 5 6 7 9 10 11 12
♂	14 14 15 15 16 16 17 17 18 19 19 20 21 21 22 22 23 23 24 25 25 26 26 27 28 28 29 29 0 1 2

♃ 1 8℞ ♓17 17 — ♄ 1 5 13 21 29 ♋8 9 10 11 12 — ♅ 1 D ♎24 — ♆ 1℞ ♐7 — ♇ 1 ♎4

8 (August)
Planet	Days
☉	9 10 11 12 13 14 15 16 17 18 19 20 21 22 23 24 25 26 27 28 29 0 1 2 3 4 5 6 7 8
☽	21 2 14 26 8 20 2 15 27 10 23 7 20 5 20 5 20 5 19 3 16 29 12 24 6 18 29 11 23
☿	22 24 26 28 0 2 4 6 8 10 12 14 16 18 20 22 24 26 28 0 2 4 6 8 9 11 13 15 17 18 20
♀	13 15 16 17 18 19 20 22 23 24 26 27 28 29 0 2 3 4 5 6 8 9 10 11 12 14 15 16 17 18 20
♂	3 4 4 5 5 6 7 7 8 8 9 9 10 11 11 12 12 13 13 14 14 15 16 16 17 17 18 19 19 20 21 22

♃ 1℞ 11 20 28 31 ♓17 16 15 14 13 — ♄ 1 6 15 24 ♋12 13 14 15 — ♅ 1 28 ♎24 25 — ♆ 1℞ 19 D ♐7 7 — ♇ 1 13 ♎4 5

9 (September)
Planet	Days
☉	9 10 11 11 12 13 14 15 16 17 18 19 20 21 22 23 24 25 26 27 28 29 0 1 2 3 4 5 6 7
☽	5 17 29 12 24 7 20 3 16 0 14 29 14 28 13 28 13 27 11 24 7 20 2 14 26 8 20 2 14 26
☿	22 24 25 27 28 29 0 2 3 5 6 8 9 11 12 14 15 16 18 19 20 21 22 23 24 26 27 28 29 0 2
♀	21 23 24 25 26 28 29 0 1 2 4 5 6 7 8 10 11 12 13 15 16 17 18 20 21 22 23 25 26 27
♂	23 23 24 24 25 26 26 27 27 28 29 29 0 0 1 2 2 3 3 4 5 5 6 6 7 8 8 9 9 10

♃ 1℞ 12 20 29 ♓13 12 11 10 — ♄ 1 3 15 30 ♋15 16 17 18 — ♅ 1 16 ♎25 26 — ♆ 1 ♐7 — ♇ 1 11 ♎5 6

10 (October)
Planet	Days
☉	8 9 10 11 12 13 14 15 16 17 18 19 20 21 22 23 24 25 26 27 28 29 0 1 2 3 4 5 6 7 8
☽	8 21 4 17 0 13 26 10 25 9 23 8 23 7 21 5 20 2 15 28 10 22 4 16 28 10 22 4 17 0 13
☿	3 4 5 6 7 8 9 9 10 10 10 10 10 10 10 10 9 9 8 7 6 5 4 2 1 0 29 29 28 27 26
♀	29 0 1 2 3 5 6 7 8 9 10 11 12 13 15 16 17 18 20 21 22 23 24 25 27 28 29 0 1 2 3
♂	12 13 14 14 15 15 16 16 17 18 18 19 19 20 21 21 22 22 23 24 24 25 25 26 27 27 28 28 29 0 1

♃ 1℞ 10 31 ♓10 9 8 — ♄ 1 ♋18 — ♅ 1 3 19 ♎26 27 28 — ♆ 1 25 ♐7 8 — ♇ 1 8 ♎6 7

11 (November)
Planet	Days
☉	9 10 11 12 13 14 15 16 17 18 19 20 21 22 23 24 25 26 27 28 29 0 1 2 3 4 5 6 7 8
☽	26 9 24 7 21 5 20 4 18 2 16 0 13 27 11 23 5 18 0 12 24 6 18 0 12 25 8 21 5 19
☿	25 25 25 25 25 25 26 27 28 29 0 1 3 4 5 7 8 10 11 13 14 16 17 19 20 22 23 25 26
♀	7 8 10 11 12 13 14 15 16 18 19 20 21 22 24 25 26 27 29 0 1 2 3 5 6 7 8 10 11 12 13
♂	3 4 5 5 6 7 7 8 9 9 10 11 11 12 13 13 14 15 15 16 17 17 18 19 19 20 21 21 22 23

♃ 1℞ 4 28 ♓8 D 9 — ♄ 1℞ ♋18 — ♅ 1 4 21 30 ♎28 29 29 0 ♏0 — ♆ 1 23 ♐8 9 — ♇ 1 ♎8

12 (December)
Planet	Days
☉	9 10 11 12 13 14 15 16 17 18 19 20 21 22 23 24 25 26 27 28 29 0 1 2 3 4 5 6 7 8 9
☽	2 16 0 15 29 12 26 10 23 6 19 1 14 26 8 20 2 14 26 8 20 3 16 29 13 27 12 27 12 27 12
☿	29 0 2 3 4 6 8 9 11 13 14 16 17 19 20 22 24 25 27 28 0 1 3 5 6 8 9 11 13 14 16
♀	15 16 17 18 20 21 22 24 25 26 27 29 0 1 2 3 5 6 7 8 10 11 12 13 14 15 16 18 19 20 21
♂	24 24 25 26 27 27 28 29 29 0 1 1 2 3 4 4 5 6 6 7 8 9 9 10 11 11 12 13 13 14 15

♃ 1 8 16 23 30 ♓9 10 11 12 13 — ♄ 1℞ 17 30 ♋18 17 16 — ♅ 1 10 ♏0 1 — ♆ 1 19 ♐9 10 — ♇ 1 13 ♎8 9

1975

1 (January)
Planet	Days
☉	♑ 10 11 12 13 14 15 16 17 18 19 20 21 22 23 24 25 26 27 28 29 ♒ 0 1 2 3 4 5 6 7 8 9 10
☽	26 11 25 10 23 7 20 3 15 28 10 22 4 16 28 10 22 4 16 28 11 24 7 21 5 20 5 20 5 20 5
☿	18 19 21 23 24 26 27 29 0 2 4 5 7 9 10 12 13 15 16 18 19 20 21 22 23 24 25 25 25 25 25
♀	24 25 26 27 29 0 1 3 4 5 6 8 9 10 11 13 14 15 16 17 19 20 21 23 24 25 26 28 29 0 1
♂	15 16 17 17 18 19 20 20 21 22 22 23 24 25 25 26 27 27 28 29 0 0 1 2 3 3 4 5 5 6 7

♃ 1 5 10 16 21 25 30 ♓13 14 15 16 17 18 19 — ♄ 1℞ 11 24 31 ♋16 15 14 13 — ♅ 1 5 ♏1 2 — ♆ 1 19 ♐10 11 — ♇ 1 14℞ ♎9 9

2 (February)
Planet	Days
☉	12 13 14 15 16 17 18 19 20 21 22 23 24 25 26 27 28 29 0 1 2 3 4 5 6 7 8 9
☽	19 3 17 29 13 25 7 19 1 13 25 7 19 1 13 25 7 20 2 15 29 13 28 13 28 13 29 14
☿	25 25 24 23 22 21 20 19 18 17 16 15 14 13 12 11 11 10 10 10 10 10 10 11 11 11 12 12
♀	3 4 5 6 8 9 10 11 13 14 15 16 18 19 20 21 23 24 25 26 27 29 0 1 2 4 5 6
♂	8 9 10 10 11 12 13 13 14 15 15 16 17 17 18 19 20 20 21 22 22 23 24 25 25 26 27 28

♃ 1 4 8 13 17 21 26 ♓19 20 21 22 23 24 25 — ♄ 1℞ 28 ♋13 12 — ♅ 1 6℞ 28 ♏2 2 2 — ♆ 1 ♐11 — ♇

3 (March)
Planet	Days
☉	10 11 12 13 14 15 16 17 18 19 20 21 22 23 24 25 26 27 28 29 0 1 2 3 4 5 6 7 8
☽	28 12 26 9 22 4 16 28 10 22 4 16 28 10 22 4 17 29 12 25 8 22 7 22 7 21 6
☿	13 14 15 16 17 18 19 20 21 22 23 24 26 27 28 0 1 3 4 6 7 8 10 11 13 15 16 18 19
♀	7 9 10 11 12 13 15 16 17 18 20 21 22 23 24 26 27 28 0 1 2 3 4 5 7 8 9 10 11
♂	28 29 0 1 1 2 3 4 4 5 6 6 7 8 9 9 10 11 11 12 13 14 14 15 16 16 17 18 19 19 20

♃ 1 6 10 14 18 23 27 31 ♓26 27 28 29 0 ♈1 2 3 — ♄ 1℞ 15 27 ♋12 D 12 — ♅ 1℞ 8 ♏2 1 — ♆ 1℞ 14℞ ♐11 11 — ♇ 1℞

4 (April)
Planet	Days
☉	11 12 13 14 15 16 17 18 19 20 21 22 23 24 25 26 27 28 29 0 1 2 3 4 5 6 7 8 9 10
☽	17 0 13 25 7 19 1 13 25 6 19 1 14 26 9 22 5 19 3 17 1 16 1 15 0 14 29 12 25
☿	24 26 28 0 1 3 5 7 9 11 13 15 17 19 21 23 25 27 29 1 3 5 7 9 10 12 14 16 18 20
♀	16 17 19 20 21 22 23 25 26 27 28 29 0 1 3 4 5 6 7 8 9 10 12 13 14 15 16 17 18 20
♂	22 23 24 24 25 26 27 27 28 29 0 0 1 2 3 3 4 5 6 6 7 8 9 9 10 11 11 12 13

♃ 1 4 8 12 17 21 25 30 ♈3 4 5 6 7 8 9 10 — ♄ 1 ♋12 13 — ♅ 1℞ 30 ♏1 0 — ♆ 1℞ ♐11 — ♇ 1℞ 30 ♎5 4

5 (May)
Planet	Days
☉	10 11 12 13 14 15 16 17 18 19 20 21 22 23 24 25 26 27 28 29 0 1 2 3 4 5 6 7 8 9 10
☽	21 3 15 27 9 21 3 15 27 10 23 5 18 2 16 29 13 28 12 26 11 25 9 23 7 20 3 16 28 10 22
☿	24 26 28 0 1 3 5 6 8 9 11 12 13 14 15 16 17 18 18 19 19 20 20 20 20 20 20 20 20 20 19
♀	20 21 22 23 24 25 26 27 28 0 1 2 3 4 5 6 7 8 9 10 11 12 13 14 15 16 17 18 19 20 21
♂	15 16 17 18 19 20 21 22 23 24 25 26 27 28 29 0 1 2 3 4 5 6 7 8 9 10 11 12 13 14 15

♃ 1 4 9 13 18 23 28 ♈10 11 12 13 14 15 16 — ♄ 1 13 23 31 ♋14 15 16 17 — ♅ 1℞ 2 ♏0 ♎29 — ♆ 1℞ 31 ♐11 10 — ♇ 1℞

6 (June)
Planet	Days
☉	10 11 12 13 14 15 16 17 18 19 20 21 22 23 24 25 26 27 28 29 0 1 2 3 4 5 6 7 8
☽	5 17 29 11 23 5 18 1 15 28 12 26 10 24 9 23 7 21 5 19 2 16 29 12 24 7 19 1 13
☿	23 22 22 21 21 20 20 19 19 18 18 17 17 16 16 16 15 15 15 15 15 15 15 15 15 16 16 16 17
♀	24 25 27 28 29 0 1 2 3 4 5 6 7 8 9 10 11 12 13 14 15 16 17 18 19 20 21 22
♂	11 12 13 13 14 15 15 16 17 18 18 19 20 21 21 22 23 24 24 25 26 27 27 28 29

♃ 1 2 8 13 20 26 ♈16 17 18 19 20 21 — ♄ 1 10 18 26 ♋17 18 19 20 — ♅ 1℞ 30 ♎29 28 — ♆ 1℞ ♐10 — ♇ 1℞ ♎4

7 (July)
Planet	Days
☉	9 10 11 12 13 14 15 16 17 18 19 20 21 22 23 24 25 26 27 28 29 0 1 2 3 4 5 6 7 8 9
☽	7 19 1 14 26 9 23 7 21 5 20 5 19 4 18 2 15 29 12 25 8 21 3 15 27 9 21 3 15
☿	18 19 20 20 21 22 23 25 26 27 28 0 1 3 5 6 8 10 12 14 15 17 20 22 24 26 28 0 2 4 6
♀	24 25 26 27 28 28 29 0 1 1 2 3 3 4 5 5 6 6 7 7 8 8 9 9 10 10 10 10 10 10 10
♂	0 1 2 3 3 4 5 6 6 7 8 9 9 10 11 11 12 13 14 14 15 16 16 17 18 19 19

♃ 1 4 13 25 ♈21 22 23 24 — ♄ 1 4 12 19 27 ♋20 21 22 23 24 — ♅ 1℞ 8 D ♎28 28 — ♆ 1℞ 31 ♐10 9 — ♇ 1

8 (August)
Planet	Days
☉	9 10 11 12 13 14 15 16 17 18 19 20 21 22 23 24 25 26 27 28 29 0 1 2 3 4 5 6 7
☽	22 4 17 1 15 29 14 29 14 29 14 28 12 26 9 22 5 18 29 12 24 6 18 0 12 24 6 19 2
☿	8 10 12 15 17 19 21 23 25 27 28 0 2 4 6 8 10 11 13 14 16 17 19 21 22 24 25 27 28
♀	11 11 11 11 11 11 11 11 11 11 11 11 10 10 10 9 9 8 8 7 7 6 6 5 5 4 4 3 3
♂	21 22 22 23 24 25 25 26 26 27 28 28 29 0 0 1 1 2 2 3 3 4 4 5 5 6 6 7

♃ 1 15℞ ♈24 24 — ♄ 1 4 12 20 28 ♋24 25 26 27 28 — ♅ 1 15 ♎28 29 — ♆ 1℞ 21 D ♐9 9 — ♇ 1

9 (September)
Planet	Days
☉	8 9 10 11 12 13 14 15 16 17 18 19 20 21 22 23 24 25 26 27 28 29 0 1 2 3 4 5 6
☽	9 23 8 23 8 23 8 22 6 19 3 15 28 10 22 4 16 28 9 21 3 15 27 9 21 4 17 1 14 28
☿	2 4 5 6 8 9 10 12 13 14 15 16 17 18 19 20 21 22 23 23 23 24 24 24 24 24 24 24 23 22
♀	0 29 29 29 29 28 28 27 27 26 26 26 26 25 25 25 25 25 25 26 26 26 26 26 26 27 27 27 28
♂	10 11 11 12 12 13 14 14 15 15 16 17 17 18 18 19 19 20 20 21 21 22 22 23 23 24

♃ 1℞ 16 25 30 ♈24 23 22 21 — ♄ 1 7 17 28 ♋28 29 ♌0 1 — ♅ 1 8 29 27 ♎29 0 ♏1 — ♆ 1 ♐9 — ♇ 1

10 (October)
Planet	Days
☉	8 9 10 11 12 13 14 15 16 17 18 19 20 21 22 23 24 25 26 27 28 29 0 1 2 3 4 5 6 7
☽	12 26 11 25 10 25 10 24 8 22 6 19 2 15 28 10 22 4 16 28 10 22 4 16 29 12 26 9 23 7
☿	16 16 16 16 16 16 17 17 18 18 19 19 20 21 22 23 24 26 27 28 0 1 3 4 6 7 9 11 12 14 15
♀	28 29 29 0 0 1 1 2 3 4 5 6 7 8 9 10 11 12 13 14 15 16 17 18 19 20 21 22 23 24 25
♂	25 25 25 26 26 26 27 27 27 28 28 28 29 29 29 29 0 0 0 1 1 1 1 1 2 2 2 2

♃ 1℞ 11 18 26 31 ♈21 20 19 18 17 — ♄ 1 13 ♌1 2 — ♅ 1 13 29 ♏1 2 3 — ♆ 1 22 ♐9 10 — ♇ 1

11 (November)
Planet	Days
☉	8 9 10 11 12 13 14 15 16 17 18 19 20 21 22 23 24 25 26 27 28 29 0 1 2 3 4 5 6 7
☽	10 25 10 24 9 22 6 20 2 14 26 8 20 2 14 26 8 20 3 16 29 12 25 9 23 6 21 5 19
☿	22 24 25 27 28 0 1 3 5 6 8 9 11 12 14 15 17 18 20 21 23 24 26 27 29 0 2 3 5 7
♀	22 23 24 25 26 28 29 0 1 3 5 6 8 9 10 11 13 14 16 17 18 19 20 22 23 24 25 26 27 29
♂	2 2 2 2 2 2 2 1 1 1 1 1 1 1 0 0 0 29 29 29 29 28 28

♃ 1℞ 13 28 ♈17 16 15 — ♄ 1 15℞ ♌2 2 — ♅ 1 14 ♏3 4 — ♆ 1 20 ♐10 11 — ♇ 1 ♎10

12 (December)
Planet	Days
☉	8 9 10 11 12 13 14 15 16 17 18 19 20 21 22 23 24 25 26 27 28 29 0 1 2 3 4 5 6 7 8
☽	18 2 17 0 14 27 10 22 4 16 28 10 22 4 16 28 10 22 4 16 29 12 25 8 22 6 21 5 19 3 17
☿	10 11 13 15 16 18 19 21 22 24 26 27 29 0 2 3 5 7 8 10 11 13 14 16 17 19 20 22 24
♀	25 26 27 28 29 0 1 2 3 4 5 7 8 9 10 11 12 13 14 16 17 18 19 20 22 23 24 25 26
♂	28 28 28 27 27 27 26 26 26 25 25 25 24 24 24 23 23 23 22 22 22 21 21 21 20 20 19 19 19 18 18

♃ 1℞ 11 D ♈15 15 — ♄ 1℞ 31 ♌2 1 — ♅ 1 22 ♏5 6 — ♆ 1 17 ♐11 12 — ♇ 1

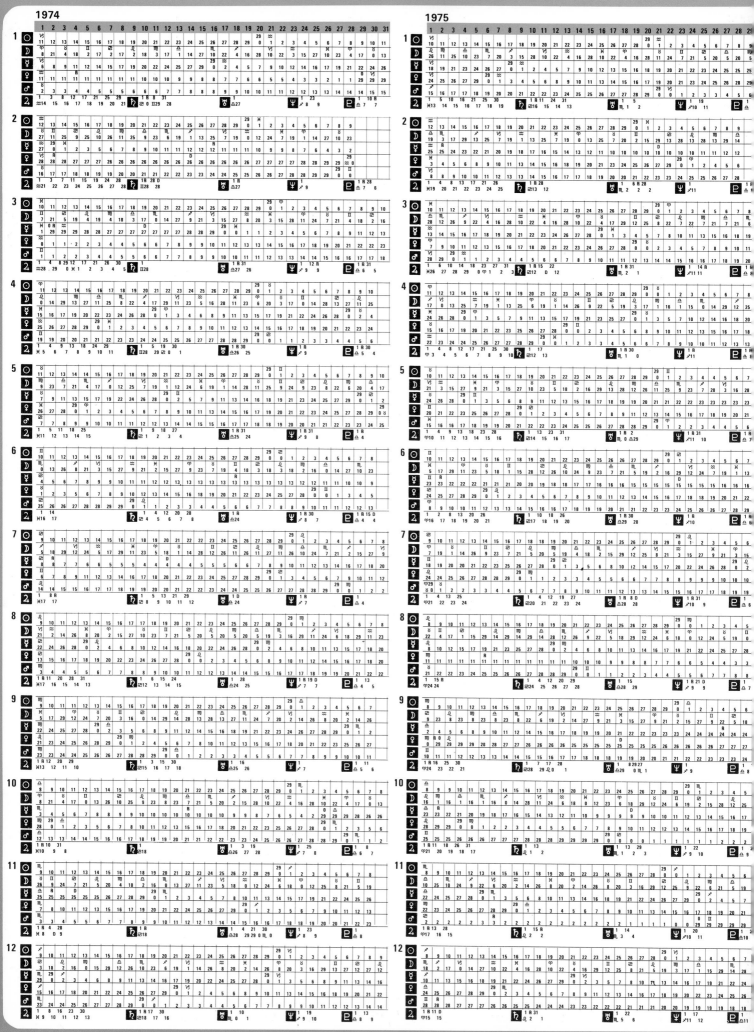

1976

1 (January)

	1	2	3	4	5	6	7	8	9	10	11	12	13	14	15	16	17	18	19	20	21	22	23	24	25	26	27	28	29	30	31
☉	♑10	11	12	13	14	15	16	17	18	19	20	21	22	23	24	25	26	27	28	29	♒0	1	2	3	4	5	6	7	8	9	10
☽	♑9	♒22	5	♓18	0	♈12	24	♉6	18	♊29	12	♋23	7	♌19	3	♍16	0	♎15	29	♏13	28	♐12	26	♑10	24	♒8	21	♓4	18	♈0	13
☿	♑27	29	♒0	1	3	4	5	6	7	8	9	9	9	9	R9	9	8	8	7	6	5	4	2	1	0	♑29	27	26	25	25	24
♀	♐0	1	2	3	4	5	6	8	9	10	11	12	14	15	16	17	19	20	21	22	24	25	26	27	28	♑0	1	2	3	4	6
♂	♊R17	17	16	16	16	16	16	16	16	16	15	15	15	15	15	15	15	15	15	15	15	D15	15	15	15	15	15	15	15	15	15

♃ 1 7 16 24 31 / ♈15 16 17 18 19 — ♄ 1R 14 29 15 31 / ♌1 0 ♋29 28 — ♅ 1 24 31 / ♏6 7 7 — ♆ 1 16 31 / ♐12 13 13 — ♇ 1 15R 31 / ♎11 11 11

2 (February)

	1	2	3	4	5	6	7	8	9	10	11	12	13	14	15	16	17	18	19	20	21	22	23	24	25	26	27	28	29
☉	♒11	12	13	14	15	16	17	18	19	20	21	22	23	24	25	26	27	28	29	♓0	1	2	3	4	5	6	7	8	9
☽	♈26	♉8	20	♊2	14	26	♋8	20	♌2	14	27	♍10	24	♎8	23	♏8	23	♐8	22	♑7	21	♒5	18	♓1	14	27	♈10	22	♉4
☿	♑R24	23	23	D23	23	23	24	24	24	25	25	26	27	27	28	29	♒0	1	2	3	4	6	7	8	9	10	12	13	14
♀	♑7	8	9	11	12	13	14	15	16	17	18	19	21	22	23	24	25	27	28	29	♒0	1	3	4	5	7	8	9	10
♂	♊15	15	16	16	16	16	16	17	17	17	17	17	18	18	18	19	19	19	19	20	20	20	20	21	21	21	22	22	22

♃ 1 6 17 26 28 29 / ♈19 20 21 22 23 24 24 — ♄ 1R 8 24 29 / ♋28 28 27 27 — ♅ 1 11R 29 / ♏7 7 7 — ♆ 1 29 / ♐13 14 — ♇ 1R 29 / ♎11 11

3 (March)

	1	2	3	4	5	6	7	8	9	10	11	12	13	14	15	16	17	18	19	20	21	22	23	24	25	26	27	28	29	30	31
☉	♓10	11	12	13	14	15	16	17	18	19	20	21	22	23	24	25	26	27	28	29	♈0	1	2	3	4	5	6	7	8	9	10
☽	♉17	29	♊11	22	4	♋16	28	♌10	22	5	♍19	2	♎16	1	♏16	1	16	♐1	16	♑1	14	28	♒11	24	♓7	19	♈1	14	26	♉8	19
☿	♒17	19	20	21	23	24	26	28	♓0	29	1	2	4	5	7	9	11	12	14	16	18	19	21	23	25	27	29	♈0	2	4	6
♀	♒13	14	15	16	18	19	20	21	22	24	25	26	27	29	♓0	1	2	3	5	6	7	9	10	11	12	13	15	16	17	18	20
♂	♊23	23	24	24	24	25	25	25	26	26	26	27	27	27	27	28	28	28	29	29	♋0	0	0	1	1	2	2	3	3	4	5

♃ 1 3 8 13 17 22 26 29 31 / ♈24 25 26 27 28 29 ♉0 1 — ♄ 1R 8 28D 31 / ♋26 26 26 — ♅ 1R 31 / ♏7 6 — ♆ 1 16R 31 / ♐14 14 14 — ♇ 1R 31 / ♎11 11

4 (April)

	1	2	3	4	5	6	7	8	9	10	11	12	13	14	15	16	17	18	19	20	21	22	23	24	25	26	27	28	29	30
☉	♈11	12	13	14	15	16	17	18	19	20	21	22	23	24	25	26	27	28	29	♉0	1	2	3	4	5	6	7	8	9	10
☽	♊1	13	25	♋7	19	♌1	14	27	♍11	25	♎9	24	♏9	25	♐10	25	♑9	24	♒7	21	♓4	16	29	♈11	23	♉5	16	28	♊10	22
☿	♈10	12	15	17	19	21	23	25	27	♉0	2	4	5	7	9	11	13	15	16	18	19	21	22	24	25	26	27	28	29	♊0
♀	♓21	22	23	24	26	27	28	♈0	1	2	3	4	6	7	8	9	11	12	13	14	15	17	18	19	20	22	23	24	25	26
♂	♋6	7	7	7	8	8	9	9	10	10	11	11	12	12	13	14	14	15	15	16	17	17	18	18	19	19	20	20	20	21

♃ 1 4 8 12 16 21 25 29 / ♉1 2 3 4 5 6 7 8 — ♄ 1 30 / ♋26 27 — ♅ 1R 30 / ♏6 5 — ♆ 1R 30 / ♐14 13 — ♇ 1R 30 / ♎10 9

5 (May)

	1	2	3	4	5	6	7	8	9	10	11	12	13	14	15	16	17	18	19	20	21	22	23	24	25	26	27	28	29	30	31
☉	♉11	12	13	14	15	16	17	18	19	20	21	22	23	24	25	26	27	28	29	♊0	0	1	2	3	4	5	6	7	8	9	10
☽	♋4	16	28	♌11	24	♍7	20	♎4	19	3	♏18	3	♐18	3	♑18	2	♒16	29	♓12	25	♈7	19	♉1	13	25	♊7	19	1	♋13	25	8
☿	♊1	1	2	3	3	3	4	4	4	R4	3	3	3	3	3	2	2	1	0	0	♉29	29	29	28	28	27	26	26	25	25	25
♀	♈29	♉0	1	3	4	5	6	8	9	10	11	13	14	15	16	18	19	20	21	22	24	25	26	27	28	♊0	1	2	3	5	6
♂	♋21	22	22	23	24	24	25	25	26	26	27	28	28	29	♌0	0	1	1	2	2	3	4	4	5	5	6	7	7	8	8	9

♃ 1 3 7 11 16 20 24 29 31 / ♉8 9 10 11 12 13 14 15 15 — ♄ 1 14 26 31 / ♋27 28 29 29 — ♅ 1R 23 31 / ♏5 4 4 — ♆ 1R 31 / ♐13 13 — ♇ 1R 31 / ♎9 9

6 (June)

	1	2	3	4	5	6	7	8	9	10	11	12	13	14	15	16	17	18	19	20	21	22	23	24	25	26	27	28	29	30
☉	♊11	12	13	14	15	16	17	18	18	19	20	21	22	23	24	25	26	27	28	29	♋0	1	2	3	4	5	6	7	8	9
☽	♋21	♌4	17	♍1	15	29	♎13	28	♏12	27	♐11	26	♑10	24	♒7	20	♓3	15	28	♈10	22	♉4	15	27	♊9	22	♋4	17	♌0	14
☿	♉D25	25	25	25	25	25	26	26	27	27	28	28	29	♊0	1	2	3	4	5	6	7	9	10	12	13	15	16	18	19	21
♀	♊6	7	8	9	11	12	13	14	16	17	18	19	21	22	23	24	25	27	28	29	♋0	2	3	4	5	7	8	9	10	11
♂	♌9	10	10	11	11	12	12	13	13	14	14	15	15	16	16	17	17	18	18	19	19	20	20	21	21	22	22	23	24	25

♃ 1 2 6 11 16 20 25 30 / ♉15 16 17 18 19 20 21 22 — ♄ 1 5 29 6 14 23 30 / ♋29 0 ♌0 1 2 2 — ♅ 1R 30 / ♏4 3 — ♆ 1R 30 / ♐12 12 — ♇ 1R 19D 30 / ♎9 9 9

7 (July)

	1	2	3	4	5	6	7	8	9	10	11	12	13	14	15	16	17	18	19	20	21	22	23	24	25	26	27	28	29	30	31
☉	♋9	10	11	12	13	14	15	16	17	18	19	20	21	22	23	24	25	26	27	28	29	♌0	1	2	3	4	5	6	7	8	9
☽	♌28	♍12	25	♎10	24	♏8	22	♐6	21	♑5	19	♒2	15	28	♓11	23	♈6	17	29	♉11	23	♊5	17	0	♋13	26	♌10	24	♍8	22	♎6
☿	♊23	25	27	29	♋0	3	5	7	9	11	13	15	18	20	22	24	26	28	♌0	2	4	6	8	10	12	14	16	18	20	22	24
♀	♋13	14	15	16	18	19	20	21	22	24	25	26	27	29	♌0	1	2	4	5	6	7	8	10	11	12	13	15	16	17	18	20
♂	♌26	27	27	28	28	29	29	♍0	0	1	2	2	3	4	4	5	5	6	7	7	8	8	9	10	10	11	11	12	13	13	14

♃ 1 5 11 16 22 29 31 / ♉22 23 24 25 26 27 27 — ♄ 1 9 17 25 31 / ♌3 4 5 6 6 — ♅ 1R 11D 31 / ♏3 3 — ♆ 1R 31 / ♐12 11 — ♇ 1 31 / ♎9 9

8 (August)

	1	2	3	4	5	6	7	8	9	10	11	12	13	14	15	16	17	18	19	20	21	22	23	24	25	26	27	28	29	30	31
☉	♌9	10	11	12	13	14	15	16	17	18	19	20	21	22	23	24	25	26	27	28	28	29	♍0	1	2	3	4	5	6	7	8
☽	♎20	♏5	19	♐3	17	♑0	14	28	♒11	24	7	♓19	2	♈13	25	♉7	19	1	♊13	25	8	♋21	4	♌18	2	♍16	1	15	♎29	13	27
☿	♌25	27	29	♍0	2	4	5	7	8	10	11	13	14	15	16	18	19	20	21	22	23	24	25	26	27	28	28	29	♎0	0	1
♀	♌21	22	23	24	26	27	28	29	♍1	2	3	4	6	7	8	9	11	12	13	14	15	17	18	19	20	22	23	24	25	26	28
♂	♍15	15	16	16	17	17	18	18	19	20	20	21	21	22	23	23	24	24	25	25	26	27	27	28	28	29	♎0	0	1	2	2

♃ 1 5 13 23 29 24 31 / ♉27 28 29 0 ♊0 0 — ♄ 1 9 17 25 31 / ♌7 8 9 10 10 — ♅ 1 31 / ♏3 4 4 — ♆ 1R 23D 31 / ♐11 11 — ♇ 1 22 31 / ♎9 10 10

9 (September)

	1	2	3	4	5	6	7	8	9	10	11	12	13	14	15	16	17	18	19	20	21	22	23	24	25	26	27	28	29	30
☉	♍9	10	11	12	13	14	15	16	17	18	19	20	21	22	23	24	25	26	27	28	29	♎0	0	1	2	3	4	5	6	7
☽	♏11	25	♐8	22	♑5	18	♒1	14	27	♓10	22	♈4	16	28	♉10	22	♊4	16	28	♋10	23	♌7	20	♍5	19	♎4	18	♏2	16	0
☿	♎1	2	2	2	R2	2	2	1	0	0	♍29	28	27	26	25	24	23	22	21	20	D20	19	19	19	20	20	21	22	23	24
♀	♍29	♎0	1	2	4	5	6	7	9	10	11	12	14	15	16	17	19	20	21	22	23	25	26	27	28	♏0	1	2	3	5
♂	♎3	4	4	5	5	6	7	7	8	8	9	10	10	11	12	12	13	14	14	15	16	16	17	18	18	19	20	20	21	22

♃ 1 8 20R 30 / ♊0 0 0 — ♄ 1 12 21 30 / ♌11 12 13 14 — ♅ 1 30 / ♏4 5 5 — ♆ 1 30 / ♐11 11 — ♇ 1 19 30 / ♎10 11 11

10 (October)

	1	2	3	4	5	6	7	8	9	10	11	12	13	14	15	16	17	18	19	20	21	22	23	24	25	26	27	28	29	30	31
☉	♎8	9	10	11	12	13	14	15	16	17	18	19	20	21	22	23	24	25	26	27	28	29	♏0	1	2	3	4	5	6	7	8
☽	♐14	27	♑10	23	♒6	18	♓0	12	24	♈6	18	♉0	12	24	♊6	18	♋0	13	25	♌8	22	♍5	19	♎4	19	♏3	17	1	♐14	27	10
☿	♍D23	23	23	24	24	25	26	27	28	♎0	1	3	5	6	8	10	11	13	15	16	18	19	21	23	24	26	28	29	♏1	2	4
♀	♏6	7	8	9	11	12	13	14	16	17	18	19	20	22	23	24	25	27	28	29	♐0	1	3	4	5	6	8	9	10	11	12
♂	♎25	25	26	26	27	28	28	29	♏0	0	1	1	2	3	3	4	5	5	6	7	7	8	9	9	10	11	11	12	13	13	14

♃ R 16 17 31 / ♊1 ♊0 ♉29 28 — ♄ 1 13 28 31 / ♌14 15 16 16 — ♅ 1 23 31 / ♏5 6 7 7 — ♆ 1 17 31 / ♐11 12 12 — ♇ 1 15 31 / ♎11 12 12

11 (November)

	1	2	3	4	5	6	7	8	9	10	11	12	13	14	15	16	17	18	19	20	21	22	23	24	25	26	27	28	29	30
☉	♏9	10	11	12	13	14	15	16	17	18	19	20	21	22	23	24	25	26	27	28	29	♐0	1	2	3	4	5	6	7	8
☽	♓21	♈3	15	27	♉9	21	♊3	15	27	♋9	21	♌3	15	27	♍9	21	4	17	♎0	14	♏28	12	27	♐12	26	♑11	25	♒9	23	6
☿	♏4	6	8	9	11	13	14	16	18	19	21	22	24	25	27	29	♐0	1	3	4	6	7	9	10	12	13	15	16	18	19
♀	♐14	15	16	17	18	20	21	22	23	24	26	27	28	29	♑0	2	3	4	5	6	8	9	10	11	12	14	15	16	17	18
♂	♏16	16	17	18	19	19	20	21	21	22	23	23	24	25	26	26	27	28	28	29	♐0	1	1	2	3	4	4	5	6	6

♃ 1R 12 19 26 30 / ♉28 27 26 25 25 — ♄ 1 28R 30 / ♌16 16 16 — ♅ 1 8 24 30 / ♏7 8 9 9 — ♆ 1 17 30 / ♐12 13 13 — ♇ 1 11 30 / ♎12 13 13

12 (December)

	1	2	3	4	5	6	7	8	9	10	11	12	13	14	15	16	17	18	19	20	21	22	23	24	25	26	27	28	29	30	31
☉	♐9	10	11	12	13	14	15	16	17	18	19	20	21	22	23	24	25	26	27	28	29	♑0	1	2	3	4	5	6	7	8	10
☽	♓12	24	♈6	18	♉0	11	24	♊6	18	♋0	12	24	♌6	18	♍1	14	27	♎10	24	♏7	21	♐6	21	♑6	20	♒5	20	♓4	17	0	13
☿	♐22	23	25	26	28	29	♑1	2	4	5	7	8	10	12	13	15	16	18	19	21	22	24	25	27	29	♒0	2	3	5	6	8
♀	♑20	21	22	23	24	26	27	28	29	♒0	1	3	4	5	6	7	8	9	10	11	13	14	15	16	17	18	19	20	21	22	23
♂	♐7	8	8	9	10	10	11	12	13	13	14	15	16	16	17	18	19	19	20	21	22	22	23	24	25	25	26	27	28	29	29

♃ 1R 13 24 31 / ♉24 23 22 21 — ♄ 1R 31 / ♌16 16 — ♅ 1 12 31 / ♏9 10 11 — ♆ 1 14 31 / ♐13 14 14 — ♇ 1 22 31 / ♎13 14 14

1977

1 (January)

	1	2	3	4	5	6	7	8	9	10	11	12	13	14	15	16	17	18	19	20	21	22	23	24	25	26	27	28	29	30	31
☉	♑11	12	13	14	15	16	17	18	19	20	21	22	23	24	25	26	27	28	29	♒0	1	2	3	4	5	6	7	8	9	10	11
☽	♉26	♊8	20	2	♋15	28	♌10	23	♍7	20	4	♎18	2	♏16	0	♐15	29	♑14	28	♒12	25	♓9	22	♈4	17	29	♉10	22	♊4	16	28
☿	♑22	21	20	19	18	17	15	14	12	11	10	9	8	8	7	7	7	D7	7	7	7	8	8	9	10	10	11	12	13	14	16
♀	♒26	27	28	29	♓0	1	2	3	4	5	6	7	8	9	10	11	12	13	14	16	17	18	19	20	21	22	23	24	25	26	27
♂	♐29	♑0	1	2	2	3	4	5	5	6	7	7	8	9	10	10	11	12	13	13	14	15	15	16	16	17	18	19	19	20	21

♃ 1R 16D 31 / ♉21 21 21 — ♄ 1R 13 26 31 / ♌16 15 14 14 — ♅ 1 31 / ♏11 11 — ♆ 1 11 31 / ♐14 15 15 — ♇ 1 16R 31 / ♎14 14 14

2 (February)

	1	2	3	4	5	6	7	8	9	10	11	12	13	14	15	16	17	18	19	20	21	22	23	24	25	26	27	28
☉	♒12	13	14	15	16	17	18	19	20	21	22	23	24	25	26	27	28	29	♓0	1	2	3	4	5	6	7	8	9
☽	♋11	23	♌6	20	♍3	17	♎1	15	29	♏13	27	♐11	25	♑9	23	♒7	20	♓4	17	29	♈12	24	♉6	18	♊0	12	24	♋6
☿	♑17	18	19	21	22	23	24	26	27	28	♒0	1	3	4	6	7	8	10	12	13	15	16	18	19	21	22	24	26
♀	♓29	♈0	1	2	3	3	4	5	6	7	8	9	10	10	11	12	13	13	14	15	15	16	17	17	18	18	19	20
♂	♑23	24	25	26	26	27	28	29	♒29	0	1	1	2	3	3	4	5	6	6	7	8	9	9	10	11	12	13	14

♃ 1 6 17 26 28 / ♉21 22 23 24 24 — ♄ 1R 20 28 / ♌13 12 11 — ♅ 1 15R 28 / ♏11 11 — ♆ 1 23 28 / ♐15 16 16 — ♇ 1R 28 / ♎14 14

3 (March)

	1	2	3	4	5	6	7	8	9	10	11	12	13	14	15	16	17	18	19	20	21	22	23	24	25	26	27	28	29	30	31
☉	♓10	11	12	13	14	15	16	17	18	19	20	21	22	23	24	25	26	27	28	29	♈0	1	2	3	4	5	6	7	8	9	10
☽	♋19	♌1	14	28	♍12	26	♎10	25	♏9	23	♐8	22	♑6	19	♒4	16	29	♓13	25	♈8	20	♉2	14	26	♊8	20	♋2	14	26	♌9	22
☿	♒28	♓29	0	1	3	5	6	8	10	12	13	15	17	19	21	23	25	27	♈29	0	1	3	5	7	9	11	13	15	17	19	21
♀	♈20	21	21	22	22	22	22	23	23	23	23	24	24	24	24	24	24	R24	24	24	24	24	24	24	23	23	23	22	22	21	20
♂	♒15	16	17	17	18	19	20	20	21	22	23	23	24	25	25	26	27	28	29	♓0	1	1	2	3	4	4	5	6	7	8	9

♃ 1 5 12 18 24 29 31 / ♉24 25 26 27 28 29 29 — ♄ 1R 31 / ♌11 10 — ♅ 1R 31 / ♏11 11 — ♆ 1 19R 31 / ♐16 16 16 — ♇ 1R 31 / ♎14 13 13

4 (April)

	1	2	3	4	5	6	7	8	9	10	11	12	13	14	15	16	17	18	19	20	21	22	23	24	25	26	27	28	29	30
☉	♈11	12	13	14	15	16	17	18	19	20	21	22	23	24	25	26	27	28	29	♉0	1	2	3	4	5	6	7	8	9	10
☽	♍6	20	♎4	19	♏4	19	3	♐18	2	♑16	0	13	♒27	9	22	♓5	17	29	♈11	23	4	♉16	28	♊10	22	♋5	17	0	♌14	28
☿	♈26	28	♉0	1	3	4	6	7	8	9	10	11	11	12	13	13	13	14	14	14	14	14	14	14	14	14	13	12	12	11
♀	♈R19	19	18	18	17	16	16	15	15	14	14	13	13	12	12	11	11	10	10	10	9	9	9	8	8	8	8	8	D8	8
♂	♓9	10	11	11	12	13	14	15	15	16	17	17	18	19	20	21	21	22	23	24	24	25	25	26	27	28	29	♈0	1	1

♃ 1 3 29 4 8 13 18 23 27 30 / ♉29 ♊0 1 2 3 4 5 5 — ♄ 1 18 11D 30 / ♌10 10 10 — ♅ 1R 24 30 / ♏11 10 10 — ♆ 1R 30 / ♐16 16 — ♇ 1R 30 / ♎13 12

5 (May)

	1	2	3	4	5	6	7	8	9	10	11	12	13	14	15	16	17	18	19	20	21	22	23	24	25	26	27	28	29	30	31
☉	♉11	12	13	14	15	16	17	18	19	20	21	22	23	24	25	26	27	28	29	♊0	1	2	3	4	5	6	7	8	9	10	10
☽	♎12	27	♏12	27	12	♐27	12	♑26	10	♒24	7	♓19	2	♈14	26	♉8	20	1	♊13	25	7	♋19	1	♌14	26	♍9	23	7	♎21	5	20
☿	♉R10	9	9	8	7	7	6	6	5	5	5	5	5	D5	5	5	5	5	6	6	7	7	8	9	10	11	12	13	14	15	16
♀	♈8	8	8	9	9	9	9	10	10	11	11	12	12	13	13	14	14	15	16	16	17	18	18	19	20	21	21	22	23	24	25
♂	♈3	3	4	5	5	6	7	8	8	9	10	11	12	12	13	14	15	15	16	17	18	18	19	20	21	22	22	23	24	25	25

♃ 1 6 11 15 19 24 28 31 / ♊6 7 8 9 10 11 12 12 — ♄ 1 15 30 31 / ♌10 11 12 12 — ♅ 1R 18 31 / ♏10 9 8 — ♆ 1R 28 31 / ♐16 15 15 — ♇ 1R 31 / ♎12 11

6 (June)

	1	2	3	4	5	6	7	8	9	10	11	12	13	14	15	16	17	18	19	20	21	22	23	24	25	26	27	28	29	30
☉	♊11	12	13	14	15	16	17	18	19	20	21	22	23	24	25	26	27	28	29	♋0	1	2	3	4	5	6	7	8	9
☽	♐6	21	♑6	21	♒5	19	3	♓16	28	♈11	23	♉5	17	28	♊10	22	4	♋16	28	♌11	23	♍6	19	♎2	16	0	♏14	29	14	29
☿	♉16	17	18	20	21	22	24	25	27	28	♊0	2	3	5	7	9	11	13	15	17	19	21	23	25	27	29	♋2	4	6	8
♀	♈26	26	27	28	29	♉0	1	2	3	4	5	6	7	8	9	10	11	12	13	14	15	16	17	18	19	20	21	22	23	23
♂	♈26	♉27	28	28	29	0	1	1	2	3	4	5	5	6	7	8	8	9	10	11	11	12	13	14	14	15	16	17	17

♃ 1 6 10 14 18 23 27 30 / ♊13 14 15 16 17 18 19 19 — ♄ 1 10 21 30 / ♌12 13 14 15 — ♅ 1R 30 / ♏8 8 — ♆ 1R 30 / ♐15 14 — ♇ 1R 21D 30 / ♎11 11 11

7 (July)

	1	2	3	4	5	6	7	8	9	10	11	12	13	14	15	16	17	18	19	20	21	22	23	24	25	26	27	28	29	30	31
☉	♋9	10	11	12	13	14	15	16	17	18	19	20	21	22	23	24	25	26	27	28	29	♌0	1	2	3	4	5	6	7	8
☽	♑14	29	♒14	28	♓12	24	♈7	19	♉2	14	25	♊7	19	1	♋13	25	7	♌19	1	♍13	25	8	♎20	3	♏16	29	13	♐26	10	24	9
☿	♋10	13	15	17	19	21	23	25	27	29	♌0	1	3	5	6	8	10	11	12	14	15	17	18	20	21	22	24	25	26	28	♍29
♀	♉24	25	26	27	28	♊29	0	1	2	3	4	5	6	7	8	9	10	11	12	13	14	15	16	17	18	19	20	21	22	23	24
♂	♉18	19	19	20	21	22	22	23	24	24	25	26	27	27	28	29	♊29	0	1	1	2	3	3	4	4	5	6	7	8	8	9

♃ 1 6 11 15 20 25 30 31 / ♊20 21 22 23 24 25 26 26 — ♄ 1 9 17 25 31 / ♌15 16 17 18 18 — ♅ 1R 17D 31 / ♏8 8 — ♆ 1R 31 / ♐14 13 — ♇ 1 31 / ♎11 12

8 (August)

	1	2	3	4	5	6	7	8	9	10	11	12	13	14	15	16	17	18	19	20	21	22	23	24	25	26	27	28	29	30	31
☉	♌9	10	11	12	13	14	15	16	17	18	19	20	21	22	23	24	25	26	27	28	29	♍0	1	2	3	4	5	6	7	8
☽	♒6	19	♓3	15	♈28	10	22	♉4	15	27	♊9	22	4	♋16	28	♌10	22	♍4	17	29	♎12	26	♏9	23	7	♐21	5	♑19	3	17	♒0
☿	♍5	6	7	8	9	11	12	13	14	15	16	17	18	18	19	20	21	21	21	21	21	R21	21	20	20	20	19	19	18	18	17
♀	♊28	29	♋0	1	2	3	5	6	7	8	9	10	11	13	14	15	16	17	19	20	21	22	23	24	26	27	28	29	♌1	2	3
♂	♊10	10	11	12	13	13	14	15	15	16	17	17	18	18	19	20	20	21	22	22	23	23	24	25	25	26	27	27	28	28	29

♃ 1 4 9 14 20 29 21 26 31 / ♊26 27 28 29 0 ♋0 1 1 — ♄ 1 10 18 26 31 / ♌19 20 21 22 22 — ♅ 1 31 / ♏8 8 — ♆ 1R 26D 31 / ♐13 13 13 — ♇ 1 31 / ♎12 12

9 (September)

	1	2	3	4	5	6	7	8	9	10	11	12	13	14	15	16	17	18	19	20	21	22	23	24	25	26	27	28	29	30
☉	♍9	10	11	12	13	14	15	16	17	18	19	20	21	22	23	24	25	26	27	28	29	♎0	1	2	3	4	5	6	7
☽	♓23	6	♈18	29	♉12	23	♊5	17	29	♋12	25	♌8	22	♍5	19	4	♎18	2	♏16	0	♐15	29	♑12	26	♒10	23	♓6	19	1	♈14
☿	♍R16	15	15	14	13	12	11	10	9	8	8	7	7	7	D7	7	7	8	9	10	11	12	13	15	16	17	19	21	22	24
♀	♌4	5	6	7	9	10	11	12	14	15	16	17	18	20	21	22	23	24	26	27	28	29	♍1	2	3	4	5	7	8	9
♂	♊29	♋0	0	1	2	2	3	4	4	5	5	6	7	7	8	9	9	10	10	11	11	12	12	13	13	14	15	15	16	17

♃ 1 9 17 28 30 / ♋2 3 4 5 5 — ♄ 1 11 19 28 30 / ♌23 24 25 26 26 — ♅ 1 30 / ♏8 9 10 — ♆ 1 30 / ♐13 13 — ♇ 1 30 / ♎13 13

10 (October)

	1	2	3	4	5	6	7	8	9	10	11	12	13	14	15	16	17	18	19	20	21	22	23	24	25	26	27	28	29	30	31
☉	♎8	9	10	11	12	13	14	15	16	17	18	19	20	21	22	23	24	25	26	27	28	29	♏0	1	2	3	4	5	6	7	8
☽	♈26	♉8	19	♊1	13	25	♋8	20	♌3	16	0	♍14	29	♎14	29	♏13	28	♐12	26	♑9	23	♒6	19	♓2	15	27	♈10	22	♉4	16	28
☿	♍24	26	28	♎0	1	3	5	6	8	10	12	13	15	17	19	20	22	24	26	27	29	♏0	2	4	5	7	9	10	12	14	15
♀	♍10	12	13	14	15	16	18	19	20	21	22	24	25	26	27	28	29	♎0	1	3	4	5	6	7	9	10	11	12	13	15	16
♂	♋17	18	18	19	19	19	20	20	21	21	22	22	23	23	24	24	25	25	26	26	27	27	28	28	28	29	♌29	0	0	1	2

♃ 1 15 25R 31 / ♋5 6 6 6 — ♄ 1 9 / ♌26 27 28 29 — ♅ 1 18 31 / ♏10 11 11 — ♆ 1 31 / ♐13 14 14 — ♇ 1 31 / ♎14 14

11 (November)

	1	2	3	4	5	6	7	8	9	10	11	12	13	14	15	16	17	18	19	20	21	22	23	24	25	26	27	28	29	30
☉	♏9	10	11	12	13	14	15	16	17	18	19	20	21	22	23	24	25	26	27	28	29	♐0	1	2	3	4	5	6	7	8
☽	♊9	21	♋3	16	28	♌11	24	♍8	22	♎7	22	♏7	22	♐7	21	♑6	19	♒3	16	29	♓12	24	♈6	18	0	♉12	24	6	♊18	0
☿	♏16	18	20	21	23	25	26	28	29	♐0	2	3	5	7	8	10	11	13	14	15	17	18	20	21	22	24	25	26	27	28
♀	♎16	18	19	20	21	22	24	25	26	27	28	29	♏0	1	3	4	5	6	8	9	10	11	13	14	15	16	18	19	20	21
♂	♌2	3	3	3	4	4	4	4	5	5	5	5	6	6	7	7	7	7	8	8	8	9	9	9	9	10	10	10	10	10

♃ 1R 26 30 / ♋6 5 4 — ♄ 1 16 17 30 / ♌29 29 ♍0 0 — ♅ 1 19 30 / ♏12 13 13 — ♆ 1 15 30 / ♐14 15 15 — ♇ 1 15 30 / ♎15 15 16

12 (December)

	1	2	3	4	5	6	7	8	9	10	11	12	13	14	15	16	17	18	19	20	21	22	23	24	25	26	27	28	29	30	31
☉	♐9	10	11	12	13	14	15	16	17	18	19	20	21	22	23	24	25	26	27	28	29	♑0	1	2	3	4	5	6	7	8	9
☽	♋12	24	♌7	19	♍2	16	♎0	15	♏0	15	0	♐15	29	♑13	27	♒10	23	♓6	18	0	♈12	24	6	♉18	0	12	♊24	6	♋18	0	12
☿	♐29	♑0	1	2	3	4	5	5	6	6	7	7	7	R7	7	6	5	4	3	2	1	♐0	29	28	27	27	26	26	26	26	26
♀	♏22	24	25	26	27	29	♐0	1	2	3	5	6	7	8	10	11	12	14	15	16	17	18	20	21	22	24	25	26	27	29	♑0
♂	♌10	10	10	10	10	10	10	R10	10	10	10	10	10	10	10	10	10	10	10	9	9	9	9	9	8	8	8	7	7	6	6

♃ 1R 8 16 23 31 29 / ♋4 3 2 1 ♊0 — ♄ 1 12R 31 / ♍0 0 0 — ♅ 1 25 31 / ♏14 15 15 — ♆ 1 12 31 / ♐15 16 16 — ♇ 1 31 / ♎16 16

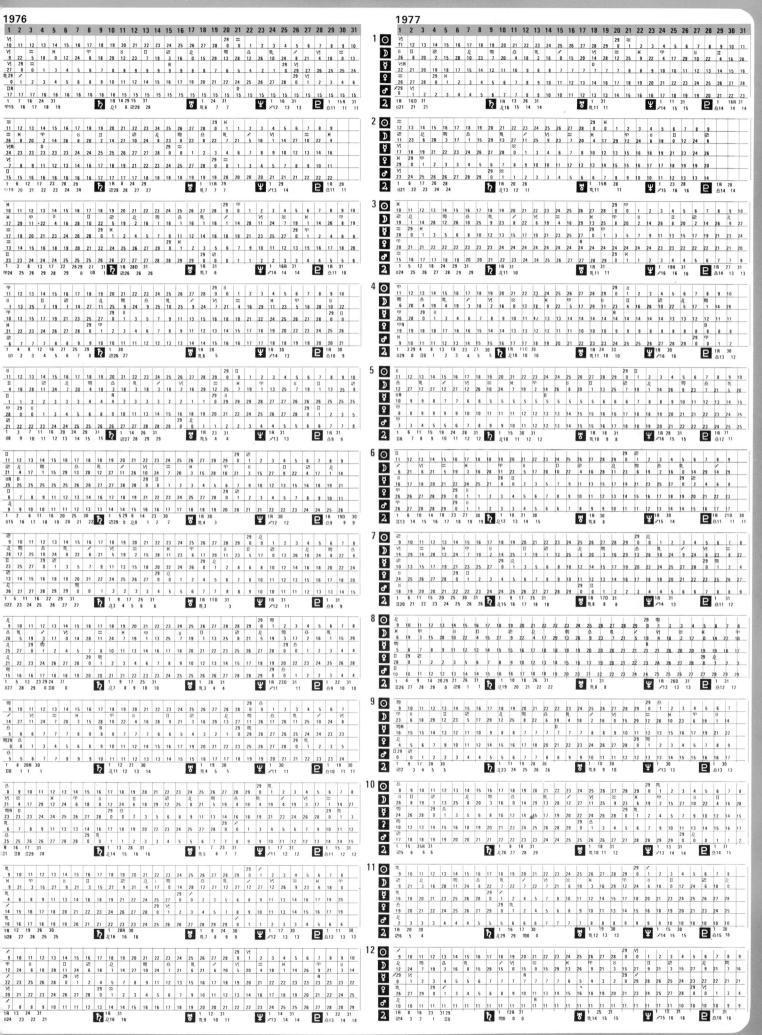

1978

Columns in the printed tables are days 1–31 of each month; values below are the degree positions as printed, in day order.

1

☉	10 11 12 13 14 15 16 17 18 19 20 21 22 23 24 25 26 27 28 29 0 1 2 3 4 5 6 7 8 9 10 11
☽	29 12 25 9 23 8 23 8 21 5 18 0 12 24 6 18 0 12 24 6 18 0 13 26 8 21 5
☿	21 21 21 22 22 23 23 24 25 26 27 28 29 0 1 3 4 5 6 7 9 10 12 13 14 16 17 19 20 21 23
♀	5 7 8 9 10 11 13 14 15 16 17 18 19 20 21 23 24 25 27 28 29 0 1 3 4 5 7 8 9 10 12 13
♂	9 9 9 8 8 8 7 7 7 6 6 6 5 5 4 4 4 3 3 2 2 1 1 0 0 29 29 29 28 28
♃	1R 16 27 31 / ♊29 28 27 27
♄	1R 5 29 6 31 / ♍0 0 ♌29 28
♅	♏15 16 16
♆	1 8 31 / ♐16 17 17
♇	1 19R 31 / ♎16 16 16

2

☉	12 13 14 15 16 17 18 19 20 21 22 23 24 25 26 27 28 29 0 1 2 3 4 5 6 7 8 9
☽	19 3 17 2 17 2 17 1 15 29 13 26 8 21 3 15 26 8 20 2 15 27 10 24 5 18 2 15
☿	25 26 28 0 1 2 4 5 7 9 10 12 13 15 17 19 21 23 24 26 28 0 1 3 5 7 8 10
♀	14 16 17 18 19 21 22 23 24 26 27 28 29 0 1 2 3 4 6 7 8 9 10 12 13 14 15 17 18 10
♂	28 27 27 27 26 26 26 25 25 25 25 24 24 24 24 23 23 23 23 23 23 22 22 22 22 22 22 22
♃	1R 20D 28 / ♊27 26 26
♄	1R 18 28 / ♌28 27 26
♅	1 20R 28 / ♏16 16 16
♆	1 15 28 / ♐17 18 18
♇	1R 28 / ♎16 16

3

☉	10 11 12 13 14 15 16 17 18 19 20 21 22 23 24 25 26 27 28 29 0 1 2 3 4 5 6 7 8 9 10
☽	29 13 28 12 26 11 25 10 23 7 20 3 16 28 10 23 4 16 28 10 23 5 18 1 14 28 12 26 10 24 9
☿	12 14 16 18 20 22 24 26 28 29 0 1 3 5 7 9 10 12 14 15 17 18 19 20 21 22 23 24 25 25 26 26
♀	19 21 22 23 24 25 26 28 29 0 1 2 3 4 5 7 8 9 11 12 13 14 15 17 18 19 20 22 23 24 25
♂	22 22 22 22 22 22 22 22 22 22 22 23 23 23 23 23 23 24 24 24 24 24 25 25 25 25 25 26 26 26
♃	1 16 27 31 / ♊26 27 28 28
♄	1R 16 31 / ♌26 25 24
♅	1R 31 / ♏16 16
♆	1 21R 31 / ♐18 18 18
♇	1R 31 / ♎16 15

4

☉	11 12 13 14 15 16 17 18 19 20 21 22 23 24 25 26 27 28 29 0 1 2 3 4 5 6 7 8 9 10
☽	23 7 21 5 18 2 15 29 11 24 6 18 0 12 24 6 18 1 13 26 9 23 7 21 6 20 5 19 4 18
☿	26 27 26 26 26 25 25 24 24 23 23 22 21 20 20 19 18 17 17 16 16 15 15 15 15 15 15 15 15 15 16
♀	28 0 0 2 3 4 5 6 8 9 10 11 12 14 15 16 18 19 20 21 22 24 25 26 27 29 0 1 2 3
♂	27 27 28 28 28 29 29 29 0 0 1 1 1 1 2 2 2 3 3 4 4 4 5 5 6 6 7 7
♃	1 4 11 12 18 24 30 / ♊28 29 29 ♋0 1 2 3
♄	1R 26D 30 / ♌24 24
♅	1R 30 / ♏15 14
♆	1R 30 / ♐18 18
♇	1R 30 / ♎15 14

5

☉	10 11 12 13 14 15 16 17 18 19 20 21 22 23 24 25 26 27 28 29 0 1 2 3 4 5 6 7 8 9 10
☽	2 15 28 12 25 7 20 2 14 26 8 20 2 14 26 9 21 4 17 1 16 0 15 0 15 29 14 28 12 25 9
☿	16 17 17 18 18 19 20 21 22 23 24 25 26 27 28 29 0 1 2 4 5 6 8 9 11 12 14 16 18 19 21 23
♀	5 6 7 8 10 11 12 13 14 15 17 18 19 20 22 23 24 25 26 28 29 0 1 2 4 5 6 7 8 10 11
♂	8 8 9 10 10 11 11 12 12 13 13 14 14 15 15 16 16 17 17 18 18 19 19 20 20 21 21 22 22 23
♃	1 6 11 16 21 26 31 / ♋3 4 5 6 7 8 9
♄	1 31 / ♌24 24
♅	1R 31 / ♏14 13
♆	1R 31 / ♐18 17
♇	1R 31 / ♎14 14

6

☉	10 11 12 13 14 15 16 17 18 19 20 21 22 23 24 25 26 27 28 29 0 1 2 3 4 5 6 7 8
☽	21 4 17 29 12 23 5 17 29 11 23 5 17 29 12 26 9 24 9 23 9 24 8 22 5 18 1 14
☿	25 27 29 0 2 4 6 8 10 12 14 16 18 21 23 25 27 29 0 2 4 6 8 10 12 14 16 18 20 22 24 25
♀	12 14 15 16 17 18 19 20 21 23 24 25 26 28 29 0 1 2 3 5 6 7 8 9 10 11 13 14 15 16
♂	23 24 24 25 25 26 26 27 27 28 28 29 29 0 0 1 1 2 2 3 3 4 4 5 5 6 6 7 7 8 8
♃	1 5 9 14 18 23 28 30 / ♋9 10 11 12 13 14 15 15
♄	1 17 28 30 / ♌25 26 27 27
♅	1R 30 / ♏13 12
♆	1R 30 / ♐17 16
♇	1R 24D 30 / ♎14 14 14

7

☉	9 10 11 12 13 14 15 16 17 18 19 20 21 22 23 24 25 26 27 28 29 0 1 2 3 4 5 6 7 8
☽	26 8 20 2 14 26 8 20 2 14 26 9 21 4 18 2 17 2 17 2 18 3 17 1 15 28 11 23 5 18 29
☿	27 29 0 1 2 4 5 7 8 10 12 13 14 16 17 18 19 20 22 23 24 25 26 27 28 29 29 0 0 1 1 1 2
♀	17 19 20 21 22 23 24 25 27 28 29 0 1 2 3 4 5 7 8 9 10 11 12 13 15 16 17 18 19 20 21
♂	9 10 10 11 11 12 12 13 13 14 15 15 16 16 17 17 18 18 19 19 20 21 22 22 23 24 24 25 25 26 27 27
♃	1 6 11 15 20 24 29 31 / ♋16 17 18 19 20 21 22 22
♄	1 8 18 26 29 27 31 / ♌27 28 29 ♍0 0
♅	1R 21D 31 / ♏12 12 12
♆	1R 31 / ♐16 16
♇	1 31 / ♎14 14

8

☉	9 10 11 12 13 14 15 16 17 18 19 20 21 22 23 24 25 26 27 28 29 0 1 2 3 4 5 6 7 8
☽	11 23 5 17 29 11 23 5 18 1 14 27 12 26 11 26 11 25 9 23 6 19 2 14 26 8 20 2 14 26 8
☿	2 3 3 3 3 3 3 3 2 2 2 1 1 0 29 29 28 27 26 25 24 24 23 22 22 21 21 20 20 20 20 21
♀	22 24 25 26 27 28 29 0 1 2 3 4 5 6 8 9 10 12 13 14 15 16 17 18 19 20 21 22 23 24
♂	28 29 29 0 0 1 2 2 3 3 4 5 5 6 7 7 8 8 9 9 10 11 11 12 13 14 14 15 15 16 17
♃	1 2 7 11 16 21 26 31 / ♋22 23 24 25 26 27 28 29
♄	1 4 12 20 28 31 / ♍0 1 2 3 4 4
♅	1 31 / ♏12 12
♆	1R 28D 31 / ♐16 15 15
♇	1 28 31 / ♎14 15 15

9

☉	9 10 11 12 13 14 15 16 17 18 19 20 21 22 23 24 25 26 27 28 29 0 1 2 3 4 5 6 7
☽	25 8 20 2 15 28 11 24 8 22 6 21 5 20 5 19 3 18 1 14 27 10 22 4 16 28
☿	21 22 22 23 24 25 26 27 28 29 0 2 4 6 8 9 11 13 15 17 19 21 22 24 26 28 29 0 2 3 5 6
♀	24 25 26 27 28 29 0 1 2 3 4 5 6 7 8 9 10 11 12 13 14 15 16 17
♂	17 18 19 19 20 21 21 22 23 23 24 25 25 26 27 28 28 29 0 1 1 2 3 3 4 5 5 6 7
♃	1 5 29 6 10 16 22 28 30 / ♋29 ♌0 1 2 3 4 4
♄	1 4 12 20 29 30 / ♍4 5 6 7 8 8
♅	1 23 30 / ♏13 14 14
♆	1 30 / ♐15 16
♇	1 25 30 / ♎15 15 16

10

☉	8 9 10 11 12 13 14 15 16 17 18 19 20 21 22 23 24 25 26 27 28 29 0 1 2 3 4 5 6 7 8
☽	29 11 24 8 22 5 19 3 17 1 15 29 14 28 12 26 9 22 5 18 0 12 24 6 18 29 12 24 7 20 3
☿	8 10 12 14 15 17 19 20 22 24 26 27 29 0 2 3 5 6 8 9 11 13 14 16 17 19 20 21 22 23 24 25
♀	18 18 19 19 20 20 20 21 21 21 21 22 22 22 22 22 22 22 21 21 21 21 20 20 20
♂	8 8 9 10 10 11 12 13 13 14 14 15 16 16 17 18 19 19 20 21 21 22 23 23 24 25 26 26 27 28
♃	1 4 12 20 31 / ♌4 5 6 7 8
♄	1 8 17 27 31 / ♍8 9 10 11 11
♅	1 12 29 31 / ♏14 15 16 16
♆	1 31 / ♐16 16
♇	1 20 31 / ♎16 17 17

11

☉	9 10 11 12 13 14 15 16 17 18 19 20 21 22 23 24 25 26 27 28 29 0 1 2 3 4 5 6 7 8
☽	17 1 15 29 14 28 12 26 10 24 8 21 4 18 0 13 25 7 19 1 13 25 8 20 3
☿	27 29 0 2 3 4 5 6 7 8 9 10 11 12 13 14 15 16 17 18 19 20 21 22 23 24 25
♀	19 18 18 17 17 16 16 16 15 15 14 14 13 13 12 12 11 10 10 10 9 9 8 8 8 7 7 7 7 7
♂	29 0 1 2 2 3 4 5 5 6 7 8 9 9 10 11 12 12 13 14 15 16 16 17 18 19 19 20
♃	1 20 26R 30 / ♌8 9 9 9
♄	1 8 23 30 / ♍11 12 13 13
♅	1 14 30 / ♏16 17 18
♆	1 12 30 / ♐16 17 17
♇	1 17 30 / ♎17 18 18

12

☉	9 10 11 12 13 14 15 16 17 18 19 20 21 22 23 24 25 26 27 28 29 0 1 2 3 4 5 6 7 8 9
☽	24 9 24 9 23 7 21 4 17 1 14 27 9 22 4 16 28 10 22 4 16 28 10 23 6 19 3 18 3 18 3
☿	19 18 17 16 14 13 12 10 9 8 7 6 5 5 5 5 5 6 6 7 7 8 9 10 11 12 13 14 15 16 17
♀	7 7 8 8 8 8 9 9 9 10 10 11 11 12 12 13 13 14 15 15 16 17 17 18 19 20 21 21 22 23 24
♂	21 22 23 23 24 25 26 26 27 28 29 0 1 2 2 3 4 5 6 7 7 8 9 10 11 11 12 13 13 14
♃	1R 21 31 / ♌9 8 7
♄	1 25R 31 / ♍13 13 13
♅	1 18 31 / ♏18 19 19
♆	1 10 31 / ♐17 18 19
♇	1 25 31 / ♎18 19 19

1979

1

☉	10 11 12 13 14 15 16 17 18 19 20 21 22 23 24 25 26 27 28 29 0 1 2 3 4 5 6 7 8 9
☽	18 3 17 1 15 28 11 24 6 19 1 13 25 7 18 0 12 24 6 18 1 14 27 12 26 11 26
☿	19 21 22 23 25 26 28 29 0 2 3 4 6 8 10 11 12 14 15 17 19 20 22 23 25 26 28 29 0
♀	24 25 26 27 28 29 0 1 2 3 4 5 6 7 8 9 10 11 13 14 15 16 17 18 19 20 21 22
♂	15 15 16 17 18 18 19 20 21 22 22 23 24 25 25 26 27 28 29 29 0 1 2 3 4 5 6
♃	1R 9 17 25 31 / ♌7 6 5 4 3
♄	1R 31 / ♍13 13
♅	1 31 / ♏20 20
♆	1 31 / ♐19 19
♇	♎19

2

☉	12 13 14 15 16 17 18 19 20 21 22 23 24 25 26 27 28 29 0 1 2 3 4 5 6 7 8 9
☽	10 24 7 21 3 16 28 10 22 4 15 27 9 21 3 15 28 10 23 6 20 5 19 4 19 4
☿	6 8 10 11 13 15 16 18 20 22 24 25 27 29 0 1 3 5 6 8 10 12 14 16 17 19 21 23 24
♀	25 27 28 29 0 1 3 4 5 6 7 9 10 11 12 13 14 15 16 17 18 19 20 21 22 23 25 26
♂	9 10 11 12 13 14 15 16 17 18 18 19 20 21 22 23 24 24 25 26 27 28 29 0 1
♃	1R 9 18 28 / ♌3 2 1 0
♄	1R 11 24 28 / ♍13 12 11 11
♅	1 20 25R 28 / ♏20 21 21 21
♆	1 28 / ♐20 20
♇	1R

3

☉	10 11 12 13 14 15 16 17 18 19 20 21 22 23 24 25 26 27 28 29 0 1 2 3 4 5 6 7 8
☽	19 2 16 29 12 25 7 19 0 12 24 6 18 0 12 25 7 20 3 17 0 14 29 13 28 13 27 12 26
☿	26 28 29 0 2 3 4 5 6 7 7 8 8 8 8 8 8 8 7 7 6 5 5 4 3 2 1 0 29
♀	27 28 29 0 1 2 3 4 5 6 7 8 10 11 12 13 14 15 16 17 18 19 20 21 23 24 25 26 28 29 0
♂	1 2 3 4 5 6 7 7 8 9 9 10 11 12 13 14 14 15 16 17 17 18 19 20 21 22 23
♃	1R 1 2 26D 31 / ♌0 ♋29 ♋29 29 29
♄	1R 22 31 / ♍10 9 8
♅	1R 31 / ♏21 20
♆	1R 24R 31 / ♐20 20 20
♇	1R

4

☉	11 12 13 14 15 16 17 18 19 20 21 22 23 24 25 26 27 28 29 0 1 2 3 4 5 6 7 8
☽	7 20 4 15 27 9 21 3 14 26 9 21 4 17 0 14 27 11 25 9 23 8 22 6 21 5 18 2 15
☿	27 27 26 26 26 26 25 25 26 26 26 27 27 28 28 29 0 1 2 3 4 5 6 7 8 10 11 12
♀	4 5 6 7 8 9 11 12 13 15 16 17 18 19 20 22 23 24 25 27 28 29 0 1 2 4 5 6 7
♂	27 26 27 28 28 29 0 1 2 3 4 5 6 7 8 9 10 11 12 13 13 14 15 15 16 17
♃	1 20 29 21 30 / ♋29 0 ♌0 1
♄	1R 30 / ♍8 7
♅	1R 30 / ♏20 19
♆	1R 30 / ♐20 20
♇	♎18

5

☉	10 11 12 13 14 15 16 17 18 19 20 21 22 23 24 25 26 27 28 29 0 1 2 3 4 5 6 7 8
☽	11 23 5 17 29 11 22 5 17 29 13 26 10 24 8 22 6 20 4 18 2 16 0 14 27 10 23 6 19
☿	15 16 18 19 21 22 24 25 27 29 0 1 2 4 5 7 9 11 13 15 17 19 21 23 26 28 29 0 2 4 6
♀	10 11 12 13 15 16 17 18 20 21 22 23 25 26 27 28 29 0 2 3 4 5 6 8 9 10 11 12 14
♂	19 20 21 21 22 23 24 24 25 26 27 28 29 29 0 1 2 3 4 5 6 6 7 8 9 10
♃	1 10 17 24 30 / ♌1 2 3 4 5
♄	1R 10D 31 / ♍7 7 7
♅	1R 31 / ♏19 18
♆	1R 31 / ♐20 19
♇	1R 31

6

☉	10 11 12 13 14 15 16 17 18 19 20 21 22 23 24 25 26 27 28 29 0 1 2 3 4 5 6 7
☽	24 6 18 0 13 25 8 21 5 19 3 18 2 17 1 15 29 13 27 10 23 7 20 2 15 27 9 21 3
☿	13 15 17 19 22 24 26 28 0 2 4 6 8 10 11 13 15 17 18 20 22 24 26 27 29 0 1
♀	17 18 20 21 22 23 25 26 27 28 29 0 1 2 3 5 6 7 8 9 10 11 12 13 14 15 16 18 19 20 21
♂	10 11 12 12 13 14 15 16 17 18 19 20 21 22 23 24 25 26 27 28 29 0 1 2
♃	1 5 11 16 22 27 30 / ♌5 6 7 8 9 10 10
♄	1 11 26 30 / ♍7 8 9 9
♅	1R 30 / ♏18 17
♆	1R 30 / ♐19 18
♇	1R / ♎16

7

☉	9 10 11 12 13 14 15 16 17 18 19 20 21 22 23 24 25 26 27 28 29 0 1 2 3 4 5 6
☽	27 8 21 3 16 29 13 27 12 27 12 27 11 25 9 22 5 17 29 11 23 5 17 29 11 24 6 18 0 12
☿	4 6 7 8 9 9 10 11 12 12 13 13 13 14 14 14 14 14 14 14 14 13 13 12 12 11 11 10
♀	24 25 26 27 28 29 0 1 2 3 5 6 7 8 9 10 11 12 13 14 15 16 17 18 19 21 22 23 24 25 26 28
♂	4 4 5 6 6 7 8 8 9 10 10 11 12 12 13 14 15 15 16 17 18 19 19 20 21 22 22 23
♃	1 7 11 16 21 26 30 31 / ♌11 12 13 14 15 16 17 17
♄	1 9 19 28 31 / ♍9 10 11 12 12
♅	1R 31 / ♏17 17
♆	1R 31 / ♐18 18
♇	1 / ♎16

8

☉	9 10 11 12 13 14 15 16 17 18 19 20 21 22 23 24 25 26 27 28 29 0 1 2 3 4 5 6
☽	11 24 8 21 6 20 5 20 5 20 4 17 1 13 26 8 20 2 14 26 8 20 2 14 26 8 20
☿	7 6 5 4 4 4 3 3 3 3 3 3 4 4 4 5 6 7 8 9 10 11 13 14 16 17 19 21
♀	2 3 4 5 6 8 9 10 11 13 14 15 16 17 19 20 21 22 24 25 26 27 28 29 0 1 3 4 5 6
♂	25 26 26 27 27 28 28 29 29 0 0 1 2 2 3 3 4 4 5 6 7 7 8 8 9 10 10 11 11
♃	1 4 8 13 17 22 27 31 / ♌17 18 19 20 21 22 23 24
♄	1 6 15 23 31 / ♍12 13 14 15 16
♅	1 31 / ♏17 17
♆	1R 31D / ♐18 18
♇	♎1

9

☉	8 9 10 11 12 13 14 15 16 17 18 19 20 21 22 23 24 25 26 27 28 29 0 1 2 3 4 5 6
☽	0 14 29 13 29 13 28 12 25 9 22 5 18 0 12 24 6 18 0 12 24 6 19 2 15 29 13 26 10
☿	27 0 1 3 5 7 8 10 12 14 16 18 20 22 24 26 27 29 0 1 3 4 6 8 10 11 13 15 16 18
♀	10 11 13 15 15 16 18 19 20 21 22 24 25 26 27 29 0 1 3 4 5 6 8 9 10 11 12
♂	15 16 16 17 18 18 19 19 20 21 21 22 23 23 24 24 25 26 26 27 28 28 29 0 0 1 1 2
♃	1 5 10 14 19 24 29 29 30 / ♌24 25 26 27 28 29 ♍0 0
♄	1 8 16 24 30 / ♍16 17 18 19 19
♅	1 15 30 / ♏17 18 18
♆	1 30 / ♐18 18
♇	♎17

10

☉	8 9 10 11 12 13 14 15 16 17 18 19 20 21 22 23 24 25 26 27 28 29 0 1 2 3 4 5
☽	8 22 7 22 7 22 7 21 5 18 1 14 26 8 20 2 14 26 8 20 2 14 27 10 23 6 20 4 18
☿	21 23 24 26 27 29 0 2 3 5 6 8 9 11 12 14 15 17 18 19 21 22 23 24 25 26 27 28
♀	17 18 20 21 22 23 25 26 27 28 0 1 2 3 5 6 7 8 10 11 12 13 15 16 17 18 20
♂	4 5 5 6 6 7 8 8 9 9 10 11 11 12 12 13 13 14 14 15 15 16 16 17 17 18 18 19 19
♃	1 4 10 15 21 27 31 / ♍0 1 2 3 4 5 5
♄	1 2 11 20 29 31 / ♍19 20 21 22 23 23
♅	1 6 20 31 / ♏18 19 19 20
♆	1 31 / ♐18 18
♇	♎1

11

☉	8 9 10 11 12 13 14 15 16 17 18 19 20 21 22 23 24 25 26 27 28 29 0 1 2 3 4 5 6
☽	1 16 0 15 29 13 26 9 22 4 16 28 10 22 4 16 28 11 23 6 20 3 17 1 15 29 13 27 11
☿	2 3 4 5 5 5 5 5 4 3 2 1 0 29 27 26 24 23 22 21 20 20 20 20 20
♀	26 27 28 0 1 2 3 5 6 7 8 10 11 12 13 15 16 17 18 20 21 22 23 25 26 27 28
♂	21 22 22 23 23 24 24 25 25 26 26 27 27 28 28 29 29 0 0 1 1 2 2 3 3 3 4
♃	1 3 10 18 28 30 / ♍5 6 7 8 9 9
♄	1 8 20 30 / ♍23 24 25 25
♅	1 9 25 30 / ♏20 21 22 22
♆	1 10 30 / ♐18 19 19
♇	♎2

12

☉	8 9 10 11 12 13 14 15 16 17 18 19 20 21 22 23 24 25 26 27 28 29 0 1 2 3 4 5 6 7
☽	9 23 7 21 4 17 29 12 24 6 18 29 12 24 6 19 2 15 29 13 27 11 25 10 24 8 22 6
☿	20 20 20 21 21 22 23 24 25 26 27 28 29 0 1 3 4 5 7 8 9 11 12 13 15 16 18 19 21 22
♀	3 5 6 7 9 10 11 12 14 15 16 17 19 20 21 22 24 25 26 27 29 0 1 2 4 5 6
♂	5 5 6 6 6 6 7 7 7 8 8 8 9 9 9 10 10 10 11 11 11 11 12 12 12 12 13 13 13
♃	1 14 27R 31 / ♍9 10 10 10
♄	1 4 31 / ♍25 26 27
♅	1 12 31 / ♏22 23 24
♆	1 31 / ♐20 21
♇	♎2

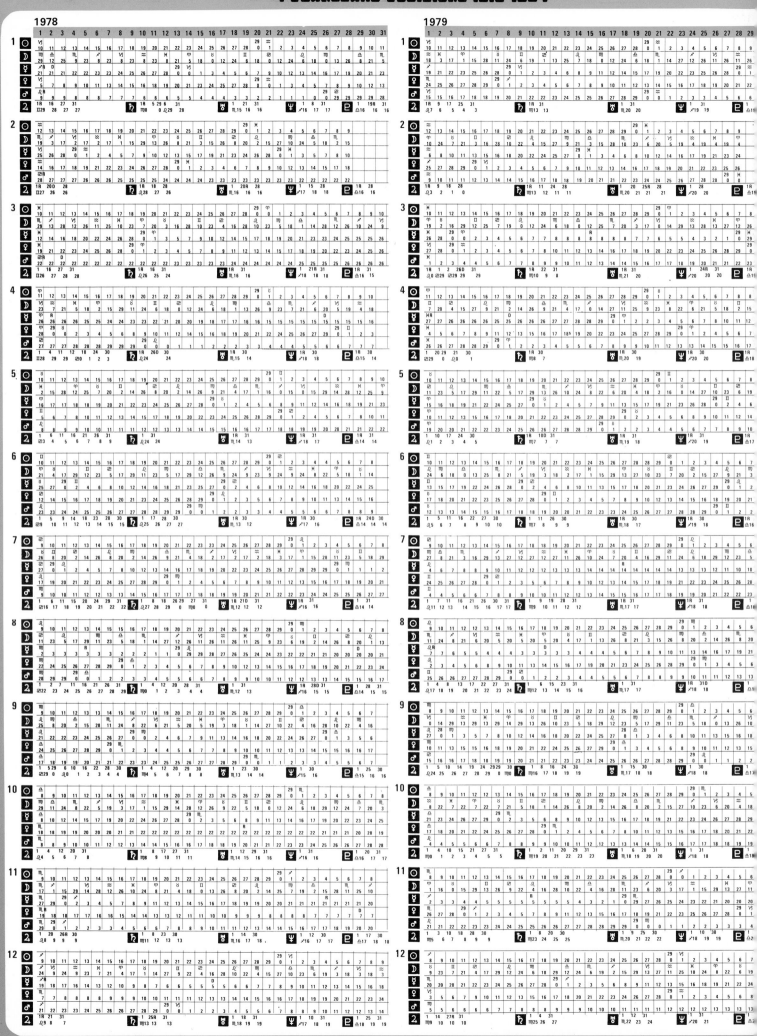

1980

1	2	3	4	5	6	7	8	9	10	11	12	13	14	15	16	17	18	19	20	21	22	23	24	25	26	27	28	29	30	31
10	11	12	13	14	15	16	17	18	19	20	21	22	23	24	25	26	27	28	29	0	1	2	3	4	5	6	7	8	9	10
[illegible]																														
28	0	2	3	5	6	8	9	11	13	14	16	17	19	21	22	24	26	27	0	1	2	4	6	7	9	11	12	14	16	18
12	13	14	16	17	18	19	20	22	23	24	25	27	28	29	0	1	3	4	5	6	8	9	10	11	12	14	15	16	17	18
14	14	14	14	14	14	15	15	15	15	15	15	15	15	15	15	15	15	15	15	15	15	15	15	15	15	14	14	14	14	14

1R 23 31 Virgo 10 9 8 · Saturn 1 7R 31 Virgo 27 26 · Uranus 1 24 31 Scorpio 24 25 25 · Neptune 1 31 Sagittarius 21 21 · Pluto 1 25R 31 Libra 21 21 21

1	2	3	4	5	6	7	8	9	10	11	12	13	14	15	16	17	18	19	20	21	22	23	24	25	26	27	28	29
12	13	14	15	16	17	18	19	20	21	22	23	24	25	26	27	28	29	0	1	2	3	4	5	6	7	8	9	10
[illegible]																												
20	21	23	25	27	28	0	2	4	5	7	8	10	12	13	14	16	17	18	19	20	20	21	21	21R	21	21	20	
20	21	22	23	24	26	27	28	29	0	1	2	3	5	6	8	9	10	11	12	13	15	16	17	18	19	20	22	23
13R	13	13	13	13	12	12	12	12	11	11	11	10	10	10	9	9	9	8	8	7	7	7	6	6	5	5	4	4

1R 11 19 25 29 Virgo 8 7 6 5 5 · Saturn 1R 25 29 Virgo 26 25 25 · Uranus 1 Scorpio 25 Scorpio 25 · Neptune 1 29 Sagittarius 22 22 · Pluto 1R 29 Libra 21 21

1	2	3	4	5	6	7	8	9	10	11	12	13	14	15	16	17	18	19	20	21	22	23	24	25	26	27	28	29	30	31
11	12	13	14	15	16	17	18	19	20	21	22	23	24	25	26	27	28	29	0	1	2	3	4	5	6	7	8	9	10	11
[illegible]																														

1R 13 22 31 Virgo 4 3 2 1 · Saturn 1R 22 31 Virgo 24 23 22 · Uranus 1R 31 Scorpio 25 25 · Neptune 1 25R 31 Sagittarius 22 22 22 · Pluto 1R 31 Libra 21 21

Months 4–12 of 1980: [illegible]

1981

	1	2	3	4	5	6	7	8	9	10	11	12	13	14	15	16	17	18	19	20	21	22	23	24	25	26	27	28	29	30	31
1 Sun	11	12	13	14	15	16	17	18	19	20	21	22	23	24	25	26	27	28	29	0	1	2	3	4	5	6	7	8	9	10	11
Moon	16	28	10	22	5	18	1	15	28	12	26	10	24	8	22	6	21	5	18	2	15	29	11	23	6	18	0	12	23	5	16
Mercury	11	12	14	16	17	19	21	22	24	26	27	29	0	2	4	6	7	9	11	12	14	16	17	19	21	22	24	25	27	28	29
Venus	17	18	19	21	22	23	24	26	27	28	29	1	2	3	4	6	7	8	9	11	12	13	15	16	17	18	20	21	22	23	24
Mars	1	2	2	3	4	5	5	6	7	8	9	9	10	11	12	12	13	14	15	16	16	17	18	19	19	20	21	22	23	23	24

Jupiter 1 9 25R 31 Libra 9 10 10 · Saturn 1 20R 31 Libra 9 9 · Uranus 1 13 31 Scorpio 28 29 29 · Neptune 1 29 31 Sagittarius 23 24 24 · Pluto 1 28R 31 Libra 24 24

	1	2	3	4	5	6	7	8	9	10	11	12	13	14	15	16	17	18	19	20	21	22	23	24	25	26	27	28
2 Sun	12	13	14	15	16	17	18	19	20	21	22	23	24	25	26	27	28	29	0	1	2	3	4	5	6	7	8	9
Moon	0	13	27	10	24	8	22	6	21	5	19	3	17	1	14	28	11	24	7	19	2	14	26	8	19	2	14	26
Mercury	0	1	2	3	4	4	4	5	5	4R	4	4	3	2	1	0	29	28	27	26	25	24	23	22	21	21	20	20
Venus	26	27	28	0	1	2	3	5	6	7	8	10	11	12	13	15	16	17	18	20	21	22	23	25	26	27	28	0
Mars	26	27	27	28	29	0	1	2	3	4	4	5	6	7	8	8	9	10	11	12	12	13	14	15	15	16	[illegible]	[illegible]

Jupiter 1R 23 28 Libra 10 9 8 · Saturn 1R 28 Libra 9 8 · Uranus 1 17 18 28 Scorpio 29 29 0 Sagittarius 0 0 · Neptune 1 28 Sagittarius 24 24 · Pluto 1R 28 Libra 24 24

	1	2	3	4	5	6	7	8	9	10	11	12	13	14	15	16	17	18	19	20	21	22	23	24	25	26	27	28	29	30	31
3 Sun	10	11	12	13	14	15	16	17	18	19	20	21	22	23	24	25	26	27	28	29	0	1	2	3	4	5	6	7	8	9	10
Moon	[illegible]																														
Mercury	20R	20	20	20	20	20	21	21	22	22	23	24	25	26	27	28	29	0	1	2	3	4	6	7	8	9	11	12	14	15	17
Venus	1	2	3	5	6	7	8	10	11	12	13	15	16	17	18	20	21	22	23	24	26	27	28	0	1	2	3	4	6	7	8
Mars	17	18	19	20	20	21	22	23	23	24	25	26	27	27	28	29	0	1	1	2	3	4	4	5	6	7	8	8	9	10	11

Jupiter 1R 14 22 30 31 Libra 8 7 6 5 5 · Saturn 1R 20 31 Libra 8 7 6 · Uranus 1 6R 20 21 31 Sagittarius 0 0 Scorpio 29 29 · Neptune 1 30R 31 Sagittarius 24 24 · Pluto 1R 31 Libra 24 23

Months 4–12 of 1981: [illegible]

1982

1

	1	2	3	4	5	6	7	8	9	10	11	12	13	14	15	16	17	18	19	20	21	22	23	24	25	26	27	28	29	30	31
☉	♑ 10	11	13	14	15	16	17	18	19	20	21	22	23	24	25	26	27	28	29	29 0	♒ 1	2	3	4	5	6	7	8	9	10	11
☽	♓ 19	♈ 3	16	♉ 1	15	29	♊ 14	29	♋ 14	29	♌ 14	28	♍ 12	25	♎ 7	20	♏ 2	14	26	♐ 8	20	♑ 2	14	26	♒ 8	21	♓ 4	17	♈ 0	13	27
☿	♑ 23	24	26	28	29 0	♒ 1	3	4	6	7	8	10	11	12	13	14	15	16	17	18	18	18	18	18R	18	18	17	16	15	14	13
♀	♒ 8R	8	8	8	8	8	8	8	7	7	7	6	6	5	5	4	4	3	2	2	1	0	0 29	♑ 29	29	28	27	27	26	26	25
♂	♎ 7	7	8	8	8	9	9	10	10	10	11	11	11	12	12	12	13	13	13	14	14	14	15	15	15	16	16	16	16	16	17

♃ 1 7 16 28 31 — ♏ 6 7 8 9 9 · ♄ 1 14 31 — ♎ 21 22 22 · ♅ 1 7 31 — ♐ 2 3 4 · ♆ 1 24 31 — ♐ 25 26 26 · ♇ 1 31 — ♎ 26 26

2

	1	2	3	4	5	6	7	8	9	10	11	12	13	14	15	16	17	18	19	20	21	22	23	24	25	26	27	28
☉	♒ 12	13	14	15	16	17	18	19	20	21	22	23	24	25	26	27	28	29 0	♓ 0	1	2	3	4	5	6	7	8	9
☽	♉ 11	25	♊ 9	23	♋ 8	23	♌ 7	21	♍ 5	19	♎ 2	15	28	♏ 10	22	♐ 5	16	28	♑ 10	22	♒ 4	17	29	♓ 13	26	♈ 10	24	♉ 8
☿	♒ 12R	10	10	8	7	6	5	4	4	3	3	3	3	D 3	3	3	4	4	4	5	6	6	7	8	9	10	11	12
♀	♑ 25R	24	24	24	24	24	23	23	23	23	23	D 23	23	23	23	24	24	24	24	25	25	25	26	26	27	27	28	28
♂	♎ 17	17	17	17	17	18	18	18	18	18	18	19	19	19	19	19	19	19	19	19	19	R 19	19	19	19	19	19	19

♃ 1 9 26R 28 — ♏ 9 10 10 · ♄ 1R 28 — ♎ 22 21 · ♅ 1 28 — ♐ 4 4 · ♆ 1 28 — ♐ 26 26 · ♇ 1R 28 — ♎ 26 26

3

	1	2	3	4	5	6	7	8	9	10	11	12	13	14	15	16	17	18	19	20	21	22	23	24	25	26	27	28	29	30	31
☉	♓ 10	11	12	13	14	15	16	17	18	19	20	21	22	23	24	25	26	27	28	29 0	♈ 0	1	2	3	4	5	6	7	8	9	10
☽	♉ 22	♊ 6	20	♋ 4	18	♌ 2	16	♍ 0	14	27	♎ 10	23	♏ 7	18	♐ 0	12	24	♑ 6	18	♒ 0	12	24	♓ 7	21	♈ 5	19	♉ 3	18	♊ 2	16	♋ 1
☿	♒ 13	15	16	17	18	19	21	22	23	25	26	28	29 0	♓ 1	2	4	5	7	8	10	11	13	15	17	18	20	22	23	25	27	29 0♈
♀	♑ 29	29 0	♒ 0	1	2	2	3	4	5	5	6	7	8	8	9	10	11	12	13	14	15	15	16	17	18	19	20	21	22	23	24
♂	♎ 18R	18	18	18	18	18	18	18	17	17	17	17	16	16	16	16	15	15	15	14	14	14	13	13	13	12	12	12	11	11	10

♃ 1R 26 31 — ♏ 10 9 8 · ♄ 1R 26 31 — ♎ 21 20 19 · ♅ 1 12R 31 — ♐ 4 4 · ♆ 1 16 31 — ♐ 26 27 27 · ♇ 1R 31 — ♎ 26 26

4

	1	2	3	4	5	6	7	8	9	10	11	12	13	14	15	16	17	18	19	20	21	22	23	24	25	26	27	28	29	30
☉	♈ 11	12	13	14	15	16	17	18	19	20	21	22	23	24	25	26	27	28	29	29 0	♉ 1	2	3	4	5	6	7	8	9	10
☽	♋ 15	29	♌ 12	26	♍ 10	23	♎ 6	19	♏ 2	14	26	♐ 8	20	♑ 2	14	26	♒ 8	20	♓ 3	16	29	♈ 13	28	♉ 13	28	♊ 13	27	♋ 11	26	♌ 10
☿	♈ 1	3	4	6	8	10	12	14	16	18	20	23	25	27	29 0	♉ 1	3	5	7	9	11	13	15	17	19	21	23	25	26	28
♀	♒ 25	26	27	28	29	29 0	♓ 1	2	3	4	5	6	7	8	9	10	11	12	13	14	15	16	17	18	19	20	22	23	24	25
♂	♎ 10R	9	9	9	8	8	8	7	7	6	6	6	5	5	5	4	4	4	3	3	3	2	2	2	2	2	1	1	1	1

♃ 1R 13 21 29 — ♏ 8 7 6 5 · ♄ 1R 21 30 — ♎ 19 17 17 · ♅ 1R 30 — ♐ 4 3 · ♆ 1R 30 — ♐ 27 27 · ♇ 1R 30 — ♎ 26 25

5

	1	2	3	4	5	6	7	8	9	10	11	12	13	14	15	16	17	18	19	20	21	22	23	24	25	26	27	28	29	30	31
☉	♉ 11	12	13	14	15	16	17	18	18	19	20	21	22	23	24	25	26	27	28	29	29 0	♊ 1	2	3	4	5	6	7	8	9	10
☽	♌ 23	♍ 6	20	♎ 3	16	28	♏ 10	23	♐ 5	17	28	♑ 10	22	♒ 4	16	28	♓ 11	24	♈ 8	22	♉ 6	21	♊ 6	21	♋ 6	21	♌ 5	19	♍ 4	17	♎ 0
☿	29♉ 0♊	♊ 1	2	4	5	6	7	9	10	10	11	12	13	13	14	14	14	15	15	15	15	15R	15	15	14	14	14	13	13	12	12
♀	♓ 26	27	29	29 0	♈ 1	2	3	4	5	6	8	9	10	11	12	13	14	15	17	18	19	20	21	22	23	24	26	27	28	29 0	♉ 0
♂	♎ 1R	1	1	0	0	0	0	0	0	0	0	0	D 0	0	0	0	0	0	0	0	1	1	1	1	1	1	1	2	2	2	2

♃ 1R 16 26 31 — ♏ 4 3 2 1 · ♄ 1R 25 31 — ♎ 17 16 15 · ♅ 1R 31 — ♐ 3 2 · ♆ 1 31 — ♐ 26 26 · ♇ 1R 31 — ♎ 25 24

6

	1	2	3	4	5	6	7	8	9	10	11	12	13	14	15	16	17	18	19	20	21	22	23	24	25	26	27	28	29	30
☉	♊ 11	12	13	14	14	15	16	17	18	19	20	21	22	23	24	25	26	27	28	29	29 0	♋ 1	2	3	4	5	6	6	7	8
☽	♎ 13	25	♏ 7	20	♐ 2	13	25	♑ 7	19	♒ 1	13	25	♓ 7	20	♈ 3	17	♉ 0	15	29	♊ 14	29	♋ 15	29	♌ 15	29	♍ 13	26	♎ 9	22	♏ 4
☿	♊ 11R	11	10	10	9	8	8	8	7	7	7	6	6	6	D 6	6	7	7	7	8	8	9	10	10	11	12	13	14	15	16
♀	♉ 2	3	4	5	6	7	8	10	11	12	13	14	15	17	18	19	20	21	23	24	25	26	27	28	29 0	♊ 1	2	3	4	5
♂	♎ 3	3	3	3	4	4	4	4	5	5	5	6	6	6	7	7	7	8	8	8	9	9	9	10	10	11	11	12	12	12

♃ 1R 29D 30 — ♏ 1 0 0 · ♄ 1R 20D 30 — ♎ 15 15 · ♅ 1R 30 — ♐ 2 1 · ♆ 1R 30 — ♐ 26 25 · ♇ 1R 30 — ♎ 24 24

7

	1	2	3	4	5	6	7	8	9	10	11	12	13	14	15	16	17	18	19	20	21	22	23	24	25	26	27	28	29	30	31
☉	♋ 9	10	11	12	13	14	15	16	17	18	19	20	21	22	23	24	25	26	26	27	28	29	29 0	♌ 1	2	3	4	5	6	7	8
☽	♏ 17	29	♐ 11	22	♑ 4	16	28	♒ 10	22	♓ 4	16	29	♈ 13	26	♉ 10	24	♊ 8	23	♋ 8	23	♌ 8	23	♍ 7	21	♎ 5	18	♏ 1	13	25	♐ 7	19
☿	♊ 17	19	20	22	23	25	26	28	29 0	♋ 1	3	5	7	9	11	13	15	17	19	21	23	25	28	29 0	♌ 1	4	6	8	10	12	14
♀	♊ 7	8	9	10	11	12	13	15	16	17	19	20	21	22	23	25	26	27	28	29 0	♋ 1	2	3	4	5	6	8	9	10	11	12
♂	♎ 13	13	14	14	15	15	16	16	16	17	17	18	18	19	19	20	20	21	21	22	22	23	24	24	25	25	26	26	27	27	28

♃ 1 17 31 — ♏ 0 1 2 · ♄ 1 13 31 — ♎ 15 16 17 · ♅ 1R 31 — ♐ 1 0 · ♆ 1 31 — ♐ 25 24 · ♇ 1R 31 — ♎ 24 24

8

	1	2	3	4	5	6	7	8	9	10	11	12	13	14	15	16	17	18	19	20	21	22	23	24	25	26	27	28	29	30	31
☉	♌ 9	10	11	12	13	14	15	16	16	17	18	19	20	21	22	23	24	25	26	27	28	29	29 0	♍ 1	2	3	4	5	6	7	8
☽	♑ 1	13	25	♒ 7	19	♓ 1	14	27	♈ 9	23	♉ 6	20	♊ 4	18	♋ 3	17	♌ 2	16	♍ 1	16	29	♎ 13	27	♏ 9	21	♐ 4	16	28	♑ 9	21	♒ 3
☿	♌ 16	18	20	22	24	26	28	29 0	♍ 1	3	5	6	8	10	11	13	15	16	18	19	21	22	23	25	26	27	29	29 0	♎ 1	3	4
♀	♋ 14	15	16	17	19	20	21	22	23	25	26	27	28	29 0	♌ 1	2	3	5	6	7	8	10	11	12	13	14	16	17	18	19	20
♂	♎ 28	29	29 0	♏ 0	1	1	2	2	3	4	4	5	5	6	7	7	8	8	9	10	10	11	11	12	13	13	14	15	15	16	17

♃ 1 9 17 24 31 — ♏ 2 3 4 5 6 · ♄ 1 13 25 31 — ♎ 17 18 19 19 · ♅ 1R 11D 31 — ♐ 0 0 · ♆ 1 31 — ♐ 24 24 · ♇ 1 30 31 — ♎ 24 25 25

9

	1	2	3	4	5	6	7	8	9	10	11	12	13	14	15	16	17	18	19	20	21	22	23	24	25	26	27	28	29	30
☉	♍ 9	10	11	12	13	14	14	15	16	17	18	19	20	21	22	23	24	25	26	27	28	29	29 0	♎ 1	2	3	4	5	6	7
☽	♒ 15	28	♓ 10	23	♈ 6	19	♉ 3	17	♊ 0	14	29	♋ 13	27	♌ 11	26	♍ 10	24	♎ 8	21	♏ 5	17	29	♐ 12	24	♑ 6	17	29	♒ 11	23	♓ 5
☿	♎ 5	6	7	8	9	10	11	12	13	14	14	15	16	16	16	17	17	17	17	17R	17	17	17	16	16	15	14	13	12	11
♀	♌ 22	23	24	25	27	28	29 0	♍ 0	2	3	4	5	6	8	9	10	12	13	14	15	17	18	19	20	21	23	24	25	26	27
♂	♏ 17	18	19	19	20	20	21	22	23	23	24	25	25	26	27	27	28	29	29	29 0	♐ 1	1	2	3	3	4	5	5	6	7

♃ 1 6 12 17 23 28 30 — ♏ 6 7 8 9 10 11 11 · ♄ 1 4 13 22 30 — ♎ 19 20 21 22 23 · ♅ 1 9 30 — ♐ 0 1 1 · ♆ 1R 9D 30 — ♐ 24 24 · ♇ 1 28 30 — ♎ 25 26 26

10

	1	2	3	4	5	6	7	8	9	10	11	12	13	14	15	16	17	18	19	20	21	22	23	24	25	26	27	28	29	30	31
☉	♎ 8	9	10	11	12	13	14	15	16	17	18	19	20	21	22	23	24	25	26	27	28	29	29 0	♏ 1	2	3	4	5	6	7	8
☽	♓ 19	♈ 2	15	29	♉ 13	27	♊ 11	25	♋ 9	24	♌ 8	22	♍ 6	20	♎ 3	16	29	♏ 12	25	♐ 7	20	♑ 2	14	25	♒ 7	19	♓ 1	14	27	♈ 10	24
☿	♎ 10R	9	8	7	5	4	4	3	2	2	2	D 2	2	3	3	4	5	6	7	8	10	11	12	14	15	17	18	20	22	23	25
♀	♍ 29	29 0	♎ 1	3	4	5	6	8	9	10	12	13	14	15	16	17	19	20	22	23	24	25	27	28	29	29 0	♏ 1	3	4	5	6
♂	♐ 8	8	9	10	11	11	12	13	13	14	15	15	16	17	18	18	19	20	21	21	22	22	24	24	25	26	27	27	28	29	29

♃ 1 3 8 13 17 22 27 31 — ♏ 11 12 13 14 15 16 17 18 · ♄ 1 9 17 25 31 — ♎ 23 24 25 26 26 · ♅ 1 7 27 31 — ♐ 1 2 3 3 · ♆ 1 28 31 — ♐ 24 25 25 · ♇ 1 23 31 — ♎ 26 27 27

11

	1	2	3	4	5	6	7	8	9	10	11	12	13	14	15	16	17	18	19	20	21	22	23	24	25	26	27	28	29	30
☉	♏ 9	10	11	12	13	14	15	16	17	18	19	20	21	22	23	24	25	26	27	28	29	29 0	♐ 1	2	3	4	5	6	7	8
☽	♉ 8	23	♊ 7	21	♋ 6	20	♌ 4	18	♍ 2	16	29	♎ 12	26	♏ 8	21	♐ 4	16	28	♑ 10	22	♒ 3	15	27	♓ 9	22	♈ 5	18	♉ 2	16	♊ 1
☿	♎ 27	29	29 0	♏ 2	4	5	7	8	10	12	13	15	17	18	20	21	23	25	26	28	29 0	♐ 1	3	4	6	7	9	10	12	13
♀	♏ 8	9	10	12	13	14	15	17	18	19	20	22	23	24	25	27	28	29 0	♐ 1	2	3	4	5	7	8	9	10	12	13	14
♂	♑ 0	1	1	2	3	4	4	5	6	7	7	8	9	10	10	11	12	13	13	14	15	16	17	17	18	19	20	20	21	22

♃ 1 5 9 14 19 23 28 30 — ♏ 18 19 20 21 22 23 24 24 · ♄ 1 3 11 20 29 30 — ♎ 26 27 28 29 0 ♏ 0 · ♅ 1 12 29 30 — ♐ 3 4 5 5 · ♆ 1 28 30 — ♐ 25 26 26 · ♇ 1 18 30 — ♎ 27 28 28

12

	1	2	3	4	5	6	7	8	9	10	11	12	13	14	15	16	17	18	19	20	21	22	23	24	25	26	27	28	29	30	31
☉	♐ 9	10	11	12	13	14	15	16	17	18	19	20	21	22	23	24	25	26	27	28	29	29 0	♑ 1	2	3	4	5	6	7	8	9
☽	♊ 16	♋ 0	15	♌ 0	14	29	♍ 10	26	♎ 10	23	♏ 5	18	♐ 0	12	24	♑ 6	18	29	♒ 12	24	♓ 5	18	♈ 0	13	26	♉ 10	24	♊ 9	24	♋ 9	24
☿	♐ 15	17	18	20	21	23	24	26	28	29 0	♑ 1	2	4	5	7	8	10	11	13	14	16	17	19	20	21	23	24	25	27	28	29
♀	♐ 15	17	18	20	21	22	23	24	25	27	28	29 0	♑ 1	2	3	4	6	7	8	9	10	12	13	14	15	17	18	19	20	22	23
♂	♑ 23	24	24	25	26	27	27	28	29	29 0	♒ 1	2	2	3	4	4	5	6	7	7	8	9	10	11	12	12	13	14	14	15	16

♃ 1 2 5 11 16 21 26 27 31 — ♏ 24 25 26 27 28 29 29 0 ♐ 0 1 · ♄ 1 9 20 31 — ♏ 0 1 2 2 · ♅ 1 15 31 — ♐ 5 6 6 · ♆ 1 25 31 — ♐ 26 27 27 · ♇ 1 20 31 — ♎ 28 29 29

1983

1

	1	2	3	4	5	6	7	8	9	10	11	12	13	14	15	16	17	18	19	20	21	22	23	24	25	26	27	28
☉	♑ 10	11	12	13	14	15	16	17	18	19	20	21	22	23	24	25	26	27	28	29 0	♒ 1	2	3	4	5	6	7	8
☽	♌ 9	24	♍ 8	23	♎ 6	19	♏ 2	15	27	♐ 9	21	♑ 3	15	27	♒ 9	20	♓ 2	14	27	♈ 9	22	♉ 5	18	♊ 2	17	♋ 2	16	♌ 2
☿	29♑ 0♒	♒ 1	1	2	2	2	2	2R	2	2	1	0 29	♑ 29	28	27	25	24	23	22	21	20	19	18	17	17	16	16	16
♀	♑ 24	25	27	28	29 0	♒ 1	2	3	4	6	7	8	10	11	12	13	15	16	17	18	19	20	22	23	24	26	27	28
♂	♒ 17	18	19	19	20	21	22	23	23	24	25	26	27	27	28	29	29 0	♓ 1	1	2	3	3	4	5	6	6	7	8

♃ 1 5 11 16 22 28 31 — ♐ 1 2 3 4 5 6 6 · ♄ 1 21 31 — ♏ 3 4 4 · ♅ 1 22 31 — ♐ 7 8 8 · ♆ 1 23 31 — ♐ 27 28 28 · ♇ 1 — ♎ 29

2

	1	2	3	4	5	6	7	8	9	10	11	12	13	14	15	16	17	18	19	20	21	22	23	24	25	26	27	28
☉	♒ 12	13	14	15	16	17	18	19	20	21	22	23	24	25	26	27	28	29	29 0	♓ 1	2	3	4	5	6	7	8	9
☽	♎ 1	15	28	♏ 12	24	♐ 6	18	♑ 0	11	24	♒ 5	17	29	♓ 11	24	♈ 6	19	♉ 2	15	28	♊ 12	26	♋ 11	25	♌ 10	25	♍ 10	25
☿	♑ 18	18	19	20	20	21	22	23	24	25	26	27	28	29 0	♒ 1	2	4	5	6	7	9	10	12	13	15	16	17	19
♀	♓ 3	4	5	7	8	9	10	12	13	14	15	17	18	19	20	22	23	24	25	26	28	29 0	♈ 0	2	3	4	5	6
♂	♓ 12	12	13	14	15	15	16	17	18	18	19	20	21	21	22	23	24	25	25	26	27	28	28	29	♈ 0	1	2	2

♃ 1 4 11 20 28 — ♐ 6 7 8 9 9 · ♄ 1 14R 28 — ♏ 4 4 · ♅ 1 27 28 — ♐ 8 9 9 · ♆ 1 28 — ♐ 28 28 · ♇ 1 — ♎ 29

3

	1	2	3	4	5	6	7	8	9	10	11	12	13	14	15	16	17	18	19	20	21	22	23	24	25	26	27	28
☉	♓ 10	11	12	13	14	15	16	17	18	19	20	21	22	23	24	25	26	27	28	29	29 0	♈ 1	2	3	4	5	6	7
☽	♎ 9	23	♏ 6	19	♐ 2	15	27	♑ 9	20	♒ 2	14	26	♓ 8	20	♈ 3	16	29	♉ 12	25	♊ 9	22	♋ 6	21	♌ 5	20	♍ 4	19	♎ 3
☿	♒ 21	22	24	25	27	28	29 0	♓ 2	4	5	7	9	10	12	14	16	18	19	21	23	25	27	28 0	♈ 1	2	5	7	9
♀	♈ 8	9	10	11	13	14	15	16	18	19	20	21	22	24	25	26	27	29	29 0	♉ 1	2	3	5	6	7	8	9	11
♂	♈ 3	4	5	5	6	7	8	8	9	10	11	11	12	13	14	14	15	16	17	17	18	19	20	20	21	22	23	23

♃ 1 3 29R 31 — ♐ 9 10 10 · ♄ 1R 25 31 — ♏ 4 3 3 · ♅ 1 16R 31 — ♐ 9 9 · ♆ 1 3 31 — ♐ 28 29 29 · ♇ 1R — ♎ 29

4

	1	2	3	4	5	6	7	8	9	10	11	12	13	14	15	16	17	18	19	20	21	22	23	24	25	26	27	28
☉	♈ 11	12	13	14	15	16	17	18	19	20	21	22	23	24	25	26	27	28	29	29 0	♉ 1	2	3	4	5	6	7	8
☽	♏ 27	♐ 10	22	♑ 5	17	28	♒ 10	22	♓ 4	17	29	♈ 12	25	♉ 8	21	♊ 5	19	♋ 3	17	♌ 1	15	♍ 0	14	28	♎ 12	26	♏ 9	22
☿	♈ 17	19	21	23	25	27	28 0	♉ 1	3	5	7	8	10	11	13	14	16	17	18	19	20	22	22	23	24	24	24	25
♀	♉ 15	17	18	19	20	21	23	24	25	26	27	28	29 0	♊ 1	2	3	4	6	7	8	9	10	11	13	14	15	16	17
♂	♈ 27	28	28	29	29 0	♉ 1	2	3	3	4	4	5	6	6	7	8	8	9	10	10	11	12	13	13	14	15	16	16

♃ 1R 30 — ♐ 10 9 · ♄ 1R 23 30 — ♏ 2 1 0 · ♅ 1R 30 — ♐ 8 8 · ♆ 1 3R 30 — ♐ 29 29 · ♇ 1R — ♎ 28

5

	1	2	3	4	5	6	7	8	9	10	11	12	13	14	15	16	17	18	19	20	21	22	23	24	25	26	27	28
☉	♉ 10	11	12	13	14	15	16	17	18	19	20	21	22	23	24	25	26	27	28	29	29 0	♊ 1	2	3	4	5	5	6
☽	♑ 0	12	24	♒ 6	18	♓ 0	12	25	♈ 7	20	♉ 3	17	♊ 1	15	29	♋ 14	28	♌ 12	27	♍ 11	25	♎ 9	22	♏ 5	18	♐ 1	14	26
☿	♉ 25	25	25R	25	25	25	24	24	23	23	22	22	21	20	20	19	19	18	18	17	17	17	16	16	16	16	D 16	16
♀	♊ 21	22	23	24	25	26	28	29	29 0	♋ 1	2	3	4	5	6	7	9	10	11	12	13	14	15	16	17	19	20	21
♂	♉ 19	20	20	21	22	22	23	24	24	25	26	27	27	28	29	29 0	♊ 0	1	2	2	3	4	4	5	6	7	7	8

♃ 1R 12 21 28 31 — ♐ 9 8 7 6 5 · ♄ 1R 6 7 31 — ♏ 0 0 29 ♎ 29 28 · ♅ 1R 31 — ♐ 8 7 · ♆ 1R 31 — ♐ 29 28 · ♇ 1R — ♎ 27

6

	1	2	3	4	5	6	7	8	9	10	11	12	13	14	15	16	17	18	19	20	21	22	23	24	25	26	27	28
☉	♊ 10	11	12	13	14	15	16	17	18	19	20	21	22	23	24	25	26	27	28	28	29 0	♋ 0	1	2	3	4	5	6
☽	♒ 14	26	♓ 8	20	♈ 2	15	28	♉ 11	25	♊ 9	24	♋ 9	24	♌ 8	23	♍ 7	21	♎ 5	19	♏ 2	15	28	♐ 10	23	♑ 5	17	29	♒ 11
☿	♉ 18	19	19	20	21	21	22	23	24	25	26	27	29	29 0	♊ 1	3	4	5	7	9	10	12	13	15	17	19	21	23
♀	♋ 25	26	27	28	29	29 0	♌ 1	2	3	4	5	6	7	8	9	10	11	12	13	14	14	15	16	17	18	19	20	20
♂	♊ 11	11	12	13	13	14	15	15	16	17	17	18	19	19	20	21	21	22	23	24	24	25	26	26	27	28	28	29

♃ 1R 13 22 30 — ♐ 5 4 3 2 · ♄ 1R 30 — ♎ 28 27 · ♅ 1R 26 30 — ♐ 7 6 6 · ♆ 1R 30 — ♐ 28 27 · ♇ 1R — ♎ 27

7

	1	2	3	4	5	6	7	8	9	10	11	12	13	14	15	16	17	18	19	20	21	22	23	24	25	26	27	28
☉	♋ 9	10	11	12	13	14	15	16	17	18	19	19	20	21	22	23	24	25	26	27	28	29	29 0	♌ 1	2	3	4	5
☽	♓ 16	28	♈ 11	23	♉ 6	20	♊ 4	18	♋ 3	17	♌ 2	17	♍ 3	17	♎ 2	15	29	♏ 12	25	♐ 7	20	♑ 2	14	26	♒ 8	19	♓ 1	13
☿	♊28 ♋0	♋ 1	3	5	7	9	12	14	16	18	20	22	25	27	28 0	♌ 1	3	5	7	9	11	13	14	16	18	20	22	23
♀	♌ 23	24	25	26	26	27	28	29	29	29 0	♍ 1	1	2	2	3	4	4	5	5	6	6	7	7	7	8	8	8	8
♂	♋ 1	2	3	3	4	4	5	6	6	7	8	9	10	10	11	12	12	13	14	14	15	16	16	17	17	18	18	19

♃ 1R 30D 31 — ♐ 2 1 · ♄ 1 3D 19 31 — ♎ 27 28 28 · ♅ 1R 31 — ♐ 6 5 · ♆ 1R 31 — ♐ 27 27 · ♇ 1R — ♎ 26

8

	1	2	3	4	5	6	7	8	9	10	11	12	13	14	15	16	17	18	19	20	21	22	23	24	25	26	27	28
☉	♌ 9	9	10	11	12	13	14	15	16	17	18	19	20	21	22	23	24	25	26	27	28	29	29 0	♍ 1	2	3	4	5
☽	♉ 2	15	28	♊ 12	26	♋ 11	26	♌ 11	26	♍ 11	26	♎ 11	25	♏ 8	22	♐ 4	17	29	♑ 11	23	♒ 5	16	28	♓ 10	22	♈ 4	17	29
☿	29♌ 0♍	♍ 1	3	4	6	7	8	10	11	13	14	15	16	17	19	20	21	22	23	24	25	26	27	27	28	28	29	29
♀	♍ 9	9	9	9	9R	9	9	9	9	8	8	8	8	7	7	6	6	5	5	4	4	3	2	2	1	1	0 29	♌ 29
♂	♋ 22	22	23	24	24	25	25	26	27	27	28	29	29 0	♌ 0	1	1	2	2	3	4	5	5	6	6	7	8	8	9

♃ 1 23 31 — ♐ 1 2 2 · ♄ 1 10 24 25 31 — ♎ 28 29 29 0 ♏ 0 0 · ♅ 1R 16D 31 — ♐ 5 5 · ♆ 1R 31 — ♐ 27 26 · ♇ 1 — ♎ 27

9

	1	2	3	4	5	6	7	8	9	10	11	12	13	14	15	16	17	18	19	20	21	22	23	24	25	26	27	28
☉	♍ 8	9	10	11	12	13	14	15	16	17	18	19	20	21	22	23	24	25	26	27	28	29	29 0	♎ 1	2	3	4	5
☽	♊ 21	♋ 5	20	♌ 5	19	♍ 5	20	♎ 5	19	♏ 3	17	♐ 0	13	25	♑ 8	20	♒ 2	13	25	♓ 7	19	♈ 1	14	26	♉ 9	22	♊ 5	18
☿	♎ 0	0	0R	0	0	0 29	♍ 29	29	28	27	27	26	25	24	23	21	20	19	19	18	17	17	16	16	16	D 16	16	17
♀	♌ 27R	26	26	25	25	25	24	24	24	24	23	23	23	23	23	23	D 23	23	23	23	23	24	24	24	25	25	25	26
♂	♌ 12	12	13	13	14	15	15	16	17	17	18	19	19	20	20	21	22	22	23	24	24	25	25	26	27	27	28	29

♃ 1 3 12 19 26 30 — ♐ 2 3 4 5 6 6 · ♄ 1 5 15 24 30 — ♏ 0 1 2 3 3 · ♅ 1 30 — ♐ 5 6 · ♆ 1R 11D 30 — ♐ 26 26 · ♇ 1 — ♎ 27

10

	1	2	3	4	5	6	7	8	9	10	11	12	13	14	15	16	17	18	19	20	21	22	23	24	25	26	27	28
☉	♎ 8	9	10	11	12	13	14	15	16	17	17	18	19	20	21	22	23	24	25	26	27	28	29 0	♏ 0	1	2	3	4
☽	♋ 29	♌ 13	28	♍ 14	28	♎ 13	27	♏ 11	25	♐ 9	21	♑ 4	16	28	♒ 10	22	♓ 4	16	28	♈ 12	23	♉ 5	18	♊ 1	15	28	♋ 12	26
☿	♍ 20	21	22	23	24	26	27	28 0	♎ 1	2	4	5	7	9	11	12	14	16	17	19	21	22	24	26	28	29 0	♏ 1	3
♀	♌ 27	28	28	29	29 0	♍ 0	1	2	2	3	3	4	5	6	7	7	8	9	10	11	12	12	13	14	15	16	17	18
♂	♍ 0	1	2	2	3	4	4	5	5	6	7	7	8	8	9	10	10	11	12	12	13	13	14	15	15	16	17	17

♃ 1 3 9 14 20 25 30 31 — ♐ 6 7 8 9 10 11 12 12 · ♄ 1 4 12 20 29 31 — ♏ 3 4 5 6 7 7 · ♅ 1 23 31 — ♐ 6 7 7 · ♆ 1 23 31 — ♐ 26 27 27 · ♇ 1 — ♎ 28

11

	1	2	3	4	5	6	7	8	9	10	11	12	13	14	15	16	17	18	19	20	21	22	23	24	25	26	27	28
☉	♏ 8	9	10	11	12	13	14	15	16	17	18	19	20	21	22	23	24	25	26	27	28	29 0	♐ 0	1	2	3	4	5
☽	♍ 23	♎ 8	22	♏ 6	20	♐ 3	16	29	♑ 12	24	♒ 6	18	29	♓ 11	23	♈ 6	18	♉ 1	14	27	♊ 11	24	♋ 8	23	♌ 7	20	♍ 5	19
☿	♏ 9	11	13	14	16	17	18	20	22	24	25	27	28	29 0	♐ 1	3	4	6	7	9	10	12	14	15	17	18	19	21
♀	♍ 22	23	24	25	26	27	28	29	29 0	♎ 1	2	3	4	5	6	7	8	9	10	11	12	14	15	16	17	18	19	20
♂	♍ 20	20	21	21	22	23	23	24	24	25	26	26	27	27	28	29	29	29 0	♎ 0	1	2	2	3	3	4	4	5	6

♃ 1 4 8 12 18 22 26 30 — ♐ 12 13 14 15 16 17 18 18 · ♄ 1 6 15 23 30 — ♏ 7 8 9 10 10 · ♅ 1 10 26 30 — ♐ 7 8 9 9 · ♆ 1 26 30 — ♐ 27 28 28 · ♇ 1 — ♎ 29

12

	1	2	3	4	5	6	7	8	9	10	11	12	13	14	15	16	17	18	19	20	21	22	23	24	25	26	27	28
☉	♐ 8	9	10	11	12	13	14	15	16	17	19	20	21	22	23	24	25	26	27	28	29	29 0	♑ 1	2	3	4	5	6
☽	♏ 1	15	28	♐ 11	24	♑ 7	19	♒ 1	14	26	♓ 7	19	♈ 1	13	26	♉ 9	22	♊ 5	19	♋ 4	18	♌ 2	17	♍ 2	16	♎ 0	14	28
☿	♐ 25	27	28	29 0	♑ 1	2	4	5	6	8	9	10	11	12	13	14	15	15	16	16	16	16	16R	16	16	15	14	13
♀	♎ 24	25	26	27	28	29 0	♏ 1	2	3	4	5	6	7	9	10	11	12	13	14	16	17	18	19	21	22	23	24	25
♂	♎ 7	8	9	9	9	10	11	11	12	12	13	13	14	15	15	16	16	17	18	18	19	19	20	20	21	21	22	22

♃ 1 6 10 15 19 24 28 31 — ♐ 19 20 21 22 23 24 25 25 · ♄ 1 12 21 31 — ♏ 11 12 13 13 · ♅ 1 13 30 31 — ♐ 9 10 11 11 · ♆ 1 22 31 — ♐ 28 29 29 · ♇ 1 — ♏ 0

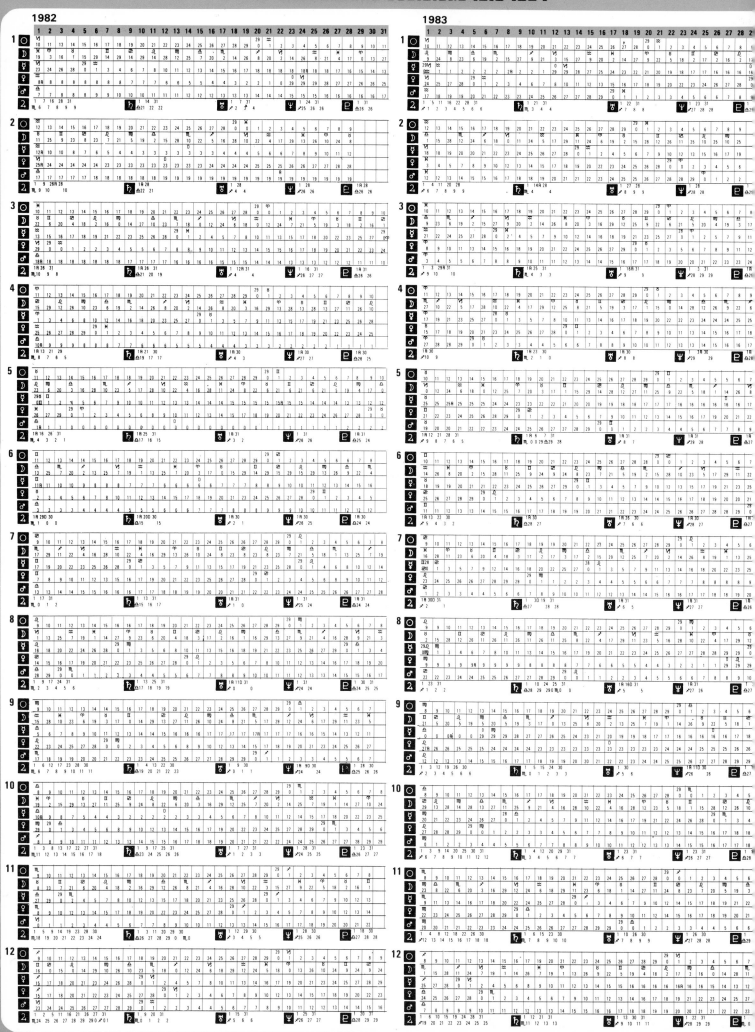

984

1	2	3	4	5	6	7	8	9	10	11	12	13	14	15	16	17	18	19	20	21	22	23	24	25	26	27	28	29	30	31
♑ 0	11	12	13	14	15	16	17	18	19	20	21	22	23	24	25	26	27	28	29 0	♒ 0	1	2	3	4	5	6	7	8	9	10
♐ 20	♑ 3	15	28	♒ 10	22	♓ 4	15	27	♈ 9	21	♉ 4	16	29	♊ 13	27	♋ 12	26	♌ 11	26	♍ 11	26	♎ 11	24	♏ 8	22	♐ 5	18	29	♑ 12	24
♑ 8R	7	5	4	3	2	1	1	0	0	0	D 0	0	1	1	2	3	3	4	5	6	7	8	9	10	11	12	13	15	16	17
♏ ♐	1	2	4	5	6	7	8	10	11	12	13	15	16	17	18	20	21	22	23	24	26	27	28	29 0	♑ 1	2	3	4	5	6
♎ 25	25	26	26	27	27	28	28	29	29	29 0	♏ 0	1	1	2	2	3	3	4	4	5	5	6	6	7	7	8	8	9	9	10

	♄	♅	♆	♇
6 11 15 19 20 25 29 31	1 15 31	1 17 31	1 18 19 31	1 14 31
26 27 28 29 29 0 ♑0 1 2 2	♏14 15 15	♐11 12 12	♐29 29 0 ♑0 0	♏1 2 2

♒ 11	12	13	14	15	16	17	18	19	20	22	23	24	25	26	27	28	29	29 0	♓ 1	2	3	4	5	6	7	8	9	10
♒ 6	18	♓ 0	12	24	♈ 6	18	♉ 0	12	25	♊ 8	21	♋ 5	20	♌ 4	19	♍ 5	20	♎ 5	20	♏ 4	18	♐ 1	14	27	♑ 9	21	♒ 3	15
♑ 19	20	22	23	24	26	27	29	29 0	♒ 1	3	5	6	8	9	11	12	14	16	17	19	21	22	24	25	27	29 0	♓ 1	3
♑ 8	9	10	12	13	14	15	17	18	19	20	21	23	24	25	26	28	29	29 0	♒ 1	2	4	5	6	7	8	10	11	12
♏ 0	11	11	11	12	12	13	13	14	14	14	15	15	16	16	16	17	17	18	18	19	19	19	20	20	20	21	21	21

	♄	♅	♆	♇
3 8 13 19 25 29	1 4 28R 29	1 11 29	1 24 29	1 6R 29
2 3 4 5 6 7 7	♏15 16 16	♐12 13 13	♑0 1 1	♏2 2

♓ 11	12	13	14	15	16	17	18	19	20	21	22	23	24	25	26	27	28	29	29 0	♈ 1	2	3	4	5	6	7	8	9	10	11
♒ 27	♓ 9	21	♈ 3	15	27	♉ 9	21	♊ 4	17	♋ 0	14	28	♌ 13	28	♍ 12	28	♎ 13	28	♏ 13	26	♐ 10	23	♑ 6	18	♒ 0	12	24	♓ 6	18	29
♓ 4	6	8	10	12	14	16	17	19	21	23	25	27	29 0	♈ 1	3	5	7	9	11	13	15	17	18	20	22	23	25	27	28	29 0♉
♒ 14	15	16	17	18	20	21	22	24	25	26	27	28	29 0	♓ 1	2	3	5	6	7	8	10	11	12	13	15	16	17	18	19	21
♏ 22	22	22	23	23	23	24	24	24	25	25	25	25	25	26	26	26	26	26	27	27	27	27	27	27	27	28	28	28	28	28

	♄	♅	♆	♇
9 16 25 31	1R 31	1 20R 31	1 31	1R 31
8 9 10 11 11	♏16 15	♐13 13	♑1 1	♏2 1

♈ 12	13	14	15	16	17	18	19	20	21	22	23	24	25	25	26	27	28	29 0	♉ 0	1	2	3	4	5	6	7	8	9	10
♈ 12	24	♉ 6	19	♊ 0	14	27	♋ 10	24	♌ 8	22	♍ 7	21	♎ 6	22	♏ 6	21	♐ 5	18	♑ 1	14	27	♒ 9	21	♓ 3	15	26	♈ 8	20	♉ 3
♉ 0	2	3	4	4	5	5	6	6	6	6	6	6R	6	6	6	5	4	4	3	3	2	1	1	0 29	♈ 29	29	28	27	27
♓ 22	23	24	26	27	28	29 0	♈ 0	2	3	4	5	7	8	9	10	12	13	14	15	16	18	19	20	21	23	24	25	26	27
♏ 28	28	28	28	28	28	28R	28	28	28	28	28	28	28	28	27	27	27	27	27	26	26	26	26	25	25	25	25	25	24

	♄	♅	♆	♇
4 30	1 21 30	1R 30	1 5R 30	1R 30
♑11 12 12	♏15 14 13	♐13 13	♑1 1	♏1 0

♉ 11	12	13	14	15	16	17	18	19	20	21	22	23	24	25	26	27	28	29	29 0	♊ 0	1	2	3	4	5	6	7	8	9	10
♉ 15	28	♊ 11	23	♋ 7	20	♌ 4	18	♍ 2	17	♎ 1	15	♏ 0	14	29	♐ 13	26	♑ 9	22	♒ 5	17	29	♓ 11	23	♈ 5	17	29	♉ 11	24	♊ 7	20
♈ 27R	26	26	26	26	26	D 26	26	27	27	27	28	28	29	29 0	♉ 1	1	2	3	4	5	6	7	8	10	11	12	13	15	16	18
♈ 29	29 0	♉ 1	2	4	5	6	7	9	10	11	12	14	15	16	17	18	20	21	22	23	25	26	27	28	29 0	♊ 1	2	3	4	6
♏ 24R	24	23	23	23	22	22	22	21	21	21	20	20	20	19	19	18	18	18	17	17	17	16	16	16	16	15	15	15	14	14

	♄	♅	♆	♇
1R 25 31	1R 18 31	1R 31	1R 31	1R 18 19 31
♑13 12 11	♏13 12 11	♐12 11	♑1 0	♏0 0 ♎29 29

♊ 11	12	13	14	15	16	17	18	19	20	21	22	23	24	25	25	26	27	28	29	29 0	♋ 1	2	3	4	5	6	7	8	9
♋ 3	17	♌ 1	15	29	♍ 13	28	♎ 12	26	♏ 10	24	♐ 7	21	♑ 4	17	♒ 0	12	25	♓ 7	19	♈ 1	13	25	♉ 7	19	♊ 2	15	28	♋ 12	26
♉ 19	21	22	24	26	27	29 0	♊ 1	3	5	7	9	11	13	15	17	19	21	23	26	28	29 0	♋ 2	4	6	9	11	13	15	17
♊ 7	8	9	10	12	13	14	15	17	18	19	20	22	23	24	25	27	28	29	29 0	♋ 1	3	4	5	6	7	9	10	11	12
♏ 14R	14	13	13	13	13	12	12	12	12	12	12	12	12	11	11	11	11	11	11	D 11	11	11	11	11	12	12	12	12	12

	♄	♅	♆	♇
1R 14 22 30	1R 22 30	1R 30	1R 22 23 30	1R 30
♑11 10 9 8	♏11 10 10	♐11 10	♑0 ♑0 ♐29 29	♎29 29

♋ 10	11	12	13	14	15	16	17	18	19	19	20	21	22	23	24	25	26	27	28	29	29 0	♌ 1	2	3	4	5	6	6	7	8
♌ 11	25	♍ 10	24	♎ 9	23	♏ 7	21	♐ 4	17	♑ 0	13	26	♒ 9	21	♓ 3	15	27	♈ 9	20	♉ 3	15	27	♊ 10	23	♋ 7	21	♌ 5	19	♍ 5	20
♋ 19	21	23	25	27	28 0	♌ 1	3	4	6	8	9	11	13	15	16	18	19	21	22	23	25	26	28	29	29 0	♍ 1	2	3	4	5
♋ 14	15	16	18	19	20	21	22	23	25	26	27	28	29 0	♌ 1	2	3	5	6	7	8	9	11	12	13	15	16	17	18	19	21
♏ 12	12	13	13	13	13	13	14	14	14	14	15	15	15	15	16	16	16	17	17	17	18	18	18	19	19	20	20	20	21	21

	♄	♅	♆	♇
1R 8 16 25 31	1R 15D 31	1R 31	1R 31	1R 11D 31
♑8 7 6 5 4	♏9 10	♐10 10	♐29 29	♎29 29

♌ 9	10	11	12	13	14	15	16	17	18	19	20	21	22	23	24	25	26	27	28	28	29 0	♍ 0	1	2	3	4	5	6	7	8
♎ 5	19	♏ 3	17	♐ 1	14	27	♑ 10	22	♒ 5	17	29	♓ 11	23	♈ 5	17	29	♉ 11	23	♊ 6	18	♋ 2	15	29	♌ 14	29	♍ 14	29	♎ 14	29	♏ 13
♍ 6	7	8	9	10	10	11	11	12	12	13	13	13	13	13	13R	13	13	12	12	11	11	10	9	8	7	7	6	5	4	3
♌ 22	23	24	25	27	28	29 0	♍ 0	2	3	4	6	7	8	9	10	11	13	14	15	16	18	19	20	22	23	24	25	26	28	29
♏ 22	22	23	23	23	24	24	25	25	26	26	27	27	28	28	29	29 0	♐ 0	0	1	2	2	3	3	4	4	5	5	6	7	7

	♄	♅	♆	♇
1R 31D	1 23 31	1R 19D 31	1 31	1 28 29 31
♑4 3	♏10 11 11	♐9 9	♐29 29	♎29 29 ♏0 0

♍ 9	10	11	12	13	14	15	16	17	18	19	20	21	22	23	24	25	26	27	28	29	29 0	♎ 0	1	2	3	4	5	6	7
♏ 27	♐ 11	24	♑ 7	20	♒ 2	14	26	♓ 8	20	♈ 2	14	25	♉ 7	20	♊ 2	14	27	♋ 10	24	♌ 8	23	♍ 7	22	♎ 7	23	♏ 8	22	♐ 7	20
♍ 2R	1	1	0	0	0	0	D 0	0	0	1	2	3	4	5	6	6	7	10	12	13	15	16	18	20	22	24	25	27	28 0♎
♍29 ♎0	♎ 1	3	4	5	6	7	9	10	11	12	14	15	16	17	18	20	21	22	23	25	26	27	28	29 0	♏ 1	2	3	4	6
♐ 8	8	9	10	10	11	11	12	13	13	14	15	15	16	16	17	18	18	19	20	20	21	22	22	23	24	24	25	26	26

	♄	♅	♆	♇
1 23 30	1 6 17 28 30	1 20 30	1R 13D 30	1 28 30
♑3 4 4	♏11 12 13 14 14	♐9 10 10	♐28 28	♏0 1 1

♎ 8	9	10	11	12	13	14	15	16	17	18	19	20	21	22	23	24	25	26	27	28	29	29 0	♏ 1	2	3	4	5	6	7	8
♑ 3	16	29	♒ 11	23	♓ 5	17	29	♈ 11	23	♉ 5	17	29	♊ 11	24	♋ 6	19	♌ 3	17	♍ 1	16	♎ 1	16	♏ 1	16	♐ 1	15	28	♑ 12	25	♒ 8
♎ 1	3	4	6	8	10	12	13	15	17	18	20	22	24	25	27	29	29 0	♏ 2	4	5	7	8	10	11	13	14	16	18	19	21
♏ 6	8	9	10	12	13	14	15	17	18	19	20	22	23	24	25	26	28	29	29 0	♐ 1	2	4	5	6	7	9	10	11	12	13
♐ 27	28	28	29	29 0	♑ 1	1	2	2	3	4	5	5	6	7	7	8	9	9	10	11	12	12	13	14	15	15	16	17	17	18

	♄	♅	♆	♇
1 4 13 20 27 31	1 7 16 25 31	1 17 31	1 15 31	1 24 31
♑4 5 6 7 8 8	♏14 15 16 17 17	♐10 11 11	♐28 29 29	♏1 2 2

♏ 9	10	11	12	13	14	15	16	17	18	19	20	21	22	23	24	25	26	27	28	29	29 0	♐ 1	2	3	4	5	6	7	8
♒ 20	♓ 2	14	26	♈ 8	19	♉ 1	14	26	♊ 8	21	♋ 4	16	29	♌ 13	27	♍ 11	25	♎ 10	25	♏ 9	24	♐ 9	23	♑ 7	20	♒ 3	16	29	♓ 10
♏ 22	24	25	26	28	29 0	♐ 1	3	4	6	7	8	9	11	12	14	15	17	18	19	20	22	23	24	25	26	27	28	29	29
♐ 14	16	17	18	20	21	22	23	24	26	27	28	29 0	♑ 0	2	3	4	5	6	8	9	10	11	12	14	15	16	17	18	20
♑ 19	20	21	21	22	23	23	24	25	26	26	27	28	29	29 0	♒ 0	1	2	2	3	4	5	5	6	7	8	8	9	10	11

	♄	♅	♆	♇
1 8 13 18 23 28 30	1 11 19 27 30	1 6 23 30	1 21 22 30	1 18 30
♑9 10 11 12 13 14 14	♏18 19 20 21 21	♐11 12 13 13	♐29 29 ♑0 0	♏2 3 3

♐ 9	10	11	12	13	14	15	16	17	18	19	20	21	22	23	24	25	26	27	28	29 0	♑ 1	2	3	4	5	6	7	8	9	10
♓ 22	♈ 4	16	28	♉ 10	22	♊ 4	17	♋ 0	13	26	♌ 10	24	♍ 8	22	♎ 6	20	♏ 5	19	♐ 3	17	♑ 1	14	28	♒ 11	24	♓ 6	18	29	♈ 12	24
♐29 ♑0	♑ 0	0	0	0	0R	0 29	♐ 29	29	28	27	26	25	23	22	21	19	18	17	16	15	15	14	14	14	D 14	15	15	16	16	17
♑ 21	22	23	24	25	27	28	29	29 0	♒ 1	3	4	5	6	7	8	10	11	12	13	14	15	16	18	19	20	21	22	23	24	26
♒ 12	12	13	14	14	15	16	17	17	18	19	20	20	21	22	23	24	24	25	26	27	27	28	29	29 0	♓ 1	2	2	3	4	4

	♄	♅	♆	♇
1 3 8 13 17 21 26 30 31	1 6 15 25 31	1 9 26 31	1 19 31	1 17 31
♑14 15 16 17 18 19 20 21 21	♏21 22 23 24 24	♐13 14 15 15	♑0 1 1	♏3 4 4

	1	2	3	4	5	6	7	8	9	10	11	12
1910	20 ♒ 21·59	19 ♓ 12·28	21 ♈ 12·03	20 ♉ 23·46	21 ♊ 23·30	22 ♋ 7·49	23 ♌ 18·43	24 ♍ 1·27	23 ♎ 22·30	24 ♏ 7·11	23 ♐ 4·11	22 ♑ 17·12
1911	21 ♒ 3·52	19 ♓ 18·21	21 ♈ 17·55	21 ♉ 5·36	22 ♊ 5·19	22 ♋ 13·36	24 ♌ 0·29	24 ♍ 7·13	24 ♎ 4·17	24 ♏ 12·59	23 ♐ 9·57	22 ♑ 22·53
1912	21 ♒ 9·29	19 ♓ 23·56	20 ♈ 23·29	20 ♉ 11·12	21 ♊ 10·57	21 ♋ 20·26	23 ♌ 6·14	23 ♍ 13·02	23 ♎ 10·08	23 ♏ 18·50	22 ♐ 15·48	22 ♑ 4·45
1913	20 ♒ 15·19	19 ♓ 5·45	21 ♈ 5·18	20 ♉ 17·03	21 ♊ 16·50	22 ♋ 1·09	23 ♌ 12·04	23 ♍ 18·48	23 ♎ 15·53	24 ♏ 0·35	22 ♐ 21·36	22 ♑ 10·35
1914	20 ♒ 21·12	19 ♓ 11·38	21 ♈ 11·11	20 ♉ 22·54	21 ♊ 22·38	22 ♋ 6·55	23 ♌ 17·47	24 ♍ 0·30	23 ♎ 21·35	24 ♏ 6·18	23 ♐ 3·21	22 ♑ 16·24
1915	21 ♒ 3·00	19 ♓ 17·23	21 ♈ 16·51	21 ♉ 4·28	22 ♊ 4·10	22 ♋ 12·29	23 ♌ 23·27	24 ♍ 6·16	24 ♎ 3·24	24 ♏ 12·10	23 ♐ 9·14	22 ♑ 22·16
1916	21 ♒ 8·54	19 ♓ 23·18	20 ♈ 22·47	20 ♉ 10·25	21 ♊ 10·06	21 ♋ 18·25	23 ♌ 5·21	23 ♍ 12·09	23 ♎ 9·15	23 ♏ 17·58	21 ♐ 14·58	22 ♑ 3·59
1917	20 ♒ 14·37	19 ♓ 5·05	21 ♈ 4·37	20 ♉ 16·17	21 ♊ 15·59	22 ♋ 0·15	23 ♌ 11·08	23 ♍ 17·54	23 ♎ 15·00	23 ♏ 23·44	22 ♐ 20·45	21 ♑ 9·46
1918	20 ♒ 20·24	19 ♓ 10·53	21 ♈ 10·26	20 ♉ 22·06	21 ♊ 21·46	22 ♋ 6·00	23 ♌ 16·52	23 ♍ 23·37	23 ♎ 20·45	24 ♏ 5·33	23 ♐ 2·38	22 ♑ 15·42
1919	21 ♒ 2·21	19 ♓ 16·48	21 ♈ 16·19	21 ♉ 3·59	22 ♊ 3·39	22 ♋ 11·54	23 ♌ 22·45	24 ♍ 5·28	24 ♎ 2·35	24 ♏ 11·21	23 ♐ 8·25	22 ♑ 21·27
1920	21 ♒ 9·05	19 ♓ 22·29	20 ♈ 22·00	20 ♉ 9·39	21 ♊ 9·22	21 ♋ 17·40	23 ♌ 4·35	23 ♍ 11·22	23 ♎ 8·28	23 ♏ 17·13	22 ♐ 14·16	22 ♑ 3·17
1921	20 ♒ 13·55	19 ♓ 4·21	21 ♈ 3·51	20 ♉ 15·32	21 ♊ 15·17	21 ♋ 23·36	23 ♌ 10·31	23 ♍ 17·15	23 ♎ 14·20	23 ♏ 23·03	22 ♐ 20·21	22 ♑ 9·08
1922	20 ♒ 19·48	19 ♓ 10·16	21 ♈ 9·49	20 ♉ 21·29	21 ♊ 21·11	22 ♋ 5·27	23 ♌ 16·20	23 ♍ 23·04	23 ♎ 10·10	24 ♏ 4·53	23 ♐ 1·55	22 ♑ 14·57
1923	21 ♒ 1·35	19 ♓ 16·00	21 ♈ 15·29	21 ♉ 3·06	22 ♊ 2·45	22 ♋ 11·03	23 ♌ 22·01	24 ♍ 4·52	24 ♎ 2·04	24 ♏ 10·51	23 ♐ 7·54	22 ♑ 20·53
1924	21 ♒ 7·29	19 ♓ 21·51	20 ♈ 21·20	20 ♉ 8·59	21 ♊ 8·41	21 ♋ 17·00	23 ♌ 3·58	23 ♍ 10·48	23 ♎ 7·58	23 ♏ 16·44	22 ♐ 13·46	22 ♑ 2·45
1925	20 ♒ 13·20	19 ♓ 3·43	21 ♈ 3·13	20 ♉ 14·51	21 ♊ 14·33	21 ♋ 22·50	23 ♌ 9·45	23 ♍ 16·33	23 ♎ 13·43	23 ♏ 22·31	22 ♐ 19·36	22 ♑ 8·37
1926	20 ♒ 19·13	19 ♓ 9·35	21 ♈ 9·01	20 ♉ 20·36	21 ♊ 20·15	22 ♋ 4·30	23 ♌ 15·25	23 ♍ 22·14	23 ♎ 19·26	24 ♏ 4·18	23 ♐ 1·28	22 ♑ 14·34
1927	21 ♒ 1·12	19 ♓ 15·35	21 ♈ 14·59	21 ♉ 2·32	22 ♊ 2·08	22 ♋ 10·21	23 ♌ 21·17	24 ♍ 4·06	24 ♎ 1·17	24 ♏ 10·07	23 ♐ 7·14	22 ♑ 20·18
1928	21 ♒ 6·57	19 ♓ 21·20	20 ♈ 20·44	20 ♉ 8·17	21 ♊ 7·53	21 ♋ 16·07	23 ♌ 3·02	23 ♍ 9·53	23 ♎ 7·06	23 ♏ 15·55	22 ♐ 13·00	22 ♑ 2·04
1929	20 ♒ 12·42	19 ♓ 3·07	21 ♈ 2·35	20 ♉ 14·11	21 ♊ 13·48	21 ♋ 22·01	23 ♌ 8·54	23 ♍ 15·41	23 ♎ 12·52	23 ♏ 21·41	22 ♐ 18·48	22 ♑ 7·53
1930	20 ♒ 18·33	19 ♓ 9·00	21 ♈ 8·30	20 ♉ 20·06	21 ♊ 19·42	22 ♋ 3·53	23 ♌ 14·42	23 ♍ 21·27	23 ♎ 18·36	24 ♏ 3·26	23 ♐ 0·34	22 ♑ 13·40
1931	21 ♒ 0·18	19 ♓ 14·40	21 ♈ 14·06	21 ♉ 1·40	22 ♊ 1·15	22 ♋ 9·28	23 ♌ 20·21	24 ♍ 3·10	24 ♎ 0·23	24 ♏ 9·15	23 ♐ 6·25	22 ♑ 19·30
1932	21 ♒ 6·07	19 ♓ 20·29	20 ♈ 19·54	20 ♉ 7·28	21 ♊ 7·07	21 ♋ 15·23	23 ♌ 2·18	23 ♍ 9·06	23 ♎ 6·16	23 ♏ 15·04	22 ♐ 12·10	22 ♑ 1·14
1933	20 ♒ 11·53	19 ♓ 2·16	21 ♈ 1·43	20 ♉ 13·19	21 ♊ 12·57	21 ♋ 21·12	23 ♌ 8·06	23 ♍ 14·53	23 ♎ 12·01	23 ♏ 20·48	22 ♐ 17·53	22 ♑ 6·58
1934	20 ♒ 17·37	19 ♓ 8·02	21 ♈ 7·28	20 ♉ 19·00	21 ♊ 18·35	22 ♋ 2·48	23 ♌ 13·42	23 ♍ 20·32	23 ♎ 17·45	24 ♏ 2·36	22 ♐ 23·44	22 ♑ 12·49
1935	20 ♒ 23·29	19 ♓ 13·52	21 ♈ 13·18	21 ♉ 0·50	22 ♊ 0·25	22 ♋ 8·38	23 ♌ 19·33	24 ♍ 2·24	23 ♎ 23·38	24 ♏ 8·29	23 ♐ 5·35	22 ♑ 18·37
1936	21 ♒ 5·12	19 ♓ 19·33	20 ♈ 18·58	20 ♉ 6·31	21 ♊ 6·08	21 ♋ 14·22	23 ♌ 1·18	23 ♍ 8·11	23 ♎ 5·26	23 ♏ 14·18	22 ♐ 11·25	22 ♑ 0·27
1937	20 ♒ 11·01	19 ♓ 1·21	21 ♈ 0·45	20 ♉ 12·20	21 ♊ 11·57	21 ♋ 20·12	23 ♌ 7·07	23 ♍ 13·58	23 ♎ 11·13	23 ♏ 20·06	22 ♐ 17·17	22 ♑ 6·22
1938	20 ♒ 16·59	19 ♓ 7·20	21 ♈ 6·43	20 ♉ 18·15	21 ♊ 17·51	22 ♋ 2·04	23 ♌ 12·57	23 ♍ 19·46	23 ♎ 17·00	24 ♏ 1·54	22 ♐ 23·06	22 ♑ 12·13
1939	20 ♒ 22·51	19 ♓ 13·10	21 ♈ 12·29	20 ♉ 23·55	21 ♊ 23·27	22 ♋ 7·40	23 ♌ 18·37	24 ♍ 1·31	23 ♎ 22·50	24 ♏ 7·46	23 ♐ 4·59	22 ♑ 18·06
1940	21 ♒ 4·44	19 ♓ 19·04	20 ♈ 18·24	20 ♉ 5·51	21 ♊ 5·23	21 ♋ 13·37	23 ♌ 0·34	23 ♍ 7·29	23 ♎ 4·46	23 ♏ 13·39	22 ♐ 10·49	21 ♑ 23·55
1941	20 ♒ 10·34	19 ♓ 0·59	21 ♈ 0·21	20 ♉ 11·51	21 ♊ 11·23	21 ♋ 19·33	23 ♌ 6·26	23 ♍ 13·30	23 ♎ 10·33	23 ♏ 19·27	22 ♐ 16·38	22 ♑ 5·44
1942	20 ♒ 16·16	19 ♓ 6·39	21 ♈ 6·03	20 ♉ 17·30	21 ♊ 17·01	22 ♋ 1·08	23 ♌ 11·59	23 ♍ 18·50	23 ♎ 16·10	23 ♏ 1·01	22 ♐ 22·23	22 ♑ 11·31
1943	20 ♒ 22·20	19 ♓ 12·41	21 ♈ 12·03	20 ♉ 23·32	21 ♊ 23·03	22 ♋ 7·13	23 ♌ 18·05	14 ♍ 0·55	23 ♎ 22·12	24 ♏ 7·09	23 ♐ 4·22	22 ♑ 17·30
1944	21 ♒ 4·09	19 ♓ 18·28	21 ♈ 17·49	20 ♉ 5·18	21 ♊ 4·51	21 ♋ 13·03	22 ♌ 23·55	23 ♍ 6·47	23 ♎ 4·02	23 ♏ 12·57	22 ♐ 10·09	21 ♑ 23·15
1945	20 ♒ 9·55	19 ♓ 0·15	20 ♈ 23·38	20 ♉ 11·08	22 ♊ 10·41	21 ♋ 18·52	23 ♌ 5·46	23 ♍ 12·36	23 ♎ 9·50	23 ♏ 18·45	22 ♐ 15·56	22 ♑ 5·04
1946	20 ♒ 15·44	19 ♓ 6·10	21 ♈ 5·34	20 ♉ 17·03	21 ♊ 16·34	22 ♋ 0·46	23 ♌ 11·37	23 ♍ 18·26	23 ♎ 15·41	24 ♏ 0·37	22 ♐ 21·47	22 ♑ 10·54
1947	20 ♒ 21·32	19 ♓ 11·53	21 ♈ 11·13	20 ♉ 22·40	21 ♊ 22·09	22 ♋ 6·19	23 ♌ 17·12	24 ♍ 0·09	23 ♎ 21·29	24 ♏ 6·27	23 ♐ 3·38	22 ♑ 16·44

	1	2	3	4	5	6	7	8	9	10	11	12
1948	21♒ 3·18	19♓17·37	20♈16·57	20♉ 4·25	21♊ 3·58	21♋12·11	22♌23·08	23♍ 6·03	23♎ 3·22	23♏12·19	22♐ 9·29	21♑22·33
1949	20♒ 9·11	18♓23·27	20♈22·49	20♉10·18	21♊ 9·51	21♋18·03	23♌ 4·58	23♍11·49	23♎ 9·06	23♏18·04	22♐15·17	22♑ 4·24
1950	20♒15·00	19♓ 5·16	21♈ 4·36	20♉16·00	21♊15·27	21♋23·37	23♌10·30	23♍17·24	23♎14·44	23♏23·48	22♐21·03	22♑10·14
1951	20♒20·53	19♓11·10	21♈10·26	20♉21·49	21♊21·15	22♋ 5·25	23♌16·21	23♍23·22	23♎20·38	23♏ 5·37	23♐ 2·52	22♑16·01
1952	21♒ 2·38	19♓16·57	20♈16·14	20♉ 3·37	21♊ 3·04	21♋11·13	22♌22·08	23♍ 5·03	23♎ 2·24	23♏11·22	22♐ 8·36	21♑21·44
1953	20♒ 8·22	18♓22·41	20♈22·01	20♉ 9·26	21♊ 8·53	21♋17·00	23♌ 3·53	23♍10·46	23♎ 8·07	23♏17·07	22♐14·23	22♑ 3·32
1954	20♒14·14	19♓ 4·33	21♈ 3·54	20♉15·20	21♊14·48	21♋22·55	23♌ 9·45	23♍16·37	23♎13·56	23♏22·58	22♐20·14	22♑ 9·25
1955	20♒20·03	19♓10·19	21♈ 9·36	20♉20·58	21♊20·25	22♋ 4·32	23♌15·25	23♍22·19	23♎19·42	23♏ 4·44	23♐ 2·02	22♑15·12
1956	21♒ 1·49	19♓16·05	20♈15·21	20♉ 2·44	21♊ 2·13	21♋10·24	22♌21·20	23♍ 4·15	23♎ 1·36	23♏10·35	22♐ 7·51	21♑21·00
1957	20♒ 7·43	18♓22·01	20♈21·17	20♉ 8·45	21♊ 8·09	21♋16·21	23♌ 3·13	23♍10·07	23♎ 7·27	23♏16·33	22♐13·45	22♑ 2·49
1958	20♒13·17	19♓ 3·49	21♈ 3·06	20♉14·28	21♊13·52	21♋21·57	23♌ 8·51	23♍15·47	23♎13·10	23♏22·12	22♐19·30	22♑ 8·40
1959	20♒19·20	19♓ 9·38	21♈ 8·55	20♉20·17	21♊19·36	22♋ 3·50	23♌14·46	23♍21·44	23♎19·09	24♏ 4·12	23♐ 1·23	22♑14·35
1960	21♒ 1·11	19♓15·26	20♈14·43	20♉ 2·06	21♊ 1·33	21♋ 9·43	22♌20·38	23♍ 3·35	23♎ 1·00	23♏10·03	22♐ 7·19	21♑20·27
1961	20♒ 7·02	18♓21·27	20♈20·27	20♉ 7·33	21♊ 6·51	21♋15·12	23♌ 2·12	23♍ 8·40	23♎ 6·26	23♏15·46	22♐13·10	22♑ 2·25
1962	20♒12·49	19♓ 3·16	21♈ 2·30	20♉13·51	21♊13·17	21♋21·24	23♌ 8·19	23♍15·13	23♎12·35	23♏21·41	22♐19·02	22♑ 8·15
1963	20♒18·55	19♓ 9·09	21♈ 8·20	20♉19·37	21♊18·59	22♋ 3·04	23♌14·00	23♍20·58	23♎18·24	24♏ 3·30	23♐ 0·50	22♑14·02
1964	20♒ 0·43	19♓15·26	20♈14·43	20♉ 2·06	21♊ 1·33	21♋ 9·43	22♌20·38	23♍ 3·35	23♎ 1·00	23♏10·03	22♐ 7·19	21♑20·27
1965	20♒ 6·30	18♓20·49	20♈20·05	20♉ 7·27	21♊ 6·51	21♋14·56	23♌ 1·49	23♍ 8·43	23♎ 6·06	23♏15·11	22♐12·30	22♑ 1·41
1966	20♒12·21	19♓ 2·39	21♈ 1·53	20♉13·12	21♊12·33	21♋20·33	23♌ 7·24	23♍14·18	23♎11·43	23♏20·52	22♐18·15	22♑ 7·29
1967	20♒18·08	19♓ 8·25	21♈ 7·37	20♉18·56	21♊18·19	22♋ 2·23	23♌13·16	23♍20·13	23♎17·38	24♏ 2·44	23♐ 0·05	22♑13·17
1968	20♒23·54	19♓14·11	20♈13·22	20♉ 0·42	21♊ 0·07	21♋ 8·13	22♌19·13	23♍ 2·02	22♎23·26	23♏ 8·30	22♐ 5·49	21♑19·00
1969	20♒ 5·30	18♓19·47	20♈19·08	20♉ 6·18	21♊ 5·41	21♋13·55	23♌ 1·05	23♍ 7·36	23♎ 5·07	23♏14·03	22♐11·23	22♑ 0·44
1970	20♒11·25	19♓ 1·43	21♈ 0·57	20♉12·16	21♊11·32	21♋19·43	23♌ 6·38	23♍13·35	23♎10·59	23♏20·05	22♐17·25	22♑ 6·36
1971	20♒17·14	19♓ 7·28	21♈ 6·38	20♉17·54	21♊17·16	22♋ 1·21	23♌12·15	23♍19·16	23♎16·47	23♏ 1·53	22♐23·15	22♑12·26
1972	20♒23·00	19♓13·12	20♈12·22	19♉23·38	20♊23·00	21♋ 7·07	22♌18·03	23♍ 1·04	22♎22·34	23♏ 7·42	22♐ 5·04	21♑18·14
1973	20♒ 4·49	18♓19·02	20♈18·13	20♉ 5·31	21♊ 4·54	21♋13·01	22♌23·56	23♍ 6·55	23♎ 4·22	23♏13·31	22♐10·55	22♑ 0·09
1974	20♒10·47	19♓ 1·00	21♈ 0·08	20♉11·19	21♊10·37	21♋18·38	23♌ 5·31	23♍12·29	23♎ 9·59	23♏19·12	22♐16·39	22♑ 5·57
1975	20♒16·37	19♓ 6·51	21♈ 5·58	20♉17·08	21♊16·25	22♋ 0·27	23♌11·23	23♍18·24	23♎15·56	24♏ 1·07	22♐22·32	22♑11·47
1976	20♒22·26	19♓12·41	20♈11·51	19♉23·04	20♊22·22	21♋ 6·25	22♌17·19	23♍ 0·19	22♎21·49	23♏ 6·59	22♐ 4·23	21♑17·36
1977	20♒ 4·15	18♓18·31	20♈17·43	20♉ 4·58	21♊ 4·15	21♋12·15	22♌23·05	23♍ 6·01	23♎ 3·30	23♏12·42	22♐10·08	21♑23·24
1978	20♒10·05	19♓ 0·22	20♈23·35	20♉10·51	21♊10·09	21♋18·10	23♌ 5·01	23♍11·58	23♎ 9·26	23♏18·38	22♐16·06	22♑ 5·22
1979	20♒16·01	19♓ 6·14	21♈ 5·23	20♉16·36	21♊15·55	21♋23·57	23♌10·50	23♍17·48	23♎15·18	24♏ 0·29	22♐21·55	22♑11·11
1980	20♒21·49	19♓12·2	20♈11·10	19♉22·24	20♊21·43	21♋ 5·48	22♌16·43	22♍23·42	22♎21·10	23♍ 6·18	22♐ 3·43	21♑16·57
1981	20♒ 3·36	18♓17·52	20♈17·3	20♉ 4·19	21♊ 3·39	21♋11·45	22♌22·40	23♍ 5·38	23♎ 3·5	23♍12·13	22♐ 9·36	21♑22·51
1982	20♒ 9·31	19♓23·47	20♈22·56	20♉10·8	21♊ 9·23	21♋17·23	23♌ 4·15	23♍11·15	23♎ 8·46	23♏17·58	22♐15·24	22♑ 4·39
1983	20♒15·17	19♓ 5·31	21♈ 4·39	20♉15·50	21♊15·7	21♋23·9	23♌10·5	23♍17·8	23♎14·42	23♏23·54	22♐21·18	22♑10·30
1984	20♒21·5	19♓11·16	20♈10·25	19♉21·38	20♊20·58	21♋ 5·2	22♌15·58	22♍23·0	22♎20·33	23♏ 5·46	22♐ 3·11	21♑16·23

		1	2	3	4	5	6	7	8	9	10	11	12
1910	1	18 41 2	20 43 15	22 33 38	0 35 52	2 34 8	4 36 22	6 34 38	8 36 52	10 39 5	12 37 21	14 39 35	16 37 51
	2	18 44 58	20 47 11	22 37 35	0 39 48	2 38 5	4 40 18	6 38 35	8 40 48	10 43 1	12 41 18	14 43 31	16 41 48
	3	18 48 55	20 51 8	22 41 32	0 43 45	2 42 1	4 44 15	6 42 31	8 44 45	10 46 58	12 45 14	14 47 28	16 45 44
	4	18 52 51	20 55 5	22 45 28	0 47 41	2 45 58	4 48 11	6 46 28	8 48 41	10 50 54	12 49 11	14 51 24	16 49 41
	5	18 56 48	20 59 1	22 49 25	0 51 38	2 49 54	4 52 8	6 50 24	8 52 38	10 54 51	12 53 8	14 55 21	16 53 37
	6	19 0 44	21 2 58	22 53 21	0 55 34	2 53 51	4 56 4	6 54 21	8 56 34	10 58 48	12 57 4	14 59 17	16 57 34
	7	19 4 41	21 6 54	22 57 18	0 59 31	2 57 48	5 0 1	6 58 18	9 0 31	11 2 44	13 1 1	15 3 14	17 1 31
	8	19 8 38	21 10 51	23 1 14	1 3 27	3 1 44	5 3 57	7 2 14	9 4 27	11 6 41	13 4 57	15 7 10	17 5 27
	9	19 12 34	21 14 47	23 5 11	1 7 24	3 5 41	5 7 54	7 6 11	9 8 24	11 10 37	13 8 54	15 11 7	17 9 24
	10	19 16 31	21 18 44	23 9 7	1 11 21	3 9 37	5 11 51	7 10 7	9 12 21	11 14 34	13 12 50	15 15 4	17 13 20
	11	19 20 27	21 22 40	23 13 4	1 15 17	3 13 34	5 15 47	7 14 4	9 16 17	11 18 30	13 16 47	15 19 0	17 17 17
	12	19 24 24	21 26 37	23 17 1	1 19 14	3 17 30	5 19 44	7 18 0	9 20 14	11 22 27	13 20 43	15 22 57	17 21 13
	13	19 28 20	21 30 34	23 20 57	1 23 10	3 21 27	5 23 40	7 21 57	9 24 10	11 26 23	13 24 40	15 26 53	17 25 10
	14	19 32 17	21 34 30	23 24 54	1 27 7	3 25 23	5 27 37	7 25 54	9 28 7	11 30 20	13 28 37	15 30 50	17 29 6
	15	19 36 13	21 38 27	23 28 50	1 31 3	3 29 20	5 31 33	7 29 50	9 32 3	11 34 16	13 32 33	15 34 46	17 33 3
	16	19 40 10	21 42 23	23 32 47	1 35 0	3 33 17	5 35 30	7 33 47	9 36 0	11 38 13	13 36 30	15 38 43	17 37 0
	17	19 44 7	21 46 20	23 36 43	1 38 56	3 37 13	5 39 26	7 37 43	9 39 56	11 42 10	13 40 26	15 42 39	17 40 56
	18	19 48 3	21 50 16	23 40 40	1 42 53	3 41 10	5 43 23	7 41 40	9 43 53	11 46 6	13 44 23	15 46 36	17 44 53
	19	19 52 0	21 54 13	23 44 36	1 46 50	3 45 6	5 47 20	7 45 36	9 47 50	11 50 3	13 48 19	15 50 33	17 48 49
	20	19 55 56	21 58 9	23 48 33	1 50 46	3 49 3	5 51 16	7 49 33	9 51 46	11 53 59	13 52 16	15 54 29	17 52 46
	21	19 59 53	22 2 6	23 52 30	1 54 43	3 52 59	5 55 13	7 53 29	9 55 43	11 57 56	13 56 12	15 58 26	17 56 42
	22	20 3 49	22 6 3	23 56 26	1 58 39	3 56 56	5 59 9	7 57 26	9 59 39	12 1 52	14 0 9	16 2 22	18 0 39
	23	20 7 46	22 9 59	0 0 23	2 2 36	4 0 52	6 3 6	8 1 23	10 3 36	12 5 49	14 4 6	16 6 19	18 4 36
	24	20 11 42	22 13 56	0 4 19	2 6 32	4 4 49	6 7 2	8 5 19	10 7 32	12 9 45	14 8 2	16 10 15	18 8 32
	25	20 15 39	22 17 52	0 8 16	2 10 29	4 8 46	6 10 59	8 9 16	10 11 29	12 13 42	14 11 59	16 14 12	18 12 29
	26	20 19 36	22 21 49	0 12 12	2 14 25	4 12 42	6 14 55	8 13 12	10 15 25	12 17 39	14 15 55	16 18 8	18 16 25
	27	20 23 32	22 25 45	0 16 9	2 18 22	4 16 39	6 18 52	8 17 9	10 19 22	12 21 35	14 19 52	16 22 5	18 20 22
	28	20 27 29	22 29 42	0 20 5	2 22 19	4 20 35	6 22 49	8 21 5	10 23 19	12 25 32	14 23 48	16 26 2	18 24 18
	29	20 31 25		0 24 2	2 26 15	4 24 32	6 26 45	8 25 2	10 27 15	12 29 28	14 27 45	16 29 58	18 28 15
	30	20 35 22		0 27 59	2 30 12	4 28 28	6 30 42	8 28 58	10 31 12	12 33 25	14 31 41	16 33 55	18 32 11
	31	20 39 18		0 31 55		4 32 25		8 32 55	10 35 8		14 35 38		18 36 8
1911	1	18 40 5	20 42 18	22 32 41	0 34 55	2 33 11	4 35 24	6 33 41	8 35 54	10 38 8	12 36 24	14 38 37	16 36 54
	2	18 44 1	20 46 14	22 36 38	0 38 51	2 37 8	4 39 21	6 37 38	8 39 51	10 42 4	12 40 21	14 42 34	16 40 51
	3	18 47 58	20 50 11	22 40 34	0 42 48	2 41 4	4 43 18	6 41 34	8 43 48	10 46 1	12 44 17	14 46 31	16 44 47
	4	18 51 54	20 54 8	22 44 31	0 46 44	2 45 1	4 47 14	6 45 31	8 47 44	10 49 57	12 48 14	14 50 27	16 48 44
	5	18 55 51	20 58 4	22 48 28	0 50 41	2 48 57	4 51 11	6 49 27	8 51 41	10 53 54	12 52 11	14 54 24	16 52 40
	6	18 59 47	21 2 1	22 52 24	0 54 37	2 52 54	4 55 7	6 53 24	8 55 37	10 57 50	12 56 7	14 58 20	16 56 37
	7	19 3 44	21 5 57	22 56 21	0 58 34	2 56 51	4 59 4	6 57 21	8 59 34	11 1 47	13 0 4	15 2 17	17 0 34
	8	19 7 40	21 9 54	23 0 17	1 2 30	3 0 47	5 3 0	7 1 17	9 3 30	11 5 44	13 4 0	15 6 13	17 4 30
	9	19 11 37	21 13 50	23 4 14	1 6 27	3 4 44	5 6 57	7 5 14	9 7 27	11 9 40	13 7 57	15 10 10	17 8 27
	10	19 15 34	21 17 47	23 8 10	1 10 24	3 8 40	5 10 53	7 9 10	9 11 23	11 13 37	13 11 53	15 14 7	17 12 23
	11	19 19 30	21 21 43	23 12 7	1 14 20	3 12 37	5 14 50	7 13 7	9 15 20	11 17 33	13 15 50	15 18 3	17 16 20
	12	19 23 27	21 25 40	23 16 3	1 18 17	3 16 33	5 18 47	7 17 3	9 19 17	11 21 30	13 19 46	15 22 0	17 20 16
	13	19 27 23	21 29 37	23 20 0	1 22 13	3 20 30	5 22 43	7 21 0	9 23 13	11 25 26	13 23 43	15 25 56	17 24 13
	14	19 31 20	21 33 33	23 23 57	1 26 10	3 24 26	5 26 40	7 24 56	9 27 10	11 29 23	13 27 40	15 29 53	17 28 9
	15	19 35 16	21 37 30	23 27 53	1 30 6	3 28 23	5 30 36	7 28 53	9 31 6	11 33 19	13 31 36	15 33 49	17 32 6
	16	19 39 13	21 41 26	23 31 50	1 34 3	3 32 20	5 34 33	7 32 50	9 35 3	11 37 16	13 35 33	15 37 46	17 36 3
	17	19 43 9	21 45 23	23 35 46	1 37 59	3 36 16	5 38 29	7 36 46	9 38 59	11 41 13	13 39 29	15 41 42	17 39 59
	18	19 47 6	21 49 19	23 39 43	1 41 56	3 40 13	5 42 26	7 40 43	9 42 56	11 45 9	13 43 26	15 45 39	17 43 56
	19	19 51 3	21 53 16	23 43 39	1 45 53	3 44 9	5 46 23	7 44 39	9 46 52	11 49 6	13 47 22	15 49 36	17 47 52
	20	19 54 59	21 57 12	23 47 36	1 49 49	3 48 6	5 50 19	7 48 36	9 50 49	11 53 2	13 51 19	15 53 32	17 51 49
	21	19 58 56	22 1 9	23 51 32	1 53 46	3 52 2	5 54 16	7 52 32	9 54 46	11 56 59	13 55 15	15 57 29	17 55 45
	22	20 2 52	22 5 6	23 55 29	1 57 42	3 55 59	5 58 12	7 56 29	9 58 42	12 0 55	13 59 12	16 1 25	17 59 42
	23	20 6 49	22 9 2	23 59 26	2 1 39	3 59 55	6 2 9	8 0 25	0 2 39	12 4 52	14 3 9	16 5 22	18 3 39
	24	20 10 45	22 12 59	0 3 22	2 5 35	4 3 52	6 6 5	8 4 22	0 6 35	12 8 48	14 7 5	16 9 18	18 7 35
	25	20 14 42	22 16 55	0 7 19	2 9 32	4 7 49	6 10 2	8 8 19	0 10 32	12 12 45	14 11 2	16 13 15	18 11 32
	26	20 18 39	22 20 52	0 11 15	2 13 28	4 11 45	6 13 58	8 12 15	0 14 28	12 16 42	14 14 58	16 17 11	18 15 28
	27	20 22 35	22 24 48	0 15 12	2 17 25	4 15 42	6 17 55	8 16 12	0 18 25	12 20 38	14 18 55	16 21 8	18 19 25
	28	20 26 32	22 28 45	0 19 8	2 21 22	4 19 38	6 21 52	8 20 8	0 22 21	12 24 35	14 22 51	16 25 5	18 23 21
	29	20 30 28		0 23 5	2 25 18	4 23 35	6 25 48	8 24 5	0 26 18	12 28 31	14 26 48	16 29 1	18 27 18
	30	20 34 25		0 27 1	2 29 15	4 27 31	6 29 45	8 28 1	0 30 15	12 32 28	14 30 44	16 32 58	18 31 14
	31	20 38 21		0 30 58		4 31 28		8 31 58	0 34 11		14 34 41		18 35 11
1912	1	18 39 8	20 41 21	22 35 41	0 37 54	2 36 11	4 38 24	6 36 41	8 38 54	10 41 7	12 39 24	14 41 37	16 39 54
	2	18 43 4	20 45 17	22 39 38	0 41 51	2 40 7	4 42 21	6 40 37	8 42 51	10 45 4	12 43 20	14 45 34	16 43 50
	3	18 47 1	20 49 14	22 43 34	0 45 47	2 44 4	4 46 17	6 44 34	8 46 47	10 49 0	12 47 17	14 49 30	16 47 47
	4	18 50 57	20 53 11	22 47 31	0 49 44	2 48 0	4 50 14	6 48 30	8 50 44	10 52 57	12 51 14	14 53 27	16 51 43
	5	18 54 54	20 57 7	22 51 27	0 53 40	2 51 57	4 54 10	6 52 27	8 54 40	10 56 53	12 55 10	14 57 23	16 55 40
	6	18 58 50	21 1 4	22 55 24	0 57 37	2 55 54	4 58 7	6 56 24	8 58 37	11 0 50	12 59 7	15 1 20	16 59 37
	7	19 2 47	21 5 0	22 59 20	1 1 33	2 59 50	5 2 3	7 0 20	9 2 33	11 4 47	13 3 3	15 5 16	17 3 33
	8	19 6 43	21 8 57	23 3 17	1 5 30	3 3 47	5 6 0	7 4 17	9 6 30	11 8 43	13 7 0	15 9 13	17 7 30
	9	19 10 40	21 12 53	23 7 13	1 9 27	3 7 43	5 9 56	7 8 13	9 10 27	11 12 40	13 10 56	15 13 10	17 11 26
	10	19 14 37	21 16 50	23 11 10	1 13 23	3 11 40	5 13 53	7 12 10	9 14 23	11 16 36	13 14 53	15 17 6	17 15 23
	11	19 18 33	21 20 46	23 15 6	1 17 20	3 15 36	5 17 50	7 16 6	9 18 20	11 20 33	13 18 49	15 21 3	17 19 19
	12	19 22 30	21 24 43	23 19 3	1 21 16	3 19 33	5 21 46	7 20 3	9 22 16	11 24 29	13 22 46	15 24 59	17 23 16
	13	19 26 26	21 28 40	23 23 0	1 25 13	3 23 29	5 25 43	7 23 59	9 26 13	11 28 26	13 26 43	15 28 56	17 27 13
	14	19 30 23	21 32 36	23 26 56	1 29 9	3 27 26	5 29 39	7 27 56	9 30 9	11 32 22	13 30 39	15 32 52	17 31 9
	15	19 34 19	21 36 33	23 30 53	1 33 6	3 31 23	5 33 36	7 31 53	9 34 6	11 36 19	13 34 36	15 36 49	17 35 6
	16	19 38 16	21 40 29	23 34 49	1 37 2	3 35 19	5 37 32	7 35 49	9 38 2	11 40 16	13 38 32	15 40 45	17 39 2
	17	19 42 12	21 44 26	23 38 46	1 40 59	3 39 16	5 41 29	7 39 46	9 41 59	11 44 12	13 42 29	15 44 42	17 42 59
	18	19 46 9	21 48 22	23 42 42	1 44 56	3 43 12	5 45 26	7 43 42	9 45 56	11 48 9	13 46 25	15 48 39	17 46 55
	19	19 50 6	21 52 19	23 46 39	1 48 52	3 47 9	5 49 22	7 47 39	9 49 52	11 52 5	13 50 22	15 52 35	17 50 52
	20	19 54 2	21 56 15	23 50 35	1 52 49	3 51 5	5 53 19	7 51 35	9 53 49	11 56 2	13 54 18	15 56 32	17 54 48
	21	19 57 59	22 0 12	23 54 32	1 56 45	3 55 2	5 57 15	7 55 32	9 57 45	11 59 58	13 58 15	16 0 28	17 58 45
	22	20 1 55	22 4 9	23 58 29	2 0 42	3 58 58	6 1 12	7 59 29	10 1 42	12 3 55	14 2 12	16 4 25	18 2 42
	23	20 5 52	22 8 5	0 2 25	2 4 38	4 2 55	6 5 8	8 3 25	10 5 38	12 7 51	14 6 8	16 8 21	18 6 38
	24	20 9 48	22 12 2	0 6 22	2 8 35	4 6 52	6 9 5	8 7 22	10 9 35	12 11 48	14 10 5	16 12 18	18 10 35
	25	20 13 45	22 15 58	0 10 18	2 12 31	4 10 48	6 13 1	8 11 18	10 13 31	12 15 45	14 14 1	16 16 14	18 14 31
	26	20 17 41	22 19 55	0 14 15	2 16 28	4 14 45	6 16 58	8 15 15	10 17 28	12 19 41	14 17 58	16 20 11	18 18 28
	27	20 21 38	22 23 51	0 18 11	2 20 25	4 18 41	6 20 55	8 19 11	10 21 25	12 23 38	14 21 54	16 24 8	18 22 24
	28	20 25 35	22 27 48	0 22 8	2 24 21	4 22 38	6 24 51	8 23 8	10 25 21	12 27 34	14 25 51	16 28 4	18 26 21
	29	20 29 31	22 31 44	0 26 4	2 28 18	4 26 34	6 28 48	8 27 4	10 29 18	12 31 31	14 29 47	16 32 1	18 30 17
	30	20 33 28		0 30 1	2 32 14	4 30 31	6 32 44	8 31 1	10 33 14	12 35 27	14 33 44	16 35 57	18 34 14
	31	20 37 24		0 33 58		4 34 27		8 34 58	10 37 11		14 37 41		18 38 11
1913	1	18 42 7	20 44 20	22 34 44	0 36 57	2 35 14	4 37 27	6 35 44	8 37 57	10 40 10	12 38 27	14 40 40	16 38 57
	2	18 46 4	20 48 17	22 38 41	0 40 54	2 39 10	4 41 24	6 39 40	8 41 54	10 44 7	12 42 24	14 44 37	16 42 53
	3	18 50 0	20 52 14	22 42 37	0 44 50	2 43 7	4 45 20	6 43 37	8 45 50	10 48 3	12 46 20	14 48 33	16 46 50
	4	18 53 57	20 56 10	22 46 34	0 48 47	2 47 3	4 49 17	6 47 34	8 49 47	10 52 0	12 50 17	14 52 30	16 50 47
	5	18 57 53	21 0 7	22 50 30	0 52 43	2 51 0	4 53 13	6 51 30	8 53 43	10 55 57	12 54 13	14 56 26	16 54 43
	6	19 1 50	21 4 3	22 54 27	0 56 40	2 54 57	4 57 10	6 55 27	8 57 40	10 59 53	12 58 10	15 0 23	16 58 40
	7	19 5 46	21 8 0	22 58 23	1 0 36	2 58 53	5 1 6	6 59 23	9 1 36	11 3 50	13 2 6	15 4 19	17 2 36
	8	19 9 43	21 11 56	23 2 20	1 4 33	3 2 50	5 5 3	7 3 20	9 5 33	11 7 46	13 6 3	15 8 16	17 6 33
	9	19 13 40	21 15 53	23 6 16	1 8 30	3 6 46	5 9 0	7 7 16	9 9 30	11 11 43	13 9 59	15 12 13	17 10 29
	10	19 17 36	21 19 49	23 10 13	1 12 26	3 10 43	5 12 56	7 11 13	9 13 26	11 15 39	13 13 56	15 16 9	17 14 26
	11	19 21 33	21 23 46	23 14 10	1 16 23	3 14 39	5 16 53	7 15 9	9 17 23	11 19 36	13 17 52	15 20 6	17 18 22
	12	19 25 29	21 27 43	23 18 6	1 20 19	3 18 36	5 20 49	7 19 6	9 21 19	11 23 32	13 21 49	15 24 2	17 22 19
	13	19 29 26	21 31 39	23 22 3	1 24 16	3 22 32	5 24 46	7 23 3	9 25 16	11 27 29	13 25 46	15 27 59	17 26 16
	14	19 33 22	21 35 36	23 25 59	1 28 12	3 26 29	5 28 45	7 26 59	9 29 12	11 31 26	13 29 42	15 31 55	17 30 12
	15	19 37 19	21 39 32	23 29 56	1 32 9	3 30 26	5 32 39	7 30 56	9 33 9	11 35 22	13 33 39	15 35 52	17 34 9
	16	19 41 16	21 43 29	23 33 52	1 36 5	3 34 22	5 36 35	7 34 52	9 37 5	11 39 19	13 37 35	15 39 48	17 38 5
	17	19 45 12	21 47 25	23 37 49	1 40 2	3 38 19	5 40 32	7 38 49	9 41 2	11 43 15	13 41 32	15 43 45	17 42 2
	18	19 49 9	21 51 22	23 41 45	1 43 59	3 42 15	5 44 29	7 42 45	9 44 59	11 47 12	13 45 28	15 47 42	17 45 58
	19	19 53 5	21 55 18	23 45 42	1 47 55	3 46 12	5 48 25	7 46 42	9 48 55	11 51 8	13 49 25	15 51 38	17 49 55
	20	19 57 2	21 59 15	23 49 39	1 51 52	3 50 8	5 52 22	7 50 38	9 52 52	11 55 5	13 53 21	15 55 35	17 53 51
	21	20 0 58	22 3 12	23 53 35	1 55 48	3 54 5	5 56 18	7 54 35	9 56 48	11 59 1	13 57 18	15 59 31	17 57 48
	22	20 4 55	22 7 8	23 57 32	1 59 45	3 58 1	6 0 15	7 58 32	10 0 45	12 2 58	14 1 15	16 3 28	18 1 45
	23	20 8 51	22 11 5	0 1 28	2 3 41	4 1 58	6 4 11	8 2 28	10 4 41	12 6 55	14 5 11	16 7 24	18 5 41
	24	20 12 48	22 15 1	0 5 25	2 7 38	4 5 55	6 8 8	8 6 25	10 8 38	12 10 51	14 9 8	16 11 21	18 9 38
	25	20 16 45	22 18 58	0 9 21	2 11 34	4 9 51	6 12 4	8 10 21	10 12 34	12 14 48	14 13 4	16 15 18	18 13 34
	26	20 20 41	22 22 54	0 13 18	2 15 31	4 13 48	6 16 1	8 14 18	10 16 31	12 18 44	14 17 1	16 19 14	18 17 31
	27	20 24 38	22 26 51	0 17 14	2 19 28	4 17 44	6 19 58	8 18 14	10 20 28	12 22 41	14 20 57	16 23 11	18 21 27
	28	20 28 34	22 30 47	0 21 11	2 23 24	4 21 41	6 23 54	8 22 11	10 24 24	12 26 37	14 24 54	16 27 7	18 25 24
	29	20 32 31		0 25 7	2 27 21	4 25 37	6 27 51	8 26 7	10 28 21	12 30 34	14 28 50	16 31 4	18 29 21
	30	20 36 27		0 29 4	2 31 17	4 29 34	6 31 47	8 30 4	10 32 17	12 34 30	14 32 47	16 35 0	18 33 17
	31	20 40 24		0 33 1		4 33 31		8 34 1	10 36 14		14 36 44		18 37 14
1914	1	18 41 10	20 43 23	22 33 47	0 36 0	2 34 17	4 36 30	6 34 47	8 37 0	10 39 13	12 37 30	14 39 43	16 38 0
	2	18 45 7	20 47 20	22 37 44	0 39 57	2 38 13	4 40 27	6 38 43	8 40 57	10 43 10	12 41 27	14 43 40	16 41 56
	3	18 49 3	20 51 17	22 41 40	0 43 53	2 42 10	4 44 23	6 42 40	8 44 53	10 47 6	12 45 23	14 47 36	16 45 53
	4	18 53 0	20 55 13	22 45 37	0 47 50	2 46 7	4 48 20	6 46 37	8 48 50	10 51 3	12 49 20	14 51 33	16 49 50
	5	18 56 56	20 59 10	22 49 33	0 51 46	2 50 3	4 52 16	6 50 33	8 52 46	10 55 0	12 53 16	14 55 29	16 53 46
	6	19 0 53	21 3 6	22 53 30	0 55 43	2 54 0	4 56 13	6 54 30	8 56 43	10 58 56	12 57 13	14 59 26	16 57 43
	7	19 4 50	21 7 3	22 57 26	0 59 40	2 57 56	5 0 9	6 58 26	9 0 39	11 2 53	13 1 9	15 3 23	17 1 39
	8	19 8 46	21 10 59	23 1 23	1 3 36	3 1 53	5 4 6	7 2 23	9 4 36	11 6 49	13 5 6	15 7 19	17 5 36
	9	19 12 43	21 14 56	23 5 19	1 7 33	3 5 49	5 8 3	7 6 19	9 8 33	11 10 46	13 9 2	15 11 16	17 9 32
	10	19 16 39	21 18 52	23 9 16	1 11 29	3 9 46	5 11 59	7 10 16	9 12 29	11 14 42	13 12 59	15 15 12	17 13 29
	11	19 20 36	21 22 49	23 13 13	1 15 26	3 13 42	5 15 56	7 14 12	9 16 26	11 18 39	13 16 56	15 19 9	17 17 25
	12	19 24 32	21 26 46	23 17 9	1 19 22	3 17 39	5 19 52	7 18 9	9 20 22	11 22 35	13 20 52	15 23 5	17 21 22
	13	19 28 29	21 30 42	23 21 6	1 23 19	3 21 36	5 23 49	7 22 6	9 24 19	11 26 32	13 24 49	15 27 2	17 25 19
	14	19 32 25	21 34 39	23 25 2	1 27 15	3 25 32	5 27 45	7 26 2	9 28 15	11 30 29	13 28 45	15 30 58	17 29 15
	15	19 36 22	21 38 35	23 28 59	1 31 12	3 29 29	5 31 42	7 29 59	9 32 12	11 34 25	13 32 42	15 34 55	17 33 12
	16	19 40 19	21 42 32	23 32 55	1 35 9	3 33 25	5 35 38	7 33 55	9 36 9	11 38 22	13 36 38	15 38 52	17 37 8
	17	19 44 15	21 46 28	23 36 52	1 39 5	3 37 22	5 39 35	7 37 52	9 40 5	11 42 18	13 40 35	15 42 48	17 41 5
	18	19 48 12	21 50 25	23 40 48	1 43 2	3 41 18	5 43 32	7 41 48	9 44 2	11 46 15	13 44 31	15 46 45	17 45 1
	19	19 52 8	21 54 21	23 44 45	1 46 58	3 45 15	5 47 28	7 45 45	9 47 58	11 50 11	13 48 28	15 50 41	17 48 58
	20	19 56 5	21 58 18	23 48 42	1 50 55	3 49 11	5 51 25	7 49 41	9 51 55	11 54 8	13 52 25	15 54 38	17 52 55
	21	20 0 1	22 2 15	23 52 38	1 54 51	3 53 8	5 55 21	7 53 38	9 55 51	11 58 4	13 56 21	15 58 34	17 56 51
	22	20 3 58	22 6 11	23 56 35	1 58 48	3 57 5	5 59 18	7 57 35	9 59 48	12 2 1	14 0 18	16 2 31	18 0 48
	23	20 7 54	22 10 8	0 0 31	2 2 44	4 1 1	6 3 14	8 1 31	10 3 44	12 5 58	14 4 14	16 6 27	18 4 44
	24	20 11 51	22 14 4	0 4 28	2 6 41	4 4 58	6 7 11	8 5 28	10 7 41	12 9 54	14 8 11	16 10 24	18 8 41
	25	20 15 48	22 18 1	0 8 24	2 10 38	4 8 54	6 11 8	8 9 24	10 11 37	12 13 51	14 12 7	16 14 21	18 12 37
	26	20 19 44	22 21 57	0 12 21	2 14 34	4 12 51	6 15 4	8 13 21	10 15 34	12 17 47	14 16 4	16 18 17	18 16 34
	27	20 23 41	22 25 54	0 16 17	2 18 31	4 16 47	6 19 1	8 17 17	10 19 31	12 21 44	14 20 0	16 22 14	18 20 30
	28	20 27 37	22 29 50	0 20 14	2 22 27	4 20 44	6 22 57	8 21 14	10 23 27	12 25 40	14 23 57	16 26 10	18 24 27
	29	20 31 34		0 24 11	2 26 24	4 24 40	6 26 54	8 25 10	10 27 24	12 29 37	14 27 54	16 30 7	18 28 24
	30	20 35 30		0 28 7	2 30 20	4 28 37	6 30 50	8 29 7	10 31 20	12 33 33	14 31 50	16 34 3	18 32 20
	31	20 39 27		0 32 4		4 32 34		8 33 4	10 35 17		14 35 47		18 36 17
1915	1	18 40 13	20 42 27	22 32 50	0 35 3	2 33 20	4 35 33	6 33 50	8 36 3	10 38 16	12 36 33	14 38 46	16 37 3
	2	18 44 10	20 46 23	22 36 47	0 39 0	2 37 16	4 39 30	6 37 46	8 40 0	10 42 13	12 40 30	14 42 43	16 40 59
	3	18 48 6	20 50 20	22 40 43	0 42 56	2 41 13	4 43 26	6 41 43	8 43 56	10 46 9	12 44 26	14 46 39	16 44 56
	4	18 52 3	20 54 16	22 44 40	0 46 53	2 45 10	4 47 23	6 45 40	8 47 53	10 50 6	12 48 23	14 50 36	16 48 53
	5	18 55 59	20 58 13	22 48 36	0 50 49	2 49 6	4 51 19	6 49 36	8 51 49	10 54 3	12 52 19	14 54 32	16 52 49
	6	18 59 56	21 2 9	22 52 33	0 54 46	2 53 2	4 55 16	6 53 33	8 55 46	10 57 59	12 56 16	14 58 29	16 56 46
	7	19 3 53	21 6 6	22 56 29	0 58 43	2 56 59	4 59 12	6 57 29	8 59 42	11 1 56	13 0 12	15 2 26	17 0 42
	8	19 7 49	21 10 2	23 0 26	1 2 39	3 0 56	5 3 9	7 1 26	9 3 39	11 5 52	13 4 9	15 6 22	17 4 39
	9	19 11 46	21 13 59	23 4 22	1 6 36	3 4 52	5 7 6	7 5 22	9 7 36	11 9 49	13 8 5	15 10 19	17 8 35
	10	19 15 42	21 17 56	23 8 19	1 10 32	3 8 49	5 11 2	7 9 19	9 11 32	11 13 45	13 12 2	15 14 15	17 12 32
	11	19 19 39	21 21 52	23 12 16	1 14 29	3 12 45	5 14 59	7 13 15	9 15 29	11 17 42	13 15 59	15 18 12	17 16 28
	12	19 23 35	21 25 49	23 16 12	1 18 25	3 16 42	5 18 55	7 17 12	9 19 25	11 21 38	13 19 55	15 22 8	17 20 25
	13	19 27 32	21 29 45	23 20 9	1 22 22	3 20 39	5 22 52	7 21 9	9 23 22	11 25 35	13 23 52	15 26 5	17 24 22
	14	19 31 28	21 33 42	23 24 5	1 26 18	3 24 35	5 26 48	7 25 5	9 27 18	11 29 32	13 27 48	15 30 1	17 28 18
	15	19 35 25	21 37 38	23 28 2	1 30 15	3 28 32	5 30 45	7 29 2	9 31 15	11 33 28	13 31 45	15 33 58	17 32 15
	16	19 39 22	21 41 35	23 31 58	1 34 12	3 32 28	5 34 42	7 32 58	9 35 12	11 37 25	13 35 41	15 37 55	17 36 11
	17	19 43 18	21 45 31	23 35 55	1 38 8	3 36 25	5 38 38	7 36 55	9 39 8	11 41 21	13 39 38	15 41 51	17 40 8
	18	19 47 15	21 49 28	23 39 51	1 42 5	3 40 21	5 42 35	7 40 51	9 43 5	11 45 18	13 43 34	15 45 48	17 44 4
	19	19 51 11	21 53 25	23 43 48	1 46 1	3 44 18	5 46 31	7 44 48	9 47 1	11 49 14	13 47 31	15 49 44	17 48 1
	20	19 55 8	21 57 21	23 47 45	1 49 58	3 48 14	5 50 28	7 48 44	9 50 58	11 53 11	13 51 28	15 53 41	17 51 57
	21	19 59 4	22 1 18	23 51 41	1 53 54	3 52 11	5 54 24	7 52 41	9 54 54	11 57 7	13 55 24	15 57 37	17 55 54
	22	20 3 1	22 5 14	23 55 38	1 57 51	3 56 8	5 58 21	7 56 38	9 58 51	12 1 4	13 59 21	16 1 34	17 59 51
	23	20 6 58	22 9 11	23 59 34	2 1 47	4 0 4	6 2 17	8 0 34	10 2 47	12 5 1	14 3 17	16 5 30	18 3 47
	24	20 10 54	22 13 7	0 3 31	2 5 44	4 4 1	6 6 14	8 4 31	10 6 44	12 8 57	14 7 14	16 9 27	18 7 44
	25	20 14 51	22 17 4	0 7 27	2 9 41	4 7 57	6 10 11	8 8 27	10 10 40	12 12 54	14 11 10	16 13 24	18 11 40
	26	20 18 47	22 21 0	0 11 24	2 13 37	4 11 54	6 14 7	8 12 24	10 14 37	12 16 50	14 15 7	16 17 20	18 15 37
	27	20 22 44	22 24 57	0 15 21	2 17 34	4 15 50	6 18 4	8 16 20	10 18 34	12 20 47	14 19 3	16 21 17	18 19 33
	28	20 26 40	22 28 54	0 19 17	2 21 30	4 19 47	6 22 0	8 20 17	10 22 30	12 24 43	14 23 0	16 25 13	18 23 30
	29	20 30 37		0 23 14	2 25 27	4 23 43	6 25 57	8 24 13	10 26 27	12 28 40	14 26 57	16 29 10	18 27 27
	30	20 34 33		0 27 10	2 29 23	4 27 40	6 29 53	8 28 10	10 30 23	12 32 36	14 30 53	16 33 6	18 31 23
	31	20 38 30		0 31 7		4 31 37		8 32 7	10 34 20		14 34 50		18 35 20
1916	1	18 39 16	20 41 29	22 35 50	0 38 3	2 36 19	4 38 33	6 36 49	8 39 3	10 41 16	12 39 32	14 41 46	16 40 2
	2	18 43 13	20 45 26	22 39 46	0 41 59	2 40 16	4 42 29	6 40 46	8 42 59	10 45 12	12 43 29	14 45 42	16 43 59
	3	18 47 9	20 49 23	22 43 43	0 45 56	2 44 12	4 46 26	6 44 42	8 46 56	10 49 9	12 47 26	14 49 39	16 47 55
	4	18 51 6	20 53 19	22 47 39	0 49 52	2 48 9	4 50 22	6 48 39	8 50 52	10 53 6	12 51 22	14 53 35	16 51 52
	5	18 55 2	20 57 16	22 51 36	0 53 49	2 52 6	4 54 19	6 52 36	8 54 49	10 57 2	12 55 19	14 57 32	16 55 49
	6	18 58 59	21 1 12	22 55 32	0 57 46	2 56 2	4 58 15	6 56 32	8 58 45	11 0 59	12 59 15	15 1 28	16 59 45
	7	19 2 56	21 5 9	22 59 29	1 1 42	2 59 59	5 2 12	7 0 29	9 2 42	11 4 55	13 3 12	15 5 25	17 3 42
	8	19 6 52	21 9 5	23 3 25	1 5 39	3 3 55	5 6 9	7 4 25	9 6 39	11 8 52	13 7 8	15 9 22	17 7 38
	9	19 10 49	21 13 2	23 7 22	1 9 35	3 7 52	5 10 5	7 8 22	9 10 35	11 12 48	13 11 5	15 13 18	17 11 35
	10	19 14 45	21 16 58	23 11 19	1 13 32	3 11 48	5 14 2	7 12 18	9 14 32	11 16 45	13 15 1	15 17 15	17 15 31
	11	19 18 42	21 20 55	23 15 15	1 17 28	3 15 45	5 17 58	7 16 15	9 18 28	11 20 41	13 18 58	15 21 11	17 19 28
	12	19 22 38	21 24 52	23 19 12	1 21 25	3 19 41	5 21 55	7 20 12	9 22 25	11 24 38	13 22 55	15 25 8	17 23 24
	13	19 26 35	21 28 48	23 23 8	1 25 21	3 23 38	5 25 51	7 24 8	9 26 21	11 28 34	13 26 51	15 29 4	17 27 21
	14	19 30 31	21 32 45	23 27 5	1 29 18	3 27 35	5 29 48	7 28 5	9 30 18	11 32 31	13 30 48	15 33 1	17 31 18
	15	19 34 28	21 36 41	23 31 1	1 33 14	3 31 31	5 33 44	7 32 1	9 34 14	11 36 28	13 34 44	15 36 57	17 35 14
	16	19 38 25	21 40 38	23 34 58	1 37 11	3 35 28	5 37 41	7 35 58	9 38 11	11 40 23	13 38 41	15 40 54	17 39 11
	17	19 42 21	21 44 34	23 38 54	1 41 8	3 39 24	5 41 38	7 39 54	9 42 8	11 44 21	13 42 37	15 44 51	17 43 7
	18	19 46 18	21 48 31	23 42 51	1 45 4	3 43 21	5 45 34	7 43 51	9 46 4	11 48 17	13 46 34	15 48 47	17 47 4
	19	19 50 14	21 52 27	23 46 48	1 49 1	3 47 17	5 49 31	7 47 47	9 50 1	11 52 14	13 50 30	15 52 44	17 51 0
	20	19 54 11	21 56 24	23 50 44	1 52 57	3 51 14	5 53 27	7 51 44	9 53 57	11 56 10	13 54 27	15 56 40	17 54 57
	21	19 58 7	22 0 21	23 54 41	1 56 54	3 55 10	5 57 24	7 55 41	9 57 54	12 0 7	13 58 24	16 0 37	17 58 53
	22	20 2 4	22 4 17	23 58 37	2 0 50	3 59 7	6 1 20	7 59 37	10 1 50	12 4 3	14 2 20	16 4 33	18 2 50
	23	20 6 0	22 8 14	0 2 34	2 4 47	4 3 4	6 5 17	8 3 34	10 5 47	12 8 0	14 6 17	16 8 30	18 6 47
	24	20 9 57	22 12 10	0 6 30	2 8 43	4 7 0	6 9 13	8 7 30	10 9 43	12 11 57	14 10 13	16 12 26	18 10 43
	25	20 13 54	22 16 7	0 10 27	2 12 40	4 10 57	6 13 10	8 11 27	10 13 40	12 15 53	14 14 10	16 16 23	18 14 40
	26	20 17 50	22 20 3	0 14 23	2 16 37	4 14 53	6 17 7	8 15 23	10 17 37	12 19 50	14 18 6	16 20 20	18 18 36
	27	20 21 47	22 24 0	0 18 20	2 20 33	4 18 50	6 21 3	8 19 20	10 21 33	12 23 46	14 22 3	16 24 16	18 22 33
	28	20 25 43	22 27 56	0 22 17	2 24 30	4 22 46	6 25 0	8 23 16	10 25 30	12 27 43	14 25 59	16 28 13	18 26 29
	29	20 29 40	22 31 53	0 26 13	2 28 26	4 26 43	6 28 56	8 27 13	10 29 26	12 31 39	14 29 56	16 32 9	18 30 26
	30	20 33 36		0 30 10	2 32 23	4 30 40	6 32 53	8 31 10	10 33 23	12 35 36	14 33 53	16 36 6	18 34 23
	31	20 37 33		0 34 6		4 34 36		8 35 6	10 37 19		14 37 49		18 38 19
1917	1	18 42 16	20 44 29	22 34 52	0 37 6	2 35 22	4 37 35	6 35 52	8 38 5	10 40 19	12 38 35	14 40 48	16 39 5
	2	18 46 12	20 48 25	22 38 49	0 41 2	2 39 19	4 41 32	6 39 49	8 42 2	10 44 15	12 42 32	14 44 45	16 43 2
	3	18 50 9	20 52 22	22 42 46	0 44 59	2 43 15	4 45 29	6 43 45	8 45 59	10 48 12	12 46 28	14 48 42	16 46 58
	4	18 54 5	20 56 19	22 46 42	0 48 55	2 47 12	4 49 25	6 47 42	8 49 55	10 52 8	12 50 25	14 52 38	16 50 55
	5	18 58 2	21 0 15	22 50 39	0 52 52	2 51 8	4 53 22	6 51 38	8 53 52	10 56 5	12 54 21	14 56 35	16 54 51
	6	19 1 58	21 4 12	22 54 35	0 56 48	2 55 5	4 57 18	6 55 35	8 57 48	11 0 1	12 58 18	15 0 31	16 58 48
	7	19 5 55	21 8 8	22 58 32	1 0 45	2 59 2	5 1 15	6 59 32	9 1 45	11 3 58	13 2 15	15 4 28	17 2 44
	8	19 9 52	21 12 5	23 2 28	1 4 41	3 2 58	5 5 11	7 3 28	9 5 41	11 7 55	13 6 11	15 8 24	17 6 41
	9	19 13 48	21 16 1	23 6 25	1 8 38	3 6 55	5 9 8	7 7 25	9 9 38	11 11 51	13 10 8	15 12 21	17 10 38
	10	19 17 45	21 19 58	23 10 21	1 12 35	3 10 51	5 13 4	7 11 21	9 13 34	11 15 48	13 14 4	15 16 17	17 14 34
	11	19 21 41	21 23 54	23 14 18	1 16 31	3 14 48	5 17 1	7 15 18	9 17 31	11 19 44	13 18 1	15 20 14	17 18 31
	12	19 25 38	21 27 51	23 18 15	1 20 28	3 18 44	5 20 58	7 19 14	9 21 28	11 23 41	13 21 57	15 24 11	17 22 27
	13	19 29 34	21 31 48	23 22 11	1 24 24	3 22 41	5 24 54	7 23 11	9 25 24	11 27 37	13 25 54	15 28 7	17 26 24
	14	19 33 31	21 35 44	23 26 8	1 28 21	3 26 37	5 28 51	7 27 7	9 29 21	11 31 34	13 29 50	15 32 4	17 30 20
	15	19 37 27	21 39 41	23 30 4	1 32 17	3 30 34	5 32 47	7 31 4	9 33 17	11 35 30	13 33 47	15 36 0	17 34 17
	16	19 41 24	21 43 37	23 34 1	1 36 14	3 34 31	5 36 44	7 35 1	9 37 14	11 39 27	13 37 44	15 39 57	17 38 13
	17	19 45 21	21 47 34	23 37 57	1 40 10	3 38 27	5 40 40	7 38 57	9 41 10	11 43 24	13 41 40	15 43 53	17 42 10
	18	19 49 17	21 51 30	23 41 54	1 44 7	3 42 24	7 42 54	5 44 37	9 45 7	11 47 20	13 45 37	15 47 50	17 46 7
	19	19 53 14	21 55 27	23 45 50	1 48 4	3 46 20	5 48 34	7 46 50	9 49 3	11 51 17	13 49 33	15 51 46	17 50 3
	20	19 57 10	21 59 23	23 49 47	1 52 0	3 50 17	5 52 30	7 50 47	9 53 0	11 55 13	13 53 30	15 55 43	17 54 0
	21	20 1 7	22 3 20	23 53 44	1 55 57	3 54 13	5 56 27	7 54 43	9 56 57	11 59 10	13 57 26	15 59 40	17 57 56
	22	20 5 3	22 7 17	23 57 40	1 59 53	3 58 10	6 0 23	7 58 40	10 0 53	12 3 6	14 1 23	16 3 36	18 1 53
	23	20 9 0	22 11 13	0 1 37	2 3 50	4 2 6	6 4 20	8 2 36	10 4 50	12 7 3	14 5 19	16 7 33	18 5 49
	24	20 12 56	22 15 10	0 5 33	2 7 46	4 6 3	6 8 16	8 6 33	10 8 46	12 10 59	14 9 16	16 11 29	18 9 46
	25	20 16 53	22 19 6	0 9 30	2 11 43	4 10 0	6 12 13	8 10 30	10 12 43	12 14 56	14 13 13	16 15 26	18 13 43
	26	20 20 50	22 23 3	0 13 26	2 15 39	4 13 56	6 16 9	8 14 26	10 16 39	12 18 53	14 17 9	16 19 22	18 17 39
	27	20 24 46	22 26 59	0 17 23	2 19 36	4 17 53	6 20 6	8 18 23	10 20 36	12 22 49	14 21 6	16 23 19	18 21 36
	28	20 28 43	22 30 56	0 21 19	2 23 33	4 21 49	6 24 3	8 22 19	10 24 32	12 26 46	14 25 2	16 27 15	18 25 32
	29	20 32 39		0 25 16	2 27 29	4 25 46	6 27 59	8 26 16	10 28 29	12 30 42	14 28 59	16 31 12	18 29 29
	30	20 36 36		0 29 12	2 31 26	4 29 42	6 31 56	8 30 12	10 32 26	12 34 39	14 32 55	16 35 9	18 33 25
	31	20 40 32		0 33 9		4 33 39		8 34 9	10 36 22		14 36 52		18 37 22

1	2	3	4	5	6	7	8	9	10	11	12
18 41 18	20 43 32	22 33 55	0 36 8	2 34 25	4 36 38	6 34 55	8 37 8	10 39 21	12 37 38	14 39 51	16 38 8
18 45 15	20 47 28	22 37 52	0 40 5	2 38 22	4 40 35	6 38 51	8 41 5	10 43 18	12 41 35	14 43 48	16 42 4
18 49 12	20 51 25	22 41 48	0 44 1	2 42 18	4 44 31	6 42 48	8 45 1	10 47 14	12 45 31	14 47 44	16 46 1
18 53 8	20 55 21	22 45 45	0 47 58	2 46 15	4 48 28	6 46 45	8 48 58	10 51 11	12 49 28	14 51 41	16 49 57
18 57 5	20 59 18	22 49 41	0 51 55	2 50 11	4 52 24	6 50 41	8 52 54	10 55 8	12 53 24	14 55 37	16 53 54
19 1 1	21 3 15	22 53 38	0 55 51	2 54 8	4 56 21	6 54 38	8 56 51	10 59 4	12 57 21	14 59 34	16 57 51
19 4 58	21 7 11	22 57 35	0 59 48	2 58 4	5 0 18	6 58 34	9 0 48	11 3 1	13 1 17	15 3 30	17 1 47
19 8 54	21 11 8	23 1 31	1 3 44	3 2 1	5 4 14	7 2 31	9 4 44	11 6 57	13 5 14	15 7 27	17 5 44
19 12 51	21 15 4	23 5 28	1 7 41	3 5 57	5 8 11	7 6 27	9 8 41	11 10 54	13 9 10	15 11 24	17 9 40
19 16 47	21 19 1	23 9 24	1 11 37	3 9 54	5 12 7	7 10 24	9 12 37	11 14 50	13 13 7	15 15 20	17 13 37
19 20 44	21 22 57	23 13 21	1 15 34	3 13 51	5 16 4	7 14 20	9 16 34	11 18 47	13 17 3	15 19 17	17 17 33
19 24 41	21 26 54	23 17 17	1 19 30	3 17 47	5 20 0	7 18 17	9 20 30	11 22 43	13 21 0	15 23 13	17 21 30
19 28 37	21 30 50	23 21 14	1 23 27	3 21 44	5 23 57	7 22 14	9 24 27	11 26 40	13 24 57	15 27 10	17 25 26
19 32 34	21 34 47	23 25 10	1 27 24	3 25 40	5 27 53	7 26 10	9 28 23	11 30 37	13 28 53	15 31 6	17 29 23
19 36 30	21 38 43	23 29 7	1 31 20	3 29 37	5 31 50	7 30 7	9 32 20	11 34 33	13 32 50	15 35 3	17 33 20
19 40 27	21 42 40	23 33 4	1 35 17	3 33 33	5 35 47	7 34 3	9 36 17	11 38 30	13 36 46	15 38 59	17 37 16
19 44 23	21 46 37	23 37 0	1 39 13	3 37 30	5 39 43	7 38 0	9 40 13	11 42 26	13 40 43	15 42 56	17 41 13
19 48 20	21 50 33	23 40 57	1 43 10	3 41 26	5 43 40	7 41 56	9 44 10	11 46 23	13 44 39	15 46 53	17 45 9
19 52 16	21 54 30	23 44 53	1 47 6	3 45 23	5 47 36	7 45 53	9 48 6	11 50 19	13 48 36	15 50 49	17 49 6
19 56 13	21 58 26	23 48 50	1 51 3	3 49 20	5 51 33	7 49 50	9 52 3	11 54 16	13 52 32	15 54 46	17 53 2
20 0 10	22 2 23	23 52 46	1 54 59	3 53 16	5 55 29	7 53 46	9 55 59	11 58 12	13 56 29	15 58 42	17 56 59
20 4 6	22 6 19	23 56 43	1 58 56	3 57 13	5 59 26	7 57 43	9 59 56	12 2 9	14 0 26	16 2 39	18 0 56
20 8 3	22 10 16	0 0 39	2 2 53	4 1 9	6 3 22	8 1 39	10 3 52	12 6 6	14 4 22	16 6 35	18 4 52
20 11 59	22 14 12	0 4 36	2 6 49	4 5 6	6 7 19	8 5 36	10 7 49	12 10 2	14 8 19	16 10 32	18 8 49
20 15 56	22 18 9	0 8 32	2 10 46	4 9 2	6 11 16	8 9 32	10 11 45	12 13 59	14 12 15	16 14 28	18 12 45
20 19 52	22 22 6	0 12 29	2 14 42	4 12 59	6 15 12	8 13 29	10 15 42	12 17 55	14 16 12	16 18 25	18 16 42
20 23 49	22 26 2	0 16 26	2 18 39	4 16 55	6 19 9	8 17 25	10 19 39	12 21 52	14 20 8	16 22 22	18 20 38
20 27 45	22 29 59	0 20 22	2 22 35	4 20 52	6 23 5	8 21 22	10 23 35	12 25 48	14 25 4	16 26 18	18 24 35
20 31 42		0 24 19	2 26 32	4 24 49	6 27 2	8 25 19	10 27 32	12 29 45	14 28 1	16 30 15	18 28 31
20 35 39		0 28 15	2 30 28	4 28 45	6 30 58	8 29 15	10 31 28	12 33 41	14 31 58	16 34 11	18 32 28
20 39 35		0 32 12		4 32 42		8 33 12	10 35 25		14 35 55		18 36 25

1	2	3	4	5	6	7	8	9	10	11	12
18 40 21	20 42 34	22 32 58	0 35 11	2 33 28	4 35 41	6 33 58	8 36 11	10 38 24	12 36 41	14 38 54	16 37 10
18 44 18	20 46 31	22 36 54	0 39 8	2 37 24	4 39 37	6 37 54	8 40 7	10 42 21	12 40 37	14 42 50	16 41 7
18 48 14	20 50 27	22 40 51	0 43 4	2 41 21	4 43 34	6 41 51	8 44 4	10 46 17	12 44 34	14 46 47	16 45 3
18 52 11	20 54 24	22 44 48	0 47 1	2 45 17	4 47 30	6 45 47	8 48 0	10 50 14	12 48 30	14 50 43	16 49 0
18 56 7	20 58 21	22 48 44	0 50 57	2 49 14	4 51 27	6 49 44	8 51 57	10 54 10	12 52 27	14 54 40	16 52 57
19 0 4	21 2 17	22 52 41	0 54 54	2 53 10	4 55 24	6 53 40	8 55 54	10 58 7	12 56 23	14 58 36	16 56 53
19 4 0	21 6 14	22 56 37	0 58 50	2 57 7	4 59 20	6 57 37	8 59 50	11 2 3	13 0 20	15 2 33	17 0 50
19 7 57	21 10 10	23 0 34	1 2 47	3 1 3	5 3 17	7 1 33	9 3 47	11 6 0	13 4 16	15 6 30	17 4 46
19 11 54	21 14 7	23 4 30	1 6 43	3 5 0	5 7 13	7 5 30	9 7 43	11 9 56	13 8 13	15 10 26	17 8 43
19 15 50	21 18 3	23 8 27	1 10 40	3 8 57	5 11 10	7 9 27	9 11 40	11 13 53	13 12 10	15 14 23	17 12 39
19 19 47	21 22 0	23 12 23	1 14 37	3 12 53	5 15 6	7 13 23	9 15 36	11 17 49	13 16 6	15 18 19	17 16 36
19 23 43	21 25 56	23 16 20	1 18 33	3 16 50	5 19 3	7 17 20	9 19 33	11 21 46	13 20 3	15 22 16	17 20 32
19 27 40	21 29 53	23 20 16	1 22 30	3 20 46	5 22 59	7 21 16	9 23 29	11 25 43	13 23 59	15 26 12	17 24 29
19 31 36	21 33 50	23 24 13	1 26 26	3 24 43	5 26 56	7 25 13	9 27 26	11 29 39	13 27 56	15 30 9	17 28 26
19 35 33	21 37 46	23 28 10	1 30 23	3 28 39	5 30 53	7 29 9	9 31 23	11 33 36	13 31 52	15 34 5	17 32 22
19 39 29	21 41 43	23 32 6	1 34 19	3 32 36	5 34 49	7 33 6	9 35 19	11 37 32	13 35 49	15 38 2	17 36 19
19 43 26	21 45 39	23 36 3	1 38 16	3 36 32	5 38 46	7 37 2	9 39 16	11 41 29	13 39 45	15 41 59	17 40 15
19 47 23	21 49 36	23 39 59	1 42 12	3 40 29	5 42 42	7 40 59	9 43 12	11 45 25	13 43 42	15 45 55	17 44 12
19 51 19	21 53 32	23 43 56	1 46 9	3 44 26	5 46 39	7 44 56	9 47 9	11 49 22	13 47 38	15 49 52	17 48 8
19 55 16	21 57 29	23 47 52	1 50 5	3 48 22	5 50 35	7 48 52	9 51 5	11 53 18	13 51 35	15 53 48	17 52 5
19 59 12	22 1 25	23 51 49	1 54 2	3 52 19	5 54 32	7 52 49	9 55 2	11 57 15	13 55 32	15 57 45	17 56 1
20 3 9	22 5 22	23 55 45	1 57 59	3 56 15	5 58 29	7 56 45	9 58 58	12 1 12	13 59 28	16 1 41	17 59 58
20 7 5	22 9 19	23 59 42	2 1 55	4 0 12	6 2 25	8 0 42	10 2 55	12 5 8	14 3 25	16 5 38	18 3 55
20 11 2	22 13 15	0 3 39	2 5 52	4 4 8	6 6 22	8 4 38	10 6 52	12 9 5	14 7 21	16 9 34	18 7 51
20 14 58	22 17 12	0 7 35	2 9 48	4 8 5	6 10 18	8 8 35	10 10 48	12 13 1	14 11 18	16 13 31	18 11 48
20 18 55	22 21 8	0 11 32	2 13 45	4 12 1	6 14 15	8 12 31	10 14 45	12 16 58	14 15 14	16 17 28	18 15 44
20 22 52	22 25 5	0 15 28	2 17 41	4 15 58	6 18 11	8 16 28	10 18 41	12 20 54	14 19 11	16 21 24	18 19 41
20 26 48	22 29 1	0 19 25	2 21 38	4 19 55	6 22 8	8 20 25	10 22 38	12 24 51	14 23 7	16 25 21	18 23 37
20 30 45		0 23 21	2 25 34	4 23 51	6 26 4	8 24 21	10 26 34	12 28 47	14 27 4	16 29 17	18 27 34
20 34 41		0 27 18	2 29 31	4 27 48	6 30 1	8 28 18	10 30 31	12 32 44	14 31 1	16 33 14	18 31 31
20 38 38		0 31 14		4 31 44		8 32 14	10 34 27		14 34 57		18 35 27

1	2	3	4	5	6	7	8	9	10	11	12
18 39 24	20 41 37	22 35 57	0 38 10	2 36 27	4 38 40	6 36 57	8 39 10	10 41 23	12 39 40	14 41 53	16 40 9
18 43 20	20 45 33	22 39 53	0 42 7	2 40 23	4 42 36	6 40 53	8 43 6	10 45 20	12 43 36	14 45 49	16 44 6
18 47 17	20 49 30	22 43 50	0 46 3	2 44 20	4 46 33	6 44 50	8 47 3	10 49 16	12 47 33	14 49 46	16 48 2
18 51 13	20 53 27	22 47 47	0 50 0	2 48 16	4 50 30	6 48 46	8 50 59	10 53 13	12 51 29	14 53 42	16 51 59
18 55 10	20 57 23	22 51 43	0 53 56	2 52 13	4 54 26	6 52 43	8 54 56	10 57 9	12 55 26	14 57 39	16 55 56
18 59 6	21 1 20	22 55 40	0 57 53	2 56 9	4 58 23	6 56 39	8 58 53	11 1 6	12 59 22	15 1 35	16 59 52
19 3 3	21 5 16	22 59 36	1 1 49	3 0 6	5 2 19	7 0 36	9 2 49	11 5 2	13 3 19	15 5 32	17 3 49
19 7 0	21 9 13	23 3 33	1 5 46	3 4 3	5 6 16	7 4 32	9 6 46	11 8 59	13 7 15	15 9 29	17 7 45
19 10 56	21 13 9	23 7 29	1 9 42	3 7 59	5 10 12	7 8 29	9 10 42	11 12 56	13 11 12	15 13 25	17 11 42
19 14 53	21 17 6	23 11 26	1 13 39	3 11 56	5 14 9	7 12 26	9 14 39	11 16 52	13 15 9	15 17 22	17 15 38
19 18 49	21 21 2	23 15 22	1 17 36	3 15 52	5 18 5	7 16 22	9 18 35	11 20 49	13 19 5	15 21 18	17 19 35
19 22 46	21 24 59	23 19 19	1 21 32	3 19 49	5 22 2	7 20 19	9 22 32	11 24 45	13 23 2	15 25 15	17 23 31
19 26 42	21 28 56	23 23 16	1 25 29	3 23 45	5 25 59	7 24 15	9 26 28	11 28 42	13 26 58	15 29 11	17 27 28
19 30 39	21 32 52	23 27 12	1 29 25	3 27 42	5 29 55	7 28 12	9 30 25	11 32 38	13 30 55	15 33 8	17 31 25
19 34 35	21 36 49	23 31 9	1 33 22	3 31 38	5 33 52	7 32 8	9 34 22	11 36 35	13 34 51	15 37 4	17 35 21
19 38 32	21 40 45	23 35 5	1 37 18	3 35 35	5 37 48	7 36 5	9 38 18	11 40 31	13 38 48	15 41 1	17 39 18
19 42 29	21 44 42	23 39 2	1 41 15	3 39 32	5 41 45	7 40 1	9 42 15	11 44 28	13 42 44	15 44 58	17 43 14
19 46 25	21 48 38	23 42 58	1 45 11	3 43 28	5 45 41	7 43 58	9 46 11	11 48 24	13 46 41	15 48 54	17 47 11
19 50 22	21 52 35	23 46 55	1 49 8	3 47 25	5 49 38	7 47 55	9 50 8	11 52 21	13 50 37	15 52 51	17 51 7
19 54 18	21 56 31	23 50 51	1 53 5	3 51 21	5 53 34	7 51 51	9 54 4	11 56 17	13 54 34	15 56 47	17 55 4
19 58 15	22 0 28	23 54 48	1 57 1	3 55 18	5 57 31	7 55 48	9 58 1	12 0 14	13 58 31	16 0 44	17 59 0
20 2 11	22 4 25	23 58 45	2 0 58	3 59 14	6 1 28	7 59 44	10 1 57	12 4 11	14 2 27	16 4 40	18 2 57
20 6 8	22 8 21	0 2 41	2 4 54	4 3 11	6 5 24	8 3 41	10 5 54	12 8 7	14 6 24	16 8 37	18 6 54
20 10 4	22 12 18	0 6 38	2 8 51	4 7 7	6 9 21	8 7 37	10 9 51	12 12 4	14 10 20	16 12 33	18 10 50
20 14 1	22 16 14	0 10 34	2 12 47	4 11 4	6 13 17	8 11 34	10 13 47	12 16 0	14 14 17	16 16 30	18 14 47
20 17 58	22 20 11	0 14 31	2 16 44	4 15 1	6 17 14	8 15 30	10 17 44	12 19 57	14 18 13	16 20 27	18 18 43
20 21 54	22 24 7	0 18 27	2 20 40	4 18 57	6 21 10	8 19 27	10 21 40	12 23 53	14 22 10	16 24 23	18 22 40
20 25 51	22 28 4	0 22 24	2 24 37	4 22 54	6 25 7	8 23 24	10 25 37	12 27 50	14 26 6	16 28 20	18 26 36
20 29 47	22 32 0	0 26 20	2 28 34	4 26 50	6 29 3	8 27 20	10 29 33	12 31 46	14 30 3	16 32 16	18 30 33
20 33 44		0 30 17	2 32 30	4 30 47	6 33 0	8 31 17	10 33 30	12 35 43	14 34 0	16 36 13	18 34 30
20 37 40		0 34 14		4 34 43		8 35 13	10 37 26		14 37 56		18 38 26

Day	1	2	3	4	5	6	7	8	9	10	11	12
1	18 42 23	20 44 36	22 34 59	0 37 12	2 35 29	4 37 42	6 35 59	8 38 12	10 40 25	12 38 42	14 40 55	16 39 12
2	18 46 19	20 48 32	22 38 56	0 41 9	2 39 26	4 41 39	6 39 56	8 42 9	10 44 22	12 42 38	14 44 52	16 43 8
3	18 50 16	20 52 29	22 42 52	0 45 6	2 43 22	4 45 35	6 43 52	8 46 5	10 48 18	12 46 35	14 48 48	16 47 5
4	18 54 12	20 56 26	22 46 49	0 49 2	2 47 19	4 49 32	6 47 49	8 50 2	10 52 15	12 50 32	14 52 45	16 51 1
5	18 58 9	21 0 22	22 50 46	0 52 59	2 51 15	4 53 29	6 51 45	8 53 58	10 56 12	12 54 28	14 56 41	16 54 58
6	19 2 5	21 4 19	22 54 42	0 56 55	2 55 12	4 57 25	6 55 42	8 57 55	11 0 8	12 58 25	15 0 38	16 58 55
7	19 6 2	21 8 15	22 58 39	1 0 52	2 59 8	5 1 22	6 59 38	9 1 52	11 4 5	13 2 21	15 4 34	17 2 51
8	19 9 59	21 12 12	23 2 35	1 4 48	3 3 5	5 5 18	7 3 35	9 5 48	11 8 1	13 6 18	15 8 31	17 6 48
9	19 13 55	21 16 8	23 6 32	1 8 45	3 7 1	5 9 15	7 7 31	9 9 45	11 11 58	13 10 14	15 12 28	17 10 44
10	19 17 52	21 20 5	23 10 28	1 12 41	3 10 58	5 13 11	7 11 28	9 13 41	11 15 54	13 14 11	15 16 24	17 14 41
11	19 21 48	21 24 1	23 14 25	1 16 38	3 14 55	5 17 8	7 15 25	9 17 38	11 19 51	13 18 7	15 20 21	17 18 37
12	19 25 45	21 27 58	23 18 21	1 20 35	3 18 51	5 21 4	7 19 21	9 21 34	11 23 47	13 22 4	15 24 17	17 22 34
13	19 29 41	21 31 55	23 22 18	1 24 31	3 22 48	5 25 1	7 23 18	9 25 31	11 27 44	13 16 1	15 28 14	17 26 30
14	19 33 38	21 35 51	23 26 15	1 28 28	3 26 44	5 28 58	7 27 14	9 29 27	11 31 41	13 29 57	15 32 10	17 30 27
15	19 37 34	21 39 48	23 30 11	1 32 24	3 30 41	5 32 54	7 31 11	9 33 24	11 35 37	13 33 54	15 36 7	17 34 24
16	19 41 31	21 43 44	23 34 8	1 36 21	3 34 37	5 36 51	7 35 7	9 37 21	11 39 34	13 37 50	15 40 3	17 38 20
17	19 45 28	21 47 41	23 38 4	1 40 17	3 38 34	5 40 47	7 39 4	9 41 17	11 43 30	13 41 47	15 44 0	17 42 17
18	19 49 24	21 51 37	23 42 1	1 44 14	3 42 30	5 44 44	7 43 0	9 45 14	11 47 27	13 45 43	15 47 57	17 46 13
19	19 53 21	21 55 34	23 45 57	1 48 10	3 46 27	5 48 40	7 46 57	9 49 10	11 51 23	13 49 40	15 51 53	17 50 10
20	19 57 17	21 59 30	23 49 54	1 52 7	3 50 24	5 52 37	7 50 54	9 53 7	11 55 20	13 53 36	15 55 50	17 54 6
21	20 1 14	22 3 27	23 53 50	1 56 4	3 54 20	5 56 33	7 54 50	9 57 3	11 59 16	13 57 33	15 59 46	17 58 3
22	20 5 10	22 7 24	23 57 47	2 0 0	3 58 17	6 0 30	7 58 47	10 1 0	12 3 13	14 1 30	16 3 43	18 1 59
23	20 9 7	22 11 20	0 1 44	2 3 57	4 2 13	6 4 27	8 2 43	10 4 56	12 7 10	14 5 26	16 7 39	18 5 56
24	20 13 3	22 15 17	0 5 40	2 7 53	4 6 10	6 8 23	8 6 40	10 8 53	12 11 6	14 9 23	16 11 36	18 9 53
25	20 17 0	22 19 13	0 9 37	2 11 50	4 10 6	6 12 20	8 10 36	10 12 50	12 15 3	14 13 19	16 15 32	18 13 49
26	20 20 57	22 23 10	0 13 33	2 15 46	4 14 3	6 16 16	8 14 33	10 16 46	12 18 59	14 17 16	16 19 29	18 17 46
27	20 24 53	22 27 6	0 17 30	2 19 43	4 17 60	6 20 13	8 18 29	10 20 43	12 22 56	14 21 12	16 23 26	18 21 42
28	20 28 50	22 31 3	0 21 26	2 23 39	4 21 56	6 24 9	8 22 26	10 24 39	12 26 52	14 25 9	16 27 22	18 25 39
29	20 32 46		0 25 23	2 27 36	4 25 53	6 28 6	8 26 23	10 28 36	12 30 49	14 29 5	16 31 19	18 29 35
30	20 36 43		0 29 19	2 31 33	4 29 49	6 32 2	8 30 19	10 32 32	12 34 45	14 33 2	16 35 15	18 33 32
31	20 40 39		0 33 16		4 33 46		8 34 16	10 36 29		14 36 59		18 37 28

Year	Day	1	2	3	4	5	6	7	8	9	10	11	12
1922	1	18 41 25	20 43 38	22 34 2	0 36 15	2 34 31	4 36 45	6 35 1	8 37 15	10 39 28	12 37 44	14 39 57	16 38 14
	2	18 45 22	20 47 35	22 37 58	0 40 11	2 38 28	4 40 41	6 38 58	8 41 11	10 43 24	12 41 41	14 43 54	16 42 11
	3	18 49 18	20 51 31	22 41 55	0 44 8	2 42 25	4 44 38	6 42 54	8 45 8	10 47 21	12 45 37	14 47 51	16 46 7
	4	18 53 15	20 55 28	22 45 51	0 48 5	2 46 21	4 48 34	6 46 51	8 49 4	10 51 17	12 49 34	14 51 47	16 50 4
	5	18 57 11	20 59 24	22 49 48	0 52 1	2 50 18	4 52 31	6 50 48	8 53 1	10 55 14	12 53 30	14 55 44	16 54 0
	6	19 1 8	21 3 21	22 53 45	0 55 58	2 54 14	4 56 27	6 54 44	8 56 57	10 59 10	12 57 27	14 59 40	16 57 57
	7	19 5 4	21 7 18	22 57 41	0 59 54	2 58 11	5 0 24	6 58 41	9 0 54	11 3 7	13 1 24	15 3 37	17 1 53
	8	19 9 1	21 11 14	23 1 38	1 3 51	3 2 7	5 4 21	7 2 37	9 4 50	11 7 4	13 5 20	15 7 33	17 5 50
	9	19 12 57	21 15 11	23 5 34	1 7 47	3 6 4	5 8 17	7 6 34	9 8 47	11 11 0	13 9 17	15 11 30	17 9 47
	10	19 16 54	21 19 7	23 9 31	1 11 44	3 10 0	5 12 14	7 10 30	9 12 44	11 14 57	13 13 13	15 15 26	17 13 43
	11	19 20 51	21 23 4	23 13 27	1 15 40	3 13 57	5 16 10	7 14 27	9 16 40	11 18 53	13 17 10	15 19 23	17 17 40
	12	19 24 47	21 27 0	23 17 24	1 19 37	3 17 54	5 20 7	7 18 23	9 20 37	11 22 50	13 21 6	15 23 20	17 21 36
	13	19 28 44	21 30 57	23 21 20	1 23 33	3 21 50	5 24 3	7 22 20	9 24 33	11 26 46	13 25 3	15 27 16	17 25 33
	14	19 32 40	21 34 53	23 25 17	1 27 30	3 25 47	5 28 0	7 26 17	9 28 30	11 30 43	13 28 59	15 31 13	17 29 29
	15	19 36 37	21 38 50	23 29 13	1 31 27	3 29 43	5 31 56	7 30 13	9 32 26	11 34 39	13 32 56	15 35 9	17 33 26
	16	19 40 33	21 42 47	23 33 10	1 35 23	3 33 40	5 35 53	7 34 10	9 36 23	11 38 36	13 36 53	15 39 6	17 37 22
	17	19 44 30	21 46 43	23 37 7	1 39 20	3 37 36	5 39 50	7 38 6	9 40 19	11 42 33	13 40 49	15 43 2	17 41 19
	18	19 48 26	21 50 40	23 41 3	1 43 16	3 41 33	5 43 46	7 42 3	9 44 16	11 46 29	13 44 46	15 46 59	17 45 16
	19	19 52 23	21 54 36	23 45 0	1 47 13	3 45 29	5 47 43	7 45 59	9 48 13	11 50 26	13 48 42	15 50 55	17 49 12
	20	19 56 20	21 58 33	23 48 56	1 51 9	3 49 26	5 51 39	7 49 56	9 52 9	11 54 22	13 52 39	15 54 52	17 53 9
	21	20 0 16	22 2 29	23 52 53	1 55 6	3 53 23	5 55 36	7 53 52	9 56 6	11 58 19	13 56 35	15 58 49	17 57 5
	22	20 4 13	22 6 26	23 56 49	1 59 2	3 57 19	5 59 32	7 57 49	10 0 2	12 2 15	14 0 32	16 2 45	18 1 2
	23	20 8 9	22 10 22	0 0 46	2 2 59	4 1 16	6 3 29	8 1 46	10 3 59	12 6 12	14 4 28	16 6 42	18 4 58
	24	20 12 6	22 14 19	0 4 42	2 6 56	4 5 12	6 7 25	8 5 42	10 7 55	12 10 8	14 8 25	16 10 38	18 8 55
	25	20 16 2	22 18 16	0 8 39	2 10 52	4 9 9	6 11 22	8 9 39	10 11 52	12 14 5	14 12 22	16 14 35	18 12 51
	26	20 19 59	22 22 12	0 12 36	2 14 49	4 13 5	6 15 19	8 13 35	10 15 48	12 18 2	14 16 18	16 18 31	18 16 48
	27	20 23 55	22 26 9	0 16 32	2 18 45	4 17 2	6 19 15	8 17 32	10 19 45	12 21 58	14 20 15	16 22 28	18 20 45
	28	20 27 52	22 30 5	0 20 29	2 22 42	4 20 58	6 23 12	8 21 28	10 23 42	12 25 55	14 24 11	16 26 24	18 24 41
	29	20 31 49		0 24 25	2 26 38	4 24 55	6 27 8	8 25 25	10 27 38	12 29 51	14 28 8	16 30 21	18 28 38
	30	20 35 45		0 28 22	2 30 35	4 28 52	6 31 5	8 29 21	10 31 35	12 33 48	14 32 4	16 34 18	18 32 34
	31	20 39 42		0 32 18		4 32 48		8 33 18	10 35 31		14 36 1		18 36 31
1923	1	18 40 27	20 42 41	22 33 4	0 35 17	2 33 34	4 35 47	6 34 4	8 36 17	10 38 30	12 36 47	14 39 0	16 37 16
	2	18 44 24	20 46 37	22 37 1	0 39 14	2 37 30	4 39 44	6 38 0	8 40 13	10 42 27	12 40 43	14 42 56	16 41 13
	3	18 48 20	20 50 34	22 40 57	0 43 10	2 41 27	4 43 40	6 41 57	8 44 10	10 46 23	12 44 40	14 46 53	16 45 10
	4	18 52 17	20 54 30	22 44 54	0 47 7	2 45 23	4 47 37	6 45 53	8 48 7	10 50 20	12 48 36	14 50 49	16 49 6
	5	18 56 14	20 58 27	22 48 50	0 51 3	2 49 20	4 51 33	6 49 50	8 52 3	10 54 16	12 52 33	14 54 46	16 53 3
	6	19 0 10	21 2 23	22 52 47	0 55 0	2 53 17	4 55 30	6 53 46	8 56 0	10 58 13	12 56 29	14 58 43	16 56 59
	7	19 4 7	21 6 20	22 56 43	0 58 57	2 57 13	4 59 26	6 57 43	8 59 56	11 2 9	13 0 26	15 2 39	17 0 56
	8	19 8 3	21 10 16	23 0 40	1 2 53	3 1 10	5 3 23	7 1 40	9 3 53	11 6 6	13 4 23	15 6 36	17 4 52
	9	19 12 0	21 14 13	23 4 37	1 6 50	3 5 6	5 7 19	7 5 36	9 7 49	11 10 3	13 8 19	15 10 32	17 8 49
	10	19 15 56	21 18 10	23 8 33	1 10 46	3 9 3	5 11 16	7 9 33	9 11 46	11 13 59	13 12 16	15 14 29	17 12 45
	11	19 19 53	21 22 6	23 12 30	1 14 43	3 12 59	5 15 13	7 13 29	9 15 42	11 17 56	13 16 12	15 18 25	17 16 42
	12	19 23 49	21 26 3	23 16 26	1 18 39	3 16 56	5 19 9	7 17 26	9 19 39	11 21 52	13 20 9	15 22 22	17 20 39
	13	19 27 46	21 29 59	23 20 23	1 22 36	3 20 52	5 23 6	7 21 22	9 23 36	11 25 49	13 24 5	15 26 18	17 24 35
	14	19 31 43	21 33 56	23 24 19	1 26 32	3 24 49	5 27 2	7 25 19	9 27 32	11 29 45	13 28 2	15 30 15	17 28 32
	15	19 35 39	21 37 52	23 28 16	1 30 29	3 28 46	5 30 59	7 29 15	9 31 29	11 33 42	13 31 58	15 34 12	17 32 28
	16	19 39 36	21 41 49	23 32 12	1 34 25	3 32 42	5 34 55	7 33 12	9 35 25	11 37 38	13 35 55	15 38 8	17 36 25
	17	19 43 32	21 45 45	23 36 9	1 38 22	3 36 39	5 38 52	7 37 9	9 39 22	11 41 35	13 39 51	15 42 5	17 40 21
	18	19 47 29	21 49 42	23 40 5	1 42 19	3 40 35	5 42 48	7 41 5	9 43 18	11 45 31	13 43 48	15 46 1	17 44 18
	19	19 51 25	21 53 39	23 44 2	1 46 15	3 44 32	5 46 45	7 45 2	9 47 15	11 49 28	13 47 45	15 49 58	17 48 14
	20	19 55 22	21 57 35	23 47 59	1 50 12	3 48 28	5 50 42	7 48 58	9 51 11	11 53 25	13 51 41	15 53 54	17 52 11
	21	19 59 18	22 1 32	23 51 55	1 54 8	3 52 25	5 54 38	7 52 55	9 55 8	11 57 21	13 55 38	15 57 51	17 56 8
	22	20 3 15	22 5 28	23 55 52	1 58 5	3 56 21	5 58 35	7 56 51	9 59 5	12 1 18	13 59 34	16 1 47	18 0 4
	23	20 7 12	22 9 25	23 59 48	2 2 1	4 0 18	6 2 31	8 0 48	10 3 1	12 5 14	14 3 31	16 5 44	18 4 1
	24	20 11 8	22 13 21	0 3 45	2 5 58	4 4 15	6 6 28	8 4 44	10 6 58	12 9 11	14 7 27	16 9 41	18 7 57
	25	20 15 5	22 17 18	0 7 41	2 9 54	4 8 11	6 10 24	8 8 41	10 10 54	12 13 7	14 11 24	16 13 37	18 11 54
	26	20 19 1	22 21 14	0 11 38	2 13 51	4 12 8	6 14 21	8 12 38	10 14 51	12 17 4	14 15 20	16 17 34	18 15 50
	27	20 22 58	22 25 11	0 15 34	2 17 48	4 16 4	6 18 17	8 16 34	10 18 47	12 21 0	14 19 17	16 21 30	18 19 47
	28	20 26 54	22 29 8	0 19 31	2 21 44	4 20 1	6 22 14	8 20 31	10 22 44	12 24 57	14 23 14	16 25 27	18 23 43
	29	20 30 51		0 23 28	2 25 41	4 23 57	6 26 11	8 24 27	10 26 40	12 28 54	14 27 10	16 29 23	18 27 40
	30	20 34 47		0 27 24	2 29 37	4 27 54	6 30 7	8 28 24	10 30 37	12 32 50	14 31 7	16 33 20	18 31 37
	31	20 38 44		0 31 21		4 31 50		8 32 20	10 34 34		14 35 3		18 35 33
1924	1	18 39 30	20 41 43	22 36 3	0 38 16	2 36 33	4 38 46	6 37 3	8 39 16	10 41 29	12 39 46	14 41 59	16 40 15
	2	18 43 26	20 45 40	22 40 0	0 42 13	2 40 29	4 42 42	6 40 59	8 43 12	10 45 26	12 43 42	14 45 55	16 44 12
	3	18 47 23	20 49 36	22 43 56	0 46 9	2 44 26	4 46 39	6 44 56	8 47 9	10 49 22	12 47 39	14 49 52	16 48 9
	4	18 51 19	20 53 33	22 47 53	0 50 6	2 48 22	4 50 36	6 48 52	8 51 6	10 53 19	12 51 35	14 53 48	16 52 5
	5	18 55 16	20 57 29	22 51 49	0 54 2	2 52 19	4 54 32	6 52 49	8 55 2	10 57 15	12 55 32	14 57 45	16 56 2
	6	18 59 12	21 1 26	22 55 46	0 57 59	2 56 15	4 58 29	6 56 45	8 58 59	11 1 12	12 59 28	15 1 42	16 59 58
	7	19 3 9	21 5 22	22 59 42	1 1 55	3 0 12	5 2 25	7 0 42	9 2 55	11 5 8	13 3 25	15 5 38	17 3 55
	8	19 7 6	21 9 19	23 3 39	1 5 52	3 4 9	5 6 22	7 4 39	9 6 52	11 9 5	13 7 21	15 9 35	17 7 51
	9	19 11 2	21 13 15	23 7 35	1 9 49	3 8 5	5 10 18	7 8 35	9 10 48	11 13 1	13 11 18	15 13 31	17 11 48
	10	19 14 59	21 17 12	23 11 32	1 13 45	3 12 2	5 14 15	7 12 32	9 14 45	11 16 58	13 15 15	15 17 28	17 15 44
	11	19 18 55	21 21 8	23 15 29	1 17 42	3 15 58	5 18 11	7 16 28	9 18 41	11 20 55	13 19 11	15 21 24	17 19 41
	12	19 22 52	21 25 5	23 19 25	1 21 38	3 19 55	5 22 8	7 20 25	9 22 38	11 24 51	13 23 8	15 25 21	17 23 38
	13	19 26 48	21 29 2	23 23 22	1 25 35	3 23 51	5 26 5	7 24 21	9 26 35	11 28 48	13 27 4	15 29 17	17 27 34
	14	19 30 45	21 32 58	23 27 18	1 29 31	3 27 48	5 30 1	7 28 18	9 30 31	11 32 44	13 31 1	15 33 14	17 31 31
	15	19 34 42	21 36 55	23 31 15	1 33 28	3 31 44	5 33 58	7 32 14	9 34 28	11 36 41	13 34 57	15 37 10	17 35 27
	16	19 38 38	21 40 51	23 35 11	1 37 24	3 35 41	5 37 54	7 36 11	9 38 24	11 40 37	13 38 54	15 41 7	17 39 24
	17	19 42 35	21 44 48	23 39 8	1 41 21	3 39 38	5 41 51	7 40 8	9 42 21	11 44 34	13 42 50	15 45 4	17 43 20
	18	19 46 31	21 48 44	23 43 4	1 45 18	3 43 34	5 45 47	7 44 4	9 46 17	11 48 30	13 46 47	15 49 0	17 47 17
	19	19 50 28	21 52 41	23 47 1	1 49 14	3 47 31	5 49 44	7 48 1	9 50 14	11 52 27	13 50 44	15 52 57	17 51 13
	20	19 54 24	21 56 37	23 50 57	1 53 11	3 51 27	5 53 40	7 51 57	9 54 10	11 56 24	13 54 40	15 56 53	17 55 10
	21	19 58 21	22 0 34	23 54 54	1 57 7	3 55 24	5 57 37	7 55 54	9 58 7	12 0 20	13 58 37	16 0 50	17 59 7
	22	20 2 17	22 4 31	23 58 51	2 1 4	3 59 20	6 1 34	7 59 50	10 2 4	12 4 17	14 2 33	16 4 46	18 3 3
	23	20 6 14	22 8 27	0 2 47	2 5 0	4 3 17	6 5 30	8 3 47	10 6 0	12 8 13	14 6 30	16 8 43	18 7 0
	24	20 10 11	22 12 24	0 6 44	2 8 57	4 7 13	6 9 27	8 7 43	10 9 57	12 12 10	14 10 26	16 12 40	18 10 56
	25	20 14 7	22 16 20	0 10 40	2 12 53	4 11 10	6 13 23	8 11 40	10 13 53	12 16 6	14 14 23	16 16 36	18 14 53
	26	20 18 4	22 20 17	0 14 37	2 16 50	4 15 7	6 17 20	8 15 37	10 17 50	12 20 3	14 18 19	16 20 33	18 18 49
	27	20 22 0	22 24 13	0 18 33	2 20 46	4 19 3	6 21 16	8 19 33	10 21 46	12 23 59	14 22 16	16 24 29	18 22 46
	28	20 25 57	22 28 10	0 22 30	2 24 43	4 23 0	6 25 13	8 23 30	10 25 43	12 27 56	14 26 13	16 28 26	18 26 42
	29	20 29 53	22 32 6	0 26 26	2 28 40	4 26 56	6 29 10	8 27 26	10 29 39	12 31 52	14 30 9	16 32 22	18 30 39
	30	20 33 50		0 30 23	2 32 36	4 30 53	6 33 6	8 31 23	10 33 36	12 35 49	14 34 6	16 36 19	18 34 36
	31	20 37 46		0 34 20		4 34 49		8 35 19	10 37 32		14 38 2		18 38 32
1925	1	18 42 29	20 44 42	22 35 5	0 37 19	2 35 35	4 37 48	6 36 5	8 38 18	10 40 31	12 38 48	14 41 1	16 39 18
	2	18 46 25	20 48 38	22 39 2	0 41 15	2 39 32	4 41 45	6 40 2	8 42 15	10 44 28	12 42 45	14 44 58	16 43 14
	3	18 50 22	20 52 35	22 42 59	0 45 12	2 43 28	4 45 41	6 43 58	8 46 11	10 48 25	12 46 41	14 48 54	16 47 11
	4	18 54 18	20 56 32	22 46 55	0 49 8	2 47 25	4 49 38	6 47 55	8 50 8	10 52 21	12 50 38	14 52 51	16 51 8
	5	18 58 15	21 0 28	22 50 52	0 53 5	2 51 22	4 53 35	6 51 51	8 54 5	10 56 18	12 54 34	14 56 47	16 55 4
	6	19 2 11	21 4 25	22 54 48	0 57 1	2 55 18	4 57 31	6 55 48	8 58 1	11 0 14	12 58 31	15 0 44	16 59 1
	7	19 6 8	21 8 21	22 58 45	1 0 58	2 59 14	5 1 28	6 59 44	9 1 58	11 4 11	13 2 27	15 4 41	17 2 57
	8	19 10 5	21 12 18	23 2 41	1 4 54	3 3 11	5 5 24	7 3 41	9 5 54	11 8 7	13 6 24	15 8 37	17 6 54
	9	19 14 1	21 16 14	23 6 38	1 8 51	3 7 8	5 9 21	7 7 38	9 9 51	11 12 4	13 10 20	15 12 34	17 10 50
	10	19 17 58	21 20 11	23 10 34	1 12 48	3 11 4	5 13 17	7 11 34	9 13 47	11 16 0	13 14 17	15 16 30	17 14 47
	11	19 21 54	21 24 7	23 14 31	1 16 44	3 15 1	5 17 14	7 15 31	9 17 44	11 19 57	13 18 14	15 20 27	17 18 43
	12	19 25 51	21 28 4	23 18 28	1 20 41	3 18 57	5 21 10	7 19 27	9 21 40	11 23 54	13 22 10	15 24 23	17 22 40
	13	19 29 47	21 32 1	23 22 24	1 24 37	3 22 54	5 25 7	7 23 24	9 25 37	11 27 50	13 26 7	15 28 20	17 26 37
	14	19 33 44	21 35 57	23 26 21	1 28 34	3 26 50	5 29 4	7 27 20	9 29 34	11 31 47	13 30 3	15 32 16	17 30 33
	15	19 37 40	21 39 54	23 30 17	1 32 30	3 30 47	5 33 0	7 31 17	9 33 30	11 35 43	13 34 0	15 36 13	17 34 30
	16	19 41 37	21 43 50	23 34 14	1 36 27	3 34 43	5 36 57	7 35 13	9 37 27	11 39 40	13 37 56	15 40 10	17 38 26
	17	19 45 34	21 47 47	23 38 10	1 40 23	3 38 40	5 40 53	7 39 10	9 41 23	11 43 36	13 41 53	15 44 6	17 42 23
	18	19 49 30	21 51 43	23 42 7	1 44 20	3 42 37	5 44 50	7 43 7	9 45 20	11 47 33	13 45 49	15 48 3	17 46 19
	19	19 53 27	21 55 40	23 46 3	1 48 16	3 46 33	5 48 46	7 47 3	9 49 16	11 51 29	13 49 46	15 51 59	17 50 16
	20	19 57 23	21 59 36	23 50 0	1 52 13	3 50 30	5 52 43	7 51 0	9 53 13	11 55 26	13 53 43	15 55 56	17 54 12
	21	20 1 20	22 3 33	23 53 56	1 56 10	3 54 26	5 56 40	7 54 56	9 57 9	11 59 23	13 57 39	15 59 52	17 58 9
	22	20 5 16	22 7 30	23 57 53	2 0 6	3 58 23	6 0 36	7 58 53	10 1 6	12 3 19	14 1 36	16 3 49	18 2 6
	23	20 9 13	22 11 26	0 1 50	2 4 3	4 2 19	6 4 33	8 2 49	10 5 3	12 7 16	14 5 32	16 7 45	18 6 2
	24	20 13 9	22 15 23	0 5 46	2 7 59	4 6 16	6 8 29	8 6 46	10 8 59	12 11 12	14 9 29	16 11 42	18 9 59
	25	20 17 6	22 19 19	0 9 43	2 11 56	4 10 12	6 12 26	8 10 42	10 12 56	12 15 9	14 13 25	16 15 39	18 13 55
	26	20 21 3	22 23 16	0 13 39	2 15 52	4 14 9	6 16 22	8 14 39	10 16 52	12 19 5	14 17 22	16 19 35	18 17 52
	27	20 24 59	22 27 12	0 17 36	2 19 49	4 18 6	6 20 19	8 18 36	10 20 49	12 23 2	14 21 18	16 23 32	18 21 48
	28	20 28 56	22 31 9	0 21 32	2 23 45	4 22 2	6 24 15	8 22 32	10 24 45	12 26 58	14 25 15	16 27 28	18 25 45
	29	20 32 52		0 25 29	2 27 42	4 25 59	6 28 12	8 26 29	10 28 42	12 30 55	14 29 12	16 31 25	18 29 42
	30	20 36 49		0 29 25	2 31 39	4 29 55	6 32 9	8 30 25	10 32 38	12 34 52	14 33 8	16 35 21	18 33 38
	31	20 40 45		0 33 22		4 33 52		8 34 22	10 36 35		14 37 5		18 37 35

		1	2	3	4	5	6	7	8	9	10	11	12
1926	1	18 41 31	20 43 44	22 34 8	0 36 21	2 34 38	4 36 51	6 35 8	8 37 21	10 39 34	12 37 51	14 40 4	16 38 20
	2	18 45 28	20 47 41	22 38 5	0 40 18	2 38 34	4 40 47	6 39 4	8 41 17	10 43 31	12 41 47	14 44 0	16 42 17
	3	18 49 24	20 51 38	22 42 1	0 44 14	2 42 31	4 44 44	6 43 1	8 45 14	10 47 27	12 45 44	14 47 57	16 46 14
	4	18 53 21	20 55 34	22 45 58	0 48 11	2 46 27	4 48 41	6 46 57	8 49 11	10 51 24	12 49 40	14 51 53	16 50 10
	5	18 57 17	20 59 31	22 49 54	0 52 7	2 50 24	4 52 37	6 50 54	8 53 7	10 55 20	12 53 37	14 55 50	16 54 7
	6	19 1 14	21 3 27	22 53 51	0 56 4	2 54 20	4 56 34	6 54 50	8 57 4	10 59 17	12 57 33	14 59 47	16 58 3
	7	19 5 11	21 7 24	22 57 47	1 0 0	2 58 17	5 0 30	6 58 47	9 1 0	11 3 13	13 1 30	15 3 43	17 2 0
	8	19 9 7	21 11 20	23 1 44	1 3 57	3 2 14	5 4 27	7 2 44	9 4 57	11 7 10	13 5 27	15 7 40	17 5 56
	9	19 13 4	21 15 17	23 5 40	1 7 53	3 6 10	5 8 23	7 6 40	9 8 53	11 11 6	13 9 23	15 11 36	17 9 53
	10	19 17 0	21 19 13	23 9 37	1 11 50	3 10 7	5 12 20	7 10 37	9 12 50	11 15 3	13 13 20	15 15 33	17 13 50
	11	19 20 57	21 23 10	23 13 33	1 15 47	3 14 3	5 16 16	7 14 33	9 16 46	11 19 0	13 17 16	15 19 29	17 17 46
	12	19 24 53	21 27 7	23 17 30	1 19 43	3 18 0	5 20 13	7 18 30	9 20 43	11 22 56	13 21 13	15 23 26	17 21 43
	13	19 28 50	21 31 3	23 21 27	1 23 40	3 21 56	5 24 10	7 22 26	9 24 40	11 26 53	13 25 9	15 27 22	17 25 39
	14	19 32 46	21 35 0	23 25 23	1 27 36	3 25 53	5 28 6	7 26 23	9 28 36	11 30 49	13 29 6	15 31 19	17 29 36
	15	19 36 43	21 38 56	23 29 20	1 31 33	3 29 49	5 32 3	7 30 19	9 32 33	11 34 46	13 33 2	15 35 16	17 33 32
	16	19 40 40	21 42 53	23 33 16	1 35 29	3 33 46	5 35 59	7 34 16	9 36 29	11 38 42	13 36 59	15 39 12	17 37 29
	17	19 44 36	21 46 49	23 37 13	1 39 26	3 37 43	5 39 56	7 38 13	9 40 26	11 42 39	13 40 56	15 43 9	17 41 25
	18	19 48 33	21 50 46	23 41 9	1 43 22	3 41 39	5 43 52	7 42 9	9 44 22	11 46 35	13 44 52	15 47 5	17 45 22
	19	19 52 29	21 54 42	23 45 6	1 47 19	3 45 36	5 47 49	7 46 6	9 48 19	11 50 32	13 48 49	15 51 2	17 49 19
	20	19 56 26	21 58 39	23 49 2	1 51 16	3 49 32	5 51 46	7 50 2	9 52 15	11 54 29	13 52 45	15 54 58	17 53 15
	21	20 0 22	22 2 36	23 52 59	1 55 12	3 53 29	5 55 42	7 53 59	9 56 12	11 58 25	13 56 42	15 58 55	17 57 12
	22	20 4 19	22 6 32	23 56 56	1 59 9	3 57 25	5 59 39	7 57 55	10 0 9	12 2 22	14 0 38	16 2 51	18 1 8
	23	20 8 15	22 10 29	0 0 52	2 3 5	4 1 22	6 3 35	8 1 52	10 4 5	12 6 18	14 4 35	16 6 48	18 5 5
	24	20 12 12	22 14 25	0 4 49	2 7 2	4 5 18	6 7 32	8 5 48	10 8 2	12 10 15	14 8 31	16 10 45	18 9 1
	25	20 16 9	22 18 22	0 8 45	2 10 58	4 9 15	6 11 28	8 9 45	10 11 58	12 14 11	14 12 28	16 14 41	18 12 58
	26	20 20 5	22 22 18	0 12 42	2 14 55	4 13 12	6 15 25	8 13 42	10 15 55	12 18 8	14 16 24	16 18 38	18 16 54
	27	20 24 2	22 26 15	0 16 38	2 18 51	4 17 8	6 19 21	8 17 38	10 19 51	12 22 4	14 20 21	16 22 34	18 20 51
	28	20 27 58	22 30 11	0 20 35	2 22 48	4 21 5	6 23 18	8 21 35	10 23 48	12 26 1	14 24 18	16 26 31	18 24 48
	29	20 31 55		0 24 31	2 26 45	4 25 1	6 27 15	8 25 31	10 27 44	12 29 58	14 28 14	16 30 27	18 28 44
	30	20 35 51		0 28 28	2 30 41	4 28 58	6 31 11	8 29 28	10 31 41	12 33 54	14 32 11	16 34 24	18 32 41
	31	20 39 48		0 32 25		4 32 54		8 33 24	10 35 38		14 36 7		18 36 37
1927	1	18 40 34	20 42 47	22 33 11	0 35 24	2 33 40	4 35 54	6 34 10	8 36 24	10 38 37	12 36 53	14 39 7	16 37 23
	2	18 44 30	20 46 44	22 37 7	0 39 20	2 37 37	4 39 50	6 38 7	8 40 20	10 42 33	12 40 50	14 43 3	16 41 20
	3	18 48 27	20 50 40	22 41 4	0 43 17	2 41 33	4 43 47	6 42 3	8 44 17	10 46 30	12 44 46	14 47 0	16 45 16
	4	18 52 23	20 54 37	22 45 0	0 47 13	2 45 30	4 47 43	6 46 0	8 48 13	10 50 26	12 48 43	14 50 56	16 49 13
	5	18 56 20	20 58 33	22 48 57	0 51 10	2 49 27	4 51 40	6 49 57	8 52 10	10 54 23	12 52 40	14 54 53	16 53 9
	6	19 0 17	21 2 30	22 52 53	0 55 6	2 53 23	4 55 36	6 53 53	8 56 6	10 58 20	12 56 36	14 58 49	16 57 6
	7	19 4 13	21 6 26	22 56 50	0 59 3	2 57 20	4 59 33	6 57 50	9 0 3	11 2 16	13 0 33	15 2 46	17 1 3
	8	19 8 10	21 10 23	23 0 46	1 3 0	3 1 16	5 3 29	7 1 46	9 3 59	11 6 13	13 4 29	15 6 42	17 4 59
	9	19 12 6	21 14 20	23 4 43	1 6 56	3 5 13	5 7 26	7 5 43	9 7 56	11 10 9	13 8 26	15 10 39	17 8 56
	10	19 16 3	21 18 16	23 8 40	1 10 53	3 9 9	5 11 23	7 9 39	9 11 53	11 14 6	13 12 22	15 14 36	17 12 52
	11	19 19 59	21 22 13	23 12 36	1 14 49	3 13 6	5 15 19	7 13 36	9 15 49	11 18 2	13 16 19	15 18 32	17 16 49
	12	19 23 56	21 26 9	23 16 33	1 18 46	3 17 2	5 19 16	7 17 32	9 19 46	11 21 59	13 20 15	15 22 29	17 20 45
	13	19 27 52	21 30 6	23 20 29	1 22 42	3 20 59	5 23 12	7 21 29	9 23 42	11 25 55	13 24 12	15 26 25	17 24 42
	14	19 31 49	21 34 2	23 24 26	1 26 39	3 24 56	5 27 9	7 25 26	9 27 39	11 29 52	13 28 9	15 30 22	17 28 38
	15	19 35 46	21 37 59	23 28 22	1 30 35	3 28 52	5 31 5	7 29 22	9 31 35	11 33 49	13 32 5	15 34 18	17 32 35
	16	19 39 42	21 41 55	23 32 19	1 34 32	3 32 49	5 35 2	7 33 19	9 35 32	11 37 45	13 36 2	15 38 15	17 36 32
	17	19 43 39	21 45 52	23 36 15	1 38 29	3 36 45	5 38 58	7 37 15	9 39 28	11 41 42	13 39 58	15 42 11	17 40 28
	18	19 47 35	21 49 48	23 40 12	1 42 25	3 40 42	5 42 55	7 41 12	9 43 25	11 45 38	13 43 55	15 46 8	17 44 25
	19	19 51 32	21 53 45	23 44 9	1 46 22	3 44 38	5 46 52	7 45 8	9 47 22	11 49 35	13 47 51	15 50 5	17 48 21
	20	19 55 28	21 57 42	23 48 5	1 50 18	3 48 35	5 50 48	7 49 5	9 51 18	11 53 31	13 51 48	15 54 1	17 52 18
	21	19 59 25	22 1 38	23 52 2	1 54 15	3 52 31	5 54 45	7 53 1	9 55 15	11 57 28	13 55 44	15 57 58	17 56 14
	22	20 3 21	22 5 35	23 55 58	1 58 11	3 56 28	5 58 41	7 56 58	9 59 11	12 1 24	13 59 41	16 1 54	18 0 11
	23	20 7 18	22 9 31	23 59 55	2 2 8	4 0 25	6 2 38	8 0 55	10 3 8	12 5 21	14 3 38	16 5 51	18 4 7
	24	20 11 15	22 13 28	0 3 51	2 6 4	4 4 21	6 6 34	8 4 51	10 7 4	12 9 17	14 7 34	16 9 47	18 8 4
	25	20 15 11	22 17 24	0 7 48	2 10 1	4 8 18	6 10 31	8 8 48	10 11 1	12 13 14	14 11 31	16 13 44	18 12 1
	26	20 19 8	22 21 21	0 11 44	2 13 58	4 12 14	6 14 28	8 12 44	10 14 57	12 17 11	14 15 27	16 17 40	18 15 57
	27	20 23 4	22 25 17	0 15 41	2 17 54	4 16 11	6 18 24	8 16 41	10 18 54	12 21 7	14 19 24	16 21 37	18 19 54
	28	20 27 1	22 29 14	0 19 38	2 21 51	4 20 7	6 22 21	8 20 37	10 22 51	12 25 4	14 23 20	16 25 34	18 23 50
	29	20 30 57		0 23 34	2 25 47	4 24 4	6 26 17	8 24 34	10 26 47	12 29 0	14 27 17	16 29 30	18 27 47
	30	20 34 54		0 27 31	2 29 44	4 28 0	6 30 14	8 28 30	10 30 44	12 32 57	14 31 13	16 33 27	18 31 43
	31	20 38 51		0 31 27		4 31 57		8 32 27	10 34 40		14 35 10		18 35 40
1928	1	18 39 37	20 41 50	22 36 10	0 38 23	2 36 40	4 38 53	6 37 10	8 39 23	10 41 36	12 39 53	14 42 6	16 40 23
	2	18 43 33	20 45 46	22 40 6	0 42 20	2 40 36	4 42 49	6 41 6	8 43 19	10 45 33	12 43 49	14 46 2	16 44 19
	3	18 47 30	20 49 43	22 44 3	0 46 16	2 44 33	4 46 46	6 45 3	8 47 16	10 49 29	12 47 46	14 49 59	16 48 16
	4	18 51 26	20 53 39	22 48 0	0 50 13	2 48 29	4 50 43	6 48 59	8 51 13	10 53 26	12 51 42	14 53 56	16 52 12
	5	18 55 23	20 57 36	22 51 56	0 54 9	2 52 26	4 54 39	6 52 56	8 55 9	10 57 22	12 55 39	14 57 52	16 56 9
	6	18 59 19	21 1 33	22 55 53	0 58 6	2 56 22	4 58 36	6 56 52	8 59 6	11 1 19	12 59 35	15 1 49	17 0 5
	7	19 3 16	21 5 29	22 59 49	1 2 2	3 0 19	5 2 32	7 0 49	9 3 2	11 5 15	13 3 32	15 5 45	17 4 2
	8	19 7 12	21 9 26	23 3 46	1 5 59	3 4 16	5 6 29	7 4 46	9 6 59	11 9 12	13 7 29	15 9 42	17 7 59
	9	19 11 9	21 13 22	23 7 42	1 9 55	3 8 12	5 10 25	7 8 42	9 10 55	11 13 9	13 11 25	15 13 38	17 11 55
	10	19 15 6	21 17 19	23 11 39	1 13 52	3 12 9	5 14 22	7 12 39	9 14 52	11 17 5	13 15 22	15 17 35	17 15 52
	11	19 19 2	21 21 15	23 15 35	1 17 49	3 16 5	5 18 18	7 16 35	9 18 48	11 21 2	13 19 18	15 21 31	17 19 48
	12	19 22 59	21 25 12	23 19 32	1 21 45	3 20 2	5 22 15	7 20 32	9 22 45	11 24 58	13 23 15	15 25 28	17 23 45
	13	19 26 55	21 29 8	23 23 29	1 25 42	3 23 58	5 26 12	7 24 28	9 26 42	11 28 55	13 27 11	15 29 25	17 27 41
	14	19 30 52	21 33 5	23 27 25	1 29 38	3 27 55	5 30 8	7 28 25	9 30 38	11 32 51	13 31 8	15 33 21	17 31 38
	15	19 34 48	21 37 2	23 31 22	1 33 35	3 31 51	5 34 5	7 32 21	9 34 35	11 36 48	13 35 4	15 37 18	17 35 34
	16	19 38 45	21 40 58	23 35 18	1 37 31	3 35 48	5 38 1	7 36 18	9 38 31	11 40 44	13 39 1	15 41 14	17 39 31
	17	19 42 41	21 44 55	23 39 15	1 41 28	3 39 45	5 41 58	7 40 15	9 42 28	11 44 41	13 42 58	15 45 11	17 43 28
	18	19 46 38	21 48 51	23 43 11	1 45 24	3 43 41	5 45 54	7 44 11	9 46 24	11 48 38	13 46 54	15 49 7	17 47 24
	19	19 50 35	21 52 48	23 47 8	1 49 21	3 47 38	5 49 51	7 48 8	9 50 21	11 52 34	13 50 51	15 53 4	17 51 21
	20	19 54 31	21 56 44	23 51 4	1 53 18	3 51 34	5 53 48	7 52 4	9 54 17	11 56 31	13 54 47	15 57 0	17 55 17
	21	19 58 28	22 0 41	23 55 1	1 57 14	3 55 31	5 57 44	7 56 1	9 58 14	12 0 27	13 58 44	16 0 57	17 59 14
	22	20 2 24	22 4 37	23 58 58	2 1 11	3 59 27	6 1 41	7 59 57	10 2 11	12 4 24	14 2 40	16 4 54	18 3 10
	23	20 6 21	22 8 34	0 2 54	2 5 7	4 3 24	6 5 37	8 3 54	10 6 7	12 8 20	14 6 37	16 8 50	18 7 7
	24	20 10 17	22 12 31	0 6 51	2 9 4	4 7 20	6 9 34	8 7 50	10 10 4	12 12 17	14 10 33	16 12 47	18 11 3
	25	20 14 14	22 16 27	0 10 47	2 13 0	4 11 17	6 13 30	8 11 47	10 14 0	12 16 13	14 14 30	16 16 43	18 15 0
	26	20 18 10	22 20 24	0 14 44	2 16 57	4 15 14	6 17 27	8 15 44	10 17 57	12 20 10	14 18 27	16 20 40	18 18 57
	27	20 22 7	22 24 20	0 18 40	2 20 53	4 19 10	6 21 23	8 19 40	10 21 53	12 24 7	14 22 23	16 24 36	18 22 53
	28	20 26 4	22 28 17	0 22 37	2 24 50	4 23 7	6 25 20	8 23 37	10 25 50	12 28 3	14 26 20	16 28 33	18 26 50
	29	20 30 0	22 32 13	0 26 33	2 28 47	4 27 3	6 29 17	8 27 33	10 29 46	12 32 0	14 30 16	16 32 29	18 30 46
	30	20 33 57		0 30 30	2 32 43	4 31 0	6 33 13	8 31 30	10 33 43	12 35 56	14 34 13	16 36 26	18 34 43
	31	20 37 53		0 34 26		4 34 56		8 35 26	10 37 40		14 38 9		18 38 39
1929	1	18 42 36	20 44 49	22 35 13	0 37 26	2 35 43	4 37 56	6 36 13	8 38 26	10 40 39	12 38 56	14 41 9	16 39 26
	2	18 46 32	20 48 46	22 39 9	0 41 22	2 39 39	4 41 52	6 40 9	8 42 22	10 44 36	12 42 52	14 45 5	16 43 22
	3	18 50 29	20 52 42	22 43 6	0 45 19	2 43 36	4 45 49	6 44 6	8 46 19	10 48 32	12 46 49	14 49 2	16 47 19
	4	18 54 26	20 56 39	22 47 2	0 49 16	2 47 32	4 49 45	6 48 2	8 50 15	10 52 29	12 50 45	14 52 59	16 51 15
	5	18 58 22	21 0 35	22 50 59	0 53 12	2 51 29	4 53 42	6 51 59	8 54 12	10 56 25	12 54 42	14 56 55	16 55 12
	6	19 2 19	21 4 32	22 54 56	0 57 9	2 55 25	4 57 39	6 55 55	8 58 9	11 0 22	12 58 38	15 0 52	16 59 8
	7	19 6 15	21 8 29	22 58 52	1 1 5	2 59 22	5 1 35	6 59 52	9 2 5	11 4 18	13 2 35	15 4 48	17 3 5
	8	19 10 12	21 12 25	23 2 49	1 5 2	3 3 18	5 5 32	7 3 48	9 6 2	11 8 15	13 6 32	15 8 45	17 7 1
	9	19 14 8	21 16 22	23 6 45	1 8 58	3 7 15	5 9 28	7 7 45	9 9 58	11 12 11	13 10 28	15 12 41	17 10 58
	10	19 18 5	21 20 18	23 10 42	1 12 55	3 11 12	5 13 25	7 11 42	9 13 55	11 16 8	13 14 25	15 16 38	17 14 55
	11	19 22 2	21 24 15	23 14 38	1 16 51	3 15 8	5 17 21	7 15 38	9 17 51	11 20 5	13 18 21	15 20 34	17 18 51
	12	19 25 58	21 28 11	23 18 35	1 20 48	3 19 5	5 21 18	7 19 35	9 21 48	11 24 1	13 22 18	15 24 31	17 22 48
	13	19 29 55	21 32 8	23 22 31	1 24 45	3 23 1	5 25 14	7 23 31	9 25 44	11 27 58	13 26 14	15 28 28	17 26 44
	14	19 33 51	21 36 4	23 26 28	1 28 41	3 26 58	5 29 11	7 27 28	9 29 41	11 31 54	13 30 11	15 32 24	17 30 41
	15	19 37 48	21 40 1	23 30 24	1 32 38	3 30 54	5 33 8	7 31 24	9 33 38	11 35 51	13 34 7	15 36 21	17 34 37
	16	19 41 44	21 43 58	23 34 21	1 36 34	3 34 51	5 37 4	7 35 21	9 37 34	11 39 47	13 38 4	15 40 17	17 38 34
	17	19 45 41	21 47 54	23 38 18	1 40 31	3 38 47	5 41 1	7 39 17	9 41 31	11 43 44	13 42 1	15 44 14	17 42 30
	18	19 49 37	21 51 51	23 42 14	1 44 27	3 42 44	5 44 57	7 43 14	9 45 27	11 47 40	13 45 57	15 48 10	17 46 27
	19	19 53 34	21 55 47	23 46 11	1 48 24	3 46 41	5 48 54	7 47 11	9 49 24	11 51 37	13 49 54	15 52 7	17 50 24
	20	19 57 31	21 59 44	23 50 7	1 52 20	3 50 37	5 52 50	7 51 7	9 53 20	11 55 34	13 53 50	15 56 3	17 54 20
	21	20 1 27	22 3 40	23 54 4	1 56 17	3 54 34	5 56 47	7 55 4	9 57 17	11 59 30	13 57 47	16 0 0	17 58 17
	22	20 5 24	22 7 37	23 58 0	2 0 14	3 58 30	6 0 44	7 59 0	10 1 13	12 3 27	14 1 43	16 3 57	18 2 13
	23	20 9 20	22 11 33	0 1 57	2 4 10	4 2 27	6 4 40	8 2 57	10 5 10	12 7 23	14 5 40	16 7 53	18 6 10
	24	20 13 17	22 15 30	0 5 53	2 8 7	4 6 23	6 8 37	8 6 53	10 9 7	12 11 20	14 9 36	16 11 50	18 10 6
	25	20 17 13	22 19 27	0 9 50	2 12 3	4 10 20	6 12 33	8 10 50	10 13 3	12 15 16	14 13 33	16 15 46	18 14 3
	26	20 21 10	22 23 23	0 13 47	2 16 0	4 14 16	6 16 30	8 14 46	10 17 0	12 19 13	14 17 30	16 19 43	18 18 0
	27	20 25 6	22 27 20	0 17 43	2 19 56	4 18 13	6 20 26	8 18 43	10 20 56	12 23 9	14 21 26	16 23 39	18 21 56
	28	20 29 3	22 31 16	0 21 40	2 23 53	4 22 10	6 24 23	8 22 40	10 24 53	12 27 6	14 25 23	16 27 36	18 25 53
	29	20 33 0		0 25 36	2 27 49	4 26 6	6 28 19	8 26 36	10 28 49	12 31 3	14 29 19	16 31 32	18 29 49
	30	20 36 56		0 29 33	2 31 46	4 30 3	6 32 16	8 30 33	10 32 46	12 34 59	14 33 16	16 35 29	18 33 46
	31	20 40 53		0 33 29		4 33 59		8 34 29	10 36 42		14 37 12		18 37 42

		1	2	3	4	5	6	7	8	9	10	11	12
1930	1	18 41 39	20 43 52	22 34 16	0 36 29	2 34 46	4 36 59	6 35 16	8 37 29	10 39 42	12 37 59	14 40 12	16 38 29
	2	18 45 35	20 47 49	22 38 12	0 40 25	2 38 42	4 40 55	6 39 12	8 41 25	10 43 39	12 41 55	14 44 8	16 42 25
	3	18 49 32	20 51 45	22 42 9	0 44 22	2 42 39	4 44 52	6 43 9	8 45 22	10 47 35	12 45 52	14 48 5	16 46 22
	4	18 53 29	20 55 42	22 46 5	0 48 19	2 46 35	4 48 48	6 47 5	8 49 18	10 51 32	12 49 48	14 52 2	16 50 18
	5	18 57 25	20 59 38	22 50 2	0 52 15	2 50 32	4 52 45	6 51 2	8 53 15	10 55 28	12 53 45	14 55 58	16 54 15
	6	19 1 22	21 3 35	22 53 58	0 56 12	2 54 28	4 56 42	6 54 58	8 57 12	10 59 25	12 57 41	14 59 55	16 58 11
	7	19 5 18	21 7 31	22 57 55	1 0 8	2 58 25	5 0 38	6 58 55	9 1 8	11 3 21	13 1 38	15 3 51	17 2 8
	8	19 9 15	21 11 28	23 1 52	1 4 5	3 2 22	5 4 35	7 2 51	9 5 5	11 7 18	13 5 35	15 7 48	17 6 4
	9	19 13 11	21 15 25	23 5 48	1 8 1	3 6 18	5 8 31	7 6 48	9 9 1	11 11 14	13 9 31	15 11 44	17 10 1
	10	19 17 8	21 19 21	23 9 45	1 11 58	3 10 15	5 12 28	7 10 45	9 12 58	11 15 11	13 13 28	15 15 41	17 13 58
	11	19 21 4	21 23 18	23 13 41	1 15 54	3 14 11	5 16 24	7 14 41	9 16 54	11 19 8	13 17 24	15 19 37	17 17 54
	12	19 25 1	21 27 14	23 17 38	1 19 51	3 18 8	5 20 21	7 18 38	9 20 51	11 23 4	13 21 21	15 23 34	17 21 51
	13	19 28 58	21 31 11	23 21 34	1 23 48	3 22 4	5 24 17	7 22 34	9 24 47	11 27 1	13 25 17	15 27 31	17 25 47
	14	19 32 54	21 35 7	23 25 31	1 27 44	3 26 1	5 28 14	7 26 31	9 28 44	11 30 57	13 29 14	15 31 27	17 29 44
	15	19 36 51	21 39 4	23 29 27	1 31 41	3 29 57	5 32 11	7 30 27	9 32 41	11 34 54	13 33 10	15 35 24	17 33 40
	16	19 40 47	21 43 0	23 33 24	1 35 37	3 33 54	5 36 7	7 34 24	9 36 37	11 38 50	13 37 7	15 39 20	17 37 37
	17	19 44 44	21 46 57	23 37 21	1 39 34	3 37 50	5 40 4	7 38 20	9 40 34	11 42 47	13 41 4	15 43 17	17 41 33
	18	19 48 40	21 50 54	23 41 17	1 43 30	3 41 47	5 44 0	7 42 17	9 44 30	11 46 43	13 45 0	15 47 13	17 45 30
	19	19 52 37	21 54 50	23 45 14	1 47 27	3 45 44	5 47 57	7 46 14	9 48 27	11 50 40	13 48 57	15 51 10	17 49 27
	20	19 56 33	21 58 47	23 49 10	1 51 23	3 49 40	5 51 53	7 50 10	9 52 23	11 54 37	13 52 53	15 55 6	17 53 23
	21	20 0 30	22 2 43	23 53 7	1 55 20	3 53 37	5 55 50	7 54 7	9 56 20	11 58 33	13 56 50	15 59 3	17 57 20
	22	20 4 27	22 6 40	23 57 3	1 59 17	3 57 33	5 59 47	7 58 3	10 0 16	12 2 30	14 0 46	16 3 0	18 1 16
	23	20 8 23	22 10 36	0 1 0	2 3 13	4 1 30	6 3 43	8 2 0	10 4 13	12 6 26	14 4 43	16 6 56	18 5 13
	24	20 12 20	22 14 33	0 4 56	2 7 10	4 5 26	6 7 40	8 5 56	10 8 10	12 10 23	14 8 39	16 10 53	18 9 9
	25	20 16 16	22 18 29	0 8 53	2 11 6	4 9 23	6 11 36	8 9 53	10 12 6	12 14 19	14 12 36	16 14 49	18 13 6
	26	20 20 13	22 22 26	0 12 50	2 15 3	4 13 19	6 15 33	8 13 49	10 16 3	12 18 16	14 16 33	16 18 46	18 17 3
	27	20 24 9	22 26 23	0 16 46	2 18 59	4 17 16	6 19 29	8 17 46	10 19 59	12 22 12	14 20 29	16 22 42	18 20 59
	28	20 28 6	22 30 19	0 20 43	2 22 56	4 21 13	6 23 26	8 21 43	10 23 56	12 26 9	14 24 26	16 26 39	18 24 56
	29	20 32 2		0 24 39	2 26 52	4 25 9	6 27 22	8 25 39	10 27 52	12 30 6	14 28 22	16 30 35	18 28 52
	30	20 35 59		0 28 36	2 30 49	4 29 6	6 31 19	8 29 36	10 31 49	12 34 2	14 32 19	16 34 32	18 32 49
	31	20 39 56		0 32 32		4 33 2		8 33 32	10 35 45		14 36 15		18 36 45
1931	1	18 40 42	20 42 55	22 33 19	0 35 32	2 33 48	4 36 2	6 34 18	8 36 32	10 38 45	12 37 1	14 39 15	16 37 31
	2	18 44 38	20 46 51	22 37 15	0 39 28	2 37 45	4 39 58	6 38 15	8 40 28	10 42 41	12 40 58	14 43 11	16 41 28
	3	18 48 35	20 50 48	22 41 12	0 43 25	2 41 41	4 43 55	6 42 11	8 44 25	10 46 38	12 44 55	14 47 8	16 45 24
	4	18 52 31	20 54 45	22 45 8	0 47 21	2 45 38	4 47 51	6 46 8	8 48 21	10 50 34	12 48 51	14 51 4	16 49 21
	5	18 56 28	20 58 41	22 49 5	0 51 18	2 49 34	4 51 48	6 50 4	8 52 18	10 54 31	12 52 48	14 55 1	16 53 18
	6	19 0 24	21 2 38	22 53 1	0 55 14	2 53 31	4 55 44	6 54 1	8 56 14	10 58 28	12 56 44	14 58 57	16 57 14
	7	19 4 21	21 6 35	22 56 58	0 59 11	2 57 28	4 59 41	6 57 58	9 0 11	11 2 24	13 0 41	15 2 54	17 1 11
	8	19 8 18	21 10 31	23 0 54	1 3 7	3 1 24	5 3 37	7 1 54	9 4 7	11 6 21	13 4 37	15 6 50	17 5 7
	9	19 12 14	21 14 27	23 4 51	1 7 4	3 5 21	5 7 34	7 5 51	9 8 4	11 10 17	13 8 34	15 10 47	17 9 4
	10	19 16 11	21 18 24	23 8 47	1 11 1	3 9 17	5 11 31	7 9 47	9 12 1	11 14 14	13 12 30	15 14 44	17 13 0
	11	19 20 7	21 22 20	23 12 44	1 14 57	3 13 14	5 15 27	7 13 44	9 15 57	11 18 10	13 16 27	15 18 10	17 16 57
	12	19 24 4	21 26 17	23 16 40	1 18 54	3 17 10	5 19 24	7 17 40	9 19 54	11 22 7	13 20 24	15 22 37	17 20 53
	13	19 28 0	21 30 14	23 20 37	1 22 50	3 21 7	5 23 20	7 21 37	9 23 50	11 26 3	13 24 20	15 26 33	17 24 50
	14	19 31 57	21 34 10	23 24 34	1 26 47	3 25 3	5 27 17	7 25 34	9 27 47	11 30 0	13 28 17	15 30 30	17 28 47
	15	19 35 53	21 38 7	23 28 30	1 30 43	3 29 0	5 31 13	7 29 30	9 31 43	11 33 57	13 32 13	15 34 26	17 32 43
	16	19 39 50	21 42 3	23 32 27	1 34 40	3 32 57	5 35 10	7 33 27	9 35 40	11 37 53	13 36 10	15 38 23	17 36 40
	17	19 43 47	21 46 0	23 36 23	1 38 36	3 36 53	5 39 6	7 37 23	9 39 37	11 41 50	13 40 6	15 42 20	17 40 36
	18	19 47 43	21 49 56	23 40 20	1 42 33	3 40 50	5 43 3	7 41 20	9 43 33	11 45 46	13 44 3	15 46 16	17 44 33
	19	19 51 40	21 53 53	23 44 16	1 46 30	3 44 46	5 47 0	7 45 16	9 47 30	11 49 43	13 47 59	15 50 13	17 48 29
	20	19 55 36	21 57 49	23 48 13	1 50 26	3 48 43	5 50 56	7 49 13	9 51 26	11 53 39	13 51 56	15 54 9	17 52 26
	21	19 59 33	22 1 46	23 52 10	1 54 23	3 52 39	5 54 53	7 53 9	9 55 23	11 57 36	13 55 52	15 58 6	17 56 22
	22	20 3 29	22 5 43	23 56 6	1 58 19	3 56 36	5 58 49	7 57 6	9 59 19	12 1 32	13 59 49	16 2 8	18 0 19
	23	20 7 26	22 9 39	0 0 3	2 2 16	4 0 33	6 2 46	8 1 3	10 3 16	12 5 29	14 3 46	16 5 59	18 4 16
	24	20 11 22	22 13 36	0 3 59	2 6 12	4 4 29	6 6 42	8 4 59	10 7 12	12 9 26	14 7 42	16 9 55	18 8 12
	25	20 15 19	22 17 32	0 7 55	2 10 9	4 8 26	6 10 39	8 8 56	10 11 9	12 13 22	14 11 39	16 13 52	18 12 9
	26	20 19 16	22 21 29	0 11 53	2 14 5	4 12 22	6 14 36	8 12 52	10 15 5	12 17 19	14 15 35	16 17 49	18 16 5
	27	20 23 12	22 25 25	0 15 49	2 18 2	4 16 19	6 18 32	8 16 49	10 19 2	12 21 15	14 19 32	16 21 45	18 20 2
	28	20 27 9	22 29 22	0 19 45	2 21 59	4 20 15	6 22 29	8 20 45	10 22 59	12 25 12	14 23 28	16 25 42	18 23 58
	29	20 31 5		0 23 42	2 25 55	4 24 12	6 26 25	8 24 42	10 26 55	12 29 8	14 27 25	16 29 38	18 27 55
	30	20 35 2		0 27 39	2 29 52	4 28 8	6 30 22	8 28 38	10 30 52	12 33 5	14 31 21	16 33 35	18 31 52
	31	20 38 58		0 31 35		4 32 5		8 32 35	10 34 48		14 35 18		18 35 48
1932	1	18 39 45	20 41 58	22 36 18	0 38 31	2 36 48	4 39 1	6 37 18	8 39 31	10 41 44	12 40 1	14 42 14	16 40 31
	2	18 43 41	20 45 55	22 40 15	0 42 28	2 40 44	4 42 58	6 41 14	8 43 28	10 45 41	12 43 58	14 46 11	16 44 27
	3	18 47 38	20 49 51	22 44 11	0 46 24	2 44 41	4 46 54	6 45 11	8 47 24	10 49 38	12 47 54	14 50 7	16 48 24
	4	18 51 34	20 53 48	22 48 8	0 50 21	2 48 37	4 50 51	6 49 8	8 51 21	10 53 34	12 51 51	14 54 4	16 52 21
	5	18 55 31	20 57 44	22 52 4	0 54 17	2 52 34	4 54 47	6 53 4	8 55 17	10 57 31	12 55 47	14 58 0	16 56 17
	6	18 59 27	21 1 41	22 56 1	0 58 14	2 56 31	4 58 44	6 57 1	8 59 14	11 1 27	12 59 44	15 1 57	17 0 14
	7	19 3 24	21 5 37	22 59 57	1 2 10	3 0 27	5 2 40	7 0 57	9 3 10	11 5 24	13 3 40	15 5 54	17 4 10
	8	19 7 21	21 9 34	23 3 54	1 6 7	3 4 24	5 6 37	7 4 54	9 7 7	11 9 20	13 7 37	15 9 50	17 8 7
	9	19 11 17	21 13 30	23 7 50	1 10 4	3 8 20	5 10 34	7 8 50	9 11 4	11 13 17	13 11 33	15 13 47	17 12 3
	10	19 15 14	21 17 27	23 11 47	1 14 0	3 12 17	5 14 30	7 12 47	9 15 0	11 17 13	13 15 30	15 17 43	17 16 0
	11	19 19 10	21 21 24	23 15 44	1 17 57	3 16 13	5 18 27	7 16 43	9 18 57	11 21 10	13 19 27	15 21 40	17 19 57
	12	19 23 7	21 25 20	23 19 40	1 21 53	3 20 10	5 22 23	7 20 40	9 22 53	11 25 6	13 23 23	15 25 36	17 23 53
	13	19 27 3	21 29 17	23 23 37	1 25 50	3 24 7	5 26 20	7 24 37	9 26 50	11 29 3	13 27 20	15 29 33	17 27 49
	14	19 31 0	21 33 13	23 27 33	1 29 46	3 28 3	5 30 16	7 28 33	9 30 46	11 33 0	13 31 16	15 33 29	17 31 46
	15	19 34 56	21 37 10	23 31 30	1 33 43	3 32 0	5 34 13	7 32 30	9 34 43	11 36 56	13 35 13	15 37 26	17 35 43
	16	19 38 53	21 41 6	23 35 26	1 37 40	3 35 56	5 38 10	7 36 26	9 38 40	11 40 53	13 39 9	15 41 23	17 39 39
	17	19 42 50	21 45 3	23 39 23	1 41 36	3 39 53	5 42 6	7 40 23	9 42 36	11 44 49	13 43 6	15 45 19	17 43 36
	18	19 46 46	21 48 59	23 43 19	1 45 33	3 43 49	5 46 3	7 44 19	9 46 33	11 48 46	13 47 2	15 49 16	17 47 32
	19	19 50 43	21 52 56	23 47 16	1 49 29	3 47 46	5 49 59	7 48 16	9 50 29	11 52 42	13 50 59	15 53 12	17 51 29
	20	19 54 39	21 56 53	23 51 13	1 53 26	3 51 42	5 53 56	7 52 12	9 54 26	11 56 39	13 54 56	15 57 9	17 55 26
	21	19 58 36	22 0 49	23 55 9	1 57 22	3 53 39	5 57 52	7 56 9	9 58 22	12 0 35	13 58 52	16 1 5	17 59 22
	22	20 2 32	22 4 46	23 59 6	2 1 19	3 59 36	6 1 49	8 0 6	10 2 19	12 4 32	14 2 49	16 5 2	18 3 19
	23	20 6 29	22 8 42	0 3 2	2 5 15	4 3 32	6 5 45	8 4 2	10 6 15	12 8 29	14 6 45	16 8 58	18 7 15
	24	20 10 25	22 12 39	0 6 59	2 9 12	4 7 29	6 9 42	8 7 59	10 10 12	12 12 25	14 10 42	16 12 55	18 11 12
	25	20 14 22	22 16 35	0 10 55	2 13 9	4 11 25	6 13 39	8 11 55	10 14 9	12 16 22	14 14 38	16 16 52	18 15 8
	26	20 18 19	22 20 32	0 14 52	2 17 5	4 15 22	6 17 35	8 15 52	10 18 5	12 20 18	14 18 35	16 20 48	18 19 5
	27	20 22 15	22 24 28	0 18 48	2 21 2	4 19 18	6 21 32	8 19 48	10 22 2	12 24 15	14 22 31	16 24 45	18 23 1
	28	20 26 12	22 28 25	0 22 45	2 24 58	4 23 15	6 25 28	8 23 45	10 25 58	12 28 11	14 26 28	16 28 41	18 26 58
	29	20 30 8	22 32 22	0 26 42	2 28 55	4 27 11	6 29 25	8 27 42	10 29 55	12 32 8	14 30 25	16 32 38	18 30 55
	30	20 34 5		0 30 38	2 32 51	4 31 8	6 33 21	8 31 38	10 33 51	12 36 4	14 34 21	16 36 34	18 34 51
	31	20 38 1		0 34 35		4 35 5		8 35 35	10 37 48		14 38 18		18 38 47
1933	1	18 42 44	20 44 58	22 35 21	0 37 34	2 35 51	4 38 4	6 36 21	8 38 34	10 40 47	12 39 4	14 41 17	16 39 34
	2	18 46 41	20 48 54	22 39 18	0 41 31	2 39 47	4 42 1	6 40 17	8 42 31	10 44 44	12 43 1	14 45 14	16 43 30
	3	18 50 37	20 52 51	22 43 14	0 45 27	2 43 44	4 45 57	6 44 14	8 46 27	10 48 41	12 46 57	14 49 10	16 47 27
	4	18 54 34	20 56 47	22 47 11	0 49 24	2 47 41	4 49 54	6 48 11	8 50 24	10 52 37	12 50 54	14 53 7	16 51 24
	5	18 58 30	21 0 44	22 51 7	0 53 20	2 51 37	4 53 50	6 52 7	8 54 20	10 56 34	12 54 50	14 57 3	16 55 20
	6	19 2 27	21 4 40	22 55 4	0 57 17	2 55 34	4 57 47	6 56 4	8 58 17	11 0 30	12 58 47	15 1 0	16 59 17
	7	19 6 24	21 8 37	22 59 0	1 1 14	2 59 30	5 1 44	7 0 0	9 2 14	11 4 27	13 2 43	15 4 57	17 3 13
	8	19 10 20	21 12 33	23 2 57	1 5 10	3 3 27	5 5 40	7 3 57	9 6 10	11 8 23	13 6 40	15 8 53	17 7 10
	9	19 14 17	21 16 30	23 6 54	1 9 7	3 7 23	5 9 37	7 7 53	9 10 7	11 12 20	13 10 36	15 12 50	17 11 6
	10	19 18 13	21 20 27	23 10 50	1 13 3	3 11 20	5 13 33	7 11 50	9 14 3	11 16 16	13 14 33	15 16 46	17 15 3
	11	19 22 10	21 24 23	23 14 47	1 17 0	3 15 16	5 17 30	7 15 47	9 18 0	11 20 13	13 18 30	15 20 43	17 19 0
	12	19 26 6	21 28 20	23 18 43	1 20 56	3 19 13	5 21 26	7 19 43	9 21 56	11 24 10	13 22 26	15 24 39	17 22 56
	13	19 30 3	21 32 16	23 22 40	1 24 53	3 23 10	5 25 23	7 23 40	9 25 53	11 28 6	13 26 23	15 28 36	17 26 53
	14	19 34 0	21 36 13	23 26 36	1 28 49	3 27 6	5 29 19	7 27 36	9 29 49	11 32 3	13 30 19	15 32 32	17 30 49
	15	19 37 56	21 40 9	23 30 33	1 32 46	3 31 3	5 33 16	7 31 33	9 33 46	11 35 59	13 34 16	15 36 29	17 34 46
	16	19 41 53	21 44 6	23 34 29	1 36 43	3 34 59	5 37 13	7 35 29	9 37 43	11 39 56	13 38 12	15 40 26	17 38 42
	17	19 45 49	21 48 2	23 38 26	1 40 39	3 38 56	5 41 9	7 39 26	9 41 39	11 43 52	13 42 9	15 44 22	17 42 39
	18	19 49 45	21 51 59	23 42 23	1 44 36	3 42 52	5 45 6	7 43 22	9 45 36	11 47 49	13 46 5	15 48 19	17 46 35
	19	19 53 42	21 55 56	23 46 19	1 48 32	3 46 49	5 49 2	7 47 19	9 49 32	11 51 45	13 50 2	15 52 15	17 50 32
	20	19 57 39	21 59 52	23 50 16	1 52 29	3 50 45	5 52 59	7 51 16	9 53 29	11 55 42	13 53 59	15 56 12	17 54 29
	21	20 1 35	22 3 49	23 54 12	1 56 25	3 54 42	5 56 55	7 55 12	9 57 25	11 59 38	13 57 55	16 0 8	17 58 25
	22	20 5 32	22 7 45	23 58 9	2 0 22	3 58 39	6 0 52	7 59 9	10 1 22	12 3 35	14 1 52	16 4 5	18 2 22
	23	20 9 29	22 11 42	0 2 5	2 4 18	4 2 35	6 4 48	8 3 5	10 5 18	12 7 32	14 5 48	16 8 1	18 6 18
	24	20 13 25	22 15 38	0 6 2	2 8 15	4 6 32	6 8 45	8 7 2	10 9 15	12 11 28	14 9 45	16 11 58	18 10 15
	25	20 17 22	22 19 35	0 9 58	2 12 12	4 10 28	6 12 42	8 10 58	10 13 12	12 15 25	14 13 41	16 15 55	18 14 11
	26	20 21 18	22 23 31	0 13 55	2 16 8	4 14 25	6 16 38	8 14 55	10 17 8	12 19 21	14 17 38	16 19 51	18 18 8
	27	20 25 15	22 27 28	0 17 51	2 20 5	4 18 21	6 20 35	8 18 51	10 21 5	12 23 18	14 21 34	16 23 48	18 22 4
	28	20 29 11	22 31 25	0 21 48	2 24 1	4 22 18	6 24 31	8 22 48	10 25 1	12 27 14	14 25 31	16 27 44	18 26 1
	29	20 33 8		0 25 45	2 27 58	4 26 15	6 28 28	8 26 45	10 28 58	12 31 11	14 29 28	16 31 41	18 29 58
	30	20 37 4		0 29 41	2 31 54	4 30 11	6 32 24	8 30 41	10 32 54	12 35 8	14 33 24	16 35 37	18 33 54
	31	20 41 1		0 33 38		4 34 8		8 34 38	10 36 51		14 37 21		18 37 51

Year	Day	1	2	3	4	5	6	7	8	9	10	11	12
	1	18 41 47	20 44 1	22 34 24	0 36 37	2 34 54	4 37 7	6 35 24	8 37 37	10 39 50	12 38 7	14 40 20	16 38 37
	2	18 45 44	20 47 57	22 38 21	0 40 34	2 38 50	4 41 4	6 39 20	8 41 34	10 43 47	12 42 4	14 44 17	16 42 33
	3	18 49 40	20 51 54	22 42 17	0 44 30	2 42 47	4 45 0	6 43 17	8 45 30	10 47 44	12 46 0	14 48 13	16 46 30
	4	18 53 37	20 55 50	22 46 14	0 48 27	2 46 44	4 48 57	6 47 14	8 49 27	10 51 40	12 49 57	14 52 10	16 50 27
	5	18 57 33	20 59 47	22 50 10	0 52 23	2 50 40	4 52 53	6 51 10	8 53 23	10 55 37	12 53 53	14 56 6	16 54 23
	6	19 1 30	21 3 43	22 54 7	0 56 20	2 54 37	4 56 50	6 55 7	8 57 20	10 59 33	12 57 50	15 0 3	16 58 20
	7	19 5 27	21 7 40	22 58 3	1 0 17	2 58 33	5 0 47	6 59 3	9 1 17	11 3 30	13 1 46	15 4 0	17 2 16
	8	19 9 23	21 11 36	23 2 0	1 4 13	3 2 30	5 4 43	7 3 0	9 5 13	11 7 26	13 5 43	15 7 56	17 6 13
	9	19 13 20	21 15 33	23 5 57	1 8 10	3 6 26	5 8 40	7 6 56	9 9 10	11 11 23	13 9 39	15 11 53	17 10 9
	10	19 17 16	21 19 30	23 9 53	1 12 6	3 10 23	5 12 36	7 10 53	9 13 6	11 15 19	13 13 36	15 15 49	17 14 6
	11	19 21 13	21 23 26	23 13 50	1 16 3	3 14 19	5 16 33	7 14 49	9 17 3	11 19 16	13 17 33	15 19 46	17 18 2
	12	19 25 9	21 27 23	23 17 46	1 19 59	3 18 16	5 20 29	7 18 46	9 20 59	11 23 12	13 21 29	15 23 42	17 21 59
	13	19 29 6	21 31 19	23 21 43	1 23 56	3 22 13	5 24 26	7 22 43	9 24 56	11 27 9	13 25 26	15 27 39	17 25 56
	14	19 33 3	21 35 16	23 25 39	1 27 52	3 26 9	5 28 22	7 26 39	9 28 52	11 31 6	13 29 22	15 31 35	17 29 52
	15	19 36 59	21 39 12	23 29 36	1 31 49	3 30 6	5 32 19	7 30 36	9 32 49	11 35 2	13 33 19	15 35 32	17 33 49
	16	19 40 56	21 43 9	23 33 32	1 35 46	3 34 2	5 36 16	7 34 32	9 36 46	11 38 59	13 37 15	15 39 29	17 37 45
	17	19 44 52	21 47 5	23 37 29	1 39 42	3 37 59	5 40 12	7 38 29	9 40 42	11 42 55	13 41 12	15 43 25	17 41 42
	18	19 48 49	21 51 2	23 41 26	1 43 39	3 41 55	5 44 9	7 42 25	9 44 39	11 46 52	13 45 8	15 47 22	17 45 38
	19	19 52 45	21 54 59	23 45 22	1 47 35	3 45 52	5 48 5	7 46 22	9 48 35	11 50 48	13 49 5	15 51 18	17 49 35
	20	19 56 42	21 58 55	23 49 19	1 51 32	3 49 48	5 52 2	7 50 18	9 52 32	11 54 45	13 53 2	15 55 15	17 53 31
	21	20 0 38	22 2 52	23 53 15	1 55 28	3 53 45	5 55 58	7 54 15	9 56 28	11 58 41	13 56 58	15 59 11	17 57 28
	22	20 4 35	22 6 48	23 57 12	1 59 25	3 57 42	5 59 55	7 58 12	10 0 25	12 2 38	14 0 55	16 3 8	18 1 25
	23	20 8 32	22 10 45	0 1 8	2 3 21	4 1 38	6 3 51	8 2 8	10 4 21	12 6 35	14 4 51	16 7 4	18 5 21
	24	20 12 28	22 14 41	0 5 5	2 7 18	4 5 35	6 7 48	8 6 5	10 8 18	12 10 31	14 8 48	16 11 1	18 9 18
	25	20 16 25	22 18 38	0 9 1	2 11 15	4 9 31	6 11 45	8 10 1	10 12 15	12 14 28	14 12 44	16 14 58	18 13 14
	26	20 20 21	22 22 34	0 12 58	2 15 11	4 13 28	6 15 41	8 13 58	10 16 11	12 18 24	14 16 41	16 18 54	18 17 11
	27	20 24 18	22 26 31	0 16 55	2 19 8	4 17 24	6 19 38	8 17 54	10 20 8	12 22 21	14 20 37	16 22 51	18 21 7
	28	20 28 14	22 30 28	0 20 51	2 23 4	4 21 21	6 23 34	8 21 51	10 24 4	12 26 17	14 24 34	16 26 47	18 25 4
	29	20 32 11		0 24 48	2 27 1	4 25 17	6 27 31	8 25 48	10 28 1	12 30 14	14 28 31	16 30 44	18 29 1
	30	20 36 7		0 28 44	2 30 57	4 29 14	6 31 27	8 29 44	10 31 57	12 34 10	14 32 27	16 34 40	18 32 57
	31	20 40 4		0 32 41		4 33 11		8 33 41	10 35 54		14 36 24		18 36 54
	1	18 40 50	20 43 3	22 33 27	0 35 40	2 33 57	4 36 10	6 34 27	8 36 40	10 38 53	12 37 10	14 39 23	16 37 40
	2	18 44 47	20 47 0	22 37 24	0 39 37	2 37 53	4 40 7	6 38 23	8 40 37	10 42 50	12 41 6	14 43 20	16 41 36
	3	18 48 43	20 50 57	22 41 20	0 43 33	2 41 50	4 44 3	6 42 20	8 44 33	10 46 46	12 45 3	14 47 16	16 45 33
	4	18 52 40	20 54 53	22 45 17	0 47 30	2 45 46	4 48 0	6 46 16	8 48 30	10 50 43	12 49 0	14 51 13	16 49 29
	5	18 56 36	20 58 50	22 49 13	0 51 26	2 49 43	4 51 56	6 50 13	8 52 26	10 54 39	12 52 56	14 55 9	16 53 26
	6	19 0 33	21 2 46	22 53 10	0 55 23	2 53 40	4 55 53	6 54 10	8 56 23	10 58 36	12 56 53	14 59 6	16 57 23
	7	19 4 30	21 6 43	22 57 6	0 59 20	2 57 36	4 59 49	6 58 6	9 0 20	11 2 33	13 0 49	15 3 2	17 1 19
	8	19 8 26	21 10 39	23 1 3	1 3 16	3 1 33	5 3 46	7 2 3	9 4 16	11 6 29	13 4 46	15 6 59	17 5 16
	9	19 12 23	21 14 26	23 4 59	1 7 13	3 5 30	5 7 43	7 6 0	9 8 13	11 10 26	13 8 42	15 10 55	17 9 12
	10	19 16 19	21 18 32	23 8 56	1 11 9	3 9 26	5 11 39	7 9 56	9 12 9	11 14 22	13 12 39	15 14 52	17 13 9
	11	19 20 16	21 22 29	23 12 53	1 15 6	3 13 22	5 15 36	7 13 52	9 16 6	11 18 19	13 16 35	15 18 49	17 17 5
	12	19 24 12	21 26 26	23 16 49	1 19 2	3 17 19	5 19 32	7 17 49	9 20 2	11 22 15	13 20 32	15 22 45	17 21 2
	13	19 28 9	21 30 22	23 20 46	1 22 59	3 21 16	5 23 29	7 21 45	9 23 59	11 26 12	13 24 29	15 26 42	17 24 58
	14	19 32 5	21 34 19	23 24 42	1 26 55	3 25 12	5 27 25	7 25 42	9 27 55	11 30 8	13 28 25	15 30 38	17 28 55
	15	19 36 2	21 38 15	23 28 39	1 30 52	3 29 9	5 31 22	7 29 39	9 31 52	11 34 5	13 32 22	15 34 35	17 32 52
	16	19 39 59	21 42 12	23 32 35	1 34 48	3 33 5	5 35 18	7 33 35	9 35 48	11 38 2	13 36 18	15 38 31	17 36 48
	17	19 43 55	21 46 8	23 36 32	1 38 45	3 37 2	5 39 15	7 37 32	9 39 45	11 41 58	13 40 15	15 42 28	17 40 45
	18	19 47 52	21 50 5	23 40 28	1 42 42	3 40 58	5 43 12	7 41 28	9 43 42	11 45 55	13 44 11	15 46 25	17 44 41
	19	19 51 48	21 54 1	23 44 25	1 46 38	3 44 55	5 47 8	7 45 25	9 47 38	11 49 51	13 48 8	15 50 21	17 48 38
	20	19 55 45	21 57 58	23 48 22	1 50 35	3 48 51	5 51 5	7 49 21	9 51 35	11 53 48	13 52 4	15 54 18	17 52 34
	21	19 59 41	22 1 55	23 52 18	1 54 31	3 52 48	5 55 1	7 53 18	9 55 31	11 57 44	13 56 1	15 58 14	17 56 31
	22	20 3 38	22 5 51	23 56 15	1 58 28	3 56 44	5 58 58	7 57 15	9 59 28	12 1 41	13 59 58	16 2 11	18 0 27
	23	20 7 34	22 9 48	0 0 11	2 2 25	4 0 41	6 2 54	8 1 11	10 3 24	12 5 37	14 3 54	16 6 7	18 4 24
	24	20 11 31	22 13 44	0 4 8	2 6 21	4 4 38	6 6 51	8 5 8	10 7 21	12 9 34	14 7 51	16 10 4	18 8 21
	25	20 15 28	22 17 41	0 8 4	2 10 17	4 8 34	6 10 47	8 9 4	10 11 17	12 13 31	14 11 47	16 14 0	18 12 17
	26	20 19 24	22 21 37	0 12 1	2 14 14	4 12 31	6 14 44	8 13 1	10 15 14	12 17 27	14 15 44	16 17 57	18 16 14
	27	20 23 21	22 25 34	0 15 57	2 18 11	4 16 27	6 18 41	8 16 57	10 19 11	12 21 24	14 19 40	16 21 54	18 20 10
	28	20 27 17	22 29 30	0 19 54	2 22 7	4 20 24	6 22 37	8 20 54	10 23 7	12 25 20	14 23 37	16 25 50	18 24 7
	29	20 31 14		0 23 51	2 26 4	4 24 20	6 26 34	8 24 50	10 27 4	12 29 17	14 27 33	16 29 47	18 28 3
	30	20 35 10		0 27 47	2 30 0	4 28 17	6 30 30	8 28 47	10 31 0	12 33 13	14 31 30	16 33 43	18 32 0
	31	20 39 7		0 31 44		4 32 13		8 32 44	10 34 57		14 35 26		18 35 56
	1	18 39 53	20 42 6	22 36 26	0 38 40	2 36 56	4 39 9	6 37 26	8 39 39	10 41 53	12 40 9	14 42 22	16 40 39
	2	18 43 50	20 46 3	22 40 23	0 42 36	2 40 53	4 43 6	6 41 23	8 43 36	10 45 49	12 44 6	14 46 19	16 44 36
	3	18 47 46	20 49 59	22 44 20	0 46 33	2 44 49	4 47 3	6 45 19	8 47 32	10 49 46	12 48 2	14 50 15	16 48 32
	4	18 51 43	20 53 56	22 48 16	0 50 29	2 48 46	4 50 59	6 49 16	8 51 29	10 53 42	12 51 59	14 54 12	16 52 29
	5	18 55 39	20 57 53	22 52 13	0 54 26	2 52 42	4 54 56	6 53 12	8 55 26	10 57 39	12 55 55	14 58 9	16 56 25
	6	18 59 36	21 1 49	22 56 9	0 58 22	2 56 39	4 58 52	6 57 9	8 59 22	11 1 35	12 59 52	15 2 5	17 0 22
	7	19 3 32	21 5 46	23 0 6	1 2 19	3 0 35	5 2 49	7 1 6	9 3 19	11 5 32	13 3 49	15 6 2	17 4 18
	8	19 7 29	21 9 42	23 4 2	1 6 15	3 4 32	5 6 45	7 5 2	9 7 15	11 9 28	13 7 45	15 9 58	17 8 15
	9	19 11 26	21 13 39	23 7 59	1 10 12	3 8 29	5 10 42	7 8 59	9 11 12	11 13 25	13 11 42	15 13 55	17 12 12
	10	19 15 22	21 17 35	23 11 55	1 14 9	3 12 25	5 14 39	7 12 55	9 15 8	11 17 22	13 15 38	15 17 51	17 16 8
	11	19 19 19	21 21 32	23 15 52	1 18 5	3 16 22	5 18 35	7 16 52	9 19 5	11 21 18	13 19 35	15 21 48	17 20 5
	12	19 23 15	21 25 28	23 19 48	1 22 2	3 20 18	5 22 32	7 20 48	9 23 2	11 25 15	13 23 31	15 25 44	17 24 1
	13	19 27 12	21 29 25	23 23 45	1 25 58	3 24 15	5 26 28	7 24 45	9 26 58	11 29 11	13 27 28	15 29 41	17 27 58
	14	19 31 8	21 33 22	23 27 42	1 29 55	3 28 11	5 30 25	7 28 41	9 30 55	11 33 8	13 31 24	15 33 38	17 31 54
	15	19 35 5	21 37 18	23 31 38	1 33 51	3 32 8	5 34 21	7 32 38	9 34 51	11 37 4	13 35 21	15 37 34	17 35 51
	16	19 39 1	21 41 15	23 35 35	1 37 48	3 36 5	5 38 18	7 36 35	9 38 48	11 41 1	13 39 17	15 41 31	17 39 47
	17	19 42 58	21 45 11	23 39 31	1 41 44	3 40 1	5 42 14	7 40 31	9 42 44	11 44 57	13 43 14	15 45 27	17 43 44
	18	19 46 55	21 49 8	23 43 28	1 45 41	3 43 58	5 46 11	7 44 28	9 46 41	11 48 54	13 47 11	15 49 24	17 47 41
	19	19 50 50	21 53 4	23 47 24	1 49 38	3 47 54	5 50 7	7 48 24	9 50 37	11 52 51	13 51 7	15 53 20	17 51 37
	20	19 54 48	21 57 0	23 51 21	1 53 34	3 51 51	5 54 4	7 52 21	9 54 34	11 56 47	13 55 4	15 57 17	17 55 34
	21	19 58 44	22 0 57	23 55 17	1 57 31	3 55 47	5 58 1	7 56 17	9 58 31	12 0 44	13 59 0	16 1 13	17 59 30
	22	20 2 41	22 4 54	23 59 14	2 1 27	3 59 44	6 1 57	8 0 14	10 2 27	12 4 40	14 2 57	16 5 10	18 3 27
	23	20 6 38	22 8 51	0 3 11	2 5 24	4 3 40	6 5 54	8 4 10	10 6 24	12 8 37	14 6 53	16 9 7	18 7 23
	24	20 10 34	22 12 47	0 7 7	2 9 20	4 7 37	6 9 50	8 8 7	10 10 20	12 12 33	14 10 50	16 13 3	18 11 20
	25	20 14 30	22 16 44	0 11 4	2 13 17	4 11 34	6 13 47	8 12 4	10 14 17	12 16 30	14 14 46	16 17 0	18 15 16
	26	20 18 27	22 20 40	0 15 0	2 17 13	4 15 30	6 17 43	8 16 0	10 18 13	12 20 26	14 18 43	16 20 56	18 19 13
	27	20 22 24	22 24 37	0 18 57	2 21 10	4 19 27	6 21 40	8 19 57	10 22 10	12 24 23	14 22 40	16 24 53	18 23 10
	28	20 26 20	22 28 33	0 22 53	2 25 7	4 23 23	6 25 36	8 23 53	10 26 6	12 28 20	14 26 36	16 28 49	18 27 6
	29	20 30 17	22 32 31	0 26 50	2 29 3	4 27 20	6 29 33	8 27 50	10 30 3	12 32 16	14 30 33	16 32 46	18 31 3
	30	20 34 13		0 30 46	2 33 0	4 31 16	6 33 30	8 31 46	10 34 0	12 36 13	14 34 29	16 36 42	18 34 59
	31	20 38 10		0 34 43		4 35 13		8 35 43	10 37 56		14 38 26		18 38 56
	1	18 42 52	20 45 6	22 35 29	0 37 42	2 35 59	4 38 12	6 36 29	8 38 42	10 40 55	12 39 12	14 41 25	16 39 42
	2	18 46 49	20 49 2	22 39 26	0 41 39	2 39 55	4 42 9	6 40 25	8 42 39	10 44 52	12 43 8	14 45 22	16 43 38
	3	18 50 45	20 52 59	22 43 22	0 45 35	2 43 52	4 46 5	6 44 22	8 46 35	10 48 48	12 47 5	14 49 18	16 47 35
	4	18 54 42	20 56 55	22 47 19	0 49 32	2 47 49	4 50 2	6 48 18	8 50 32	10 52 45	12 51 1	14 53 15	16 51 31
	5	18 58 39	21 0 52	22 51 15	0 53 28	2 51 45	4 53 58	6 52 15	8 54 28	10 56 41	12 54 58	14 57 11	16 55 28
	6	19 2 35	21 4 48	22 55 12	0 57 25	2 55 42	4 57 55	6 56 12	8 58 25	11 0 38	12 58 55	15 1 8	16 59 24
	7	19 6 32	21 8 45	22 59 8	1 1 22	2 59 38	5 1 51	7 0 8	9 2 21	11 4 35	13 2 51	15 5 4	17 3 21
	8	19 10 28	21 12 42	23 3 5	1 5 18	3 3 35	5 5 48	7 4 5	9 6 18	11 8 31	13 6 48	15 9 1	17 7 18
	9	19 14 25	21 16 38	23 7 2	1 9 15	3 7 31	5 9 45	7 8 1	9 10 15	11 12 28	13 10 44	15 12 57	17 11 14
	10	19 18 21	21 20 35	23 10 58	1 13 11	3 11 28	5 13 41	7 11 58	9 14 11	11 16 24	13 14 41	15 16 54	17 15 11
	11	19 22 18	21 24 31	23 14 55	1 17 8	3 15 24	5 17 38	7 15 54	9 18 8	11 20 21	13 18 37	15 20 51	17 19 7
	12	19 26 14	21 28 28	23 18 51	1 21 4	3 19 21	5 21 34	7 19 51	9 22 4	11 24 17	13 22 34	15 24 47	17 23 4
	13	19 30 11	21 32 24	23 22 48	1 25 1	3 23 18	5 25 31	7 23 48	9 26 1	11 28 14	13 26 30	15 28 44	17 27 0
	14	19 34 8	21 36 21	23 26 44	1 28 57	3 27 14	5 29 27	7 27 44	9 29 57	11 32 10	13 30 27	15 32 40	17 30 57
	15	19 38 4	21 40 17	23 30 41	1 32 54	3 31 11	5 33 24	7 31 41	9 33 54	11 36 7	13 34 24	15 36 37	17 34 53
	16	19 42 1	21 44 14	23 34 37	1 36 51	3 35 7	5 37 20	7 35 37	9 37 50	11 40 4	13 38 20	15 40 33	17 38 50
	17	19 45 57	21 48 10	23 38 34	1 40 47	3 39 4	5 41 17	7 39 34	9 41 47	11 44 0	13 42 17	15 44 30	17 42 47
	18	19 49 54	21 52 7	23 42 31	1 44 44	3 43 0	5 45 14	7 43 30	9 45 44	11 47 57	13 46 14	15 48 26	17 46 43
	19	19 53 50	21 56 4	23 46 27	1 48 40	3 46 57	5 49 10	7 47 27	9 49 40	11 51 53	13 50 10	15 52 23	17 50 40
	20	19 57 47	22 0 0	23 50 24	1 52 37	3 50 53	5 53 7	7 51 23	9 53 37	11 55 50	13 54 6	15 56 20	17 54 36
	21	20 1 43	22 3 57	23 54 20	1 56 33	3 54 50	5 57 3	7 55 20	9 57 33	11 59 46	13 58 3	16 0 16	17 58 33
	22	20 5 40	22 7 53	23 58 17	2 0 30	3 58 47	6 1 0	7 59 17	10 1 30	12 3 43	14 2 0	16 4 13	18 2 29
	23	20 9 37	22 11 50	0 2 13	2 4 26	4 2 43	6 4 56	8 3 13	10 5 26	12 7 39	14 5 56	16 8 9	18 6 26
	24	20 13 33	22 15 46	0 6 10	2 8 23	4 6 40	6 8 53	8 7 10	10 9 23	12 11 36	14 9 53	16 12 6	18 10 23
	25	20 17 30	22 19 43	0 10 6	2 12 20	4 10 36	6 12 49	8 11 6	10 13 19	12 15 33	14 13 49	16 16 2	18 14 19
	26	20 21 26	22 23 39	0 14 3	2 16 16	4 14 33	6 16 46	8 15 3	10 17 16	12 19 29	14 17 46	16 19 59	18 18 16
	27	20 25 23	22 27 36	0 18 0	2 20 13	4 18 29	6 20 43	8 18 59	10 21 12	12 23 26	14 21 42	16 23 55	18 22 12
	28	20 29 19	22 31 33	0 21 56	2 24 9	4 22 26	6 24 39	8 22 56	10 25 9	12 27 22	14 25 39	16 27 52	18 26 9
	29	20 33 16		0 25 53	2 28 6	4 26 22	6 28 36	8 26 52	10 29 6	12 31 19	14 29 35	16 31 49	18 30 5
	30	20 37 13		0 29 49	2 32 2	4 30 19	6 32 32	8 30 49	10 33 2	12 35 15	14 33 32	16 35 45	18 34 2
	31	20 41 9		0 33 46		4 34 16		8 34 46	10 36 59		14 37 28		18 37 58

Year	Day	1	2	3	4	5	6	7	8	9	10	11	12
1938	1	18 41 55	20 44 8	22 34 32	0 36 45	2 35 1	4 37 15	6 35 32	8 37 45	10 39 58	12 38 14	14 40 28	16 38 44
	2	18 45 52	20 48 5	22 38 28	0 40 41	2 38 58	4 41 11	6 39 28	8 41 41	10 43 54	12 42 11	14 44 24	16 42 41
	3	18 49 48	20 52 1	22 42 25	0 44 38	2 42 55	4 45 8	6 43 25	8 45 38	10 47 51	12 46 7	14 48 21	16 46 37
	4	18 53 45	20 55 58	22 46 22	0 48 35	2 46 51	4 49 4	6 47 21	8 49 34	10 51 47	12 50 4	14 52 17	16 50 34
	5	18 57 41	20 59 54	22 50 18	0 52 31	2 50 48	4 53 1	6 51 18	8 53 31	10 55 44	12 54 1	14 56 14	16 54 30
	6	19 1 38	21 3 51	22 54 14	0 56 28	2 54 44	4 56 57	6 55 14	8 57 27	10 59 41	12 57 57	15 0 10	16 58 27
	7	19 5 34	21 7 48	22 58 11	1 0 24	2 58 41	5 0 54	6 59 11	9 1 24	11 3 37	13 1 54	15 4 7	17 2 24
	8	19 9 31	21 11 44	23 2 8	1 4 21	3 2 37	5 4 51	7 3 7	9 5 21	11 7 34	13 5 50	15 8 3	17 6 20
	9	19 13 27	21 15 41	23 6 4	1 8 17	3 6 34	5 8 47	7 7 4	9 9 17	11 11 30	13 9 47	15 12 0	17 10 17
	10	19 17 24	21 19 37	23 10 1	1 12 14	3 10 30	5 12 44	7 11 0	9 13 14	11 15 27	13 13 43	15 15 57	17 14 13
	11	19 21 21	21 23 34	23 13 57	1 16 10	3 14 27	5 16 40	7 14 57	9 17 10	11 19 23	13 17 40	15 19 53	17 18 10
	12	19 25 17	21 27 31	23 17 54	1 20 7	3 18 24	5 20 37	7 18 54	9 21 7	11 23 20	13 21 36	15 23 50	17 22 6
	13	19 29 14	21 31 27	23 21 50	1 24 3	3 22 20	5 24 33	7 22 50	9 25 3	11 27 16	13 25 33	15 27 46	17 26 3
	14	19 33 10	21 35 23	23 25 47	1 28 0	3 26 17	5 28 30	7 26 47	9 29 0	11 31 13	13 29 30	15 31 43	17 29 59
	15	19 37 7	21 39 20	23 29 43	1 31 57	3 30 13	5 32 26	7 30 43	9 32 56	11 35 10	13 33 26	15 35 39	17 33 56
	16	19 41 3	21 43 17	23 33 40	1 35 53	3 34 10	5 36 23	7 34 40	9 36 52	11 39 6	13 37 22	15 39 36	17 37 53
	17	19 45 0	21 47 13	23 37 37	1 39 50	3 38 6	5 40 20	7 38 36	9 40 49	11 43 3	13 41 19	15 43 32	17 41 49
	18	19 48 56	21 51 10	23 41 33	1 43 46	3 42 3	5 44 16	7 42 33	9 44 46	11 46 59	13 45 16	15 47 29	17 45 46
	19	19 52 53	21 55 6	23 45 30	1 47 43	3 45 59	5 48 13	7 46 29	9 48 43	11 50 56	13 49 12	15 51 26	17 49 42
	20	19 56 50	21 59 3	23 49 26	1 51 39	3 49 56	5 52 9	7 50 26	9 52 39	11 54 52	13 53 9	15 55 22	17 53 39
	21	20 0 46	22 3 0	23 53 23	1 55 36	3 53 53	5 56 6	7 54 23	9 56 36	11 58 49	13 57 5	15 59 19	17 57 35
	22	20 4 43	22 6 56	23 57 19	1 59 32	3 57 49	6 0 2	7 58 19	10 0 32	12 2 46	14 1 2	16 3 15	18 1 32
	23	20 8 39	22 10 52	0 1 16	2 3 29	4 1 46	6 3 59	8 2 16	10 4 29	12 6 42	14 4 59	16 7 12	18 5 28
	24	20 12 36	22 14 49	0 5 12	2 7 26	4 5 42	6 7 55	8 6 12	10 8 25	12 10 39	14 8 55	16 11 8	18 9 25
	25	20 16 32	22 18 46	0 9 9	2 11 22	4 9 39	6 11 52	8 10 9	10 12 22	12 14 35	14 12 52	16 15 5	18 13 22
	26	20 20 29	22 22 42	0 13 6	2 15 19	4 13 35	6 15 49	8 14 5	10 16 19	12 18 32	14 16 48	16 19 1	18 17 18
	27	20 24 25	22 26 39	0 17 2	2 19 15	4 17 32	6 19 45	8 18 2	10 20 15	12 22 28	14 20 45	16 22 58	18 21 15
	28	20 28 22	22 30 35	0 20 59	2 23 12	4 21 28	6 23 42	8 21 58	10 24 12	12 26 25	14 24 41	16 26 55	18 25 11
	29	20 32 19		0 24 55	2 27 8	4 25 25	6 27 38	8 25 55	10 28 8	12 30 22	14 28 38	16 30 51	18 29 8
	30	20 36 15		0 28 52	2 31 5	4 29 22	6 31 35	8 29 52	10 32 5	12 34 18	14 32 34	16 34 48	18 33 4
	31	20 40 12		0 32 48		4 33 18		8 33 48	10 36 1		14 36 31		18 37 1
1939	1	18 40 57	20 43 11	22 33 34	0 35 47	2 34 4	4 36 17	6 34 34	8 36 47	10 39 0	12 37 17	14 39 30	16 37 47
	2	18 44 54	20 47 7	22 37 31	0 39 44	2 38 0	4 40 14	6 38 30	8 40 44	10 42 57	12 41 13	14 43 27	16 41 43
	3	18 48 51	20 51 4	22 41 27	0 43 40	2 41 57	4 44 10	6 42 27	8 44 40	10 46 53	12 45 10	14 47 23	16 45 40
	4	18 52 47	20 55 0	22 45 24	0 47 37	2 45 54	4 48 7	6 46 24	8 48 37	10 50 50	12 59 6	14 51 20	16 49 36
	5	18 56 44	20 58 57	22 49 20	0 51 34	2 49 50	4 52 3	6 50 20	8 52 33	10 54 46	12 53 3	14 55 16	16 53 33
	6	19 0 40	21 2 54	22 53 17	0 55 30	2 53 47	4 56 0	6 54 17	8 56 30	10 58 43	12 57 0	14 59 13	16 57 29
	7	19 4 37	21 6 50	22 57 14	0 59 27	2 57 43	4 59 56	6 58 13	9 0 26	11 2 40	13 0 56	15 3 9	17 1 26
	8	19 8 33	21 10 47	23 1 10	1 3 23	3 1 40	5 3 53	7 2 10	9 4 23	11 6 36	13 4 53	15 7 6	17 5 22
	9	19 12 30	21 14 44	23 5 7	1 7 20	3 5 36	5 7 50	7 6 6	9 8 20	11 10 33	13 8 49	15 11 2	17 9 19
	10	19 16 26	21 18 40	23 9 3	1 11 16	3 9 33	5 11 46	7 10 3	9 12 16	11 14 29	13 12 46	15 14 59	17 13 16
	11	19 20 23	21 22 36	23 13 0	1 15 13	3 13 29	5 15 43	7 13 59	9 16 13	11 18 26	13 16 42	15 18 55	17 17 12
	12	19 24 20	21 26 33	23 16 56	1 19 9	3 17 26	5 19 39	7 17 56	9 20 9	11 22 22	13 20 39	15 22 52	17 21 9
	13	19 28 16	21 30 29	23 20 53	1 23 6	3 21 23	5 23 36	7 21 53	9 24 6	11 26 19	13 24 35	15 26 49	17 25 5
	14	19 32 13	21 34 26	23 24 49	1 27 3	3 25 19	5 27 32	7 25 49	9 28 2	11 30 15	13 28 32	15 30 45	17 29 2
	15	19 36 9	21 38 22	23 28 46	1 30 59	3 29 16	5 31 29	7 29 46	9 31 59	11 34 12	13 32 29	15 34 42	17 32 58
	16	19 40 6	21 42 19	23 32 43	1 34 56	3 33 12	5 35 25	7 33 42	9 35 55	11 38 9	13 36 25	15 38 38	17 36 55
	17	19 44 2	21 46 16	23 36 39	1 38 52	3 37 9	5 39 22	7 37 39	9 39 52	11 42 5	13 40 22	15 42 35	17 40 52
	18	19 47 59	21 50 12	23 40 36	1 42 49	3 41 5	5 43 19	7 41 35	9 43 49	11 46 2	13 44 18	15 46 31	17 44 48
	19	19 51 55	21 54 9	23 44 32	1 46 45	3 45 2	5 47 15	7 45 32	9 47 45	11 49 58	13 48 15	15 50 28	17 48 45
	20	19 55 52	21 58 5	23 48 29	1 50 42	3 48 58	5 51 12	7 49 28	9 51 42	11 53 55	13 52 11	15 54 24	17 52 41
	21	19 59 49	22 2 2	23 52 25	1 54 38	3 52 55	5 55 8	7 53 25	9 55 38	11 57 51	13 56 8	15 58 21	17 56 38
	22	20 3 45	22 5 58	23 56 22	1 58 35	3 56 52	5 59 5	7 57 22	9 59 35	12 1 48	14 0 4	16 2 18	18 0 34
	23	20 7 42	22 9 55	0 0 18	2 2 31	4 0 48	6 3 1	8 1 18	10 3 31	12 5 44	14 4 1	16 6 14	18 4 31
	24	20 11 38	22 13 51	0 4 15	2 6 28	4 4 45	6 6 58	8 5 15	10 7 28	12 9 41	14 7 58	16 10 11	18 8 27
	25	20 15 35	22 17 48	0 8 11	2 10 25	4 8 41	6 10 55	8 9 11	10 11 24	12 13 38	14 11 54	16 14 7	18 12 24
	26	20 19 31	22 21 45	0 12 8	2 14 21	4 12 38	6 14 51	8 13 8	10 15 21	12 17 34	14 15 51	16 18 4	18 16 21
	27	20 23 28	22 25 41	0 16 5	2 18 18	4 16 34	6 18 48	8 17 4	10 19 18	12 21 31	14 19 47	16 22 0	18 20 17
	28	20 27 24	22 29 38	0 20 1	2 22 14	4 20 31	6 22 44	8 21 1	10 23 14	12 25 27	14 23 44	16 25 57	18 24 14
	29	20 31 21		0 23 58	2 26 11	4 24 27	6 26 41	8 24 57	10 27 11	12 29 24	14 27 40	16 29 53	18 28 10
	30	20 35 18		0 27 54	2 30 7	4 28 24	6 30 37	8 28 54	10 31 7	12 33 20	14 31 37	16 33 50	18 32 7
	31	20 39 14		0 31 51		4 32 21		8 32 51	10 35 4		14 35 33		18 36 3
1940	1	18 40 0	20 42 13	22 36 33	0 38 46	2 37 3	4 39 16	6 37 33	8 39 46	10 41 59	12 40 16	14 42 29	16 40 46
	2	18 43 56	20 46 10	22 40 30	0 42 43	2 40 59	4 43 13	6 41 29	8 43 43	10 45 56	12 44 12	14 46 25	16 44 42
	3	18 47 53	20 50 6	22 44 26	0 46 39	2 44 56	4 47 9	6 45 26	8 47 39	10 49 52	12 48 9	14 50 22	16 48 39
	4	18 51 50	20 54 3	22 48 23	0 50 36	2 48 53	4 51 6	6 49 22	8 51 36	10 53 49	12 52 5	14 54 19	16 52 35
	5	18 55 46	20 57 59	22 52 19	0 54 33	2 52 49	4 55 2	6 53 19	8 55 32	10 57 45	12 56 2	14 58 15	16 56 32
	6	18 59 43	21 1 56	22 56 16	0 58 29	2 56 46	4 58 59	6 57 16	8 59 29	11 1 42	12 59 58	15 2 12	17 0 28
	7	19 3 39	21 5 52	23 0 13	1 2 26	3 0 42	5 2 55	7 1 12	9 3 25	11 5 38	13 3 55	15 6 8	17 4 25
	8	19 7 36	21 9 49	23 4 9	1 6 22	3 4 39	5 6 52	7 5 9	9 7 22	11 9 35	13 7 52	15 10 5	17 8 21
	9	19 11 32	21 13 46	23 8 6	1 10 19	3 8 35	5 10 49	7 9 5	9 11 18	11 13 32	13 11 48	15 14 1	17 12 18
	10	19 15 29	21 17 42	23 12 2	1 14 15	3 12 32	5 14 45	7 13 2	9 15 15	11 17 28	13 15 45	15 17 58	17 16 15
	11	19 19 25	21 21 39	23 15 59	1 18 12	3 16 28	5 18 42	7 16 58	9 19 12	11 21 25	13 19 41	15 21 54	17 20 11
	12	19 23 22	21 25 35	23 19 55	1 22 8	3 20 25	5 22 38	7 20 55	9 23 8	11 25 21	13 23 38	15 25 51	17 24 8
	13	19 27 19	21 29 32	23 23 52	1 26 5	3 24 22	5 26 35	7 24 51	9 27 5	11 29 18	13 27 34	15 29 48	17 28 4
	14	19 31 15	21 33 28	23 27 48	1 30 1	3 28 18	5 30 31	7 28 48	9 31 1	11 33 14	13 31 31	15 33 44	17 32 1
	15	19 35 12	21 37 25	23 31 45	1 33 58	3 32 15	5 34 28	7 32 45	9 34 58	11 37 11	13 35 27	15 37 41	17 35 57
	16	19 39 8	21 41 21	23 35 41	1 37 55	3 36 11	5 38 24	7 36 41	9 38 54	11 41 7	13 39 24	15 41 37	17 39 54
	17	19 43 5	21 45 18	23 39 38	1 41 51	3 40 8	5 42 21	7 40 38	9 41 51	11 45 4	13 43 21	15 45 34	17 43 50
	18	19 47 1	21 49 15	23 43 35	1 45 48	3 44 4	5 46 18	7 44 34	9 46 47	11 49 1	13 47 17	15 49 30	17 47 47
	19	19 50 58	21 53 11	23 47 31	1 49 44	3 48 1	5 50 14	7 48 31	9 50 44	11 52 57	13 51 14	15 53 27	17 51 44
	20	19 54 54	21 57 8	23 51 28	1 53 41	3 51 57	5 54 11	7 52 27	9 54 41	11 56 54	13 55 10	15 57 23	17 55 40
	21	19 58 51	22 1 4	23 55 24	1 57 37	3 55 54	5 58 7	7 56 24	9 58 37	12 0 50	13 59 7	16 1 20	17 59 37
	22	20 2 48	22 5 1	23 59 21	2 1 34	3 59 51	6 2 4	8 0 20	10 2 34	12 4 47	14 3 3	16 5 17	18 3 33
	23	20 6 44	22 8 57	0 3 17	2 5 30	4 3 47	6 6 0	8 4 17	10 6 30	12 8 43	14 7 0	16 9 13	18 7 30
	24	20 10 41	22 12 54	0 7 14	2 9 27	4 7 44	6 9 57	8 8 14	10 10 27	12 12 40	14 10 56	16 13 10	18 11 26
	25	20 14 37	22 16 50	0 11 10	2 13 24	4 11 40	6 13 53	8 12 10	10 14 23	12 16 36	14 14 53	16 17 6	18 15 23
	26	20 18 34	22 20 47	0 15 7	2 17 20	4 15 37	6 17 50	8 16 7	10 18 20	12 20 33	14 18 50	16 21 3	18 19 19
	27	20 22 30	22 24 44	0 19 4	2 21 17	4 19 33	6 21 47	8 20 3	10 22 16	12 24 30	14 22 46	16 24 59	18 23 16
	28	20 26 27	22 28 40	0 23 0	2 25 13	4 23 30	6 25 43	8 24 0	10 26 13	12 28 26	14 26 43	16 28 56	18 27 13
	29	20 30 23	22 32 37	0 26 57	2 29 10	4 27 26	6 29 40	8 27 56	10 30 10	12 32 23	14 30 39	16 32 52	18 31 9
	30	20 34 20		0 30 53	2 33 6	4 31 23	6 33 36	8 31 53	10 34 6	12 36 19	14 34 36	16 36 49	18 35 6
	31	20 38 17		0 34 50		4 35 20		8 35 49	10 38 3		14 38 32		18 39 2
1941	1	18 42 59	20 45 12	22 35 36	0 37 49	2 36 5	4 38 18	6 36 35	8 38 48	10 41 2	12 39 18	14 41 31	16 39 48
	2	18 46 55	20 49 9	22 39 32	0 41 45	2 40 2	4 42 15	6 40 32	8 42 45	10 44 58	12 43 15	14 45 28	16 43 44
	3	18 50 52	20 53 5	22 43 29	0 45 42	2 43 58	4 46 12	6 44 28	8 46 41	10 48 55	12 47 11	14 49 24	16 47 41
	4	18 54 48	20 57 2	22 47 25	0 49 38	2 47 55	4 50 8	6 48 25	8 50 38	10 52 51	12 51 8	14 53 21	16 51 38
	5	18 58 45	21 0 58	22 51 22	0 53 35	2 51 51	4 54 5	6 52 21	8 54 35	10 56 48	12 55 4	14 57 17	16 55 34
	6	19 2 42	21 4 55	22 55 18	0 57 31	2 55 48	4 58 1	6 56 18	8 58 31	11 0 44	12 59 1	15 1 14	16 59 31
	7	19 6 38	21 8 51	22 59 15	1 1 28	2 59 45	5 1 58	7 0 14	9 2 28	11 4 41	13 2 57	15 5 11	17 3 27
	8	19 10 35	21 12 48	23 3 11	1 5 25	3 3 41	5 5 54	7 4 11	9 6 24	11 8 37	13 6 54	15 9 7	17 7 24
	9	19 14 31	21 16 44	23 7 8	1 9 21	3 7 38	5 9 51	7 8 8	9 10 21	11 12 34	13 10 50	15 13 4	17 11 20
	10	19 18 28	21 20 41	23 11 5	1 13 18	3 11 34	5 13 47	7 12 4	9 14 17	11 16 30	13 14 47	15 17 0	17 15 17
	11	19 22 24	21 24 38	23 15 1	1 17 14	3 15 31	5 17 44	7 16 1	9 18 14	11 20 27	13 18 44	15 20 57	17 19 13
	12	19 26 21	21 28 34	23 18 58	1 21 11	3 19 27	5 21 41	7 19 57	9 22 10	11 24 24	13 22 40	15 24 53	17 23 10
	13	19 30 17	21 32 31	23 22 54	1 25 7	3 23 24	5 25 37	7 23 54	9 26 7	11 28 20	13 26 37	15 28 50	17 27 7
	14	19 34 14	21 36 27	23 26 51	1 29 4	3 27 20	5 29 34	7 27 50	9 30 4	11 32 17	13 30 33	15 32 46	17 31 3
	15	19 38 11	21 40 24	23 30 47	1 33 0	3 31 17	5 33 30	7 31 47	9 34 0	11 36 13	13 34 30	15 36 43	17 35 0
	16	19 42 7	21 44 20	23 34 44	1 36 57	3 35 14	5 37 27	7 35 43	9 37 57	11 40 10	13 38 26	15 40 40	17 38 56
	17	19 46 4	21 48 17	23 38 40	1 40 53	3 39 10	5 41 23	7 39 40	9 41 53	11 44 6	13 42 23	15 44 36	17 42 53
	18	19 50 0	21 52 13	23 42 37	1 44 50	3 43 7	5 45 20	7 43 37	9 45 50	11 48 3	13 46 19	15 48 33	17 46 49
	19	19 53 57	21 56 10	23 46 33	1 48 47	3 47 3	5 49 16	7 47 33	9 49 46	11 51 59	13 50 16	15 52 29	17 50 46
	20	19 57 54	22 0 7	23 50 30	1 52 43	3 51 0	5 53 13	7 51 30	9 53 43	11 55 56	13 54 13	15 56 26	17 54 42
	21	20 1 50	22 4 3	23 54 27	1 56 40	3 54 56	5 57 10	7 55 26	9 57 39	11 59 53	13 58 9	16 0 22	17 58 39
	22	20 5 47	22 8 0	23 58 23	2 0 36	3 58 53	6 1 6	7 59 23	10 1 36	12 3 49	14 2 6	16 4 19	18 2 36
	23	20 9 43	22 11 56	0 2 20	2 4 33	4 2 49	6 5 3	8 3 19	10 5 33	12 7 46	14 6 2	16 8 15	18 6 32
	24	20 13 40	22 15 53	0 6 16	2 8 29	4 6 46	6 8 59	8 7 16	10 9 29	12 11 42	14 9 59	16 12 12	18 10 29
	25	20 17 36	22 19 49	0 10 13	2 12 26	4 10 43	6 12 56	8 11 12	10 13 26	12 15 39	14 13 55	16 16 9	18 14 25
	26	20 21 33	22 23 46	0 14 9	2 16 22	4 14 39	6 16 52	8 15 9	10 17 22	12 19 35	14 17 52	16 20 5	18 18 22
	27	20 25 29	22 27 42	0 18 6	2 20 19	4 18 36	6 20 49	8 19 6	10 21 19	12 23 32	14 21 48	16 24 2	18 22 18
	28	20 29 26	22 31 39	0 22 2	2 24 16	4 22 32	6 24 45	8 23 2	10 25 15	12 27 28	14 25 45	16 27 58	18 26 15
	29	20 33 22		0 25 59	2 28 12	4 26 29	6 28 42	8 26 59	10 29 12	12 31 25	14 29 42	16 31 55	18 30 11
	30	20 37 19		0 29 56	2 32 9	4 30 25	6 32 39	8 30 55	10 33 8	12 35 22	14 33 38	16 35 51	18 34 8
	31	20 41 15		0 33 52		4 34 22		8 34 52	10 37 5		14 37 35		18 38 5

Year	Day	1	2	3	4	5	6	7	8	9	10	11	12
1942	1	18 42 1	20 44 14	22 34 38	0 36 51	2 35 8	4 37 21	6 35 38	8 37 51	10 40 4	12 38 20	14 40 34	16 38 50
	2	18 45 58	20 48 11	22 38 34	0 40 48	2 39 4	4 41 17	6 39 34	8 41 47	10 44 0	12 42 17	14 44 30	16 42 47
	3	18 49 54	20 52 8	22 42 31	0 44 44	2 43 1	4 45 14	6 43 31	8 45 44	10 47 57	12 46 14	14 48 27	16 46 43
	4	18 53 51	20 56 4	22 56 28	0 48 41	2 46 57	4 49 10	6 47 27	8 49 40	10 51 54	12 50 10	14 52 23	16 50 40
	5	18 57 47	21 0 1	22 50 24	0 52 37	2 50 54	4 53 7	6 51 24	8 53 37	10 55 50	12 54 7	14 56 20	16 54 36
	6	19 1 44	21 3 57	22 54 21	0 56 34	2 54 50	4 57 4	6 55 20	8 57 33	10 59 47	13 58 3	15 0 16	16 58 33
	7	19 5 40	21 7 54	22 58 17	1 0 30	2 58 47	5 1 0	6 59 17	9 1 30	11 3 43	13 2 0	15 4 13	17 2 30
	8	19 9 37	21 11 50	23 2 14	1 4 27	3 2 43	5 4 57	7 3 13	9 5 27	11 7 40	13 5 56	15 8 9	17 6 26
	9	19 13 34	21 15 47	23 6 10	1 8 23	3 6 40	5 8 53	7 7 10	9 9 23	11 11 36	13 9 53	15 12 6	17 10 23
	10	19 17 30	21 19 43	23 10 7	1 12 20	3 10 37	5 12 50	7 11 6	9 13 20	11 15 33	13 13 49	15 16 3	17 14 19
	11	19 21 27	21 23 40	23 14 3	1 16 17	3 14 33	5 16 46	7 15 3	9 17 16	11 19 29	13 17 46	15 19 59	17 18 16
	12	19 25 23	21 27 36	23 18 0	1 20 13	3 18 30	5 20 43	7 19 0	9 21 13	11 23 26	13 21 43	15 23 56	17 22 12
	13	19 29 20	21 31 33	23 21 57	1 24 10	3 22 26	5 24 39	7 22 56	9 25 9	11 27 23	13 25 39	15 27 52	17 26 9
	14	19 33 16	21 35 30	23 25 53	1 28 6	3 26 23	5 28 36	7 26 53	9 29 6	11 31 19	13 29 36	15 31 49	17 30 5
	15	19 37 13	21 39 26	23 29 50	1 32 3	3 30 19	5 32 33	7 30 49	9 33 2	11 35 16	13 33 32	15 35 45	17 34 2
	16	19 41 9	21 43 23	23 33 46	1 35 59	3 34 16	5 36 29	7 34 46	9 36 59	11 39 12	13 37 29	15 39 42	17 37 59
	17	19 45 6	21 47 19	23 37 43	1 39 56	3 38 12	5 40 26	7 38 42	9 40 56	11 43 9	13 41 25	15 43 38	17 41 55
	18	19 49 3	21 51 16	23 41 39	1 43 52	3 42 9	5 44 22	7 42 39	9 44 52	11 47 5	13 45 22	15 47 35	17 45 52
	19	19 52 59	21 55 12	23 45 36	1 47 49	3 46 6	5 48 19	7 46 36	9 48 49	11 51 2	13 49 18	15 51 32	17 49 48
	20	19 56 56	21 59 9	23 49 32	1 51 45	3 50 2	5 52 15	7 50 32	9 52 45	11 54 58	13 53 15	15 55 28	17 53 45
	21	20 0 52	22 3 5	23 53 29	1 55 42	3 53 59	5 56 12	7 54 29	9 56 42	11 58 55	13 57 12	15 59 25	17 57 41
	22	20 4 49	22 7 2	23 57 25	1 59 39	3 57 55	6 0 8	7 58 25	10 0 38	12 2 51	14 1 8	16 3 21	18 1 38
	23	20 8 45	22 10 59	0 1 22	2 3 35	4 1 52	6 4 5	8 2 22	10 4 35	12 6 48	14 5 5	16 7 18	18 5 35
	24	20 12 42	22 14 55	0 5 19	2 7 32	4 5 48	6 8 2	8 6 18	10 8 31	12 10 45	14 9 1	16 11 14	18 9 31
	25	20 16 38	22 18 52	0 9 15	2 11 28	4 9 45	6 11 58	8 10 15	10 12 28	12 14 41	14 12 58	16 15 11	18 13 28
	26	20 20 35	22 22 48	0 13 12	2 15 25	4 13 41	6 15 55	8 14 11	10 16 25	12 18 38	14 16 54	16 19 7	18 17 24
	27	20 24 32	22 26 45	0 17 8	2 19 21	4 17 38	6 19 51	8 18 8	10 20 21	12 22 34	14 20 51	16 23 4	18 21 21
	28	20 28 28	22 30 41	0 21 5	2 23 18	4 21 35	6 23 48	8 22 5	10 24 18	12 26 31	14 24 47	16 27 1	18 25 17
	29	20 32 25		0 25 1	2 27 14	4 25 31	6 27 44	8 26 1	10 28 14	12 30 27	14 28 44	16 30 57	18 29 14
	30	20 36 21		0 28 58	2 31 11	4 29 28	6 31 41	8 29 58	10 32 11	12 34 24	14 32 40	16 34 54	18 33 10
	31	20 40 18		0 32 54		4 33 24		8 33 54	10 36 7		14 36 37		18 37 7
1943	1	18 41 4	20 43 17	22 33 40	0 35 53	2 34 10	4 36 23	6 34 40	8 36 53	10 39 6	12 37 23	14 39 36	16 37 53
	2	18 45 0	20 47 13	22 37 37	0 39 50	2 38 7	4 40 20	6 38 36	8 40 50	10 43 3	12 41 19	14 43 33	16 41 49
	3	18 48 57	20 51 10	22 41 33	0 43 46	2 42 3	4 44 16	6 42 33	8 44 46	10 46 59	12 45 16	14 47 29	16 45 46
	4	18 52 53	20 55 6	22 45 30	0 47 43	2 46 0	4 48 13	6 46 30	8 48 43	10 50 56	12 49 13	14 51 26	16 49 42
	5	18 56 50	20 59 3	22 49 26	0 51 40	2 49 56	4 52 9	6 50 26	8 52 39	10 54 53	12 53 9	14 55 22	16 53 39
	6	19 0 46	21 3 0	22 53 23	0 55 36	2 53 53	4 56 6	6 54 23	8 56 36	10 58 49	12 57 6	14 59 19	16 57 35
	7	19 4 43	21 6 56	22 57 20	0 59 33	2 57 49	5 0 3	6 58 19	9 0 32	11 2 46	13 1 2	15 3 15	17 1 33
	8	19 8 39	21 10 53	23 1 16	1 3 29	3 1 46	5 3 59	7 2 16	9 4 29	11 6 42	13 4 59	15 7 12	17 5 29
	9	19 12 36	21 14 49	23 5 13	1 7 26	3 5 42	5 7 56	7 6 12	9 8 26	11 10 39	13 8 55	15 11 8	17 9 25
	10	19 16 33	21 18 46	23 9 9	1 11 22	3 9 39	5 11 52	7 10 9	9 12 22	11 14 36	13 12 52	15 15 5	17 13 22
	11	19 20 29	21 22 42	23 13 6	1 15 19	3 13 36	5 15 49	7 14 5	9 16 19	11 18 32	13 16 48	15 19 2	17 17 18
	12	19 24 26	21 26 39	23 17 2	1 19 15	3 17 32	5 19 45	7 18 2	9 20 15	11 22 28	13 20 45	15 22 58	17 21 15
	13	19 28 22	21 30 35	23 20 59	1 23 12	3 21 29	5 23 42	7 21 59	9 24 12	11 26 25	13 24 41	15 26 55	17 25 11
	14	19 32 19	21 34 32	23 24 55	1 27 9	3 25 25	5 27 38	7 25 55	9 28 8	11 30 21	13 28 38	15 30 51	17 29 8
	15	19 36 15	21 38 29	23 28 52	1 31 5	3 29 22	5 31 35	7 29 52	9 32 5	11 34 18	13 32 35	15 34 48	17 33 4
	16	19 40 12	21 42 25	23 32 49	1 35 2	3 33 18	5 35 32	7 33 48	9 36 1	11 38 15	13 36 31	15 38 44	17 37 1
	17	19 44 8	21 46 22	23 36 45	1 38 58	3 37 15	5 39 28	7 37 45	9 39 58	11 42 11	13 40 28	15 42 41	17 40 58
	18	19 48 5	21 50 18	23 40 42	1 42 55	3 41 11	5 43 25	7 41 41	9 43 55	11 46 8	13 44 24	15 46 37	17 44 55
	19	19 52 2	21 54 15	23 44 38	1 46 51	3 45 8	5 47 21	7 45 38	9 47 51	11 50 4	13 48 21	15 50 34	17 48 51
	20	19 55 58	21 58 11	23 48 35	1 50 48	3 49 4	5 51 18	7 49 34	9 51 48	11 54 1	13 52 17	15 54 31	17 52 47
	21	19 59 55	22 2 8	23 52 31	1 54 44	3 53 1	5 55 14	7 53 31	9 55 44	11 57 57	13 56 14	15 58 27	17 56 44
	22	20 3 51	22 6 4	23 56 28	1 58 41	3 56 58	5 59 11	7 57 28	9 59 41	12 1 54	14 0 10	16 2 24	18 0 40
	23	20 7 48	22 10 1	0 0 24	2 2 38	4 0 54	6 3 7	8 1 24	10 3 37	12 5 50	14 4 7	16 6 20	18 4 37
	24	20 11 44	22 13 57	0 4 21	2 6 34	4 4 51	6 7 4	8 5 21	10 7 34	12 9 47	14 8 4	16 10 17	18 8 33
	25	20 15 41	22 17 54	0 8 18	2 10 31	4 8 47	6 11 1	8 9 17	10 11 30	12 13 44	14 12 0	16 14 13	18 12 30
	26	20 19 37	22 21 51	0 12 14	2 14 27	4 12 44	6 14 57	8 13 14	10 15 27	12 17 40	14 15 57	16 18 10	18 16 27
	27	20 23 34	22 25 47	0 16 11	2 18 24	4 16 40	6 18 54	8 17 10	10 19 24	12 21 37	14 19 53	16 22 6	18 20 24
	28	20 27 31	22 29 44	0 20 7	2 22 20	4 20 37	6 22 50	8 21 7	10 23 20	12 25 33	14 23 50	16 26 3	18 24 20
	29	20 31 27		0 24 4	2 26 17	4 24 34	6 26 47	8 25 3	10 27 17	12 29 30	14 27 46	16 30 0	18 28 16
	30	20 35 24		0 28 0	2 30 13	4 28 30	6 30 43	8 29 0	10 31 14	12 33 26	14 31 43	16 33 56	18 32 13
	31	20 39 20		0 31 57		4 32 27		8 32 57	10 35 10		14 35 39		18 36 9
1944	1	18 40 6	20 42 20	22 36 39	0 38 52	2 37 9	4 39 22	6 37 39	8 39 52	10 42 5	12 40 22	14 42 35	16 40 52
	2	18 44 3	20 46 13	22 40 36	0 42 49	2 41 6	4 43 19	6 41 35	8 43 49	10 46 2	12 44 18	14 46 32	16 44 48
	3	18 47 59	20 50 12	22 44 32	0 46 46	2 45 2	4 47 15	6 45 32	8 47 45	10 49 58	12 48 15	14 50 28	16 48 45
	4	18 51 56	20 54 9	22 48 29	0 50 42	2 48 59	4 51 12	6 49 29	8 51 42	10 53 55	12 52 12	14 54 25	16 52 41
	5	18 55 52	20 58 5	22 52 25	0 54 39	2 52 55	4 55 8	6 53 25	8 55 38	10 57 52	12 56 8	14 58 21	16 56 38
	6	18 59 49	21 2 2	22 56 22	0 58 35	2 56 52	4 59 5	6 57 22	8 59 35	11 1 48	13 0 5	15 2 18	17 0 35
	7	19 3 45	21 5 59	23 0 19	1 2 32	3 0 48	5 3 2	7 1 18	9 3 32	11 5 45	13 4 1	15 6 14	17 4 31
	8	19 7 42	21 9 55	23 4 16	1 6 28	3 4 45	5 6 58	7 5 15	9 7 28	11 9 41	13 7 58	15 10 11	17 8 28
	9	19 11 38	21 13 52	23 8 12	1 10 25	3 8 41	5 10 55	7 9 11	9 11 25	11 13 38	13 11 54	15 14 8	17 12 24
	10	19 15 35	21 17 48	23 12 8	1 14 21	3 12 38	5 14 51	7 13 8	9 15 21	11 17 34	13 15 51	15 18 4	17 16 21
	11	19 19 32	21 21 45	23 16 5	1 18 18	3 16 35	5 18 48	7 17 5	9 19 18	11 21 31	13 19 47	15 22 1	17 20 17
	12	19 23 28	21 25 41	23 20 1	1 22 14	3 20 31	5 22 44	7 21 1	9 23 14	11 25 27	13 23 44	15 25 57	17 24 14
	13	19 27 25	21 29 38	23 23 58	1 26 11	3 24 28	5 26 41	7 24 58	9 27 11	11 29 24	13 27 41	15 29 54	17 28 10
	14	19 31 21	21 33 34	23 27 54	1 30 8	3 28 24	5 30 37	7 28 54	9 31 7	11 33 21	13 31 37	15 33 50	17 32 7
	15	19 35 18	21 37 31	23 31 51	1 34 4	3 32 21	5 34 34	7 32 51	9 35 4	11 37 17	13 35 34	15 37 47	17 36 4
	16	19 39 14	21 41 28	23 35 48	1 38 1	3 36 17	5 38 31	7 36 47	9 39 1	11 41 14	13 39 30	15 41 43	17 40 0
	17	19 43 11	21 45 24	23 39 44	1 41 57	3 40 14	5 42 27	7 40 44	9 42 57	11 45 10	13 43 27	15 45 40	17 43 57
	18	19 47 7	21 49 21	23 43 41	1 45 54	3 44 10	5 46 24	7 44 40	9 46 54	11 49 7	13 47 23	15 49 37	17 47 53
	19	19 51 4	21 53 18	23 47 37	1 49 50	3 48 7	5 50 20	7 48 37	9 50 50	11 53 3	13 51 20	15 53 33	17 51 50
	20	19 55 0	21 57 14	23 51 34	1 53 47	3 52 4	5 54 17	7 52 34	9 54 47	11 57 0	13 55 16	15 57 30	17 55 46
	21	19 58 57	22 1 10	23 55 30	1 57 43	3 56 0	5 58 13	7 56 30	9 58 43	12 0 56	13 59 13	16 1 26	17 59 43
	22	20 2 51	22 5 7	23 59 27	2 1 40	3 59 57	5 2 10	8 0 27	10 2 40	12 4 53	14 3 10	16 5 23	18 3 39
	23	20 6 50	22 9 3	0 3 23	2 5 37	4 3 53	6 6 6	8 4 23	10 6 36	12 8 50	14 7 6	16 9 20	18 7 36
	24	20 10 47	22 13 0	0 7 20	2 9 33	4 7 50	6 10 3	8 8 20	10 10 33	12 12 46	14 11 3	16 13 16	18 11 33
	25	20 14 43	22 16 57	0 11 17	2 13 30	4 11 46	6 14 0	8 12 16	10 14 29	12 16 43	14 14 59	16 17 12	18 15 29
	26	20 18 40	22 20 53	0 15 13	2 17 26	4 15 43	6 17 56	8 16 13	10 18 26	12 20 39	14 18 56	16 21 9	18 19 26
	27	20 22 36	22 24 50	0 19 10	2 21 23	4 19 39	6 21 53	8 20 9	10 22 23	12 24 36	14 22 52	16 25 6	18 23 22
	28	20 26 33	22 28 46	0 23 6	2 25 19	4 23 36	6 25 49	8 24 6	10 26 19	12 28 32	14 26 49	16 29 2	18 27 19
	29	20 30 30	22 32 43	0 27 3	2 29 16	4 27 33	6 29 46	8 28 3	10 30 16	12 32 29	14 30 45	16 32 59	18 31 15
	30	20 34 26		0 30 59	2 33 12	4 31 29	6 33 42	8 31 59	10 34 12	12 36 25	14 34 42	16 36 55	18 35 12
	31	20 38 23		0 34 56		4 35 26		8 35 56	10 38 9		14 38 39		18 39 9
1945	1	18 43 5	20 45 18	22 35 42	0 37 55	2 36 12	4 38 25	6 36 42	8 38 55	10 41 8	12 39 25	14 41 38	16 39 54
	2	18 47 2	20 49 15	22 39 38	0 41 52	2 40 8	4 42 21	6 40 38	8 42 51	10 45 5	12 43 21	14 45 34	16 43 51
	3	18 50 58	20 53 11	22 43 35	0 45 48	2 44 5	4 46 18	6 44 35	8 46 48	10 49 1	12 47 18	14 49 31	16 47 48
	4	18 54 55	20 57 8	22 47 31	0 49 45	2 48 1	4 50 14	6 48 31	8 50 44	10 52 58	12 51 14	14 53 27	16 51 44
	5	18 58 51	21 1 5	22 51 28	0 53 41	2 51 58	4 54 11	6 52 28	8 54 41	10 56 54	12 55 11	14 57 24	16 55 41
	6	19 2 48	21 5 1	22 55 25	0 57 38	2 55 54	4 58 8	6 56 24	8 58 38	11 0 51	12 59 7	15 1 20	16 59 38
	7	19 6 44	21 8 58	22 59 21	1 1 34	2 59 51	5 2 4	7 0 21	9 2 34	11 4 47	13 3 4	15 5 17	17 3 34
	8	19 10 41	21 12 54	23 3 18	1 5 31	3 3 47	5 6 1	7 4 17	9 6 31	11 8 44	13 7 0	15 9 14	17 7 30
	9	19 14 38	21 16 51	23 7 14	1 9 27	3 7 44	5 9 57	7 8 14	9 10 27	11 12 40	13 10 57	15 13 10	17 11 27
	10	19 18 34	21 20 47	23 11 11	1 13 24	3 11 40	5 13 54	7 12 11	9 14 24	11 16 37	13 14 54	15 17 7	17 15 23
	11	19 22 31	21 24 44	23 15 7	1 17 21	3 15 37	5 17 50	7 16 7	9 18 20	11 20 34	13 18 50	15 21 3	17 19 20
	12	19 26 28	21 28 40	23 19 4	1 21 17	3 19 33	5 21 47	7 20 4	9 22 17	11 24 30	13 22 47	15 25 0	17 23 17
	13	19 30 24	21 32 37	23 23 0	1 25 14	3 23 30	5 25 44	7 24 0	9 26 13	11 28 27	13 26 44	15 28 56	17 27 13
	14	19 34 20	21 36 34	23 26 57	1 29 10	3 27 27	5 29 40	7 27 57	9 30 10	11 32 24	13 30 40	15 32 53	17 31 10
	15	19 38 17	21 40 30	23 30 54	1 33 7	3 31 23	5 33 37	7 31 53	9 34 7	11 36 20	13 34 36	15 36 50	17 35 6
	16	19 42 13	21 44 27	23 34 50	1 37 3	3 35 20	5 37 33	7 35 50	9 38 3	11 40 16	13 38 33	15 40 46	17 39 3
	17	19 46 10	21 48 24	23 38 47	1 41 0	3 39 16	5 41 30	7 39 47	9 42 0	11 44 13	13 42 29	15 44 43	17 42 59
	18	19 50 7	21 52 20	23 42 43	1 44 56	3 43 13	5 45 26	7 43 43	9 45 56	11 48 9	13 46 26	15 48 40	17 46 56
	19	19 54 3	21 56 16	23 46 40	1 48 53	3 47 10	5 49 23	7 47 40	9 49 53	11 52 6	13 50 23	15 52 36	17 50 52
	20	19 58 0	22 0 13	23 50 36	1 52 49	3 51 6	5 53 19	7 51 36	9 53 49	11 56 2	13 54 19	15 56 32	17 54 49
	21	20 1 56	22 4 9	23 54 33	1 56 46	3 55 3	5 57 16	7 55 33	9 57 46	11 59 59	13 58 16	16 0 29	17 58 46
	22	20 5 53	22 8 6	23 58 29	2 0 43	3 58 59	6 1 13	7 59 29	10 1 42	12 3 56	14 2 12	16 4 25	18 2 42
	23	20 9 49	22 12 3	0 2 26	2 4 39	4 2 56	6 5 9	8 3 26	10 5 39	12 7 52	14 6 9	16 8 22	18 6 39
	24	20 13 46	22 15 59	0 6 23	2 8 36	4 6 52	6 9 6	8 7 22	10 9 36	12 11 49	14 10 5	16 12 19	18 10 35
	25	20 17 42	22 19 56	0 10 19	2 12 32	4 10 49	6 13 2	8 11 19	10 13 32	12 15 45	14 14 2	16 16 15	18 14 32
	26	20 21 39	22 23 52	0 14 16	2 16 29	4 14 45	6 16 59	8 15 15	10 17 29	12 19 42	14 17 58	16 20 12	18 18 28
	27	20 25 36	22 27 49	0 18 12	2 20 25	4 18 42	6 20 55	8 19 12	10 21 25	12 23 38	14 21 55	16 24 8	18 22 25
	28	20 29 32	22 31 45	0 22 9	2 24 22	4 22 39	6 24 52	8 23 9	10 25 22	12 27 35	14 25 52	16 28 5	18 26 21
	29	20 33 29		0 26 5	2 28 18	4 26 35	6 28 48	8 27 5	10 29 18	12 31 31	14 29 48	16 32 1	18 30 18
	30	20 37 25		0 30 2	2 32 15	4 30 32	6 32 45	8 31 2	10 33 15	12 35 28	14 33 45	16 35 58	18 34 15
	31	20 41 22		0 33 58		4 34 28		8 34 58	10 37 11		14 37 42		18 38 11

Year	Day	1	2	3	4	5	6	7	8	9	10	11	12
1946	1	18 42 8	20 44 21	22 34 45	0 36 58	2 35 14	4 37 28	6 35 44	8 37 58	10 40 11	12 38 27	14 40 40	16 38 57
	2	18 46 4	20 48 18	22 38 41	0 40 54	2 39 11	4 41 24	6 39 41	8 41 54	10 44 7	12 42 24	14 44 37	16 42 54
	3	18 50 1	20 52 14	22 42 38	0 44 51	2 43 7	4 45 21	6 43 37	8 45 51	10 48 4	12 46 20	14 48 34	16 46 50
	4	18 53 57	20 56 11	22 46 34	0 48 47	2 47 4	4 49 17	6 47 34	8 49 47	10 52 0	12 50 17	14 52 30	16 50 47
	5	18 57 54	21 0 7	22 50 31	0 52 44	2 51 0	4 53 14	6 51 30	8 53 44	10 55 57	12 54 14	14 56 27	16 54 43
	6	19 1 51	21 4 4	22 54 27	0 56 40	2 54 57	4 57 10	6 55 27	8 57 40	10 59 53	12 58 10	15 0 23	16 58 40
	7	19 5 47	21 8 0	22 58 24	1 0 37	2 58 54	5 1 7	6 59 24	9 1 37	11 3 50	13 2 7	15 4 20	17 2 37
	8	19 9 44	21 11 57	23 2 20	1 4 34	3 2 50	5 5 3	7 3 20	9 5 33	11 7 47	13 6 3	15 8 16	17 6 33
	9	19 13 40	21 15 53	23 6 17	1 8 30	3 6 47	5 9 0	7 7 17	8 9 30	11 11 43	13 10 0	15 12 13	17 10 30
	10	19 17 37	21 19 50	23 10 13	1 12 27	3 10 43	5 12 57	7 11 13	9 13 27	11 15 40	13 13 56	15 16 9	17 14 26
	11	19 21 33	21 23 47	23 14 10	1 16 23	3 14 40	5 16 53	7 15 10	9 17 23	11 19 36	13 17 53	15 20 6	17 18 23
	12	19 25 30	21 27 43	23 18 7	1 20 20	3 18 36	5 20 50	7 19 6	9 21 20	11 23 33	13 21 49	15 24 3	17 22 19
	13	19 29 26	21 31 40	23 22 3	1 24 16	3 22 33	5 24 46	7 23 3	9 25 16	11 27 29	13 25 46	15 27 59	17 26 16
	14	19 33 23	21 35 36	23 26 0	1 28 13	3 26 29	5 28 43	7 27 0	9 29 13	11 31 26	13 29 42	15 31 56	17 30 12
	15	19 37 20	21 39 33	23 29 56	1 32 9	3 30 26	5 32 39	7 30 56	9 33 9	11 35 22	13 33 39	15 35 52	17 34 9
	16	19 41 16	21 43 29	23 33 53	1 36 6	3 34 23	5 36 36	7 34 53	9 37 6	11 39 19	13 37 36	15 39 49	17 38 6
	17	19 45 13	21 47 26	23 37 49	1 40 3	3 38 19	5 40 32	7 38 49	9 41 2	11 43 16	13 41 32	15 43 45	17 42 2
	18	19 49 9	21 51 22	23 41 46	1 43 59	3 42 16	5 44 29	7 42 46	9 44 59	11 47 12	13 45 29	15 47 42	17 45 59
	19	19 43 6	21 55 19	23 45 42	1 47 56	3 46 12	5 48 26	7 46 42	9 48 56	11 51 9	13 49 25	15 51 39	17 49 55
	20	19 57 2	21 59 16	23 49 39	1 51 52	3 50 9	5 52 22	7 50 39	9 52 52	11 55 5	13 53 22	15 55 35	17 53 52
	21	20 0 59	22 3 12	23 53 36	1 55 49	3 54 5	5 56 19	7 54 35	9 56 49	11 59 2	13 57 18	15 59 32	17 57 49
	22	20 4 55	22 7 9	23 57 32	1 59 45	3 58 2	6 0 15	7 58 32	10 0 45	12 2 58	14 1 15	16 3 28	18 1 45
	23	20 8 52	22 11 5	0 1 29	2 3 42	4 1 59	6 4 12	8 2 29	10 4 42	12 6 55	14 5 12	16 7 25	18 5 42
	24	20 12 48	22 15 2	0 5 25	2 7 38	4 5 55	6 8 8	8 6 25	10 8 38	12 10 51	14 9 8	16 11 21	18 9 38
	25	20 16 45	22 18 58	0 9 22	2 11 35	4 9 52	6 12 5	8 10 22	10 12 35	12 14 48	14 13 5	16 15 18	18 13 35
	26	20 20 42	22 22 55	0 13 18	2 15 32	4 13 48	6 16 1	8 14 18	10 16 31	12 18 45	14 17 1	16 19 14	18 17 31
	27	20 24 38	22 26 51	0 17 15	2 19 28	4 17 45	6 19 58	8 18 15	10 20 28	12 22 41	14 20 58	16 23 11	18 21 28
	28	20 28 35	22 30 48	0 21 11	2 23 25	4 21 41	6 23 55	8 22 11	10 24 25	12 26 38	14 24 54	16 27 8	18 25 24
	29	20 32 31		0 25 8	2 27 21	4 25 38	6 27 51	8 26 8	10 28 21	12 30 35	14 28 51	16 31 4	18 29 21
	30	20 36 28		0 29 5	2 31 18	4 29 34	6 31 48	8 30 5	10 32 18	12 34 31	14 32 47	16 35 1	18 33 17
	31	20 40 24		0 33 1		4 33 31		8 34 1	10 36 14		14 36 44		18 37 14
1947	1	18 41 10	20 43 24	22 33 47	0 36 0	2 34 17	4 36 30	6 34 47	8 37 0	10 39 14	12 37 30	14 39 43	16 38 0
	2	18 45 7	20 47 20	22 37 44	0 39 57	2 38 14	4 40 27	6 38 44	8 40 57	10 43 10	12 41 27	14 43 40	16 41 57
	3	18 49 4	20 51 17	22 41 40	0 43 54	2 42 10	4 44 23	6 42 40	8 44 53	10 47 7	12 45 24	14 47 38	16 45 53
	4	18 53 0	20 55 13	22 45 37	0 47 50	2 46 7	4 48 20	6 46 37	8 48 50	10 51 3	12 49 20	14 51 33	16 49 50
	5	18 56 57	20 59 10	22 49 34	0 51 47	2 50 3	4 52 17	6 50 33	8 52 47	10 55 0	12 53 16	14 55 30	16 53 46
	6	19 0 53	21 3 7	22 53 30	0 55 43	2 54 0	4 56 13	6 54 30	8 56 43	10 58 56	12 57 13	14 59 26	16 57 43
	7	19 4 50	21 7 3	22 57 27	0 59 40	2 57 56	5 0 10	6 58 26	9 0 40	11 2 53	13 1 10	15 3 23	17 1 39
	8	19 8 46	21 11 0	23 1 23	1 3 36	3 1 53	5 4 6	7 2 23	9 4 36	11 6 49	13 5 6	15 7 19	17 5 36
	9	19 12 43	21 14 56	23 5 20	1 7 33	3 5 50	5 8 3	7 6 20	9 8 33	11 10 46	13 9 3	15 11 16	17 9 33
	10	19 16 40	21 18 53	23 9 16	1 11 29	3 9 46	5 11 59	7 10 16	9 12 30	11 14 43	13 12 59	15 15 12	17 13 29
	11	19 20 36	21 22 49	23 13 13	1 15 26	3 13 43	5 15 56	7 14 13	9 16 26	11 18 39	13 16 56	15 19 9	17 17 26
	12	19 24 33	21 26 46	23 17 9	1 19 23	3 17 39	5 19 52	7 18 9	9 20 22	11 22 36	13 20 52	15 23 5	17 21 22
	13	19 28 29	21 30 42	23 21 6	1 23 19	3 21 36	5 23 49	7 22 6	9 24 19	11 26 32	13 24 49	15 27 2	17 25 19
	14	19 32 26	21 34 39	23 25 3	1 27 16	3 25 32	5 27 46	7 26 2	9 28 16	11 30 29	13 28 45	15 30 59	17 29 15
	15	19 36 22	21 38 36	23 28 59	1 31 12	3 29 29	5 31 42	7 29 59	9 32 12	11 34 25	13 32 42	15 34 55	17 33 12
	16	19 40 19	21 42 32	23 32 56	1 35 9	3 33 25	5 35 39	7 33 55	9 36 9	11 38 22	13 36 38	15 38 52	17 37 8
	17	19 44 15	21 46 29	23 36 52	1 39 5	3 37 22	5 39 35	7 37 52	9 40 5	11 42 18	13 40 35	15 42 48	17 41 5
	18	19 48 12	21 50 25	23 40 49	1 43 2	3 41 19	5 43 32	7 41 49	9 44 2	11 46 15	13 44 32	15 46 45	17 45 2
	19	19 52 9	21 54 22	23 44 45	1 46 59	3 45 15	5 47 28	7 45 45	9 47 59	11 50 12	13 48 28	15 50 41	17 48 58
	20	19 56 5	21 58 18	23 48 42	1 50 55	3 49 12	5 51 25	7 49 42	9 51 55	11 54 8	13 52 25	15 54 38	17 52 55
	21	20 0 2	22 2 15	23 52 38	1 54 52	3 53 8	5 55 22	7 53 38	9 55 51	11 58 5	13 56 21	15 58 34	17 56 51
	22	20 3 58	22 6 11	23 56 35	1 58 48	3 57 5	5 59 18	7 57 35	9 59 48	12 2 1	14 0 18	16 2 31	18 0 48
	23	20 7 55	22 10 8	0 0 31	2 2 45	4 1 1	6 3 15	8 1 31	10 3 45	12 5 58	14 4 14	16 6 28	18 4 44
	24	20 11 51	22 14 5	0 4 28	2 6 41	4 4 58	6 7 11	8 5 28	10 7 41	12 9 54	14 8 11	16 10 24	18 8 41
	25	20 15 48	22 18 1	0 8 25	2 10 38	4 8 54	6 11 8	8 9 24	10 11 38	12 13 51	14 12 7	16 14 21	18 12 37
	26	20 19 44	22 21 58	0 12 21	2 14 34	4 12 51	6 15 4	8 13 21	10 15 34	12 17 47	14 16 4	16 18 17	18 16 34
	27	20 23 41	22 25 54	0 16 18	2 18 31	4 16 48	6 19 1	8 17 18	10 19 31	12 21 44	14 20 1	16 22 14	18 20 31
	28	20 27 38	22 29 51	0 20 14	2 22 27	4 20 44	6 22 57	8 21 14	10 23 27	12 25 41	14 23 57	16 26 10	18 24 27
	29	20 31 34		0 24 11	2 26 24	4 24 41	6 26 54	8 25 11	10 27 24	12 29 37	14 27 54	16 30 7	18 28 24
	30	20 35 31		0 28 7	2 30 21	4 28 37	6 30 51	8 29 7	10 31 20	12 33 34	14 31 51	16 34 3	18 32 20
	31	20 39 27		0 32 4		4 32 34		8 33 4	10 35 17		14 35 47		18 36 17
1948	1	18 40 13	20 42 27	22 36 47	0 39 0	2 37 17	4 39 30	6 37 47	8 40 0	10 42 13	12 40 30	14 42 43	16 41 0
	2	18 44 10	20 46 23	22 40 43	0 42 56	2 41 13	4 43 26	6 41 43	8 43 56	10 46 10	12 44 26	14 46 39	16 44 56
	3	18 48 7	20 50 20	22 44 40	0 46 53	2 45 10	4 47 23	6 45 40	8 47 53	10 50 6	12 48 23	14 50 36	16 48 53
	4	18 52 3	20 54 16	22 48 36	0 50 50	2 49 6	4 51 19	6 49 36	8 51 50	10 54 3	12 52 19	14 54 33	16 52 49
	5	18 56 0	20 58 13	22 52 33	0 54 46	2 53 3	4 55 16	6 53 33	8 55 46	10 57 59	12 56 16	14 58 29	16 56 46
	6	18 59 56	21 2 9	22 56 30	0 58 43	2 56 59	4 59 13	6 57 29	8 59 43	11 1 56	13 0 12	15 2 26	17 0 42
	7	19 3 53	21 6 6	23 0 26	1 2 39	3 0 56	5 3 9	7 1 26	9 3 39	11 5 52	13 4 9	15 6 22	17 4 39
	8	19 7 49	21 10 3	23 4 23	1 6 36	3 4 52	5 7 6	7 5 22	9 7 36	11 9 49	13 8 6	15 10 19	17 8 36
	9	19 11 46	21 13 59	23 8 19	1 10 32	3 8 49	5 11 2	7 9 19	9 11 32	11 13 46	13 12 2	15 14 15	17 12 32
	10	19 15 42	21 17 56	23 12 16	1 14 29	3 12 46	5 14 59	7 13 16	9 15 29	11 17 42	13 15 59	15 18 12	17 16 29
	11	19 19 39	21 21 53	23 16 12	1 18 25	3 16 42	5 18 55	7 17 12	9 19 26	11 21 39	13 19 55	15 22 8	17 20 25
	12	19 23 36	21 25 49	23 20 9	1 22 22	3 20 39	5 22 52	7 21 9	9 23 22	11 25 35	13 23 52	15 26 5	17 24 22
	13	19 27 32	21 29 46	23 24 5	1 26 19	3 24 35	5 26 49	7 25 5	9 27 19	11 29 32	13 27 48	15 30 2	17 28 18
	14	19 31 29	21 33 42	23 28 2	1 30 15	3 28 32	5 30 45	7 29 2	9 31 15	11 33 28	13 31 45	15 33 58	17 32 15
	15	19 35 25	21 37 38	23 31 59	1 34 12	3 32 28	5 34 42	7 32 59	9 35 12	11 37 25	13 35 41	15 37 55	17 36 11
	16	19 39 22	21 41 35	23 35 55	1 38 8	3 36 25	5 38 38	7 36 55	9 39 8	11 41 21	13 39 38	15 41 51	17 40 8
	17	19 43 18	21 45 32	23 39 52	1 42 5	3 40 21	5 42 35	7 40 52	9 43 5	11 45 18	13 43 35	15 45 48	17 44 5
	18	19 47 15	21 49 28	23 43 48	1 46 1	3 44 18	5 46 32	7 44 48	9 47 1	11 49 14	13 47 31	15 49 44	17 48 1
	19	19 51 11	21 53 25	23 47 45	1 49 58	3 48 15	5 50 28	7 48 45	9 50 58	11 53 11	13 51 28	15 53 41	17 51 58
	20	19 55 8	21 57 21	23 51 41	1 53 54	3 52 11	5 54 24	7 52 41	9 54 54	11 57 8	13 55 24	15 57 37	17 55 54
	21	19 59 5	22 1 18	23 55 38	1 57 51	3 56 8	5 58 21	7 56 38	9 58 51	12 1 4	13 59 21	16 1 34	17 59 51
	22	20 3 1	22 5 14	23 59 34	2 1 48	4 0 4	6 2 18	8 0 34	10 2 48	12 5 1	14 3 17	16 5 31	18 3 47
	23	20 6 58	22 9 11	0 3 31	2 5 44	4 4 1	6 6 14	8 4 31	10 6 44	12 8 57	14 7 14	16 9 27	18 7 44
	24	20 10 54	22 13 7	0 7 28	2 9 41	4 7 58	6 10 11	8 8 27	10 10 41	12 12 54	14 11 10	16 13 24	18 11 40
	25	20 14 51	22 17 4	0 11 24	2 13 37	4 11 54	6 14 7	8 12 24	10 14 37	12 16 50	14 15 7	16 17 20	18 15 37
	26	20 18 47	22 21 1	0 15 21	2 17 34	4 15 50	6 18 4	8 16 21	10 18 34	12 20 47	14 19 4	16 21 17	18 19 34
	27	20 22 44	22 24 57	0 19 17	2 21 30	4 19 47	6 22 0	8 20 17	10 22 30	12 24 43	14 23 0	16 25 13	18 23 30
	28	20 26 40	22 28 54	0 23 14	2 25 27	4 23 44	6 25 57	8 24 14	10 26 27	12 28 40	14 26 57	16 29 10	18 27 27
	29	20 30 37	22 32 50	0 27 10	2 29 23	4 27 40	6 29 53	8 28 10	10 30 23	12 32 37	14 30 53	16 33 6	18 31 23
	30	20 34 34		0 31 7	2 33 20	4 31 37	6 33 50	8 32 7	10 34 20	12 36 33	14 34 50	16 37 3	18 35 20
	31	20 38 30		0 35 3		4 35 33		8 36 3	10 38 17		14 38 46		18 39 16
1949	1	18 43 13	20 45 26	22 35 50	0 38 3	2 36 20	4 38 33	6 36 50	8 39 3	10 41 16	12 39 33	14 41 46	16 40 3
	2	18 47 9	20 49 23	22 39 46	0 41 9	2 40 16	4 42 29	6 40 46	8 42 59	10 45 13	12 43 29	14 45 42	16 43 59
	3	18 51 6	20 53 19	22 43 43	0 45 56	2 44 13	4 46 26	6 44 43	8 46 56	10 49 9	12 47 26	14 49 39	16 47 56
	4	18 55 3	20 57 16	22 47 39	0 49 53	2 48 9	4 50 23	6 48 39	8 50 53	10 53 6	12 51 22	14 53 36	16 51 52
	5	18 58 59	21 1 12	22 51 36	0 53 49	2 52 6	4 54 19	6 52 36	8 54 49	10 57 2	12 55 19	14 57 32	16 55 49
	6	19 2 56	21 5 9	22 55 33	0 57 46	2 56 2	4 58 16	6 56 32	8 58 46	11 0 59	12 59 15	15 1 29	16 59 45
	7	19 6 52	21 9 6	22 59 29	1 1 42	2 59 59	5 2 12	7 0 29	9 2 42	11 4 55	13 3 12	15 5 25	17 3 42
	8	19 10 49	21 13 2	23 3 26	1 5 39	3 3 55	5 6 9	7 4 25	9 6 39	11 8 52	13 7 9	15 9 22	17 7 39
	9	19 14 45	21 16 59	23 7 22	1 9 35	3 7 52	5 10 5	7 8 22	9 10 35	11 12 49	13 11 5	15 13 18	17 11 35
	10	19 18 42	21 20 55	23 11 19	1 13 32	3 11 49	5 14 2	7 12 19	9 14 32	11 16 45	13 15 2	15 17 15	17 15 32
	11	19 22 38	21 24 52	23 15 15	1 17 28	3 15 45	5 17 58	7 16 15	9 18 28	11 20 42	13 18 58	15 21 11	17 19 28
	12	19 26 35	21 28 48	23 19 12	1 21 25	3 19 42	5 21 55	7 20 12	9 22 25	11 24 38	13 22 55	15 25 8	17 23 25
	13	19 30 32	21 32 45	23 23 8	1 25 22	3 23 38	5 25 52	7 24 8	9 26 22	11 28 35	13 26 51	15 29 5	17 27 21
	14	19 34 28	21 36 41	23 27 5	1 29 18	3 27 35	5 29 48	7 28 5	9 30 18	11 32 31	13 30 48	15 33 1	17 31 18
	15	19 38 25	21 40 38	23 31 2	1 33 15	3 31 31	5 33 45	7 32 1	9 34 15	11 36 28	13 34 44	15 36 58	17 35 14
	16	19 42 21	21 44 35	23 34 58	1 37 11	3 35 28	5 37 41	7 35 58	9 38 11	11 40 24	13 38 41	15 40 54	17 39 11
	17	19 46 18	21 48 31	23 38 55	1 41 8	3 39 24	5 41 38	7 39 55	9 42 8	11 44 21	13 42 38	15 44 51	17 43 8
	18	19 50 14	21 52 28	23 42 51	1 45 4	3 43 21	5 45 34	7 43 51	9 46 4	11 48 18	13 46 34	15 48 47	17 47 4
	19	19 54 11	21 56 24	23 46 48	1 49 1	3 47 18	5 49 31	7 47 48	9 50 1	11 52 14	13 50 31	15 52 44	17 51 1
	20	19 58 8	22 0 21	23 50 44	1 52 57	3 51 14	5 53 27	7 51 44	9 53 57	11 56 11	13 54 27	15 56 40	17 54 57
	21	20 2 4	22 4 17	23 54 41	1 56 54	3 55 11	5 57 24	7 55 41	9 57 54	12 0 7	13 58 24	16 0 37	17 58 54
	22	20 6 1	22 8 14	23 58 37	2 0 51	3 59 7	6 1 21	7 59 37	10 1 51	12 4 4	14 2 20	16 4 34	18 2 50
	23	20 9 57	22 12 10	0 2 34	2 4 47	4 3 4	6 5 17	8 3 34	10 5 47	12 8 0	14 6 17	16 8 30	18 6 47
	24	20 13 54	22 16 7	0 6 31	2 8 44	4 7 0	6 9 14	8 7 30	10 9 44	12 11 57	14 10 13	16 12 27	18 10 43
	25	20 17 50	22 20 4	0 10 27	2 12 40	4 10 57	6 13 10	8 11 27	10 13 40	12 15 53	14 14 10	16 16 23	18 14 40
	26	20 21 47	22 24 0	0 14 24	2 16 37	4 14 53	6 17 7	8 15 24	10 17 37	12 19 50	14 18 7	16 20 20	18 18 37
	27	20 25 43	22 27 57	0 18 20	2 20 33	4 18 50	6 21 3	8 19 20	10 21 33	12 23 46	14 22 3	16 24 16	18 22 33
	28	20 29 40	22 31 53	0 22 17	2 24 30	4 22 47	6 25 0	8 23 17	10 25 30	12 27 43	14 26 0	16 28 13	18 26 30
	29	20 33 37		0 26 13	2 28 26	4 26 43	6 28 56	8 27 13	10 29 26	12 31 40	14 29 56	16 32 10	18 30 26
	30	20 37 33		0 30 10	2 32 23	4 30 40	6 32 53	8 31 10	10 33 23	12 35 36	14 33 53	16 36 6	18 34 23
	31	20 41 30		0 34 6		4 34 36		8 35 6	10 37 20		14 37 49		18 38 19

1	2	3	4	5	6	7	8	9	10	11	12
18 42 16	20 44 29	22 34 53	0 37 6	2 35 23	4 37 36	6 35 53	8 38 6	10 40 19	12 38 36	14 40 49	16 39 6
18 46 12	20 48 26	22 38 49	0 41 3	2 39 19	4 41 32	6 39 49	8 42 2	10 44 16	12 42 32	14 44 46	16 43 2
18 50 9	20 52 22	22 42 46	0 44 59	2 43 16	4 45 29	6 43 46	8 45 59	10 48 12	12 46 29	14 48 42	16 46 59
18 54 6	20 56 19	22 46 42	0 48 56	2 47 12	4 49 26	6 47 42	8 49 56	10 52 9	12 50 25	14 52 39	16 50 55
18 58 2	21 0 15	22 50 39	0 52 52	2 51 9	4 53 22	6 51 39	8 53 52	10 56 5	12 54 22	14 56 35	16 54 52
19 1 59	21 4 12	22 54 36	0 56 49	2 55 5	4 57 19	6 55 35	8 57 49	11 0 2	12 58 19	15 0 32	16 58 48
19 5 55	21 8 9	22 58 32	1 0 45	2 59 2	5 1 15	6 59 32	9 1 45	11 3 58	13 2 15	15 4 28	17 2 45
19 9 52	21 12 5	23 2 29	1 4 42	3 2 59	5 5 12	7 3 29	9 5 42	11 7 55	13 6 12	15 8 25	17 6 42
19 13 48	21 16 2	23 6 25	1 8 38	3 6 55	5 9 8	7 7 25	9 9 38	11 11 52	13 10 8	15 12 21	17 10 38
19 17 45	21 19 58	23 10 22	1 12 35	3 10 52	5 13 5	7 11 22	9 13 35	11 15 48	13 14 5	15 16 18	17 14 35
19 21 42	21 23 55	23 14 18	1 16 32	3 14 48	5 17 1	7 15 18	9 17 31	11 19 45	13 18 1	15 20 14	17 18 31
19 25 38	21 27 51	23 18 15	1 20 28	3 18 45	5 20 58	7 19 15	9 21 28	11 23 41	13 21 58	15 24 11	17 22 28
19 29 35	21 31 48	23 22 11	1 24 25	3 22 41	5 24 55	7 23 11	9 25 25	11 27 38	13 25 54	15 28 8	17 26 24
19 33 31	21 35 44	23 26 8	1 28 21	3 26 38	5 28 51	7 27 8	9 29 21	11 31 34	13 29 51	15 32 4	17 30 21
19 37 28	21 39 41	23 30 5	1 32 18	3 30 34	5 32 48	7 31 4	9 33 18	11 35 31	13 33 48	15 36 1	17 34 18
19 41 24	21 43 38	23 34 1	1 36 14	3 34 31	5 36 44	7 35 1	9 37 14	11 39 27	13 37 44	15 39 57	17 38 14
19 45 21	21 47 34	23 37 58	1 40 11	3 38 27	5 40 41	7 38 58	9 41 11	11 43 24	13 41 41	15 43 54	17 42 11
19 49 17	21 51 31	23 41 54	1 44 7	3 42 24	5 44 37	7 42 54	9 45 7	11 47 21	13 45 37	15 47 50	17 46 7
19 53 14	21 55 27	23 45 51	1 48 4	3 46 21	5 48 34	7 46 51	9 49 4	11 51 17	13 49 34	15 51 47	17 50 4
19 57 11	21 59 24	23 49 47	1 52 0	3 50 17	5 52 30	7 50 47	9 53 0	11 55 14	13 53 30	15 55 44	17 54 0
20 1 7	22 3 20	23 53 44	1 55 57	3 54 14	5 56 27	7 54 44	9 56 57	11 59 10	13 57 27	15 59 40	17 57 57
20 5 4	22 7 17	23 57 40	1 59 54	3 58 10	6 0 24	7 58 40	10 0 54	12 3 7	14 1 23	16 3 37	18 1 53
20 9 0	22 11 13	0 1 37	2 3 50	4 2 7	6 4 20	8 2 37	10 4 50	12 7 3	14 5 20	16 7 33	18 5 50
20 12 57	22 15 10	0 5 34	2 7 47	4 6 3	6 8 17	8 6 33	10 8 47	12 11 0	14 9 17	16 11 30	18 9 47
20 16 53	22 19 7	0 9 30	2 11 43	4 10 0	6 12 13	8 10 30	10 12 43	12 14 56	14 13 13	16 15 26	18 13 43
20 20 50	22 23 3	0 13 27	2 15 40	4 13 57	6 16 10	8 14 27	10 16 40	12 18 53	14 17 10	16 19 23	18 17 40
20 24 46	22 27 0	0 17 23	2 19 36	4 17 53	6 20 6	8 18 23	10 20 36	12 22 50	14 21 6	16 23 19	18 21 36
20 28 43	22 30 56	0 21 20	2 23 33	4 21 50	6 24 3	8 22 20	10 24 33	12 26 46	14 25 3	16 27 16	18 25 33
20 32 40		0 25 16	2 27 29	4 25 46	6 28 0	8 26 16	10 28 29	12 30 43	14 28 59	16 31 13	18 29 29
20 36 36		0 29 13	2 31 26	4 29 43	6 31 56	8 30 13	10 32 26	12 34 39	14 32 56	16 35 9	18 33 26
20 40 33		0 33 9		4 33 39		8 34 9	10 36 23		14 36 52		18 37 22
18 41 19	20 43 32	22 33 56	0 36 9	2 34 26	4 36 39	6 34 56	8 37 9	10 39 22	12 37 39	14 39 52	16 38 9
18 45 16	20 47 29	22 37 52	0 40 6	2 38 22	4 40 35	6 38 52	8 41 6	10 43 19	12 41 35	14 43 49	16 42 5
18 49 12	20 51 25	22 41 49	0 44 2	2 42 19	4 44 32	6 42 49	8 45 2	10 47 15	12 45 32	14 47 45	16 46 2
18 53 9	20 55 22	22 45 46	0 47 59	2 46 15	4 48 29	6 46 45	8 48 59	10 51 12	12 49 28	14 51 42	16 49 58
18 57 5	20 59 19	22 49 42	0 51 55	2 50 12	4 52 25	6 50 42	8 52 55	10 55 8	12 53 25	14 55 38	16 53 55
19 1 2	21 3 15	22 53 39	0 55 52	2 54 8	4 56 22	6 54 38	8 56 52	10 59 5	12 57 22	14 59 35	16 57 52
19 4 58	21 7 12	22 57 35	0 59 49	2 58 5	5 0 18	6 58 35	9 0 48	11 3 1	13 1 18	15 3 31	17 1 48
19 8 55	21 11 8	23 1 32	1 3 45	3 2 2	5 4 15	7 2 32	9 4 45	11 6 58	13 5 15	15 7 28	17 5 45
19 12 51	21 15 5	23 5 28	1 7 41	3 5 58	5 8 11	7 6 28	9 8 41	11 10 55	13 9 11	15 11 24	17 9 41
19 16 48	21 19 1	23 9 25	1 11 38	3 9 55	5 12 8	7 10 25	9 12 38	11 14 51	13 13 8	15 15 21	17 13 38
19 20 45	21 22 58	23 13 21	1 15 35	3 13 51	5 16 5	7 14 21	9 16 35	11 18 48	13 17 4	15 19 18	17 17 34
19 24 41	21 26 54	23 17 18	1 19 31	3 17 48	5 20 1	7 18 18	9 20 31	11 22 44	13 21 1	15 23 14	17 21 31
19 28 38	21 30 51	23 21 14	1 23 28	3 21 44	5 23 58	7 22 14	9 24 28	11 26 41	13 24 57	15 27 11	17 25 27
19 32 34	21 34 48	23 25 11	1 27 24	3 25 41	5 27 54	7 26 11	9 28 24	11 30 37	13 28 54	15 31 7	17 29 24
19 36 31	21 38 44	23 29 8	1 31 21	3 29 37	5 31 51	7 30 7	9 32 21	11 34 34	13 32 51	15 35 4	17 33 21
19 40 27	21 42 41	23 33 4	1 35 17	3 33 34	5 35 47	7 34 4	9 36 17	11 38 31	13 36 47	15 39 0	17 37 17
19 44 24	21 46 37	23 37 1	1 39 14	3 37 31	5 39 44	7 38 1	9 40 14	11 42 27	13 40 44	15 42 57	17 41 14
19 48 20	21 50 34	23 40 57	1 43 10	3 41 27	5 43 40	7 41 57	9 44 10	11 46 24	13 44 40	15 46 53	17 45 10
19 52 17	21 54 30	23 44 54	1 47 7	3 45 24	5 47 37	7 45 54	9 48 7	11 50 20	13 48 37	15 50 50	17 49 7
19 56 14	21 58 27	23 48 50	1 51 4	3 49 20	5 51 34	7 49 50	9 52 4	11 54 17	13 52 33	15 54 47	17 53 3
20 0 10	22 2 23	23 52 47	1 55 0	3 53 17	5 55 30	7 53 47	9 56 0	11 58 13	13 56 30	15 58 43	17 57 0
20 4 7	22 6 20	23 56 43	1 58 57	3 57 13	5 59 27	7 57 43	9 59 57	12 2 10	14 0 26	16 2 40	18 0 56
20 8 3	22 10 17	0 0 40	2 2 53	4 1 10	6 3 23	8 1 40	10 3 53	12 6 6	14 4 23	16 6 36	18 4 53
20 12 0	22 14 13	0 4 37	2 6 50	4 5 6	6 7 20	8 5 37	10 7 50	12 10 3	14 8 20	16 10 33	18 8 50
20 15 56	22 18 10	0 8 33	2 10 46	4 9 3	6 11 16	8 9 33	10 11 46	12 13 59	14 12 16	16 14 29	18 12 46
20 19 53	22 22 6	0 12 30	2 14 43	4 13 0	6 15 13	8 13 30	10 15 43	12 17 56	14 16 13	16 18 26	18 16 43
20 23 50	22 26 3	0 16 26	2 18 39	4 16 56	6 19 9	8 17 26	10 19 39	12 21 53	14 20 9	16 22 22	18 20 39
20 27 46	22 29 59	0 20 23	2 22 36	4 20 53	6 23 6	8 21 23	10 23 36	12 25 49	14 24 6	16 26 19	18 24 36
20 31 43		0 24 19	2 26 33	4 24 49	6 27 3	8 25 19	10 27 33	12 29 46	14 28 2	16 30 16	18 28 32
20 35 39		0 28 16	2 30 29	4 28 46	6 30 59	8 29 16	10 31 29	12 33 42	14 31 59	16 34 12	18 32 29
20 39 36		0 32 12		4 32 42		8 33 12	10 35 26		14 35 55		18 36 25
18 40 22	20 42 35	22 36 57	0 39 9	2 37 25	4 39 39	6 37 55	8 40 9	10 42 22	12 40 38	14 42 52	16 41 8
18 44 19	20 46 32	22 40 52	0 43 5	2 41 22	4 43 35	6 41 52	8 44 5	10 46 18	12 44 35	14 46 48	16 45 5
18 48 15	20 50 28	22 44 49	0 47 2	2 45 18	4 47 32	6 45 48	8 48 2	10 50 15	12 48 31	14 50 45	16 49 1
18 52 12	20 54 25	22 48 45	0 50 58	2 49 15	4 51 28	6 49 45	8 51 58	10 54 11	12 52 28	14 54 41	16 52 58
18 56 8	20 58 22	22 52 42	0 54 55	2 53 11	4 55 25	6 53 41	8 55 55	10 58 8	12 56 25	14 58 38	16 56 55
19 0 5	21 2 18	22 56 38	0 58 51	2 57 8	4 59 21	6 57 38	8 59 51	11 2 5	13 0 21	15 2 34	17 0 51
19 4 1	21 6 15	23 0 35	1 2 48	3 1 5	5 3 18	7 1 35	9 3 48	11 6 1	13 4 18	15 6 31	17 4 48
19 7 58	21 10 11	23 4 31	1 6 44	3 5 1	5 7 14	7 5 31	9 7 44	11 9 58	13 8 14	15 10 27	17 8 44
19 11 54	21 14 8	23 8 28	1 10 41	3 8 58	5 11 11	7 9 28	9 11 41	11 13 54	13 12 11	15 14 24	17 12 41
19 15 51	21 18 4	23 12 24	1 14 38	3 12 54	5 15 8	7 13 24	9 15 38	11 17 51	13 16 7	15 18 21	17 16 37
19 19 48	21 22 1	23 16 21	1 18 34	3 16 51	5 19 4	7 17 21	9 19 34	11 21 47	13 20 4	15 22 17	17 20 34
19 23 44	21 25 57	23 20 18	1 22 31	3 20 47	5 23 1	7 21 17	9 23 31	11 25 44	13 24 0	15 26 14	17 24 30
19 27 41	21 29 54	23 24 14	1 26 27	3 24 44	5 26 57	7 25 14	9 27 27	11 29 40	13 27 57	15 30 10	17 28 27
19 31 37	21 33 51	23 28 11	1 30 24	3 28 40	5 30 54	7 29 11	9 31 24	11 33 37	13 31 54	15 34 7	17 32 24
19 35 34	21 37 47	23 32 7	1 34 20	3 32 37	5 34 50	7 33 7	9 35 20	11 37 34	13 35 50	15 38 3	17 36 20
19 39 30	21 41 44	23 36 4	1 38 17	3 36 34	5 38 47	7 37 4	9 39 17	11 41 30	13 39 47	15 42 0	17 40 17
19 43 27	21 45 40	23 40 0	1 42 13	3 40 30	5 42 43	7 41 0	9 43 13	11 45 27	13 43 43	15 45 56	17 44 13
19 47 24	21 49 37	23 43 57	1 46 10	3 44 27	5 46 40	7 44 57	9 47 10	11 49 23	13 47 40	15 49 53	17 48 10
19 51 20	21 53 33	23 47 53	1 50 7	3 48 23	5 50 37	7 48 53	9 51 7	11 53 20	13 51 36	15 53 50	17 52 6
19 55 17	21 57 30	23 51 50	1 54 3	3 52 20	5 54 33	7 52 50	9 55 3	11 57 16	13 55 33	15 57 46	17 56 3
19 59 13	22 1 26	23 55 47	1 58 0	3 56 16	5 58 30	7 56 46	9 59 0	12 1 13	13 59 29	16 1 43	17 59 59
20 3 10	22 5 23	23 59 43	2 1 56	4 0 13	6 2 26	8 0 43	10 2 56	12 5 9	14 3 26	16 5 39	18 3 56
20 7 6	22 9 20	0 3 40	2 5 53	4 4 9	6 6 23	8 4 40	10 6 53	12 9 6	14 7 23	16 9 36	18 7 53
20 11 3	22 13 16	0 7 36	2 9 49	4 8 6	6 10 19	8 8 36	10 10 49	12 13 2	14 11 19	16 13 32	18 11 49
20 14 59	22 17 13	0 11 33	2 13 46	4 12 3	6 14 16	8 12 33	10 14 46	12 16 59	14 15 16	16 17 29	18 15 46
20 18 56	22 21 9	0 15 29	2 17 42	4 15 59	6 18 12	8 16 29	10 18 42	12 20 56	14 19 12	16 21 25	18 19 42
20 22 53	22 25 6	0 19 26	2 21 39	4 19 56	6 22 9	8 20 26	10 22 39	12 24 52	14 23 9	16 25 22	18 23 39
20 26 49	22 29 2	0 23 22	2 25 36	4 23 52	6 26 6	8 24 22	10 26 36	12 28 49	14 27 5	16 29 19	18 27 35
20 30 46	22 32 59	0 27 19	2 29 32	4 27 49	6 30 2	8 28 19	10 30 32	12 32 45	14 31 2	16 33 15	18 31 32
20 34 42		0 31 15	2 33 29	4 31 45	6 33 59	8 32 15	10 34 29	12 36 42	14 34 58	16 37 12	18 35 28
20 38 39		0 35 12		4 35 42		8 36 12	10 38 25		14 38 55		18 39 25
18 43 22	20 45 35	22 35 58	0 38 12	2 36 28	4 38 41	6 36 58	8 39 11	10 41 25	12 39 41	14 41 55	16 40 11
18 47 18	20 49 31	22 39 55	0 42 8	2 40 25	4 42 38	6 40 55	8 43 8	10 45 21	12 43 38	14 45 51	16 44 8
18 51 15	20 53 28	22 43 52	0 46 5	2 44 21	4 46 35	6 44 51	8 47 5	10 49 18	12 47 34	14 49 48	16 48 4
18 55 11	20 57 25	22 47 48	0 50 1	2 48 18	4 50 31	6 48 48	8 51 1	10 53 14	12 51 31	14 53 44	16 52 1
18 59 8	21 1 21	22 51 45	0 53 58	2 52 14	4 54 28	6 52 44	8 54 58	10 57 11	12 55 28	14 57 41	16 55 57
19 3 4	21 5 18	22 55 41	0 57 54	2 56 11	4 58 24	6 56 41	8 58 54	11 1 7	12 59 24	15 1 37	16 59 54
19 7 1	21 9 14	22 59 38	1 1 51	3 0 8	5 2 21	7 0 38	9 2 51	11 5 4	13 3 21	15 5 34	17 3 51
19 10 57	21 13 11	23 3 34	1 5 47	3 4 4	5 6 17	7 4 34	9 6 47	11 9 1	13 7 17	15 9 30	17 7 47
19 14 54	21 17 7	23 7 31	1 9 44	3 8 1	5 10 14	7 8 31	9 10 44	11 12 57	13 11 14	15 13 27	17 11 44
19 18 51	21 21 4	23 11 27	1 13 41	3 11 57	5 14 10	7 12 27	9 14 41	11 16 54	13 15 10	15 17 23	17 15 40
19 22 47	21 25 0	23 15 24	1 17 37	3 15 54	5 18 7	7 16 24	9 18 37	11 20 50	13 19 7	15 21 20	17 19 37
19 26 44	21 28 57	23 19 21	1 21 34	3 19 50	5 22 4	7 20 20	9 22 34	11 24 47	13 23 3	15 25 17	17 23 33
19 30 40	21 32 54	23 23 17	1 25 30	3 23 47	5 26 0	7 24 17	9 26 30	11 28 43	13 27 0	15 29 13	17 27 30
19 34 37	21 36 50	23 27 14	1 29 27	3 27 43	5 29 57	7 28 13	9 30 27	11 32 40	13 30 56	15 33 10	17 31 26
19 38 33	21 40 47	23 31 10	1 33 23	3 31 40	5 33 53	7 32 10	9 34 23	11 36 36	13 34 53	15 37 6	17 35 23
19 42 30	21 44 43	23 35 7	1 37 20	3 35 37	5 37 50	7 36 7	9 38 20	11 40 33	13 38 50	15 41 3	17 39 20
19 46 27	21 48 40	23 39 3	1 41 16	3 39 33	5 41 46	7 40 3	9 42 16	11 44 30	13 42 46	15 44 59	17 43 16
19 50 23	21 52 36	23 43 0	1 45 13	3 43 30	5 45 43	7 44 0	9 46 13	11 48 26	13 46 43	15 48 56	17 47 13
19 54 20	21 56 33	23 46 56	1 49 10	3 47 26	5 49 40	7 47 56	9 50 9	11 52 23	13 50 39	15 52 52	17 51 9
19 58 16	22 0 29	23 50 53	1 53 6	3 51 23	5 53 36	7 51 53	9 54 6	11 56 19	13 54 36	15 56 49	17 55 6
20 2 13	22 4 26	23 54 49	1 57 3	3 55 19	5 57 33	7 55 49	9 58 3	12 0 16	13 58 32	16 0 46	17 59 2
20 6 9	22 8 23	23 58 46	2 0 59	3 59 16	6 1 29	7 59 46	10 1 59	12 4 12	14 2 29	16 4 2	18 2 59
20 10 6	22 12 19	0 2 43	2 4 56	4 3 12	6 5 26	8 3 43	10 5 56	12 8 9	14 6 25	16 8 39	18 6 55
20 14 2	22 16 16	0 6 39	2 8 52	4 7 9	6 9 22	8 7 39	10 9 52	12 12 5	14 10 22	16 12 35	18 10 52
20 17 59	22 20 12	0 10 36	2 12 49	4 11 6	6 13 19	8 11 36	10 13 49	12 16 2	14 14 19	16 16 32	18 14 49
20 21 56	22 24 9	0 14 32	2 16 45	4 15 2	6 17 15	8 15 32	10 17 45	12 19 59	14 18 15	16 20 28	18 18 45
20 25 52	22 28 5	0 18 29	2 20 42	4 18 59	6 21 12	8 19 29	10 21 42	12 23 55	14 22 12	16 24 25	18 22 42
20 29 49	22 32 2	0 22 25	2 24 39	4 22 55	6 25 9	8 23 25	10 25 38	12 27 52	14 26 8	16 28 22	18 26 38
20 33 45		0 26 22	2 28 35	4 26 52	6 29 5	8 27 22	10 29 35	12 31 48	14 30 5	16 32 18	18 30 35
20 37 42		0 30 18	2 32 32	4 30 48	6 33 2	8 31 18	10 33 32	12 35 45	14 34 1	16 36 15	18 34 31
20 41 38		0 34 15		4 34 45		8 35 15	10 37 28		14 37 58		18 38 28

		1	2	3	4	5	6	7	8	9	10	11	12
1954	1	18 42 24	20 44 38	22 35 1	0 37 14	2 35 31	4 37 44	6 36 1	8 38 14	10 40 28	12 38 44	14 40 57	16 39 14
	2	18 46 21	20 48 34	22 38 58	0 41 11	2 39 28	4 41 41	6 39 58	8 42 11	10 44 24	12 42 41	14 44 54	16 43 11
	3	18 50 18	20 52 31	22 42 54	0 45 8	2 43 24	4 45 37	6 43 54	8 46 7	10 48 21	12 46 37	14 48 50	16 47 7
	4	18 54 14	20 56 27	22 46 51	0 49 4	2 47 21	4 49 34	6 47 51	8 50 4	10 52 17	12 50 34	14 52 47	16 51 4
	5	18 58 11	21 0 24	22 50 48	0 53 1	2 51 17	4 53 31	6 51 47	8 54 1	10 56 14	12 54 30	14 56 44	16 55 0
	6	19 2 7	21 4 21	22 54 44	0 56 57	2 55 14	4 57 27	6 55 44	8 57 57	11 0 10	12 58 27	15 0 40	16 58 57
	7	19 6 4	21 8 17	22 58 41	1 0 54	2 59 10	5 1 24	6 59 40	9 1 54	11 4 7	13 2 23	15 4 37	17 2 53
	8	19 10 0	21 12 14	23 2 37	1 4 50	3 3 7	5 5 20	7 3 37	9 5 50	11 8 3	13 6 20	15 8 33	17 6 50
	9	19 13 57	21 16 10	23 6 34	1 8 47	3 7 4	5 9 17	7 7 34	9 9 47	11 12 0	13 10 17	15 12 30	17 10 46
	10	19 17 54	21 20 7	23 10 30	1 12 43	3 11 0	5 13 13	7 11 30	9 13 43	11 15 57	13 14 13	15 16 26	17 14 43
	11	19 21 50	21 24 3	23 14 27	1 16 40	3 14 57	5 17 10	7 15 27	9 17 40	11 19 53	13 18 10	15 20 23	17 18 40
	12	19 25 47	21 28 0	23 18 23	1 20 37	3 18 53	5 21 6	7 19 23	9 21 36	11 23 50	13 22 6	15 24 19	17 22 36
	13	19 29 43	21 31 56	23 22 20	1 24 33	3 22 50	5 25 3	7 23 20	9 25 33	11 27 46	13 26 3	15 28 16	17 26 33
	14	19 33 40	21 35 53	23 26 17	1 28 30	3 26 46	5 29 0	7 27 16	9 29 30	11 31 43	13 29 59	15 32 13	17 30 29
	15	19 37 36	21 39 50	23 30 13	1 32 26	3 30 43	5 32 56	7 31 13	9 33 26	11 35 39	13 33 56	15 36 9	17 34 26
	16	19 41 33	21 43 46	23 34 10	1 36 23	3 34 39	5 36 53	7 35 9	9 37 23	11 39 36	13 37 52	15 40 6	17 38 22
	17	19 45 29	21 47 43	23 38 6	1 40 19	3 38 36	5 40 49	7 39 6	9 41 19	11 43 32	13 41 49	15 44 2	17 42 19
	18	19 49 26	21 51 39	23 42 3	1 44 16	3 42 33	5 44 46	7 43 3	9 45 16	11 47 29	13 45 46	15 47 59	17 46 15
	19	19 53 23	21 55 36	23 45 59	1 48 12	3 46 29	5 48 42	7 46 59	9 49 12	11 51 26	13 49 42	15 51 55	17 50 12
	20	19 57 19	21 59 32	23 49 56	1 52 9	3 50 26	5 52 39	7 50 56	9 53 9	11 55 22	13 53 39	15 55 52	17 54 9
	21	20 1 16	22 3 29	23 53 52	1 56 6	3 54 22	5 56 35	7 54 52	9 57 5	11 59 19	13 57 35	15 59 48	17 58 5
	22	20 5 12	22 7 25	23 57 49	2 0 2	3 58 19	6 0 32	7 58 49	10 1 2	12 3 15	14 1 32	16 3 45	18 2 2
	23	20 9 9	22 11 22	0 1 45	2 3 59	4 2 15	6 4 29	8 2 45	10 4 59	12 7 12	14 5 28	16 7 42	18 5 58
	24	20 13 5	22 15 19	0 5 42	2 7 55	4 6 12	6 8 25	8 6 42	10 8 55	12 11 8	14 9 25	16 11 38	18 9 55
	25	20 17 2	22 19 15	0 9 39	2 11 52	4 10 8	6 12 22	8 10 38	10 12 52	12 15 5	14 13 21	16 15 35	18 13 51
	26	20 20 58	22 23 12	0 13 35	2 15 48	4 14 5	6 16 18	8 14 35	10 16 48	12 19 1	14 17 18	16 19 31	18 17 48
	27	20 24 55	22 27 8	0 17 32	2 19 45	4 18 2	6 20 15	8 18 32	10 20 45	12 22 58	14 21 15	16 23 28	18 21 45
	28	20 28 52	22 31 5	0 21 28	2 23 41	4 21 58	6 24 11	8 22 28	10 24 41	12 26 54	14 25 11	16 27 24	18 25 41
	29	20 32 48		0 25 25	2 27 38	4 25 55	6 28 8	8 26 25	10 28 38	12 30 51	14 29 8	16 31 21	18 29 38
	30	20 36 45		0 29 21	2 31 35	4 29 51	6 32 5	8 30 21	10 32 34	12 34 48	14 33 4	16 35 17	18 33 34
	31	20 40 41		0 33 18		4 33 48		8 34 18	10 36 31		14 37 1		18 37 31
1955	1	18 41 27	20 43 41	22 34 4	0 36 17	2 34 34	4 36 47	6 35 4	8 37 17	10 39 30	12 37 47	14 40 0	16 38 17
	2	18 45 24	20 47 47	22 38 1	0 40 14	2 38 30	4 40 44	6 39 0	8 41 14	10 43 27	12 41 43	14 43 57	16 42 13
	3	18 49 20	20 51 34	22 41 57	0 44 10	2 42 27	4 44 40	6 42 57	8 45 10	10 47 23	12 45 40	14 47 53	16 46 10
	4	18 53 17	20 55 30	22 45 54	0 48 7	2 46 24	4 48 37	6 46 53	8 49 7	10 51 20	12 49 36	14 51 50	16 50 6
	5	18 57 14	20 59 27	22 49 50	0 52 3	2 50 20	4 52 33	6 50 50	8 53 3	10 55 16	12 53 33	14 55 46	16 54 3
	6	19 1 10	21 3 23	22 53 47	0 56 0	2 54 17	4 56 30	6 54 47	8 57 0	10 59 13	12 57 30	14 59 43	16 57 59
	7	19 5 7	21 7 20	22 57 43	0 59 57	2 58 13	5 0 26	6 58 43	9 0 56	11 3 10	13 1 26	15 3 39	17 1 56
	8	19 9 3	21 11 16	23 1 40	1 3 53	3 2 10	5 4 23	7 2 40	9 4 53	11 7 6	13 5 23	15 7 36	17 5 53
	9	19 13 0	21 15 13	23 5 37	1 7 50	3 6 6	5 8 20	7 6 36	9 8 50	11 11 3	13 9 19	15 11 32	17 9 49
	10	19 16 56	21 19 10	23 9 33	1 11 46	3 10 3	5 12 16	7 10 33	9 12 46	11 14 59	13 13 16	15 15 29	17 13 46
	11	19 20 53	21 23 6	23 13 30	1 15 43	3 13 59	5 16 13	7 14 29	9 16 43	11 18 56	13 17 12	15 19 26	17 17 42
	12	19 24 49	21 27 3	23 17 26	1 19 39	3 17 56	5 20 9	7 18 26	9 20 39	11 22 52	13 21 9	15 23 22	17 21 39
	13	19 28 46	21 30 59	23 21 23	1 23 36	3 21 53	5 24 6	7 22 22	9 24 36	11 26 49	13 25 5	15 27 19	17 25 35
	14	19 32 43	21 34 56	23 25 19	1 27 32	3 25 49	5 28 2	7 26 19	9 28 32	11 30 45	13 29 2	15 31 15	17 29 32
	15	19 36 39	21 38 52	23 29 16	1 31 29	3 29 46	5 31 59	7 30 16	9 32 29	11 34 42	13 32 59	15 35 12	17 33 29
	16	19 40 36	21 42 49	23 33 12	1 35 26	3 33 42	5 35 55	7 34 12	9 36 25	11 38 39	13 36 55	15 39 8	17 37 25
	17	19 44 32	21 46 45	23 37 9	1 39 22	3 37 39	5 39 52	7 38 9	9 40 22	11 42 35	13 40 52	15 43 5	17 41 22
	18	19 48 29	21 50 42	23 41 6	1 43 19	3 41 35	5 43 49	7 42 5	9 44 19	11 46 32	13 44 48	15 47 1	17 45 18
	19	19 52 25	21 54 39	23 45 2	1 47 15	3 45 32	5 47 45	7 46 2	9 48 15	11 50 28	13 48 45	15 50 58	17 49 15
	20	19 56 22	21 58 35	23 48 59	1 51 12	3 49 28	5 51 42	7 49 58	9 52 12	11 54 25	13 52 41	15 54 55	17 53 11
	21	20 0 18	22 2 32	23 52 55	1 55 8	3 53 25	5 55 38	7 53 55	9 56 8	11 58 21	13 56 38	15 58 51	17 57 8
	22	20 4 15	22 6 28	23 56 52	1 59 5	3 57 22	5 59 35	7 57 52	10 0 5	12 2 18	14 0 34	16 2 48	18 1 4
	23	20 8 12	22 10 25	0 0 48	2 3 1	4 1 18	6 3 31	8 1 48	10 4 1	12 6 14	14 4 31	16 6 44	18 5 1
	24	20 12 8	22 14 21	0 4 45	2 6 58	4 5 15	6 7 28	8 5 45	10 7 58	12 10 11	14 8 28	16 10 41	18 8 58
	25	20 16 5	22 18 18	0 8 41	2 10 55	4 9 11	6 11 24	8 9 41	10 11 54	12 14 8	14 12 24	16 14 37	18 12 54
	26	20 20 1	22 22 14	0 12 38	2 14 51	4 13 8	6 15 21	8 13 38	10 15 51	12 18 4	14 16 21	16 18 34	18 16 51
	27	20 23 58	22 26 11	0 16 34	2 18 48	4 17 4	6 19 18	8 17 34	10 19 48	12 22 1	14 20 17	16 22 30	18 20 47
	28	20 27 54	22 30 8	0 20 31	2 22 44	4 21 1	6 23 14	8 21 31	10 23 44	12 25 57	14 24 14	16 26 27	18 24 44
	29	20 31 51		0 24 28	2 26 41	4 24 57	6 27 11	8 25 27	10 27 41	12 29 54	14 28 10	16 30 24	18 28 40
	30	20 35 47		0 28 24	2 30 37	4 28 54	6 31 7	8 29 24	10 31 37	12 33 50	14 32 7	16 34 20	18 32 37
	31	20 39 44		0 32 21		4 32 51		8 33 21	10 35 34		14 36 3		18 36 33
1956	1	18 40 30	20 42 43	22 37 3	0 39 16	2 37 33	4 39 46	6 38 3	8 40 16	10 42 29	12 40 46	14 42 59	16 41 16
	2	18 44 27	20 46 40	22 41 0	0 43 13	2 41 30	4 43 43	6 42 0	8 44 13	10 46 26	12 44 43	14 46 56	16 45 12
	3	18 48 23	20 50 36	22 44 56	0 47 10	2 45 26	4 47 39	6 45 56	8 48 9	10 50 23	12 48 39	14 50 52	16 49 9
	4	18 52 20	20 54 33	22 48 53	0 51 6	2 49 23	4 51 36	6 49 53	8 52 6	10 54 19	12 52 36	14 54 49	16 53 6
	5	18 56 16	20 58 29	22 52 50	0 55 3	2 53 19	4 55 33	6 53 49	8 56 2	10 58 16	12 56 32	14 58 45	16 57 2
	6	19 0 13	21 2 26	22 56 46	0 58 59	2 57 16	4 59 29	6 57 46	8 59 59	11 2 12	13 0 29	15 2 42	17 0 59
	7	19 4 9	21 6 23	23 0 43	1 2 56	3 1 12	5 3 26	7 1 42	9 3 56	11 6 9	13 4 25	15 6 38	17 4 55
	8	19 8 6	21 10 19	23 4 39	1 6 52	3 5 9	5 7 22	7 5 39	9 7 52	11 10 5	13 8 22	15 10 35	17 8 52
	9	19 12 2	21 14 16	23 8 36	1 10 49	3 9 5	5 11 19	7 9 35	9 11 49	11 14 2	13 12 18	15 14 32	17 12 48
	10	19 15 59	21 18 12	23 12 32	1 14 45	3 13 2	5 15 15	7 13 32	9 15 45	11 17 58	13 16 15	15 18 28	17 16 45
	11	19 19 56	21 22 9	23 16 29	1 18 42	3 16 59	5 19 12	7 17 29	9 19 42	11 21 55	13 20 12	15 22 25	17 20 41
	12	19 23 52	21 26 5	23 20 25	1 22 39	3 20 55	5 23 8	7 21 25	9 23 38	11 25 52	13 24 8	15 26 21	17 24 38
	13	19 27 49	21 30 2	23 24 22	1 26 35	3 24 52	5 27 5	7 25 22	9 27 35	11 29 48	13 28 5	15 30 18	17 28 35
	14	19 31 45	21 33 58	23 28 19	1 30 32	3 28 48	5 31 2	7 29 18	9 31 31	11 33 45	13 32 1	15 34 14	17 32 31
	15	19 35 42	21 37 55	23 32 15	1 34 28	3 32 45	5 34 58	7 33 15	9 35 28	11 37 41	13 35 58	15 38 11	17 36 28
	16	19 39 38	21 41 52	23 36 12	1 38 25	3 36 41	5 38 55	7 37 11	9 39 25	11 41 38	13 39 54	15 42 7	17 40 24
	17	19 43 35	21 45 48	23 40 8	1 42 21	3 40 38	5 42 51	7 41 8	9 43 21	11 45 34	13 43 51	15 46 4	17 44 21
	18	19 47 31	21 49 45	23 44 5	1 46 18	3 44 35	5 46 48	7 45 4	9 47 18	11 49 31	13 47 47	15 50 1	17 48 17
	19	19 51 28	21 53 41	23 48 1	1 50 14	3 48 31	5 50 44	7 49 1	9 51 14	11 53 27	13 51 44	15 53 57	17 52 14
	20	19 55 25	21 57 38	23 51 58	1 54 11	3 52 28	5 54 41	7 52 58	9 55 11	11 57 24	13 55 40	15 57 54	17 56 10
	21	19 59 21	22 1 34	23 55 54	1 58 8	3 56 24	5 58 37	7 56 54	9 59 7	12 1 20	13 59 37	16 1 50	18 0 7
	22	20 3 18	22 5 31	23 59 51	2 2 4	4 0 21	6 2 34	8 0 51	10 3 4	12 5 17	14 3 34	16 5 47	18 4 4
	23	20 7 14	22 9 27	0 3 47	2 6 1	4 4 17	6 6 31	8 4 47	10 7 0	12 9 14	14 7 30	16 9 43	18 8 0
	24	20 11 11	22 13 24	0 7 44	2 9 57	4 8 14	6 10 27	8 8 44	10 10 57	12 13 10	14 11 27	16 13 40	18 11 57
	25	20 15 7	22 17 21	0 11 41	2 13 54	4 12 10	6 14 24	8 12 40	10 14 54	12 17 7	14 15 23	16 17 36	18 15 53
	26	20 19 4	22 21 17	0 15 37	2 17 50	4 16 7	6 18 20	8 16 37	10 18 50	12 21 3	14 19 20	16 21 33	18 19 50
	27	20 23 0	22 25 14	0 19 34	2 21 47	4 20 4	6 22 17	8 20 33	10 22 47	12 25 0	14 23 16	16 25 30	18 23 46
	28	20 26 57	22 29 10	0 23 30	2 25 43	4 24 0	6 26 13	8 24 30	10 26 43	12 28 56	14 27 13	16 29 26	18 27 43
	29	20 30 54	22 33 7	0 27 27	2 29 40	4 27 57	6 30 10	8 28 27	10 30 40	12 32 53	14 31 10	16 33 23	18 31 39
	30	20 34 50		0 31 23	2 33 37	4 31 53	6 34 6	8 32 23	10 34 36	12 36 49	14 35 6	16 37 19	18 35 36
	31	20 38 47		0 35 20		4 35 50		8 36 20	10 38 33		14 39 3		18 39 33
1957	1	18 43 29	20 45 42	22 36 6	0 38 19	2 36 36	4 38 49	6 37 6	8 39 19	10 41 32	12 39 49	14 42 2	16 40 18
	2	18 47 26	20 49 39	22 40 2	0 42 16	2 40 32	4 42 45	6 41 2	8 43 15	10 45 28	12 43 45	14 45 58	16 44 15
	3	18 51 22	20 53 35	22 43 59	0 46 12	2 44 29	4 46 42	6 44 59	8 47 12	10 49 25	12 47 42	14 49 55	16 48 11
	4	18 55 19	20 57 32	22 47 56	0 50 9	2 48 25	4 50 38	6 48 55	8 51 8	10 53 22	12 51 38	14 53 51	16 52 8
	5	18 59 15	21 1 29	22 51 52	0 54 5	2 52 22	4 54 35	6 52 52	8 55 5	10 57 18	12 55 35	14 57 48	16 56 5
	6	19 3 12	21 5 25	22 55 49	0 58 2	2 56 18	4 58 32	6 56 48	8 59 2	11 1 15	12 59 31	15 1 44	17 0 1
	7	19 7 8	21 9 22	22 59 45	1 1 58	3 0 15	5 2 28	7 0 45	9 2 58	11 5 11	13 3 28	15 5 41	17 3 58
	8	19 11 5	21 13 18	23 3 42	1 5 55	3 4 11	5 6 25	7 4 41	9 6 55	11 9 8	13 7 24	15 9 38	17 7 54
	9	19 15 2	21 17 15	23 7 38	1 9 51	3 8 8	5 10 21	7 8 38	9 10 51	11 13 4	13 11 21	15 13 34	17 11 51
	10	19 18 58	21 21 11	23 11 35	1 13 48	3 12 5	5 14 18	7 12 35	9 14 48	11 17 1	13 15 17	15 17 31	17 15 47
	11	19 22 55	21 25 8	23 15 31	1 17 45	3 16 1	5 18 14	7 16 31	9 18 44	11 20 57	13 19 14	15 21 27	17 19 44
	12	19 26 51	21 29 4	23 19 28	1 21 41	3 19 58	5 22 11	7 20 28	9 22 41	11 24 54	13 23 11	15 25 24	17 23 40
	13	19 30 48	21 33 1	23 23 25	1 25 38	3 23 54	5 26 8	7 24 24	9 26 37	11 28 51	13 27 7	15 29 20	17 27 37
	14	19 34 44	21 36 58	23 27 21	1 29 34	3 27 51	5 30 4	7 28 21	9 30 34	11 32 47	13 31 4	15 33 17	17 31 34
	15	19 38 41	21 40 54	23 31 18	1 33 31	3 31 47	5 34 1	7 32 17	9 34 31	11 36 44	13 35 0	15 37 13	17 35 30
	16	19 42 37	21 44 51	23 35 14	1 37 27	3 35 44	5 37 57	7 36 14	9 38 27	11 40 40	13 38 57	15 41 10	17 39 27
	17	19 46 34	21 48 47	23 39 11	1 41 24	3 39 40	5 41 54	7 40 10	9 42 24	11 44 37	13 42 53	15 45 7	17 43 23
	18	19 50 31	21 52 44	23 43 7	1 45 20	3 43 37	5 45 50	7 44 7	9 46 20	11 48 33	13 46 50	15 49 3	17 47 20
	19	19 54 27	21 56 40	23 47 4	1 49 17	3 47 34	5 49 47	7 48 4	9 50 17	11 52 30	13 50 46	15 53 0	17 51 16
	20	19 58 24	22 0 37	23 51 0	1 53 14	3 51 30	5 53 43	7 52 0	9 54 13	11 56 26	13 54 43	15 56 56	17 55 13
	21	20 2 20	22 4 33	23 54 57	1 57 10	3 55 27	5 57 40	7 55 57	9 58 10	12 0 23	13 58 40	16 0 53	17 59 9
	22	20 6 17	22 8 30	23 58 53	2 1 7	3 59 23	6 1 36	7 59 53	10 2 6	12 4 20	14 2 36	16 4 49	18 3 6
	23	20 10 13	22 12 27	0 2 50	2 5 3	4 3 20	6 5 33	8 3 50	10 6 3	12 8 16	14 6 33	16 8 46	18 7 3
	24	20 14 10	22 16 23	0 6 47	2 9 0	4 7 16	6 9 30	8 7 46	10 10 0	12 12 13	14 10 29	16 12 42	18 10 59
	25	20 18 6	22 20 20	0 10 43	2 12 56	4 11 13	6 13 26	8 11 43	10 13 56	12 16 9	14 14 26	16 16 39	18 14 56
	26	20 22 3	22 24 16	0 14 40	2 16 53	4 15 9	6 17 23	8 15 39	10 17 53	12 20 6	14 18 22	16 20 36	18 18 52
	27	20 26 0	22 28 13	0 18 36	2 20 49	4 19 6	6 21 19	8 19 36	10 21 49	12 24 2	14 22 19	16 24 32	18 22 49
	28	20 29 56	22 32 9	0 22 33	2 24 46	4 23 3	6 25 16	8 23 33	10 25 46	12 27 59	14 26 15	16 28 29	18 26 45
	29	20 33 53		0 26 29	2 28 42	4 26 59	6 29 12	8 27 29	10 29 42	12 31 55	14 30 12	16 32 25	18 30 42
	30	20 37 49		0 30 26	2 32 39	4 30 56	6 33 9	8 31 26	10 33 39	12 35 52	14 34 9	16 36 22	18 34 38
	31	20 41 46		0 34 22		4 34 52		8 35 22	10 37 35		14 38 5		18 38 35

Year	Day	1	2	3	4	5	6	7	8	9	10	11	12
1958	1	18 42 32	20 44 45	22 35 8	0 37 21	2 35 38	4 37 51	6 36 8	8 38 21	10 40 34	12 38 51	14 41 4	16 39 21
	2	18 46 28	20 48 41	22 39 5	0 41 18	2 39 35	4 41 48	6 40 5	8 42 18	10 44 31	12 42 48	14 45 1	16 43 17
	3	18 50 25	20 52 38	22 43 1	0 45 15	2 43 31	4 45 44	6 44 1	8 46 14	10 48 27	12 46 44	14 48 57	16 47 14
	4	18 54 21	20 56 35	22 46 58	0 49 11	2 47 28	4 49 41	6 47 58	8 50 11	10 52 24	12 50 41	14 52 54	16 51 10
	5	18 58 18	21 0 31	22 50 55	0 53 8	2 51 24	4 53 37	6 51 54	8 54 7	10 56 21	12 54 37	14 56 50	16 55 7
	6	19 2 14	21 4 28	22 54 51	0 57 4	2 55 21	4 57 34	6 55 51	8 58 4	11 0 17	12 58 34	15 0 47	16 59 3
	7	19 6 11	21 8 24	22 58 48	1 1 1	2 59 17	5 1 31	6 59 47	9 2 1	11 4 14	13 2 30	15 4 43	17 3 0
	8	19 10 7	21 12 21	23 2 44	1 4 57	3 3 14	5 5 27	7 3 44	9 5 57	11 8 10	13 6 27	15 8 40	17 6 57
	9	19 14 4	21 16 17	23 6 41	1 8 54	3 7 10	5 9 24	7 7 40	9 9 54	11 12 7	13 10 24	15 12 36	17 10 53
	10	19 18 1	21 20 14	23 10 37	1 12 50	3 11 7	5 13 20	7 11 37	9 13 50	11 16 3	13 14 20	15 16 33	17 14 50
	11	19 21 57	21 24 10	23 14 34	1 16 47	3 15 4	5 17 17	7 15 34	9 17 47	11 20 0	13 18 16	15 20 30	17 18 46
	12	19 25 54	21 28 7	23 18 30	1 20 44	3 19 0	5 21 13	7 19 30	9 21 43	11 23 56	13 22 13	15 24 26	17 22 43
	13	19 29 50	21 32 3	23 22 27	1 24 40	3 22 57	5 25 10	7 23 27	9 25 40	11 27 53	13 26 10	15 28 23	17 26 39
	14	19 33 47	21 36 0	23 26 24	1 28 37	3 26 53	5 29 6	7 27 23	9 29 36	11 31 50	13 30 6	15 32 19	17 30 36
	15	19 37 43	21 39 57	23 30 20	1 32 33	3 30 50	5 33 3	7 31 20	9 33 33	11 35 46	13 34 3	15 36 16	17 34 33
	16	19 41 40	21 43 53	23 34 17	1 36 30	3 34 46	5 37 0	7 35 16	9 37 30	11 39 43	13 37 59	15 40 12	17 38 29
	17	19 45 36	21 47 50	23 38 13	1 40 26	3 38 43	5 40 56	7 39 13	9 41 26	11 43 39	13 41 56	15 44 9	17 42 26
	18	19 49 33	21 51 46	23 42 10	1 44 23	3 42 39	5 44 53	7 43 9	9 45 23	11 47 36	13 45 52	15 48 5	17 46 22
	19	19 53 30	21 55 43	23 46 6	1 48 19	3 46 36	5 48 49	7 47 6	9 49 19	11 51 32	13 49 49	15 52 2	17 50 19
	20	19 57 26	21 59 39	23 50 3	1 52 16	3 50 33	5 52 46	7 51 3	9 53 16	11 55 29	13 53 45	15 55 59	17 54 15
	21	20 1 23	22 3 36	23 53 59	1 56 12	3 54 29	5 56 42	7 54 59	9 57 12	11 59 25	13 57 42	15 59 55	17 58 12
	22	20 5 19	22 7 32	23 57 56	2 0 9	3 58 26	6 0 39	7 58 56	10 1 9	12 3 22	14 1 39	16 3 52	18 2 8
	23	20 9 16	22 11 29	0 1 53	2 4 6	4 2 23	6 4 35	8 2 52	10 5 5	12 7 19	14 5 35	16 7 48	18 6 5
	24	20 13 12	22 15 26	0 5 49	2 8 2	4 6 19	6 8 32	8 6 49	10 9 2	12 11 15	14 9 32	16 11 45	18 10 2
	25	20 17 9	22 19 22	0 9 46	2 11 59	4 10 15	6 12 29	8 10 45	10 12 59	12 15 12	14 13 28	16 15 42	18 13 58
	26	20 21 5	22 23 19	0 13 42	2 15 55	4 14 12	6 16 25	8 14 42	10 16 55	12 19 8	14 17 25	16 19 38	18 17 55
	27	20 25 2	22 27 15	0 17 39	2 19 52	4 18 8	6 20 22	8 18 38	10 20 52	12 23 5	14 21 22	16 23 34	18 21 51
	28	20 28 59	22 31 12	0 21 35	2 23 48	4 22 5	6 24 18	8 22 35	10 24 48	12 27 1	14 25 18	16 27 31	18 25 48
	29	20 32 55		0 25 32	2 27 45	4 26 2	6 28 15	8 26 32	10 28 45	12 30 58	14 29 14	16 31 28	18 29 44
	30	20 36 52		0 29 28	2 31 41	4 29 58	6 32 11	8 30 28	10 32 41	12 34 54	14 33 11	16 35 24	18 33 41
	31	20 40 48		0 33 25		4 33 55		8 34 25	10 36 38		14 37 7		18 37 37
1959	1	18 41 34	20 43 47	22 34 11	0 36 24	2 34 40	4 36 54	6 35 10	8 37 24	10 39 37	12 37 53	14 40 6	16 38 23
	2	18 45 31	20 47 44	22 38 7	0 40 20	2 38 37	4 40 50	6 39 7	8 41 20	10 43 33	12 41 50	14 44 3	16 42 20
	3	18 49 27	20 51 40	22 42 4	0 44 17	2 42 34	4 44 47	6 43 3	8 45 17	10 47 30	12 45 46	14 47 59	16 46 16
	4	18 53 24	20 55 37	22 46 0	0 48 13	2 46 30	4 48 43	6 47 0	8 49 13	10 51 26	12 49 43	14 51 56	16 50 13
	5	18 57 20	20 59 33	22 49 57	0 52 10	2 50 27	4 52 40	6 50 57	8 53 10	10 55 23	12 53 39	14 55 53	16 54 9
	6	19 1 17	21 3 30	22 53 53	0 56 7	2 54 23	4 56 36	6 54 53	8 57 6	10 59 19	12 57 36	14 59 49	16 58 6
	7	19 5 13	21 7 27	22 57 50	1 0 3	2 58 20	5 0 33	6 58 50	9 1 3	11 3 16	13 1 33	15 3 46	17 2 2
	8	19 9 10	21 11 23	23 1 47	1 4 0	3 2 16	5 4 30	7 2 46	9 4 59	11 7 13	13 5 29	15 7 42	17 5 59
	9	19 13 6	21 15 20	23 5 43	1 7 56	3 6 13	5 8 26	7 6 43	9 8 56	11 11 9	13 9 26	15 11 39	17 9 56
	10	19 17 3	21 19 16	23 9 40	1 11 53	3 10 9	5 12 23	7 10 39	9 12 53	11 15 6	13 13 22	15 15 35	17 13 52
	11	19 21 0	21 23 13	23 13 36	1 15 49	3 14 6	5 16 19	7 14 36	9 16 49	11 19 2	13 17 19	15 19 32	17 17 49
	12	19 24 56	21 27 9	23 17 33	1 19 46	3 18 2	5 20 16	7 18 32	9 20 46	11 22 59	13 21 15	15 23 28	17 21 45
	13	19 28 53	21 31 6	23 21 29	1 23 42	3 21 59	5 24 12	7 22 29	9 24 42	11 26 55	13 25 12	15 27 25	17 25 42
	14	19 32 49	21 35 2	23 25 26	1 27 39	3 25 56	5 28 9	7 26 26	9 28 39	11 30 52	13 29 8	15 31 22	17 29 38
	15	19 36 46	21 38 59	23 29 22	1 31 36	3 29 52	5 32 5	7 30 22	9 32 35	11 34 48	13 33 5	15 35 18	17 33 35
	16	19 40 42	21 42 56	23 33 19	1 35 32	3 33 49	5 36 2	7 34 19	9 36 32	11 38 45	13 37 2	15 39 15	17 37 31
	17	19 44 39	21 46 52	23 37 16	1 39 29	3 37 45	5 39 59	7 38 15	9 40 28	11 42 42	13 40 58	15 43 11	17 41 28
	18	19 48 35	21 50 49	23 41 12	1 43 25	3 41 42	5 43 55	7 42 12	9 44 25	11 46 38	13 44 55	15 47 8	17 45 25
	19	19 52 32	21 54 45	23 45 9	1 47 22	3 45 38	5 47 52	7 46 8	9 48 22	11 50 35	13 48 51	15 51 4	17 49 21
	20	19 56 29	21 58 42	23 49 5	1 51 18	3 49 35	5 51 48	7 50 5	9 52 18	11 54 31	13 52 48	15 55 1	17 53 18
	21	20 0 25	22 2 38	23 53 2	1 55 15	3 52 31	5 55 45	7 54 1	9 56 15	11 58 28	13 56 44	15 58 57	17 57 14
	22	20 4 22	22 6 35	23 56 58	1 59 11	3 57 28	5 59 41	7 57 58	10 0 11	12 2 24	14 0 41	16 2 54	18 1 11
	23	20 8 18	22 10 31	0 0 55	2 3 8	4 1 25	6 3 38	8 1 55	10 4 8	12 6 21	14 4 37	16 6 51	18 5 7
	24	20 12 15	22 14 28	0 4 51	2 7 5	4 5 21	6 7 34	8 5 51	10 8 4	12 10 17	14 8 34	16 10 47	18 9 4
	25	20 16 11	22 18 25	0 8 48	2 11 1	4 9 18	6 11 31	8 9 48	10 12 1	12 14 14	14 12 31	16 14 44	18 13 0
	26	20 20 8	22 22 21	0 12 45	2 14 58	4 13 14	6 15 28	8 13 44	10 15 57	12 18 11	14 16 27	16 18 40	18 16 57
	27	20 24 4	22 26 18	0 16 41	2 18 54	4 17 11	6 19 24	8 17 41	10 19 54	12 22 7	14 20 24	16 22 37	18 20 54
	28	20 28 1	22 30 14	0 20 38	2 22 51	4 21 7	6 23 21	8 21 37	10 23 50	12 26 4	14 24 20	16 26 33	18 24 50
	29	20 31 58		0 24 34	2 26 47	4 25 4	6 27 17	8 25 34	10 27 47	12 30 0	14 28 17	18 30 30	18 28 47
	30	20 35 54		0 28 31	2 30 44	4 29 1	6 31 14	8 29 30	10 31 44	12 33 57	14 32 13	16 34 26	18 32 43
	31	20 39 51		0 32 27		4 32 57		8 33 27	10 35 40		14 36 10		18 36 40
1960	1	18 40 36	20 42 50	22 37 10	0 39 23	2 37 39	4 39 53	6 38 9	8 40 22	10 42 36	12 40 52	14 43 5	16 41 22
	2	18 44 33	20 46 46	22 41 6	0 43 19	2 41 36	4 43 49	6 42 6	8 44 19	10 46 32	12 44 49	14 47 2	16 45 19
	3	18 48 29	20 50 43	22 45 3	0 47 16	2 45 32	4 47 46	6 46 2	8 48 16	10 50 29	12 48 45	14 50 58	16 49 15
	4	18 52 26	20 54 39	22 48 59	0 51 12	2 49 29	4 51 42	6 49 59	8 52 12	10 54 25	12 52 42	14 54 55	16 53 12
	5	18 56 23	20 58 36	22 52 56	0 55 9	2 53 26	4 55 39	6 53 55	8 56 9	10 58 22	12 56 38	14 58 52	16 57 8
	6	19 0 19	21 2 32	22 56 52	0 59 5	2 57 22	4 59 35	6 57 52	9 0 5	11 2 18	13 0 35	15 2 48	17 1 5
	7	19 4 16	21 6 29	23 0 49	1 3 2	3 1 19	5 3 32	7 1 49	9 4 2	11 6 15	13 4 31	15 6 45	17 5 1
	8	19 8 12	21 10 25	23 4 45	1 6 59	3 5 15	5 7 28	7 5 45	9 7 58	11 10 11	13 8 28	15 10 41	17 8 58
	9	19 12 9	21 14 22	23 8 42	1 10 55	3 9 12	5 11 25	7 9 42	9 11 55	11 14 8	13 12 25	15 14 38	17 12 54
	10	19 16 5	21 18 19	23 12 39	1 14 52	3 13 8	5 15 22	7 13 38	9 15 51	11 18 5	13 16 21	15 18 34	17 16 51
	11	19 20 2	21 22 15	23 16 35	1 18 48	3 17 5	5 19 18	7 17 35	9 19 48	11 22 1	13 20 18	15 22 31	17 20 48
	12	19 23 58	21 26 12	23 20 32	1 22 45	3 21 1	5 23 15	7 21 31	9 23 45	11 25 58	13 24 14	15 26 27	17 24 44
	13	19 27 55	21 30 8	23 24 28	1 26 41	3 24 58	5 27 11	7 25 28	9 27 41	11 29 54	13 28 11	15 30 24	17 28 41
	14	19 31 52	21 34 5	23 28 25	1 30 38	3 28 55	5 31 8	7 29 24	9 31 38	11 33 51	13 32 7	15 34 21	17 32 37
	15	19 35 48	21 38 1	23 32 21	1 34 34	3 32 51	5 35 4	7 33 21	9 35 34	11 37 47	13 36 4	15 38 17	17 36 34
	16	19 39 45	21 41 58	23 36 18	1 38 31	3 36 48	5 39 1	7 37 18	9 39 31	11 41 44	13 40 0	15 42 14	17 40 30
	17	19 43 41	21 45 54	23 40 14	1 42 28	3 40 44	5 42 57	7 41 14	9 43 27	11 45 40	13 43 57	15 46 10	17 44 27
	18	19 47 38	21 49 51	23 44 11	1 46 24	3 44 41	5 46 54	7 45 11	9 47 24	11 49 37	13 47 54	15 50 7	17 48 23
	19	19 51 34	21 53 48	23 48 8	1 50 21	3 48 37	5 50 51	7 49 8	9 51 20	11 53 34	13 51 50	15 54 3	17 52 20
	20	19 55 31	21 57 44	23 52 4	1 54 17	3 52 34	5 54 47	7 53 4	9 55 17	11 57 30	13 55 47	15 58 0	17 56 17
	21	19 59 27	22 1 41	23 56 1	1 58 14	3 56 30	5 58 44	7 57 0	9 59 14	12 1 27	13 59 43	16 1 56	18 0 13
	22	20 3 24	22 5 37	23 59 57	2 2 10	4 0 27	6 2 40	8 0 57	10 3 10	12 5 23	14 3 40	16 5 53	18 4 10
	23	20 7 21	22 9 34	0 3 54	2 6 7	4 4 24	6 6 37	8 4 53	10 7 7	12 9 20	14 7 36	16 9 50	18 8 6
	24	20 11 17	22 13 30	0 7 50	2 10 3	4 8 20	6 10 33	8 8 50	10 11 3	12 13 16	14 11 33	16 13 46	18 12 3
	25	20 15 14	22 17 27	0 11 47	2 14 0	4 12 17	6 14 30	8 12 47	10 15 0	12 17 13	14 15 29	16 17 43	18 15 59
	26	20 19 10	22 21 23	0 15 43	2 17 57	4 16 13	6 18 26	8 16 43	10 18 56	12 21 9	14 19 26	16 21 39	18 19 56
	27	20 23 7	22 25 20	0 19 40	2 21 53	4 20 10	6 22 23	8 20 40	10 22 53	12 25 6	14 23 23	16 25 36	18 23 52
	28	20 27 3	22 29 17	0 23 37	2 25 50	4 24 6	6 26 20	8 24 36	10 26 49	12 29 3	14 27 19	16 29 32	18 27 49
	29	20 31 0	22 33 13	0 27 33	2 29 47	4 28 3	6 30 16	8 28 33	10 30 46	12 32 59	14 31 16	16 33 29	18 31 46
	30	20 34 56		0 31 30	2 33 43	4 31 59	6 34 13	8 32 29	10 34 42	12 36 56	14 35 12	16 37 25	18 35 42
	31	20 38 53		0 35 26		4 35 56		8 36 26	10 38 39		14 39 9		18 39 39
1961	1	18 43 35	20 45 48	22 36 12	0 38 25	2 36 42	4 38 55	6 37 12	8 39 25	10 41 38	12 39 55	14 42 8	16 40 24
	2	18 47 32	20 49 45	22 40 9	0 42 22	2 40 38	4 42 51	6 41 8	8 43 21	10 45 35	12 43 51	14 46 4	16 44 21
	3	18 51 28	20 53 42	22 44 5	0 46 18	2 44 35	4 46 48	6 45 5	8 47 18	10 49 31	12 47 48	14 50 1	16 48 17
	4	18 55 25	20 57 38	22 48 2	0 50 15	2 48 31	4 50 45	6 49 1	8 51 14	10 53 28	12 51 44	14 53 57	16 52 14
	5	18 59 21	21 1 35	22 51 58	0 54 11	2 52 28	4 54 41	6 52 58	8 55 11	10 57 24	12 55 41	14 57 54	16 56 11
	6	19 3 18	21 5 31	22 55 55	0 58 8	2 56 24	4 58 38	6 56 54	8 59 8	11 1 21	12 59 37	15 1 50	17 0 7
	7	19 7 15	21 9 28	22 59 51	1 2 4	3 0 21	5 2 34	7 0 51	9 3 4	11 5 17	13 3 34	15 5 47	17 4 4
	8	19 11 11	21 13 24	23 3 48	1 6 1	3 4 18	5 6 31	7 4 47	9 7 1	11 9 14	13 7 30	15 9 44	17 8 0
	9	19 15 8	21 17 21	23 7 44	1 9 58	3 8 14	5 10 27	7 8 44	9 10 57	11 13 10	13 11 27	15 13 40	17 11 57
	10	19 19 4	21 21 17	23 11 41	1 13 54	3 12 11	5 14 24	7 12 41	9 14 54	11 17 7	13 15 24	15 17 37	17 15 53
	11	19 23 1	21 25 14	23 15 37	1 17 51	3 16 7	5 18 20	7 16 37	9 18 50	11 21 4	13 19 20	15 21 33	17 19 50
	12	19 26 57	21 29 11	23 19 34	1 21 47	3 20 4	5 22 17	7 20 34	9 22 47	11 25 0	13 23 17	15 25 30	17 23 46
	13	19 30 54	21 33 7	23 23 31	1 25 44	3 24 0	5 26 14	7 24 30	9 26 43	11 28 57	13 27 13	15 29 26	17 27 43
	14	19 34 50	21 37 4	23 27 27	1 29 40	3 27 57	5 30 10	7 28 27	9 30 40	11 32 53	13 31 10	15 33 23	17 31 40
	15	19 38 47	21 41 0	23 31 24	1 33 37	3 31 53	5 34 7	7 32 23	9 34 37	11 36 50	13 35 6	15 37 19	17 35 36
	16	19 42 44	21 44 57	23 35 20	1 37 33	3 35 50	5 38 3	7 36 20	9 38 33	11 40 45	13 39 3	15 41 16	17 39 33
	17	19 46 40	21 48 53	23 39 17	1 41 30	3 39 47	5 42 0	7 40 16	9 42 30	11 44 43	13 42 59	15 45 13	17 43 29
	18	19 50 37	21 52 50	23 43 13	1 45 26	3 43 43	5 45 56	7 44 13	9 46 26	11 48 39	13 46 56	15 49 9	17 47 26
	19	19 54 33	21 56 46	23 47 10	1 49 23	3 47 40	5 49 53	7 48 10	9 50 23	11 52 36	13 50 52	15 53 6	17 51 22
	20	19 58 30	22 0 43	23 51 6	1 53 20	3 51 36	5 53 49	7 52 6	9 54 19	11 56 32	13 54 49	15 57 2	17 55 19
	21	20 2 26	22 4 40	23 55 3	1 57 16	3 55 33	5 57 46	7 56 3	9 58 16	12 0 29	13 58 46	16 0 59	17 59 15
	22	20 6 23	22 8 36	23 59 0	2 1 13	3 59 29	6 1 43	7 59 59	10 2 12	12 4 26	14 2 42	16 4 55	18 3 12
	23	20 10 19	22 12 33	0 2 56	2 5 9	4 3 26	6 5 39	8 3 56	10 6 9	12 8 22	14 6 39	16 8 52	18 7 9
	24	20 14 16	22 16 29	0 6 53	2 9 6	4 7 22	6 9 36	8 7 52	10 10 6	12 12 19	14 10 35	16 12 48	18 11 5
	25	20 18 13	22 20 26	0 10 49	2 13 2	4 11 19	6 13 32	8 11 49	10 14 2	12 16 15	14 14 32	16 16 45	18 15 2
	26	20 22 9	22 24 22	0 14 46	2 16 59	4 15 16	6 17 29	8 15 45	10 17 59	12 20 12	14 18 28	16 20 42	18 18 58
	27	20 26 6	22 28 19	0 18 42	2 20 55	4 19 12	6 21 25	8 19 42	10 21 55	12 24 8	14 22 25	16 24 38	18 22 55
	28	20 30 2	22 32 15	0 22 39	2 24 52	4 23 9	6 25 22	8 23 39	10 25 52	12 28 5	14 26 21	16 28 35	18 26 51
	29	20 33 59		0 26 35	2 28 49	4 27 5	6 29 18	8 27 35	10 29 48	12 32 1	14 30 18	16 32 31	18 30 48
	30	20 37 55		0 30 32	2 32 45	4 31 2	6 33 15	8 31 32	10 33 45	12 35 58	14 34 15	16 36 28	18 34 45
	31	20 41 52		0 34 29		4 34 58		8 35 28	10 37 41		14 38 11		18 38 41

Year	Day	1	2	3	4	5	6	7	8	9	10	11	12
1962	1	18 42 38	20 44 51	22 35 14	0 37 28	2 35 44	4 37 57	6 36 14	8 38 27	10 40 40	12 38 57	14 41 10	16 39 27
	2	18 46 34	20 48 47	22 39 11	0 41 24	2 39 41	4 41 54	6 40 11	8 42 24	10 44 37	12 42 54	14 45 7	16 43 23
	3	18 50 31	20 52 44	22 43 7	0 45 21	2 43 37	4 45 50	6 44 7	8 46 20	10 48 34	12 46 50	14 49 3	16 47 20
	4	18 54 27	20 56 41	22 47 4	0 49 17	2 47 34	4 49 47	6 48 4	8 50 17	10 52 30	12 50 47	14 53 0	16 51 16
	5	18 58 24	21 0 37	22 51 1	0 53 14	2 51 30	4 53 44	6 52 0	8 54 13	10 56 27	12 54 43	14 56 56	16 55 13
	6	19 2 20	21 4 34	22 54 57	0 57 10	2 55 27	4 57 40	6 55 57	8 58 10	11 0 23	12 58 40	15 0 53	16 59 10
	7	19 6 17	21 8 30	22 58 54	1 1 7	2 59 23	5 1 37	6 59 53	9 2 7	11 4 20	13 2 36	15 4 49	17 3 6
	8	19 10 14	21 12 27	23 2 50	1 5 3	3 3 20	5 5 33	7 3 50	9 6 3	11 8 16	13 6 33	15 8 46	17 7 3
	9	19 14 10	21 16 23	23 6 47	1 9 0	3 7 17	5 9 30	7 7 46	9 10 0	11 12 13	13 10 29	15 12 43	17 10 59
	10	19 18 7	21 20 20	23 10 43	1 12 56	3 11 13	5 13 26	7 11 43	9 13 56	11 16 9	13 14 26	15 16 39	17 14 56
	11	19 22 3	21 24 16	23 14 40	1 16 53	3 15 10	5 17 23	7 15 40	9 17 53	11 20 6	13 18 23	15 20 36	17 18 52
	12	19 26 0	21 28 13	23 18 36	1 20 50	3 19 6	5 21 19	7 19 36	9 21 49	11 24 3	13 22 19	15 24 32	17 22 49
	13	19 29 56	21 32 10	23 22 33	1 24 46	3 23 3	5 25 16	7 23 33	9 25 46	11 27 59	13 26 16	15 28 29	17 26 46
	14	19 33 53	21 36 6	23 26 30	1 28 43	3 26 59	5 29 13	7 27 29	9 29 42	11 31 56	13 30 12	15 32 25	17 30 42
	15	19 37 49	21 40 3	23 30 26	1 32 39	3 30 56	5 33 9	7 31 26	9 33 39	11 35 52	13 34 9	15 36 22	17 34 39
	16	19 41 46	21 43 59	23 34 23	1 36 36	3 34 52	5 37 6	7 35 22	9 37 36	11 39 49	13 38 5	15 40 18	17 38 35
	17	19 45 43	21 47 56	23 38 19	1 40 32	3 38 49	5 41 2	7 39 19	9 41 32	11 43 45	13 42 2	15 44 15	17 42 32
	18	19 49 39	21 51 52	23 42 16	1 44 29	3 42 46	5 44 59	7 43 15	9 45 29	11 47 42	13 45 58	15 48 12	17 46 28
	19	19 53 36	21 55 49	23 46 12	1 48 25	3 46 42	5 48 55	7 47 12	9 49 25	11 51 38	13 49 55	15 52 8	17 50 25
	20	19 57 32	21 59 45	23 50 9	1 52 22	3 50 39	5 52 52	7 51 9	9 53 22	11 55 35	13 53 52	15 56 5	17 54 21
	21	20 1 29	22 3 42	23 54 5	1 56 19	3 54 35	5 56 48	7 55 5	9 57 18	11 59 31	13 57 48	16 0 1	17 58 18
	22	20 5 25	22 7 39	23 58 2	2 0 15	3 58 32	6 0 45	7 59 2	10 1 15	12 3 28	14 1 45	16 3 58	18 2 15
	23	20 9 22	22 11 35	0 1 59	2 4 12	4 2 28	6 4 42	8 2 58	10 5 11	12 7 25	14 5 41	16 7 54	18 6 11
	24	20 13 18	22 15 32	0 5 55	2 8 8	4 6 25	6 8 38	8 6 55	10 9 8	12 11 21	14 9 38	16 11 51	18 10 8
	25	20 17 15	22 19 28	0 9 52	2 12 5	4 10 21	6 12 35	8 10 51	10 13 5	12 15 18	14 13 34	16 15 47	18 14 4
	26	20 21 12	22 23 25	0 13 48	2 16 1	4 14 18	6 16 31	8 14 48	10 17 1	12 19 14	14 17 31	16 19 44	18 18 1
	27	20 25 8	22 27 21	0 17 45	2 19 58	4 18 15	6 20 28	8 18 44	10 20 58	12 23 11	14 21 27	16 23 41	18 21 57
	28	20 29 5	22 31 18	0 21 41	2 23 54	4 22 11	6 24 24	8 22 41	10 24 54	12 27 7	14 25 24	16 27 37	18 25 54
	29	20 33 1		0 25 38	2 27 51	4 26 8	6 28 21	8 26 38	10 28 51	12 31 4	14 29 20	16 31 34	18 29 50
	30	20 36 58		0 29 34	2 31 48	4 30 4	6 32 17	8 30 34	10 32 47	12 35 0	14 33 17	16 35 30	18 33 47
	31	20 40 54		0 33 31		4 34 1		8 34 31	10 36 44		14 37 14		18 37 44
1963	1	18 41 40	20 43 53	22 34 17	0 36 30	2 34 47	4 37 0	6 35 17	8 37 30	10 39 43	12 38 0	14 40 13	16 38 29
	2	18 45 37	20 47 50	22 38 13	0 40 27	2 38 43	4 40 56	6 39 13	8 41 26	10 43 40	12 41 56	14 44 9	16 42 26
	3	18 49 33	20 51 46	22 42 10	0 44 23	2 42 40	4 44 53	6 43 10	8 45 23	10 47 36	12 45 53	14 48 6	16 46 23
	4	18 53 30	20 55 43	22 46 7	0 48 20	2 46 36	4 48 49	6 47 6	8 49 19	10 51 33	12 49 49	14 52 2	16 50 19
	5	18 57 26	20 59 40	22 50 3	0 52 16	2 50 33	4 52 46	6 51 3	8 53 16	10 55 29	12 53 46	14 55 59	16 54 16
	6	19 1 23	21 3 36	22 54 0	0 56 13	2 54 29	4 56 43	6 54 59	8 57 13	10 59 26	12 57 42	14 59 55	16 58 12
	7	19 5 19	21 7 33	22 57 56	1 0 9	2 58 26	5 0 39	6 58 56	9 1 9	11 3 22	13 1 39	15 3 52	17 2 9
	8	19 9 16	21 11 29	23 1 53	1 4 6	3 2 22	5 4 36	7 2 52	9 5 6	11 7 19	13 5 35	15 7 49	17 6 5
	9	19 13 13	21 15 26	23 5 49	1 8 2	3 6 19	5 8 32	7 6 49	9 9 2	11 11 15	13 9 32	15 11 45	17 10 2
	10	19 17 9	21 19 22	23 9 46	1 11 59	3 10 16	5 12 29	7 10 46	9 12 59	11 15 12	13 13 29	15 15 42	17 13 58
	11	19 21 6	21 23 19	23 13 42	1 15 56	3 14 12	5 16 25	7 14 42	9 16 55	11 19 9	13 17 25	15 19 38	17 17 55
	12	19 25 2	21 27 15	23 17 39	1 19 52	3 18 9	5 20 22	7 18 39	9 20 52	11 23 5	13 21 22	15 23 35	17 21 52
	13	19 28 59	21 31 12	23 21 35	1 23 49	3 22 5	5 24 19	7 22 35	9 24 48	11 27 2	13 25 18	15 27 31	17 25 48
	14	19 32 55	21 35 9	23 25 32	1 27 45	3 26 2	5 28 15	7 26 32	9 28 45	11 30 58	13 29 15	15 31 28	17 29 45
	15	19 36 52	21 39 5	23 29 29	1 31 42	3 29 58	5 32 12	7 30 28	9 32 42	11 34 55	13 33 11	15 35 24	17 33 41
	16	19 40 48	21 43 2	23 33 25	1 35 38	3 33 55	5 36 8	7 34 25	9 36 38	11 38 51	13 37 8	15 39 21	17 37 38
	17	19 44 45	21 46 58	23 37 22	1 39 35	3 37 51	5 40 5	7 38 21	9 40 35	11 42 48	13 41 4	15 43 18	17 41 34
	18	19 48 42	21 50 55	23 41 18	1 43 31	3 41 48	5 44 1	7 42 18	9 44 31	11 46 44	13 45 1	15 47 14	17 45 31
	19	19 52 38	21 54 51	23 45 15	1 47 28	3 45 45	5 47 58	7 46 15	9 48 28	11 50 41	13 48 58	15 51 11	17 49 27
	20	19 56 35	21 58 48	23 49 11	1 51 25	3 49 41	5 51 54	7 50 11	9 52 24	11 54 37	13 52 54	15 55 7	17 53 24
	21	20 0 31	22 2 44	23 53 8	1 55 21	3 53 38	5 55 51	7 54 8	9 56 21	11 58 34	13 56 51	15 59 4	17 57 21
	22	20 4 28	22 6 41	23 57 4	1 59 18	3 57 34	5 59 48	7 58 4	10 0 17	12 2 31	14 0 47	16 3 0	18 1 17
	23	20 8 24	22 10 38	0 1 1	2 3 14	4 1 31	6 3 44	8 2 1	10 4 14	12 6 27	14 4 44	16 6 57	18 5 14
	24	20 12 21	22 14 34	0 4 58	2 7 11	4 5 27	6 7 41	8 5 57	10 8 11	12 10 24	14 8 40	16 10 54	18 9 10
	25	20 16 17	22 18 31	0 8 54	2 11 7	4 9 24	6 11 37	8 9 54	10 12 7	12 14 20	14 12 37	16 14 50	18 13 7
	26	20 20 14	22 22 27	0 12 51	2 15 4	4 13 20	6 15 34	8 13 50	10 16 4	12 18 17	14 16 33	16 18 47	18 17 3
	27	20 24 11	22 26 24	0 16 47	2 19 0	4 17 17	6 19 30	8 17 47	10 20 0	12 22 13	14 20 30	16 22 43	18 21 0
	28	20 28 7	22 30 20	0 20 44	2 22 57	4 21 14	6 23 27	8 21 44	10 23 57	12 26 10	14 24 27	16 26 40	18 24 56
	29	20 32 4		0 24 40	2 26 54	4 25 10	6 27 23	8 25 40	10 27 53	12 30 6	14 28 23	16 30 36	18 28 53
	30	20 36 0		0 28 37	2 30 50	4 29 7	6 31 20	8 29 37	10 31 50	12 34 3	14 32 20	16 34 33	18 32 50
	31	20 39 57		0 32 33		4 33 3		8 33 33	10 35 46		14 36 16		18 36 46
1964	1	18 40 43	20 42 56	22 37 16	0 39 29	2 37 46	4 39 59	6 38 16	8 40 29	10 42 42	12 40 59	14 43 12	16 41 29
	2	18 44 39	20 46 53	22 41 13	0 43 26	2 41 42	4 43 56	6 42 12	8 44 26	10 46 39	12 44 55	14 47 9	16 45 25
	3	18 48 36	20 50 49	22 45 9	0 47 22	2 45 39	4 47 52	6 46 9	8 48 22	10 50 35	12 48 52	14 51 5	16 49 22
	4	18 52 32	20 54 46	22 49 6	0 51 19	2 49 36	4 51 49	6 50 5	8 52 19	10 54 32	12 52 48	14 55 2	16 53 18
	5	18 56 29	20 58 42	22 53 2	0 55 15	2 53 32	4 55 45	6 54 2	8 56 15	10 58 28	12 56 45	14 58 58	16 57 15
	6	19 0 26	21 2 39	22 56 59	0 59 12	2 57 29	4 59 42	6 57 59	9 0 12	11 2 25	13 0 42	15 2 55	17 1 11
	7	19 4 22	21 6 35	23 0 55	1 3 8	3 1 25	5 3 38	7 1 55	9 4 8	11 6 22	13 4 38	15 6 51	17 5 8
	8	19 8 19	21 10 32	23 4 52	1 7 5	3 5 22	5 7 35	7 5 52	9 8 5	11 10 18	13 8 35	15 10 48	17 9 5
	9	19 12 15	21 14 28	23 8 48	1 11 2	3 9 18	5 11 31	7 9 48	9 12 1	11 14 15	13 12 31	15 14 44	17 13 1
	10	19 16 12	21 18 25	23 12 45	1 14 58	3 13 15	5 15 28	7 13 45	9 15 58	11 18 11	13 16 28	15 18 41	17 16 58
	11	19 20 8	21 22 22	23 16 42	1 18 55	3 17 11	5 19 25	7 17 42	9 19 55	11 22 8	13 20 24	15 22 38	17 20 54
	12	19 24 5	21 26 18	23 30 38	1 22 51	3 21 8	5 23 21	7 21 38	9 23 51	11 26 4	13 24 21	15 26 34	17 24 51
	13	19 28 1	21 30 15	23 24 35	1 26 48	3 25 4	5 27 18	7 25 35	9 27 48	11 30 1	13 28 17	15 30 31	17 28 47
	14	19 31 58	21 34 11	23 28 31	1 30 44	3 29 1	5 31 14	7 29 31	9 31 44	11 33 57	13 32 14	15 34 27	17 32 44
	15	19 35 55	21 38 8	23 32 28	1 34 41	3 32 58	5 35 11	7 33 28	9 35 41	11 37 54	13 36 11	15 38 24	17 36 40
	16	19 39 51	21 42 4	23 36 24	1 38 37	3 36 54	5 39 7	7 37 24	9 39 37	11 41 51	13 40 7	15 42 20	17 40 37
	17	19 43 48	21 46 1	23 40 21	1 42 34	3 40 51	5 43 4	7 41 21	9 43 34	11 45 47	13 44 4	15 46 17	17 44 34
	18	19 47 44	21 49 57	23 44 17	1 46 31	3 44 47	5 47 1	7 45 17	9 47 30	11 49 44	13 48 0	15 50 13	17 48 30
	19	19 51 41	21 53 54	23 48 14	1 50 27	3 48 44	5 50 57	7 49 14	9 51 27	11 53 40	13 51 57	15 54 10	17 52 27
	20	19 55 37	21 57 50	23 52 11	1 54 24	3 52 40	5 54 54	7 53 10	9 55 24	11 57 37	13 55 53	15 58 7	17 56 23
	21	19 59 34	22 1 47	23 56 7	1 58 20	3 56 37	5 58 50	7 57 7	9 59 20	12 1 33	13 59 50	16 2 3	18 0 20
	22	20 3 30	22 5 44	0 0 4	2 2 17	4 0 33	6 2 47	8 1 3	10 3 17	12 5 30	14 3 46	16 6 0	18 4 16
	23	20 7 27	22 9 40	0 4 0	2 6 13	4 4 30	6 6 43	8 5 0	10 7 13	12 9 27	14 7 43	16 9 56	18 8 13
	24	20 11 23	22 13 37	0 7 57	2 10 10	4 8 27	6 10 40	8 8 57	10 11 10	12 13 23	14 11 40	16 13 53	18 12 10
	25	20 15 20	22 17 33	0 11 53	2 14 6	4 12 23	6 14 36	8 12 53	10 15 6	12 17 19	14 15 36	16 17 49	18 16 6
	26	20 19 17	22 21 30	0 15 50	2 18 3	4 16 20	6 18 33	8 16 50	10 19 3	12 21 16	14 19 33	16 21 46	18 20 3
	27	20 23 13	22 25 26	0 19 46	2 22 0	4 20 16	6 22 30	8 20 46	10 22 59	12 25 13	14 23 29	16 25 42	18 23 59
	28	20 27 10	22 29 23	0 23 43	2 25 56	4 24 13	6 26 26	8 24 43	10 26 56	12 29 9	14 27 26	16 29 39	18 27 56
	29	20 31 6	22 33 19	0 27 40	2 29 53	4 28 9	6 30 23	8 28 40	10 30 53	12 33 6	14 31 22	16 33 36	18 31 52
	30	20 35 3		0 31 36	2 33 49	4 32 6	6 34 19	8 32 36	10 34 49	12 37 2	14 35 19	16 37 32	18 35 49
	31	20 38 59		0 35 33		4 36 2		8 36 32	10 38 46		14 39 15		18 39 45
1965	1	18 43 42	20 45 56	22 36 19	0 38 32	2 36 49	4 39 2	6 37 19	8 39 32	10 41 45	12 40 2	14 42 15	16 40 32
	2	18 47 39	20 49 52	22 40 16	0 42 29	2 40 45	4 42 59	6 41 15	8 43 29	10 45 42	12 43 58	14 46 12	16 44 28
	3	18 51 35	20 53 49	22 44 12	0 46 25	2 44 42	4 46 55	6 45 12	8 47 25	10 49 38	12 47 55	14 50 8	16 48 25
	4	18 55 32	20 57 45	22 48 8	0 50 22	2 48 38	4 50 52	6 49 8	8 51 22	10 53 35	12 51 52	14 54 5	16 52 21
	5	18 59 28	21 1 42	22 52 5	0 54 18	2 52 35	4 54 48	6 53 5	8 55 18	10 57 31	12 55 48	14 58 1	16 56 18
	6	19 3 25	21 5 38	22 56 2	0 58 15	2 56 32	4 58 45	6 57 2	8 59 15	11 1 28	12 59 45	15 1 58	17 0 15
	7	19 7 22	21 9 35	22 59 58	1 2 11	3 0 28	5 2 41	7 0 58	9 3 11	11 5 25	13 3 41	15 5 54	17 4 11
	8	19 11 18	21 13 31	23 3 55	1 6 8	3 4 25	5 6 38	7 4 55	9 7 8	11 9 21	13 7 38	15 9 51	17 8 8
	9	19 15 15	21 17 28	23 7 51	1 10 5	3 8 21	5 10 35	7 8 51	9 11 5	11 13 18	13 11 34	15 13 47	17 12 4
	10	19 19 12	21 21 24	23 11 48	1 14 1	3 12 18	5 14 31	7 12 48	9 15 1	11 17 14	13 15 31	15 17 44	17 16 1
	11	19 23 8	21 25 21	23 15 45	1 17 58	3 16 14	5 18 28	7 16 44	9 18 58	11 21 11	13 19 27	15 21 41	17 19 57
	12	19 27 4	21 29 18	23 19 41	1 21 54	3 20 11	5 22 24	7 20 41	9 22 54	11 25 7	13 23 24	15 25 37	17 23 54
	13	19 31 1	21 33 14	23 23 38	1 25 51	3 24 7	5 26 21	7 24 37	9 26 51	11 29 4	13 27 20	15 29 34	17 27 50
	14	19 34 57	21 37 11	23 27 34	1 29 47	3 28 4	5 30 17	7 28 34	9 30 47	11 33 0	13 31 17	15 33 30	17 31 47
	15	19 38 54	21 41 7	23 31 31	1 33 44	3 32 1	5 34 14	7 32 31	9 34 44	11 36 57	13 35 14	15 37 27	17 35 44
	16	19 42 51	21 45 4	23 35 27	1 37 40	3 35 57	5 38 10	7 36 27	9 38 40	11 40 54	13 39 10	15 41 23	17 39 40
	17	19 46 47	21 49 0	23 39 24	1 41 37	3 39 54	5 42 7	7 40 24	9 42 37	11 44 50	13 43 7	15 45 20	17 43 37
	18	19 50 44	21 52 57	23 43 20	1 45 34	3 43 50	5 46 4	7 44 20	9 46 33	11 48 47	13 47 3	15 49 16	17 47 33
	19	19 54 40	21 56 53	23 47 17	1 49 30	3 47 47	5 50 0	7 48 17	9 50 30	11 52 43	13 51 0	15 53 13	17 51 30
	20	19 58 37	22 0 50	23 51 14	1 53 27	3 51 43	5 53 57	7 52 14	9 54 27	11 56 40	13 54 56	15 57 9	17 55 26
	21	20 2 33	22 4 47	23 55 10	1 57 23	3 55 40	5 57 53	7 56 10	9 58 23	12 0 36	13 58 53	16 1 6	17 59 23
	22	20 6 30	22 8 43	23 59 7	2 1 20	3 59 36	6 1 50	8 0 6	10 2 20	12 4 33	14 2 49	16 5 3	18 3 19
	23	20 10 26	22 12 40	0 3 3	2 5 16	4 3 33	6 5 46	8 4 3	10 6 16	12 8 29	14 6 46	16 8 59	18 7 16
	24	20 14 23	22 16 36	0 7 0	2 9 13	4 7 29	6 9 43	8 8 0	10 10 13	12 12 26	14 10 43	16 12 56	18 11 13
	25	20 18 19	22 20 33	0 10 56	2 13 9	4 11 26	6 13 39	8 11 56	10 14 9	12 16 23	14 14 39	16 16 52	18 15 9
	26	20 22 16	22 24 29	0 14 53	2 17 6	4 15 23	6 17 36	8 15 53	10 18 6	12 20 19	14 18 36	16 20 49	18 19 6
	27	20 26 13	22 28 26	0 18 49	2 21 3	4 19 19	6 21 33	8 19 49	10 22 3	12 24 16	14 22 32	16 24 45	18 23 2
	28	20 30 9	22 32 22	0 22 46	2 24 59	4 23 16	6 25 29	8 23 46	10 25 59	12 28 12	14 26 29	16 28 42	18 26 59
	29	20 34 6		0 26 43	2 28 56	4 27 12	6 29 26	8 27 42	10 29 56	12 32 9	14 30 25	16 32 39	18 30 55
	30	20 38 2		0 30 39	2 32 52	4 31 9	6 33 22	8 31 39	10 33 52	12 36 5	14 34 22	16 36 35	18 34 52
	31	20 41 59		0 34 36		4 35 5		8 35 36	10 37 49		14 38 18		18 38 48

1	2	3	4	5	6	7	8	9	10	11	12
18 42 45	20 44 58	22 35 22	0 37 35	2 35 52	4 38 5	6 36 22	8 38 35	10 40 48	12 39 5	14 41 18	16 39 35
18 46 42	20 48 55	22 39 18	0 41 32	2 39 48	4 42 1	6 40 18	8 42 32	10 44 45	12 43 1	14 45 14	16 43 31
18 50 38	20 52 51	22 43 15	0 45 28	2 43 45	4 45 58	6 44 15	8 46 28	10 48 41	12 46 58	14 49 11	16 47 28
18 54 35	20 56 48	22 47 12	0 49 25	2 47 41	4 49 55	6 48 11	8 50 25	10 52 38	12 50 54	14 53 8	16 51 24
18 58 31	21 0 45	22 51 8	0 53 21	2 51 38	4 53 51	6 52 8	8 54 21	10 56 34	12 54 51	14 57 4	16 55 21
19 2 28	21 4 41	22 55 5	0 57 18	2 55 34	4 57 48	6 56 4	8 58 18	11 0 31	12 58 48	15 1 1	16 59 17
19 6 24	21 8 38	22 59 1	1 1 14	2 59 31	5 1 44	7 0 1	9 2 14	11 4 27	13 2 44	15 4 57	17 3 14
19 10 21	21 12 34	23 2 58	1 5 11	3 3 28	5 5 41	7 3 58	9 6 11	11 8 24	13 6 41	15 8 54	17 7 11
19 14 18	21 16 31	23 6 54	1 9 7	3 7 24	5 9 37	7 7 54	9 10 7	11 12 21	13 10 37	15 12 50	17 11 7
19 18 14	21 20 27	23 10 51	1 13 4	3 11 21	5 13 34	7 11 51	9 14 4	11 16 17	13 14 34	15 16 47	17 15 4
19 22 11	21 24 24	23 14 47	1 17 1	3 15 17	5 17 31	7 15 47	9 18 0	11 20 14	13 18 30	15 20 43	17 19 0
19 26 7	21 28 20	23 18 44	1 20 57	3 19 14	5 21 27	7 19 44	9 21 57	11 24 10	13 22 27	15 24 40	17 22 57
19 30 4	21 32 17	23 22 41	1 24 54	3 23 10	5 25 24	7 23 40	9 25 54	11 28 7	13 26 23	15 28 37	17 26 53
19 34 0	21 36 14	23 26 37	1 28 50	3 27 7	5 29 20	7 27 37	9 29 50	11 32 3	13 30 20	15 32 33	17 30 50
19 37 57	21 40 10	23 30 34	1 32 47	3 31 3	5 33 17	7 31 33	9 33 47	11 36 0	13 34 17	15 36 30	17 34 46
19 41 53	21 44 7	23 34 30	1 36 43	3 35 0	5 37 13	7 35 30	9 37 43	11 39 56	13 38 13	15 40 26	17 38 43
19 45 50	21 48 3	23 38 27	1 40 40	3 38 57	5 41 10	7 39 27	9 41 40	11 43 53	13 42 10	15 44 23	17 42 40
19 49 47	21 52 0	23 42 23	1 44 36	3 42 53	5 45 6	7 43 23	9 45 36	11 47 50	13 46 6	15 48 19	17 46 36
19 53 43	21 55 56	23 46 20	1 48 33	3 46 50	5 49 3	7 47 20	9 49 33	11 51 46	13 50 3	15 52 16	17 50 33
19 57 40	21 59 53	23 50 16	1 52 30	3 50 46	5 53 0	7 51 16	9 53 29	11 55 49	13 53 59	15 56 13	17 54 29
20 1 36	22 3 49	23 54 13	1 56 26	3 54 43	5 56 56	7 55 13	9 57 26	11 59 39	13 57 56	16 0 9	17 58 26
20 5 33	22 7 46	23 58 9	2 0 23	3 58 39	6 0 53	7 59 9	10 1 23	12 3 36	14 1 52	16 4 5	18 2 22
20 9 29	22 11 43	0 2 6	2 4 19	4 2 36	6 4 49	8 3 6	10 5 19	12 7 32	14 5 49	16 8 2	18 6 19
20 13 26	22 15 39	0 6 3	2 8 16	4 6 32	6 8 46	8 7 2	10 9 16	12 11 29	14 9 46	16 11 59	18 10 15
20 17 22	22 19 35	0 9 59	2 12 12	4 10 29	6 12 42	8 10 59	10 13 12	12 15 25	14 13 42	16 15 55	18 14 12
20 21 19	22 23 32	0 13 56	2 16 9	4 14 26	6 16 39	8 14 56	10 17 9	12 19 22	14 17 39	16 19 52	18 18 9
20 25 16	22 27 29	0 17 52	2 20 9	4 48 22	6 20 35	8 18 52	10 21 5	12 23 19	14 21 35	16 23 48	18 22 5
20 29 12	22 31 25	0 21 49	2 24 2	4 22 19	6 24 32	8 22 49	10 25 2	12 27 15	14 25 32	16 27 45	18 26 2
20 33 9		0 25 45	2 27 59	4 26 15	6 28 29	8 26 45	10 28 59	12 31 12	14 29 28	16 31 42	18 29 58
20 37 5		0 29 42	2 31 55	4 30 12	6 32 25	8 30 42	10 32 55	12 35 8	14 33 25	16 35 38	18 33 55
20 41 2		0 33 38		4 34 8		8 34 38	10 36 52		14 37 21		18 37 51

1	2	3	4	5	6	7	8	9	10	11	12
18 41 48	20 44 1	22 34 25	0 36 38	2 34 55	4 37 8	6 35 25	8 37 38	10 39 51	12 38 8	14 40 21	16 38 38
18 45 45	20 47 58	22 38 21	0 40 35	2 38 51	4 41 4	6 39 21	8 41 34	10 43 48	12 42 4	14 44 17	16 42 34
18 49 41	20 51 54	22 42 18	0 44 31	2 42 48	4 45 1	6 43 18	8 45 31	10 47 44	12 46 1	14 48 14	16 46 31
18 53 38	20 55 51	22 46 14	0 48 28	2 46 44	4 48 58	6 47 14	8 49 28	10 51 41	12 49 57	14 52 11	16 50 27
18 57 34	20 59 47	22 50 11	0 52 24	2 50 41	4 52 54	6 51 11	8 53 24	10 55 37	12 53 54	14 56 7	16 54 24
19 1 31	21 3 44	22 54 8	0 56 21	2 54 37	4 56 51	6 55 7	8 57 21	10 59 34	12 57 51	15 0 4	16 58 20
19 5 27	21 7 41	22 58 4	1 0 17	2 58 34	5 0 47	6 59 4	9 1 17	11 3 30	13 1 47	15 4 0	17 2 17
19 9 24	21 11 37	23 2 1	1 4 14	3 2 30	5 4 44	7 3 1	9 5 14	11 7 27	13 5 44	15 7 57	17 6 14
19 13 20	21 15 34	23 5 57	1 8 10	3 6 27	5 8 40	7 6 57	9 9 10	11 11 24	13 9 40	15 11 53	17 10 10
19 17 17	21 19 30	23 9 54	1 12 7	3 10 24	5 12 37	7 10 54	9 13 7	11 15 20	13 13 37	15 15 50	17 14 7
19 21 14	21 23 27	23 13 50	1 16 4	3 14 20	5 16 33	7 14 50	9 17 3	11 19 17	13 17 33	15 19 47	17 18 3
19 25 10	21 27 23	23 17 47	1 20 0	3 18 17	5 20 30	7 18 47	9 21 0	11 23 13	13 21 30	15 23 43	17 22 0
19 29 7	21 31 20	23 21 43	1 23 57	3 22 13	5 24 27	7 22 43	9 24 57	11 27 10	13 25 26	15 27 40	17 25 56
19 33 3	21 35 16	23 25 40	1 27 53	3 26 10	5 28 23	7 26 40	9 28 53	11 31 6	13 29 23	15 31 36	17 29 53
19 37 0	21 39 13	23 29 37	1 31 50	3 30 6	5 32 20	7 30 36	9 32 50	11 35 3	13 33 20	15 35 33	17 33 49
19 40 56	21 43 10	23 33 33	1 35 46	3 34 3	5 36 16	7 34 33	9 36 46	11 38 59	13 37 16	15 39 29	17 37 46
19 44 53	21 47 6	23 37 30	1 39 43	3 38 0	5 40 13	7 38 30	9 40 43	11 42 56	13 41 13	15 43 26	17 41 43
19 48 49	21 51 3	23 41 26	1 43 39	3 41 56	5 44 9	7 42 26	9 44 39	11 46 53	13 45 9	15 47 22	17 45 39
19 52 46	21 54 59	23 45 23	1 47 36	3 45 53	5 48 6	7 46 23	9 48 36	11 50 49	13 49 6	15 51 19	17 49 36
19 56 43	21 58 56	23 49 19	1 51 33	3 49 49	5 52 2	7 50 19	9 52 32	11 54 46	13 53 2	15 55 16	17 53 32
20 0 39	22 2 52	23 53 16	1 55 29	3 53 46	5 55 59	7 54 16	9 56 29	11 58 42	13 56 59	15 59 12	17 57 29
20 4 36	22 6 49	23 57 12	1 59 26	3 57 42	5 59 56	7 58 12	10 0 26	12 2 39	14 0 55	16 3 9	18 1 25
20 8 32	22 10 46	0 1 9	2 3 22	4 1 39	6 3 52	8 2 9	10 4 22	12 6 35	14 4 52	16 7 5	18 5 22
20 12 29	22 14 42	0 5 6	2 7 19	4 5 35	6 7 49	8 6 5	10 8 19	12 10 32	14 8 48	16 11 2	18 9 18
20 16 25	22 18 39	0 9 2	2 11 15	4 9 32	6 11 45	8 10 2	10 12 15	12 14 28	14 12 45	16 14 58	18 13 15
20 20 22	22 22 35	0 12 59	2 15 12	4 13 29	6 15 42	8 13 59	10 16 12	12 18 25	14 16 42	16 18 55	18 17 12
20 24 18	22 26 32	0 16 55	2 19 8	4 17 25	6 19 38	8 17 55	10 20 8	12 22 22	14 20 38	16 22 51	18 21 8
20 28 15	22 30 28	0 20 52	2 23 5	4 21 22	6 23 35	8 21 52	10 24 5	12 26 18	14 24 35	16 26 48	18 25 5
20 32 12		0 24 48	2 27 2	4 25 18	6 27 32	8 25 48	10 28 1	12 30 15	14 28 31	16 30 45	18 29 1
20 36 8		0 28 45	2 30 58	4 29 15	6 31 28	8 29 45	10 31 58	12 34 11	14 32 28	16 34 41	18 32 58
20 40 5		0 32 41		4 33 11		8 33 41	10 35 55		14 36 24		18 36 54

1	2	3	4	5	6	7	8	9	10	11	12
18 40 51	20 43 4	22 37 24	0 39 38	2 37 54	4 40 7	6 38 24	8 40 37	10 42 51	12 41 7	14 43 21	16 41 37
18 44 48	20 47 1	22 41 21	0 43 34	2 41 51	4 44 4	6 42 21	8 44 34	10 46 47	12 45 4	14 47 17	16 45 34
18 48 44	20 50 57	22 45 17	0 47 31	2 45 47	4 48 1	6 46 17	8 48 31	10 50 44	12 49 0	14 51 14	16 49 30
18 52 41	20 54 54	22 49 14	0 51 27	2 49 44	4 51 57	6 50 14	8 52 27	10 54 40	12 52 57	14 55 10	16 53 27
18 56 37	20 58 50	22 53 11	0 55 24	2 53 40	4 55 54	6 54 10	8 56 24	10 58 37	12 56 54	14 59 7	16 57 23
19 0 34	21 2 47	22 57 7	0 59 20	2 57 37	4 59 50	6 58 7	9 0 20	11 2 34	13 0 50	15 3 3	17 1 20
19 4 30	21 6 44	23 1 4	1 3 17	3 1 34	5 3 47	7 2 4	9 4 17	11 6 30	13 4 47	15 7 0	17 5 17
19 8 27	21 10 40	23 5 0	1 7 13	3 5 30	5 7 43	7 6 0	9 8 13	11 10 27	13 8 43	15 10 56	17 9 13
19 12 23	21 14 37	23 8 57	1 11 10	3 9 27	5 11 40	7 9 57	9 12 10	11 14 23	13 12 40	15 14 53	17 13 10
19 16 20	21 18 33	23 12 53	1 15 7	3 13 23	5 15 36	7 13 53	9 16 7	11 18 20	13 16 36	15 18 50	17 17 6
19 20 17	21 22 30	23 16 50	1 19 3	3 17 20	5 19 33	7 17 50	9 20 3	11 22 16	13 20 33	15 22 46	17 21 3
19 24 13	21 26 26	23 20 46	1 23 0	3 21 16	5 23 30	7 21 46	9 24 0	11 26 13	13 24 29	15 26 43	17 24 59
19 28 10	21 30 23	23 24 43	1 26 56	3 25 13	5 27 26	7 25 43	9 27 56	11 30 9	13 28 26	15 30 39	17 28 56
19 32 6	21 34 20	23 28 40	1 30 53	3 29 9	5 31 23	7 29 39	9 31 53	11 34 6	13 32 23	15 34 36	17 32 53
19 36 3	21 38 16	23 32 36	1 34 49	3 33 6	5 35 19	7 33 36	9 35 49	11 38 2	13 36 19	15 38 32	17 36 49
19 39 59	21 42 13	23 36 33	1 38 46	3 37 3	5 39 16	7 37 33	9 39 46	11 41 59	13 40 16	15 42 29	17 40 46
19 43 56	21 46 9	23 40 29	1 42 42	3 40 59	5 43 12	7 41 29	9 43 42	11 45 56	13 44 12	15 46 25	17 44 42
19 47 52	21 50 6	23 44 26	1 46 39	3 44 56	5 47 9	7 45 26	9 47 39	11 49 52	13 48 9	15 50 22	17 48 39
19 51 49	21 54 2	23 48 22	1 50 36	3 48 52	5 51 6	7 49 22	9 51 36	11 53 49	13 52 5	15 54 19	17 52 35
19 55 46	21 57 59	23 52 19	1 54 32	3 52 49	5 55 2	7 53 19	9 55 32	11 57 45	13 56 2	15 58 15	17 56 32
19 59 42	22 1 55	23 56 15	1 58 29	3 56 45	5 58 59	7 57 15	9 59 29	12 1 42	13 59 58	16 2 12	18 0 28
20 3 39	22 5 52	0 0 12	2 2 25	4 0 41	6 2 55	8 1 12	10 3 25	12 5 38	14 3 55	16 6 8	18 4 25
20 7 35	22 9 49	0 4 9	2 6 22	4 4 38	6 6 52	8 5 8	10 7 22	12 9 35	14 7 52	16 10 5	18 8 22
20 11 32	22 13 45	0 8 5	2 10 18	4 8 35	6 10 48	8 9 5	10 11 18	12 13 31	14 11 48	16 14 1	18 12 18
20 15 28	22 17 42	0 12 2	2 14 15	4 12 32	6 14 45	8 13 2	10 15 15	12 17 28	14 15 45	16 17 58	18 16 15
20 19 25	22 21 38	0 15 58	2 18 11	4 16 28	6 18 41	8 16 58	10 19 11	12 21 25	14 19 41	16 21 54	18 20 11
20 23 21	22 25 35	0 19 55	2 22 8	4 20 25	6 22 38	8 20 55	10 23 8	12 25 21	14 23 38	16 25 51	18 24 8
20 27 18	22 29 31	0 23 51	2 26 5	4 24 21	6 26 35	8 24 51	10 27 4	12 29 18	14 27 34	16 29 48	18 28 4
20 31 15	22 33 28	0 27 48	2 30 1	4 28 18	6 30 31	8 28 48	10 31 1	12 33 14	14 31 31	16 33 44	18 32 1
20 35 11		0 31 44	2 33 58	4 32 14	6 34 28	8 32 44	10 34 58	12 37 11	14 35 27	16 37 41	18 35 57
20 39 8		0 35 41		4 36 11		8 36 41	10 38 54		14 39 24		18 39 54

1	2	3	4	5	6	7	8	9	10	11	12
18 43 51	20 46 4	22 36 27	0 38 41	2 36 57	4 39 10	6 37 27	8 39 41	10 41 54	12 40 10	14 42 24	16 40 40
18 47 47	20 50 0	22 40 24	0 42 37	2 40 54	4 43 7	6 41 24	8 43 37	10 45 50	12 44 7	14 46 20	16 44 37
18 51 44	20 53 57	22 44 21	0 46 34	2 44 50	4 47 4	6 45 20	8 47 34	10 49 47	12 48 3	14 50 17	16 48 33
18 55 40	20 57 54	22 48 17	0 50 30	2 48 47	4 51 0	6 49 17	8 51 30	10 53 43	12 52 0	14 54 13	16 52 30
18 59 37	21 1 50	22 52 14	0 54 27	2 52 43	4 54 57	6 53 14	8 55 27	10 57 40	12 55 57	14 58 10	16 56 27
19 3 33	21 5 47	22 56 10	0 58 23	2 56 40	4 58 53	6 57 10	8 59 23	11 1 37	12 59 53	15 2 6	17 0 23
19 7 30	21 9 43	23 0 7	1 2 20	3 0 37	5 2 50	7 1 7	9 3 20	11 5 33	13 3 50	15 6 3	17 4 20
19 11 26	21 13 40	23 4 3	1 6 16	3 4 33	5 6 46	7 5 3	9 7 16	11 9 30	13 7 46	15 9 59	17 8 16
19 15 23	21 17 36	23 8 0	1 10 13	3 8 30	5 10 43	7 9 0	9 11 13	11 13 26	13 11 43	15 13 56	17 12 13
19 19 20	21 21 33	23 11 56	1 14 10	3 12 26	5 14 40	7 12 56	9 15 10	11 17 23	13 15 39	15 17 53	17 16 9
19 23 16	21 25 29	23 15 53	1 18 6	3 16 23	5 18 36	7 16 53	9 19 6	11 21 19	13 19 36	15 21 49	17 20 6
19 27 13	21 29 26	23 19 50	1 22 3	3 20 19	5 22 33	7 20 49	9 23 3	11 25 16	13 23 32	15 25 46	17 24 2
19 31 9	21 33 23	23 23 46	1 25 59	3 24 16	5 26 29	7 24 46	9 26 59	11 29 12	13 27 29	15 29 42	17 27 59
19 35 6	21 37 19	23 27 43	1 29 56	3 28 12	5 30 26	7 28 43	9 30 56	11 33 9	13 31 26	15 33 39	17 31 56
19 39 2	21 41 16	23 31 39	1 33 52	3 32 9	5 34 22	7 32 39	9 34 52	11 37 6	13 35 22	15 37 35	17 35 52
19 42 59	21 45 12	23 35 36	1 37 49	3 36 6	5 38 19	7 36 36	9 38 49	11 41 2	13 39 19	15 41 32	17 39 49
19 46 56	21 49 9	23 39 32	1 41 45	3 40 2	5 42 15	7 40 32	9 42 45	11 44 59	13 43 15	15 45 28	17 43 45
19 50 52	21 53 5	23 43 29	1 45 42	3 43 59	5 46 12	7 44 29	9 46 42	11 48 55	13 47 12	15 49 25	17 47 42
19 54 49	21 57 2	23 47 25	1 49 39	3 47 55	5 50 9	7 48 25	9 50 39	11 52 52	13 51 8	15 53 22	17 51 38
19 58 45	22 0 58	23 51 22	1 53 35	3 51 52	5 54 5	7 52 22	9 54 35	11 56 48	13 55 5	15 57 18	17 55 35
20 2 42	22 4 55	23 55 18	1 57 32	3 55 48	5 58 2	7 56 18	9 58 32	12 0 45	13 59 1	16 1 15	17 59 31
20 6 38	22 8 52	23 59 15	2 1 28	3 59 45	6 1 58	8 0 15	10 2 28	12 4 41	14 2 58	16 5 11	18 3 28
20 10 35	22 12 48	0 3 12	2 5 25	4 3 41	6 5 55	8 4 12	10 6 25	12 8 38	14 6 55	16 9 8	18 7 25
20 14 31	22 16 45	0 7 8	2 9 21	4 7 38	6 9 51	8 8 8	10 10 21	12 12 35	14 10 51	16 13 4	18 11 21
20 18 28	22 20 41	0 11 5	2 13 18	4 11 35	6 13 48	8 12 5	10 14 18	12 16 31	14 14 48	16 17 1	18 15 18
20 22 25	22 24 38	0 15 1	2 17 14	4 15 31	6 17 44	8 16 1	10 18 14	12 20 28	14 18 44	16 20 58	18 19 14
20 26 21	22 28 34	0 18 58	2 21 11	4 19 28	6 21 41	8 19 58	10 22 11	12 24 24	14 22 41	16 24 54	18 23 11
20 30 18	22 32 31	0 22 54	2 25 8	4 23 24	6 25 38	8 23 54	10 26 8	12 28 21	14 26 37	16 28 51	18 27 7
20 34 14		0 26 51	2 29 4	4 27 21	6 29 34	8 27 51	10 30 4	12 32 17	14 30 34	16 32 47	18 31 4
20 38 11		0 30 47	2 33 1	4 31 17	6 33 31	8 31 47	10 34 1	12 36 14	14 34 30	16 36 44	18 35 1
20 42 7		0 34 44		4 35 14		8 35 44	10 37 57		14 38 27		18 38 57

		1	2	3	4	5	6	7	8	9	10	11	12
1970	1	18 42 54	20 45 7	22 35 30	0 37 44	2 36 0	4 38 14	6 36 30	8 38 44	10 40 57	12 39 13	14 41 27	16 39 43
	2	18 46 50	20 49 3	22 39 27	0 41 40	2 39 57	4 42 10	6 40 26	8 42 40	10 44 53	12 43 10	14 45 23	16 43 40
	3	18 50 47	20 53 0	22 43 24	0 45 37	2 43 53	4 46 7	6 44 24	8 46 37	10 48 50	12 47 5	14 49 20	16 47 36
	4	18 54 43	20 56 57	22 47 20	0 49 33	2 47 50	4 50 3	6 48 20	8 50 33	10 52 46	12 51 3	14 53 16	16 51 33
	5	18 58 40	21 0 53	22 51 17	0 53 30	2 51 46	4 54 0	6 52 17	8 54 30	10 56 43	12 55 0	14 57 13	16 55 30
	6	19 2 36	21 4 50	22 55 13	0 57 26	2 55 43	4 57 56	6 56 13	8 58 26	11 0 40	12 58 56	15 1 9	16 59 26
	7	19 6 33	21 8 46	22 59 10	1 1 23	2 59 40	5 1 53	7 0 10	9 2 23	11 4 36	13 2 53	15 5 6	17 3 23
	8	19 10 30	21 12 43	23 3 6	1 5 20	3 3 36	5 5 49	7 4 6	9 6 19	11 8 33	13 6 49	15 9 3	17 7 19
	9	19 14 26	21 16 39	23 7 3	1 9 16	3 7 33	5 9 46	7 8 3	9 10 16	11 12 29	13 10 46	15 12 59	17 11 16
	10	19 18 23	21 20 36	23 10 59	1 13 13	3 11 29	5 13 43	7 11 59	9 14 13	11 16 26	13 14 42	15 16 56	17 15 12
	11	19 22 19	21 24 32	23 14 56	1 17 9	3 15 26	5 17 39	7 15 56	9 18 9	11 20 22	13 18 39	15 20 52	17 19 9
	12	19 26 16	21 28 29	23 18 53	1 21 6	3 19 22	5 21 36	7 19 52	9 22 6	11 24 19	13 22 36	15 24 49	17 23 5
	13	19 30 12	21 32 26	23 22 49	1 25 2	3 23 19	5 25 32	7 23 49	9 26 2	11 28 15	13 26 32	15 28 45	17 27 2
	14	19 34 9	21 36 22	23 26 46	1 28 59	3 27 16	5 29 29	7 27 46	9 29 59	11 32 12	13 30 29	15 32 42	17 30 59
	15	19 38 5	21 40 19	23 30 42	1 32 55	3 31 12	5 33 25	7 31 42	9 33 55	11 36 9	13 34 25	15 36 38	17 34 55
	16	19 42 2	21 44 15	23 34 39	1 36 52	3 35 9	5 37 22	7 35 39	9 37 52	11 40 5	13 38 22	15 40 35	17 38 52
	17	19 45 59	21 48 12	23 38 35	1 40 49	3 39 5	5 41 18	7 39 35	9 41 49	11 44 2	13 42 18	15 44 32	17 42 48
	18	19 49 55	21 52 8	23 42 32	1 44 45	3 43 2	5 45 15	7 43 32	9 45 45	11 47 58	13 46 15	15 48 28	17 46 45
	19	19 53 52	21 56 5	23 46 28	1 48 42	3 46 58	5 49 12	7 47 28	9 49 42	11 51 55	13 50 11	15 52 25	17 50 41
	20	19 57 48	22 0 1	23 50 25	1 52 38	3 50 55	5 53 8	7 51 25	9 53 38	11 55 51	13 54 8	15 56 21	17 54 38
	21	20 1 45	22 3 58	23 54 22	1 56 35	3 54 51	5 57 5	7 55 21	9 57 35	11 59 48	13 58 5	16 0 18	17 58 34
	22	20 5 41	22 7 55	23 58 18	2 0 31	3 58 48	6 1 1	7 59 18	10 1 31	12 3 44	14 2 1	16 4 14	18 2 31
	23	20 9 38	22 11 51	0 2 15	2 4 28	4 2 45	6 4 58	8 3 15	10 5 28	12 7 41	14 5 58	16 8 11	18 6 28
	24	20 13 34	22 15 48	0 6 11	2 8 24	4 6 41	6 8 54	8 7 11	10 9 24	12 11 38	14 9 54	16 12 7	18 10 24
	25	20 17 31	22 19 44	0 10 8	2 12 21	4 10 38	6 12 51	8 11 8	10 13 21	12 15 34	14 13 51	16 16 4	18 14 21
	26	20 21 28	22 23 41	0 14 4	2 16 18	4 14 34	6 16 48	8 15 4	10 17 17	12 19 31	14 17 47	16 20 1	18 18 17
	27	20 25 24	22 27 37	0 18 1	2 20 14	4 18 31	6 20 44	8 19 1	10 21 14	12 23 27	14 21 44	16 23 57	18 22 14
	28	20 29 21	22 31 34	0 21 57	2 24 11	4 22 27	6 24 41	8 22 57	10 25 11	12 27 24	14 25 40	16 27 54	18 26 10
	29	20 33 17		0 25 54	2 28 7	4 26 24	6 28 37	8 26 54	10 29 7	12 31 20	14 29 37	16 31 50	18 30 7
	30	20 37 14		0 29 51	2 32 4	4 30 20	6 32 34	8 30 50	10 33 4	12 35 17	14 33 33	16 35 47	18 34 4
	31	20 41 10		0 33 47		4 34 17		8 34 47	10 37 0		14 37 30		18 38 0
1971	1	18 41 57	20 44 10	22 34 33	0 36 47	2 35 3	4 37 17	6 35 33	8 37 47	10 40 0	12 38 16	14 40 30	16 38 46
	2	18 45 53	20 48 6	22 38 30	0 40 43	2 39 0	4 41 13	6 39 30	8 41 43	10 43 56	12 42 13	14 44 26	16 42 43
	3	18 49 50	20 52 3	22 42 27	0 44 40	2 42 56	4 45 10	6 43 26	8 45 40	10 47 53	12 46 10	14 48 23	16 46 39
	4	18 53 46	20 56 0	22 46 23	0 48 36	2 46 53	4 49 6	6 47 23	8 49 36	10 51 49	12 50 6	14 52 19	16 50 36
	5	18 57 43	20 59 56	22 50 20	0 52 33	2 50 50	4 53 3	6 51 20	8 53 33	10 55 46	12 54 3	14 56 16	16 54 33
	6	19 1 39	21 3 53	22 54 16	0 56 29	2 54 46	4 56 59	6 55 16	8 57 29	10 59 43	12 57 59	15 0 12	16 58 29
	7	19 5 36	21 7 49	22 58 13	1 0 26	2 58 43	5 0 56	6 59 13	9 1 26	11 3 39	13 1 56	15 4 9	17 2 26
	8	19 9 33	21 11 46	23 2 9	1 4 23	3 2 39	5 4 52	7 3 9	9 5 22	11 7 36	13 5 52	15 8 5	17 6 22
	9	19 13 29	21 15 42	23 6 6	1 8 19	3 6 36	5 8 49	7 7 6	9 9 19	11 11 32	13 9 49	15 12 2	17 10 19
	10	19 17 26	21 19 39	23 10 2	1 12 16	3 10 32	5 12 46	7 11 2	9 13 16	11 15 29	13 13 45	15 15 59	17 14 15
	11	19 21 22	21 23 36	23 13 59	1 16 12	3 14 29	5 16 42	7 14 59	9 17 12	11 19 25	13 17 42	15 19 55	17 18 12
	12	19 25 19	21 27 32	23 17 56	1 20 9	3 18 25	5 20 39	7 18 55	9 21 9	11 23 22	13 21 39	15 23 52	17 22 8
	13	19 29 15	21 31 29	23 21 52	1 24 5	3 22 22	5 24 35	7 22 52	9 25 5	11 27 18	13 25 35	15 27 48	17 26 5
	14	19 33 12	21 35 25	23 25 49	1 28 2	3 26 19	5 28 32	7 26 49	9 29 2	11 31 15	13 29 32	15 31 45	17 30 2
	15	19 37 8	21 39 22	23 29 45	1 31 58	3 30 15	5 32 28	7 30 45	9 32 58	11 35 12	13 33 28	15 35 41	17 33 58
	16	19 41 5	21 43 18	23 33 42	1 35 55	3 34 12	5 36 25	7 34 42	9 36 55	11 39 8	13 37 25	15 39 38	17 37 55
	17	19 45 2	21 47 15	23 37 38	1 39 52	3 38 8	5 40 21	7 38 38	9 40 51	11 43 5	13 41 21	15 43 34	17 41 51
	18	19 48 58	21 51 11	23 41 35	1 43 48	3 42 5	5 44 18	7 42 35	9 44 48	11 47 1	13 45 18	15 47 31	17 45 48
	19	19 52 55	21 55 8	23 45 31	1 47 45	3 46 1	5 48 15	7 46 31	9 48 45	11 50 58	13 49 14	15 51 28	17 49 44
	20	19 56 51	21 59 4	23 49 28	1 51 41	3 49 58	5 52 11	7 50 28	9 52 41	11 54 54	13 53 11	15 55 24	17 53 41
	21	20 0 48	22 3 1	23 53 24	1 55 38	3 53 54	5 56 8	7 54 24	9 56 38	11 58 51	13 57 7	15 59 21	17 57 37
	22	20 4 44	22 6 58	23 57 21	1 59 34	3 57 51	6 0 4	7 58 21	10 0 34	12 2 47	14 1 4	16 3 17	18 1 34
	23	20 8 41	22 10 54	0 1 18	2 3 31	4 1 48	6 4 1	8 2 18	10 4 31	12 6 44	14 5 1	16 7 14	18 5 31
	24	20 12 37	22 14 51	0 5 14	2 7 27	4 5 44	6 7 57	8 6 14	10 8 27	12 10 41	14 8 57	16 11 10	18 9 27
	25	20 16 34	22 18 47	0 9 11	2 11 24	4 9 41	6 11 54	8 10 11	10 12 24	12 14 37	14 12 54	16 15 7	18 13 24
	26	20 20 31	22 22 44	0 13 7	2 15 21	4 13 37	6 15 51	8 14 7	10 16 20	12 18 34	14 26 50	16 19 4	18 17 20
	27	20 24 27	22 26 40	0 17 4	2 19 17	4 17 34	6 19 47	8 18 4	10 20 17	12 22 30	14 20 47	16 23 0	18 21 17
	28	20 28 24	22 30 37	0 21 0	2 23 14	4 21 30	6 23 44	8 22 0	10 24 14	12 26 27	14 24 43	16 26 57	18 25 13
	29	20 32 20		0 24 57	2 27 10	4 25 27	6 27 40	8 25 57	10 28 10	12 30 23	14 28 40	16 30 53	18 29 10
	30	20 36 17		0 28 54	2 31 7	4 29 23	6 31 37	8 29 53	10 32 7	12 34 20	14 32 36	16 34 50	18 33 6
	31	20 40 13		0 32 50		4 33 20		8 33 50	10 36 3		14 36 33		18 37 3
1972	1	18 40 59	20 43 13	22 37 33	0 39 46	2 38 2	4 40 16	6 38 33	8 40 46	10 42 59	12 41 16	14 43 29	16 41 45
	2	18 44 56	20 47 9	22 41 29	0 43 42	2 41 59	4 44 12	6 42 29	8 44 42	10 46 56	12 45 12	14 47 25	16 45 42
	3	18 48 52	20 51 6	22 45 26	0 47 39	2 45 56	4 48 9	6 46 26	8 48 39	10 50 52	12 49 9	14 51 22	16 49 39
	4	18 52 49	20 55 2	22 49 22	0 51 36	2 49 52	4 52 5	6 50 22	8 52 35	10 54 49	12 53 5	14 55 18	16 53 35
	5	18 56 45	21 58 59	22 53 19	0 55 32	2 53 49	4 56 2	6 54 19	8 56 32	10 58 45	12 57 2	14 59 15	16 57 32
	6	19 0 42	21 2 55	22 57 15	0 59 29	2 57 45	4 59 59	6 58 15	9 0 29	11 2 42	13 0 58	15 3 12	17 1 28
	7	19 4 39	21 6 52	23 1 12	1 3 25	3 1 42	5 3 55	7 2 12	9 4 25	11 6 38	13 4 55	15 7 8	17 5 25
	8	19 8 35	21 10 49	23 5 9	1 7 22	3 5 38	5 7 52	7 6 8	9 8 22	11 10 35	13 8 51	15 11 5	17 9 21
	9	19 12 32	21 14 45	23 9 5	1 11 18	3 9 35	5 11 48	7 10 5	9 12 18	11 14 31	13 12 48	15 15 1	17 13 18
	10	19 16 28	21 18 42	23 13 2	1 15 15	3 13 32	5 15 45	7 14 2	9 16 15	11 18 28	13 16 45	15 18 58	17 17 14
	11	19 20 25	21 22 38	23 16 58	1 19 11	3 17 28	5 19 41	7 17 58	9 20 11	11 22 25	13 20 41	15 22 54	17 21 11
	12	19 24 21	21 26 35	23 20 55	1 23 8	3 21 25	5 23 38	7 21 55	9 24 8	11 26 21	13 24 38	15 26 51	17 25 8
	13	19 28 18	21 30 31	23 24 51	1 27 5	3 25 21	5 27 34	7 25 51	9 28 4	11 30 18	13 28 34	15 30 47	17 29 4
	14	19 32 15	21 34 28	23 28 48	1 31 1	3 29 18	5 31 31	7 29 49	9 32 1	11 34 14	13 32 31	15 34 44	17 33 1
	15	19 36 11	21 38 24	23 32 44	1 34 58	3 33 14	5 35 28	7 33 44	9 35 58	11 38 11	13 36 27	15 38 41	17 36 57
	16	19 40 8	21 42 21	23 36 41	1 38 54	3 37 11	5 39 24	7 37 41	9 39 54	11 42 7	13 40 24	15 42 37	17 40 54
	17	19 44 4	21 46 18	23 40 38	1 42 51	3 41 7	5 43 21	7 41 37	9 43 51	11 46 4	13 44 20	15 46 34	17 44 50
	18	19 48 1	21 50 14	23 44 34	1 46 47	3 45 4	5 47 17	7 45 34	9 47 47	11 50 0	13 48 17	15 50 30	17 48 47
	19	19 51 57	21 54 11	23 48 31	1 50 44	3 49 1	5 51 14	7 49 31	9 51 44	11 53 57	13 52 14	15 54 27	17 52 43
	20	19 55 54	21 58 7	23 52 27	1 54 40	3 52 57	5 55 10	7 53 27	9 55 40	11 57 54	13 56 10	15 58 23	17 56 40
	21	19 59 50	22 2 4	23 56 24	1 58 37	3 56 54	5 59 7	7 57 24	9 59 37	12 1 50	14 0 7	16 2 20	18 0 37
	22	20 3 47	22 6 0	0 0 20	2 2 34	4 0 50	6 3 3	8 1 20	10 3 33	12 5 47	14 4 3	16 6 16	18 4 33
	23	20 7 44	22 9 57	0 4 17	2 6 30	4 4 47	6 7 0	8 5 17	10 7 30	12 9 43	14 8 0	16 10 13	18 8 30
	24	20 11 40	22 13 53	0 8 13	2 10 27	4 8 43	6 10 57	8 9 13	10 11 27	12 13 40	14 11 56	16 14 10	18 12 26
	25	20 15 37	22 17 50	0 12 10	2 14 23	4 12 40	6 14 53	8 13 10	10 15 23	12 17 36	14 15 53	16 18 6	18 16 23
	26	20 19 33	22 21 47	0 16 7	2 18 20	4 16 36	6 18 50	8 17 6	10 19 20	12 21 33	14 19 49	16 22 3	18 20 19
	27	20 23 30	22 25 43	0 20 3	2 22 16	4 20 33	6 22 46	8 21 3	10 23 16	12 25 29	14 23 46	16 25 59	18 24 16
	28	20 27 26	22 29 40	0 24 0	2 26 13	4 24 30	6 26 43	8 25 0	10 27 13	12 29 26	14 27 43	16 29 56	18 28 13
	29	20 31 23	22 33 36	0 27 56	2 30 9	4 28 26	6 30 39	8 28 56	10 31 9	12 33 22	14 31 39	16 33 52	18 32 9
	30	20 35 20		0 31 53	2 34 6	4 32 23	6 34 36	8 32 53	10 35 6	12 37 19	14 35 36	16 37 49	18 36 6
	31	20 39 16		0 35 49		4 36 19		8 36 49	10 39 2		14 39 32		18 40 2
1973	1	18 43 59	20 46 12	22 36 36	0 38 49	2 37 5	4 39 19	6 37 35	8 39 49	10 42 2	12 40 18	14 42 32	16 40 48
	2	18 47 55	20 50 9	22 40 32	0 42 45	2 41 2	4 43 15	6 41 32	8 43 45	10 45 58	12 44 15	14 46 28	16 44 45
	3	18 51 52	20 54 5	22 44 29	0 46 42	2 44 58	4 47 12	6 45 28	8 47 42	10 49 55	12 48 11	14 50 25	16 48 41
	4	18 55 48	20 58 2	22 48 25	0 50 38	2 48 55	4 51 8	6 49 25	8 51 38	10 53 51	12 52 8	14 54 21	16 52 38
	5	18 59 45	21 1 58	22 52 22	0 54 35	2 52 52	4 55 5	6 53 22	8 55 35	10 57 48	12 56 5	14 58 18	16 56 34
	6	19 3 42	21 5 55	22 56 18	0 58 31	2 56 48	4 59 1	6 57 18	8 59 31	11 1 45	13 0 1	15 2 14	17 0 31
	7	19 7 38	21 9 51	23 0 15	1 2 28	3 0 45	5 2 58	7 1 15	9 3 28	11 5 41	13 3 58	15 6 11	17 4 28
	8	19 11 35	21 13 48	23 4 11	1 6 25	3 4 41	5 6 55	7 5 11	9 7 24	11 9 38	13 7 54	15 10 7	17 8 24
	9	19 15 31	21 17 44	23 8 8	1 10 21	3 8 38	5 10 51	7 9 8	9 11 21	11 13 34	13 11 51	15 14 4	17 12 21
	10	19 19 28	21 21 41	23 12 5	1 14 18	3 12 34	5 14 48	7 13 4	9 15 18	11 17 31	13 15 47	15 18 1	17 16 17
	11	19 23 24	21 25 38	23 16 1	1 18 14	3 16 31	5 18 44	7 17 1	9 19 14	11 21 27	13 19 44	15 21 57	17 20 14
	12	19 27 21	21 29 34	23 19 58	1 22 11	3 20 27	5 22 41	7 20 57	9 23 11	11 25 24	13 23 40	15 25 54	17 24 10
	13	19 31 17	21 33 31	23 23 54	1 26 7	3 24 24	5 26 37	7 24 54	9 27 7	11 29 20	13 27 37	15 29 50	17 28 7
	14	19 35 14	21 37 27	23 27 51	1 30 4	3 28 21	5 30 34	7 28 51	9 31 4	11 33 17	13 31 34	15 33 47	17 32 3
	15	19 39 11	21 41 24	23 31 47	1 34 0	3 32 17	5 34 30	7 32 47	9 35 0	11 37 14	13 35 30	15 37 43	17 36 0
	16	19 43 7	21 45 20	23 35 44	1 37 57	3 36 14	5 38 27	7 36 44	9 38 57	11 41 12	13 39 27	15 41 40	17 39 57
	17	19 47 4	21 49 17	23 39 40	1 41 54	3 40 10	5 42 24	7 40 40	9 42 53	11 45 7	13 43 23	15 45 36	17 43 53
	18	19 51 0	21 53 13	23 43 37	1 45 50	3 44 7	5 46 20	7 44 37	9 46 50	11 49 3	13 47 20	15 49 33	17 47 50
	19	19 54 57	21 57 10	23 47 34	1 49 47	3 48 3	5 50 17	7 48 33	9 50 47	11 53 0	13 51 16	15 53 30	17 51 46
	20	19 58 53	22 1 7	23 51 30	1 53 43	3 52 0	5 54 13	7 52 30	9 54 43	11 56 56	13 55 13	15 57 26	17 55 43
	21	20 2 50	22 5 3	23 55 27	1 57 40	3 55 56	5 58 10	7 56 26	9 58 40	12 0 53	13 59 9	16 1 23	17 59 39
	22	20 6 46	22 9 0	23 59 23	2 1 36	3 59 53	6 2 6	8 0 23	10 2 36	12 4 49	14 3 6	16 5 19	18 3 36
	23	20 10 43	22 12 56	0 3 20	2 5 33	4 3 50	6 6 3	8 4 20	10 6 33	12 8 46	14 7 3	16 9 16	18 7 33
	24	20 14 40	22 16 53	0 7 16	2 9 29	4 7 46	6 9 59	8 8 16	10 10 29	12 12 43	14 10 59	16 13 12	18 11 29
	25	20 18 36	22 20 49	0 11 13	2 13 26	4 11 43	6 13 56	8 12 13	10 14 26	12 16 39	14 14 56	16 17 9	18 15 26
	26	20 22 33	22 24 46	0 15 9	2 17 23	4 15 39	6 17 53	8 16 9	10 18 22	12 20 36	14 18 52	16 21 5	18 19 22
	27	20 26 29	22 28 42	0 19 6	2 21 19	4 19 36	6 21 49	8 20 6	10 22 19	12 24 32	14 22 49	16 25 2	18 23 19
	28	20 30 26	22 32 39	0 23 3	2 25 16	4 23 32	6 25 46	8 24 2	10 26 16	12 28 29	14 26 45	16 28 59	18 27 15
	29	20 34 22		0 26 59	2 29 12	4 27 29	6 29 42	8 27 59	10 30 12	12 32 25	14 30 42	16 32 55	18 31 12
	30	20 38 19		0 30 56	2 33 9	4 31 25	6 33 39	8 31 55	10 34 9	12 36 22	14 34 38	16 36 52	18 35 8
	31	20 42 15		0 34 52		4 35 22		8 35 52	10 38 5		14 38 35		18 39 5

Year	Day	1	2	3	4	5	6	7	8	9	10	11	12
1974	1	18 43 2	20 45 15	22 35 38	0 37 51	2 36 8	4 38 21	6 36 38	8 38 51	10 41 4	12 39 21	14 41 34	16 39 51
	2	18 46 58	20 49 11	22 39 35	0 41 48	2 40 5	4 42 18	6 40 35	8 42 48	10 45 1	12 43 18	14 45 31	16 43 47
	3	18 50 55	20 53 8	22 43 31	0 45 45	2 44 1	4 46 14	6 44 31	8 46 44	10 48 58	12 47 14	14 49 27	16 47 44
	4	18 54 51	20 57 4	22 47 28	0 49 41	2 47 58	4 50 11	6 48 28	8 50 41	10 52 54	12 51 11	14 53 24	16 51 41
	5	18 58 48	21 1 1	22 51 25	0 53 38	2 51 54	4 54 8	6 52 24	8 54 38	10 56 51	12 55 7	14 57 20	16 55 37
	6	19 2 44	21 4 58	22 55 21	0 57 34	2 55 51	4 58 4	6 56 21	8 58 34	11 0 47	12 59 4	15 1 17	16 59 34
	7	19 6 41	21 8 54	22 59 18	1 1 31	2 59 47	5 2 1	7 0 17	9 2 31	11 4 44	13 3 0	15 5 14	17 3 30
	8	19 10 37	21 12 51	23 3 14	1 5 27	3 3 44	5 5 57	7 4 14	9 6 27	11 8 40	13 6 57	15 9 10	17 7 27
	9	19 14 34	21 16 47	23 7 11	1 9 24	3 7 41	5 9 54	7 8 10	9 10 24	11 12 37	13 10 53	15 13 7	17 11 23
	10	19 18 31	21 20 44	23 11 7	1 13 20	3 11 37	5 13 50	7 12 7	9 14 20	11 16 33	13 14 50	15 17 3	17 15 20
	11	19 22 27	21 24 40	23 15 4	1 17 17	3 15 34	5 17 47	7 16 4	9 18 17	11 20 30	13 18 47	15 21 0	17 19 16
	12	19 26 24	21 28 37	23 19 0	1 21 14	3 19 30	5 21 43	7 20 0	9 22 13	11 24 27	13 22 43	15 24 56	17 23 13
	13	19 30 20	21 32 33	23 22 57	1 25 10	3 23 27	5 25 40	7 23 57	9 26 10	11 28 23	13 26 40	15 28 53	17 27 10
	14	19 34 17	21 36 30	23 26 54	1 29 7	3 27 23	5 29 37	7 27 53	9 30 7	11 32 20	13 30 36	15 32 49	17 31 6
	15	19 38 13	21 40 27	23 30 50	1 33 3	3 31 20	5 33 33	7 31 50	9 34 3	11 36 16	13 34 33	15 36 46	17 35 3
	16	19 42 10	21 44 23	23 34 47	1 37 0	3 35 16	5 37 30	7 35 46	9 38 0	11 40 13	13 38 29	15 40 43	17 38 59
	17	19 46 6	21 48 20	23 38 43	1 40 56	3 39 13	5 41 26	7 39 43	9 41 56	11 44 9	13 42 26	15 44 39	17 42 56
	18	19 50 3	21 52 16	23 42 40	1 44 53	3 43 10	5 45 23	7 43 40	9 45 53	11 48 6	13 46 22	15 48 36	17 46 52
	19	19 54 0	21 56 13	23 46 36	1 48 49	3 47 6	5 49 19	7 47 36	9 49 49	11 52 2	13 50 19	15 52 32	17 50 49
	20	19 57 56	22 0 9	23 50 33	1 52 46	3 51 3	5 53 16	7 51 33	9 53 46	11 55 59	13 54 16	15 56 29	17 54 45
	21	20 1 53	22 4 6	23 54 29	1 56 43	3 54 59	5 57 12	7 55 29	9 57 42	11 59 56	13 58 12	16 0 25	17 58 42
	22	20 5 49	22 8 2	23 58 26	2 0 39	3 58 56	6 1 9	7 59 26	10 1 39	12 3 52	14 2 9	16 4 22	18 2 39
	23	20 9 46	22 11 59	0 2 22	2 4 36	4 2 52	6 5 6	8 3 22	10 5 35	12 7 49	14 6 5	16 8 18	18 6 35
	24	20 13 42	22 15 56	0 6 19	2 8 32	4 6 49	6 9 2	8 7 19	10 9 32	12 11 45	14 10 2	16 12 15	18 10 32
	25	20 17 39	22 19 52	0 10 16	2 12 29	4 10 45	6 12 59	8 11 15	10 13 29	12 15 42	14 13 58	16 16 12	18 14 28
	26	20 21 35	22 23 49	0 14 12	2 16 25	4 14 42	6 16 55	8 15 12	10 17 25	12 19 38	14 17 55	16 20 8	18 18 25
	27	20 25 32	22 27 45	0 18 9	2 20 22	4 18 39	6 20 52	8 19 9	10 21 22	12 23 35	14 21 51	16 24 5	18 22 21
	28	20 29 29	22 31 42	0 22 5	2 24 18	4 22 35	6 24 48	8 23 5	10 25 18	12 27 31	14 25 48	16 28 1	18 26 18
	29	20 33 25		0 26 2	2 28 15	4 26 32	6 28 45	8 27 2	10 29 15	12 31 28	14 29 45	16 31 58	18 30 15
	30	20 37 22		0 29 58	2 32 12	4 30 28	6 32 41	8 30 58	10 33 11	12 35 25	14 33 41	16 35 54	18 34 11
	31	20 41 18		0 33 55		4 34 25		8 34 55	10 37 8		14 37 38		18 38 8
1975	1	18 42 4	20 44 17	22 34 41	0 36 54	2 35 11	4 37 24	6 35 40	8 37 54	10 40 7	12 38 24	14 40 37	16 38 53
	2	18 46 1	20 48 14	22 38 37	0 40 51	2 39 7	4 41 20	6 39 37	8 41 50	10 44 4	12 42 20	14 44 33	16 42 50
	3	18 49 57	20 52 11	22 42 34	0 44 47	2 43 4	4 45 17	6 43 34	8 45 47	10 48 0	12 46 17	14 48 30	16 46 47
	4	18 53 54	20 56 7	22 46 31	0 48 44	2 47 0	4 49 14	6 47 30	8 49 44	10 51 57	12 50 13	14 52 26	16 50 43
	5	18 57 50	21 0 4	22 50 27	0 52 40	2 50 57	4 53 10	6 51 27	8 53 40	10 55 53	12 54 10	14 56 23	16 54 40
	6	19 1 47	21 4 0	22 54 24	0 56 37	2 54 53	4 57 7	6 55 23	8 57 37	10 59 50	12 58 6	15 0 20	16 58 36
	7	19 5 44	21 7 57	22 58 20	1 0 33	2 58 50	5 1 3	6 59 20	9 1 33	11 3 46	13 2 3	15 4 16	17 2 33
	8	19 9 40	21 11 53	23 2 17	1 4 30	3 2 47	5 5 0	7 3 17	9 5 30	11 7 43	13 5 59	15 8 13	17 6 29
	9	19 13 37	21 15 50	23 6 13	1 8 26	3 6 43	5 8 56	7 7 13	9 9 26	11 11 39	13 9 56	15 12 9	17 10 26
	10	19 17 33	21 19 46	23 10 10	1 12 23	3 10 40	5 12 53	7 11 10	9 13 23	11 15 36	13 13 53	15 16 6	17 14 22
	11	19 21 30	21 23 43	23 14 6	1 16 20	3 14 36	5 16 49	7 15 6	9 17 19	11 19 33	13 17 49	15 20 2	17 18 19
	12	19 25 26	21 27 40	23 18 3	1 20 16	3 18 33	5 20 46	7 19 3	9 21 16	11 23 29	13 21 46	15 23 59	17 22 16
	13	19 29 23	21 31 36	23 22 0	1 24 13	3 22 29	5 24 43	7 22 59	9 25 13	11 27 26	13 25 42	15 27 55	17 26 12
	14	19 33 19	21 35 33	23 25 56	1 28 9	3 26 26	5 28 39	7 26 56	9 29 9	11 31 22	13 29 39	15 31 52	17 30 9
	15	19 37 16	21 39 29	23 29 53	1 32 6	3 30 22	5 32 36	7 30 52	9 33 6	11 35 19	13 33 35	15 35 49	17 34 5
	16	19 41 13	21 43 26	23 33 49	1 36 2	3 34 19	5 36 32	7 34 49	9 37 2	11 39 15	13 37 32	15 39 45	17 38 2
	17	19 45 9	21 47 22	23 37 46	1 39 59	3 38 16	5 40 29	7 38 46	9 40 59	11 43 12	13 41 28	15 43 42	17 41 58
	18	19 49 6	21 51 19	23 41 42	1 43 55	3 42 12	5 44 25	7 42 42	9 44 55	11 47 8	13 45 25	15 47 38	17 45 55
	19	19 53 2	21 55 15	23 45 39	1 47 52	3 46 9	5 48 22	7 46 39	9 48 52	11 51 5	13 49 22	15 51 35	17 49 51
	20	19 56 59	21 59 12	23 49 35	1 51 49	3 50 5	5 52 18	7 50 35	9 52 48	11 55 2	13 53 18	15 55 31	17 53 48
	21	20 0 55	22 3 9	23 53 32	1 55 45	3 54 2	5 56 15	7 54 32	9 56 45	11 58 58	13 57 15	15 59 28	17 57 45
	22	20 4 52	22 7 5	23 57 29	1 59 42	3 57 58	6 0 12	7 58 28	10 0 42	12 2 55	14 1 11	16 3 24	18 1 41
	23	20 8 48	22 11 2	0 1 25	2 3 38	4 1 55	6 4 8	8 2 25	10 4 38	12 6 51	14 5 8	16 7 21	18 5 38
	24	20 12 45	22 14 58	0 5 22	2 7 35	4 5 51	6 8 5	8 6 21	10 8 35	12 10 48	14 9 4	16 11 18	18 9 34
	25	20 16 42	22 18 55	0 9 18	2 11 31	4 9 48	6 12 1	8 10 18	10 12 31	12 14 44	14 13 1	16 15 14	18 13 31
	26	20 20 38	22 22 51	0 13 15	2 15 28	4 13 45	6 15 58	8 14 15	10 16 28	12 18 41	14 16 57	16 19 11	18 17 27
	27	20 24 35	22 26 48	0 17 11	2 19 24	4 17 41	6 19 54	8 18 11	10 20 24	12 22 37	14 20 54	16 23 7	18 21 24
	28	20 28 31	22 30 44	0 21 8	2 23 21	4 21 38	6 23 51	8 22 8	10 24 21	12 26 34	14 24 50	16 27 4	18 25 20
	29	20 32 28		0 25 4	2 27 18	4 25 34	6 27 48	8 26 4	10 28 17	12 30 31	14 28 47	16 31 0	18 29 17
	30	20 36 24		0 29 1	2 31 14	4 29 31	6 31 44	8 30 1	10 32 14	12 34 27	14 32 44	16 34 57	18 33 14
	31	20 40 21		0 32 58		4 33 27		8 33 57	10 36 10		14 36 40		18 37 10
1976	1	18 41 7	20 43 20	22 37 40	0 39 53	2 38 10	4 40 23	6 38 40	8 40 53	10 43 6	12 41 23	14 43 36	16 41 52
	2	18 45 3	20 47 17	22 41 37	0 43 50	2 42 6	4 44 20	6 42 36	8 44 49	10 47 3	12 45 19	14 47 32	16 45 49
	3	18 49 0	20 51 13	22 45 33	0 47 46	2 46 3	4 48 16	6 46 33	8 48 46	10 50 59	12 49 16	14 51 29	16 49 46
	4	18 52 56	20 55 10	22 49 30	0 51 43	2 49 59	4 52 13	6 50 29	8 52 43	10 54 56	12 53 12	14 55 25	16 53 42
	5	18 56 53	20 59 6	22 53 26	0 55 39	2 53 56	4 56 9	6 54 26	8 56 39	10 58 52	12 57 9	14 59 22	16 57 39
	6	19 0 49	21 3 3	22 57 23	0 59 36	2 57 53	5 0 6	6 58 22	9 0 36	11 2 49	13 1 5	15 3 19	17 1 35
	7	19 4 46	21 6 59	21 1 19	1 3 32	3 1 49	5 4 2	7 2 19	9 4 32	11 6 45	13 5 2	15 7 15	17 5 32
	8	19 8 43	21 10 56	23 5 16	1 7 29	3 5 46	5 7 59	7 6 16	9 8 29	11 10 42	13 8 58	15 11 12	17 9 28
	9	19 12 39	21 14 53	23 9 12	1 11 26	3 9 42	5 11 55	7 10 12	9 12 25	11 14 38	13 12 55	15 15 8	17 13 25
	10	19 16 36	21 18 49	23 13 9	1 15 22	3 13 39	5 15 52	7 14 9	9 16 22	11 18 35	13 16 52	15 19 5	17 17 21
	11	19 20 32	21 22 45	23 17 6	1 19 19	3 17 35	5 19 49	7 18 5	9 20 18	11 22 32	13 20 48	15 23 1	17 21 18
	12	19 24 29	21 26 42	23 21 2	1 23 15	3 21 32	5 23 45	7 22 2	9 24 15	11 26 28	13 24 45	15 26 58	17 25 15
	13	19 28 25	21 30 39	23 24 59	1 27 12	3 25 28	5 27 42	7 25 58	9 28 12	11 30 25	13 28 41	15 30 54	17 29 11
	14	19 32 22	21 34 35	23 28 55	1 31 8	3 29 25	5 31 38	7 29 55	9 32 8	11 34 21	13 32 38	15 34 51	17 33 8
	15	19 36 18	21 38 32	23 32 52	1 35 5	3 33 21	5 35 35	7 33 51	9 36 5	11 38 18	13 36 34	15 38 48	17 37 4
	16	19 40 15	21 42 28	23 36 48	1 39 1	3 37 18	5 39 31	7 37 48	9 40 1	11 42 14	13 40 31	15 42 44	17 41 1
	17	19 44 12	21 46 25	23 40 45	1 42 58	3 41 15	5 43 28	7 41 45	9 43 58	11 46 11	13 44 27	15 46 41	17 44 57
	18	19 48 8	21 50 21	23 44 41	1 46 54	3 45 11	5 47 24	7 45 41	9 47 54	11 50 7	13 48 24	15 50 37	17 48 54
	19	19 52 5	21 54 18	23 48 38	1 50 51	3 49 8	5 51 21	7 49 38	9 51 51	11 54 4	13 52 21	15 54 34	17 52 50
	20	19 56 2	21 58 14	23 52 34	1 54 48	3 53 4	5 55 18	7 53 34	9 55 47	11 58 1	13 56 17	15 58 30	17 56 47
	21	19 59 58	22 2 11	23 56 31	1 58 44	3 57 1	5 59 14	7 57 31	9 59 44	12 1 57	14 0 14	16 2 27	18 0 44
	22	20 3 54	22 6 8	0 0 28	2 2 41	4 0 57	6 3 11	8 1 27	10 3 41	12 5 54	14 4 10	16 6 23	18 4 40
	23	20 7 51	22 10 4	0 4 24	2 6 37	4 4 54	6 7 7	8 5 24	10 7 37	12 9 50	14 8 7	16 10 20	18 8 37
	24	20 11 48	22 14 1	0 8 21	2 10 34	4 8 50	6 11 4	8 9 20	10 11 34	12 13 47	14 12 3	16 14 17	18 12 33
	25	20 15 44	22 17 57	0 12 17	2 14 30	4 12 47	6 15 0	8 13 17	10 15 30	12 17 43	14 16 0	16 18 13	18 16 30
	26	20 19 41	22 21 54	0 16 14	2 18 27	4 16 44	6 18 57	8 17 14	10 19 27	12 12 40	14 19 56	16 22 10	18 20 26
	27	20 23 37	22 25 50	0 20 10	2 22 24	4 20 40	6 22 53	8 21 10	10 23 23	12 25 36	14 23 53	16 26 6	18 24 23
	28	20 27 34	22 29 47	0 24 7	2 26 20	4 24 37	6 26 50	8 25 7	10 27 20	12 29 33	14 27 50	16 30 3	18 28 19
	29	20 31 30	22 33 43	0 28 3	2 30 17	4 28 33	6 30 47	8 29 3	10 31 16	12 33 30	14 31 46	16 33 59	18 32 16
	30	20 35 27		0 32 0	2 34 13	4 32 30	6 34 43	8 33 0	10 35 13	12 37 26	14 35 43	16 37 56	18 36 13
	31	20 39 23		0 35 57		4 36 26		8 36 56	10 39 9		14 39 39		18 40 9
1977	1	18 44 6	20 46 19	22 36 42	0 38 56	2 37 12	4 39 25	6 37 42	8 39 55	10 42 8	12 40 25	14 42 38	16 40 55
	2	18 48 2	20 50 15	22 40 39	0 42 52	2 41 9	4 43 22	6 41 39	8 43 52	10 46 5	12 44 22	14 46 35	16 44 51
	3	18 51 59	20 54 12	22 44 36	0 46 49	2 45 5	4 47 18	6 45 35	8 47 48	10 50 2	12 48 18	14 50 31	16 48 48
	4	18 55 55	20 58 9	22 48 32	0 50 45	2 49 2	4 51 15	6 49 32	8 51 45	10 53 58	12 52 15	14 54 28	16 52 44
	5	18 59 52	21 2 5	22 52 29	0 54 42	2 52 58	4 55 12	6 53 28	8 55 41	10 57 55	12 56 11	14 58 24	16 56 41
	6	19 3 48	21 6 2	22 56 25	0 58 38	2 56 55	4 59 8	6 57 25	8 59 38	11 1 51	13 0 8	15 2 21	17 0 38
	7	19 7 45	21 9 58	23 0 22	1 2 35	3 0 51	5 3 5	7 1 21	9 3 35	11 5 48	13 4 4	15 6 17	17 4 34
	8	19 11 42	21 13 55	23 4 18	1 6 31	3 4 48	5 7 1	7 5 18	9 7 31	11 9 44	13 8 1	15 10 14	17 8 31
	9	19 15 38	21 17 51	23 8 15	1 10 28	3 8 45	5 10 58	7 9 14	9 11 28	11 13 41	13 11 57	15 14 11	17 12 27
	10	19 19 35	21 21 48	23 12 11	1 14 25	3 12 41	5 14 54	7 13 11	9 15 24	11 17 37	13 15 54	15 18 7	17 16 24
	11	19 23 31	21 25 44	23 16 8	1 18 21	3 16 38	5 18 51	7 17 8	9 19 21	11 21 34	13 19 51	15 22 4	17 20 20
	12	19 27 28	21 29 41	23 20 5	1 22 18	3 20 34	5 22 47	7 21 4	9 23 17	11 25 31	13 23 47	15 26 0	17 24 17
	13	19 31 24	21 33 38	23 24 1	1 26 14	3 24 31	5 26 44	7 25 1	9 27 14	11 29 27	13 27 44	15 29 57	17 28 13
	14	19 35 21	21 37 34	23 27 58	1 30 11	3 28 27	5 30 41	7 28 57	9 31 10	11 33 24	13 31 40	15 33 53	17 32 10
	15	19 39 17	21 41 31	23 31 54	1 34 7	3 32 24	5 34 37	7 32 54	9 35 7	11 37 20	13 35 37	15 37 50	17 36 7
	16	19 43 14	21 45 27	23 35 51	1 38 4	3 36 20	5 38 34	7 36 50	9 39 4	11 41 17	13 39 33	15 41 46	17 40 3
	17	19 47 11	21 49 24	23 39 47	1 42 0	3 40 17	5 42 30	7 40 47	9 43 0	11 45 13	13 43 30	15 45 43	17 44 0
	18	19 51 7	21 53 20	23 43 44	1 45 57	3 44 14	5 46 27	7 44 44	9 46 57	11 49 10	13 47 26	15 49 40	17 47 56
	19	19 55 4	21 57 17	23 47 40	1 49 53	3 48 10	5 50 23	7 48 40	9 50 53	11 53 6	13 51 23	15 53 36	17 51 53
	20	19 59 0	22 1 13	23 51 37	1 53 50	3 52 7	5 54 20	7 52 37	9 54 50	11 57 3	13 55 20	15 57 33	17 55 49
	21	20 2 57	22 5 10	23 55 33	1 57 47	3 56 3	5 58 16	7 56 33	9 58 46	12 0 59	13 59 16	16 1 29	17 59 46
	22	20 6 53	22 9 7	23 59 30	2 1 43	4 0 0	6 2 13	8 0 30	10 2 43	12 4 56	14 3 13	16 5 26	18 3 42
	23	20 10 50	22 13 3	0 3 27	2 5 40	4 3 56	6 6 10	8 4 26	10 6 39	12 8 53	14 7 9	16 9 22	18 7 39
	24	20 14 46	22 17 0	0 7 23	2 9 36	4 7 53	6 10 6	8 8 23	10 10 36	12 12 49	14 11 6	16 13 19	18 11 36
	25	20 18 43	22 20 56	0 11 20	2 13 33	4 11 49	6 14 3	8 12 19	10 14 33	12 16 46	14 15 2	16 17 15	18 15 32
	26	20 22 40	22 24 53	0 15 16	2 17 29	4 15 46	6 17 59	8 16 16	10 18 29	12 20 42	14 18 59	16 21 12	18 19 29
	27	20 26 36	22 28 49	0 19 13	2 21 26	4 19 43	6 21 56	8 20 13	10 22 26	12 24 39	14 22 55	16 25 9	18 23 25
	28	20 30 33	22 32 46	0 23 9	2 25 22	4 23 39	6 25 52	8 24 9	10 26 22	12 28 35	14 26 52	16 29 5	18 27 22
	29	20 34 29		0 27 6	2 29 19	4 27 36	6 29 49	8 28 6	10 30 19	12 32 32	14 30 48	16 33 2	18 31 18
	30	20 38 26		0 31 2	2 33 16	4 31 32	6 33 45	8 32 2	10 34 15	12 36 28	14 34 45	16 36 58	18 35 15
	31	20 42 22		0 34 59		4 35 29		8 35 59	10 38 12		14 38 42		18 39 12

Year	Day	1	2	3	4	5	6	7	8	9	10	11	12
1978	1	18 43 8	20 45 21	22 35 45	0 37 58	2 36 15	4 38 28	6 36 44	8 38 58	10 41 11	12 39 27	14 41 40	16 39 57
	2	18 47 5	20 49 18	22 39 41	0 41 54	2 40 11	4 42 24	6 40 41	8 42 54	10 45 7	12 43 24	14 45 37	16 43 54
	3	18 51 1	20 53 14	22 43 38	0 45 51	2 44 8	4 46 21	6 44 38	8 46 51	10 49 4	12 47 20	14 49 34	16 47 50
	4	18 54 58	20 57 11	22 47 34	0 49 48	2 48 4	4 50 17	6 48 34	8 50 47	10 53 0	12 51 17	14 53 30	16 51 47
	5	18 58 54	21 1 8	22 51 31	0 53 44	2 52 1	4 54 14	6 52 31	8 54 44	10 56 57	12 55 14	14 57 27	16 55 43
	6	19 2 51	21 5 4	22 55 28	0 57 41	2 55 57	4 58 10	6 56 27	8 58 40	11 0 54	12 59 10	15 1 23	16 59 40
	7	19 6 47	21 9 1	22 59 24	1 1 37	2 59 54	5 2 7	7 0 24	9 2 37	11 4 50	13 3 7	15 5 20	17 3 36
	8	19 10 44	21 12 57	23 3 21	1 5 34	3 3 50	5 6 4	7 4 20	9 6 34	11 8 47	13 7 3	15 9 16	17 7 33
	9	19 14 41	21 16 54	23 7 17	1 9 30	3 7 47	5 10 0	7 8 17	9 10 30	11 12 43	13 11 0	15 13 13	17 11 30
	10	19 18 37	21 20 50	23 11 14	1 13 27	3 11 44	5 13 57	7 12 13	9 14 27	11 16 40	13 14 56	15 17 9	17 15 26
	11	19 22 34	21 24 47	23 15 10	1 17 23	3 15 40	5 17 53	7 16 10	9 18 23	11 20 36	13 18 53	15 21 6	17 19 23
	12	19 26 30	21 28 43	23 19 7	1 21 20	3 19 37	5 21 50	7 20 7	9 22 20	11 24 33	13 22 49	15 25 3	17 23 19
	13	19 30 27	21 32 40	23 23 3	1 25 17	3 23 33	5 25 46	7 24 3	9 26 16	11 28 29	13 26 46	15 28 59	17 27 16
	14	19 34 23	21 36 36	23 27 0	1 29 13	3 27 30	5 29 43	7 28 0	9 30 13	11 32 26	13 30 43	15 32 56	17 31 12
	15	19 38 20	21 40 33	23 30 57	1 33 10	3 31 26	5 33 39	7 31 56	9 34 9	11 36 23	13 34 39	15 36 52	17 35 9
	16	19 42 16	21 44 30	23 34 53	1 37 6	3 35 23	5 37 36	7 35 53	9 38 6	11 40 19	13 38 36	15 40 49	17 39 5
	17	19 46 13	21 48 26	23 38 50	1 41 3	3 39 19	5 41 33	7 39 49	9 42 3	11 44 16	13 42 32	15 44 45	17 43 2
	18	19 50 10	21 52 23	23 42 46	1 44 59	3 43 16	5 45 29	7 43 46	9 45 59	11 48 12	13 46 29	15 48 42	17 46 59
	19	19 54 6	21 56 19	23 46 43	1 48 56	3 47 12	5 49 26	7 47 42	9 49 56	11 52 9	13 50 25	15 52 38	17 50 55
	20	19 58 3	22 0 16	23 50 39	1 52 52	3 51 9	5 53 22	7 51 39	9 53 52	11 56 5	13 54 22	15 56 35	17 54 52
	21	20 1 59	22 4 12	23 54 36	1 56 49	3 55 6	5 57 19	7 55 36	9 57 49	12 0 2	13 58 18	16 0 32	17 58 48
	22	20 5 56	22 8 9	23 58 32	2 0 45	3 59 2	6 1 15	7 59 32	10 1 45	12 3 58	14 2 15	16 4 28	18 2 45
	23	20 9 52	22 12 5	0 2 29	2 4 42	4 2 59	6 5 12	8 3 29	10 5 42	12 7 55	14 6 12	16 8 25	18 6 41
	24	20 13 49	22 16 2	0 6 25	2 8 39	4 6 55	6 9 9	8 7 25	10 9 38	12 11 51	14 10 8	16 12 21	18 10 38
	25	20 17 45	22 19 59	0 10 22	2 12 35	4 10 52	6 13 5	8 11 22	10 13 35	12 15 48	14 14 5	16 16 18	18 14 34
	26	20 21 42	22 23 55	0 14 19	2 16 32	4 14 48	6 17 2	8 15 18	10 17 31	12 19 45	14 18 1	16 20 14	18 18 31
	27	20 25 39	22 27 52	0 18 15	2 20 28	4 18 45	6 20 58	8 19 15	10 21 28	12 23 41	14 21 58	16 24 11	18 22 28
	28	29 29 35	22 31 48	0 22 12	2 24 25	4 22 41	6 24 55	8 23 11	10 25 25	12 27 38	14 25 54	16 28 7	18 26 24
	29	20 33 32		0 26 8	2 28 21	4 26 38	6 28 51	8 27 8	10 29 21	12 31 34	14 29 51	16 32 4	18 30 21
	30	20 37 28		0 30 5	2 32 18	4 30 35	6 32 48	8 31 5	10 33 18	12 35 31	14 33 47	16 36 1	18 34 17
	31	20 41 25		0 34 1		4 34 31		8 35 1	10 37 14		14 37 44		18 38 14
1979	1	18 42 10	20 44 24	22 34 47	0 37 0	2 35 17	4 37 30	6 35 47	8 38 0	10 40 13	12 38 30	14 40 43	16 38 59
	2	18 46 7	20 48 20	22 38 44	0 40 57	2 39 13	4 41 27	6 39 43	8 41 57	10 44 10	12 42 26	14 44 39	16 42 56
	3	18 50 4	20 52 17	22 42 40	0 44 53	2 43 10	4 45 23	6 43 40	8 45 53	10 48 6	12 46 23	14 48 36	16 46 53
	4	18 54 0	20 56 13	22 46 37	0 48 50	2 47 7	4 49 20	6 47 36	8 49 50	10 52 3	12 50 19	14 52 32	16 50 49
	5	18 57 57	21 0 10	22 50 33	0 52 46	2 51 3	4 53 16	6 51 33	8 53 46	10 55 59	12 54 16	14 56 29	16 54 46
	6	19 1 53	21 4 6	22 54 30	0 56 43	2 55 0	4 57 13	6 55 30	8 57 43	10 59 56	12 58 12	15 0 26	16 58 42
	7	19 5 50	21 8 3	22 58 26	1 0 40	2 58 56	5 1 9	6 59 26	9 1 39	11 3 52	13 2 9	15 4 22	17 2 39
	8	19 9 46	21 12 0	23 2 23	1 4 36	3 2 53	5 5 6	7 3 23	9 5 36	11 7 49	13 6 6	15 8 19	17 6 35
	9	19 13 43	21 15 56	23 6 20	1 8 33	3 6 49	5 9 2	7 7 19	9 9 32	11 11 46	13 10 2	15 12 15	17 10 32
	10	19 17 39	21 19 53	23 10 16	1 12 29	3 10 46	5 12 59	7 11 16	9 13 29	11 15 42	13 13 59	15 16 12	17 14 29
	11	19 21 36	21 23 49	23 14 13	1 16 26	3 14 42	5 16 56	7 15 12	9 17 26	11 19 39	13 17 55	15 20 8	17 18 25
	12	19 25 33	21 27 46	23 18 9	1 20 22	3 18 39	5 20 52	7 19 9	9 21 22	11 23 35	13 21 52	15 24 5	17 22 22
	13	19 29 29	21 31 42	23 22 6	1 24 19	3 22 35	5 24 49	7 23 5	9 25 19	11 27 32	13 25 48	15 28 1	17 26 18
	14	19 33 26	21 35 39	23 26 2	1 28 15	3 26 32	5 28 45	7 27 2	9 29 15	11 31 28	13 29 45	15 31 58	17 30 15
	15	19 37 22	21 39 35	23 29 59	1 32 12	3 30 29	5 32 42	7 30 59	9 33 12	11 35 25	13 33 41	15 35 54	17 34 11
	16	19 41 19	21 43 32	23 33 55	1 36 9	3 34 25	5 36 38	7 34 55	9 37 8	11 39 21	13 37 38	15 39 51	17 38 8
	17	19 45 15	21 47 29	23 37 52	1 40 5	3 38 22	5 40 35	7 38 52	9 41 5	11 43 18	13 41 35	15 43 48	17 42 4
	18	19 49 12	21 51 25	23 41 49	1 44 2	3 42 18	5 44 32	7 42 48	9 45 1	11 47 15	13 45 31	15 47 44	17 46 1
	19	19 53 8	21 55 22	23 45 45	1 47 58	3 46 15	5 48 28	7 46 45	9 48 58	11 51 11	13 49 28	15 51 41	17 49 58
	20	19 57 5	21 59 18	23 49 42	1 51 55	3 50 11	5 52 25	7 50 41	9 52 55	11 55 8	13 53 24	15 55 37	17 53 54
	21	20 1 2	22 3 15	23 53 38	1 55 51	3 54 8	5 56 21	7 54 38	9 56 51	11 59 4	13 57 21	15 59 34	17 57 51
	22	20 4 58	22 7 11	23 57 35	1 59 48	3 58 4	6 0 18	7 58 34	10 0 48	12 3 1	14 1 17	16 3 30	18 1 47
	23	20 8 55	22 11 8	0 1 31	2 3 44	4 2 1	6 4 14	8 2 31	10 4 44	12 6 57	14 5 14	16 7 27	18 5 44
	24	20 12 51	22 15 4	0 5 28	2 7 41	4 5 58	6 8 11	8 6 28	10 8 41	12 10 54	14 9 10	16 11 24	18 9 40
	25	20 16 48	22 19 1	0 9 24	2 11 38	4 9 54	6 12 7	8 10 24	10 12 37	12 14 50	14 13 7	16 15 20	18 13 37
	26	20 20 44	22 22 58	0 13 21	2 15 34	4 13 51	6 16 4	8 14 21	10 16 34	12 18 47	14 17 4	16 19 17	18 17 33
	27	20 24 41	22 26 54	0 17 18	2 19 31	4 17 47	6 20 1	8 18 17	10 20 30	12 22 44	14 21 0	16 23 13	18 21 30
	28	20 28 37	22 30 51	0 21 14	2 23 27	4 21 44	6 23 57	8 22 14	10 24 27	12 26 40	14 24 57	16 27 10	18 25 27
	29	20 32 34		0 25 11	2 27 24	4 25 40	6 27 54	8 26 10	10 28 23	12 30 37	14 28 53	16 31 6	18 29 23
	30	20 36 31		0 29 7	2 31 20	4 29 37	6 31 50	8 30 7	10 32 20	12 34 33	14 32 50	16 35 3	18 33 20
	31	20 40 27		0 33 4		4 33 34		8 34 3	10 36 17		14 36 46		18 37 16
1980	1	18 41 13	20 43 26	22 37 46	0 39 59	2 38 16	4 40 29	6 38 46	8 40 59	10 43 12	12 41 29	14 43 42	16 41 59
	2	18 45 10	20 47 23	22 41 43	0 43 56	2 42 13	4 44 26	6 42 43	8 44 56	10 47 9	12 45 26	14 47 39	16 45 55
	3	18 49 6	20 51 19	22 45 39	0 47 53	2 46 9	4 48 22	6 46 39	8 48 52	10 51 5	12 49 22	14 51 35	16 49 52
	4	18 53 3	20 55 16	22 49 36	0 51 49	2 50 6	4 52 19	6 50 36	8 52 49	10 55 2	12 53 19	14 55 32	16 53 48
	5	18 56 59	20 59 13	22 53 33	0 55 46	2 54 2	4 56 16	6 54 32	8 56 45	10 58 59	12 57 15	14 59 28	16 57 45
	6	19 0 56	21 3 9	22 57 29	0 59 42	2 57 59	5 0 12	6 58 29	9 0 42	11 2 55	13 1 12	15 3 25	17 1 42
	7	19 4 52	21 7 6	23 1 26	1 3 39	3 1 55	5 4 9	7 2 25	9 4 39	11 6 52	13 5 8	15 7 21	17 5 38
	8	19 8 49	21 11 2	23 5 22	1 7 35	3 5 52	5 8 5	7 6 22	9 8 35	11 10 48	13 9 5	15 11 18	17 9 35
	9	19 12 46	21 14 59	23 9 19	1 11 32	3 9 48	5 12 2	7 10 18	9 12 32	11 14 45	13 13 1	15 15 15	17 13 31
	10	19 16 42	21 18 55	23 13 15	1 15 28	3 13 45	5 15 58	7 14 15	9 16 28	11 18 41	13 16 58	15 19 11	17 17 28
	11	19 20 39	21 22 52	23 17 12	1 19 25	3 17 42	5 19 55	7 18 12	9 20 25	11 22 38	13 20 54	15 23 8	17 21 24
	12	19 24 35	21 26 48	23 21 8	1 23 22	3 21 38	5 23 51	7 22 8	9 24 21	11 26 34	13 24 51	15 27 4	17 25 21
	13	19 28 32	21 30 45	23 25 5	1 27 18	3 25 35	5 27 48	7 26 5	9 28 18	11 30 31	13 28 48	15 31 1	17 29 17
	14	19 32 28	21 34 42	23 29 2	1 31 15	3 29 31	5 31 45	7 30 1	9 32 14	11 34 28	13 32 44	15 34 57	17 33 14
	15	19 36 25	21 38 38	23 32 58	1 35 11	3 33 28	5 35 41	7 33 58	9 36 11	11 38 24	13 36 41	15 38 54	17 37 11
	16	19 40 21	21 42 35	23 36 55	1 39 8	3 37 24	5 39 38	7 37 54	9 40 8	11 42 21	13 40 37	15 42 50	17 41 7
	17	19 44 18	21 46 31	23 40 51	1 43 4	3 41 21	5 43 34	7 41 51	9 44 4	11 46 17	13 44 34	15 46 47	17 45 4
	18	19 48 15	21 50 28	23 44 48	1 47 1	3 45 17	5 47 31	7 45 47	9 48 1	11 50 14	13 48 30	15 50 44	17 49 0
	19	19 52 11	21 54 24	23 48 44	1 50 57	3 49 14	5 51 27	7 49 44	9 51 57	11 54 10	13 52 27	15 54 40	17 52 57
	20	19 56 8	21 58 21	23 52 41	1 54 54	3 53 11	5 55 24	7 53 41	9 55 54	11 58 7	13 56 23	15 58 37	17 56 53
	21	20 0 4	22 2 17	23 56 37	1 58 51	3 57 7	5 59 20	7 57 37	9 59 50	12 2 3	14 0 20	16 2 33	18 0 50
	22	20 4 1	22 6 14	0 0 34	2 2 47	4 1 4	6 3 17	8 1 34	10 3 47	12 6 0	14 4 17	16 6 30	18 4 46
	23	20 7 57	22 10 10	0 4 30	2 6 44	4 5 0	6 7 14	8 5 30	10 7 43	12 9 57	14 8 13	16 10 26	18 8 43
	24	20 11 54	22 14 7	0 8 27	2 10 40	4 8 57	6 11 10	8 9 27	10 11 40	12 13 53	14 12 10	16 14 23	18 12 40
	25	20 15 50	22 18 4	0 12 24	2 14 37	4 12 53	6 15 7	8 13 23	10 15 37	12 17 50	14 16 6	16 18 19	18 16 36
	26	20 19 47	22 22 0	0 16 20	2 18 33	4 16 50	6 19 3	8 17 20	10 19 33	12 21 46	14 20 3	16 22 16	18 20 33
	27	20 23 44	22 25 57	0 20 17	2 22 30	4 20 46	6 23 0	8 21 16	10 23 30	12 25 43	14 23 59	16 26 13	18 24 29
	28	20 27 40	22 29 53	0 24 13	2 26 26	4 24 43	6 26 56	8 25 13	10 27 26	12 29 39	14 27 56	16 30 9	18 28 26
	29	20 31 37	22 33 50	0 28 10	2 30 23	4 28 40	6 30 53	8 29 10	10 31 23	12 33 36	14 31 52	16 34 6	18 32 22
	30	20 35 33		0 32 6	2 34 19	4 32 36	6 34 49	8 33 6	10 35 19	12 37 32	14 35 49	16 38 2	18 36 19
	31	20 39 30		0 36 3		4 36 33		8 37 3	10 39 16		14 39 46		18 40 15
1981	1	18 44 11	20 46 25	22 36 49	0 39 2	2 37 18	4 39 32	6 37 48	8 40 1	10 42 15	12 40 31	14 42 44	16 41 1
	2	18 48 8	20 50 22	22 40 45	0 42 58	2 41 15	4 43 28	6 41 45	8 43 58	10 46 11	12 44 28	14 46 41	16 46 58
	3	18 52 5	20 54 18	22 44 42	0 46 55	2 45 11	4 47 25	6 45 41	8 47 55	10 50 8	12 48 24	14 50 37	16 48 54
	4	18 56 1	20 58 15	22 48 38	0 50 51	2 49 8	4 51 21	6 49 38	8 51 51	10 54 4	12 52 21	14 54 34	16 52 51
	5	18 59 58	21 2 11	22 52 35	0 54 48	2 53 4	4 55 18	6 53 34	8 55 47	10 58 1	12 56 17	14 58 31	16 56 47
	6	19 3 54	21 6 8	22 56 31	0 58 44	2 57 1	4 59 14	6 57 31	8 59 44	11 1 57	13 0 14	15 2 27	17 0 44
	7	19 7 51	21 10 4	23 0 28	1 2 41	3 0 58	5 3 11	7 1 27	9 3 41	11 5 54	13 4 11	15 6 24	17 4 40
	8	19 11 47	21 14 1	23 4 24	1 6 38	3 4 54	5 7 7	7 5 24	9 7 37	11 9 51	13 8 7	15 10 20	17 8 37
	9	19 15 44	21 17 57	23 8 21	1 10 34	3 8 51	5 11 4	7 9 21	9 11 34	11 13 47	13 12 4	15 14 17	17 12 34
	10	19 19 41	21 21 54	23 12 17	1 14 30	3 12 47	5 15 0	7 13 17	9 15 30	11 17 44	13 16 0	15 18 13	17 16 30
	11	19 23 37	21 25 51	23 16 14	1 18 27	3 16 44	5 18 57	7 17 14	9 19 27	11 21 40	13 19 57	15 22 10	17 20 27
	12	19 27 34	21 29 47	23 20 11	1 22 24	3 20 40	5 22 54	7 21 10	9 23 24	11 25 37	13 23 53	15 26 6	17 24 23
	13	19 31 30	21 33 44	23 24 7	1 26 20	3 24 37	5 26 50	7 25 7	9 27 20	11 29 33	13 27 50	15 30 3	17 28 20
	14	19 35 27	21 37 40	23 28 4	1 30 17	3 28 33	5 30 47	7 29 3	9 31 17	11 33 30	13 31 46	15 34 0	17 32 16
	15	19 39 24	21 41 37	23 32 0	1 34 13	3 32 30	5 34 43	7 33 0	9 35 13	11 37 26	13 35 43	15 37 56	17 36 13
	16	19 43 20	21 45 33	23 35 57	1 38 10	3 36 27	5 38 40	7 36 56	9 39 10	11 41 23	13 39 40	15 41 53	17 40 9
	17	19 47 16	21 49 29	23 39 53	1 42 6	3 40 23	5 42 36	7 40 53	9 43 6	11 45 19	13 43 36	15 45 49	17 44 6
	18	19 51 13	21 53 26	23 43 50	1 46 3	3 44 20	5 46 33	7 44 50	9 47 3	11 49 16	13 47 33	15 49 46	17 48 2
	19	19 55 10	21 57 23	23 47 46	1 49 59	3 48 16	5 50 30	7 48 46	9 51 0	11 53 13	13 51 29	15 53 42	17 51 59
	20	19 59 6	22 1 19	23 51 43	1 53 56	3 52 13	5 54 26	7 52 43	9 54 56	11 57 9	13 55 26	15 57 39	17 55 56
	21	20 3 2	22 5 16	23 55 40	1 57 53	3 56 9	5 58 23	7 56 39	9 58 53	12 1 6	13 59 22	16 1 35	17 59 52
	22	20 7 0	22 9 13	23 59 36	2 1 49	4 0 6	6 2 19	8 0 36	10 2 49	12 5 2	14 3 19	16 5 32	18 3 49
	23	20 10 56	22 13 9	0 3 33	2 5 46	4 4 2	6 6 16	8 4 32	10 6 46	12 8 59	14 7 15	16 9 29	18 7 45
	24	20 14 52	22 17 6	0 7 29	2 9 42	4 7 59	6 10 12	8 8 29	10 10 42	12 12 55	14 11 12	16 13 25	18 11 42
	25	20 18 49	22 21 2	0 11 26	2 13 39	4 11 56	6 14 9	8 12 26	10 14 39	12 16 52	14 15 8	16 17 22	18 15 38
	26	20 22 46	22 24 58	0 15 22	2 17 35	4 15 52	6 18 5	8 16 22	10 18 35	12 20 48	14 19 5	16 21 18	18 19 35
	27	20 26 42	22 28 55	0 19 19	2 21 32	4 19 49	6 22 2	8 20 19	10 22 32	12 24 45	14 23 1	16 25 15	18 23 31
	28	20 30 39	22 32 52	0 23 15	2 25 29	4 23 45	6 25 59	8 24 15	10 26 28	12 28 42	14 26 58	16 29 11	18 27 28
	29	20 34 35		0 27 12	2 29 25	4 27 42	6 29 55	8 28 12	10 30 25	12 32 38	14 30 55	16 33 8	18 31 25
	30	20 38 32		0 31 9	2 33 22	4 31 38	6 33 52	8 32 8	10 34 22	12 36 35	14 34 51	16 37 4	18 35 21
	31	20 42 28		0 35 5		4 35 35		8 36 5	10 38 18		14 38 48		18 39 18

Day	1	2	3	4	5	6	7	8	9	10	11	12
1	18 43 14	20 45 28	22 35 51	0 38 4	2 36 21	4 38 34	6 36 51	8 39 4	10 41 17	12 39 34	14 41 47	16 40 4
2	18 47 11	20 49 24	22 39 48	0 42 1	2 40 17	4 42 31	6 40 47	8 43 1	10 45 14	12 43 30	14 45 44	16 44 0
3	18 51 7	20 53 21	22 43 44	0 45 57	2 44 14	4 46 27	6 44 44	8 46 57	10 49 10	12 47 27	14 49 40	16 47 57
4	18 55 4	20 57 17	22 47 41	0 49 54	2 48 10	4 50 24	6 48 40	8 50 54	10 53 7	12 51 23	14 53 37	16 51 53
5	18 59 1	21 1 14	22 51 37	0 53 50	2 52 6	4 54 20	6 52 37	8 54 50	10 57 3	12 55 20	14 57 33	16 55 50
6	19 2 57	21 5 10	22 55 34	0 57 47	2 56 3	4 58 17	6 56 33	8 58 47	11 1 0	12 59 17	15 1 30	16 59 46
7	19 6 54	21 9 7	22 59 30	1 2 44	3 0 0	5 2 13	7 0 30	9 2 43	11 4 57	13 3 13	15 5 26	17 3 43
8	19 10 50	21 13 3	23 3 27	1 5 40	3 3 57	5 6 10	7 4 27	9 6 40	11 8 53	13 7 10	15 9 23	17 7 40
9	19 14 47	21 17 0	23 7 23	1 9 37	3 7 53	5 10 6	7 8 23	9 10 36	11 12 50	13 11 6	15 13 19	17 11 36
10	19 18 43	21 20 56	23 11 20	1 13 33	3 11 50	5 14 3	7 12 20	9 14 33	11 16 46	13 15 3	15 17 16	17 15 33
11	19 22 40	21 24 53	23 15 17	1 17 30	3 15 46	5 18 0	7 16 16	9 18 30	11 20 43	13 19 0	15 21 12	17 19 29
12	19 26 36	21 28 50	23 19 13	1 21 26	3 19 43	5 21 56	7 20 13	9 22 26	11 24 39	13 22 57	15 25 9	17 23 26
13	19 30 33	21 32 46	23 23 10	1 25 23	3 23 39	5 25 53	7 24 9	9 26 23	11 28 36	13 26 53	15 29 6	17 27 22
14	19 34 30	21 36 43	23 27 6	1 29 19	3 27 36	5 29 49	7 28 6	9 30 19	11 32 32	13 30 49	15 33 2	17 31 19
15	19 38 26	21 40 39	23 31 3	1 33 16	3 31 33	5 33 46	7 32 3	9 34 16	11 36 29	13 34 46	15 36 58	17 35 15
16	19 42 23	21 44 36	23 35 0	1 37 13	3 35 29	5 37 42	7 36 0	9 38 12	11 40 25	13 38 42	15 40 55	17 39 12
17	19 46 19	21 48 32	23 38 56	1 41 9	3 39 26	5 41 39	7 39 56	9 42 9	11 44 22	13 42 38	15 44 52	17 43 8
18	19 50 16	21 52 29	23 42 52	1 45 5	3 43 22	5 45 35	7 43 52	9 46 5	11 48 19	13 46 35	15 48 48	17 47 5
19	19 54 12	21 56 26	23 46 49	1 49 2	3 47 19	5 49 32	7 47 49	9 50 2	11 52 15	13 50 32	15 52 45	17 51 1
20	19 58 9	22 0 22	23 50 46	1 52 58	3 51 15	5 53 28	7 51 45	9 53 58	11 56 12	13 54 28	15 56 42	17 54 58
21	20 2 5	22 4 19	23 54 42	1 56 55	3 55 12	5 57 25	7 55 42	9 57 55	12 0 8	13 58 25	16 0 38	17 58 55
22	20 6 2	22 8 15	23 58 39	2 0 52	3 59 8	6 1 22	7 59 38	10 1 52	12 4 5	14 2 21	16 4 35	18 2 51
23	20 9 58	22 12 12	0 2 35	2 4 48	4 3 5	6 5 18	8 3 35	10 5 48	12 8 1	14 6 18	16 8 31	18 6 48
24	20 13 55	22 16 8	0 6 32	2 8 45	4 7 2	6 9 15	8 7 32	10 9 45	12 11 58	14 10 14	16 12 28	18 10 44
25	20 17 52	22 20 5	0 10 28	2 12 41	4 10 58	6 13 11	8 11 28	10 13 41	12 15 54	14 14 11	16 16 24	18 14 41
26	20 21 48	22 24 1	0 14 25	2 16 38	4 14 55	6 17 8	8 15 25	10 17 38	12 19 51	14 18 8	16 20 21	18 18 38
27	20 25 45	22 27 58	0 18 21	2 20 35	4 18 51	6 21 5	8 19 21	10 21 34	12 23 48	14 22 4	16 24 17	18 22 34
28	20 29 41	22 31 54	0 22 18	2 24 31	4 22 48	6 25 1	8 23 18	10 25 31	12 27 44	14 26 1	16 28 14	18 26 31
29	20 33 38		0 26 14	2 28 28	4 26 44	6 28 58	8 27 14	10 29 28	12 31 41	14 29 57	16 32 11	18 30 27
30	20 37 34		0 30 11	2 32 24	4 30 41	6 32 54	8 31 11	10 33 24	12 35 37	14 33 54	16 36 7	18 34 24
31	20 41 31		0 34 8		4 34 38		8 35 7	10 37 21		14 37 50		18 38 20
1	18 42 17	20 44 30	22 34 54	0 37 7	2 35 23	4 37 37	6 35 53	8 38 7	10 40 20	12 38 37	14 40 49	16 39 6
2	18 46 13	20 48 27	22 38 50	0 41 3	2 39 20	4 41 33	6 39 50	8 42 3	10 44 16	12 42 33	14 44 46	16 43 3
3	18 50 10	20 52 23	22 42 47	0 45 0	2 43 17	4 45 30	6 43 46	8 46 0	10 48 13	12 46 30	14 48 43	16 47 0
4	18 54 7	20 56 20	22 46 43	0 48 56	2 47 13	4 49 26	6 47 43	8 49 56	10 52 10	12 50 26	14 52 39	16 50 56
5	18 58 3	21 0 16	22 50 40	0 52 53	2 51 10	4 53 23	6 51 40	8 53 53	10 56 6	12 54 23	14 56 36	16 54 53
6	19 2 0	21 4 13	22 54 37	0 56 50	2 55 6	4 57 20	6 55 36	8 57 49	11 0 3	12 58 19	15 0 32	16 58 49
7	19 5 56	21 8 10	22 58 33	1 0 46	2 59 3	5 1 16	6 59 33	9 1 46	11 4 0	13 2 16	15 4 29	17 2 46
8	19 9 53	21 12 6	23 2 30	1 4 43	3 3 0	5 5 13	7 3 29	9 5 43	11 7 57	13 6 12	15 8 26	17 6 42
9	19 13 49	21 16 3	23 6 26	1 8 39	3 6 56	5 9 9	7 7 26	9 9 39	11 11 53	13 10 9	15 12 22	17 10 39
10	19 17 46	21 19 59	23 10 23	1 12 36	3 10 52	5 13 6	7 11 22	9 13 36	11 15 49	13 14 5	15 16 19	17 14 35
11	19 21 42	21 23 56	23 14 19	1 16 32	3 14 49	5 17 2	7 15 19	9 17 32	11 19 45	13 18 2	15 20 15	17 18 32
12	19 25 39	21 27 52	23 18 16	1 20 29	3 18 46	5 20 58	7 19 16	9 21 29	11 23 42	13 21 58	15 24 12	17 22 28
13	19 29 36	21 31 49	23 22 12	1 24 25	3 22 42	5 24 55	7 23 12	9 25 25	11 27 39	13 25 55	15 28 8	17 26 25
14	19 33 32	21 35 45	23 26 9	1 28 22	3 26 39	5 28 52	7 27 9	9 29 22	11 31 35	13 29 52	15 32 5	17 30 22
15	19 37 29	21 39 42	23 30 5	1 32 19	3 30 35	5 32 48	7 31 5	9 33 18	11 35 32	13 33 48	15 36 1	17 34 18
16	19 41 25	21 43 38	23 34 2	1 36 15	3 34 32	5 36 45	7 35 2	9 37 15	11 39 28	13 37 45	15 39 58	17 38 15
17	19 45 22	21 47 35	23 37 58	1 40 12	3 38 28	5 40 42	7 38 58	9 41 12	11 43 25	13 41 41	15 43 54	17 42 11
18	19 49 18	21 51 32	23 41 55	1 44 8	3 42 25	5 44 38	7 42 55	9 45 8	11 47 21	13 45 38	15 47 51	17 46 8
19	19 53 15	21 55 28	23 45 52	1 48 5	3 46 21	5 48 35	7 46 51	9 49 5	11 51 18	13 49 34	15 51 48	17 50 4
20	19 57 12	21 59 25	23 49 48	1 52 1	3 50 18	5 52 31	7 50 48	9 53 1	11 55 14	13 53 31	15 55 44	17 54 1
21	20 1 8	22 3 21	23 53 45	1 55 58	3 54 15	5 56 28	7 54 45	9 56 58	11 59 11	13 57 28	15 59 41	17 57 57
22	20 5 5	22 7 18	23 57 41	1 59 54	3 58 11	6 0 24	7 58 41	10 0 54	12 3 7	14 1 24	16 3 37	18 1 54
23	20 9 1	22 11 14	0 1 38	2 3 51	4 2 8	6 4 21	8 2 38	10 4 51	12 7 4	14 5 21	16 7 34	18 5 51
24	20 12 58	22 15 11	0 5 34	2 7 48	4 6 4	6 8 17	8 6 34	10 8 47	12 11 1	14 9 17	16 11 30	18 9 47
25	20 16 54	22 19 7	0 9 31	2 11 44	4 10 1	6 12 14	8 10 31	10 12 44	12 14 57	14 13 14	16 15 27	18 13 44
26	20 20 51	22 23 4	0 13 28	2 15 41	4 13 57	6 16 11	8 14 27	10 16 41	12 18 54	14 17 10	16 19 23	18 17 40
27	20 24 47	22 27 1	0 17 24	2 19 37	4 17 54	6 20 7	8 18 24	10 20 37	12 22 50	14 21 7	16 23 20	18 21 37
28	20 28 44	22 30 57	0 21 21	2 23 34	4 21 50	6 24 4	8 22 20	10 24 34	12 26 47	14 25 3	16 27 17	18 25 33
29	20 32 41		0 25 17	2 27 30	4 25 47	6 28 0	8 26 17	10 28 30	12 30 43	14 29 0	16 31 13	18 29 30
30	20 36 37		0 29 14	2 31 27	4 29 44	6 31 58	8 30 14	10 32 27	12 34 40	14 32 58	16 35 10	18 33 26
31	20 40 34		0 33 10		4 33 40		8 34 10	10 36 23		14 36 53		18 37 23

		1	2	3	4	5	6	7	8	9	10	11	12
1984	1	18 41 20	20 43 33	22 37 53	0 40 6	2 38 23	4 40 36	6 38 53	8 41 6	10 43 19	12 41 36	14 43 49	16 42 6
	2	18 45 16	20 47 30	22 41 50	0 44 3	2 42 19	4 44 33	6 42 49	8 45 2	10 47 16	12 45 33	14 47 46	16 46 2
	3	18 49 13	20 51 26	22 45 46	0 48 0	2 46 16	4 48 29	6 46 46	8 48 59	10 51 12	12 49 29	14 51 42	16 49 59
	4	18 53 9	20 55 23	22 49 43	0 51 57	2 50 12	4 52 26	6 50 43	8 52 56	10 55 9	12 53 25	14 55 39	16 53 55
	5	18 57 6	20 59 19	22 53 39	0 55 53	2 54 9	4 56 22	6 54 39	8 56 53	10 59 5	12 57 22	14 59 35	16 57 52
	6	19 1 2	21 3 16	22 57 36	0 59 49	2 58 6	5 0 19	6 58 36	9 0 49	11 3 2	13 1 19	15 3 32	17 1 48
	7	19 4 59	21 7 12	23 1 32	1 3 45	3 2 2	5 4 15	7 2 32	9 4 45	11 6 58	13 5 15	15 7 28	17 5 45
	8	19 8 56	21 11 9	23 5 29	1 7 42	3 5 58	5 8 12	7 6 29	9 8 42	11 10 55	13 9 12	15 11 25	17 9 42
	9	19 12 52	21 15 5	23 9 25	1 11 38	3 9 55	5 12 8	7 10 25	9 12 38	11 14 52	13 13 8	15 15 22	17 13 38
	10	19 16 49	21 19 2	23 13 22	1 15 35	3 13 52	5 16 5	7 14 22	9 16 35	11 18 48	13 17 5	15 19 18	17 17 35
	11	19 20 45	21 22 58	23 17 18	1 19 32	3 17 48	5 20 2	7 18 18	9 20 32	11 22 46	13 21 1	15 23 15	17 21 31
	12	19 24 42	21 26 55	23 21 15	1 23 28	3 21 45	5 23 58	7 22 15	9 24 28	11 26 41	13 24 58	15 27 11	17 25 28
	13	19 28 38	21 30 52	23 25 12	1 27 27	3 25 41	5 27 55	7 26 11	9 28 25	11 30 38	13 28 54	15 31 8	17 29 24
	14	19 32 35	21 34 48	23 29 8	1 31 21	3 29 38	5 31 51	7 30 8	9 32 21	11 34 34	13 32 51	15 35 4	17 33 21
	15	19 36 32	21 38 45	23 33 5	1 35 18	3 33 34	5 35 48	7 34 5	9 36 18	11 38 31	13 36 48	15 39 1	17 37 18
	16	19 40 28	21 42 41	23 37 1	1 39 14	3 37 31	5 39 44	7 38 1	9 40 14	11 42 27	13 40 44	15 42 57	17 41 14
	17	19 44 25	21 46 38	23 40 58	1 43 11	3 41 28	5 43 41	7 41 58	9 44 11	11 46 24	13 44 41	15 46 54	17 45 11
	18	19 48 21	21 50 34	23 44 54	1 47 7	3 45 24	5 47 37	7 45 54	9 48 7	11 50 21	13 48 37	15 50 50	17 49 7
	19	19 52 18	21 54 31	23 48 51	1 51 4	3 49 21	5 51 34	7 49 51	9 52 4	11 54 17	13 52 34	15 54 47	17 53 4
	20	19 56 14	21 5 27	23 52 48	1 55 1	3 53 17	5 55 31	7 53 47	9 56 1	11 58 14	13 56 30	15 58 43	17 57 0
	21	20 0 11	22 2 24	23 56 44	1 58 57	3 57 14	5 59 27	7 57 44	9 59 57	12 2 10	14 0 27	16 2 40	18 0 57
	22	20 4 7	22 6 21	0 0 41	2 2 54	4 1 10	6 3 24	8 1 40	10 3 54	12 6 7	14 4 23	16 6 37	18 4 53
	23	20 8 4	22 10 17	0 4 37	2 6 50	4 5 7	6 7 20	8 5 37	10 7 52	12 10 3	14 8 20	16 10 33	18 8 50
	24	20 12 0	22 14 14	0 8 34	2 10 47	4 9 3	6 11 17	8 9 33	10 11 47	12 14 0	14 12 17	16 14 30	18 12 47
	25	20 15 57	22 18 10	0 12 30	2 14 43	4 13 0	6 15 13	8 13 31	10 15 43	12 17 56	14 16 13	16 18 26	18 16 43
	26	20 19 54	22 22 7	0 16 27	2 18 40	4 16 57	6 19 10	8 17 27	10 19 40	12 21 53	14 20 10	16 22 23	18 20 40
	27	20 23 50	22 26 3	0 20 23	2 22 37	4 20 53	6 23 7	8 21 23	10 23 36	12 25 50	14 24 6	16 26 20	18 24 36
	28	20 27 47	22 30 0	0 24 20	2 26 33	4 24 50	6 27 3	8 25 20	10 27 33	12 29 46	14 28 3	16 30 16	18 28 33
	29	20 31 43	22 33 57	0 28 16	2 30 30	4 28 46	6 30 59	8 29 16	10 31 30	12 33 43	14 32 0	16 34 13	18 32 29
	30	20 35 40		0 32 13	2 34 26	4 32 43	6 34 56	8 33 13	10 35 26	12 37 39	14 35 57	16 38 9	18 36 26
	31	20 39 36		0 36 10		4 36 39		8 37 10	10 39 23		14 39 53		18 40 22

3 HOUSES FOR NORTHERN LATITUDES

A = Sidereal time
10 = Midheaven (10th House)
B = Ascendant

A	10	B 2° 0′	B 4° 0′	B 7° 0′	B 11° 0′	B 14° 0′	B 18° 0′	B 21° 59′	B 25° 19′	B 28° 40′	B 30° 2′	B 31° 46′	B 33° 20′	B 35° 39′	B 37° 58′	B 40° 43′	B 41° 54′	B 45° 30′	B 48° 50′	B 50° 22′	B 51° 32′	B 52° 57′	B 54° 34′	B 56° 28′	B 57° 29′	B 59° 00′	B 59° 56′
	°	° ′	° ′	° ′	° ′	° ′	° ′	° ′	° ′	° ′	° ′	° ′	° ′	° ′	° ′	° ′	° ′	° ′	° ′	° ′	° ′	° ′	° ′	° ′	° ′	° ′	° ′
0 0 0	0♈	0♋48	1♋36	2♋48	4♋25	5♋40	7♋22	9♋8	10♋40	12♋16	12♋57	13♋50	14♋40	15♋56	17♋15	18♋53	19♋39	22♋3	24♋28	25♋40	26♋36	27♋48	29♋13	0♌59	1♌58	3♌31	4♌31
0 3 40	1	1 38	2 26	3 38	5 16	6 30	8 12	9 57	11 28	13 5	13 45	14 38	15 28	16 42	18 1	19 38	20 24	22 46	25 10	26 21	27 17	28 27	29 51	1 36	2 35	4 6	5 5
0 7 20	2	2 29	3 16	4 29	6 6	7 20	9 1	10 46	12 17	13 53	14 33	15 26	16 15	17 29	18 47	20 23	21 8	23 29	25 52	27 2	27 56	29 7	0♌30	2 13	3 11	4 41	5 39
0 11 0	3	3 19	4 7	5 19	6 56	8 9	9 51	11 35	13 5	14 41	15 21	16 13	17 1	18 15	19 33	21 12	21 53	24 12	26 33	27 42	28 42	29 46	1 8	2 50	3 47	5 16	6 14
0 14 41	4	4 10	4 58	6 9	7 46	8 59	10 40	12 24	13 54	15 29	16 8	17 0	17 48	19 2	20 19	21 55	22 37	24 55	27 15	28 23	29 17	0♌25	1 46	3 27	4 23	5 51	6 48
0 18 21	5	5 0	5 48	6 59	8 36	9 49	11 29	13 13	14 42	16 16	16 56	17 47	18 35	19 48	21 4	22 40	23 22	25 38	27 56	29 3	29 55	1 4	2 24	4 4	4 59	6 26	7 22
0 22 2	6	5 51	6 39	7 50	9 26	10 39	12 19	14 2	15 31	17 4	17 43	18 34	19 22	20 34	21 50	23 24	24 6	26 21	28 37	29 44	0♌34	1 43	3 2	4 40	5 35	7 1	7 56
0 25 42	7	6 41	7 29	8 41	10 16	11 29	13 8	14 51	16 19	17 52	18 31	19 22	20 9	21 20	22 35	24 8	24 50	27 3	29 19	0♌24	1 14	2 22	3 40	5 17	6 11	7 35	8 30
0 29 23	8	7 32	8 20	9 31	11 6	12 19	13 57	15 40	17 7	18 40	19 18	20 9	20 55	22 6	23 20	24 54	25 34	27 46	0♌0	1 5	1 55	3 1	4 18	5 54	6 47	8 10	9 4
0 33 4	9	8 23	9 10	10 21	11 56	13 9	14 47	16 29	17 56	19 28	20 6	20 56	21 42	22 52	24 6	25 37	26 18	28 29	0 41	1 45	2 33	3 40	4 56	6 30	7 23	8 45	9 38
0 36 45	10	9 14	10 1	11 11	12 46	13 58	15 36	17 18	18 44	20 15	20 53	21 42	22 28	23 38	24 51	26 22	27 6	29 11	1 22	2 25	3 14	4 19	5 34	7 7	7 59	9 20	10 12
0 40 26	11	10 5	10 51	12 2	13 37	14 48	16 26	18 7	19 32	21 3	21 40	22 29	23 15	24 24	25 36	27 5	27 46	29 54	2 3	3 5	3 54	4 57	6 12	7 43	8 35	9 54	10 46
0 44 8	12	10 56	11 42	12 53	14 27	15 38	17 15	18 55	20 20	21 50	22 27	23 16	24 1	25 9	26 21	27 50	28 29	0♌36	2 44	3 46	4 33	5 36	6 49	8 20	9 11	10 29	11 20
0 47 50	13	11 47	12 33	13 44	15 18	16 29	18 5	19 44	21 8	22 37	23 15	24 2	24 48	25 55	27 6	28 33	29 13	1 19	3 25	4 26	5 12	6 15	7 27	8 57	9 47	11 4	11 54
0 51 32	14	12 39	13 24	14 35	16 8	17 19	18 54	20 33	21 57	23 25	24 2	24 49	25 34	26 41	27 51	29 18	29 57	2 1	4 5	5 6	5 52	6 54	8 5	9 33	10 22	11 39	12 28
0 55 14	15	13 30	14 16	15 26	16 59	18 9	19 44	21 22	22 45	24 12	24 49	25 36	26 20	27 27	28 36	0♌3	0♌41	2 43	4 46	5 56	6 30	7 32	8 43	10 10	10 58	12 13	13 2
0 58 57	16	14 21	15 7	16 16	17 49	18 59	20 33	22 10	23 33	25 0	25 36	26 23	27 6	28 13	29 22	0 46	1 24	3 26	5 27	6 26	7 9	8 11	9 10	10 46	11 34	12 48	13 36
1 2 40	17	15 13	15 58	17 7	18 39	19 49	21 23	22 59	24 22	25 47	26 24	27 9	27 53	28 59	0♌6	1 31	2 8	4 8	6 8	7 6	7 50	8 50	9 48	11 23	12 10	13 23	14 10
1 6 23	18	16 4	16 50	17 58	19 30	20 40	22 13	23 49	25 10	26 35	27 11	27 56	28 39	29 44	0 52	2 14	2 52	4 50	6 49	7 46	8 30	9 29	10 36	12 0	12 46	13 58	14 45
1 10 7	19	15 56	17 41	18 50	20 21	21 30	23 3	24 38	25 58	27 23	27 58	28 44	29 26	0♌30	1 37	2 58	3 36	5 33	7 30	8 26	9 9	10 7	11 14	12 36	13 22	14 33	15 19
1 13 51	20	17 48	18 33	19 41	21 12	22 20	23 53	25 27	26 47	28 11	28 46	29 31	0♌13	1 6	2 22	3 43	4 20	6 15	8 11	9 6	9 48	10 46	11 52	13 13	13 58	15 8	15 53
1 17 35	21	18 40	19 25	20 33	22 3	23 11	24 43	26 16	27 35	28 59	29 13	0♌18	0 59	2 2	3 7	4 27	5 3	6 57	8 51	9 47	10 28	11 25	12 29	13 49	14 34	15 43	16 27
1 21 20	22	19 32	20 17	21 25	22 54	24 2	25 33	27 5	28 24	29 47	0♌21	1 5	1 46	2 48	3 52	5 12	5 47	7 40	9 32	10 27	11 8	12 4	13 7	14 26	15 10	16 18	17 2
1 25 6	23	20 25	21 9	22 17	23 46	24 53	26 23	27 55	29 13	0♌35	1 8	1 52	2 33	3 34	4 37	5 56	6 31	8 22	10 13	11 7	11 48	12 42	13 45	15 3	15 46	16 53	17 36
1 28 52	24	21 18	22 2	23 9	24 37	25 44	27 13	28 45	0♌2	1 23	1 56	2 39	3 20	4 21	5 23	6 40	7 15	9 5	10 54	11 47	12 28	13 21	14 23	15 40	16 22	17 28	18 11
1 32 38	25	22 11	22 55	24 1	25 29	26 35	28 4	29 34	0 51	2 11	2 44	3 26	4 6	5 7	6 8	7 25	7 59	9 47	11 35	12 28	13 8	14 0	15 1	16 17	16 59	18 3	18 45
1 36 25	26	23 4	23 48	24 53	26 20	27 26	28 54	0♌24	1 40	2 59	3 32	4 14	4 53	5 53	6 54	8 9	8 43	10 30	12 17	13 8	13 48	14 39	15 39	16 54	17 35	18 39	19 20
1 40 12	27	23 57	24 41	25 46	27 13	28 18	29 45	1 14	2 29	3 47	4 20	5 1	5 40	6 39	7 39	8 53	9 27	11 13	12 58	13 48	14 28	15 18	16 18	17 31	18 11	19 14	19 55
1 44 0	28	24 50	25 34	26 39	28 5	29 9	0♌36	2 4	3 18	4 35	5 8	5 49	6 27	7 25	8 25	9 38	10 11	11 56	13 39	14 29	15 8	15 58	16 56	18 8	18 48	19 49	20 29
1 47 48	29	25 44	26 28	27 32	28 57	0♌1	1 27	2 54	4 7	5 23	5 56	6 36	7 14	8 11	9 11	10 24	10 56	12 38	14 20	15 10	15 48	16 37	17 34	18 45	19 24	20 25	21 4
1 51 37	30	26 38	27 21	28 25	29 49	0 53	2 18	3 44	4 57	6 12	6 44	7 24	8 2	8 58	9 56	11 8	11 40	13 21	15 2	15 50	16 28	17 16	18 13	19 22	20 1	21 1	21 39

1 51 37	0♉	26♋38	27♋21	28♋25	29♋49	0♌53	2♌18	3♌44	4♌57	6♌12	6♌44	7♌24	8♌2	8♌58	9♌56	11♌8	11♌40	13♌21	15♌2	15 50	16♌28	17♌16	18♌13	19♌22	20♌1	21♌1	21♌39
1 55 27	1	27 32	28 15	29 19	0♌43	1 45	3 9	4 35	5 47	7 1	7 32	8 13	8 49	9 45	10 42	11 53	12 25	14 4	15 43	16 31	17 8	17 56	18 51	19 59	20 38	21 36	22 14
1 59 17	2	28 27	29 9	0♌13	1 35	2 37	4 1	5 25	6 36	7 50	8 21	9 1	9 37	10 32	11 28	12 38	13 9	14 47	16 25	17 12	17 48	18 35	19 30	20 37	21 14	22 12	22 49
2 3 8	3	29 22	0♌4	1 7	2 29	3 30	4 53	6 16	7 26	8 40	9 10	9 49	10 25	11 19	12 14	13 22	13 54	15 31	17 6	17 53	18 28	19 15	20 8	21 14	21 51	22 48	23 25
2 6 59	4	0♌17	0 59	2 1	3 22	4 23	5 45	7 7	8 16	9 29	9 58	10 37	11 13	12 6	13 1	14 8	14 39	16 14	17 48	18 34	19 9	19 54	20 47	21 52	22 28	23 24	24 0
2 10 51	5	1 13	1 54	2 55	4 16	5 16	6 37	7 58	9 7	10 18	10 47	11 26	12 0	12 53	13 47	14 53	15 23	16 57	18 30	19 15	19 49	20 34	21 26	22 30	23 5	24 0	24 36
2 14 44	6	2 8	2 49	3 50	5 10	6 9	7 29	8 49	9 57	11 7	11 36	12 14	12 48	13 40	14 33	15 39	16 8	17 41	19 12	19 56	20 29	21 14	22 5	23 8	23 42	24 36	25 11
2 18 37	7	3 4	3 44	4 44	6 4	7 3	8 21	9 41	10 48	11 57	12 25	13 3	13 36	14 27	15 20	16 24	16 54	18 25	19 54	20 37	21 10	21 54	22 44	23 45	24 20	25 13	25 47
2 22 31	8	4 1	4 40	5 39	5 58	7 57	9 14	10 33	11 38	12 47	13 15	13 51	14 25	15 15	16 7	17 10	17 39	19 8	20 36	21 19	21 51	22 34	23 23	24 23	24 57	25 49	26 22
2 26 25	9	4 57	5 37	6 35	7 52	8 50	10 7	11 25	12 29	13 36	14 4	14 40	15 13	16 3	16 54	17 56	18 24	19 52	21 18	22 0	22 32	23 14	24 2	25 2	25 35	26 26	26 58
2 30 20	10	5 54	6 33	7 31	8 47	9 44	11 0	12 17	13 20	14 26	14 54	15 29	16 2	16 51	17 40	18 41	19 10	20 36	22 1	22 42	23 14	23 54	24 42	25 40	26 12	27 2	27 34
2 34 16	11	6 51	7 29	8 27	9 42	10 38	11 53	13 9	14 12	15 17	15 44	16 18	16 50	17 39	18 28	19 27	19 55	21 20	22 43	23 24	23 55	24 35	25 21	26 18	26 50	27 39	28 10
2 38 13	12	7 48	8 26	9 24	10 38	11 33	12 47	14 1	15 3	16 7	16 34	17 8	17 39	18 27	19 15	20 14	20 41	22 4	23 26	24 5	24 36	25 15	26 1	26 57	27 28	28 16	28 47
2 42 10	13	8 46	9 24	10 20	11 34	12 28	13 41	14 54	15 55	16 58	17 24	17 57	18 28	19 15	20 2	21 0	21 27	22 48	24 9	24 47	25 17	25 56	26 40	27 35	28 6	28 53	29 23
2 46 8	14	9 44	10 22	11 17	12 29	13 23	14 35	15 47	16 47	17 49	18 15	18 47	19 17	20 3	20 50	21 47	22 13	23 33	24 52	25 30	25 58	26 37	27 20	28 14	28 44	29 30	29 59
2 50 7	15	10 43	11 20	12 14	13 26	14 19	15 29	16 40	17 39	18 40	19 5	19 31	20 6	20 52	21 37	22 33	22 59	24 17	25 35	26 12	26 40	27 17	28 0	28 53	29 22	0♍7	0♍36
2 54 7	16	11 42	12 19	13 12	14 22	15 14	16 23	17 33	18 31	19 31	19 56	20 28	20 56	21 40	22 25	23 20	23 45	25 2	26 18	26 54	27 22	27 58	28 40	29 32	0♍0	0 45	1 13
2 58 7	17	12 41	13 17	14 10	15 19	16 10	17 18	18 27	19 24	20 22	20 47	21 18	21 46	22 29	23 13	24 7	24 32	25 47	27 1	27 37	28 4	28 40	29 21	0♍11	0 39	1 22	1 50
3 2 8	18	13 40	14 15	15 8	16 16	17 6	18 13	19 20	20 16	21 14	21 38	22 8	22 36	23 19	24 2	24 54	25 18	26 32	27 45	28 19	28 46	29 21	0♍1	0 50	1 18	2 0	2 27
3 6 9	19	14 40	15 14	16 6	17 13	18 2	19 8	20 14	21 9	22 6	22 29	22 59	23 27	24 8	24 50	25 42	26 5	27 17	28 28	29 2	29 29	0♍2	0 41	1 29	1 56	2 37	3 4
3 10 12	20	15 40	16 13	17 5	18 11	18 59	20 4	21 8	22 2	22 58	23 21	23 50	24 17	24 58	25 38	26 29	26 52	28 3	29 12	29 45	0♍12	0 44	1 22	2 9	2 35	3 15	3 41
3 14 15	21	16 41	17 14	18 4	19 8	19 56	21 0	22 3	22 56	23 50	24 13	24 41	25 8	25 47	26 27	27 17	27 39	28 48	29 56	0♍28	0 54	1 25	2 3	2 49	3 14	3 53	4 18
3 18 19	22	17 42	18 15	19 3	20 7	20 54	21 56	22 58	23 49	24 43	25 4	25 32	25 59	26 37	27 16	28 4	28 26	29 33	0♍40	1 11	1 36	2 7	2 44	3 28	3 53	4 31	4 56
3 22 23	23	18 43	19 16	20 3	21 5	21 51	22 52	23 53	24 43	25 35	25 57	26 24	26 49	27 27	28 5	28 52	29 14	0♍19	1 24	1 55	2 20	2 49	3 25	4 8	4 32	5 10	5 34
3 26 29	24	19 44	20 17	21 3	22 4	22 49	23 48	24 48	25 37	26 28	26 49	27 16	27 40	28 17	28 54	29 40	0♍1	1 5	2 8	2 38	3 2	3 31	4 6	4 48	5 12	5 48	6 11
3 30 35	25	20 46	21 18	22 4	23 3	23 47	24 45	25 43	26 31	27 21	27 41	28 8	28 31	29 7	29 44	0♍29	0 49	1 51	2 53	3 22	3 45	4 14	4 47	5 28	5 51	6 27	6 49
3 34 41	26	21 49	22 19	23 4	24 2	24 45	25 42	26 39	27 26	28 14	28 34	29 0	29 23	29 58	0♍34	1 17	1 37	2 37	3 37	4 6	4 28	4 56	5 29	6 9	6 31	7 5	7 27
3 38 49	27	22 51	23 21	24 5	25 2	25 44	26 39	27 35	28 20	29 7	29 27	29 52	0♍14	0♍49	1 24	2 6	2 25	3 24	4 22	4 50	5 11	5 38	6 10	6 49	7 11	7 44	8 5
3 42 57	28	23 54	24 23	25 6	26 1	26 42	27 36	28 31	29 15	0♍1	0♍20	0♍44	1 6	1 39	2 14	2 55	3 13	4 10	5 7	5 34	5 54	6 21	6 52	7 30	7 51	8 23	8 44
3 47 6	29	24 57	25 26	26 8	27 1	27 41	28 34	29 27	0♍10	0 55	1 13	1 37	1 58	2 31	3 4	3 43	4 1	4 57	5 52	6 18	6 38	7 4	7 34	8 10	8 31	9 2	9 22
3 51 15	30	26 0	26 29	27 10	28 3	28 41	29 33	0♍23	1 6	1 49	2 7	2 30	2 50	3 21	3 54	4 32	4 50	5 44	6 37	7 2	7 21	7 47	8 16	8 51	9 11	9 41	10 1

3 51 15	0♊	26♌0	26♌29	27♌10	28♌3	28♌41	29♌33	0♍23	1♍6	1♍49	2♍7	2♍30	2♍50	3♍21	3♍54	4♍32	4♍50	5♍44	6♍37	7♍2	7♍21	7♍47	8♍16	8♍51	9♍11	9♍41	10♍1
3 55 25	1	27 5	27 32	28 12	29 3	29 41	0♍31	1 20	2 1	2 43	3 0	3 23	3 42	4 13	4 44	5 22	5 39	6 30	7 22	7 47	8 5	8 30	8 58	9 32	9 51	10 20	10 39
3 59 36	2	28 10	28 36	29 14	0♍4	0♍41	1 29	2 17	2 57	3 38	3 54	4 16	4 35	5 4	5 35	6 10	6 27	7 17	8 7	8 31	8 49	9 13	9 40	10 13	10 32	11 0	11 18
4 3 48	3	29 15	29 40	0♍17	1 6	1 41	2 28	3 14	3 53	4 32	4 48	5 9	5 28	5 56	6 26	7 0	7 16	8 5	8 53	9 16	9 33	9 56	10 22	10 54	11 12	11 39	11 57
4 8 0	4	0♍20	0♍44	1 20	2 7	2 41	3 27	4 11	4 49	5 27	5 43	6 2	6 21	6 48	7 17	7 49	8 5	8 52	9 39	10 1	10 17	10 39	11 5	11 36	11 53	12 19	12 36
4 12 13	5	1 25	1 49	2 24	3 9	3 42	4 26	5 9	5 45	6 22	6 37	6 56	7 14	7 40	8 8	8 40	8 55	9 40	10 24	10 46	11 2	11 23	11 47	12 17	12 33	12 59	13 15
4 16 26	6	2 31	2 54	3 28	4 11	4 43	5 25	6 7	6 42	7 17	7 32	7 50	8 7	8 33	8 59	9 30	9 44	10 27	11 10	11 31	11 46	12 7	12 30	12 58	13 14	13 39	13 54
4 20 40	7	3 37	3 59	4 32	5 13	5 44	6 25	7 5	7 38	8 13	8 26	8 44	9 0	9 25	9 50	10 19	10 34	11 15	11 56	12 16	12 30	12 50	13 13	13 40	13 55	14 19	14 34
4 24 55	8	4 43	5 5	5 36	6 16	6 46	7 25	8 3	8 35	9 8	9 21	9 39	9 54	10 18	10 42	11 10	11 23	12 3	12 43	13 1	13 15	13 34	13 56	14 22	14 36	14 59	15 13
4 29 10	9	5 50	6 11	6 41	7 20	7 48	8 25	9 2	9 32	10 4	10 16	10 33	10 47	11 10	11 33	12 0	12 13	12 51	13 29	13 47	14 0	14 18	14 39	15 4	15 18	15 39	15 53
4 33 26	10	6 56	7 16	7 45	8 23	8 50	9 25	10 0	10 30	10 59	11 12	11 27	11 41	12 3	12 25	12 51	13 3	13 39	14 15	14 32	14 45	15 2	15 22	15 46	15 59	16 19	16 32
4 37 42	11	8 3	8 22	8 50	9 26	9 52	10 25	10 59	11 27	11 55	12 7	12 22	12 35	12 56	13 17	13 41	13 53	14 28	15 2	15 18	15 30	15 46	16 5	16 28	16 40	17 0	17 12
4 41 59	12	9 11	9 29	9 56	10 29	10 54	11 26	11 58	12 24	12 51	13 3	13 16	13 29	13 49	14 9	14 32	14 43	15 16	15 48	16 4	16 15	16 31	16 48	17 10	17 22	17 40	17 52
4 46 16	13	10 19	10 36	11 1	11 33	11 56	12 27	12 57	13 22	13 48	13 58	14 11	14 23	14 42	15 1	15 23	15 33	16 4	16 35	16 50	17 0	17 15	17 32	17 52	18 3	18 21	18 32
4 50 34	14	11 27	11 43	12 7	12 38	12 59	13 28	13 56	14 20	14 44	14 54	15 6	15 18	15 35	15 53	16 14	16 24	16 53	17 22	17 36	17 45	18 0	18 15	18 34	18 45	19 1	19 12
4 54 52	15	12 36	12 51	13 13	13 41	14 2	14 29	14 56	15 18	15 41	15 50	16 1	16 12	16 28	16 45	17 5	17 14	17 42	18 9	18 22	18 30	18 44	18 59	19 17	19 27	19 42	19 52
4 59 10	16	13 44	13 58	14 19	14 46	15 5	15 30	15 56	16 16	16 37	16 46	16 57	17 7	17 22	17 38	17 56	18 5	18 30	18 56	19 8	19 16	19 29	19 43	19 59	20 9	20 23	20 32
5 3 29	17	14 52	15 6	15 25	15 50	16 8	16 31	16 55	17 15	17 34	17 42	17 53	18 2	18 16	18 30	18 47	18 55	19 19	19 43	19 54	20 3	20 14	20 26	20 42	20 51	21 4	21 12
5 7 49	18	16 1	16 14	16 32	16 55	17 11	17 33	17 55	18 13	18 31	18 39	18 48	18 57	19 10	19 23	19 39	19 46	20 8	20 30	20 40	20 49	20 58	21 10	21 24	21 33	21 45	21 53
5 12 9	19	17 10	17 22	17 39	18 0	18 15	18 35	18 55	19 11	19 28	19 35	19 44	19 52	20 3	20 16	20 30	20 37	20 57	21 17	21 27	21 35	21 43	21 54	22 7	22 15	22 26	22 33
5 16 29	20	18 20	18 30	18 46	19 5	19 19	19 37	19 55	20 10	20 25	20 32	20 40	20 47	20 57	21 9	21 22	21 28	21 46	22 5	22 13	22 20	22 28	22 38	22 50	22 57	23 7	23 13
5 20 49	21	19 30	19 39	19 53	20 10	20 22	20 39	20 55	21 9	21 23	21 28	21 35	21 42	21 52	22 2	22 13	22 19	22 35	22 52	23 0	23 6	23 13	23 22	23 33	23 39	23 48	23 54
5 25 9	22	20 40	20 48	21 0	21 15	21 26	21 41	21 55	22 8	22 20	22 25	22 31	22 37	22 46	22 55	23 5	23 10	23 25	23 39	23 46	23 51	23 58	24 6	24 16	24 21	24 29	24 35
5 29 30	23	21 50	21 57	22 7	22 21	22 30	22 44	22 56	23 6	23 17	23 22	23 27	23 32	23 40	23 48	23 57	24 1	24 14	24 27	24 33	24 37	24 43	24 50	24 59	25 3	25 10	25 15
5 33 51	24	23 0	23 5	23 15	23 26	23 34	23 46	23 56	24 5	24 14	24 18	24 23	24 27	24 34	24 41	24 49	24 52	25 3	25 14	25 20	25 23	25 29	25 34	25 42	25 46	25 52	25 56
5 38 12	25	24 9	24 14	24 22	24 31	24 38	24 48	24 57	25 4	25 12	25 15	25 19	25 22	25 28	25 34	25 40	25 44	25 52	26 2	26 6	26 9	26 14	26 19	26 25	26 28	26 33	26 36
5 42 34	26	25 19	25 23	25 29	25 37	25 42	25 50	25 57	26 3	26 9	26 12	26 16	16 17	26 22	26 27	26 32	26 35	26 42	26 49	26 53	26 55	26 59	27 3	27 8	27 10	27 14	27 17
5 46 55	27	26 29	26 32	26 36	26 43	26 47	26 52	26 58	27 3	27 7	27 9	27 12	27 13	27 16	27 20	27 25	27 26	27 31	27 37	27 40	27 41	27 44	27 47	27 51	27 53	27 56	27 58
5 51 17	28	27 39	27 42	27 44	27 49	27 51	27 55	27 58	28 2	28 5	28 6	28 8	28 9	28 11	28 13	28 16	28 17	28 20	28 25	28 26	28 27	28 29	28 31	28 34	28 35	28 37	28 39
5 55 38	29	28 50	28 51	28 52	28 55	28 56	28 58	28 59	29 1	29 2	29 3	29 4	29 4	29 6	29 7	29 8	29 9	29 10	29 12	29 13	29 13	29 15	29 16	29 17	29 18	29 19	29 19
6 0 0	30	30 0	30 0	30 0	30 0	30 0	30 0	30 0	30 0	30 0	30 0	30 0	30 0	30 0	30 0	30 0	30 0	30 0	30 0	30 0	30 0	30 0	30 0	30 0	30 0	30 0	30 0

3 HOUSES FOR NORTHERN LATITUDES

A = Sidereal time
10 = Midheaven (10th House)
B = Ascendant

A	10	B 2° 0′	B 4° 0′	B 7° 0′	B 11° 0′	B 14° 0′	B 18° 0′	B 21° 59′	B 25° 19′	B 28° 40′	B 30° 2′	B 31° 46′	B 33° 20′	B 35° 39′	B 37° 58′	B 40° 43′	B 41° 54′	B 45° 30′	B 48° 50′	B 50° 22′	B 51° 32′	B 52° 57′	B 54° 34′	B 56° 28′	B 57° 29′	B 59° 00′	B 59° 56′
	°	° ′	° ′	° ′	° ′	° ′	° ′	° ′	° ′	° ′	° ′	° ′	° ′	° ′	° ′	° ′	° ′	° ′	° ′	° ′	° ′	° ′	° ′	° ′	° ′	° ′	° ′
6 0 0	0♋	0♎ 0	0♎ 0	0♎ 0	0♎ 0	0♎ 0	0♎ 0	0♎ 0	0♎ 0	0♎ 0	0♎ 0	0♎ 0	0♎ 0	0♎ 0	0♎ 0	0♎ 0	0♎ 0	0♎ 0	0♎ 0	0♎ 0	0♎ 0	0♎ 0	0♎ 0	0♎ 0	0♎ 0	0♎ 0	0♎ 0
6 4 22	1	1 10	1 9	1 8	1 5	1 4	1 2	1 1	0 59	0 58	0 57	0 56	0 56	0 54	0 53	0 52	0 51	0 50	0 48	0 47	0 47	0 45	0 44	0 43	0 42	0 41	0 41
6 8 43	2	2 21	2 18	2 16	2 11	2 9	2 5	2 2	1 58	1 55	1 54	1 52	1 51	1 49	1 47	1 44	1 43	1 40	1 35	1 34	1 33	1 31	1 29	1 26	1 25	1 23	1 21
6 13 5	3	3 31	3 28	3 24	3 17	3 13	3 8	3 2	2 57	2 53	2 51	2 48	2 47	2 44	2 40	2 35	2 34	2 29	2 23	2 20	2 19	2 16	2 13	2 9	2 7	2 4	2 2
6 17 26	4	4 41	4 37	4 31	4 23	4 18	4 10	4 3	3 57	3 51	3 48	3 44	3 43	3 38	3 33	3 28	3 25	3 18	3 11	3 7	3 5	3 1	2 57	2 52	2 50	2 46	2 43
6 21 48	5	5 51	5 46	5 38	5 29	5 22	5 12	5 3	4 56	4 48	4 45	4 41	4 38	4 32	4 26	4 20	4 16	4 8	3 58	3 54	3 51	3 46	3 41	3 35	3 32	3 27	3 24
6 26 9	6	7 0	6 55	6 45	6 34	6 26	6 14	6 4	5 55	5 46	5 42	5 37	5 33	5 26	5 19	5 11	5 8	4 57	4 46	4 40	4 37	4 31	4 26	4 18	4 14	4 8	4 4
6 30 30	7	8 10	8 3	7 53	7 39	7 30	7 16	7 4	6 54	6 43	6 38	6 33	6 28	6 20	6 12	6 3	5 59	5 46	5 33	5 27	5 23	5 17	5 10	5 1	4 57	4 50	4 45
6 34 51	8	9 20	9 12	9 0	8 45	8 34	8 19	8 5	7 52	7 40	7 35	7 29	7 23	7 14	7 5	6 55	6 50	6 35	6 21	6 14	6 9	6 2	5 54	5 44	5 39	5 31	5 26
6 39 11	9	10 30	10 21	10 7	9 50	9 38	9 21	9 5	8 51	8 37	8 32	8 25	8 18	8 8	7 58	7 47	7 41	7 25	7 8	7 0	6 55	6 47	6 38	6 27	6 21	6 12	6 6
6 43 31	10	11 40	11 30	11 14	10 55	10 41	10 23	10 5	9 50	9 35	9 28	9 20	9 13	9 3	8 51	8 38	8 32	8 14	7 55	7 47	7 40	7 32	7 22	7 10	7 3	6 53	6 47
6 47 51	11	12 50	12 38	12 21	12 0	11 45	11 25	11 5	10 49	10 32	10 25	10 16	10 8	9 57	9 44	9 30	9 23	9 3	8 43	8 33	8 26	8 17	8 6	7 53	7 45	7 34	7 27
6 52 11	12	13 59	13 46	13 28	13 5	12 49	12 27	12 5	11 47	11 29	11 21	11 12	11 3	10 50	10 37	10 21	10 14	9 52	9 30	9 20	9 12	9 2	8 50	8 36	8 27	8 15	8 8
6 56 31	13	15 8	14 54	14 35	14 10	13 52	13 29	13 5	12 45	12 26	12 18	12 7	11 58	11 44	11 30	11 13	11 5	10 41	10 17	10 6	9 58	9 46	9 34	9 18	9 9	8 56	8 48
7 0 50	14	16 16	16 2	15 41	15 14	14 55	14 30	14 4	13 44	13 23	13 14	13 3	12 53	12 38	12 22	12 4	11 55	11 30	11 4	10 52	10 43	10 31	10 17	10 1	9 51	9 37	9 28
7 5 8	15	17 24	17 9	16 47	16 19	15 58	15 31	15 4	14 42	14 19	14 10	13 59	13 48	13 32	13 15	12 55	12 46	12 18	11 51	11 38	11 28	11 16	11 1	10 43	10 33	10 18	10 8
7 9 26	16	18 33	18 17	17 53	17 22	17 1	16 32	16 3	15 40	15 16	15 6	14 54	14 42	14 25	14 7	13 46	13 36	13 7	12 38	12 24	12 14	12 0	11 45	11 26	11 15	10 59	10 48
7 13 44	17	19 41	19 24	18 59	18 27	18 4	17 33	17 3	16 38	16 12	16 2	15 49	15 37	15 18	14 59	14 37	14 27	13 56	13 25	13 10	12 59	12 45	12 28	12 8	11 57	11 39	11 28
7 18 1	18	20 49	20 31	20 4	19 31	19 6	18 34	18 2	17 36	17 9	16 57	16 44	16 31	16 11	15 51	15 28	15 17	14 44	14 12	13 56	13 45	13 29	13 12	12 50	12 38	12 20	12 8
7 22 18	19	21 57	21 38	21 10	20 34	20 8	19 35	19 1	18 33	18 5	17 53	17 38	17 25	17 4	16 43	16 19	16 7	15 32	14 58	14 42	14 30	14 14	13 55	13 32	13 20	13 0	12 48
7 26 34	20	23 4	22 44	22 15	21 37	21 10	20 35	20 0	19 30	19 1	18 48	18 33	18 19	17 57	17 35	17 9	16 57	16 21	15 45	15 28	15 15	14 58	14 38	14 14	14 1	13 41	13 28
7 30 50	21	24 10	23 49	23 19	22 40	22 12	21 35	20 58	20 28	19 56	19 44	19 27	19 13	18 50	18 27	18 0	17 47	17 9	16 31	16 13	16 0	15 42	15 21	14 56	14 42	14 21	14 7
7 35 5	22	25 17	24 55	24 24	23 44	23 14	22 35	21 57	21 25	20 52	20 39	20 21	20 6	19 42	19 18	18 50	18 37	17 57	17 17	16 59	16 45	16 26	16 4	15 38	15 24	15 1	14 47
7 39 20	23	26 23	26 1	25 28	24 47	24 16	23 35	22 55	22 22	21 47	21 34	21 16	21 0	20 35	20 10	19 41	19 26	18 45	18 4	17 44	17 30	17 10	16 47	16 20	16 5	15 41	15 27
7 43 34	24	27 29	27 6	26 32	25 49	25 17	24 35	23 53	23 18	22 43	22 28	22 10	21 53	21 27	21 1	20 30	20 16	19 33	18 50	18 29	18 15	17 53	17 30	17 2	16 46	16 21	16 6
7 47 47	25	28 35	28 11	27 36	26 51	26 18	25 34	24 51	24 15	23 38	23 23	23 4	22 46	22 20	21 52	21 20	21 5	20 20	19 36	19 14	18 59	18 37	18 13	17 43	17 27	17 1	16 45
7 52 0	26	29 40	29 16	28 40	27 53	27 19	26 33	25 49	25 11	24 33	24 17	23 58	23 39	23 12	22 43	22 11	21 55	21 8	20 21	19 59	19 43	19 21	18 55	18 24	18 7	17 41	17 24
7 56 12	27	0♏45	0♏20	29 43	28 54	28 19	27 32	26 46	26 7	25 28	25 12	24 51	24 32	24 4	23 34	23 0	22 44	21 55	21 7	20 44	20 27	20 4	19 38	19 6	18 48	18 21	18 3
8 0 24	28	1 50	1 24	0♏46	29 56	29 19	28 31	27 43	27 3	26 22	26 6	25 44	25 25	24 56	24 25	23 50	23 33	22 44	21 55	21 29	21 11	20 47	20 20	19 47	19 28	19 0	18 42
8 4 35	29	2 55	2 28	1 48	0♏57	0♏19	29 29	28 40	27 59	27 17	27 0	26 37	26 18	25 47	25 16	24 38	24 21	23 30	22 38	22 13	21 56	21 30	21 2	20 28	20 9	19 40	19 21
8 8 45	30	4 0	3 31	2 50	1 57	1 19	0♏27	29 37	28 54	28 11	27 53	27 30	27 10	26 39	26 6	25 28	25 10	24 16	23 23	22 58	22 40	22 13	21 44	21 9	20 49	20 19	19 59

A	10	B 2° 0′	B 4° 0′	B 7° 0′	B 11° 0′	B 14° 0′	B 18° 0′	B 21° 59′	B 25° 19′	B 28° 40′	B 30° 2′	B 31° 46′	B 33° 20′	B 35° 39′	B 37° 58′	B 40° 43′	B 41° 54′	B 45° 30′	B 48° 50′	B 50° 22′	B 51° 32′	B 52° 57′	B 54° 34′	B 56° 28′	B 57° 29′	B 59° 00′	B 59° 56′
8 8 45	0♌	4♏ 0	3♏31	2♏50	1♏57	1♏19	0♏27	29♎37	28♎54	28♎11	27♎53	27♎30	27♎10	26♎39	26♎ 6	25♎28	25♎10	24♎16	23♎23	22♎58	22♎40	22♎13	21♎44	21♎ 9	20♎49	20♎19	19♎59
8 12 54	1	5 3	4 34	3 52	2 59	2 19	1 26	0♏33	29 50	29 5	28 47	28 23	28 2	27 29	26 56	26 17	25 59	25 3	24 8	23 42	23 24	22 56	22 26	21 50	21 29	20 58	20 38
8 17 3	2	6 6	5 37	4 54	3 59	3 18	2 24	1 29	0♏45	29 59	29 40	29 16	28 54	28 21	27 46	27 5	26 47	25 50	24 53	24 26	24 7	23 39	23 8	22 30	22 9	21 37	21 16
8 21 11	3	7 9	6 39	5 55	4 58	4 16	3 21	2 25	1 40	0♏53	0♏33	0♏ 8	29 46	29 11	28 36	27 54	27 35	26 36	25 38	25 10	24 50	24 22	23 50	23 11	22 49	22 16	21 55
8 25 19	4	8 11	7 41	6 56	5 58	5 15	4 18	3 21	2 34	1 46	1 26	1 0	0♏37	0♏ 2	29 26	28 43	28 23	27 23	26 23	25 54	25 34	25 4	24 31	23 51	23 29	22 55	22 33
8 29 26	5	9 14	8 42	7 56	6 57	6 13	5 15	4 17	3 39	2 39	2 19	1 52	1 29	0 53	0♏16	29 31	29 11	28 9	27 7	26 38	26 18	25 46	25 13	24 32	24 9	23 33	23 11
8 33 31	6	10 16	9 43	8 57	7 56	7 11	6 12	5 12	4 23	3 32	3 11	2 44	2 20	1 43	1 6	0♏20	29 59	28 55	27 52	27 22	27 1	26 29	25 54	25 12	24 48	24 12	23 49
8 37 37	7	11 17	10 44	9 57	8 55	8 9	7 8	6 7	5 17	4 25	4 3	3 36	3 11	2 33	1 55	1 8	0♏46	29 41	28 36	28 5	27 44	27 11	26 35	25 52	25 28	24 50	24 26
8 41 41	8	12 18	11 45	10 57	9 53	9 6	8 4	7 2	6 11	5 17	4 56	4 28	4 1	3 28	2 44	1 56	1 34	0♏27	29 20	28 49	28 26	27 53	27 16	26 32	26 7	25 29	25 4
8 45 45	9	13 19	12 46	11 56	10 52	10 4	9 0	7 57	7 4	6 10	5 47	5 19	4 52	4 13	3 33	2 43	2 21	1 12	0♏ 4	29 32	29 8	28 35	27 57	27 11	26 46	26 7	25 42
8 49 48	10	14 20	13 47	12 55	11 49	11 1	9 56	8 51	7 58	7 2	6 39	6 10	5 43	5 2	4 22	3 31	3 8	1 57	0 48	0♏15	29 50	29 16	28 38	27 51	27 25	26 45	26 19
8 53 51	11	15 20	14 46	13 54	12 47	11 58	10 52	9 46	8 51	7 54	7 31	7 1	6 33	5 52	5 10	4 18	3 55	2 43	1 32	0 58	0♏32	29 58	29 19	28 31	28 4	27 23	26 56
8 57 52	12	16 20	15 45	14 52	13 44	12 54	11 47	10 40	9 44	8 46	8 22	7 52	7 24	6 41	5 58	5 6	4 42	3 28	2 15	1 41	1 15	0♏39	29 59	29 10	28 42	28 0	27 33
9 1 53	13	17 19	16 43	15 50	14 41	13 50	12 42	11 33	10 36	9 38	9 13	8 42	8 14	7 31	6 47	5 53	5 28	4 13	2 59	2 23	1 58	1 20	0♏39	29 49	29 21	28 38	28 10
9 5 53	14	18 18	17 41	16 48	15 38	14 46	13 37	12 27	11 29	10 29	10 4	9 32	9 4	8 20	7 35	6 40	6 15	4 58	3 42	3 6	2 39	2 2	1 20	0♏28	0♏ 0	29 15	28 47
9 9 53	15	19 17	18 40	17 46	16 34	15 41	14 31	13 20	12 21	11 20	10 55	10 23	9 54	9 8	8 23	7 27	7 1	5 43	4 25	3 48	3 21	2 43	2 0	1 7	0 38	29 53	29 24
9 13 52	16	20 16	19 38	18 43	17 31	16 37	15 25	14 13	13 13	12 11	11 45	11 13	10 43	9 57	9 10	8 13	7 47	6 27	5 8	4 30	4 3	3 23	2 40	1 46	1 16	0♏30	0♏ 1
9 17 50	17	21 14	20 36	19 40	18 26	17 32	16 19	15 6	14 5	13 2	12 36	12 3	11 32	10 45	9 58	9 0	8 33	7 12	5 51	5 13	4 44	4 4	3 20	2 25	1 54	1 7	0 37
9 21 47	18	22 12	21 34	20 36	19 22	18 27	17 13	15 59	14 57	13 53	13 26	12 52	12 21	11 33	10 45	9 46	9 19	7 56	6 34	5 55	5 56	4 45	3 59	3 3	2 32	1 44	1 13
9 25 44	19	23 9	22 31	21 33	20 18	19 22	18 7	16 51	15 48	14 43	14 16	13 42	13 10	12 21	11 32	10 33	10 5	8 40	7 17	6 36	6 7	5 25	4 39	3 42	3 10	2 21	1 50
9 29 40	20	24 6	23 27	22 29	21 13	20 16	19 0	17 43	16 40	15 34	15 6	14 31	13 58	13 9	12 20	11 19	10 50	9 24	7 59	7 18	6 48	6 6	5 18	4 20	3 48	2 58	2 26
9 33 35	21	25 3	24 23	23 25	22 8	21 10	19 53	18 35	17 31	16 24	15 56	15 20	14 47	13 57	13 6	12 4	11 37	10 8	8 42	8 0	7 29	6 46	5 58	4 58	4 25	3 34	3 2
9 37 29	22	25 59	25 20	24 21	23 2	22 3	20 46	19 27	18 22	17 13	16 45	16 9	15 35	14 45	13 53	12 50	12 21	10 52	9 24	8 41	8 9	7 26	6 37	5 37	5 3	4 11	3 38
9 41 23	23	26 56	26 16	25 16	23 56	22 57	21 39	20 19	19 12	18 3	17 35	16 57	16 24	15 33	14 40	13 36	13 6	11 35	10 6	9 23	8 50	8 6	7 16	6 15	5 40	4 47	4 13
9 45 16	24	27 52	27 11	26 10	24 50	23 51	22 31	21 11	20 3	18 53	18 24	17 46	17 12	16 20	15 27	14 21	13 52	12 19	10 48	10 4	9 31	8 46	7 55	6 52	6 18	5 34	4 49
9 49 9	25	28 47	28 6	27 5	25 44	24 44	23 23	22 2	20 53	19 42	19 13	18 34	18 0	17 7	16 13	15 7	14 37	13 3	11 30	10 45	10 11	9 26	8 34	7 30	6 55	6 0	5 24
9 53 1	26	29 43	29 1	27 59	26 38	25 37	24 15	22 53	21 44	20 31	20 2	19 23	18 47	17 54	16 59	15 52	15 21	13 46	12 12	11 26	10 51	10 6	9 13	8 8	7 32	6 36	6 0
9 56 52	27	0♐38	29 56	28 53	27 31	26 30	25 7	23 44	22 34	21 20	20 50	20 11	19 35	18 41	17 46	16 38	16 6	14 29	12 54	12 7	11 32	10 45	9 52	8 46	8 9	7 12	6 35
10 0 42	28	1 33	0♐51	29 47	28 25	27 23	25 59	24 35	23 24	22 10	21 39	20 59	20 23	19 28	18 32	17 22	16 51	15 13	13 35	12 48	12 12	11 25	10 30	9 23	8 46	7 48	7 11
10 4 33	29	2 28	1 45	0♐41	29 17	28 15	26 51	25 25	24 13	22 59	22 28	21 47	21 11	20 15	19 18	18 7	17 35	15 56	14 17	13 29	12 53	12 4	11 9	10 1	9 22	8 24	7 46
10 8 23	30	3 22	2 39	1 35	0♐11	29 7	27 42	26 16	25 3	23 48	23 16	22 36	21 58	21 2	20 4	18 52	18 20	16 39	14 58	14 10	13 33	12 44	11 47	10 38	9 59	8 59	8 21

A	10	B 2° 0′	B 4° 0′	B 7° 0′	B 11° 0′	B 14° 0′	B 18° 0′	B 21° 59′	B 25° 19′	B 28° 40′	B 30° 2′	B 31° 46′	B 33° 20′	B 35° 39′	B 37° 58′	B 40° 43′	B 41° 54′	B 45° 30′	B 48° 50′	B 50° 22′	B 51° 32′	B 52° 57′	B 54° 34′	B 56° 28′	B 57° 29′	B 59° 00′	B 59° 56′
10 8 23	0♍	3♐22	2 39	1♐35	0♐11	29♐ 7	27♏42	26♏16	25♏ 3	23♏48	26♏16	22♏36	21♏58	21♏ 2	20♏ 4	18♏52	18♏20	16♏39	14♏58	14♏10	13♏33	12♏44	11♏47	10♏38	9♏59	8♏59	8♏21
10 12 12	1	4 16	3 32	2 28	1 3	29 59	28 33	27 6	25 53	24 37	24 4	23 24	22 46	21 49	20 49	19 36	19 4	17 22	15 40	14 50	14 13	13 23	12 26	11 15	10 36	9 35	8 56
10 16 0	2	5 10	4 26	3 21	1 55	0♐51	29 24	27 56	26 42	25 25	24 52	24 11	23 33	22 35	21 35	20 22	19 49	18 4	16 21	15 31	14 53	14 2	13 4	11 52	11 12	10 11	9 31
10 19 48	3	6 3	5 19	4 14	2 47	1 42	0♐15	28 46	27 31	26 13	25 40	24 59	24 20	23 21	22 21	21 7	20 33	18 47	17 2	16 12	15 33	14 42	13 42	12 29	11 49	10 46	10 5
10 23 35	4	6 56	6 12	5 7	3 40	2 34	1 6	29 36	28 20	27 1	26 28	25 46	25 7	24 7	23 6	21 51	21 17	19 30	17 43	16 52	16 13	15 21	14 21	13 6	12 25	11 21	10 40
10 27 22	5	7 49	7 5	5 59	4 31	3 25	1 56	0♐26	29 9	27 49	27 16	26 34	25 54	24 53	23 52	22 35	22 1	20 13	18 25	17 32	16 52	16 0	14 59	13 43	13 1	11 57	11 15
10 31 8	6	8 42	7 58	6 51	5 23	4 16	2 47	1 15	29 58	28 37	28 4	27 21	26 40	25 39	24 37	23 20	22 45	20 55	19 6	18 13	17 32	16 39	15 37	14 20	13 38	12 32	11 49
10 34 54	7	9 35	8 51	7 43	6 14	5 7	3 37	2 5	0♐47	29 25	28 52	28 8	27 27	26 26	25 23	24 4	23 29	21 38	19 47	18 53	18 12	17 18	16 15	14 57	14 14	13 7	12 24
10 38 40	8	10 28	9 43	8 35	7 6	5 58	4 27	2 55	1 36	0♐13	29 39	28 55	28 14	27 12	26 8	24 48	24 13	22 20	20 28	19 33	18 52	17 56	16 53	15 34	14 50	13 42	12 58
10 42 25	9	11 20	10 35	9 27	7 57	6 49	5 17	3 44	2 25	1 1	0♐27	29 42	29 1	27 58	26 53	25 33	24 57	23 3	21 9	20 13	19 31	18 35	17 31	16 11	15 26	14 17	13 33
10 46 9	10	12 12	11 27	10 19	8 48	7 40	6 7	4 33	3 13	1 49	1 14	0♐29	29 47	28 44	27 38	26 17	25 40	23 45	21 50	20 54	20 11	19 14	18 8	16 47	16 2	14 52	14 7
10 49 53	11	13 4	12 19	11 10	9 39	8 30	6 57	5 22	4 2	2 37	2 2	1 16	0♐34	29 30	28 23	27 2	26 24	24 27	22 30	21 34	20 50	19 53	18 46	17 23	16 38	15 27	14 41
10 53 37	12	13 56	13 10	12 2	10 30	9 20	7 47	6 11	4 50	3 25	2 49	2 4	1 21	0♐16	29 8	27 46	27 8	25 10	23 11	22 14	21 30	20 32	19 24	18 0	17 14	16 2	15 15
10 57 20	13	14 47	14 2	12 53	11 21	10 11	8 37	7 1	5 38	4 13	3 36	2 51	2 7	1 1	29 54	28 29	27 52	25 52	23 52	22 54	22 9	21 10	20 2	18 37	17 50	16 37	15 50
11 1 3	14	15 39	14 53	13 44	12 11	11 1	9 27	7 50	6 27	5 0	4 24	3 37	2 54	1 47	1♐38	29 14	28 36	26 34	24 33	23 34	22 49	21 49	20 40	19 14	18 26	17 12	16 24
11 4 46	15	16 30	15 44	14 34	13 1	11 51	10 16	8 38	7 15	5 48	5 11	4 24	3 40	2 33	1 24	29 57	29 19	27 17	25 14	4 14	23 28	22 28	21 17	19 50	19 2	17 47	16 58
11 8 28	16	17 21	16 36	15 25	13 52	12 41	11 6	9 27	8 3	6 35	5 58	5 11	4 26	3 19	2 9	0♐42	0♐ 3	27 59	25 55	24 54	24 8	23 6	21 55	20 27	19 38	18 21	17 32
11 12 10	17	18 13	17 27	16 16	14 42	13 31	11 55	10 16	8 52	7 23	6 45	5 58	5 12	4 5	2 54	1 27	0 47	28 41	26 36	25 34	24 47	23 45	22 33	21 3	20 13	18 56	18 6
11 15 52	18	19 4	18 18	17 7	15 33	14 22	12 45	11 5	9 40	8 10	7 23	6 44	5 59	4 51	3 39	2 10	1 31	29 24	27 16	26 14	25 27	24 24	23 11	21 40	20 49	19 31	18 40
11 19 34	19	19 55	19 9	17 58	16 23	15 12	13 34	11 53	10 28	8 57	8 20	7 31	6 45	5 30	4 24	2 55	2 14	0♐ 6	27 57	26 55	26 6	25 3	23 48	22 17	21 25	20 6	19 14
11 23 15	20	20 46	19 59	18 49	17 14	16 2	14 24	12 42	11 16	9 45	9 7	8 18	7 32	6 22	5 9	3 38	2 58	0 49	28 38	27 35	26 45	25 41	24 26	22 53	22 1	20 40	19 48
11 26 56	21	21 37	20 50	19 39	18 4	16 51	15 13	13 31	12 4	10 32	9 54	9 4	8 18	7 8	5 54	4 23	3 32	1 31	29 19	28 15	27 25	26 20	25 4	23 30	22 37	21 15	20 22
11 30 37	22	22 28	21 40	20 29	18 54	17 41	16 3	14 20	12 53	11 20	10 42	9 51	9 5	7 54	6 40	5 6	4 26	2 14	0♐ 0	28 55	28 5	26 59	25 42	24 6	23 13	21 50	20 56
11 34 18	23	23 19	22 31	21 19	19 44	18 31	16 52	15 9	13 41	12 8	11 29	10 38	9 51	8 40	7 25	5 52	5 10	2 57	0 41	29 36	28 44	27 38	26 20	24 43	23 49	22 25	21 30
11 37 58	24	24 9	23 21	22 10	20 34	19 21	17 41	15 58	14 29	12 56	12 17	11 26	10 38	9 26	8 10	6 36	5 54	3 39	1 23	0♐16	29 24	28 17	26 58	25 20	24 25	22 59	22 4
11 41 39	25	25 0	24 12	23 1	21 24	20 11	18 31	16 47	15 18	13 44	13 4	12 13	11 25	10 12	8 56	7 20	6 38	4 22	2 4	0 57	0♐ 3	28 56	27 36	25 56	25 1	23 34	22 38
11 45 19	26	25 50	25 2	23 51	22 14	21 1	19 20	17 36	16 6	14 31	13 52	13 0	12 12	10 58	9 41	8 5	7 23	5 5	2 45	1 37	0 43	29 35	28 14	26 33	25 37	24 9	23 12
11 49 0	27	26 41	25 53	24 41	23 4	21 51	20 9	18 24	16 55	15 19	14 39	13 47	12 59	11 45	10 27	8 48	8 7	5 48	3 27	2 18	1 23	0♐14	28 52	27 10	26 13	24 44	23 46
11 52 40	28	27 31	26 44	25 31	23 54	22 40	20 59	19 14	17 43	16 7	15 27	14 34	13 45	12 31	11 13	9 37	8 52	6 31	4 8	2 58	2 3	0 53	29 30	27 47	26 49	25 19	24 21
11 56 20	29	28 22	27 34	26 22	24 44	23 30	21 48	20 3	18 32	16 55	16 15	15 22	14 32	13 18	11 59	10 22	9 36	7 14	4 50	3 39	2 43	1 33	0♐ 9	28 24	27 25	25 54	24 55
12 0 0	30	29 12	28 24	27 12	25 35	24 20	22 38	20 52	19 20	17 44	17 3	16 10	15 20	14 4	12 45	11 7	10 21	7 57	5 32	4 20	3 13	2 12	0 47	29 1	28 2	26 29	25 29

A = Sidereal time
10 = Midheaven (10th House)
B = Ascendant

A	10	B 2° 0′	B 4° 0′	B 7° 0′	B 11° 0′	B 14° 0′	B 18° 0′	B 21° 59′	B 25° 19′	B 28° 40′	B 30° 2′	B 31° 46′	B 33° 20′	B 35° 39′	B 37° 58′	B 40° 43′	B 41° 54′	B 45° 30′	B 48° 50′	B 50° 22′	B 51° 32′	B 52° 57′	B 54° 34′	B 56° 28′	B 57° 29′	B 59° 00′	B 59° 56′
	°	° ′	° ′	° ′	° ′	° ′	° ′	° ′	° ′	° ′	° ′	° ′	° ′	° ′	° ′	° ′	° ′	° ′	° ′	° ′	° ′	° ′	° ′	° ′	° ′	° ′	° ′
12 0 0	0♎	29♐12	28♐24	27♐12	25♐25	24♐20	22♐38	20♐52	19♐20	17♐44	17♐ 3	16♐10	15♐20	14♐ 4	12♐45	11♐ 7	10♐21	7♐57	5♐32	4♐20	3♐23	2♐12	0♐47	29♏ 1	28♏ 2	26♏29	25♏29
12 3 40	1	0♑ 3	29 15	28 2	26 25	25 10	23 27	21 41	20 9	18 32	17 51	16 57	16 7	14 51	13 31	11 52	11 6	8 40	6 13	5 1	4 4	2 52	1 25	29 38	28 38	27 4	26 3
12 7 20	2	0 53	0♑ 5	28 53	27 15	26 0	24 17	22 31	20 58	19 20	18 39	17 44	16 54	15 38	14 17	12 37	11 51	9 24	6 55	5 43	4 45	3 31	2 4	0♐15	29 14	27 39	26 38
12 11 0	3	1 44	0 56	29 43	28 5	26 50	25 7	23 20	21 47	20 9	19 27	18 32	17 42	16 25	15 3	13 19	12 36	10 8	7 38	6 24	5 26	4 11	2 43	0 53	29 51	28 15	27 12
12 14 41	4	2 34	1 46	0♑34	28 56	27 40	25 57	24 10	22 36	20 57	20 15	19 21	18 30	17 12	15 50	14 7	13 21	10 52	8 20	7 5	6 7	4 51	3 22	1 30	0♐28	28 50	27 47
12 18 21	5	3 25	2 37	1 24	29 46	28 31	26 47	24 59	23 26	21 46	21 4	20 9	19 18	17 59	16 37	14 52	14 7	11 36	9 3	7 47	6 48	5 31	4 1	2 8	1 4	29 25	28 21
12 22 2	6	4 15	3 27	2 15	0♑37	29 21	27 39	25 49	24 15	22 35	21 53	20 57	20 6	18 47	17 24	15 38	14 52	12 20	9 45	8 29	7 29	6 12	4 40	2 46	1 41	0♐ 1	28 56
12 25 42	7	5 6	4 18	3 5	1 28	0♑12	28 27	26 40	25 5	23 24	22 42	21 46	20 54	19 34	18 11	16 23	15 38	13 5	10 28	9 11	8 10	6 52	5 19	3 24	2 18	0 37	29 31
12 29 23	8	5 57	5 9	3 56	2 19	1 3	29 18	27 29	25 55	24 13	23 31	22 35	21 43	20 22	18 58	17 11	16 24	13 50	11 11	9 53	8 51	7 33	5 59	4 2	2 56	1 13	0♐ 6
12 33 4	9	6 48	6 0	4 47	3 9	1 53	0♑ 8	28 20	26 45	25 3	24 20	23 24	22 32	21 10	19 46	17 58	17 11	14 35	11 55	10 36	9 33	8 13	6 39	4 40	3 33	1 49	0 41
12 36 45	10	7 39	6 51	5 38	4 0	2 44	0 58	29 10	27 35	25 52	25 10	24 13	23 21	21 59	20 33	18 45	17 57	15 19	12 38	11 18	10 15	8 55	7 19	5 18	4 11	2 25	1 16
12 40 26	11	8 30	7 43	6 30	4 52	3 35	1 50	0♑ 1	28 25	26 42	25 59	25 2	24 10	22 48	21 21	19 32	18 44	16 5	13 22	12 1	10 57	9 36	7 59	5 57	4 48	3 1	1 51
12 44 8	12	9 21	8 34	7 21	5 43	4 27	2 42	0 52	29 16	27 33	26 49	25 52	24 59	23 37	22 10	20 20	19 31	16 51	14 6	12 45	11 40	10 17	8 39	6 36	5 26	3 37	2 27
12 47 50	13	10 13	9 26	8 13	6 35	5 19	3 34	1 43	0♑ 7	28 23	27 40	26 42	25 49	24 26	22 58	21 8	20 19	17 37	14 50	13 28	12 22	10 59	9 19	7 15	6 4	4 14	3 2
12 51 32	14	11 4	10 17	9 4	7 26	6 10	4 25	2 34	0 58	29 14	28 30	27 32	26 39	25 15	23 47	21 57	21 6	18 22	15 35	14 12	13 4	11 41	10 0	7 54	6 42	4 51	3 38
12 55 14	15	11 56	11 9	9 56	8 18	7 2	5 17	3 26	1 49	0♑ 5	29 21	28 23	27 29	26 4	24 36	22 43	21 54	19 9	16 20	14 56	13 47	12 23	10 41	8 33	7 21	5 28	4 14
12 58 57	16	12 47	12 0	10 48	9 10	7 54	6 9	4 18	2 41	0 56	0♑12	29 14	28 19	26 54	25 25	23 33	22 43	19 56	17 5	15 40	14 30	13 6	11 23	9 13	8 0	6 5	4 50
13 2 40	17	13 39	12 52	11 40	10 2	8 46	7 1	5 10	3 32	1 48	1 3	0♑ 5	29 10	27 45	26 16	24 22	23 31	20 43	17 50	16 25	15 14	13 49	12 4	9 53	8 39	6 42	5 27
13 6 23	18	14 31	13 44	12 33	10 55	9 39	7 53	6 1	4 24	2 39	1 55	0 56	0♑ 1	28 35	27 5	25 11	24 20	21 31	18 37	17 10	15 59	14 32	12 46	10 33	9 18	7 20	6 3
13 10 7	19	15 23	14 36	13 25	11 47	10 32	8 46	6 54	5 17	3 32	2 47	1 48	0 52	29 26	27 56	26 1	25 10	22 19	19 23	17 55	16 44	15 16	13 28	11 14	9 57	7 58	6 40
13 13 51	20	16 16	15 29	14 18	12 40	11 25	9 39	7 47	6 10	4 24	3 39	2 39	1 44	0♑18	28 47	26 51	25 59	23 7	20 9	18 41	17 29	15 59	14 11	11 54	10 57	8 36	7 17
13 17 35	21	17 8	16 22	15 10	13 33	12 18	10 32	8 41	7 3	5 17	4 31	3 32	2 36	1 10	29 38	27 40	26 49	23 56	20 56	19 27	18 14	16 44	14 54	12 35	11 17	9 14	7 54
13 21 20	22	18 1	17 15	16 3	14 26	13 11	11 26	9 34	7 56	6 10	5 24	4 24	3 29	2 2	0♑30	28 32	27 40	24 45	21 44	20 13	19 0	17 28	15 37	13 17	11 57	9 53	8 32
13 25 6	23	18 54	18 8	16 57	15 21	14 5	12 20	10 28	8 50	7 3	6 18	5 18	4 22	2 55	1 22	29 23	28 31	25 34	22 31	21 0	19 45	18 13	16 21	13 59	12 38	10 32	9 9
13 28 52	24	19 47	19 1	17 51	16 14	14 59	13 14	11 22	9 44	7 57	7 11	6 11	5 15	3 48	2 14	0♑14	29 22	26 24	23 20	21 47	20 31	18 59	17 5	14 41	13 19	11 11	9 47
13 32 38	25	20 41	19 55	18 45	17 8	15 53	14 8	12 16	10 38	8 51	8 6	7 5	6 9	4 41	3 7	1 7	0♑14	27 15	24 8	22 35	21 18	19 44	17 49	15 23	14 1	11 51	10 26
13 36 25	26	21 34	20 49	19 38	18 2	16 48	15 3	13 11	11 33	9 46	9 0	7 59	7 3	5 35	4 1	2 0	1 6	28 6	24 58	23 23	22 6	20 31	18 34	16 6	14 43	12 31	11 4
13 40 12	27	22 28	21 43	20 33	18 57	17 43	15 58	14 6	12 28	10 41	9 55	8 54	7 58	6 30	4 55	2 52	1 59	28 57	25 47	24 12	22 54	21 18	19 19	16 50	15 25	13 11	11 43
13 44 0	28	23 22	22 37	21 28	19 52	18 38	16 53	15 2	13 24	11 36	10 50	9 49	8 53	7 24	5 49	3 46	2 52	29 49	26 38	25 1	23 42	22 5	20 5	17 34	16 7	13 52	12 23
13 47 48	29	24 16	23 31	22 22	20 47	19 33	17 49	15 58	14 20	12 32	11 46	10 45	9 49	8 19	6 44	4 41	3 46	0♑42	27 28	25 51	24 31	22 53	20 51	18 18	16 50	14 33	13 2
13 51 37	30	25 10	24 26	23 17	21 43	20 29	18 45	16 54	15 16	13 28	12 43	11 41	10 45	9 15	7 39	5 35	4 41	1 35	28 20	26 42	25 20	23 41	21 38	19 3	17 34	15 14	13 42
13 51 37	0♏	25♑10	24♑26	23♑17	21♑43	20♑29	18♑45	16♑54	15♑16	13♑28	12♑43	11♑41	10♑45	9♑15	7♑39	5♑35	4♑41	1♑35	28♐20	26♐42	25♐20	23♐41	21♐38	19♐ 3	17♐34	15♐14	13♐42
13 55 27	1	26 5	25 22	24 13	22 39	21 26	19 42	17 51	16 13	14 25	13 39	12 38	11 41	10 11	8 35	6 30	5 36	2 28	29 12	27 33	26 10	24 30	22 26	19 48	18 18	15 56	14 23
13 59 17	2	27 0	26 17	25 9	23 35	22 23	20 39	18 48	17 10	15 23	14 37	13 35	12 38	11 8	9 32	7 27	6 31	3 23	0♑ 4	28 24	27 2	25 19	23 14	20 34	19 2	16 38	15 4
14 3 8	3	27 56	27 13	26 5	24 32	23 20	21 36	19 46	18 8	16 20	15 · 34	14 33	13 36	12 6	10 29	8 23	7 27	4 18	0 57	29 16	27 53	26 10	24 2	21 20	19 47	17 21	15 45
14 6 59	4	28 52	28 9	27 2	25 29	24 17	22 34	20 44	19 6	17 19	16 33	15 31	14 34	13 4	11 26	9 20	8 24	5 14	1 51	0♑ 9	28 45	27 0	24 51	22 7	20 33	18 4	16 27
14 10 51	5	29 48	29 5	27 59	26 27	25 14	23 32	21 43	20 5	18 18	17 32	16 30	15 33	14 2	12 24	10 18	9 22	6 10	2 46	1 3	29 36	27 52	25 41	22 55	21 19	18 48	17 9
14 14 44	6	0♒45	0♒ 2	28 56	27 24	26 12	24 31	22 42	21 4	19 17	18 31	17 30	16 33	15 1	13 23	11 16	10 20	7 7	3 41	1 57	0♑29	28 44	26 32	23 43	22 6	19 33	17 52
14 18 31	7	1 41	0 59	29 53	28 22	27 11	25 30	23 41	22 4	20 17	19 31	18 30	17 33	16 1	14 23	12 15	11 19	8 4	4 37	2 52	1 23	29 37	27 23	24 32	22 54	20 18	18 35
14 22 31	8	2 38	1 56	0♒51	29 21	28 10	26 30	24 41	23 4	21 18	20 32	19 30	18 33	17 1	15 23	13 15	12 19	9 3	5 34	3 48	2 18	0♑31	28 15	25 21	23 42	21 4	19 19
14 26 25	9	3 35	2 54	1 49	0♒20	29 9	27 30	25 42	24 5	22 19	21 33	20 31	19 34	18 3	16 24	14 16	13 19	10 2	6 32	4 45	3 14	1 25	29 8	26 12	24 30	21 50	20 4
14 30 20	10	4 33	3 52	2 48	1 19	0♒ 9	28 30	26 43	25 7	23 21	22 35	21 33	20 36	19 4	17 26	15 17	14 20	11 2	7 30	5 42	4 11	2 20	0♑ 1	27 3	25 20	22 37	20 49
14 34 16	11	5 31	4 51	3 47	2 19	1 10	29 31	27 44	26 9	24 23	23 37	22 35	21 39	20 7	18 29	16 19	15 22	12 3	8 30	6 41	5 9	3 17	0 56	27 55	26 11	23 25	21 35
14 38 13	12	6 30	5 50	4 47	3 19	2 11	0♒33	28 46	27 11	25 26	24 40	23 39	22 42	21 10	19 32	17 23	16 25	13 5	9 30	7 40	6 7	4 14	1 51	28 48	27 2	24 13	22 21
14 42 10	13	7 29	6 49	5 47	4 20	3 12	1 35	29 49	28 15	26 29	25 44	24 43	23 46	22 15	20 36	18 27	17 29	14 8	10 32	8 40	7 6	5 12	2 48	29 41	27 54	25 2	23 9
14 46 8	14	8 28	7 48	6 47	5 21	4 13	2 37	0♒52	29 18	27 34	26 49	25 47	24 51	23 19	21 41	19 32	18 33	15 12	11 34	9 42	8 6	6 11	3 45	0♑36	28 48	25 53	23 57
14 50 7	15	9 27	8 48	7 47	6 23	5 15	3 40	1 56	0♒23	28 39	27 54	26 53	25 57	24 25	22 47	20 37	19 39	16 17	12 37	10 44	9 8	7 11	4 43	1 32	29 41	26 44	24 46
14 54 7	16	10 27	9 49	8 48	7 25	6 18	4 44	3 1	1 28	29 45	29 0	27 59	27 3	25 32	23 53	21 44	20 45	17 22	13 42	11 48	10 11	8 13	5 43	2 29	0♑36	27 36	25 36
14 58 7	17	11 27	10 50	9 50	8 27	7 22	5 48	4 6	2 34	0♒51	0♒ 6	29 6	28 10	26 39	25 1	22 51	21 53	18 29	14 47	12 52	11 15	9 15	6 44	3 27	1 32	28 29	26 27
14 2 8	18	12 27	11 50	10 51	9 30	8 25	6 52	5 11	4 0	1 58	1 14	0♒14	29 18	27 48	26 9	23 59	23 1	19 37	15 54	13 58	12 20	10 19	7 46	4 24	2 30	29 23	27 18
15 6 9	19	13 28	12 51	11 53	10 33	9 29	7 57	6 17	4 47	3 6	2 22	1 22	0♒27	28 56	27 18	25 9	24 11	20 46	17 2	15 5	13 27	11 24	8 49	5 26	3 28	0♑18	28 11
15 10 12	20	14 29	13 53	12 56	11 37	10 34	9 3	7 24	5 55	4 14	3 30	2 31	1 36	0♒ 7	28 29	26 19	25 21	21 56	18 11	16 14	14 35	12 30	9 53	6 28	4 28	1 15	29 5
15 14 15	21	15 31	14 55	13 59	12 40	11 39	10 10	8 32	7 3	5 23	4 40	3 42	2 46	1 18	29 41	27 31	26 33	23 8	19 22	17 24	15 43	13 38	10 59	7 31	5 29	2 12	0♑ 0
15 18 19	22	16 33	15 58	15 3	13 46	12 45	11 17	9 40	8 12	6 33	5 51	4 53	3 57	2 30	0♒53	28 43	27 46	24 21	20 34	18 35	16 52	14 47	12 7	8 36	6 32	3 11	0 57
15 22 23	23	17 36	17 1	16 7	14 51	13 51	12 24	10 49	9 22	7 44	7 2	6 4	5 9	3 43	2 6	29 57	29 0	25 34	21 47	19 48	18 3	15 58	13 16	9 42	7 36	4 12	1 55
15 26 29	24	18 38	18 5	17 12	15 57	14 58	13 32	11 59	10 32	8 56	8 14	7 17	6 23	4 57	3 21	1♒14	0♒15	26 50	23 2	21 2	19 16	17 11	14 27	10 49	8 42	5 14	2 54
15 30 35	25	19 42	19 9	18 17	17 4	16 5	14 41	13 9	11 44	10 8	9 27	8 31	7 37	6 11	4 36	2 28	1 31	28 7	24 19	22 18	20 32	18 25	15 39	11 59	9 49	6 18	3 55
15 34 41	26	20 45	20 13	19 22	18 10	17 12	15 49	14 19	12 55	11 22	10 40	9 45	8 52	7 27	5 53	3 46	2 49	29 25	25 37	23 35	21 48	19 41	16 53	13 10	10 58	7 23	4 58
15 38 49	27	21 49	21 17	20 27	19 17	18 21	16 59	15 30	14 8	12 36	11 55	11 0	10 8	8 44	7 11	5 5	4 8	0♒45	26 56	24 54	23 8	20 59	18 9	14 24	12 10	8 31	6 2
15 42 57	28	22 54	22 22	21 33	20 25	19 29	18 10	16 42	15 21	13 50	13 10	12 16	11 25	10 1	8 29	6 25	5 28	2 6	28 18	26 15	24 29	22 19	19 28	15 39	13 23	9 40	7 8
15 47 6	29	23 59	23 28	22 40	21 32	20 38	19 21	17 55	16 36	15 6	14 27	13 33	12 43	11 20	9 49	7 46	6 50	3 28	29 41	27 39	25 51	23 40	20 48	16 57	14 39	10 52	8 17
15 51 15	30	25 4	24 34	23 48	22 42	21 49	20 33	19 8	17 50	16 22	15 44	14 51	14 1	12 40	11 10	9 8	8 13	4 53	1♒ 6	29 4	27 15	25 4	22 11	18 17	15 57	12 6	9 28
15 51 15	0♐	25♒ 4.	24♒34	23♒48	22♒42	21♒49	20♒33	19♒ 8	17♒50	16♒22	15♒44	14♒51	14♒ 1	12♒40	11♒10	9♒ 8	8♒13	4♒53	1♒ 6	29♑ 4	27♑15	25♑ 4	22♑11	18♑17	15♑57	12♑ 6	9♑28
15 55 25	1	26 10	25 41	24 55	23 50	22 59	21 45	20 22	19 6	17 40	17 2	16 10	15 21	14 1	12 32	10 31	9 37	6 19	2 33	0♒31	28 42	26 31	23 36	19 39	17 17	13 22	10 41
15 59 36	2	27 16	26 48	26 3	25 0	24 10	22 58	21 36	20 22	18 58	18 20	17 30	16 42	15 23	13 56	11 56	11 3	7 47	4 1	2 0	0♒11	27 59	25 3	21 4	18 40	14 41	11 56
16 3 48	3	28 22	27 55	27 11	26 11	25 22	24 11	22 51	21 39	20 17	19 40	18 51	18 4	16 46	15 20	13 23	12 30	9 16	5 32	3 31	1 42	29 30	26 34	22 32	20 6	16 3	13 15
16 8 0	4	29 28	29 2	28 20	27 21	26 33	25 25	24 7	22 57	21 36	21 1	20 13	19 26	18 10	16 46	14 50	13 59	10 47	7 5	5 4	3 16	1♒ 4	28 7	24 3	21 36	17 28	14 36
16 12 13	5	0♓35	0♓ 9	29 29	28 32	27 45	26 39	25 24	24 15	22 56	22 22	21 35	20 49	19 36	18 13	16 9	15 29	12 20	8 40	6 40	4 53	2 40	29 42	25 37	23 8	18 56	16 1
16 16 26	6	1 43	1 18	0♓39	29 44	28 59	27 54	26 41	25 35	24 18	23 44	22 58	22 14	21 2	19 41	17 50	17 0	13 54	10 17	8 18	6 32	4 19	1♒21	27 15	24 44	20 28	17 30
16 20 40	7	2 51	2 27	1 49	0♓55	0♓12	29 9	27 59	26 55	25 40	25 7	24 23	23 39	22 29	21 11	19 22	18 33	15 31	11 57	9 59	8 13	6 1	3 4	28 56	26 23	22 5	19 2
16 24 55	8	3 59	3 36	3 0	2 8	1 26	0♓26	29 18	28 15	27 3	26 31	25 48	25 6	23 58	22 41	20 56	20 8	17 9	13 39	11 42	9 57	7 47	4 49	0♒41	28 7	23 45	20 39
16 29 10	9	5 8	4 45	4 10	3 21	2 41	1 43	0♓37	29 36	28 27	27 56	27 14	26 33	25 28	24 13	22 30	21 43	18 49	15 23	13 28	11 44	9 35	6 38	2 29	29 55	25 29	22 20
16 33 26	10	6 17	5 55	5 21	4 34	3 56	3 0	1 57	0♓58	29 51	29 22	28 41	28 2	26 58	25 46	24 7	23 21	20 31	17 9	15 16	13 34	11 26	8 31	4 22	1♒47	27 19	24 7
16 37 42	11	7 26	7 5	6 33	5 48	5 11	4 17	3 17	2 20	1♓17	0♓48	0♓ 9	29 32	28 30	27 21	25 44	25 0	22 14	18 58	17 7	15 26	13 21	10 27	6 20	3 44	29 14	25 58
16 41 59	12	8 35	8 15	7 45	7 2	6 26	5 35	4 38	3 44	2 43	2 15	1 38	1♓ 2	0♓ 3	28 56	27 23	26 40	24 0	20 49	19 1	17 20	15 19	12 28	8 22	5 46	1♒14	27 56
16 46 16	13	9 44	9 26	8 57	8 16	7 42	6 54	5 59	5 8	4 9	3 43	3 8	2 33	1 36	0♓33	29 4	28 22	25 48	22 43	20 58	19 18	17 20	14 32	10 29	7 54	3 21	0♒ 1
16 50 34	14	10 54	10 37	10 9	9 31	8 59	8 13	7 21	6 32	5 37	5 12	4 38	4 5	3 11	2 10	0♓45	0♓ 5	27 37	24 38	22 57	21 22	19 26	16 41	12 41	10 7	5 34	2 13
16 54 52	15	12 4	11 48	11 22	10 45	10 16	9 32	8 43	7 57	7 4	6 41	6 9	5 38	4 46	3 49	2 27	1 50	29 28	26 37	24 59	23 29	21 34	18 54	14 58	12 26	7 54	4 32
16 59 10	16	13 14	13 0	12 35	2 1	11 33	10 52	10 6	9 23	8 33	8 11	7 40	7 12	6 23	5 28	4 11	3 36	1♓21	28 38	27 4	25 36	23 47	21 11	17 22	14 52	10 22	7 0
17 3 29	17	14 25	14 11	13 48	13 16	12 50	12 12	11 29	10 49	10 2	9 42	9 13	8 46	8 0	7 9	5 56	5 23	3 16	0♓41	29 11	27 46	26 3	23 33	19 50	17 24	12 58	9 37
17 7 49	18	15 36	15 23	15 2	14 32	14 8	13 22	12 53	12 16	11 32	11 13	10 46	10 21	9 39	8 51	7 43	7 11	5 12	2 46	1♓21	0♓ 0	28 22	25 59	22 25	20 3	15 43	12 23
17 12 9	19	16 47	16 35	16 16	15 49	15 26	14 53	14 17	13 43	13 2	12 45	12 20	11 57	11 37	10 33	9 30	9 1	7 10	4 53	3 34	2 19	0♓45	28 30	25 5	22 48	18 36	15 21
17 16 29	20	17 59	17 48	17 30	17 5	16 45	16 15	15 42	15 10	14 34	14 17	13 54	13 33	12 57	12 16	11 18	10 52	9 10	7 3	5 49	4 40	3 12	1♓ 5	27 52	25 42	21 39	18 29
17 20 49	21	19 11	19 1	18 44	18 22	18 3	17 37	17 6	16 38	16 5	15 50	15 30	15 10	14 37	14 0	13 8	12 43	11 10	9 14	8 7	7 2	5 42	3 44	0♓44	28 42	24 52	21 49
17 25 9	22	20 23	20 14	19 58	19 39	19 22	18 59	18 32	18 6	17 36	17 23	17 5	16 47	16 19	15 44	14 57	14 36	13 13	11 28	10 27	9 26	8 15	6 27	3 42	1♓49	28 14	25 21
17 29 30	23	21 35	21 27	21 14	20 57	20 42	20 21	19 57	19 35	19 9	18 57	18 41	18 25	18 0	17 30	16 48	16 29	15 16	13 43	12 49	11 54	10 51	9 14	6 45	5 3	1♓46	29 6
17 33 51	24	22 46	22 40	22 29	22 14	22 2	21 43	21 23	21 3	20 41	20 31	20 18	20 4	19 42	19 16	18 41	18 24	17 20	16 0	15 13	14 24	13 30	12 5	9 54	8 23	5 27	3♓ 2
17 38 12	25	23 58	23 53	23 44	23 31	23 21	23 6	22 49	22 32	22 14	22 5	21 54	21 43	21 24	21 2	20 33	20 19	19 25	18 17	17 38	17 0	16 11	14 59	13 7	11 49	9 17	7 10
17 42 34	26	25 11	25 6	24 59	24 48	24 40	24 28	24 15	24 2	23 47	23 40	23 31	23 22	23 6	22 49	22 25	22 14	21 31	20 37	20 4	19 33	18 54	17 56	16 24	15 20	13 15	11 30
17 46 55	27	26 23	26 20	26 14	26 7	26 1	25 51	25 41	25 31	25 20	25 15	25 8	25 1	24 50	24 37	24 19	24 10	23 38	22 57	22 32	22 6	21 39	20 55	19 45	18 56	17 20	15 58
17 51 17	28	27 35	27 33	27 29	27 24	27 20	27 14	27 7	27 1	26 53	26 50	26 45	26 40	26 33	26 24	26 12	26 7	25 45	25 17	25 1	24 40	24 25	23 56	23 9	22 35	21 30	20 34
17 55 38	29	28 48	28 46	28 45	28 43	28 41	28 37	28 33	28 30	28 26	28 25	28 22	28 20	28 17	28 12	28 7	28 3	27 53	27 39	27 30	27 20	27 12	26 58	26 34	26 17	25 44	25 16
18 0 0	30	30 0	30 0	30 0	30 0	30 0	30 0	30 0	30 0	30 0	30 0	30 0	30 0	30 0	30 0	30 0	30 0	30 0	30 0	30 0	30 0	30 0	30 0	30 0	30 0	30 0	30 0

3 HOUSES FOR NORTHERN LATITUDES

A = Sidereal time
10 = Midheaven (10th House)
B = Ascendant

A	10	B 2° 0′	B 4° 0′	B 7° 0′	B 11° 0′	B 14° 0′	B 18° 0′	B 21° 59′	B 25° 19′	B 28° 40′	B 30° 2′	B 31° 46′	B 33° 20′	B 35° 39′	B 37° 58′	B 40° 43′	B 41° 54′	B 45° 30′	B 48° 50′	B 50° 22′	B 51° 32′	B 52° 57′	B 54° 34′	B 56° 28′	B 57° 29′	B 59° 00′	B 59° 56′
	°	° ′	° ′	° ′	° ′	° ′	° ′	° ′	° ′	° ′	° ′	° ′	° ′	° ′	° ′	° ′	° ′	° ′	° ′	° ′	° ′	° ′	° ′	° ′	° ′	° ′	° ′
18 0 0	0 ♑	0 ♈ 0	0 ♈ 0	0 ♈ 0	0 ♈ 0	0 ♈ 0	0 ♈ 0	0 ♈ 0	0 ♈ 0	0 ♈ 0	0 ♈ 0	0 ♈ 0	0 ♈ 0	0 ♈ 0	0 ♈ 0	0 ♈ 0	0 ♈ 0	0 ♈ 0	0 ♈ 0	0 ♈ 0	0 ♈ 0	0 ♈ 0	0 ♈ 0	0 ♈ 0	0 ♈ 0	0 ♈ 0	0 ♈ 0
18 4 22	1	1 12	1 14	1 15	1 17	1 19	1 23	1 27	1 30	1 34	1 35	1 38	1 40	1 43	1 48	1 53	1 57	2 7	2 21	2 30	2 39	2 48	3 2	3 36	3 43	4 16	4 44
18 8 43	2	2 25	2 27	2 31	2 36	2 40	2 46	2 53	2 59	3 7	3 10	3 15	3 20	3 27	3 36	3 48	3 53	4 15	4 43	4 59	5 19	5 35	6 4	6 51	7 25	8 30	9 26
18 13 5	3	3 37	3 40	3 46	3 53	3 59	4 9	4 19	4 29	4 40	4 45	4 52	4 59	5 10	5 23	5 41	5 50	6 22	7 3	7 28	7 55	8 21	9 5	10 15	11 4	12 40	14 2
18 17 26	4	4 49	4 54	5 1	5 12	5 20	5 32	5 45	5 58	6 13	6 20	6 29	6 38	6 54	7 11	7 35	7 46	8 29	9 23	9 56	10 29	11 6	12 4	13 36	14 40	16 45	18 30
18 21 48	5	6 2	6 7	6 16	6 29	6 39	6 54	7 11	7 28	7 46	7 55	8 6	8 17	8 36	8 58	9 27	9 41	10 35	11 43	12 22	13 2	13 49	15 1	16 53	18 11	20 43	22 50
18 26 9	6	7 14	7 20	7 31	7 46	7 56	8 17	8 37	8 57	9 19	9 29	9 42	9 56	10 18	10 44	11 19	11 36	12 40	14 0	14 47	15 36	16 30	17 55	20 6	21 37	24 33	26 58
18 30 30	7	8 25	8 33	8 46	9 3	9 18	9 39	10 3	10 25	10 51	11 3	11 19	11 35	12 0	12 30	13 12	13 31	14 44	16 17	17 11	18 6	19 9	20 46	23 15	24 57	28 14	0 ♉ 54
18 34 51	8	9 37	9 46	10 1	10 21	10 38	11 1	11 28	11 54	12 24	12 37	12 55	13 13	13 41	14 16	15 3	15 24	16 47	18 32	19 33	20 34	21 45	23 33	26 18	28 11	1 ♉ 46	4 39
18 39 11	9	10 49	10 59	11 16	11 38	11 57	12 23	12 54	13 22	13 55	14 10	14 30	14 50	15 23	16 0	16 52	17 17	18 50	20 46	21 53	22 59	24 18	26 16	29 16	1 ♉ 18	5 8	8 11
18 43 31	10	12 1	12 12	12 30	12 55	13 15	13 45	14 18	14 50	15 26	15 43	16 6	16 27	17 3	17 44	18 42	19 8	20 50	22 57	24 11	25 22	26 48	28 55	2 ♉ 8	4 18	8 21	11 31
18 47 51	11	13 13	13 25	13 44	14 11	14 34	15 7	15 43	16 17	16 58	17 15	17 40	18 3	18 43	19 27	20 30	20 59	22 50	25 7	26 26	27 42	29 15	1 ♉ 30	4 55	7 12	11 24	14 39
18 52 11	12	14 24	14 37	14 58	15 28	15 52	16 28	17 7	17 44	18 28	18 47	18 14	19 39	20 21	21 9	22 17	22 49	24 48	27 14	28 39	29 58	1 ♉ 38	4 1	7 35	9 57	14 17	17 37
18 56 31	13	15 35	15 49	16 12	16 44	17 10	17 48	18 31	19 11	19 58	20 18	20 47	21 14	22 0	22 51	24 4	24 37	26 44	29 19	0 ♉ 19	2 ♉ 13	3 57	6 27	10 10	12 36	17 2	20 23
19 0 50	14	16 46	17 0	17 25	17 59	18 27	19 8	19 54	20 37	21 27	21 49	22 20	22 48	23 37	24 32	25 49	26 24	28 39	1 ♉ 22	2 56	4 24	6 13	8 49	12 38	15 8	19 38	23 0
19 5 8	15	17 56	18 12	18 38	19 15	19 44	20 28	21 17	22 3	22 56	23 19	23 51	24 22	25 14	26 11	27 33	28 10	0 ♉ 32	3 23	5 1	6 30	8 26	11 6	15 2	17 34	22 6	25 28
19 9 26	16	19 6	19 23	19 51	20 29	21 1	21 47	22 39	23 28	24 23	24 48	25 22	25 55	26 49	27 50	29 15	29 55	2 23	5 22	7 3	8 36	10 34	13 19	17 19	19 53	24 26	27 48
19 13 44	17	20 16	20 34	21 3	21 44	22 18	23 6	24 1	24 52	25 51	26 17	26 52	27 27	28 24	29 27	0 ♉ 56	1 ♉ 38	4 12	7 17	9 2	10 40	12 40	15 28	19 31	22 6	26 39	29 59
19 18 1	18	21 25	21 45	22 15	22 58	23 34	24 25	25 22	26 16	27 17	27 45	28 22	28 58	29 57	1 ♉ 4	2 37	3 20	6 0	9 11	10 59	12 39	14 41	17 32	21 38	24 14	28 46	2 ♊ 4
19 22 18	29	22 34	22 55	23 27	24 12	24 49	25 43	26 43	27 39	28 43	29 12	29 51	0 ♉ 28	1 ♉ 30	2 39	4 16	5 0	7 46	11 2	12 53	14 35	16 39	19 33	23 40	26 16	0 ♊ 46	4 2
19 26 34	20	23 43	24 5	24 39	25 26	26 4	27 0	28 3	29 2	0 ♉ 9	0 ♉ 38	1 ♉ 19	1 58	3 2	4 14	5 53	6 39	9 29	12 51	14 44	16 28	18 34	21 29	25 38	28 13	2 41	5 53
19 30 50	21	24 52	25 15	25 50	26 39	27 19	28 17	29 23	0 ♉ 24	1 33	2 4	2 46	3 27	4 32	5 47	7 30	8 17	11 11	14 37	16 32	18 17	20 25	23 22	27 31	0 ♊ 5	4 31	7 40
19 35 5	22	26 1	26 24	27 0	27 52	28 34	29 34	0 ♉ 42	1 45	2 57	3 29	4 12	4 54	6 2	7 19	9 4	9 52	12 51	16 21	18 18	20 3	22 13	25 11	29 19	1 53	6 15	9 21
19 39 20	23	27 9	27 33	28 11	29 5	29 48	0 ♉ 51	2 1	3 5	4 20	4 53	5 37	6 21	7 31	8 49	10 38	11 27	14 29	18 3	20 1	21 48	23 59	26 56	1 ♊ 4	3 37	7 55	10 58
19 43 34	24	28 17	28 42	29 21	0 ♉ 16	1 ♉ 1	2 6	3 19	4 25	5 42	6 16	7 2	7 46	8 58	10 19	12 10	13 0	16 6	19 43	21 42	23 29	25 41	28 39	3 45	5 16	9 32	12 30
19 47 47	25	29 25	29 51	0 ♉ 31	1 28	2 15	3 21	4 36	5 45	7 4	7 38	8 25	9 11	10 24	11 47	13 41	14 31	17 40	21 20	23 20	25 9	27 20	0 ♊ 18	4 23	6 52	11 4	13 59
19 52 0	26	0 ♉ 32	0 ♉ 58	1 40	2 39	3 27	4 35	5 53	7 3	8 24	8 59	9 47	10 34	11 50	13 14	15 10	16 1	19 13	22 55	24 56	26 45	28 56	1 53	5 57	8 24	12 32	15 24
19 56 12	27	1 38	2 5	2 49	3 49	4 38	5 49	7 9	8 21	9 43	10 20	11 9	11 56	13 14	14 40	16 37	17 30	20 44	24 28	26 29	28 18	0 ♊ 30	3 26	7 28	9 54	13 57	16 45
20 0 24	28	2 44	3 12	3 57	5 0	5 50	7 2	8 24	9 38	11 2	11 40	12 30	13 18	14 37	16 4	18 4	18 57	22 13	25 59	28 0	29 49	2 1	4 57	8 56	11 20	15 19	18 4
20 4 35	29	3 50	4 19	5 5	6 10	7 1	8 15	9 38	10 54	12 20	12 58	13 50	14 39	15 59	17 28	19 29	20 23	23 41	27 27	29 29	1 ♊ 19	3 29	6 24	10 21	12 43	16 38	19 19
20 8 45	30	4 56	5 26	6 12	7 18	8 11	9 27	10 52	12 10	13 38	14 16	15 9	15 59	17 20	18 50	20 52	21 47	25 7	28 54	0 ♊ 56	2 45	4 56	7 49	11 43	14 3	17 54	20 32
20 8 45	0 ♒	4 ♉ 56	5 ♉ 26	6 ♉ 12	7 ♉ 18	8 ♉ 11	9 ♉ 27	10 ♉ 52	12 ♉ 10	13 ♉ 38	14 ♉ 16	15 ♉ 9	15 ♉ 59	17 ♉ 20	18 ♉ 50	20 ♉ 52	21 ♉ 47	25 ♉ 7	28 ♉ 54	0 ♊ 56	2 ♊ 45	4 ♊ 56	7 ♊ 49	11 ♊ 43	14 ♊ 3	17 ♊ 54	20 32
20 12 54	1	6 1	6 32	7 20	8 28	9 22	10 39	12 5	13 24	14 54	15 33	16 27	17 17	18 40	20 11	22 14	23 10	26 32	0 ♊ 19	2 21	4 9	6 20	9 12	13 3	15 21	19 8	21 43
20 17 3	2	7 6	7 38	8 27	9 35	10 31	11 50	13 18	14 39	16 10	16 50	17 44	18 35	19 59	21 31	23 35	24 32	27 54	1 42	3 45	5 32	7 41	10 32	14 21	16 37	20 20	22 52
20 21 11	3	8 11	8 43	9 33	10 43	11 39	13 1	14 30	15 52	17 24	18 5	19 0	19 52	21 16	22 49	24 55	25 52	29 15	3 4	5 6	6 53	9 1	11 51	15 36	17 50	21 29	23 58
20 25 19	4	9 15	9 47	10 38	11 50	12 48	14 11	15 41	17 5	18 38	19 20	20 15	21 8	22 33	24 7	26 14	27 11	0 ♊ 35	4 23	6 25	8 12	10 19	13 7	16 50	19 2	22 37	25 2
20 29 26	5	10 18	10 51	11 43	12 56	13 55	15 19	16 51	18 16	19 52	20 33	21 29	22 23	23 49	25 24	27 32	28 29	1 53	5 41	7 42	9 27	11 35	14 21	18 1	20 11	23 42	26 5
20 33 31	6	11 22	11 55	12 48	14 3	15 2	16 28	18 1	19 28	21 4	21 46	22 43	23 37	25 3	26 39	28 46	29 45	3 10	6 58	8 58	10 43	12 49	15 33	19 11	21 18	24 46	27 6
20 37 37	7	12 24	12 59	13 53	15 9	16 9	17 36	19 11	20 38	22 16	22 58	23 56	24 51	26 17	27 54	0 ♊ 3	1 ♊ 0	4 26	8 13	10 12	11 58	14 2	16 44	20 18	22 24	25 48	28 5
20 41 41	8	13 27	14 2	14 57	16 14	17 15	18 43	20 20	21 48	23 27	24 9	25 7	26 3	27 30	29 7	1 17	2 14	5 39	9 26	11 25	13 9	15 12	17 53	21 24	23 28	26 49	29 3
20 45 45	9	14 29	15 5	16 1	17 20	18 21	19 50	21 28	22 57	24 37	25 20	26 18	27 14	28 42	0 ♊ 19	2 29	3 27	6 52	10 38	12 36	14 18	16 22	19 1	22 29	24 31	27 48	0 ♋ 0
20 49 48	10	15 31	16 7	17 4	18 23	19 26	20 57	22 36	24 5	25 46	26 30	27 29	28 24	29 53	1 31	3 41	4 39	8 4	11 49	13 46	15 25	17 30	20 7	23 32	25 32	28 45	0 55
20 53 51	11	16 32	17 9	18 7	19 27	20 31	22 3	23 43	25 13	26 54	27 38	28 38	29 33	1 ♊ 4	2 42	4 51	5 49	9 14	12 58	14 55	16 32	18 36	21 11	24 34	26 32	29 42	1 49
20 57 52	12	17 33	18 10	19 9	20 30	21 35	23 8	24 49	26 20	28 2	28 46	29 46	0 ♊ 42	2 12	3 51	6 1	6 59	10 23	14 6	16 2	17 39	19 41	22 14	25 35	27 30	0 ♋ 37	2 42
21 1 53	13	18 33	19 10	20 10	21 33	22 38	24 12	25 54	27 26	29 9	29 54	0 ♊ 54	1 50	3 21	4 59	7 9	8 7	11 31	15 13	17 8	18 44	20 45	23 16	26 33	28 28	1 31	3 33
21 5 53	14	19 33	20 11	21 12	22 35	23 42	25 16	26 59	28 32	0 ♊ 15	1 ♊ 0	2 1	2 57	4 28	6 7	8 16	9 15	12 38	16 18	18 12	19 48	21 47	24 17	27 31	29 34	2 24	4 24
21 9 53	15	20 33	21 12	22 13	23 37	24 45	26 20	28 4	29 37	1 21	2 6	3 7	4 3	5 35	7 13	9 23	10 21	13 43	17 23	19 16	20 51	22 49	25 17	28 28	0 ♋ 19	3 16	5 14
21 13 52	16	21 32	22 12	23 13	24 39	25 47	27 23	29 8	0 ♊ 42	2 26	3 11	4 13	5 9	6 41	8 19	10 30	11 27	14 48	18 26	20 18	21 53	23 49	26 15	29 24	1 12	4 7	6 3
21 17 50	17	22 31	23 11	24 13	25 40	26 48	28 25	0 ♊ 11	1 45	3 31	4 16	5 17	6 14	7 45	9 24	11 33	12 31	15 52	19 29	21 20	22 53	24 48	27 12	0 ♋ 19	2 6	4 58	6 51
21 21 47	18	23 30	24 10	25 13	26 41	27 49	29 27	1 14	2 49	4 34	5 20	6 21	7 18	8 50	10 28	12 37	13 35	16 55	20 30	22 20	23 52	25 46	28 9	1 12	2 58	5 47	7 39
21 25 44	19	24 29	25 9	26 13	27 41	28 50	0 ♊ 29	2 16	3 51	5 37	6 23	7 25	8 21	9 53	11 31	13 41	14 38	17 57	21 30	23 19	24 51	26 43	29 4	2 5	3 49	6 35	8 25
21 29 40	20	25 27	26 8	27 12	28 41	29 51	1 30	3 17	4 53	6 39	7 25	8 27	9 24	10 56	12 34	14 43	15 40	18 58	22 30	24 18	25 48	27 40	29 59	2 57	4 40	7 23	9 11
21 33 35	21	26 25	27 6	28 11	29 40	0 ♊ 51	2 30	4 18	5 55	7 41	8 27	9 29	10 26	11 57	13 36	15 44	16 41	19 58	23 28	25 15	26 44	28 35	0 ♋ 52	3 48	5 30	8 10	9 56
21 37 29	22	27 22	28 4	29 9	0 ♊ 39	1 50	3 30	5 19	6 56	8 42	9 28	10 30	11 27	12 59	14 37	16 45	17 41	20 57	24 26	26 12	27 40	29 29	1 45	4 39	6 18	8 56	10 41
21 41 23	23	28 19	29 1	0 ♊ 7	1 38	2 49	4 30	6 19	7 56	9 43	10 29	11 30	12 27	13 59	15 37	17 45	18 41	21 56	25 23	27 8	28 34	0 ♋ 23	2 37	5 28	7 6	9 42	11 25
21 45 16	24	29 15	29 58	1 4	2 36	3 48	5 29	7 18	8 56	10 43	11 29	12 30	13 27	14 59	16 37	18 44	19 40	22 53	26 19	28 3	29 29	1 16	3 29	6 17	7 54	10 27	12 8
21 49 9	25	0 ♊ 12	0 ♊ 55	2 1	3 33	4 46	6 28	8 17	9 55	11 42	12 28	13 30	14 27	15 58	17 36	19 42	20 38	23 50	28 14	28 51	0 ♋ 22	2 8	4 19	7 5	8 41	11 12	12 51
21 53 1	26	1 8	1 51	2 58	4 31	5 43	7 26	9 16	10 54	12 41	13 27	14 29	15 26	16 56	18 34	20 40	21 36	24 46	28 9	29 51	1 15	3 0	5 0	7 53	9 27	11 56	13 33
21 56 52	27	2 4	2 47	3 55	5 28	6 40	8 24	10 14	11 52	13 40	14 26	15 27	16 24	17 54	19 31	21 37	22 33	25 42	29 3	0 ♋ 44	2 7	3 50	5 58	8 40	10 13	12 39	14 15
22 0 43	28	3 0	3 43	4 51	6 25	7 37	9 21	11 12	12 50	14 37	15 23	16 25	17 22	18 52	20 28	23 33	23 29	26 37	29 56	1 36	2 57	4 41	6 46	9 26	10 58	13 22	14 56
22 4 33	29	3 55	4 38	5 47	7 21	8 34	10 18	12 9	13 47	15 35	16 21	17 22	18 19	19 49	21 25	23 30	24 24	27 32	0 ♋ 48	2 27	3 48	5 30	7 34	10 12	11 42	14 4	15 37
22 8 23	30	4 50	5 34	6 43	8 17	9 31	11 15	13 6	14 44	16 32	17 17	18 19	19 15	20 45	22 21	24 25	25 19	28 25	1 40	3 18	4 38	6 19	8 22	10 57	12 26	14 46	16 18
22 8 23	0 ♓	4 ♊ 50	5 ♊ 34	6 ♊ 43	8 ♊ 17	9 ♊ 31	11 ♊ 15	13 ♊ 6	14 ♊ 44	16 ♊ 32	17 ♊ 17	18 ♊ 19	19 ♊ 15	20 ♊ 45	22 ♊ 21	24 ♊ 25	25 ♊ 19	28 ♊ 25	1 ♊ 40	3 ♋ 18	4 ♋ 38	6 ♋ 19	8 ♋ 22	10 ♋ 57	12 ♋ 26	14 ♋ 46	16 ♋ 18
22 12 12	1	5 44	6 29	7 38	9 13	10 27	12 11	14 2	15 40	17 28	18 14	19 15	20 11	21 41	23 16	25 19	26 14	29 18	2 32	4 9	2 28	7 7	9 9	11 42	13 10	15 27	16 58
22 16 0	2	6 38	7 23	8 32	10 8	11 22	13 7	14 58	16 36	18 24	19 10	20 11	21 7	22 36	24 11	26 14	27 8	0 ♋ 11	3 22	4 59	6 17	7 55	9 55	12 26	13 53	16 8	17 37
22 19 48	3	7 32	8 17	9 27	11 3	12 17	14 2	15 54	17 32	19 19	20 5	21 6	22 2	23 30	25 5	27 8	28 1	1 3	4 13	5 48	7 5	8 42	10 41	13 10	14 35	16 49	18 17
22 23 35	4	8 26	9 11	10 22	11 58	13 12	14 57	16 49	18 27	20 14	21 0	22 1	22 57	24 25	25 59	28 0	28 54	1 54	5 2	6 37	7 53	9 29	11 26	13 54	15 17	17 29	18 56
22 27 22	5	9 19	10 5	11 15	12 52	14 7	15 52	17 44	19 22	21 9	21 54	22 55	23 51	25 19	26 53	28 53	29 46	2 45	5 52	7 25	8 42	10 16	12 11	14 37	15 59	18 9	19 34
22 31 8	6	10 13	10 59	12 9	13 46	15 1	16 46	18 38	20 16	22 3	22 49	23 49	24 45	26 12	27 46	29 46	0 ♋ 38	3 36	6 40	8 13	9 29	11 1	12 55	15 19	16 41	18 49	20 13
22 34 54	7	11 6	11 52	13 3	14 39	15 55	17 40	19 32	21 10	22 57	23 42	24 42	25 38	27 5	28 38	0 ♋ 37	1 29	4 26	7 29	9 0	10 16	11 47	13 39	16 1	17 22	19 28	20 51
22 38 40	8	11 59	12 45	13 57	15 34	16 49	18 34	20 26	22 4	23 50	24 36	25 36	26 31	27 58	29 30	1 28	2 20	5 15	8 16	9 47	11 2	12 32	14 23	16 43	18 3	20 7	21 28
22 42 25	9	12 52	13 38	14 50	16 27	17 42	19 28	21 19	22 57	24 43	25 29	26 28	27 24	28 50	0 ♋ 22	2 20	3 11	6 4	9 4	10 33	11 47	13 16	15 6	17 25	18 43	20 46	22 6
22 46 9	10	13 44	14 31	15 42	17 20	18 35	20 21	22 13	23 50	25 36	26 21	27 21	28 16	29 42	1 13	3 39	4 1	6 53	9 51	11 19	12 31	14 1	15 47	18 6	19 23	21 24	22 43
22 49 53	11	14 37	15 24	16 35	18 13	19 28	21 14	23 6	24 43	26 28	27 13	28 12	29 8	0 ♋ 34	2 4	3 59	4 50	7 41	10 37	12 5	13 16	14 44	16 32	18 46	20 3	22 2	23 20
22 53 37	12	15 29	16 16	17 27	19 5	20 21	22 7	23 59	25 36	27 21	28 5	29 4	29 59	1 25	2 55	4 49	5 40	8 29	11 23	12 50	14 1	15 28	17 14	19 27	20 42	22 40	23 57
22 57 20	13	16 21	17 8	18 20	19 58	21 14	22 59	24 50	26 28	28 12	28 57	29 55	0 ♋ 50	2 15	3 44	5 38	6 29	9 17	12 10	13 35	14 45	16 11	17 56	20 7	21 21	23 18	24 33
23 1 3	14	17 13	18 0	19 12	20 50	22 6	23 51	25 42	27 19	29 4	29 48	0 ♋ 46	1 41	3 6	4 35	6 27	7 17	10 4	12 55	14 20	15 28	16 54	18 37	20 47	22 0	23 55	25 10
23 4 46	15	18 4	18 51	20 4	21 42	22 58	24 43	26 34	28 11	29 55	0 ♋ 39	1 37	2 31	3 56	5 24	7 17	8 6	10 51	13 40	15 4	16 11	17 37	19 19	21 27	22 39	24 32	25 46
23 8 28	16	18 56	19 43	20 56	22 34	23 50	25 35	27 26	29 2	0 ♋ 46	1 30	2 28	3 21	4 45	6 13	8 3	8 54	11 38	14 25	15 48	16 54	18 19	20 0	22 6	23 18	25 9	26 22
23 12 10	17	19 47	20 34	21 47	23 25	24 41	26 26	28 17	29 53	1 37	2 20	3 18	4 11	5 34	7 2	8 52	9 41	12 23	15 10	16 32	17 37	19 1	20 41	22 45	23 56	25 46	26 58
23 15 52	18	20 39	21 26	22 39	24 17	25 33	27 18	29 8	0 ♋ 44	2 27	3 11	4 8	5 1	6 23	7 50	9 40	10 29	13 9	15 54	17 15	18 20	19 43	21 21	23 24	24 34	26 23	27 33
23 19 34	19	21 30	22 17	23 30	25 8	26 25	28 10	29 59	1 35	3 18	4 1	4 58	5 50	7 12	8 39	10 28	11 16	13 55	16 38	17 59	19 3	20 24	22 1	24 3	25 12	26 59	28 9
23 23 15	20	22 21	23 9	24 22	26 0	27 16	29 2	0 ♋ 50	2 25	4 8	4 50	5 47	6 39	8 1	9 27	11 15	12 3	14 41	17 22	18 42	19 45	21 5	22 41	24 42	25 49	27 35	28 44
23 26 56	21	23 12	24 0	25 13	26 51	28 7	29 52	1 40	3 15	4 57	5 40	6 36	7 28	8 50	10 14	12 2	12 49	15 25	18 5	19 24	20 26	22 47	23 21	25 20	26 27	28 11	29 19
23 30 37	22	24 3	24 51	26 4	27 41	28 57	0 ♋ 42	2 31	4 5	5 47	6 29	7 25	8 17	9 38	11 2	12 49	13 36	16 10	18 49	20 7	21 8	22 27	24 1	25 58	27 4	28 47	29 54
23 34 18	23	24 54	25 42	26 55	28 32	29 48	1 33	3 20	4 55	6 36	7 18	8 14	9 6	10 36	11 49	13 37	14 22	16 55	19 32	20 49	21 50	23 8	24 41	26 36	27 42	29 23	0 ♌ 29
23 37 58	24	25 45	26 33	27 45	29 23	0 ♋ 39	2 23	4 11	5 45	7 25	8 7	9 3	9 54	11 13	12 36	14 22	15 8	17 40	20 15	21 31	22 31	23 48	25 20	27 14	28 19	29 59	1 4
23 41 39	25	26 35	27 23	28 36	0 ♋ 14	1 29	3 13	5 1	6 34	8 14	8 56	9 51	10 42	12 1	13 23	15 8	15 53	18 24	20 57	22 13	23 12	24 29	25 59	27 52	28 56	0 ♌ 35	1 39
23 45 19	26	27 26	28 14	29 26	1 4	2 20	4 3	5 50	7 24	9 3	9 45	10 39	11 30	12 48	14 10	15 53	16 39	19 8	21 40	22 55	23 53	25 9	26 38	28 30	29 32	1 10	2 13
23 49 0	27	28 16	29 4	0 ♋ 17	1 55	3 10	4 53	6 40	8 13	9 51	10 33	11 28	12 18	13 35	14 57	16 41	17 24	19 52	22 22	23 36	24 32	25 48	27 17	29 7	0 ♌ 9	1 45	2 48
23 52 40	28	29 7	29 55	1 7	2 45	4 0	5 43	7 29	9 2	10 40	11 21	12 16	13 6	14 22	15 43	17 23	18 9	20 36	23 5	24 17	25 15	26 29	27 56	29 45	0 46	2 21	3 22
23 56 20	29	29 57	0 ♋ 45	1 58	3 35	4 50	6 33	8 19	9 51	11 28	12 9	13 3	13 53	15 9	16 29	18 8	18 54	21 20	23 47	24 59	25 56	27 8	28 35	0 ♌ 22	1 22	2 56	3 57
24 0 0	30	0 ♋ 48	1 36	2 48	4 25	5 40	7 22	9 8	10 40	12 16	12 57	13 50	14 40	15 56	17 15	18 53	19 39	22 3	24 28	25 40	26 36	27 48	29 13	0 59	1 58	3 31	4 31

	1910	1911	1912	1913	1914	1915	1916	1917	1918	1919	1920	1921	1922	1923	1924	1925	1926	1927	1928
1	1♊6	1♉16	1♈27	1♈8	1♓18	1♒29	1♒10	1♑20	1♑1	1♐12	1♏22	1♏3	1♎14	1♍24	1♍5	1♌16	1♋26	1♋7	1♊18
	6 5	19 15	12 26	5 7	18 17	12 28	6 9	17 19	11♑0	5 11	18 21	10 2	4 13	17 23	11 4	3 15	16 25	10 6	4 17
	25 4		31 25	24 6		31 27	24 8		30♐29	24 10		29 1	23 12		29 3	22 14		29 5	23 16
2	1♊4	1♉15	1♈25	1♈6	1♓17	1♒27	1♒8	1♑19	1♐29	1♐10	1♏21	1♏1	1♎12	1♍23	1♍3	1♌14	1♋25	1♋5	1♊16
	13 3	7 14	19 24	12 5	6 16	19 26	12 7	5 18	18 28	12 9	5 20	17 0	11 11	5 22	17 2	10 13	4 24	17 4	11 15
		25 13			25 15			24 17			24 19			24 21			23 23		29 14
3	1♊3	1♉13	1♈24	1♈5	1♓15	1♒26	1♒7	1♐28	1♑17	1♐9	1♏19	1♏0	1♎11	1♍21	1♍2	1♌12	1♋23	1♋4	1♊14
	4 2	16 12	9 23	3 4	16 14	9 25	2 6	15 16	9 27	3 8	14 18	8♎29	2 10	15 20	7 1	20 11	14 22	8 3	19 13
	22 1		28 22	22 3		28 24	21 5		28 26	21 7		27 28	21 9		26 0			26 2	
4	1♊1	1♉12	1♈22	1♈3	1♓14	1♒24	1♒5	1♑16	1♐26	1♐7	1♏18	1♎28	1♎9	1♍20	1♍0	1♌11	1♋22	1♋2	1♊13
	10♊0	4 11	16 21	10 2	3 13	16 23	9 4	3 15	15 25	9 6	2 17	15 27	9 8	2 19	14♌29	8 10	2 21	14 1	7 12
	29♉29	23 10		29 1	22 12		28 3	22 14		28 5	21 16		27 7	21 18		27 9	21 20		26 11
5	1♉29	1♉10	1♈21	1♈1	1♓12	1♒23	1♒3	1♑14	1♐25	1♐5	1♏16	1♎27	1♎7	1♍18	1♌28	1♌9	1♋20	1♋1	1♊11
	18 28	10 9	5 20	17 0	11 11	5 22	17 2	11 13	4 24	17 4	10 15	4 26	16 6	10 17	22 27	16 8	9 19	3♋0	15 10
		31 8	24 19		30 10	24 21		29 12	23 23		29 14	23 25		29 16			28 18	22♊29	
6	1♉28	1♉8	1♈19	1♈0	1♓10	1♒21	1♒2	1♑12	1♐23	1♐4	1♏14	1♎25	1♎6	1♍16	1♌27	1♌8	1♋18	1♊29	1♊10
	6 27	19 7	11 18	5♓29	18 9	12 20	5 1	17 11	11 22	5 3	17 13	10 24	4 5	17 15	10 26	3 7	16 17	10 28	3 9
	25 26		30 17	24 28			23 0		30 21	24 2		29 23	23 4		28 25	22 6		29 27	22 8
7	1♉26	1♉7	1♈17	1♓28	1♓9	1♒19	1♒0	1♑11	1♐21	1♐2	1♏13	1♎23	1♎4	1♍15	1♌25	1♌6	1♋17	1♊27	1♊8
	14 25	8 6	19 16	13 27	7 8	20 18	12♑29	6 10	19 20	13 1	5 12	18 22	12 3	6 14	17 24	11 5	5 16	18 26	11 7
		26 5			26 7		31 28	25 9			24 11		31 21	25 13		30 4	24 15		29 6
8	1♉25	1♉5	1♈16	1♓26	1♓7	1♒18	1♑28	1♑9	1♐20	1♐0	1♏11	1♎22	1♎2	1♍13	1♌24	1♌4	1♋15	1♊26	1♊6
	2 24	14 4	7 15	20 25	14 6	7 17	19 27	13 8	7 19	19♏29	12 10	6 21	19 1	13 12	5 23	18 3	12 14	6 25	17 5
	21 23		26 14			26 16			26 18		31 9	25 20		31 11	24 22		31 13	25 24	
9	1♉23	1♉4	1♈14	1♓25	1♓6	1♒16	1♑27	1♑7	1♐18	1♏29	1♏9	1♎20	1♎1	1♍11	1♌22	1♌3	1♋13	1♊24	1♊5
	8 22	2 3	14 13	8 24	2 5	14 15	7 26	20 6	13 17	7 28	19 8	13 19	7 0	19 10	12 21	6 2	19 12	12 23	5 4
	27 21	21 2		27 23	20 4		26 25			26 27			25♍29			25 1			24 3
10	1♉21	1♉2	1♈13	1♓23	1♓4	1♒15	1♑25	1♑6	1♐17	1♏27	1♏8	1♎19	1♍29	1♍10	1♌20	1♌1	1♋12	1♊22	1♊3
	17 20	10 1	3 12	15 22	9 3	2 14	15 24	9 5	2 16	15 26	8 7	2 18	14 28	8 9	20 19	14 0	7 11	20 21	13 2
		29 0	22 11		28 2	22 13		27 4	21 15		27 6	21 17		27 8			26 10		
11	1♉20	1♉0	1♈11	1♓22	1♓2	1♒13	1♑24	1♑4	1♐15	1♏26	1♏6	1♎17	1♍28	1♍8	1♌19	1♌0	1♋10	1♊21	1♊1
	4 19	17♈29	10 10	3 21	16 1	10 12	3 23	15 3	9 14	3 25	15 5	9 16	2 27	15 7	8 18	2♋29	14 9	8 20	20 0
	23 18		28 9	22 20		29 11	22 22		28 13	22 24		27 15	21 26		27 17	20 28		26 19	
12	1♉18	1♈9	1♈9	1♓20	1♓1	1♒11	1♑22	1♑3	1♐13	1♏24	1♏5	1♎15	1♍26	1♍7	1♌17	1♋28	1♋9	1♊19	1♊0
	12 17	6 28	17 8	11 19	5 0	18 10	10 21	4 2	17 12	11 23	4 4	16 14	10 25	4 6	16 16	9 27	3 8	16 18	9♉29
	31 16	25 27		30 18	24♒29		29 20	23 1		30 22	22 3		29 24	23 5		28 26	22 7		27 28

	1929	1930	1931	1932	1933	1934	1935	1936	1937	1938	1939	1940	1941	1942	1943	1944	1945	1946	1947
1	1♉28	1♉9	1♈20	1♈0	1♓11	1♒22	1♒2	1♑13	1♐24	1♐4	1♏15	1♎26	1♎6	1♍17	1♌27	1♌8	1♋19	1♊29	1♊10
	15 27	9 8	3 19	16♓29	9 10	2 21	15 1	9 12	2 23	14 3	8 14	2 25	14 5	7 16	20 26	14 7	7 18	19 28	13 9
		28 7	22 18		27 9	21 20		28 11	11 22		27 13	21 24		26 15			26 17		
2	1♉27	1♉7	1♈18	1♓29	1♓9	1♒20	1♒1	1♑11	1♐22	1♐3	1♏13	1♎24	1♎4	1♍15	1♌26	1♌7	1♋17	1♊28	1♊8
	3 26	16 6	10 17	4 28	15 8	9 19	3 0	16 10	8 21	2 2	15 12	9 23	20 3	14 14	8 25	2 6	13 16	7 27	20 7
	22 25			22 27		28 18	22♑29		27 20	21 1		27 22			27 24	21 5		26 26	
3	1♉25	1♉6	1♈16	1♓27	1♓8	1♒18	1♑29	1♐10	1♐20	1♐1	1♏12	1♎22	1♎3	1♍14	1♌24	1♌5	1♋16	1♊26	1♊7
	13 24	7 5	20 15	12 26	6 7	19 17	13 28	5 9	18 19	12♐0	6 11	17 21	11 2	5 13	18 23	11 4	4 15	17 25	11 6
		26 4		31 25	25 6		31 27	24 8		31♏29	25 10		30 1	24 12		29 3	23 14		30 5
4	1♉23	1♉4	1♈15	1♓25	1♓6	1♒17	1♑27	1♑8	1♐19	1♏29	1♏10	1♎21	1♎1	1♍12	1♌23	1♌3	1♋14	1♊15	1♊5
	20 22	14 3	7 14	19 24	13 5	7 16	19 26	12 7	6 18	19 28	13 9	5 20	18 0	12 11	6 22	17 2	11 13	5 24	18 4
			26 13			26 15			24 17			24 19			25 21		30 12	24 23	
5	1♉22	1♉3	1♈13	1♓24	1♓5	1♒15	1♑26	1♑6	1♐17	1♏28	1♏8	1♎19	1♎0	1♍10	1♌21	1♌2	1♋12	1♊23	1♊4
	28 21	3 2	15 12	8 23	2 4	15 14	8 25	20 5	14 16	8 27	19 7	13 18	7♍29	20 9	13 20	6 1	19 11	13 22	6 3
		21 1		27 22	21 3		27 24			26 26			26 28			25 0			25 2
6	1♉20	1♉1	1♈12	1♓22	1♓3	1♒14	1♑24	1♑5	1♐16	1♏26	1♏7	1♎17	1♍28	1♍9	1♌19	1♌0	1♋11	1♊21	1♊2
	15 19	9♉0	3 11	15 21	9 2	2 13	15 23	8 4	2 15	14 25	8 6	20 16	14 27	7 8	20 18	13♋29	7 10	19 20	13 1
		28♈29	22 10		27 1	21 12		27 3	21 14		27 5			26 7			26 9		
7	1♉19	1♈29	1♈10	1♓21	1♓1	1♒12	1♑23	1♑3	1♐14	1♏25	1♏5	1♎16	1♍27	1♍7	1♌18	1♋29	1♋9	1♊20	1♊1
	4 18	17 28	11 9	4 20	16 0	10 11	4 22	16 2	9 13	4 24	16 4	9 15	3 26	15 6	9 17	2 28	15 8	8 19	21♉29
	23 17		30 8	23 19		29 10	23 21		28 12	22 23		28 14	21 25		28 16	21 27		27 18	
8	1♉17	1♈28	1♈8	1♓19	1♓0	1♒10	1♑21	1♑2	1♐12	1♏23	1♏4	1♎14	1♍25	1♍6	1♌16	1♋27	1♋8	1♊18	1♉29
	11 16	5 27	18 7	11 18	4♒29	17 9	11 20	3 1	16 11	10 22	4 3	15 13	9 24	3 5	16 15	9 26	2 7	15 17	9 28
	30 15	24 26		29 17	23 28		30 19	22 0		29 21	23 2		28 23	22 4		27 25	21 6		28 27
9	1♉15	1♈26	1♈7	1♓17	1♒28	1♒9	1♑19	1♑0	1♐11	1♏21	1♏2	1♎13	1♍23	1♍4	1♌15	1♋25	1♋6	1♊17	1♉27
	18 14	12 25	5 6	17 16	11 27	5 8	17 18	10♐29	4 10	17 20	11 1	3 12	16 22	10 3	4 14	15 24	9 5	3 16	16 26
			24 5		30 26	24 7		29 28	23 9		29 0	22 11		29 2	23 13		28 4	22 15	
10	1♉14	1♈24	1♈5	1♓16	1♒26	1♒7	1♑18	1♐28	1♐9	1♏20	1♏0	1♎11	1♍22	1♍2	1♌13	1♋24	1♋4	1♊15	1♉26
	7 13	19 23	13 4	6 15	19 25	13 6	6 17	18 27	12 8	6 19	18♎29	11 10	24 21	18 1	11 12	4 23	17 3	11 14	5 25
	26 12			25 14		31 5	25 16		31 7	25 18		30 9			30 11	23 22		30 13	23 24
11	1♉12	1♈23	1♈3	1♓14	1♒25	1♒5	1♑16	1♐27	1♐7	1♏18	1♎29	1♎9	1♍20	1♍1	1♌11	1♋22	1♋3	1♊13	1♉24
	14 11	7 22	20 2	13 13	7 24	19 4	13 15	6 26	19 6	12 17	6 28	18 8	12 19	5 0	18 10	11 21	5 2	17 12	11 23
		26 21			25 23			25 25			25 27			24♌29		30 20	24 1		30 22
12	1♉11	1♈21	1♈2	1♓13	1♒23	1♒4	1♑15	1♐25	1♐6	1♏16	1♎27	1♎8	1♍18	1♌29	1♌10	1♋20	1♋1	1♓12	1♉22
	2 10	15 20	9 1	3 12	14 22	8 3	2 14	14 24	7 5	20 15	14 26	7 7	19 17	13 28	7 9	19 19	13 0	6 11	19 21
	21 9		28 0	21 11		27 2	21 13		26 4			26 6			26 8		31♊29	25 10	

	1948	1949	1950	1951	1952	1953	1954	1955	1956	1957
1	1♉21 7 20 26 19	1♉1 19 0	1♈12 12 11 31 10	1♓23 6 22 25 21	1♓3 19 2	1♒14 12 13 31 12	1♑25 6 24 24 23	1♑5 18 4	1♐16 12 15 31 14	1♏27 5 26 24 25
2	1♉19 14 18	1♉0 7♈29 25 28	1♈10 19 9	1♓21 13 20	1♓2 7 1 26 0	1♒12 19 11	1♑23 12 22	1♑4 6 3 25 2	1♐14 19 13	1♏25 12 24
3	1♉18 4 17 23 16	1♈28 16 27	1♈9 10 8 29 7	1♓20 4 19 23 18	1♓0 16♒29	1♒11 9 10 28 9	1♑22 3 21 22 20	1♑2 16 1	1♐13 9 12 28 11	1♏24 3 23 21 22
4	1♉16 10 15 29 14	1♈27 4 26 23 25	1♈7 17 6	1♓18 11 17 30 16	1♒29 3 28 22 27	1♒9 16 8	1♑20 10 19 29 18	1♑1 4 0 23♐29	1♐11 15 10	1♏22 9 21 28 20
5	1♉14 18 13	1♈25 12 24 31 23	1♈6 6 5 25 4	1♓16 18 15	1♒27 11 26 30 25	1♒8 5 7 24 6	1♑18 18 17	1♐29 12 28 30 27	1♐10 4 9 23 8	1♏20 17 19
6	1♉13 6 12 25 11	1♈23 19 22	1♈4 13 3	1♓15 6 14 25 13	1♒25 18 24	1♒6 12 5	1♑17 6 16 25 15	1♐27 18 26	1♐8 11 7 30 6	1♏19 5 18 24 17
7	1♉11 14 10	1♈22 8 21 27 20	1♈2 20 1	1♓13 14 12	1♒24 7 23 26 22	1♒4 20 3	1♑15 13 14	1♐26 7 25 26 24	1♐6 19 5	1♏17 13 16
8	1♉10 2 9 21 8	1♈20 14 19	1♈1 8 0 27♓29	1♓12 2 11 21 10	1♒22 14 21	1♒3 7 2 26 1	1♑12 20 11	1♐24 14 23	1♐5 7 4 26 3	1♏15 19 14
9	1♉8 8 7 27 6	1♈19 2 18 21 17	1♓29 15 28	1♓10 9 9 28 8	1♒21 2 20 20 19	1♒1 14 0	1♑12 8 11 27 10	1♐23 2 22 21 21	1♐3 13 2	1♏14 7 13 26 12
10	1♉6 16 5	1♈17 10 16 29 15	1♓28 4 27 23 26	1♓a 17 7	1♒19 9 18 28 17	1♒0 3♑29 22 28	1♑10 16 9	1♐21 10 20 29 19	1♐2 2 1 21 0	1♏12 15 11
11	1♉5 4 4 23 3	1♈15 17 14	1♓26 11 25 29 24	1♓7 4 6 23 5	1♒17 16 16	1♑28 10 27 29 26	1♑9 4 8 23 7	1♐19 16 18	1♐0 9♏29 28 28	1♏11 3 10 22 9
12	1♉3 12 2 31 1	1♈14 6 13 25 12	1♓24 18 23	1♓5 12 4 31 3	1♒16 5 15 24 14	1♑26 18 25	1♑7 11 6 30 5	1♐18 5 17 24 16	1♏28 17 27	1♏9 11 8 30 7

	1958	1959	1960	1961	1962	1963	1964	1965	1966
1	1♏7 17 6	1♎18 11 17 30 16	1♍29 5 28 24 27	1♍9 17 8	1♌20 11 19 25 18	1♌1 4 0 24♋29	1♋11 17 10	1♓22 10 21 29 20	1♓3 4 2 23 1
2	1♏6 5 5 24 4	1♎16 18 15	1♍27 12 26	1♎8 5 7 24 6	1♌18 17 17	1♋29 11 28	1♋10 5 9 24 8	1♊20 17 19	1♊1 11 0
3	1♏4 15 3	1♎15 9 14 28 13	1♍26 2 25 21 24	1♍6 14 5	1♌17 8 16 27 15	1♋28 2 27 21 26	1♋8 14 7	1♊19 8 18 26 17	1♉29 20 28
4	1♏3 3 2 22 1	1♎13 16 12	1♍24 9 23 27 22	1♍5 2 4 21 3	1♌15 15 14	1♋26 9 25 28 24	1♋7 2 6 21 5	1♊17 14 16	1♉18 8 27 27 26
5	1♏1 11 0 30♎29	1♎12 5 11 23 10	1♍22 16 21	1♍3 10 2 29 1	1♌14 4 13 23 12	1♋24 17 23	1♋5 9 4 28 3	1♊16 3 15 22 14	1♉26 16 25
6	1♎29 18 28	1♎10 11 9 30 8	1♍21 4 20 23 19	1♍1 17 0	1♌12 11 11 30 10	1♋23 5 22 23 21	1♋3 16 2	1♊14 10 13 29 12	1♉25 4 24 23 23
7	1♎28 7 27 25 26	1♎8 19 7	1♍19 12 18 31 17	1♍0 6♌29 25 28	1♌10 18 9	1♋21 12 20 31 19	1♋2 4 1 24 0	1♊12 18 11	1♉23 12 22 30 21
8	1♎26 13 25	1♎7 7 6 26 5	1♍17 19 16	1♌28 13 27 31 26	1♌9 6 8 25 7	1♋19 19 18	1♋0 12♊29 31 28	1♊11 6 10 25 9	1♉21 18 20
9	1♎24 20 23	1♎5 14 4	1♍16 7 15 25 14	1♌26 19 25	1♌7 13 6	1♋18 7 17 26 16	1♊28 19 27	1♊9 12 8	1♉20 6 19 25 18
10	1♎23 9 22 28 21	1♎4 3 3 22 2	1♍14 14 13	1♌25 8 24 27 23	1♌6 2 5 21 4	1♋16 15 15	1♊27 7 26 26 25	1♊7 20 6	1♉18 14 17
11	1♎21 16 20	1♎2 9 1 28 0	1♍13 2 12 21 11	1♌23 15 22	1♌4 9 3 28 2	1♋15 3 14 21 13	1♊25 14 24	1♊6 8 5 27 4	1♉17 2 16 21 15
12	1♎20 5 19 23 18	1♎0 17♍29	1♍11 10 10 29 9	1♌22 4 21 23 20	1♌2 17 1	1♋13 10 12 29 11	1♊24 3 23 23 22	1♊4 16 3	1♉15 10 14 29 13

	1967	1968	1969	1970	1971	1972	1973	1974	1975
1	1♉13 16 12	1♈24 10 23 29 22	1♈5 31 4 22 3	1♓15 16 14	1♒26 9 25 28 24	1♒6 31 5	5♑17 25 16	18♐27	12♐8 31 7
2	1♉12 4 11 23 10	1♈22 17 21	1♈3 10 2	1♓14 4 13 22 12	1♒24 16 23	21♒4	12♑15	6♐26 25 25	19♐6
3	1♉10 14 9	1♈21 7 20	1♈1 20 0 26 19	1♓12 13 11	1♒23 7 22	9♒3 29 2 26 21	3♑14 22 13	16♐24	10♐5 29 4
4	1♉9 2 8 21 7	1♈19 14 18	1♈0 7♓29 26 28	1♓10 20 9	1♒21 14 20	16♒1	10♑12 29 11	4♐23 23 22	17♐3
5	1♉7 10 6 29 5	1♈18 3 17 21 16	1♓28 15 27	1♓9 9 8 28 7	1♒20 2 19 22 18	5♒0 6♑29	18♑10	12♐21 30 20	6♐2 24 1
6	1♉5 17 4	1♈16 9 15 28 14	1♓27 3 26 22 25	1♓7 16 6	1♒18 10 17 28 16	12♑28	6♑9 25 8	18♐19	12♐0 12♏29
7	1♉4 5 3 24 2	1♈14 17 13	1♓25 11 24 30 23	1♓6 5 5 24 4	1♒16 17 15	1♑27 19 26	14♑7	7♐18 26 17	1♏29 20 28
8	1♉2 12 1 31 0	1♈13 4 12 24 11	1♓23 18 22	1♓4 11 3 30 2	1♒15 5 14 24 13	7♑25 26 24	1♑6 20 5	14♐16	8♏27 27 26
9	1♉0 19♈29	1♈11 12 10	1♓22 5 21 24 20	1♓2 18 1	1♒13 12 12	14♑23	8♑4 27 3	2♐15 21 14	15♏25
10	1♈29 8 28 27 27	1♈9 19 8	1♓20 13 19	1♓1 7 0 26♒29	1♒11 20 10	3♑22 22 21	16♑2	10♐13 29 12	4♏24 22 23
11	1♈27 15 26	1♈8 7 7 26 6	1♓18 20 17	1♒29 14 28	1♒10 8 9 27 8	10♑20 29 19	4♑1 22 0 22♐29	17♐11	10♏22 29 21
12	1♈26 3 25 22 24	1♈6 15 5	1♓17 9 16 28 15	1♒28 3 27 22 26	1♒8 15 7	18♑18	29♐28	5♐10 24 9	18♏20

	1976	1977	1978	1979	1980	1981	1982	1983	1984
1	6♏19 25 18	1♎29	11♎10 30 9	5♍21 24 20	17♍1	10♌12 29 11	4♋23 23 22	17♋3	11♊14 30 13
2	13♏17	5♎28 24 27	18♎8	12♍19	5♍0 6♌29	17♌10	12♋21 28 20	5♋2 24 1	18♊12
3	3♏16 21 15	15♎26	9♎7 28 6	3♍18 22 17	14♌28	8♌9 27 8	16♋20 21 19	14♋0 15♊29	7♊11 26 10
4	9♏14 28 13	3♎25 22 24	16♎5	10♍16 29 15	2♌27 21 26	15♌7	9♋18 28 17	21♊28	14♊9
5	17♏12	11♎23 30 22	4♎4 23 3	17♍14	10♌25 29 24	3♌6	16♋16	10♊27 29 26	3♊8 22 7
6	5♏11 24 10	17♎21	11♎2 30 1	5♍13 24 12	16♌23	11♌4 30 3	5♋15 23 14	18♊25	10♊6 29 5
7	13♏9 31 8	7♎20 25 19	19♎0 19♍29	13♍11	5♌22 24 21	19♌2	12♋13 31 12	7♊24 25 23	18♊4
8	19♏7	13♎18	7♍29 26 28	1♍10 20 9	12♌20 31 19	6♌1 25 0 26♋29	19♋11	13♊22	6♊3 24 2
9	7♏6 26 5	1♎17 20 16	14♍27	7♍8 26 7	19♌18	13♋29	7♋10 26 9	1♊21 20 20	12♊1 30 0
10	15♏4	9♎15 28 14	3♍26 22 25	15♍6	8♌17 27 16	2♋28 21 27	15♋8	8♊19 27 18	1♉29
11	3♏3 22 2	16♎13	10♍24 29 23	3♍5 22 4	15♌15	9♋26 28 25	2♋7 21 6	15♊17	8♉28 27 27
12	11♏1 30 0 31♎29	4♎12 23 11	17♍22	11♍3 30 2	3♌14 22 13	16♋24 31 23	10♋5 30 4	4♊16 23 15	16♉26 31 25

1980	1	2	3	4	5	6	7	8	9	10	11	12
♂	14♍	14	3	26♌	29	10♍	25	13♎	2♏	22	14♐	7♑
♃	10♍	8	4	1	0	2	6	12	18	25	1♎	6
♄	27♍	25	23	21	20	20	22	25	28	2♎	6	8
♅	24♏	25	26	25	24	23	22	21	22	23	25	27
♆	19♐	20	21	21	21	20	19	19	18	19	19	20
♇	21♎	21	21	20	19	19	19	19	20	21	22	23

1981	1	2	3	4	5	6	7	8	9	10	11	12
♂	1♒	25	17♓	12♈	5♉	27	18♊	9♋	29	19♌	6♍	22
♃	9♎	10	8	5	1	0	2	6	12	18	25	1♏
♄	9♎	9	7	5	3	3	4	6	10	13	17	19
♅	29♏	0♐	0	0	29♏	28	27	26	26	27	29	1♐
♆	22♐	23	23	23	23	22	21	21	21	21	21	22
♇	24♎	24	24	23	22	21	21	21	22	23	24	25

1982	1	2	3	4	5	6	7	8	9	10	11	12
♂	7♎	17	19	10	1	3	13	29	17♏	8♐	0♑	23
♃	6♏	9	10	8	5	1	0	2	6	12	18	25
♄	21♎	22	20	18	16	15	16	18	21	24	28	1♏
♅	3♐	4	5	4	3	2	1	1	1	2	3	5
♆	24♐	25	25	25	25	25	24	23	23	23	24	25
♇	26♎	26	26	25	25	24	24	24	25	26	27	9

1983	1	2	3	4	5	6	7	8	9	10	11	12
♂	17♒	12♓	4♈	28	20♉	12♊	3♋	23	13♌	2♍	20	8♎
♃	1♐	7	10	11	9	5	2	1	3	7	13	19
♄	3♏	4	3	2	0	28♎	28	29	2♏	5	8	11
♅	7♐	8	9	9	8	7	6	5	5	6	8	9
♆	26♐	27	27	28	27	27	26	25	25	25	26	27
♇	29♎	29	29	28	27	27	26	26	27	28	29	0♏

1984	1	2	3	4	5	6	7	8	9	10	11	12
♂	26♎	11♏	23	28	24	15	13	22	8♐	27	19♑	12♒
♃	26♐	3♑	8	12	13	12	8	5	3	5	9	15
♄	14♏	16	16	14	12	11	10	10	12	15	19	22
♅	11♐	13	13	13	13	12	10	10	10	10	12	14
♆	28♐	29	0♑	0	0	29♐	28	27	27	27	28	29
♇	1♏	2	1	1	0	29♎	29	29	0♏	1	2	3

1985	1	2	3	4	5	6	7	8	9	10	11	12
♂	5♓	29	20♈	13♉	4♊	25	15♋	5♌	25	14♍	3♎	22
♃	22♑	29	5♒	11	15	17	16	13	9	7	9	13
♄	25♏	27	28	27	25	23	22	22	23	26	29	2♐
♅	15♐	17	18	18	17	16	15	14	14	15	16	18
♆	0♑	1	2	2	2	1	0	0	29♐	29	0♑	1
♇	4♏	4	4	3	3	2	1	2	2	3	4	6

1986	1	2	3	4	5	6	7	8	9	10	11	12
♂	11♏	0♐	16	2♑	15	23	21	13	15	25	13♒	4♓
♃	18♒	25	2♓	9	16	20	23	23	20	16	14	14
♄	5♐	8	9	9	8	6	4	4	4	6	9	12
♅	20♐	21	22	22	22	21	20	19	18	19	20	22
♆	2♑	3	4	4	4	3	3	2	2	2	2	3
♇	6♏	7	7	6	5	5	4	4	5	6	7	8

1987	1	2	3	4	5	6	7	8	9	10	11	12
♂	25♓	17♈	6♉	28	18♊	9♋	28	18♌	7♍	26	16♎	5♏
♃	18♓	24	0♈	8	15	21	26	0♉	0	27♈	23	21
♄	16♐	19	20	20	20	18	16	15	15	17	19	22
♅	24♐	25	26	27	26	25	24	23	23	23	24	26
♆	4♑	5	6	6	6	6	5	4	4	4	4	5
♇	9♏	9	9	9	8	7	7	7	7	8	9	11

1988	1	2	3	4	5	6	7	8	9	10	11	12
♂	26♏	17♐	6♑	26	16♒	5♓	23	6♈	10	3	29♓	7♈
♃	21♈	24	29	5♉	12	20	26	2♊	6	6	4	0
♄	26♐	29	1♑	2	2	0	28♐	27	27	28	0♑	2
♅	28♐	29	0♑	1	1	0	29♐	28	27	27	28	0♑
♆	6♑	7	8	9	8	8	7	6	6	6	6	7
♇	12♏	12	12	11	11	10	9	9	10	11	12	13

1989	1	2	3	4	5	6	7	8	9	10	11	12
♂	19♈	7♉	24	13♊	2♋	21	10♌	29	19♍	8♎	28	18♏
♃	27♉	27	29	4♊	10	17	24	0♋	6	10	11	9
♄	6♑	9	11	13	13	12	10	9	8	8	10	13
♅	2♑	4	5	5	5	4	3	2	1	1	2	4
♆	8♑	9	10	11	11	10	9	8	8	8	8	9
♇	14♏	15	15	14	13	13	12	12	12	13	14	16

1990	1	2	3	4	5	6	7	8	9	10	11	12
♂	10♐	3♑	24	16♒	9♓	2♈	23	13♉	0♊	12	13	4
♃	5♋	2	1	3	7	13	20	26	3♌	8	12	14
♄	16♑	19	22	24	25	24	23	21	20	20	21	23
♅	6♑	8	9	9	9	9	8	6	6	6	6	8
♆	10♑	12	12	13	13	12	12	11	10	10	11	11
♇	17♏	17	17	17	16	15	15	15	15	16	17	18

1991	1	2	3	4	5	6	7	8	9	10	11	12
♂	28♉	4♊	14	0♋	16	4♌	22	12♍	1♎	21	12♏	3♐
♃	12♌	8	5	4	5	9	14	21	28	4♍	9	13
♄	26♑	0♒	2	5	6	6	5	3	1	1	1	3
♅	10♑	12	13	14	14	13	12	11	10	10	11	12
♆	13♑	14	14	15	15	15	14	13	12	12	13	14
♇	19♏	20	20	20	19	18	17	17	17	18	19	21

1992	1	2	3	4	5	6	7	8	9	10	11	12
♂	25♐	19♑	10♒	4♓	27	20♈	12♉	4♊	23	11♋	24	28
♃	14♍	13	9	6	4	6	10	15	21	28	4♎	9
♄	6♒	10	13	15	18	18	17	16	14	13	12	14
♅	14♑	16	17	18	18	17	16	15	14	14	15	16
♆	15♑	16	17	17	17	17	16	15	15	15	15	16
♇	22♏	22	22	22	21	21	20	20	20	21	22	23

1993	1	2	3	4	5	6	7	8	9	10	11	12
♂	21♋	11	10	19	2♌	18	5♍	24	14♎	3♏	25	17♐
♃	13♎	14	13	9	6	4	6	9	15	21	28	4♏
♄	16♒	20	23	26	29	0♓	0	28♒	26	25	24	25
♅	18♑	20	21	22	22	21	20	19	18	18	19	20
♆	17♑	18	19	19	19	19	18	17	17	17	17	18
♇	24♏	25	25	25	24	23	23	22	23	23	24	26

1994	1	2	3	4	5	6	7	8	9	10	11	12
♂	10♑	4♒	27	21♓	14♈	7♉	29	21♊	11♋	29	15♌	26
♃	9♏	13	14	13	9	6	5	6	10	15	22	28
♄	27♒	0♓	3	7	10	12	12	11	9	7	6	6
♅	22♑	23	25	26	26	26	25	23	22	22	23	24
♆	19♑	20	21	21	22	21	21	20	19	19	19	20
♇	27♏	27	28	27	27	26	25	25	25	26	27	28

1995	1	2	3	4	5	6	7	8	9	10	11	12
♂	3♍	26♌	16	14	20	3♍	19	7♎	27	18♏	10♐	2♑
♃	5♐	10	14	15	14	10	7	5	7	10	16	23
♄	8♓	11	14	18	21	23	24	24	22	20	18	18
♅	25♑	27	29	0♒	0	0	29♑	28	27	26	27	28
♆	21♑	22	23	24	24	24	23	22	21	21	21	22
♇	29♏	0♐	0	0	29♏	28	28	27	27	28	29	0♐

1996	1	2	3	4	5	6	7	8	9	10	11	12
♂	26♑	20♒	12♓	7♈	0♉	22	14♊	5♋	25	14♌	1♍	17
♃	0♑	6	12	16	18	17	13	10	8	9	13	18
♄	19♓	22	25	29	2♈	5	7	7	6	3	1	0
♅	29♑	1♒	3	4	5	4	3	2	1	0	1	2
♆	23♑	24	25	26	26	26	25	24	24	23	24	24
♇	1♐	2	3	2	2	1	0	0	0	1	2	3

1997	1	2	3	4	5	6	7	8	9	10	11	12
♂	29♍	6♎	3	21♍	17	24	6♎	22	12♏	2♐	25	17♑
♃	25♑	3♒	9	15	20	22	22	19	15	13	13	17
♄	1♈	3	6	10	14	17	19	20	19	17	15	13
♅	3♒	5	7	8	9	9	8	6	5	5	5	6
♆	25♑	26	27	28	28	28	27	27	26	26	26	26
♇	4♐	5	5	5	4	4	3	2	2	3	4	5

1998	1	2	3	4	5	6	7	8	9	10	11	12
♂	12♒	6♓	29	22♈	15♉	7♊	28	19♋	9♌	27	16♍	3♎
♃	23♒	29	6♓	14	20	25	28	28	26	22	19	19
♄	13♈	15	17	21	25	29	2♉	3	3	1	29♈	27
♅	7♒	9	11	12	13	13	12	11	9	9	9	9
♆	27♑	28	29	0♒	0	0	0	29♑	28	28	28	28
♇	6♐	7	8	7	7	6	5	5	5	5	6	8

1999	1	2	3	4	5	6	7	8	9	10	11	12
♂	22♎	6♏	11	12	2	25♎	29	11♏	0♐	20	12♑	5♒
♃	23♓	28	4♈	12	19	26	1♉	5	6	3	29♈	26
♄	26♈	27	29	3♉	7	11	14	16	17	16	13	11
♅	11♒	13	14	16	17	17	16	15	14	13	13	13
♆	29♑	1♒	2	2	3	2	2	1	0	0	0	1
♇	9♐	10	10	10	9	9	8	7	7	8	9	10

2000	1	2	3	4	5	6	7	8	9	10	11	12
♂	29♒	23♓	14♈	7♉	29	20♊	10♋	1♌	21	9♍	29	17♎
♃	26♈	29	3♉	10	17	24	0♊	6	10	12	10	6
♄	9♉	10	11	15	19	23	26	29	1♊	0	28♉	25
♅	15♒	16	18	20	21	21	20	19	18	17	17	17
♆	2♒	3	4	4	5	5	4	3	3	2	2	3
♇	11♐	12	12	12	12	11	10	10	10	10	11	12

DEGREES OR HOURS

0	1	2	3	4	5	6	7	8	9	10	11	12	13	14	15
3·1584	1·3802	1·0792	9031	7781	6812	6021	5351	4771	4260	3802	3388	3010	2663	2341	2041
3·1584	1·3730	1·0756	9007	7763	6798	6009	5341	4762	4252	3795	3382	3004	2657	2386	2036
2·8573	1·3660	1·0720	8983	7745	6784	5997	5330	4753	4244	3788	3375	2998	2652	2330	2032
2·6812	1·3590	1·0685	8959	7728	6769	5985	5320	4744	4236	3780	3368	2992	2646	2325	2027
2·5563	1·3522	1·0649	8935	7710	6755	5973	5310	4735	4228	3773	3362	2986	2640	2320	2022
2·4594	1·3454	1·0614	8912	7692	6741	5961	5300	4726	4220	3766	3355	2980	2635	2315	2017
2·3802	1·3388	1·0580	8888	7674	6726	5949	5280	4717	4212	3759	3349	2974	2629	2310	2012
2·3133	1·3323	1·0546	8865	7657	6712	5937	5279	4708	4204	3752	3342	2968	2624	2305	2008
2·2553	1·3258	1·0511	8842	7639	6698	5925	5269	4699	4196	3745	3336	2962	2618	2300	2003
2·2041	1·3195	1·0478	8819	7622	6684	5913	5259	4690	4188	3737	3329	2956	2613	2295	1998
2·1584	1·3133	1·0444	8796	7604	6670	5902	5249	4682	4180	3730	3323	2950	2607	2280	1993
2·1170	1·3071	1·0411	8773	7587	6656	5890	5239	4673	4172	3723	3316	2944	2602	2284	1988
2·0792	1·3010	1·0378	8751	7570	6642	5878	5229	4664	4164	3716	3310	2938	2596	2279	1984
2·0444	1·2950	1·0345	8728	7552	6628	5866	5219	4655	4156	3709	3303	2933	2591	2274	1979
2·0122	1·2891	1·0313	8706	7535	6614	5855	5209	4646	4148	3702	3297	2927	2585	2269	1974
1·9823	1·2833	1·0280	8683	7518	6600	5843	5199	4638	4141	3695	3291	2921	2580	2264	1969
1·9542	1·2775	1·0248	8661	7501	6587	5832	5189	4629	4133	3688	3284	2915	2574	2259	1965
1·9279	1·2719	1·0216	8639	7484	6573	5820	5179	4620	4125	3681	3278	2909	2569	2254	1960
1·9031	1·2663	1·0185	8617	7467	6559	5809	5169	4611	4117	3674	3271	2903	2564	2249	1955
1·8796	1·2607	1·0153	8595	7451	6546	5797	5159	4603	4109	3667	3265	2897	2558	2244	1950
1·8573	1·2553	1·0122	8573	7434	6532	5786	5149	4594	4102	3660	3258	2891	2553	2239	1946
1·8361	1·2499	1·0091	8552	7417	6519	5774	5139	4585	4094	3653	3252	2885	2547	2234	1941
1·8159	1·2445	1·0061	8530	7401	6505	5763	5129	4577	4086	3646	3246	2880	2542	2229	1936
1·7966	1·2393	1·0030	8509	7384	6492	5752	5120	4568	4079	3639	3239	2874	2536	2223	1932
1·7781	1·2341	1·0000	8487	7368	6478	5740	5110	4559	4071	3632	3233	2868	2531	2218	1927
1·7604	1·2289	0·9970	8466	7351	6465	5729	5100	4551	4063	3625	3227	2862	2526	2213	1922
1·7434	1·2239	0·9940	8445	7335	6451	5718	5090	4542	4055	3618	3220	2856	2520	2208	1917
1·7270	1·2188	0·9910	8424	7318	6438	5706	5081	4534	4048	3611	3214	2850	2515	2203	1913
1·7112	1·2139	0·9881	8403	7302	6425	5695	5071	4525	4040	3604	3208	2845	2509	2198	1908
1·6960	1·2090	0·9852	8382	7286	6412	5684	5061	4516	4032	3597	3201	2839	2504	2193	1903
1·6812	1·2041	0·9823	8361	7270	6398	5673	5051	4508	4025	3590	3195	2833	2499	2188	1890
1·6670	1·1993	0·9794	8341	7254	6385	5662	5042	4499	4017	3583	3189	2827	2493	2183	1894
1·6532	1·1946	0·9765	8320	7238	6372	5651	5032	4491	4010	3576	3183	2821	2488	2178	1889
1·6398	1·1899	0·9737	8300	7222	6359	5640	5023	4482	4002	3570	3176	2816	2483	2173	1885
1·6269	1·1852	0·9708	8279	7206	6346	5629	5013	4474	3994	3563	3170	2810	2477	2168	1880
1·6143	1·1806	0·9680	8259	7190	6333	5618	5003	4466	3987	3556	3164	2804	2472	2164	1875
1·6021	1·1761	0·9652	8239	7174	6320	5607	4994	4457	3979	3549	3157	2798	2467	2159	1871
1·5902	1·1716	0·9625	8219	7159	6307	5596	4984	4449	3972	3542	3151	2793	2461	2154	1866
1·5786	1·1671	0·9597	8199	7143	6294	5585	4975	4440	3964	3535	3145	2787	2456	2149	1862
1·5673	1·1627	0·9570	8179	7128	6282	5574	4965	4432	3957	3529	3139	2781	2451	2144	1857
1·5563	1·1584	0·9542	8159	7112	6269	5563	4956	4424	3949	3522	3133	2775	2445	2139	1852
1·5456	1·1540	0·9515	8140	7097	6256	5552	4947	4415	3942	3515	3126	2770	2440	2134	1848
1·5351	1·1498	0·9488	8120	7081	6243	5541	4937	4407	3934	3508	3120	2764	2435	2129	1843
1·5249	1·1455	0·9462	8101	7066	6231	5531	4928	4399	3927	3501	3114	2758	2430	2124	1838
1·5149	1·1413	0·9435	8081	7050	6218	5520	4918	4390	3919	3495	3108	2753	2424	2119	1834
1·5051	1·1372	0·9409	8062	7035	6205	5509	4909	4382	3912	3488	3102	2747	2419	2114	1829
1·4956	1·1331	0·9383	8043	7020	6193	5498	4900	4374	3905	3481	3096	2741	2414	2109	1825
1·4863	1·1290	0·9356	8023	7005	6180	5488	4890	4365	3897	3475	3089	2736	2409	2104	1820
1·4771	1·1249	0·9330	8004	6990	6168	5477	4881	1357	3890	3468	3083	2730	2403	2099	1816
1·4682	1·1209	0·9305	7985	6975	6155	5466	4872	4349	3882	3461	3077	2724	2398	2095	1811
1·4594	1·1170	0·9279	7966	6960	6143	5456	4863	4341	3875	3454	3071	2719	2393	2090	1806
1·4508	1·1130	0·9254	7947	6945	6131	5445	4853	4333	3868	3448	3065	2713	2388	2085	1802
1·4424	1·1091	0·9228	7929	6930	6118	5435	4844	4324	3860	3441	3059	2707	2382	2080	1797
1·4341	1·1053	0·9203	7910	6915	6106	5424	4835	4316	3853	3434	3053	2702	2377	2075	1793
1·4260	1·1015	0·9178	7891	6900	6094	5414	4826	4308	3846	3428	3047	2696	2372	2070	1788
1·4180	1·0977	0·9153	7873	6885	6081	5403	4817	4300	3838	3421	3041	2691	2367	2065	1784
1·4102	1·0939	0·9128	7854	6871	6069	5393	4808	4292	3831	3415	3034	2685	2362	2061	1779
1·4025	1·0902	0·9104	7836	6856	6057	5382	4798	4284	3824	3408	3028	2679	2356	2056	1774
1·3949	1·0865	0·9079	7818	6841	6045	5372	4789	4276	3817	3401	3022	2674	2351	2051	1770
1·3875	1·0828	0·9055	7800	6827	6033	536b	4780	4268	3809	3395	3016	2668	2346	2046	1765

ADJUSTED CALCULATION DATE (A.C.D.)

The adjusted calculation date, or noon date as it is otherwise known, is based on the fact that as 24 hours = 1 day = 1 year, then any given proportion of 1 day will equal a corresponding proportion of a year. A Chart is progressed for *x* number of days after birth corresponding to the age of the person, i.e. progressions for the 20th year of life will be computed for the 20th day after the birth-date.

In order to avoid calculating the progressed Chart for the time at which birth occurred, the planetary positions as at noon are listed, but these positions will correspond to a different date in the year, depending upon the time of birth.

An additional verification that the adjusted date is correct, is that when the listings of the progressed Moon's position are noted, the Moon should be in an identical position on the adjusted date, with its position calculated on the progressed day for the birth-time.

	1	2	3	4	5	6	7	8	9	10	11	12
1	1	32	60	91	121	152	182	213	244	274	305	335
2	2	33	61	92	122	153	183	214	245	275	306	336
3	3	34	62	93	123	154	184	215	246	276	307	337
4	4	35	63	94	124	155	185	216	247	277	308	338
5	5	36	64	95	125	156	186	217	248	278	309	339
6	6	37	65	96	126	157	187	218	249	279	310	340
7	7	38	66	97	127	158	188	219	250	280	311	341
8	8	39	67	98	128	159	189	220	251	281	312	342
9	9	40	68	99	129	160	190	221	252	282	313	343
10	10	41	69	100	130	161	191	222	253	283	314	344
11	11	42	70	101	131	162	192	223	254	284	315	345
12	12	43	71	102	132	163	193	224	255	285	316	346
13	13	44	72	103	133	164	194	225	256	286	317	347
14	14	45	73	104	134	165	195	226	257	287	318	348
15	15	46	74	105	135	166	196	227	258	288	319	349
16	16	47	75	106	136	167	197	228	259	289	320	350
17	17	48	76	107	137	168	198	229	260	290	321	351
18	18	49	77	108	138	169	199	230	261	291	322	352
19	19	50	78	109	139	170	200	231	262	292	323	353
20	20	51	79	110	140	171	201	232	263	293	324	354
21	21	52	80	111	141	172	202	233	264	294	325	355
22	22	53	81	112	142	173	203	234	265	295	326	356
23	23	54	82	113	143	174	204	235	266	296	327	357
24	24	55	83	114	144	175	205	236	267	297	328	358
25	25	56	84	115	145	176	206	237	268	298	329	359
26	26	57	85	116	146	177	207	238	269	299	330	360
27	27	58	86	117	147	178	208	239	270	300	331	361
28	28	59	87	118	148	179	209	240	271	301	332	362
29	29		88	119	149	180	210	241	272	302	333	363
30	30		89	120	150	181	211	242	273	303	334	364
31	31		90		151		212	243		304		365

HOURS & MINUTES

HOURS	DAYS	MINUTES	DAYS	MINUTES	DAYS	MINUTES	DAYS
1	15·2	1	0·2	24	6·1	35	8·9
2	30·4	2	0·5	25	6·3	40	10·1
3	45·6	3	0·7	26	6·6	45	11·4
4	60·8	4	1·0	27	6·8	50	12·7
5	76·0	5	1·3	28	7·1	55	13·9
6	91·2	6	1·5	29	7·3		
7	106·5	7	1·8	30	7·6		
8	121·6	8	2·0				
9	136·8	9	2·3				
10	152·1	10	2·5				
11	167·3	11	2·8				
12	182·5	12	3·0				
13	197·7	13	3·3				
14	212·9	14	3·5				
15	228·1	15	3·8				
16	243·3	16	4·0				
17	258·5	17	4·3				
18	273·7	18	4·6				
19	288·9	19	4·8				
20	304·2	20	5·1				
21	319·4	21	5·3				
22	334·6	22	5·6				
23	349·8	23	5·8				

NOTE

Greenwich time to be taken in all cases, if using a Greenwich based ephemeris.

A.M. Births. *Add.*
P.M. Births. *Subtract.*

Deduct 1 day if 29 February in leap year enters calculation.

Places fast on GMT (mainly those East of Greenwich)
The times given below should be added to GMT to give Standard Time, subtracted from Standard Time to give GMT

	h	m
Aden (Southern Yemen)	03	
Admiralty Islands	10	
Afghanistan	04	30
Albania*	01	
Amirante Islands	04	
Andaman Islands	05	30
Angola (Portuguese West Africa)	01	
Annobon Island‡	01	
Arabian Emirates, Federation of	04	
Australia		
Australian Capital Territory	10	
New South Wales[2]	10	
Northern Territory	09	30
Queensland	10	
South Australia	09	30
Tasmania*	10	
Victoria	10	
Western Australia	08	
Austria	01	
Balearic Islands‡	01	
Belgium	01	
Botswana, Republic of	02	
British New Guinea	10	
Brunei	08	
Bulgaria	02	
Burma	06	30
Cambodia	07	
Cameroun Republic	01	
Central African Republic‡	01	
Ceylon	05	30
Chad	01	
Channel Islands[1]	01	
Chatham Islands‡	12	45
China[3]	08	
Christmas Island, Indian Ocean	07	
Congo Republic	01	
Congolese Republic		
eastern part	02	
western part	01	
Corsica‡	01	
Crete	02	
Cyprus	02	
Cyrenaica‡	02	
Czechoslovakia	01	
Dahomey, Republic of	01	
Denmark	01	
Egypt* (United Arab Republic)	02	
Ellice Islands	12	
Equatorial Guinea, Republic of	01	
Estonia	03	
Ethiopia	03	
Fernando Poo‡	01	
Fiji	12	
Finland	02	
Formosa* (Taiwan)	08	
France‡	01	
French Territory of the Afars and Issas	03	
Friendly Islands	13	
Gabon	01	
Germany	01	
Gibraltar‡	01	
Gilbert and Ellice Islands	12	
Great Britain[1]	01	
Greece	02	
Holland (The Netherlands)	01	
Hong Kong*	08	
Hungary	01	
India	05	30
Indonesia, Republic of		
Bali, Bangka, Billiton, Java, Madurá, Sumatra	07	
Borneo, Celebes, Flores, Lombok, Sumba, Sumbawa, Timor	08	
Aru, Kei, Moluccas, Tanimbar, West Irian	09	
Iran	03	30
Iraq	03	
Ireland, Northern[1]	01	
Irish Republic	01	
Israel	02	
Italy*	01	
Japan	09	
Jordan	02	
Kenya	03	
Korea	09	
Kuwait	03	
Laos	07	
Latvia	03	
Lebanon*	02	
Lesotho	02	
Libya	02	
Liechtenstein	01	
Lithuania	03	
Luxembourg‡	01	
Macao*	08	
Malagasy Republic	03	
Malawi	02	
Malaysia		
Malaya	07	30
Sabah, Sarawak	08	
Maldive Republic	05	
Malta	01	
Manchuria	09	
Mauritius	04	
Monaco‡	01	
Mozambique (Portuguese East Africa)	02	
Muscat and Oman, Sultanate of	04	
New Caledonia	11	
New Guinea, British	10	
New Hebrides	11	
New Zealand	12	
Nigeria, Republic of	01	
Norfolk Island	11	30
North Vietnam	07	
Norway*	01	
Ocean Island	11	
Okinawa	09	
Pakistan, East	06	
West	05	
Papua	10	
Persia (Iran)	03	30
Philippine Republic	08	
Poland*	01	
Portugal	01	
Portuguese West Africa (Angola)	01	
Reunion	04	
Rhodesia	02	
Rumania	02	
Santa Cruz Islands	11	
Sardinia	01	
Saudi Arabia	04	
Dhahran, Jedda	03	
Seychelles	04	
Siam (Thailand)	07	
Sicily	01	
Singapore	07	30
Solomon Islands	11	
Somali Republic	03	
South Africa, Republic of	02	
Southern Yemen	03	
South Vietnam	08	
South West Africa	02	
Spain‡	01	
Spitsbergen (Svalbard)	01	
Sudan, Republic of	02	
Swaziland	02	
Sweden	01	
Switzerland	01	
Syria (Syrian Arab Republic)*	02	
Taiwan* (Formosa)	08	
Taiwan (Formosa)*	08	
Thailand	07	
Timor	08	
Tonga Islands	13	
Tripolitania	02	
Tunisia	01	
Turkey*	02	
Uganda	03	
Union of Soviet Socialist Republics[4]		
west of long. E.40°	03	
long E.40° to E.52°30′	04	
long E.52°30′ to E.67°30′	05	
long E.67°30′ to E.82°30′	06	
long. E.82°30′ to E.97°30′	07	
long. E.97°30′ to E.112°30′	08	
long. E.112°30′ to E.127°30′	09	
long. E.127°30′ to E.142°30′	10	
long. E.142°30′ to E.157°30′	11	
long. E.157°30′ to E.172°30′	12	
east of long. E.172°30′	13	
Vietnam, North	07	
South	08	
West Irian	09	
Yugoslavia	01	
Zambia, Republic of	02	

*Summer time may be kept in these countries.
‡This time is used throughout the year, but may differ from the legal time.
Great Britain reverts to Greenwich Mean Time on 31 October 1971.

[2]Except Broken Hill Area, which keeps $09^h\ 30^m$.
[3]All the coast, but some areas may keep summer time.
[4]The boundaries between the zones are irregular; the longitudes given are approximate only.

Places normally keeping GMT

Algeria
Ascension Island
Canary Islands‡
Channel Islands[1]
Faeroes, The
Gambia
Ghana
Great Britain[1]
Guinea Republic
Iceland
Ifni
Ireland, Northern[1]
Ivory Coast
Madeira
Mali
Mauritania
Morocco*
Niger
Principe
Rio de Oro‡
St. Helena
Sao Tome
Sierra Leone
Spanish Sahara
Tangier
Togo Republic
Tristan da Cunha
Upper Volta

*Summer time may be kept in these countries.
‡GMT is in general use throughout the year, but the legal standard time differs from GMT.

[1]The British Standard Time Act, 1968, which states that the standard time shall be one hour in advance of GMT, allows for the possibility of revision to GMT on 31 October 1971. See list 1.

Places slow on GMT (West of Greenwich)
The times given below should be subtracted from GMT to give Standard Time, added to Standard Time to give GMT

	h	m	s
Argentina*	04		
Azores	01		
Bahamas*	05		
Barbados	04		
Bermuda	04		
Bolivia	04		
Brazil* eastern[1]	03		
Territory of Acre	05		
western	04		
British Honduras‡	06		
Canada			
Alberta	07		
British Columbia*	08		
Labrador*	03	30	
Manitoba*	06		
New Brunswick*	04		
Newfoundland*	03	30	
Northwest, Territories*			
east of long. W.68°	04		
long. W.68° to W.85°	05		
long. W.85° to W.102°	06		
long. W.102° to W.120°	07		
west of long. W.120°	08		
Nova Scotia*	04		
Ontario*			
east of long. W.90°	05		
west of long. W.90°	06		
Prince Edward Island*	04		
Quebec*,			
east of long. W.68°	04		
west of long. W.68°	05		
Saskatchewan*	07		
Yukon*	09		
Cape Verde Islands	02		
Cayman Islands	05		
Chile*	04		
Colombia	05		
Costa Rica	06		
Cuba*	05		
Curaçao Island	04		
Dominican Republic‡	05		
Dutch Guiana (Surinam)	03	30	
Ecuador	05		
Falkland Islands[2]	04		
French Guiana	04		
Galapagos Islands	05		
Grenada*	04		
Guadeloupe	04		
Guatemala	06		
Guiana, Dutch	03	30	
French	04		
Guyana	03	45	
Haiti	05		
Honduras	06		
Honduras, British‡	06		
Jamaica	05		
Leeward Islands	04		
Liberia	00	44	30
Marquesas Islands[3]	09	30	
Martinique	04		
Mexico[4]	06		
Midway Islands	11		
Nicaragua	06		
Panama Canal Zone	05		
Panama, Republic of	05		
Paraguay	04		
Peru	05		
Portuguese Guinea	01		
Puerto Rico	04		
St Pierre and Miquelon	03		
Salvador, El	06		
Samoa	11		
Tobago	04		
Trinidade Island, South Atlantic	02		
Trinidad	04		
Turks and Caicos Islands	05		
United States of America			
Alabama[5]	06		
Alaska[5],			
E. of long. W.137°	08		
long. W.137° to W.141°	09		
long W.141° to W.161°	10		
long W.161° to W.172°30′	11		
Arizona	07		
Arkansas[5]	06		
California[5]	08		
Colorado[5]	07		
Connecticut[5]	05		
Delaware[5]	05		
District of Columbia[5]	05		
Florida[5,6]	05		
Georgia[5]	05		
Hawaii	10		
Idaho[5,6]	07		
Illinois[5]	06		
Indiana[5]	06		
Iowa[5]	06		
Kansas[5,6]	06		
Kentucky[5,6]	05		
Louisiana[5]	06		
Maine[5]	05		
Maryland[5]	05		
Massachusetts[5]	05		
Michigan[5,6]	05		
Minnesota[5]	06		
Mississippi[5]	06		
Missouri[5]	06		
Montana[5]	07		
Nebraska[5,6]	06		
Nevada[5]	08		
New Hampshire[5]	05		
New Jersey[5]	05		
New Mexico[5]	07		
New York[5]	05		
North Carolina[5]	05		
North Dakota,[5,6]	06		
Ohio[5]	05		
Oklahoma[5]	06		
Oregon[5,6]	08		
Pennsylvania[5]	05		
Rhode Island[5]	05		
South Carolina[5]	05		
South Dakota[5],			
eastern part	06		
western part	07		
Tennessee[5,6]	06		
Texas[5]	06		
Utah[5,6]	07		
Vermont[5]	05		
Virginia[5]	05		
Washington D.C.[5]	05		
Washington[5]	08		
West Virginia[5]	05		
Wisconsin[5]	06		
Wyoming[5]	07		
Uruguay*	03	30	
Venezuela	04		
Virgin Islands	04		
Windward Islands	04		

*Summer time may be kept in these countries.
‡Winter time may be kept in these countries.
[1]Including all the coast.
[2]Port Stanley keeps summer time September to March.
[3]This is the legal standard time, but local mean time is generally used.

[4]Except the states of Sonora, Sinaloa, Nayarit, and the Southern District of Lower California which keep 07^h, and the Northern District of Lower California which keeps 08^h.
[5]Summer (daylight-saving) time, one hour fast on the time given, is kept in these states from the last Sunday in April to the last Sunday in October changing at $02^h\ 00^m$ local clock time.
[6]This applies to the greater portion of the state.

INDEX

Page numbers in italics refer to illustrations, also to relevant text appearing on the same page.

TECHNICAL INDEX

This shorter index is intended as a reference guide for use in calculating and interpreting natal and progressed Birth Charts. Page numbers in italics refer to illustrations, also to relevant text appearing on the same page.